THE BRITISH YEAR BOOK OF INTERNATIONAL LAW

THE BRITISH YEAR BOOK OF INTERNATIONAL LAW

1995

SIXTY-SIXTH YEAR OF ISSUE

OXFORD
AT THE CLARENDON PRESS

OXFORD
UNIVERSITY PRESS

Great Clarendon Street, Oxford OX2 6DP

Oxford University Press is a department of the University of Oxford.
It furthers the University's objective of excellence in research, scholarship,
and education by publishing worldwide in

Oxford New York

Auckland Cape Town Dar es Salaam Hong Kong Karachi
Kuala Lumpur Madrid Melbourne Mexico City Nairobi
New Delhi Shanghai Taipei Toronto
With offices in
Argentina Austria Brazil Chile Czech Republic France Greece
Guatemala Hungary Italy Japan South Korea Poland Portugal
Singapore Switzerland Thailand Turkey Ukraine Vietnam

Oxford is a registered trade mark of Oxford University Press
in the UK and in certain other countries

Published in the United States
by Oxford University Press Inc., New York

Reprinted 2008

ISBN 978-0-19-825882-7

Editorial Communications should be addressed as follows:

Articles and Notes:
PROFESSOR IAN BROWNLIE
All Souls College, Oxford, OX1 4AL

Books for Review:
PROFESSOR J. G. MERRILLS
University of Sheffield Faculty of Law,
Crookesmoor Building, Conduit Road,
Sheffield, S10 1FL.

The Editors and members of the Editorial Committee do not make themselves in any way responsible for the views expressed by contributors, whether the contributions are signed or not.

The British Year Book of International Law is indexed in *Current Law Index*, published by Information Access Company, and in *Legal Journals Index*, published by Legal Information Resources Limited.

CONTENTS

PROFESSOR KENNETH SIMMONDS—A MEMOIR

Professor Kenneth Simmonds, who died in London on 29 April 1995, had been a member of the Editorial Committee of the *British Year Book of International Law* since 1967. His career as an international lawyer had four features of particular distinction. First, he took a wide view of international law, including, from an early stage of its development, European law. Secondly, he developed a special expertise in two fields of international law, namely the international regional treaties of Central and South America and the international law of the sea. Thirdly, he not only himself carried out research into international law but was equally active as an editor of international materials and an organizer of international conferences encouraging its further study. Fourthly, he put his learning to practical use as an international practitioner.

Kenneth Royston Simmonds was born in Watford on 11 November 1927, and educated at Watford Grammar School and Exeter College, Oxford, where he obtained an Amelia Jackson Senior Fellowship and was awarded a D Phil. with a thesis on Alberico Gentili. Subsequently he obtained teaching posts successively at the University College of Wales (1953–58), the University of Liverpool (1958–61) and Queen's University, Belfast (1961–63). In 1963 the present writer, then Director of the British Institute of International and Comparative Law, heard Simmonds making very pertinent interventions in fluent French and German in the Hamburg Conference of the International Academy of Comparative Law and recommended his appointment to the Governing Body of the Institute as Assistant Director with special responsibility for international law. In 1965 he succeeded the present writer as Director and remained in that post until 1982 (after 1976 in an honorary capacity). From 1970–72 he was Professor of Law in the University of Kent. From 1976–92 he was Professor of International Law in the University of London, during which period from 1980–84 he was Dean to the Faculty of Law of Queen Mary College, London. It should be added that in the course of his career Simmonds held a number of visiting professorships; these included McGill (1968); Wyoming (1967); the Free University of Brussels (1972 and 1973); Amsterdam (annually from 1979); Kentucky (1985); and Texas at Austin (1986–87). In 1989 he was invited to give lectures at the Hague Academy of International Law, and from 1986–92 he was Gresham Professor of Law at Gresham College in the City of London.

The wide view which Simmonds took of international law, especially in its relation with European law, is most strikingly illustrated by his Editorship of the *Common Market Law Review* which he held for twenty-four years, from 1967 to 1991; thereafter until his death he remained a member of the Advisory Board of the *Review*. And he was also from 1972 to 1993 the General Editor of the three volumes of the *Encyclopaedia of European Community Law*. Another topic, not directly relating to but raising problems of international law, with which Simmonds was concerned, was the law governing multinational corporations. In 1976, as Director of the British Institute of International and Comparative Law, he organized a major conference in London on the legal problems of multinational corporations and prepared for the conference an impressive collection of material on the subject.

Simmonds' special study of international regional organizations is evident from the yearly report which he himself made on his personal activities as Director of the British Institute of International and Comparative Law. Thus, for example, he reports that in 1968 he lectured at the National University of Mexico and in 1970 in Barbados and Venezuela in connection with the state of regional organizations in Central and South America. Also in 1970 he published an article in the *International and Comparative Law Quarterly* in the light of his travels; its title was 'International Economic Organisations in Central and Latin America and the Caribbean: Regionalism and Sub-regionalism in the Integration Process'. In another sphere of Simmonds' special interests, the international law of the sea, he published *Resources of the Ocean Bed* in 1970, *New Directions in the Law of the Sea*, 1972 to 1981 (with a further volume in 1982), *Cases in the Law of the Sea*, 1976–84 (with a second series in 1990), *The United Nations Convention on the Law of the Sea 1982*, and, in a related field, *The International Maritime Organisation*, 1994. It was no doubt his publications in this field that led to his practice as an international lawyer to which reference is made below.

An outstanding example of Simmonds' organizing capacity and editing skill was the large scale and very successful conference, already mentioned, on the legal problems of multinational corporations held under the auspices of the British Institute of International and Comparative Law in 1976 in the newly-acquired headquarters of the Institute at Charles Clore House, Russell Square. In 1978 Simmonds produced two volumes of documents and papers on the subject. His work on the law of the sea is also an example of a mixture of original work and editorial arrangement. At the time of his death, which by today's standards must be regarded as sadly premature, Simmonds was entering a further stage beyond the editorial in joining a publishing partnership covering international law and related fields.

The detail and extent of the practice of an international lawyer may be difficult to ascertain owing to the condition of confidentiality subject to which it has been conducted. However, the *International Law Reports* (vol. 91) has published the decision of a Court of Arbitration in 1981 concerning the boundaries of Dubai and Sharjah in which Simmonds agreed with the President (Cahier) of the Court but did not give a separate opinion and where his fellow arbiter (Simpson) dissented. About the time of this case Simmonds was consulted by the Pope in connection with the Beagle Channel dispute between Argentina and Chile. The long-running difference had evidently been referred to the Pope as a confidential method of settlement without restraints of time. It appears that Simmonds gave advice to the Cardinal, to whom the Pope had delegated the matter, on the issues of procedure involved in the case. It is also known that Simmonds was one of the lawyers consulted by the Turkish Government in their dispute with Greece about certain islands in the Aegean Sea.

A memoir is not a biography or a bibliography. All it has been possible to provide, within the usual editorial restraints, is some impression of the extraordinary width of Professor Simmonds' achievement in the international law field. It may well be that this has been underestimated, at least in the United Kingdom, by reason of a failure to appreciate its multifarious nature and also, perhaps, because Simmonds, although an easy and sociable colleague, tended to be reticent about his many activities and projects. He was, however, widely known and respected abroad, being made a Commander of the German Order of Merit and a Chevalier of the Order of Merit, and an Officier of the Ordres des Palmes Académiques, of France.

NORMAN S. MARSH

THE LAW AND PROCEDURE OF THE INTERNATIONAL COURT OF JUSTICE 1960–1989*

PART SEVEN

By HUGH THIRLWAY‡

III. Points of Substantive Law, 1960–1989 (*continued*)

Division B: State Sovereignty, Territory and Frontiers

Division C: State Responsibility and International Claims

‡ Professor of International Law, Graduate Institute of International Studies, Geneva; formerly Principal Legal Secretary, International Court of Justice.

In the preparation of this, the seventh in the series of articles begun in 1989 to continue the magisterial survey of the work of the International Court of Justice up to 1959 by Sir Gerald Fitzmaurice, a problem foreseen at the outset has become a very real one. Since 1989, the 'cut-off date' for the present series, the jurisprudence of the Court has by no means stood still; many areas of law have been clarified or illumined, and in particular a number of matters dealt with during the period under review have been re-examined in decisions subsequent to that date. To include those decisions in the survey would contradict its title, and would also cause an imbalance inasmuch as previous articles in the series, written before such decisions were taken, have for that reason taken no account of them. On the other hand, to discuss a given topic in 1996 while ignoring what the Court may have said about it since 1990 looks like pedantic historicism, and may be misleading.

The solution adopted is, frankly, empirical and a compromise. It should be recalled that the purpose of these articles, like those of Sir Gerald, is not to give a complete *tour d'horizon* of the state of international law, even confined to the particular period examined; it is merely to draw attention to what the Court has contributed, by way of decision or dicta, to the various fields of international law, arranged analytically for reference and comparison.[1] Accordingly, the attempt will be made to make some mention of decisions since 1989 which afford a gloss on, or an extension or even contradiction of, decisions given between 1960[2] and 1989; but all other decisions or aspects of those decisions will be left aside, however great their contribution to the law, as being outside the writer's present remit. In the previous article of the series, it was in effect this approach which led to the inclusion of the case concerning *Maritime Delimitation in the Area between Jan Mayen and Greenland*; in the present article, mention will be made particularly of the *Land, Island and Maritime Frontier Dispute* (El Salvador/Honduras/Nicaragua) and the *Territorial Dispute* (Chad/Libya), with some allusion to other recent cases.

[1] This point should perhaps be stressed in particular in relation to the treatment in the present article of State responsibility, in view of the apparently wide-ranging structure adopted; what is offered is not a survey of the law on the topic, but merely a commentary on the decisions of the Court in the field.

[2] In some cases earlier decisions need to be covered: see the first article in this series, this *Year Book*, 60 (1989), p. 5.

Division B: State Sovereignty, Territory and Frontiers

CHAPTER I

STATE SOVEREIGNTY[3]

A Subject and a Sovereign are clear different things.

King Charles I, Speech on the scaffold, 30 January 1649

1. *Sovereignty and International Legal Personality*

In the *Western Sahara* case the Court had to ascertain whether there were legal ties between the Territory of Western Sahara and 'the Mauritanian entity', which, it was explained by Mauritania, was the term used by the United Nations General Assembly

> to denote the cultural geographical and social entity which existed at the time [of Spanish colonization—i.e. around 1884] in the region of Western Sahara and within which the Islamic Republic of Mauritania was later to be created.[4]

It was supplied with considerable information about this entity, alternatively known as the 'Bilad Shinguitti', and described as 'a distinct human unit, characterized by a common language, way of life and religion'.[5] After examining the entity's legal nature, the Court concluded that 'it did not have the character of a personality or corporate entity distinct from the several emirates and tribes which composed it'; but this conclusion served as support for the finding that

> The proposition, therefore that the Bilad Shinguitti should be considered as having been a Mauritanian 'entity' *enjoying some form of sovereignty* in Western Sahara is not one that can be sustained.[6]

The question addressed was not: was the Bilad Shinguitti a State in international law?—but rather: Was the Bilad Shinguitti an entity capable of exercising sovereignty in international law? Applying the intertemporal principle, however, it may be questioned whether in 1884 there would have been any distinction between the two questions.

When addressing itself to the issue of legal personality, the Court first recalled the observation made in the *Reparation for Injuries* case that 'The subjects of law in any legal system are not necessarily identical in

[3] See Fitzmaurice in this *Year Book*, 27 (1959), p. 11; 30 (1953), pp. 1–3, *Collected Edition*, I, pp. 11, 132–4.

[4] *ICJ Reports*, 1975, p. 57, para. 131.

[5] *ICJ Reports*, 1975, p. 58, para. 132(*b*).

[6] *ICJ Reports*, 1975, p. 63, para. 149, emphasis added.

their nature or in the extent of their legal rights, and their nature depends upon the needs of the community'.[7] It continued:

Some criterion has, however, to be employed to determine in any particular case whether what confronts the law is or is not legally an 'entity'. The Court, moreover, notes that in the *Reparation* case the criterion which it applied was to enquire whether the United Nations Organization—the entity involved—was in 'such a position that it possesses, in regard to its Members, rights which it is entitled to ask them to respect' *(ibid.)*. In that Opinion, no doubt, the criterion was applied in a somewhat special context. Nevertheless, it expresses the essential test where a group, whether composed of States, of tribes or of individuals, is claimed to be a legal entity distinct from its members.[8]

The Court referred to the facts, which in its view showed the independence of the emirates and many of the tribes, whose people dwelt in the Sahara region, in relation to one another, and, 'despite some forms of common activity, the absence among them of any common institutions or organs, even of a quite minimal character'.

Accordingly, the Court is unable to find that the information before it provides any basis for considering the emirates and tribes which existed in the region to have constituted, in another phrase used by the Court in the *Reparation* case, 'an entity capable of availing itself of obligations incumbent upon its Members' *(ibid.)*. Whether the Mauritanian entity is described as the Bilad Shinguitti, or as the Shinguitti 'nation', as Mauritania suggests, or as some form of league or association, the difficulty remains that it did not have the character of a personality or corporate entity distinct from the several emirates and tribes which composed it.[9]

The latter quotation from the *Reparation* case is slightly confusing; presumably the Court was not drawing an analogy between the enforcement of obligations owed to an entity by the units composing it (i.e. in the case of the Bilad Shinguitti, the emirates and tribes), by analogy to the Members of the United Nations; it was considering the relations between the entity and other subjects of international law, outsiders, who happened however to be, in the case of the United Nations, *also* the units composing the entity.[10]

The Court went on to emphasize that its conclusion as to legal personality did not mean that there were no legal ties between the Territory and the Mauritanian entity, but merely that there were no ties of sovereignty. It was able to find that there were such ties, by treating the 'Mauritanian entity' not as a 'legal entity', but as an expression 'taken to denote the various tribes living in the territories of the Bilad Shinguitti

[7] *ICJ Reports*, 1949, p. 178, quoted in *ICJ Reports*, 1975, p. 63, para. 148.
[8] *ICJ Reports*, 1975, p. 63, para. 148.
[9] *ICJ Reports*, 1975, p. 63, para. 149.
[10] This is clear if one looks at the context; in the 1949 advisory opinion the Court was discussing the hypothesis of the Organization bringing a claim against one of its Members, not in respect of any breach of its obligations as a Member, but in respect of its responsibility as a State.

which are now comprised within the Islamic Republic of Mauritania',[11] considered, presumably, *ut singuli*. This also serves to emphasize, *a contrario*, the close link discerned by the Court between sovereignty and international legal personality, normally expressed in the character of being a State.

2. *Territorial and Political Sovereignty*

In the case concerning *Military and Paramilitary Activities in and against Nicaragua*, the Court discussed the principles of non-intervention and the prohibition of the use of the force against the background of the 'principle of respect for State sovereignty', with which, in its view, those principles were closely linked. In this connection it spelled out the spatial extent of the sovereignty of the State:

> The basic legal concept of State sovereignty in customary international law, expressed in, *inter alia*, Article 2, paragraph 1, of the United Nations Charter, extends to the internal waters and territorial sea of every State and to the air space above its territory.

In this respect it quoted the 1944 Chicago Convention on Civil Aviation, the 1958 Geneva Convention on the Territorial Sea, and the Montego Bay Convention, and added:

> The Court has no doubt that these prescriptions of treaty-law merely respond to firmly established and longstanding tenets of customary international law.[12]

The practical impact on the decision is that the Court condemned certain overflights of Nicaraguan territory by United States aircraft, and certain attacks on, and the mining of, Nicaraguan ports, as breaches of the obligation of the United States not to violate the sovereignty of Nicaragua.[13] Except in the case of the overflights, these acts were however also found to be unlawful as the use of force against another State; which leaves the relationship between the two principles not entirely clear. The Court stated that

> The effects of the principle of respect for territorial sovereignty inevitably overlap with those of the principles of the prohibition of the use of force and of non-intervention,[14]

but this observation refers only to the *effects* of the various principles. Is

[11] *ICJ Reports*, 1975, pp. 64–5, para. 152.

[12] *ICJ Reports*, 1986, p. 111, para. 212.

[13] *ICJ Reports*, 1986, pp. 52–3, para. 91; p. 112, para. 214; pp. 127–8, paras. 250–2; p. 147, para. 292(5) and (6). In paragraph 251 the Court also includes 'the assistance to the *contras*' as one of the acts which 'not only amount to an unlawful use of force, but also constitute infringements of the territorial sovereignty of Nicaragua'; but this is not reflected elsewhere in either the reasoning or the operative clause of the decision.

[14] *ICJ Reports*, 1986, p. 128, para. 251.

the use of force a special and more aggravated form of violation of sovereignty—in which case there would seem to have been no need to condemn the same acts under both headings? Or are these two distinct rules of law? It is difficult to conceive of a use of force which would not at the same time constitute a violation of the sovereignty of the victim State.

Infringement of sovereignty need not of course necessarily involve infringement of territory. In the *Nicaragua* case the Court also analysed the content of the principle of non-intervention in the internal or external affairs of other States. It deduced from this definition of the principle that

> A prohibited intervention must accordingly be one bearing on matters in which each State is permitted, by the principle of State sovereignty, to decide freely. One of these is the choice of a political, economic, social and cultural system, and the formulation of a foreign policy. Intervention is wrongful when it uses methods of coercion in regard to such choices, which must remain free ones.[15]

Similarly the Court observed that

> However the regime in Nicaragua be defined, adherence by a State to any particular doctrine does not constitute a violation of customary international law; to hold otherwise would make nonsense of the fundamental principle of State sovereignty, on which the whole of international law rests, and the freedom of choice of the political, social, economic and cultural system of a State.
>
> . . .
>
> Similar considerations apply to the criticisms expressed by the United States of the external policies and alliances of Nicaragua . . . it is sufficient to say that State sovereignty evidently extends to the area of its foreign policy, and that there is no rule of customary international law to prevent a State from choosing and conducting a foreign policy in co-ordination with that of another State.[16]

The fixing of a frontier by agreement is also clearly a matter of State sovereignty: in the *Territorial Dispute* case between Chad and Libya the Court observed that 'the fixing of a frontier depends on the will of the sovereign States directly concerned'.[17]

[15] *ICJ Reports*, 1986, p. 108, para. 205. It does not appear that this was intended as an exhaustive definition; forms of interference in internal affairs can be imagined which would not go so far as to seek to coerce the State in the formulation of *policy*, but merely to influence specific decisions. In its 1984 order indicating provisional measures, the Court had referred to 'the right to sovereignty *and* to political independence possessed by the Republic of Nicaragua'(*ICJ Reports*, 1984, p. 187, para. 41, subpara. 2), as though these were distinct; but too much importance should not be attached to these discrepancies of wording in a preliminary order issued as a matter of urgency.

[16] *ICJ Reports*, 1986, p. 133, paras. 263, 265; the reference is of course to the alleged Communist leanings of the Nicaraguan Government, which displeased the United States.

[17] *ICJ Reports*, 1994, p. 23, para. 45 (a case outside the period covered by these articles).

3. *Domestic Jurisdiction*[18]

The passage quoted above from the *Nicaragua* case irresistibly recalls Fitzmaurice's definition of the criterion for determining whether a matter is or is not one of domestic jurisdiction; in his view the issue

> turns simply on whether the matters involved are or are not the subject of international *obligations*, whether arising under a treaty or other international agreement, or under a rule of customary international law. Thus, matters of domestic jurisdiction might be said to comprise all matters (but only those) which are not the subject of some international obligation.[19]

If the issue is raised defensively, to prevent a particular matter being litigated, it is treated as a question of domestic jurisdiction; if it is raised offensively, in order to assert that another State has sought to interfere in such a matter, it is treated as a matter of intervention in the affairs of another State; but in either case what is really being raised is the scope of a State's sovereignty.

In the article quoted, Fitzmaurice dealt with the judgment at the preliminary objection stage of the *Right of Passage* case; soon after his article appeared, the Court gave judgment on the merits in that case, and ruled very much on the lines that he had suggested. In a comparatively brief treatment of the relevant objection raised by India,[20] it noted that Portugal was claiming a right of passage over Indian territory, and asserting the existence of a correlative obligation upon India; in support of its claims it was relying on a treaty, a bilateral practice, international custom and the principles of international law.

To contend that such a right of passage is one which can be relied upon as

[18] This question was dealt with by Fitzmaurice first under the main heading 'International Organizations and Tribunals': this *Year Book*, 29 (1952), pp. 34–37; *Collected Edition*, I, pp. 103–6; and later under the main heading 'General Principles and Sources of International Law': this *Year Book*, 35 (1959), pp. 204–14; *Collected Edition*, II, pp. 599–609; as he explained in the latter article, the matter has both a substantive and a procedural aspect. It seems convenient to treat the substantive aspect here in relation to the question of sovereignty, of which, it is suggested, the principle of domestic jurisdiction is an emanation. The procedural aspect may well call for comment in a later article; it was dealt with at length by G. Arangio-Ruiz in his 1984 General Course at the Hague Academy, 'Le Domaine réservé', *Recueil des cours*, 225 (1990–VI).

[19] This *Year Book*, 35 (1959), p. 204; *Collected Edition*, II, p. 599. It might of course be claimed, in relation to an obligation said to have been imposed by treaty, that such obligation was excluded by a reservation made to that treaty; but the question of the validity and scope of the reservation would, once again, be a matter of international law. If the reservation were to the jurisdictional clause of the treaty, the point would be covered by the principle of *la compétence de la compétence*; but see the problem raised by such a reservation in an advisory case: *Applicability of Article VI, Section 22, of the Convention on the Privileges and Immunities of the United Nations* (the '*Mazilu*' case), *ICJ Reports*, 1989, pp. 190–1.

[20] So brief, direct and to the point that one might wonder why the Court could not at the outset have applied what Fitzmaurice called the 'provisional principle' as had been urged at the preliminary objections stage by Judge Klaestad (*ICJ Reports*, 1957, p. 277), on the basis that, whether Portugal's contentions were or were not correct, they involved considerations of international law. The Court was however in 1960 speaking with a much fuller knowledge of what those contentions in fact were, and the nature of India's repudiation of them.

against India, to claim that such an obligation is binding upon India, to invoke, whether rightly or wrongly, such principles is to place oneself on the plane of international law . . . To decide upon the validity of those principles, upon the existence of such a right of Portugal as against India, upon such obligation of India towards Portugal, and upon the alleged failure to fulfil that obligation, does not fall exclusively within the jurisdiction of India.[21]

Matters of domestic jurisdiction may of course be intertwined with matters not of domestic jurisdiction; but the distinction continues to exist, and matters in the latter category are not attracted into the former category, so as to be immune to international jurisdiction. Thus in the case of the *United States Diplomatic and Consular Staff in Tehran*, Iran, in an informal communication to the Court, had asserted that the question of the embassy hostages formed only a 'marginal and secondary aspect of an overall problem', and that 'any examination of the numerous repercussions of the Islamic revolution of Iran is essentially and directly a matter within the national sovereignty of Iran'.[22] The Court, in its order indicating provisional measures, observed that

it is no doubt true that the Islamic revolution of Iran is a matter 'essentially and directly within the national sovereignty of Iran'; . . . however a dispute which concerns diplomatic and consular premises and the detention of internationally protected persons, and involves the interpretation or application of multilateral conventions codifying the international law governing diplomatic and consular relations, is one which by its very nature falls within international jurisdiction.[23]

An unexpected reference to domestic jurisdiction is to be found in the *Barcelona Traction* judgment, in the context of the question whether the injury to Belgian shareholders in the company was an infringement of rights. The Court considered that the rights of the shareholders to be referred to were the rights conferred by municipal law:

. . . international law has had to recognize the corporate entity as an institution created by States *in a domain essentially within their domestic jurisdiction*. This in turn requires that, whenever legal issues arise concerning the rights of States with regard to the treatment of companies and shareholders, as to which rights international law has not established its own rules, it has to refer to the relevant rules of municipal law.[24]

To regard the domain of legal corporations under the municipal law of States as 'essentially within their domestic jurisdiction' would seem to imply that no claim for injury to an alien resulting from the exercise of

[21] *ICJ Reports*, 1960, p. 33. Note the expression 'whether rightly or wrongly', which looks like an *ex post facto* consideration of the 'provisional principle'.

[22] Order on provisional measures, *ICJ Reports*, 1979, p. 15, para. 22.

[23] *ICJ Reports*, 1979, pp. 15–16, para. 25. In its judgment on the merits the Court noted that Iran had merely repeated its earlier observations on this point, and found it sufficient to 'recall and confirm its previous statement': *ICJ Reports*, 1980, p. 18, para. 34.

[24] *ICJ Reports*, 1970, pp. 32–3, para. 38, emphasis added.

the powers of the State in this domain would be receivable, which seems a doubtful proposition. It seems that the point the Court intended to make is no more than a factual one: the rules governing the creation, operation, and extinction of private-law corporations are necessarily matters of municipal law, because such corporations are the creation of municipal law.

Chapter II

Acquisition of Territory[24a]

Territory: an area occupied more or less exclusively by an animal or group of animals by means of repulsion through overt defense or advertisement.

Edward O. Wilson, *Sociobiology: The New Synthesis* 1975

1. *Occupation and* terra nullius

In the *Western Sahara* case in 1975 the Court was invited to give an advisory opinion on, first of all, the question 'Was Western Sahara (Rio de Oro and Sakiet El Hamra) at the time of colonization by Spain a territory belonging to no one (*terra nullius*)?' The Court decided on the facts that the 'time of colonization by Spain' referred to in the question was the period beginning in the year 1884. It then observed that the words of the question clearly

have to be interpreted by reference to the law in force at that period. The expression '*terra nullius*' was a legal term of art employed in connection with 'occupation' as one of the accepted legal methods of acquiring sovereignty over territory. 'Occupation' being legally an original means of peaceably acquiring sovereignty otherwise than by cession or succession, it was a cardinal condition of a valid 'occupation' that the territory should be *terra nullius*—a territory belonging to no one—at the time of the act alleged to constitute the 'occupation' (cf. *Legal Status of Eastern Greenland, P.C.I.J. Series A/B, No.* 53, pp. 44 f. and 63 f.). In the view of the Court, therefore, a determination that Western Sahara was a '*terra nullius*' at the time of colonization by Spain would be possible only if it were established that at that time the territory belonged to no one in the sense that it was then open to acquisition through the legal process of 'occupation'.[25]

[24a] A means of acquisition of territory which did not fall to be considered by the Court during the period under consideration was accretion; the effect of the shifting of a river-bed was considered by the Chamber in the *Land, Island and Maritime Frontier Dispute*, but the point was found by the Chamber to be, in the circumstances of the case, one of Spanish colonial law, not international law: *ICJ Reports*, 1992, p. 547, para. 311.

[25] *ICJ Reports*, 1975, p. 39, para. 79.

Since the Court was dealing with a period almost a century before, it was appropriate to recall the principle of intertemporal law; but the emphasis on that aspect given by the consistent use of the past tense in the passage quoted may give the impression that the Court was impliedly indicating a view that acquisition of territory by occupation was no longer possible in 1975.

This, it is suggested, was not the Court's intention, even though by the date of its opinion there was very little scope left for the practical application of the concept of 'occupation', there being virtually no land undiscovered, and practically all the land areas of the world being under the sovereignty of some State.[26] Its emphasis on the point was in the first place explained by its rejection of a contention advanced during the proceedings[27] as to the interpretation of the question. It had been suggested that, since the Court was asked, if it concluded that the territory had not been *terra nullius*, to say what were the legal ties between the Territory and the Kingdom of Morocco and 'the Mauritanian entity', the meaning of *terra nullius* was a territory not having legal ties with either of those entities (or any other sovereign State). As to the use of the past tense, what the Court probably was anxious to do was to avoid giving the impression, through its application of 1884 law, that there had been no change in the meantime in the definition of *terra nullius*; and to make clear in particular that the possibility, recognized in 1884, of acquiring territory by occupation, even if it was not wholly empty of population,[28] was no longer in harmony with current law, with its emphasis on the right of self-determination of peoples.

This clarification was unnecessary for the purposes of the advisory opinion, since the Court found that Western Sahara had, in 1884, not been a *terra nullius* even according to the contemporary definition:

Whatever differences of opinion there may have been among jurists, the State practice of the relevant period indicates that territories inhabited by tribes or peoples having a social or political organization were not regarded as *terrae nullius* . . .

In the present instance, the information furnished to the Court shows that at the time of colonization Western Sahara was inhabited by peoples which, if

[26] There still remains the theoretical possibility of acquisition by occupation of territory which has been abandoned, but if this ever occurs, it is very difficult to prove.

[27] Principally by Spain, but traceable also in the arguments of Morocco and Mauritania: cf. separate opinion of Judge de Castro, *ICJ Reports*, 1975, p. 134.

[28] On this point, note the views of Judge Dillard in his separate opinion: he attached considerable importance to the fact that the Spanish agreements with the local chiefs were treaties of protection, and apparently might have been ready to find that, under 1884 law, the territory was *terra nullius*, had a different form of agreement been employed—despite the presence of socially organized tribes in the area: *ICJ Reports*, 1975, p. 124.

nomadic, were socially and politically organized in tribes and under chiefs competent to represent them.[29]

Its political significance should not however be under-rated.[30]

Similarly the Court took pains to emphasize that the practice of entering into agreements with local rulers, which had been much criticized as open to great abuses in view of the different degrees of sophistication on each side, and consequent misunderstanding of the true effects of such agreements, was not a mere 'occupation', simply over-riding the titles of the local population.

On occasion, it is true, the word 'occupation' was used in a non-technical sense

> denoting simply acquisition of sovereignty; but that did not signify that the acquisition of sovereignty through such agreements with authorities of the country was regarded as an 'occupation' of a '*terra nullius*' in the proper sense of these terms. On the contrary, such agreements with local rulers, whether or not considered as an actual 'cession' of the territory, were regarded as derivative roots of title, and not original titles obtained by occupation of *terra nullius*.[31]

The Court declined to go further into the question of the nature and legal value of agreements between a State and local chiefs, since in its view the questions put for advisory opinion did not require it 'to pronounce upon the legal character or the legality of the titles which led to Spain becoming the administering Power of Western Sahara'.[32]

2. *Acquisitive Prescription*

In the *Right of Passage* case between Portugal and India, the central issue was whether India, by restricting passage between the Portuguese colony of Goa and Portuguese enclaves within Indian territory further inland, had acted in breach of an established legal right of passage. India however based its defence on (*inter alia*) a challenge to the existence of Portuguese sovereignty over the enclaves themselves. Portuguese title to these rested initially on a 1779 Treaty between itself and the Maratha ruler of the relevant part of India, coupled with decrees issued by the ruler in 1783 and 1785, assigning certain villages to the Portuguese. India however contended that the effect of the Treaty and the decrees was not to transfer sovereignty over the villages to Portugal, but only to confer,

[29] *ICJ Reports*, 1975, p. 39, paras. 80–1. The Court also noted that Spain had not in 1884 purported to acquire the territory by occupation, but relied rather on agreements with chiefs of the local tribes (ibid.).

[30] Note the approval given to paragraph 80 of the advisory opinion in the separate opinion of Judge Ammoun, a fierce (and somewhat undiscriminating) opponent of the whole concept of *terra nullius*: *ICJ Reports*, 1975, pp. 86–7.

[31] *ICJ Reports*, 1975, p. 39, para. 80.

[32] *ICJ Reports*, 1975, pp. 39–40, para. 82.

'with respect to the villages, a revenue grant of the value of 12,000 rupees per annum called a *jagir* or *saranjam*'.[33] This grant entailed the right to collect revenues from the villages, and the right (and perhaps the duty) to put down revolt or rebellion in the villages, apparently in exercise of a delegated authority from the Maratha ruler. The Court upheld this contention, with the result that during the period of Maratha rule, Portugal's rights did not amount to sovereignty. The subsequent history of the villages, and the legal implications, were stated by the Court as follows:

the situation underwent a change with the advent of the British as sovereign of that part of the country in place of the Marathas. The British found the Portuguese in occupation of the villages and exercising full and exclusive administrative authority over them. They accepted the situation as they found it and left the Portuguese in occupation of, and in exercise of exclusive authority over, the villages. The Portuguese held themselves out as sovereign over the villages. The British did not, as successors of the Marathas, themselves claim sovereignty, nor did they accord express recognition of Portuguese sovereignty, over them. The exclusive authority of the Portuguese over the villages was never brought in question. Thus Portuguese sovereignty over the villages was recognized by the British in fact and by implication and was subsequently tacitly recognized by India. As a consequence the villages comprised in the Maratha grant acquired the character of Portuguese enclaves within Indian territory.[34]

There is a certain ambiguity in the last sentence: what was the relevance of India's tacit recognition? In other words, did the villages 'acquire the character of Portuguese enclaves' before or after the independence of India? It seems that the Court's view was that by that date Portugal had already acquired sovereignty over them against the British, so that India's title by succession was already subject to the existence of that Portuguese sovereignty; on that basis any subsequent tacit recognition could only be confirmatory.[35] The actual process of acquisition of the territory of the villages is difficult to pin down in legal terms: Portugal's continued occupation against the British must presumably be equated with prescription, but there is the unusual feature

[33] *ICJ Reports*, 1960, p. 38.

[34] *ICJ Reports*, 1960, p. 39. It should be noted that while the Court based the existence of the right of passage to the enclaves on a bilateral local custom which had come into existence between Portugal and the successive territorial sovereigns, it treated the existence of Portuguese sovereignty over the villages as a preliminary question, on the basis that such a right as was claimed could not come into existence if the enclaves to which access was required were not the sovereign territory of Portugal. The finding in favour of sovereignty was based on the reasoning in the passage quoted, and not on the idea of bilateral custom. The possibility does not seem to have been considered that what was acquired prescriptively was sovereignty over the enclaves, *coupled with* an appropriate right of passage.

[35] Thus when the Court, having thus established Portuguese sovereignty over the enclaves, turned to the asserted right of passage, it observed that it 'must have regard to what happened during the British and post-British periods' (*ICJ Reports*, 1960, p. 39); if sovereignty was only acquired after Indian independence, the British period would have been irrelevant—and the time-scale of the exercise of the right would probably have been too short.

that Portugal's actual occupation and its exercise of at least some administrative authority were attributable to a lesser title, so that there was no open adverse possession, except to the extent that Portugal may have exercised wider authority than was accorded it in the 1779 Treaty and the Maratha decrees. It seems also highly probable that the British were not aware of the details, at least, of the events of 1779–1785, and simply assumed that Portugal already had full sovereignty over the villages, by grant or cession from the Marathas.

The situation nevertheless seems to fall within the definition of prescription given in the latest edition of a well-known and authoritative work of reference:

> the acquisition of sovereignty over a territory through continuous and undisturbed exercise of sovereignty over it during such a period as is necessary to create under the influence of historical development the general conviction that the present condition of things is in conformity with international order.[36]

The case in fact serves to emphasize the weakness of analogies between the operation of prescription in relation to territory in international law, and municipal law concepts of adverse possession which has generally to be asserted *nec vi, nec clam, nec precario*. The precariousness (in the technical sense) of the Portuguese title to the villages and the fact that it involved mere delegated authority were not elements which prevented the simple running of time, and the lack of protest or objection from the 'true' sovereign by succession, from consolidating the Portuguese possession and exercise of authority into full sovereignty.[37]

An alternative characterization is that of 'novation', defined by Verzijl as 'the gradual transformation of a right *in territorio alieno*, for example, a lease, or a pledge, or certain concessions of a territorial nature, into full sovereignty without any formal or unequivocal instrument to that effect intervening'; but to affix this label to the process does not assist in determining the conditions in which it is legally possible for a State which has been given an inch to take an ell.[38]

[36] *Oppenheim's International Law* (9th edn., by Jennings and Watts, 1992), vol. 1, p. 706. The case is mentioned as an example of prescription in *Droit international* (Nguyen Quoc Dinh) (5th edn., by Daillier and Pellet, 1994), p. 511, § 354, though apparently on the basis that the Court used the term in its judgment, which in fact it did not.

[37] 'Prescription . . . comprehends both a possession of which the origin is unclear or disputed, and an adverse possession which is in origin demonstrably unlawful': Jennings, *The Acquisition of Territory in International Law* (Manchester, 1963), p. 23.

[38] Verzijl, *International Law in Historical Perspective*, vol. 3, p. 384, referring *inter alia* to the *Right of Passage* case, this being one where the Court 'in my opinion in fact invented' such a process of tacit novation. Brownlie, *Principles of Public International Law* (4th edn., 1990), pp. 162–3, adopts Verzijl's category, and links it with acquisition, prescription, acquiescence, recognition and estoppel.

3. *Succession and the Principle of* uti possidetis[38a]

In the *Frontier Dispute* case, the parties had requested the Chamber to decide the matter on the basis of, in particular, the 'principle of the intangibility of frontiers inherited from colonization', and the Chamber took this as text for a lengthy disquisition on the subject of the principle of *uti possidetis*. After noting the origins of the principle in Spanish America, the Chamber declared:

Nevertheless the principle is not a special rule which pertains solely to one specific system of international law. It is a general principle, which is logically connected with the phenomenon of the obtaining of independence, wherever it occurs. Its obvious purpose is to prevent the independence and stability of new States being endangered by fratricidal struggles provoked by the challenging of frontiers following the withdrawal of the administering power.[39]

As a matter of legal history, this statement cannot but prompt doubts. In the first place, the purpose of the principle mentioned by the Chamber was only one of the original purposes in Latin America; another, if not the primary purpose, was, as pointed out by Judge *ad hoc* Abi-Saab in his separate opinion,

a defensive purpose towards the rest of the world, in the form of an outright denial that there was any land without a sovereign (or *terra nullius*) in the decolonized territories, even in unexplored areas or those beyond the control of the colonizers.[40]

Secondly, the Chamber passes over in silence the fact that in Latin America there were two rival versions of the principle: that of the *uti possidetis juris*, contended for by the former Spanish possessions, and that of the *uti possidetis de facto*, advanced by Brazil.[41] Thirdly, in Africa, the principle enshrined in the Cairo resolution was applicable frequently, if not primarily, in relations between new States which had not formerly belonged to the same colonizer—precisely the situation which in Latin America had not been capable of resolution by a single recognized principle.[42]

The question of stability of boundaries between colonial possessions of two different powers, fixed by treaty between them, is strictly a quite separate issue from the application of the principle of *uti possidetis*. The

[38a] The first of the present series of articles contained some remarks on this matter: this *Year Book*, 60 (1989), pp. 105–6.

[39] *ICJ Reports*, 1986, p. 565, para. 20.

[40] *ICJ Reports*, 1986, p. 661. See also the arbitral award of the Swiss Federal Council of 24 March 1922, between Colombia and Venezuela, *Reports of International Arbitral Awards*, vol. 1, p. 228, quoted in the judgment in the *Land, Island and Maritime Frontier Dispute, ICJ Reports*, 1992, p. 387, para. 42.

[41] See the separate opinion of Judge Torres Bernárdez in the *Land, Island and Maritime Frontier Dispute, ICJ Reports*, 1992, pp. 633 ff., particularly foot of p. 635.

[42] As was pointed out by the Arbitral Tribunal formed to deal with the maritime delimitation dispute between Guinea-Bissau and Senegal: decision, para. 61. Cf. also Abi-Saab, 'La pérennité des frontières en droit international', *Relations internationales*, 64 (1990), pp. 347–8.

determination and the stability of the boundary is there ensured by the rules of succession of *States* in respect of boundary treaties; whereas the primary role of *uti possidetis* is to provide a criterion for the creation of a new international frontier, namely the transformation of the old internal administrative boundary. The *Temple of Preah Vihear* case, for example, related to the interpretation of such a treaty, and thus not to the application of *uti possidetis*;[43] nor, strictly, did a case concerning a maritime boundary, the *Continental Shelf* case between Tunisia and Libya. There the Court found that for purposes of delimitation of the continental shelf between the parties, 'the undisputed land frontier between the Parties established by a convention becomes a circumstance of considerable relevance'.[44] It therefore examined the history of that frontier, which dated from a period before the independence of the two countries, and could be traced back to a 1910 Convention between the Bey of Tunis and the Ottoman Empire.[45] No mention was made of the principle of *uti possidetis*, but the Court stated that the boundary 'exemplifies the principle declared in the 1964 Cairo Resolution of the Organization of African Unity', and noted that 'This rule of continuity *ipso jure* of boundary and territorial treaties was later embodied in the 1978 Vienna Convention on Succession of States in respect of Treaties'.[46]

For a boundary treaty to bind a successor State in respect of maritime boundaries, it must be established that the treaty did in fact deal with maritime boundaries. It was argued by Libya that 'it was the effect of the 1910 Boundary Convention, which defined the land frontier, to delimit also the maritime areas off Ras Ajdir' (the point at which that frontier reached the coast), but the Court rejected this submission. The Court was however ready to treat as one of the 'relevant criteria to be taken into account in selecting a line of delimitation calculated to ensure an equitable solution' (*inter alia*) 'the concept of prolongation of the general direction of the land boundary'.[47]

Since the principle of *uti possidetis* (or at least that of *uti possidetis juris*) requires that pre-independence administrative divisions be respected,

[43] *Contra*, Brownlie, *Principles of Public International Law* (4th edn., 1990), p. 135, n. 50.

[44] *ICJ Reports*, 1982, p. 65, para. 82.

[45] It later appeared, when the question of the frontiers of Libya was directly before the Court in the *Territorial Dispute* between Libya and Chad, that the matter was not quite so simple, particularly as regards the effect of a 1955 Franco-Libyan Treaty: see the decision in that case, *ICJ Reports*, 1994, p. 18, para. 30, and pp. 20 ff., paras. 37 ff.

[46] *ICJ Reports*, 1982, p. 66, para. 84. It was strongly urged by Guinea-Bissau in its dispute with Senegal that the rule of succession to land boundaries established by treaty did not apply to maritime boundaries, but the Arbitral Tribunal was unable to accept this: decision, paras. 63–6. Arbitrator Bedjaoui put in a strong dissent on this point.

[47] *ICJ Reports*, 1982, p. 85, para. 120. Judge Jiménez de Aréchaga, in his separate opinion, drew attention to documents suggesting that when the land boundary was modified, by a subsequent treaty, no new line was claimed seaward from the endpoint of the land boundary: ibid., p. 127, para. 91.

some reference to the pre-independence legal position will be required. For the Chamber seised of the *Frontier Dispute* between Burkina Faso and Mali this was a sensitive point, since the pre-independence law was evidently that of the colonial power, and the Chamber was clearly anxious to avoid anything that might be interpreted as a defence or approval of colonialism. It therefore found it necessary to include in the judgment a 'clarification . . . as concerns the application of French *droit d'outre-mer*':

By becoming independent, a new State acquires sovereignty with the territorial base and boundaries left to it by the colonial power. This is part of the ordinary machinery of State succession. International law—and consequently the principle of *uti possidetis*—applies to the new State (as a State) not with retroactive effect, but immediately and from that moment onwards. It applies to the State *as it is*, i.e. to the 'photograph'of the territorial situation then existing. The principle of *uti possidetis* freezes the territorial title; it stops the clock, but does not put back the hands. Hence international law does not effect any renvoi to the law established by the colonizing State, nor indeed to any legal rule unilaterally established by any State whatever; French law—especially legislation enacted by France for its colonies and *territoires d'outre-mer*—may play a role not in itself (as if there were a sort of *continuum juris*, a legal relay between such law and international law), but only as one factual element among others, or as evidence indicative of what has been called the 'colonial heritage', i.e., the 'photograph of the territory' at the critical date.[48]

It may be thought that it was hardly necessary to emphasize that the principle of *uti possidetis* implies neither retroactive effect to a time *before* the moment of independence,[49] nor any continued application of colonial law as such after independence. But it is impossible to escape the fact, whether the process be referred to as one of *renvoi* or not, that the boundaries 'photographed' at the moment of independence are what they are and where they are through the operation of the law of the colonial power, not as matters of 'pure' fact. As the Chamber seised of the *Land, Island and Maritime Frontier Dispute* was to observe, more robustly:

It should be recalled that when the principle of the *uti possidetis juris* is involved, the *jus* referred to is not international law but the constitutional or administrative law of the pre-independence sovereign, in this case Spanish colonial law . . . .[50]

[48] *ICJ Reports*, 1986, p. 568, para. 30, emphasis original. The motivation behind this paragraph is clear from the separate opinion of Judge *ad hoc* Abi-Saab, who refers to it with approval, adding that 'there can therefore be no question of even circuitously finding in contemporary international law any retroactive legitimation whatever of colonialism as an institition': ibid., p. 659.

[49] Yet, as the Chamber observed in the *Land, Island and Maritime Frontier* case, '*uti possidetis juris* is essentially a retrospective principle, investing as international boundaries administrative limits intended originally for quite other purposes': *ICJ Reports*, 1992, p. 388, para. 43.

[50] *ICJ Reports*, 1992, p. 559, para. 333. In view of the greater antiquity of the decolonization process in Latin America, there was less embarrassment in emphasizing the importance of the colonial law.

CHAPTER III

LAND FRONTIERS

Glendower: Come, here's the map: shall we divide our right
According to our threefold order ta'en?

William Shakespeare, *Henry IV, Part I*, Act III, Sc. 1.

1. *Fully Delimited Frontiers Not Essential*

In the *North Sea Continental Shelf* cases, in the unlikely context of an examination of the law relating to maritime delimitation, the Court had occasion to restate the proposition that the existence of a State, while dependent on (*inter alia*) the possession of a territory, does not require that all the territorial boundaries be defined.

> The appurtenance of a given area, considered as an entity, in no way governs the precise delimitation of its boundaries, any more than uncertainty as to boundaries can affect territorial rights. There is for instance no rule that the land frontiers of a State must be fully delimited and defined, and often in various places and for long periods they are not . . . [51]

It may be noted also that when in the *Western Sahara* case the Court had to ascertain whether there were legal ties between the Territory of Western Sahara and 'the Mauritanian entity', and concluded, after examining the legal nature of this entity, that 'it did not have the character of a personality or corporate entity distinct from the several emirates and tribes which composed it',[52] the Court was not influenced, in reaching that conclusion, by the fact that, as a result of the nomadic nature of the tribes which composed it, the boundaries of the Bilad Shinguitti were very far from clear and determinable.

Similarly in the *Territorial Dispute* between Chad and Libya, it was contended by Libya that at the time of Libyan independence, and at the time of the conclusion of a Franco-Libyan Treaty of 1955, the effect of which was the key element of the case, the only frontiers of Libya which had been created by international instruments binding on Libya were frontiers which related to territories other than those in issue in the case. In the area essentially in dispute, there was, according to Libya, only a line deriving from a Franco-British Declaration 'delimiting spheres of influence'.[53] It was never suggested that the absence of a frontier affected

[51] *ICJ Reports*, 1969, p. 32, para. 46, quoting *Monastery of Saint Naoum*, *PCIJ*, Series B, No. 9, at p. 10.

[52] *ICJ Reports*, 1975, p. 63, para. 149.

[53] *ICJ Reports*, 1994, p. 22, para. 44.

Libya's existence as a State, or that its accession to independence necessarily converted this line into a frontier.[54] The Court did observe in its judgment that 'to "define" a territory is to define its frontiers',[55] but this was in the context of a (somewhat strained) interpretation of a provision of the 1955 Treaty as indicating that the purpose of the Treaty was to define Libya's frontiers.

2. *Distinction between Terrestrial and Maritime Boundaries*

The Special Agreement by which the Court was seised of the *Gulf of Maine* case asked that a Chamber of the Court decide 'What is the course of the single maritime boundary (*frontière maritime unique*) that divides the continental shelf and fisheries zones . . . '. The Chamber in its judgment expressed doubt as to this terminology, at least in French:

A la rigueur, une question pourrait surgir du fait de l'emploi, dans le texte français du compromis, des termes 'frontière maritime', lesquels pourraient évoquer l'idèe erronée d'une véritable frontière entre deux souverainetés. Mais il est évident, pour la Chambre, que la tâche dont elle se trouve chargée ne concerne que la délimitation entre les différentes formes de juridiction partielle, à savoir entre les 'droits souverains' que le droit international . . . reconnaît aujourd'hui aux Etats côtiers . . . [56]

The French text of the judgment is the authoritative text; the English translation at this point uses the French term '*frontière maritime*', adding in brackets the English version used in the Special Agreement ('maritime boundary'). The problem identified by the Chamber does not seem to arise in relation to the English term 'boundary': it may be observed that in the *Aegean Sea Continental Shelf* case in 1978 the Court had defined the act of delimiting the continental shelves of neighbouring States as being 'to establish the boundary or boundaries (*la limite ou les limites*) between neighbouring States, that is to say, to draw the exact line or lines where the extensions in space of the sovereign powers and rights of Greece meet those of Turkey'.[57] This terminology seems as appropriate for a terrestrial frontier as for a maritime line of delimitation.

For the Chamber, this was not however a mere matter of looseness of terminology, but a question of substance, since it proceeded to draw the conclusion that

The rights of third States in the areas in question cannot *therefore* be in any way affected by the delimitation which the Chamber is required to effect.[58]

[54] It was contended by Chad, and denied by Libya, that Libya had, subsequently to independence, acquiesced in the line as a frontier, thus 'consolidating' it; but this contention was not examined by the Court.

[55] *ICJ Reports*, 1994, p. 26, para. 52.

[56] *ICJ Reports*, 1984, p. 265, para. 19.

[57] *ICJ Reports*, 1978, p. 35, para. 85.

[58] Ibid., emphasis added.

The implication is clearly that if the Chamber had been requested to trace an actual *frontière*, and assuming that it had the power to do so, the line drawn would have been opposable to third States, whereas a mere delimitation of sovereign rights over maritime areas would not have been so opposable.[59]

Reserving for the present the question of the *erga omnes* effect of a land frontier, the dictum quoted may be contrasted with the attitude of the Court in the following year to the problem of the interests of Italy in the *Continental Shelf (Libya/Malta)* case. The Court there was asked to delimit the areas of continental shelf which 'appertained' to each of the parties; the Court referred to Article 59 of the Statute, and continued:

> If therefore the decision is to be stated in absolute terms, in the sense of permitting the delimitation of the areas of shelf which 'appertain' to the Parties, as distinct from the areas to which one of the Parties has shown a better title than the other, but which might nevertheless prove to 'appertain' to a third State if the Court had jurisdiction to enquire into the entitlement of that third State, the decision must be limited to a geographical area in which no such claims exist.[60]

The rights whose geographical extent was to be defined were however the same in each case, and it is not clear how the difference in wording of the two special agreements could have affected the matter.[61] It therefore appears that in 1985 the Court rejected the distinction drawn by the *Gulf of Maine* Chamber between a *frontière*, effective against third States, and a delimitation of the extent of maritime rights, sovereign or otherwise, which could not affect the rights of third States. The two types of boundary were rendered equivalent in effect by up-grading the maritime boundary to the rank of a *frontière*, which was taken to be effective *erga omnes*, and which could therefore not be drawn without taking account of the claims or interests of other States in the area. (Whether this was a correct assessment of the effect of a territorial frontier is a point to be examined in a moment.)

[59] In the arbitration between Guinea-Bissau and Senegal, Guinea-Bissau argued similarly 'qu'il était illégitime d'assimiler les délimitations maritimes aux frontières terrestres', in order to contend that successor States were not bound by such delimitations. The Tribunal rejected this contention (decision, para. 63), as did Arbitrator Bedjaoui (dissenting opinion annexed to decision, p. 22), who disagreed with his colleagues on other grounds.

[60] *ICJ Reports*, 1985, p. 25, para. 21. The Court did in fact express its judgment in terms of areas 'appertaining' to each Party, and thus, according to its own terminology, in 'absolute' terms, having therefore limited its geographical reach to areas where no claim had been made by Italy. This has of course the interesting implication that a State can have no rights over maritime areas beyond the areas to which it has laid claim, despite the recognized rule, codified in Article 2, paragraph 3, of the 1958 Continental Shelf Convention, that 'The rights of the coastal State over the continental shelf do not depend on occupation, effective or notional, or on any express proclamation'. What would have been the position if Italy had made no continental shelf claims at all?

[61] The *Gulf of Maine* special agreement referred to the boundary between the continental shelf and fisheries zones 'of' Canada and the US, which must surely mean the shelf and zones which 'appertained' to those States.

A different interpretation of the *Libya/Malta* judgment was offered a year later by the Chamber in the *Frontier Dispute* case between Burkina Faso and Mali. Dealing, as explained below, with the problem whether it could draw a frontier between the two parties right up to what would in effect be a tripoint with Niger, not a party to the case, it referred to the position taken up by the Court in the *Libya/Malta* case, and distinguished 'the process by which a court determines the line of a land boundary between two States' from 'the process by which it identifies the principles and rules applicable to the delimitation of the continental shelf'.[62]

The legal considerations which have to be taken into account in determining the location of the land boundary between parties are in no way dependent on the position of the boundary between the territory of either of those parties and the territory of a third State, even where, as in the present case, the rights in question for all three States derive from one and the same predecessor State. On the other hand, in continental shelf delimitations, an agreement between the parties which is perfectly valid and binding on the treaty level may, when the relations between the parties and a third State are taken into consideration, prove to be contrary to the rules of international law governing the continental shelf.[63]

The Chamber here refers to the equidistance line agreed between Denmark and the Netherlands 'over the head' of the Federal Republic of Germany in the *North Sea Continental Shelf* cases, as to which the Court found that 'its validity *erga omnes* including the Federal Republic . . . presupposes both the delimitation and the validity' of equidistance boundaries to be drawn by Denmark and the Netherlands with the Federal Republic.[64] The Chamber therefore concludes that

a court dealing with a request for the delimitation of a continental shelf must decline, even if so authorized by the disputant parties, to rule upon rights relating to areas in which third States have such claims as may contradict the legal considerations—especially in regard to equitable principles—which would have formed the basis of its decision.[65]

The distinction is a subtle one—perhaps over-subtle. The idea appears to be that if Niger had been a party to the proceedings, the Chamber might have fixed the endpoint of the Burkina Faso/Mali frontier differently, in order to respect the rights of Niger; but that otherwise Niger's claims and interests would not have affected the course of the line up to that point. In the context of a continental shelf delimitation, on the other hand, knowledge of the claims, and ascertainment of the rights, of a third State might affect not merely the extent of the delimitation line, but the

[62] *ICJ Reports*, 1986, p. 578, para. 47.
[63] *ICJ Reports*, 1986, p. 578, para. 47.
[64] *ICJ Reports*, 1969, p. 20, para. 14; pp. 27–8, paras. 35–6.
[65] *ICJ Reports*, 1986, p. 578, para. 47.

legal basis on which it was to be drawn, and thus its whole position. While there is much to be said for this distinction, what is perhaps less convincing is the idea that in this regard there is a difference between the areas of shelf claimed only by the two parties before the court and areas in which a third State also has claims, since it could apparently also be the case that the position of the boundary line of the third State's rights in the triply disputed area might be relevant for the determination of the line in the area subject only to the two-sided dispute.

3. *The* erga omnes *Character of a Territorial Frontier*

It is sometimes said that, since the course of a territorial boundary is a matter to be determined by the two adjacent States, 'in this sense, the two adjacent States create an objective situation which is valid *erga omnes*'.[66] It is possibly this way of expressing the point that the *Gulf of Maine* Chamber had in mind when emphasizing that it was not called upon to fix a *frontière.* A boundary treaty is however only effective *erga omnes* to the same extent as is any other bilateral treaty which deals solely with matters entirely within the sphere of action of the two contracting States: if two States conclude a treaty providing for cultural exchanges, or reciprocal rights of establishment, it is not so much that such a treaty is valid against non-party States as that there is no point of contact between those States and the treaty.[67] If a territorial boundary is fixed by agreement between two adjacent States in a region in which a third State has territorial claims, the agreement is clearly non-opposable to that third State.

This evident truth emerges from the decision of the Chamber in the *Frontier Dispute* case between Burkina Faso and Mali. The area in which the Chamber was asked to define the frontier between the parties bordered to the east on the territory of Niger, so that the endpoint of the frontier would be, in effect, a tripoint; but there had never been any agreement between the three States as to its position, and even the extent of Niger's claims was unascertained. Mali therefore argued that that tripoint 'cannot be determined by the two Parties without Niger's agreement, nor can it be determined by the Chamber, which may not affect the rights of a third State not a party to the proceedings',[68] it concluded that the line should stop before reaching the area of possible claims of Niger, rather as the Libya/Malta maritime delimitation line had

[66] Bothe, 'Boundaries', in R. Bernhardt (ed.), *Encyclopedia of Public International Law*, vol. 10 (1987), p. 22; cf. *Oppenheim's International Law* (9th edn., by Jennings and Watts), vol. 1, p. 669.

[67] This is clear if one considers the situation if, exceptionally, there *is* some such point of contact: if for example the effect of the treaty is to produce a situation in conflict with a prior treaty with the other State.

[68] *ICJ Reports*, 1986, p. 576, para. 44.

done. Burkina Faso disagreed, but its arguments in reply to Mali's point seem semantic rather than helpful.[69]

The Chamber's solution to the problem was elegant. After referring to the protection afforded the neighbouring State by Article 59 of the Statute, it observed:

> The Parties could at any time have concluded an agreement for the delimitation of their frontier, according to whatever perception they might have had of it, and an agreement of this kind, although legally binding upon them by virtue of the principle *pacta sunt servanda*, would not be opposable to Niger. A judicial decision, which 'is simply an alternative to the direct and friendly settlement' of the dispute between the Parties (*P.C.I.J., Series A, No. 22*, p. 13), merely substitutes for the solution stemming directly from their shared intention, the solution arrived at by a court under the mandate which they have given it. In both instances, the solution only has legal and binding effect as between the States which have accepted it, either directly or as a consequence of having accepted the court's jurisdiction to decide the case. Accordingly, on the supposition that the Chamber's judgment specifies a point which it finds to be the easternmost point of the frontier, there would be nothing to prevent Niger from claiming rights, vis-à-vis either of the Parties, to territories lying west of the point identified by the Chamber.[70]

The Chamber however then proceeded to complicate matters, first by distinguishing the case of a maritime delimitation (see above), and then by continuing:

> The Chamber is in fact required, not to fix a tripoint, which would necessitate the consent of all States concerned, but to ascertain, in the light of the evidence which the Parties have made available to it, how far the frontier which they inherited from the colonial power extends. Certainly such a finding implies, as a logical corollary, both that the territory of a third State lies beyond the end-point, and that the Parties have exclusive sovereign rights up to that point. However, this is no more than a twofold presumption which underlies any boundary situation. This presumption remains in principle irrebuttable in the judicial context of a given case, in the sense that neither of the disputant parties, having contended that it possesses a common frontier with the other as far as a specific point, can change its position to rely on the alleged existence of sovereignty pertaining to a third State; but this presumption does not thereby create a ground of opposability outside that context and against the third State. Indeed, this is the whole point of the above-quoted Article 59 of the Statute.[71]

[69] It contended that although the endpoint of the Chamber's line would be a tripoint, 'the determination of that point will be a consequence and not the object of the Chamber's judgment' (*ICJ Reports*, 1986, p. 576, para. 44).

[70] *ICJ Reports*, 1986, pp. 577–8, para. 45. This point is expressed hypothetically since the passage appears in a preliminary paragraph of the judgment, before the Chamber has begun on the actual task of drawing the line.

[71] *ICJ Reports*, 1986, p. 579, para. 49.

The obscurity of this passage lies primarily in the uncertainty as to when the 'presumption' referred to arises: in the first sentence, it appears that it is a presumption attaching to a judicial finding, one which it is not open to the parties to the case to question, but which is no more than a rebuttable presumption as against a third State. The third sentence however seems to suggest that there is a presumption (or perhaps two distinct presumptions) that an area attributed by either party, either to itself or to the other party, is not in fact territory of the third State; and the party which has so claimed cannot go back on its assertion. Presumably the case envisaged is that in which State A's alleged titles to a particular area are shown by its opponent, State B, to be unsound; State A cannot then contend, as an alternative, that the area belongs to State C. Is it then necessary for State B to produce *some* proof of a conflicting title? or could a court deduce simply from the invalidity of State A's title that the territory appertained to State B? The Chamber seems to be saying that a court could so act, *even* where there was a possibility that the territory in question appertained to State C.[72] However, the whole passage lacks sufficient clarity for any firm conclusion to be based upon it.

4. *The Intangibility of Land Frontiers*

In the *Temple of Preah Vihear* case,[73] the Court observed that

> In general, when two countries establish a frontier between them, one of the primary objects is to achieve stability and finality. This is impossible if the line so established can, at any moment, and on the basis of a continuously available process, be called in question, and its rectification claimed, whenever any inaccuracy by reference to a clause in the parent treaty is discovered. Such a process could continue indefinitely, and finality would never be reached so long as possible errors still remained to be discovered. Such a frontier, far from being stable, would be completely precarious.[74]

This is of course the philosophy underlying the recognized rule, stated in Article 62 of the Vienna Convention on the Law of Treaties, that 'a fundamental change of circumstances may not be invoked as a ground for terminating or withdrawing from a treaty . . . if the treaty establishes a boundary . . . '. In an earlier passage of the judgment in the *Temple* case, the Court had referred to a claim by Thailand concerning the attention

[72] The result would seem to be that, as pointed out by Sir Gerald Fitzmaurice (in this *Year Book*, 30 (1953), pp. 7–8; 34 (1958), p. 151; *Collected Edition*, I, pp. 138–9; II, p. 576), a question of burden of proof might operate to determine the result of the whole case.

[73] The facts of the case are summarized in previous articles in this series: this *Year Book*, 62 (1991), p. 54, and 63 (1992), p. 23.

[74] *ICJ Reports*, 1962, p. 34. The same line of thought led the Court to consider that Thailand was precluded from challenging the line because it had enjoyed the benefits of the 1904 Treaty, 'if only the benefit of a stable frontier': ibid., p. 32.

given at the time to the map which it received showing what it later contended was an incorrect line purporting to correspond to the provisions of the Treaty establishing its frontier with Cambodia, and stated:

The Court moreover considers that there is no legal foundation for the consequence it is attempted to deduce from the fact that no-one in Thailand at that time may have known of the importance of the Temple or have been troubling about it. Frontier rectifications cannot in law be claimed on the ground that a frontier area has turned out to have an importance not known or suspected when the frontier was established.[75]

The purpose of the general statement in the first passage quoted above was however rather different. The Court, as it emphasized, was dealing at this point in the judgment solely with a question of treaty interpretation. Article 1 of the relevant Treaty stated that the frontier between Siam and Cambodia (in the relevant area) 'follows the watershed between the basins of the Nam Sen and the Mekong'; Article 3 provided that 'There shall be a delimitation of the frontiers' between the two States, to be carried out by Mixed Commissions. If then the line as traced in accordance with Article 3 did *not* follow the watershed referred to in Article 1, and putting aside questions of acceptance of the line by subsequent conduct, where did the Treaty-frontier run? Taking into account the general philosophy of frontier treaties quoted above, the Court held that the reason why the parties had included Article 3 was 'because they regarded a watershed indication [in the Treaty] as insufficient in itself to achieve certainty and finality':[76]

There is . . . no reason to think that the Parties attached any special importance to the line of the watershed as such, as compared with the overriding importance, in the interests of finality, of adhering to the map line as eventually delimited and as accepted by them. The Court, therefore, feels bound, as a matter of treaty interpretation, to pronounce in favour of the line as mapped in the disputed area.[77]

[75] *ICJ Reports*, 1962, p. 25. This observation, while sound in itself, seems rather to miss the point of the contention of Thailand: it was not asking for a rectification of the frontier on the ground of the unexpected importance of the area; it was denying that the frontier represented on the map had ever been accepted by Thailand, *inter alia* on the ground that it had not examined, and could not have been expected to examine, in detail a line in an area which was not thought to be of any importance.

For a parallel in the domain of maritime boundaries, cf. *Continental Shelf (Tunisia/Libya)*, *ICJ Reports*, 1982, p. 77, para. 107.

[76] *ICJ Reports*, 1962, p. 34.

[77] *ICJ Reports*, 1962, p. 35. The inclusion of the phrase 'and as accepted by them' slightly weakens the argument, since the map line, provided it was produced in accordance with the procedure laid down by Article 3, would, on this interpretation, be definitive even in the absence of express or tacit acceptance by the parties. On the other hand, Judge Fitzmaurice in his separate opinion observed that even if the map was accepted, and thus 'became part of the treaty settlement', Thailand could still argue that the conflict between text and map was to be resolved by application of the rules of treaty interpretation, which in his view would not necessarily give preference to the map: ibid., p. 65.

The Court was not therefore saying that in principle a line purporting to represent a frontier established by treaty could not be challenged on the ground that it did not correctly represent the purport of the treaty on its proper interpretation, and thus that any frontier line actually drawn should be intangible, in order to ensure finality. A discrepancy between the frontier line and the text of the treaty might well be covered by estoppel (as in the *Temple* case), or by appeal to the subsequent conduct of the parties as an interpretation, or a modification, of the treaty;[78] but in the absence of such circumstances, the desirability of finality could not override the need to apply the treaty according to its terms.

In the *Territorial Dispute* between Chad and Libya, the Court had found that a 1955 Franco-Libyan Treaty had fixed the frontier between the two countries; however, the Treaty in question provided that it was concluded for a period of twenty years, and could thereafter be terminated; did this affect the permanency of the frontier? The Court stated that, notwithstanding the provision referred to,

> the Treaty must, in the view of the Court, be taken to have determined a permanent frontier. There is nothing in the 1955 Treaty to indicate that the boundary agreed was to be provisional or temporary; on the contrary it bears all the hallmarks of finality. The establishment of this boundary is a fact which, from the outset, has had a legal life of its own, independently of the fate of the 1955 Treaty. Once agreed, the boundary stands, for any other approach would vitiate the fundamental principle of the stability of boundaries, the importance of which has been repeatedly emphasized by the Court (*Temple of Preah Vihear, I.C.J. Reports 1962*, p. 34; *Aegean Sea Continental Shelf, I.C.J. Reports 1978*, p. 36).
>
> A boundary established by treaty thus achieves a permanence which the treaty itself does not necessarily enjoy. The treaty can cease to be in force without in any way affecting the continuance of the boundary. In this instance the Parties have not exercised their option to terminate the Treaty, but whether or not the option be exercised, the boundary remains. This is not to say that two States may not by mutual agreement vary the border between them; such a result can of course be achieved by mutual consent, but when a boundary has been the subject of agreement, the continued existence of that boundary is not dependent upon the continuing life of the treaty under which the boundary is agreed.[79]

This must apparently be read as no more than the statement of a *presumption* in the interpretation of a boundary treaty; States must, it is to be supposed, retain the possibility of concluding a treaty which, in express terms, establishes a boundary to exist so long as it and the treaty are not simultaneously terminated on conditions laid down in the treaty.

[78] See a previous article, this *Year Book*, 62 (1991), pp. 48 ff., especially p. 54.

[79] *ICJ Reports*, 1994, p. 37, paras. 72–3 The opposite conclusion was arrived at by Judge *ad hoc* Sette-Camara in his dissenting opinion: ibid., p. 98. He did not however dispute the existence of the rule relied on by the Court, but considered that its application to the 1955 Treaty had not been established.

An alternative view is that provisions for denunciation in a treaty which deals with a frontier must be taken to relate only to the other provisions of the treaty, not to the article or articles establishing the boundary.[79a]

Chapter IV

Territorial Disputes and the Critical Date

Hamlet: Goes it against the main of Poland, sir,
Or for some frontier?

Captain: Truly to speak sir, and without addition,
We go to gain a little patch of ground
That hath in it no profit but the name.

William Shakespeare, *Hamlet*, Act IV, Sc. 4

1. *'Frontier Disputes', 'Delimitation Disputes' and Attribution of Territory*

A recognized distinction exists in international law between boundary questions and questions of territorial sovereignty.[80] In many instances, the distinction is so evident that to make it might seem to be merely the statement of a truism: for example, if two States each claim sovereignty over the same island, on a basis of discovery and occupation, since the island is a unit, the issue is whether the one or the other has the better title, not how far in space the title of each extends.[81] In other cases, the distinction is less clear-cut, and the issue arises whether it is legally

[79a] In this sense, Kohn, 'Le Règlement des différends territoriaux à la lumière de l'arrêt de la C.I.J. dans l'affaire Libye/Tchad', *Revue générale de droit international public*, 1995, p. 324; but the severance of the denunciation provisions in this way seems awkward.

A question not dealt with by the Court is the fate of any provisions in the treaty which are linked to the boundary, for example provisions for trans-frontier movements by nomadic tribes. There were in fact such provisions contained, not in the 1955 Treaty itself, but in a simultaneous Convention of Good Neighbourliness: see *ICJ Reports*, 1994, pp. 26–7, paras. 53–4.

[80] See *Oppenheim's International Law* (9th edn., by Jennings and Watts), vol. 1, pp. 668–9.

[81] As was noted by Munkman, 'Adjudication and Adjustment: International Judicial Decisions and the Settlement of Territorial Boundary Disputes', this *Year Book*, 46 (1972–3), p. 1, most territorial disputes based on claims of *occupation* have in fact related to islands.

Even where an island is at stake, there may however be 'frontier' questions, e.g. if the island lies off the mainland coasts of two adjacent States just opposite what is found to be the endpoint of the land frontier: see *Land, Island and Maritime Frontier Dispute, ICJ Reports*, 1992, pp. 552–3, paras. 320–1; and in the same case the problem of sovereignty over a small island (Meanguerita) as a 'dependency' of a larger island (Meanguera), ibid., p. 570, para. 356, and the separate opinion of Judge Torres Bernárdez, pp. 709–11, paras. 169–76.

necessary or useful to make it.[82] During the period under review the Court has made a number of pertinent observations in this field.

In its judgment on the preliminary objections raised in the case concerning the *Temple of Preah Vihear*, the Court defined the dispute before it as follows:

In the present case, Cambodia alleges a violation on the part of Thailand of Cambodia's territorial sovereignty over the region of the Temple of Preah Vihear and its precincts. Thailand replies by affirming that the area in question lies on the Thai side of the common frontier between the two countries, and is under the sovereignty of Thailand. *This is a dispute about territorial sovereignty;* . . . [83]

In its place, this observation appears to be merely the introduction to an explanation that the Court had, at that stage, only to deal with preliminary objections; however, the Court found it appropriate to quote the passage from its earlier judgment at the beginning of its judgment on the merits, and to reiterate that it was a 'question of territorial sovereignty'.[84] In neither context, however, did the distinction between a delimitation dispute and a territorial dispute have any impact on the Court's decision.[85]

The distinction was stated, in different words, in the *North Sea Continental Shelf* cases, in a passage already quoted above:

The appurtenance of a given area, considered as an entity, in no way governs the precise delimitation of its boundaries, any more than uncertainty as to boundaries can affect territorial rights. There is for instance no rule that the land frontiers of a State must be fully delimited and defined, and often in various places and for long periods they are not . . . [86]

However, the Court was there defending the view that there existed a rule of law ascribing certain areas (i.e., continental shelf) to a State as a matter of inherent and original right, which nevertheless did not include or entail a rule by which those areas could be obligatorily delimited;[87] its dictum does not throw any light on the relationship between territorial and boundary issues on land territory.

In another case relating to the continental shelf, the Court made a

[82] Cf. the *Rann of Kutch* arbitration, *International Legal Materials*, 7 (1968), pp. 633 ff., in which it was argued by Pakistan that the Rann of Kutch formed a broad belt of boundary, and that the Tribunal had no competence to reduce it to a 'widthless line': loc. cit., pp. 669, 695.

[83] *ICJ Reports*, 1961, p. 22, emphasis added.

[84] *ICJ Reports*, 1962, p. 14.

[85] It apparently derives from Thailand's preliminary objection to an alternative basis of jurisdiction, not examined by the Court, for which it was material that the dispute should be one over frontiers: see *ICJ Pleadings, Oral Arguments, Documents*, vol. 2, pp. 79–80 (Reuter).

[86] *ICJ Reports*, 1969, p. 32, para. 46, quoting *Monastery of Saint Naoum, PCIJ*, Series B, No. 9, at p. 10.

[87] The opposite view had been advanced by, in particular, Judge Morelli: see *ICJ Reports*, 1969, p. 200, and a previous article in this series: this *Year Book*, 64 (1993), p. 45.

further observation as to the relationship between delimitation and territory:

Any disputed delimitation of a boundary entails some determination of entitlement to the areas to be delimited . . . [88]

The context was the question whether the expression 'disputes relating to the territorial status of Greece' in that State's accession to the 1928 General Act for the Pacific Settlement of International Disputes applied to a dispute over the continental shelves of Greece and Turkey, and the phrase quoted supported the Court's view that 'it would be difficult to accept the broad proposition that delimitation is entirely extraneous to the notion of territorial status'. Taken in isolation, however, the statement clearly envisages the fact that it is normally impossible to define the *where* of a boundary line without considering the *why* of it.

One case in which the parties did consider that something of moment turned on the distinction between 'frontier disputes', 'delimitation disputes', and 'disputes as to attribution of territory' was the case to which the Court had in fact attributed the title *Frontier Dispute*, between Burkina Faso and Mali.[89] The judgment does not explain the significance which the parties attached to the distinction: it observes that

Both Parties seem ultimately to have accepted that the present dispute belongs rather to the category of delimitation disputes, even though they fail to agree on the conclusions to be drawn from this,[90]

but again these conclusions are not spelled out. It appears,[91] however, that in the view of Burkina Faso, it followed from the classification of the dispute as a delimitation dispute, first that it was for the Court to choose between the lines claimed by the two parties, and not indicate any different line of its own;[92] and secondly that it was only the position as it was when France withdrew and the two States became independent

[88] *Aegean Sea Continental Shelf, ICJ Reports*, 1978, p. 35, para. 84.

[89] This notwithstanding the fact that they had concluded a Special Agreement in order to seise the Court of what was therein described as a 'différend frontalier': see *ICJ Reports*, 1986, p. 557. For the case (falling strictly outside the period here under examination) of the Chad/Libya dispute, in which the document treated as the Special Agreement referred to a 'territorial dispute', see below, pp. 30–1.

[90] *ICJ Reports*, 1986, p. 563, para. 17.

[91] The pleadings and oral arguments in the case have not yet been published in the Court's series of *Pleadings, Oral Arguments, Documents*, and the original pleadings and verbatim records lack detailed tables of contents.

[92] Cf. the 1831 award in the *North-Eastern Boundary Question* between Great Britain and the United States (Moore, *International Arbitrations*, vol. 1, p. 119), where the Arbitrator found the arguments insufficient to sustain either of the two lines claimed by the parties, and substituted his own line, with the result that the award was rejected (see *British and Foreign State Papers*, vol. 22 (1833–4), pp. 772–5).

which should be taken into account, not any subsequent conduct of either State.[93]

The Chamber observed, for its own part, that

In fact, however, in the great majority of cases, including this one, the distinction outlined above is not so much a difference in kind but rather a difference of degree as to the way in which the operation in question is carried out. The effect of any delimitation, no matter how small the disputed area crossed by the line, is an apportionment of the areas of land lying on either side of the line . . . In both cases, a clarification is made of a given legal situation with declaratory effect from the date of the legal title upheld by the Court.[94]

The Chamber did deal specifically, though somewhat indirectly, with the question whether the nature of the dispute affected the relevance or otherwise of post-colonial *effectivités*: it went on to refer to

a misunderstanding which might arise from this distinction between 'delimitation disputes' and 'disputes as to attribution of territory'. One of the effects of this distinction is to contrast 'legal titles' and '*effectivités*'. In this context, the term 'legal title' appears to denote documentary evidence alone . . . In fact, the concept of title may also, and more generally, comprehend both any evidence which may establish the existence of a right, and the actual source of that right.[95]

It therefore found itself free to rely both on French administrative documents, on the basis of *uti possidetis*, and on post-independence conduct, without having to opt for the one definition of the nature of the dispute rather than the other.

In the case which the International Court designated, on the basis of the terminology used in the 'Accord-Cadre' by which the case was submitted to it, the *Territorial Dispute* between Chad and Libya, the parties were nevertheless at odds over the same question of definition:

Libya proceeds on the basis that there is no existing boundary, and asks the Court to determine one. Chad proceeds on the basis that there is an existing boundary, and asks the Court to declare what that boundary is. Libya considers that the case concerns a dispute regarding attribution of territory, while in Chad's view it concerns a dispute over the location of a boundary.[96]

[93] '[I]l ne s'agit pas d'allouer ou de partager un territoire mais bien de décider, entre les lignes présentées par les Parties, celle qui répond, ou correspond le mieux, aux exigences du droit international': ICJ C 2/CR 86/3, p. 11. '[I]l ne s'agit en aucune manière d'un conflit d'attribution dont le règlement aurait pu privilégier d'éventuels actes d'administration des Parties dans la zone revendiquée, mais d'un conflit de délimitation à propos duquel les Parties sollicitent la chambre d'examiner les titres légués par l'ancienne puissance coloniale afin de leur indiquer où passe la ligne de la frontière': ibid., p. 12.

[94] *ICJ Reports*, 1986, p. 563, para. 17. This passage may be compared with the distinction made by the Court in the *North Sea Continental Shelf* cases between delimitation and apportionment—two different things 'even though in a number of cases the results may be comparable, or even identical' (*ICJ Reports*, 1969, p. 22, para. 18).

[95] *ICJ Reports*, 1986, p. 564, para. 18.

[96] *ICJ Reports*, 1994, pp. 14–15, para. 19.

Both parties however recognized that a 1955 Franco-Libyan Treaty, which according to Chad had fixed the relevant boundary, was 'the logical starting-point for consideration of the issues before the Court';[97] and since the Court upheld the contentions of Chad as to the effect of the Treaty, it thereby found that the case was a boundary dispute, not a dispute as to attribution of territory, after all. Perhaps conscious of this, the Court states towards the end of the judgment:

> It will be evident from the preceding discussion that the dispute before the Court, *whether described as a territorial dispute or a boundary dispute*, is conclusively determined by a Treaty to which Libya is an original party and Chad a party in succession to France.[98]

The conclusion which may be drawn from the Court's jurisprudence in this field seems therefore to be a negative one: it does not appear that the terms 'delimitation dispute' (or 'question'), 'frontier dispute', 'dispute as to attribution of territory' are anything more than labels, practically interchangeable, or at least lying at different positions along a spectrum so as to shade into one another, and thus usually without substantive or procedural significance.

2. *The 'Critical Date' in Territorial Disputes*

The concept of the 'critical date' in the context of territorial disputes was the subject of lengthy examination by Sir Gerald Fitzmaurice, in one of his articles[99] in the series to which this paper is a sequel, in the light of the decision in the *Minquiers and Ecrehos* case. However, that analysis has come under criticism as over-elaborate and artificial;[100] and it does perhaps rest more on the theoretical approach to the problem put forward by Sir Gerald as counsel in that case than on what the Court actually decided. Before examining the references made to the concept by the Court in the period under review, the *Minquiers* case will be briefly noticed.

97 *ICJ Reports*, 1994, p. 20, para. 36.

98 *ICJ Reports*, 1994, p. 38, para. 75, emphasis added. In view of the sensitivity shown by governments in recent years over the titles given by the Court, purely for practical working purposes, to the cases before it, this is a salutary reminder that such titles have no effective significance; this is not however to deny the psychological impact they may have. On this decision, see Kohn, 'Le Règlement des différends territoriaux à la lumière de l'arrêt de la C.I.J. dans l'affaire Libye/Tchad', *Revue générale de droit international public*, 1995, pp. 303–8.

99 This *Year Book*, 32 (1955–6), pp. 20 ff.; *Collected Edition*, I pp. 260 ff.

100 See for example Jennings, *The Acquisition of Territory in International Law* (Manchester, 1963), pp. 31, 34–5; 'General Course on International Law', *Recueil des cours*, 121 (1967–II), pp. 423–4; Mengel, 'Der entscheidungsrelevante Zeitpunkt für die völkerrechtliche Beurteilung von Streitigkeiten territorialer Souveränität', *German Yearbook of International Law*, 24 (1981), pp. 92 ff. (criticizing in particular the idea that there is any need to limit the historical material available to a tribunal); *Oppenheim's International Law* (9th edn. by Jennings and Watts), vol. 1, pp. 710–12.

Each of the parties, the United Kingdom and France, contended that it had an ancient or original title, and that such title had always been maintained and never lost. After examining the claims of original title, the Court expressed the view that

What is of decisive importance . . . is not indirect presumptions deduced from events in the Middle Ages, but the evidence which relates directly to the possession of the Ecrehos and Minquiers groups.[101]

The Court then examined, and rejected, a claim by France that the matter was determined by an 1839 Fishery Convention between the parties which had, in France's contention, subjected (*inter alia*) the disputed islets to a common fishery zone, from which France deduced that acts performed by either party after that date in relation to the islets could not be relied on as manifestations of territorial sovereignty.

At this point in the judgment the Court deals with the question of the 'critical date':

The United Kingdom Government submits that, though the Parties have for a long time disagreed as to the sovereignty over the two groups, the dispute did not become 'crystallized' before the conclusion of the Special Agreement of December 29th 1950, and that therefore this date should be considered as the critical date, with the result that all acts before that date must be taken into consideration by the Court. The French Government, on the other hand, contends that the date of the Convention of 1839 should be selected as the critical date, and that all subsequent acts must be excluded from consideration.

At the date of the Convention of 1839, no dispute as to the sovereignty over the Ecrehos and Minquiers groups had yet arisen. The Parties had for a considerable time been in disagreement with regard to the exclusive right to fish oysters, but they did not link that question to the question of sovereignty over the Ecrehos and the Minquiers. In such circumstances there is no reason why the conclusion of that Convention should have any effect on the question of allowing or ruling out evidence relating to sovereignty. A dispute as to sovereignty over the groups did not arise before the years 1886 and 1888, when France for the first time claimed sovereignty over the Ecrehos and Minquiers respectively. But in view of the special circumstances of the present case, subsequent acts should also be considered by the Court, unless the measure in question was taken with a view to improving the legal position of the Party concerned. In many respects activity in regard to these groups had developed gradually long before the dispute as to sovereignty arose, and it has continued without interruption and in a similar manner. In such circumstances there would be no justification for ruling out all events which during this continued development occurred after the years 1886 and 1888 respectively.[102]

The definition of the concept of the critical date given by Sir Gerald Fitzmaurice in commenting on the decision is 'the date after which the

[101] *ICJ Reports*, 1953, p. 57.
[102] *ICJ Reports*, 1953, pp. 59–60.

actions of the parties can no longer affect the issue';[103] and this is clearly correct, since the Court implies that, had it not been for 'special circumstances', it would have declined to take account of acts performed after the dispute had, in its view, arisen in 1886–8. This definition was offered in relation in particular to disputed claims to territorial sovereignty, but Sir Gerald observed at the same time that 'Such a date must obviously exist in all litigated disputes, if only for the reason that it can never be later than the date on which the legal proceedings are commenced'. He then analysed the concept in relation to a wide range of territorial disputes, which he divided into three classes: questions of occupation, involving considerations of *res nullius*; questions of acquisitive prescription; and claims of ancient or immemorial right. He did not deal with territorial disputes turning on, for example, the interpretation of a Convention, or the application of the *uti possidetis* principle; these were in effect excluded by his definition, since in relation to disputes of those kinds it is not normally possible to affect the issue by acts of asserted territorial sovereignty; but later confusion might have been avoided had he spelled the point out.

The Court in fact pinpointed the essential element when it declared its intention of excluding measures after 1886–8 which were 'taken with a view to improving the legal position of the Party concerned'.[104] The purpose of the critical date doctrine is exactly that: to enable a judge to exclude from consideration acts which are likely to have been performed in order to consolidate a State's own view as to its rights in an area where it is known that these are disputed. The critical date is the date on which it became apparent that there was a dispute, so that acts on the ground can no longer be attributed to the State's *bona fide* beliefs as to its legal rights, as having been performed *in tempore non suspecto*. The Court's exception to the rule is then clearly self-justifying: it concerns a continuous process, begun *in tempore non suspecto* and continuing consistently after the appearance of the dispute.

The French contention as to the 1839 Convention was in fact a borderline case: on the issue of whether or not the Convention created a common fishery zone, subsequent acts of either party were only relevant in so far as they might throw light on the common interpretation of the Convention; thus, for purposes of this aspect of the case, no issue as to 'critical date' arose. Had the Court upheld the French contention, no acts subsequent to 1839 could have been relied on, but that did not mean that 1839 was the 'critical date' in the sense of Fitzmaurice's definition; simply that the issue became such that no acts of purported territorial sovereignty *could* have affected the issue, so that there was no need to

[103] This *Year Book*, 32 (1955–6), p. 20; *Collected Edition*, I, p. 260; see eod. loc., footnote 1, for alternative definitions.

[104] Criticized by Sir Gerald Fitzmaurice in his article: see this *Year Book*, 32 (1955–6), pp. 40–4; *Collected Edition*, I, pp. 280–4.

divide them temporally into those that could, and those that could not, be taken into account.

In subsequent cases, however, it has been apparently assumed that in *all* territorial disputes there is a 'critical date' which it is necessary, or at least desirable, to determine, in order to include or exclude evidence of certain acts. This, it is suggested, is not so, unless one adopts a wider definition of 'critical date', one which leads to confusion. For purposes of discussion, it is suggested that, in territorial questions, a distinction be made between two uses of the term. The critical date *stricto sensu* is only relevant where successive State acts may be constitutive or confirmatory of title, in particular in cases of occupation or prescription; such date 'sets a term to the span of time during which, in a given case, right-creating facts can be availed of in order to perfect a title'.[105] The critical date *lato sensu* is the date by reference to which it is necessary to determine the rights of the parties, regardless of whether the nature of their claims is such that acts subsequent to that date might have to be taken into account as evidence of assertions of sovereignty.[106]

Sir Gerald Fitzmaurice himself may have contributed to this confusion; in the article referred to, he treated the French proposed date of 1839 as a 'critical date' (as France had presented it); and he cites his own speech as counsel in the *Minquiers* case:

> the theory of the critical date involves . . . that, whatever was the position at the date determined to be the critical date, such is still the position now. Whatever were the rights of the Parties then, those are still the rights of the Parties now.[107]

In either sense, the term is one whose use is (or should be) confined to territorial *disputes*; thus in the *Western Sahara* case, the Court, when considering the question of the date which should be treated as the 'time of colonization by Spain', at which date the Court was to determine the status of the territory (as *terra nullius* or otherwise), emphasized that

> it is not here concerned to establish a 'critical date' in the sense given to this term in territorial disputes; for the questions [put to the Court] do not ask the Court to adjudicate between conflicting legal titles to Western Sahara.[108]

[105] Goldie, 'The Critical Date', *International and Comparative Law Quarterly*, 12 (1963), p. 1251.

[106] It is in this wide sense that the French term 'date critique' was, for example, used by the PCIJ to refer to the date, in an acceptance of jurisdiction under the 'optional clause', defining the *terminus a quo* for ascertaining the disputes to which the acceptance applied: *Electricity Company of Sofia and Bulgaria, PCIJ*, Series A/B, No. 77, p. 82; the English translation, interestingly, uses 'material date'.

[107] *Minquiers and Ecrehos, ICJ Pleadings, Oral Arguments, Documents*, vol. 2, p. 64, quoted in this *Year Book*, 32 (1955–6), pp. 20–1, *Collected Edition*, I, pp. 260–1.

[108] *ICJ Reports*, 1975, p. 38, para. 76. In the same sense, Judge de Castro in his separate opinion, though he does think it appropriate to speak of a 'critical period': ibid., p. 137.

The key date in a territorial dispute is thus not necessarily the critical date *stricto sensu*: in the *Temple of Preah Vihear* case, it was events occurring *before* the key date which were not to be taken into account,[109] because it was common ground between the parties that the dispute originated from a boundary settlement in the period 1904–8, and depended in particular on a boundary treaty of 1904.[110] No question was there raised of acts on the ground having to be disregarded as posterior to the critical date; the Court took note of acts of occupation as late as 1954, but attached no significance to them, not because they were subsequent to the appearance of the dispute, but because they did not affect the question of the effect of the boundary treaty, which was the substance of the dispute. The judgment does not use the expression 'critical date',[111] and that for the very good reason that the date of 1904 was not a 'critical date' *stricto sensu*, in the sense of the *Minquiers* decision as expounded by Fitzmaurice.[112]

It is significant in this respect that in many cases, including the *Temple* case, the question whether there is a critical date *lato sensu*, and if so what it is, is not a subject of controversy between the parties; in the *Frontier Dispute* between Burkina Faso and Mali, the parties were in agreement that the frontier between them was the frontier which existed at the moment of independence from France. They also agreed, accordingly, that 'no legal validity attaches to any subsequent acts of administration which may have been performed by either of them on the territory of the other'.[113] The views of the parties did diverge as to what exactly *was* the moment of independence, but fortunately they both 'ultimately admitted that the point has no practical implications for the case'.[114] Both parties relied on what were referred to as '*effectivités*', i.e. acts of effective administration in the disputed area, but those were solely the 'colonial *effectivités*', i.e. 'the conduct of the administrative authorities as proof of the effective exercise of territorial jurisdiction in the region *during the*

[109] But see the comments on this of Judge Fitzmaurice in his separate opinion, *ICJ Reports*, 1962, p. 52.

[110] *ICJ Reports*, 1962, p. 16.

[111] Although writers have attributed the concept of critical date to this judgment also: see for example Sanchez Rodriguez, 'El problema de la fecha critica en los litigios relativos a la atribución de la soberania territorial', *Anuario de derecho internacional*, 4 (1977–8), pp. 77–8, 87.

[112] Who of course took part in the decision, and wrote a separate opinion discussing (*inter alia*) the 'relevance of the pre-1904 position' without using the term 'critical date'.

[113] *ICJ Reports*, 1986, p. 570, para. 34. The phrase 'on the territory of the other' comes as rather a surprise, as apparently begging the whole question of the position of the frontier! Presumably what is meant is 'on the territory on the other side of the line inherited from France'.

[114] *ICJ Reports*, 1986, p. 570, para. 33. The two States had become independent on two different dates, two months apart; but in addition Mali argued that it was necessary to go back to the 'last date on which the French colonial authorities participated in the exercise of jurisdiction for administrative organization'.

colonial period'.[115] Thus there was no 'critical date' *stricto sensu*;[116] the key date remained the date of independence; which did not prevent the Chamber in fact taking into account, in the name of equity , a subsequent agreement, reached at low level and admitted to be non-binding, between local administrators on each side as to the position and division of a frontier pool.[117] (Even had the rule as to the critical date been applicable, this would, it is suggested, not have been in conflict with that concept, since it was not a question of allowing either party to take advantage unilaterally of acts performed in the disputed area after the appearance of the dispute.)

The case of the *Land, Island and Maritime Frontier Dispute* between El Salvador and Honduras, although it falls strictly outside the period here considered, requires to be mentioned in this connection. As in the *Frontier Dispute* case, the Chamber seised of the case was required to establish the position of the frontier at the time of independence of the two States; as in that case, in order to arrive at a conclusion as to the position of the *uti possidetis* boundary, 'it cannot but take into account . . . the colonial *effectivités* as reflected in the documentary evidence of the colonial period submitted by the Parties'.[118] It went further, however:

> The Chamber may have regard also, in certain instances, to documentary evidence of post-independence *effectivités* when it considers that they afford indications in respect of the 1821 *uti possidetis juris* boundary, providing a relationship exists between the *effectivités* concerned and the determination of that boundary.[119]

For the reasons just explained, this does not mean that, in *uti possidetis* cases, the date of independence is the 'critical date' in the proper sense of the term; and for this reason, it is perhaps unfortunate that the Chamber used the expression 'critical date' when it went on to make a general

[115] *ICJ Reports*, 1986, p. 586, para. 63, emphasis added. It is important to note this limitation of the concept of *effectivités* in the case, since the term was later used in a different sense, in particular by the parties in the *Land, Island and Maritime Frontier Dispute* (*El Salvador/Honduras*).

[116] In fact the Chamber only uses the expression 'critical date' to refer to the date of independence, and this may have been *per incuriam*: *ICJ Reports*, 1986, p. 568, para. 30. Judge *ad hoc* Abi Saab echoes this paragraph, and uses the expression at one other point (ibid., pp. 662, 659); Judge *ad hoc* Luchaire uses the expression in relation to an argument from *effectivités* in the form of the exercise of voting rights, a context where it is more appropriate (ibid., p. 656).

[117] *ICJ Reports*, 1986, pp. 631–3, paras. 145–50. On the use of equity in the settlement of boundary questions, see Bardonnet, 'Equité et frontières terrestres', *Le Droit international: unité et diversité (Mélanges Reuter)* (1981), pp. 35 ff.; and, specifically in relation to *uti possidetis*, pp. 56–66.

[118] *ICJ Reports*, 1992, p. 399, para. 62.

[119] *ICJ Reports*, 1992, p. 399, para. 62. The Chamber, while rejecting any idea of 'natural frontiers', was even ready to recognize that the convenience of a particular boundary might suggest that it was that boundary, rather than another, that had been contemplated in 1821: *ICJ Reports*, 1992, p. 390, para. 46: for comment, see Decaux, 'Le Différend frontalier, terrestre, insulaire et maritime: la délimitation terrestre', *Annuaire français de droit international*, 1992, p. 407.

statement on the subject in its judgment in the *El Salvador/Honduras* case:

The principle of *uti possidetis juris* is sometimes stated in almost absolute terms, suggesting that the position at the date of independence is always determinative; in short, that no other critical date can arise. As appears from the discussion above, this cannot be so. A later critical date clearly may arise, for example, either from adjudication or from a boundary treaty. Thus, in the previous Latin American boundary arbitrations it is the award that is now determinative, even though it be based upon a view of the *uti possidetis juris* position. The award's view of the *uti possidetis juris* position prevails and cannot now be questioned juridically, even if it could be questioned historically. So for such a boundary the date of the award has become a new and later critical date. Likewise there can be no question that the parts of the El Salvador/Honduras boundary fixed by the General Treaty of Peace of 1980 now constitute the boundary and 1980 is now the critical date. If the *uti possidetis juris* position can be qualified by adjudication and by treaty, the question then arises whether it can be qualified in other ways, for example by acquiescence or recognition. There seems to be no reason in principle why these factors should not operate, where there is sufficient evidence to show that the parties have in effect clearly accepted a variation, or at least an interpretation, of the *uti possidetis juris* position.[120]

In the event of a dispute over a territory which had been the subject of a treaty or an arbitral award, the issue would presumably be what was the precise effect, or the correct interpretation, of the treaty or the award.[121] Thus the possible effect, as acts of asserted sovereignty over the territory, of events before or after the treaty or the award, would not be in question, and no 'critical date' would be needed to distinguish those which could be taken into account and those which could not.

The Chamber's cautious recognition that a boundary fixed by *uti possidetis* might be found to have been modified by later events amounting to acquiescence was not necessary to justify taking into account, in relation to the disputed land boundary, the 'post-colonial *effectivités*', since this was done solely where they threw light on the position of the 1821 boundary. If one recalls the purpose intended to be served by the doctrine of the critical date, as conceived by Sir Gerald Fitzmaurice, namely that

The whole point, the whole *raison d'être*, of the critical date rule is, in effect, that time is deemed to stop at that date. Nothing that happens afterwards can operate

[120] *ICJ Reports*, 1992, p. 401, para. 67. This passage of the 1992 judgment has been criticized as using the expression 'the critical date' in two senses of which one, it is suggested, rests on a false analogy: Decaux, loc. cit. above (n. 119), pp. 400–1.

[121] Cf. in this respect the later cases of the *Territorial Dispute* between Chad and Libya (interpretation of a 1955 Franco-Libyan Treaty), and *Arbitral Award of 31 July 1989* (validity of an arbitral award determining the effect of an international maritime boundary agreement).

to change the situation that then existed. Whatever that situation was, it is deemed in law still to exist; and the rights of the Parties are governed by it,[122]

it will be seen that there can be no contradiction with that doctrine in using evidence of later acts to ascertain what was the position on the critical date, rather than as assertions of an effective modification of that position. When it came to the disputed islands, however, the Chamber was bolder: in particular, this was its finding concerning the island of Meanguera:

while the *uti possidetis juris* position in 1821 cannot be satisfactorily ascertained on the basis of colonial titles and *effectivités*, the fact that El Salvador asserted a claim to the island of Meanguera in 1854, and was thereafter in effective possession and control of the island, justifies the conclusion that El Salvador may be regarded as sovereign over the island. If there remained any doubt, its position in respect of Meanguera is made definitive by the acquiescence of Honduras in its exercise of sovereignty in the island since the later years of the last century.[123]

No clearer demonstration could be required that the date of 1821, as regards the island dispute, was not the 'critical date', since on that basis, not merely the extensive dossier of comparatively recent exercise of sovereignty by El Salvador,[124] but even the evidence of the 1854 claim, would have had to be excluded. The judgment does not however appear to contemplate the possibility that a true 'critical date', later than 1821, did exist, namely the date at which the dispute appeared (or 'crystallized'), with the consequence that all acts relied on by El Salvador after that date should have been excluded from consideration. Whether this results from concentration on 1821 as 'critical date' having the effect of obscuring the point, or whether the Chamber was applying and extending the *Minquiers* exception of the 'continuous process', does not appear. It does not seem that the Chamber was rejecting the whole principle of exclusion of evidence of events after the 'critical date', in view of the attention paid to the point earlier in the judgment.

Division C: State Responsibility and International Claims

During the period covered by Sir Gerald Fitzmaurice's articles in the *Year Book*, it chanced that the Court gave few decisions touching on matters of State responsibility and international claims; accordingly, it

[122] *Minquiers and Ecrehos, ICJ Pleadings, Oral Arguments, Documents*, vol. 2, p. 64 (Fitzmaurice), quoted in this *Year Book*, 32 (1955–6), pp. 20–1, *Collected Edition*, I, pp. 260–1.

[123] *ICJ Reports*, 1992, p. 579, para. 367.

[124] The so called 'Meanguera dossier': see *ICJ Reports*, 1992, pp. 572–4, paras. 359–60. In this sense Kohen, '*L'uti possidetis* revisité', *Revue générale de droit international public*, 97 (1993), pp. 939, 941, who observes that the Chamber appears to have adopted the hostile stance toward the 'critical date' expressed, prior to his election to the Court, by Judge Jennings: cf. references in n. 100, above.

was unnecessary for him to set aside a major division of his structure to accommodate such questions. The period now under review, in contrast, offers a wealth of material in the field. For purposes of analysis, a convenient structure is afforded by the Draft Articles on State Responsibility adopted by the International Law Commission in 1980,[125] which were, of course, drafted taking into account decisions of the Court given prior to that date. The Court has never expressly referred in a decision to those Articles, nor has its terminology in matters of responsibility been wholly consistent with the Commission's work,[126] but for that very reason it is interesting to confront the jurisprudence with the system of concepts embodied in the Draft Articles.[127]

CHAPTER I

THE 'ACT OF THE STATE' UNDER INTERNATIONAL LAW

My words are my own, but my actions are my Ministers'.

King Charles II

1. *Imputability in General*

In the *Nicaragua* case, the Court had before it certain declarations by (among others) responsible authorities of the United States, and took the opportunity to recall that 'such declarations may involve legal effects'; as one of those effects, it referred to their being regarded as 'evidence that [certain] facts are attributable to the States the authorities of which are the authors of these declarations'.[128] Specifically, the Court noted that it was argued by the applicant that the United States had in effect admitted 'direct and substantial involvement in the military and paramilitary operations' complained of, by raising a contention of collective self-defence. The Court refused to treat the mere general invocation of self-defence as equivalent to a blanket admission of the conduct complained of, indicating that something more specific would be required for this to be possible; but while declining to 'consider reliance on self-defence to be

[125] *ILC Yearbook*, 1980, vol. 2, pp. 30 ff.

[126] But see pp. 42–3, below. The influence of the analytical structure of the Commission's drafts is clear: cf. Condorelli, 'L'Imputation à l'Etat d'un fait internationalement illicite: solutions classiques et nouvelles tendances', *Recueil des cours*, 189 (1984–VI), pp. 94–5.

[127] Like the International Law Commission, the present Division of these articles will concentrate on 'the principles which govern the responsibility of States for internationally wrongful acts' as distinct from 'the rules that place obligations on States, the violation of which may generate responsibility'; see Report of the ILC, *ILC Yearbook*, 1970, vol. 2, p. 306, para. 66(c).

[128] *ICJ Reports*, 1986, p. 43, para. 71.

an implied general admission on the part of the United States', it did observe that 'it is certainly a recognition of the imputability of some of the activities complained of'.[129]

The question thus arises whether imputability is to be determined purely objectively, or whether the State's own view of its relationship with the authors of the wrongful act may be relevant.[130] In the case in question the Court, while finding the United States responsible under other heads of claim, did not consider that the evidence supported a finding 'attributing to the United States the acts committed by the *contras* in the course of their military or paramilitary operations in Nicaragua'.[131] Leaving out of account the other charges which were upheld against the United States, in relation to which the question of self-defence might also have been relevant, if the objective evidence for imputability of the *contras* actions was insufficient, would it be legitimate to invoke the subjective element of an implied admission resulting from the invocation of self-defence? It is suggested that it would not; that the 'legal effects' referred to by the Court could only attach to a *specific* admission of imputability.

2. *Responsibility Flowing from Control of a Territory*

In the *Corfu Channel* case, discussed by Fitzmaurice in the first of his articles,[132] the Court in effect found that there is some general responsibility of States for acts occurring in their territory, but that such responsibility is not absolute, nor even prima facie. That responsibility was not attributed to sovereignty as such, but rather to the 'mere fact of the control exercised by a State over its territory'.[133] In the *Namibia* case, the Court, when enunciating the legal consequences of the presence of South Africa in Namibia, which it had found to be illegal, emphasized the same point:

> The fact that South Africa no longer has any title to administer the Territory does not release it from its obligations and responsibilities under international law towards other States in respect of the exercise of its powers in relation to the Territory. Physical control of a territory, and not sovereignty or legitimacy of title, is the basis of State liability for acts affecting other States.[134]

This observation appears to have been included *ex abundanti cautela*, to prevent South Africa suggesting that another State which disputed the

[129] *ICJ Reports*, 1986, p. 45, para. 74.

[130] It should go without saying that the State's view that the acts in question were *not* imputable to it would carry no weight; it is only anything in the nature of an admission or a statement against interest that might be taken into account: see *ICJ Reports*, 1986, p. 43, para. 69.

[131] *ICJ Reports*, 1986, p. 64, para. 115.

[132] This *Year Book*, 27 (1950), pp. 19–23; *Collected Edition*, I, pp. 19–23.

[133] *ICJ Reports*, 1949, p. 18.

[134] *ICJ Reports*, 1971, p. 54, para. 118.

legitimacy of its presence in Namibia could not at the same time assert its responsibility for what happened there; but in so far as responsibility was attributed to an act of the South African Government 'in respect of the exercise of its powers' in the Territory, as opposed to responsibility of the *Corfu Channel* type, it would in many cases, if not most, be an act of agents or organs of the South African Government, for which it would have to answer, irrespective of where it occurred.

The principle laid down in the *Corfu Channel* case was also applied in the *Nicaragua* case, in relation to the contention of the United States that Nicaragua was involved in the supply of arms to insurgents in neighbouring countries, a contention that was relied on in order to justify the United States' own activities as acts of collective self-defence:

> even supposing it well established that military aid is reaching the armed opposition in El Salvador from the territory of Nicaragua, it still remains to be proved that this aid is imputable to the authorities of the latter country. Indeed, the applicant State has in no way sought to conceal the possibility of weapons en route to the armed opposition in El Salvador crossing its territory but it denies that this is the result of any deliberate official policy on its part.[135]

The Court then cited the relevant passage from the *Corfu Channel* judgment; and after considering various other factual aspects confirming its approach, concluded that, for the period under consideration, 'the evidence is insufficient to satisfy the Court that . . . the Government of Nicaragua was responsible for any flow of arms' to the armed opposition in El Salvador.[136]

3. *Attribution of Conduct to the State*

(1) *Action by agents or organs of the State*

The Court in the *Nicaragua* case was faced with the problem whether or not the United States was to be held responsible for all the activities of the *contras* in Nicaragua. It defined the question as follows:

> What the Court has to determine at this point is whether or not the relationship of the *contras* to the United States Government was so much one of dependence on the one side and control on the other that it would be right to equate the *contras*, for legal purposes, with an organ of the United States Government, or as acting on behalf of that Government.[137]

The test of 'dependence and control' is, in those terms, an unfamiliar one. So far as 'dependence' is concerned, it would presumably have been

[135] *ICJ Reports*, 1986, pp. 83–4, para. 155.
[136] *ICJ Reports*, 1986, p. 86, para. 160.
[137] *ICJ Reports*, 1986, p. 62, para. 109.

insufficient, for the purpose of fixing the United States with responsibility for the acts of the *contras*, to show merely that they would have been impotent without the financial support, and supply of arms and equipment, of the United States. Nicaragua had argued that the fact that each *contra* offensive followed a legislative authorization of funds by the United States showed that the United States was determining *contra* strategy; but the Court ruled that

> In the sense that an offensive could not be launched until the funds were available, that may well be so; but, in the Court's view, it does not follow that each provision of funds by the United States was made in order to set in motion a particular offensive, and that that offensive was planned by the United States.[138]

As to 'control', would it have been sufficient to show that the United States had the power of control, that its agents *could* have determined the policies and objectives of the *contras*, or would it not have been necessary to show that it *did* exercise this power in a manner inimical to Nicaragua? The Court in fact went on to say that

> Whether the United States Government at any stage devised the strategy and directed the tactics of the *contras* depends on the extent to which the United States made use of the potential for control inherent in that dependence,[139]

and found that it had insufficient evidence to determine the point.

A more traditional view, expressly linked with the ILC Draft Articles, of the definition of agents or organs of the State, from an expert in the field, is to be found in the separate opinion of Judge Ago,[140] who endorsed the Court's findings on

> the question of the imputability to the Respondent of those [acts] which must undeniably be construed as the conduct of United States agents or organs in the proper sense of the terms, namely acts performed by persons or groups directly belonging to the State apparatus of that country and acting as such. . . . This is in conformity with the provisions of Article 5 (*Attribution to the State of the conduct of its organs*) of the draft articles adopted on the subject by the International Law Commission. The Court was also right to consider as acts of the United States of America the conduct of persons or groups that, without strictly being agents or organs of that State, belong nevertheless to public entities empowered within its domestic legal order to exercise certain elements of the government authority. Here I note conformity with the provisions of Article 7 (*Attribution to the State of the conduct of other entities empowered to*

[138] *ICJ Reports*, 1986, p. 60, para. 103.
[139] *ICJ Reports*, 1986, p. 62, para. 110.
[140] Who was, of course, the author of a whole series of Reports on State Responsibility for the ILC, on the basis of which the bulk of the Draft Articles on State Responsbility were adopted.

exercise elements of the government authority) of the International Law Commission's draft.[141]

Judge Ago also agreed with the decision to reject the suggestion 'that the misdeeds committed by some members of the *contra* forces should be considered as acts imputable to the United States', citing in support of that decision Articles 11 and 8 of the ILC Draft Articles; he observed in this respect that

> Only in cases where certain members of those forces happened to have been specifically charged by United States authorities to commit a particular act, or carry out a particular task of some kind on behalf of the United States, would it be possible so to regard them. Only in such instances does international law recognize, as a rare exception to the rule, that the conduct of persons or groups which are neither agents nor organs of the State, nor members of its apparatus even in the broadest acceptation of that term, may be held to be acts of that State.[142]

In this connection, Judge Ago expressed regret that the Court had not quoted what in his view was the relevant precedent of the case of the *United States Diplomatic and Consular Staff in Tehran*, to be examined below; in both cases, in his view, it was a matter of 'the imputability to [the respondent State] of such conduct as can be duly proved to be that of the organs' of that State 'in connection with' the misdeeds of groups not themselves organs or agents of the State.[143]

(2) *Inaction by agents or organs of the State*

It is evident that the 'conduct' of a State which is in breach of an obligation of the State and thus amounts to an unlawful act does not have to be a positive act, which is in breach of, in effect, a negative obligation (not to do something); an obligation may require that a State take specific action in certain circumstances, and the unlawful act may thus be constituted by the failure to act in such circumstances.[144] The classic case of this is the case concerning *United States Diplomatic and Consular Staff in Tehran*. As first step in its reasoning, the Court in that case considered whether the attacks on the United States Embassy and consulates were attributable to Iran on the basis that they were carried out by agents of the Iranian State; it concluded that these attacks were 'executed by militants not having an official character', and that the initiation of those

[141] *ICJ Reports*, 1986, p. 188, para. 15. Judge Ago explained that the first hypothesis applied to 'members of the government administration or armed forces of the United States', and the second to 'activities of members of the CIA, or of the UCLAs or of other bodies of the same kind'. For explanation of the term 'UCLAs', see the judgment at p. 45, para. 75.

[142] *ICJ Reports*, 1986, pp. 188–9, para. 16.

[143] *ICJ Reports*, 1986, p. 189, paras. 18–19.

[144] The distinction is referred to as an important element in the analysis of the obligation of cessation of a wrongful act, in the Preliminary Report on State Responsibility of Arangio-Ruiz, *ILC Yearbook*, 1988, vol. 2, part 1, p. 16, para. 44.

attacks accordingly 'cannot be considered as in itself imputable to the Iranian State'. That however 'does not mean that Iran was, in consequence, free of any responsibility in regard to those attacks; for its own conduct was in conflict with its international obligations'.[145] The Court referred to a number of provisions of the Vienna Conventions on Diplomatic and Consular Relations of 1961 and 1963 requiring Iran, as the 'receiving State', to take appropriate steps to ensure the protection of the embassy and consulates, their staff, their archives, their means of communication, and the freedom of movement of members of their staffs. It was satisfied that the Iranian Government failed altogether to take any 'appropriate steps' of this kind, despite urgent and repeated requests for help from the embassy, and concluded that 'This inaction of the Iranian Government by itself constituted clear and serious violation of Iran's obligations to the United States' under a number of provisions of the two Vienna Conventions.[146]

In the *Nicaragua* case, most of the obligations which the United States was found to have breached were obligations to refrain from particular action—not to threaten or use force, not to intervene in the affairs of Nicaragua, etc. However, in relation to the mines laid in Nicaraguan ports, the Court found that United States responsibility was twofold. In the first place, it was found that the act of laying mines was imputable to the United States, and that it constituted an unlawful use of force against another State; but secondly the Court took note of the existence in international law of an obligation to issue a warning or notification of the presence of mines:

> in peacetime for one State to lay mines in the internal or territorial waters of another is an unlawful act; but in addition, if a State lays mines in any waters whatever in which the vessels of another State have rights of access or passage, and fails to give any warning or notification whatsoever, in disregard of the security of peaceful shipping, it commits a breach of the principles of humanitarian law underlying the specific provisions of [Hague] Convention No. VIII of 1907.[147]

The distinction between an obligation to refrain from specific conduct and an obligation to take positive steps is however by no means clear and precise in all cases. At the least, an obligation to do something positive may involve the corollary that there is also a negative obligation, not to take any action which would contradict the positive obligation, and so compound the offence. The Court in the *Tehran Hostages* case did not find that, at the initial stage of the attacks on the embassy, the Iranian Government had committed any positive breach of its obligations, by

[145] *ICJ Reports*, 1980, p. 30, para. 60–1.

[146] *ICJ Reports*, 1980, p. 32, para. 67.

[147] *ICJ Reports*, 1986, p. 112, para. 215. On the question to whom this obligation was owed, see below, pp. 54–5.

acts, as opposed to failure to act, contrary to its obligations; when it did begin to act in that way (by endorsing the militants' actions) this was treated as affecting the imputability of the militants' subsequent actions; they became what they had not been before, agents of the Iranian State.[148] The existence of mirror-image obligations, one positive, one negative, was however a further feature of the *Nicaragua* case.

The Court found that the United States was under an obligation 'in the terms of Article 1 of the Geneva Conventions' of 12 August 1949 to 'respect' the Conventions and 'to ensure respect' for them.[149] In form this is an obligation to act, to do whatever is necessary to ensure respect for the Conventions; but this may be taken to entail a negative obligation, *not* to act in such a way as to encourage disregard of the Conventions. In most circumstances, any act which would be contrary to that negative obligation would also constitute a breach of the Conventions themselves,[150] but in the *Nicaragua* case the Court was of course inhibited from any finding of a simple breach of the Conventions by the existence of the 'multilateral treaty reservation'. It therefore fell back on a finding that the obligation to 'ensure respect' imposed on the United States 'an obligation not to encourage persons or groups engaged in the conflict in Nicaragua to act in violation of the provisions of Article 3 common to the four 1949 Geneva Conventions'.[151]

In the *Elettronica Sicula (ELSI)* case, the obligations of Italy under the relevant treaty were of both kinds; one provision relied on laid down that the property of United States nationals 'shall not be taken . . . without due process of law';[152] others referred to what nationals and corporations of each party should be 'permitted' to do in the territory of the other party.[153] Even in the absence of treaty provisions, cases of diplomatic protection may be hard to categorize one way or the other; in the case of, for example, expropriation, is the obligation not to expropriate (negative), or to afford adequate compensation (positive), or to ensure that there is no denial of justice (probably positive)? Fortunately, in most circumstances the distinction is academic and without practical effects.

[148] See sub-section (4) below.

[149] *ICJ Reports*, 1986, p. 114, para. 220. In view of the 'multilateral treaty reservation' in the United States acceptance of jurisdiction, the Court explained that such obligation did not 'derive only from the Conventions themselves, but from the general principles of humanitarian law to which the Conventions merely give specific expression' (ibid.).

[150] But note the Court's finding, also in the *Nicaragua* case, that there is a general obligation not to act in such a way as to deprive a treaty of its object and purpose, and that conduct not actually constituting a breach of the treaty itself may yet violate this distinct obligation: see *ICJ Reports*, 1986, pp. 136–8, paras. 271–6.

[151] *ICJ Reports*, 1986, p. 114, para. 220.

[152] Article V, paragraph 2, of the Treaty of Friendship, Commerce and Navigation, quoted at *ICJ Reports*, 1989, p. 67, para. 113.

[153] Article III of the FCN Treaty, quoted in *ICJ Reports*, 1989, p. 49, para. 68.

(3) *Possible conditions of a positive obligation: the* Hostages *case*

It was however in relation to an obligation to take positive action, and a consequent breach of that obligation resulting from passivity, that the Court, in the *Hostages* case, stated what apparently are conditions of responsibility of this kind. It observed that, in regard to the first phase of the attack on the embassy,

> the Iranian authorities:
> (*a*) were fully aware of their obligations under the conventions in force to take appropriate steps to protect the premises of the United States Embassy and its diplomatic and consular staff from any attack and from any infringement of their inviolability, and to ensure the security of such other persons as might be present on the said premises;
> (*b*) were fully aware, as a result of the appeals for help made by the United States Embassy, of the urgent need for action on their part;
> (*c*) had the means at their disposal to perform their obligations;
> (*d*) completely failed to comply with these obligations.[154]

It appears, *a contrario*, that if conditions (*a*) to (*c*) had not been fulfilled, there would have been no responsibility of Iran. In general, is it sufficient for a State to say that it was unaware of, or did not have means at its disposal to perform, an obligation? In the *Temple of Preah Vihear* case, Thailand had removed cultural objects from the Temple in the conviction that it had sovereignty over it; could it therefore have claimed that it was 'unaware' of its obligation not to do so?[155] In respect of ability to perform the obligation, the ILC Draft Articles go no further than recognizing *force majeure*, distress and necessity as circumstances precluding wrongfulness. It is therefore interesting to speculate whether the Court intended, specifically in the case of responsibility for inaction, in breach of a positive obligation, to go further than the International Law Commission in recognizing either lack of awareness that the obligation had become due,[156] or simple inability to comply, as circumstances excluding wrongfulness.

(4) *Action by persons or groups other than agents of the State*

In the *Tehran Hostages* case, the Court recognized the possibility that private persons who caused injury to a foreign State might, as a result of

[154] *ICJ Reports*, 1980, pp. 32–3, para. 68.

[155] It must be conceded that, as from the moment of the Court's decision, it became aware of such an obligation; but it is interesting that the Court, at Cambodia's request, made an order (or declaration—see Chapter V below) for return of the objects, without waiting to see whether Thailand would do so of its own accord, which suggests that it regarded the obligation as *already* breached.

[156] P.-M. Dupuy cites this passage as relevant to the question, pertinent in the case of some kinds of obligation, of the intention of the State author of the act: 'Le fait générateur de la responsabilité internationale des Etats', *Recueil des cours*, 183 (1984–V), p. 38; but it is not apparent in what respect intention was relevant when there was a simple failure to carry out a straightforward obligation, enshrined in a treaty. Dupuy also suggests that the text 'permet d'établir non seulement l'existence de l'illicite et son imputation à l'Etat, mais aussi son degré de gravité' (ibid.).

subsequent conduct by the authorities of the State of which they were nationals, become transformed into organs of that State, with consequent responsibility owed by it to the injured State. The Court found that when the US embassy in Tehran was stormed by militants on 4 November 1979, they had no official status as recognized 'agents' or organs of the Iranian State.

Their conduct might be considered as itself directly imputable to the Iranian State only if it were established that, in fact, on the occasion in question the militants acted on behalf of the State, having been charged by some competent organ of the Iranian State to carry out a specific operation. The information before the Court does not, however, suffice to establish with the requisite certainty the existence at that time of such a link between the militants and any competent organ of the State.[157]

At a later stage, however, the Iranian Government, as the Court found, announced its approval and endorsement of the action of the militants, and itself maintained in existence the illegal situation which had been created.

The result of that policy was fundamentally to transform the legal nature of the situation created by the occupation of the Embassy and the detention of its diplomatic and consular staff as hostages. The approval given to these facts by the Ayatollah Khomeini and other organs of the Iranian State, and the decision to perpetuate them, translated continuing occupation of the Embassy and detention of the hostages into acts of that State. The militants, authors of the invasion and jailers of the hostages, had now become agents of the Iranian State for whose acts the State itself was internationally responsible.[158]

The first question raised by this finding is a temporal one: did the transformation of the militants into agents of the State only take effect *ex tunc*,[159] or did it have the effect of rendering attributable to the Iranian State the whole operation which began on 4 November 1979?[160] The point is obscured in the judgment by the fact that, while Iran was not vicariously responsible for the acts of the militants prior to the endorsement of their actions by the Government, it was at the same time responsible for the failure of its own organs to prevent the attack, to protect the Embassy, and to respond to the appeals for help made by the United States diplomats.[161] It is for this reason that the operative clause of the judgment contains a decision that Iran was under an obligation to

157 *ICJ Reports*, 1980, p. 29, para. 58.

158 *ICJ Reports*, 1980, p. 35, para. 74.

159 This is the interpretation preferred by Condorelli, 'L'Imputation á l'Etat d'un fait internationalement illicite; solutions classiques et nouvelles tendances', *Recueil des cours*, 189 (1984–VI), pp. 102–3.

160 An interesting parallel in ancient common law terms is the doctrine of 'trespass *ab initio*'; see the *Six Carpenters*' case, (1610) 8 Co. Rep. 146a.

161 This is exactly the situation provided for in Article 11, paragraph 2, of the ILC Draft Articles on State Responsibility (1980).

make reparation to the United States 'for the injury caused to the latter *by the events of 4 November 1979* and what followed from these events'.[162]

Secondly, a problem may well arise, if a private person becomes transformed into an agent of the State by an *ex post facto* endorsement by that State of his actions, in determining the scope of his authority as such an agent. It is of course well established that the conduct of an organ of a State is only to be considered as an act of that State 'provided that organ was acting in that capacity in the case in question'.[163] If the militants in the United States embassy, without authorization or instruction from the Government, had taken it into their heads to mount an attack on an embassy next door, of some third State, would their action have been attributable to Iran as an act of an organ of the State? It is suggested that in deciding that the militants 'had now become agents of the Iranian State' the Court may have gone slightly too far; that it was sufficient to have ruled that Government approval had 'translated continuing occupation of the Embassy and detention of the hostages into acts of that State'. In terms of the ILC Draft Articles, the case might have been better met by finding that, with effect from the moment of Iranian Government approval, the militants were 'in fact acting on behalf of that State' (Article 8 (*a*)), rather than that they had been transformed into agents of the State, to be classified as (presumably) 'an organ of an entity which is not part of the formal structure of the State', which is treated as an organ of the State under Article 7(2).

In the *Nicaragua* case, the emphasis of the pleadings and of the judgment was on the question whether the acts of the *contras* could be attributed to the United States on the basis that their relationship with the United States was such that 'it would be right to equate the *contras*, for legal purposes, with an organ of the United States Government', but in the same breath the Court added 'or as acting on behalf of that Government',[164] the terminology of Articles 8 and 11 of the ILC Draft Articles. Paragraph 2 of the latter Article provides that the provision in paragraph 1 that the conduct of a person or a group of persons not acting on behalf of the State is not to be considered an act of that State

> is without prejudice to the attribution to the state of any other conduct which is related to that of the persons or groups of persons referred to in that paragraph and which is to be considered as an act of the State by virtue of Articles 5 to 10.

[162] *ICJ Reports*, 1980, p. 45, para. 95(5), emphasis added. Judge Lachs voted against this paragraph (as did those who disagreed with the whole decision), but his reason was simply that he thought it unnecessary, as a matter of 'sound judicial economy' (ibid., p. 47). Underlying his approach was probably concern not to provoke Iran unnecessarily, in the hope of a diplomatic solution to the dispute.

[163] Article 5 of the ILC Draft Articles on State Responsibilty (1980).

[164] *ICJ Reports*, 1986, p. 62, para. 109.

It is in effect in application of the rule so stated that the Court found the United States had incurred responsibility by encouraging the *contras*, in particular by issuing the notorious guerilla manual (*'Operaciones sicológicas en guerra de guerillas'*), to commit acts contrary to general principles of humanitarian law.[165]

(5) *Responsibility for acts of another State*

No case before the Court has involved the hypothesis of the responsibility of one State for the internationally wrongful act of another State, as contemplated by Article 28 of the International Law Commission's Draft Articles. The question was however alluded to in passing in the judgment in the *Nicaragua* case, when the Court was dealing with the possible responsibility of the United States for encouragement of groups to commit breaches of humanitarian law.

> The question here does not of course relate to the definition of the circumstances in which one State may be regarded as responsible for acts carried out by another State, which probably do not include the possibility of incitement.[166]

All that can be said in this respect is that Article 28 certainly does not extend so far as to cover cases of incitement, being directed more to questions of direction, control or coercion.

Chapter II

The Breach of an International Obligation

1. *Inter-State Obligations*

The essence of an international obligation is that it is something owed by one or more subjects of international law to one or more subjects of international law; and excluding the special case of the so-called 'obligations *erga omnes*', international responsibility only arises in relation to the State or States to whom the obligation alleged to have been breached was owed.[167] The point arose in the *Nicaragua* case in the parallel context of the lawfulness of counter-measures: the United States had purported to justify its actions toward Nicaragua on the grounds (*inter alia*) of

[165] See *ICJ Reports*, 1986, pp. 66–9, paras. 118–22; pp. 129–30, paras. 254–6; p. 148, para. 292(9).

[166] *ICJ Reports*, 1986, p. 129, para. 255.

[167] It is of course possible that an obligation may be owed to more than one State or entity, so that the corresponding right is enjoyed in common; cf. the view of Judge Wellington Koo in the *Northern Cameroons* case, below, p. 58. The opposite situation, of an obligation owed to one State by several States, jointly, or jointly and severally, is also possible; for the procedural problems when it is sought to enforce such an obligation, see the case of *Certain Phosphate Lands in Nauru*, *ICJ Reports*, 1992, *passim*.

alleged breaches by the Government of Nicaragua of its 'solemn commitments to the Nicaraguan people, the United States, and the Organization of American States'. Those breaches were stated to involve questions such as the composition of the government, its political ideology and alignment, totalitarianism, human rights, militarization and aggression.[168]

With regard specifically to commitments said to have been made towards the OAS, the Court pointed out that

> even supposing that such a political pledge had the force of a legal commitment, it could not have justified the United States insisting on the fulfilment of a commitment made not directly towards the United States, but towards the Organization, the latter alone being empowered to monitor its implementation,[169]

and, one might add, to complain of a breach of an international obligation in that respect.

This principle was the essence of the much criticized decision of the Court in 1966 in the *South West Africa* cases: the decision 'to reject the claims of the Empire of Ethiopia and the Republic of Liberia'[170] was based on the conclusion that:

> the Court finds that the Applicants cannot be considered to have established any legal right or interest appertaining to them in the subject-matter of the present claims, and that, accordingly, the Court must decline to give effect to them.[171]

The Court fully recognized that under the Mandate for South West Africa, South Africa was (or had been[172]) under very specific obligations as regards its administration of the Territory—what became known as the 'conduct' provisions. A system of supervision of the discharge of those obligations by the Council of the League of Nations was provided for in the mandates system. In these circumstances,

> the question is whether the various mandatories had any direct obligation towards the other members of the League individually, as regards the carrying out of the 'conduct' provisions of the mandates.[173]

The Court concluded that they did not; and whether or not that decision was a correct interpretation of the specific Mandate, and a correct analysis of the mandates system, it is impossible not to recognize that the existence of an obligation does not imply the possession of a right by any

[168] *ICJ Reports*, 1986, p. 130, para. 257.
[169] *ICJ Reports*, 1986, p. 132, para. 262.
[170] *ICJ Reports*, 1966, p. 51, para. 100.
[171] *ICJ Reports*, 1966, p. 51, para. 99.
[172] In the 1966 judgment, the Court expressly reserved the question whether the Mandate, as a treaty, was still in force: *ICJ Reports*, 1966, p. 19, para. 7. Most observers supposed that this question had been decided in the affirmative, if not by the Court's advisory opinion of 1950, at least by the decision on the preliminary objections in 1962.
[173] *ICJ Reports*, 1966, p. 22, para. 14.

subject of international law other than that, or those, in favour of whom the obligation was created. Whether an obligation can be created in favour of all States, the so-called obligations *erga omnes*, is another matter, already discussed in a previous article.[174]

The point could be presented as a matter purely of *jus standi*, and as such treated as one of the law of international claims, or even of procedure, rather than one of State responsibility. The Court was however at some pains to demonstrate that the question it was deciding was one of the merits of the case, not a matter of jurisdiction or admissibility. The reason for its emphasis on this was simply that issues of jurisdiction and admissibility had already been argued and settled at the stage of the preliminary objections and the 1962 judgment rejecting them. Thus the Court emphasized that

> there can be no contradiction between a decision allowing that the Applicants had the capacity to invoke the jurisdictional clause [of the Mandate]—this being the only question which, so far as this point goes, the Court was then called upon to decide, or could decide,—and a decision that the Applicants have not established the legal basis of their claim on the merits,[175]

and that the question was not one of admissibility, that no question of admissibility had been disposed of by the 1962 judgment, and finally that

> If therefore any question of admissibility were involved, it would fall to be decided now, . . . and all that the Court need say is that if this were so, it would determine the question in exactly the same way, and for the same reasons, as in the present judgment.[176]

In any event, it is suggested that the point is clearly the existence *vel non* of an international obligation owed by the respondent State to the applicant State, and of the corresponding right appertaining to the applicant State.

Identification of the beneficiary of an international obligation, and thus the holder of an international right, may coincide with identification of the entity suffering injury from the act complained of; but the two are not necessarily synonymous. In the *Nuclear Tests* case, there was at one stage a suggestion by Australia that the mere fact of the conduct of atmospheric nuclear tests by France justified its claims, but it later emphasized that the essential element of its claim was responsibility for the deposit of

[174] This *Year Book*, 60 (1989), 92–102; see also below, pp. 58–9.

[175] *ICJ Reports*, 1966, p. 38, para. 61.

[176] *ICJ Reports*, 1966, p. 43, para. 76. This part of the judgment is probably the weakest, and caused the most astonishment to those who supposed that the question, regarded as one of *jus standi*, had been settled in 1962. It is also interesting to note that Judges Spender and Fitzmaurice, who voted in favour of the 1966 decision, and are generally regarded as having been its authors, made the same point as to the absence of an individual interest, though in relation to a Trusteeship Agreement, in the *Northern Cameroons* case; but there they each treated the matter as one of *jurisdiction*: see *ICJ Reports*, 1963, pp. 65 and 84 (Spender), 111 and 121 (Fitzmaurice).

fall-out on Australian territory.[177] In the *Barcelona Traction* case,[178] on the other hand, there was no doubt about the existence of injury suffered by Belgian interests, but the existence of an obligation to respect those interests was successfully disputed. It was asserted by Belgium that, as a result of bankruptcy proceedings improperly conducted in Spain relating to the Barcelona Traction company, incorporated in Canada, Belgian nationals with substantial investments as shareholders in the company had suffered loss, for which Spain was thus internationally responsible. The Court dealt first with

> the question of the right of Belgium to exercise diplomatic protection of Belgian shareholders in a company which is a juristic entity incorporated in Canada, the measures complained of having been taken in relation not to any Belgian national but to the company itself,[179]

and stated the issue as being

> whether the losses allegedly suffered by Belgian shareholders in Barcelona Traction were the consequence of the violation of obligations of which they were the beneficiaries. In other words: has a right of Belgium been violated on account of its nationals' having suffered infringement of their rights as shareholders in a company not of Belgian nationality?[180]

Thus the Court was saying that Spain was under an obligation to Belgium not to violate the rights of Belgian nationals, such rights being enjoyed not as a matter of international law, but as a matter of (some system of) municipal law.[181] It similarly had an obligation toward Canada not to violate the rights of the Canadian company, but whether it had done so or not was a matter the Court had no jurisdiction to determine; the case was argued on the assumption that a wrong had been done to the company. This would seem to imply that a State can cause any degree of injury to the *interests* of foreign nationals, without exposing itself to diplomatic claims, provided the *rights* of those persons under municipal law are respected. Yet, as declared in the ILC Draft Articles (Article 4), the characterization of the act of a State as internationally wrongful 'cannot be affected by the characterization of the same act as lawful by internal law'; this is a point to be examined further below.

Although the matter was dealt with as one of *jus standi*, it was, as in the

[177] *ICJ Pleadings, Oral Arguments, Documents*, vol. 1, pp. 324–5 (memorial of Australia) and p. 479 (oral argument). See further section 5 below.

[178] *ICJ Reports*, 1970, p. 3; discussed in the previous articles in this series, this *Year Book*, 60 (1989), pp. 93 ff., 61 (1990), pp. 14 ff., 61 ff.

[179] *ICJ Reports*, 1970, p. 32, para. 32.

[180] *ICJ Reports*, 1970, pp. 32–3, para. 35. On the question of nationality of claims generally, see Fitzmaurice, this *Year Book*, 27 (1950), pp. 24–6; 37 (1961), pp. 37–8; *Collected Edition*, I, pp. 24–6; II, pp. 670–1.

[181] See the passage from the judgment quoted above, text and n. 24. As observed in a previous article in this series, it is a weakness of the judgment that 'it treats "municipal law" not as a concept which, to be meaningful, has to be attached to a specific national legal order, but as a sort of pool of legal ideas common to municipal legal systems': this *Year Book*, 60 (1989), p. 122.

South West Africa cases, really a substantive question: had there been a breach of an obligation owed by Spain to Belgium? The Court's answer was that there had not: not because there was no obligation on Spain to respect the rights of Belgian shareholders in a foreign company, but because there was only an obligation to respect their *rights*, not an obligation to respect their interests. The fact that the *rights* of the Canadian company had (*semble*) not been respected was irrelevant if the only obligation in that respect was owed to Canada. While the judgment has its unsatisfactory aspects, it does make the point that State responsibility flows from the breach of an obligation owed to the complainant State, not to some other entity.

Judge Fitzmaurice did not however see the case as turning on

> any consideration of to whom, or to what entity, was the obligation owed in this case, not to act in a manner contrary to international law. This does not seem to me to be the right question to ask where the issue involved is not one of treaty or other particular obligations, but of general international law obligations in the sphere of the treatment of foreigners. If in the latter area a State, either directly or through its agencies or authorities, acts illicitly, it stands in breach of international law irrespective of whether any other State is qualified to take the matter up. For instance if an individual were concerned, he might be stateless . . . Nor is the question of the entity to which the obligation is due helpful even for the purpose of identifying the party entitled to claim, for such entity would itself previously need to be identified, and the discussion would turn in a circle.[182]

For Judge Fitzmaurice,

> The material and only pertinent question is who or what entity, if any, is entitled to claim in respect of damage accruing to *shareholders* in consequence of illicit treatment of the *company*; . . . [183]

This approach however seems to lead to the conclusion that an act of a State may be illicit in international law even though no obligation owed to any other subject of international law has been breached. Thus Judge Fitzmaurice observes that

> If in the present case there have been contraventions of international law, they are in no way legitimized, nor do they become less illicit, because Canada has not (or even possibly could not) pursue the matter, and because Belgium is held to possess no *locus standi in judicio* for doing so.[184]

This might be said to have been the situation in and at the time of the *South West Africa* cases, on the assumption that South Africa's activities in the Territory were a breach of the Mandate; and *a fortiori* after the

[182] *ICJ Reports*, 1970, p. 66, para. 5.

[183] Ibid., emphasis original. Judge Fitzmaurice came however to the same conclusion as the Court, and in essence for the same reason, the nature in municipal law of the status and rights of shareholders.

[184] *ICJ Reports*, 1970, p. 66, para. 4.

Court in the *Namibia* case had ruled both that the presence of South Africa in Namibia was illegal following the termination of the Mandate by General Assembly Resolution 2145 (XXI), and that the application of *apartheid* to the territory was a breach of the United Nations Charter.

By maintaining the present illegal situation, and occupying the Territory without title, South Africa incurs international responsibilities arising from the continuing violation of an international obligation. It also remains accountable for any violations of its international obligations, or of the rights of the people of Namibia.[185]

If it is asked, to whom were these international responsibilities owed? it is not easy to reply. Normally, if a State is in occupation of a territory unlawfully, there is another State which has the legitimate title, to whom is owed the obligation of the trespasser State to withdraw and make reparation. Thus in the *Temple of Preah Vihear* case, the consequence of the Court's finding that the Temple was situate in Cambodian territory was the existence of an obligation on Thailand to withdraw its forces from the area and restore any cultural objects removed from the Temple. This was clearly an obligation owed to Cambodia. In the case of the Territory of Namibia, difficult questions of legal personality (of the people of Namibia, or of the United Nations Council for Namibia) are raised.[186] The situation was however an exceptional one, the reason for which was the unusual if not unique circumstance of the disappearance of the entity to which the Mandate obligations were owed. In principle and in general, the concept of an act which infringes no one's rights under international law, and is yet internationally illicit, is intellectually unattractive and, it is suggested, a suitable candidate for the application of Occam's razor.

It is of course true that an obligation may be owed to all, or to a large number of States, in the sense that as soon as one or other of them is actually injured (if only in a non-material sense), responsibility arises towards that State. Thus in the *Nicaragua* case, the Court found that there was an obligation on a State which had laid mines at sea in peacetime to give notification of the position of the minefield. Since, as regards Nicaragua, the minelaying constituted a breach of an obligation not to violate sovereignty over internal and territorial waters, the Court did not spell out the implications; and indeed, it had no jurisdiction to find that the United States had incurred responsibility to any of the third States whose vessels struck mines and were damaged. It does not however appear that the Court was holding that the United States had

[185] *ICJ Reports*, 1971, p. 54, para. 118.

[186] See, for example, the legal complications in obtaining admission of Namibia, represented by the UN Council for Namibia, to the ILO, described by Zacklin, 'The Problem of Namibia in International Law', *Recueil des cours*, 171 (1981–I), pp. 311–18.

incurred responsibility towards all States, or even all maritime States; responsibility had to await the event—*in casu* the explosion.[187]

A further curious aspect of the situation in the *Barcelona Traction* case is that the non-existence of an obligation owed to Belgium rested upon the existence of an obligation toward Canada, since the Court recognized that 'the general rule might not take effect' in the situation of 'the company's national State lacking capacity to take action on its behalf'.[188] After examining the relationship between the Barcelona Traction company and Canada, and the steps actually taken by Canada by way of diplomatic protection of the company, the Court concluded that

> This cannot be regarded as amounting to a situation where a violation of law remains without a remedy: in short, a legal vacuum. There is no obligation upon the possessors of rights to exercise them. Sometimes no remedy is sought, though rights are infringed.[189]

This approach is not entirely consistent with the finding that Belgium's *jus standi* depended on whether or not injury had been done to the shareholders' rights conferred by municipal law (in the sense of 'general municipal law'[190]). Whether those rights existed or not, or had or had not been infringed by Spain, could not depend on the quite distinct question whether or not the company's national State had capacity to take action on its behalf. The idea seems to be that there is, at the international law level, an obligation not to cause unlawful injury (if the question-begging term may be permitted!) to the economic entity constituted by the company and its investors; that obligation is owed primarily to the national State of incorporation of the company itself, but if for some reason that State *cannot* enforce the obligation (not merely does not choose to enforce it), then to avoid a 'legal vacuum', there is a secondary or contingent obligation owed to the shareholders' national State. This is a workable conception because it lies all on the plane of international law; but if the underlying criterion is said to be the existence of rights under municipal law, the implication is that rights under municipal law may vary according to whether there is or is not a legal vacuum at the level of international law.

In the *Elettronica Sicula (ELSI)* case a claim was also made to exercise diplomatic protection on behalf of shareholders: it was based on the treatment by Italy of two United States corporations in relation to the

[187] Cf. Ago, Second Report on State Responsibility, *ILC Yearbook*, 1973, vol. 2, pp. 182–4, paras. 11–12.

[188] *ICJ Reports*, 1970, p. 40, para. 64. The point was that it was contended that there was no 'genuine link' between the company and Canada so as to satisfy the test laid down in the *Nottebohm* case, so that Canada could not have exercised diplomatic protection, and, in consequence, Belgium should be permitted to do so. See in particular the separate opinion of Judge Fitzmaurice, *ICJ Reports*, 1970, pp. 79 ff.

[189] *ICJ Reports*, 1970, pp. 44–5, para. 80.

[190] See above, and the previous article referred to in n. 181, above.

Italian corporation ELSI which was wholly owned by the United States corporations, the specific act complained of being the requisition by Italian authorities of the assets of ELSI. No argument was however based by Italy on the ruling in the *Barcelona Traction* case; the claim was based on breach of a treaty-obligation[191] rather than an obligation under customary law, but this does not seem to be a determining element. The case was also one in which the injury inflicted on the company was the act of the national State of the company; according to one view, this constitutes an exceptional case in which customary practice admits the possibility of diplomatic protection exercised by the national State of shareholders.[192] At all events, the Court also made no reference whatever to the *Barcelona Traction* decision; it was left to Judge Oda, in a separate opinion, to raise the matter.

Judge Oda observed, with undisputable correctness, that the United States had espoused the cause of its two national corporations, not that of ELSI,[193] and recalled the limitation described in the 1970 judgment of injury to the direct rights of the shareholders; he pointed out that 'no infringement of any of these rights has been alleged in connection with the events that occurred in Sicily in 1968'.[194] He continued:

> The general principle of law concerning the rights or status of shareholders, which underlies not only Italian company law but also the company law of some other civil law countries, may not be altered by any treaty aimed at the protection of investments unless that treaty contains some express provision to that end. A question which should therefore be asked is whether Italy and the United States agreed, by means of the 1948 FCN Treaty or the 1951 Supplementary Agreement, to modify such a general principle of law or to grant any additional rights to foreign shareholders. It is difficult to see how an affirmative answer can be given to this question.[195]

What for the Court in 1970 was the common core of municipal systems relating to corporations is thus presented by Judge Oda as a general

[191] A Treaty of Friendship, Commerce and Navigation between the two States, dated 2 February 1948, and a Supplementary Agreement, dated 26 September 1951.

[192] See in particular the separate opinion of Judge Fitzmaurice in the *Barcelona Traction* case, *ICJ Reports*, 1970, pp. 72–5, and that of Judge Jessup, ibid., pp. 191–3, paras. 50–2, and the authorities cited. It has to be observed however that the judgment in that case, while mentioning certain other exceptions to the rule against diplomatic protection of shareholders, did not mention this one; since Barcelona Traction was not a Spanish company, it may have been regarded as of too little relevance to be mentioned. *Oppenheim's International Law* (9th edn., by Jennings and Watts) does not mention this exception (see the discussion at vol. 1, pp. 519–20).

[193] *ICJ Reports*, 1989, p. 83. The judgment (para. 46) noted that the original claim was presented on behalf of the US companies, and (para. 56) that the damage alleged was suffered by those companies, but did not deal expressly with the distinction between the Italian company and its shareholders.

[194] *ICJ Reports*, 1989, p. 85, quoting *ICJ Reports*, 1970, p. 36.

[195] *ICJ Reports*, 1989, p. 86. For criticisms of Judge Oda's approach, see Mann, 'Foreign Investment in the International Court of Justice', *American Journal of International Law*, 86 (1992), pp. 97, 99.

principle of law.[196] In the *Barcelona Traction* case, the Court quite openly appealed, by way of *renvoi*, as it were,[197] to municipal law, to something which was not itself part of international law. In which system does Judge Oda's general principle have its being? Not in any specific system of municipal law, nor even in all;[198] but the subject-matter of the principle is 'the rights and status of shareholders', not the right of exercising diplomatic protection on behalf of shareholders, so the 'general principle', governing as it does the subjects of municipal law, not subjects of international law, cannot be a principle of international law.

The conclusion in fact reached by Judge Oda is that a right to exercise diplomatic protection on behalf of shareholders for injury done, not to their 'direct rights', but to the company, since it does not exist in customary international law, can only be conferred by treaty; and, *semble*, such a treaty must be interpreted restrictively,[199] so as not to recognize such a right unless it is clearly intended. The only issue on which Judge Oda effectively differed from his colleagues was thus on how the actual FCN Treaty should be interpreted;[200] the reference to a general principle, it is suggested, merely confuses the issue.

In the *Barcelona Traction* case, at a later stage of the judgment, the Court defined a different aspect of the case: could Belgium claim for injury, through the Barcelona Traction shareholders, to its own economic interests? In this context, the Court stated that

> the Belgian Government would be entitled to bring a claim if it could show that one of its rights had been infringed and that the acts complained of involved the breach of an international obligation arising out of a treaty or a general rule of law.[201]

[196] He also refers to the United States corporations as not being entitled to claim, as shareholders of ELSI, any rights 'other than those rights of shareholders guaranteed to them under Italian law as well as under the general principles of law concerning companies': ibid., pp. 87–8.

It was suggested in an earlier article in this series that the Court in the *Barcelona Traction* case did not base, and indeed could not have based, its decision on 'general principles of law': see this *Year Book*, 61 (1990), pp. 124–6.

[197] This was not how the judgment expressed the process, but was the term used by Judge Gros (*ICJ Reports*, 1970, p. 272, para. 9), and seems to be an accurate description.

[198] Note the reference to Italy and to '*some* other civil law countries': is this sufficient to found a 'general principle of law'?

[199] This seems to have been the view also of the majority of the Chamber, though on a different question of interpretation: see *ICJ Reports*, 1989, p. 65, para. 108; p. 74, para. 124. Judge Oda's restrictive approach is apparently based on the idea that 'It is a great privilege to be able to engage in business in a country other than one's own': *ICJ Reports*, 1989, p. 90.

[200] Judge Oda also held, for reasons not here material, that the claim could however have been brought on the basis of other provisions of the FCN Treaty, not relied on by the United States; but that even so, the claim would have failed on the facts, as the majority of the Chamber concluded on the basis of the articles of the Treaty that *were* relied on.

[201] *ICJ Reports*, 1970, p. 46, para. 86.

There is a certain tautology in this statement, since in the context of this aspect of the case, the possible right of the Belgian Government could apparently only be a right conferred directly by international law; and if so, the breach of an international obligation and the infringement of the right would be one and the same thing. It does however serve to reiterate that State responsibility flows from infringement of a right (the corollary of the respondent State's obligation) appertaining to the State claiming to enforce responsibility.[202]

It is of course evident that responsibility will only flow from a breach of obligation if the obligation was in existence at the time of the alleged breach, and this requirement is stated in Article 18 of the ILC Draft Articles. In the *Northern Cameroons* case, Judge Wellington Koo held that the interest of the Republic of Cameroon in the proper performance by the United Kingdom of its obligations under the Trusteeship for Northern Cameroon was held in common with the United Nations and its other Members, and that all questions relating to that common interest had been disposed of and settled when the General Assembly terminated the Trusteeship by a resolution which Cameroon voted against.

It would be a different matter if the Applicant were complaining of violations of certain of its individual rights or those of its nationals under the Trusteeship Agreement. For such a question might not have been necessarily included in a settlement of all the questions relating to the promotion of the general interests of the trust territory or its inhabitants by the Administering Authority in conformity with its obligations under the Agreement.[203]

2. *Obligations* erga omnes

This matter was fully treated in the first article in this series.[204] In the present context, it should simply be recalled that there has yet been no case before the Court in which responsibility has been found to exist on the basis of an obligation of this type, let alone a case in which the applicant State had not itself suffered direct injury as a result of the act

[202] Cf. the *Barcelona Traction* judgment at pp. 32–3, para. 35. '[T]he idea of the breach of an international obligation can be regarded as the exact equivalent of the idea of the violation of the subjective rights of others': Ago, Third Report on State Responsibility, *ILC Yearbook*, 1971, vol. 2, part 1, pp. 220–1, para. 65.

[203] *ICJ Reports*, 1963, p. 55, para. 39.

[204] This *Year Book*, 60 (1989), pp. 92 ff. The current state of the matter is well surveyed by Claudia Annacker, *Die Durchsetzung von* erga omnes *Verpflichtungen vor dem Internationalen Gerichtshof* (Kovac, Hamburg, 1994), and 'The Legal Regime of *erga omnes* Obligations in International Law', *Austrian Journal of Public International Law*, 46 (1994), p. 131.

alleged to constitute a violation of such an obligation.[205] One of the most difficult questions surrounding the idea of obligations *erga omnes* is in fact the implementation of State responsibility *vis-à-vis* a State which has not itself suffered any direct injury to its individual rights. Is the distinguishing mark of an obligation *erga omnes* the fact that it opens a sort of *actio popularis*, or is it the case, as suggested in Oppenheim, that

> Although the notion of *actio popularis* is in some respects associated with that of rights and obligations *erga omnes*, the two are distinct and, to the extent that they are accepted, each may exist independently of the other.[206]?

3. *Relevance or Irrelevance of Municipal Law*[207]

Mention has already been made of the established rule, enshrined in Article 4 of the ILC Draft Articles on State Responsibility, that the characterization of an act of a State as internationally wrongful by international law 'cannot be affected by the characterization of the same act as lawful by internal law'. This of course is one of the best-established principles in the field; and it applies whether the international obligation said to have been breached is one of customary law or one imposed by treaty.[208] What is the situation if the treaty itself refers to municipal law as the standard for determining the obligation of the State party?

The point was raised in the *Elettronica Sicula* case. The Treaty of Friendship, Commerce and Navigation between Italy and the United States provided that the nationals, corporations and associations of either party were to be permitted to organize, manage and control corporations and associations of the other party 'in conformity with the applicable laws and regulations within the territories' of that other party.[209] The assets of an Italian subsidiary (ELSI) of two United States corporations were requisitioned, and as a result, it was claimed, the subsidiary became

[205] In the *East Timor* case, Portugal argued that, the right of self-determination being a right *erga omnes*, the obligation to respect it was an obligation *erga omnes*, and that therefore Portugal was entitled to bring proceedings against Australia alleging that the conclusion by Australia of a treaty with Indonesia affecting East Timor's continental shelf was an infringement of the right of self-determination of the people of East Timor, in view of the alleged unlawfulness of Indonesia's presence in the territory. The Court refused to hear the case in the absence of Indonesia, on the precedent of the *Monetary Gold* decision. While this was clearly correct, it is a pity that the Court did not have the opportunity to point out the logical error in the very first step in Portugal's argument. To say that a right is enforceable against all the world does not mean necessarily that anyone other than the beneficiary of the right can so enforce it.

[206] *Oppenheim's International Law* (9th edn., by Jennings and Watts), vol. 1, p. 5.

[207] See also Fitzmaurice in this *Year Book*, 29 (1952), pp. 25–6, and 35 (1959), p. 183; *Collected Edition*, I, pp. 156–7, II, p. 587; and the present writer, ibid., 60 (1989), pp. 117–25 and 127–8.

[208] 'It is a generally accepted principle of international law that in the relations between powers who are contracting parties to a treaty, the provisions of municipal law cannot prevail over those of the treaty': *Greek and Bulgarian Communities*, PCIJ, Series B, No. 17, p. 32.

[209] For the text of the Treaty on this point, see *ICJ Reports*, 1989, p. 49, para. 68.

insolvent, causing loss to the United States corporations. It was argued by Italy that the clause quoted confirmed that the correct interpretation of the text of the Treaty was that

> it was not intended to confer upon United States nationals any rights of control and management more extensive, or more extensively protected, than those enjoyed by other stockholders, of whatever nationality, in Italian companies,[210]

and that since the requisition 'was issued by the competent authority on a regular legal basis', no breach of the Treaty had occurred. The Court however declined to read the Treaty in that sense:

> But, in the Chamber's view, the reference to conformity with 'the applicable laws and regulations' cannot mean that, if an act is in conformity with the municipal law and regulations, that would of itself exclude any possibility that it was an act in breach of the FCN Treaty.[211]

The Court was here not laying down a principle of general law, but simply interpreting a specific treaty; and there would seem no reason why a treaty should not provide in terms that the nationals of each party should have the same rights as local nationals, but no more or wider rights, so that diplomatic protection could only be exercised if there were discriminatory treatment; whether this would add anything to the customary rules as to the 'international minimum standard' is another matter. At the same time, the Court's dictum seems to imply at the least a presumption against the interpretation advanced by Italy, so that only a clear and unambiguous treaty provision in that sense would have the effect contended for; and in so holding, it appears to have been influenced by the idea that municipal law may not be cited as a justification for failure to perform international law obligations. Strictly, that aspect is irrelevant: the question is, what was the extent of the international law obligations that were undertaken?

In other words, in some cases the question whether there has been an act internationally wrongful by international law may depend on the lawfulness of the same or related acts under internal law. It also appears that this possibility is not limited to treaty-obligations: the *Barcelona Traction* judgment expressly contemplates that a customary-law obligation may be so dependent on municipal law. This follows from the distinction drawn by the Court between 'injury in respect of a right and injury to a simple interest' of foreign nationals:

> evidence that damage was suffered does not *ipso facto* justify a diplomatic claim. Persons suffer damage or harm in most varied circumstances. This in itself does not involve the obligation to make reparation. Not a mere interest affected, but solely a right infringed involves responsibility, so that an act directed against and

[210] *ICJ Reports*, 1989, p. 50, para. 71.
[211] *ICJ Reports*, 1989, pp. 50–1, para. 71.

infringing only the company's rights does not involve responsibility towards the shareholders, even if their interests are affected.[212]

What system of law defines the rights whose infringement involves responsibility? The Court had already stated that

> whenever legal issues arise concerning the rights of States with regard to the treatment of companies and shareholders, as to which rights international law has not established its own rules, it has to refer to the relevant rules of municipal law.[213]

It would therefore seem to follow that if a foreign company or a foreign shareholder is injured by an act attributable to a State, the question whether that act is internationally wrongful depends on whether the act infringed a municipal law right, i.e. whether the act is to be characterized as wrongful in municipal law.

This makes clear why the Court in 1970 was discreetly vague about *which* municipal law is to determine whether it is rights or 'simple interests' that have been infringed; if it were the municipal law of the respondent State, or indeed the law of (for example) the national State of the company, the result would be to allow that internal law to prevail over international law. Hence the idea of a sort of common law of corporations, according to which no right of shareholders is infringed if the company is rendered bankrupt by improper means. In a sense, the 1970 judgment appeals to a sort of international minimum standard in the field of company law; presumably if Canada had brought proceedings, on the grounds of injury to the company, the Court would have accepted that the international minimum standard had not been attained, that there had been a breach of the *rights* of the company under this common municipal law, so that, assuming the case against Spain could be established on the facts, Canada would have been able to recover.

In the first of this series of articles[214] attention was drawn to the finding in the *Elettronica Sicula* case that the reverse is also true: the fact that injury is suffered by foreign nationals as a result of an act which is found, by a municipal court, to be contrary to internal law does not of itself signify that that act is an internationally wrongful act. The general dictum of the Court in that case:

> the fact that an act of a public authority may have been unlawful in municipal law does not necessarily mean that that act was unlawful in international law, as a breach of treaty or otherwise,[215]

[212] *ICJ Reports*, 1970, p. 36, para. 46.

[213] *ICJ Reports*, 1970, pp. 33–4, para. 38.

[214] This *Year Book*, 60 (1989), pp. 116–17.

[215] *ICJ Reports*, 1989, p. 74, para. 124. This finding was criticized by Mann as a 'discrepancy' which 'introduces a new aspect into the law of state responsibility': 'Foreign Investment in the International Court of Justice: the *ELSI* case', *American Journal of International Law*, 86 (1992), p. 95.

was in fact rather wider than the case required. The contention of the United States was that a requisition order made by the Italian authorities against the ELSI company, which was the origin of injury suffered by the United States parent company, was a breach of a treaty[216] which provided that

> The nationals, corporations and associations of either High Contracting Party shall not be subjected to arbitrary or discriminatory measures within the territories of the other High Contracting Party . . . [217]

and that since the requisition order was later quashed (on grounds, apparently, of 'excess of power'[218]), this demonstrated that it had been an 'arbitrary measure' within the meaning of the treaty. The United States was thus not arguing that municipal-law illegality entailed breach of treaty, but simply that the revocation of the requisition on grounds of *ultra vires* was overwhelming proof that it was arbitrary, which was forbidden by the treaty. Whether any conclusion could safely be drawn from the revocation of the order as to its international unlawfulness outside the regime of the treaty must be regarded as doubtful.

A question raised in the *Barcelona Traction* proceedings but which, being part of the merits, was not examined by the Court was the allegation by Belgium that 'a large number of decisions of the Spanish courts' in relation to the company were 'vitiated by gross and manifest error in the application of Spanish law, by arbitrariness or discrimination' and that these thus constituted 'in international law denials of justice *lato sensu*'.[219] It is of course recognized that the international minimum standard in this field requires protection against arbitrary or discriminatory treatment of aliens, but Belgium appears to have suggested that 'gross and manifest error' by the judge in the application of internal law would be in itself sufficient to constitute denial of justice, at least if the error resulted in the assumption of jurisdiction contrary to the requirements of internal law.[220]

4. *Obligations of Means and Obligations of Result*

The ILC Draft Articles on State Responsibility introduced into this field of the law a distinction which, though probably previously latent in

[216] A Supplementary Agreement, dated 26 Septmber 1951, to a Treaty of Friendship, Commerce and Navigation between the two countries, dated 2 February 1948.

[217] Quoted in *ICJ Reports*, 1989, p. 72, para. 120.

[218] The Chamber had some difficulty in ascertaining exactly what were, in Italian law, the grounds for revoking the order; but see *ICJ Reports*, 1989, p. 76, para. 127.

[219] Final submissions of Belgium, quoted in *ICJ Reports*, 1970, p. 18.

[220] See in particular Mann, counsel for Belgium, who argued the question: 'did the Spanish court in pronouncing the bankruptcy of Barcelona Traction act so grossly in disregard of Spanish law that Spain committed a denial of justice by acting without jurisdiction in Spanish law?': *ICJ Pleadings, Oral Arguments, Documents, Barcelona Traction*, vol. 8, pp. 400 ff.

State practice and abitral decisions, had not previously been stated explicitly as recognized in international law: the distinction between '*obligations de moyens*' (obligations of means, or of conduct) and '*obligations de résultat*' (obligations of result).[221] The Court has not so far found it necessary to state this distinction expressly for purposes of analysis of cases before it, but in the *Elettronica Sicula (ELSI)* case, Judge Schwebel employed it in his dissenting opinion to find Italy responsible for a breach of the Treaty relied on in that case.

The distinction appears in Articles 20 and 21 of the ILC Draft:

Article 20.
Breach of an international obligation requiring the adoption of a particular course of conduct

There is a breach by a State of an international obligation requiring it to adopt a particular course of conduct when the conduct of that State is not in conformity with that required of it by that obligation.

Article 21.
Breach of an international obligation requiring the achievement of a specified result

1. There is a breach by a State of an international obligation requiring it to achieve, by means of its own choice, a specified result if, by the conduct adopted, the State does not achieve the result required of it by that obligation.
2. When the conduct of the State has created a situation not in conformity with the result required of it by an international obligation, but the obligation allows that this or an equivalent result may nevertheless be achieved by subsequent conduct of the State, there is a breach of the obligation only if the State also fails by its subsequent conduct to achieve the result required of it by that obligation.[222]

The obligation in question in the case was the requirement of the Supplemental Agreement to the Treaty of Friendship, Commerce and Navigation between Italy and the United States that the nationals,

[221] The distinction was suggested by Ago in his Sixth Report to the ILC on State Responsibility, *ILC Yearbook*, 1977, vol. 2, part 1, p. 8, para. 12, refining an idea advanced by Reuter, *Droit international public* (1955), pp. 56 ff. The Report of the ILC also attributes some credit for the concept to Donati, *I trattati internazionali nel diritto costituzionale* (Turin, 1906): see ibid., part 2, p. 12, n. 23.

It appears that the distinction as expressed in the ILC Draft Articles is not identical to the distinction designated by the same terminology in municipal law, in particular French law: see Combacau, 'Obligations de résultat et obligations de comportement: quelques questions et pas de réponse', *Le Droit international, unité et diversité (Mélanges Reuter)* (1981), pp. 186–7. The distinction is in fact fairly long-established in French law: see Demogue, *Traité des obligations en général* (1923), tome V, no. 1237; tome VI, no. 599; and Tung, 'La Distinction des obligations de résultat et des obligations de diligence', *Jurisclasseurs périodiques*, 1945, pp. 1, 449.

[222] *ILC Yearbook*, 1980, vol. 2, p. 32.

corporations and associations of either party should not be subjected to 'arbitrary or discriminatory measures' within the territories of the other party.[223] Judge Schwebel took the view that a requisition by the Mayor of Palermo of the assets of the ELSI company amounted to an arbitrary measure *vis-à-vis* the two United States corporations of which ELSI was a wholly-owned subsidiary. The requisition was however annulled by the Prefect of Palermo, though only after considerable delay, never satisfactorily explained; and Judge Schwebel was concerned to refute the argument that

> since ELSI . . . had access to processes of justice, and since the procedures and results of that process cannot be seen as tantamount to a denial of justice, that is the end of the matter, that, even if the order of requisition was arbitrary and hence initially engaged Italy's responsibility under the Treaty, that responsibility was never consummated by reason of the fact that, in the end, ELSI's case was dealt with by Italy's internal processes.[224]

The Chamber did not go into these matters, because it did not consider that the original order of requisition was 'a measure which could reasonably be said to earn the qualification "arbitrary", as it is employed in Article I'.[225] In reply to the argument thus stated, Judge Schwebel considered the treaty requirement in the light of the ILC distinction between the two sorts of obligation, and concluded that, in terms of the Commission's analysis, 'the obligation of Article I would seem to be an obligation not of means but of result, as international treaty obligations concerning the protection of aliens and their interests normally are'.[226] Accordingly, Italy had achieved neither the 'specified result' laid down by the Treaty, nor the 'equivalent result' contemplated by Article 21, paragraph 2, of the ILC Draft; the 'specified result' being, 'namely, relieving ELSI of the effects of the arbitrary measure of requisition', since although the requisition was annulled, by the time the Prefect of Palermo made his decision, irreparable damage had been done.

It is difficult to fault Judge Schwebel's analysis of the obligation under Article I as being an obligation of result; and his opinion thus offers a

[223] See the text of the Article at p. 72 of *ICJ Reports*, 1986.

[224] This is Judge Schwebel's own statement of the objection which might be made to his view, as set out in his dissenting opinion, *ICJ Reports*, 1986, pp. 115–16.

[225] *ICJ Reports*, 1986, p. 77, para. 130.

[226] Ibid., p. 117. The ILC classified rules as to treatment of aliens generally as obligations of result: Report of the ILC, *Yearbook of the ILC*, 1977, vol. 2, part 2, p. 24, para. 17. Note however the view expressed by some judges in the *Ambatielos* case that a claim of denial of justice is essentially a claim arising under, and founded on, general international law, not a matter of commercial treaty rights; see the discussion by Fitzmaurice in this *Year Book*, 32 (1955–6), pp. 81–2; *Collected Edition*, I, pp. 321–2. The treaty involved in that case was however of a different nature, and played a different role, from the US-Italian FCN Treaty in the *ELSI* case.

useful gloss, if one of no great significance, on the distinction drawn in the ILC Draft Articles. Yet the result of his argument in the specific case is perhaps surprising, and prompts hesitations. This need not however cast doubts on the validity or appropriateness of the distinction between the two classes of obligation; if one is to disagree with Judge Schwebel's conclusion, it may rather be a disagreement with his view of what the actual obligation of result entailed. Was there a duty to 'relieve ELSI of the effects of the arbitrary measure of requisition'? If it is assumed that the belated action of the Prefect, however regrettable, was not in itself 'arbitrary or discriminatory' (and it is not Judge Schwebel's argument that it was), then was the treaty obligation anything more than to ensure that, if an arbitrary measure was taken with regard to a United States national, that measure was corrected by the normal judicial or administrative means, operating themselves in a non-arbitrary and non-discriminatory way? There is also the fact that if the effects of the requisition order were peculiarly disastrous, and in effect irretrievable, so that the revocation of the order did not restore the *status quo*, this was because of the critical financial position of the company, for which the Italian authorities were not responsible.[226a] In other words, one should perhaps guard against being led by the neatness of the distinction between obligations of conduct and obligations of result to assume that that distinction must always be a sharp one; that the 'specified result' must always be seen in absolute terms,[227] rather than in terms of its context, which may imply some qualification, particularly in the field of protection of aliens, on the lines of 'in accordance with the normal judicial and administrative procedures'.

5. *The Impact of the State Act: The Relevance of Damage*

On the basis that State responsibility arises from the breach by one State of an obligation owed to another, the controversy over the question whether damage or prejudice suffered by the latter State is an essential element for the existence of responsibility has not entirely been laid to

[226a] The problem is not unknown in municipal law: in England, cf. the litigation following the sinking of the dredger *Liesbosch*: *The Edison*, [1931] P 230; [1932] P 52; *Owners of dredger Liesbosch* v. *Owners of steamship Edison*, [1933] AC 449.

[227] 'La distinction des deux types d'obligations ne porte pas sur le degré de précision de la norme juridique. Il est des obligations de résultat "floues" ou ambiguës, comme il est des obligations de comportement qui impose des résultats très précis . . . L'opposition réside dans la "permissivité quant aux moyens" laissée initialement au destinataire de la norme ou dans la possibilité qui lui est laissée de corriger les effets pervers de la mise en oeuvre initiale de son obligation': *Droit international public* (Nguyen Quoc Dinh) (5th edn. by Daillier and Pellet, 1994), p. 735, § 484.

rest.[228] The Reports of Ago to the International Law Commission took the view that the existence of prejudice was not an essential element for the existence of responsibility, only for its *mise en oeuvre*, i.e., in effect, that *injuria sine damnum* is nonetheless *injuria*, and the Commission adopted that view;[229] it has however been suggested that the current Rapporteur, Arangio-Ruiz, is moving rather in the direction of reinstating prejudice as a precondition to the existence of responsibility.[230] Even in the original Ago/ILC approach, however, it was recognized that a 'theoretical' breach of an international obligation, which has no impact at all on the beneficiary of the obligation, does not give rise to responsibility; and by coincidence, the hypothetical case which Ago put forward, and the Commission adopted, to illustrate the point became reality a few years later, and came before the Court as the case concerning *United States Diplomatic and Consular Staff in Tehran.*

In the Commission's report it was explained that in the case of some obligations, a necessary condition of responsibility would be the occurrence of a certain external event.

> For a State to be said to have failed in its duty to protect the premises of a foreign embassy against injurious acts of third parties, it is not sufficient to show that the State was negligent in not providing adequate police protection; some injurious event must also have taken place as a result of that negligence, such as damage by hostile demonstrators or an attack on the embassy premises by private individuals.[231]

When an attack of precisely that kind was made on the United States embassy, the Court found that it was the 'inaction' of the Iranian Government which 'constituted clear and serious violations of Iran's

[228] Thus P.-M. Dupuy has suggested that in excluding the idea of damage from its conception of the condition for creation of international responsibility, the ILC has merely made its own task more difficult: see 'Le fait générateur de la responsabilité internationale des Etats', *Recueil des cours*, 188 (1984–V), pp. 54–5.

One way of expressing the point is by asking whether in international law, and specifically international litigation, there exists a *contentieux de légalité* as well as a *contentieux de responsabilité* or *contentieux de la réparation*; cf. Bollecker-Stern, *Le Préjudice dans la théorie de la responsabilité internationale* (Paris, 1973). In the view of Judge Gros, the proceedings brought by Australia and New Zealand in the *Nuclear Tests* cases were the former rather than the latter: separate opinion, *ICJ Reports*, 1974, p. 277, para. 2. The Court's power to give a declaratory judgment is well recognized, indeed 'indisputable' (*Northern Cameroons, ICJ Reports*, 1963, p. 37), but would it conclude and declare that there had been an internationally unlawful act in the absence of any prejudice? *Contra*, P.-M. Dupuy, op. cit., pp. 91–2.

[229] Ago in *ILC Yearbook*, 1970, vol. 2, pp. 194–5, paras. 50–4; Report of the Commission, ibid., 1973, vol. 2, pp. 182–4, paras. 10–11. The Commission indeed held that 'To refer to "damage" as a constituent element of the internationally wrongful act separate from the breach of an obligation could even be dangerous, because it might give the impression that in the Commission's opinion, where there was breach of an international obligation without "damage", there was no wrongful act and no responsibility': ibid., p. 183, footnote 97. In the same sense, Graefrath, 'Responsibility and Damages Caused: Relationship between Responsibility and Damages', *Recueil des cours*, 185 (1984–II), pp. 34–6.

[230] See *Droit international public* (Nguyen Quoc Dinh), p. 753, para. 495.

[231] *ILC Yearbook*, 1973, vol. 2, p. 182, para. 11.

obligations to the United States' under the Vienna Conventions on Diplomatic and Consular Relations, and under 'general international law'.[232] Those obligations were 'to take all appropriate steps to protect the premises of the mission against any intrusion or damage' (1961 Convention, Article 22) and to 'take all appropriate steps to prevent any attack' on the person of a diplomatic agent (ibid., Article 29). Clearly it would only be possible to establish indisputably that such steps had *not* been taken if an intrusion, damage or attack were actually to occur; but this, strictly, only goes to proof. Iran could say that, so long as no such event had occurred, the steps it was taking, however inadequate in theory or in appearance, could not be said to fall short of the standard of 'appropriateness'.[233] Furthermore, the Court laid some stress on the fact that, after the attack had begun, the embassy called for help, and nothing was done by the Iranian Government; this also goes rather to a question of proof.

At all events, the distinction between the Commission's 'external event' and actual 'damage' is a fine one; but it is certainly possible, in the context of the *Hostages* case, to imagine an external event which would reveal that insufficient protection was being given to an embassy, even without the embassy premises or staff suffering any injury.[234]

One of the stock examples mentioned to show that a breach of an international obligation may occur without any material damage or prejudice being caused is that of an unauthorized overflight of State territory by an aircraft of another State.[235] In the *Nicaragua* case this was one of the complaints addressed to the United States by Nicaragua, and the Court found that by authorizing such overflights the United States had acted 'in breach of its obligation under customary international law not to violate the sovereignty of another State'.[236] It is curious that both Nicaragua and the Court devoted some attention to the question whether or not some of the overflights had produced 'sonic booms', intended, in Nicaragua's view, to exert psychological pressure on the population and government,[237] since this allegation, even if true, would be irrelevant to the establishment of United States responsibility.

Another stock problem in the discussion of this subject is the effect of a State's internal legislation which is in conflict with its international

[232] *ICJ Reports*, 1980, p. 31, para. 62; p. 32, para. 67.

[233] In this negative sense, *post hoc* and *propter hoc* are indistinguishable; the corollary is that the host State has to accept that the converse argument is also legitimate: the occurrence of an attack shows, or constitutes a presumption that, the protection was insufficient.

[234] This may be illustrated by an incident which occurred at The Hague in the writer's experience; a shot was fired, intended for a particular embassy, but the marksman had mistaken the address, and shattered the window of the house next door. There was no damage suffered by the embassy; was there a breach of the obligation of protection?

[235] Graefrath, 'Responsibility and Damages Caused: Relationship between Responsibility and Damages', *Recueil des cours*, 185 (1984–II), pp. 34–5.

[236] *ICJ Reports*, 1986, p. 147, para. 292(5); see also p. 128, para. 251.

[237] *ICJ Reports*, 1986, pp. 51–3, paras. 87–91.

obligations; is the mere adoption of such legislation a breach of obligation, or only its active implementation? (There is also the parallel problem of a failure to adopt legislation required by a treaty commitment.) In the *Nicaragua* case legislation was passed in the United States authorizing financial aid to the *contras*; the Court found that 'by training, arming, equipping, *financing* and supplying the *contra* forces'[238] the United States was in breach of the obligation not to intervene in the affairs of another State; but it does not appear that the mere passage of the legislation amounted to a breach, but only its implementation—the actual supply of funds to the *contras*.

In the case concerning the *Applicability of the Obligation to Arbitrate under Section 21 of the United Nations Headquarters Agreement of 26 June 1947*, the Court was asked to say whether the United States was under an obligation to enter into arbitration with the United Nations under the treaty provision referred to, which covered 'any dispute between the United Nations and the United States concerning the interpretation or application of this agreement . . . '. The United States had adopted legislation requiring the closure of the office of the Palestine Liberation Organization in New York; it was contended by the Secretary-General (and in fact accepted by the State Department) that implementation of this legislation would constitute a breach of the provisions of the Agreement concerning free movement of persons invited to Headquarters by the United Nations. The legislation was 'signed into law' by the United States President on 22 December 1987; it was to come into effect on 21 March 1988. On 14 January 1988 the Secretary-General formally invoked the dispute settlement procedure in Article 21 of the Agreement. On 11 March 1988 the United States Attorney-General notified the PLO of the legislation, and indicated that if the PLO failed to comply with it, 'the Department of Justice will forthwith take action in United States federal court to ensure your compliance'.

The Court was not asked whether the United States was in fact in breach of the Agreement, but only whether there was a dispute such that the arbitration clause would come into effect.[239] The Court was undoubtedly correct in holding that a dispute had arisen 'concerning the interpretation or implementation of' the Agreement; but it is noticeable that it was cautious on the question of timing. The Secretary-General had contended that there was a dispute 'from the moment the Anti-Terrorism Act was signed into law by the President';[240] but he did not suggest that there had been a breach of the Agreement until the date of the Attorney-General's letter of 11 March 1988. The Court at one point referred to the situation as being one in which 'one party to a treaty

[238] *ICJ Reports*, 1986, p. 146, para. 292(3), emphasis added; for the details of the legislation see ibid., pp. 55–9, paras. 95–9.

[239] *ICJ Reports*, 1988, p. 26, para. 33.

[240] *ICJ Reports*, 1988, p. 28, para. 36.

protests against the behaviour or a decision of another party, and claims that such behaviour *constitutes a breach of the treaty*',[241] but finally avoided linking the existence of a dispute to the claim that there had already been a breach of the treaty, or any statement as to when the dispute arose:

For the purposes of the present advisory opinion there is no need to seek to determine the date at which the dispute came into existence, once the Court has reached the conclusion that there is such a dispute at the date on which its opinion is given.[242]

There may be situations in which the existence of material damage may be required, if not directly to establish the breach of an obligation, at least to identify the victim of the State act impugned, and thus establish in which direction an obligation is owed.[243] The evident example is the *Barcelona Traction* case; if the bankruptcy of the company in Spain had not caused financial injury to the Belgian shareholders, the question whether there was an obligation owed to, and enforceable by, Belgium to respect their interests, would simply not have arisen. If the shareholders had had appropriate rights, and not merely interests, under general municipal law, such an obligation would have existed; but if the shareholders had all been Spanish, it would not. Unless there has been material damage, it is impossible to say what has been infringed, and therefore impossible to say whether it was a right or an interest.

A parallel situation arises where an act is said to be in breach of an obligation owed to all States, but only one particular State, or certain States, have suffered harm. An illustration is the contention of France in the *Nuclear Tests* cases: it in effect conceded that fall-out from its atmospheric tests was received on Australian territory, but adduced evidence to show that this did not constitute a danger to the health of the population, from which it concluded that 'in the absence of ascertained damage attributable to its nuclear experiments, they did not violate any rule of international law'.[244] The complainant States in that case relied on an alleged general rule of illegality of atmospheric nuclear tests; but Australia did not assert an obligation *erga omnes* in the sense of an obligation, breach of which would open universal responsibility without proof of injury. Australia recognized that it had to show special damage, or at least special impact;[245] it did mention the *Barcelona Traction* dictum

[241] *ICJ Reports*, 1988, p. 28, para. 38, emphasis added.

[242] *ICJ Reports*, 1988, p. 30, para. 44.

[243] *Contra*, Graefrath, 'Responsibility and Damages Caused: Relationship between Responsibility and Damages', *Recueil des cours*, 185 (1984–II), pp. 42–7.

[244] Quoted in order on provisional measures, *ICJ Reports*, 1973, p. 105, para. 28. But note the possibility that infringement of sovereignty by the fall-out was in itself damage to Australia.

[245] The contrary interpretation advanced by Graefrath, 'Responsibility and Damages Caused: Relationship between Responsibility and Damages', *Recueil des cours*, 185 (1984–II), pp. 44–5, does not appear to distinguish sufficiently between the positions of Australia and New Zealand.

in its memorial, but later disclaimed any intention of arguing that France incurred legal responsibility merely by conducting the tests; the essential element was responsibility for the fall-out on Australian territory.[246] New Zealand on the other hand did advance the *erga omnes* view,[247] and maintained it to the end; the Court however appears to have treated its submissions in this respect as ancillary to the main objective of achieving an end to the tests, so that the French unilateral undertaking to stop them was treated as rendering the whole claim 'moot'.[248]

Chapter III

Circumstances Precluding Wrongfulness

1. *Preliminary*

In the conceptual structure of the ILC Draft Articles, it is clear that consideration of the question whether any circumstances are present precluding the wrongfulness of a particular State act is postponed to the establishment of the illicit nature of that act in itself, assuming the absence of any such circumstances. Circumstances peculiar to the nature of the obligation may render lawful, and no breach of the obligation, an act which in other factual circumstances, or perhaps in most, would have been such a breach. These are however not the 'circumstances precluding wrongfulness' of Chapter V of the Draft Articles, which are of general application, irrespective of the source or nature of the obligation relied on.

This is illustrated by the decision in the *Right of Passage* case. The Court concluded that with regard to private persons, civil officials and goods in general there existed in favour of Portugal a right of passage between Daman and the Portuguese enclaves in Indian territory, but that no such right existed in respect of armed forces, armed police and arms and ammunition.[249] It had thus to consider 'whether India has acted contrary to its obligation resulting from Portugal's right of passage'; it was admitted that after the overthrow of Portuguese authority in the enclave of Dadra on 21–22 July 1954, all passage between Daman and the

[246] *Pleadings, Oral Arguments, Documents*, vol. 1 pp. 334–5; ibid., p. 479.

[247] See in particular *Pleadings, Oral Arguments, Documents*, vol. 2, pp. 263 ff.

[248] See paras. 30–1 of the judgment in the New Zealand case, *ICJ Reports*, 1974, pp. 466–7, and the dissent of Judges Onyeama, Dillard, Jiménez de Aréchaga and Waldock, ibid., pp. 474–500. One may in fact suspect that the decision in the New Zealand case was forced into the mould set by the Australian case, the 're-interpretation' of the intentions of the applicant being easier in relation to the claims of Australia than in relation to those of New Zealand. The latter State was therefore in a slightly stronger position to try to recommence proceedings in 1995; in its order of 22 September 1995 the Court simply treated the 're-interpretation' as *res judicata*, as of course it was, without seeking to justify it; *ICJ Reports*, 1995, p. 305, para. 59.

[249] *ICJ Reports*, 1960, pp. 40, 43.

enclaves was suspended by India,[250] so that prima facie there had been a breach of India's obligation. However, the Court held that 'in view of the tension then prevailing in Indian territory' (which had been mentioned by India in a diplomatic note as a ground for refusing a specific request by Portugal for passage), India's action was not 'action contrary to its obligation resulting from Portugal's right of passage'.[251]

There is an obvious affinity between this reasoning and the hypothesis of a state of necessity mentioned in Article 33 of the ILC Draft Articles as a circumstance precluding wrongfulness; and this is emphasized by the fact that in Portugal's view the Government of India had contributed to the creation of the situation of tension which it relied upon as an excuse.[252] But the Court's reasoning was that on a proper interpretation of the obligation itself, no breach had occurred:

> Portugal's claim to a full right of passage is subject to full recognition and exercise of Indian sovereignty over the intervening territory and without any immunity in favour of Portugal. The Court is of the view that India's refusal of passage in those cases was, in the circumstances, covered by its power of regulation and control of the right of passage of Portugal.[253]

Similarly in the *Elettronica Sicula (ELSI)* case, when called upon to decide whether the requisition of the company's plant and equipment by the Mayor of Palermo was an 'arbitrary' measure, and thus contrary to Italy's treaty obligations toward the United States, the Chamber seised of the case observed that

> one must remember the situation in Palermo at the moment of the requisition, with the threatened sudden unemployment of some 800 workers at one factory. It cannot be said to have been unreasonable or merely capricious for the Mayor to seek to use the powers conferred on him by the law in an attempt to do something about a difficult and distressing situation.[254]

This again is a question of determination whether there had been a breach of an international obligation at all, rather than ascertaining whether such a breach, although committed, was excused by a situation of necessity. The Court had already noted that

> Every system of [municipal] law must provide, for example, for interferences with the normal exercise of rights during public emergencies and the like.[255]

[250] *ICJ Reports*, 1960, p. 44.

[251] *ICJ Reports*, 1960, p. 45.

[252] See, for example, Portuguese reply, *ICJ Pleadings, Oral Arguments, Documents*, vol. 2, pp. 569–70, para. 385; the Court appears to have tacitly rejected this argument. But cf. Article 33, para. 2 (*b*), of the ILC Draft Articles, whereby a state of necessity may not be invoked 'if the State in question has contributed to the occurrence of the state of necessity'.

[253] *ICJ Reports*, 1960, p. 45.

[254] *ICJ Reports*, 1989, p. 76, para. 129.

[255] *ICJ Reports*, 1989, p. 51, para. 74.

At the same time, it must be recognized that the structure of the ILC Draft Articles, whereby such matters as necessity and self-defence operate, not to excuse a State from the consequences of a recognized breach of obligation, but to render the relevant act innocent by 'excluding unlawfulness', results in a very fine dividing line between a finding that the obligation on its terms, did not arise in (for example) a case of necessity, and deciding that although there was a breach of obligation, there was no unlawfulness because of the existence of a state of necessity.

A problem of some theoretical interest, but which need only be touched on here, is the relevance of 'circumstances excluding unlawfulness' to the exercise of the Court's power under Article 41 of the Statute to indicate provisional measures. In the *Nicaragua* case, the United States contended (*inter alia*) at the stage of the Nicaraguan request for provisional measures that

> Nicaragua's armed forces have conducted open armed attacks across its borders, as a result of which Honduras and Costa Rica have repeatedly protested; and that Nicaragua's neighbours have turned to the United States for security assistance, and there has been increased co-operation among those countries in collective self-defence measures.[256]

Assuming this to be an unambiguous reliance on collective self-defence, as a 'circumstance excluding unlawfulness', it amounted to a direct denial that any rights of Nicaragua had been infringed, even if all Nicaragua's allegations as to what the United States had done were upheld. This consideration was surely relevant to the question whether the circumstances required the indication of measures 'to preserve the respective rights of either party' under Article 41. If self-defence were regarded as a justification whereby a breach of an obligation (and thus an infringement of a right) would not entail the normal consequences of responsibility, while still remaining a breach of the obligation, the Court would be in a stronger position to protect what would, on that hypothesis, be an undoubted right to be free from the threat or use of force by the United States. In view however of the reference in the Statute to the rights of either party, the United States could insist on equal attention being paid, even on the *summaria cognitio*, to the possibility that it was acting perfectly lawfully, unlawfulness being excluded by collective self-defence.

In practice, the Court of course relies in provisional measures cases on the consideration that at that stage it 'cannot make definitive findings of fact', and the reservation of the right of the respondent 'to dispute the facts alleged and to submit arguments in respect of the merits',[257] and would probably do so, and to the same extent, whatever the view it took

[256] *ICJ Reports*, 1984, p. 182, para. 30.

[257] *Nicaragua* case, *ICJ Reports*, 1984, p. 182, para. 31.

as to the exact legal nature and operation of such elements as self-defence.

2. *Consent*

Article 29 of the International Law Commission's Draft Articles enshrines the well-established, if not self-evident, principle that consent precludes wrongfulness of the act consented to.[258] An instance of this was alluded to in passing in the judgment in the *Nicaragua* case: it was concerned to show that even if the United States had been requested by the *contras*, as an opposition group in Nicaragua, to support them in their struggle, this would not have justified United States intervention.

> Indeed, it is difficult to see what would remain of the principle of non-intervention in international law if intervention, which is already allowable at the request of the government of a State, were also to be allowed at the request of the opposition.[259]

Aside from this pragmatic justification, the essential difference between the two cases is surely that the legitimate government has status to give consent to what would otherwise be an unlawful act against the State, while the opposition has not.

In the case concerning *Certain Phosphate Lands in Nauru*, Nauru claimed from Australia rehabilitation of phosphate lands on the island worked out prior to independence, during a United Nations Trusteeship administered by Australia, New Zealand and the United Kingdom. Australia raised a preliminary objection that 'the Nauruan authorities, even before acceding to independence, waived all claims relating to rehabilitation of the phosphate lands'.[260] This however is not so much a claim of consent negativing international unlawfulness, but rather that, assuming there to have been responsibility (which Australia denied) arising from a breach of an obligation toward Nauru, that responsibility had been voluntarily waived. The question is not one of a 'circumstance excluding unlawfulness'; it is mentioned here only to mark the distinction.

3. *Self-Defence*

In the *Nicaragua* case, the Court had occasion to examine the law of self-defence, in particular collective self-defence, as it exists in customary

[258] Paragraph 1: 'The consent validly given by a State to the commission by another State of a specified act not in conformity with an obligation of the latter State towards the former State precludes the wrongfulness of the act in relation to that State to the extent that the act remains within the limits of that consent'. Paragraph 2 reserves the question of *jus cogens*.

[259] *ICJ Reports*, 1986, p. 126, para. 246.

[260] *ICJ Reports*, 1992, p. 247, para. 12.

law, as distinct from the regime of Article 51 of the United Nations Charter.[261] It did not employ the ILC terminology whereby the 'wrongfulness' of the acts attributed to the United States would have been 'precluded' if they had been shown to have been acts of self-defence; it referred to the point as one of the 'arguments advanced by the United States to justify the acts of which it is accused',[262] and also examined the possibility whether other rules might afford 'any justification for the acts in question'.[263] The result appears to be the same; if an act otherwise wrongful under international law is 'justified' by another rule of law, the act presumably will not be wrongful.

(1) *The condition of the existence of an armed attack*

The essential condition was stated by the Court unambiguously:

> In the case of individual self-defence, the exercise of this right is subject to the State concerned having been the victim of an armed attack. Reliance on collective self-defence of course does not remove the need for this.[264]

This finding disposes, as far as the Court is concerned, of the controversy whether self-defence may justify measures taken in response to activities falling short of an armed attack.[265] It was therefore necessary to define the meaning of 'armed attack', at least sufficiently to determine whether the acts attributed by the United States to Nicaragua in relation to its Central American neighbours amounted to an 'armed attack'. The Court regarded the definition as clearly established, since there appeared 'to be general agreement on the nature of the acts which can be treated as constituting armed attacks'.[266]

The Court treated as part of customary law the element from the General Assembly's definition of aggression[267] whereby

> an armed attack must be understood as including not merely action by regular armed forces across an international border, but also 'the sending by or on behalf of a State of armed bands, groups, irregulars or mercenaries, which carry out acts of armed force against another State of such gravity as to amount to' (*inter alia*) an actual armed attack conducted by regular forces, 'or its substantial involvement therein' . . . But the Court does not believe that the concept of 'armed attack' includes not only acts by armed bands where such acts occur on

[261] It will be recalled that, in view of the existence, in the United States' acceptance of jurisdiction, of the 'multilateral treaty reservation', the Court regarded itself as precluded from examining and applying the Charter as such.

[262] *ICJ Reports*, 1986, p. 102, para. 193.

[263] *ICJ Reports*, 1986, p. 106, para. 201.

[264] *ICJ Reports*, 1986, p. 103, para. 195.

[265] See the comments of Judge Schwebel in his dissenting opinion, *ICJ Reports*, 1986, pp. 347–8, paras. 172–3, and the authorities there cited.

[266] *ICJ Reports*, 1986, p. 103, para. 195.

[267] Resolution 3314 (XXIX) of 14 December 1974.

a significant scale but also assistance to rebels in the form of the provision of weapons or logistical or other support.[268]

What of the relationship between the State victim of an armed attack and a third State claiming to act in response by way of collective self-defence? Obviously, in requiring the existence of an armed attack in the case of collective self-defence as much as in the case of individual self-defence, the Court was not meaning to imply that every State asserting the right of collective self-defence must itself have been the victim of armed attack; that would be a contradiction of the whole concept of collective self-defence. In the first place,

It is also clear that it is the State which is the victim of an armed attack which must form and declare the view that it has been so attacked. There is no rule in customary international law permitting another State to exercise the right of collective self-defence on the basis of its own assessment of the situation. Where collective self-defence is invoked, it is to be expected that the State for whose benefit this right is used will have declared itself to be the victim of an armed attack.[269]

The most likely scenario will be that the victim State will not merely identify what is being done to it as an armed attack, but will actively request help from its friends and allies in the form of collective self-defence; and the Court then turned to the question

whether the lawfulness of the use of collective self-defence by the third State for the benefit of the attacked State also depends on a request addressed by that State to the third State.[270]

The Court's examination of this point is, as a matter of judicial enquiry, somewhat disappointing; being a matter of customary law, it was presumably to be determined by reference to State practice. The Court however merely refers[271] to the OAS Charter and the Rio Treaty of Reciprocal Assistance, before concluding:

At all events, the Court finds that in customary international law, whether of a general kind or that particular to the inter-American legal system, there is no rule permitting the exercise of collective self-defence in the absence of a request by the State which regards itself as the victim of an armed attack. The Court concludes that the requirement of a request by the State which is the victim of

[268] *ICJ Reports*, 1986, pp. 103–4, para. 195. The Court added that such action might be regarded as a threat or use of force or amount to intervention in the internal or external affairs of the victim State. The Court's narrow definition of 'armed attack' was strongly criticized by Judge Jennings: *ICJ Reports*, 1986, pp. 542–4.

[269] *ICJ Reports*, 1986, p. 104, para. 195.

[270] *ICJ Reports*, 1986, p. 104, para. 196.

[271] In a rather embarrassed fashion, in view of the existence of the multilateral treaty reservation.

the alleged attack is additional to the requirement that such State should declare itself to have been attacked.[272]

It is difficult to see what circumstances the Court had in mind as raising the distinction as a practical issue: one would expect that the very request for help as a matter of collective self-defence would in itself constitute a declaration by the victim that it had been attacked.

Later in the judgment, when the Court was engaged in applying the legal principles stated to the facts of the case, it retained the distinction, but appeared to argue on the basis that the declaration by the victim, and its separate request for help, were not so much legal conditions for the exercise of collective self-defence, as elements proving that an armed attack had in fact occurred.

The exercise of the right of collective self-defence presupposes that an armed attack has occurred; and it is evident that it is the victim State, being the most directly aware of that fact, which *is likely to* draw general attention to its plight. It is also evident that if the victim State wishes another State to come to its help in the exercise of the right of collective self-defence, it will *normally* make an express request to that effect. Thus in the present instance, the Court is entitled to take into account, in judging the asserted justification of the exercise of collective self-defence by the United States, of the actual conduct of El Salvador, Honduras and Costa Rica at the relevant time, *as indicative of a belief* by the State in question that it was the victim of an armed attack by Nicaragua, and of the making of a request by the victim State to the United States for help in the exercise of collective self-defence.[273]

Furthermore, the point is treated in the same breath as the significance to be attached to the fact that the United States had not reported the matter to the Security Council under Article 51 of the Charter. Since the Court found expressly that there was no *customary law* obligation to do so, all the Court deduced from it was that

this conduct of the United States hardly conforms with the latter's avowed conviction that it was acting in the context of collective self-defence as consecrated by Article 51 of the Charter.[274]

In other words, the whole point of this section of the judgment is to deduce that there had been no armed attack, justifying collective self-defence, from the conduct of the States concerned, by showing that they did not behave as though there had been an armed attack. This is evidently not the same as requiring specific conduct as a *precondition* to

[272] *ICJ Reports*, 1986, p. 105, para. 199. There is much to be said for the more common-sense approach of Judge Jennings: 'It may readily be agreed that the victim State must both be in real need of assistance and must want it and that the fulfilment of both these conditions must be shown. But to ask that these requirements take the form of some sort of formal declaration and request might sometimes be unrealistic': *ICJ Reports*, 1986, p. 545.

[273] *ICJ Reports*, 1986, p. 120, para. 232, emphasis added.

[274] *ICJ Reports*, 1986, p. 121, para. 235.

the invocation of collective self-defence. It is therefore suggested that, despite the statements of principle in the earlier paragraphs of the judgment, both the declaration by the victim State and (possibly) the request for assistance might be dispensed with in a proper case, where it was clear *aliter* that an armed attack had occurred, and the third State's intervention was welcomed by the victim as a matter of collective self-defence.

While Nicaragua's conduct was treated by the United States Government as threatening to the security interests of the United States,[275] its activities did not of course directly involve armed attack, or the use of force, against the sovereignty or territory of the United States itself. In this respect, Judge Jennings drew attention to the nature of self-defence, as embodied specifically in the English expression 'self-defence'.[276] He pointed out that when collective self-defence is invoked,

> whatever collective self-defence means, it does not mean vicarious defence; for that way the notion is indeed open to abuse. The assisting State is not an authorized champion, permitted under certain conditions to go to the aid of a favoured State. The assisting State surely must, by going to the victim State's assistance, be also, and in *addition* to other requirements, in some measure defending itself. There should even in 'collective self-defence' be some real element of self involved with the notion of defence.[277]

Judge Jennings did not however go so far as to suggest that it should be required that the assisting State should itself have been attacked, but simply that what was visualized was a system of collective security whereby 'the security of each member State' of an organization 'is meant to be involved with the security of the others; not merely as a result of a contractual arrangement but by the real consequences of the system and its organization'; this for him was typified by the system of Article 27 of the OAS Charter.[278]

(2) *Necessity and proportionality*

In the *Nicaragua* case, the Court made some observations concerning the recognized conditions of the invocation of the right of reprisals, i.e. that the measures taken were necessary, and were proportional to the acts responded to, as being relevant also to self-defence.[279] These were strictly *obiter dicta*,[280] since the Court had found that there had not been

[275] See in particular the Executive Order of 1 May 1985, quoted in the judgment, *ICJ Reports*, 1986, p. 70, para. 125.

[276] As Judge Jennings notes, the French expression 'légitime défense' is unhelpful, since 'it does no more than beg the question of what is "légitime" ': *ICJ Reports*, 1986, p. 545, footnote.

[277] *ICJ Reports*, 1986, p. 545, emphasis original.

[278] Ibid.

[279] *ICJ Reports*, 1986, p. 122, para. 237; cf. also ibid., p. 127, para. 249.

[280] They may have been included in order to counter the opposing views expressed, in the context of self-defence, by Judge Schwebel in his dissenting opinion, *ICJ Reports*, 1986, pp. 362–9, paras. 201–14.

the 'armed attack' which was the essential precondition for recourse to self-defence, individual or collective. In the light of that decision,

> the appraisal of the United States activities in relation to the criteria of necessity and proportionality takes on a different significance. As a result of this conclusion of the Court, even if the United States activities in question had been carried on in strict compliance with the canons of necessity and proportionality, they would not thereby become lawful. If however they were not, this may constitute an additional ground of wrongfulness.[281]

On the question of necessity, the Court ruled out as possible measures of self-defence measures taken, purportedly in defence of El Salvador, which were only taken, and began to produce their effects, after the major offensive of the armed opposition to the government of that country had been completely repulsed:

> Thus it was possible to eliminate the main danger to the Salvadorian Government without the United States embarking on activities in and against Nicaragua. Accordingly, it cannot be held that these activities were undertaken in the light of necessity.[282]

On proportionality, the Court identified certain activities attributable to the United States which, it considered, 'could not have been proportionate' to the aid received by the Salvadorian armed opposition from Nicaragua: the mining of Nicaraguan ports and the attacks on ports, oil installations, etc. It finally observed that

> the reaction of the United States in the context of what it regarded as self-defence was continued long after the period in which any presumed armed attack by Nicaragua could reasonably be contemplated.[283]

It is not clear whether this is presented as non-compliance with a further condition of lawful self-defence; it might be thought to be no more than a temporal aspect of the test of necessity.

There is in any event a certain unreality, or question-begging character, in these observations, given that there was, as the Court found, no 'armed attack'. As was explained by Ago in his Reports to the ILC, 'The reason for stressing that action taken in self-defence must be *necessary* is that the State attacked . . . must not, in the particular circumstances, have had any means of halting the attack other than recourse to armed force';[284] if then there was no attack, the question whether there was any means of halting it other than armed force becomes academic and, in many circumstances, meaningless. The same is true of the test of

[281] *ICJ Reports*, 1986, p. 122, para. 237. The meaning of the last sentence is extremely obscure; does wrongfulness admit of degrees (excluding the hypothesis of an international crime, as contemplated by Article 19 of the ILC Draft Articles on State Responsibility)?

[282] *ICJ Reports*, 1986, p. 122, para. 237.

[283] *ICJ Reports*, 1986, pp. 122–3, para. 237

[284] Addendum to 8th Report on State Responsibility, *ILC Yearbook*, 1980, vol. 2, part 1, p. 69; quoted by Judge Schwebel in his dissenting opinion, *ICJ Reports*, 1986, p. 363, para. 201.

proportionality: virtually any measures might be regarded as lacking in proportionality, in the context of self-defence against armed attack, in relation to activities which had unsuccessfully been invoked as constituting an armed attack. Although not so presented, the observations made by the Court seem really to be addressed to the question whether the actions of the United States, if examined as counter-measures to unlawful acts of Nicaragua, met conditions of necessity and proportionality, with the consequent implication that those tests are equally applicable to counter-measures.[285]

It would seem that proportionality does not necessarily imply identity of the measures taken with the acts complained of, a strict compliance with the *lex talionis*, or even a close similarity. Judge Schwebel, in his dissenting opinion, raised an interesting point in this respect: he understood the Court as indicating by implication that the United States might have been justified in replying by overt action to certain covert activities of Nicaragua, and asked 'where is it prescribed that, in response to covert measures of aggression, defensive measures must be open?'[286]

4. *Legitimate Counter-Measures*

Although this question is closely related to State responsibility, as witness its treatment in Article 30 of the ILC Draft Articles, it can also be regarded as a matter of more general international law, and as such it has already been treated in the present series of articles.[287] All that might be added at this point, other than the observations made at the end of the preceding section on the relevance of the conditions of necessity and proportionality, is a reminder[288] of the fact that counter-measures can only lawfully be taken in response to an act which is unlawful and in some way directed against the State taking those measures, and not in reaction to something which is a breach of an obligation owed solely to another State or States. This also emerges from the judgment in the *Nicaragua* case: after disposing of self-defence and collective counter-measures in face of an armed intervention, the Court considered 'whether there is anything [else] in the conduct of Nicaragua which

[285] This appears to be the recognized position as regards non-armed reprisals: see *Droit international public* (Nguyen Quoc Dinh) (5th edn. by Daillier and Pellet), p. 899, § 585; *Air Services Agreement of 27 March 1946* (*USA* v. *France*) (1978), 54 ILR 304, at p. 338; see also Articles 11 (Counter-measures by an injured State) and 13 (Proportionality) provisionally adopted by the ILC in 1994: *Report of the ILC on the work of its 46th Session* (A/49/10), pp. 364–5.

[286] *ICJ Reports*, 1986, pp. 366–7, paras. 209–10. Proportionality in self-defence is something of a neglected topic: cf. Brownlie, 'Non-use of Force in Contemporary International Law', *Non-Use of Force in International Law* (ed. Butler, 1989), p. 25; Gardam, 'Proportionality and Force in International Law', *American Journal of International Law*, 87 (1993), p. 391, at p. 404, n. 72.

[287] This *Year Book*, 60 (1989), pp. 107–13.

[288] The point was briefly dealt with in the earlier article: loc. cit., p. 113.

warrant counter-measures by the United States'.[289] It considered breaches, alleged by the United States to have been committed by Nicaragua, of various 'commitments', which, however, it found to have been made (if they were legally effective at all) not in favour of the United States, but to the Organization of American States. Accordingly, such pledges 'could not have justified the United States insisting on the fulfilment of a commitment made not directly towards the United States, but towards the Organization'.[290]

Chapter IV

The Rule of Exhaustion of Local Remedies

As Sir Gerald Fitzmaurice observed in 1961 of the rule as to the requirement for the exhaustion of local remedies,

> The rule—known for short as the local remedies rule—is accepted as one of the best established and, in principle, least questioned rules of international law: yet its precise scope and application can be highly controversial.[291]

The Court in the *Interhandel* case stated that

> The rule that local remedies must be exhausted before international proceedings may be instituted is a well-established rule of customary international law,[292]

and in the *Elettronica Sicula (ELSI)* case the Court referred to it as not merely a rule, but 'an important principle of customary international law'.[293] Nevertheless in both those cases the Court found itself faced with questions of application of the rule which were not free from difficulty.

1. *A Rule of Substance or of Procedure?*

One of the controversial aspects of the local remedies rules is its categorization as a rule of substance or a rule of procedure;[294] this is not

[289] *ICJ Reports*, 1986, p. 130, para. 257.

[290] *ICJ Reports*, 1986, p. 132, para. 262.

[291] 'Hersch Lauterpacht—The Scholar as Judge', this *Year Book*, 37 (1961), p. 53; *Collected Edition*, II, p. 686. The literature on the subject is immense; it is well surveyed by Amerasinghe, *Local Remedies in International Law* (Grotius, 1990).

[292] *ICJ Reports*, 1959, p. 27. For the view that it might also be regarded as a 'general principle of law', see the separate opinion of Judge Ammoun in *Barcelona Traction*, *ICJ Reports*, 1970, p. 301.

[293] *ICJ Reports*, 1989, p. 42, para. 50.

[294] For an up-to-date survey of doctrinal authority on each side of the controversy, see Amerasinghe, *Local Remedies in International Law* (Grotius, 1990), pp. 321–30.

a mere matter of terminology but determines the view taken of its operation.

Sometimes the rule is explained on the theory that until municipal remedies have been exhausted there has been no breach of international law in relation to the treatment of individuals. At others it is based on the argument that although a breach of international law has been committed as soon as the act complained of is done, there is a jurisdictional rule permitting the formulation of a claim only when this is the only available recourse.[295]

The International Law Commission has accepted the view of Roberto Ago as Rapporteur that the rule is a substantive one, no international responsibility arising until local remedies have been exhausted without success.[296] Fitzmaurice took the view that there was one rule with two aspects, one substantive and one procedural, and that it depended on the facts of the case which aspect was applicable: it might be that the act complained of was a breach of international law in itself, in which case the rule would merely operate procedurally; or it might be that the only breach of international law lay in a denial of justice to the injured national, which denial would not occur until all local means of redress had been exhausted.[297]

This issue was presented in a slightly different form in the *Norwegian Loans* case: Norway contended that the payment of French bondholders in the manner complained of by France, as not in accordance with the terms of the Norwegian loan issue, was a matter within the domestic jurisdiction of Norway. As one of the arguments in favour of this view, it contended that it was the failure to observe local remedies which prevented the dispute from acquiring the complexion of a dispute concerning international law. The Court did not deal with the point, since it upheld a different preliminary objection to jurisdiction advanced by Norway. Judge Lauterpacht however, in his separate opinion, rejected the Norwegian argument:

The crucial point is that, assuming that Norwegian law operates in a manner injurious to French bondholders, there are various questions of international law involved. To introduce in this context the question of exhaustion of local remedies is to make the issue revolve in a circle. The exhaustion of local

[295] O'Connell, *International Law* (Stevens, 1970), vol. 2, p. 1053. He continues, however, 'It matters not which attitude is adopted . . . '!

[296] See Ago, Sixth Report on State Responsibility, *ILC Yearbook*, 1977, vol. 2, part 1, pp. 22–33; Report of the ILC, ibid., part 2, pp. 35–6, para. 15.

[297] This *Year Book*, 37 (1961), p. 32; *Collected Edition*, II, p. 686; note also his brief reference to the subject in ibid., 27 (1950), p. 27; *Collected Edition*, I, p. 27. A similar approach was taken by García Amador: 'State Responsibility—Some New Problems', *Recueil des cours*, 94 (1958–II), p. 449. The question is linked with the distinction, discussed above, between obligations of conduct and obligations of result; for Ago, in the case of injury to an alien, the obligation is complied with if reparation is afforded the victim (*ILC Yearbook*, 1977, vol. 2, part 1, p. 12, para. 23); thus there is no unlawful act *until* the possibility of reparation is excluded by unsuccessful exhaustion of local remedies.

remedies cannot in itself bring within the province of international law a dispute which is otherwise outside its sphere. The failure to exhaust local remedies may constitute a bar to the jurisdiction of the Court; it does not affect the intrinsically international character of a dispute.[298]

With all respect to Judge Lauterpacht, the conclusion only follows from the initial assumption, which is that the case falls into the category identified by Fitzmaurice where the act complained of is already a breach of international law. If the essence of the French claim were denial of justice to its bondholders (which, of course, Lauterpacht did not think it was), denial of local remedies would *create* the international dispute; it would not 'bring within the province of international law' a dispute otherwise outside its sphere, but give rise to a new dispute. Thus Lauterpacht's finding is perhaps too widely expressed, and leaves open the possibility of cases in which the local remedies rule would be substantive and not procedural.

The Court upheld a preliminary objection based on the local remedies rule in the *Interhandel* case, but did not have occasion to distinguish between the substantive and procedural aspects of the rule. Judge Córdova, in his separate opinion, though referring to the rule as 'procedural', in fact clearly favoured the view that the rule is always a substantive one:

the well-settled principle of international procedure of the exhaustion of local remedies is based on the fundamental idea that a claim is not ripe, that there is no international claim, until the damaged foreigner has complied with such principle.[299]

The *Barcelona Traction* case involved an objection on the ground of non-exhaustion of local remedies, which was first joined to the merits,[300] and then left aside in the ultimate judgment, which rejected the Belgian claim on other grounds. Judge Fitzmaurice commented in his separate opinion on some aspects of the rule; in the context of an examination of the possibility that the proceedings in Spain had been, internationally, wholly invalid, he reverted to the distinction between the two classes of case, that where the rule operates procedurally, and that where it is a matter of substance:

a clear distinction must be drawn between [municipal court] proceedings which, if invalid, are so *ab initio*, and proceedings the complaint as to which concerns their *outcome*, e.g., that they *resulted* in a denial of justice. As regards the latter

[298] *ICJ Reports*, 1957, p. 38. For the discussion of Lauterpacht's views by Fitzmaurice, see this *Year Book*, 37 (1961), pp. 56–7; *Collected Edition*, II, pp. 689–90.

[299] *ICJ Reports*, 1959, p. 46.

[300] *ICJ Reports*, 1964, p. 46; it was found to be 'inextricably interwoven with the issues of denial of justice which constitute the major part of the merits'. In a dissenting opinion, Judge Morelli expressed the view that the rule was 'substantive and not procedural': *ICJ Reports*, 1964, p. 114; quoted with approval by Ago, Sixth Report on State Responsibility, *ILC Yearbook*, 1977, vol. 2, part 1, p. 31, para. 75.

kind of proceedings, it is evident, that, in principle at least, local remedies must be exhausted. The case is different, at any rate as regards the substance of the issues involved, where the alleged vice relates not to the outcome but to the very inception of the proceedings.[301]

In this context, Fitzmaurice made an interesting suggestion concerning the circumstances which give rise to an international claim to which the rule of exhaustion of local remedies is applicable. He held that in that case the bankruptcy proceedings in Spain against the Barcelona Traction company which were complained of by Belgium, '*considered at the international level*, . . . did involve an excess of legitimate, or at least normal, Spanish jurisdiction—internationally'.[302] After elaborating on this view, he concluded that 'the whole bankruptcy proceedings were, for excess of jurisdiction, internationally null and void *ab initio*, and without effect on the international plane', and continued:

> The conclusion just indicated would also be of importance as regards the question of exhausting local remedies, in so far as it might tend to suggest that, strictly, this question did not arise at all,—for there should be no necessity to exhaust such remedies in respect of proceedings which, for excess of jurisdiction were, internationally, a nullity and void *ab initio*. At least, in respect of the *substance* of the proceedings, there could be no such obligation if—internationally—the proceedings were vitiated from the start.[303]

Fitzmaurice does not press the point—his opinion continues 'Be that as it may . . . ', and turns to other considerations. He may have been conscious of the difficulty of this line of argument constituted by the fact that the proceedings in Spain were effective, in terms of local law, to dispossess the Barcelona Traction company, and *were* therefore effective internationally, on the premisses of Belgium's argument, to create an international wrong. If those proceedings were really 'without effect on the international plane', what, one might ask, was there for Belgium to complain of? It is not possible, by invoking the ideas of nullity and voidness *ab initio*, to treat what ought not to have happened as not having happened;[304] and if an act on the domestic level results in an international wrong, the local remedies rule normally requires that any means of redress afforded by the local law be tried.

Judge Tanaka also discussed the *raison d'être* of the rule in his separate opinion, but in terms which would seem to be equally consistent with the

[301] *ICJ Reports*, 1970, p. 107, para. 75.
[302] *ICJ Reports*, 1970, pp. 103–4, para. 68; emphasis original.
[303] Ibid., p. 106, paras. 72, 73; emphasis original.
[304] Like Palström in Christian Morgenstern's poem *Die unmögliche Tatsache*:

> Und er kommt zu dem Ergebnis:
> Nur ein Traum was das Erlebnis,
> Weil, so schließt er messerscharf,
> Nicht sein *kann*, was nicht sein *darf*.

substantive or the procedural interpretation.[304a] Judge Bustamante indicated in his separate opinion why he would have upheld the objection based on non-exhaustion of local remedies, but also without spelling out his interpretation of the rule as procedural or substantive. A hint of the latter interpretation perhaps emerges from his observation that

On voit donc comment, du point de vue international, les résultats du recours en revision revêtent une importance capitale quand il s'agit ultérieurement d'établir l'existence ou la non-existence de la responsabilité de l'Etat.[304b]

In the *Elettronica Sicula (ELSI)* case, an objection was raised of non-exhaustion of local remedies; the Court did not indicate whether it saw the matter as procedural or substantive. Since the claim was based on treaty, however, the Court had occasion to observe in passing, *inter alia*, that it had no doubt that parties to a treaty can 'agree [in the treaty] that the local remedies rule shall not apply to claims based on alleged breaches of that treaty'.[304c] It has however been questioned whether a *substantive* rule of local remedies can be waived in this way.[305] If the rule is procedural, such a treaty would simply amount to renouncing in advance the benefit of the procedural rule; but can the parties to a treaty decide to agree that action which would ordinarily not be a breach of international law unless and until it had given rise to a subsequent denial of justice, should, as between those parties, be treated *ab initio* as a breach of the treaty? Since the obligation to act in a particular way in regard to the other party's nationals is itself (*ex hypothesi*) created by the treaty, it could of course be argued that, in relation to that manner of acting, the local remedies rule is necessarily procedural; but the question is by no means free from difficulty.

Similar considerations apply to the question whether a State can be estopped from raising an objection based on non-exhaustion of local remedies.[306] Two kinds of estoppel can however be distinguished. In the *Interhandel* case, it was observed that the United States had admitted that Interhandel had exhausted the remedies available to it in the United States; this was advanced as an estoppel preventing the United States from alleging that some remedies remained available but untried. In the *ELSI* case, similarly, the United States had, when presenting a diplomatic claim to Italy in 1974, expressed the view that local remedies had

[304a] *ICJ Reports*, 1970, pp. 141 ff. He refers at one point to the exhaustion of local remedies as 'a condition of a procedural nature', but this apparently refers to the procedures of the *municipal* courts, since he continues: 'which is imposed on an individual whose interests his national State wants to protect by international proceedings': loc. cit., p. 144.

[304b] *ICJ Reports*, 1970, p. 63 (original French); the English translation is somewhat stilted and therefore less clear.

[304c] *ICJ Reports*, 1989, p. 42, para. 50; it did not however consider that the treaty before it had that effect.

[305] This is doubted, to say the least, by Amerasinghe: *Local Remedies in International Law*, pp. 335–7.

[306] See Amerasinghe, *Local Remedies in International Law*, p. 337.

been exhausted by the company in Italy; Italy did not comment on the point, nor did it raise the question of local remedies until proceedings had been brought in 1987. Thus in neither case did the alleged estoppel relate to the question whether the local remedies rule was *applicable* to the case, but only to the factual question whether the condition imposed by the rule had been complied with. It is suggested that it is only an alleged estoppel on the former question that might have implications for the attribution to the rule of a substantive or procedural character.

For this reason, in neither of the two cases referred to did the Court's ruling take the matter any further; in both it rejected estoppel on the facts, holding in the *Interhandel* case simply that the United States' statements relied on were 'based upon a view [of the situation in the US courts] which has proved unfounded';[307] and in the *ELSI* case that 'there are obvious difficulties in constructing an estoppel from a mere failure to mention a matter at a particular point in somewhat desultory diplomatic exchanges'.[308]

2. *The Case of an Alleged Breach of State Rights*

Fitzmaurice regarded as one of the most controversial questions in this field the problem whether the rule applies 'not only where the claim is made on behalf of a private person or entity, but also where it is made, either in whole or in part, in respect of an alleged direct breach of international law as between State and State'.[309] There are arbitral precedents in support of the view that a claim limited to a request for a declaration of the existence of a breach of direct inter-State obligations is not subject to the local remedies rule.[310] This has also recently been confirmed by the Court: in the case concerning *Applicability of the Obligation to Arbitrate under Section 21 of the United Nations Headquarters Agreement* (the 'PLO case'), the Court observed that the alleged dispute arising out of the United States legislation directed to closing the PLO office

> relates solely to what the United Nations considers to be its rights under the Headquarters Agreement. The purpose of the arbitration procedure envisaged

[307] *ICJ Reports*, 1959, p. 27.

[308] *ICJ Reports*, 1986, p. 44, para. 54, a view strongly endorsed by Mann, 'Foreign Investment in the International Court of Justice', *American Journal of International Law*, 86 (1992), p. 101.

[309] 'Hersch Lauterpacht—The Scholar as Judge', this *Year Book*, 37 (1961), p. 54; *Collected Edition*, II, p. 687. Ago however regarded the hypothesis of such a judgment as 'more a theoretical than a practical possibility since it has never actually happened': Sixth Report on State Responsibility, *ILC Yearbook*, 1977, vol. 2, part 1, pp. 32–3, para. 80. On the difficulty of reconciling the possibility of a declaratory judgment with the basis of the rule, see Ago, ibid., and Jeancolas, 'L'Arrêt Elettronica Sicula S.p.a. (ELSI) du 20 juillet 1989', *Revue générale de droit international public*, 94 (1990), pp. 715–16.

[310] See *Swiss Confederation* v. *Federal Republic of Germany* (1958), 25 ILR 33, at p. 38; *Air Services Agreement of 27 March 1946* (*USA* v. *France*) (1978), 54 ILR 304.

by that Agreement is precisely the settlement of such disputes as may arise between the Organization and the host country without any prior recourse to municipal courts, and it would be against both the letter and the spirit of that Agreement for the implementation of that procedure to be subjected to such prior recourse. It is evident that a provision of the nature of section 21 of the Headquarters Agreement cannot require the exhaustion of local remedies as a condition of its implementation.[311]

There is also good doctrinal authority for saying that the rule does not apply to any case in which a State interest is being invoked, even if reparation is sought (sometimes referred to as a 'mixed case');[312] and Fitzmaurice interpreted Judge Lauterpacht's separate opinion in the *Interhandel* case as being to the same effect. The decision of the Court in that case is however to be understood in the opposite sense. Switzerland in that case had presented two submissions: by the principal submission, the Court was asked to adjudge and declare that the United States was under an obligation to restore the confiscated assets of Interhandel, a Swiss company adjudged (wrongly, it was alleged) to be under enemy (German) control. By an alternative submission, the Court was asked to adjudge and declare that the United States was under an obligation, by virtue of a treaty between the parties, to submit the dispute to arbitration or conciliation. Proceedings instituted by Interhandel were pending in the United States, and the Court found that these had not yet been finally determined. In regard to the application of the rule to the first submission, the Court stated:

the rule has been generally observed in cases in which a State has adopted the cause of its national whose rights are claimed to have been disregarded in another State in violation of international law. Before resort may be had to an international court in such a situation, it has been considered necessary that the State where the violation occurred should have an opportunity to redress it by its own means, within the framework of its own domestic legal system. *A fortiori* the rule must be observed when domestic proceedings are pending, as in the case of Interhandel, and when the two actions, that of the Swiss company in the United States courts and that of the Swiss Government in this Court, in its principal Submission, are designed to obtain the same result: the restitution of the assets of Interhandel vested in the United States.[313]

The Court therefore found the principal submission inadmissible for lack of exhaustion of local remedies. On the alternative submission, the Court ruled as follows:

[311] *ICJ Reports*, 1988, p. 29, para. 41. The case is of course an exceptional one since the right asserted by the United Nations was simply to have a matter arbitrated; but the principle appears the same.

[312] See, for example, *Oppenheim's International Law* (9th edn., by Jennings and Watts), vol. 1, p. 523, n. 3, quoting Fawcett, 'The Exhaustion of Local Remedies; Substance or Procedure?', this *Year Book*, 31 (1954), at pp. 454 ff.

[313] *ICJ Reports*, 1959, p. 27.

The Court considers that one interest, and one alone, that of Interhandel, which has led the latter to institute and to resume proceedings before the United States courts, has induced the Swiss Government to institute international proceedings. This interest is the basis for the present claim and should determine the scope of the action brought before the Court by the Swiss Government in its alternative form as well as in its principal form. On the other hand, the grounds upon which the rule of exhaustion of local remedies is based are the same, whether in the case of an international court, arbitral tribunal or conciliation commission. In these circumstances, the Court considers that any distinction so far as the rule of exhaustion of local remedies is concerned between the various claims or between the various tribunals is unfounded.[314]

The 'interest' of Interhandel in question was presumably its interest in recovering its assets in the United States; thus, it is suggested, a simpler way of expressing the Court's view would be to note that, if the proceedings in the United States courts were successful, both the principal and the alternative submission of Switzerland would cease to have any *raison d'être*; the latter since there would no longer be any dispute to be submitted to arbitration.[315] On this basis, the Court's ruling seems to be a matter of common sense.

Judge Klaestad however saw the matter differently: for him, the point was that the Swiss alternative submission was something which 'cannot in any case be determined by local courts in the United States'.[316] Other judges observed that, if there were to be arbitration, the question of exhaustion of local remedies would be one for the arbitrators.[317] Judge Winiarski specifically took the point discussed by Fitzmaurice in the article referred to above; after agreeing with the Court as to the reason for the rule (in the passage quoted above), he continued:

But where the rights and obligations of the two States flow directly from their treaties and agreements there can be no question of settling such dispute by recourse to local remedies. The American courts are competent to adjudicate on the rights of a Swiss national; they have no competence to adjudicate on the existence of an obligation on the part of the United States to submit to

314 *ICJ Reports*, 1959, p. 29.

315 This observation is however linked to the —equally controversial—question whether the local remedies rule is one of procedure or substance (see above); if there is no breach of international law unless and until the court of last instance of the respondent State has ruled against the foreign national, the point made here is, it is suggested, valid as it stands. If however there has been a breach of international law at an earlier stage, but international litigation is excluded until local remedies have been unsuccessfully exhausted, it might be argued that a request for a declaratory judgment would not be barred by the fact that the individual injured had ultimately been vindicated by the local courts. But would the claim for a declaratory judgment necessarily be capable of having what the Court in *Northern Cameroons* called any 'forward reach', even if the treaty continued in force? See the judgment in that case, *ICJ Reports*, 1963, p. 36–8.

316 *ICJ Reports*, 1959, p. 82.

317 Judge *ad hoc* Carry, *ICJ Reports*, 1959, p. 32; Judge Winiarski, ibid., p. 84; Judge Lauterpacht, ibid., pp. 120–1.

arbitration or conciliation. The legal problems are on different planes and their solution must be different.[318]

Judge Lauterpacht disagreed with the majority decision, apparently on this same ground, though he expresses his view in slightly different terms; he drew attention to the judgment of the PCIJ in the *Chorzów Factory* case, to the effect that, different rules being applicable,

The damage suffered by an individual is never therefore identical in kind with that which will be suffered by a State; it can only afford a convenient scale for calculation of the reparation due to the State,[319]

and observed that

That principle is not a mere doctrinal refinement. An international award may give to a State satisfaction different from restitution of the property seized; a State may have a legal interest, independent of any material compensation and restitution, in vindicating the remedy of arbitration provided for in the Treaty.[320]

At all events, in view of the clear statement of the other view in the dissenting opinion of Judge Winiarski, the Court must be taken, by its decision to uphold the preliminary objection, to have rejected that view, at least in the special circumstances of the *Interhandel* case.

A parallel problem arose in the *Elettronica Sicula (ELSI)* case, where the claim of the United States against Italy was for damage suffered by two United States corporations as a result of the treatment of their wholly-owned Italian subsidiary in Sicily, ELSI; the claim was however based not on customary international law, but on the provisions of a Treaty of Friendship, Commerce and Navigation between the two States. Italy raised an objection on the ground of the alleged failure of the United States corporations to exhaust local remedies in Italy. The United States first relied on the absence of any reference in the Treaty to the local remedies rules, but the Chamber of the Court seised of the case rejected this argument:

The Chamber has no doubt that the parties to a treaty can therein agree that the local remedies rule shall not apply to claims based on alleged breaches of that treaty; or confirm that it shall apply. Yet the Chamber finds itself unable to accept that an important principle of customary international law should be held

[318] *ICJ Reports*, 1959, p. 84.

[319] *PCIJ*, Series A, No. 17, p. 28. To quote this passage in this context still appears to overlook the fact that, if the domestic proceedings are successful, the question of reparation to the State will not arise.

[320] *ICJ Reports*, 1959, p. 120.

to have been tacitly dispensed with, in the absence of any words making clear an intention to do so.[321]

The United States had however included in its submissions a request for a declaratory judgment finding that the FCN Treaty had been violated; and contended that the local remedies rule did not apply to that submission.

The argument of the United States is that such a judgment would declare that the United States own rights under the FCN Treaty had been infringed; and that to such a direct injury the local remedies rule, which is a rule of customary international law developed in the context of the espousal by a State of the claim of one of its nationals, would not apply. The Chamber, however, has not found it possible in the present case to find a dispute over alleged violation of the FCN Treaty resulting in direct injury to the United States, that is both distinct from, and independent of, the dispute over the alleged violation in respect of [the US corporations].[322]

The Court referred to the judgment in the *Interhandel* case, and found that the 'matter which colours and pervades the United States claim as a whole, is the alleged damage to' the two United States corporations; it accordingly rejected the argument that 'there is a part of the Applicant's claim which can be severed so as to render the local remedies rule inapplicable to that part'.[323]

It appears therefore that, in the Court's jurisprudence, what counts for the applicability or otherwise of the local remedies rule is the nature of the principal element of the claim.[324] Obviously if the claim is such that it does not involve injury of a kind which could be remedied by recourse to the local courts, the rule is totally excluded; not however because purely inter-State rights are involved, but because the claim is of such a kind that redress *could* not be obtained in local courts. But if the essence of the matter is injury to nationals, whose claim is being espoused by their State, and redress by the local courts will effectively put an end to the dispute, then the rule will apply to render inadmissible also any subsidiary aspects of the claim which might be regarded as strictly

[321] *ICJ Reports*, 1989, p. 42, para. 50. The position may be different in the field of protection of human rights; see Cançado Trindade, *The Application of the Rule of Exhaustion of Local Remedies in International Law* (1983), pp. 131 ff. For an example of a treaty expressly confirming the applicability of the local remedies rule, see the 1927 Treaty of Conciliation, Judicial Settlement and Arbitration between Belgium and Spain, relied on in the *Barcelona Traction* case; quoted in the separate opinion of Judge Tanaka, *ICJ Reports*, 1970, pp. 141–2.

[322] *ICJ Reports*, 1989, pp. 42–3, para. 51.

[323] *ICJ Reports*, 1989, p. 43, para. 52.

[324] For a parallel in a different field, note the decision in the case of *Nuclear Tests (New Zealand* v. *France)* to treat the claim as 'moot' as a result of the French announcement that it was stopping tests, on the basis that New Zealand's ultimate objective was to obtain a termination of the tests. The request of New Zealand for a declaration that the tests were illegal was allowed to share the fate of the more concrete claims: see *ICJ Reports*, 1974, pp. 466–7, paras. 30–1; and the strong dissent of Judges Onyeama, Dillard, Jiménez de Aréchaga and Waldock, ibid., pp. 494–500.

matters of direct inter-State relations.[325] Obviously the mere fact that nationals of the claimant State have been injured is not determining: thus in the case of the *United States Diplomatic and Consular Staff in Tehran*, no-one suggested that the staff members concerned should first seek redress from the Iranian courts,[326] and that not merely because such a suggestion would probably have been regarded as adding insult to injury! The breaches of obligation complained of were violations of duties owed directly to the United States, as sending State of the diplomats, not to the diplomats as United States nationals,[327] and accordingly no adequate redress could be obtained from the local courts. Almost as outrageous was the contention of Bulgaria in the case concerning the *Aerial Incident of 27 July 1955 (Israel* v. *Bulgaria)* that the passengers on the El Al flight shot down by Bulgaria (or their personal representatives) should have exhausted local remedies before international proceedings were brought. In reply Rosenne, as counsel for Israel, pointed out that 'The rule regarding exhaustion of local remedies applies solely to the case of so-called diplomatic protection, where a State adopts the cause of its nationals whose rights have been disregarded by another State in violation of international law'; the case in question was not one of diplomatic protection, but one of the 'unity of the aircraft with every person and everything on board, and the link of that unity with the sovereignty of Israel'.[328] The Court dismissed the case on jurisdictional grounds, and therefore did not deal with the points raised.

[325] It has been suggested that the *ELSI* judgment modifies or extends the *ratio decidendi* of the *Interhandel* judgment: 'where *Interhandel* and other authorities may have suggested that the ultimate test was the remedy sought, *ELSI* suggests that the real test is a "but for" analysis that focuses on the origin of the claim. If the claim would not have been brought without an accompanying claim for damages, the Court will make the State await the national's exhaustion of local remedies before addressing the State's own claim': Adler, 'The Exhaustion of Local Remedies Rule after the International Court of Justice's Decision in ELSI', *International and Comparative Law Quarterly*, 39 (1990), pp. 651–2.

[326] There was also the fact that, as diplomats, they were entitled to immunities; cf. Fitzmaurice: 'a person entitled to diplomatic immunity does not lose that immunity through ignoring proceedings against him in the local courts,—nor is it a condition of his government's right to complain that he should have exhausted local means of recourse in the assertion or defence of his immunity': separate opinion in *Barcelona Traction*, *ICJ Reports*, 1970, p. 106, para. 74.

[327] A question might however have been raised in respect of the two United States nationals who were among the victims of the Embassy raid but who were *not* diplomatic or consular staff: their seizure was found to be a breach of a Treaty of Amity, Economic Relations and Consular Rights between Iran and the United States, requiring the parties to ensure 'the most constant protection and security' of each other's nationals (see *ICJ Reports*, 1980, pp. 26–7, para. 50; p. 32, para. 67. However, the predominant element of the United States claim was of course the sanctity of embassies, diplomats and consular staff.

[328] *ICJ Pleadings, Oral Arguments, Documents*, p. 531. The Bulgarian objection did however have some reasonable justification since Israel was claiming reparation for the relatives of the victims: see Cot at ibid., p. 450. Rosenne also put forward the interesting suggestion that the local remedies rule only applies when the injured alien has voluntarily established a connection between the respondent State and himself, e.g. by residence or trade activities, and therefore could not apply to the unfortunate passengers on the El Al flight: ibid., pp. 531–2. On this, cf. Jennings, 'General Course of International Law', *Recueil des cours*, 121 (1967–II), p. 485.

3. *The Nature of the Municipal Claim and the Burden of Proof*

When reference is made to 'local remedies' in the terminology of the rule requiring their exhaustion, what is meant is not merely that it is to the courts (or administrative organs of redress) of the respondent State that application must be made, but also that it is the remedies offered by the municipal law under which those courts or organs operate which must be pursued, not the rules of State responsibility of international law, nor yet the specific international norms in force between the two States concerned. In the *ELSI* case, the United States was invoking the responsibility of Italy under treaties in force between the two States. As part of its case on local remedies, Italy contended

> that it was possible for the matter to have been brought before the municipal courts, citing the provisions of the treaties themselves, and alleging their violation.[329]

This was never done—in the various proceedings in Italy, the treaties were never mentioned; one reason for this, as the Chamber noted, was that ELSI was in the hands of a trustee in bankruptcy, and it was he, and not the United States parent companies, who decided how the matter was to be pleaded before the local courts. The Chamber continued, however:

> Furthermore, the local remedies rule does not, indeed cannot, require that a claim be presented to the municipal courts in a form, and with arguments, suited to an international tribunal, applying different law to different parties: for an international claim to be admissible, it is sufficient if the essence of the claim has been brought before the competent tribunals and pursued as far as permitted by local law and procedures, and without success.[330]

At first sight, this reads like a considerable softening of the traditional rule. Setting aside the practical problem that the litigation strategy was in the hands of the trustee, the claim of Italy was that, under Italian law, it was *possible* to rely on the treaties before the local courts. The question is not whether, in general, the local remedies rule requires international law to be invoked before the local courts; but if, in a given jurisdiction, the claim *can* be framed in that way, and has not been, can it not be said that there has been a failure to use a remedy that was available, and hence that the local remedies rule is not complied with?[331] The Chamber did however proceed, in the following paragraphs of its judgment, to deal

[329] *ICJ Reports*, 1989, p. 46, para. 59.

[330] Ibid. Note the sardonic comment of Mann that 'That the breach by a state of an obligation arising from a treaty incorporated into municipal law could be actionable is unlikely to cause surprise to lawyers familiar with continental law': 'Foreign Investment in the International Court of Justice: the *ELSI* case', *American Journal of International Law*, 86 (1992), p. 101.

[331] The question may be whether reliance on the treaties must be said to be included in what the Institut de droit international referred to as 'l'usage normal des voies de recours': Granada Resolution, *Annuaire de l'Institut de droit international*, 46 (1956), p. 358.

with that very question. It seems therefore that the Chamber was simply anxious to emphasize that what matters is that the '*essence* of the claim' (presumably, of the international claim as later presented[332]) has been brought before the competent tribunals; if this can be done by asserting international law (in the form of a treaty or otherwise), then it should be, but it cannot be expected that this option will be available.

Whether this option was available in Italy proved to be a complex question, depending on whether the relevant provisions of the FCN Treaty would have been treated by the Italian courts as self-executing. The Chamber ultimately resolved the matter on the basis of burden of proof:

> It thus appears to the Chamber to be impossible to deduce, from the recent [Italian] jurisprudence cited, what the attitude of the Italian courts would have been had [the United States corporations] brought an action, some 20 years ago, in reliance on Article 2043 of the Civil Code in conjunction with the provisions of the FCN Treaty and the Supplementary Agreement . . . In the present case, . . . it was for Italy to show, as a matter of fact, the existence of a remedy which was open to the United States stockholders and which they failed to employ. The Chamber does not consider that Italy has discharged that burden.[333]

This conclusion is not consistent with the views expressed by Judge Lauterpacht in his separate opinion in the *Norwegian Loans* case, and quoted with approval by Sir Gerald Fitzmaurice in one of his articles devoted to Lauterpacht's judicial achievements:[334]

> (1) As a rule, it is for the plaintiff State to prove that there are no effective remedies to which recourse can be had . . .
>
> . . .
>
> (4) the degree of burden of proof thus to be adduced ought not to be so stringent as to render the proof unduly exacting.[335]

There was however a special aspect of the case, namely that extensive use had in fact been made of the Italian courts.

> With such a deal of litigation in the municipal courts about what is in substance the claim now before the Chamber, it was for Italy to demonstrate that there was nevertheless some local remedy that had not been tried; or at least, not exhausted. *This burden Italy never sought to deny.*[336]

The acceptance by Italy of the burden of proof may leave open the question whether the mere existence of some attempts to exhaust local remedies throws on to the respondent the burden of showing there are

[332] Cf. the *Finnish Ships* arbitration, *Reports of International Arbitral Awards*, vol. 3, p. 1502.
[333] *ICJ Reports*, 1989, p. 47, para. 62.
[334] This *Year Book*, 37 (1961), p. 61; *Collected Edition*, II, p. 694.
[335] *ICJ Reports*, 1957, p. 39.
[336] *ICJ Reports*, 1989, p. 46, para. 59, emphasis added.

others untried. The dictum may on the other hand be regarded as in line with precedent inasmuch as the Chamber did not require Italy to show the existence of an *effective* remedy, this aspect being for the applicant to disprove.[337]

Chapter V

Reparation[338] and Restitution

I never meet a Pennsylvanian at a London dinner without feeling a disposition to seize and divide him; to allot his beaver to one sufferer and his coat to another; to appropriate his pocket handkerchief to the orphan, and to comfort the widow with his silver watch . . .

Rev. Sidney Smith (1843, after the State of Pennsylvania had repudiated its external debt), *Works*, vol. 2, p. 329.

In the period under consideration the Court has not had to determine the amount of pecuniary compensation for any breach of an international obligation which it has judicially declared; it has however made findings of the existence in principle of a duty to make reparation, and on one occasion has given directions for specific reparation. These have however been treated as matters logically subordinate to the establishment of the existence of the breach of an international obligation, and indeed, where appropriate, to the declaration of an obligation to cease an unlawful activity. The pattern of the operative clauses of the judgments in the *Tehran Hostages* case and the *Nicaragua* case clearly owes something to the analytical structure of the work of the International Law Commission,[339] even if only indirectly, through the pattern of the submission in those cases, themselves influenced by the ILC Draft Articles. In each judgment, the Court first finds that there have been breaches of international obligations owed by one State to another, then decides that the guilty State must 'take all steps to redress the situation' or to 'cease and refrain from all such actions as may constitute breaches' of those obligations,[340] and that that State 'is under an obligation to make reparation' to the other State for the injury caused, and finally that the form and amount of the reparation, failing agreement between the parties, will be fixed by the Court.[341]

337 Cf. Amerasinghe, *Local Remedies in International Law*, p. 289.

338 See Fitzmaurice in this *Year Book*, 27 (1950), pp. 6–8; 37 (1961), pp. 37–8; *Collected Edition*, I, pp. 6–8; II, pp. 670–1.

339 In this sense Condorelli, 'L'Imputation à l'Etat d'un fait internationalement illicite; solutions classiques et nouvelles tendances', *Recueil des cours*, 189 (1984–VI), pp. 94–5.

340 *ICJ Reports*, 1980, p. 44, para. 95(3); *ICJ Reports*, 1986, p. 149, para. 292(12).

341 *ICJ Reports*, 1980, p. 45, para. 95(5) and (6); *ICJ Reports*, 1986, p. 149, paras. (13), (14) and (15). It should not be overlooked that even a declaratory judgment may be regarded as a form of reparation: cf. Migliorino, 'Sur la déclaration d'illicéité comme forme de satisfaction', *Revue générale de droit international public*, 96 (1992), pp. 72–3.

In the *Fisheries Jurisdiction* cases, no direction was made for cessation of Icelandic interference with United Kingdom and German fishing activities, although this might have been expected to be the logical corollary of the finding that the Icelandic Fisheries Regulations were not opposable to the applicant States.[342] It would have been difficult to include such a direction, since the Court held that the parties were under an obligation to negotiate an equitable solution of their difficulties, taking into account, *inter alia*, the Icelandic preferential rights. As to reparation, the United Kingdom withdrew its claim in this sense. On a submission of the Federal Republic of Germany that Iceland should make reparation for the acts of interference of Icelandic patrol boats committed in the enforcement of the extension of Icelandic fisheries jurisdiction which the Court had found to be not opposable to the Federal Republic, the Court refused to make a finding. The principle that 'the breach of an engagement involves an obligation to make reparation in an adequate form'[343] of course remained intact; as Judge de Castro observed, 'To say that an illegal act which has caused injury gives rise to an obligation to make reparation is a mere truism', and from this he deduced that for the Court 'there is no point in saying it'.[344] The refusal of the majority of the Court to rule on the German submission was based on procedural grounds, which do not require examination here, not on any denial of the principle.

Of more interest in that respect is the division in the Court on the point whether the Court had jurisdiction to deal with the submission, on the basis of the title of jurisdiction relied on, an Exchange of Notes between Germany and Iceland of 1961 by which Iceland was to give notice of any extension of its fisheries jurisdiction, and

> in case of a dispute relating to such an extension, the matter shall, at the request of either party, be referred to the International Court of Justice.

The point did not arise until the merits stage of the case,[345] and the Court's finding in favour of jurisdiction over compensation is brief.

[342] The United Kingdom in its submission in the memorial had asked the Court to say that Icelandic activities interfering with British fishing were 'unlawful', and that Iceland was under a duty to make compensation, but did not ask for a direction that they should cease. At the stage of the oral proceedings, this submission was withdrawn: see *ICJ Reports*, 1974, p. 7, paras. 11 and 12. The Federal Republic made similar submissions, but did not withdraw that relating to a declaration of unlawfulness and the obligation to make compensation: ibid., p. 179, paras. 12–13.

[343] *Chorzów Factory*, *PCIJ*, Series A, No. 9, p. 21; quoted in the *Reparation for Injuries* case, *ICJ Reports*, 1949, p. 184.

[344] *ICJ Reports*, 1974, p. 225.

[345] Because the submission in question was only included in the memorial on the merits, by which time there had been a number of incidents involving Icelandic patrol boats and German fishing vessels. This produced the curious result that, having decided in 1973 in absolute terms that 'it has jurisdiction to entertain the Application', the Court had to re-open the question of jurisdiction in 1974. See the present writer's comments in *Non-Appearance before the International Court of Justice* (Cambridge, 1985), p. 173.

The Court cannot accept the view that it would lack jurisdiction to deal with this submission. The matter raised therein is part of the controversy between the Parties, and constitutes a dispute relating to Iceland's extension of its fisheries jurisdiction. The submission is one based on facts subsequent to the filing of the Application, but arising directly out of the question which is the subject-matter of that Application. As such it falls within the scope of the Court's jurisdiction defined in the compromissory clause of the Exchange of Notes of 19 July 1961.[346]

The opposition of the dissenting judges to this finding was based on the consideration that the parties, and in particular Iceland, would not have contemplated the question of compensation being referred to the Court under their Exchange of Notes, and would not have agreed to it if they had.[347] It is suggested that Judge Onyeama was in the right of it when he observed that 'claims for compensation for acts done in breach of the agreement . . . must be deemed to be in the contemplation of the Parties when they conferred jurisdiction on the Courts',[348] and the reason for this is simply the existence of the principle stated in the *Chorzów Factory* and *Reparation for Injuries* cases. In fact, as Judge Waldock pointed out, the Permanent Court in the former case had drawn the express conclusion that

Differences relating to reparations, which may be due by reason of failure to apply a convention, are consequently differences relating to its application;[349]

and, as Judge Waldock observed, 'by parity of reasoning', a similar conclusion should be drawn in respect of the Exchange of Notes. This aspect of the decision in the *Fisheries Jurisdiction* case may accordingly be regarded as a re-affirmation of the principle that reparation is the automatic consequence of the breach of an obligation.

In the *Nicaragua* case, the Court was, as already noted, ready to make a finding on a general submission as to reparation, which had been cast in a different form from that of the Federal Republic in the earlier case; in dealing with the question of its jurisdiction to do so, it observed that 'In general, jurisdiction to determine the merits of a dispute entails jurisdiction to determine reparation', and quoted the PCIJ dictum referred to above.[350] It made two declarations that the United States was 'under an obligation to make reparation' to Nicaragua for the breaches of customary law determined in the judgment, and the breaches of a Treaty of Friendship, Commerce and Navigation similarly determined, respectively; it then decided that the form and amount of such reparation, failing agreement between the parties, would be settled by the Court in

346 *ICJ Reports*, 1974, p. 203, para. 72.

347 See disssenting opinion of Judge Gros, *ICJ Reports*, 1974, pp. 236–7; dissenting opinion of Judge Petrén, ibid., pp. 242–3.

348 *ICJ Reports*, 1974, p. 250.

349 *PCIJ*, Series A, No. 9, p. 21, quoted in *ICJ Reports*, 1974, pp. 230–1.

350 *ICJ Reports*, 1986, p. 142, para. 283.

a subsequent procedure.[351] The case was however discontinued before such the reparations phase had proceeded beyond the filing of a memorial by Nicaragua.[352]

Nicaragua had also endeavoured to get a sort of 'payment on account' or interim judgment; it asked for an award of $370,200,000 as the 'minimum (and in that sense provisional) valuation of direct damages'; the Court refused to make any order in this sense, for reasons which are purely procedural, and therefore not here relevant.[353]

An order for specific restitution,[354] as distinct from monetary compensation, was made by the Court in the case of the *Temple of Preah Vihear*; having found that sovereignty over the disputed area of the Temple belonged to Cambodia, the Court briefly examined a submission by Cambodia that Thailand should return various objects which it claimed had been removed from the Temple by Thailand since 1954. In the absence of specific evidence, the Court indicated that it could only give 'a finding of principle in favour of Cambodia, without relating it to any particular objects'.[355] The obligation which had been breached was presumably an obligation not to remove items of property from an area under the sovereignty of another State, and the fact that Thailand had so removed them in the conviction that the area was under its own sovereignty did not affect the matter.

[351] Ibid., p. 149, para. 292, sub-paras. (13), (14) and (15).

[352] See the President's order of 26 September 1991, *ICJ Reports*, 1991, p. 47.

[353] *ICJ Reports*, 1986, p. 143, para. 285.

[354] On the theoretical distinction to be drawn between cessation of unlawful activity and restitution, cf. Arangio-Ruiz, 1st Report on State Responsibility, *ILC Yearbook*, 1988, vol. 2, part. 1, p. 19.

[355] *ICJ Reports*, 1962, p. 36. It has been argued that the Court had in fact no power to award restitution, and that this part of the judgment was declaratory rather than mandatory: Christine Gray, 'Is there an International Law of Remedies?', this *Year Book*, 56 (1985), pp. 25 ff., at p. 37, n. 52; *contra*, Mann, 'The Consequences of an International Wrong', this *Year Book*, 48 (1976–7), p. 13. The wording of the *Temple* judgment is certainly declaratory in form, but there seems no reason why the Court should not direct specific restitution, as the PCIJ did in the *Peter Pázmány University* case, *PCIJ*, Series A/B, No. 61, p. 249. Cf. also the Lagergren award in the *British Petroleum* v. *Libya* case, and the comments of Christopher Greenwood in this *Year Book*, 53 (1982), p. 76.

EMPLOYMENT CONTRACTS AS AN EXCEPTION TO STATE IMMUNITY: IS ALL PUBLIC SERVICE IMMUNE?*

By HAZEL FOX‡

INTRODUCTION

The restrictive rule of State immunity was adopted to render subject to the jurisdiction of the national courts of the forum State commercial transactions or private law acts entered into by a foreign State. In principle, the general exception to State immunity for such commercial transactions or private law relationships is broad enough to include employment. The employment contract is one in which a private person may engage both as an employer and as an employee, and the appointment, employment, use and dismissal of personnel is an incidental feature of any business operation, and hence one might assume, to be categorized, like the business itself, as a commercial or private law transaction.

This thinking would seem to be supported by the construction of the employment relationship in civil law countries. Thus, the Austrian Supreme Court accepted jurisdiction over a claim against the French Government made by a French national, head of the visa section in Innsbruck, for breach of contract and unpaid salary, stating:

> Where the foreign State acts as the holder of private rights and concludes a contract of employment for work to be performed on the territory of the State of the forum, that foreign State can also be subjected to proceedings concerning the employment relationship.[1]

Similarly the Amsterdam Court of Appeal recognized an exception to immunity 'as soon as the defendant performs acts which it performs on the same footing as a natural or legal person'.[2]

‡ QC; Hon. Fellow, Somerville College, Oxford; formerly Director of the British Institute of International and Comparative Law.

[1] *French Consular Employee* case, *Journal de droit international*, 1993, vol. 2, p. 387; 86 ILR 583.

[2] *MK* v. *Republic of Turkey*, *Netherlands Yearbook of International Law*, 19 (1984), p. 435; see also *Republic of Portugal* v. *De Sousa*, where the District Court of Amsterdam confirmed the lower court's assumption of jurisdiction: 'The conclusion of a contract of employment in which the employee is appointed a teacher is an act which, by its nature, can also be performed by a private individual as a normal legal dealing. What is involved here is an act in the sphere of normal social dealings governed by private law, in respect of which as the Lower Court rightly observed, Portugal entered into a legal relationship with De Sousa on a footing of equality. There is no question, therefore, of an exception to the jurisdiction of Dutch courts acknowledged under international law as it is currently interpreted': 94 ILR 314 at 315.

A similar approach has been adopted in US federal courts in construing the legislative enactment in the Foreign Sovereign Immunities Act (FSIA), section 1605(*a*)(2), of the exception to State immunity for 'commercial activity'; on the basis of that section jurisdiction was assumed over a claim for wrongful dismissal against Spain brought by an Argentine national, permanently resident in the United States, marketing Spanish wines on behalf of the Commercial Office attached to the Spanish embassy.[3]

These cases exercising local jurisdiction over employment claims against a foreign State are misleading. They convey the impression that under the restrictive rule, all employees of a foreign State, performing work abroad of a nature similar to that in the private sector, may have access to local courts. Such an impression is false. In many respects the absolute immunity previously enjoyed by a foreign State with regard to claims of its employees still continues under the restrictive rule. The true position, however, is obscured by the complexity of the treatment of the employment exception in immunity law, diversity of application in national jurisdictions and divergence in theory. There is, currently, no uniformity of approach. This state of affairs is reflected in the fact that out of some 1200 cases brought annually in 1993 against the United States in 80 countries raising an issue of State immunity, over 80 per cent involved disputes with staff.[4] This general confusion makes uncertain the scope of immunity of public service abroad in international law to be applied by local courts.[5]

A number of models can be identified in the treatment of employment and these will be examined in turn. Model I, already identified in the US legislation and also to be found in the Canada State Immunity Act, gives no special treatment to employment but includes employment contracts within the general exception relating to commercial or private law transactions; the case law demonstrates the difficulty which courts have had in fitting employment into either of these categories. A second model, frequently combined with Models I and III, is to identify

[3] *Segni* v. *Commercial Office of Spain*, 835 F 2d 160 (7th Cir., 1987).

[4] David Epstein, Director of Foreign Litigation, Civil Division, United States Department of Justice, paper given at the Lawyers in Europe Conference on State Immunity, 30 June–2 July 1994.

[5] The employment exception had been researched and debated by the International Law Commission: Fifth Report of S. Sucharitkul, Special Rapporteur, *ILC Yearbook*, 1993, vol. 2, part 1, pp. 32–8; Commentary to Article 13 on contracts of employment, ibid., 1984, vol. 2, part 2, pp. 63–6; and see further ILC documentation in Section II.(e), below. See also ILA, *The ILA Montreal Draft Convention on State Immunity* (1983), pp. 51–2, para. 22; Reports of International Committee on State Immunity (Chairman Monroe Leigh; Rapporteur Professor Georg Ress), ILA Cairo Conference (1992), pp. 25–7, paras. 77–9; ILA Buenos Aires Conference (1994), pp. 51, 58; Institut de droit international, draft resolution, *Annuaire de l'Institut de droit international*, 62–II (1987), p. 241; Brownlie, preliminary report, ibid., 62–I (1987), p. 13, definitive report, ibid., p. 45; Seyersted, *International and Comparative Law Quarterly*, 14 (1965), pp. 33–82, 493–527; Australian Law Reform Commission Report No. 24 *Foreign State Immunity* (1984), pp. 94–100; Lewis, *State and Diplomatic Immunity* (3rd edn., 1990), pp. 48–51.

specified categories of foreign State employees, such as diplomats, consuls and visiting armed forces, to design special regimes of jurisdiction for such categories shared between sending and receiving States, and to exclude them from the general law of State immunity. Differing practice of States as to whether the immunity should include all grades employed in diplomatic and consular posts has complicated the use of this model. A third model, designed to preserve in large measure immunity for employment with a foreign State despite the adoption of a restrictive law of State immunity, is to enact a special exception for contracts of employment additional to the general exception for commercial transactions. This approach is derived from the introduction of a special article devoted to employment contracts in the European Convention on State Immunity (ECSI) in 1972 and is adopted in the legislation of the UK, Australia and some other Commonwealth countries. ECSI Article 5 employs the private international law connexion of place of performance of the work to remove immunity in its first paragraph, but by a series of provisos restores it to the employer State where the connexion of nationality or habitual residence to the forum State is absent or where the terms of employment have so provided.

It might be thought that universal adoption by States of this specific exception in Model III would promote the emergence of a single uniform rule of international law. But an independent line taken by the Swiss Federal Tribunal in *S* v. *India*[6] rejecting ECSI Article 5 as customary international law, and continued discussions in the International Law Commission, the Institut de droit international and the International Law Association as to the scope of the employment exception, suggest otherwise. In place of the nationality/habitual residence of the employee used in the European Convention to distinguish public service from private employment, the ILC draft article proposes a test of the performance of 'functions closely related to the exercise of government authority', whereas the ILA Montreal draft Convention addresses the problem as a question of exclusive competence of the employing State over disputes determinable by its administrative law, that is, over relations within its own administration. Thus it is apparent that the subject continues to provoke argument as to the theoretical basis of any criterion. Some writers base immunity solely on international law and principles of State responsibility and non-intervention, whilst others support analysis in terms of competences of administrative and private law and of jurisdictional factors derived from private international law. However, if treated as a question of private international law, further complexity is introduced by uncertainty as to the principle by which the applicable law of employment involving a foreign country is to be

[6] *Arrêts du tribunal fédéral suisse*, 110 II 255 (1984), 82 ILR 14, commented on by Vischer, *Annuaire suisse de droit international*, 1986, p. 26; see also Monnier, ibid., 1985, p. 235.

determined, whether by autonomy of the parties, territorial connexion, or the principle of the law most favourable to the employee (as adopted in the EEC Rome Convention on Contractual Obligations 1980).[7]

These differences of theoretical and practical approach and diversity of rule are not surprising in a topic so directly connected with labour law and more specifically the treatment of public service within that law. Labour law is not static; the employment relationship can be variously analysed as one of contract—'the personal and voluntary exchange of freely bargained promises'—or status, of master with prerogative power over his servant, or a movement from one to the other resulting in an institution of public law enforcing minimum standards of employment protection.[8] These notions of employment relationship underlie the adoption of an interventionist or abstentionist approach to labour issues; current debates concerning the British opt-out of the Social Chapter in the EC Maastricht Treaty show that different States and different groups within a single State may differ on the degree to which the parties to an employment relationship should be required to conform to common conditions of work and pay.[9]

The international dimension is provided by UN and ILO standard setting; the freedom of association declared in the UN Covenant on Civil and Political Rights and the right to work, to the enjoyment of just and favourable conditions of work including health and safety conditions and equal opportunity, and the right to social security proclaimed in the UN Covenant on Economic Social and Cultural Rights, have been elaborated in individual conventions of the ILO.[10] Human rights law, UN and regional, also introduces into employment law requirements of equality of treatment, non-discrimination by race, gender or on the other grounds, and a procedural right of access to a court to enforce the employee's human rights.[11] For members of the European Union there are further pressures to modify national conditions of employment to meet the requirements of freedom of movement of workers and establishment.

Employment within the public service remains largely excluded from these EC developments, yet, though still largely restricted to nationals of the employing State, public service is undergoing change by privatiza-

[7] Gamillscheg, 'Conflicts of Laws in Employment Contracts and Industrial Relations', in Blanchpain and Engels, *Comparative Labour Law and Industrial Relations in Industrialised Market Economies* (5th ed., 1993), p. 183 at p. 186.

[8] P. Davies and M. Freedland, *Labour Law: Text and Materials* (2nd edn., 1984), pp. 106–11.

[9] P. Davies and M. Freedland, *Labour Legislation and Public Policy* (1993), pp. 526, 574.

[10] N. Valticos and K. Samson, 'International Labour Law', in Blanchpain and Engels, op. cit. above (n. 7), p. 77; Convention No. 151 concerning the Protection of the Right to Organize and Procedures for Determining Conditions of Employment in the Public Service, 27 June 1978, *UN Treaty Series*, vol. 1218, p. 87.

[11] See Section III, below.

tion of many of its functions and application of the employment protection rules of the private sector to its employees. In some respects the situation of employment abroad exacerbates differences of approach and rule, and highlights the conflicting interests of the three parties involved, the employer State, the forum State and the employee. A State pursuing interventionist employment policies at home may wish to apply the same rules to its overseas labour force and be unwilling to accept adjudication of labour disputes in courts other than its own. The employing State has an additional ground—independence in the conduct of foreign relations—which may in part be shared by the forum State so far as treatment of its own foreign service is concerned. The forum State, however, along with the employee himself and any trade union or association supporting his interests, may also be mindful of the need to ensure fair and reasonable conditions of work for the local labour force, non-discrimination and access to the forum State's courts.

The present article will examine how the tensions observable in the law relating to employment and public service affect the application of the employment exception to State immunity. Section I describes the proceedings which may be brought in respect of employment by a foreign State; it considers their scope, the parties to the proceedings and remedies sought. Section II contains a description and analysis of the three models of an employment exception to immunity. This is followed by an account of the work of the International Law Commission which led to Article 11 of the draft articles on jurisdictional immunity submitted in 1991 to United Nations. Section III contains an excursus on EC law relating to the exclusion of public service from the freedom of movement of workers and an outline of the organization of the British Foreign Service, being that part of the public service which is most directly involved in disputes relating to employment by the United Kingdom abroad. Section IV sets out a summary of findings, conclusions and some recommendations.

I. Types of Proceedings for which the Employer State Seeks Immunity

Proceedings relating to employment disputes with a foreign State may cover issues wider than the initial contract of employment, involve parties other than the immediate employer and employee, distinguish between work rendered by an employee and one by an independent contractor and vary in the remedy sought. Where the legislation relating to the employment exception to State immunity is worded by reference to the employment contract between the foreign State and the employee as in Model III,[12] claims not falling within that framework may either have to be brought within the general exceptions for commercial transaction or tort[13] or remain immune.

(a) *The Contract of Employment*

Claims relating to the contract of employment and its terms for performance, wages, severance pay, sick pay, overtime and other benefits including notice and other procedures for dismissal as provided in the individual contract or imported from standard service regulations or collective bargaining agreements will fall within the exception. As already stated, and as the experience of foreign ministries confirms, the majority of claims brought against foreign States include proceedings of this nature.

The employment exception is primarily formulated in contractual terms since the basis of the restrictive approach to immunity is the State's voluntary consent to a commercial or private law act. But this seriously neglects the overlay of statutory and mandatory provisions which labour law imposes, and which form the reasonable expectation of the employee in undertaking employment. Labour laws in many countries identify the employee as the weaker bargaining party in employment and provide a special body of law to protect the worker, a body of law which concerns, first, the individual contract with the employer, second, collective bargaining arrangements between employers and organized representatives of employees in a particular sector of employment, such as trade unions or work councils, and third, the social security requirements of the State in relation to its national work force.[14]

In industrialized States special labour courts have become quite usual, but the range of competence and types of case treated vary considerably.[15] Similar systems of labour laws exist in other countries. In the United States, the National Labour Relations Act establishes a board and

[12] The ILA Montreal draft articles narrow the employment exception even further by including the words 'and the proceedings relate to the (employment) contract': Article IIIC, ILA Montreal Draft Convention on State Immunity, 1983.

[13] An early claim for personal injuries sustained on embassy premises failed by reason of the jurisdictional inviolability of the diplomatic premises: *Foreign Status (Legation Buildings) Immunities* case (1928), *Annual Digest*, 4 (1927–8), No. 113; cf. *Stapledon* v. *First Lord of the Admiralty* (1923), *Annual Digest*, 2 (1923–4), No. 74 (accident causing death of Egyptian national on merchant ship chartered for transport of troops; claim immune).

[14] Gamillscheg writes of three categories of norms in substantive labour law: contractual norms, as established by the employment contract; 'protective rules' enforced by public law penal sanctions relating to safety at work and protection of vulnerable workers such as children, pregnant women, or handicapped persons; and hybrid industrial or collective norms, contained in collective agreements, but not enforced by public law: Blanchpain and Engels, op. cit. above (n. 7), p. 183.

[15] A. Gladstone, 'Settlement of Disputes over Rights', in Blanchpain and Engels, op. cit. above (n. 7), p. 455.

special administrative procedures for the enforcement of trade union rights. In France, labour laws were created in the 1950s setting up a *conseil de prud'hommes* consisting of two representatives drawn from employers and two from employees to determine disputes, with appeal to the Labour Law Chamber of the Court of Appeal and hence to the Social and Economic Chamber of the Court of Cassation. These labour courts are not a section of the administrative courts, but a branch of the civil law courts; and their specialist nature makes them unfamiliar with considerations of foreign relations when they arise concerning contracts of employment made by a foreign State.

The wording in the legislation providing an employment exception to State immunity may reflect the contractual concept of employment and consequently apply only to complaints relating to statutory conditions of employment which occur in the actual period of employment, excluding claims relating to events before or after. Thus, complaints relating to negotiations prior to entry into an employment contract may not fall within the employment exception. In England racially discriminatory advertisements for employment issued by a High Commission, which resulted in no contract of employment with the complainant, were held to be pre-contractual acts and not to come within the employment exception of the State Immunity Act 1978.[16] Yet there may be statutory

[16] *Banai* v. *Canadian High Commission* (1990), EAT 65/90. SIA 1978 s. 4 reads:

'(1) A State is not immune as respects proceedings relating to a contract of employment between the State and an individual where the contract was made in the United Kingdom or the work is to be wholly or partly performed there.

(2) Subject to subsections (3) and (4) below, this section does not apply if:

- (*a*) at the time when the proceedings are brought the individual is a national of the State concerned; or
- (*b*) at the time when the contract was made the individual was neither a national of the United Kingdom nor habitually resident there; or
- (*c*) the parties to the contract have otherwise agreed in writing.

(3) Where the work is for an office, agency or establishment maintained by the State in the United Kingdom for commercial purposes, subsection (2)(*a*) and (*b*) above do not exclude the application of this section unless the individual was, at the time when the contract was made, habitually resident in the State.

(4) Subsection (2)(*c*) above does not exclude the application of this section when the law of the United Kingdom requires the proceedings to be brought before a court of the United Kingdom.

(5) In subsection (2)(*b*) above "national of the United Kingdom" means

- (*a*) a British citizen, a British Dependent Territories citizen, a British National (Overseas) or a British Overseas citizen; or
- (*b*) a person who under the British Nationality Act 1981 is a British subject; or
- (*c*) a British protected person within the meaning of that Act.

(6) In this section "proceedings relating to a contract of employment" includes proceedings brought between the parties to such a contract in respect of any statutory rights or duties to which they are entitled or subject as employer or employee.'

(Commencement Order, SI 1978, No. 1572. Subsection (5) amended by the British Nationality Act 1981, s. 52(6), Sch. 7; and the Hong Kong (British Nationality) Order 1986, SI 1986, No. 948, Art. 8, Schedule.)

rights of the employee under forum law extending to this period covering the obligation to negotiate in good faith, discrimination against job-seekers and prohibition of anti-competitive treatment of tenders. The UK Act expressly extends the employment exception to cover statutory rights by defining 'proceedings relating to a contract of employment' to include 'proceedings between the parties to such a contract in respect of any statutory rights or duties to which they are entitled or subject as employer or employee'.[17] These words would seem wide enough to cover statutory rights which subsist alongside the contractual relationship such as those relating to conditions of work, equality of pay, disciplinary procedures, health, safety and protection of the workforce. *Banai's* case, however, suggests that they are not wide enough to cover pre-contractual statutory rights.

In England the common law has enlarged the employer's liability by a duty of care relating to the place, manner and equipment provided for work. The employment exception in the SIA seems wide enough to cover this type of claim, although the personal injuries exception in section 5 may also be available. A minority opinion in *Saudi Arabia* v. *Nelson*[18] was prepared to find the employer under a duty to warn of the risks of employment abroad.

(b) *Claimants other than the Employee*

Dependants have on occasion been allowed to sue on a non-immune contract of employment for loss sustained from employment.[19] In England a system of industrial tribunals with appeal to an Employment Appeals Tribunal now deals with disputes arising out of employment protection, complaints of discrimination on grounds of sex or race, disciplinary powers of management and rights of trade unions and their members, and attachment of wages under a maintenance agreement.[20] Claims as to nature and amount of employment or social security benefits may be made by the labour or social security authority on behalf of the employee against the foreign State. The Dutch cases relating to entitlement to unemployment benefit on proof of non-consensual termination

[17] SIA section 4(6).

[18] 113 S Ct. 1471 (1993).

[19] For failure to provide a safe place of work, to insure the employee and his family: *Stichtung de Revalidatie Centrum 'de Trappenberg'* v. *Morocco*, *Netherlands Yearbook of International Law*, 18 (1987), p. 354; 65 ILR 375; for retention of passport and imprisonment in hotel: *Alicog* v. *Saudi Arabia*, 850 F Supp. 379 (1994, US Dis.).

[20] In the *British Embassy Driver* case (1978), 65 ILR 20, as a consequence of the non-immune nature of the driver's employment with the embassy, an Austrian court held that his earnings were also subject to attachment under the forum law at the instance of his dependants.

of employment illustrate this type of claim.[21] Third parties may bring proceedings by reference to a contract of employment, as, for example, a claim for injury caused by the negligent driving of an employee,[22] or failure to train an ambassador or other staff in their duties.[23]

Trade unions or workers' associations from time to time have sought to bring proceedings against the foreign State employer; proceedings may relate to the right to represent the employee, to collective bargaining agreements, strikes or lockouts in violation of such agreements and collective dismissal. Such proceedings are more readily recognized as direct intervention in the internal administration of a State than claims by individual employees for basic fair conditions of work. Certainly this was the view of the Pretore of Milan who refused an order sought against the United States by an Italian trade union for embassy and consular staff:

> In particular should a court order a foreign state—as has been requested in the case in hand—to modify preordained procedures for employment of staff (even of persons employed in an administrative or clerical capacity), to suppress those aspects considered harmful to the collective interests of trade union, then the court would undoubtedly infringe upon the State's power to organise its own offices and act *in jure imperii*. In such a case the court's decision would amount to a judicial interference that is not allowed even vis-à-vis the Italian public administration . . . thereby violating the principle of good faith.[24]

Intervention in internal administration has not, however, barred as immune claims by trade unions against a foreign State employer in US courts. Claims for union representation have successfully been brought under FSIA section 1605(*a*)(2) in respect of employees in a branch of a nationalized bank[25] and a cultural centre of a foreign government.[26] In the *Goethe House* case, the District Court held immune the Board's claim

[21] By bringing proceedings against the foreign employer to show that it has failed to obtain the consent of the Regional Labour Director, the employee hopes to establish this non-consensual termination; after some hesitation and debate (*Gootges* v. *Kingdom of Belgium* (Rotterdam court, 1978), 65 ILR 373; cf. *Republic of Portugal* v. *De Sousa* (Amsterdam court, 1981), 94 ILR 314), the Dutch courts accepted that the Director's consent to proceedings was necessary. Thus, to give the employee access to local State benefits, the Dutch courts accepted jurisdiction over a private law relationship and applied a Dutch statutory requirement of the Director's consent: *MK* v. *Republic of Turkey* (Hague court, 1985), *Netherlands Yearbook of International Law*, 19(1988), p. 435 (see Professor Maas, ibid., 10 (1979), p. 442). As to whether such consent was required for employment or its termination in foreign embassies and consulates, see *BV* v. *Istituto Italiano* (1990, reversed 1991), *Netherlands Yearbook of International Law*, 23 (1992), p. 447. The Dutch court accepted that the director's consent was necessary: *Republic of Portugal* v. *De Sousa* (Hague court, 1981), confirmed by Court of Appeal, 94 ILR 314.

[22] *Castro* v. *Saudi Arabia*, 510 F Supp. 309 (DC, 1986); 63 ILR 419.

[23] *Travel Associates* v. *Kingdom of Swaziland* (DC, 1990), Lexis 11455; *Guzel* v. *State of Kuwait* (US DC Col., 1993), Lexis 3793.

[24] *Italian Trade Union for Embassy and Consular Staff* v. *United States* (Italy, pretore of Milan, 1981), 65 ILR 339 at 342–3.

[25] *State Bank of India* v. *NRLB*, 808 F 2d 526.

[26] *Goethe House* v. *NRLB*, 685 F Supp. 427 (SDNY, 1988), reversed 689 F 2d 75 (2nd Cir., 1989).

to allow union representation for 7 non-German (among up to 40 German) employees, and as constituting intervention by a US agency in 'the underlying employment structure of [an] arm of a foreign State that is [conceded as] not involved in commercial activity'. The same view was taken by Circuit Judge Lumbard in a strong dissent on appeal; the majority, however, refused to stay the Board's proceedings, influenced no doubt by the prior unionization of the German employees in Goethe House, which indicated that the employer had already lost the power unilaterally to determine the working conditions of its employees. These US cases are to be contrasted with the Canadian case of *Re Canada Labour Code*,[27] where the Canadian Supreme Court refused to allow trade representation of civilian craftsmen on the US naval base in Newfoundland. The Canadian court distinguished the *Goethe House* case; unlike a cultural centre the operations of embassies and offshore military posts were 'quintessential examples of State activity'.

The definition of the contract of employment as confined to the State employer and individual employee excludes proceedings brought by trade unions from the express employment exception under the ECSI, SIA and other legislation; SIA section 3(3) proviso excludes the same narrowly defined employment contracts from the general exception for commercial transactions. It would, therefore, seem to follow that proceedings brought by a trade union in the UK, if allowed at all, would have to be brought, as they have been under Model I in the US and Canadian courts, under the general exception for commercial transactions.

This differentiation of treatment by which immunity is more readily withdrawn from a claim brought by an individual employee than one by a trade union may have some immediate practical significance for the employer's conduct of the office; a claim by an individual may relate to one hard case whereas a claim by a trade union may affect a whole sector of the work force. Yet many labour lawyers would consider there to be a common continuity of purpose shared between arrangements achieved by collective bargaining and mandatory employment protection requirements written into an individual contract; intrusion into the internal administration of a State may not be so obvious when a court enforces an individual employee's contract, but the end-result, the restriction of the employer's freedom to control the conditions of work, may not be much different.

It is obvious that only one party to the employment relationship, the employee and those representing him or deriving rights through him, will bring proceedings under the employment exception to State immunity. Any claim made by the State employer, such as, for example, to

[27] [1990] 1 FC 332; (1992) 91 DLR (4th) 449 at 468; *International Legal Materials*, 32 (1993), p. 1.

enforce a covenant in restraint of trade, or to restrain a worker inciting others to breach of employment, will inevitably constitute submission by the employer State to the jurisdiction of the forum court.

(c) *Contract of Services*

Common law jurisdictions make a distinction between a contract for service and one for services, the former involving an employment relationship, the second that of an independent contractor.[28] Originally based on a test of control, the courts have moved to a test embracing multiple factors and in part influenced by the purpose for which the question is asked.[29] If this distinction is applicable, independent contractors, such as architects, surveyors or accountants for work done at embassy premises, are not to be categorized as employees; claims made by such persons would not, therefore, fall within a special employment exception, but would have to be brought within the general exception for commercial transactions.[30]

(d) *Employment in the Territory of the Employing State*

In both Model I and Model III-type legislation relating to the employment exception it is possible for two separate types of proceedings to arise. The State which employs workers abroad may be summoned by the employee before a court of the country where the work is performed; alternatively a complaint may be brought before the court of the country where the employee was recruited by a foreign State in respect of work to be performed in the territory of the recruiting State. The employer State's claim to immunity is clearly stronger in the second situation, for the reason that the work is to be performed in the territory over which the employer State exercises jurisdiction. The preference for a decision in favour of the employer State in this second situation illustrates how

[28] The Wages Act 1986 s. 8 defines a contract of employment as 'a contract whereby the individual undertakes to do or perform any work or services for another party to the contract whose status is not by virtue of the contract that of a client or customer of any profession or business undertaking carried on by that individual'. Cf. EC law, where a worker is defined as 'any person performing for remuneration work the nature of which is not determined by himself for and under control of another, regardless of the employment relationship': *Lawrie-Blum* v. *Land Baden-Wurtemberg*, Case 66/85, [1986] ECR 2121.

[29] Selwyn, *Law of Employment* (7th edn., 1991), p. 35; I.T. Smith and J.C. Wood, *Industrial Law* (5th edn., 1993), p. 10.

[30] Arguably, on this ground, an architect's claim for unpaid fees in making preliminary sketches for the Congo's national pavilion at EXPO 67 in *Venne* v. *Republic of the Congo* (1971), 22 DLR (3d) 1912, did not concern an employment contract; the point, however, was not raised; the case was decided under the common law and by majority decision, 7–2, the Canadian Supreme Court held immune, even if the restrictive rule was applicable, the preparation of the construction of a national pavilion at an international exhibition as a public act. See also *Prentice Shaw and Schiess* v. *Republic of Bolivia*, 64 ILR 685; cf. *Tsakos* v. *USA* (1972, Labour Tribunal, Geneva), 75 ILR 78.

linked to private international law questions of jurisdiction and applicable law is the application of a rule of immunity.

(e) *Remedies*

Remedies for breach of an employment contract include payment of unpaid contracted salary, recovery of remuneration for overtime, loss of promotion and other contracted or statutory benefits, declaration as to future liability in respect of disability, retirement or redundancy payment, and order for reinstatement. Even if successfully obtained, all may then be met by a plea of immunity from execution. Both general labour law and State immunity law construe an order for reinstatement or injunction not to dismiss the employee as an order requiring the performance of a personal act by the employer and hence as one difficult to enforce in law; an order for specific performance or an injunction continues to attract absolute immunity[31] and the Australian Act specifically enacts that 'a court may not make an order that a foreign state employ a person or re-instate a person in employment'.[32] Indeed, in English employment law it was due to the inability under the common law to obtain an order for specific performance of a contract for personal services that a statutory right was introduced in 1971 not to be unfairly dismissed with a right to reinstatement; however, orders for reinstatement are in fact rarely granted and the statutory remedy in the main entitles the employee to a higher level of compensation for the employer's refusal to reinstate.[33] Whilst forum courts might similarly increase the compensation awarded against a foreign State employer where an order for reinstatement is justified in law but debarred from personal enforcement against a State, even money orders obtained by employees against a State remain largely worthless. A judgment for monies due, failing co-operation of the State, will only be satisfied if the employee can locate an account of the employer State which is not immune from attachment.[34]

II. Three Models and the ILC'S Draft Article on the Employment Exception

The treatment of the exception for employment in the restrictive rule of State immunity can be analysed into a number of models. The general

[31] SIA s. 13(2)(*a*).

[32] Australian Foreign States Immunities Act 1985 s. 29(2).

[33] It is not available for workers with less than two years' service or over the retirement age, nor where there is no termination of employment.

[34] *Abbot* v. *Republic of South Africa* (Spanish Constitutional Court, 1 July 1992), 177 BOE Sup. 24 July 1992, p. 34.

exception to immunity made under the restrictive rule for trading activities of the State in common law countries is expressed as an exception for commercial transactions, whereas in civil law countries it turns on the civil court's competence over private law acts. For the purposes of the present discussion Model I is employed to cover both types of act, whether commercial or private law, because employment contracts in this model are considered under the general exception and given no special treatment. Model II identifies specified categories of State employees, designs special regimes of jurisdiction for such categories and excludes them from the general law of immunity. While it rarely stands alone, being often combined with Model I or III, it operates independently as an exclusion of a special regime from the general law of immunity. Model III provides a special exception for contracts of employment additional to the general exception for commercial transactions or private law acts. In addition under Conclusions it will be seen that a fourth model is suggested, a variant of Model III, which allows full play to all the jurisdictional connexions which private international law recognizes as relevant to the employment relationship.

(a) *Model IA: Employment as a Commercial Act within the General Exception*

In the legislation introducing restrictive immunity in the United States and Canada there is no express exception dealing specifically with employment contracts. These countries are, therefore, examples of Model I legislation. In addition there may also be considered under this heading common law countries which, having no specific State immunity legislation in force, observe a restrictive approach and apply a general commercial test, and also civil code countries which, again in the absence of legislation, apply a general private law test.

Diplomatic exchanges dating back to the nineteenth century show the US Government active in maintaining immunity for its officials employed abroad in embassies and consulates.[35] Prior to the enactment of the immunity legislation, reported cases relating to public employment suggest that both US and Canadian courts were prepared to extend immunity to a wide category of State employees. The Canadian case of *Venne* has already been referred to, where an architect's fee for drawings for a national pavilion at an international exhibition was held irrecoverable as immune, and a similar result was reached in *Heaney* v. *Government of Spain*[36] and *Gittler* v. *German Information Service*[37] where,

[35] Hackworth, *Digest of International Law*, vol. 4 (1942), p. 730.
[36] 445 F 2d 507, 57 ILR 153.
[37] 408 New York Supp. 2d Ser. 600 (1980).

despite advice to the contrary from the State Department, a claim for work for making documentary films to foster cultural relations and to promote understanding between Germany and the United States was held immune.

US Law

The legislative history of the US Foreign Sovereign Immunities Act 1976 (FSIA) makes it clear that it was the intention of the legislator to apply to employment disputes the general exception to immunity for commercial activity contained in section 1605(*a*)(2). That section provides that a foreign State shall not be immune from the jurisdiction of a court of the United States in any case in which

> the action is based upon a commercial activity carried on in the United States by the foreign State; or by an act performed in the United States in connection with a commercial activity of the foreign State elsewhere; or upon an act outside the territory of the United States in connection with a commercial activity of the foreign State elsewhere and that act causes a direct effect in the United States.

Section 1605(*a*)(2), thus, contains three basic requirements. The plaintiff's action must be (i) 'based upon' (ii) 'a commercial activity', or an act in connection with a commercial activity, (iii) with a sufficient 'nexus' or jurisdictional link to the United States.

Commerciality. Employment, to come within the section, must be classified as a 'commercial activity'. Section 1603(3)(*f*) defines 'commercial activity' as

> a regular course of commercial conduct or a particular commercial transaction or act. The commercial character of an activity shall be determined by reference to the nature of the course of conduct or particular transaction, rather than by reference to its purpose.

As many critics have observed, the circularity of this definition deprives it of much value. Some guidance, however, can be obtained from the legislative history. The House Report explains that among activities to be classified as:

> public or governmental would be the employment of diplomatic, civil service, or military personnel, but not the employment of American citizens or third country nationals by the foreign State in the United States. The courts would have a good deal of latitude in determining what is a 'commercial activity' for the purposes of the bill. It has seemed unwise to attempt an excessively precise definition of the term even if that were practical. Activities such as a foreign government's sale of a service or product, . . . its employment or engagement of labourers, clerical staff or public relations or market agents, . . . would be among those included within the definition.[38]

[38] Foreign Sovereign Immunities Act 1976, House Report No. 94–1487, p. 6604 at p. 6615.

Two contrasting notions are here introduced but little assistance is given on how to relate them. Employment in the public service is to remain immune but otherwise the commerciality of the employment in terms of a sale of a service will bring it within the general commercial transaction exception to immunity. Some attempt to relate the two notions is found in the US courts declining jurisdiction which involves supervision of the internal administration or policy-making of the employer State. 'The employment by a foreign State or an international organization of internal administrative personnel – civil servants – is not properly characterized as "doing business" ', the Appeals Court held in *Broadbent* v. *Organization of American States*.[39] Although this case related to employment in an international organization, it is relevant because the organization's immunity in respect of its employees was construed by analogy to the immunity afforded under the FSIA to employment by a foreign State; the court relied on the above quoted passage in the House Report to declare that 'this report clearly marks employment of civil servants as non-commercial for the purposes of restrictive immunity'. 'Internal administration' in the international organization cases has been construed as covering the following proceedings:

(i) wrongful dismissal by staff members of the general secretariat, OAS having an elaborate internal grievance procedure with an appeal to an administrative tribunal;[40]
(ii) alleged racial discrimination and interference with the attorney/client relationship of the employee (a lawyer) with the other employees; the court characterized these claims as 'arising from PAHO's supervision of its civil service personnel and from its provision and allocation of office space';[41]
(iii) complaints relating to forcible detention and investigation for theft, characterized as arising directly from the World Bank's employment practices;[42]
(iv) a claim of sexual harassment and failure to promote women employees by an Argentine woman employed as a researcher.[43]

[39] 628 F 2d 27 (DC Cir., 1980) at 33.
[40] *Broadbent*, loc. cit. above (n. 39).
[41] *Tuck* v. *Pan-American Health Organization*, 668 F 2d 547 (DC Cir., 1981).
[42] *Morgan* v. *International Bank for Reconstruction and Development*, 752 F Supp. 492 (DDC 1990). The temporary nature of the services of Morgan, who was hired as a temporary worker from an outside agency, was held of no significance, the immunity applying to all employment contracts. Morgan also sought to rely by analogy on the tort exception in FSIA s. 1605(*a*)(5) in respect of alleged libel and slander by the World Bank as to his theft of money. However, the District Court held this tort exception to be inapplicable as 'the continuous process of investigation into missing money which involved the participation of higher level World Bank Security and Ethics department officials' involved 'the exercise of policy judgment' and fell within the discretionary function for which the FSIA preserves immunity.
[43] *Mendaro* v. *The World Bank*, 717 F 2d 610 (DC Cir., 1983).

The ruling in *Broadbent* is comprehensive, embracing all employees' disputes by reason of the vulnerability of an international organization to intervention; without the attributes which a State enjoys of its own territory or population, such an organization is dependent for its efficient functioning on the goodwill of the receiving State where it has its headquarters and the restraint of its courts.[44] A further reason given in that case was:

denial of immunity opens the door to divided decisions of the courts of different member States passing judgment on the rules, regulations and decisions of international bodies. Underwriting uniformity in the application of staff rules or regulations would undermine the ability of the organization to function effectively.[45]

The same reasoning does not necessarily apply to employment disputes concerning a foreign State employer.[46] US courts have shown themselves more ready to equate a foreign State with a private employer with all the inconvenience of 'conforming their employment practice to the laws of each country in which they retain staff', particularly where justified by the similarity of the nature of the work to the private sector and by the employee's inferior position in the decision-making structure. In *Segni* v. *Commercial Office of Spain* an Argentinian national, permanently resident in the United States, was employed by the Commercial Office to develop the marketing of Spanish wines in mid-western United States. The written contract was made in the United States on behalf of the Commercial Office, which itself was located in the Spanish embassy, by a member of the diplomatic mission, and was for three years. Segni was to receive a monthly salary, thirty days' vacation with US and Spanish holidays, and he was entitled to choose between US and Spanish social security. After six months he was dismissed and brought proceedings for salary due under the terminated contract. The court found the

[44] 'The law of international immunities [of international organizations] has been founded on three basic propositions, namely (1) that international organisations should have a status which protects them against control or unilateral interference by any one government in the performance of functions for the effective discharge of which they are responsible to the democratically constituted international bodies in which all the nations concerned are represented, (2) that no country should derive any national financial advantage by laying fiscal charges on common international funds, and (3) that international organisations should, as collectivities of States, be accorded the facilities for the conduct of their official business customarily extended to each other by their individual member States': Jenks *The Proper Law of International Organisations* (1962), p. xxxiii.

[45] Loc. cit. above (n. 39), at p. 35.

[46] Civil lawyers frequently attribute the immunity before local courts of international organizations concerning the employment disputes of their employees to incompetence *ratione materiae* of the local court with regard to acts of internal administration, and argue that the same incompetence exists in respect of a foreign State's internal administration, e.g. on the question of the administrative status in his home country of a foreign official (Cassese, 'Immunity from Civil Jurisdiction of International Organisations in Italian Case-law', *Annuaire français de droit international*, 30 (1984), p. 556 at p. 557; Dominice, in a paper presented to the Saarbrucken meeting of ILA International Committee on State Immunity, 1992). US courts do not appear to accept this distinction.

commerciality test unhelpful, first as to the nature of the transaction – the Court of Appeals rejected as too simple 'to define Segni's contract as merely the purchase of services'.[47] Indeed the commerciality test here seemed rather to go to purpose; the public purpose behind the employee's hiring was itself related to commerce, the promotion of foreign sales of wine to increase the health of the Spanish economy: 'Thus, confusingly enough, we must decide whether the *nature* of Segni's hiring is commercial, conscious of the fact that the *purpose* is both commercial and public.'[48] Similarly the fact that the work was 'diplomatic activity', the direct execution of a policy to increase Spanish exports, again related to purpose and was rejected by the court as providing no guidance. The court, however, departed from the *Broadbent* approach under which all employment in the civil service was to be treated as immune by reformulating the *nature* test so as to apply it, not to the nature of the employer, but to the nature of the duties undertaken by the employee. On examination the court decided that they could not be considered as those either of a civil servant or of a diplomatic officer:

> He had no role in the creation of the government policy or its administration; rather, he simply carried it out. There is no indication in the record that he was so supervised or monitored by the Commercial Office, or so privy to its political deliberations, as to be considered a part of the Spanish government, as a civil servant or diplomat would be.

The court concluded that the contract should be described as a contract to 'provide services in the area of product marketing' and as such was commercial, within the exception and non-immune.[49]

In this case the employee was not a national of the employing State. The commerciality test places no weight upon nationality of the employee, yet it is plain that US courts have regard to nationality as an ancillary ground for immunity. The FSIA makes no mention of nationality in applying the commercial exception. But both the House Report

[47] *Segni* v. *Commercial Office of Spain*, 835 F 2d 160 (7th Cir., 1987) at 164.

[48] Ibid.

[49] This case is to be contrasted with *Practical Concepts* v. *Republic of Bolivia* which shows that, even where the provider of services is a private person, courts may differ in their application of the commercial test. The District Court held a three-year written contract of a private enterprise to design and implement a comprehensive programme for the development of Bolivian rural areas to be immune: 'The text of the contract includes numerous terms which only a soverign State could perform and which no private firm or individual going into the market place could ever offer . . . Where, as here, a State exempts a private party from taxation, grants preferential bureaucratic treatment, and diplomatic privileges it is acting in a sovereign (as distinguished from a commercial) capacity' (615 F Supp. at p. 93). The Court of Appeals reversed, holding the contract for services non-immune as a commercial activity: 'The [district] court focused on the auxiliary provisions rather than the agreement's core to classify the contract as "governmental" rather than "commercial". It is more sensible, and faithful to the probable intent of Congress, we believe, generally to center on the basic exchange (e.g. the sale of goods or services), not on the facilitating features (e.g. expediting entrance of personnel and supplies), in determining whether an obligation qualifies as a "commercial activity" for FSIA purposes' (811 F 2d 1594). See *Princz* v. *Germany*, 26 F 3d 1166 (1994), on whether leasing of POW slave labour is 'commercial'.

and the Court of Appeals in *Broadbent* base a distinction between commercial and public service on the nationality of the employee:

The Committee Reports establish an exception from the general rule in the case of employment of American citizens or third country nationals by foreign States. The exception leaves foreign States free to conduct 'governmental matters' through their own citizens.[50]

Nationality of the foreign State is thus used, much more than non-commerciality, in cases under FSIA section 1605(*a*)(2), as an indicator that the employee belongs to that section of the labour force, the civil service of the State, which should be immune.

A similar, though more articulated, approach is taken in the employment exception to immunity in the European Convention under Model III.

Employment in the territory of the employer State. As already noted, FSIA section 1605(*a*)(2) is broad enough to cover claims arising out of employment by a foreign State where the work is to be performed outside the United States. Here again the activity must satisfy the commercial test; US courts have classified as commercial employment abroad as an air pilot,[51] as an engineer in highway construction,[52] engineer in a public hospital,[53] and in a tourist centre.[54] For work performed in the territory of the employer State the two further requirements of the section may serve to exclude US jurisdiction, namely that the claim be based on the commercial activity and have sufficient nexus with the United States. This latter requirement goes more to the use of jurisdictional connections as a criterion of non-immunity in place of commerciality and will be considered under Model III in that context. The requirement that the claim be 'based' on employment has general relevance in that both in respect of transactions found by the court to be commercial or (by a civil court) a private law act, it introduces an additional focusing of the complaint so as to reduce the employment relationship to the context or 'factual matrix' of the claim and to characterize the proceedings, not by that relationship, but by subsequent factors. In the US cases the loss complained of is characterized as a third party act or event extraneous to the employment. Thus, proceedings failed for personal injuries allegedly caused by Air France to the plaintiff while working with a US firm in France,[55] and for loss of dependency against Iran following the murder of a US citizen by a revolutionary group while working in Iran.[56] Even

[50] 628 F 2d 27 (1980), at 34.
[51] *Forsythe* v. *Saudi Arabian Airlines*, 885 F 2d 285 (6th Cir., 1989).
[52] *Zedan* v. *Saudi Arabia*, 849 F 2d 1511 (DC Cir., 1988).
[53] *Saudi Arabia* v. *Nelson*, 123 L Ed 2d 47, 113 S Ct. 1471 (1993).
[54] *Brewer* v. *Republic of Iraq*, 890 F 2d 97 (8th Cir., 1989).
[55] *Santos* v. *Air France*, 935 F 2d 890 (7th Cir., 1991).
[56] *Berkovitz* v. *Iran*, 735 F 2d 329 (1984).

where the State is also the employer, the injury must be shown to arise by way of breach of that employment, not by reason of some other public act of the State.[57]

In the leading case of *Saudi Arabia* v. *Nelson* the Supreme Court, by five to four, held that a claim for alleged detention in prison, torture and beating by Saudi police of a systems monitoring engineer, a US national, employed in a hospital in Riyadh, was a sovereign public act under FSIA and Saudi Arabia was immune from exercise of jurisdiction of the American courts. It was conceded that the appellant hospital and agency with an office in the United States, along with Saudi Arabia, all qualified as a 'foreign State' within the meaning of FSIA. Three constructions were advanced as to the conduct on which the claim was based. Souter J, who delivered the majority opinion, held that the tortious intentional infliction of personal injuries was the basis of the claim and it was not of a commercial nature. He held that the fact that the mistreatment was in retaliation for the manner in which Nelson performed his commercial contract with the hospital was irrelevant as motivation and went to purpose rather than the nature of the act. It was not the type of action by which a private person engages in trade (*Weltover*[58]); 'The conduct boils down to abuse of the power of the police by the Saudi Government and . . . a foreign State's exercise of the power of its police has long been understood for the purposes of the restrictive theory as peculiarly sovereign in nature'.[59] White and Blackmun JJ, in a concurring dissent, held that Nelson's injuries arose from the operation of a commercial hospital, and no distinction should be made as to whether the hospital resorted to thugs or government officers to carry on its business; 'As countless cases attest, retaliation for whistle blowing is not a practice foreign to the market place'.[60] However, these two justices concurred with the majority in upholding immunity as the identified commercial activity was not carried on in the United States. The remaining two justices, Kennedy and Stevens JJ, put forward a third construction. In their view Nelson's claim could properly be said to be based on the advertisement, recruiting and signature of his contract of employment in the United States (the interview took place in Saudi Arabia); these acts were commercial and occurred in the United States and were accordingly not immune. Kennedy J considered that the failure to warn of the risks of employment in Saudi Arabia was a ground of claim which further investigation might prove to be both commercial as a breach of the contract and to take place in the United States;[61] but the majority

[57] *Saudi Arabia* v. *Nelson*, loc. cit. above (n. 53).

[58] *Republic of Argentina* v. *Weltover Inc.*, 112 S Ct. 3160 (1992), *International Legal Materials*, 31 (1992), p. 1220.

[59] *Nelson*, loc. cit. above (n. 53), at p. 61.

[60] Ibid., at p. 64.

[61] Ibid., at p. 68.

dismissed such a duty to warn as 'a semantic ploy': 'For aught we can see a plaintiff could recast virtually any claim of international tort committed by a sovereign act as a claim of failure to warn, simply by charging the defendant with an obligation to announce its own tortious propensity before indulging it'.[62]

Saudi Arabia v. *Nelson* confines the employment exception even when conceived in general commercial terms to the employment relationship. It provides support for the drawing of a distinction between claims for remuneration arising from the employment relationship, which may be subject to local jurisdiction, and claims relating to treatment of the employee subsequent to his engagement where immunity should be retained provided the State employer can convincingly establish that it relates to the exercise of governmental powers, as in the case of dismissal for security, and more questionably for compulsory redundancy due to budget constraints.

Other common law countries

Respect for autonomy of the employer State in its internal administration and exercise of public powers was acknowledged by courts applying a restrictive rule of immunity under the common law.

In England, following the House of Lord's adoption of a restrictive common law rule of immunity in *I Congreso del Partido*,[63] Browne-Wilkinson VC in *Sengupta* v. *Republic of India*[64] had to apply the rule to a contract of an Indian national employed on low-grade clerical duties in the Indian High Commission in London; he enjoyed no diplomatic immunities. The judge reached his decision by posing four questions. The first, 'Was the contract of a kind which a private individual could enter into?', he answered in the affirmative but held it irrelevant:

> It is true that any private individual can employ another i.e. can enter into a contract of employment. Therefore in that sense the entry into a contract of employment is a private act. But when one looks to see what is involved in the performance of Mr Sengupta's contract, it is clear that the performance of the contract is part of the discharge by the foreign State of its sovereign functions in which Mr Sengupta himself, at however lowly a level, is under the terms of his contract necessarily engaged.[65]

He went on to say that the dismissal was an act done in the running of the mission and

> the fairness of any such dismissal is very likely to involve an investigation by the industrial tribunal into the internal management of the diplomatic representation in the United Kingdom of the Republic of India, an investigation wholly

[62] Ibid., at p. 63.

[63] [1983] 1 AC 244.

[64] [1983] ICR 221; 64 ILR 352.

[65] *Sengupta* v. *Republic of India*, [1983] ICR 221; 64 ILR 352 at p. 360.

inconsistent with the dignity of the foreign State and an interference with its sovereign functions.[66]

These passages also provided answers to the three further questions posed by the judge: namely that the performance of the contract involved the participation of both parties in the public functions of the foreign State, that the nature of the alleged breach was wrongful dismissal and that the investigation of that breach would involve an investigation into the public acts of the foreign State.

Sengupta thus established (and its ruling has not since been displaced) that, under the restrictive rule at English common law, employment contracts of *all* persons working on diplomatic premises and engaged in the work of the mission are immune. The breach of contract was alleged to occur and the claim was brought after the date of the entry into force of the UK State Immunity Act, but the conclusion of the contract took place before that date. The latter event was the relevant one under the transitional provisions, SIA section 23(3)(*b*),[67] and accordingly the case was decided under the common law, not the statute. The court did, however, construe sections 4 and 16(1)(*a*) of the Act to conclude that the proceedings would have been immune had the Act applied. It seems probable that this construction influenced the decision to reach a similar outcome under the common law.[68] The court acknowledged the possibility that employees 'solely concerned with providing the physical environment in which the diplomatic mission operates might be able to claim', but left it for a future occasion.

A similar comprehensive view was taken by the Irish Supreme Court in *Canada* v. *Burke*[69] (the first case in Irish law to apply a restrictive rule of immunity under the common law). The Supreme Court held immune a claim for wrongful dismissal brought against Canada by an Irish national employed as a chauffeur in the Canadian embassy in Dublin as an activity which 'truly touched the actual business or policy of the foreign government . . . the element of trust and confidentiality reposed in the driver of an embassy car created a bond with his employer that had the effect of involving him in the employing government's public business organisation and interests.' It is suggested that the true ground of this case may lie in the security aspect of a post of Ambassador's chauffeur, not in the extension of immunity to all service staff employed at the embassy.

These cases demonstrate that the UK and Irish construction of the commerciality test is to treat it as having no application to employment of whatever nature in diplomatic or consular posts. Other common law

[66] Ibid., at p. 361.

[67] SIA s. 23(3) excludes from the operation of the Act all contracts of employment entered into before 22 November 1978: Commencement Order, State Immunity Act 1978, SI 1978, No. 1572.

[68] Crawford, this *Year Book*, 54 (1983), p. 279 at p. 282.

[69] *Canada* v. *Employment Appeals Tribunal and Burke*, [1992] ILRM 325.

jurisdictions have disagreed, preferring the more selective US approach seeking, where possible, ground for exercise of local jurisdiction.

The Canadian Federal Court of Appeal held non-immune under the general exception for commercial transactions a trade union's application for certification as bargaining agent for all Canadian civilians employed on the US naval base in Newfoundland. It noted there to be a distinction between proceedings brought to enforce employer's obligations and the certification process to achieve bargaining status for a collective agreement. But, disregarding as irrelevant the purpose of the employment to serve the defence requirements of the United States, the appellate court held the nature of the employment contracts to be commercial: 'If . . . a supplier of electricity or groceries to the (US) base is entitled to sue the United States for breach of contract in a Canadian court, there is no reason why a Canadian civilian employee there should not have the like entitlement'.[70] However, the Canadian Supreme Court was not prepared, on a matter closely relating to the employer State's power of defence, to take such a narrow focus; it reversed the appellate court by a majority of three to two. Declaring the employment contracts to be of a hybrid nature – the right to be paid being commercial in nature, the power to dismiss without notice for security reasons being public in nature –, the Supreme Court stated that in structuring the work at the base it was impossible to ignore its sovereign purposes and that the United States must be given unfettered control to manage and employ at the base.[71] The US case of *Goethe House*[72] was distinguished; unlike a cultural centre, the operations of embassies and offshore military posts were 'a quintessential example of State activity'.[73]

The application of the commercial test in the Canadian case was complicated by two factors: the alleged public purpose concerned defence, an area where States are particularly sensitive and assertive of their exclusive jurisdiction, and the proceedings were brought by a trade union, not the individual employee. Absent these elements, the commercial transaction can be used, as the Canadian appellate court sought to do, to distinguish routine office duties performed by staff and participation in public acts.

The focus on the immediate duties of the employee to the disregard of the larger purpose for which it is performed was adopted by an Australian court applying a restrictive common law rule of immunity to a wrongful dismissal claim which predated the entry into force of the Australian Foreign States Immunities Act 1985. The Supreme Court of Victoria held it had jurisdiction to hear an air pilot's claim arising out of his employment with the State airline of Nauru, even though the

[70] *In re the Canada Labour Code*, [1990] 1 FC 332 at 637.
[71] *In re the Canada Labour Code*, (1992) 91 DLR (4th) 449 at 467.
[72] 869 F 2d 75.
[73] 91 DLR (4th) 449 at 468.

airline was run at a loss to provide essential transport to support the island's population of 10,000.[73a]

Even if the operation of the airline could not be regarded itself as an essentially commercial exercise by reason of the important function which it carried out, it did not follow that every activity incidental to it must be encompassed by the concept of sovereign immunity, e.g. such things as the purchase of equipment or fuel, the cost of catering, or, indeed, the engagement of staff, save in some circumstances would not generally be elevated to the status of acts *jure imperii*.

The advantage of treating employment under a general commercial exception is that it can be stretched to cover all types of employer, State, corporate or individual; all types of employment, governmental or private, and of performance in or outside the United States, provided a sufficient nexus is established; all types of claim relating to the contract including tortious conduct provided it is based on the commercial activity; and to collective agreements. This generality, however, is its very disadvantage; it contains within itself no clear criterion to distinguish between types of State employment which are and are not immune and consequently leads, as *Practical Concepts* and *Nelson* show, to different conclusions by courts. There is a fumbling attempt to use nationality as a criterion but it is not worked through.

(b) *Model IB: Employment as a Private Law Transaction within the General Exception*

The general test which civil law courts apply so as to bring them under Model I turns on the private law nature of the act, not its commerciality. This test derives from the competence of courts, relations between private individuals being dealt with in the civil court whereas relations between the State and the individual come within the administrative court.

This distinction has both doctrinal and practical implications. The 1982 ILA draft Montreal Convention expressed the doctrinal aspect of the notion by including a clause at the end of the employment exception: 'This provision shall not confer on tribunals in the forum State competence in respect of employees appointed under the public (administrative) law of the foreign State.' Civil lawyers describe the forum court as incompetent *ratione materiae*. Instead of treating State immunity as a plea to bar the exercise of territorial jurisdiction by the courts of the forum State, which derives from the forum State's duty in international law to respect the independence of a sovereign State and to abstain from intervention in its internal affairs, this approach bases the plea of State

[73a] *Reid* v. *Republic of Nauru* (Supreme Court of Victoria, 1992), *Australian Industrial Law Review*, 34 (10) (1992), p. 188. Cf. *Governor of Pitcairn* v. *Sutton*, [1995] NZLR 426 (CA).

immunity on the right of the immune State to exercise a jurisdiction, distinct from territorial or personal jurisdiction, described as 'functional' or 'organic',[74] or by Rousseau as '*compétences aux services publics*'.[75] This jurisdiction is said to include all relations between the State, its organs and officials as determined by the public law of the State and to be exclusive and autonomous from the jurisdiction of other States. Whilst the attribution of such a jurisdiction may usefully complement the self-restraint which States, on the grounds of comity, non-justiciability, act of State or lack of competence, do in fact exercise so as to prevent them from pronouncing on the constitutional validity or administrative propriety of the public acts of another State,[76] whether it amounts to anything more than territorial or personal jurisdiction of the State seems questionable.[77] In any event, international and regional obligations undertaken by the State have reduced the exclusivity of its jurisdiction over constitutional matters.[78]

The use of organic jurisdiction to support withdrawal of employment disputes of all foreign officials from the jurisdiction of the courts of the State where the work is performed is even more dubious. Historically, as discussed below, the position of officials in their own country lacked legal protection, giving rise to no right or at most a complaint under administrative law, and it is, therefore, not surprising to find courts unwilling to give more extensive legal remedies to officials in the employ of a foreign State. But the mandatory requirements of private labour law, and the reasonable expectations of good administration to which administrative or public law now gives rise and recognition, have much reduced the exclusivity of such 'organic' jurisdiction within the State. Further, the treatment of public service abroad raises the difficult issue of the extent to which the courts of another State are under obligation to recognize or otherwise give effect to foreign public law; in the recent *Spycatcher* case, the Australian High Court refused to enforce an obligation of confidentiality arising out of his employment on a former civil servant of the British Secret Service.[79] Public law is territorial in scope; as a matter of public law any question of competing jurisdictions

[74] Seyersted, *International and Comparative Law Quarterly*, 14 (1965), p. 31, at pp. 33 and 522.

[75] Rousseau, *Droit international public* (1953), p. 241.

[76] Brownlie, *Principles of Public International Law* (4th edn, 1990), p. 324, citing Diplock LJ in *Buck* v. *Attorney-General*, [1965] Ch. 745 at 770–1.

[77] Seyersted in elaborating his theory of 'organic' jurisdiction was chiefly concerned to establish a basis for international organizations to exercise exclusive jurisdiction, independent of the territorial jurisdiction of the State where the organization had its headquarters or the personal jurisdiction of a State in relation to nationals serving as officials: loc. cit. above (n. 74), at p. 47.

[78] See, for example, UN Security Council Resolution 827 (1993) establishing a war crimes tribunal for the former Yugoslavia: para. 4 decides that all States shall take the necessary measures under their domestic law to implement the resolution 'including the obligation to comply with the requests for assistance or orders issued by a Trial Chamber' of the tribunal.

[79] *HM Attorney-General for the UK* v. *Heinemann Publishers Australia Pty. Ltd. (No. 2)*, (1988) 165 CLR 30, discussed in Collier, *Conflict of Laws* (2nd edn., 1994), at p. 368.

is not open to solution by private international law principles. Finally, civil lawyers who base immunity of public service on organic jurisdiction may find it proves too much. It excludes *all* public service with a foreign State, and to achieve some forum State jurisdiction over the work of low-grade employees or nationals of the forum State, they are driven to introduce some private international law connexions. Thus, as will be seen, ECSI Article 5 in Model III confines the exclusivity of organic jurisdiction over the officials of a State to nationals of that State or of a third State.

This line of argument is largely unfamiliar to common lawyers. If they recognize the incompetence of the forum court based on the exclusive organic jurisdiction of the employing State, which is questionable, since civil courts assert jurisdiction by way of judicial review over administrative acts of the State, they might describe the bar to local court jurisdiction as a jurisdictional form of non-justiciability or act of State. It is, however, as regards employment questionable whether the issue is properly characterized as non-justiciable given that consent of the foreign State to the proceedings in the local court appears to remove any obstacle to the local court's exercising jurisdiction.[80]

The treatment of employment in civil law courts, particularly Italian courts, throws up into sharp relief the difficulties of the theoretical position. Whilst the categorization as a legal transaction under private laws has provided the reasoning for civil law courts to develop a restrictive rule of immunity, its application to the employment relationship has proved more controversial. In *S* v. *India* the Swiss court was prepared to place employment contracts 'in the same category as the contracts of sale and lease' and to treat them as 'acts governed by the *jus gestionis* even if they relate to the premises of the mission'. It did so on the ground that 'the activities of the sending State in foreign territory, in particular, are never hindered by the submission of disputes arising from such contracts to the jurisdiction of the receiving state'.[81] The Italian Court of Cassation disagreed. As it has noted more than once:

> Legal transactions falling under the private law . . . necessary for the establishment, organisation and good operation of the office belonging to a foreign State such as a lease concerning a building destined to be a consulate or contracts for the purchase of tools and materials [are exempted from the general immunity of States but] more delicate problems arise with regard to pre-existing employment relations which involve the citizens of both states. In this case the foreign organization does not deal with an object, but with a human who carries out an

[80] cf. *Kuwait Airways Corp.* v. *Iraqi Airways Co.*, [1995] 3 All ER 694. Lord Goff of Chieveley ruled that 'the principle [in *Buttes*' case [1982] AC 888, 934] that such public acts will not be called into question does, as I understand the position, raise a question of jurisdiction' (p. 713), and 'a party is not precluded from invoking the principle by reason of his having taken a step in the action or otherwise having submitted to the jurisdiction' (p. 714).

[81] On the facts, the tribunal was not prepared to find the employment governed by Indian public law as the administrative regulations were not produced: 82 ILR 14 at 20–1.

activity necessary for the achieving of the institutional purpose of the foreign state.[82]

A distinction between trading activities and contracts with employees was early appreciated by Italian courts in relation to the Russian Trade Delegation before the Second World War. The Italian Court of Cassation accepted that it had jurisdiction to determine a claim brought by a trader on a contract made by the Russian Trade Delegation,[83] but declared immune a claim for wrongful dismissal brought by a member of the staff of the delegation employed as a correspondent in Milan.[84] The underlying principle was well explained in the later case of *Tani*:

> Even if according to Italian law the exercise of commerce in general and, in particular, trading between the Union [of Soviet Socialist Republics] and individuals in Italy is a matter of private law, this does not affect the public law character of the relationship of employment created between the Union and the staff which the Union engages in order to carry on commerce in Italy and all the other activities connected therewith designed to protect Russian interests. These two activities differ greatly from each other. The relations which may arise between individual private persons on a footing of equality cannot be regarded as identical with those arising under public law where the State exercises sovereign powers towards a subject. In the present case a foreign State is affected which enjoys international immunity in respect of the organisation of its offices. These are called upon to carry out not only commercial contracts but also studies, propaganda, initiation and surveillance of commerce, in short all the activities which come within the function of the State according to the law of the Union.[85]

The public act of a State is held extraneous to the legal order of the territorial State and hence the official participating in that public act is equally outside the local court's jurisdiction.[86] By a public act of the State the Italian court seems to understand both acts governed by international law and acts given effect by the foreign State's law. The main function of a State abroad is representation of the State.[87] The Vienna Convention on Diplomatic Relations 1961, Article 3, defines very broadly the activities included within such representation. In addition to representing the sending State in the receiving State, they include protecting the interests of the sending State and its nationals, negotiating with the government of the receiving State, ascertaining conditions and develop-

[82] *Royal Embassy of Norway* v. *Quattri Monika*, Italy, Court of Cassation, No. 2521/90, L/12771, 13 December 1990. The Australian court in *Reid* (above, n. 73a) appears to be applying a similar exception to an employment contract of an air pilot necessary to the operation of a publicly owned airline but in no way involved in the public function which it served.

[83] *Russian Trade Delegation in Italy* v. *De Castro*, *Annual Digest*, 7 (1933–4), p. 179.

[84] *Russian Trade Delegation in Italy* v. *Kazmann*, ibid., p. 178.

[85] *Tani* v. *Russian Trade Delegation in Italy* (1947), ibid., 15 (1948), p. 141 at p. 144.

[86] *Rubin* v. *Consul of the Republic of Panama* (Italy, Court of Cassation, 1977), 77 ILR 593.

[87] Salmon, 'Immunités et actes de la fonction', *Annuaire français de droit international*, 38 (1992), p. 314 at p. 327.

ments and reporting thereon, promoting friendly relations between the receiving and sending State, and developing their economic, cultural and scientific relations. From this, it may be said that any participation by an employee in an activity falling within Article 3 of the Vienna Convention for the purpose of representation of the employer State abroad involves performance of a public act and hence is immune. Such an approach would bring all types of employees in diplomatic and consular posts of whatever grade, nationality, residence, and regardless of place where engaged, within immunity and would also cover employees in press and information offices and cultural and education institutes where the grant of immunity has seemed most unjustifiable. To justify extension to these peripheral State activities Italian courts have either construed the activity as one which the diplomat or consul is capable of performing in the course of his official duties or as one which a bilateral treaty between employer and forum State recognizes as a public function of the State. In *Little* v. *Riccio*, on appeal from the Naples court, the Court of Cassation, declaring itself incompetent, held 'the cemetery was maintained by Great Britain *de jure imperii* as a consular function for the benefit of her nationals as such and not for them as individuals',[88] and in *Mazzucchi*,[89] as regards a task of disinfecting emigrants, 'although his duties were simple, they were nevertheless still relative to a service of a political nature which the American State carries on'. In other cases the Italian court, relying on the NATO treaty, or conventions relating to cultural relations or educational institutes, declared immune employment disputes relating to a civilian worker at a US military base in Livorno,[90] an administrator in the Hungarian Institute[91] and a teacher in a French lycée in Rome.[92]

More recently Italian courts have sought ways to avoid such comprehensive extension of immunity, particularly where the staff has been locally engaged under a private law form of contract.[93] In *Piccoli* it was noted that the Supreme Court had excluded immunity for menial and casual workers such as manual and catering staff.[94] One alternative test has been to consider whether the work of the employee involves lawmaking or regulatory duties. If it does, the employee's claim concerning employment will be held immune, even though participation is at a

[88] *Annual Digest*, 7 (1933–4), p. 176 at p. 177.

[89] *Mazzucchi* v. *American Consulate*, *Annual Digest*, 6 (1931–2), p. 336.

[90] *Department of Army USA* v. *Gori Savellini* (1956), 23 ILR 201.

[91] *Hungarian People's Republic* v. *Oneri* (1956), 23 ILR 203; cf. *Hungarian Papal Institute* v. *Hungarian Institute of Rome* (1957), 24 ILR 218.

[92] *Republic of France and Lycée Chateaubriand* v. *Jacuzio* (1987), 87 ILR 53. The setting up of a resthome for US sailors in Naples, where the complainant carried out duties of an interpreter and cashier, was, however, held not intended by the US as an act of sovereignty appurtenant to the State's essentially military activity (*Novaco* (1957), 24 ILR 219).

[93] *Bari Institute of the International Centre for Advanced Mediterranean Agronomic Studies* v. *Jasbez* (Italy, Court of Cassation, 1977), 77 ILR 602 at 608.

[94] *Association of Italian Knights of Malta* v. *Piccoli* (1974), 65 ILR 308.

low level; so Mrs Rubin, a clerk and translator working in the Panamanian consulate in Venice, who was responsible for drafting letters and drawing up ships' licences, exercised a regulatory function and her claim was held immune.[95] Service staff such as chauffeurs, catering staff and low grade clerical staff would not exercise such a regulatory function and hence their claims would be within the local court's jurisdiction.[96] In applying this criterion it would seem irrelevant whether the function relates to public acts on the international plane such as negotiation and conclusion of a treaty, or acts with effect under the employer State's law, such as a consul's registration of a birth.

Another test has been to separate the 'economic aspects of the employment relation' from the 'organizational'; and thereby permit the local court to exercise jurisdiction where the claim relates to an amount of wages which has been agreed but not paid or payment has been delayed.[97] As noted in *Trobbiani*, the scope of such a remedy is very limited because the court will not permit any 'investigation of the internal and sovereign activities of the employer state'; consequently, enquiry into the manner in which the duties were allocated by the employer or performed by the employee is excluded, as being an intrusion on the employer State's independence.[98]

The above criteria have been developed to meet the situation where, as in Italy, the employment contract is not of itself categorized as a private law relationship and hence subject to private law courts of the forum country. The more usual approach in civil law countries is to draw the immunity line between public service and private employment.

Public service is subject to different treatment in municipal law from private employment. At its most extreme, employment in the public service is not treated as a relationship giving rise to enforceable legal rights. This was certainly the historic position under English law,[99] which treated officials as office holders under the Crown without an

[95] *Rubin*, loc. cit. above (n. 86), at p. 595.

[96] *Rubin*, ibid. In *Jasbez*, loc. cit. above (n. 93), a case relating to an international organization, its employee, a simultaneous interpreter, was refused immunity on the ground that she was entrusted with responsibilities which consisted of the mechanical repetition in a foreign language of words spoken or written by others: 'These responsibilities were, therefore, unconnected with the intellectual process of taking decisions in furtherance of the organisation's aims, nor did they form part of the public function of that process (in contrast to the case of embassy interpreters or state officials on duty abroad whose responsibilities constitute an essential and indispensable medium for the performance of the state's public functions)' (p. 609).

[97] *Royal Embassy of Norway* v. *Quattri Monika*, Italy, Court of Cassation, No. 2521/90, L/12771, 13 December 1990. The Court of Cassation allowed the claim to proceed 'on the ulterior salary-related claims, relative to the payment of the "cashier risk" allowance, of the advance notice, the end of employment pay, the accrued Christmas and summer bonuses and the unused 1989 leave. This examination does not interfere with the untouchable public powers of the Foreign State.'

[98] *Libyan Arab Republic* v. *Trobbiani, Il Foro Italiano*, 113 (1990).

[99] *R* v. *Civil Service Appeals Board, ex parte Bruce*, [1989] 3 All ER 686, where para. 14 of the Civil Service Pay and Conditions Code stating that a civil servant does not have a contract of employment enforceable in the courts was construed as evidence of the Crown's lack of intention to be bound.

enforceable contract of employment in the ordinary courts.[100] It would also seem true of US armed forces who have no legal rights enforceable against the United States.[101]

A more usual treatment is for the relationship to be governed by a different law from private law. This difference in treatment of public service is widely adopted in civil law countries and stems from the separation of powers, and in France the separate system of supervision of the administration by the *Conseil d'Etat*. In civil law countries a contract for public work of a public body or body providing a public service and containing a power to vary or rescind or some other *clause exorbitante* is governed by administrative law. Consequently a distinction is made between the public service, where the official is appointed under regulations of the service subject to administrative law, and employment under a private law contract governed by private law. It is somewhat curious that Browne-Wilkinson VC in *Sengupta*, in reaching his decision that employment disputes in all grades of staff of the diplomatic mission were immune,[102] cited Belgian,[103] Italian [104] and German[105] decisions in support without noting that in all these cases the employees were officials appointed under public service regulations and not engaged, as Sengupta appeared to be, under a private law contract of employment.

This distinction between administrative and civil law provided a ready-made solution for application by analogy to employment disputes with a foreign State employer. When a claim relating to such an employment dispute was brought against a foreign State, the civil or commercial court, in the same way that it would dispose of a claim by a home civil servant, ruled that it had no jurisdiction. Thus the Italian Court of Cassation stated:

> In Italy relations arising out of public employment are not subject to the jurisdiction of the ordinary courts. All the more must they be exempt from the jurisdiction of the Italian courts if the relationship was created by a foreign State.[106]

The position, however, is complicated by the fact that both French and German law recognize two types of employment by the State, one governed by public law, that of officials in public service (*fonctionnaires*) regulated by administrative law and departmental regulations, and the other by private law, by contract of employment used for manual staff

[100] *Halsbury's Laws of England* (4th edn.), vol. 8, para. 97; *CSSU* v. *Minister for the Civil Service*, [1985] AC 374.

[101] *Feres* v. *USA*, 340 US 135 (1950).

[102] *Sengupta* v. *Republic of India*, [1983] ICR 221, 64 ILR 352 at 360.

[103] *De Decker* v. *USA*, 23 ILR 209 (decided by the Appeal Court of the Belgian Congo, not of Belgium as stated in the English judgment).

[104] *Luna* v. *Republic of Rumania* (Italy, Court of Cassation, 1974), 54 ILR 313.

[105] *Courades* v. *Government of the UK* (Hanover Labour Court, 1981), 65 ILR 205.

[106] *Tani* v. *Russian Trade Delegation* (1947), 15 ILR 141 at 154.

(*ouvriers*), and office staff (*employés*). From the EC cases discussed below, it would also appear that on occasion even functions similar to those of high level *fonctionnaires* relating to policy-making may be performed by individuals employed under contracts of employment, although they do not enjoy the status or permanence of post of a public official.

Public service may thus give rise to no legally enforceable rights or be governed by a separate administrative law. A third method of legal differentiation of public service is to treat it as a private law relationship but attach different rights and obligations to the relationship. This would seem to be the somewhat hybrid position which English law has now reached.[107]

To conclude this section, civil law courts' use of the Model I produces no certainty in relation to a criterion of the private law act. The use of a concept of organic jurisdiction on the part of the employing State is unhelpful, being self-contradictory and excluding too much. There is too much diversity of practice in the use of the private law contracts for the employment of public officials; courts lack uniformity in treating such employment as indicative of local jurisdiction, and have applied alternative criteria to enable them to exercise jurisdiction over low-grade officials, even where engaged under service regulations, and employed in diplomatic and consular posts.

(c) *Model II: Exclusion of Certain Categories of Foreign State Employment*

This model identifies special categories of foreign State employee and by exclusion confers special treatment on them. It is not unusual for a treaty on a general topic, whether bilateral or multilateral, to contain exclusion clauses relating to a particular category of transaction or person which is separately covered in special legislation. Such an exclusionary approach is, perhaps, more surprising in a 'public law' convention purporting to regulate conduct of sovereign States but it, none the less, is to be found in varying degrees of specificity in all the legislation relating to State immunity.

The European Convention on State Immunity adopts the Model II approach to exclude certain categories of State officials, diplomats and consuls (Article 32), visiting forces (Article 31); certain types of transaction, namely, social security, damage or injury in nuclear matters, customs duties, taxes or penalties (Article 29), the operation of State

[107] See Section III.(b), below.

ships in the carriage of goods or passengers (Article 30); and certain international agreements 'in special fields which relate to matters dealt with' in the Convention (Article 33).

If all these exclusions are to be construed as covering employment by the State in connection with them, a very wide swathe of State employment is removed and reserved for special treatment.[108] The mere presence of a saving clause does not, however, bring into effect Model II. Model II envisages exclusion from the general law of State immunity of *employment* disputes relating to a particular class of transaction or person, and its treatment under a special regime or applicable law. To operate satisfactorily it is necessary that the wording of the exclusion relating to the special class of persons, e.g. staff of diplomatic and consular posts, should clearly cover employment disputes of such persons so as to remove them from the scope of the general law of State immunity, and that the special regime or law referred to provides rules by which to settle such employment disputes. Unfortunately, as will be noted, these two requirements of Model II are rarely achieved, despite legislation on State immunity, with or without an express employment exception, generally containing such exclusionary clauses.

It will be useful to look at each of the excluded matters in turn.

Other international agreements

This wide form of exclusion is found in the European Convention: 'nothing in this Convention shall affect existing or future international agreements which relate to matters dealt with in the present Convention' (Article 33). The commentary includes in its list of treaties likely to come within this article 'agreements dealing specifically (i.e. otherwise than in a general manner) with State immunity'. Similarly, the US Act in enacting the general rule of immunity makes it 'subject to "existing" international agreements to which the United States is a party at the time of enactment of this Act' (section 1604) The House Report states that 'all immunity provisions are made subject to "existing" and other international agreements to which the United States is a party. In the event that an international agreement expressly conflicts with this bill, the international agreement would control'[109] (see also section 1330). Applying the legislative purpose of the Act as here indicated in the House Report, the international agreement will only control where it expressly conflicts *with the immunity provisions* of the FSIA. The Supreme Court

[108] Cf. the comprehensive formula in Article IIIC of the ILA 1995 draft Montreal Convention: 'or 4. the employee was appointed under the public (administrative) law of the foreign State, such as, inter alia members of the mission, diplomatic, consular or military staff'.

[109] Above, n. 18.

has construed this section as excluding the operation of the FSIA *only where* the international agreement provides conflicting immunities.[110]

Diplomatic and consular staff

The European Convention on State Immunity contains a similar exclusion clause in respect of other treaties; it provides that 'nothing in this Convention shall affect privileges and immunities relating to the functions of diplomatic and consular posts and of persons connected with them' (Article 32). It gives as its reason in the commentary that these immunities are already covered by the Diplomatic and Consular Relations Conventions of 1961 (VCD) and 1963 (VCC), that they are based on different considerations and that in the event of conflict the provisions of the latter should prevail.

This approach is carried forward in all State immunity legislation by saving clauses of varying specificity giving effect to these Conventions. The House Report on the effect of FSIA section 1604 states that 'the bill is not intended to affect either diplomatic or consular immunity'.[111]

Does diplomatic immunity debar proceedings relating to employment disputes in local courts? This Model II approach has the demerit of over-comprehensiveness. Without express reference to employment in the exclusion clause, it is not self-evident that the immunities accorded to diplomatic missions and consular posts are in conflict with general State immunity legislation. Reliance on diplomatic immunity as a basis for immunity for employment with a foreign State, it is suggested, is mistaken for a number of reasons.

First, it is by no means generally accepted that the immunities

[110] A very broad construction of this phrase was initially given by a first instance US court so as to set aside the immunity granted a State under the FSIA in a situation where that State could be shown to be in breach of a treaty to which the United States was a party. A US District Court in *Von Dardel* v. *USSR* applied the Vienna Convention on Diplomatic Relations 1961 as such an existing international agreement, and construed that Convention by virtue of section 1604 not merely to remove a diplomatic agent from the scope of the FSIA but positively to confer jurisdiction on American courts over a foreign State which violated the 1961 Convention. The District Court held the USSR not immune for the tort of unlawful detention in Russia of Raoul Wallenberg, a Swedish diplomat who had aided the escape of Jewish victims from Nazi persecution. It found that '. . . the FSIA incorporates preexisting standards of international law, under which a government is not immune for certain acts in clear violation of the universally accepted law of nations': 623 F Supp. 246 (1985), at 252.

This construction is not supported by the House Report and has been overruled in *Amerada Hess Shipping Corp.* v. *Argentine Republic*, 102 L Ed. 2d 818. The House Report explains that the exclusion applies when international agreements 'expressly conflict' with immunity provisions of the FSIA; and was construed by the Supreme Court to refer to treaties providing conflicting immunities, not to 'conventions that only set forth substantive rules of conduct and state that compensation shall be paid for certain wrongs. They do not create private rights of action for foreign corporations to recover compensation from foreign states in US courts.' (The House Report states: 'Treaties of friendship, commerce and navigation often contain provisions relating to the immunity of foreign States. To the extent such agreements are silent on a question of immunity, the bill would control; the international agreement would only control where a conflict was manifest' (p. 6616).

[111] p. 6616.

conferred in the Vienna Conventions are intended to be used by the foreign State itself against its employees. In the *French Consular Employee* case the Austrian Supreme Court treated the immunity of the consul and his employees from local jurisdiction under the 1963 Convention as 'inapplicable because the proceedings are brought against the contractual partner of the plaintiff in the employment relationship, which is not the General Consulate of the defendant State or an official of that Consulate, but rather the Defendant as the sending State'.[112] The Swiss Federal Tribunal came to a similar conclusion in *S* v. *India* in respect of a clerical worker in the Indian embassy at Berne; the Swiss tribunal rejected the contention of the lower court that because the employee was entitled as a member of the administrative and technical staff to diplomatic immunity he was prevented by the Vienna Convention from bringing proceedings without the consent of the sending State, his employer.[113] The tribunal construed VCD Article 32(2) as contemplating the institution of proceedings by diplomatic staff against the employer State and that the conferment of immunity from jurisdiction in Article 31 and from giving evidence as a witness (Article 31(2)) was confined to proceedings brought against and not by diplomatic staff. This view was criticized by Monnier as contrary to the majority of authorities and to VCD Article 32(1), which requires waiver to be made by the sending State and to be express. This supports, in his view, a general curtailment of any right of submission to local jurisdiction, whether by way of institution of proceedings or defence, of diplomatic staff save with the consent of the employing State.[114] Monnier here transfers the ambit of waiver as a method of submission by which the State may change its own position as a party before the court to a restriction on the conduct of proceedings generally by a member of the mission. Politically this has much sense in that the appearance in a local court of a diplomatic officer may well be misunderstood as appearance on behalf of and with the authority of the State. It appears to be the line adopted in UK missions abroad as illustrated by the rules relating to local employment in the private sector of spouses of diplomatic staff. As such employment may be construed to represent a loss of immunity (either as a change of status as a dependent of a member of the mission or by submission to local jurisdiction by the terms of the employment), Foreign Service regulations require approval of the head of the mission to be obtained.[115] This somewhat cautious position is however qualified by the general injunction to heads of mission that 'immunity from jurisdiction does not mean

[112] 86 ILR 585. Cf. *MDDA* v. *Australian Embassy*, *Netherlands Yearbook of International Law*, 19 (1988), p. 438, where a Dutch court originally allowed a claim by a butler against Australia but then reversed, as the claimant was employed by the ambassador, on the ground that he could not be sued by reason of diplomatic immunity. Nor could the embassy as it had no legal persona.

[113] 82 ILR 14 at 18.

[114] *Annuaire suisse de droit international*, 41 (1985), p. 235.

[115] Foreign Service Regulations, vol. I, Diplomatic Status and Immunities, para. 20.1.

a general immunity from compliance with local laws',[116] and 'immunity is not maintained if the individual will be fairly treated and the work of the mission not prejudiced'.[117]

Legally, however, to give such a wide scope to VCD Article 32 is questionable. The purpose of the privileges and immunities conferred in the convention 'is not to benefit individuals but to ensure the efficient performance of the function of the diplomatic missions as representing States' (the preamble), and, as the Swiss Federal Tribunal said, 'the activities of the sending state on foreign territory in particular are never hindered by the submission of disputes arising from such contracts'.[118]

Secondly, there is an underlying ambiguity in the 1961 Vienna Convention as to whether the immunities conferred are those of the sending State, the diplomatic mission or the individual member of the diplomatic staff. Certainly the purpose of diplomatic immunity differs from State immunity in that, in addition to conferring immunity *ratione materiae* for the public acts of the sending State performed by the diplomatic agent in the exercise of his official functions, a more generous immunity *ratione personae* for the personal non-official acts of the diplomat is conferred to ensure that he will not be impeded in his function of representation of the sending State abroad (*ne impediatur legatio*).[119] That legal proceedings may be an impediment to performance of public acts is not, however, a ground of State immunity. The Swiss tribunal expressed the point well in likening contracts of employment to contracts of sale and lease, which State immunity treats as acts governed by the *jus gestionis* and hence subject to local jurisdiction:

> Whilst it is true that the sending state has a certain interest in seeing that legal disputes involving members of its missions with relatively senior functions are not subject to the jurisdiction of foreign courts, the situation is quite different in respect of junior employees. In the latter case the subjection of such employees to the jurisdiction of the local courts can always be accepted if the employee does not enjoy the nationality of the sending state and has been recruited on the spot . . . The sending State is in no way impeded in the performance of its tasks by such decisions.[120]

A US decision in *Tabion* v. *Mufti*[121] aptly illustrates the broader scope of diplomatic immunity. A Jordanian diplomat in Washington pleaded diplomatic immunity to proceedings brought by his domestic servant, a Philippine national, for violation of Fair Labour standards in failing to pay her a minimum wage, providing no reasonable work schedule and

[116] Ibid., para. 20.8.

[117] Ibid., para. 20.15.

[118] *S* v. *India*, 82 ILR 14 at 19.

[119] Salmon, 'Immunites et actes de la fonction', *Annuaire français de droit international*, 37 (1992), p. 314.

[120] 82 ILR 14 at 20.

[121] 63 LW 2537 (1995).

confiscating her passport. On behalf of the domestic servant it was contended that the claim came within the exception to immunity in Article 31(1)(*c*) of the 1961 Vienna Convention for 'professional or commercial activity exercised by the diplomatic agent in the receiving State outside his official functions'. The US District Court dismissed the claim and held that, unlike the commercial activities exception to FSIA 'where a foreign State is not immune from suit for debts relating to private acts, including an employment contract such as the one at issue here', Article 31(1)(*c*) did not 'deprive diplomats of immunity from commercial transactions that are merely incidental to day-to-day life'; the exception related solely to business transactions for profit. The same issue arose in *Bayani* v. *Russel* before the English Employment Appeals Tribunal in respect of an employee of a Canadian diplomat stationed in London. The Tribunal was referred to the definition of commercial activity in section 3 of the UK State Immunity Act 1978. The Tribunal held the exception in Article 31 of the Vienna Convention did not apply so as to confer jurisdiction on the court:

> Article 31 must relate to some form of trading activity entered into by the agent in question in which he does not enter in his diplomatic capacity but as a private trader.

The diplomat accordingly was entitled to immunity in respect of the employment claim but the tribunal held he had waived the immunity by a choice of English jurisdiction and law clause in the contract of employment.[122]

These cases demonstrate that unlike State immunity there can be no exception for private law or ordinary commercial transactions including the employment of personal servants by diplomats. Litigation in local courts concerning the diplomat employer's treatment of his employee is likely to impede him carrying out his diplomatic functions and hence is held immune. The restrictive version of State immunity, on the other hand, is precisely based on the assumption that litigation relating to commercial acts of the State is compatible with the performance of public functions. In principle, as Model III seeks to recognize, employment contracts should not be immune, but difficulty arises where the work is to be performed in the diplomatic mission involving functions and supervising staff which the VCD and VCC recognize as entitled to immunity from investigation by local courts.

[122] *Bayani* v. *Russel*, 15 October 1986, Industrial Tribunal, Case No. 1812/67. The submission clause in the employment contract read: 'The parties to this contract during the performance of the contract shall be subject to the law of England. In case of disputes arising from this contract the matter shall be submitted to an appropriate and competent body or government agency in England in accordance with the laws of the said country.' The tribunal held itself to be an appropriate and competent body set up by statute for the resolution of such disputes. The case did not proceed beyond a preliminary ruling, being withdrawn by the applicant, 9 December 1986, Case No. 1047/86.

Third, the reliance on diplomatic immunity in Model II as excluding employment disputes of all grades of employees within the diplomatic or consular mission is not supported by the conventions themselves which, even in the public function of representation of the State, introduce grades of immunities. Three categories of officials, compositely referred to as the head of the mission and members of the staff of the mission, are identified in Article 1 of the VCD: (i) the head of the mission and members of the staff having diplomatic rank; (ii) the administrative and technical staff of the mission; and (iii) the members of the service staff.

As is well known, the first category alone enjoys full immunity from the jurisdiction of the courts of the receiving State in respect of criminal matters and civil matters subject to three specified exceptions (VCD Article 31). The second category, the administrative and technical staff, enjoy the same immunity from the jurisdiction of the courts of the receiving State 'except that the immunity from civil and administrative jurisdiction of the receiving State . . . shall not extend to acts performed outside the course of their duties' (VCD Article 37(2)). The third category, members of the service staff of the mission, only enjoy immunity from the local jurisdiction 'in respect of acts performed in the course of their duties' (VCD Article 37(3)).

Prima facie, then, the VCD recognized that even within the public function of representation of the State there were grades of work. The VCD treats the grades as indicative of the degree to which the member of the diplomatic staff participates in the public function of the State, so as to require more immunity for the policy-making grade of the diplomat, functional immunity for the administrative and technical staff, and a lesser degree of immunity for service staff. It is true, as discussed below,[123] that it qualified the grant of such immunities where members of the staff of the mission were nationals of the receiving State, but this does not affect the general distinction based on the type of work undertaken. Here consent of the receiving State was necessary for appointment to a post as diplomat within that State and only functional immunity was conferred. Administrative and technical and service staff who were nationals of the receiving State under VCD Article 38(2) enjoy immunity only to the extent admitted by the receiving State. International law, then, permits the receiving State, or possibly its courts by construction of VCD, to confer no immunity as regards employment disputes for such grades. The second paragraph of VCD Article 38(2) might inhibit the receiving State from so doing, should the exercise of jurisdiction by the local courts over these persons interfere unduly with the performance of the functions of the mission.

Unlike the VCD, the use of Model II makes no distinction between employment of senior rank and subordinate officials. This ambiguity as

[123] Section II.(d)(iv).

to whether, despite Model II's exclusion clause, some staff, and particularly subordinate staff employed in a mission, may take advantage of the employment exception, has been clarified in the subsequent British and Australian legislation though in different senses. The UK Act, section 16(1), provides that the Act shall not affect any privilege or immunity conferred by the Diplomatic Privileges Act 1964 or the Consular Relations Act 1968, and expressly enacts that the employment exception shall not apply to 'proceedings concerning the employment of the members of the diplomatic mission . . . or consular post' within the meaning of the VCD and VCC (section 16(1)(*a*)). In *Sengupta* v. *Republic of India*[124] the court construed these words by reference to Article 1 of the 1961 Convention to 'exclude jurisdiction over claims relating to the employment not only of diplomatic staff but also of lower grade administrative, technical, and domestic staff irrespective of their nationality'.

The Australian Foreign States Immunities Act 1985 also excludes by reference to immunities conferred in its legislation implementing the 1961 and 1963 Conventions, but in the enactment of the express exception for employment limits it to 'employment of a member of the diplomatic staff of a mission as defined in the 1961 Convention, [or] of a consular officer as defined in the 1963 Convention, irrespective of nationality'; it thus draws a distinction between these officials and those in more subordinate positions, and 'administrative or technical staff . . . or a consular employee' who at the time of the contract of employment were permanent residents of Australia.

It will be seen below that the second rapporteur to the ILC, Ogiso, proposed, as a reference point to distinguish immune from non-immune grades of employees, 'administrative and technical staff of a diplomatic or consular mission who is associated with the exercise of governmental authority', but this formula was not adopted; the more general criterion of 'the employee who has been recruited to perform functions closely related to the exercise of governmental authority' was included in the final draft of Article 11 which was submitted to United Nations.

It is to be noted that UK practice relating to its missions abroad is more flexible than SIA section 16(1). Instructions to heads of mission accept such a differentiation in treatment, stating: 'it is unsustainable to claim absolute immunity over employment of all locally employed staff irrespective of the nature of their duties and how close (or far) those are from central or diplomatic functions'. Flexibility in British practice, however, consists in authorizing waiver in respect of lower grades but not in conceding that no immunity exists in respect of employment disputes relating to these grades.

[124] (1983), 64 ILR 352.

Visiting forces

Model II has the merit of identifying as immune a particular class of employees. It can be extended to other particularly sensitive areas of foreign State employment. Thus the European Convention also has an exclusion clause so as not to affect 'anything done or omitted to be done by, or in relation to, its armed forces when on the territory of another contracting State' (Article 31). The UK Act, section 16(2), gives effect to this provision by the exclusion from the operation of the Act of proceedings in relation to the armed forces of a State while present in the UK and 'has effect subject to the Visiting Forces Act 1952'.[125]

As already noted, the US Act in enacting the general rule of immunity makes it 'subject to existing international agreements to which the United States is a party at the time of enactment of this Act' (section 1604), and the House Report commenting on this section notes:

> In the event an international agreement expressly conflicts with this bill, the international agreement would control. Thus the bill would not alter the rights or duties of the United States under the Nato Status of Forces Agreement or similar agreements with other countries.[126]

To determine whether the exclusion covers employment disputes between all types of employees of the visiting State, some understanding of the NATO Agreement is necessary.

It is a complex negotiated agreement and its history of application in the courts of contracting States shows that its application to particular facts is not always straightforward.[127] Its main purpose is to eliminate or reduce cause for friction between visiting and receiving States, and its provisions seek, where possible, to achieve friendly out-of-court settlement of any disputes. Briefly, its main components consist of the conferment of privileges relating to arms, uniform, driving licences, customs and local taxes and the allocation of jurisdiction over certain disputes. As regards criminal matters, jurisdiction is exclusive for certain offences, shared for others. As regards civil jurisdiction concerning tortious acts (contractual claims being excluded), a distinction is made between acts done in the course of official duties and those not so performed, with a provision for arbitration to determine in which category a particular act falls. For claims relating to damage to property and death or personal injuries suffered in the course of official duties, there is a system of waiver of claims against the other State, compensa-

[125] Curiously, the presence of a similar provision in the Canadian State Immunity Act does not seem to have avoided the application of the general commercial transaction test to the question of whether trade union representation of the Canadian civilian work force at the US naval base in Newfoundland was a public activity.

[126] p. 6616.

[127] Lazareff, *Status of Visiting Forces under Current International Law* (1971); Woodliffe, *The Peacetime Use of Foreign Military Installations under Modern International Law* (1992), p. 135.

tion payable by the claimant State and access to a hardship fund. For tortious acts not performed in the course of official duties the courts of the receiving State have jurisdiction, but an *ex gratia* payment made by the sending State is to be treated as full satisfaction of the claim. A further distinction is made in respect of the second category between claims by a State or by a member of the armed forces and claims by third parties.

The NATO Agreement does not expressly mention claims or jurisdiction relating to employment disputes. Essentially it is an agreement to allocate jurisdiction and responsibility which arises in respect of disputes between the visiting and receiving States, not to resolve disputes between the visiting State and members of its own forces. Article II of the Agreement, however, requires the visiting force and its civilian component to respect the laws of the receiving State; French laws applicable to employers of domestic personnel on French territory are applicable to NATO personnel.[128]

English law. Certainly the view that the NATO Agreement does not cover employment disputes is supported by the English decision in *Littrell* v. *USA*. A member of the US air force sued the USA in the English courts for the medical negligence of another member of the US force. In the lower court it was held that the waiver of claims in Article 4 of the NATO Agreement for acts causing personal injuries debarred the complainant from suing. In the Court of Appeal, however, it was held that this article of the NATO Agreement had never been incorporated into English law by statute, and the matter accordingly fell to be determined by the common law relating to State immunity at the time of the entry into force of the NATO Agreement.[129] This was in 1952, and an absolute rule of immunity then applied. Accordingly the Court of Appeal held the claim against the USA for medical negligence to be immune.

It was a surprising result, particularly so in that to an event occurring in 1989 after the enactment of the UK SIA, the court applied the previous common law. That previous common law, on the authority of *Littrell* and *Sengupta*, has now been applied by the English and Scottish industrial tribunals in respect of employment claims by US nationals employed in a civilian capacity by US armed forces based in the United Kingdom; claims of a bowling equipment repairer in a bowling alley[130] and a woman bar-tender[130a] were held immune by reason that, as US nationals, both were employed under US military regulations, and both

[128] Lazareff, op. cit. above (n. 127), p. 102.

[129] [1992] 3 All ER 218 (12 November 1993, CA).

[130] *United States of America* v. *Hicks*, Employment Appeal Tribunal (Tuckey J, S.M. Springer, R.N. Straker), 28 July 1995, EAT/1021/94.

[130a] *Larson* v. *United States of America*, Industrial Tribunal (Scotland), 30 January 1994, S/3362/95.

were employed in 'recreational facilities to sustain the effectiveness of the [US] central military activity or capability'. In the latter case the tribunal was told that immunity in US practice depended on the nationality of the employee; that it was not the policy of the United States to assert immunity in disputes relating to employment contracts with non-US nationals,[131] particularly bearing in mind Article IX(4) of the NATO Agreement. which provides that conditions of employment and work of nationals of the receiving State are to be in accordance with the law of that State; but that as regards US nationals a system had been established of 'employment remedies which was uniform for all US civilian employees of the US military and its agencies worldwide. . . . Any interference or review of this system would necessarily involve a challenge to or an inquiry into a sovereign act.'[131a] The outcome of these cases, and of *Littrell*, is that immunity in English law of employment claims relating to visiting forces depends first on nationality of the employee and second on a general commerciality test as in Model I. The special exclusion clause in SIA section 16(2) seems a roundabout way to achieve this result.

To sum up, Model II has the demerit of over-comprehensiveness and ambiguity. Some jurisdictions, whilst accepting that employees in diplomatic and consular posts require immunity themselves to enable them to discharge their duties, have not accepted that it bars them from bringing proceedings against the foreign State in respect of their employment.[132] The Vienna Conventions relating to diplomats and consuls recognize some grading of immunity according to the nature of the work of the staff, and such immunity is not wholly exclusive of local jurisdiction; respect for the laws and regulations of the receiving State is expressed as a duty on all persons enjoying immunities (Article 41(1)). Indeed, in relation to social security, provision under the home State or compliance with local law is required.[133]

[131] In *Tai* v. *USA* (1986), Case 3151/86, a cashier, married to a sergeant in the US air force, stationed in England, brought proceedings in an English industrial tribunal for wrongful dismissal. The tribunal assumed jurisdiction on the basis that the applicant was a British national, which brought her within the employment exception to State immunity in section 4 of the SIA. In its decision it referred to evidence given by the deputy staff judge advocate on behalf of the United States showing that it was the US practice to employ personnel under two sets of employment conditions. 'American personnel', which included wives and adult children of serving US military personnel, were employed under a set of regulations similar to those obtaining for employees in mainland America and paid in dollars. 'British personnel', who fell within the UK employment protection legislation, were employed under a different set of conditions, were paid in sterling and had the right, in appropriate circumstances, to complain to an industrial tribunal of unfair dismissal, whereas American personnel did not have that right (p. 2). Morgenstern dryly comments on this difference: 'The case law of European countries . . . shows that people happy to enjoy during service the terms of employment governed by US law seek the protection of a European system of law when it comes to a problem of dismissal': *International Conflicts of Labour Law* (ILO, 1984), p. 2.

[131a] *Larson*, loc. cit. above (n. 130a), at p. 3.

[132] *S* v. *India*, 82 ILR 14.

[133] VCD Art. 32; VCC Art. 48. See Section II.(d)(iv), below.

(d) *Model III: An Exception for Employment Additional to the General Exception*

This model provides an exception to immunity for employment contracts additional to the general exception for commercial transactions. The European Convention and the UK Act and other legislation modelled on the UK Act contain an express exception to State immunity for employment contracts. The ILC's draft convention on jurisdictional immunities also contains such an express exception, though it has been much debated and several States (China, East Germany prior to unification, Algeria and other African States) remain opposed to it.

A legislative exception for contracts of employment first appears in Article 5 of the European Convention on State Immunity 1972.

Although the preamble to the treaty states that 'there is in international law a tendency to restrict the cases in which a State may claim immunity before foreign courts', it is clear from the earlier survey of the case law and from the ILC's work that Article 5 was not reflecting any such previous restrictive tendency as regards claims by employees of foreign States. Whilst the Italian court might be right in describing Article 5 as 'the recognition of the most authoritative and recent trends in learned opinion and case laws',[134] it was not a codification of existing law but introduced a new and 'special regime', one which was included in the Convention at the express wish of the Contracting States.[135]

The Convention represented a considerable advance in the treatment of exceptions to immunity from the rather general proposition to be found in juristic writing and case law, and illustrated, by the Model I approach, that a restrictive theory of State immunity required an exception for private law or commercial transactions. It achieved this advance by being a regional arrangement, where on the whole, unlike in the ILC's work, there was majority support for a restrictive rule of immunity. The Convention was a regional convention open for signature by any member State of the Council of Europe, and to non-member States by invitation of the unanimous vote of the Committee of Ministers of the Council of Europe, and within that membership were included countries whose courts supported an absolute doctrine of immunity, others slowly moving to a restrictive approach and others whose courts already applied a very restrictive approach.[136]

Two consequences resulted from these negotiating positions. First, the one general exception for commercial transactions was broken up into specific categories of activity of a generally accepted commercial nature and spread over eight articles. Second, all the exceptions, other than those involving waiver (where the State was deemed to consent to local

[134] *Bari Institute* v. *Jasbez* (Court of Cassation, 1977), 77 ILR 602.

[135] *S* v. *India*, loc. cit. above (n. 132), at p. 21.

[136] Sinclair, *International and Comparative Law Quarterly*, 22 (1973), p. 254; Wiedekehr, *Annuaire français de droit international*, 20 (1974), p. 925.

jurisdiction) were given jurisdictional links with the territory of the forum State. By limiting the exceptions to situations where the forum court had a firm basis for exercising jurisdiction, there would be good grounds, it was hoped, to justify the court's assumption of jurisdiction and the making of judgments against a State.

These general considerations underlying the drafting of the ECSI had an effect on the formulation of the exception relating to contracts of employment. Article 5 reads:

1. A Contracting State cannot claim immunity from the jurisdiction of another Contracting State if the proceedings relate to a contract of employment between the State and an individual where the work has to be performed on the territory of the State of the forum.
2. Paragraph 1 shall not apply where:
 (*a*) the individual is a national of the employing State at the time when the proceedings are brought;
 (*b*) at the time when the contract was entered into the individual was neither a national of the State of the forum nor habitually resident in that State; or
 (*c*) the parties to the contract have otherwise agreed in writing, unless, in accordance with the law of the State of the forum, the courts of that State have exclusive jurisdiction by reason of the subject-matter.
3. Where the work is done for an office, agency or other establishment referred to in Article 7, paragraphs 2(*a*) and (*b*) of the present Article apply only if, at the time the contract was entered into, the individual had his habitual residence in the Contracting State which employs him.

Every subsequent enactment of an employment exception has been based on and follows fairly closely this wording.[136a] It is, therefore, of first importance to understand the thinking behind Article 5.

This exception is remarkable for the following characteristics:
(i) it relates to employment contracts made by the State as employer;
(ii) it covers employment contracts whether relating to governmental or commercial activity;
(iii) it introduces jurisdictional links additional to those required in the other exceptions relating to commercial activity;
(iv) it uses some of these additional jurisdictional links as a means to distinguish the type of employment which is to remain immune; and
(v) the removal of immunity is subject to the parties agreeing otherwise in writing, but in that event any mandatory provisions of the forum law will prevail.

Each of these characteristics will be further examined.

(i) *Employment contracts with the foreign State as employer*

The employment envisaged in the article is defined in contractual terms and in relation to narrowly defined parties. The foreign State is

[136a] See SIA, s. 4 (at n. 16, above).

cast always in the role of employer and the employee is an individual.[137] The wording of Article 5 would seem to remove immunity solely for proceedings relating to a contract of *service* between a foreign State and an individual employee; contracts with independent contractors for *services*, or arrangements in which a corporation or even the foreign State itself provides services, would fall outside Article 5's scope and have to be considered by reference to the general exception for contracts in Article 4, or the more specialist exceptions in Article 6 (participation in a company), Article 7 (commercial activity carried on in an establishment in the forum State), Article 8 (patents, trade marks and copyright), etc. It is not clear whether Article 5 would render non-immune proceedings brought by a trade union in respect of collective employment arrangements; certainly in the UK the SIA would appear to clarify and exclude this type of proceedings by defining the non-immune proceedings as 'proceedings *between* the parties to such a contract' (section 4(6), emphasis added).

The emphasis on the employment relationship between employer and employee equally excludes claims under this article based on vicarious liability of the State for acts of its employees. If such acts cause personal injuries or tangible loss in the forum State, they would be non-immune under the less restricted tort exception in Article 11, less restricted in that the tortious acts may be of a governmental nature; otherwise it would be necessary to characterize such acts as contractual under Article 4 or carried out in an establishment of the foreign State in the forum territory under Article 7.

(ii) *Employment contracts may relate to governmental or commercial activity*

The employment exception in Article 5 contains no overt criterion based on the nature of the employment or the functions of either the State employer or the employee. The legislative history shows that, at an early stage, a suggestion, by reference to a recent decision of an Italian court,[138] was made that immunity should be retained for employment if the functions were exercised with a view to performing international tasks of the foreign authority; this suggestion was not pursued. Instead, the first draft of Article 5 included a specific exclusion from non-immune employment of foreign nationals who were members of the staff other than service staff of an embassy or consulate,[138a] and there was a subsequent attempt to limit the proviso so as to permit administrative and technical staff as well as service staff to bring employment disputes

[137] The Australian Foreign States Immunities Act expressly states in enacting the employment exception that it applies to 'the State as employer'.

[138] *Italian Naval Mission* v. *Bernardini* (Italian Court of Appeal, 28 November 1959), *Rivista di diritto internazionale*, 1960, p. 526; *Journal de droit international*, 1961, p. 838.

[138a] Text considered at the 6th Meeting of the Committee of Legal Experts in 1967. Employees who were nationals of the forum State were not included in this proviso.

to the local courts of the forum State. In the end the majority voted that the whole subject of diplomatic immunities and privileges was better dealt with by an exclusion clause, and the Convention, as has been noted in the discussion of Model II, contains saving clauses relating to diplomatic and consular staff, visiting forces and State employees engaged in other excluded matters. Whilst the majority may have thought that the retention of immunity for these categories would confine Article 5 to such employees as fell outside those categories, several legal experts at the time expressed doubts that Article 5 sufficiently safeguarded the proper functioning of embassies from interference of local courts, and one delegate commented that the Convention text perpetuated the tendency to confuse State with diplomatic immunity. These doubts were justified for, as has been shown, the saving clauses in relation to the staff of diplomatic and consular missions do not expressly exclude employment disputes, nor does the special law relating to those categories always deal with them. Accordingly, it is possible, and some courts of Contracting States have so concluded, to apply Article 5 to persons employed in diplomatic missions[139] and consular posts[139a] and by visiting forces.[140]

Article 5 omits any express criterion by reference to the type of duties of the employee. It was this omission that the ILC sought to remedy by inserting an express proviso excluding the non-immunity conferred by paragraph 1 in respect of 'the employee recruited to perform functions closely relating to the exercise of governmental authority'. Possibly there is implicit reference to such a criterion for employees in a commercial State office or agency. ECSI Article 5(3) extends to employment contracts of such agencies the removal of immunity which ECSI Article 7 provides for proceedings in respect of commercial activity carried on by a State in the territory of the forum State through an office, agency, or other establishment. Arguably the duties of an employee in such a commercial establishment are similar to those in private employment and hence justify the removal of immunity.[141] Even in such establishments which engage 'in the same manner as a private person, in an industrial, commercial, or financial activity', a differentiation is made between proceedings involving third parties, i.e. traders, which are non-immune, and proceedings relating to contracts of employment with employees in such establishments. Article 5 preserves immunity here only in respect of habitual residents of the employer State. Nationality is not a sufficient

[139] *Diana Abbot* v. *Republic of South Africa*, 86 ILR 512 (Spanish Supreme Court); *Canada* v. *Employment Appeals Tribunal and Burke*, [1992] ILRM 325 (Irish Supreme Court).

[139a] *French Consular Employee Claim*, 86 ILR 583 (Austrian Supreme Court).

[140] *Novaco* v. *US Navy* (1957), 24 ILR 219 (Athens Court, No. 55/1991) (Greek lawyer employed by US military base, held not immune).

[141] Lewis suggests that a State tourist office would be a 'commercial' State agency for the purposes of SIA s. 4(3), a parallel provision, but possibly not, where it acted merely as an information service taking no bookings and charging no fees: *State and Diplomatic Immunity* (3rd edn., 1990), p. 50.

bar; immunity is preserved only if the individual employee at the time the contract was entered into had his habitual residence in the contracting State which employs him.

(iii) *Additional jurisdictional links*

Place of performance of work. The general exception to immunity for commercial acts appears in the Convention at Article 4 and is confined to 'an obligation of the State, which, by virtue of a contract, falls to be discharged in the territory of the State of the forum'. Performance within the forum State is also the jurisdictional link used in the employment exception in Article 5, but it is more narrowly defined, reflecting the one-sided nature of the contract of employment which that article purports to cover. The nexus required is performance of work in the forum State territory; mere payment of wages in that territory is insufficient; and it is performance of the employee's obligation, not that of the employer, which is relevant.

Article 5 is an over-ambitious provision in that it purports to embrace in one provision different types of employment relationship – the long-term appointment of a career diplomat as well as local engagement for domestic duties of migrant labour – and workers with different bargaining power; home-appointed staff are well-served by trade unions and workers' associations, whereas local courts may be the only effective remedy available to low-paid migrant workers. The article seeks to achieve this comprehensive coverage by adopting in its first paragraph for all employment with a foreign State the jurisdictional connection of 'place of performance'.

It is a peculiarity of ECSI that each of its listed exceptions to immunity is given a jurisdictional link to the territory of the forum State. Whilst this ties in with the general system for exercise of jurisdiction and enforcement of judgments to be found in the Brussels Convention of 1968, it is contrary to the underlying notion of State immunity, which is that, either by reason of the nature of the participant, a sovereign State, or the act, an exercise of governmental power, the transaction is not capable of determination by a municipal court. In the analogous case of an international organization, jurisdictional links such as the place at which the work is performed or the location of the employment undertaking do not render its employment contracts subject to the jurisdiction of the courts of the country where it has its headquarters; that jurisdiction is excluded by the international personality and function of the organization. Similarly, the State, as a subject of international law, performing acts with effect in international law, should remove any dispute from local court jurisdiction save where the employment relationship resembles one which the municipal law regulates. This incompetence of the local court has already been discussed in relation to Model IB.

However, as Model I has shown, the identification of an independent criterion to distinguish State employment from private employment has proved particularly elusive. ECSI Article 5, in Model III, adopts instead a private international law approach to the problem. Such an approach may be challenged at the outset in its applicability to public service. Nonetheless, Article 5 appears to adopt this approach using the jurisdictional connection of the place of performance of the work to separate off the type of State employment to be made subject to forum State jurisdiction, qualified by the link of common or third State nationality or habitual residence in the provisos to clawback categories of that employment which are to remain immune.

In preferring the 'place of performance' over other connecting factors of place of conclusion, common nationality, domicile or residence, or the employer's principal place of business, ECSI Article 5 follows the usual pattern of labour legislation. The place of performance is adopted for 'typical' employment relations as 'the place where the employee is integrated into the working community', and 'recourse to its law then permits both the equal treatment of employees working together and the operation of a coherent system of rules', including mandatory provisions.[142] The jurisdictional connection of place of performance is employed in the Brussels Convention on Jurisdiction and Judgments, 1968, to which the UK is a party. The general jurisdictional rule of this convention, that proceedings may be brought in the country where the defendant, that is the employer, is domiciled (Article 2), is supplemented by rules of special jurisdiction relating to employment; in so far as the proceedings are based on the contract of employment, jurisdiction is given to the courts of the country of the place of performance of the contract (Article 5(1)). The case law of the ECJ identifies the place of performance of the contract as the place where the employee habitually carries out his work, or, if there is no such place, the place of business through which he is engaged.[143]

Place of conclusion of contract. The conclusion of a contract of employment is not given as an alternative jurisdictional link in ECSI Article 5.[144] The UK SIA, however, introduces this additional basis of jurisdiction – 'where the contract was made in the United Kingdom' – and thereby opens the door to proceedings by employees for wrongful

[142] Morgenstern, op. cit. above (n. 131), p. 24.

[143] *De Bloos* v. *Boyer*, Case 14/76, [1976] ECR 1497, [1977] CMLR 60.

[144] The Commentary to Article 5 seems to infer that the place of performance will also usually be the place of conclusion for those contracts of employment rendered non-immune by paragraph 1. Contracts of persons not nationals or habitual residents of that forum State *at the time when the contract was entered into* are excluded by proviso (*b*) from that paragraph and the Commentary thereby seems to assume that the recruitment of such persons, i.e. of nationals or residents of the employing or third State, will take place *outside* the forum State. This seems a rather over-broad assumption.

dismissal for work contracted in the United Kingdom but performed abroad.

Here, as with Model I, the application of the employment exception to State immunity to work performed abroad introduces a wholly different set of interests requiring protection. The connection with the foreign State is closer; the home base or centre of operations of the employer State coincides with the place of work of the employee, and even for private employment the law of the foreign State is likely to be the applicable law. A strong case can, therefore, be made that the primary, if not the exclusive, jurisdiction over the employment relationship should be with the foreign State's courts. Provisos (*a*) and (*b*) of the second subsection, however, by excluding nationals and residents of the employing or a third State, effectively allow only UK nationals to bring suit in an English court for a claim arising out of employment in another country and to benefit from section 4's removal of immunity; this is surely discriminatory, particularly in respect of nationals of other EC member States.[145]

(iv) *The use of additional jurisdictional links to the sending State to exclude forum State jurisdiction*

The test of place of performance used in paragraph 1, however, is generally unsuitable for non-typical employment, that is temporary or long-term detachment for work abroad, or services in many countries where links with the home base seem more relevant. A considerable element of a State's work force abroad may be made up of persons engaged on such temporary or long-term detachment.

Somewhat surprisingly, the ECSI provides separate treatment for these non-typical or home-based workers by employing a principle of nationality (extended to include habitual residence[146]) to distinguish immune from non-immune employment. Article 5(2) operates to exclude employees who are nationals of the employer State or a third State from suing in respect of their employment in the courts of the State where they work. To sue in the local court the employee must hold at the date of making of the contract nationality or permanent residence of the forum State (thus excluding nationals of a third State), and also at the date of the commencement of proceedings not be a national of the employer State. Article 5 goes further in applying a continuity of nationality rule so

[145] In this connection see the current debate over the EC Directive relating to workers posted abroad.

[146] The UK, Singapore and Pakistan Acts refer to habitual residence, the South African Act to ordinary residence; the Australian Act uses one term, 'permanent residence', which it defines to include '(*a*) an Australian citizen or (*b*) a person resident in Australia whose continued presence is not subject to a limitation as to time imposed by or under a law of Australia' (s. 12(7)). For the meaning of 'habitual residence' in SIA s. 4 see Lewis, *State and Diplomatic Immunity* (3rd edn., 1990), p. 50: 'Whether the employee could show that he was not habitually resident in the State would probably depend on how long he had spent there in recent years, how long his period of sojourn in the UK was, and what homes he maintained in the two countries.'

as to bar a national of the forum State from bringing a claim if the nationality was not held at either the conclusion of the employment contract or the bringing of proceedings. Even in respect of employment in a State establishment operated for commercial purposes (Article 5(3)), the harshness of the nationality rule is only modified to permit proceedings to be brought by an employee who at the time the contract was entered into was not a permanent resident of the employer State.

The ECSI appears to employ the nationality/residence test to provide an indication of the closeness of the association of the employee with the governmental authority of the foreign State.[146a]

As the Commentary to Article 5 says:

> In certain circumstances it may be justifiable to accord immunity to a defendant State under a contract of employment particularly when the employee is a national of the employing State (see paragraph 2, sub-paragraph (*a*)). The same is true when the employee is a national neither of the State for whom he works, nor of the State where he works, and where the contract of employment was not concluded in the territory of the latter State – namely where the employee is a foreign worker who has not been locally recruited (see paragraph 2, sub-paragraph (*b*)). In both cases the links between the employee and the employing State (in whose courts the employee may always bring proceedings) are generally closer than those between the employee and the State of the forum.[147]

Private international law rules. The use of the nationality/residence test on its own as a connecting factor is not in conformity with usual private international law rules relating to jurisdiction and applicable law concerning disputes arising out of employment involving temporary or long-term detachment abroad. States diverge considerably in the criteria used; it is true that, while not given much weight in the common law, this factor is considered relevant in France, whereas Austria, Germany, Switzerland, Japan and other countries employ the habitual residence of the defendant. In employment cases this may well equate to the employer's principal place of business. Whereas common law countries treat jurisdiction as a procedural matter based on service of process, both they and civil law countries in matters of employment have regard to territorial connections of the work.[148] The broad result is that the connecting factor generally adopted for private employment involving detachment abroad, particularly where the employee does not perform his work in one country alone, is, in the absence of agreement of the

[146a] The legislative history of the ECSI shows that the exclusion of nationals of the employing State from recourse to the courts of the forum State in relation to their employment disputes was accepted unanimously and without discussion.

[147] Explanatory Report to the European Convention on State Immunity and Additional Protocol, Misc. No. 31 (1972), Cmnd. 5081.

[148] Morgenstern, op. cit. above (n. 131), pp. 47–51.

parties to the contrary, that of the location of the employing undertaking, the undertaking's principal place of business.[149]

Private international lawyers are divided as to whether autonomy of the parties or territorial connection should be the determinative principle in respect of the applicable law of employment with a foreign element, but the recent trend, by reason of the perceived weaker bargaining position of the employee, appears to favour a compromise based on the principle of the law most favourable to the employee.[150] The 'balance' which the two paragraphs in ECSI Article 5 attempt to achieve between the 'ordinary' work force, using place of performance, and home-based staff, using nationality/habitual residence as an indicator, is contrary to this current trend to the use of jurisdictional factors in private international law to identify the country which best affords the worker protection. This absence of 'neutrality' in the operation of private international law is well illustrated by the Rome Convention on Contractual Obligations 1980, enacted into English law by the Contracts (Applicable Law) Act 1990, which determines applicable law in contracts. For employment contracts in the private sector, in the absence of choice (given effect by Article 3), the governing law of a contract of employment may be one of three possibilities, the law of the country of habitual performance, the law of the employer's place of business or the law of the closest connection. These possibilities also apply, despite the choice of the parties, so as not to deprive the employee of the mandatory laws afforded to him by any of these governing laws (Article 6(2)). The conclusion, therefore, in the present context, applying conflict of laws principles, must be that section 5 makes a selective use of jurisdictional connections contrary to conflict of laws rules relating to private employment, and does so in a way which prevents an application of the principle of the law most favourable to the employee.

Criteria derived from the Vienna Conventions on Diplomatic and Consular Relations. Criteria of nationality and permanent residence[151] appear

[149] Ibid., p. 28; Dicey and Morris, *The Conflict of Laws* (11th edn., 1987), pp. 1297–303.

[150] Gammillscheg, 'Conflicts of Laws in Employment Contracts and Industrial Relations', in Blanchpain and Engels, op. cit. above (n. 7), p. 183 at pp. 186–93.

[151] The inclusion of permanent residence alongside the jurisdictional link of nationality is probably explained by the perception of that status as a stage in the entitlement to nationality. A *note verbale* dated 6 April 1961 of the United States relating to the drafting of the Vienna Convention on Consular Relations stated: 'The draft articles should not distinguish the status of permanent residents from that of nationals of the receiving State. Persons in the receiving State as immigrants or stateless persons recruited locally should enjoy no more favourable status than nationals of the receiving state in which they reside': *ILC Yearbook*, 1961, vol. 2, p. 164. The inclusion of permanent residence as a criterion has caused considerable problems of construction; unlike nationality, which all States accept as a matter to be determined by the law of the country whose nationality is claimed, there is no universal definition of permanent residence nor any universal acceptance of the receiving State's right to determine it unilaterally. The ECSI, when adopting such a concept, used the term 'habitual residence' and thereby incorporated the definition, varied for each member State, for this term which is to be found in the Brussels Convention on Jurisdiction and Judgments 1968.

in the Vienna Conventions on Diplomatic and Consular Relations to reflect the general international law principle that a diplomat or consular officer should owe allegiance to only one State. After extensive investigation into State practice and discussion in the International Law Commission, which prepared drafts for the codifying conferences,[152] the Vienna Conventions reconciled this principle with the functional need for immunity by allowing members of the mission or consular post to have nationality or permanent residence of the receiving State, but then conferred more restricted immunities. In discussing Model II, reference has already been made to the three grades of work performed by members of the diplomatic mission recognized in the VCD. For the first category of diplomatic agent or consular officer, immunity from jurisdiction and inviolability were restricted to the performance of official acts (VCD Article 38(1); VCC Article 71(1)). For the other staff of administrative or service rank in the diplomatic mission or for other members of the consular post, immunity was accorded only to the extent admitted by the receiving State (VCD Article 38(2); VCC Article 71(2)). Thus, a considerable reduction in immunity was brought about where a sending State chose to appoint as diplomat or consul a national or permanent resident of the receiving State. The immunity of the diplomat or consular officer was reduced to the level of service staff, and for other members of the mission was determinable at the will of the receiving State.

By these provisions the VCD introduced degrees based on function and on intensity of relationship with the sending State, with corresponding degrees of immunity or subjection to local jurisdiction. The functional and nationality classifications used in the Vienna Conventions support an increase in the exercise of local jurisdiction over an employee of the sending State based on *both* the nature of his work and the employee's possession of the receiving State's nationality or permanent residence. Thus, both in respect of the comprehensiveness of the immunities accorded to members of the sending State, and to those members who are nationals or permanent residents of the receiving State, the degree of participation in the public service is given weight; the diplomatic agent is identified most closely with policy-making and as such enjoys the highest degree of immunity from civil jurisdiction, and even when a national or permanent resident of the State in which he is posted, his diplomatic function confers on him an immunity (though much reduced).

The conclusion must be that, unlike the ECSI, the Vienna Convention does not rely on a principle of nationality/residence of the sending State

[152] 2nd Report of J. Zourek, Special Rapporteur, *ILC Yearbook*, 1960, vol. 2, pp. 28, 154.

alone to retain immunity, and certainly contains no provision to apply such a principle to third State nationals and residents.

Qualification for public service. If the Vienna Conventions fail to provide a basis for the use of nationality as a criterion to distinguish immune from non-immune employment, it may be that its use as a qualification for entry to public service justifies its adoption in ECSI Article 5(2). A comparative survey of the twelve member States of the European Union shows that they all impose a nationality/citizenship requirement for entry to public office; entry to the British civil service is slightly less restricted being, for the higher grades, by merit on the basis of competition, open to British subjects (including Commonwealth citizens) and citizens of the Republic of Ireland, who fulfil certain conditions regarding birth, parentage and residence.[153] The emphasis on nationality stresses the special relationship of allegiance to the State and that the work is for the community to which the civil servant himself belongs; but extended, as it is in ECSI Article 5, to habitual residents in the employing State and third State nationals and residents, it undermines uniformity of treatment of persons working in the same establishment; and, as regards third State nationals and residents, substitutes no other effective jurisdiction for that of the forum State.

Further, the use of nationality and habitual residence alone to distinguish immune from non-immune employment as a basis for selection of public officials is under attack as discrimination in EC law, as will be shown below.

The principle of nationality is used in treaty contexts to indicate what persons come within the purview of the treaty and in particular, as in investment and protection treaties, to stipulate for certain privileges and advantages on behalf of a State's nationals. It is rare to use nationality, as ECSI Article 5 appears to do, as a means to deprive nationals of benefits otherwise provided in the treaty. ECSI Article 5(2)(*b*) purports to go further by depriving third State nationals of access to local courts.

The manner of the use of a continuity of nationality rule is similar to that to be found in State responsibility, where a State may only espouse a claim against another State in respect of an individual who held its nationality both at the time of the cause of action (the conclusion of the contract) and the bringing of proceedings. Under ECSI Article 5 there is no question of a State making a claim against another: rather the nationality rules are used to delimit jurisdiction, to restrict the employee holding the employer State's nationality to seeking redress solely from the employer State.

[153] Civil Service Commission General Regulations 1969, as amended. See generally J.P. Gardner, *Hallmarks of Citizenship: A Green Paper* (1994), p. 32.

In conclusion, as already noted, conflict of laws rules relating to place of performance or place of employer's business lack neutrality in their application. They are adopted with the objective of providing protection for the employee as the weaker bargaining party to the contract. This raises fundamental questions: first, the suitability of jurisdictional connexions designed to protect the employee for use as indicators of immunity. It is questionable whether they can be adapted to serve another purpose, i.e. the segregation of governmental service from private employment. But, more fundamentally, the question arises whether, in the light of the wide recognition of the need to protect the employee, it is appropriate or possible for States by international law to remove by a plea of immunity a category of employee from such protection solely by reason of the fact of his working for a foreign State.

(v) *The parties' agreement and mandatory provisions of the labour law of the forum State*

Agreement of the parties would seem to be an obvious criterion to distinguish immune from non-immune employment. Such agreement could be directed both to choice of jurisdiction and of law and, if not express, could be implicit by making the terms of the employment subject to settlement by the law of the employer State, i.e. under public service regulations which provide for dispute settlement in the employer State. Consent of the parties to exclude forum State jurisdiction in this way would then constitute a converse form of State waiver, namely a positive exercise of choice to retain immunity as opposed to a choice to waive it. The legislative history shows that the first draft of the Convention made provision for such exclusion by consent of the parties.

Employment law, however, is generally not favourable to choice of jurisdiction or law. By reason of the weaker bargaining power of the employee, the need for uniformity, and the community interest in labour protection, it tends to give effect to the choice of the parties only in so far as it is more favourable to the employee than the law otherwise applicable. Unlike Article 5 as a whole, where the legislative history shows that, in adopting the jurisdictional links of place of performance of the work and nationality of the employee, little account was taken of municipal labour laws, proviso (*c*) in paragraph 2 of ECSI Article 5 was amended at a late stage to take account of the weaker bargaining position of the employee. Provisos (*a*) and (*b*) excluding nationals and residents of the employing or third State operate so as to make proviso (*c*) applicable only to the nationals and habitual residents of the forum State whose contracts of employment are prima facie rendered non-immune by the operation of paragraph 1.[154] Proviso (*c*) permits such persons to agree terms of employment including its immunity, but only so as not to conflict with mandatory forum law. Instead of using consent of the parties as an independent ground of immunity – which would be the converse form of waiver – proviso (*c*) demotes such consent to a restricted choice of law clause, overridden or displaced by mandatory law of the forum State where some positive or negative policy of its labour law requires. For example, the UK Employment Protection (Consolidation) Act 1978 overrides express choice of forum clauses where the employee ordinarily works within Great Britain, and assumes competence over the labour relationship.[155] The SIA section 4(4) makes this plain, identifying as a UK mandatory rule 'where the law of the United Kingdom requires the proceedings to be brought before a court of the UK'.[156]

The effect is to emasculate a State's right of waiver; the freedom of the State by the terms of employment to retain its immunity is overridden by the mandatory law of the forum State. It should, however, be noted that such overriding effect only occurs where the forum State law confers *exclusive* jurisdiction on its courts. As stated in the Explanatory Report, paragraph 30, jurisdiction is not exclusive if resort may be had to arbitration.[157] Whether the provision is mandatory is determined by the national law of which it is part, and frequently the employment protection legislation applies if the relevant employment takes place in the enacting country, whatever law may be applicable to the employment contract.[158]

Proviso (*c*), though restricting the application of mandatory forum State law to provisions relating to exclusive jurisdiction, has the effect of regulating the applicable law of the employment with the foreign State.

[154] This reading of ECSI Article 5 assumes each of the provisos is phrased in the alternative; the omission of 'or' between provisos (*a*) and (*b*) and its insertion between (*b*) and (*c*) gives ground for an alternate reading by which provisos (*a*) and (*b*) relating to status are cumulative, a reading in some degree supported by the different points in time at which the required status is to be determined. The UK SIA s. 4(2) makes it plain that the provisos should be read as alternatives by inserting an 'or' between provisos (*a*) and (*b*) as well as between (*b*) and (*c*). The Australian Act s. 12 omits any requirement as to status at the time of the proceedings.

[155] It should, however, be noted that there is a qualification period of two years' continuous work for the same employer before the employee comes within this statutory protection.

[156] Lewis, op. cit. above (n. 141), p. 51. An English industrial tribunal has held, in respect of an employment claim brought under the Diplomatic Privileges Act 1964 (not the SIA) that prior written agreement containing a general waiver of immunity from the jurisdiction of the English court is sufficient provided it is authorized by the foreign State: *Bayani* v. *Russel*, 5 October 1986, Case No. 1812/67. Another English tribunal has construed the phrase 'prior written agreement' in SIA s. 2(1) by reference to the more explicit wording in ECSI Article 3 – 'international agreement, express term contained in a contract of writing', and as requiring 'a written agreement in the nature of a contract'. It accordingly rejected as constituting no submission a solicitor's letter setting out the position under English law circulated by the military attaché to employees in the Saudi mission in London: *Saudi Arabia* v. *Ahmed*, EAT, 8 October 1993 (Knox J), affirmed [1996] ICR 25 (CA).

[157] Sinclair, *Recueil des cours*, 167 (1980–II), p. 280.

[158] Morse, 'Consumer Contracts, Employment Contracts and the Rome Convention', *International and Comparative Law Quarterly*, 41 (1992), p. 1 at p. 15.

Just as paragraph 1 departs from immunity to apply private international law criteria, so this proviso moves from a jurisdictional issue into identification of the law to determine the relationship. While this discussion shows the complexity of the laws which govern a private law contract of employment, the general effect is to enable the employee, as the party in the weaker bargaining position, to bring proceedings in and to apply the laws of the country which best affords him protection. This will, in general, enable him to resort to the courts and law of the country in which he works, even if the contract specifies another governing law or his employer's business is centred in another country. Further, he enjoys this entitlement regardless of his status as a national or permanent resident.

(e) *The International Law Commission's Draft Article on Contracts of Employment*

No discussion of the practice relating to the employment exception is complete without some reference to the work of the International Law Commission (ILC). The ILC began its consideration of the topic, 'jurisdictional immunities of States and their property', in 1979 when it had the First Report of the Special Rapporteur, Mr Sompong Sucharitkul, before it. The exception relating to contracts of employment was not addressed until his Fourth Report prepared for the 1982 session of the Commission and the first draft of Article 13 (renumbered 12 in 1986, and 11 in 1991), entitled 'Contracts of Employment', appeared in the Fifth Report dated 22 March and 11 April 1983.[159] Despite the absence of State practice, and partly in response to legislation such as the UK SIA, the Rapporteur declared there to be an emerging trend favouring 'the application of local labour law in regard to recruitment of the available labour force within a country, and consequently to encourage the exercise of territorial jurisdiction at the expense of the jurisdictional immunities of foreign States'. He advocated the drafting of a 'flexible and balanced' exception which should not constitute 'any intrusion into the sphere of administrative law or the administrative functions of government officials'. He hoped it would provide a 'mild incentive to encourage conformity with local labour law and improve social conditions, labour relations and the employment outlook'.

He accordingly prepared a draft exception narrowly limited to work performed in the forum State by persons who from the commencement of the work to the date of the proceedings were nationals or permanent

[159] *ILC Yearbook*, 1983, vol. 2, part 1, p. 25.

residents of the forum State.[160] Questions of appointment and dismissal were kept immune. The layout was in two paragraphs, with the exception stated in the first paragraph and the second paragraph containing four clauses excluding the operation of the exception. This layout was preserved in the later drafts but with additions and subtractions to both the exception and the exclusionary clauses. This first draft was severely criticized on all sides in a week-long debate at the 1983 session (18 to 25 May) with every phrase and possible alternative canvassed.[161]

In his Sixth Report of the following year the Special Rapporteur noted 'the lack of enthusiasm' for the exception (along with his proposed exception for acts of the foreign State causing personal injuries or damage to property) 'since they found no support in the general procedure of States'. In consequence he submitted a revised draft[162] introducing a further requirement that for a contract of employment to be non-immune the foreign State must have 'effectively placed the employee under the social security system' of the forum State.[163] This revised version was substantially redrafted by the Drafting Committee,

[160] 'Article 13. *Contracts of Employment*
1 Unless otherwise agreed, a State is not immune from the jurisdiction of the courts of another State in respect of proceedings relating to a "contract of employment" of a national or resident of that other state for work to be performed there.
2 Paragraph 1 does not apply if:
(*a*) the proceedings relate to failure to employ an individual or dismissal of an employee;
(*b*) the employer is a national of the employing State at the time the proceedings are brought;
(*c*) the employee is neither a national nor a resident of the State of the forum at the time of the employment; or
(*d*) the employer has otherwise agreed in writing, unless, in accordance with the law of the State of the forum, the courts of that State have exclusive jurisdiction by reason of the subject-matter': *ILC Yearbook*, 1983, vol. 1, p. 43.

[161] Ibid., p. 50.

[162] 'Article 13. *Contracts of Employment*
1 Unless otherwise mutually agreed between the States concerned a State which employs an individual for services to be performed, in whole or in part, in the territory of another State, and has effectively placed the employee under the social security system of that other State, is considered to have consented to the exercise of jurisdiction by a court of that other State in a proceeding relating to the contract of employment.
2 Paragraph 1 does not apply if:
(*a*) the individual has been appointed under the administrative law of the employer State and is performing functions in the exercise of governmental authority;
(*b*) the proceedings relate to non-appointment or dismissal of an individual seeking employment or re-employment;
(*c*) the individual is a national of the employer State at the time the proceeding is instituted;
(*d*) the individual was neither a national nor a habitual resident of the State of the forum at the time when the contract of employment was concluded, unless otherwise agreed in writing between the parties to the contract of employment;
(*e*) the individual has otherwise agreed in writing, and the court of the State of the forum does not retain exclusive jurisdiction by reason of the subject-matter of the proceeding or the subordinate rank of the employee performing services of a solely domestic or non-governmental nature': ILC Sixth Report (A/CN.4/376, 31 January 1984), p. 17, revised version proposed by the Special Rapporteur.

[163] A/CN.4/376, 31 January 1984, p. 17.

discussed at the 1868th Meeting on 20 July 1984,[164] and went forward for inclusion in the provisional draft articles of 1986.

The reception of the Special Rapporteur's proposal for the employment exception was unenthusiastic. In 1983 and subsequently there have always been several States, not always the same ones (though China, Algeria and the former USSR and GDR were fairly consistently opposed to the exception), who expressed the opinion that State practice did not support such an exception and that it should be deleted from the draft.

However, sufficient support was expressed for a revised article (now numbered Article 12) to be agreed and included in the provisional draft of the convention adopted by the ILC on a first reading on 20 July 1984. In this draft two additional conditions were added to the first paragraph, and the exclusionary clauses in paragraph 2 now numbered five.[165]

Not surprisingly, this complex piece of drafting came in for considerable criticism when in 1987 it was circulated for comments by governments. The second Special Rapporteur, Motoo Ogiso, in his First Report dated 28 May 1988,[166] summarized the criticisms, and proposed fairly radical revision. He suggested deletion of the condition in the first paragraph requiring the contract of employment to be covered by social security provisions of the forum State, and thereby abandoned one of the initial grounds in 1984 for the adoption of such an employment exception as a whole, and also proposed the deletion of two of the exclusionary clauses in the second paragraph, exclusions considered by opponents of the exception to remove two safeguards protecting public employment in the foreign State from local judicial supervision. The total effect of these

[164] *Yearbook of the ILC*, 1984, vol. 1, pp. 321–4.

[165] 'Article 13. *Contracts of Employment*

1 Unless otherwise agreed between the States concerned, the immunity of a State cannot be invoked before a court of another State which is otherwise competent in a proceeding which relates to a contract of employment between the State and an individual for services performed or to be performed in whole or in part, in the territory of that other State, if the employee has been recruited in that other State and is covered by the social security provisions which may be in force in that other State.

2 Paragraph 1 does not apply if:

(*a*) the employee has been recruited to perform services associated with the exercise of governmental authority;

(*b*) the proceedings relate to the recruitment, renewal of employment or reinstatement of an individual;

(*c*) the employee was neither a national nor a habitual resident of the State of the forum at the time when the contract of employment was concluded;

(*d*) the employee is a national of the employer State at the time the proceeding is instituted;

(*e*) the employee and the employer State have otherwise agreed in writing, subject to any considerations of public policy conferring on the courts of the State of the forum exclusive jurisdiction by reason of the subject-matter of the proceeding': ILC Drafting Committee revised draft, 1868th Meeting, 20 July 1984 (*ILC Yearbook*, 1984, vol. 1, p. 321).

[166] A/CN.4/415.

deletions was considerably to enlarge the scope of the exception,[167] and incidentally to follow closely the form of the employment exception in Article 5 of the ECSI.

His Second Report and revised draft was discussed by the ILC in 1989 and 1990, as a result of which Ogiso restored the two excised provisos but kept the deletion of any reference to social security. He prepared an amended version of proviso (*a*), restricting its application to administrative and technical staff of the diplomatic mission or consular post,[168] but this not being favourably received, the Drafting Committee reverted to its 1984 revised draft with five provisos but omitting the social security reference.

In 1989 in the ILC debate over Ogiso's revised draft Article 12, ILC members drawn from the Federal Republic of Germany, the United States and France (somewhat reluctantly) supported its inclusion in the convention, whilst members from China, Poland and East Germany opposed it.

In this form, Article 11 relating to contracts of employment was included in the draft articles adopted on the second reading in 1991, which went forward to the UNGA Sixth Committee with a recommendation for the convening of an international conference to adopt and sign a convention on jurisdictional immunities. It reads as follows:

Article 11, Contracts of Employment

1. Unless otherwise agreed between the States concerned, a State cannot invoke immunity from jurisdiction before a court of another State which is otherwise competent in a proceeding which relates to a contract of employment between the State and an individual for work performed or to be performed, in whole or in part, in the territory of that other State.
2. Paragraph 1 does not apply if:
(*a*) the employee has been recruited to perform functions closely related to the exercise of government authority;

[167] 'Article 12. *Contracts of Employment*
1 Unless otherwise agreed between the States concerned, the immunity of a State cannot be invoked before a court of another State which is otherwise competent in a proceeding which relates to a contract of employment between the State and an individual for services performed or to be performed, in whole or in part, in the territory of that other State, if the employee has been recruited in that other State.
2 Paragraph 1 does not apply if:
(*a*) the employee was neither a national nor a habitual resident of the State of the forum at the time when the contract of employment was concluded;
(*b*) the employee is a national of the employer State at the time the proceeding is instituted;
(*c*) the employee and the employer State have otherwise agreed in writing, subject to any considerations of public policy conferring on the courts of the State of the forum exclusive jurisdiction by reason of the subject-matter of the proceedings': Ogiso, 2nd Rapporteur, revised draft after governments' comments, 1988, A/CN.4/415.

[168] '2(*a*) The employee is a member of the administrative or technical staff of a diplomatic or consular mission who is associated with the exercise of governmental authority': 1990 Ogiso proposal, 3rd Report, A/CN.4/L.448, p. 10.

(*b*) the subject of the proceedings is the recruitment, renewal of employment or reinstatement of an individual;

(*c*) the employee was neither a national nor a habitual resident of the State of the forum at the time when the contract of employment was concluded;

(*d*) the employee is a national of the employer State at the time when the proceeding is instituted;

(*e*) the employer State and the employee have otherwise agreed in writing, subject to any considerations of public policy conferring on the courts of the State of the forum exclusive jurisdiction by reason of the subject-matter of the proceeding.[169]

Dissatisfaction continued to be expressed with the formulation of the exception in the 1990 and 1991 discussions in the Sixth Committee of the UN General Assembly; in 1990 Puissochet (France) said his delegation considered legitimate a restriction on immunity in the case of labour disputes but it was necessary 'to strike a balance between two equally valid concerns, that of protecting the interests of the employees of a foreign State and respect for the social legislation of the forum State on the one hand, and that of avoiding abusive intervention into activities connected with the exercise of governmental authority by the foreign State on the other'.[170]

By Resolution 48/55 of 9 December 1991 the General Assembly took note of the draft articles of the Convention on Jurisdictional Immunities of States and their Property approved by the ILC on its second reading in 1991 and resolved that a working group should be set up to consider issues of substance which would facilitate the successful conclusion of the convention and the question of continuing an international conference to negotiate and adopt a final text of the convention.

In November 1992 the contract of employment exception was identified in the Working Party set up by the UN General Assembly's Sixth Committee as 'a matter of substance' giving rise to difficulties which required resolution prior to the convening of such an international conference.[171] Opinions expressed in the 1992 and 1993 Working Party were again very divided. Belgium, China, France, India and Iran in 1992 and other countries in 1993 continued to advocate the deletion of the exception. Others supported the inclusion of an exception for contracts of employment in the draft convention but were concerned that it was undermined by the numerous exceptions in paragraph 2. Renewed objection to the proviso in paragraph 2(*b*) led the Chairman to reformulate it to read: 'the purpose of the claim is to obtain the recruitment, renewal of employment or reinstatement of an individual'. In the 1984 discussion in the Working Party, reservations were again expressed as to

[169] 1991, second reading of Articles, A/CN.4/L.457; A/46/405.

[170] UNGA 6th Committee, discussions on the report of the ILC, 1990, A/C.6/45/SR.28, p. 9.

[171] UNGA 6th Committee, Convention on Jurisdictional Immunities, Report of the Working Group, A/C.6/47/L10, 3 November 1992.

provisos (*a*) and (*c*) in the second paragraph as affecting 'the overriding interest of the forum state in matters of domestic policy and law affording protection to its local labour force'. A challenge for the first time was made to proviso (*c*) on the ground that it 'could not be reconciled with the principle of non-discrimination based on nationality'.[172]

The discussions in the ILC air every type of objection and solution to the relationship of immunity to public employment, from members who favoured preserving immunity for all foreign State employment, to those, such as Thiam (Senegal), who questioned the permissibility under international law of depriving State employees of their basic rights to employment protection:

> A State could not waive regulations concerning wages, work by children or women, nightwork, or weekly working hours. The forum State did not enjoy complete freedom in its relations with its workers for it was subject to the control of its own courts; what was more at the international level there were conventions on the subject and organisations which ensured their observance. Certain principles might even be considered to form part of *jus cogens*. Consequently the sending State could not invoke the principle of jurisdictional immunity for the purpose of inserting in contracts of employment provisions that were contrary to the public policy of the forum State.[173]

On the assumption that some reservation of employment matters was to be accorded to the employer State, the Special Rapporteur also examined criteria of nationality, permanent residence, local recruitment, function of the employee, governmental purpose of the employment, and type of proceeding. A novel criterion not appearing in Models I, II or III was the proposal to link immunity to employees 'performing functions closely related to the exercise of governmental authority'. This proposal, which appeared as paragraph 2(*a*) in the 1986 draft, was criticized by governments. Belgium, the Federal Republic of Germany and the UK considered the proposal to be 'imprecise', 'extra-ordinarily broad' and 'dangerously vague'. Germany stated that 'a link with the exercise of "governmental authority" can probably be established in practically all contracts of employment'. The UK was unconvinced by the arguments in support in the ILC's commentary on this article:[174]

> While there can be no objection to such an exception being made for 'officials of established accreditation', it is not apparent, in the case of many other instances given, why questions relating to the contracts of these employees should be thought to have, invariably, a closer connection with the legal system of the employing State than with the State of the forum, given that (by definition) the basic criteria for non-immunity set out in paragraph 1 of the article have been satisfied and that none of the other exceptions specified in

[172] UNGA Documents A/C.6/49/L.2, 4 October 1994, para. 9.
[173] Thiam, Senegal, *ILC Yearbook*, 1983, vol. 1, p. 57.
[174] ILC's Report, 36th Session.

paragraph 2 (eg as to nationality and residence) are applicable. It is also relevant that there is no question of the employing State being compelled to engage or retain or re-employ any particular person.

Reference was here made to paragraph 2(*b*) of the article and also to Article 26, which appeared in the 1986 draft and gave a State immunity from 'any measure of coercion requiring it to perform or to refrain from performing a specific act on pain of suffering a monetary penalty'.[175]

The second Rapporteur accepted these criticisms and deleted paragraph 2(*a*) from the revised draft, but in the subsequent debates in the ILC (1989) and the Sixth Committee, strong support for its retention was expressed by Third World States including Algeria, Brazil, Iraq and Turkey. In the 1992 Working Party discussions it was suggested that the drafting be tightened to exclude such professions as librarians and translators, which seemed to have little to do with the exercise of governmental authority, and attention was drawn to the Australian FSIA, section 12, which drew a line between diplomatic staff and other staff.

An alternative approach was employed in his first draft by the first Rapporteur; on the basis, somewhat questionably, of Italian case law, he drew a distinction between the acts of appointment and dismissal which, as exercise of governmental authority, should not be subject to local courts' jurisdiction – a State could never be compelled to re-employ or reinstate an employee – and the consequences of dismissal or breach of employment on which he considered the local courts might adjudicate.[176]

The basis for such a distinction was challenged by both the UK and the Federal Republic of Germany in their comments in 1987; the latter suggested that if it covered the validity of a dismissal, which was the key issue of numerous labour disputes, it would result in all major cases of labour disputes being subject to immunity. The second Rapporteur, Ogiso, was clearly impressed and deleted this exclusion.

In proposing these tests he at times confused the issue of connecting links to establish jurisdiction with indicia of applicable law. For this he was sharply rebuked by Ushakov, USSR. He criticized the use of applicable law as a criterion of immunity, saying it raised numerous questions:

First was the court to apply the law of the employer State or that of the forum State? If the applicable law was that of the forum State, why would the case be brought before the court of the forum State rather than of the employer State? If the applicable law was that of the forum State, why did the article provide for

[175] This draft Article 26 does not appear in the 1991 version.

[176] The words 'failure to employ' were criticized by Evensen (Norway) as too wide and not designed to cover a State which had no employment vacancies to offer: *ILC Yearbook*, 1983, vol. 1, p. 50.

two different regimes for a single category of employees, depending on whether they were nationals of the employer State or of the forum State? Secondly, where the applicable law was that of the forum State, it was because it was considered to be more favourable to the employee in question than the law of the employer State. However, what evidence was there that assumption rather than the contrary was valid?'[177]

Social security provisions

In the course of the International Law Commission's consideration of the employment exception, a criterion depending on a reference to social security provisions was introduced into the draft article. During the 1983 debate on his first draft, the Special Rapporteur, Dr Sucharitkul, noted the exemption from social security provisions in the receiving State of diplomats and consuls under the Vienna Convention (and also in the Conventions relating to Special Missions 1969 and Representation of States with International Organizations 1975) but observed that these Conventions made no mention of locally recruited staff.[178] He considered the practice of States favoured the application of the local social security system to nationals of the State where the work was to be performed, who might also be locally recruited. Indeed Mr Jenks, Assistant Director-General of the ILO, had specifically drawn the Law Commission's attention to this group when he had addressed the UN Conference on Diplomatic Immunities:

> For members of diplomatic missions and their families continuity of protection could only be secured by the sending state; in general, it was secured by applying to them the social security arrangements applicable to the public service of the sending state. The servants and employees of diplomatic missions, on the other hand, generally spent their whole working lives in one country, but not necessarily in the service of a particular diplomatic mission. Unless, therefore, they were covered by the social security system of the receiving state, they were liable to be without adequate social security protection in the event of invalidity, bereavement or old age,

and he urged governments

> which were committed to the general concept of comprehensiveness of coverage . . . to provide adequate protection for the local staff of their own diplomatic missions in the only manner in which that protection could be satisfactorily provided, namely, by cooperating in the arrangements necessary to secure continued participation by such staff in the social security scheme of the country where they were employed. Any such hesitation would involve a departure from the principle enunciated in the Universal Declaration of Human Rights that 'everyone, as a member of society, has the right to social security'.[179]

[177] Ibid., 1984, vol. 1, p. 322, para. 15.
[178] Ibid., 1983, vol. 1, p. 56, para. 54.
[179] *UN Conference on Diplomatic Intercourse and Immunities, Vienna 1961, Official Records*, vol. 1, 25th meeting (22 March 1961), paras. 6 and 7.

Following this advice, Rapporteur Sucharitkul recommended a revised draft 'narrowly confined to a small area where the employer State, of its own free will, decides or chooses to place the locally recruited non-national employees under the social security system of the host State in preference to its own'. His reason ('this may constitute a clear indication of intention to consent to the exercise of local jurisdiction and the applicability of local labour law in regard to the particular contract of employment') was an attempt to treat the application of social security provisions as based on implied consent of the foreign State, and hence to meet the objections of States who favoured no exception to State immunity without consent. The commentary of the ILC similarly justified the requirements relating to the social security provisions 'especially in cases where the employer state has chosen or opted to place the employee under the social security system of the state of the forum in preference to its own', and included an explicit reference to VDC Article 33(1).

The 1984 revised draft proposed by the Special Rapporteur contained the requirement:

> A state which . . . has effectively placed the employee under the social security system of that other State is considered to have consented to the exercise of jurisdiction by a court of that other State.

The approach based on waiver or implied consent was, however, lost in the Drafting Committee's revision, which changed the words to 'if the employee has been recruited in that other State and is covered by the social security provisions which may be in force in that other State'.[180] The basis of the exception to immunity by reason of the changed wording was not made clear. Whilst it no longer depended on consent of the foreign State to local jurisdiction, the place of recruitment and inclusion within the local social security scheme could be treated as connecting factors to the forum State; alternatively the basis of the exception could be seen as a determination of applicable law to a particular category of foreign State employees.

The reference to social security provisions came in for criticism on diverse grounds in the 1987 comments of governments on the first 1986 ILC draft and the ILC 1989 debate on the second reading of the articles. Some, like Shi (China) and Graefrath (East Germany), thought there should be no question of subjecting a foreign State's employees to the social legislation of the forum State; such disputes, the Chairman Graefrath (East Germany) stated, were normally settled by mutual

[180] The Chairman of the Drafting Committee, Mr Mahiou (Algeria), justified the inclusion of the words 'may be in force' on the ground of flexibility to take account of the fact that coverage in a social security system might be compulsory in some States but optional in others, and also of the Vienna Convention on Diplomatic Relations, Article 33.

agreement or insurance coverage.[181] Pawlak (Poland) considered the matter appropriate for inclusion in bilateral agreements but out of place in an international convention.[182] Calero Rodriguez (Brazil), Al-Qaysi (Iraq) and Njenga (Kenya) favoured deletion,[183] but other members, Reuter (France), with Mahiou (Algeria) and Razafindralambo (Madagascar) speaking positively in favour, supported its retention.[184] The Second Rapporteur concluded that the criterion of 'social security' is neither an effective reference nor a necessary limitation on the exception to State immunity, and deleted the reference to social security provisions.[185]

Subsequent debates both in the ILC and in the Sixth Committee indicated some support for reference to social security provisions, but its omission was confirmed in the version of Article 11 adopted on the second reading which went forward to the UN Sixth Committee. The 1991 commentary to the article summarizes the reasons for the omission:

> Reference to the coverage of the social security provisions incorporated in the original text has been deleted on second reading, since not all States have social security systems in the strict sense of the term and some foreign States may prefer that their employees not be covered by the social security system of the forum State. Furthermore, there were social security systems whose benefits did not cover persons employed for very short periods. If the reference to social security provisions was retained in article 11, such persons would be deprived of the protection of the courts of the forum State. However, it was precisely those persons who were in the most vulnerable position and who most needed effective judicial remedies.[185a]

III. European Community Law, and the Organization of the British Diplomatic Service

In this penultimate section an excursus is made to give an account of EC law's treatment of public service and, as a factual background to the discussion, an outline of the organization of the British Diplomatic Service.

(a) *Nationality as a Ground of Discrimination in EC Law*

Nationality as a condition of eligibility for work runs counter to the freedom of movement of workers guaranteed by Article 48 of the Treaty

181 *ILC Yearbook*, 1989, vol. 1, p. 138, para. 25, and p. 181, para. 34.
182 Ibid., p. 165, para. 51.
183 Ibid., p. 168, para. 14, p. 155, para. 46, and p. 154, para. 35.
184 Ibid., p. 175, para. 74.
185 Preliminary Report, Motoo Ogiso, A/CN.4/415 (20 May 1988), p. 74.
185a A/CN.4/L462 Add. 2 (26 June 1991), p. 48.

of Rome of the European Community.[186] Article 48(2) requires 'the abolition of any discrimination between workers of the Member States as regards employment, remuneration and other conditions of work and employment'. An exemption in Article 48(4) excludes public service and has led to construction by the European Court of Justice of the type of work which by reason of performance of public duties may properly be restricted to nationals of the employing State. This EC law has consequently relevance to the issue under discussion in this paper; factually it may establish a correlation between public duties and their performance by nationals of the employing State sufficient to use nationality as a criterion of public and hence immune employment, and it may provide criteria by which to identify 'the performance of duties in the exercise of governmental authority'. It should, however, be borne in mind that the Court's definition of public employment may expand or contract according to the purpose in hand: 'an interpretation is sought of each measure which is most in keeping with its place in the Treaty and thus with the purpose of the concept of public authority which is used'.[187] Thus, with regard to the application of unimplemented directives the Court was prepared to construe the definition of State to cover State trading agencies, discarding criteria of form, function or capacity as employer. It defined the State to include

> . . . a body, whatever its legal form, which has been made responsible pursuant to a measure adopted by the State for providing a public service under the control of the State and which has for that purpose special powers beyond those which result from the normal rules applied in relations between individuals . . .[188]

The result is to produce an all embracing definition of the State totally at odds with the international rule of restrictive immunity distinguishing between governmental and commercial functions.

There is no definition of public service in the Treaty; a parallel provision relating to self-employed and the right of establishment restricts the exemption to activities which in the Member State 'are connected, even occasionally, with the exercise of official authority'. The European Commission successfully challenged in the Court Member States' inclusion within the public service exemption of certain lower and middle levels of employment relating to nursing staff (*Commission* v. *France*), railway workers (*Commission* v. *Belgium*), university researchers and junior posts (*Commission* v. *Italy*, *Commission* v. *Allue*), and secon-

[186] The Treaty provides for an employed person and family the right to accept offers of employment actually made, to move freely within the territory of Member States for this purpose, to stay in the Member State for the purpose of employment, and to remain in a Member State after having been employed there.

[187] *Foster* v. *British Gas*, Case C–188/89, [1990] 2 All ER 897 at 913.

[188] Ibid. See also *Marshall* v. *Southampton and SW Hampshire Area Health Authority*, Case 152/84, [1986] 2 All ER 584 at 594, *per* Advocate General Slynn.

dary school teachers (*Lawrie-Blum, Bleis*).[189] The Court, in activist mode, mindful that a wide definition of public service would exclude a large swathe of workers from EC Article 48's protection, and despite much opposition from Member States, ruled in *Commission* v. *Belgium* that employment in the public service was restricted to:

> . . . those posts which involve direct or indirect participation in the exercise of powers conferred by public law and duties designed to safeguard the general interests of the State or of other public authorities.

The Court gave as its justification:

> Such posts in fact presume on the part of those occupying them the existence of a special relationship of allegiance to the State and reciprocity of rights and duties which form the foundation of the bond of nationality.

In arriving at this conclusion the court applied a uniform EC definition 'unaffected by public national criteria'. It disregarded provisions in some Member States' constitutions containing a principle of non-admission of aliens to public posts,[190] and classic international law, which allows the operation of a principle of nationality between States.[191] Whilst recognizing that every State has the power to define the field of action of its own administration and to assert its own concept of State intervention in national life,[192] the Court held that the Treaty of Rome as an instrument of economic and social integration required a uniform approach.

A criterion of form based on administrative and civil law categories of employment was also rejected, in part on the practical ground that in some cases the identical work was performed by nationals under administrative regulation and by non-nationals under private law contracts of employment, but also on the broader ground that such national distinctions were arbitrary.

As the Court said in *Sotgiu*:

> It is of no interest whether a worker is engaged as a workman (ouvrier), a clerk (employé), or an official (fonctionnaire) or even whether the terms on which he is employed come under public or private law.[193]

Advocate-General Mayras in his opinion noted:

[189] *Commission* v. *France*, Case 307/84, [1986] ECR 1725; *Commission* v. *Belgium*, Case 149/79, [1980] ECR 3881; *Commission* v. *Italy*, Case 225/85, [1987] ECR 2625; *Commission* v. *Allue*, Case 259/91, [1993] ECR I–4309; *Commission* v. *Lawrie-Blum*, Case 66/85, [1986] ECR 2121; *Commission* v. *Bleis*, Case 4/91, [1991] ECR 5627.

[190] Belgium relied on a provision in its constitution restricting to Belgians civil and military posts except in special cases.

[191] e.g. European Convention on Establishment, 13 December 1955, Article 13: 'Any contracting State may reserve for its own nationals the exercise of public functions or of occupations connected with national security or defence'.

[192] European Parliament Resolution of 17 January 1972, *Official Journal*, 1972, C 10, p. 4.

[193] *Sotgiu* v. *Deutsches Bundespost*, Case 152/73, [1974] ECR 153.

The distinction between on the one hand officials subject to legislative provisions whose position as regards the administration is governed by statutes and regulations and on the other hand employees of the public service of an industrial or commercial nature whose relationship with their employees is subject to contracts of employment under private law is of significance inasmuch as the legal nature of the employment relationship determines the type of court with jurisdiction to take cognisance of law suits concerning them and moreover involves important consequences of substantive law,

but declared it to be of little relevance to the task in hand of deciding the scope of non-discrimination between workers based on nationality.[194]

The Member States argued strongly for the retention of the nationality principle: it ensured that the civil servant 'works for the community to which he belongs'; it preserved the unitary and career structure of public service whereby on entry (often subject to competition or prior qualification) the official was afforded permanence of tenure, and opportunity for promotion to the highest posts in exchange for loyalty and compliance with discipline, and the State employer was given flexibility to transfer employees to posts involving security. The court disregarded such an institutional approach.

Unlike the Court's ruling on unimplemented directives, the criterion of function was given more weight in applying the public service exemption. Mancini in his opinion in *Commission* v. *France*, taking account of the condition previously laid down by the Court that the powers exercised should be for protection of general interests, listed powers relating to policing, defence of the State, the administration of justice and assessments to tax. In drawing up such a list he relied on the reference to 'exercise of official authority' in Article 55's exemption, and Advocate-General Mayras' view that such authority

is that which arises from the sovereignty . . . of the State; for him who exercises it, it implies the power of enjoying the prerogatives outside the general law, privileges of official power and powers of coercion over citizens.[195]

The European Court's ruling has necessitated some amendment to the administrative practice of Member States. In directions to the British civil service the Court's ruling has been interpreted to exclude '(*a*) any post of a type for example where the work has been put out to an outside agency without restrictions on nationality for the staff employed and (*b*) any post where the activities are such that they are also carried out in fields outside the public service and which do not involve direct or indirect participation in' the core functions of the State as described by the Court; an appended list identifies, as those outside public service, doctors, teachers, researchers, caterers, librarians, translators and clerical

[194] Ibid., at p. 163.
[195] *Reyners*, [1974] ECR at 664.

and service staff. Curators' D–G posts in national museums have been agreed with the European Commission to be 'non-public service' posts.[196]

This implementation of EC Article 48's prohibition of discrimination based on nationality illustrates the entrenched practice in Member States of reserving public administration posts to nationals. There is a deep-rooted conviction that public service is an area in which the State should exercise full sovereignty, and a widespread tendency, particularly in times of high unemployment, to see the public service as a convenient reservoir of posts.[197]

(b) *The British Diplomatic Service*

The Diplomatic Service (DS), like the home civil service, is set up by prerogative Order in Council which gives the Secretary of State for Foreign Affairs the power to issue regulations regarding conditions of service, salary, promotion and, in uniformity with statute and concurrence of the Treasury, retirement and pensions.[198]

A number of distinctions can be drawn between the staff employed in the Diplomatic Service and by heads of mission abroad, and some of these distinctions resemble the criteria in the three Models discussed earlier when applying the employment exception from immunity.

Place of recruitment

The Diplomatic Service covers home-recruited personnel for service both within the UK and abroad, and heads of missions abroad may engage local staff (locally engaged staff, LE). Home-based staff are covered by the regulations whereas locally engaged staff are subject to decision of the head of the mission in accordance with the Diplomatic Service procedure.

Eligibility

Only British subjects (including Commonwealth citizens) and citizens of the Republic of Ireland (who fulfil certain conditions as to birth, parentage and residence) are eligible for appointment for permanent

[196] Civil Service Personal Management Compendium (1992), Annex C to Chapter I.2. The following appear in the list: bookbinders, catering staff, civil research, cleaners, dentists, doctors, driving examiners, electricians, gardeners, joiners, librarians, messengers, nurses, paperkeepers, porters, plumbers, reprographic staff, staff maintaining stamp machines, teachers, translators.

[197] Mancini in *France* at p. 1728.

[198] Diplomatic Service Order 1991, re-enacting DS Orders 1964–1982.

posts in the higher grades of the home-based Diplomatic Service.[199] No such restriction exists for locally engaged staff though, on grounds of cost due to treasury tax abatement rules and British social security, British citizens may be preferred over other equally qualified candidates.

Selection

By Diplomatic Service Order 1991, permanent appointment to the higher grades of DS, and of all legal and senior research officers, is to be with written approval of the Civil Service Commission by selection on merit on the basis of fair and open competition. Promotion is based on performance and in the light of promotability assessments.[200] Since 1982, lower DS and other branches and part-time or temporary (one-year) appointments in higher DS grades have not been subject to this selection requirement.

Locally engaged staff are appointed by the head or other member of the mission.

Method of appointment

The general method for home-based staff is by letter of appointment referring to the conditions of service set out in the Diplomatic Service regulations.

In England public service so defined derives from the concept of private servants of the Crown who as office-holders served the monarch in the exercise of the classic tasks of police, defence, administration of justice and the collection of taxes. In legal theory all civil servants form part of the personal staff of the sovereign, and it is still true to say that on appointment civil servants as servants of the Crown hold office during the pleasure of the Crown.[201]

The Crown was considered constitutionally incapable of binding itself by contract with servants, who were regarded historically as members of the sovereign's household, and its ability to dismiss its servants at will was also thought incompatible with a contractual relationship. Over time these positions have been eroded by case law: 'There is nothing unconstitutional about civil servants being employed by the Crown pursuant to contracts of service';[202] the Crown's power to dismiss at will 'is not inconsistent with the existence of a contract until so deter-

[199] The Aliens Employment Act 1955 empowers the Minister to issue a certificate of employment to an alien where there is no suitably qualified candidate who satisfies nationality rules and the alien possesses exceptional qualifications or experience. Alien certificates are not required for those taking up posts not designated as public service.

The Race Relations Act 1976, section 75(5), specifically exempts the operation of civil service nationality rules from its scope. An officer has the right to go to an industrial tribunal if he considers there has been discrimination against him.

[200] FCO Code of Management, p. 4.

[201] The Civil Service Pay and Conditions of Service Code, 1982, Article 4.

[202] *R* v. *Civil Service Appeals Board, ex parte Bruce*, [1988] 3 All ER 686, *per* May LJ at p. 694.

mined'.[203] It was further maintained until the 1990s in the Civil Service Code that 'A civil servant does not have a contract of employment enforceable in the Courts but rather a letter of appointment'. However, as the later edition of the same Code noted:

> The legal position of civil servants has been radically changed by the growing trend for legislation to apply to the civil service either directly by the provisions of the Acts themselves or by the Government's assurances that the conditions applying to civil servants will not be less favourable than those applying to other employees.

This change has led to a succession of cases challenging the classic position.[204] Following *ex parte Nangle* it can now be accepted that a civil servant is capable of having a legally enforceable contract of employment.[205] Indeed the government is proposing to introduce explicit written employment contracts for members of the senior civil service (current grade 5 and upwards). The contracts of employment would be for an indefinite term but with specified periods of notice, three months for the case of resignation and six months for compulsory retirement and severance.[206] Accordingly, diplomatic staff in the senior grades (DS 4 upwards) are likely to receive employment contracts in the future.

Locally engaged staff receive a letter of appointment setting out the grade, date of appointment, period of probation, normal notice of termination (one month), starting salary scale, increments, bonus payments and tax liability, social security arrangements, and other conditions. The instructions to heads of mission state that the letter of appointment should be considered as a bona fide offer of employment, the terms of which will be honoured, but it should be made clear in the letter that the right is reserved to change them as necessary and care taken to see that the letter in no way constitutes a waiver of diplomatic or State immunity.

Terms of contract

Social security. Home-based staff are insured under UK legislation. Within the EU, LE staff employed in diplomatic missions in EC countries are insurable under the legislation of the member State in which they are employed. If British nationals, they may opt to be subject to UK legislation,[207] the option to be exercised within three months of entry into employment and renewed each year. Outside the European Union, Foreign Office instructions, in accordance with VCD Article 33,

[203] *Reilly* v. *The King*, [1934] AC 176, *per* Lord Atkin at p. 180.

[204] P. Davies and M. Freedland, *Labour Law: Text and Materials* (2nd edn., 1984), pp. 435, 513.

[205] *R* v. *Lord Chancellor's Department, ex parte Nangle*, [1992] 1 All ER 897.

[206] *The Civil Service: Continuity and Change*, Cm. 2627, para. 4.31–2; *The Civil Service: Taking Forward Continuity and Change*, Cm. 2748, para. 4.8–9.

[207] Full Class I contributions being payable.

require the LE employee to be insured under the social security laws of the receiving State or in accordance with the provisions of any bilateral social security agreement between the UK and the receiving State.

Security

Diplomatic officers owe allegiance to the Crown. In its executive capacity the authority of the government is exercised through the government of the day. Diplomatic Service Officers are therefore required to discharge loyally duties assigned to them by the government of the day, of whatever political persuasion.[208]

Home-based and locally engaged staff are employed under the terms of the Official Secrets Acts 1911–89, which in addition to dismissal for security reasons may also authorize criminal prosecution. For home-based staff, the obligations of confidentiality and loyalty to the Crown are enforced by positive security vetting on entry of all candidates for posts involving access to highly classified information; if at any time thereafter the necessary positive judgment of the employee's trustworthiness cannot be made, the vetting clearance will be withdrawn, the officer suspended, and, subject to successful appeal, required to leave the service. Restrictions on political activities, contacts with the media and publications are also imposed, with staff being ranked in three categories of 'politically sensitive', 'politically free' and intermediate; the 'politically sensitive' group are debarred from both national and political activities, but the intermediate may engage in such activities except to stand for the British or European Parliament.

Summary dismissal. Gross and deliberate misconduct or conduct which brings the Service into gross disrepute or seriously affects the UK Government's relations with another government is ground for summary dismissal, with a right of internal appeal to a disciplinary board. Similarly, early retirement severance in the public interest is to be considered by the retirement board in consultation with the trade unions; compensation may be payable.

Grading

Home-based staff regulations categorize the posts into diplomatic, grades 1–10, legal, research, communications and technical including Queen's messengers, secretarial, executive assistant, and security. For locally engaged staff, the Diplomatic Service procedure grades them from DS 6–10, beginning with senior commercial officers at the top (DS6), commercial officers, vice-consuls, information and management officers (DS7), assistant information officers, senior translators, accountants (DS9), senior clerks, secretaries, shorthand typists, commercial

[208] DS Reg. 15: political activities.

assistants, translators in the immigration department, bookkeepers, junior clerks and routine clerical, copy-typing work (GD10).

Immunity

Officers at DS7 and above, and DS8 in the Diplomatic Branch, serving at diplomatic posts, are given diplomatic rank and are automatically members of the mission as defined in the VCD. Other officers are accorded the status of the administrative and technical class but the head of mission has discretion to accord them full diplomatic status, if necessary to enable them to carry out their duties or by reason of local conditions. Heads of mission are reminded that there should be consistency between the policy applied to foreign diplomats in the UK and to HMG's own overseas staff, and that immunity from jurisdiction does not mean a general immunity from compliance with local laws. In practice, however, as already noted, not all States are prepared to concede the complete exemption for employment matters concerning diplomatic or consular missions which the SIA section 16 affords. Thus, British posts abroad may be exposed to a more narrowly construed immunity. Immunity may be waived where the individual will be treated fairly and the work of the mission not prejudiced (e.g. security may be at risk where an officer privy to sensitive information is imprisoned or exposed to questioning by local police). In practice immunity is most unlikely to be waived in respect of a home-based member of staff.[209] Spouses may present problems on immunity grounds; marriage to a foreign national may affect promotion prospects; where a spouse wishes to work in a post abroad the regulations require approval of the head of the mission; by working she (and in most cases it is wives that are in issue) may lose her dependency status and hence her immunity; alternatively, local employment may require her to submit any dispute to local courts and hence constitute a waiver of immunity.

As regards locally engaged staff, the same principles govern in that the instructions to heads of mission declare that it is not acceptable that posts should use their immunity as a means of evading due compliance with local laws and legal obligations.[210] The preamble of the VCD is cited to the effect that immunity is not to benefit individuals but to ensure the efficient performance of the functions of diplomatic missions as representing States. In conformity with Model III these instructions declare that 'it is unsustainable to claim absolute immunity over employment of all LE staff irrespective of the nature of their duties and how close (or far) those are from central diplomatic and consular functions'. Where a dispute arises, advice from a local lawyer is essential; where a general plea

[209] 'The State's Response', paper given by Sir Franklin Berman KCMG at a Conference on Sovereign Immunity, St John's College, Cambridge, 30 June–2 July 1994, under the auspices of Lawyers in Europe.

[210] *Diplomatic Service Procedure: 1989 Review*, Part I, paras. 1–9.

of immunity is not likely to be accepted by the local court as necessarily excluding its jurisdiction over an employment claim, certain matters are to be taken into consideration by the head of the mission in deciding whether or not to waive immunity. First, whether the proper defendant should be the UK, not the mission; second, whether the exercise of jurisdiction by the local court relates to a particular individual rather than all LE staff; third, whether the particular job is held to be a 'public function'; fourth, even in this case the cost of adducing evidence to establish the public function is to be compared to the amount of the claim and, if in excess, serious consideration is to be given to settlement of the case out of court. The determination of whether a particular job is a 'public function' is recognized as difficult and a matter for local legal advice as to what is relevant, as well as consultation with the Foreign Office, particularly the legal advisers; no criteria are offered but some examples illustrate where to draw the line. Vice-consuls and commercial officers clearly do have public functions whereas drivers and clerks do not; the position of an accountant may be borderline.

The overall legal position of an employee in the English public service is well described by Fredman and Morris:

> We find that no consistent distinction has been drawn between the State and private employers. Unlike some systems, there is no separate body of administrative law which exclusively governs public service employment. In some contexts, public and private employees are treated alike. For example most of the statutory protection rights specifically apply to civil servants. In the sphere of industrial action, English law stands out from other systems in giving public service workers largely the same freedoms as those in the private sector. In other respects, however, public service workers, particularly civil servants and police, are set apart from private sector employees. For example, obligations of loyalty and confidentiality in relation to their employment are enforced by the criminal as well as the civil law . . . the concept of dismissal at will still applies.[211]

In any event the legal position fails to reflect accurately the present factual relationship between the civil servant and the British State. The same authors identify five distinguishing criteria for public service in England: the power to initiate legislation and to govern, funding from taxation, the justification of activities in the 'national interest' with consequent constraints on private rights, accountability to Parliament and review by the courts in a manner not required from private employment and finally by the bureaucratic structure. The outline of some of these features is blurring as the effect of the Thatcher reforms introduced in the 1980s takes effect.[212] These reforms include a severe retrenchment of the public service and privatization of its activities, internally by setting targets with tightly controlled budgets and putting

[211] *The State as Employer* (1989), p. 2.

[212] P. Davies and M. Freedland, *Labour Legislation and Public Policy* (1993), p. 628.

out to competitive tender a range of services, and externally by the establishment of executive agencies or outright transfer of function to the private sector.[213] Modification of the nationality, confidentiality and accountability requirements have been necessitated by these reforms.

IV. Conclusions

Model I

The first conclusion to be drawn from the above survey of the operation of the employment exception to immunity is that a restrictive theory in simple form does not work. Under that theory, if the work is identical to that performed in the private sector, the test of the *nature* of the work should render the claim subject to the local court's jurisdiction. But as the House Report on the US FSIA, the US and other common law jurisdictions in Model I show, public service continues immune by taking into account the public status of the employer and the *purpose* of the work, the achievement of the classic functions of government, thus largely preserving a rule of absolute immunity for civil servants abroad. Whilst this goal may be the desired result, the distortion of the commerciality test to achieve it undermines its use elsewhere in restrictive immunity.

The civil law test of a private law contract of employment seems a more promising approach. It is supported by a juridical theory of incompetence of the forum court *ratione materiae*, by which international law prohibits the exercise of jurisdiction of another State over the acts of internal administration of a State. On occasion the private law contract of employment undoubtedly reflects a factual difference in place of recruitment, nature of duties, nationality of employee, and conditions of work and employment protection. But neither theory nor practice provide clear or consistent guidance as to location of the line dividing internal administration from 'external' employment by a State. There can be no efficacy, and hence no acceptance, in the use of the private law act as a test when not all jurisdictions recognize a distinction between administrative and private law competencies, and those that do, determine the distinction by reference to domestic municipal law, not international law, and finally apply it to the employment of labour in the public sector with differing consequences. Thus, Belgium may use the contract for low-grade manual or clerical workers, France for high-grade non-national employees and the UK for locally recruited staff, so as to make its use as a uniform test unreliable.

[213] Cm. 2748, para. 3.8; Deregulation and Contracting Out Act 1994.

Model II

Model II, then, seems to offer a preferable solution, namely the exclusion of listed categories of workers closely associated with the classic functions of the State such as defence (military), law and order (police), collection of revenue and representation abroad (diplomatic and consular staff). This approach also can be faulted; it suffers from two defects. First, it is over-comprehensive, excluding from local jurisdiction all grades of duties and levels of responsibility; second, the exclusion itself rarely provides an alternative regime by which to settle the employment disputes of the excluded category of workers. Both these defects could be remedied by greater particularity, if not in the exclusion clause, in specific protocols to the general conventions, such as the VCD or NATO Status of Forces Agreement, which regulate the excluded category. The different constructions placed on the Vienna Convention on Diplomatic Relations to give or deny a right to the individual member of the diplomatic staff to bring proceedings against the employing State indicates a *lacuna* calling for such a protocol. Nevertheless, there is probably insufficient awareness of the severity of the problem to produce support for a multilateral convention to achieve such an end, and States are more likely by bilateral exchange to clarify individual difficulties which arise.

Model III

One then turns to Model III which undoubtedly has the merit, unlike Models I and II, of recognizing the complexity of the issues involved—the need to accommodate different types of employment, 'ordinary' work, long- or short-term assignment abroad, different nationalities and residences held by employees, and competing claims of forum and employing State to jurisdiction and applicable law. It is a complex piece of drafting to deal with a complex situation but probably not over difficult to apply in a straightforward case. (For the purposes of the discussion, reference will be made to SIA section 4.) Beginning with the general assumption of State immunity, that section removes immunity for work performed wholly or in part in the forum State; 'partly performed' introduces uncertainty for employees engaged from a home base, or whose work takes them to a number of countries (the qualification of the conclusion of the contract in the forum country adds a further complexity to the construction of the first subsection). The second subsection then restores immunity for nationals of the employing or third State. In borderline situations, where the nationality or habitual residence of the employee is in issue, the section can prove difficult to apply. Nationality is determined by the country of the nationality. In cases of double nationality, or as may often occur, where the employee is in process of changing his nationality, the employing and forum State may hold different views as to the nationality possessed by the employee at the relevant times, and consequent uncertainty as to whether he is or is not excluded by the provisions of the second paragraph. Uncertainty may also arise from the exclusion of immunity in proviso (*c*) of the second subsection by agreement in writing; the parties are free to exclude local jurisdiction and law at any time during the employment, but the extent to which such an arrangement falls foul of local mandatory labour law may undermine its clarity or usefulness. Arrangements for the employee to take advantage of the local social security system may create a false impression that he is protected by forum courts, an impression particularly misleading for third State nationals who have had lengthy periods of residence in the forum country. Subsection 3 refers to work 'for an office . . . for commercial purposes', and thereby introduces confusion as to whether the work in subsection 1 is limited to non-commercial purposes.

The merit, then, of Model III broadly lies in its recognition of the variety of the types of employment which a State may provide and its treatment in a manner which accommodates both locally engaged and home based staff. It is, however, as has been shown, seriously flawed. Model III uses the connecting factors of 'place of performance' and 'choice of jurisdiction by the parties'. A theoretical objection can be made that, by so doing, it predetermines the issue as one of competing jurisdictions of the municipal courts of the employing and the forum States, not of international versus municipal law. In this respect, Model III may be subject to the same criticism as that levelled against Model I, that it seeks to solve an international law issue of immunity by rules derived from municipal law systems, such rules of necessity lacking uniformity by reason of their diverse national origin. However, this criticism has been formally disposed of,[214] as with the rest of the jurisdictional factors identified in the ECSI, by describing international law as selecting the jurisdictional connexions as the most appropriate means to indicate the absence of immunity.

A more serious complaint, as already noted in Section II.(d), is Model III's use of these connecting factors as alternatives to nationality and residence, as alternative and not cumulative connexions in a way contrary to current trends in private international law. All connecting factors in conflicts of law relating to employment with a foreign element are used, in a non-neutral manner, to afford to the employee the most favourable protection under any available jurisdiction. The application of Model III, thus, frequently produces a result—the exclusion from forum State jurisdiction of other States' nationals, particularly nationals of the employing or third State engaged in 'ordinary' duties—which is the opposite of the object which private international law rules seek to achieve.

[214] Dominice, 'The Relationship between Immunity and Jurisdiction of Courts', paper written for the ILA International Committee on State Immunity, Saarbrucken meeting, 1992. See also Dominice, 'Immunités de juridiction et d'execution des états et chefs d'état étrangers', *Fiches juridiques suisses*, 934 (1992), pp. 12–14.

The core objection to Model III must arise from its use of nationality/habitual residence. That use lays the model open to attack as discriminatory and providing unequal conditions of work between workers in the same working place. Where staff enjoy different conditions of work, remuneration, health, safety and social security under service regulations from those afforded to home-based employees engaged under private law contracts or locally engaged staff, it may be shown on the individual facts that they are placed in a more, or less, favourable position than the category of workers who by operation of the first paragraph of Model III, ECSI Article 5, have access to forum courts. Such complaints of lack of equal treatment, discrimination, inadequate representation by trade association or provision of social security may be based on the standards to be found in United Nations[215] and ILO[216] conventions, universal and regional human rights conventions[217] and conventions of the Council of Europe.[218] The European Community's prohibition on discrimination between workers by nationality has already been mentioned. ECSI Article 5(1) and SIA section 4(1) appear to run counter to EC Article 48 in that they may confer jurisdiction in favour of one Member State's nationals, those of the forum State, at the expense of nationals of the employing or third State. To argue that EC Article 48 is excluded by the derogation in favour of public service begs the question; the legislative intent underlying the 'place of performance' indicator in ECSI Article 5(1) is to remove a category of workers from the scope of public service.

Some idea of the challenges that must be expected to the legality of ECSI Article 5 and national legislation modelled on it is to be found in the English decision of *Jayetilleke* v. *High Commission for the Bahamas.*[219] Under ECSI Article 5 the nationality rules are used to restrict the employee holding the employer State's nationality to seeking redress solely from the employer State. In situations where no remedy exists in the employer State, this may represent a denial of procedural rights to the individual (e.g. Article 6 of the European Convention on Human Rights (ECHR)); this would seem to be particularly true where a third State national is deprived of redress in the State where he is employed. Such a claim was indeed made in *Jayetilleke*, where a British citizen of Asian origin employed as senior accounts clerk in the Bahamas High Commission, and hence employed in diplomatic premises within the

[215] UN ICCPR, 1966, Article 22 (freedom of association), UN ICESCR, 1966, Articles 6–9 (right to work and social security); CERDS, 1966; CEDAW, 1967; Convention on Protection of Rights of All Migrant Workers and Members of their Families, 1990.

[216] N. Valticos and K. Samson, 'International Labour Law', in Blanchpain and Engels (ed.), *Comparative Labour Law and Industrial Relations in Industrialised Market Economies* (3rd edn., 1993), p. 77 at pp. 83–9.

[217] e.g. ECHR, Articles 6 and 11.

[218] The 1961 European Social Charter and 1987 and 1991 Protocols.

[219] EAT, 14 December 1994 (Mummery J, Lord Gladwyn, J. Ramsey), EAT 741/94.

meaning of SIA section 16(1)(*a*), sought to overcome this bar to suing under the employment exception in SIA section 4 by relying on Article 6 of the ECHR. Her claim was dismissed on the ground that the ECHR had not been enacted into English law and no common law right of access to the courts could abrogate immunity given by the primary legislation of the SIA. The ground of rejection was a technical one applicable only to English law. To rebut such a charge in other jurisdictions may cause the employer State greater difficulty.

The general conclusion is that Model I is unsatisfactory, Model II incomplete and Model III, though a workable compromise, open to attack as discriminatory.

It must also be noted that none of the models addresses the lack of effective means in the forum State to enforce any judgment or award for a monetary sum obtained by the employee against the foreign State. For such employees of the foreign State as do manage to come within the exception to State immunity, inability to enforce the judgment against State property still deprives them of an effective remedy. One has sympathy with the Sub-District Court of The Hague who declared the Republic of Zaire bankrupt when it failed to discharge a judgment for the wages of a secretary who had worked at its embassy in The Hague. The Court of Appeal, however, allowed the appeal holding the appointment of a trustee in bankruptcy to constitute a substantial infringement of Zaire's independence and allowed Zaire's claim to immunity.[220]

However, non-execution of employment judgments or awards is but one aspect of the much larger, independent and intransigent issue of immunity from enforcement of States, and of State property from forcible attachment in the forum State. As such it is beyond the scope of this article.[221]

In the face of the criticisms of the models, is there an alternative or some method of reform? A number of courses seem open:

(i) *The private international law solution*

This solution follows through the route adopted in ECSI Article 5 but so as to allow all private international law connexions rather than the single test of nationality/residence, thereby avoiding any charge of discrimination, to determine whether the court of the forum State or the employing State shall exercise jurisdiction. To give jurisdiction to the forum court in no way determines the applicable law which in cases of

[220] *Republic of Zaire* v. *Duclaux*, *Netherlands Yearbook of International Law*, 20 (1989), p. 196; 94 ILR 368.

[221] One incremental way forward, if the arbitration solution under (iii) were adopted, might be to require at the time of reference to arbitration and as a stay of forum jurisdiction payment into an escrow account by the employer State of a sum such as represents two to three years' salary payable to the claimaint employee. See Fox, 'State Immunity and Enforcement of Arbitral Awards; do we need an UNCITRAL Model Law Mark II for Execution against State Property?' (forthcoming in *Arbitration International*).

appointment under service regulations would remain that of the employing State. This approach has been adopted in Austrian,[222] Netherlands[223] and Swiss courts when they have assumed jurisdiction over foreign State employees. Further they have shown themselves prepared to declare their incompetence *ratione materiae* on facts relating not to engagement but to performance of employment, where dismissal is justified on grounds of the security of the State or, more controversially, compulsory redundancy is sought on the ground of budget cuts). Even in these cases it is well to bear in mind the decision of the House of Lords, approved by the European Commission of Human Rights, in the *GCHQ* case, ruling that 'although the Government is in a better position than the courts to determine the requirements of national security, if a decision is challenged . . . , it is for the Government to adduce evidence to satisfy the court that the decision under challenge is founded on grounds of national security'.[224]

The case of *S* v. *India* decided by the Swiss Federal Tribunal in 1984 illustrates both the advantages and demerits of this private international law solution. Although Switzerland had ratified the ECSI (subject to a declaration under Article 24[225]), the case was decided by reference to international customary law and the tribunal showed some unwillingness to accept ECSI Article 5 as accurately representing international law. The Swiss court declared immune the claim for salary following dismissal of a radio telegraphist (his duties were later reduced to translator and office clerk) employed in the Indian embassy at Berne. The tribunal first decided that the employee did not require the consent of the employing State to bring proceedings in the local court (discussed in Section II.(c)). It then decided that the claim was not immune on a number of grounds: recruitment and entry into the employment contract in the territory of the forum State; the private law nature of the employment relationship, at least for 'junior staff' in 'subordinate functions' not engaged in the accomplishment of tasks at the diplomatic level; the form of the employment, 'under standing administrative regulations governed by Indian public law' as alleged by India, was held not supported by evidence and not sufficiently brought to the notice of the employee at the time of the contract's conclusion; as an Italian citizen, national of a third State, he enjoyed 'no initial connection linking him with India, and his activities at the mission . . . were not such as to

[222] *Handicapped and Security Risk Cases* v. *USA* (Austrian Supreme Court), *Journal de droit international*, 1993, vol. 2, p. 388.

[223] *M.K.B. van der Hulst* v. *USA* (Netherlands Supreme Court, 1991), *Netherlands Yearbook of International Law*, 22 (1991), p. 379.

[224] *CSSU* v. *UK*, Application No. 11603/85, 10 EHRR 269 at 280.

[225] Article 24 permits, in addition to the exceptions to immunity set out in ECSI Articles 1–13, a contracting State to entertain proceedings against another contracting State 'to the extent that its courts are entitled to entertain proceedings against States not party to the Convention' (subject to no exercise of jurisdiction on an exorbitant ground).

give rise to such a connection'; that the unproven fact of habitual residence in Italy could not be invoked in respect of an employment relationship of long duration (22 years in the present case); reciprocity, in that Swiss practice was to treat the engagement of locally recruited personnel in its missions abroad of foreign nationality as governed by private law (the contracts being governed by Swiss law in the absence of other applicable laws). A further argument deployed was that the entry of a foreign State into relations with an individual beyond its frontiers was a serious indication that an act was performed *jure gestionis*.

The Swiss Federal Tribunal, thus, based its ruling of non-immunity on an accumulation of indicators. Recruitment and work outside the territory of the employing State predisposed it to rule against immunity; this was confirmed by residence, even if not habitual, in Switzerland, long-term duration of the employment and third State nationality; the subordinate nature of the work was supportive but, it is suggested, not conclusive.[226] Its ruling was in conformity with ECSI Article 5(1) in holding the employment by its performance in the forum State not to be immune, but contrary in that it refused to apply the nationality/habitual residence test to a third State national and introduced further tests of local recruitment, duration, grade and level of responsibility of the employment, to confirm its overall view that the forum court had jurisdiction over the employment dispute.

Whilst the outcome of the case was to give full weight to every factor linking the dispute to the forum jurisdiction and to provide a remedy to a third State national, the progress of the case through the Swiss courts and the decision itself show that the process is an uncertain one. As Gamillscheg comments about this method, which 'endeavours to find the suitable connecting factor for every single contract as such':

> This theory aspires to a maximum of individual case justice, purchased, to be honest, with a high measure of uncertainty; for, in the final analysis, it is the judge who subsequently decides on the predominating connecting factor and with it on the proper law.[227]

(ii) *The listed categories*

Exclusion of the categories of employees under Model II could be refined so as to (*a*) provide an alternative regime for settlement of employment disputes (which could be arbitration: see (iii) below); and (*b*)

[226] The decision was criticized by Monnier as wrongly construing the VCD to permit an employee without consent to sue the employing State in the courts of the forum State; as disregarding the claimant's status as one of the administrative and technical staff of the Indian embassy and consequently identified with the performance of diplomatic work, and as selectively applying parts of ECSI Article 5 and disregarding others.

[227] Op. cit. above (n. 7), at p. 188.

restrict the excluded category to senior grades[228] with an overall residuary clause that other grades should only be treated as immune in respect of employment proceedings where the responsibility of their duties or national security so require. In drafting such a modification of Model II, regard might be had to the various phraseology devised in the ILC drafts set out in Section II.(e).

Alternatively a compromise between Models I and III might be to introduce a version of the above amended listed approach alongside the general commercial transaction exception.

(iii) *Arbitration*

International organizations, as the price of immunity in employment disputes with their officials from the jurisdiction of the host State or State of the nationality of the employee, provide an alternative settlement system for all their employees. Model III fails to do this. It assumes that a non-national of the forum State will have ready recourse against the employing State in its own national system or courts. Whilst this may generally be true in respect of the higher grades of the diplomatic service recruited in the home State, it is not true as regards the lower grades, the locally engaged and third State nationals. The deficiencies of Model III to which this article has drawn attention would be reduced by the acceptance on the part of the employing State of compulsory arbitration for all employment which is immune from the exercise of jurisdiction by courts of the country where the work is performed. Such arbitration would involve no submission to forum State jurisdiction by the employing State; at most it might give rise to an award enforceable under the New York Arbitration Convention 1958. It would be a minimalist solution, leaving ECSI Article 5 and legislation based on it in its present form, but make the 'opt out' provisos of the second paragraph all conditional on the employing State making available an arbitral process, and one in which the arbitral tribunal will have regard to equality of treatment and non-discrimination between workers. This condition of arbitration could in the first instance form part of the bilateral arrangements between the receiving and employing State; but one would hope that in due course it would come to be seen as a requirement of international customary law for the conferment of immunity for public service with a State.

[228] i.e. those 'whose functions are normally considered as policy-making or managerial, or to employees whose duties are of a highly confidential nature': ILO Convention on the Right to Organize and Procedures for Determining Conditions of Work in the Public Service (No. 151), *UN Treaty Series*, vol. 1218, p. 87, Article 1(2).

THE SUBJECTIVE ELEMENT IN CUSTOMARY INTERNATIONAL LAW*

By MAURICE MENDELSON[1]

Article 38(1) of the Statute of the International Court of Justice provides that 'The Court, whose function is to decide in accordance with international law such disputes as are submitted to it, shall apply . . . (*b*) international custom, as evidence of a general practice accepted as law'. The orthodox approach, which finds expression in this provision, is that there are two components of general[2] customary international law: State practice, which is known as the 'material element'[3], and a 'subjective element'—a state of mind in relation to that conduct, sometimes unhelpfully called the 'psychological element'—which the Statute renders as 'acceptance as law'. Whilst there is relatively little disagreement that State practice is an indispensable element,[4] considerable controversy surrounds the nature of the subjective element. As Thirlway put it:

> The precise definition of . . . the psychological element in the formation of custom, the philosopher's stone which transmutes the inert mass of accumulated usage into the gold of binding legal rules, has probably caused more academic controversy than all the actual contested claims made by States on the basis of alleged custom, put together.[5]

One reason why these controversies have continued for so long without resolution is that the holders of different theories are able to find in the phenomenon what they want to see, thereby strengthening their preconceptions. Thus, those who place a lot of stress on the subjectivities of

[1] QC, MA, D Phil. (Oxon.); Professor of International Law, University College London.

[2] This article does not deal, except in passing, with local, regional or other forms of particular customary law. Neither does it deal with *jus cogens* (which may be a special type of customary law) nor (except, again, incidentally) with the question whether new methods of custom-formation may have come into being—e.g. through resolutions of the United Nations General Assembly. The focus here is on 'traditional', general customary law, a form which is still very much current.

[3] It has been submitted elsewhere that this includes, in certain circumstances, omissions and statements: see Mendelson, 'State Acts and Omissions as Explicit or Implicit Claims', in *Le Droit international au service de la paix, de la justice et du développement: Mélanges Michel Virally* (1991), p. 373 (also reprinted in International Law Association, *Report of the Cairo Conference* (1992), pp. 366, 370).

[4] *Pace* Cheng, for whom practice is merely evidence of *opinio juris*, the latter being the only and essential element of a customary rule: see his 'United Nations Resolutions on Outer Space: "Instant" International Customary Law?', *Indian Journal of International Law*, 5 (1965), p. 23.

[5] Thirlway, *International Customary Law and Codification* (1972), p. 47.

the actors are not daunted by the fact that often the only information one has is the external conduct of States: for them, conduct is merely the evidence of those subjectivities. Similarly, those who consider that consent is the key to customary law are not downcast by the undisputed fact that general customary rules bind States who have given no intimation of such consent: such States, they say, are deemed to have agreed tacitly. Because these are matters of judgement, inference and interpretation, it is not to be expected that scientific methods of proof (examination of empirical evidence and logical analysis) will definitively establish the correctness or otherwise of particular theories. The only tools we can use here are an understanding of international decision-makers, common sense and, perhaps, Occam's razor—'entities [in this case legal concepts and fictions] are not to be multiplied unnecessarily'.

A deeper reason for the knottiness of the problem lies in the approach adopted to it. Discussion of custom usually takes place in the context of discourse about sources. For a positivist (and most international lawyers are more or less positivists today), what this means is process: we seek to identify the types of procedure which, if carried out by authorized actors, create law for members of the society in question. In developed municipal societies, these rules may be complex (e.g. the rules about the binding force of precedent in common-law jurisdictions), but they are at least for the most part discoverable and describable. In international law, the same could be said about the treaty process. There are rules of recognition which help us to identify the authorized decision-makers in the system (principally States), and the law of treaties tells us what steps undertaken by them will result in legal obligations, by what means and in what circumstances these obligations can be suspended or terminated, and so on.

The trouble is that custom is not really like that. What characterizes it, above all, is its very lack of formality. So to discuss customary law in terms of elements, steps in its creation, and so on is to impose on it a framework which in a sense falsifies its nature. The problem is exacerbated by the modern jurist's unfamiliarity with customary law outside the international sphere. Not so very long ago, the general custom of the realm, the region, or the municipality was an important source of law throughout Europe, as well as in other places; but it came to be replaced by statute law and (to a greater or lesser extent) judicial precedent. True, customary law lingers on in parts of Africa and elsewhere, but even there it has become somewhat subordinated to the modern, 'Western' approach. So most commentators about the sources of international law slip easily into a formalistic mode of analysis without stopping to ask themselves whether the technique is suitable to the phenomenon under consideration. It is submitted that, *mutatis mutandis*, the study of domestic customary law societies, past and present, can afford useful insights into the nature of customary law.[6]

Recognizing these differences between treaty law and customary international law, Ago characterized the latter as 'spontaneous law'.[7] The term may be somewhat inappropriate: it is redolent of the now discredited 'historical school' about which more will be said later; and much customary law today emerges as the result of careful calculation on the part of its instigators and is thus far from spontaneous. Nevertheless, Ago's description does serve to remind us that, in trying to fit wild[8] custom into the formalistic clothing of 'civilized' lawmaking, we may deform its nature.[9]

There is another methodological trap of which one should beware. Because in modern municipal societies jurisdiction is compulsory, it is at least feasible (if not wholly correct) to think of law in terms of what a judge will do; and in few areas is this more marked than in the doctrine of sources, where the question is often reduced to an investigation of what processes a judge would regard as capable of creating binding law. But it should not be forgotten that, in the international system, where jurisdiction is not compulsory, adjudication is the exception, not the rule. The more typical decision-maker is the government official, engaged either in advising his or her own government, or in negotiating with others. The difference in the observational standpoint[10] has the following consequence for our topic. At least in theory, if the status of an alleged rule as customary law is challenged before a tribunal, the judge or arbitrator has to decide whether the processes for the creation of custom had been completed by the critical date. Government decision-makers,

[6] See, e.g., Brutails, *La Coutume d'Andorre* (2nd edn., 1965); Allen, *Law in the Making* (7th edn., 1964), p. 148; Gluckman, *Ideas in Barotse Jurisprudence* (rev. edn., 1965); Allott, Epstein and Gluckman, Introduction to Gluckman (ed.), *Ideas and Processes in African Customary Law* (1969), esp. at pp. 1–15; Mittlebeer, *African Custom and Western Law* (1976); Goldin and Gelfand, *African Law and Custom in Rhodesia* (1975); Holleman, *Shona Customary Law* (1952); Watson, *The Evolution of Law* (1985), chap. 2; id., *Sources of Law, Legal Change and Ambiguity* (1985), chap. 2.

[7] 'Diritto positivo e diritto internazionale', in *Scritti di Diritto internazionale in onore di Tomaso Perassi* (1957), vol. 1, pp. 1, 44; cf. Barberis, 'Réflexions sur la coutume internationale', *Annuaire français de droit international*, 36 (1990), pp. 15–17. Abi-Saab has even gone so far as to call the process 'mysterious': 'La coutume dans tous ses états', in *Le droit international à l'heure de sa codification, Etudes en l'honneur de Roberto Ago* (1987), vol. 1, pp. 55, 58 ff.

[8] The phrase, though not its signification, is borrowed from R.-J. Dupuy, 'Coutume sage et coutume sauvage', *Mélanges offerts à Charles Rousseau* (1974), p. 75.

[9] The artificiality of formal analysis is perhaps particularly evident if one tries to determine the exact moment at which a customary rule becomes law. Although this can be done in the case of legislation or a treaty, it is normally impossible where custom is concerned. (Admittedly, in practical terms it seldom matters: a court need only decide whether the rule had come into being for the parties at the 'critical date' (or equivalent)—in other words, whether the fruit is ripe, not when it ripened. For a national decision-maker, such as a government legal adviser, the question is, likewise, 'Is there already a rule?' or 'Shall we contribute to the formation of the rule?', not 'When did the rule come into being?'.)

[10] Cf. Mendelson, 'Formation of International Law and the Observational Standpoint' in International Law Association, *Record of the 63rd Conference* (Warsaw, 1988), pp. 935, 941.

however, need not be so objective; whilst they may well want to find out how much support the practice has attracted up until now, if it is one which they wish to follow on its merits they will probably simply do so, even if the rule has not yet 'crystallized'.[11]

This fact would of itself, it is submitted, provide sufficient justification for not engaging here in a minute and exhaustive analysis of the judicial pronouncements.[12] But there is another reason. The International Court (like other tribunals) has given relatively little useful guidance on this subject.[13] Although it has on several occasions stated that the two elements of custom are needed, the cases tend to be somewhat special ones, as will be shown. Moreover, it has not made it clear exactly what it understands the subjective element to be: agreement or belief. And, most importantly, its own practice is in various respects inconsistent with its pronouncements. Thus, although on occasion stressing the need for the two elements to be present, it has often held that something is a rule of customary or general law after a discussion of only one element (be it practice or the subjective element). Indeed, not infrequently it has come to its conclusion without discussion of *either* element. The Court's tendency, indeed, is to invoke the formal requirements mainly when it wants to say that an alleged customary rule is not one.

Despite all of these serious methodological and practical difficulties, it is suggested that there is some use in trying to analyse the components of custom, so long as the limitations of the method are not lost sight of. After all, there is something uncomfortable for a lawyer in having to say 'I cannot define custom, but I know it when I see it'.

The present article focuses on the subjective element, leaving to one side the material element, practice. This is partly for reasons of space but also because the topic of the material element is regarded as rather less problematic. It is conceded, though, that as a practical matter, it is often difficult to separate the two components.[14] But they are at least to some extent distinguishable, and we are told on the highest authority that there are indeed two distinct elements.

Some identify the subjective element in custom as the State's will (or several or all States' will) that the practice become a rule of law: in other words, with consent to the (would-be) rule. Proponents of this, volun-

[11] See further below, p. 203.

[12] Fuller analyses of the case law can in any case be found in, for example, Haggenmacher, 'La doctrine des deux éléments du droit coutumier dans la pratique de la Cour internationale', *Revue générale de droit international public*, 90 (1986), p. 5; Thirlway, 'The Law and Procedure of the International Court of Justice, 1960–89', this *Year Book*, 61 (1990), pp. 1, 31–110.

[13] See Mendelson, 'The International Court of Justice and the Sources of International Law', in *Fifty Years of the International Court of Justice: Essays in Honour of Sir Robert Jennings* (1996), p. 63.

[14] Cf. Salvioli, 'Les règles générales du droit de la paix', *Recueil des cours*, 46 (1933–IV), pp. 1, 20; Stern, 'La coutume au coeur du droit international: quelques réflexions', in *Mélanges offerts à Paul Reuter: le droit international, unité et diversité* (1981), pp. 479, 482; and Haggenmacher, loc. cit. above (n. 12).

tarist, approach tend to equate the creation of custom with tacit agreement: just as treaties are the written, formal expression of States' will, so custom is its informal manifestation. Others reject the voluntarist thesis, preferring to regard the subjective element as a *belief*—a belief in the legally permissible or obligatory character (as the case may be) of the conduct in question: *opinio juris sive necessitatis*, or *opinio juris* as it is known for short.[15]

The jurisprudence of the World Court has certainly failed to still the controversy, and proponents of both theories can cite judgments which expressly or impliedly support (or appear to support) their contentions. A few examples on either side will make the point.

The Permanent Court of International Justice in *The SS 'Lotus'* gave some encouragement to voluntarists by observing that

> International law governs relations between independent States. The rules of law binding upon States therefore emanate from their own free will as expressed in conventions or by usages generally accepted as expressing principles of law . . . [16]

though it should be noted that the phrase 'generally accepted' suggests that the consent of each and every State is not necessary, and it will be seen shortly that the judgment also appears to lend support to the 'belief' approach. In the *Asylum* case the International Court of Justice observed that 'The Party which relies on a [regional or local] custom of this kind must prove that this custom is established in such a manner that it has become binding on the other Party', and went on to rely on non-acceptance by Peru as a (subsidiary and perhaps *obiter*) ground for rejecting the claims of Colombia.[17] In the *Fisheries* case the Court relied heavily on the absence of protest by interested States generally, and the

[15] Stern neatly describes this distinction as one between *opinio juris assentiment* and *opinio juris sentiment*: loc. cit. above (n. 14). The dualism is in a sense a manifestation of two opposing currents in international law: that of individualism and that of collectivism. Cf. Koskenniemi, *From Apology to Utopia* (1989); Kennedy, *International Legal Structures* (1987).

The controversy between supporters of the two approaches to the subjective element goes back at least two hundred years, and has continued unabated. In 1950, members of the International Law Commission were very much in disagreement about the issue: *Yearbook of the International Law Commission*, 1950, vol. 2, pp. 25–6 and 367–74; ibid., vol. 1, pp. 4–6. A recent issue of the *International and Comparative Law Quarterly* (44 (1995)) contains two articles adopting diametrically opposed views on this subject: O. Elias, 'The Nature of the Subjective Element in Customary International Law', loc. cit., p. 501; and Lobo de Souza, 'The Role of State Consent in the Customary Process', ibid., p. 521. What perhaps makes this opposition of views all the more striking is that the two doctors did their research at the same institution under the same supervisor.

[16] *PCIJ*, Series A, No. 10 (1927), pp. 4, 18.

[17] *ICJ Reports*, 1950, pp. 266, 276–8. On the other hand, there is also language which has been invoked in aid of the belief approach, e.g. 'respected by the territorial States as a duty incumbent on them'.

United Kingdom in particular;[18] and in the *Right of Passage* case it referred to the practice in question being 'accepted' by the parties.[19]

On the other hand, there is no shortage of case law relying on general opinion rather than the consent of the parties. Thus, in the *SS 'Wimbledon'* case the Permanent Court alluded to the fact that passage of belligerent warships and ships carrying contraband through the Suez Canal 'had never been regarded by anyone as violating the neutrality of the Ottoman Empire' and to the absence of objections by anybody to the like passage through the Panama Canal, and went on to say that these precedents were 'merely illustrations of the general opinion according to which . . . such a waterway is assimilated to natural straits . . . '.[20] In *Nottebohm (Second Phase)* the Court relied on what it held to be general rules, without any reference to acceptance or the like on the part of Guatemala;[21] similarly in *Barcelona Traction (Second Phase)*.[22] Indeed, there have even been express holdings that *opinio juris* is required. In the *Lotus* case the Permanent Court, in repudiating French reliance on the relative absence of prosecutions of the crew of foreign ships involved in collisions on the high seas, said that

> only if such abstention were based on [States'] being conscious of having a duty to abstain would it be possible to speak of an international custom. The alleged fact [of general abstention, with some exceptions] does not allow one to infer that States have been conscious of having such a duty . . . [23]

In the *North Sea Continental Shelf* cases[24] the ICJ cited this pronouncement and, referring to the assertion by Denmark and the Netherlands that certain delimitation agreements by non-parties to the Geneva Convention on the Continental Shelf, 1958, evidenced the existence of a new rule of customary law regarding delimitation, observed that

> even if these instances . . . were much more numerous than they in fact are, they would not, even in the aggregate, suffice to constitute the *opinio juris*;—for, in order to achieve this result, two conditions must be fulfilled. Not only must the acts concerned amount to a settled practice, but they must also be such, or be

[18] Ibid., 1951, pp. 116, 136–9; cf. also its reliance on the agreement of the parties as to the breadth of the territorial sea, at p. 128.

[19] Ibid., 1960, pp. 6, 39–40. The language is, however, somewhat ambiguous: 'acceptance as law' could mean acknowledgment of an existing legal position, which is not an implausible interpretation when it is recalled that India was a successor State. On the other hand, where a bilateral (local) custom is concerned, both parties will need to have known about the practice and (if only by implication) to have agreed to it.

[20] *PCIJ*, Series A, No. 1, pp. 15, 26–8.

[21] *ICJ Reports*, 1955, pp. 4, 12–26.

[22] Ibid., 1970, p. 3.

[23] *PCIJ*, Series A, No. 10, pp. 4, 28. But note the reference to tacit consent on the next page.

[24] *ICJ Reports*, 1969, p. 3, at p. 44, para. 77. See also p. 42, para. 71.

carried out in such a way, as to be evidence of a belief that this practice is rendered obligatory by the existence of a rule requiring it. The need for such a belief, i.e. the existence of a subjective element, is implicit in the very notion of the *opinio juris sive necessitatis*. The States concerned must therefore feel that they are conforming to what amounts to a legal obligation. The frequency, or even habitual character of the acts is not in itself enough. There are many international acts, e.g., in the field of ceremonial and protocol, which are performed almost invariably, but which are motivated only by considerations of courtesy, convenience or tradition, and not by any sense of legal duty.[25]

In the *Continental Shelf (Libya* v. *Malta*) case[26] the Court said that

It is of course axiomatic that the material of customary international law is to be looked for primarily in the actual practice and *opinio juris* of States, even though multilateral conventions [such as the Law of the Sea Convention 1982] may have an important role to play in recording and defining rules deriving from custom, or indeed in developing them.

It did not, however, go on to develop the point in issue here. In the *Nicaragua (Merits)* case the Court made repeated reference to its need to establish, not only the practice, but also the *opinio juris* of States.[27] It will, however, be submitted below that even these clear statements of support for the 'belief' approach are not conclusive.[28]

One of the purposes of this article is to suggest that the dichotomy between these two approaches has been drawn too sharply, and that neither school has a monopoly of wisdom. Consent plays a role in some conditions, but belief in others. The context in which one poses the question is crucial.[29] It will also be suggested that the interplay between consent and belief is better understood if one differentiates between *necessary* conditions and *sufficient* conditions. It will finally be submitted that (contrary to the prevailing belief) it is not an invariable requirement

[25] It is curious that the Court thought that the need for a notion (in this case, *opinio juris*) can be implicit in its content. The Man in the Moon is a notion, but this does not prove his existence or his necessity. As a matter of logic, the most than can be deduced from the content of the notion of *opinio juris* is that some have thought it to be relevant or necessary, not that it is in fact relevant or necessary.

[26] Ibid., 1985, p. 13, at pp. 29–30, para. 27.

[27] Ibid., 1986, pp. 14, 97–8 (paras. 183–5), 99–100 (paras. 188–9), 101 (para. 191), and 108–10 (paras. 206–7 and 211).

[28] Pp. 204–7.

[29] This is not the same as Haggenmacher's ingenious espousal of a sort of *gestalt* approach to the problem (loc. cit. above (n. 12), pp. 111 ff.). His reliance on overarching principles of international law seems overstated; and whilst there is obviously a good deal of truth in his view (shared with many other authors) that the opinion of the judge is decisive, this seems to overlook the fact that custom (like law in general) is not merely what the judge declares (cf. Hart, *The Concept of Law* (1st edn., 1961), pp. 121–50). *A fortiori* when it is recalled that, in the international system, the role of the judge is somewhat sporadic and peripheral: see above, pp. 179–80.

that the subjective element be present (in one or other of its forms) for a practice to constitute or reflect a rule of customary international law.

The Voluntarist Approach

The consent or will theory of custom is mainly concerned with the stage at which the custom is being formed. This approach has a considerable antiquity. Thus, there are frequently cited Roman law texts which indicate that what the people wills expressly is law (legislation), and what it wills or consents to implicitly is customary law.[30] And in the field of public international law, writers from at least Grotius[31] onwards echo these maxims, asserting that what States agree to expressly is treaty law, and what they agree to implicitly is customary law.[32] But it is the rise of positivism, with its rejection of natural law and emphasis on the sovereign will of States, that brought the voluntarist approach to the fore.[33]

To begin with, it may be observed that the waters are muddied by those adherents of the consent theory who, like Tunkin, want to fit their voluntarist approach into the traditional framework and language of practice plus *opinio juris*. They therefore subvert the literal meaning of the phrase *opinio juris sive necessitatis* to mean consent.[34] But although, as

[30] 'Consuetudine ius esse putatur id, quod voluntate omnium sine lege vetustas comprobavit': Cicero, *de invent.*, 2.22.67; 'inveterata consuetudo pro lege non immerito custoditur et hoc est ius quod dicitur moribus constitutum. nam cum ipsae leges nulla alia ex causa nos teneant quod iudicio populi receptae sunt, merito et ea quae sine ullo scripto populus probavit tenebunt onmes: nam quid interest suffragio populus voluntatem suam declaret an rebus ipsis et factis?': *Digest*, 1.3.32.1 (Julian, 84 Dig.). Cf. h.t. 35 (Hermogenian, *libro I iuris epitomarum*)—'tacit agreement of the citizens'; h.t. 36 (Paul *ad Sabinum VII*)—especial weight is to be given to custom because it has received such approval that it was not necessary to reduce it to writing.

[31] *De jure belli ac pacis* (1646 ed.), *Prolegomena*, §§ 1, 17 and 40.

[32] Another strand of thought found in Grotius and other classical authors (though the way they put it varied) was that customary law was the working out in practice of the precepts of natural law, or the filling in of gaps in natural law, from which customary law ultimately derived its validity. Such theories are generally regarded today as outmoded and philosophically untenable, but it will be necessary to revert to this topic briefly below (pp. 196–7).

[33] See, e.g., Oppenheim, *International Law*, vol. 1 (1st edn., 1905), pp. 15–18—though it should be noted that there are strong traces here of a Rousseauesque *volonté générale*; Hall, *A Treatise on International Law* (8th edn., 1924), p. 5; Triepel, 'Les rapports entre le droit interne et le droit international', *Recueil des cours*, 1 (1923), pp. 77, 82–3; Anzilotti (tr. Gidel), *Cours de droit international* (1929), p. 67; Cavaglieri 'Règles générales du droit de la paix', *Recueil des cours*, 26 (1929–I), pp. 315, 322; Strupp, 'Les règles générales du droit de la paix', ibid., 47 (1934–I), pp. 257, 301 ff.

[34] Tunkin, *Theory of International Law* (tr. Butler, 1974), pp. 123–33. Wolfke, *Custom in Present International Law* (2nd rev. edn., 1993), appears in places to equate *opinio juris* with State will (e.g. at p. 47), but in other places speaks of express or tacit acceptance or recognition. Terms like 'recognition' or 'acceptance' are somewhat ambiguous. They may connote an act of choice, or merely the act of taking cognizance of what is already the position: see below, p. 203, n. 99.

will be explained below, there are difficulties in translating that phrase, it is clear that the word *opinio* denotes a *belief*, not an act of will.[35]

In principle the voluntarist approach requires every State bound by a rule of customary international law to have individually agreed to it, for sovereignty means, it is said, that States cannot acquire obligations without their consent. This seems inconsistent with reality. When one examines the emergence of such universally applicable customary rules and principles as those relating to diplomatic immunities, the prohibition of piracy and privateering, and sovereign rights over the continental shelf, it is impossible to show that every State positively consented to the emergence of the rule in question. Yet it is virtually unanimously accepted by the authorities that these rules have come to bind all States.[36]

The nature of the process by which these customary rules emerged seems to be more along the following lines. Some States actively created the practice, some by initiating it, some by imitating it, and others still, who were directly affected by the claims in question, by acquiescing in it. This initiation, imitation and acquiescence may plausibly be described in terms of consent. But others still, who were not directly affected, sat by and did nothing, and in due course found themselves bound by the emerging rule. One can actually observe this process with regard to the continental shelf, for example. To say that all States gave their consent, in any normal sense of the word 'consent', is simply untrue. In this context, it is helpful to recall that the international community is not the only customary law society that has ever existed. In domestic societies where customary law has played an important part, its creation and maintenance or replacement, and especially its formulation and recognition, often seem to result from the activities of a relatively few leading 'movers and shakers' (not necessarily the same for every area of activity), with others eventually finding themselves bound without having consciously consented to the particular rule, or at any rate that formulation of it.[37] The same seems to be true of international society.

Voluntarists such as Strupp, Tunkin, Wolfke and Danilenko do not regard this objection as fatal. They say that the States who do nothing impliedly consent or are deemed to do so: their passivity is a form of

[35] Olufemi Elias has recently made a sophisticated attempt to equate *opinio juris* with State will: loc. cit. above (n. 15). But this is not entirely convincing. In particular, once a custom is mature, a State which observes it does so less because it freely so wills than because it considers itself bound. To describe this as an act of will is to use the term in a sense completely different from its use if one is describing the action of those who pioneer a particular practice.

[36] One cannot *a priori* rule out the possibility of a *communis error* on the part of the writers. But many of them have been legal advisers of governments or otherwise engaged in the practice of international law, and might be expected to know how things operate in the real world of international relations. See also below, pp. 201–2.

[37] See the sources cited at n. 6 above, especially Brutails and Watson.

acquiescence.[38] This is superficially an attractive explanation; but it is a mere fiction. In other words, it does not describe what actually happens.

Several authors who equate silence with tacit consent distinguish between 'specially affected States' and others. In principle, it is only the former who, if their interests are affected, are expected to protest, with the result that, if they do not, they are bound by the rule. But even those who, like MacGibbon, go into acquiescence quite deeply, rarely take the analysis very far on this point.[39]

First, it is said that only affected States who knew, or might have been expected to know,[40] of the practice can be said to acquiesce tacitly in it. But it is far from clear that, in the past, all of those who found themselves bound by a general customary rule knew of the practice in question. Admittedly, this is less likely to be the case today, given the expansion of international communications and the fact that a good deal of diplomacy is carried out in international organizations and conferences. But indeed, this very dissemination of information may, in the not-too-distant future, render presumed knowledge even more of a fiction than it is today: it may well be that, with the proliferation of publications reporting State behaviour (often failing to distinguish between the trivial and the important) and with more and more information becoming available electronically, many States who are technically in possession of the relevant data will have insufficient means to process or evaluate them.

Secondly, the notion 'specially affected States' is not very precise. Every time a State makes a claim *erga omnes*, or relies on a purported general rule, every other State is potentially affected, because the claim is a brick in the edifice of a (new) customary rule. But what is the degree to which it needs to be affected? Suppose that State A asserts a new form of jurisdiction over fishing in waters adjacent to it. States B, C and D, whose nationals already fish there, might reasonably be expected to protest and, if they do not, can be presumed to have acquiesced. Perhaps States E, F, and G, whose nationals do not at present fish in those waters, but who might do so in the foreseeable future, should also protest. But what of States H to Z, who have no interest, actual or potential, in these particular waters? For one of them to protest, simply on the ground that the precedent might be invoked in the future by one of its own

[38] Respectively op cit. above (nn. 33 and 34); Danilenko, 'The Theory of Customary International Law', *German Yearbook of International Law*, 31 (1988), p. 9. This approach has a long pedigree: see, e.g., Rachel, *De Iure Naturae et Gentium Dissertationes* (1676): *De Iure Gentium*, X and XXXVII.

[39] MacGibbon, 'The Scope of Acquiescence in International Law', this *Year Book*, 31 (1954), p. 143. A partial exception is Villiger, *Customary International Law and Treaties* (1985), pp. 18–22.

[40] Cf. *Fisheries* case, *ICJ Reports*, 1951, pp. 116, 138–9.

neighbours, might be thought unnecessary and unfriendly, and it does not seem that such protests are at all common.[40a] Yet these States are not really acquiescing either. Again, suppose that State A enacts legislation claiming a right of extra-territorial jurisdiction which might be thought exorbitant. Those directly affected by the application of such laws may be expected to protest—as have the trading partners of the United States on various occasions. But would it be appropriate for States whose nationals are only potentially liable under these laws to protest? And what of those countries which do not have significant commercial relations with the country enacting the legislation? Should they protest, merely on the grounds that this would otherwise constitute a precedent which might be invoked against them in the future, perhaps by an entirely different State? It is not clear that they either would or should. But if that is so, then it is simply not true that all of those who failed to protest can reasonably be taken to have acquiesced.[41]

Danilenko asserts that even 'indirectly affected' States must be taken to acquiesce.[42] But this is a pure fiction or, to put it differently, a presumption of law. And if it is a presumption of law, it seems to be a reinstatement of the 'objectivist' approach to which voluntarists object: it is not due to the exercise of their will that these States are bound; *a fortiori* for those authors who make such presumptions of law irre-buttable in certain cases.

[40a] This is not to say that such protests can never occur, just that they do not seem at all common. Professor Ian Brownlie has kindly drawn the author's attention to the protests against allegedly illegal extensions of maritime jurisdiction set out in Mouton, *The Continental Shelf* (1952), pp. 89–96, 214 and 319. But most or all of these were by States who were, or could have been, directly affected by the decrees in question. Many of the protests were by the United States against the decrees of its Latin American neighbours, and it is reasonable to assume that its fishing vessels and warships actually did or might in future use those waters. (The legislation in question in many cases involved the extension of territorial waters, and not just the establishment of fishery zones.) At least so far as concerns fishing, the same is true of the British (and probably the Netherlands and Belgian) protests against the Icelandic baselines. Similarly, the Japanese protest against the extension of Korean sovereignty to certain waters adjacent to the peninsula. It is less certain that British boats were fishing in the waters off Ecuador, Peru, Chile and so on (though British colonies in the area should not be overlooked). But in so far as the protested decrees of these States constituted or were tantamount to extensions of territorial waters, British naval interests would have been affected. And even if could be shown that, on occasion, major Powers who are particularly vigilant protest simply to preserve the position in general law, even when their actual or prospective interests are not directly affected by the specific legislation protested against, this would appear to be the exception rather than the rule.

Of course, it is difficult to be categorical on this point, because many protests remain confidential: see Mendelson, 'Practice, Propaganda and Principle in International Law', *Current Legal Problems*, 1989, pp. 1, 12.

[41] It is not suggested that single precedents can themselves create general law; and admittedly, the requirement that the practice attain a certain level of generality and representativeness before all States are bound means that, at some point (even if not at the outset), quite a few States will be presented with a proper occasion on which to protest or (truly) acquiesce. But not necessarily all.

[42] Loc. cit. above (n. 38).

There is no indication in the jurisprudence of the International Court on the subject of general, as opposed to local and (possibly) regional, custom, that it is necessary to prove the existence of express or tacit consent on the part of the particular State concerned. If it has consented (as the UK was held to have done in the *Fisheries* case in relation to the Norwegian straight baseline system),[43] so much the better; but whilst consent in such instances is a *sufficient* condition for being bound, it has never yet been held to be a *necessary* condition.[44]

Another problem for the voluntarist theory is how new States come to be constrained by rules of customary law which arose before they came into being, and the analogous problem of how a State which is new to a particular type of activity (for example, a landlocked State which acquires access to the sea) can be bound by pre-existing customary rules.[45] It is of course *possible* to argue, with Redslob, Tunkin and others,[46] that new States are in fact free to repudiate existing customary law *en bloc*, but that they choose not to do so in order to gain the benefits of full participation in the international community that they have just joined, and can be presumed to consent to existing custom as soon as they enter that community. *Mutatis mutandis*, the same could be argued in the case of States participating for the first time in a particular activity. It is difficult, if not impossible, to disprove this argument.[47] Nevertheless, it strikes one as rather artificial. If there is a better explanation, i.e. one more consistent with the observable phenomena of social behaviour, it is to be preferred. It is submitted that in reality the new State is entering an

[43] *ICJ Reports*, 1951, p. 116, at pp. 138–9.

[44] There are quite a few examples of international and municipal tribunals assuming that a party would be bound if there was a rule of general law, without seeking the consent of that party. See, e.g., the *Wimbledon* case (1923), *PCIJ*, Series A, No. 1, pp. 15, 25–8; *Nottebohm* case (*Second phase*), *ICJ Reports*, 1955, pp. 12, 22 ff.; *North Sea Continental Shelf* cases, ibid., 1969, pp. 3, 42–3; *Gulf of Maine* case, ibid., 1984, pp. 246, 292–3; *The Regolo Attilio* case, *UN Reports of International Arbitral Awards*, vol. 12, pp. 1, 8–9; *The Scotia*, 14 Wallace 170 (US Supreme Court, 1871).

Local and regional customs may well be different. Bilateral (local) customs obviously require the assent (express or tacit) of the State whom it is sought to burden (cf. *Right of Passage* case, *ICJ Reports*, 1960, p. 6); and there is some authority that this is also so in the case of regional customs (*Asylum* case, ibid. 1950, p. 266).

[45] See, e.g., Accioly, *Tratado de Direito Internacional Publico* (2nd edn., 1956), vol. 1, pp. 38–9.

[46] Redslob, *Histoire des grands principes du droit des gens* (1923), pp. 12–13; Tunkin, 'Remarks on the Juridical Nature of Customary Norms of International Law', *Columbia Law Review*, 49 (1961), pp. 419, 426–8.

[47] Sørensen, 'Principes de droit international public', *Recueil des cours*, 101 (1960–III), pp. 45–6, argues that, if the thesis in question were correct, existing States would be equally free to decide not to apply established customary rules to a new State. Lobo de Souza, loc. cit. above (n. 15), at pp. 533–4, points out that it is unconvincing to argue that new States consent to certain rules which they immediately try to have reformed because they do not like them. The article as a whole is a strong attack on the voluntarist thesis.

existing legal system and is simply expected (and expects) to conform.[48] Similarly with the new actor. The fact is that, in the practice of States and of tribunals, it is simply taken for granted that new entrants are bound by the existing customary rules.[49] Certainly, they are free to try and change them through contrary practice which obtains the acquiescence of others (or through amendment by treaty). But that is equally true for existing members of the community. And until the existing customary rules are changed, they continue to oblige old and new members alike. Here, too, the voluntarist thesis does not seem to accord with reality; and to call in aid a legal fiction begs the question why it is needed at all.

In the face of these difficulties, one might ask why supporters of the consent theory are so wedded to it. In some cases, writers may have been consciously or unconsciously persuaded by the requirements of ideology or the political position of their Government. Thus communist ideology and the policy of the Soviet State (at any rate until just before its demise) was rather antipathetic to customary international law, which was regarded as the product of an outmoded system dominated by bourgeois States. The preferred mode of rule-creation was the treaty, individual consent to which was the indispensable condition of being individually bound.[50]

Another reason why some favour the voluntarist approach is, it is submitted, based on assumptions—usually not articulated or carefully analysed—that they make about the role of consent in the international legal system *as a whole*.[51] It is commonly said that international law is based on the consent of sovereign States; *ergo* customary law, which is part of that *corpus*, must equally depend on consent. Now, undoubtedly, consent plays a very important part in the system, at different levels; but to argue from this premiss that the consent of each and every State is necessary to the formation of a rule of general international law is

[48] As Cheng points out, it would be wrong to invoke the analogy of the child born into municipal society. The child is certainly bound by the rules of that society without its consent. But there are major differences between the power structure of municipal society and that of the international society: 'Custom: The Future of General State Practice in a Divided World', in Macdonald and Johnston, *The Structure and Process of International Law* (1983), pp. 513, 516. What one might perhaps say, however, is that participation in a society generally entails participation in its legal system, for the two are necessarily intertwined.

[49] Waldock, 'General Course on Public International Law', *Recueil des cours*, 106 (1962–II), points out that in the cases in which they participated in the PCIJ and ICJ, respectively, neither Poland nor India sought to rely on the fact that they were new States, and that it seems to have been assumed that they would be bound by existing rules: see *German Settlers in Poland* case (1923), *PCIJ*, Series B, No. 6, at p. 36; *Certain German Interests in Polish Upper Silesia* case (1926), ibid., Series A, No. 7, at pp. 22 and 42; *Right of Passage* case, *ICJ Reports*, 1960, p. 6.

[50] The Western observer should beware of priding himself or herself on a lack of a corresponding ideological and political motivation. A legal system in which States can find themselves bound without their positive consent (expressly or tacitly given) is one which may tend (though not invariably) to favour the most active and influential, i.e. the West.

[51] Cf. Reuter, *Droit international public* (6th edn., 1983), p. 111.

misconceived. The error can be better understood by considering the role of consent at different levels of analysis, or in different contexts.

At the most general, *systemic level*, it is certainly true that, if States chose to dispense with international law as a whole, and to operate on anarchic principles (or—what might very well amount to the same thing—to allow force to take the place of legal compulsion), they could do so. In that sense, it is true that international law as a whole is dependent on consent. But given that States have in fact consented to the existence of a system of international law as a whole, and continue to do so, it does not necessarily follow that the creation and binding force of each individual rule in the system is dependent on the consent of each and every subject at each and every moment.

Descending from the most general, systemic level to the sources of international law, it may be thought that these, at least, are dependent on the consent of States. Now, in one sense they are. It is States, as the principal subjects of the system, who decide what processes will be recognized as generating rules of law. If they chose, they could recognize papal pronouncements or the randomly generated choices of a computer, say, as sources of legal obligation. Less fancifully, if they chose to treat resolutions of the General Assembly as *ipso facto* creating rules of law, such resolutions would be a source of legal obligation for States. But once again, to say that the consent of States is needed for a particular process to be accepted as a source of law is not *necessarily* to say that the only such process recognized by them is one which involves the individual consent of each and every State. For example, if States as a whole recognized the binding force of papal pronouncements (as once Western rulers did), such pronouncements would not entail any act of State will as a part of the law-making process. *Mutatis mutandis*, the binding force of General Assembly resolutions would not, in the hypothetical situation, depend on the will of the minority States. Maybe we will discover that each of the recognized sources does require the manifestation of consent; but this must be determined empirically, without preconceptions. (For convenience, the context just discussed might be called the *identification of sources level*. What has yet to be established is that consent is an indispensable part of the content of the individual source: the *particular-source-content level*.)

Coming down one more level, then, and looking at the sources which actually are recognized, we find that the Statute of the ICJ essentially recognizes three: treaties, custom, and what it describes as 'general principles of law recognized by civilized nations'.[52] *Is* consent an indispensable element of each?

[52] For present purposes, the judicial decisions and writings of the most highly qualified publicists referred to in Art. 38(1)(*d*) may be discounted as being merely evidence of the law rather than formal sources of it, though this may be something of an over-simplification: see, e.g., Mendelson, loc. cit. above (n. 13).

The meaning of the third source recognized in Article 38(1) of the Court's Statute, 'general principles of law recognized by civilized nations', is not entirely clear. The Court has not elucidated its meaning, and the commentators differ. Indeed, it seems that even those who drafted the Statute differed as to what it meant, and in some cases were not clear in their own minds. However, in practice at least, one of the things it does mean is general principles of national law which are suitable for transplantation to international society. Now, in this sense of the term, it should be noted, there is no requirement of individual consent. If a principle is found in main municipal legal systems, and there is no reason of principle militating against transplantation to international society, then the principle is one of international law, *ipso facto* and without the need for consent.[53] This would also be true if, as some would argue, the phrase in Article 38(1)(*c*) denotes concepts inherent in the idea of any or all kinds of legal system—not just municipal law. So here, at least, one finds a source which does not include individual consent as part of the rule-generating process.

Turning from general principles to the first item listed in the Statute of the Court, treaties certainly seem at first sight to require individual consent. Above all, it is a well-recognized principle that they bind only the States which actively consent to them by signature, ratification, accession, etc. But this is not the whole story. Once a State has consented to be bound by a treaty which has come into force, it is universally accepted that it cannot release itself from its obligations merely by withdrawing its consent. More generally, the rules concerning treaties' identity, creation, validity, application, interpretation, amendment, modification, suspension and termination all depend on rules outside States' individual and continuing consent. But in any case, even if treaties as a source of international law *were* wholly dependent on consent, this would prove nothing about the other main source of international law, custom, unless we were to make the assumption that only agreement can be a source of international law—which assumption, as has already been seen, has no *a priori* justification and is, indeed, question-begging.

One is therefore obliged to examine empirically whether the creation of customary rules is indeed treated by States as requiring individual consent. And in fact, as has already been submitted, neither the decisions of international tribunals nor the overwhelming generality of State practice seem to require the individual consent of each and every State,

[53] The fact that the State can be said to have consented to the rule's forming part of its *municipal* system is no answer to this point.

or even of the State alleged to be bound by a generally accepted rule.[54] (Still less is there evidence that the continuing validity of a customary obligation is dependent on continuing individual consent to it.) And for what it is worth, the drafting history of Article 38(1)(*b*) of the Statute seems to bear out the conclusion that its authors were not thinking in terms of tacit consent.[55]

Does this mean that the voluntarist approach has no value at all as an explanation of the creation of customary law obligations? It is submitted that it does not, and this is one place where the distinction between *necessary* and *sufficient* conditions may be useful.

(*a*) It is a necessary condition of the creation of a customary rule that at least some States should have willed the existence of the rule: the State or States initiating the practice, and the State or States imitating, or genuinely acquiescing in it.[56] Customs do not nowadays grow up by themselves, if ever they did.[57] In short, *someone's* will needs to be actively engaged before a customary rule can even begin to be created.

(*b*) If it can be shown that the State allegedly bound by a customary rule actually imitated the claim made by the originators of the practice, this act of will is sufficient to make the rule binding on it: whether as general, or as particular, customary law need not concern us here. For instance, the United Kingdom followed the lead given by the Truman Proclamation on the continental shelf by making its own, similar claims.[58]

(*c*) Similarly, if a State actually does acquiesce in a practice, this is equivalent to consent and will be sufficient to bind it. The most obvious form of such acquiescence is where State A requires State B, on legal grounds, to do or refrain from doing something, and State B complies. For instance, State A demands compensation from State B for some act, and B pays; or A demands the release of an arrested diplomat, and he is released. But real acquiescence (as opposed to that presumed by a

[54] Above, pp. 185 and 188. A stronger argument in favour of the voluntarist approach than the one just analysed would be that, to dispense with the consent of each and every State would be to violate the principle of sovereign equality. However, this is far from being the only derogation from that principle; and one of the strengths of customary international law in its traditional form is that it reflects the realities of power.

[55] For a particularly full account, see Haggenmacher, loc. cit. above (n. 12), pp. 18–32.

[56] This author's concept of 'genuine acquiescence' will be explained very shortly.

[57] Cf. R.-J. Dupuy, loc. cit. above (n. 8), pp. 75, 77.

[58] Admittedly, in the *Nicaragua* case (*Merits*), *ICJ Reports*, 1986, pp. 14, 97–8, the Court expressly refused to accept the recognition by the two parties of certain rules as customary law as sufficient: it had to examine the *opinio juris* of States in general. This seems to suggest that acceptance by the individual party is not in fact sufficient. An interesting discussion is possible as to whether, as a matter of procedure, the Court ought to go beyond a concession of the party which is alleged to be bound by the rule in question. But even if it is thought that the Court was right to do so here, the case seems to be an exception to the general principle, well recognized in its jurisprudence, that if a party does consent to an alleged customary rule it will be bound by it. Cf. *Fisheries* case, ibid., 1951, pp. 116, 128 (regarding the 4-mile limit of Norway's territorial sea); *Fisheries Jurisdiction (Merits)* case, ibid., 1974, pp. 3, 24 (para. 54). Cf. Thirlway, loc. cit. above (n. 12), pp. 51–2.

voluntarist fiction) also occurs if a State's interests are directly engaged by some innovative conduct on the part of another State, but the first State does not protest or take other action. See, for example, the *Fisheries* case, where the Court held that the United Kingdom's failure to protest against the Norwegian straight baseline system, of which it must have known and which directly affected its national interests, precluded it from complaining about the application of those rules to its nationals.[59] In such cases, consent is, once again, a *sufficient* condition for the imposition of a customary rule on the State concerned.[60]

(*d*) If a State expressly refuses to accept an emerging rule of customary international law, the prevailing view is that it is able to opt out. This is the 'persistent objector' or 'persistent dissenter' rule. According to it, a State which clearly indicates, whilst a customary rule is in the process of emerging, that it refuses to accept it, will not be bound by the rule.[61] In this sense, it can be said that the absence of consent *at the relevant time* is a sufficient condition for the State not to be bound.[62]

In short, whilst consent is always a sufficient condition for the creation of a customary obligation, it is not a necessary one. Though the voluntarist approach is plausible and hard to disprove definitively, there are important respects in which it does not furnish a convincing answer. At the theoretical level, it is often based on a logical error concerning the

[59] *ICJ Reports*, 1951, pp. 116, 136–9. The strands in the Court's reasoning here are notoriously difficult to disentangle. The broad context was a discussion of whether a rule of general international law existed of the type contended for by the United Kingdom. However, the Court was at the same time considering whether Norway had made out an historic title to the waters in question (in which case acquiescence by others, amongst them the UK, was relevant). There seems to be a third strand to the reasoning, too, which is that the acquiescence of the UK, as the foreign State principally affected, *precluded* it from complaining. Reliance is placed here especially on the words 'The notoriety of the facts, the general toleration of the international community, Great Britain's position in the North Sea, her own interest in the question, and her prolonged abstention would *in any case* warrant Norway's enforcement of her system against the United Kingdom' (p. 139, emphasis added).

[60] Some of these instances might be said to amount to tacit agreements. Wolfke (op. cit. above (n. 34), pp. 96–100) objects that tacit agreements are not customary international law. This is perhaps unduly restrictive: it is certainly convenient and common to treat all forms of rule-making based on practice rather than on express agreement as custom.

[61] 'The persistent objector rule' is a term also frequently used to describe the phenomenon that, if a State or a group of States which plays an important part in a particular area of activity refuses to accept an emerging rule of customary law, that dissent will prevent its becoming rule of general law. However, this is really only the converse of the doctrine that, for such a rule to be created, there must be a sufficiently wide participation, including all 'representative groups'.

In either its wider or its narrower signification, the persistent objector rule is generally thought not to apply to States who object only after the customary rule has come into being: there is no 'subsequent objector' rule enabling them to escape from customary law obligations.

[62] The existence of the rule is well-supported in State practice and the literature: cf. Akehurst, 'Custom as a Source of International Law', this *Year Book*, 47 (1974–5), pp. 1, 23–7; Brownlie, *Principles of Public International Law* (4th edn., 1990), p. 10. It has not gone unchallenged: see esp. Charney, 'The Persistent Objector Rule and the Development of Customary International Law', this *Year Book*, 56 (1985), p. 1. However, the author's arguments seem on the whole unconvincing, and work in progress is likely to lead to a detailed refutation. See Hulton, *The Persistent Dissenter Rule in Customary International Law: Survey of the Case-Law and Other Literature*, paper circulated by the British Branch of the International Law Association at the Cairo Conference (1992).

level of analysis; and empirically it postulates a will which is often lacking in fact. It seeks to overcome these deficiencies by relying on a presumption of consent, a sort of legal fiction. But if there is some other explanation that fits better, it seems appropriate to dispense with the fiction and the theory that it supports. The time has therefore come to consider whether an approach which emphasizes belief rather than consent is preferable.

Opinio Juris Sive Necessitatis

Literally, the phrase means 'belief (or opinion) of law or of necessity'. This does not make much sense in English, and in fact its clumsiness as a piece of Latin arouses the suspicion that it is not Roman at all. The present author has not found it in the *Digest* or other classical writings on Roman law, and although the Glossators and Post-Glossators have not been exhaustively combed through, the expression does not appear to have much of a pedigree in Roman law. The first person to use the complete phrase seems to have been Gény in 1919,[63] though, as Guggenheim noted,[64] one finds parts of the phrase or something like it in the writings of the German historical school in the late eighteenth and early nineteenth centuries.[65] We shall return to the historical school later. So far as specifically international law is concerned, the expression does not seem to have been used by any of the so-called 'fathers' of international law, and the earliest use of the concept—though not the precise phrase—that the present writer has found in this context is in Rivier in 1896.[66] The idea was quickly adopted by many others, however.[67]

It is quite common to dress up legal maxims and the like in Roman robes in order to give them an air of respectability, though only too often the toga can muffle thought. In this case, the robes seem not even to be genuine, and it is submitted that the linguistic incoherence of the phrase *opinio juris sive necessitatis* reflects a certain incoherence of the thought behind it.

[63] *Méthode d'interprétation et sources en droit privé positif* (2nd edn., 1919), pp. 319–24, 360.

[64] 'Contribution à l'histoire des sources du droit des gens', *Recueil des cours*, 94 (1958–II), pp. 1, 52; id., 'L'origine de la notion de la *opinio juris sive necessitatis* comme deuxième élément de la coutume dans l'histoire du droit des gens', in *Hommage d'une génération de juristes au Président Basdevant* (1960), p. 258.

[65] Cf. Glück, *Ausfürliche Erläuterung der Pandekten* (1797), p. 461; Puchta, *Das Gewohnheitsrecht* (2 vols, 1828 and 1837), vol. 2, book 3, chap. 2, pp. 29–30 and 33–9; von Savigny, *System des heutigen Römischen Rechts* (1840), vol. 1, pp. 32–4. Compare the rather similar school of so-called 'objective law': e.g. Duguit, *Traité de droit constitutionnel* (2nd edn., 1921), vol. 1, pp. 65 and 73–4.

Walden, 'The Subjective Element in the Formation of Customary International Law', *Israel Law Review*, 12 (1977), pp. 344, 358 n. 47, appears to be correct when he states that Allen's attribution of the concept of *opinio necessitatis* to Blackstone is mistaken.

[66] *Principes du droit des gens*, vol. 1, p. 35. But there are perhaps earlier hints of this in Savigny, *System des heutigen Römischen Rechts* (1840), vol. 1, pp. 32–4. Cf. Kosters, 'Les fondements du droit des gens', *Bibliotheca Visseriana*, 9 (1925), p. 115.

[67] See, e.g., Accioly, op. cit. above (n. 45), pp. 38–40.

What does *opinio juris sive necessitatis* mean, or what should it mean, in the context of international law? At this point, it may be helpful to offer a provisional working translation or definition. It is a *belief in (or claim as to) the legally permissible or obligatory nature of the conduct in question,*[68] *or of its necessity*. We shall return later to the part of this definition which relates to necessity.

On the subject of belief, it may also be convenient at this juncture to refer to an observation made by Virally,[69] and echoed by D'Amato[70] and Akehurst,[71] amongst others. We cannot know what States believe, it is suggested. First of all States, being abstractions or institutions, do not have minds of their own; and in any case, since much of the decision-making within governments takes place in secret, we cannot know what States (or those who direct or speak for them) really think, but only what they say they think. There may be something of an exaggeration here. In some instances, we can discover their views because the opinions of their legal advisers or governments are published.[72] Furthermore, it will be suggested later that the express or presumptive understandings and beliefs of the international legal community about the rules of international law are in certain circumstances relevant. But, with these qualifications, Virally's observation is a useful one. We should not speak of a *psychological* element in custom, but of a *subjective* one, for it is more a question of the *positions* taken by the organs of States about inter-

[68] The bipolar nature of legal relations means that if X has a legal right (e.g. to compensation), Y will have a duty to pay; and if X has a liberty (e.g. of innocent passage through Y's territorial sea), Y will have no right to complain and an obligation not to interfere with that passage. These ideas can be expressed in terms of obligatoriness and permissibility. Cf. Mendelson, loc. cit. above (n. 3). It is hard to follow MacGibbon's suggestion (loc. cit. above (n. 39), pp. 127–8) that the role of *opinio juris* should be limited to claims to positive conduct.

[69] 'The Sources of International Law' in Sørensen (ed.), *Manual of Public International Law* (1968), pp. 116, 133–4.

[70] *The Concept of Custom in International Law* (1971), pp. 35–9. This volume, which enjoyed a considerable vogue, particularly in the United States, for some years after its publication, propounds a number of unconventional ideas, but unfortunately not a few of them seem unfounded or overstated. Reasons of space preclude a complete examination here; but amongst these questionable ideas are the following. (1) The equation or substitution of *opinio juris* with a theory of articulation, whereby if any entity, be it a State, international organization, or scholar, has articulated what it, he or she considers to be a new rule of customary law, and that articulation is followed at any time thereafter by an act of State practice—apparently even a single one—then that will found the rule, even if the State which performed the act made no connection between its own conduct and the articulation by another—so long as it was aware of it, or had reason to be (pp. 74–87). (2) So far as concerns the material element, the author appears to consider that treaty promises constitute (without more) qualifying State practice, but unilateral acts, such as legislation, cannot—a strange reversal (pp. 89–91). (3) A mechanistic form of reasoning (pp. 91–8) leads him to suggest that just two precedents can constitute a (*semble* general) customary rule. This seems far too crude: *a fortiori* the suggestion that, in litigation, a single precedent might well suffice. (4) The legal significance of protest is downgraded (pp. 98–102) in a manner belied by the practice of States and the decisions of international tribunals.

[71] Loc. cit. above (n. 62), at pp. 36–7.

[72] Though admittedly this is done only on a partial and selective basis and often only long after the event; and though it must also be conceded that the opinion of a government legal adviser does not invariably become that of the government.

national law, in their internal processes[73] and in their interaction with other States, than of their *beliefs*. This viewpoint is not unrelated to the well-known observation of McDougal that the customary process is one of claim and response, where the legal claims and the responses thereto can be implied in the conduct concerned without necessarily being expressed.

Supplied with our working definition, we can now return to the question: What part does or should the notion of *opinio juris sive necessitatis* play in the context of customary international law?

To begin with, it is important to appreciate that the phrase has been used in different contexts to express different things. These usages may be perfectly comprehensible, or even correct, in their own context: however, confusion and error arise when a concept which makes perfectly good sense in one framework is moved to another, or when the same concept is made to perform many different types of task. Once again, it is helpful to adopt a 'level-of-analysis' approach.

(*a*) In the first place, the concept of *opinio juris* may be used to try to explain why the substantive rules of a legal system are what they are, and not something different. This brings us back to the so-called historical school of jurisprudence. In the nineteenth century, Savigny and his colleagues and followers wanted to explain why, say, German law was (and should be) different from French law, Italian law, and so on. What they said was that law—especially customary law—represented the national spirit, the *Volksgeist* of the particular people concerned. Customary rules were not the result of a formal, law-making process: they just emerged out of the juridical consciousness of the people.[74] This product of romantic nationalism has long been discredited as a legal theory; and it seems particularly inappropriate to public international law, where no *Volk* with common traditions and culture yet exists, and where customary rules these days do not just grow up, but come into being through the deliberate conduct of the principal actors, for the most part.

(*b*) Somewhat akin to the historical school's approach is the idea that customary law comes about because of the social necessity of a practice—an *opinio necessitatis*.[75] As an explanation of *why* customary rules come about, there is no doubt something in this idea. For instance, in issuing the Truman Proclamation, the United States invoked a sort of *opinio*

[73] Including the communications of governments to national legislatures and courts, and the express or implicit *prises de position* about rules of international law by national courts and legislatures in the exercise of their functions.

[74] Cf. Ago's 'spontaneous law', n. 7 above.

[75] There are several variants of this approach. Cf., e.g., Duguit, *Traité de droit constitutionnel* (2nd edn., 1921), vol. 1, p. 65; Scelle, 'Règles générales du droit de la paix', *Recueil des cours*, 46 (1933–IV), pp. 327, 434; Basdevant, 'Règles générales du droit de la paix', ibid., 58 (1936–IV), pp. 471, 516; Judge Negulesco's dissenting opinion in the *European Commission of the Danube* case, *PCIJ*, Series B, No. 14 (1927), pp. 84, 105 and 114.

necessitatis. It claimed that it was 'reasonable and just' for the coastal State to have jurisdiction and control over adjacent continental shelf resources, since its co-operation was needed for them to be conserved or exploited; since the shelf might be regarded as an extension of its land-mass; since these resources might be an extension of a pool or deposit already lying within its territory; and since self-protection made it necessary for the coastal State to keep a close watch over offshore activities. This was not the expression of a belief in the existence of a *legal* necessity imposed by current law: it was, rather, an assertion of political necessity and reasonableness. But as a means of attempting to persuade other States to accept this new claim, it was prudent to proceed in this manner. In short, *opinio necessitatis* in this sense can play a part in the law-creating process, even though extra-legal necessity and reasonableness are not themselves sufficient to make law. It is, however, important to stress that an alleged rule is not law just because it is (alleged to be) socially necessary: here be the lions (as maps used to say) of natural law[76] and policy-oriented jurisprudence.[77]

(*c*) Returning to strict law, though, the concept of *opinio juris* is of some use in helping us distinguish rules which are legally binding from those which are not. This is not a phenomenon confined to custom, but is found in international agreements as well. It is well known that the Final Act of the Helsinki Conference on Security and Co-operation in Europe was not intended to be legally binding as such.[78] There are in fact many other examples of non-binding international agreements.[79] But the distinction is particularly useful in the context of customary law, and it is here that the concept of *opinio juris* (or something similar) can be of assistance. The Court itself referred to this function in the *North Sea Continental Shelf* cases.[80] It will be helpful, however, to analyse this function rather more closely. In doing so, it is submitted that it is useful to think of this criterion as a means of distinguishing, not so much (or only) one class of rules from another, but those precedents which *count* towards the formation of law from those which do not.

(i) First, there are those practices which, although regularly observed, might be said to fall into a class of actions which can *not* give rise to

[76] For a thoughtful account of a possible limited return to a natural law approach, cf. Dominicé, 'Le grand retour au droit naturel en droit des gens', in *Mélanges en l'honneur de Jacques-Michel Grossen* (1992), p. 399.

[77] Gihl also rightly points out that by no means all new customary rules come into being out of a common sense of necessity or reasonableness—power politics also plays a part: *Scandinavian Studies in Law*, 1 (1957), pp. 51, 81.

[78] *International Legal Materials*, 14 (1975), p. 1292.

[79] See, e.g., Aust, 'The Theory and Practice of Informal International Instruments', *International and Comparative Law Quarterly*, 35 (1986), p. 787.

[80] *ICJ Reports*, 1969, p. 3, at p. 44, para. 77.

customary obligations: for example, sending condolences on the death of a head of State. It might seem inevitable that these rules of etiquette should not be considered legally obligatory; but given the importance which has been attached to protocol in other times and other societies, it is not entirely axiomatic.[81] If forced to explain why these practices amount merely to comity, we would probably say that it is generally *believed* in the international community that they do not give rise to legal obligations (a sort of *opinio non juris*), or—to put it differently—no-one *claims* performance of these duties as a matter of legal right. But the truth is that the absence of legal obligation *in such a context* is regarded as self-evident, just as, in municipal law, social invitations are treated as self-evidently not a matter for legal regulation.[82]

(ii) Secondly, there are cases where the usage is of such a nature that it could perfectly well give rise to legal rights and duties, but it happens not to do so because of a common belief that such is the case (again, the *opinio non juris*) or, to put it differently, because such claims are never made. A frequently-cited example is the exemption from customs duties of goods imported for the personal use of diplomats. Article 36 of the Vienna Convention on Diplomatic Relations 1961 shows that this exemption is perfectly capable of being the subject of legal regulation; but before the adoption of the Convention the exemption was regarded as being merely a matter of comity.[83]

(iii) Thirdly, there are the disclaimer cases. Here we have acts of State practice which would be perfectly capable of creating precedents which could in the future be invoked against the State performing the act or against others, but for an accompanying statement of the government concerned that it is, for example, making payment *ex gratia* or without prejudice. Here it is perhaps not very useful to talk in terms of belief, but rather in the language of claims: indeed, the natural term to describe this type of conduct is dis*claim*er.

(iv) Fourthly, there are those cases where the conduct in question is *ambiguous*; here the language of *opinio juris* is commonly employed, not least by the International Court, to explain why it is that it does not

[81] Quadri, 'Cours général du droit international public', *Recueil des cours*, 113 (1964–III), p. 237, at p. 328, seems mistaken when he says that the distinction between legal usages and rules of mere comity depends on the relative importance of the subject-matter.

[82] This seems to meet Akehurst's point (loc. cit. above (n. 62), at p. 34) that States do not normally issue disclaimers about the obligatoriness of this kind of conduct.

[83] Reference may also be made here to the observation of the ICJ in the *Nicaragua* case (*Merits*), to the effect that precedents ostensibly contrary to the principle of non-intervention should not count if the evidence suggested that States were not so acting under a claim of right; and *a fortiori* if they accept the legal rule, but seek to justify their conduct on other grounds: *ICJ Reports*, 1986, pp. 14, 98 (para. 186) and 109 (para. 207).

count as a precedent. Conduct which is not clearly referable to an existing or potential legal rule should not count.

(a) One such case is *omissions*. The present author has sought to show elsewhere that omissions are perfectly capable, if they are sufficiently unambiguous, of constituting acts of State practice.[84] But even though it is possible for such omissions to count, in many cases the evidence is more ambiguous. Take, for example, the *'Lotus'* case.[85] There, France argued that the rarity of prosecutions for collisions on the high seas (other than by the flag State of the ship on board which the wrongful act took place) was evidence of an obligation not to institute such prosecutions. The Permanent Court disagreed, on the ground that there was no evidence of a 'conscious-[ness] of having a duty to abstain'. What it seems to have been saying is this. There are all sorts of possible reasons why a State might refrain from prosecution in such a case. One possibility, admittedly, is that customary international law prohibits it. But there may be other reasons: for example, lack of jurisdiction under *municipal* law, lack of interest, or a belief that the courts of the flag State are a more convenient forum. In the absence of evidence that those who refrained from prosecuting did so by reference to perceived constraints of an international legal kind, the omissions simply do not count as precedents. In other words, the conduct was too ambiguous in the absence of evidence of *opinio juris*.[86]

(b) Omissions are not the only kind of ambiguous conduct, however. Another occurred in the *North Sea Continental Shelf* cases.[87] There, it will be recalled, the alternative argument of Denmark and the Netherlands was that, even if Article 6 of the Geneva Convention on the Continental Shelf 1958 did not embody pre-existing customary law or crystallize an emerging rule, State practice had grown up since 1958 along the same lines, so that a new rule of customary international law had come into being. In support of this contention they referred to a number of bilateral treaties whereby the continental shelf had been apportioned on the basis of equidistance. The International Court of Justice rejected this contention, relying

[84] Loc. cit. above (n. 3). For example, State A does something which gives rise to protests by other States on legal grounds. Henceforth, it does not perform such acts, even though this is inconvenient; and there is no evidence that it is desisting merely *ex gratia* or because it is simply yielding to extra-legal pressure. In such circumstances, it is submitted that it is reasonable to count, not only the other States' protests, but also State A's omission, as a precedent or precedents vindicating the rule in question.

[85] *PCIJ*, Series A, No. 10, at p. 28. Cf. the dissenting opinion of Judge Nyholm, pp. 59 and 60.

[86] It may be noted in passing that here, the language of claims is less appropriate.

[87] *ICJ Reports*, 1969, p. 3.

once again (amongst other things) on the notion of *opinio juris*.[88] What the Court was apparently saying was the following. Yes, one of the conceivable reasons why States might decide to delimit their overlapping continental shelf on the basis of equidistance is the existence of a legal obligation necessitating it. But there are other possible explanations. For example, to divide a resource equally is an obvious common-sense way of settling a dispute over entitlement; but just because two States decide to 'go halves', this does not necessarily mean that either of them thought that this was the limit of its entitlement, or that it was obliged to determine the matter in this way. The conduct, in short, was ambiguous, and in such cases it will only be if there is an accompanying *opinio juris* or, to put it in different words, an unambiguous claim and response based on international law, that the conduct in question will count as a precedent.[89]

The uses of *opinio juris* which have been identified so far[90] essentially concern the *dis*qualification of certain forms of State practice as rule-creating precedents, because of an *opinio non juris* or a disclaimer, or because of the ambiguity of the conduct in question. But these are all special, and comparatively unusual, cases. In particular, they do not tell

[88] The Court found that over half of the States which had delimited on the basis of equidistance were already, or were shortly to become, parties to the Geneva Convention on the Continental Shelf. Their practice could therefore be discounted, as they had a treaty obligation so to act. It went on:

> 'As regards those States, on the other hand, which were not, and have not become parties to the Convention, the basis of their action can only be problematical and must remain entirely speculative. . . . [N]o inference could justifiably be drawn that they believed themselves to be applying a mandatory rule of customary international law. . . . The essential point in this connection . . . is that even if these instances of action by non-parties to the Convention were much more numerous than they in fact are, they would not, even in the aggregate, suffice in themselves to constitute the *opinio juris*.'

(Ibid., at pp. 43–4, paras. 76–7.)

[89] Indeed, the *North Sea Continental Shelf* cases offer us another example of ambiguity. Before it came to consider whether a new rule of customary international law had come into being, the ICJ had to consider whether Art. 6 of the Convention on the Continental Shelf codified an existing customary rule making equidistance the starting-point. The article might have done so, but not necessarily—yet another type of ambiguity. To resolve it, the Court looked at what the drafters of the Convention, and particularly the International Law Commission, *believed* to be the state of existing customary law. And, as is well known, the Court rejected the contention on the grounds that the Commission had included the provision as a measure of progressive development of the law, rather than as an expression of what it believed to be *lex lata* or inherent in the concept of the continental shelf: ibid., pp. 32–6, paras. 47–56.

One further use of *opinio juris* to resolve ambiguities may be mentioned here, though a full exploration is beyond the scope of the present article. As a general rule, resolutions of the UN General Assembly are not binding in and of themselves; and whilst they may articulate existing customary law, they do not necessarily do so. In determining which is the case, it is necessary to examine the circumstances surrounding the adoption of the resolution, including the votes and the explanations of vote. Cf., e.g., Brownlie, op. cit. above (n. 62), p. 15.

[90] Leaving aside dubious explanations of a Savignian type or appeals to social necessity and suchlike.

us whether, in the more typical instance of a constant and uniform practice by many States, unopposed by others including those directly affected by the practice, it is necessary to demonstrate some sort of *opinio juris*. Of course, in such a case it might be relatively easy to infer the existence of the subjective element from the practice, if one so desired. But this begs the question why it is necessary to look for it at all.[91]

Opinio juris might be invoked as the explanation of why States conform to an established customary rule. If, for example, a new State instructs its military aircraft to respect the airspace of others in time of peace, we may, if we wish, explain this in terms of an *opinio juris*. It should, however, be noted that this explanation is in a sense superfluous: all we are really saying is that the State follows the practice because it is the law. But this would be true of the observance of the State's treaty obligations also: it obeys the law because it is the law. Here the concept of *opinio juris* is being used as part of a general theory of legal obligation—and possibly not a very useful part, because it seems tautologous.

But in any case, it should be noted that this last instance concerned cases of *established* customary law. The concept of *opinio juris*, as traditionally formulated, is definitely unhelpful when it comes to the creation of *new* rules of customary international law. For if the practice is a new one involving a departure from (and breach of) previous law, as with the Truman Proclamation regarding the continental shelf, how can the State concerned possibly entertain the opinion that it is acting in accordance with the law?[92] As Kelsen pointed out, in theory one might try to circumvent this difficulty by saying that the State is acting in error; but this is plainly improbable in the case of the United States in that case, and in most other instances, too. Kelsen himself dismissed the suggestion as implausible,[93] though other supporters of the *opinio juris* approach have from time to time been tempted by it.[94] The truth is that the State which introduces a new practice has in these cases no belief that its conduct is permitted or required by existing law, and neither have the first States to respond positively or negatively to its conduct. No *opinio juris*, then, but a *claim* and the acceptance of a claim—express in the case of the Truman Proclamation, and implicit in some other instances where

[91] There is a good deal of truth in Brownlie's observation (op. cit. above (n. 62), p. 7) that 'The essential problem is surely one of proof, and especially the incidence of the burden of proof'.

[92] A difficult and controversial passage in the Digest, attributed to Celsus, raises this issue: D.1.3.39.

[93] 'Théorie du droit coutumier', *Revue internationale de la théorie du droit (NS)*, 1 (1939), pp. 253, 263.

[94] Stern attempts to resurrect this notion by saying that 'Il suffit parfois de croire à l'amour pour qu'il existe' (loc. cit. above (n. 14), p. 487). But this charming analogy is misleading: States are far more calculating (even) than lovers, and usually better-informed.

States simply act by initiating conduct or by responding to the conduct of others.[95]

Thus, we have found that *opinio juris* is helpful in resolving some problems and explaining some answers the law gives; but it is far from providing an answer in all—or even the normal—cases. In particular, it provides an explanation—if one is needed—as to why certain types of precedent do not count, and a somewhat tautologous explanation of obedience to established customary rules. But, in particular, it does not provide a very helpful explanation of the *creation* of these rules. In this regard, it is in a sense the mirror image of the voluntarist approach, which adequately explains the inception of the process by which new rules are created, but does not really help us understand how it is that they come to bind non-participants. Both approaches offer a partial, but not a complete, solution.

A Synthesis or an Alternative Hypothesis?

Given that both the voluntarist and the *opinio juris* approaches have their deficiencies and that each offers at best a partial explanation of the creation and existence of customary rules, it may at first sight seem tempting to attempt a synthesis, for example by arguing that, whilst the voluntarist thesis is the better approach to the question of the *formation* of customary rules, the approach which emphasizes belief better explains why mature customary rules are observed.[96] Up to a point it is certainly helpful to distinguish between different stages in the formation of customary law: for instance, whilst States may believe themselves bound by an *established* customary rule, the State which first engages in a new practice can hardly be said to share this belief.[97] But the approach is hardly a panacea.

For one thing, custom-creation and custom-application are not entirely alternative categories: the customary process is a continuing one, where every act which conforms to an established practice helps to strengthen it, and every act which violates it helps to undermine it.[98] In other words, at the mature stage of a customary rule, practice is constitutive as well as evidential. Another objection is that, as has been

[95] As Judge Lachs observed in his dissenting opinion in the *North Sea Continental Shelf* cases, to postulate otherwise is to resort to a legal fiction, and to require a conviction that the conduct is already a matter of legal obligation is to deny the possibility of developing new rules of customary law: *ICJ Reports*, 1969, pp. 218, 231.

[96] Cf. Fitzmaurice, 'The General Principles of International Law Considered from the Standpoint of the Rule of Law', *Recueil des cours*, 92 (1957–II), pp. 1, 98–9, 103; MacGibbon, loc. cit. above (n. 39), pp. 115, 137.

[97] For elaborate forms of stages analysis, cf. Bos, *A Methodology of International Law* (1984), and Van Hoof, *Rethinking the Sources of International Law* (1983).

[98] Unless the violation is objected to, in which case the violation is in a sense neutralized. If the objection is successful, the rule is actually strengthened.

argued above, consent is a *sufficient* (even if not a necessary) basis of obligation at *all* stages. Thirdly, and more importantly, the problem is not so much the initiation of a customary rule or the reasons for obeying it when it is mature. Rather, the difficulty is with the intermediate stage. After a limited number of important actors have initiated a practice (whether by originating it, imitating it, or 'genuinely acquiescing'), what effects the transformation (which undoubtedly occurs) from particular law to general law binding even the passive bystander? As has been argued above, to say that the magic ingredient is consent is possible only by the use of fictions and presumptions which in fact negative (at least to some extent) the idea of consent. And yet, at this intermediate stage, it may well be premature to speak of an *opinio juris*.[99]

One way of dealing with this difficulty is to ignore it. Often, the 'consumer' of legal rules does not need to know when the fruit ripened, but simply whether it is ripe when he comes to eat it, or is still too hard or sour to eat.[100] Indeed (to change the metaphor), to ask a follower of fashion at what point exactly something became the mode is in a sense to miss the point of informal rule-systems.[100a] Secondly, it can be pointed out that, in practical terms, there is often little to choose between the two

[99] It is interesting to note, however, that if a synthesis of the two approaches is desired, this would be consistent with the use of the words 'a general practice accepted as law' in Article 38(1)(*b*) of the Statute. The 'acceptance' might be consent in some cases, and in others an acknowledgment that something is already the law—an acknowledgement, incidentally, that need not come from States alone, but could emanate from a tribunal, for instance.

[100] For a somewhat different approach, based on the idea of 'crystallization', see Thirlway, loc. cit. above (n. 12), pp. 93–6.

[100a] The efforts of Crawford and Viles to determine the state of international law on the day after the Truman Proclamations on the continental shelf and coastal fisheries highlight (as they intend) the difficulty of determining the exact status of customary rule at certain (but, it is submitted, not all) stages of its evolution: 'International Law on a Given Day', in *Völkerrecht zwischen normativen Anspruch und politischer Realität: Festschrift für Karl Zemanek zum 65. Geburtstag* (1994), p. 45. It seems, however, that they exaggerate some of the difficulties, and that the elaborate investigation does not ultimately advance the discussion of the problem of *opinio juris* beyond the point at which it was left by previous writings. Thus, to say (at p. 67) that the United States' *opinio juris* about its new claim to the continental shelf was not that it already was the law, but simply that it should become the law in the future, is a well-known response to the question how it could have believed that what it was doing was permissible under existing law, when manifestly it was not. But this is rather far from the normal signification of the phrase *opinio juris*, and in addition begs the question why we need to have recourse to the notion of *opinio juris* at all in such a case. Neither is it helpful to invoke the maxim *ex injuria jus non oritur* in order to cast doubt on how the Truman Proclamation could have given rise to new law (ibid.). The existing law of the sea on this subject (as on most others) was *jus dispositivum*, which means that States were free both to vary it by treaty and to replace it with new customary rules by means of recognition, acquiescence and imitation. Finally, to say that how a court might have answered a question about the continental shelf on the day after the Proclamation 'would have depended, *inter alia*, on the wisdom of the Court' seems a little vague, even if possible responses are suggested: are the authors saying that a court would have had a discretion, or simply that some judges are more adept at finding the right answer than others? They may also exaggerate the degree to which this question was an open one for the hypothetical court on the date selected: even in the light of the copious background material which they deploy, it is hard to see how any reasonable court could have upheld the United States' claim before there had been any clear acceptance or concordant practice by other States, and when *ex hypothesi* the other party to the ligitation, in particular, had not accepted it.

approaches. Whether or not an inactive State is said to be bound by an *opinio juris generalis*, or by a consent which is presumed, is to some extent a matter of taste. Another avoidance technique is to emphasize the discretion of the judge in deciding on the existence and extent of the customary rule.[101] There is undoubtedly a good deal of truth in such an approach. And yet, judges are supposed to apply the law, not make it; and, in any case, as already observed, the chances of a dispute coming before an international tribunal are, in the absence of compulsory jurisdiction, small. If no such tribunal is available, it is somewhat unsatisfactory (though perhaps realistic up to a point) to say that the question whether there is a customary rule is left to the auto-interpretation of States.

In short, neither an amalgam of the two interpretations of the subjective element, nor avoidance techniques, wholly solve the problem. It is time to consider a different approach.

In the present author's submission, and contrary to the prevailing orthodoxy, it is unnecessary, either in theory or (particularly) in practice, to seek proof of *opinio juris*, any more than it is necessary to prove consent, in all cases. It is of course true that the International Court has on several occasions solemnly said that *opinio juris* is one of the two elements of custom (the other being practice). But first of all, in most of these cases there was some ambiguity or other uncertainty in the practice, so that *opinio juris* was a necessary tool in resolving the uncertainty in those particular circumstances. (See, for example, the omissions in the *Lotus* case,[102] or the equivocal bilateral delimitation treaties in *North Sea Continental Shelf*.[103]) This is not true of the *Libya/Malta* case,[104] but the reference there is easily explained away: the Court was expounding why it could not rely on the Law of the Sea Convention as such (it not being in force), and the point could have been made without recourse to the notion of *opinio juris*. That leaves only the *Nicaragua* case (*Merits*), where the Court's insistence on the two elements was put in general terms.[105]

[101] Cf., e.g., H. Lauterpacht, *The Development of International Law by the International Court* (1958), pp. 368–93; Sørensen, *Les sources du droit international* (1946), p. 24.

[102] *PCIJ*, Series A, No. 10, at p. 28.

[103] *ICJ Reports*, 1969, p. 3, at p. 44, paras. 76–8.

[104] Ibid., 1985, p. 13, at pp. 29–30, para. 27.

[105] The key references to the need for the subjective element are the following:

'183. [T]he Court has next to consider what are the rules of customary international law applicable to the present dispute. For this purpose, it has to direct its attention to the practice and *opinio juris* of States; as the Court recently observed,

> "It is of course axiomatic that the material of customary international is to be looked for primarily in the actual practice and *opinio juris* of States, even though multilateral conventions may have an important role to play in recording and defining rules deriving from custom, or indeed in developing them" [citing the above-mentioned *Libya/Malta* case].

But in fact, in their context the pronoucements in question are probably not fundamentally inconsistent with the thesis presented in this article.

In this respect, the Court must not lose sight of the Charter of the United Nations and that of the [Organization of American States], notwithstanding the operation of the multilateral treaty reservation. Although the Court has no jurisdiction to determine whether the conduct of the United States constitutes a breach of those conventions, it can and must take them into account in ascertaining the content of the customary international law which the United States is also alleged to have infringed.

184. The Court notes that there is in fact evidence . . . of a considerable degree of agreement between the Parties as to the content of the customary international law relating to the non-use of force and non-intervention. This concurrence of their views does not however dispense the Court from having itself to ascertain what rules of customary international law are applicable. The mere fact that States declare their recognition of certain rules is not sufficient for the Court to consider these as being part of customary international law, and as applicable as such to those States. Bound as it is by Article 38 of its Statute to apply, *inter alia*, international custom "as evidence of a general practice accepted as law", the Court may not disregard the essential role played by general practice. Where two States agree to incorporate a particular rule in a treaty, their agreement suffices to make that rule a legal one, binding upon them; but in the field of customary international law, the shared view of the Parties as to the content of what they regard as the rule is not enough. The Court must satisfy itself that the existence of the rule in the *opinio juris* is confirmed by practice.

185. . . . [I]n the present case, apart from the treaty commitments binding the Parties to the rules in question, there are various instances of their having expressed recognition of the validity thereof as customary international law in other ways. It is therefore in the light of this "subjective element"—the expression used by the Court in its 1969 Judgment in the *North Sea Continental Shelf* cases (*ICJ Reports 1969*, p. 44)—that the Court has to appraise the relevant practice.' (*ICJ Reports*, 1986, pp. 14, 97–8.)

'188. The Court thus finds that both Parties take the view that the principles as to the use of force incorporated into the United Nations Charter correspond, in essentials, to those found in customary international law. . . . The Court has however to be satisfied that there exists in customary international law an *opinio juris* as to the binding character of such abstention. This *opinio juris* may, though with all due caution, be deduced from, *inter alia*, the attitude of the Parties and the attitude of States towards certain General Assembly resolutions, and particularly resolution 2625 (XXV) entitled "Declaration on Principles of International Law concerning Friendly Relations and Co-operation among States in accordance with the Charter of the United Nations". The effect of consent to the text of such resolutions cannot be understood as merely that of a "reiteration or elucidation" of the treaty commitment undertaken in the Charter. On the contrary, it may be understood as an acceptance of the validity of the rule or set of rules declared by the resolution by themselves. . . . It would therefore seem apparent that the attitude referred to expresses an *opinio juris* respecting such rule (or set of rules), to be thenceforth treated separately from the provisions, especially those of an institutional kind, to which it is subject on the treaty-law plane of the Charter.' (Ibid., pp. 99–100.)

'202. . . . Expressions of an *opinio juris* regarding the existence of the principle of non-intervention in customary international law are numerous and not difficult to find. Of course, statements whereby States avow their recognition of the principles of international law set forth in the United Nations Charter cannot strictly be interpreted as applying to the principle of non-intervention . . . since this principle is not, as such, spelt out in the Charter. But it was never intended that the Charter should embody written confirmation of every essential principle of international law in force. The existence in the *opinio juris* of the principle of non-intervention is backed by established and substantial practice. . . . ' (Ibid., p. 106.)

'207. In considering the instance of [foreign intervention in support of forces opposed to their government], the Court has to emphasize that, as was observed in the *North Sea Continental Shelf* cases, for a new customary rule to be formed, not only must the acts concerned "amount to a settled practice", but they must be accompanied by the *opinio juris sive necessitatis*. Either the States taking such action or other States in a position to react to it, must have behaved so that their conduct is

"evidence of a belief that this practice is rendered obligatory by the existence of a rule of law requiring it. The need for such a belief, i.e., the existence of a subjective element, is implicit in the very notion of the *opinio juris sive necessitatis*" (*ICJ Reports 1969*), p. 44, para. 77.)'
(Ibid., pp. 108–9.)

In so far as the Court was relying on what it regarded as acceptance of the relevant principles as customary law by the parties and others, it has already been submitted that acceptance is a sufficient condition for a practice to constitute a rule of customary law. And in so far as it used the concept of *opinio juris* to explain why certain apparent departures from the non-intervention rule did not really undermine it, because the purported justifications were given either in terms of the rule, or on non-legal grounds, this is compatible with what has been said above about the role of *opinio juris*—and especially of *opinio non juris*—in helping to determine what practice counts towards the formation of custom. To put it differently, it is a matter of deciding what is being *claimed* in a legal context. The only passage which cannot so easily be explained away is the above-quoted paragraph 202; but even there the instances cited by the Court constituted either practice or a recognition of the binding force of the rule. Note also that the rules in question entailed *abstention* (cf. the *Lotus* case). And in any case, it seems fair to point out that the Court's handling of custom in that case has been criticized, with varying degrees of severity, both in separate and dissenting opinions, and in the literature.[106] And, leaving these rather special cases aside, we find that, where there is a well-established practice, the Court and other international tribunals, not to mention States themselves, tend to conclude that there is a customary rule without looking for proof of *opinio juris* (or any other subjective element), whether individual or general, at any rate overtly. They have simply relied on the practice.[107] The cases are indeed legion in which these bodies have simply asserted that such-and-such

[106] The principal criticisms of the Court's use of customary law in that case are as follows: (1) It dealt unsatisfactorily with the question whether the customary law was 'subsumed and supervened' by the Charter and other treaties. (2) Although clearly indicating that there are two separate elements of customary law, the Court appears to have 'double-counted' General Assembly resolutions and participation in treaties as evidence both of practice and of *opinio juris*. (3) It dealt unsatisfactorily with the question whether and how far participation in, and practice under, a treaty counts towards the formation or evidencing of customary law. (4) It is questionable whether some of the treaties and resolutions relied on by the Court in fact supported the conclusions it drew from them. See the separate opinion of Judge Ago, ibid., pp. 181, 183–4; and the dissenting opinions of Judges Oda (pp. 212, 215–19), Schwebel (pp. 259, 302–6) and Jennings (pp. 528, 529–37). Criticisms in the literature include Charlesworth, 'Customary International Law and the Nicaragua Case', *Australian Yearbook of International Law*, 11 (1984–7), p. 1; D'Amato, 'Trashing Customary International Law', *American Journal of International Law*, 81(1987), p. 101; Panel discussion, 'The Jurisprudence of the Court in the Nicaragua Decision', *Proceedings of the American Society of International Law*, 81 (1987), p. 258; Thirlway, loc. cit. above (n. 12), pp. 46–50; and Mendelson, 'The *Nicaragua* Case and Customary International Law', *Coexistence*, 26(1989), p. 85 (also reprinted in Butler (ed.), *The Non-Use of Force in International Law* (1989), p. 85).

[107] e.g. *Fisheries* case, *ICJ Reports*, 1949, pp. 116, 128 (low- as opposed to high-water mark the starting point for measurement of the territorial sea); *Nottebohm* case (*Second Phase*), ibid., 1955, pp. 4, 23 (definition of nationality); *Barcelona Traction* case, ibid., 1970, pp. 3, 42 (para. 70, attribution of nationality to corporations); *Continental Shelf (Libya/Malta)* case, ibid., 1985, pp. 13, 33 (para. 34—exclusive economic zone now a part of customary law).

is the rule, without explicit reference to either of the famous two elements.[108] In short, in standard cases there is often no real search for *opinio juris* (or, if it comes to that, consent): the subjective element is superfluous. It only comes into its own if evidence of consent happens to be forthcoming (it being a sufficient condition); or if the circumstances are such as to suggest that the precedents should perhaps not count (because of the general context, ambiguity, or disclaimers); or (probably) where the State whom it is sought to bind can show that it was a persistent objector.

In its broad outlines, the submission that the subjective element is superfluous is not a new one: it was made over fifty years ago by Kelsen,[109] Guggenheim[110] and Kopelmanas.[111] But Kelsen[112] and Guggenheim[113] later recanted (at least to some extent), seemingly because of the need to find a criterion for distinguishing comity from law. Perhaps that recantation was premature and unnecessary. Provided that we allow a limited and exceptional role for the subjective element in the way previously outlined, there seems to be no particular reason why it should be looked for in the standard, run-of-the-mill case.

Summary and Conclusions

1. A State's consent to a rule will be a sufficient explanation of its being bound by it, and its refusal at the formative stage of a rule a reason why it is (probably) *not* bound. But the voluntarist approach does not provide a satisfactory explanation of the whole of customary law. In particular, it does not provide a convincing reason why States who have not truly participated in the formation of a rule should be bound by it—though undoubtedly they are.

2. *Opinio juris sive necessitatis*, for its part, is a phrase of dubious provenance and uncertain meaning. The concept was originally used by the historical school of jurisprudence to explain the content of substantive national law, and was transferred to the context of international law around the turn of the present century. It does have a role to perform

[108] See, for example, the *Corfu Channel* case (*Merits*), *ICJ Reports*, 1949, pp. 4, 22; *Nicaragua* case (*Merits*), ibid., 1986, pp. 14, 113–14 (para. 218—elementary considerations of humanity); ibid., p. 94 (para. 176, proportionality and necessity); ibid., p. 111 (para. 212, sovereignty over air space); *Barcelona Traction* case (*Second Phase*), ibid., 1970, pp. 3, 32 (para. 33—duties of host States). In several cases, the Court did not even expressly identify the rule as one of *customary* law.

The author acknowledges the contribution of Dr Stephen Neff, of Edinburgh University, in identifying some of the instances cited in this and the preceding footnote.

[109] Loc. cit. above (n. 93).

[110] 'Les deux éléments de la coutume en droit international', in *Les techniques et les principes du droit public: Etudes en honneur de G. Scelle* (1950), vol. 1, p. 275.

[111] 'Custom as a Means of the Creation of International Law', this *Year Book*, 18 (1937), p. 127.

[112] *General Theory of Law and State* (1949), p. 114.

[113] *Traité de droit international public*, vol. 1 (2nd edn., 1967), pp. 104–5.

in explaining why certain types of conduct constitute mere comity or otherwise do not count as precedents. It is not certain, however, that these functions could not be as well or better performed by using the language of claim and response.

3. In any case, there seems analytically to be no particular reason to insist on proof of the presence of *opinio juris* in the standard type of case, where there is a constant, uniform and unambiguous practice of sufficient generality, clearly taking place in a legal context and unaccompanied by disclaimers, with no evidence of opposition at the time of the rule's formation by the State which it is sought to burden with the customary obligation, or by another State or group of States sufficiently important to have prevented a general rule coming into existence at all.

The adoption of the present thesis would bring doctrine more into line with the practice of States and of international tribunals than the mechanical repetition of the necessity of the two elements. As a matter of theory, too, it is submitted that this approach could be justified in terms of the creation of legitimate expectations. This is not the place for a complete explanation of this author's theory of legitimate expectations, which underlie the sources of international law. Perhaps it will suffice for the present to say that if a State actually consents to a rule, a legitimate expectation will be created that it will comply with it, just as a disclaimer or persistent dissent at the appropriate time will prevent such an expectation being created. And where there is a constant and uniform practice of sufficient generality, in a legal context, it seems legitimate for members of the community to expect all others to continue to observe that practice. And finally, as a matter of policy, the solution proposed seems a reasonable one. If a relevant practice is sufficiently widespread, it ought to become law, because otherwise the convoy will have to move at the pace of the slowest. To require proof of consent—or even *opinio juris* on the part of each and every State—seems excessive and unnecessary. At the same time, the sovereignty and the reasonable interests of States can be safeguarded. If a sufficient number of like-minded States object to a new practice, they can prevent its ever becoming general law. And in addition, the individual State can individually opt out, at the formative stage, by becoming a persistent objector. By these means, customary law can continue to make a useful contribution to the formation of international law; and given that the treaty process has disadvantages as well as advantages, it is essential that custom continues to make that contribution.

THE EUROPEAN CONVENTION ON HUMAN RIGHTS AND ITS 'DEMOCRATIC SOCIETY'*

By SUSAN MARKS‡

The European Convention on Human Rights famously recites in its Preamble that the fundamental freedoms it takes to be the 'foundation of justice and peace in the world' are 'best maintained on the one hand by an effective political democracy and on the other by . . . observance of the human rights upon which they depend'. As with many preambles, the peremptory language no doubt belied a complex mixture of history, ideology, aspiration and cant. But it also touched on issues—about the relationship between rights and freedoms and democracy, and about the defining features of an 'effective political democracy'—that have framed the law of the Convention in enduring ways. In what follows, the writer explores evolving perceptions of the Convention's relationship with democracy,[1] and seeks to identify, and draw out some of the implications of, the image of democracy upon which those perceptions rest.

In addressing these themes, it will first be instructive to examine, by reference to both drafting debates and case law, the Convention's encounter with democracy over three areas. Section I will survey some generalized indications concerning democracy. It will highlight in particular those rights and freedoms which have been marked out as expressions, or essential concomitants, of democracy. Democracy is also assumed to justify limitations on individual rights and freedoms for the

‡ Lecturer, Faculty of Law, University of Cambridge; Fellow, Emmanuel College, Cambridge.

[1] See further on this subject O. Jacot-Guillarmod, 'The Relationship Between Democracy and Human Rights', in *Democracy and Human Rights*, Proceedings of a Colloquy organized by the Government of Greece and the Council of Europe (Kehl: N. P. Engel, 1987), p. 43, along with other contributions to the same volume. See also J. G. Merrills, *The Development of International Law by the European Court of Human Rights* (Manchester: Manchester University Press, 2nd edn., 1993); P. Vegleris, 'La Fonction de la notion de 'démocratie' dans le texte de la Convention européenne des droits de l'homme', in *Der Missbrauch von Grundrechten in der Demokratie* (Baden-Baden: Nomos Verlagsgesellschaft, 1989), p. 61; F. Ost, 'The Original Canons of Interpretation of the European Court of Human Rights', in M. Delmas-Marty (ed.), *The European Convention for the Protection of Human Rights: International Protection Versus National Restrictions* (Dordrecht: Kluwer Academic Publishers, 1992), p. 283; and M. Delmas-Marty, 'The Richness of Underlying Reasoning', in M. Delmas-Marty (ed.), *The European Convention for the Protection of Human Rights: International Protection Versus National Restrictions* (Dordrecht: Kluwer Academic Publishers, 1992), p. 319. For illuminating discussions of the relationship between human rights generally and democracy, and between international law generally and democracy, see respectively A. Rosas, 'Democracy and Human Rights', in A. Rosas and J. Helgesen (eds.), *Human Rights in a Changing East-West Perspective* (London and New York: Pinter Publishers, 1990), p. 17; and J. Crawford, 'Democracy and International Law', this *Year Book*, 64 (1993), p. 113.

common good or to protect more compelling rights of others. Thus, the Convention in a number of provisions permits limitations where 'necessary in a democratic society'. Section II will investigate the implications of this assumption for the Convention, and the understanding of 'democratic' necessity that has informed Convention case law. The Western liberal conception of a 'democratic society' gives a pre-eminent place to elections, and yet electoral rights were not included in the Convention. It was not until two years after the Convention had been adopted that electoral guarantees were provided in the First Protocol, Article 3. Section III will examine the controversy in the drafting debates surrounding electoral rights, and will consider the scope and limits of the First Protocol, Article 3.

For several decades Western societies have seen calls for a more participatory, more substantial, more far-reaching kind of democracy than that which is currently the norm. Section IV will draw together the various elements in the first three sections, to assess what image of a 'democratic society' they add up to. It will be suggested that the image is largely, though not entirely, unresponsive to these demands. Finally, section V will address the debate concerning the 'globalization' of democracy. Against a background of broadening adherence to the Convention, this last section will seek to highlight the role the Convention does, and could, play in this 'globalization' process.

I. 'Democratic' Rights and Freedoms

The Convention is, of course, a product of the immediate post-War era. For the framers democracy was given a vivid significance, in the contrast with recent, personal, experiences of 'fascism, hitlerism, communism'.[2] A bold line distinguished the democratic 'we' from the totalitarian 'they',[3] and a major, perhaps the major, aim of the Convention was now to keep things that way. The French delegate Pierre-Henri Teitgen put the point forcefully:

> We are less concerned to set up a European judicial authority capable of righting isolated wrongs, isolated illegal acts committed in our countries, than to prevent, from the outset, the setting up in one or other of these countries of a regime of the Fascist or Nazi type.[4]

Thus, the Convention was to 'prevent a rebirth of totalitarianism',[5] to 'defend our peoples against dictatorship',[6] and to 'strengthen the resis-

[2] Council of Europe, *Collected Edition of the 'Travaux Préparatoires' of the European Convention on Human Rights* (hereafter *Travaux*), vol. 1, p. 40 (Teitgen).

[3] See, e.g., *Travaux*, vol. 2, p. 90 (Sweetman).

[4] *Travaux*, vol. 5, p. 294.

[5] *Travaux*, vol. 1, p. 192 (Teitgen).

[6] *Travaux*, vol. 5, p. 332 (Hedlund).

tance in all our countries against insidious attempts to undermine our way of life'.[7] More positively, and in so far as 'we' were concerned, the Convention was to 'define and guarantee the political basis of this association of European nations',[8] to 'ensure that the States of the Members of the Council of Europe are democratic, and remain democratic',[9] and to set forth a 'code of law for the democracies'.[10] The Convention was to do these things by providing a collective guarantee, if not of all pertinent rights and freedoms, then at least of those deemed 'essential for a democratic way of life'.[11]

From this perspective, the Convention, the additional Protocols and the entire corpus of Strasbourg case law can be seen as articulating the scope and limits of democracy. If rights and freedoms are to be protected in so far as they safeguard the 'democratic way of life', then the boundaries of the protection granted will reflect (without necessarily being fully co-extensive with) the boundaries of democracy. Purely institutional stipulations[12] may be an exception, though even these may be seen to play a part in the articulation inasmuch as they affect the character of review of national law and practice, and hence the protection ultimately afforded to rights and freedoms. On the other hand, it would be neither feasible nor helpful here to re-state Convention law in its entirety. Instead, two lines of enquiry will be pursued, the first investigating some of the ways in which the Convention organs characterize democracy generally; the second investigating the rights and freedoms identified in Convention jurisprudence as especially vital to democracy. In this way it may be possible to build up an illustrative picture at least of some of the key features of the conception of democracy that informs the Convention.

A striking—if, in the light of the drafting debates, unsurprising—feature of the Convention organs' early jurisprudence is that, when democracy was evoked, it was evoked in terms of a starkly drawn contrast with 'totalitarianism'. Thus, for instance, democratic societies which strayed from the Convention were said to be in danger of '[sliding] imperceptibly towards totalitarianism'.[13] Hallmarks of 'totalitarian

[7] *Travaux*, vol. 1, p. 30 (Layton).

[8] *Travaux*, vol. 2, p. 50 (Layton).

[9] *Travaux*, vol. 2, p. 60 Ungoed-Thomas).

[10] *Travaux*, vol. 2, p. 4 (Edberg).

[11] *Travaux*, vol. 1, pp. 43–4 (Teitgen). The contradiction between such a guarantee and the continued status of many of the Convention's proponents as colonial powers does not appear to have troubled the drafters. Article 63 of the Convention permits parties that are colonial powers to extend the Convention's application to their dependent territories. It does not, however, require them to do so, nor does it cast any doubt on the democratic legitimacy of colonial rule *per se*.

[12] i.e., those concerned with the role of the European Commission and Court of Human Rights and Council of Europe Committee of Ministers and Secretary-General in relation to the Convention.

[13] *Klass*, 6 September 1978, Publications of the European Court of Human Rights (hereinafter ECHR), Series A, No. 28, para. 47 (submission of the applicants, endorsed by the Court).

regimes' were noted and opposed to the more homely attributes of democratic societies.[14] For some judges this led them to question whether rights such as privacy could be extended beyond ensuring that people and their families 'were no longer to be subjected to the four o-clock in the morning rat-a-tat on the door'.[15]

If privacy has been extended well beyond protection from the secret policeman's knock,[16] democracy has also come to be more delicately contrasted with the absence of adequate safeguards against arbitrary exercises of power, even by the more benign welfare State.[17] Further generalized characterizations of democracy have highlighted as distinctive features the 'separation of powers',[18] as well as the principle of accountability. Citizens, it has been said, are entitled in a democracy to keep 'critical control of the exercise of public power'.[19] The Strasbourg organs have also insisted that 'democracy does not simply mean that the views of the majority must always prevail'; rather, 'a balance must be achieved which ensures fair and proper treatment of minorities and avoids abuse of a dominant position'.[20] And the view has been expressed that the 'democratic process is dependent on the interplay of a wide variety of group interests'.[21]

Amongst particular rights and freedoms identified in Convention jurisprudence as integrally linked with democracy, freedom of expression is the right most often singled out. Thus, in the *Handyside* case, the Court, in a much cited statement, asserted that '[f]reedom of expression constitutes one of the essential foundations of [a democratic society], one of the basic conditions for its progress and for the development of every man'. Faced with an issue of obscenity law, the Court went on:

[Freedom of expression] is applicable not only to 'information' or 'ideas' that are favourably received, but also to those that offend, shock or disturb the State or

[14] *Le Compte, Van Leuven and De Meyere* v. *Belgium*, 23 June 1981, ECHR, Series A, No. 43, para. 65.

[15] Fitzmaurice, dissenting opinion, para. 7, *Marckx* v. *Belgium*, 13 June 1979, ECHR, Series A, No. 31.

[16] See P. van Dijk and G. van Hoof, *Theory and Practice of the European Convention on Human Rights* (Deventer: Kluwer Law and Taxation, 2nd edn., 1990), p. 368, and the references there cited.

[17] *Feldbrugge* v. *Netherlands*, Appl. 8562/79, Commission, 9 May 1984, 7 EHRR 279, dissenting opinion of Mr Melchior, para. 27; endorsed by Court, 29 May 1986, ECHR, Series A, No. 99.

[18] *Klass*, 6 September 1978, ECHR, Series A, No. 28, separate opinion of Judge Pinheiro Farinha, p. 35.

[19] *Barfod* v. *Denmark*, Appl. 11508/85, Commission, 16 July 1987, 11 EHRR 559, para. 64. The Commission's decision was reversed by the Court, but without comment on this point: 22 February 1989, ECHR, Series A, No. 149.

[20] *Young, James and Webster* v. *UK*, 13 August 1981, ECHR, Series A, No. 44, para. 63.

[21] *Markt Intern and Beerman* v. *Germany*, Appl. 10572/83, Commission, 18 December 1987, 11 EHRR 212, para. 203. The Commission's decision was reversed before the Court with narrowest of margins, and without comment on this point: 20 November 1989, ECHR, Series A, No. 164.

any sector of the population. Such are the demands of that pluralism, tolerance and broadmindedness without which there is no 'democratic society'.[22]

In other cases, where critical or revelatory comment on public officials or policy has been at issue, the Court has stressed that 'freedom of political debate is at the very core of the concept of a democratic society which prevails throughout the Convention'.[23] It has underlined that '[i]n a democratic system the actions or omissions of the Government must be subject to the close scrutiny not only of the legislative and judicial authorities but also of the press and public opinion'.[24] The Court has attributed particular significance to the function of the press in this regard, as 'public watchdog', imparting to the public 'information and ideas on matters of public interest', which the public moreover 'has a right to receive'.[25] The Court has also expressed the view that this necessarily entails that ownership not just of the press but of all media be 'grounded in the principle of pluralism', as distinct from monopoly.[26]

To note these indications of the centrality of freedom of expression for democracy is not, of course, to say anything about what counts as freedom of expression or what distinguishes an acceptable restriction on freedom of expression from an unacceptable one. For present purposes there is no need to delve into the large body of case law and commentary which addresses these matters.[27] What is important is simply the strong connection made between this freedom and democracy, and the basis of the connection, resting as it apparently does on the impulse for self-fulfilment, the liberal values of tolerance and broadmindedness, and the democratic concern with securing the accountability of those who exercise public power.

A number of further rights and freedoms are also marked out in Convention jurisprudence as fundamental to democracy, though generally without explanation or elaboration. These include the right of peaceful assembly,[28] freedom to form and join professional associations,[29] freedom from State indoctrination in education,[30] the fair

[22] 7 December 1976, ECHR, Series A, No. 24, para. 49.

[23] *Lingens* v. *Austria*, 8 July 1986, ECHR, Series A, No. 103, para. 42.

[24] *Castells* v. *Spain*, 23 April 1992, ECHR, Series A, No. 236, para. 46.

[25] *Observer and Guardian* v. *UK*, 26 November 1991, ECHR, Series A, No. 216, para. 59; see also *Thorgeirson* v. *Iceland*, 25 June 1992, ECHR, Series A, No. 239, para. 63.

[26] *Informationsverein Lentia* v. *Austria*, 24 November 1993, ECHR, Series A, No. 276, para. 38.

[27] For a survey of this, see P. van Dijk and G. van Hoof, *Theory and Practice of the European Convention on Human Rights* (Deventer: Kluwer Law and Taxation, 2nd edn., 1990), p. 407, and the references there cited.

[28] *H* v. *Austria*, Appl. 15225/89, Commission, EHRR Commission Supplement No. 1, CD 70.

[29] *Le Compte, Van Leuven and De Meyere* v. *Belgium*, 23 June 1981, ECHR, Series A, No. 43, para. 65.

[30] *Kjeldsen, Busk Madsen and Pedersen*, 7 December 1976, ECHR, Series A, No. 23, para. 53.

administration of justice,[31] the right to personal liberty and security[32] and the associated freedom from arbitrary detention.[33]

This first section has canvassed features and rights which the Convention organs appear, in principle, to associate with democracy. But it has revealed little of what happens when this abstract position confronts cases and is translated into argument, and little of its relation to the outcomes actually produced. To grasp something of these matters, it is worthwhile to give some attention to the various limitation clauses in the Convention that permit restriction of rights and freedoms where, amongst other things, necessary 'in a democratic society'.

II. Limitation Clauses and 'Democratic' Necessity

In the drafting debates concerning the Convention there was a shared assumption that limitation of the rights and freedoms otherwise guaranteed would be justified in some circumstances. However, a division of opinion emerged as to how these limitations should be provided for. Should they be expressed in a general, overarching proviso, as in the Universal Declaration,[34] or should specific limitations clauses be attached to particular rights and freedoms? This was related to a larger debate between those who were content with a relatively spare enumeration of the rights and freedoms to be protected and those who favoured a precise definition of the scope of those rights and freedoms.[35] In turn this debate was seemingly bound up with the influence of divergent legal traditions, some at ease with broadly expressed principles, others preferring to aim for the most detailed stipulation possible.[36] At stake was also the issue of whether all the rights and freedoms in the Convention would be susceptible of limitation (or of limitation on a uniform basis), or whether distinctions would be drawn between categories of rights and freedoms *a priori*. The Convention is to some extent a compromise between the two approaches, though overall the voice of the precise definitionists is perhaps stronger. Certainly, they held sway as regards specific limitations clauses, albeit that these were modelled on the Universal Declaration's general proviso. Whereas many of the Convention's provisions set parameters and build in qualifications and exceptions, by limitations clauses are here meant the limiting conditions

[31] *Delcourt* v. *Belgium*, 17 January 1970, ECHR, Series A, No. 11, para. 25; *Kostovski* v. *Netherlands*, 20 November 1989, ECHR, Series A, No. 166, para. 44.

[32] *De Wilde, Ooms and Versyp*, 18 June 1971, ECHR, Series A, No. 12, para. 65.

[33] *Winterwerp* v. *Netherlands*, 24 October 1979, ECHR, Series A, No. 33, para. 39.

[34] Art. 29, para. 2.

[35] For a summary of the positions, see *Travaux*, vol. 3, p. 252.

[36] Those governments in favour of precise definition were the United Kingdom (the most vocal on this subject), Greece, Norway and Denmark. Those in favour of enumeration included France, Italy, Ireland and Turkey. See *Travaux*, vol. 4, pp. 178 ff.

included in, principally, Articles 8–11 of the Convention as well as Article 1 of the First Protocol, Article 2 of the Fourth Protocol and Article 1 of the Seventh Protocol.[37]

These limiting conditions follow (with some significant differences to be noted) a characteristic pattern. This lays down three criteria for a justifiable restriction on rights and freedoms. First, the restriction (or penalty, interference or other measure denying protection) must be provided for by law. This has been understood to require not only that the restriction have a basis in domestic law but also that that law be both adequately accessible and formulated with sufficient precision to enable people to foresee the way in which it will apply to given conduct.[38] Secondly, each of the provisions concerned sets forth a catalogue of aims or interests, to at least one of which the restriction must be directed. To illustrate the range, freedom of expression (Article 10) may be limited

> in the interests of national security, territorial integrity or public safety, for the prevention of disorder or crime, for the protection of health or morals, for the protection of the reputation or the rights of others, for preventing the disclosure of information received in confidence, or for maintaining the authority and impartiality of the judiciary.

The peaceful enjoyment of possessions (Article 1, Protocol 1) may only be denied—that is to say, expropriation may only take place—for a single, if wide-ranging, aim: 'the public interest'. Respondent governments have rarely had difficulty persuading the Convention organs that a restriction was for one of the accepted aims or interests.

Thirdly, and more demandingly, it is provided in all the provisions cited, with the exception of Article 1, Protocol 1,[39] that the restriction must not just be for one of the stated aims or interests. It must be 'necessary' for them 'in a democratic society'.[40] It was the application of

[37] See Art. 8, para. 2; Art. 9, para. 2; Art. 10, para. 2; Art. 11, para. 2; First Protocol, Art. 1; Fourth Protocol, Art. 2, paras. 3–4; Seventh Protocol, Art. 1, paras. 1–2. See also Art. 6, para. 1.

[38] *Sunday Times*, 26 April 1979, ECHR, Series A, No. 30, para. 49. For further elaboration, see, regarding the basis in domestic law, *Campbell* v. *UK*, 25 March 1992, ECHR, Series A, No. 233; *Barthold* v. *Germany*, 25 March 1985, ECHR, Series A, No. 90; *Kruslin* v. *France*, 24 April 1990, ECHR, Series A, No. 176A; and regarding accessibility and foreseeability, *Groppera Radio AG and others* v. *Switerland*, 28 March 1990, ECHR, Series A, No. 173; *Leander* v. *Sweden*, 26 March 1987, ECHR, Series A, No. 116; *Kruslin* v. *France*, 24 April 1990, ECHR, Series A, No. 176A; *Gillow* v. *UK*, 24 November 1986, ECHR, Series A, No. 109; and *Open Door and Dublin Well Woman* v. *Ireland*, 29 October 1992, ECHR, Series A, No. 246.

[39] Article 2, Protocol 4 also differs slightly from the other provisions under consideration. It uses the phrase 'justified by the public interest in a democratic society'. Notwithstanding these differences, the substantive considerations addressed under the rubric of democratic necessity are regularly addressed in cases concerning Article 1, Protocol 1, and Article 2, Protocol 4.

[40] For discussions of this stipulation see P. Vegleris, 'Valeur et signification de la clause "dans une société démocratique" dans la Convention européenne des droits de l'homme', *Human Rights Journal*, 1 (1968), p. 219; O. Garibaldi, 'On the Ideological Content of Human Rights Instruments: the Clause "In a Democratic Society" ', in T. Buergenthal (ed.), *Contemporary Issues in International Law. Essays in Honour of Louis B. Sohn* (Kehl: N. P Engel, 1984), p. 23; and P. van Dijk and G. van Hoof, *Theory and Practice of the European Convention on Human Rights* (Deventer: Kluwer Law and Taxation, 2nd edn., 1990). p. 583.

this stipulation that provided the occasion for many of the observations about democracy and 'democratic' rights and freedoms mentioned in section I above. And it is clearly this stipulation which is of greatest interest here. Necessity in this context has been identified with a 'pressing social need',[41] while the reference to 'democratic society' has been seen as qualifying this by insisting that the restriction must be 'proportionate' to the aim or interest pursued.[42] The aesthetic metaphor perhaps signals the kind of rationality we should expect to encounter in this domain. Proportion is self-evident to one who sees it, and can acceptably be asserted, without elaborations.

The emphasis on proportion also indicates that the issue here is above all about how relationships are to be drawn—relationships between what are taken to be discrete parts within some whole, the 'democratic society'. One relationship to which argument is invariably addressed is that between community interests (or, where applicable, the 'rights of others') and the individual's rights which are the subject of the restriction. The Court expressed the view in the *Klass* case[43] that both have a role in play in a 'democratic society'. Discussing secret surveillance measures sought to be justified in terms of the community interest in national security, the Court attached importance to the safeguards provided to protect the individual's right to privacy. To fail to provide adequate safeguards was, the Court warned, to risk 'undermining or even destroying democracy on the ground of defending it'.[44] But if democracy resides as much in individual rights as in community interests, it is striking that the Convention organs appear more concerned to accommodate both where the outcome is favourable to the applicant's rights than where it is favourable to the respondent State's claim regarding community interest.

Where the organs find in favour of the respondent State, they make little effort to disguise the fact that the individual's rights have, up to a point, been subordinated. Where, however, the organs find in favour of the applicant, they often seek to reconcile their decision with *some* community interest, even if not that which the respondent State (drawing on the relevant catalogue of legitimate aims or interests for restriction) has advanced. The way this is done in a number of cases is to re-state, or generalize, the individual rights in issue as, in themselves, a community interest. Thus, for instance, in the well-known *Sunday Times* case the Court, dismissing the government's argument based on 'maintaining the authority of the judiciary',[45] drew attention to the 'public

[41] *Handyside*, 7 December 1976, ECHR, Series A, No. 24, para. 48.
[42] Ibid., para. 49.
[43] 6 September 1978, ECHR, Series A., No. 28.
[44] Ibid., para. 49.
[45] See Art. 10, para. 2.

interest in freedom of expression'.[46] In the case of *Ezelin*, involving disciplinary action taken against a participant in a demonstration, the respondent government sought to justify the interference with the applicant's freedom of assembly by reference to the 'prevention of disorder'.[47] Rejecting the justification, the Court referred to 'the requirements of . . . the free expression of opinions . . . by persons assembled in the streets or in other public places'. It was adamant that 'the pursuit of a just balance must not result in [those in the position of the applicant] being discouraged . . . from making clear their beliefs'.[48]

Argument concerning 'democratic' necessity has led to enquiry into other relationships as well. The Convention organs have discussed that long-standing preoccupation of liberal democracy, the relationship between majorities and minorities within countries. Thus, for instance, in the case of *Dudgeon*, concerning Northern Irish legislation affecting homosexuality, it was observed that the opinion of the majority in Northern Ireland concerning homosexuality merited serious consideration, but '[could not] of itself be decisive'.[49] In *Young, James and Webster* it was stressed, in connection with the 'closed shop', that a proportion must be found between respect for a minority wish to disassociate and a majority wish to associate.[50]

Inasmuch as the Convention is intended to set common standards for all its States parties, the Convention organs have also addressed the relationship between the majority and the minority of those States parties. Thus, in *Dudgeon*, the Court said that it '[could not] overlook the marked changes which have occurred in . . . regard [to homosexuality] in the domestic law of the [other] member States'.[51] In *Informationsverein Lentia*, concerning a State broadcasting monopoly, the Court dismissed the respondent government's concerns on the footing that these were 'contradicted by the experience of several European States of a comparable size'.[52] One member of the Commission has recently gone so far as to suggest that, in the context of the limitation clauses, the notion of 'democratic society' should take as its 'model' 'European democratic society', on the basis that 'what is necessary for the State concerned cannot be decisive'.[53]

And finally, the Convention organs have given attention to their own relationship with respondent governments. The organs have repeatedly

[46] 26 April 1979, ECHR, Series A, No. 30, para. 42.

[47] See Art. 11, para. 2.

[48] 26 April 1991, ECHR. Series A, No. 202, para. 52.

[49] 22 October 1981, ECHR, Series A, No. 45, para. 59.

[50] 13 August 1981, ECHR, Series A, No. 44.

[51] 22 October 1981, ECHR, Series A, No. 45, para. 60.

[52] 24 November 1993, ECHR, Series A, No. 276, para. 42.

[53] See *Open Door and Dublin Well Woman* v. *Ireland*, Commission Report, partly concurring and partly dissenting opinion of Sir Basil Hall, 14 EHRR 115, p. 142. Sir Basil Hall appears to have intended this as an exhortation to take into account European Community law, including—in the particular context of this case—free movement of persons.

emphasized that, in deciding issues of 'democratic necessity', their task is 'not to take the place of the competent national authorities but rather to review under [the Convention] the decisions [the national authorities] delivered'. In this regard the national authorities have a 'margin of appreciation', but one which 'goes hand in hand with a European supervision'.[54] The organs have acknowledged that the scope of the margin of appreciation—that is to say, the deference paid to national decisions—is not always identical,[55] and that factors which affect its 'width' include 'the importance . . . of the rights in question',[56] 'the nature of the aim of the restriction [and] the nature of the activities involved'.[57] Commentators have sought to elaborate these criteria and relate them to outcomes in cases, but have found precise threads of principle disturbingly elusive.[58]

The significance of the margin of appreciation doctrine for present purposes lies in what it reveals about 'democratic societies' and the Convention organs' relationship with them. The question how, from a perspective of democracy, to justify review of legislation by unelected and unaccountable judges is one with which constitutional courts and commentators have long grappled.[59] In the case of the Convention, a somewhat similar issue arises. The restrictive measure must, as noted, be provided for by law; arbitrary executive action is relatively easy to condemn. But if the measure is provided for by law, on what basis and to what extent should it be questioned by the European Commission and Court?

Indications from the Strasbourg organs suggest that one way of understanding this issue may be in terms of the respect due to the 'democratic process'. In the *Mellacher* case, a complaint under Article 1, Protocol 1, concerning rent control legislation, the Commission noted that the

> proportionality of [the rent control measures] was disputed both in Parliament and in general public debate . . . . However, it is inherent in the democratic process that different political views on social justice prevail in various sectors of the population and will be reflected in the law-making process . . . . It . . .

[54] *Observer and Guardian* v. *UK*, 26 November 1991, ECHR, Series A, No. 216, para. 59.

[55] *Sunday Times*, 26 April 1979, ECHR, Series A, No. 30, para. 59.

[56] *Informationsverein Lentia* v.*Austria*, 24 November 1993, ECHR, Series A, No. 276, para. 35.

[57] *Dudgeon* v. *UK*, 22 October 1981, ECHR, Series A, No. 45, para. 52.

[58] See T. O'Donnell, 'The Margin of Appreciation Doctrine: Standards in the Jurisprudence of the European Court of Human Rights', *Human Rights Quarterly*, 4 (1982), p. 474; R. Macdonald, 'The Margin of Appreciation in the Jurisprudence of the European Court of Human Rights', in *International Law at the Time of its Codification. Essays in Honour of Roberto Ago* (1987), vol. 3, p. 187; and J. G. Merrills, *The Development of International Law by the European Court of Human Rights* (Manchester: Manchester University Press, 2nd edn., 1993), chap. 7.

[59] For a valuable perspective on the issues, see C. Sunstein, 'Constitutions and Democracies: An Epilogue', in J. Elster and R. Slagstad (eds.), *Constitutionalism and Democracy* (Cambridge: Cambridge University Press, 1988), p. 327.

remains the legitimate task of the competent legislative body to determine the measures which it considers to be necessary in the general interest.[60]

The Court, while departing from the Commission in the ultimate result, appeared to agree with this, and found in it an argument for a very wide margin of appreciation. In relation to 'social and economic policies', it said, the 'court will respect the legislature's judgement as to what is in the general interest unless that judgement be manifestly without reasonable foundation'.[61] In the case of *Open Door and Dublin Well Woman*[62] the Court held that a restraint on the provision in Ireland of information about abortion abroad violated freedom of expression and information under the Convention. The constitutional provision on which the restraint was based had been enacted by the Irish legislature following a referendum in 1983. A number of dissenting judges seized on this point. The provision, as one judge put it, was 'merely the legislature's response to the democratically expressed will of the Irish people'. 'That choice must be respected', he insisted, adding that 'it is not even necessary in this connection to have recourse to the notion of the margin of appreciation'.[63]

The passages cited appear to suggest that the 'width' of the margin of appreciation, at least in the view of some judges, is a function of the level of respect due to the 'democratic process' within the respondent State—not, of course, generally, but as regards the restrictive measure. Returning to the earlier metaphor, the width of the margin may thus be understood as referring to the extent to which the respondent government ought to be master of its own 'proportions'—the extent, in other words, to which the national polity should be left to manage the various relationships discussed above in its own way. The *Mellacher* case demonstrates that in relation to widely debated legislation concerning 'social and economic', or at any rate housing, policy a wide margin of appreciation is indicated.[64] The national 'democratic process' is to be questioned sparingly.

But *Mellacher* and the dissenting judgments in *Open Door and Dublin Well Woman* are not the only cases to reveal a correlation between the margin of appreciation and the national 'democratic process'. Other cases imply such a correlation, even if they make it less explicit. The Convention organs have, for instance, considered an exacting scrutiny

[60] Commission, Appl. 10522/83, 11 July 1988, 12 EHRR 97, para. 211.

[61] 19 December 1989, ECHR, Series A, No. 169, para. 45. See also *Lithgow and others* v. *UK*, 8 July 1986, ECHR, Series A, No. 102, para. 122, and *James and others* v. *UK*, 21 February 1986, ECHR, Series A, No. 98, para. 46.

[62] 29 October 1992, ECHR, Series A, No. 246.

[63] Partly dissenting opinion of Judge Matscher. In a similar vein Judge Cremona laid emphasis on the fact that the principle enshrined in the provision had been affirmed 'by the direct will of a strong majority of the people by means of the eminently democratic process of a comparatively recent national referendum'.

[64] 19 December 1989, ECHR, Series A, No. 169, para. 45.

appropriate where freedom of expression has been in issue, at least in cases bearing upon public affairs. On this footing a narrow margin of appreciation has applied in, amongst others, cases concerning the administration of justice,[65] as well as cases concerning defamation.[66] With regard to the latter the Court expressed particular commitment to a narrow margin of appreciation in one case in which an opposition Member of Parliament was prosecuted, and convicted, for insulting the Government. The Court said that

> [w]hile freedom of expression is important for everybody, it is especially so for an elected representative of the people. He represents his electorate, draws attention to their preoccupations and defends their interests. Accordingly, interferences with the freedom of expression of an opposition Member of Parliament . . . call for the closest scrutiny on the part of the Court.[67]

The Court seemingly found little reason to defer to the State's 'democratic process' when that very process was seen to be under attack. Where, as here, the organs apply a narrow margin of appreciation, they can be read as giving notice of grounds for reservation about the 'democratic process' in its relation to the restrictive measure.

In cases of freedom of expression in economic affairs, by contrast, the Convention organs have generally been disposed to adopt a rather wider margin of appreciation. Thus, for instance, the Court has underscored that the 'margin of appreciation is particularly essential in the complex and fluctuating' areas of unfair competition[68] and professional advertising.[69] This seems to be not so much because the Court has no reservations about the quality of the 'democratic process' in relation to the restrictive measures. Rather, the wide margin seems attributable to a perception that generally the 'democratic process' plays little part in these commercial contexts.

A wide margin has also been deemed appropriate where 'national security' is implicated.[70] Again, this may be explicable on the basis of an assumption that, where protection of the democratic society itself is in issue, the 'democratic process' steps aside. Those who reject this assumption and hold that, where government secrecy is in issue, a wide

[65] See, e.g., *Sunday Times*, 26 April 1979, ECHR, Series A, No. 30.

[66] See, e.g., *Lingens* v. *Austria*, 8 July 1986, ECHR, Series A, No. 103; *Thorgeirson* v.*Iceland*, 25 June 1992, ECHR, Series A, No. 239; and *Castells* v. *Spain*, 23 April 1992, ECHR, Series A, No. 236, para. 42.

[67] *Castells* v. *Spain*, 23 April 1992, ECHR, Series A, No. 236, para. 42.

[68] *Markt Intern and Beermann* v. *Germany*, 20 November 1989, ECHR, Series A, No. 164, para. 33.

[69] *Casado Coca* v. *Spain*, 24 February 1994, ECHR, Series A, No. 285, para. 50. Notwithstanding the Court's statement that 'restrictions [of the kind in issue] must . . . be closely scrutinised by the Court' (para. 51), the width of the margin actually applied is indicated by the Court's final decision that there was no violation because the relevant authorities' reaction 'could not be considered unreasonable and disproportionate' (para. 57). This 'not unreasonable' test is the least exacting test the Court uses.

[70] See, e.g., *Leander* v. *Sweden*, 26 March 1987, ECHR, Series A, No. 116.

margin is inadequate to protect individual rights can be understood as questioning whether an exclusionary and opaque 'democratic process' merits respect. And, to give a final example, the view was taken in the early Convention jurisprudence that a wide margin is to be accorded in matters of morals, at least where no common European standards exist.[71] It may be that the organs are becoming more willing to discover common European standards. In any event, the Court has affirmed that this wide margin might be reduced or contra-indicated where issues arise of individual rights and freedoms touching on 'intimate aspect[s] of private life'.[72] Closer investigation might then be called for to ensure that these have been given due consideration.

This discussion of the 'democratic process' has sought to highlight the relevance of the concept for the operation of the Convention's limitation clauses. But it has left assumptions about the character of the 'process' virtually unanalysed, save to cite comments in a few cases associating it with Parliament, legislation, referenda and public debate. To grasp an element perceived as central to this 'process', it is necessary to turn to the question of elections.

III. Democracy and Elections[73]

The first draft of the Convention included an undertaking on the part of member States

> to respect the fundamental principles of democracy in all good faith and, in particular, as regards their metropolitan territory: 1) to hold free elections at reasonable intervals, with universal suffrage and secret ballot, so as to ensure that Government action and legislation is, in fact, an expression of the will of the people; 2) to take no action which shall interfere with the right of criticism and the right to organize a political opposition.[74]

This provision was, however, immediately controversial and, over the course of the drafting period, increasingly so. When the draft was first debated, a proposal was made that the words 'so as to ensure that Government action and legislation is, in fact, an expression of the will of the people' be omitted. This was countered with the assertion that 'this was not a theory of political philosophy and therefore a subject of dispute

[71] See *Sunday Times*, distinguishing *Handyside*: 26 April 1979, ECHR, Series A, No. 30, para. 59.

[72] *Norris* v. *Ireland*, 26 October 1988, ECHR, Series A, No. 142, para. 46 (concerning homosexuality).

[73] On electoral rights generally, see further T. Franck, 'The Emerging Right to Democratic Governance', *American Journal of International Law*, 86 (1992), p. 46. For an engaging discussion of wider participation rights, see H. Steiner, 'Political Participation as a Human Right', *Harvard Human Rights Yearbook*, 1 (1988), p. 77 (where the major focus is on the Universal Declaration of Human Rights and the International Covenant on Civil and Political Rights).

[74] The draft is attached to Teitgen report, *Travaux*, vol. 1, pp. 296 ff.

but rather a fundamental requirement of democracy'.[75] Later, one expert advanced the argument that the entire provision should be deleted on the ground that the issues concerned were of a 'constitutional and political character'. He objected to the vagueness of the reference to 'fundamental principles of democracy' and observed that universal suffrage and the secret ballot could not always and of necessity ensure that Governmental action and legislation were expressions of the will of the people. He also raised practical difficulties which, he warned, would attend the provision. Amongst these were the compatibility with the notion of 'universal suffrage' of diverse qualifications attached to voting rights.[76] Others opposed the provision on the basis that it went 'outside the traditional domain of human rights'.[77]

Supporters of the provision defended it as 'a very important part of the general plan for safeguarding democratic rights'.[78] Some linked it with the limitation clauses which, in their reference to 'democratic' necessity, were said to illustrate 'the vital importance of democratic principles in this matter'.[79] To 'guarantee individual freedoms without guaranteeing democracy and the fundamental principles of its institutions' was, it was contended, 'utter nonsense', for they are 'indissolubly linked'.[80] Thus, it was argued, '[t]he freedoms we wish to defend and to protect have no existence, no meaning, no practical content save within the framework of democracy and through its organs'.[81] For Pierre-Henri Teitgen what was at stake was the very purpose of the Convention:

> . . . [O]ur concern was not with . . . isolated illegal actions. In every country there exist tribunals which themselves correct the illegality in the immense majority of cases . . . . [W]hat we want to prevent is the re-establishment or establishment in some countries, of totalitarian dictatorships such as we saw in Italy and Germany before the war . . . . We are seeking an international procedure capable of active intervention from the start. But what in fact happens in such a case? They begin by suppressing democratic institutions, by suppressing the secret ballot and universal suffrage, by suppressing elected Parliaments. Then when the dictatorship is firmly established, it suppresses, one after the other, the freedoms defined by earlier laws . . . .It is from the very first day, from the day of the assassination of a Matteotti, from the day of a Reichstag fire . . . that [the European Commission or Court] must be able to intervene . . . .If we reject that possibility, our system would lose the greater part of its political efficacy.[82]

[75] *Travaux*, vol. 1, p. 202 (Teitgen).
[76] *Travaux*, vol. 3, p. 182 (Dowson).
[77] *Travaux*, vol. 4, p. 140.
[78] *Travaux*, vol. 5, p. 210 (Layton).
[79] Letter dated 24 June 1950 from the Committee on Legal and Administrative Questions to the Committee of Ministers, reproduced in *Travaux*, vol. 7, p. 152.
[80] *Travaux*, vol. 5, p. 288 (Teitgen).
[81] Ibid.
[82] *Travaux*, vol. 5, pp. 292–3 (Teitgen).

It proved impossible to reconcile these two positions before the Convention was signed.[83] The provision was omitted from the Convention on the basis that it would be included in the First Protocol. In its final form Article 3, Protocol 1, provides:

The High Contracting Parties undertake to hold free elections at reasonable intervals by secret ballot, under conditions which will ensure the free expression of the opinion of the people in the choice of legislature.

Responding to objections mentioned, this eschews any reference both to the 'fundamental principles of democracy' and to 'universal suffrage'. Successive drafts indicate that the framers had difficulty grappling with the purpose, or role, of elections as regards the relationship between government and the electors. Should elections be seen as significant for 'government action and legislation'?[84] Or was their significance to be only for institutions, for 'government and legislature',[85] or even just for the 'choice of the legislature'?[86] And what should be the nature of Convention parties' obligations regarding elections? Could, and should, Convention parties be expected to hold elections 'so as to ensure that government action and legislation is, *in fact*, an expression of the will of the people', as in the first draft?[87] Or should States parties merely be required to hold elections 'under *conditions* which will ensure' the legitimacy of government?[88] If the latter, in what circumstances will the conditions be taken to ensure the legitimacy of government? Should the conditions be expected to ensure that 'government and legislature *represent* the people'?[89] Should they be expected simply to ensure that government and legislature '*represent the opinion of* the people'?[90] Or was it to be enough if they ensured the '*free expression of the people in the choice of* the legislature'?[91] The drafters appear to have been minded to accept a formulation which would have required States parties to hold elections under conditions that ensure 'that the government and legislature shall represent the opinion of the people'. This was amended in the final version to allay fears that the provision might otherwise be taken to

[83] By way of compromise, it was proposed that the provision concerning elections could, at a State's option, be specially excluded from the scope of the Court's jurisdiction. See *Travaux*, vol. 5, p. 12. It was also proposed that the provision be re-cast to take account of some of the objections raised. See, e.g., Alternatives A and A/2, draft Article 3, *Travaux*, vol. 4, p. 54.

[84] Draft 1 (approved by Consultative Assembly during first session) in the compilation of the various drafts, *Travaux*, vol. 7, pp. 150–1.

[85] Drafts II (incorporating modifications of Committee of Experts) and III (adopted by Committee on Legal and Administrative Questions and approved by Consultative Assembly during second session), ibid.

[86] Art. 3, Protocol 1.

[87] Emphasis added; Draft 1 in the compilation of the various drafts, *Travaux*, vol. 7, pp. 150–1.

[88] Emphasis added; Drafts II and III, ibid., and Art. 3, Protocol 1.

[89] Emphasis added; Draft II, ibid.

[90] Emphasis added; Draft III, ibid.

[91] Emphasis added; Art. 3, Protocol 1.

demand some form of proportional representation.[92] Contenting themselves with a claim about the 'choice of the legislature', along with a claim about 'conditions' that ensure the 'free expression of the opinion of the people' in that choice, the drafters thus ultimately endorsed a relatively modest account of the role of elections as regards the relationship between government and the people.

Contrary to M. Teitgen's expectations, or apprehensions, the Convention organs have found themselves mainly confronted with what he might have regarded as 'isolated illegal actions'. These actions have, of course, almost invariably been neither isolated incidents nor illegal acts under national law; rather, they have generally been systematic departures from Convention standards. But the Convention organs have not had to deal with the assassination of a Matteotti or a Reichstag fire.[93] The Convention has come to protect people not just from dictatorship but also from unfreedom, indignities and abuses of power in States with governments of firm liberal democratic commitment. Article 3, Protocol 1, has been invoked in relatively few cases,[94] only one of which—*Mathieu-Mohin and Clerfayt*[95]—has been referred to the Court. None has led to a finding of a violation.[96]

Even so, to the extent that the Commission and Court have had to address Article 3, they have attached considerable significance to it. Linking the provision with the Convention's preambular assertion that human rights and freedoms are best maintained by an 'effective political democracy', the Court has said that Article 3 'enshrines a characteristic principle of democracy . . . and is accordingly of prime importance in the Convention system'.[97] As regards the scope of Article 3, three principal issues have been discussed.

First, the organs have examined the rights and obligations to which Article 3 gives rise. As the provision is couched in terms of an '[undertaking] to hold free elections at reasonable intervals by secret ballot', an early question arose as to whether universal suffrage was required. In view of the reference to a State undertaking rather than to rights—an unusual formulation for the Convention—a further question

[92] Secretary-General's comments, *Travaux*, vol. 7, p. 130. See further *Travaux*, vol. 7, pp. 202, 212, and vol. 8, p. 14.

[93] The *Greek* case, arising out of the colonels' coup in 1967, might be seen as an exception: Commission Report, 5 November 1969, *Yearbook of the European Convention on Human Rights*, 12 (1969). In its report (at p. 179) the Commission expressed the view that Art. 3, Protocol 1, 'presupposes the existence of a representative legislature elected at reasonable intervals as the basis of a democratic society'.

[94] For a detailed examination of the case law, see P. van Dijk and G. van Hoof, *Theory and Practice of the European Convention on Human Rights* (Deventer: Kluwer Law and Taxation, 2nd edn., 1990), p. 478.

[95] 2 March 1987, ECHR, Series A, No. 113.

[96] In *Mathieu-Mohin and Clerfayt* v. *Belgium*, the Commission found in favour of the applicants. This was reversed, however, when the case went to the Court: Appl. 9267/81; Court, 2 March 1987, ECHR, Series A, No. 113.

[97] Para. 47.

arose as to whether correlative individual rights were entailed. The Commission's views in this regard have evolved over time. Initially, the Commission was reluctant to find in Article 3 more than an institutional guarantee of free elections.[98] In later cases, however, the Commission came to accept that the Article implied universal suffrage (notwithstanding the reservations expressed about that concept in the drafting debates)[99] and what the Court in *Mathieu-Mohin and Clerfayt* later characterized as 'subjective rights of participation':[100] the right to vote and the right to stand for election to the legislature.[101] The Commission at the same time recognized that 'States can attach conditions to the right to vote and the right to stand as a candidate as long as they are not arbitrary and do not infringe the free expression of the opinion of the people'.[102] Thus, for instance, the Commission in one case accepted conditions attached to candidature which demanded adherence to a party with an elected executive, a written programme and a minimal level of demonstrable public support.[103] The Court in *Mathieu-Mohin and Clerfayt* confirmed both that Article 3 implies the right to vote and the right to stand for election, and that those rights may be made subject to conditions. In this, the Court said, States have a 'wide margin of appreciation', though it is for the Court ultimately to verify that the conditions 'do not curtail the rights . . . to such an extent as to impair their very essence . . . ; that they are imposed in pursuance of a legitimate aim; and that the means employed are not disproportionate'.[104] Thus the Court drew on the approach adopted in relation to limitation clauses elsewhere in the Convention, finding appropriate a high degree of deference to the national 'democratic process'.

The undertaking in Article 3 is, it will be recalled, to hold elections 'under conditions which ensure the free expression of the opinion of the people in the choice of the legislature'. The Convention organs have addressed, secondly, the 'legislature' to which this applies. In *Edwards* the Commission confronted an application arising out of the disbanding of, and cancellation of elections to, the Greater London Council in 1985. The application failed because the Commission did not consider that the GLC formed part of the United Kingdom 'legislature'. For the Commission, a body only counts as the 'legislature' if it '[possesses] an inherent primary rulemaking power and those powers which have been delegated

[98] Appl. 1028/61, *X* v. *Belgium*, *Yearbook of the European Convention on Human Rights*, 4 (1961), p. 338.

[99] Appl. 2728/66, *X* v. *Germany*, *Yearbook of the European Convention on Human Rights*, 10 (1967), p. 338.

[100] Para. 51.

[101] Appl. 6850/74, *X, Y and Z* v. *Germany*, *Decisions and Reports of the European Commission of Human Rights* (hereinafter *Decisions and Reports*), vol. 5, p. 90, at p. 93.

[102] Ibid.

[103] Appl. 6850/74, *X, Y and Z* v. *Germany*, *Decisions and Reports*, vol. 5, p. 90.

[104] Para. 52.

to it by the Parliament of the United Kingdom are exercised subject to Parliament's ultimate control'.[105] On the other hand, in *Mathieu-Mohin and Clerfayt*,[106] the Court noted that this does not mean Article 3 applies only to national Parliaments. Rather, it applies to all parts of a State's legislature, as understood in the light of the State's particular constitutional structure.[107] At issue in that case were electoral arrangements in Belgium concerning the Flemish Council, a regional body with wide-ranging legislative powers. The Court had no doubt that this body formed part of the Belgian 'legislature'.

The Commission subsequently applied this approach in *Tete*,[108] where the complaint related to arrangements in France for the election of French representatives to the European Parliament. Just as 'legislature' may include sub-national legislative organs, so—the Commission here observed—it may also include supra-national legislative organs:

> The international obligations of States which could affect the legislative competence of national Parliaments had to be taken into consideration . . . . The High Contracting Parties could not by means of a transfer of competence render the guarantees of the Convention inapplicable in areas which normally fall within its ambit.[109]

With regard to the European Parliament, the Commission acknowledged that the Parliament's role had been progressively enlarged,[110] but expressed the view that the Parliament 'did not as yet constitute a legislative body in the ordinary sense of that term'.[111] Considering that further evolution was likely, the Commission eventually preferred to leave open the question whether the European Parliament should be seen as part of the French 'legislature'.

A third matter which has preoccupied the Convention organs is the manner in which a State may fulfil its obligation to 'ensure the free expression of the opinion of the people in the choice of the legislature'. In a number of cases before the Commission, the argument was adduced that the simple majority electoral system in use in the United Kingdom was incompatible with Article 3, Protocol 1, and that only some form of proportional representation would suffice. Rejecting this argument, the Commission adopted the view taken in the drafting debates that propor-

[105] *Edwards* v. *UK*, Appl. 11377/85, 8 EHRR 96, at p. 98. See also *X* v. *UK*, Appl. 5155/71, *Decisions and Reports*, vol. 6, p. 13 (deciding that local authorities were not part of the Northern Irish 'legislature') and *Booth-Clibborn and others* v. *UK*, Appl. 11391/85, *Decisions and Reports*, vol. 43, p. 236 (deciding that metropolitan county councils were not part of the UK 'legislature').

[106] 2 March 1987, ECHR, Series A, No. 113.

[107] Para. 53.

[108] *Tete* v. *France*, Appl. 1123/84, 11 EHRR 91.

[109] Ibid.

[110] The Commission referred to the Single European Act. To this could now be added (though seemingly with little effect on the Commission's ultimate decision) the Treaty on European Union, Maastricht.

[111] Ibid., at p. 92.

tional representation was not to be required.[112] In *Mathieu-Mohin and Clerfayt*, the Court confirmed that Article 3 does not create an obligation to introduce any specific electoral system, provided that the system employed ensures 'equality of treatment of all citizens in the exercise of their right to vote and their right to stand for election'. Here too, the Court said, States have a 'wide margin of appreciation'. In exercising its ultimate supervision the Court thought it appropriate to take into account the 'political evolution' of the country concerned, on the basis that 'features that would be unacceptable in the context of one system may . . . be justified in the context of another'.[113]

The circumstances of *Mathieu-Mohin and Clerfayt* raised the question of equality of treatment of citizens in particularly acute form. The Flemish Council's legislative powers extended over the predominantly Dutch-speaking Halle-Vivoorde district, amongst others. Membership of the Council was confined by law to members of Parliament who had taken their parliamentary oath in Dutch. The applicants, two members of Parliament from the Halle-Vivoorde district who had taken their parliamentary oath in French, and who were therefore ineligible for membership of the Flemish Council, complained that the system violated Article 3, Protocol 1. In substance, their claim was that the system excluded representation of the French-speaking electors of Halle-Vivoorde. The Court dismissed this charge, insisting that '[t]he French-speaking electors in the district of Halle-Vivoorde enjoy the right to vote and the right to stand for election on the same legal footing as the Dutch-speaking electors'.[114] The Court was satisfied—bearing in mind the State's 'wide margin of appreciation'—that the conditions that were attached to the right to stand for election to the Flemish Council fulfilled the stated criteria. It also considered that they could be justified in terms of the 'political evolution' of Belgium and the concern to diffuse language disputes. In reaching this conclusion, the Court addressed a number of the issues characteristically addressed in the context of 'democratic necessity'. It showed concern for the relationship between minorities and majorities, noting that the arrangements do 'not necessarily threaten the interest of the minorities'.[115] And it stressed that the arrangements were consistent with 'the organisation of elections in a good many States'.[116] Finally, it observed that the policy which the arrangements implemented

[112] *X* v. *UK*, Appl. 7140/75, *Decisions and Reports*, vol. 7, p. 95; *Kennedy Lindsay and others* v. *UK*, Appl. 8364/78, *Decisions and Reports*, vol. 15, p. 247. See also *Liberal Party and others* v. *UK*, Appl. 8765/79. *Decisions and Reports*, vol. 21, p. 211 (arguing on the basis of Article 3, Protocol 1, read in conjunction with Article 14). The Commission has also dismissed a complaint concerning discrepancies in the size of constituencies in Iceland: *X* v. *Iceland*, Appl. 8941/80, *Decisions and Reports*, vol. 27, p. 145.

[113] Para. 54.

[114] Para. 57.

[115] Para. 57.

[116] Ibid.

'emerges from the debates in the democratic national Parliament and is borne out by the massive majorities achieved in favour of [the relevant electoral legislation]'.[117] As argued in section II above, this consideration may have been significant for the Court's willingness to extend the State a wide margin of appreciation.

IV. The Convention's 'Democratic Society'

It is now possible to begin reconstructing the picture of a 'democratic society' that emerges from the Convention jurisprudence. This reconstruction necessarily takes place against a background of constant debate about the meaning and possibilities of democracy. Without an indication of some of the main lines of this debate, at least in its contemporary form and at least in so far as it bears upon Western liberal democracy, our picture's shape and significance will fail to appear. A detailed, historical account of the debate is a life-long preoccupation of many political theorists and, it hardly needs stating, will not be attempted here.

The starting point for current disputes about liberal democracy is the familiar representative democracy of modern Western capitalist polities, the heir to traditions of liberal democratic theory and political strategy established in the eighteenth and nineteenth centuries. It is worth recalling some of the key postulates of this.[118] Sovereignty belongs to the citizenry, but is vested in representatives. Periodic elections, supported by political rights and freedoms and competition between parties, ensure the accountability of representatives. The legal circumscription of State powers and the separation of legislative, judicial and executive functions enhance protection against abuses. State and civil society are distinct domains: the former a political realm of decision-making about the production and distribution of resources; the latter a non-political arena of economic relations, culture, family life. Citizens are individuals pursuing their private utility in civil society.

A vigorous debate centres on the adequacy of these postulates for realising the democratic ideal of self-rule by a free and equal citizenry.[119]

[117] Ibid.

[118] This account is drawn principally from C. B. Macpherson, *The Life and Times of Liberal Democracy* (Oxford: Oxford University Press, 1977), and D. Held, *Models of Democracy* (Cambridge: Polity Press, 1987).

[119] Illuminating perspectives on this debate can be found in P. Corcoran, 'The Limits of Democratic Theory', in G. Duncan (ed.), *Democratic Theory and Practice* (Cambridge: Cambridge University Press, 1983), p. 13; J. Dunn, 'Conclusion', in J. Dunn (ed.), *Democracy, The Unfinished Journey, 503 BC to AD 1993* (Oxford: Oxford University Press, 1992), p. 239; J. Dunn, *Western Political Theory in the Face of the Future* (Cambridge: Cambridge University Press, 2nd edn, 1993), chap. 1; D. Held, 'Democracy: From City-States to Cosmopolitan Order?', in D. Held (ed.), *Prospects for Democracy* (Cambridge: Polity Press, 1993), p. 13; and D. Beetham, 'Liberal Democracy and the Limits of Democratisation', in D. Held (ed.), *Prospects for Democracy* (Cambridge: Polity Press, 1993), p. 55.

This ideal has been part of democratic thought since ancient Athens, and its implications have been pursued in the modern era by, amongst others, Rousseau,[120] Marx[121] and John Stuart Mill.[122] Contemporary critics draw inspiration from these sources (amongst others) for two principal lines of argument. One is that current liberal democratic practice is decisively flawed in the extent to which it alienates citizens from involvement in decision-making.[123] Substantially oligarchical government, legitimated by an occasional vote, is incompatible with self-rule. More than that, it deprives citizens of the chance to participate in setting the terms of their common life. Citizen participation in public affairs can be evaluated in a variety of ways. For some, participation affords valuable opportunities for self-development.[124] For others, participation is an essential element in the good life.[125] For still others, participation has, above all, a prudential value, as a method of enhancing accountability and guarding against self-interested rule by those who wield political power.[126] Whichever position is taken, the assertion is that democracy should be much more than just a procedure for choosing governments. The assumption that greater participation, more 'direct' democracy, is inconsistent with the realities of complex, large-scale, industrialized societies is forcefully rejected. Advances in communications technology are said to heighten the possibilities for more active citizen involvement in public decision-making.[127] On this view, then, the relevance of democracy should be extended beyond formal political institutions to

[120] Rousseau, *The Social Contract* (trans. and ed. M. Cranston, London: Penguin, 1968).

[121] D. Held, *Models of Democracy* (Cambridge: Polity Press, 1987), chap. 4, gives a useful summary of the implications for democracy of Marx's thought.

[122] J. S. Mill, 'Considerations on Representative Government' in *On Liberty and Other Essays* (ed. J. Gray, Oxford: Oxford University Press, 1991).

[123] For early formulations of this argument, see C. Pateman, *Participation and Democratic Theory* (Cambridge: Cambridge University Press, 1970); C. B. Macpherson, *The Life and Times of Liberal Democracy* (Oxford: Oxford University Press, 1977), chap. 5; and B. Barber, *Strong Democracy* (Berkeley: University of California Press, 1984). More recent theorists have shifted the focus somewhat, from participatory democracy to revitalised citizenship. See, e.g., R. Bellamy, *Liberalism and Modern Society* (Cambridge: Polity Press, 1992), and C. Mouffe, 'Democratic Citizenship and Political Community', in C. Mouffe (ed.), *Dimensions of Radical Democracy* (London and New York: Verso, 1992), p. 225.

[124] This was the rationale for the 'participatory' theorists of the 1960s, 70s and early 80s. See, e.g., C. Pateman, *Participation and Democratic Theory* (Cambridge: Cambridge University Press, 1970); C. B. Macpherson, *The Life and Times of Liberal Democracy* (Oxford: Oxford University Press, 1977), chap. 5; and B. Barber, *Strong Democracy* (Berkeley: University of California Press, 1984).

[125] This is the rationale of recent theorists who draw inspiration from Aristotle and the civic humanist tradition. See, e.g., A. MacIntyre, *After Virtue* (London: Duckworth, 2nd edn., 1985).

[126] This is the rationale of recent theorists who draw inspiration from Machiavelli and the classical republican tradition. See, e.g., Q. Skinner, 'On Justice, the Common Good and the Priority of Liberty', in C. Mouffe (ed.), *Dimensions of Radical Democracy* (London and New York: Verso, 1992), p. 211; and R. Bellamy, *Liberalism and Modern Society* (Cambridge: Polity Press, 1992).

[127] For a discussion on the impact of technological advances on the possibilities for more 'direct' democracy, see I. Budge, 'Direct Democracy: Setting Appropriate Terms of Debate', in D. Held (ed.), *Prospects for Democracy* (Cambridge: Polity Press, 1993), p. 136, and the references there cited.

political and social processes, and urgent attention should be given to devising ways of achieving this.

A second line of criticism is that liberal democratic practice fails to live up to its commitment to treat citizens as free and equal.[128] Formal civil and political rights—rights to vote and to stand for public office, freedoms of expression, assembly and association, amongst others—are inadequate because they are radically compromised by social and economic inequalities. Systematic asymmetries of power and resources in the 'private' sphere—patterns of domination based on class, race and sex—prevent people from taking full advantage of their rights and realizing themselves equally as citizens. Thus, for example, feminist theorists have argued that the political equality of women is substantially undercut by, and perhaps actually premised on, arrangements of sexual inequality in civil society.[129] Unless democracy is extended to the sphere of civil society—indeed, unless democracy permeates everywhere that power resides—the promise of freedom and equality for all citizens will remain hollow. While democracy is limited to the 'public' sphere, the State will continue to provide for 'private' inequalities the congenial framework which currently sustains them. Thus, it is argued, democracy must be put into practice in the workplace, as well as 'in the kitchen, the nursery and the bedroom'.[130]

To summarize, the two trajectories seek respectively more democracy—more active citizenship through 'strong'[131] democracy in 'public' affairs—and democracy in more settings—equal citizenship through democratization of the 'private' sphere. Together, they add up to a call for what one theorist terms a 'double democratization':[132] the simultaneous, and mutually reinforcing, restructuring of State power and transformation of civil society. This brief survey by no means exhausts all the

[128] For detailed presentations of this argument, see R. Dahl, *Democracy and its Critics* (New Haven: Yale University Press, 1989), chap. 23; D. Held, *Political Theory and the Modern State* (Cambridge: Polity Press, 1989), chap. 7; and C. Mouffe, 'Democratic Citizenship and Political Community', in C. Mouffe (ed.), *Dimensions of Radical Democracy* (London and New York: Verso, 1992), p. 225.

[129] See C. Pateman, *The Disorder of Women* (Cambridge: Cambridge University Press, 1989), especially chap. 9; A. Phillips, *Engendering Democracy* (Cambridge: Polity Press, 1991); A. Phillips, 'Must Feminists Give Up on Liberal Democracy?', in D. Held (ed.), *Prospects for Democracy* (Cambridge: Polity Press, 1993), p. 92; and S. Mendus, 'Losing the Faith: Feminism and Democracy', in J. Dunn (ed.), *Democracy, The Unfinished Journey, 503 BC to AD 1993* (Oxford: Oxford University Press, 1992), p. 207.

[130] C. Pateman, *The Disorder of Women* (Cambridge: Cambridge University Press, 1989), p. 222.

[131] 'Strong' democracy is Benjamin Barber's phrase. See B. Barber, *Strong Democracy* (Berkeley: University of California Press, 1984).

[132] D. Held, 'Democracy: From City-States to Cosmopolitan Order?', in D. Held (ed.), *Prospects for Democracy* (Cambridge: Polity Press, 1993), p. 24. See further the discussion of 'democratic autonomy' in D. Held, *Models of Democracy* (Cambridge: Polity Press, 1987), pp. 283–9. For a variation on this theme, see also Michael Walzer's concept of 'critical associationalism', in M. Walzer, 'The Civil Society Argument', in C. Mouffe (ed.), *Dimensions of Radical Democracy* (London and New York: Verso, 1992), pp. 105–7.

proposals for reform and areas of contestation within contemporary liberal democratic thought. It is perhaps sufficient, none the less, to indicate the existence of competing conceptions of the nature of democratic life, the proper scope of democracy and the institutional forms democracy might take—each proceeding from a differing understanding of the significance of freedom and equality, and each leading to a different distribution of power in society.

Returning to the European Convention, it follows that a 'democratic society' is no technical matter, no fixed archetype. The contention, advanced during the Convention's drafting debates, that democracy is 'not a theory of political philosophy and therefore not a subject of dispute'[133] cannot be accepted. Nor, on the other hand, can the notion be endorsed that the 'political' and contestable character of democracy renders it inappropriate to the Convention.[134] As demonstrated above, democracy was in fact given a variety of tasks within the Convention, and the Strasbourg organs have had to confront those tasks, even if they have preferred to adopt the conventional liberal posture of reticence as regards their political implications.

In reconstructing the image of a 'democratic society' that informs the Convention, it will be convenient to consider separately these various tasks and the clues they have thrown up. The three-fold categorization adopted above will be followed. In this, it will be recalled, democracy's role in the Convention is taken to be first, to justify and lend shape to, and priority among, the rights and freedoms guaranteed; secondly, to distinguish between acceptable and unacceptable restrictions of particular rights and freedoms; and thirdly, to ground certain rights and institutions directly connected with elections.

With regard to the first of these tasks, it was noted in section I that early perspectives on democracy in this context dwelt on the line separating democracy from totalitarianism. This can be a useful analytical move.[135] In the hands of those associated with the Convention, however, it suggested an extremely narrow, protective view of democracy, in which democracy was a means for protecting citizens from the worst abuses of State power and enabling them to carry on with their lives in time-honoured fashion in civil society. If more recent understandings of democracy in this context have adopted a wider view of the

[133] *Travaux*, vol. 1, p. 202 (Teitgen).

[134] *Travaux*, vol. 3, p. 182 (Dowson).

[135] Claude Lefort builds a theory of democracy on the distinction between democracy, where the place of power is symbolically empty, and totalitarianism, where the place of power is symbolically filled by those claiming to embody the people. In his conception human rights operate primarily to protect the empty space that is the necessary concomitant of popular sovereignty by securing the separation of power from justice. Nonetheless, Lefort's theory leads him to a generous, developmental vision of democracy rather than a purely protective one. See C. Lefort, *The Political Forms of Modern Society* (ed. J. Thompson, Cambridge: Polity Press, 1986), chaps. 7 and 8; C. Lefort, *Democracy and Political Theory* (trans. D. Macey, Cambridge: Polity Press, 1988), chaps. 1 and 2.

accountability of public power, they have none the less remained within substantially similar terrain. Democracy is associated with the separation of public powers, the interplay of group interests, public debate, faith in the media and the freedoms of expression, association, assembly and security. At the same time, democracy is also identified with the liberal virtues of 'pluralism, tolerance and broadmindedness', the urge to constrain the majoritarian tendencies of liberal democracy to respect individual difference.

These features are crucial elements in any liberal democratic order. But they contain little that would hearten those seeking the further democratization of actually existing liberal democracy. Democracy is seen as primarily about government. Government is assumed to be properly conducted by professionals, with citizens' interest limited to protection from misuse of State power and accountability in 'public' affairs. Questions about active citizenship, participation in decision-making and the enabling conditions for that participation do not figure. Perhaps the most encouraging sign for the critics is the Court's early acknowledgement in *Handyside*[136] that freedom of expression is not just a precondition for elections and competition between parties but is also a condition for self-development. The Court here implies—though it does not pursue the implications of—a vision of democratic life that tends in the direction of 'strong' democracy.

As regards democracy's second function, its work concerning restrictions on rights and freedoms, it will be recalled that argument has often been in terms of a tension between community rights and individual rights or between the rights of different individuals. The Convention organs have sought to resolve the tension by achieving a 'proportion'. The latitude the organs claim to have allowed themselves in achieving this proportion is seemingly dependent, at least in part, on the respect the organs consider is due to the political process from which the restriction emerged.

While in this context the Convention organs have largely avoided grappling substantively with what a 'democratic society' might be, their pronouncements reflect assumptions largely consonant with the conventional tenets of liberal democracy. Democracy is taken to be about institutions and procedures of public decision-making. The main issue is invariably the extent to which the organs will call into question those institutions and procedures, the acts of the 'national authorities'. Statements by the minority of the Court in *Open Door and Dublin Well Woman*[137] to the effect that a decision endorsed by national referendum should not be called into question may please the advocates of 'strong' democracy. These statements tend to suggest that decisions are most

[136] 7 December 1976, ECHR, Series A, No. 24, para. 49.
[137] 29 October 1992, ECHR, Series A, No. 246.

worthy of respect when they have engaged (relatively speaking) the most citizen participation. If the majority of the Court side-stepped this issue in *Open Door and Dublin Well Woman*, the organs have been even more reticent in taking the correlative point, that decisions are not worthy of respect where they have been made in an environment of unconstrained secrecy.

The case law in this context also appears to confirm the organs' attachment to the separation between public and private spheres.[138] Thus, in cases involving freedom of expression in a commercial context,[139] the Convention organs have opted for a wide margin of appreciation, in marked contrast to their attitude in cases involving free speech in the public sphere. While this may be explained in a variety of ways, it is certainly consistent with a conventional liberal assumption about private and public domains. That is to say, it is consistent with an assumption that, whereas public affairs are essentially 'political', economic relations are essentially 'non-political' and do not engage democracy to the same extent.

It is in democracy's third, election-oriented, context that the 'thinnest' conception of liberal democracy appears. It will be recalled that Protocol 1, Article 3, envisages elections solely for the choice of members of the legislature, who are then taken to 'represent' the electors. The Convention organs have understood 'legislature' in this context to include organs other than national parliaments, but only to the extent that they have 'primary rule-making capacity'.[140] The Commission and Court have thus given little encouragement to moves for more local democracy. If a State party wishes to minimize its obligations under Article 3, it need only avoid devolving power.

Moreover, Protocol 1, Article 3, requires only that elections be held 'under conditions which will ensure the free expression of the opinion of the people'. In drafting debates it appears to have been recognized that conventional electoral processes in Western polities cannot be said to ensure in any real sense that the legislature, much less the government, 'is an expression of the will of the people', 'represents the people' or even 'represents the opinion of the people'.[141] This was not, however, taken as a signal that the polities themselves were less democratic than they might be; rather it was taken to indicate that the draft article was pitched too

[138] Regarding this attachment, and particularly its implications for the *Drittwirkung*, see A. Clapham, *Human Rights in the Private Sphere* (Oxford: Oxford University Press, 1993).

[139] e.g., *Markt Intern and Beermann* v. *Germany*, 20 November 1989, ECHR, Series A, No. 164, and *Casado Coca* v. *Spain*, 24 February 1994, ECHR, Series A, No. 285.

[140] See *Edwards* v. *UK*, Appl. 11377/85, 8 EHRR 96; and *Mathieu-Mohin and Clerfayt*, 2 March 1987, ECHR, Series A, No. 113.

[141] This can be inferred from the rejection of successive drafts of Protocol 1, Art. 3, in favour of the final formulation. See compilation of drafts, reproduced in *Travaux*, vol. 7, pp. 150–1. It can also, to an extent, be inferred from observations such as those of Sir Oscar Dowson, UK member of Committee of Experts, that the first draft of Art. 3 was, in a variety of respects, 'a rather misleading over-simplification': *Travaux*, vol. 3, p. 182.

high and needed amending. The Convention organs have understood Article 3 to require that the State must operate an electoral system which ensures equality of treatment of all citizens in the exercise of the right to vote. Applying the margin of appreciation doctrine, however, they have so far declined to examine closely the conditions necessary to render that equality effective.[142]

Protocol 1, Article 3, thus envisages democracy as entailing a formal right of citizens to vote in national—and in some polities, regional—elections. Democracy, in this conception, is about professional government, legitimated by periodic elections. It envisages no further citizen involvement in decision-making, and assumes no need, and no role, for democracy within civil society.

From these three contexts, a picture of a 'democratic society' emerges that adheres closely to the conventional postulates of Western liberal democracy as regards the nature of democratic life, the proper scope of democracy and the institutional forms democracy is assumed to take. Democratic life appears as an undemanding, and of itself unsatisfying, existence. Voting in periodic national elections is the principal opportunity people have to act in their capacity as citizens. The structuring of common life is given over to the professionals and experts, while ordinary people live out their lives in a 'private' sphere assumed to be autonomous and non-political. The proper scope of democracy is taken to be the 'public' realm. Asymmetries of power in the realm of civil society, affecting the efficacy and genuineness of formal freedom and equality, are largely invisible to the Convention's eye. And, finally, democracy is taken, above all, to be about formal political institutions and the formal rights and freedoms directly associated with them. Institutional forms designed to enhance local, unmediated, informal decision-making by citizens over issues affecting them are not part of this conception of democracy. While some hints in the direction of a less instrumental, more empowering picture of a 'democratic society' have been noted, it is apparent that, overall, the Convention remains substantially in the camp of 'thin' liberal democracy.

V. Globalizing Democracy: What Role for the Convention?

The previous section examined the Convention in the light of calls for a 'double democratization' or, as it is sometimes put, a deepening of democracy on two levels, from formal political institutions to political and social processes and from State to civil society. In addition, political

[142] See *Liberal Party and others* v. *UK*, Appl. 8765/79, 18 December 1980, 4 EHRR 106; and *Mathieu-Mohin and Clerfayt*, 2 March 1987, ECHR, Series A, No. 113.

theory has recently seen calls for a deepening of democracy along a third axis: a deepening from the level of each nation-State to that of global society.[143] Political analysts relate the need for a 'globalization' of democracy to a more general phenomenon of globalization in social, political and economic relations.[144] National and international affairs have always been connected, but globalization refers to an exponential and increasingly institutionalized intensification of these connections. It refers to the emergence of a global economic system and military order; to the recognition of social, security, environmental and resource distributional problems that demand transnational solutions; to the spread of world-wide communications and transport networks. Equally, it refers to the expanding agenda of international law; to the establishment of regional and international organizations with programmes that range more and more widely; and to efforts at fostering a moral community extending beyond national boundaries. Each of these (inter-related) developments eludes the control of any single State. Yet because the developments themselves testify to a world in which events in one State produce outcomes in others, each also limits the policy choices that are, or at any rate should be, available to national polities. From this perspective, globalization is a name for the evident strains on the sovereignty of nation-States.

In view of this globalizing turn, it is argued that democracy too must 'become a transnational affair'.[145] By this appears to be meant that those who govern nationally should assume accountability to a constituency consonant with the impact of their decisions. Regional and international organizations should be strengthened in their capacity effectively to address common problems, especially those that transcend national boundaries. These organizations ought also to become more accountable and more transparent; the balance within them between 'parliamentary' and 'bureaucratic' procedures should shift in favour of the former. Attention must be given to finding ways of unsettling, and reducing the impact of, entrenched disparities of power in international relations. Non-governmental actors should be integrated into the processes of regional and international governance.

[143] David Held develops this argument furthest, casting it in terms of his own powerful and highly suggestive concept of 'cosmopolitan' democracy. See *Political Theory and the Modern State* (Cambridge: Polity Press, 1989), chap. 8; 'Democracy, the Nation-State and the Global System', in D. Held (ed.), *Political Theory Today* (Cambridge: Polity Press, 1991), p. 197; 'Democracy: From City-States to Cosmopolitan Order?', in D. Held (ed.), *Prospects for Democracy* (Cambridge: Polity Press, 1993), p. 24; and, most recently, 'Democracy and the New International Order', in D. Archibugi and D. Held (eds.), *Cosmopolitan Democracy* (Cambridge: Polity Press, 1995), p. 96. The case for a globalization of democracy is also advanced in Y. Sakamoto, 'Introduction: The Global Context of Democratization', *Alternatives*, 16 (1991), p. 119.

[144] Concerning this phenomenon, see A. Giddens, *The Consequences of Modernity* (Cambridge: Polity Press, 1990), pp. 64 ff.

[145] D. Held, 'Democracy: From City-States to Cosmopolitan Order?', in D. Held (ed.), *Prospects for Democracy* (Cambridge: Polity Press, 1993), p. 24, at p. 40.

Those who argue for a globalization of democracy insist that it is in no way at odds with calls for more local democracy and for the infusion of democracy in the 'private' sphere. On the contrary, global democracy would be partial indeed if it were not accompanied by processes of internal deepening, just as those internal processes could ultimately achieve little without a sympathetic framework of global democracy. The very point of globalization is that the diverse settings of social, political and economic life are interlinked. Thus, it is said, 'democracy can be deepened only if it is globalized, and it can be globalized only if it is deepened'.[146]

As a treaty which sets, and seeks to enforce, common standards between States parties, the European Convention is an obvious part of the globalization phenomenon. All the more so, given that it has influenced legal developments in other regions in the world.[147] As a human rights treaty, its main thrust is towards internal arrangements within nation-States. In section IV above, the conclusion was reached that the conception of a 'democratic society' that informs the Convention is relatively unresponsive to calls for more democracy in more settings. This may, in turn, limit the extent to which the Convention, as currently understood by the supervisory organs, can contribute towards the internal deepening—and thus ultimately, to the globalization—of democracy.

Focusing on the globalizing axis, the case of *Tete*[148] suggests that the Strasbourg organs are cognisant of the potential impact on Convention commitments of other forces for globalization affecting European States, such as the European Union. This is so, even if the Commission was in that case unsure precisely how to characterize the European Parliament. In certain fundamental respects, however, the significance of globalization for the interpretation and application of the Convention remains unclear. It will be recalled that in the context of limitation clauses, the Convention organs have expressed concern to achieve a 'proportion' between minority and majority opinions within countries. In particular, they have attached importance to the protection of the former. The organs' attitude has frequently been different as regards divergences of law and practice among national societies within the Council of Europe. Thus in *Dudgeon*[149] and *Norris*[150] the Court was strongly influenced by the position with regard to homosexuality in the majority of member States, a position to which, it appeared to think, Northern Ireland and

[146] Y. Sakamoto, 'Introduction: The Global Context of Democratization', *Alternatives*, 16 (1991), p. 119, at p. 122.

[147] The European Convention has influenced both national constitutions (e.g., those of a number of African States, former British colonies) and regional human rights treaties (notably, the American Convention on Human Rights and the African Charter of Human and Peoples' Rights).

[148] Appl. 1123/84, 11 EHRR 91.

[149] *Dudgeon* v. *UK*, 22 October 1981, ECHR, Series A, No. 45.

[150] *Norris* v. *Ireland*, 26 October 1988, ECHR, Series A, No. 142.

Ireland should respectively conform. And in *Open Door and Dublin Well Woman*[151] the Court showed how one right (in that case freedom of information) could be used indirectly to compel a measure of conformity to the European norm with regard to another matter (abortion). The Court's stance illustrates a seemingly unresolved tension within globalization between homogenization on the one hand and respect for pluralism and group difference on the other. The issue is rendered all the more urgent with the adherence to the Convention of Central and Eastern European States. As the character of the Council of Europe majority shifts, and its coincidence with hierarchies of power within Europe abates, the Court will need, more than ever, to confront the meaning of 'common' standards.

VI. Concluding Reflections

Investigating the European Convention's multifaceted relationship with democracy, the writer has suggested that the Convention is currently premised on a relatively thin conception of a 'democratic society'. While the Convention undoubtedly contributes to the phenomenon of globalization, this conception may constrain the extent to which it can assist in globalizing *democracy*. For the Convention to play a larger role in the globalization of democracy, Convention law would need to impose on States obligations to widen access to public decision-making and to eliminate systematic obstacles that undercut formal rights, including those which widened access to public decision-making would offer.[152] To the extent that the Convention organs apply a conception of a 'democratic society' in the various contexts discussed above, there is no reason why they could not apply one that is animated by these obligations. As 'guardians of the Convention',[153] the organs have both the responsibility and the power to take bold interpretative positions that challenge States parties to live up to their commitments and deny governments the luxury of complacency. The fear that the organs might, by adopting exacting standards, provoke governments to denounce the Convention or revoke their acceptance of the Commission's competence, or that they might

[151] *Open Door and Dublin Well Woman* v. *Ireland*, 29 October 1992, ECHR, Series A, No. 246.

[152] With regard to the elimination of systematic obstacles, the European Social Charter is no doubt to be seen as the Council of Europe's primary vehicle for pressing pertinent State obligations. This does not, however, affect the suggestion made below that the Convention organs should reinforce the Charter's work. Reinforcement is all the more necessary given that the Charter currently affords no right of individual petition.

[153] See Art. 19.

discourage parallel developments in other regions of the world, has surely diminished in practical force.[154]

Were these changes to be implemented, the Convention's 'democratic society' would still—it seems safe to predict—be open to further democratization. Political philosophers and activists will not stop rethinking and debating the conditions, and strategies, for achieving a more substantial liberal democracy than that currently on offer. Certainly, reports of the death of all alternatives to actually existing Western liberal democracy[155] seem very greatly exaggerated. Indeed, these reports appear only to have served to revivify the reformers.[156] The question posed in this article is whether the members of the European Commission and Court of Human Rights, inevitably political philosophers too of a sort,[157] will follow this example.

[154] Judge Fitzmaurice attached much importance to this concern in a series of dissenting and separate opinions in the 1970s. See, especially, *Golder*, 21 February 1975, ECHR, Series A, No. 18, separate opinion, paras. 32–46, and *National Union of Belgian Police*, 27 October 1975, ECHR, Series A, No. 19, separate opinion, para. 8.

[155] See F. Fukuyama, 'The End of History', *The National Interest*, 1989, p. 16; 'A Reply to My Critics', *The National Interest*, 1989–90, p. 18; and *The End of History and the Last Man* (New York: Free Press, 1992), reflecting upon the revolutionary changes in Central and Eastern Europe beginning in 1989.

[156] Francis Fukuyama's writings provoked an avalanche of responses. Alex Callinicos captures the spirit of many of them when he writes: 'It is strange that 1989/91, so dramatic a demonstration that "nothing has to be the way it is", should have instead reinforced a restriction of the political imagination to the confines imposed by the market. To me it seems rather to be a time to think big.' See A. Callinicos, 'Socialism and Democracy', in D. Held (ed.), *Prospects for Democracy* (Cambridge: Polity Press, 1993), p. 200, at p. 211.

[157] Thus, Karl Klare, in an inspiring article on democratic reconstruction in Eastern Europe, notes that the rights foundation of democratic reconstruction 'is an invitation to make political philosophy, not only initially in promulgating the initial charters, but at every step along the way of articulating and interpreting rights concepts and filling them with concrete legal and institutional meaning'. See K. Klare, 'Legal Theory and Democratic Reconstruction: Reflections on 1989', *University of British Columbia Law Review*, 25 (1991), p. 69, at pp. 101–2.

THE DESTRUCTION OF AIRCRAFT IN FLIGHT OVER SCOTLAND AND NIGER: THE QUESTIONS OF JURISDICTION AND EXTRADITION UNDER INTERNATIONAL LAW*

By SAMI SHUBBER‡

Two aircraft exploded in flight, namely a US-registered aircraft (Pan Am 103) over the Scottish town of Lockerbie on 21 December 1988, and a French-registered aircraft (UTA 772) over Niger on 19 September 1989. The two explosions killed 440 persons.[1] Investigators of the debris of the US-registered aircraft in Lockerbie found a few fragments of a bomb. From these fragments, the UK and USA say that a twisting trail led to the Libyan secret service, so the two States issued arrest warrants for two persons alleged to be employees of the Libyan secret service.[2] France also accused a group of Libyans of destroying the French-registered aircraft, demanding their extradition. The UK, USA and France referred the matter to the Security Council, which adopted Resolution 731 on 21 January 1992, Resolution 748 on 31 March 1992 and Resolution 883 on 11 November 1993, applying sanctions not involving the use of force under Chapter VII of the UN Charter against Libya. Libya, on the other hand, instituted proceedings on 3 March 1992 against the UK and USA before the International Court of Justice (ICJ)[3] in respect of a dispute with the USA and the UK over the interpretation

‡ Lic-en-Dr. (Baghdad), Postgraduate Dip. in Law, LLM (London), Ph.D (Cantab.); Barrister of Gray's Inn.

[1] See *The Economist*, 28 March-3 April 1992, p. 55.

[2] Ibid.

[3] See *Questions of Interpretation and Application of the 1971 Montreal Convention arising from the Aerial Incident at Lockerbie, Libya* v. *UK, ICJ Reports*, 1992, p. 3, and *Libya* v. *US, ICJ Reports*, 1992, p. 114. On the Lockerbie case, see M. Weller, 'The Lockerbie Case: A Premature End to the "New World Order"?', *Journal of the African Society of International and Comparative Law*, 4 (1992), p. 302; F. Beveridge, 'The Lockerbie Affair', *International and Comparative Law Quarterly*, 41 (1992), p. 907; C. Tomuschat, 'The Lockerbie Case before the International Court of Justice', *Review of the International Commission of Jurists*, 48 (1992), p. 38; T. Franck, ' "The Powers of Appreciation": Who is the Ultimate Guardian of UN Legality?', *American Journal of International Law*, 86 (1992), p. 519; id., 'UN Checks and Balances: The Roles of the ICJ and the Security Council', in American Society of International Law/Nederlandse Vereniging voor International Recht, *Contemporary International Law Issues: Opportunities at a Time of Momentous Change* (1993), p. 280; J.M. Sorel, 'Les Ordonnances de la Cour International de Justice du 14 avril 1992 dans l'affaire relative à des questions d'interprétation et d'application de la Convention de Montreal de 1971 résultant de l'incident aérien de Lockerbie (Libye c. Royaume Uni et Libye c. Etats-Unis), *Revue générale de droit international public*, 97 (1993), p. 690; and V. Gowlland-Debbas, 'The Relationship between the International Court of Justice and the Security Council in the Light of the *Lockerbie* Case', *American Journal of International Law*, 88 (1994), p. 643.

and application of the Montreal Convention for the Suppression of Unlawful Acts against the Safety of Civil Aviation, 1971 (hereinafter referred to as the 'Montreal Convention').[4] The UN Secretary-General and the Arab League were also involved in an attempt to find an amicable solution to the dispute.

The Montreal Convention was adopted at an international diplomatic conference, held under the auspices of ICAO, on 23 September 1971. The purpose of the Convention is to protect the safety of international civil aviation and its facilities and to increase the confidence of people all over the world in the safety of international civil air transport.[5] The Montreal Convention is the applicable treaty in the cases of aircraft sabotage dealt with in this article, and it is in force among a very large number of States, including Libya, France, the UK and the USA. It has been supplemented by the Montreal Protocol for the Suppression of Unlawful Acts of Violence at Airports Serving Civil Aviation, 1988[6] (hereinafter referred to as the 'Montreal Protocol'). This article will deal with the following questions within the context of the Montreal Convention: first, the offence of aircraft sabotage; secondly, the exercise of jurisdiction over that offence; and thirdly, the extradition arrangements and the action of the Security Council relating thereto. A comparison with other relevant international conventions will be made when appropriate.

I. The Offence of Aircraft Sabotage

In accordance with Article 1, paragraph 1, of the Montreal Convention,

> any person commits an offence if he unlawfully and intentionally:
>
> ...
>
> (*b*) destroys an aircraft in service or causes damage to such an aircraft which renders it incapable of flight or which is likely to endanger its safety in flight.

The provision does not give a specific name to the offence, nor does it

[4] The text of the Montreal Convention is to be found in *International Legal Materials*, 10 (1971), pp. 1151–6.

[5] See the statement of the Delegate of Japan to the Montreal Conference: '. . . acts of violence against international civil air transport and its facilities no doubt jeopardize the safety of civil aviation, seriously affect the operation of international air services and undermine the confidence of the people of the world in the safety of international civil air transport': International Conference on Air Law, Montreal, September 1971, ICAO Document 9081–LC/170–1, p. 5, paragraph 10. The Acting President of the Conference said: 'Acts such as sabotage, and similar offences, which interfered with the safety of international civil aviation were a threat to the development of a vital means of transportation in a modern world': ibid., p. 1, paragraph 3.

[6] See Article 1 of the Protocol; the text of the Protocol is reproduced in *International Legal Materials*, 27 (1988), pp. 627–30.

define the offence. It merely describes the elements of the offence. It is to be noted that Article 1 of the Montreal Convention deals with other offences, such as acts of violence on board an aircraft, the placing of destructive substances on board an aircraft damage to, air navigation facilities and so on. But for the purposes of this article, only the offence of aircraft sabotage will be treated.

The elements of the offence of aircraft sabotage are:

(1) Destruction of, or causing damage to, an aircraft.
(2) the aircraft must be in service; and
(3) the action must be unlawful and intentional.

1. *Destruction of, or causing damage to, an aircraft*

Any act resulting in the destruction of an aircraft in service, or causing damage to it, constitutes the first element of the offence of aircraft sabotage. This element constitutes the *actus reus* of the offence in the sense of English criminal law.[7] Such an act can be committed by the placing of a bomb in a suitcase which explodes in the aircraft, firing at the aircraft, or causing fire on board the aircraft itself. The destruction of both the Pan Am aircraft in Scotland and UTA aircraft in Niger appear to have been caused by the explosion of destructive devices placed in the luggage carried in the aircraft.[8] It is to be noted, however, that any damage to an aircraft has to be of such a nature that 'it renders it incapable of flight or which is likely to endanger its safety in flight'. Damage of a lesser extent may not be subject to the Montreal Convention. During the deliberations of the Montreal Conference, 1971, the French[9] and UK[10] Delegates expressed the view that the Convention should apply only to grave offences.

Any of the acts mentioned above may be characterized as an offence against penal law, though created by an international convention. Therefore, they could be covered by the Tokyo Convention on Offences and Certain Other Acts Committed on Board Aircraft, 1963[11] (hereinafter referred to as the 'Tokyo Convention'). This point may be relevant from the point of view of jurisdiction, as will be seen later. A similar offence with respect to ships was created by the Rome Convention for the Suppression of Unlawful Acts against the Safety of Maritime Navigation, 1988 (hereinafter referred to as the 'Rome Convention').[12] This is

[7] See G. Williams, *Textbook of Criminal Law* (1978), p. 30.

[8] See above, n. 1.

[9] See International Conference on Air Law, Montreal, loc. cit. above (n. 5), p. 21, paragraph 11.

[10] Ibid., p. 23, paragraph 21.

[11] The text of the Tokyo Convention is to be found in *International Legal Materials*, 2 (1963), pp. 1042–6. On the Tokyo Convention see Shubber, *Jurisdiction over Crimes on Board Aircraft* (1973).

[12] See Article 3 of the Rome Convention. The text of the Rome Convention is to be found in *International Legal Materials*, 27 (1988), pp. 672–84.

not surprising, for the Rome Convention is essentially based on the Hague and Montreal Conventions.[13]

2. *The aircraft must be in service*

The second element of the offence is that the destroyed or damaged aircraft must be 'in service'. The Montreal Convention defines the term as follows:

Article 2

For the purposes of this Convention:

. . .

(*b*) an aircraft is considered to be in service from the beginning of the preflight preparation of the aircraft by ground personnel or by the crew for a specific flight until twenty-four hours after any landing; the period of service shall, in any event, extend for the entire period during which the aircraft is in flight as defined in paragraph (*a*) of this article.

'In service', therefore, includes various stages of preparing the aircraft for a flight, even while the aircraft is in the hangar or in flight as defined in the Convention,[14] and extends 24 hours after the aircraft lands. This is a very wide coverage in terms of time and place. Accordingly, aircraft sabotage can be committed when the aircraft is not yet airborne, or 'in flight' in the sense of the Montreal Convention. However, in accordance with Article 4, paragraph 2, the Convention applies, 'irrespective of whether the aircraft is engaged in an international or domestic flight, only if: (*a*) the place of take-off or landing, actual or intended, of the aircraft is situated outside the territory of the State of registration of the aircraft; or (*b*) the offence is committed in the territory of a State other than the State of registration of the aircraft.' Therefore, if an aircraft registered in State A is being prepared for a flight between that State and State B, and is destroyed by a group of terrorists in State A, even before take-off, the Convention applies. The same applies if the aircraft is destroyed in the territory of State B, whether on the ground or in the airspace of State B. It may be recalled that the Pan Am aircraft and the UTA aircraft were destroyed while they were in flight, in the airspace of States, other than the States of registration, en route for the latter States.

The notion of 'in service' is wider than that of 'in flight' used in the Tokyo Convention[15] and the Convention for the Suppression of Unlaw-

[13] See International Maritime Organization (IMO) Document C57/25, 1 October 1986, Annex, p. 3, paragraph 1. For the Hague Convention, see below, p. 243.

[14] Article 2, paragraph (*a*), of the Montreal Convention defines 'in flight' as follows:

'An aircraft is considered to be in flight at any time from the moment when all its external doors are closed following embarkation until the moment when any such door is opened for disembarkation; in the case of a forced landing the flight shall be deemed to continue until the competent authorities take over the responsibility for the aircraft and for persons and property on board.'

[15] Article 1, paragraph 3, of the Tokyo Convention reads: 'For the purposes of this Convention, an aircraft is considered to be in flight from the moment when power is applied for the purpose of take-off until the moment when the landing run ends'.

ful Seizure of Aircraft, 1970 (hereinafter referred to as the 'Hague Convention').[16] The wide scope of the Montreal Convention can be justified by the nature of the offences covered by it and the place where such offences can be committed. While under the Tokyo and Hague Conventions the offences can be committed only when the external doors of the aircraft are closed after embarkation, an aircraft can be the subject of sabotage, even before the embarkation of passengers, which justifies the different treatment of the Montreal Convention.

3. *The action must be unlawful and intentional*

The destruction of an aircraft, or the causing of damage to it, must be intentional and unlawful, in order to fall within the scope of the Montreal Convention. This element constitutes the *mens rea* of the offence, in the sense of English criminal law.[17] If a person unintentionally leaves a destructive device in his hand luggage, and the aircraft is damaged as a result, the offence of aircraft sabotage would not be committed, though another offence under the relevant jurisdiction would probably be committed. During the discussion of the provision at the Montreal Conference, the UK Delegate made the following comment on this point:

> . . . His Delegation wished to be sure that the convention would apply only to deliberate acts of sabotage (that is, to acts where it was the intention or purpose to endanger the aircraft, or to cause danger, etc.). Everyone was aware of how easily one could, quite intentionally, do something that had the effect of endangering safety, without in any way intending that result.[18]

The unlawfulness of the action needs no labouring, as it is hardly likely that any person would destroy or damage an aircraft in service for lawful purposes, except, perhaps in the exercise of self-defence. In this case, the conditions of self-defence must be present.[19] This element of intentional and unlawful act is common in all international conventions on terrorism.[20]

[16] See Article 3, paragraph 1, of the Hague Convention, which is identical with Article 2 of the Montreal Convention quoted in n. 14 above. The text of the Hague Convention is to be found in *International Legal Materials*, 10 (1971), pp. 133–6.

[17] See Williams, op. cit. above (n. 7).

[18] International Conference on Air Law, Montreal, loc. cit. above (n. 5), p. 23, paragraph 21.

[19] See Article 51 of the UN Charter; for different views on the conditions of self-defence, see the two leading authorities on the subject: Bowett, *Self-Defence in International Law* (1958), and Brownlie, *International Law and the Use of Force by States* (1963).

[20] For examples, see the International Convention against the Taking of Hostages, 1979 (hereinafter referred to as the 'Convention against Hostage-Taking'), Article 1, paragraph 1; and Article 3, paragraph 1, of the Rome Convention. On the Convention against Hostage-Taking, see Shubber, 'The International Convention against the Taking of Hostages', this *Year Book*, 52 (1981), pp. 205 ff., and on the Rome Convention, see Shubber, 'Sabotage and Attacks against Ships, Cargoes and Persons on Board—The Rome Convention 1988', *Austrian Journal of Public and International Law*, 43 (1992), pp. 139 ff.

When the three elements are met, the offence of aircraft sabotage is committed under the Montreal Convention. This appears to be the case with respect to the Pan Am and UTA aircraft. It should be pointed out that not only is the commission of the offence subject to the Convention, but also an attempt to commit the offence is covered, in accordance with Article 1, paragraph 2(*a*). Furthermore, not only is the perpetrator of the offence subject to the Convention, but also his accomplice, as well as the accomplice of a person who attempts to commit the offence of aircraft sabotage, in accordance with Article 1, paragraph 2(*b*). However, it is unfortunate that the Montreal Convention does not deal with threats to commit aircraft sabotage. For it is possible that someone may threaten to blow up an aircraft, unless his demands are met, be it for a ransom or for something else. There have been cases of such threats. For example, in 1971, a threat to blow up a TWA aircraft was made, unless the sum of US$2,000,000 were paid by the airline; a bomb was discovered in the cockpit of the aircraft.[21] This omission has been avoided in the Rome Convention, which is based on the Montreal Convention.[22]

Finally, the destruction of an aircraft, or the causing of damage to it, can be committed by 'any person', irrespective of his status or position. That is to say, a passenger, a member of the crew, a person at an airport, a government official[23] and so on can be the perpetrator of the offence, and as such, will be subject to the Montreal Convention. For the provision does not contain any qualification, or condition, as to who may be subject to it. It simply says 'any person' will commit the offences enumerated in Article 1, paragraph 1, of the Convention.

II. Jurisdiction over the Offence of Aircraft Sabotage

Article 5 of the Montreal Convention provides the legal basis for the exercise of jurisdiction by States under the Convention; it reads as follows:

1. Each Contracting State shall take such measures as may be necessary to establish its jurisdiction over the offences in the following cases:
   (*a*) when the offence is committed in the territory of that State;

[21] See *International Herald Tribune*, 8 March 1971. A similar threat was made against an Air Lingus aircraft in 1971: see *The Times*, 19 July 1971.

[22] See Article 3, paragraph 2(*c*), of the Rome Convention.

[23] During the hearing of the Libyan application for provisional measures, the question was raised as to whether Libya could try the accused Libyans, who were described as 'officers of the Libyan Intelligence Services'. Judge Schwebel asked: 'Does the [Montreal] Convention cover such an accusation, i.e., of acts of persons in official service carrying out official purposes? Would the trial by a State of persons alleged to be its own officials . . . be the prosecution by a Contracting State which is contemplated by the Montreal Convention?': *ICJ Oral Hearings* (hereinafter referred to as *Oral Hearings*), CR92/6 (28 March 1992), p. 48, paragraph 1.

(*b*) when the offence is committed against or on board an aircraft registered in that State;
(*c*) when the aircraft on board which the offence is committed lands in its territory with the alleged offender still on board;
(*d*) when the offence is committed against or on board an aircraft leased without crew to a lessee who has his principal place of business or, if the lessee has no such place of business, his permanent residence, in that State.

2. Each Contracting State shall likewise take such measures as may be necessary to establish its jurisdiction over the offences mentioned in Article 1, paragraph 1 (*a*), (*b*) and (*c*), and in Article 1, paragraph 2, in so far as that paragraph relates to those offences, in the case where the alleged offender is present in its territory and it does not extradite him pursuant to Article 8 to any of the States mentioned in paragraph 1 of this article.
3. This Convention does not exclude any criminal jurisdiction exercised in accordance with national law.

Article 5 provides the same bases for the exercise of jurisdiction over the offence of aircraft sabotage as those provided under Article 4 of the Hague Convention against aircraft hijacking, and is probably based on the latter provision. Furthermore, the provision does not speak of the competence of the States enumerated in it to exercise jurisdiction, but merely states that 'each Contracting State shall take such measures as may be necessary to establish its jurisdiction over the offence'. The same language was used in other international conventions adopted to combat other aspects of terrorism, such as the New York Convention on the Prevention and Punishment of Crimes against Internationally Protected Persons, including Diplomatic Agents, 1973 (hereinafter referred to as the 'New York Convention'),[24] the Convention against Hostage-Taking,[25] and the Rome Convention.[26] The question then arises: is the provision intended merely to establish a basis for jurisdiction, e.g., enacting national legislation, or is it intended for the establishment of such a basis and the exercise of it?[27] It is submitted that what is intended

[24] See Article 3, paragraph 1, of the Convention; the text of the Convention is to be found in *International Legal Materials*, 13 (1974), pp. 41–9.

[25] See Article 5, paragraph 1, of the Convention.

[26] See Article 6, paragraph 1, of the Convention.

[27] On a similar point with respect to the Hague Convention, see Shubber, 'Aircraft Hijacking under the Hague Convention 1970—A New Regime?', *International and Comparative Law Quarterly*, 22 (1973), pp. 706–7. Jurisdiction in the sense of international law has three aspects: executive jurisdiction, legislative jurisdiction and curial (or judicial) jurisdiction. See Sir Robert Jennings, 'The Limits of State Jurisdiction' *Nordisk Tidsskrift for International Ret*, 32 (1962), p. 209. The American Law Institute divides jurisdiction into thee categories: 'a) *jurisdiction to prescribe*, i.e., the authority of a state to make its law applicable to persons or activities; b) *jurisdiction to adjudicate*, i.e., the authority of a state to subject particular persons or things to its judicial process; and c) *jurisdiction to enforce*, i.e., the authority of a state to use the resources of government to induce or compel compliance with its law': *Restatement of the Law Third* (1986), vol. 1, Introductory Note, p. 231, and sec. 401, p. 232.

is probably the establishment of the basis for jurisdiction and the exercise thereof. This interpretation appears to be in line with the objective of the Convention, as declared in its preamble, of providing a deterrent against aircraft sabotage and appropriate measures for the punishment of the offenders.[28]

This article will now deal with the States entitled to exercise jurisdiction over the offence of aircraft sabotage under the Montreal Convention. However, reference will also be made to the bases of jurisdiction under international customary law.

1. *The territorial State*

In accordance with Article 5, paragraph 1(*a*), of the Montreal Convention, the State in whose territory an act of sabotage against an aircraft is committed has the right to exercise jurisdiction over the offender. Territory includes the land, airspace and territorial sea of the State concerned. Therefore, if a bomb placed on board an aircraft registered in State A explodes in the airspace of State B, or the aircraft is attacked and damaged by gunfire while preparing for take-off at an airport in State B, the latter has the right to try the offenders in its courts, apply its laws to the offence and enforce whatever penalty may be imposed by its courts. The basis for the exercise of this jurisdiction is, of course, the territorial principle under international customary law, and the provision is merely declaratory of that principle.[29] The territorial principle '. . . has received universal recognition, and is but a single application of the essential territoriality of the sovereignty, the sum of legal competences, which a state has'.[30] Applying this principle to the case of sabotage of Pan Am Flight 103 over Lockerbie, Scotland, the UK is competent, subject to its outstanding treaty obligations, to exercise jurisdiction over the offenders, because the offence took place in its airspace. Similarly, Niger has the

[28] During the hearing of the Libyan application for provisional measures, Counsel for the UK, Professor Higgins, argued that Article 5(2) of the Montreal Convention '. . . imposes upon each party to the Convention a *duty* to ensure that its law provides for jurisdiction over the offences listed in Article 1, irrespective of where, or by whom, they were committed, so that a State has the capacity under its own law to try an offender if it does not extradite him. The text of Article 5(2) makes clear that what is involved is the *creation* of jurisdiction, and not its exercise in an individual case': *Oral Hearings*, CR92/3 (26 March 1992), p. 45. It is submitted with respect that while it is possible to interpret Article 5(2) of the Montreal Convention in the way advanced by Professor Higgins, this interpretation would probably not be in line with the objective of the Convention nor with the intention of the drafters of it. After all, the Montreal Convention was intended to discourage and, eventually, stop all acts of aircraft sabotage; hence jurisdiction covers all aspects under international law.

[29] The Solicitor General of Scotland, Mr A. Rodger, QC, said the following, during the Oral Hearings of Libya's application for provisional measures, in relation to the destruction of Pan Am flight 103: 'the Scottish Courts have jurisdiction, of course, on the basis that they are the courts of the locus of the offences. That basis of jurisdiction is one of the most fundamental recognized in customary international law . . . ': ibid., p. 14.

[30] Brownlie, *Principles of Public International Law* (4th edn., 1990), p. 300.

right to exercise jurisdiction over the offenders who caused the destruction of UTA Flight 772 in its airspace.

Subsequent conventions adopted by the international community, under the auspices of the United Nations or other international organizations, in order to combat terrorism, torture, illicit traffic in drugs and sabotage of ships and cargoes, contain a similar basis of jurisdiction.[31]

2. *The State of registration of the aircraft*

Article 5, paragraph 1(*b*), gives the State of registration of an aircraft the right to exercise jurisdiction over acts of sabotage committed against, or on board, an aircraft registered in that State. An aircraft registered in a given State bears the nationality of that State, by virtue of Article 17 of the Chicago Convention on Civil Aviation, 1944. Thus, registration confers the nationality of the registering State on the aircraft, as is the case with ships.[32] The basis of the exercise of jurisdiction is the nationality of the aircraft. This is in accordance with international customary law, which permits the flag State to exercise jurisdiction over crimes committed on board aircraft, and ships, registered in that State on the basis of assimilation of aircraft, and ships, to territory.[33] Accordingly, the US and France, the two States in which the destroyed aircraft of Pan Am and UTA were registered, are entitled to try the offenders in their courts and apply their national laws on the subject. In fact, the Lord Advocate of Scotland and a Grand Jury of the US District Court for the District of Columbia brought charges against two Libyan nationals in connection with the destruction of Pan Am Flight 103. This was followed by a declaration by the British and American Governments on 27 November 1991 to the effect that the Government of Libya must

[31] See the New York Convention, Article 3, paragraph 1(*a*); the Convention against Hostage-Taking, Article 5, paragraph 1(*a*); the Convention against Torture and other Cruel, Inhuman or Degrading Treatment or Punishment (hereinafter referred to as the 'Convention against Torture'), Article 5, paragraph 1(*a*) (for the text of the Convention, see *International Legal Materials*, 23 (1984), pp. 1027–37); the Rome Convention, Article 6, paragraph 1(*b*); and the Convention against Illicit Traffic in Drugs, Article 4, paragraph 1(*a*)(i).

[32] See Article 5(1) of the Geneva Convention on the High Seas, 1958, and Article 91 of the UN Convention on the Law of the Sea, 1982.

[33] See Sir Robert Jennings: '... The courts of the flag State are justified in international law in exercising jurisdiction for [the reason] ... that an aircraft like a ship may, for the purposes of jurisdiction, be regarded as being in the same position as territory': 'Note on *Regina* v. *Martin and others* (1956)', *International and Comparative Law Quarterly*, 5 (1956), pp. 604–5. See also the comment on Article 4 of the Harvard Research Draft Convention on Jurisdiction with respect to Crime: 'Ships and aircraft are not territory. It is recognized, nevertheless, that a State has with respect to such ships or aircraft a jurisdiction which is similar to its jurisdiction over its territory. Thus the State's jurisdiction includes crimes committed in whole or in part upon such ships or aircraft': *American Journal of International Law*, 29 (1935), Supplement, p. 509. See also Shubber, *Jurisdiction over Crimes on Board Aircraft* (1973), pp. 51–4. The American Law Institute takes the following position: 'A state may apply its law to activities, persons, or things aboard a vessel, aircraft, or spacecraft registered in the state ... The application of law to activities on board a state's vessels, aircraft, or spacecraft has sometimes been supported as an extension of the territoriality principle but it is better seen as an independent basis of jurisdiction': *Restatement of the Law Third*, vol. 1, comment (h), pp. 240–1.

surrender for trial all those charged with the crime.[34] A French magistrate issued arrest warrants against four Libyan nationals, and sought two others for questioning, in connection with the destruction of UTA Flight 772.[35]

It is to be noted that the State of registration of the aircraft can exercise jurisdiction, wherever the offence of sabotage is committed, be it over the high seas, the airspace of another State or on its territory. There appears to be no limitation on the exercise of jurisdiction under the provision. This is a form of extra-territorial jurisdiction based on the principle of nationality of the aircraft, as is the case with ships, which is declaratory of international customary law.

A pertinent point under this heading is the question of joint registration of aircraft. The Montreal Convention regulates in a reasonable manner the question of jurisdiction when an aircraft, the subject of an attack, is subject to joint or international registration and is operated by joint air transport operating organizations or international operating agencies.[36] Article 9 of the Montreal Convention requires the designation of the State among the parties to the Convention which shall exercise jurisdiction and have the attributes of the State of registration for the purpose of the Convention. The provision requires notice of such designation to be given to the ICAO for the purpose of communication to the other parties to the Convention. This is a very useful device for avoiding any gap, or confusion, in the exercise of jurisdiction, which could otherwise arise, and was used first in the Tokyo Convention,[37] and later repeated in the Hague Convention.[38] Provisions similar to Article 5, paragraph 1(*b*), of the Montreal Convention are to be found in the Tokyo Convention,[39] the Hague Convention,[40] the Convention against Hostage-Taking,[41] the Convention against Torture,[42] the Rome Convention[43] (for the flag State) and the Convention against Illicit Traffic in Drugs.[44]

3. *The State where the aircraft lands with the alleged offender on board*

In accordance with Article 5, paragraph 1(*c*), the State where an aircraft lands with the alleged offender still on board has the right to exercise jurisdiction over him. This is so, it would appear, wherever the

[34] *ICJ Reports*, 1992, p. 11, paragraph 28, and p. 122, paragraph 30.

[35] *Oral Hearings*, CR92/4 (27 March 1992), p. 19.

[36] On joint air transport operating organizations and international operating agencies, see Cheng, *The Law of International Air Transport*, (1962), pp. 252–9; also his memorandum to the International Law Association (52nd Conference, 1966), p. 270, paragraphs 5 and 6.

[37] Article 18.

[38] Article 5.

[39] Article 3, paragraph 1.

[40] Article 4, paragraph 1(*a*).

[41] Article 5, paragraph 1(*a*).

[42] Article 5, paragraph 1(*a*).

[43] Article 6, paragraph 1(*a*).

[44] Article 4, paragraph 1(*a*)(ii).

offence might have been committed, be it over the high seas or the territory or airspace of another State. Furthermore, the State can exercise jurisdiction in this case, it would appear, irrespective of whether the offender is a national of that State or not, or whether any of its nationals has been a victim or not. In other words, the State in question can exercise jurisdiction, even though it may have no links at all with the offence, the offender or the aircraft, as long as the aircraft lands with the offender still on board in that State's territory. This may be considered as a new basis of extra-territorial jurisdiction,[45] based on a treaty, as is the case with respect to hijacking of aircraft under the Hague Convention.[46] This basis is similar to the exercise of jurisdiction under the universality principle, under international customary law, over piracy.[47] The extension of jurisdiction appears to be in line with the purposes of the Montreal Convention of deterring acts of aircraft sabotage and providing appropriate punishment of offenders.

4. *The State where the charterer of an aircraft has his principal place of business or permanent residence*

An aircraft registered in State A and leased without crew to a person in State B may be the subject of an act of sabotage. In this case, there may be a problem of jurisdiction if the offence is committed outside the territory of State B, as State B, not being the State of registration, has no legal links with the aircraft that can entitle it to exercise jurisdiction. Article 5, paragraph 1(*d*), of the Montreal Convention takes care of this situation by giving the State where the charterer of such an aircraft has his principal place of business, or his permanent residence, the right to exercise jurisdiction over the offence. If, for example, X, whose principal place of business is in State B, charters an aircraft registered in State A, without crew, and the aircraft is sabotaged by a national of State C while outside the territory of State B, the latter has jurisdiction under the Montreal Convention to try the alleged offender and subject him to its law. The same applies if X has his permanent residence in State B. Therefore, it would seem that the Montreal Convention puts State B in the same position as State A (the State of registration of the aircraft) and

[45] International customary law provides the following bases of extra-territorial jurisdiction: 1) the nationality principle; 2) the passive personality principle; 3) the security principle; and 4) the universality principle. On this question with respect to crimes on board aircraft, see Shubber, *Jurisdiction over Crimes on Board Aircraft* (1973), pp. 76 ff.

[46] See Article 4, paragraph 1(*b*), of the Hague Convention. Indeed, Article 5, paragraph 1(*c*), was proposed by the Delegates of Australia and Ireland, as an incorporation of Article 4, paragraph 1(*b*), of the Hague Convention: International Conference on Air Law, Montreal, loc. cit. above (n. 5), p. 57, paragraph 44.

[47] See Article 19 of the Geneva Convention on the High Seas, 1958, and Article 105 of the UN Convention on the Law of the Sea, 1982.

the State where an aircraft lands with the alleged offender still on board, from the point of view of exercising jurisdiction. This is a very interesting development in the area of jurisdiction, as State B, in this example, has no legal links with the aircraft whatsoever, the offence having been committed by a foreign national, against an aircraft bearing the nationality of another State and outside the territory of State B. And yet State B has been given the right to exercise jurisdiction over the offence by the Montreal Convention. Of course, if the offence is committed within the territory of State B, it can claim the right to exercise jurisdiction on the basis of the territorial principle under international customary law. Hence the Montreal Convention has established a new basis for the exercise of extra-territorial jurisdiction, which does not fall within the traditional extra-territorial bases of jurisdiction under international customary law.

This principle is similar to that contained in the Hague Convention (Article 4, paragraph 1(*c*)) and is intended to close any gap which may otherwise exist in respect of those who commit acts of sabotage in the situation described above.

The Montreal Convention limits the application of its Article 5, paragraph 1(*d*), to aircraft leased without crew. The wisdom of this limitation is open to question, as the problem, from the point of view of jurisdiction, may be the same whether an aircraft is leased with or without crew.

5. *The State where the alleged offender is found*

In accordance with Article 5, paragraph 2, of the Montreal Convention, a contracting State where an alleged saboteur of an aircraft is found is competent to exercise jurisdiction over him, irrespective of where the offence is committed, and irrespective of the existence or otherwise of a legal link between the alleged offender and the State. For example, if X, a national of State Y, destroys an aircraft registered in State A while it was in service in State B, and then escapes to State C, the latter is competent to arrest him, try him before its courts and enforce any judgment against him. It is, of course, assumed that States A, B, C and Y are all parties to the Montreal Convention. State C has no legal link either with the aircraft or the offender or the place where the offence was committed, and yet it has been given the right to exercise jurisdiction over the offender. The same holds true even if X is a national of State C, because the wording of the provision does not appear to impose any restriction or qualification as regards the nationality of the offender, the nationality of the aircraft or the place where the offence is committed (though State C can exercise jurisdiction over X under the nationality principle). The only conditions imposed by the provision are: (1) that the alleged offender is physically in the territory of a contracting State; and (2) that State does not extradite him to any of the States mentioned in paragraph 1, namely the State where the offence is committed, the State of registration of the aircraft, the State where the aircraft lands with the alleged offender and the State where the charterer of the aircraft has his principal place of business or his permanent residence.

It would therefore be possible to argue that, on the basis of Article 5, paragraph 2, of the Montreal Convention, Libya has jurisdiction to try its two nationals accused of the destruction of Pan Am flight 103. It could also try those accused of destroying UTA flight 772. They are on its territory and it has, so far, refused to extradite them to the US or the UK, respectively the State of registration of the destroyed aircraft and the State where the offence was committed in the first case, or to France, the State of registration in the second case. As has been pointed out earlier, the nationality of the alleged offender does not affect the right to exercise jurisdiction in this situation.

The question of whether Libya can rely on Article 5, paragraph 2, to exercise jurisdiction over the accused in the Lockerbie incident, was hotly disputed during the Oral Hearings of Libya's request for interim measures. Counsel for Libya, Professor Salmon, after referring to Article 1(*b*) of the Montreal Convention (which deals with the offences covered by the Convention), said: 'In such an offence, Libya has carried out all its obligations under Article 5(2) and (3) of the [Montreal] Convention, in other words, it has taken the measures necessary to establish its jurisdiction over the offences'. He went on: 'The rights that Libya means to preserve are . . . the right to establish its own jurisdiction over the two alleged offenders (Article 5(2) of the Convention)'.[48] Moreover, Professor Suy, for Libya, stated that ' . . . the 1971 Montreal Convention provides for the jurisdiction of the State in the territory of which the suspects are found. The jurisdiction of the Libyan court is, therefore, unquestionable and judicial proceedings are in progress in Libya.'[49]

On the other hand, Professor Higgins, Counsel for the UK, argued that Article 5, paragraph 2, of the Montreal Convention ' . . . imposes upon each party to the Convention a *duty* to ensure that its law provides for jurisdiction over the offences listed in Article 1, irrespective of where, or by whom, they were committed, so that a State has the capacity under its own law to try an offender if it does not extradite him. The text of Article 5(2) makes clear that what is involved is the *creation* of jurisdiction, and not its *exercise* in an individual case.' She went on to say:

[48] *Oral Hearings*, CR92/2 (translation) (26 March 1992), pp. 50 and 52.
[49] Ibid., p. 71.

'regarding Article 5, paragraph 2, the United Kingdom has not prevented Libya from establishing its jurisdiction'.[50]

This basis of jurisdiction is similar to that provided under Article 4, paragraph 2, of the Hague Convention *vis-à-vis* hijackers of aircraft and represents a very interesting development. This basis could be considered as a new principle in the area of extra-territorial jurisdiction under international law, derived from a treaty. It may be worthwhile mentioning that the same principle has been incorporated in the New York Convention,[51] the Convention against Hostage-Taking,[52] the Rome Convention,[53] the Convention against Torture[54] and the Convention against Illicit Traffic in Drugs.[55] In view of such provisions, would it be possible now to argue that this principle has been incorporated into international customary law? It is submitted that such an argument can succeed only if the two elements of an international custom (i.e. practice and *opinio juris*) are established.[56] It might be possible to establish practice, but it would be difficult to establish *opinio juris*. Therefore it would be reasonable to suggest that this basis of jurisdiction rests on a treaty basis.[57]

Finally, a State where the alleged offender is found is obliged by Article 7 of the Montreal Convention, if it does not extradite him, to submit the case to its competent authorities for the purpose of prosecution.[58] Accordingly, since Libya has so far refused to extradite its nationals accused of the destruction of a US and a French aircraft, it is under the obligation to submit their case 'to its competent authorities for the purpose of prosecution'. Once it does that, Libya would appear to

[50] Ibid., CR92/3 (26 March 1992), pp. 45 and 55–6.

[51] Article 3, paragraph 2.

[52] Article 5, paragraph 2.

[53] Article 6, paragraph 4.

[54] Article 5, paragraph 2.

[55] Article 4, paragraph 2(*b*).

[56] *Asylum* case, *ICJ Reports*, 1950, p. 276; *North Sea Continental Shelf* cases, ibid., 1969, p. 42, paragraph 73; and *Military and Paramilitary Activities in and against Nicaragua* (*Merits*), ibid., 1986, p. 97, paragraph 183. For discussion of a similar point under the Rome Convention, see Shubber, *Austrian Journal of Public and International Law*, 43 (1992), pp. 173–5.

[57] The position of the American Law Institute with respect to the Hague, Montreal, New York and Hostage-Taking Conventions is that 'such agreements are effective only among the parties, unless customary law comes to accept these offences as subject to universal jurisdiction': *Restatement of the Law Third*, vol. 1, p. 257, paragraph 404.

[58] Similar provisions are to be found in the Hague Convention (Article 7), the New York Convention (Article 7), the Convention against Hostage-Taking (Article 8, paragraph 1), the Convention against Torture (Article 7, paragraph 1), the Rome Convention (Article 10, paragraph 1) and the Convention against Illicit Traffic in Drugs (Article 6, paragraph 9(*a*)).

A Greek court sentenced a Palestinian to 18 years in jail for a mid-air bomb explosion on board a Pan Am flight to Hawaii in 1982, which resulted in the death of a Japanese teenager and the wounding of 15 other passengers. The offender was arrested at Athens airport in May 1988, on a US tip off: *International Herald Tribune*, 9 January 1992, p. 8. According to the press report, the Greek Government rejected a US request for the extradition of the person concerned, made in September 1990, but tried him in its courts.

have complied with all its obligations under the Montreal Convention.[59]

The meaning of the expression 'to submit the case to its competent authorities for the purpose of prosecution' will now be considered. It would be reasonable to interpret the expression according to its ordinary meaning and within its context.[60] Accordingly, the expression can be interpreted to mean that the State where the offender is found, if it refuses to extradite him, must refer the case of the alleged saboteur, together with all relevant information, documents and evidence, to its competent authorities, be they judicial or police authorities, for the purpose of prosecution. By doing so, the State concerned would fulfil its obligations under the Montreal Convention, irrespective of whether or not those authorities decide to prosecute or not. The International Law Commission made the following comment on a similar provision in the New York Convention, during its preparatory stages:

> As the article is drafted, it is clear that no obligation is created thereunder to punish or to conduct a trial. The obligation of the State where the alleged offender is present will have been fulfilled once it has submitted the case to its competent authorities, which will, in most States, be judicial in character, for the purpose of prosecution. It will be up to those authorities to decide whether to prosecute or not, subject to the normal requirement of treaty law that the decision be taken in good faith in the light of all the circumstances involved. The obligation of the State party in such a case will be fulfilled under the article even if the decision which those authorities may take is not to commence criminal trial proceedings.[61]

6. *Criminal jurisdiction according to national law*

A general basis for the exercise of jurisdiction is recognized in Article 5, paragraph 3, namely any criminal jurisdiction exercised in accordance with national law. It is not clear what is intended by this provision. However, an argument might be advanced to the effect that the provision is intended to recognize criminal jurisdiction that may be provided by the

[59] Libya claimed that it had submitted the case of the accused Libyans to its competent authorities for the purpose of prosecution; see *Libya* v. *UK*, *ICJ Reports*, 1992, p. 5, paragraph 5; and *Libya* v. *US*, ibid., p. 116, paragraph 5. Counsel for Libya insisted, during the Oral Hearings of Libya's application for provisional measures, on Libya's right under Article 7 of the Montreal Convention: loc. cit. above (n. 48), p. 53. Professor Higgins, for the UK, argued that '. . . Article 7 stipulates obligations for Libya, but no rights for Libya arise thereunder': loc. cit. above (n. 50), p. 47.

[60] Article 31(1) of the Vienna Convention on the Law of Treaties reads: 'A treaty shall be interpreted in good faith in accordance with the ordinary meaning to be given to the terms of the treaty in their context and in the light of its object and purpose'.

[61] Report of the International Law Commission on the work of its twenty-fourth session to the General Assembly, *Yearbook of the International Law Commission*, 1972, vol. 2, p. 318, paragraph 2. The report is reproduced in *International Legal Materials*, 11 (1972), pp. 977–99. See also Rozakis, 'Terrorism and the Internationally Protected Persons in the Light of the ILC's Draft Articles', *International and Comparative Law Quarterly*, 23 (1974), p. 56; also Kearney, 'The Twenty-Fourth Session of the International Law Commission', *American Journal of International Law*, 67 (1973), pp. 84 ff.

national law of a State party to the Montreal Convention on a basis other than that provided in the Convention,[62] perhaps with different definitions of the offences, or with more categories than those covered by the Convention. This argument may be supported by the rule that '. . . it is a fundamental rule in interpreting legal texts that one should not lightly admit that they contain superfluous words: the right course, whenever possible, is to seek for an interpretation which allows a reason and a meaning to every word in the text'.[63]

Article 5, paragraph 3, of the Montreal Convention is identical with Article 3, paragraph 3, of the Tokyo Convention[64] and Article 4, paragraph 3, of the Hague Convention. All conventions adopted by the international community dealing with various acts of terrorism and drug-trafficking contain provisions identical with Article 5, paragraph 3, of the Montreal Convention.[65]

7. *Conflict of jurisdictions*

As has been seen above, under Article 5 of the Montreal Convention, several States have been given the right to exercise jurisdiction over the offence of aircraft sabotage, but there is no indication as to how this operates if two or more States wish to exercise jurisdiction over the same offence. If, for example, the State of registration of the aircraft and the State where the offence occurred both wish to exercise jurisdiction over the accused, would one of them have a prior entitlement to do so? Or would they both have the same right? If so, a conflict of jurisdiction would arise. The Montreal Convention is silent on the question, though this is not unexpected. For the system of jurisdiction under the Montreal Convention is similar to, and is indeed based on, that of the Hague Convention, which is also silent on the matter. The drafters of the

[62] During the deliberations of the Montreal Convention, the Delegate of Zambia made the following comments *vis-à-vis* Article 5, paragraph 3: he said the latter provision '. . . did not exclude any criminal jurisdiction exercised in accordance with national law. Those countries which had the principle of extra-territorial jurisdiction could take jurisdiction over an offender who was a national or if the offence had been committed against that national': International Conference on Air Law, Montreal, loc.cit. above (n. 5), p. 56, paragraph 39. Professor Higgins described Article 5, paragraph 3, as '. . . a saving provision, designed to do nothing more than make clear that any basis for criminal jurisdiction which already existed in the law of a State prior to the adoption of the Montreal Convention . . . is not excluded or superseded by the other provisions of the Convention': loc.cit. above (n. 50), p. 46.

[63] See Judge Anziloti's separate opinion in the *Lighthouses* case (1934), *PCIJ*, Series A/B, No. 62, p. 31.

[64] On a detailed treatment of Article 3, paragraph 3, of the Tokyo Convention, see Shubber *Jurisdiction over Crimes on Board Aircraft*, pp. 71–4.

[65] See Article 3, paragraph 3, of the New York Convention; Article 3, paragraph 3, of the Convention against Hostage-Taking; Article 5, paragraph 3, of the Convention against Torture; Article 6, paragraph 5, of the Rome Convention; Article 3, paragraph 5, of the Protocol to the Rome Convention; and Article 4, paragraph 3, of the Convention against Illicit Traffic in Drugs.

Montreal Convention were aware of this problem, as the Delegate of the then USSR referred to the question of competitive jurisdiction which might lead to conflict of jurisdictions: 'In his Delegation's opinion, it was the State of registry that should have the right of prior jurisdiction'. He proposed that the State of registration of the aircraft 'should have primary jurisdiction'. But the proposal was rejected.[66] A concrete illustration of this problem arose in the Lockerbie incident and the UTA flight 772, where the UK, US, France and Libya claimed the right to try the Libyans accused of the destruction of the aircraft in question. During the oral hearings relating to Libya's request for provisional measures before the ICJ, all the parties concerned recognized that the Montreal Convention does not provide for priority of jurisdiction, and any of the States which can claim the right to exercise jurisdiction under the Convention may do so, regardless of the claims of others.[67]

Another problem may arise in connection with the system of jurisdiction under the Montreal Convention, namely the possibility of conflict with the Tokyo Convention. For there are situations where an act covered by the Montreal Convention, such as carrying explosives on

[66] See International Conference on Air Law, Montreal, loc.cit. above (n. 5), p. 58, paragraph 49, p. 61, paragraph 3, and p. 62, paragraph 11.

[67] Counsel for the US, Mr Schwartz, said: ' . . . The [Montreal] Convention does not address how to sort out which State should be given priority in exercising jurisdiction in a given case. Under international law, several States may have authority to prosecute—here, the States whose nationals were killed, the State of registry of the aircraft, the State where the offence occurred, and the State where the suspects are in custody. The purpose of the prosecute or extradite formula is to ensure that one of these States will exercise authority to prosecute, but it does not dictate which. The negotiating history of the Montreal Convention confirms this . . . There an effort to create such a priority of jurisdiction failed, as did a similar effort in The Hague Hijacking Convention negotiations . . . ': *Oral Hearings*, CR92/4 (27 March 1992), pp. 60–1.

Counsel for Libya, Professor Salmon, agreed that the Montreal Convention does not provide for exclusive jurisdiction or priority of jurisdiction. He said: 'Comme l'a dit justement à cet égard notre confrère americain, M. Schwartz, la convention n'institue ni priorité, ni exclusivité de compétence. La Libye a le droit de juger les suspects au même titre que le Royaume-Uni et les Etats-Unis': ibid., CR92/5 (28 March 1992), p. 41.

Professor Higgins, for the UK, said: 'Article 5(3) [of the Montreal Convention] does not address the question of which State should exercise jurisdiction when more than one has a basis for doing so'. Further on in the proceedings, she observed: 'Counsel for Libya agreed, and we are interested to hear this, that there was under the Montreal Convention no priority as to permissible jurisdictions and no exclusivity'. She went on to say in relation to Article 11 of the Convention: 'But, once it is conceded that within the Montreal provisions there is nothing which tells us which of several possible jurisdictions shall in fact have competence in a particular case over a trial, Article 11 has to be an ancillary right . . . ': ibid., CR92/3, p. 46, and CR92/6, p. 19. (Article 11 of the Montreal Convention deals with the question of provision of assistance by the parties to the Convention in connection with criminal proceedings brought in respect of the offences covered by it.)

It may be interesting to note that the ILC has formulated a draft statute for an international criminal court, whose jurisdiction covers, *inter alia*, aircraft hijacking and sabotage and other acts of terrorism. For a lucid treatment of the subject, see Professor James Crawford, 'The ILC's Draft Statute for an International Criminal Tribunal', *American Journal of International Law*, 88 (1994), p. 140.

board an aircraft, is also covered by the Tokyo Convention.[68] Both Conventions apply, in this case, and while this would not result in the offender escaping punishment, each Convention has its own jurisdiction and requirements. For example, the aircraft commander has the right to arrest the offender on board an aircraft and deliver him to authorities of the contracting parties, under the Tokyo Convention, which is not the case under the Montreal Convention. This is not the place for going into the differences between the two Conventions. But the point is raised to draw attention to this problem.

III. Extradition under the Montreal Convention

Extradition has been defined as '. . . the delivery of an accused or a convicted individual to the state where he is accused of, or has been convicted of, a crime, by the state on whose territory he happens for the time to be'.[69] It is defined by the American Law Institute as 'the process by which a person charged with or convicted of a crime under the law of one state is arrested in another state and returned for trial or punishment'.[70] It would appear that under international customary law there is no obligation to extradite a person accused of an offence, such as aircraft sabotage, in the absence of treaty obligations to do so. According to Oppenheim, 'although Grotius held that every state has the duty either to punish, or to surrender to the prosecuting state, such individuals within its boundaries as have committed a crime abroad, no such rule forms part of customary international law.'[71] According to the American Law Institute, 'extradition is not required by customary law, and many states do not extradite except as bound to do so by treaty.'[72] Shearer observes that '. . . the common law countries, on the whole, do not

[68] According to Article 1 of the Tokyo Convention:
'This Convention shall apply in respect of:
(*a*) offences against penal law;
(*b*) acts which, whether or not they are offences, may or do jeopardize the safety of the aircraft or of persons or property therein or which jeopardize good order and discipline on board'.

On the question of absence of a rule on priority of jurisdiction under the Hague Convention, see Shubber, *International and Comparative Law Quarterly*, 22 (1973), p. 715.

In his dissenting opinion in the case of *Interpretation and Application of the 1971 Montreal Convention*, Judge Ajibola, referring, *inter alia*, to Article 5 of the Montreal Convention, observed: 'The hydra-headed problem or conflict of jurisdiction to prosecute which must clearly be borne in mind in this case, is that the two Parties have the right/obligation to prosecute offences listed in the Convention in their respective States. Article 5(1) enumerates such options thus . . . ', and he goes on to quote the provision. See *ICJ Reports*, 1992, p. 81, paragraph 3, and p. 186, paragraph 3.

[69] Oppenheim, *International Law*, vol. 1 (9th edn., 1992, edited by Sir Robert Jennings and Sir Arthur Watts), parts 2 to 4, pp. 948–9.

[70] American Law Institute, *Restatement of the Law Third*, vol. 1, Introductory Note, pp. 556–7.

[71] Oppenheim, op.cit. above (n. 69), p. 950.

[72] Op.cit. above (n. 70), p. 559, Comment (a).

extradite in the absence of a treaty'.[73] O'Connell is of the opinion that 'by its very nature extradition is not a matter regulated by international law—though the consequences of extradition . . . may be—and hence the duty to surrender cannot arise except under treaty'.[74]

So far as the Montreal Convention is concerned, it contains extradition arrangements concerning persons accused of committing the offences covered by it. These arrangements are identical with those contained in Article 8 of the Hague Convention[75] (apart from some minor words), and are laid down in Article 8 of the Montreal Convention, which reads as follows:

1. The offences shall be deemed to be included as extraditable offences in any extradition treaty existing between Contracting States. Contracting States undertake to include the offences as extraditable offences in every extradition treaty to be concluded between them.
2. If a Contracting State which makes extradition conditional on the existence of a treaty receives a request for extradition from another Contracting State with which it has no extradition treaty, it may at its option consider this Convention as the legal basis for extradition in respect of the offences. Extradition shall be subject to the other conditions provided by the law of the requested State.
3. Contracting States which do not make extradition conditional on the existence of a treaty shall recognize the offences as extraditable offences between themselves subject to the conditions provided by the law of the requested State.
4. Each of the offences shall be treated, for the purpose of extradition between Contracting States, as if it had been committed not only in the place in which it occurred but also in the territories of the States required to establish their jurisdiction in accordance with Article 5, paragraph 1(b), (c) and (d).

The following points will be considered: (1) aircraft sabotage as an extraditable offence, (2) bilateral extradition arrangements, (3) multilateral extradition arrangements, (4) the place of commission of aircraft sabotage, (5) extradition of nationals, and (6) multiple requests for extradition.

[73] Shearer, *Extradition in International Law* (1971), p. 28.

[74] O'Connell, *International Law* (2nd edn., 1970), vol. 2, p. 721.

[75] The Legal Committee of ICAO, which was responsible for the preparation of the first draft of the Montreal Convention, said: 'the Committee decided to adopt in the new draft convention similar provisions as in Article 8 of the draft convention on unlawful seizure of aircraft . . . ': International Conference on Air Law, Montreal, loc.cit. above (n. 5), Documents, vol. 2, ICAO Doc. 9081–LC/170–2, p. 33, paragraph 15. During the Montreal Conference, the Commission of the Whole ' . . . *agreed* to retain the wording of Article 8 of the Hague Convention for Article 8 [of the Montreal Convention], it being understood that the appropriate adjustment should be made to the reference in paragraph 4': ibid., vol. 1, p. 63, paragraph 22. In the light of the foregoing, it may be permissible to refer to the *travaux préparatoires* of the Hague Convention, when appropriate, in order to ascertain the meaning of Article 8 of the Montreal Convention.

1. *Aircraft sabotage as an extraditable offence*

Article 8, paragraph 1, describes the offence of aircraft sabotage as an extraditable offence, which is deemed to be included in existing extradition treaties, and is to be included in any future treaties of this nature. This means that a person accused of sabotage of an aircraft can be the subject of extradition on the basis of an existing treaty of extradition between two States parties to the Convention, even though it is not expressly included in such a treaty. For example, in a treaty of extradition concluded in 1960 (aircraft sabotage not having existed as an offence in a treaty then) between States A and B, which are now parties to the Montreal Convention, the offence would now be considered as included in that treaty by virtue of Article 8, paragraph 1.[76] This is so, irrespective of whether State A or B considers that that offence has some political elements, or might be motivated by political considerations.

The effect of this provision is to amend existing treaties, immediately and automatically,[77] in a way that may not correspond to the rules mentioned in Article 39[78] of the Vienna Convention on the Law of Treaties, even though it is based on consent of the parties. The rules referred to in Article 39 deal with, *inter alia*, the question of capacity, adoption of the text and authentication thereof, and so forth. These processes represent the usual procedure which is necessary to amend treaties, which, it could be argued, may not have been observed in the immediate amendment of extradition treaties brought about by the Montreal Convention. It could be argued, on the other hand, that the participation of States in the Montreal Conference 1971, and their deliberations on the wording, substance and various aspects of the Convention, including the question of extradition, and their subsequent ratification or adherence thereto, constitute the various steps and measures embodied in Part II of the Vienna Convention. Therefore there is, perhaps, nothing objectionable about the means of amending existing extradition treaties by Article 8, paragraph 1, of the Montreal Conven-

[76] Sir Robert Jennings and Sir Arthur Watts have said the following on this point: 'the specification of extraditable crimes in a bilateral treaty may be extended not only by a further bilateral treaty but also by multilateral treaties dealing with the suppression of certain offences, which may provide for those offences to be deemed included in extradition treaties concluded by the contracting parties'. They go on to give, *inter alia*, Article 8, paragraph 1, of the Montreal Convention as an example: Oppenheim, op.cit. above (n. 69), p. 957 and n. 3.

[77] It is interesting to note the direct way in which the European Convention on the Suppression of Terrorism 1977 deals with this point. Article 3 thereof reads: 'The provisions of all extradition treaties and arrangements applicable between Contracting States, including the European Convention on Extradition, are modified as between Contracting States to the extent that they are incompatible with this Convention'. For the text of the Convention, see *International Legal Materials*, 15 (1976), p. 1272.

[78] See Article 39 of the Vienna Convention, which reads: 'A treaty may be amended by agreement between the parties. The rules laid down in Part II apply to such an agreement except in so far as the treaty may otherwise provide.' Part II contains rules relating to the capacity of the parties, adoption of the text and authentication thereof, consent and so on (see Articles 6–25 of the Vienna Convention).

tion. Moreover, States parties to the Montreal Convention have undertaken to include the offence of aircraft sabotage in any future extradition treaties to be concluded between them. Such States will therefore be in breach of their treaty obligations if they fail to include the offence in their future extradition treaties. The intention here, as well as in the immediate and automatic amendment of existing extradition treaties, is to ensure that offenders should not escape punishment, because a State party to an existing extradition treaty can no longer claim that such an offence is not covered by an existing treaty, or that the offence has a political element, or the motive for its commission is political, and is therefore excluded from the scope of such a treaty. It may be interesting to point out that such arguments have been relied upon in the past by some States to refuse the extradition of aircraft hijackers.[79]

Subsequent conventions dealing with other aspects of terrorism have followed the approach of the Montreal Convention, i.e., the New York Convention,[80] the Convention against Hostage-Taking,[81] the Convention against Torture,[82] the Rome Convention[83] and the Convention against Illicit Traffic in Drugs.[84]

To apply the rule laid down in Article 8, paragraph 1, of the Montreal Convention to the situation arising from the destruction of the American and French aircraft will require the existence of extradition treaties between Libya, on the one hand, and the US, the UK and France, on the other, or the conclusion of such treaties in the future. If such treaties already exist, and assuming that they contain no reference to the offence of aircraft sabotage, they would be considered as having been amended by Article 8, paragraph 1, and the offence included therein. However, it would appear that no treaties of extradition existed at the time of adoption of the Montreal Convention between the US, UK, France and

[79] The US refused to extradite the Czechoslovakian hijackers of three Czechoslovakian aircraft in March 1950. See Whiteman, *Digest of International Law*, vol. 6, p. 810. Italy refused to extradite a US national of Italian origin who hijacked a US aircraft to Italy in November 1969; Algeria did the same with respect to some US nationals (Black Panthers) who hijacked some American aircraft; a Swiss court held that the hijackers of a Yugoslavian aircraft in 1952 to Switzerland could not be extradited because of the political nature of the offence. For references and other examples, see Shubber, loc.cit. above (n. 27), p. 716 and p. 717, notes 111 and 112.

[80] Article 8, paragraph 1.

[81] Article 10, paragraph 1.

[82] Article 8, paragraph 1.

[83] Article 11, paragraph 1.

[84] Article 6, paragraph 2. The Convention to Prevent and Punish the Acts of Terrorism taking the form of Crimes against Persons and Related Extortion that are of International Significance, 1971, (hereinafter referred to as the 'Washington Convention') contains a provision providing for the inclusion of the offences dealt with thereunder 'giving rise to extradition in any treaty on the subject to which they agree among themselves in the future'. See Article 7 of the Convention. The text of the convention is reproduced in UN Doc. A/AC. 188/L.2 (10 August 1977).

Libya, nor have any such treaties been concluded since then.[85] Therefore, Libya is not obliged under the Montreal Convention to extradite the accused Libyans to France, the UK or the US. As Judges Evensen, Tarassov, Guillaume and Aguilar Mawdsley said in their joint declaration in the case of the *Interpretation and Application of the 1971 Montreal Convention*, '. . . the Montreal Convention, which in our opinion was applicable in this case, did not prohibit Libya from refusing to extradite the accused to the United Kingdom or the United States. It implied that, in the absence of extradition, Libya had to submit the case to its competent authorities for the purpose of prosecution.'[86]

2. *The requirement of an extradition treaty—the Convention as a bilateral treaty*

As has been pointed out earlier, there is no obligation to extradite an offender under international customary law, as such an obligation arises only from extradition treaties or arrangements. The Montreal Convention therefore provides a device whereby, in the absence of a treaty of extradition between two States parties to it, the Convention can be considered as a substitute for such a treaty. This device is to be found in Article 8, paragraph 2, of the Convention, which reads as follows:

> If a Contracting State which makes extradition conditional on the existence of a treaty receives a request for extradition from another Contracting State with which it has no extradition treaty, it may at its option consider this Convention as the legal basis for extradition in respect of the offences. Extradition shall be subject to the other conditions provided by the law of the requested State.

Accordingly, if State A, which requires an extradition treaty in order to accede to a request for the extradition of a person accused of destroying an aircraft, receives a request for the extradition of such a person from State B, with which it has no such treaty, State A 'may at its option' consider the Montreal Convention as such a treaty for the purposes of extraditing the accused to State B. This is a very useful device for facilitating the extradition of aircraft saboteurs and bringing them before competent courts, though there are some weak aspects of the provision. The absence of a treaty of extradition can often be invoked by unwilling States as an excuse for refusal to accede to a request for extradition. The provision then, it may be argued, in effect, creates a bilateral treaty of extradition between States A and B in the above example, although not a perfect one. It is not a perfect bilateral treaty for the following reasons. First, State A, in the example, is not obliged to accede to a request for

[85] This is clearly stated in Libya's application to the ICJ for provisional measures, in so far as the UK and the US are concerned: see *ICJ Reports*, 1992, p. 6, paragraph 5, and p. 117, paragraph 5. However, it is clear from the proceedings of the ICJ that no extradition treaty exists between Libya and France.

[86] Ibid., pp. 24–5, paragraph 3, and pp. 136–7, paragraph 3.

extradition, as is the case under the normal treaty obligation, but 'may at its option' consider the Montreal Convention as the legal basis for extradition. The expression 'may at its option' is *permissive* and leaves the requested State a large measure of discretion to reject the request. Secondly, the provision subjects the extradition to other conditions provided by the law of the requested State[87] (State A in the example). Therefore, even if State A agrees to consider the Montreal Convention as a treaty between itself and State B, the conditions laid down in its law will come into play here, and may frustrate compliance with a request for extradition: for example, State A's law may require that where there is reasonable ground to believe that the accused is not likely to have a fair trial in State B, or that there may be prejudice against him,[88] State A may refuse to extradite the accused on that ground. Nevertheless, the accused is not likely to escape punishment on the ground of lack of jurisdiction, because Article 7 of the Montreal Convention obliges State A '. . . without exception whatsoever and whether or not the offence was committed in its territory, to submit the case to its competent authorities for the purpose of prosecution'. Furthermore, the provision requires the offence to be treated as any 'ordinary offence of a serious nature under the law of that State'. Thus, there can be no excuse to treat the offence as a political one, which may require a different treatment.

If Article 8, paragraph 2, is applied to the dispute between the UK, US, France and Libya concerning the Lockerbie incident and UTA flight, then it could be argued that since Libya requires the existence of extradition treaties between itself and the States in question, Libya could have considered the Montreal Convention as such a treaty and extradited the persons concerned to the US, UK or France. On the other hand, it could be argued that Libya is not under a legal obligation to extradite those persons to any of the States in question, on the basis of the wording of Article 8, paragraph 2. The latter provides that 'it may at its option consider' the Montreal Convention as the legal basis for extradition. This

[87] In connection with the Hague Convention's extradition arrangements under its Article 8, the ICAO Subcommittee on Unlawful Seizure of Aircraft in 1969 said in this respect: 'At the present session [second Session], the Subcommittee was unanimous in thinking that the Convention should not attempt to prevent any State to refuse extradition of the person concerned in conformity with its law': Report of the Subcommittee, ICAO Doc. 8838–LC/157, p. 6, paragraph 18. During the discussion of Article 8 of the Hague Convention by the ICAO Legal Committee in 1970, the UK Delegate said: '. . . the Subcommittee had found that the national laws relating to extradition differed from State to State and that in many cases they had been hallowed by antiquity. It would be difficult for many States to depart from the established principles of extradition laid down in their national law. For these reasons, she considered it desirable that the Convention should include no obligation to extradite, but that the national law on this subject should be applied': ICAO Legal Committee, 17th session, ICAO Doc. 8877–LC/161, p. 58, paragraph 31.

[88] Article 9 of the Convention against Hostage-Taking allows the requested State to refuse a request for the extradition of a hostage-taker if it has substantial grounds for believing, *inter alia*, that his position may be prejudiced on account of race, religion, nationality, ethnic origin or political opinion. See to the same effect Article 6, paragraph 6, of the Convention against Illicit Traffic in Drugs.

expression, as stated above, leaves a large measure of discretion,[89] it would seem, for Libya to refuse to consider the Montreal Convention as such a legal basis. Moreover, Libya has invoked before the ICJ its national law, which does not allow the extradition of nationals, as a basis to refuse the extradition of the accused Libyans.[90]

Conventions adopted subsequent to the Montreal Convention dealing with other aspects of terrorism and other international offences have included similar extradition arrangements. Thus the Convention on Hostage-Taking and the Rome Convention contain identical provisions,[91] while the New York Convention contains a similar provision.[92]

3. *The absence of the requirement of an extradition treaty—the Convention as a basis of extradition*

Article 8, paragraph 3, of the Montreal Convention has a different type of extradition arrangement whereby the Convention provides the legal basis for recognizing the offence of aircraft sabotage as an extraditable offence. The provision reads as follows:

> Contracting States which do not make extradition conditional on the existence of a treaty shall recognize the offences as extraditable offences between themselves subject to the conditions provided by the law of the requested State.

According to this provision, if States A, B, C and D, which are parties to the Montreal Convention, do not require the existence of a treaty for the purposes of extradition, they undertake to recognize the offence of aircraft sabotage (and the other offences created by the Convention) as an extraditable offence, merely on the basis of the Convention. Therefore, it would be reasonable to say that the Montreal Convention has the effect of creating a treaty link between those States for the purpose of extraditing aircraft saboteurs. This link may be said to amount to the

[89] Counsel for Libya argued before the ICJ that 'it is true that Article 8, paragraph 2 provides further latitude, but this is a discretionary right not applicable here'. He went on: 'Libya also intends to preserve the following rights . . . : the latitude under Article 8 . . . ': *Oral Hearing*, CR92/2 (translation) (26 March 1992), p. 51 and p. 53.

It is interesting to note the observation made by Professor Higgins, for the UK, in this respect. She said Article 8(2) ' . . . provides a mechanism by which extradition may be effected, if the States concerned wish to make use of it. The United Kingdom has not, however, sought the extradition of the two accused under Article 8(2)—indeed, it has not sought their *extradition* (in the technical sense of the term) at all—but has instead maintained that Libya should, for reasons unrelated to the Montreal Convention, surrender the two accused': ibid., CR92/3, p. 48. This observation might be construed as an implicit admission that Libya is not required to extradite the accused, under the Montreal Convention.

[90] See *ICJ Reports*, 1992, p. 6, paragraph 5, and p. 117, paragraph 5.

[91] See Article 10, paragraph 2, of the Convention against Hostage-Taking and Article 11, paragraph 2, of the Rome Convention.

[92] See Article 8, paragraph 2, of the New York Convention; see also Article 8, paragraph 2, of the Convention against Torture and Article 6, paragraph 3, of the Convention against Illicit Traffic in Drugs. The difference between these Conventions and those mentioned in n. 91 is that the latter have dropped the expression 'at its option'. The latter term weakens further the undertaking of the parties to the conventions concerned.

creation of a multilateral international instrument[93] between the parties to the Montreal Convention. Therefore, it could be argued that States A, B, C and D have, implicitly, undertaken to comply with a request for the extradition of aircraft saboteurs, subject to the procedure and other conditions required by the national law of the requested State. The significance of this point may be that those States would no longer be in a position to plead that such an offence is a political one or is not regulated by an extradition treaty, and as such is not extraditable. They clearly recognize the extraditable nature of the offence. It is to be noted that Article 8, paragraph 3, uses mandatory language, whereas paragraph 2 of the provision, as we have seen above, uses the permissive language 'may at its option'. Nevertheless, any of those States can still invoke the national law requirements, if applicable, to justify refusal to comply with a request for extradition.

If Article 8, paragraph 3, is applied to the dispute between the US, UK, France and Libya, then it could be argued that Libya should comply with the request to extradite the persons concerned, provided that it does not make extradition conditional on the existence of a treaty. However, if Libya requires the existence of such a treaty, as is the case, as has been seen above, then it would not be under an obligation to surrender those persons, in the absence of extradition treaties between itself, the US, UK or France. Indeed, as has been shown above,[94] Libya pleaded before the ICJ the absence of extradition treaties between itself and the UK, the US and France, and invoked its national law, which does not permit the extradition of its nationals, as bases for refusing to extradite the Libyans accused of the destruction of Pan Am flight 103 and UTA flight 772.

Article 8, paragraph 3, of the Montreal Convention is identical with Article 8, paragraph 3, of the Hague Convention, and identical provisions are to be found in subsequent conventions, namely, the New York Convention,[95] the Convention against Hostage-Taking,[96] the Convention against Torture,[97] the Rome Convention[98] and the Convention against Illicit Traffic in Drugs.[99]

4. *The place of commission of aircraft sabotage*

Another point pertinent to the extradition arrangements under the Montreal Convention is the treatment of the offence as being committed

[93] Cheng proposed to the Royal Aeronautical Society (Air Law Group), as long ago as 1962, a multilateral extradition clause, in connection with crimes on board aircraft: see Study Group on Crimes on Board Aircraft, p. 22, paragraph G.

[94] See above, p. 261.

[95] See Article 8, paragraph 3, of the Convention.

[96] See Article 10, paragraph 3, of the Convention.

[97] See Article 8, paragraph 3, of the Convention.

[98] See Article 11, paragraph 3, of the Convention.

[99] See Article 6, paragraph 4, of the Convention.

in the territories of the States competent to exercise jurisdiction under the Convention, as well as in the place where it occurred. According to Article 8, paragraph 4, of the Montreal Convention,

> each of the offences shall be treated, for the purpose of extradition between Contracting States, as if it had been committed not only in the place in which it occurred but also in the territories of the States required to establish their jurisdiction in accordance with article 5, paragraph 1(*b*), (*c*) and (*d*).

Accordingly, if an act of sabotage is committed against an aircraft registered in State A, while it is flying in the airspace of State B, the offence will be treated, for the purpose of extradition, as if it was committed in the territory of State A, besides being committed in State B. For example, in the Lockerbie and UTA incidents, the offence would be treated as if it was committed in US territory, as well as in UK airspace, and as if it was committed in French territory as well as Niger airspace, for the purpose of extradition. The rationale for this treatment is probably that, for the purpose of extradition, the offence should have been committed in the territory of the requesting State in order to justify a request for the extradition of the offender.

This is a useful device and is similar to the one contained in the Tokyo Convention[100] and identical with that contained in the Hague Convention.[101] It has been followed in the New York Convention,[102] the Convention against Hostage-Taking,[103] the Convention against Torture[104] and the Rome Convention.[105]

5. *Extradition of nationals*

The extradition arrangements contained in Article 8 of the Montreal Convention do not specifically deal with the question of the extradition of nationals of the requested State. For example, if State A, a contracting party to the Montreal Convention, requests the extradition of a saboteur who is a national of State B, from State B, another contracting party to the Convention, Article 8 does not describe the position of State B. But there appears to be no reason why State B could refuse to extradite the saboteur on the ground that he is one of its nationals. It would be reasonable to argue that Article 8 does not envisage any distinction between nationals and non-nationals of the requested State for the purposes of extradition. Therefore it could be maintained that if the conditions laid down in the provisions are met, the requested State cannot justify a refusal to extradite on the basis of the nationality of the

[100] See Article 16, paragraph 1.
[101] See Article 8, paragraph 4.
[102] See Article 8, paragraph 4.
[103] See Article 10, paragraph 4.
[104] See Article 8, paragraph 4.
[105] See Article 11, paragraph 4; the provision uses the term 'if necessary', which is not used in any of the other conventions.

saboteur. It is a rule of treaty interpretation that 'account is taken of any relevant rules of international law not only as constituting the background against which the treaty's provisions must be viewed, but in the presumption that the parties intend something not inconsistent with generally recognized principles of international law . . . '.[106] According to the American Law Institute, 'no rule of international law prohibits extradition of nationals of the requested state'.[107] It would, nevertheless, appear, again according to the American Law Institute, that 'as a matter of policy, some states will not extradite their own nationals; other states, including the United States and Great Britain, do not draw such a distinction'.[108] According to Sir Robert Jennings and Sir Arthur Watts,

> in principle, any individual, whether he is a national of the prosecuting state, or of the state which is required to extradite him, or of a third state, may be extradited. Many states, however, such as France and Germany, never extradite one of their own nationals to a foreign state, but themselves have the power to punish them for grave crimes committed abroad. Other states, including the United Kingdom, have not adopted this principle, and, in the absence of treaty provisions to the contrary, make no distinction between their own nationals and other persons whose extradition from their territory is requested.[109]

Applying the above principles to the Lockerbie incident and UTA flight 772, it could be argued that Libya cannot refuse to extradite the Libyans accused of the sabotage of the US and French aircraft, solely on the ground that they are her nationals. However, Libya can do so on the basis of the absence of an extradition treaty between her and the UK, the US and France or on the basis of national law.[110] Indeed, as we have seen above, Libya pleaded before the ICJ that ' . . . Libyan law prohibits the extradition of Libyan nationals'.[111] In their joint declaration, Judges Evensen, Tarassov, Guillaume and Aguilar Mawdsley said:

> The United Kingdom and the United States were entitled to request Libya to extradite the two Libyan nationals charged by the American and British authorities with having contributed to the destruction of the aeroplane lost in the Lockerbie incident. For this purpose they could take any action consistent with

[106] Oppenheim, op.cit. above (n. 69), p. 1275. See the *Right of Passage (Preliminary Objections)* case, where the ICJ said: 'it is a rule of interpretation that a text emanating from a Government must, in principle, be interpreted as producing and as intended to produce effects in accordance with existing law and not in violation of it': *ICJ Reports*, 1957, p. 142.

[107] Op.cit. above (n. 70), p. 561(f).

[108] Ibid., p. 558. See also O'Connell: 'the United States, unless exempted by treaty from surrendering its own nationals, does so as a matter of obligation and in pursuance of its territoriality conception of jurisdiction. Great Britain likewise has always been prepared to surrender her own nationals': op.cit. above (n. 74), pp. 725–6.

[109] See Oppenheim, op.cit. above (n. 69), pp. 955–6.

[110] Counsel for Libya argued that 'there is . . . no obligation in international law to surrender nationals in the absence of specific extradition agreements, which did not exist in the present case': *Oral Hearings*, CR92/2 (translation) (26 March 1992), p. 71.

[111] See *ICJ Reports*, 1992, p. 6, paragraph 5, and p. 117, paragraph 5.

international law. For its part, Libya was entitled to refuse such an extradition and to recall in that connection that, in common with the law of many other countries, its domestic law prohibits the extradition of nationals.[112]

But in that case, as mentioned earlier, Libya is bound by virtue of Article 7 of the Montreal Convention to submit their case 'to its competent authorities for the purpose of prosecution'.

6. *Multiple requests for extradition*

Under the extradition arrangements of the Montreal Convention, several States may request the extradition of the same saboteur, and yet there is no indication in Article 8 of the Convention as to which of these States is more entitled than the others to receive the saboteur. For example, if an act of sabotage is committed on board an aircraft registered in State B, while in the territory of State C, and then the aircraft lands in State D, where the saboteur escapes to State F, States B, C, D and F are all entitled to exercise jurisdiction over the saboteurs.[113] Suppose that States B, C and D request the extradition of the saboteur from State F, what is the position under the Convention? Does any of these States have priority over the others for this purpose? What would be the position of State F? No answer can be found in the Montreal Convention, and there appears to be no indication in the *travaux préparatoires* as to how the problem could be solved. However, the situation prevailing under the Montreal Convention is the same as that prevailing under the Hague Convention. With respect to the latter, the drafters were aware of the difficulty, as during the Hague Conference a proposal was submitted by the US providing for priority to be given to a request for extradition from the State of registration of the hijacked aircraft, in the absence of a treaty obligation to a non-contracting State. However, the proposal was withdrawn because of the problems it raised for other delegates at the Conference.[114] It would, therefore, be reasonable to assume that the drafters of the Montreal Convention adopted the same attitude to the problem, since they based Article 8 of the Montreal Convention on Article 8 of the Hague Convention.[115] It follows that when the US and the UK have requested the extradition of the accused Libyans, it is difficult to decide whether the US request should have priority over the UK request. The same applies if Niger decides to ask for the extradition of the accused Libyans in connection with UTA flight 772, besides France. In the absence of any guidance under the Convention, it may be suggested that Libya could probably, under the circumstances, itself decide to which one of these States it extradites the accused

[112] Ibid., p. 24, paragraph 1, and p. 136, paragraph 1.

[113] For the bases of jurisdiction, see above, pp. 244–53.

[114] See International Conference on Air Law, The Hague, December 1970, vol. 1, ICAO Doc. 8979-LC/165-1, p. 112, paragraph 29 and p. 113, paragraph 37.

[115] See above, n. 75.

Libyans, should it reverse its current position concerning its refusal to extradite them. Another possibility for Libya would be to decide to accede to the request that came first. The question of a fair trial[116] for the accused would be a relevant factor in both situations.

An important legal aspect, in this respect, is the question of human rights standards applicable to the process of extradition and the likelihood of the accused receiving a fair trial. The discussions of the Institute of International Law, at its Cambridge session in 1983, on extradition, and the resolution adopted, provide some indications of what these standards might be. Members of the Institute were concerned about the protection of the human rights of the person whose extradition is being sought. The Rapporteur of the Commission dealing with the subject stated that 'if in a given case extradition could factually result in the violation of human rights then extradition should not be granted even through [though ?] the individual was himself accused of violating human rights'.[117] Mr Mosler suggested the insertion, in the draft resolution, of the expression 'basic rights of the human person', 'which . . . took account of the dignity of the human person and the needs closely linked with the development of man as a human being. In his view, it would not be an exaggeration to state that the protection that this basic human position justified might prevail over treaties as a norm of *jus cogens*.'[118] The presumption of innocence,[119] the identity of penal legislation (where there is no death penalty in the requested State but it exists in the requesting State), and even mob violence covertly encouraged by the State,[120] were among the concerns expressed in connection with the protection of the human rights of the person whose extradition has been requested. And finally, the Institute adopted a resolution, paragraph IV of which reads as follows:

The Protection of the Fundamental Rights of the Human Person

In cases where there is a well-founded fear of the violation of the fundamental human rights of an accused in the territory of the requesting State, extradition may be refused, whosoever the individual whose extradition is requested and whatever the nature of the offence of which he is accused.[121]

This resolution clearly shows the importance the Institute of International Law attaches to the protection of the fundamental human

[116] On the question of a fair trial, see the observation made by *ad hoc* Judge El-Kosheri, in his dissenting opinion, below, p. 282.

[117] *Yearbook of the Institute of International Law*, 60 (1983), part 2, p. 219.

[118] Ibid., p. 234.

[119] Ibid., p. 231, intervention of Ténékides.

[120] Ibid., p. 232, intervention of Mareк, and p. 259, intervention of Seidl-Hohenveldern.

[121] Ibid., p. 306. Article 9 of the Convention against Hostage-Taking allows the requested State to refuse a request for the extradition of a hostage-taker if it has substantial grounds for believing, *inter alia*, that his position may be prejudiced on account of race, religion, nationality, ethnic origin or political opinion. See to the same effect Article 6, paragraph 6, of the Convention against Illicit Traffic in Drugs.

rights'[122] of an accused, whose extradition is requested, whatever the nature of the offence of which he is accused. The Institute recommends that if there is a well-founded fear of violation of such rights, the requested State may refuse extradition. It is to be noted that the resolution speaks of 'well-founded fear', and not, for example, 'suspicion'. 'Fear', according to *The Concise Oxford Dictionary*, means 'an unpleasant emotion caused by exposure to danger, expectation of pain etc.'.[123]

IV. The Security Council's Action against Libya

As has been shown earlier, there is no obligation for Libya to extradite Libyan nationals accused of involvement in the destruction of Pan Am flight 103 and UTA flight 772, either under the Montreal Convention, or under customary international law. Therefore the question arises: is it possible for the Security Council, from a legal point of view, to consider Libya's failure to surrender its nationals to France, the UK or US as a threat to international peace and security? Let it first be recalled that in its Resolution 731 (1992), adopted on 21 January 1992, the Council stated that it was deeply disturbed by the worldwide acts of international terrorism in all its forms, and that it was deeply concerned by all illegal activities directed against international civil aviation. It then referred to the requests of France, the UK and the US[124] to Libya. The UK and the US requested Libya 'to surrender for trial all those charged with the crime [of the destruction of Pan Am 103 and UTA 772]; and accept responsibility for the actions of Libyan officials; disclose all it knows of this crime, including the names of all those responsible, and allow full

[122] See Article 10 of the Universal Declaration of Human Rights: 'everyone is entitled in full equality to a fair and public hearing by an independent and impartial tribunal, in the determination of his rights and obligations and of any criminal charge against him'. See also Article 11(1): 'everyone charged with a penal offence has the right to be presumed innocent until proved guilty according to law in a public trial at which he has had all the guarantees necessary for his defence'. See to the same effect Article 14, paragraphs (1) and (2), of the International Covenant on Civil and Political Rights, 1966. The Declaration and the Covenant are reproduced in *Human Rights—A Compilation of International Instruments* (United Nations, 1978), pp. 1 and 8.

[123] *The Concise Oxford Dictionary* (8th edn., 1990), p. 427; 'to suspect' means '1. having an impression of the existence or presence of . . . 2. believe tentatively, without clear ground': ibid., p. 1229.

[124] The requests of France, the UK and US are to be found in UN Doc. S/23306, 31 December 1991; UN Doc. S/23307, 31 December 1991; UN Doc. S/23308, 20 December 1991, and UN Doc. S/23309, 20 December 1991. On the position of Libya, see UN Doc. S/23221, 16 November 1991; UN Doc. S/23396, 9 January 1992; and UN Doc. S/23417, 13 January 1992. Most of these documents are reproduced in *International Legal Materials*, 31 (1992), pp. 717 ff. It is to be noted that while France requested Libya only for co-operation with the French authorities in order to help establish responsibility for the terrorist act, it could be argued that it, implicitly, went along with the UK and US requests mentioned above. This could be supported by the wording of the French statement and the French, UK and US joint statement. See UN Doc. S/23306; and UN Doc. S/23309.

access to all witnesses, documents and other material evidence, including all remaining timers; pay appropriate compensation. We expect Libya to comply promptly and in full.' It went on to urge 'the Libyan Government immediately to provide a full and effective response to those requests [of France, the UK and the US] so as to contribute to the elimination of international terrorism'.[125] In its Resolution 748 (1992), adopted on 31 March 1992, the Security Council expressed its deep concern about Libya's failure to provide a full and effective response to the requests in its Resolution 731 (1992) (i.e., the French, UK and US requests), and went on to determine that ' . . . the failure by the Libyan Government to demonstrate by concrete actions its renunciation of terrorism and in particular its continued failure to respond fully and effectively to the requests in resolution 731 (1992), constitute a threat to international peace and security'.[126] The Council went on to apply sanctions, not involving the use of force, under Article 41 of Chapter VII of the Charter, against Libya.[127] Now the questions are: does Libya's failure to hand over the accused Libyans to France, the UK and the US constitute a threat to international peace and security? Is Security Council Resolution 748 (1992) contrary to international law, as contended by Libya?[128] If so, is there a possibility of a judicial review by the ICJ? And what is the relationship between the ICJ and the Security Council? An attempt to answer these questions will be made.

In accordance with Article 24, paragraph 1, of the Charter, Members of the UN conferred on the Security Council the 'primary responsibility for the maintenance of international peace and security'. Furthermore, in accordance with Article 39 of the Charter, 'the Security Council shall determine the existence of any threat to the peace, breach of the peace, or act of aggression[129] and shall make recommendations, or decide what measures shall be taken in accordance with Articles 41 and 42, to maintain or restore international peace and security'. Accordingly, the Security Council has the responsibility to maintain international peace and security, and the authority to determine the existence of any threat to the peace, breach of the peace or act of aggression, and recommend, or decide upon, any appropriate measure, in accordance with Articles 41

[125] Resolutionn 731 (1992), operative paragraph 3.

[126] Resolution 748 (1992), seventh preambular paragraph.

[127] Ibid., operative paragraph 3. In a third resolution adopted by the Security Council on 11 November 1993, Resolution 883 (1993), the Council reaffirmed its previous resolutions and repeated its determination that Libya's failure to respond to the requests and decisions in Resolutions 731 (1992) and 748 (1992) constitutes a threat to international peace and security. It decided, again acting under Chapter VII of the Charter, to widen the sanctions applied under previous resolutions, by requiring the freezing of Libyan assets abroad, except for financial resources derived from the sale of oil. See first and sixth preambular paragraphs and operative paragraphs 3 and 4.

[128] See *ICJ Reports*, 1992, p. 14, paragraph 36, and p. 126, paragraph 39.

[129] The General Assembly adopted Resolution 2314 (XXIX) on 14 December 1974 on the Definition of Aggression; see *General Assembly Official Records*, 29th session, Supplement No. 31 (A/9631), pp. 142–4.

and 42, to remedy the situation. However, Article 39 of the Charter does not define what situation may be considered as a threat to international peace or an act of aggression, nor does it impose any qualifications on the power of the Council to do so. It seems to leave it to the discretion of the Security Council to characterize, subject to the limitations[130] imposed by the relevant Charter provisions, what may be considered a threat to international peace or a breach of the peace. It might therefore be argued that the Security Council could decide that Libya's refusal to hand over the alleged offenders involved in the destruction of Pan Am 103 and UTA 772 constitutes a threat to international peace. By the same token, it could decide what measures are appropriate to use in order to maintain or restore international peace. In his dissenting opinion in the case of the *Interpretation and Application of the 1971 Montreal Convention* Judge Weeramantry said: '. . . for the determination under Article 39 of the existence of any threat to the peace, breach of the peace or act of aggression, is one entirely within the discretion of the Council. It would appear that the Council and no other is the judge of the existence of the state of affairs which brings Chapter VII into operation.'[131]

According to this standpoint then, the action of the Security Council and the adoption of Resolution 748 (1992) are in conformity with the Charter and international law. As Acting President Oda said in his declaration in the *Interpretation and Application of the 1971 Montreal Convention*, 'the [Security] Council appears, in fact, to have been acting within its competence when it discerned a threat against international peace and security in Libya's refusal to deliver up the two Libyan accused'. He went on say: '. . . I feel bound to point out that Security Council resolution 748 (1992) was adopted in line with the Council's determination to eliminate international terrorism, the extradition of the two Libyan accused serving basically as a convenient focus for that determination . . . '.[132]

On the other hand, it can be argued that while the Security Council has the authority just mentioned, its actions should be measured by the provisions of the Charter and its own practice. So far as the practice of the Security Council is concerned, it does not appear to show that it

[130] In his separate opinion Judge Shahabuddeen raised the question '. . . whether there are any limitations on the power of the [Security] Council to characterize a situation as one justifying the making of a decision . . . [which may override the legal rights of States]. Are there any limits to the Council's powers of appreciation?' He went on to say: 'If there are any limits, what are those limits and what body, if other than the Security Council, is competent to say what those limits are?': *ICJ Reports*, 1992, p. 32, and p. 142. Judge Bedjaoui, President of the ICJ, says: '. . . On doit reconnaître que le caractère peu précis et/ou controversé dans leur portée des termes employés à l'article 39 de la Charte (par exemple celui de '*menace contre la paix*') donne au Conseil une très large liberté dans l'appréciation des situations auxquelles il est confronté. La liberté d'appréciation du Conseil évoquée souvent ici, qu'on y soit favorable ou pas, se fonde clairement sur le texte de la Charte': *Nouvel ordre mondial et contrôle de la légalité des actes du Conseil de Sécurité* (1994), p. 67.

[131] *ICJ Reports*, 1992, p. 66, and p. 176.

[132] Ibid., p. 17, and p. 129.

considered the action of individuals, in contrast to that of States as such, as a threat to international peace. A few examples of the Security Council's actions in this area may be given: Korea 1950,[133] the Congo 1960,[134] Rhodesia 1966,[135] Iraq 1990,[136] Bosnia 1991[137] and Somalia 1993.[138] In these situations, the Council took action against States resorting to armed force against other States (North Korea, Iraq and Serbia and Montenegro), military intervention by a State (Belgium in the Congo), unilateral declaration of independence (Rhodesia) and civil strife (Somalia). In Somalia, however, the Security Council, acted under Chapter VII in relation to individuals when it called for the arrest of those responsible for attacking and killing some members of the UN forces.[139] But such attacks and killing of members of the UN forces were a deliberate move against the UN forces and their operations in Somalia carried out by organized groups belonging to the United Somalia Congress. None of the situations described above, it would seem, can be considered as similar to the refusal to extradite those accused of involvement in the destruction of Pan Am 103 and UTA 772, and thus justify action under Chapter VII of the UN Charter.[140]

So far as the Charter is concerned, according to Article 24, paragraph 1, the Security Council has 'primary responsibility' for the maintenance of international peace and security. According to Article 24, paragraph 2, 'in discharging these duties the Security Council shall act in accordance with the Purposes and Principles of the United Nations'. The purposes and principles of the UN are laid down in Articles 1 and 2 of the Charter. They deal with the maintenance of international peace and security, collective measures, settlement of disputes by peaceful means, non-use of force and so on. But it could be argued that none of them could be considered as a basis to justify the application of Chapter VII of the Charter against Libya for its refusal to surrender its accused nationals. Moreover, Libya's refusal to do so could be based on an international treaty, i.e., the Montreal Convention, and international customary law. It could therefore be argued that the action of the Security Council under Chapter VII, and its Resolution 748, might not be in conformity with the UN Charter and the practice of the Council itself. In his dissenting opinion in the *Interpretation and Application of the 1971 Montreal Convention*, Judge El-Kosheri said: '. . . it is possible to consider that the

[133] See Security Council Resolutions of 25 June and 27 June 1950.

[134] See Security Council Resolutions of 14, 22 July and 9 August 1960.

[135] See Security Council Resolution 232 (1966) of 16 December 1966.

[136] See Security Council Resolutions 660 (1990) of 2 August 1990 and 678 (1990) of 29 November 1990.

[137] See Security Council Resolution 757 (1992) of 30 May 1992.

[138] See Security Council Resolution 733 (1992) of 23 January 1992.

[139] See Security Council Resolution 837 (1993), operative paragraph 5.

[140] As one commentator on the Lockerbie case put it, '. . . No form of terrorism had previously been found to constitute a threat or use of force within the meaning of Article 39 of the Charter': Beveridge, loc.cit. above (n. 3), p. 912.

Security Council, when adopting paragraph 1 of resolution 748 (1992), impeded the Court's jurisdiction freely to exercise its inherent judicial function . . . and that by doing so the Security Council committed an act of *excès de pouvoir* which amounts to a violation of Article 92 of the Charter . . . '.[141] He went on to say: 'The *ultra vires* character of paragraph 1 of resolution 748 (1992) appears even more serious considering that a number of delegates at the Security Council meeting of 31 March 1992 are reported to have warned those pushing for a hasty adoption of the draft then under discussion against the negative effects of such failure to observe due respect for the Court's credibility and the integrity of its judicial functions'.[142]

Indeed, even in the case of the American hostages in Teheran in 1979, the Security Council did not act in a similar way, even though the Secretary-General referred the matter to it under Article 99 of the Charter,[143] because in his opinion the crisis between Iran and the US relating to the American hostages posed a serious threat to international peace and security. The Security Council did adopt resolutions on the subject showing its concern over the same danger,[144] but no measure under Chapter VII of the Charter was adopted. It could therefore be argued that the Security Council has not acted 'in accordance with the Purposes and Principles of the United Nations'. In Resolution 748, the Security Council has asked Libya to do something she is not obliged to do under general international law. Members of the United Nations, when they become members of the Organisation, agree to carry out the decisions of the Security Council taken in conformity with the Charter provisions. As Professor Bowett so eloquently put it:

> Are members to be treated as having accepted, *in advance*, whatever decisions the Council might take, so that such decisions have the very same force as the Charter provisions themselves? It may be doubted whether States ratifying the Charter ever believed they were granting to the Council a blank cheque to modify their legal rights.

He went on:

> This is why the last phrase of Article 25—'in accordance with the present Charter'—is so important. The Council decisions are binding only in so far as

[141] See *ICJ Reports*, 1992, p. 105, paragraph 33, and p. 210, paragraph 33.

[142] Ibid., paragraph 36 and paragraph 36.

[143] Article 99 reads as follows: 'the Secretary-General may bring to the attention of the Security Council any matter which in his opinion may threaten the maintenance of international peace and security'.

[144] See Security Council Resolution 461 (1979) of 31 December 1979, fifth preambular paragraph.

they are in accordance with the Charter. They may spell out, or particularise, the obligations of members, that arise from the Charter. But they may not create totally new obligations that have no basis in the Charter, for the Council is an executive organ, not a legislature. In short, the Council does not have a blank cheque.[145]

Furthermore, as Judge Bedjaoui says:

Le Conseil de sécurité, comme tous les autres organes politiques des Nations Unies, doit se conformer dans ses actes aux dispositions de la Charte. Les Etats parties à ce traité international qu'est la Charte ont exprimé leur volonté de créer un organe qui leur doit son existence et qui dispose de pouvoirs précis et de moyens bien déterminés pour atteindre des buts qui lui ont été clairement assignés. Cet organe doit naturellement servir cette volonté exprimée et s'abstenir dans ses actes de tout dépassement de son mandat. La Charte, donc les Etats parties au traité, l'exige.[146]

It would be reasonable to suppose that there are limits on the powers of the Security Council. As Professor Franck says in relation to the *Lockerbie* case:

The majority and dissenting opinions seem to be in agreement that there are such limits and that they cannot be left exclusively to the Security Council to interpret. The legality of actions by any UN organ must be judged by reference to the Charter as a 'constitution' of *delegated* powers. In extreme cases, the Court may have to be the last-resort defender of the system's legitimacy if the United Nations is to continue to enjoy the adherence of its members. This seems to be tacitly acknowledged judicial common ground.[147]

The relationship between the ICJ and the political organs of the UN, and the issue of judicial review, will now be surveyed.

The ICJ, the General Assembly and the Security Council are principal organs of the UN (Article 7 of the Charter). Furthermore, the ICJ is the principal judicial organ of the UN (Article 92 of the Charter), whereas the Security Council has primary responsibility for the maintenance of

[145] 'The Impact of Security Council Decisions on Dispute Settlement Procedures', *European Journal of International Law*, 5 (1994), pp. 92–3.
See also Tomuschat: commenting on the *Lockerbie* case and whether the Security Council is bound to respect general rules of international law, in connection with the extradition of nationals he said: '. . . No one contested the empirical finding that many states do not extradite their own nationals. . . . Such reluctance accords perfectly with present-day international law. Therefore, it may seen unacceptable to impose on a state a duty which is not derived from general international law and which openly seeks to restrict sovereign powers normally held by a state': loc.cit. above (n. 3), p. 46.

[146] Op.cit. above (n. 130), pp. 39–40.

[147] *American Journal of International Law*, 86 (1992), pp. 522–3.

international peace and security (Article 24 of the Charter), while the General Assembly has the power to make recommendations with respect to international peace and security (Articles 10, 11, 12 with certain limitations and 14).[148] Moreover, there is no hierarchy between these organs under the Charter, nor does the ICJ possess a review function over acts of the Security Council or the General Assembly, under the Charter.[149] So what is the relationship between the ICJ and the political organs of the UN?[150] The relationship between the ICJ and the Security Council has been clearly described by the ICJ in the case of *Military and Paramilitary Activities in and against Nicaragua*: 'the [Security] Council has functions of a political nature assigned to it, whereas the Court exercises purely judicial functions. Both organs can therefore perform their separate but complementary functions with respect to the same events.'[151] The Court went on to say: 'it must also be remembered that, as the *Corfu Channel* case . . . shows, the Court has never shied away from a case brought before it merely because it had political implications or because it involved serious elements of the use of force'. The Court then cited a passage from its judgment in the *Corfu Channel* case and said: 'what is also significant is that the Security Council itself in that case had "undoubtedly intended that the whole dispute should be decided by the Court" '.[152] The Court added that ' . . . even after a determination under Article 39, there is no necessary inconsistency between Security

[148] The ICJ, in the case of *Certain Expenses of the United Nations* (1962), found that the General Assembly was entitled to claim residual responsibility in questions affecting international peace and security: *ICJ Reports*, 1962, p. 163.

[149] ' . . . [A]t the San Francisco Conference the proposal to confer the point of preliminary determination [of each organ's competence] upon the International Court of Justice was rejected. The view was preferred that each organ would interpret its own competence': Higgins, *The Development of International Law through the Political Organs of the United Nations* (1963), p. 66 and n. 27, quoted by Franck, *American Journal of International Law*, 86 (1992), p. 520.

[150] For a thorough and detailed treatment of the relationship between the ICJ and the Security Council, see Gowlland-Debbas, loc.cit. above (n. 3).

[151] *ICJ Reports*, 1984, p. 435, paragraph 95.

[152] Ibid., paragraph 96; Gowlland-Debbas maintains that the *Lockerbie* case ' . . . created a potential for conflict between two organs of the United Nations seized by *different* parties to a dispute': loc.cit. above (n. 3), p. 644 (original emphasis). Judge Bedjaoui believes that the *Lockerbie* case could turn into an open conflict between the ICJ and the Security Council. He says: 'Le différend purement *entre Etats* (Royaume-Uni, Etats-Unis, Libye) soumis à la fois au Conseil (auquel la France a aussi recouru) et à la Cour, risquait de se muer en *conflit ouvert entre le Conseil et la Cour*. C'est ce qui se produisit en fait lorsque le 31 mars 1992 et alors que l'affaire était *sub judice*, le Conseil de sécurité a maintenu et renouvelé sa demande d'extradition par sa résolution 748 prise en vertu du Chapitre VII et assortie d'un embargo contre la Libye pour les transports aériens et le commerce des armes . . . ': op.cit. above (n. 130), p. 85 (original emphasis). The ICJ, itself, in the *Lockerbie* case, declined to deal with the question of relationship between itself and the Security Council, which had been raised by the parties. The Court, having declined to indicate provisional measures, simply stated that ' . . . it is not called upon to determine any of the other questions which have been raised in the present proceedings': *ICJ Reports*, 1992, p. 15, paragraph 42, and p. 127, paragraph 45.

Council action and adjudication by the Court'.[153] The Court's position is that its functions and those of the Security Council complement each other. It would be reasonable to apply the same, by analogy, to the functions of the General Assembly. But if a Security Council resolution affects the legal rights of a State, for example when the Council '. . . has framed its resolutions not in terms of directives as to conduct but in language resembling a judicial determination of the law and of the legal consequences said to flow from the conduct of the State that is arraigned',[154] what is the legal position? Furthermore, when a political organ of the UN acts *ultra vires* its functions, where does one turn for assessment of the validity of such actions?

In Libya's request for interim measures, it argued that by its Resolution 748 (1992), 'the Security Council infringes, or threatens to infringe, the enjoyment and the exercise of the rights conferred on Libya by the Montreal Convention and its economic, commercial and diplomatic rights'.[155] Libya also contended that Security Council Resolution 748 (1992) was contrary to international law.[156] It is to be recalled that in its Resolution 748 (1992) the Security Council called upon Libya, *inter alia*, to surrender for trial all those charged with the crimes of destruction of Pam Am flight 103 and UTA flight 772, accept responsibility for actions of its officials, pay appropriate compensation, and comply promptly and fully. In doing so, the Council appears to have ruled on legal matters arising under general international law, namely the rights and duties of Libya in relation to its nationals, the responsibility of Libya and its obligation to make reparation. But has the Council ascertained the facts of the case or verified the evidence, in an objective and impartial way, in order to engage Libya's responsibility?[157] Has it observed the standards of fairness in this exercise? As Professor Bowett has pointed out,

[153] *ICJ Reports*, 1984, p. 432, paragraph 90.

[154] See Professor E. Lauterpacht, *Aspects of the Administration of International Justice* (1991), p. 39. He gives some examples: the case of South West Africa, Security Council Resolution 276 (1970); Southern Rhodesia, Security Council Resolution 217 (1965), 20 November 1965; the Iraqi 'annexation' of Kuwait, Security Council Resolution 662 (1990), 9 August 1990.

[155] *ICJ Reports*, 1992, p. 14, paragraph 35, and p. 125, paragraph 38.

[156] Ibid., p. 14, paragraph 36, and p. 126, paragraph 39.

[157] A commentator on the *Lockerbie* case observed that '. . . by endorsing the demand for compensation the Security Council apparently endorses the view that Libya has breached international law and should make reparations. Since the object of the previous demand was to allow criminal trials to proceed this could be regarded as prejudicial (in the strict sense of the word)': Beveridge, loc.cit. above (n. 3), p. 911. See also Gowlland-Debbas: '. . . In Resolution 748 the Council established Libyan responsibility for international terrorism under the Charter by linking terrorist acts to Article 2(4). It did this *by implicitly endorsing the accusations of individual member states* expressed in Security Council documents that Libya had breached international law and in consequence should make reparations': loc.cit. above (n. 3), p. 660 (emphasis added). See also Sorel:

Where the Council decides under Article 39 that Chapter VII applies, and in addition decides that State X . . . must pay compensation, the latter finding is not simply a matter of political judgment. It is a finding based upon an assessment of the facts and the application of a norm of international law, based on that assessment of the facts. So, too, where the Council decides that Member States must apply economic sanctions against State X because of its violation of the right of self-determination. The obligation to apply sanctions arises because of the delict by State X, and a finding of delict is not a purely political decision: it is a finding of fact and law.[158]

There appears to be no evidence that the Council had decided Libya's guilt on a finding of fact and law. Professor Lauterpacht's apt description of the major concern of the Council in such situations might be appropriate to quote here:

It is evident that in reaching its conclusions about the law the Security Council has not acted in a way that would normally be recognized as judicial. Though it may have given the 'defendant' party an opportunity to put its case, it certainly will not have heard evidence presented in the systematic manner associated with court proceedings; there will have been no cross-examination of witnesses; there will have been no detailed assessment of the legal background and the legal factors; and, above all, the assessment of the evidence and the determination of the law will not have been free from collateral political considerations in the same way as the process of reaching a truly judicial conclusion would or should have been. The usual procedure is that a draft resolution expressing the conclusions of the Council will have been circulated at an early stage in the debate, perhaps even before its actual commencement, and activity in the Council will have been aimed at negotiating the final text of the resolution and securing political adhesion to it, rather than at reaching an impartial conclusion based upon unbiased consideration of the facts and objective examination of the

commenting on the US-UK demand that Libya should surrender the accused Libyans and pay compensation, he said: 'De même, la formulation très discutée et pour le moins maladroite du texte américano-britannique qui demande la livraison des deux "accusés" et le versement immédiat d'indemnités méritera éclaircissements. En effet, la présomption d'innocence disparaît et la qualification "d'accusé" est donnée non par un jury populaire mais par des Etats. Le versement d'indemnités exigé semble faire fi de toute la procédure de la responsabilité internationale. C'est réclamer la réparation avant d'avoir établi la culpabilité des suspects qui—si elle est reconnue—apporte un élément de preuve de la culpabilité de la Libye comme Etat terroriste': loc.cit. above (n. 3), p. 721. Judge Shahabuddeen, in his separate opinion, made the following observation on the issue of prior determination of the guilt of the accused Libyans: 'Since the ground on which the United Kingdom made its demand for payment of compensation was that Libya had engaged international responsibility for the crimes allegedly committed by its two accused nationals, the making of the demand for payment "promptly and in full" constituted a public and widely publicized announcement by the Respondent State of a prior determination by it, as a State, that the two accused were in fact guilty of the offences charged. . . . The Solicitor General for Scotland affirmed to the Court that "their guilt or innocence will be determined not by the Lord Advocate, nor by the Government of the United Kingdom . . . ". True, in the sense that guilt is for the courts; but it is nevertheless clear that guilt has already been determined by the United Kingdom as a State': *ICJ Reports*, 1992, p. 31; 'The United States demand that Libya "must . . . pay appropriate compensation . . . promptly and in full" presupposes a determination by the United States that the accused are guilty, since the responsibility of the Libyan State is premised on the guilt of the accused': ibid., p. 141.

[158] Loc.cit. above (n. 145), pp. 94–5.

law. Certainly, there will be no statement by the Council as such presenting a reasoned explanation of its conclusions of law and fact in a manner comparable to that of a judgment of a court of law.[159]

In respect of Resolution 731 (1992) Weller observed: 'It was adopted unanimously, on the strength of allegations made by three permanent members of the Council. The evidence in support of these allegations was never made public and, indeed, the claimants had refused to submit evidence to an impartial investigatory body.'[160] There is some force in the views of Tomuschat: ' . . . it may be extremely difficult to prove that the Libyan government—or some agencies forming part of the governmental structure—is behind the bombing. It is only by a thorough investigation and trial that full light may be shed on the destruction of the Pan Am jet.'[161] It could therefore be argued that by adopting Resolution 748, the Security Council has prejudged the question of guilt, and as such, the resolution is flawed: 'It is one of the peculiar features of the Lockerbie case that the Security Council, by adopting Resolution 748, acted at the last minute to provide support to the case of the two defendant states, certainly not in ignorance of their delicate procedural situation before the [ICJ]'.[162]

In what direction can one move to eliminate the flaw in the actions of the political organs of the UN, which Professor Lauterpacht calls 'quasi-judicial activity'? He suggests that 'the answer would appear to lie in the direction of judicial review'.[163] The doctrine of *ultra vires* has been advanced by Professor Bowett as one of the valid grounds for judicial review of Security Council resolutions that can be raised in an inter-State dispute.[164] There appears to be support from a number of writers for the view that the ICJ is qualified to review decisions of the political organs of the UN.[165] The Court, it is hoped, would not shy away from doing so, at the merits phase of the Lockerbie incident.[166]

[159] Op.cit. above (n. 154), pp. 42–3.
[160] See Weller, loc.cit. above (n. 3), p. 313.
[161] Loc.cit. above (n. 3), p. 43.
[162] Ibid.
[163] Op.cit. above (n. 154), p. 113.
[164] Loc.cit. above (n. 145), pp. 95 and 98.
[165] See Weller, loc.cit. above (n. 3), p. 324; Franck, loc.cit. above (n. 3), pp. 523 (1992) and 283 (1993); Beveridge, loc.cit. above (n. 3), p. 916; Tomuschat, loc.cit. above (n. 3), p. 48; and Gowlland-Debbas, loc.cit. above (n. 3), p. 664; see also Bowett, loc.cit. above (n. 145), p. 97. It must be pointed out that the UK does not seem to consider the ICJ competent to exercise review power over Security Council resolutions. Higgins stated, during the oral hearings of the Libyan request for provisional measures, that 'the International Court [of Justice] is not in any general sense an appeal tribunal, available to Member States who have not been able to make their views prevail in the Security Council': *Oral Hearings*, CR92/3, p. 69. T. Gill believes that 'the ICJ is not a constitutional court of the UN system. It has no power of judicial review of the decisions or actions of either the Security Council or of any other organ or agency of the UN system': American Society of International Law, op.cit. above (n. 3), p. 284.
[166] Judge Bedjaoui believes that the ICJ should have considered the validity of Security Council Resolutions 731 and 748 at the stage of the Libyan request for provisional measures. He says: 'Le

V. Extradition and Security Council Resolutions

As has been seen earlier, Libya is under no obligation, either under the Montreal Convention or under customary international law, to extradite its accused nationals to the UK, US or France in connection with the destruction of Pan Am flight 103 and UTA flight 772. But can the Security Council still order Libya to surrender those accused Libyans? And if the Security Council does so, is Libya bound by such a resolution? In Resolution 748 (1992), as has been shown earlier, the Security Council, acting under Chapter VII, decided, in operative paragraph 1, '. . . that the Libyan Government must now comply without any further delay with paragraph 3 of resolution 731 (1992) regarding the requests [from France, the UK and US] . . . '. These demands were for the surrender for trial of all those charged with the crime of destruction of Pan Am flight 103 and UTA flight 772; acceptance by Libya of responsibility for actions of its officials; disclosure of Libya's knowledge of the crime; payment of appropriate compensation; and prompt and full compliance.[167] The first element, namely, the surrender of Libyans accused of the crime, is the relevant one for this enquiry. The first thing to be noted is the use of the term 'surrender' and not 'extradite' in the requests. The former is not a technical term and, according to *The Concise Oxford Dictionary*, it means 'hand over, relinquish possession of' ('to surrender' in French is: 'livrer, . . . mettre à la discrétion, au pouvoir de (qqn)').[168] It could therefore be argued that the Security Council has intended to act outside the scope of the Montreal Convention. Secondly, besides the surrender of the accused Libyans, the requests in question relate to State responsibility and payment of compensation, promptly and in full, for wrongful acts. Such matters fall outside the scope of the Montreal Convention. It could therefore be argued that the Security Council has envisaged its action, under Chapter VII of the Charter, in fulfilment of its functions under Article 24 of the Charter. If so, then obligations of UN members under Article 25 of the Charter 'to accept and carry out the decisions of the Security Council' come into operation. Such obligations prevail over other obligations under other international agreements undertaken by UN members in accordance with Article 103

problème véritable de validité des résolutions 731 et surtout 748 se posait immédiatement et devait être tranché même à ce stade préliminaire de la procédure, dans la mesure où la manière du Conseil d'exercer là sa compétence mettait radicalement en échec celle de la Cour. Les pouvoirs respectifs des deux organes devenaient incompatibles. Dès lors que la résolution 748 (1992) avait eu pour objet, ou pour effet, . . . d'empêcher en fait la Cour elle-même de s'acquitter de la fonction judiciaire dont la Charte l'a investie, *la Cour aurait dû s'interroger sérieusement et prioritairement sur la légalité de cette résolution, même à ce stade des mesures conservatoires*': op.cit. above (n. 130), pp. 87–8 (original emphasis).

[167] See *ICJ Reports*, 1992, p. 11, paragraph 28, and pp. 122–3, paragraph 30. See also above, n. 124.

[168] See *The Concise Oxford Dictionary* (8th edn., 1990), p. 1228; see also le Robert, *Dictionnaire de la langue française* (2nd edn., 1985), vol. 6, p. 39. See what Professor Higgins said during the oral hearings of Libya's application for provisional measures: above, n. 89.

of the Charter. The ICJ considered prima facie that the obligation of UN members under Article 25 of the Charter '. . . extends to the decision contained in resolution 748 (1992); and . . . in accordance with Article 103 of the Charter, the obligations of the Parties in that respect prevail over their obligations under any other international agreement, including the Montreal Convention'.[169] According to this point of view, Libya would be under its Charter obligation to carry out Security Council Resolution 748 (1992) and thus, *inter alia*, to surrender the Libyans accused of the destruction of Pan Am flight 103 and UTA flight 772 to France, the UK or the US.[170]

A countervailing argument might be advanced to the effect that the sanctions imposed by the Security Council under Resolution 748 (1992) could not be considered as an *intra vires* exercise of the Council's functions under the Charter. The State against which the sanctions were imposed (Libya) was not in breach of the Charter or international law in general. It did not commit a wrong. It merely refused to surrender its nationals, because it claimed the right to exercise jurisdiction over them, in conformity with an international treaty, namely the Montreal Convention. Therefore, it might be doubted that the Security Council has exercised its functions in conformity with 'the Purposes and Principles of the United Nations', as required by Article 24, paragraph 2, of the Charter. If so, then it could be argued that there has been *excès de pouvoir* on the part of the Security Council. In this case, its action might be considered *ultra vires*, and as such the resolution imposing the sanctions against Libya might not be capable of imposing obligations on it that would prevail over other obligations imposed by the Montreal Convention. As Judge Bedjaoui says, 'En principe toute manière d'agir de l'Organisation ou de l'un de ses organes, qui serait contraire aux dispositions de la Charte régissant ses fonctions, constituerait un excès de pouvoir'. He goes on:

> Un organe créé par un traité est d'évidence soumis à celui-ci dans son existence, sa mission et ses pouvoirs. Le Conseil de sécurité doit obéir aux dispositions de la Charte dans sa mission au service de l'Organisation des Nations Unies. L'article 24, paragraph 2, paraît bien consacrer cette évidence: '*Dans l'accomplissement de (ses) devoirs, le Conseil de sécurité agit conformément aux buts et principes des Nations Unies*'.[171]

[169] See *ICJ Reports*, 1992, p. 15, paragraph 39, and p. 126, paragraph 42.

[170] It is interesting to observe that Judge Weeramantry, in his dissenting opinion, agrees with the majority of the Court on this point. He said: '. . . I take the view that resolution 748 (1992) must be treated as binding on Libya . . . in terms of Article 25 of the United Nations Charter and that, in terms of Article 103, the obligations it lays down prevail over the obligations flowing from any other international agreement. In specific terms, this means that Libya is, prima facie, bound by the provisions of that resolution even if they should conflict with the rights Libya claims under the Montreal Convention': ibid., p. 67, and p. 177.

[171] Op.cit. above (n. 130), pp. 22 and 24 (original emphasis).

The dissenting opinion of the late Judge Sir Gerald Fitzmaurice in the *Namibia* case of 1971 may also be relied upon to support this proposition. Referring to Article 25 of the Charter and its proviso ' in accordance with the present Charter', he said:

If, under the relevant chapter or article of the Charter, the decision is *not* binding, Article 25 cannot make it so. If the effect of that Article were automatically to make *all* decisions of the Security Council binding, then the words 'in accordance with the present Charter' would be quite superfluous. They would add nothing to the preceding and only other phrase in the Article, namely 'The Members of the United Nations agree to accept and carry out the decisions of the Security Council', which they are clearly intended to qualify. They effectively do so only if the decisions referred to are those which *are* duly binding 'in accordance with the present Charter'.[172]

Accordingly Article 103 of the Charter would not be applicable in this situation and Libya's conduct remains governed by the provisions of the Montreal Convention in respect of the exercise of jurisdiction over the accused Libyans. As noted earlier, in his dissenting opinion in the *Interpretation and Application of the 1971 Montreal Convention*, Judge El-Kosheri considered that ' . . . the Security Council, when adopting paragraph 1 of resolution 748 (1992), impeded the Court's jurisdiction freely to exercise its inherent judicial function . . . , and that by doing so the Security Council committed an act of *excès de pouvoir* which amounts to a violation of Article 92 of the Charter . . . '.[173] He also described paragraph 1 of Resolution 748 (1992) as of '*ultra vires* character'.[174] As Judge Bedjaoui says, 'si l'organe ne respecte pas la Charte et spécialement "l'économie interne" de l'Organisation, . . . c'est-à-dire la répartition interne des compétence des organes, il est manifeste que sa décision est prise *ultra vires* et doit être tenue pour irrégulière. *La fin même la plus noble ne peut justifier n'importe quel moyen.*'[175] Furthermore, obligations

[172] Advisory opinion on the *Legal Consequences for States of the Continued Presence of South Africa in Namibia, ICJ Reports*, 1971, p. 293, paragraph 113. See also Tomuschat, commenting on Resolution 748: 'It might also be argued that the Security Council has no authority to deal with individual cases, its primary function being to ensure international peace and security in interstate relationships (Articles 24 and 39 of the Charter)': loc.cit. above (n. 3), p. 45.

[173] See *ICJ Reports*, 1992, p. 105, paragraph 33, and p. 210, paragraph 33.

[174] Ibid., paragraph 36, and paragraph 36. Counsel for Libya (Mr Suy) made the following observation: referring to ten international conventions against international terrorism, recalled by the UN General Assembly in its resolution of 9 December 1991 entitled 'Measures to Eliminate International Terrorism', he said: 'at this moment these ten conventions constitute the code of international law concerning the elimination of international terrorism. What right does the Security Council have to ignore this important result of work done during the last 30 years to develop international law? What is it that inspires the Respondents with the idea of claiming that the 1971 Montreal Convention . . . is not to be applied? How do these Parties dare maintain that from now on the struggle against international terrorism is no longer within the framework of the provisions of international law that have been specifically adopted to that end and that this series of ten conventions is no longer to be applied?': *Oral Hearings*, CR92/2 (translation) (26 March 1992), pp. 73–4.

[175] Op.cit. above (n. 130), p. 38 (original emphasis).

under Article 103 of the Charter apply in cases of inconsistency between the Charter and any other international agreement. But if a Member State relies on general international law, would the Charter obligations still apply? Libya's rights could be said to derive from general international law.[176] Professor Bowett, referring to the ICJ ruling in the *Lockerbie* case concerning the application of Article 103 of the Charter, says:

It is true that this reasoning is confined to the supremacy of a Council decision over inconsistent *treaty* rights or obligations, because Article 103 is concerned solely with compatibility between Charter obligations and obligations 'under any other international agreement'. Accordingly, the reasoning would not apply where a member relied on its rights under general international law . . . . But even in relation to Article 103 the Court's reasoning is unconvincing. It involves the following propositions.

i) By virtue of Article 103, a Charter obligation prevails over any other inconsistent treaty provision. (Correct).
ii) Under Article 25 members have an obligation to accept Security Council decisions. (Correct).
iii) Therefore a Security Council decision prevails over any other inconsistent treaty right or obligation. (Incorrect).

The last step in the Court's reasoning is that it equates a Council decision with a Charter *treaty* obligation, and that is incorrect. A Council decision is *not* a treaty obligation. The obligation to comply may be, but the decision *per se* is not.[177]

VI. Conclusion

The offence of aircraft sabotage is an international offence created by the Montreal Convention 1971, like other international offences created by treaties, such as aircraft hijacking and hostage-taking. The destruction of Pan Am flight 103 and UTA flight 772 demonstrates, beyond doubt, the great danger to international civil aviation arising from acts of aircraft sabotage. This offence can also threaten relations between States. The response of the international community to that danger by the adoption of the Montreal Convention has therefore been timely and reasonable.

However, the regime of jurisdiction under the Montreal Convention is not free from difficulties, as unfortunately the Convention, though it provides for several jurisdictions, does not contain any sort of order in the exercise of jurisdiction. This state of affairs can lead, and has actually led, to more than one State claiming, rightly, the competence to exercise

[176] See Judge Oda's declaration, *ICJ Reports*, 1992, pp. 17–18, and pp. 130–1.

[177] Loc.cit. above (n. 145), p. 92; Bowett quotes Combaceau, *Le Pouvoir de sanction de l'ONU* (1974), on this issue of conflict between Article 103 and a treaty.

jurisdiction at the same time and over the same offence. This state of affairs could frustrate the purpose and object of the Montreal Convention. Furthermore, the extradition arrangements under the Convention are optional, and subject to some qualifications. Therefore Libya can claim, and has claimed, the right not to extradite its accused nationals. Such a claim is tenable under the Montreal Convention. This may lead one to question whether or not the Security Council was justified in applying Chapter VII of the UN Charter (measures not involving the use of force) against Libya for its refusal to surrender its accused nationals to France, the UK or the US.

The problems which have arisen in the areas of jurisdiction and extradition in the Lockerbie incident and the UTA flight 772 may draw the attention of the international community to the need to find some solutions thereto. One such solution could be the adoption of another protocol to the Montreal Convention,[178] perhaps devoted to the regulation of the conflict of jurisdiction demonstrated by the Lockerbie and the UTA incidents. Such a protocol could either provide for a rule on priority of jurisdiction, or establish some criteria that would tilt the balance in favour of one jurisdiction rather than another. It could also provide for some binding extradition arrangements under the Montreal Convention, with some guarantees for the protection of the fundamental rights of the accused. After all, the Montreal Convention was adopted more than twenty-three years ago, and it is not unreasonable to find some solutions to problems, which have arisen from concrete examples, in its operation. A very important guarantee in this respect would be the assurance of a fair trial to the accused, which, unfortunately, might not be possible for those accused of the Lockerbie and UTA incidents, owing to the publicity and wide coverage of the two incidents by the mass media. Indeed, Judge El-Kosheri observed in his dissenting opinion in the *Interpretation and Application of the 1971 Montreal Convention*, '... in the light of the special circumstance of the present case ... the two Libyans suspected to be the authors of the Lockerbie massacre could not possibly receive a fair trial, neither in the United States or in the United Kingdom, nor in Libya'.[179] Another solution may be found in the International Criminal Tribunal envisaged under the ILC Draft Statute, under the regime of 'opting in to jurisdiction'.[180]

[178] See above, n. 6.

[179] *ICJ Reports*, 1992, p. 111, paragraph 60, and p. 216, paragraph 60.

[180] See Article 22 of the Draft Statute, and Professor Crawford's explanation of the system of jurisdiction, *American Journal of International Law*, 88 (1994), p. 144.

NEGOTIATING SOVEREIGNTY: THE PRACTICE OF THE UNITED KINGDOM IN REGARD TO THE RIGHT OF SELF-DETERMINATION*

By ROBERT MCCORQUODALE‡

It is true that we [the United Kingdom] took the position in the 1960s that self-determination was a principle and not a right. However, in 1966 the two International Covenants—on Economic, Social and Cultural Rights, and on Civil and Political Rights—were adopted. . . . Not only has my country endorsed the right to self-determination in the sense of the [United Nations] Charter, the [International] Covenants and the Friendly Relations Declaration [1970], but we have gone a great deal further to disprove the allegation that we are the colonial Power *par excellence*. Since General Assembly Resolution 1514 (XV) was adopted at the end of 1960, we have brought to sovereign independence and membership of this Organisation no less than 28 States. We are proud of our record, and I think we have every right to be.[1]

The role of the United Kingdom has been central in the development of the right of self-determination. As the above statement indicates, from an initial rejection of the right as merely a 'political principle' with 'strong moral force'[2] to subsequent endorsement of the right as an 'inalienable right . . . which cannot be taken away',[3] the practice of the United Kingdom with regard to the right of self-determination has been of considerable significance in international law. It was once the 'colonial power *par excellence*', as it administered the majority of non-self-governing territories, but it has now acknowledged the role of the right of self-determination in its decolonization process.

In its practice a number of the difficult issues concerning the right of self-determination have been dealt with by the United Kingdom. The

‡ Senior Lecturer, Faculty of Law, Australian National University; formerly Fellow and Lecturer in Law, St John's College, University of Cambridge.

[1] Permanent Representative of the United Kingdom (UK) to the United Nations (UN) (Sir Anthony Parsons), 25 May 1982, S/PV.2366, pp. 71–2, as quoted in G. Marston (ed.), 'United Kingdom Materials on International Law' (UKMIL), this *Year Book*, 53 (1982), pp. 371–2.

[2] Statement by the UK representative to the General Assembly (GA) (Mr Hoare), Third Committee, 642nd meeting (1954), p. 90, paras. 11–12. The author is grateful to Sally Morphet of the UK Foreign and Commonwealth Office (FCO) for her assistance in indicating materials on UK practice.

[3] Letter from Permanent Representative of the UK to the UN (Sir Anthony Parsons) to the President of the Security Council (SC), 28 April 1982, *SC Official Records (SCOR)*, 37th Session, Supplement for April, May, June, p. 47.

ones which will be considered in this article are: whether self-determination is a right or a moral principle; who are the 'peoples' entitled to the right; the application of the right beyond the colonial context; how the wishes of the 'peoples' are to be determined; what types of exercise of the right there are; and the impact of territorial claims by other States on the exercise of the right. The United Kingdom's practice and its impact on these aspects of the right of self-determination will be analysed. In the course of this examination it will be possible to consider whether the United Kingdom's practice has been consistent.

I. A 'Principle' or a 'Right'?

(a) *Prior to the International Human Rights Covenants*

Self-determination has been referred to as an aspect of United Kingdom policy at least since 1918, when the then Prime Minister (Lloyd George) declared that one reason for the United Kingdom entering the First World War had been the 'principle of self-determination' and that future territorial questions should be resolved by respecting 'the consent of the governed'.[4] The United Kingdom acknowledged 'the right of all peoples to choose the form of government under which they will live' when it signed the Atlantic Charter in 1941.[5] After the Second World War it ratified the Charter of the United Nations (UNC), which includes references to 'the principle of equal rights and self-determination of peoples'.[6]

Moreover, Article 73 of the UNC placed an obligation on those States which administered non-self-governing territories to provide information about those territories[7] and also

> to develop self-government, to take account of the political aspirations of the peoples, and to assist them in the progressive development of their free political institutions, according to the particular circumstances of each territory and its peoples and their varying stages of advancement.[8]

This obligation was rapidly acknowledged by the United Kingdom.[9] But the obligation was not one the United Kingdom considered to be based on the right of self-determination, as self-determination was considered

[4] Address to the Trade Union Conference, 5 January 1918, reported in *The New York Times Current History* (New York), p. 270.

[5] United States, *Department of State Bulletin*, 16 August 1941, p. 125.

[6] Arts. 1(2) and 55.

[7] Art. 73(*e*).

[8] Art. 73(*b*). For similar obligations related to Trust Territories, see UNC, Chapter XII.

[9] The UK Minister of State for Foreign Affairs (Mr Ormsby Gore), in a speech to the GA on 28 November 1960, said: 'I find it hard to improve upon the terms of article 73 of the Charter as a description of the British concept of the modern colonial relationship': Report of the Proceedings of the 50th Session of the GA, Cmnd. 1456 (HMSO, 1961), p. 121.

by it to be merely a 'formative principle of great potency',[10] having 'strong moral force' only.[11] In fact, it resisted the inclusion of an article on the right of self-determination in the International Human Rights Covenants (the Covenants)—what became the International Covenant on Civil and Political Rights (ICCPR) and the International Covenant on Economic, Social and Cultural Rights (ICESCR)—because it 'would in the name of a great principle introduce political dynamite into a troubled world'.[12]

(b) *Subsequent to the International Human Rights Covenants*

Nevertheless, once the article on the right of self-determination was included in both the Covenants, the United Kingdom did ratify those Covenants.[13] Common Article 1 of these Covenants provides:

> 1. All peoples have the right of self-determination. By virtue of that right they freely determine their political status and freely pursue their economic, social and cultural development.
> 2. All peoples may, for their own ends, freely dispose of their natural wealth and resources without prejudice to any obligations arising out of international economic co-operation, based upon the principle of mutual benefit, and international law. In no case may a people be deprived of its means of subsistence.
> 3. The States Parties to the present Covenant, including those having responsibility for the administration of Non-Self-Governing and Trust Territories, shall promote the realization of the right of self-determination, and shall respect that right, in conformity with the provisions of the Charter of the United Nations.

Upon the signature by the United Kingdom of both Covenants in 1968, it stated that

> the Government of the United Kingdom declare their understanding that, by virtue of article 103 of the Charter of the United Nations, in the event of any conflict between their obligations under article 1 of the Covenant and their obligations under the Charter (in particular articles 1, 2 and 73 thereof) their obligations under the Charter shall prevail.[14]

[10] Submission by the UK, 22 September 1964, during consideration of the drafting of the Declaration on Principles of International Law, UN Doc. A/5725/Add. 4 (1964), p. 74.

[11] Statement by the UK representative to the GA (Mr Hoare), Third Committee, 642nd meeting (1955), p. 90, para. 12.

[12] Ibid., para. 13.

[13] As at 1 February 1996, the ICESCR had been ratified by 134 States and the ICCPR by 132 States (information provided by the United Nations Centre for Human Rights, Geneva). Thus they have been ratified by more than two-thirds of the member States of the UN.

[14] *United Nations Treaty Series*, vols. 993 and 999, as printed in United Nations, *Multilateral Treaties Deposited with the Secretary-General: Status as at 31 December 1993* (United Nations, 1994), pp. 118 and 132.

This interpretative declaration[15] was maintained when the United Kingdom ratified both Covenants in 1976.[16]

It would seem that the purpose of this declaration was to try to assert the priority of obligations under Article 73 of the UNC, which contemplated the progressive implementation of self-government, over the more immediate obligations under Article 1 of the Covenants. The justification for this was that obligations under the UNC prevail, as is provided in Article 103 of the UNC.[17] But the effect of the declaration was that the United Kingdom expressly accepted that there was a right of self-determination which placed legal obligations upon the United Kingdom, even if the United Kingdom wished to comply with those obligations at a gradual pace. Yet the declaration appears to have been unnecessary, at least by the time of the United Kingdom's ratification, for a number of reasons: the obligations under Article 1 of the Covenants could not be immediate as the freely expressed wishes of the peoples had to be ascertained first; Article 1(3) of the Covenants clarified that a State's obligations were to be in conformity with its obligations under the UNC; and the Covenants were expressly intended to give effect to the principles proclaimed in the UNC.[18] In any event, any possible conflict between Article 1 of the Covenants and the obligations under the UNC was largely resolved by the Declaration on Principles of International Law in 1970—to which the United Kingdom consented[19]—where the right of self-determination was restated and applied expressly to non-self-governing territories:

> the territory of a colony or other non-self-governing territory has, under the Charter of the United Nations, a status separate and distinct from the territory of the State administering it; and such . . . status . . . shall exist until the people of the colony or other non-self-governing territory have exercised their right of self-determination in accordance with the Charter, and particularly its purposes and principles.[20]

[15] When the Human Rights Committee (HRC) was considering the UK's Third Report, the UK representative (Mr Beamish) stated that this declaration 'did not constitute a reservation': UN Doc. CCPR/C/SR. 1046, p. 9, para. 40. However, in *Belilos* v. *Switzerland* (1988), ECHR, Series A, No. 132 (particularly at para. 49), the European Court of Human Rights held that an 'interpretative declaration' was in reality a reservation where its substantive content was to limit the obligations of the State and avoid the strictures of the reservation obligations of a human rights treaty. The HRC has taken the same view: General Comment 24(52), para. 3, UN Doc.CCPR/C/21/Rev. 1/Add. 6 (*International Human Rights Reports*, 2 (1995), p. 10). In the light of this position, it would be possible to consider the UK's declaration as a reservation.

[16] *UK Treaty Series*, No. 6 (1977), p. 44, Cmnd. 6702 (HMSO, 1977).

[17] In the consideration by the HRC of the UK's Second Report, the UK representative (Frank Berman), in response to questions about whether the UK would withdraw its declaration about Article 1, said that 'he would, however, note unofficially that the reservation [sic] seemed to do no more than what was already provided in the Charter, namely that in any conflict between obligations under the Charter and any other international obligations, those under the Charter would in any event take priority': UN Doc.CCPR/C/SR. 594, p. 11, para. 50.

[18] Preambles to the ICCPR and the ICESCR.

[19] The resolution was adopted by the GA without a vote.

[20] GA Resolution 2625 (XXV), 24 October 1970.

Therefore, the declaration made by the United Kingdom relating to the Covenants does not limit its obligations to uphold the right of self-determination for its non-self-governing territories. This conclusion is now accepted by the United Kingdom, as seen in its endorsement of the right of self-determination in the statement quoted at the beginning of this article and by its comment in 1986 that

> we have constantly upheld the right of all peoples to determine their own future. Our policy towards non-self-governing territories for which the United Kingdom is itself responsible continues to be founded on respect for this inalienable right.[21]

The United Kingdom has also said that the right of self-determination forms a 'fundamental' part of its foreign policy.[22] Indeed, it has called the right an 'inalienable right':

> Inalienable is a very strong word. It means birthright; it means you cannot get rid of it; it means that . . . [peoples] have a right of self-determination which no one can take from them.[23]

So the United Kingdom now accepts that self-determination is a right, not merely a principle with strong moral force, which places legal obligations on the United Kingdom.

These obligations have been further acknowledged by the United Kingdom with the extension of the application of the Covenants to almost all the territories it administers ('dependent territories').[24] In 1994 there were thirteen territories to which these Covenant obligations were extended—less than a quarter of the number in 1950—the Bailiwick of Guernsey, the Bailiwick of Jersey, the Isle of Man, Bermuda, the British Virgin Islands, the Cayman Islands, the Falkland Islands and Dependencies,[25] Gibraltar, Hong Kong, Montserrat, the Pitcairn Group, St Helena and Dependencies, and the Turks and Caicos Islands. These Covenant obligations have not been extended to Anguilla, though it remains on the list of UN non-self-governing territories, or to the dependent territories[26] of British Antarctic Territory, British Indian Ocean Territory and the United Kingdom Sovereign Bases on Cyprus,

[21] Statement in letter by UK Permanent Representative to the UN (Sir John Thomson), 31 January 1986, UKMIL, this *Year Book*, 57 (1986), p. 513.

[22] Foreign Secretary (Francis Pym) in statement to the GA, 29 September 1982, UKMIL, this *Year Book*, 54 (1983), p. 397.

[23] Statement by the UK Permanent Representative to the UN (Sir John Thomson) at the GA's Special Committee (the Decolonization Committee), 2 September 1983, UN Doc. A/AC.109/PV. 1238, UKMIL, this *Year Book*, 54 (1983), p. 404.

[24] The term 'dependent territories' is the name given to territories to which application of the Covenants has been extended and includes non-self-governing territories and other colonies; see the discussion of the difference in these terms in section II(b), below.

[25] The term 'Falkland Islands' will be used here and not the more usual term 'Falkland (Malvinas) Islands', as the islands are referred to solely as the 'Falkland Islands' by the UK.

[26] The list of UK overseas dependent territories is given in UKMIL, this *Year Book*, 63 (1992), p. 652.

with no clear reason given for this exclusion.[27] In the extension of the Covenants to the above territories the United Kingdom has made a number of reservations, though none of these are to Article 1. A reservation to Article 25 of the ICCPR (the right to participate in government) concerning Hong Kong has some relevance to Article 1 and is dealt with below.[28] As it is obliged to do under Article 40 of the ICCPR[29] and Article 16 of the ICESCR, the United Kingdom submits periodic reports on its compliance with these Covenants, including protecting the right of self-determination in common Article 1. It is not a party to the First Optional Protocol to the ICCPR and so no complaints against the United Kingdom can be brought by an individual to the Human Rights Committee (HRC), the body which reviews compliance with the ICCPR.

II. The 'Peoples' Protected by the Right

(a) *Non-Self-Governing Territories*

Who are the 'peoples' entitled to the protection of the right of self-determination has been a much debated issue.[30] The uncertainty of finding a definition to be applied by the United Kingdom is seen in the response by the Legal Adviser to the United Kingdom Foreign and Commonwealth Office to the question as to what is meant by 'peoples':

> This is a very difficult question . . . [and] there is no internationally accepted definition of the term 'peoples'. What one needs to consider are the circumstances of each particular case in which the [right of self-determination] may be invoked. Amongst the considerations to which we for our part attach importance . . . is whether the people in a particular territory constitute a settled and self-sustaining community with its own institutions and civil administration

[27] The UK has dealt with questions from the Human Rights Committee (HRC) about these latter territories by simply stating that it 'had not ratified the Covenant in respect of those . . . Territories': First Report to the HRC by the UK, UN Doc. CCPR/C/SR. 164, para. 56.

[28] See section V(b), expecially the text at n. 177.

[29] Hereafter all the reports to the HRC by the UK, including the supplementary reports, are referred to as the 'First Report', the 'Second Report', the 'Third Report' and the 'Fourth Report'.

[30] See, for example, M. Pomerance, *Self-Determination in Law and Practice: The New Doctrine in the UN* (Martinus Nijhoff, London, 1982), pp. 18–23, R. Kiwanuka. 'The Meaning of "People" in the African Charter of Human and Peoples' Rights', *American Journal of International Law*, 82 (1988), p. 80, and Article 1(2) of the International Labour Organization (ILO) Convention concerning Indigenous and Tribal People in Independent Countries 1989, *International Legal Materials*, 28 (1989), p. 1382. Who are a 'people' may be really more an issue of procedure (i.e. who is a victim of the abuse of the right) than of the substance of the right: see R. McCorquodale, 'Human Rights and Self-Determination', in M. Sellers (ed.), *New World Order: Sovereignty, Human Rights and the Self-Determination of Peoples* (Berg Publishers, Providence, RI, 1996).

built up over many years . . . [that is] our own working definition or rule of thumb.[31]

This 'working definition' has the benefit of being very flexible but contains problems. It ignores any 'self-identity', i.e. whether a group identifies themselves as a 'people', and, in regard to its dependent territories, that the United Kingdom itself largely determines if a people has its own institutions and civil administration. Nevertheless, in practice the United Kingdom has decided that all the inhabitants of its dependent territories are 'peoples' for the purpose of the right of self-determination, no matter the degree of development of the institutions or of civil administration, as evidenced by its reports to the HRC on Article 1 for each of its dependent territories.

This stance by the United Kingdom has proved to be contentious in relation to the Falkland Islands. There are only about 2,000 inhabitants of the Falkland Islands[32] and they are a 'settler' community and not indigenous.[33] This led Argentina to claim that the inhabitants of the Falkland Islands were not a 'people' and also to object to the inclusion of the Falkland Islands as a dependent territory of the United Kingdom under the Covenants.[34] The United Kingdom has adamantly rejected the view that the Falkland Islanders are not a 'people':

> The consistent practice of the United Nations shows that there is no minimum figure for a population to qualify for the right to self-determination: it suffices to cite the case of St Helena, another South Atlantic island with about 4,000 people whose right to self-determination has been consistently upheld.[35]

Other cases of small populations exercising self-determination include Tuvalu, with a population of 6,000, and Niue, with a population of 4,000. In respect of the nature of the population of the Falkland Islands, the United Kingdom has shown that it is a permanent, not a transient, population, more than half of the inhabitants having been there for over twenty years and some families having achieved their seventh generation

[31] Evidence by Sir Ian Sinclair to the House of Commons Foreign Affairs Committee, UKMIL, this *Year Book*, 54 (1983), pp. 399–400.

[32] Supplementary Report to the Third Report, para. 3.

[33] The term 'indigenous' is usually applied to tribal peoples and others who are descendants of populations which inhabited a territory at the time of the conquest or colonization of that territory: see Article 1, ILO Convention, loc. cit. above (n. 30).

[34] Argentina 'rejects and considers null and void the [UK's declaration] of territorial extension': *Multilateral Treaties Deposited with the Secretary-General*, op. cit. above (n. 14), p. 122. However, Argentina has not objected to the status of the Falkland Islands as a non-self-governing territory: see F. Hassan, 'The Sovereignty Dispute over the Falkland Islands', *Virginia Journal of International Law*, 23 (1982), p. 53, at pp. 69–70.

[35] Letter from the Permanent Representative of the UK to the UN (Sir Anthony Parsons) to the President of the SC, 28 April 1982, *SCOR*, 37th Session, Supplement for April, May, June, p. 48.

of residence.[36] Similarly, the United Kingdom has defended the position that the people of Gibraltar are a 'people' even though their territory is less than six square miles (with a population of 30,000).

The application by the United Kingdom of the concept of 'peoples' to the inhabitants of the Falkland Islands and Gibraltar is consistent with the general State practice according to which the inhabitants of each non-self-governing territory constitute a 'people' entitled to the right of self-determination as one unit. The International Court of Justice confirmed this general State practice in the *Namibia* case, when it held that

> the subsequent development of international law in regard to non-self-governing territories, as enshrined in the Charter of the United Nations, made the principle of self-determination applicable to all of them.[37]

So, whatever the size of its population, in principle the inhabitants of a non-self-governing territory are a 'people' entitled to the right of self-determination. Whether there are any exceptions to this practice or any limitations on the exercise of this right are considered in sections V and VI below but, even if there are some limitations on the exercise of the right, they do not affect the entitlement to the right. In addition, general State practice shows that the right has been applied to non-self-governing territories even where there are only long-established, independent settler populations or mixed indigenous and settler communities. A restriction of the right to indigenous populations alone would be

> a dangerous assertion, for if it was taken literally, it would apply to the majority of the world's population, beginning with the descendants of the conquistadores, who could also be considered as an imported population.[38]

However, there needs to be clarification of whether the term 'peoples' can be applied to the inhabitants of a territory which is not described as 'non-self-governing', such as Hong Kong and within the United Kingdom itself.

(b) *Hong Kong*

The term 'non-self-governing territories' is a term of art, arising from its use as a heading in Chapter XI (Articles 73 and 74) of the UNC. It

[36] See Second Report, UN Doc. CCPR/C/32/Add. 14, p. 38, Annex D, para. 42, and letter from the Permanent Representative of the UK to the UN (Sir Anthony Parsons) to the President of the SC, 29 April 1982, UN Doc. S/15010, UKMIL, this *Year Book*, 53 (1982), p. 369.

[37] Advisory opinion on the *Legal Consequences for States of the Continued Presence of South Africa in Namibia (South West Africa) Notwithstanding Security Council Resolution 276 (1970)* (*Namibia* case), *ICJ Reports*, 1971, p. 16, at p. 31, para. 52.

[38] Statement by the Jamaican representative in the Fourth Committee of the UN (Mr Barnett), *General Assembly Official Records* (*GAOR*), 22nd Session, Fourth Committee, UN Doc. A/C.4/SR. 1746 (1968), at p. 473.

refers to those territories on the United Nations' list of non-self-governing territories for which States must make regular reports under Article 73(*e*) to the Special Committee on the Situation with regard to the Implementation of the Declaration on the Granting of Independence to Colonial Countries and Peoples (the Special Committee).[39] Most territories are removed from that list when they achieve 'a full measure of self-government', which is defined by General Assembly Resolution 1541 (XV)[40] as being independence, free association with another State or integration with another State.

Hong Kong was removed from the list of non-self-governing territories in 1972. This removal occurred shortly after the change in China's representation in the United Nations—from Taiwan to the People's Republic of China (PRC)[41]—when China wrote to the Special Committee that

> the settlement of the questions of Hong Kong and Macao is entirely within China's sovereign right and does not at all fall under the ordinary category of colonial territories.[42]

The Special Committee recommended to the General Assembly, as part of its annual report, that Hong Kong be removed from the list of non-self-governing territories. The General Assembly adopted the report of the Special Committee in its Resolution 2908 (XXVII) but made no explicit mention of Hong Kong in the resolution.[43] This removal occurred with very limited consideration of the legal issues involved and with no apparent protest by the United Kingdom (probably because it was about to commence diplomatic relations with the PRC). However, the United Kingdom did state that the removal 'in no way affects the legal status of Hong Kong'.[44]

This latter statement by the United Kingdom can be supported. First, the list of non-self-governing territories is not conclusive as to which territories are actually non-self-governing. For example, New Caledonia

[39] It is sometimes also known as the Decolonization Committee or the Committee of 24, as it has 24 members.

[40] Principle VI. This Resolution concerned the 'Principles which should guide members in determining whether or not an obligation exists to transmit information called for under Article 73(e) of the Charter'. It was passed on 15 December 1960, the day after the Declaration on Granting of Indpendence to Colonial Countries and Peoples.

[41] The term 'China' will be used for the State of China, unless the context requires a distinction between the governments of China.

[42] Letter from Chinese Ambassador (Huang Hua) to Chairman of the Special Committee, 10 March 1972, reprinted in D. Jones, 'A Leg to Stand On? Post-1997 Hong Kong Courts as a Constraint on PRC Abridgement of Individual Rights and Local Autonomy', *Yale Journal of International Law*, 12 (1987), p. 250, at p. 255.

[43] The GA resolution was passed on 2 November 1972.

[44] Letter dated 19 December 1972 from the UK's Permanent Representative to the UN to the Secretary-General of the UN: see N. Jayawickrama, 'The Right of Self-Determination', in P. Wesley-Smith (ed.), *Hong Kong's Basic Law: Problems and Prospects* (Faculty of Law, University of Hong Kong, 1990), p. 85, at pp. 91–3.

was removed from the list unilaterally by France in 1947 but was reinscribed in the list in 1986 by a resolution of the General Assembly, which also reaffirmed the right of self-determination of the people of New Caledonia.[45] In the interim period New Caledonia remained a non-self-governing territory even though France did not provide reports under Article 73(*e*). The General Assembly made this clear in a 1986 resolution, which stated that:

> in the absence of a decision by the General Assembly itself that a Non-Self-Governing Territory has attained a full measure of self-government in terms of Chapter XI of the Charter, the administering Power concerned should continue to transmit information under Article 73e of the Charter with respect to that Territory.[46]

Thus the administering State, or any other State alone, could not decide whether or not a territory was non-self-governing. Therefore, as the General Assembly had never itself decided that Hong Kong had attained a full measure of self-government (and neither had the Special Committee), Hong Kong has remained a non-self-governing territory but is simply not on the list of non-self-governing territories.

Secondly, Chapter XI of the UNC is concerned with 'territories whose people have not yet attained a full measure of self-government'[47] and, as explained by Resolution 1541(XV), this was intended to refer to all 'colonies' because

> the authors of the Charter of the United Nations had in mind that Chapter XI should be applicable to territories which were then known to be of the colonial type.[48]

Indeed, that resolution defined the territories to which Chapter XI related as being ones which are 'geographically separate and . . . distinct ethnically and/or culturally from the country administering' them.[49] Hong Kong must fall within that latter definition and its people have not yet attained a 'full measure of self-government'. The United Kingdom

[45] GA Resolution 41/41A of 2 December 1986, passed by 89 in favour, 34 against and 24 abstentions. See the discussion in *Proceedings of the American Society of International Law*, 82 (1988), p. 429. A similar situation had arisen with French Somaliland (now Djibouti) and the Comoros, which were reinscribed in 1965 and 1972 respectively. E. Gayim, *The Eritrean Question: Conflict between the Right of Self-Determination and the Interests of States* (Iustus Forlag, Uppsala, 1993), at pp. 462–3, argues that Eritrea became a non-self-governing territory again once the federation with Ethiopia was terminated.

[46] GA Resolution 41/13 of 31 October 1986, passed by 149 in favour, 3 against (France, UK and United States) and no abstentions. The UK had argued that the status was determined by the administering State and the local government.

[47] Article 73.

[48] Loc. cit. above (n. 40), Principle 1.

[49] Ibid., Principle IV. Other elements may be brought into consideration about a territory to place an obligation on a State under Article 73(*e*), such as administrative, political, juridical, economic and historical considerations: Principle V.

administers Hong Kong as a colony[50] and it reports to the HRC on the application of Article 1 of the ICCPR in regard to Hong Kong in exactly the same way as it reports on its (listed) non-self-governing territories. In addition, other States treat the United Kingdom as the colonial administrator of Hong Kong by, for example, seeking the United Kingdom's permission to enter any agreement concerning Hong Kong's territory.[51] All these factors indicate that, for the purpose of looking at the status of Hong Kong, there is no distinction between a territory on the list of non-self-governing territories and a geographically separate and ethnically distinct territory which is administered by a State as a colony.

This lack of distinction in the status of these two types of territory coincides with a lack of distinction in entitlement of the inhabitants of each type of territory to the right of self-determination, as the Declaration on Principles of International Law indicates:

> the territory of a colony or other non-self-governing territory has, under the Charter of the United Nations, a status separate and distinct from the territory of the State administering it; and such . . . status . . . shall exist until the people of the colony or other non-self-governing territory have exercised their right of self-determination in accordance with the Charter, and particularly its purposes and principles.[52]

For both types of territory, colonies and non-self-governing territories, the inhabitants are a 'people' entitled to the right of self-determination. Indeed, the Declaration provides that this territorial status remains until the people of the territory have exercised their right. Thus, a simple removal from the list of non-self-governing territories without any exercise of the right, or at least without the General Assembly deciding that the right has been exercised, does not remove the entitlement of the people of a territory to the right of self-determination.

As will be seen,[53] the people of Hong Kong have not exercised their right of self-determination at all and certainly had not by 1972 when Hong Kong was removed from the list. This removal of Hong Kong from the list without its people's consent does not change Hong Kong's status as a non-self-governing territory. Even if it did, Hong Kong is still a colony and so its inhabitants are a 'people' entitled to the right of self-determination. It could also be argued that the inhabitants of Hong Kong are distinct from the people of China, despite the high percentage of ethnic Chinese living in Hong Kong, because the economic, political and social structure in Hong Kong is profoundly different from that of

[50] Hong Kong is described as an 'Overseas Dependent Territory' by the UK: UKMIL, this *Year Book*, 63 (1992), p. 652.

[51] For example, the UK approved a series of air services agreements between Hong Kong and, amongst others, Switzerland, the Netherlands, Canada and Brunei Darussalam: see UKMIL, this *Year Book*, 60 (1989), pp. 593–5.

[52] Loc. cit. above (n. 20).

[53] See section IV(a), below.

China, as evidenced by the concept of 'one country: two systems' in the United Kingdom-China agreements and the special citizenship given to Hong Kong residents by the British Nationality Act 1981.[54]

(c) *Within the United Kingdom*

The United Kingdom manifestly accepts that there can be different 'peoples' within a State. For example, in its colonial administration it has, at times, participated in the division of a colony because the colony contained different 'peoples', as in the case of its organization of the referendum in 1961 where the northern part of British Cameroon voted to become part of Nigeria and the southern part voted to become part of (French) Cameroun; in its actions in pressing for 'safe havens' for the Kurds in Iraq;[55] and in its voting on GA resolutions, such as the resolution supporting the right of self-determination of the Tibetans.[56] Above all, in its reports to the HRC the United Kingdom asserts

> its support in United Nations bodies for the right of self-determination and the exercise of that right within the United Kingdom itself.[57]

Thus it reports on its actions concerning the right in Scotland, Wales and Northern Ireland,[58] as well as within those territories which the United Kingdom considers to be 'internally self-governing dependencies': that is, Guernsey, Jersey and the Isle of Man.[59] There is the definite assumption by the United Kingdom that there exist different 'peoples' within its territory.

While there may be some debate about whether the only 'peoples' in the United Kingdom are those within England, Scotland, Wales and

[54] British Dependent Territories Citizenship. For discussion, see International Commission of Jurists, *Countdown to 1997: Report of a Mission to Hong Kong* (ICJ, Geneva, 1992), chapter VI. Hong Kong is also economically viable, even though it has no natural resources.

[55] SC Resolution 688 of 5 April 1991 created 'safe havens' for the Kurds north of the 36th parallel in Iraq. See further O. Schachter, 'United Nations Law in the Gulf Conflict', *American Journal of International Law*, 85 (1991), p. 452, at pp. 468–9.

[56] The UK voted for GA Resolution 2079 (XX), 18 December 1965, upholding the right of self-determination of the Tibetan people; see also R. McCorquodale and N. Orosz (eds.). *Tibet: The Position in International Law* (Hansjorg Mayer, London, 1994).

[57] Fourth Report, para. 12.

[58] For example, para. 19 and Addendum of the Third Report and para. 3 of the First Report.

[59] An 'internally self-governing dependency' is one where the UK 'is ultimately responsible for the good government of the islands and the UK is directly responsible for their defence and international relations': Reply by Minister of State, Home Office, HC Debs., vol. 210, WA, cols. 517–18, 30 June 1992, UKMIL, this *Year Book*, 63 (1992), pp. 650–1. The convention is that the UK does not legislate for these islands without their consent on domestic matters: first conclusion of the Royal Commission on the Constitution (Kilbrandon Commission) 1973, Cmnd. 5460, p. 465, para. 1539. Reports on the islands are given as annexes to the main UK Reports to the HRC.

Northern Ireland,[60] this division is largely reflective of the constitution and legislation of the United Kingdom. It was by treaties that the separate States of Wales (in 1536) and Scotland (in 1707) joined England; by legislation that Scotland has a separate legal and education system and the Welsh have a separate language;[61] and by administrative practice that the affairs of Northern Ireland, Scotland and Wales are dealt with by central government institutions devoted exclusively to that purpose.[62] There is also a consciousness of separate Scottish and Welsh identities. As one commentator noted:

the claim of Scottish [and Welsh] distinctiveness . . . is aided by the State having conceded that Scotland [and Wales] is a political entity through its establishment of central institutions and some measure of policy distinctiveness.[63]

This separate nature of the Scots and the Welsh was also formally acknowledged by the United Kingdom by offering referenda on devolution in 1979 to the inhabitants of those regions.[64]

In respect of Northern Ireland, the United Kingdom has sought by legislation[65] to treat the inhabitants of Northern Ireland as a 'people' entitled to the right of self-determination.[66] This determination is also seen in its international dealings with Ireland. The signature by the United Kingdom and Ireland of the Anglo-Irish Agreement of 1985, by which it was agreed that Ireland would be consulted about the affairs of Northern Ireland, affirmed

[60] A. Macartney, 'Autonomy in the British Isles', *Nordisk Tidsskrift for International Ret*, 54 (1984), p. 10, at p. 11, sets out 'the following nationalities [in the British Isles] in order of size: England; Scotland; Ireland; Wales; Jersey; Guernsey; Man; Alderney; and Sark. Two problem areas are left out of [this] scheme—the six counties of NE Ireland which form part of the UK, and the ancient Celtic territory of Cornwall. It will be further noted that the Northern and Western Isles are here subsumed in the Scottish nation, albeit as a very distinctive part of the Scottish realm.'

[61] Welsh may be used in court proceedings and for statutory documents and forms: Welsh Court Act 1942, Welsh Language Act 1967; see A. Samuels, 'Legal Recognition and Protection of Minority Customs in a Plural Society in England', *Anglo-American Law Review*, 10 (1981), p. 241, at p. 248.

[62] See further, the Royal Commission on Devolution to Scotland and Wales, *Our Changing Democracy*, Cmnd. 6348 (1975), Part III.

[63] J. Mitchell, 'The 1992 Election in Scotland in Context', *Parliamentary Affairs*, 45 (1992), p. 612, at p. 613. See also J. Brand, 'Scotland: The Politics of Devolution', *Parliamentary Affairs*, 46 (1993), p. 38.

[64] See paras. 18–20 of the Third Report.

[65] This legislation has been primarily in response to the alleged state of emergency in Northern Ireland, for example, in setting up the Diplock Courts (no jury), prohibiting incitement to religious hatred, and in the anti-terrorist legislation. See, generally, K. Boyle, T. Hadden and P. Hillyard, *Ten Years On in Northern Ireland: The Legal Control of Political Violence* (Cobden Trust, London, 1980). Also a House of Commons Northern Ireland Select Committee was set up in 1994: *The Guardian*, 10 March 1994, p. 8.

[66] A clear example is the UK's Northern Ireland Constitution Act 1973, as s. 1 provides that 'in no event will the United Kingdom or any part of it cease to be part of Her Majesty's dominions and of the United Kingdom without the consent of the majority of the people of the United Kingdom voting in a poll'.

that any change in the status of Northern Ireland would only come about with the consent of a majority of the people of Northern Ireland.[67]

The then Prime Minister (Margaret Thatcher) considered that this affirmation

is fully consistent with the commitment of the two Governments under the Helsinki accords in regard to the inviolability of frontiers, the territorial integrity of participating States and the right of self-determination of peoples.[68]

This practice by the United Kingdom was developed further in another agreement between the two States—known as the Downing Street Declaration—in December 1993. In this agreement it was stated:

The British Government agree that it is for the people of the island of Ireland alone, by agreement between the two parts respectively, to exercise their right of self-determination on the basis of consent, freely and concurrently given, North and South, to bring about a united Ireland, if that is their wish . . .

[I]t would be wrong to attempt to impose a united Ireland, in the absence of the freely given consent of the people of Northern Ireland . . . [T]he Irish Government [accepts] that the democratic right of self-determination by the people of Ireland as a whole must be achieved and exercised with the consent of a majority of the people of Northern Ireland.[69]

From these international agreements it is clear that the United Kingdom considers that both the entire people of Ireland and the people of Northern Ireland—as the people of Northern Ireland must 'consent' to any change in sovereignty—each have the right of self-determination. Thus, in the view of the United Kingdom, the inhabitants of Northern Ireland are a sufficiently separate unit to be a 'people' entitled to the right of self-determination, even if that right has a limited exercise in the form of a veto.[70]

This practice by the United Kingdom whereby the Northern Irish are considered a 'people' for the purposes of the right of self-determination is open to some criticism.[71] While it is possible that both the inhabitants of the island of Ireland as a whole and the inhabitants of Northern Ireland are each a 'people', as most individuals are part of more than one 'people' at the same time, there is very little consciousness or self-identity by the inhabitants of Northern Ireland as being 'Northern Irish'. Instead it is a divided society, with most of its inhabitants

[67] Article 1 of the Anglo-Irish Agreement, 15 November 1985.

[68] HC Debs., vol. 98, WA, cols. 561–2, 4 June 1986, UKMIL, this *Year Book*, 57 (1986), p. 515. The 'Helsinki accords' refers to the CSCE process, especially the Helsinki Final Act 1979.

[69] Downing Street Declaration, 15 December 1993, paras. 4 and 5.

[70] The means of implementation of these agreements are considered in Northern Ireland Office, *Frameworks for the Future* (HMSO, 1995).

[71] J. Cole, 'In Blood Red Hands', *The Guardian*, 17 December 1993, p. 22, points out that the Downing Street Declaration does not expressly state that the peoples of Northern Ireland have the right of self-determination.

considering themselves 'British' or 'Irish' and not 'Northern Irish'.[72] This perception is not surprising considering that Northern Ireland has only been a defined, separate territory for about seventy-five years and it is a 'created' society, with few common historical, social or cultural characteristics. While who are a 'people' does change and develop over time[73] and a 'created' society may be a 'people' with the right of self-determination, as seen with the acceptance of people within the arbitrary colonial boundaries being a 'people', the international community has been unreceptive to the idea that created societies within a State may constitute a 'people'. For example, the international community has declared that neither the inhabitants of the created societies of the South African 'homelands' nor the inhabitants of the Turkish Republic of Northern Cyprus were, in international law, 'peoples' entitled to the right of self-determination,[74] and there are very few islands that are recognized as having divided sovereignty other than by reason of colonial action.[75]

In Northern Ireland's case, it could be surmised that the inhabitants have been categorized by the United Kingdom as a 'people' for political or social ends,[76] for example to enable the United Kingdom Government to involve the Irish Government in negotiations over the territory.[77] By this categorization, international law governing the right of self-determination (and all other human rights) applies to Northern Ireland and so any action by Ireland in Northern Ireland cannot be characterized as an unlawful interference in the United Kingdom's domestic affairs.[78] The benefit of the application of the right of self-determination of the inhabitants of Northern Ireland should be that there is some legal justification for international scrutiny (for example, by the HRC) of actions by the United Kingdom in that territory which infringe the

[72] See H. Hannum, *Autonomy, Sovereignty and Self-Determination: The Accommodation of Conflicting Rights* (University of Pennsylvania Press, Philadelphia, 1990), chapter 11, especially p. 230.

[73] See P. Allott, 'The Nation as Mind Politic', *New York University Journal of International Law and Politics*, 24 (1992), p. 1361, and N. Berman, 'Sovereignty in Abeyance: Self-Determination in International Law', *Wisconsin International Law Journal*, 7 (1988), p. 51.

[74] For example, SC Resolutions 402 (1976) (22 December 1976) and 407 (1977) (25 May 1977) with regard to South Africa, and SC Resolution 541 (1983) with regard to Northern Cyprus. See J. Dugard, *Recognition and the United Nations* (Grotius Publications, Cambridge, 1987), pp. 98–111. For a comparison of the UK with South Africa in regard to Northern Ireland, see A. Guelke, 'International Legitimacy, Self-Determination, and Northern Ireland', *Review of International Studies*, 11 (1985), p. 37.

[75] Only Haiti and Dominican Republic (on the island of Hispaniola) were to any extent independent before they divided, but their division was based on previous colonial boundaries.

[76] This is not uncommon, as can be seen in J. Sharp, 'Introduction: Constructing Social Reality', in E. Boonzaier and J. Sharp (eds.), *South African Keywords: The Uses and Abuses of Political Concepts* (David Philip, Cape Town, 1988), p. 1, particularly at p. 4, and E. Hobsbawm, *Nations and Nationalism since 1780: Programme, Myth, Reality* (Cambridge, CUP, 1990).

[77] See A. Guelke, *Northern Ireland, The International Perspective* (Dublin, Gill and Macmillan, 1988), and K. Boyle and T. Hadden, *Northern Ireland—The Choices* (Penguin, London, 1995).

[78] Article 4 of the Vienna Declaration and Programme of Action arising from the 1993 United Nations World Conference on Human Rights, *International Legal Materials*, 32 (1993), p. 1661, provides that 'the promotion and protection of all human rights is a legitimate concern of the international community'.

wishes of the inhabitants. However, the consequence of the United Kingdom applying the right of self-determination to the inhabitants of the created society of Northern Ireland, where there is little objective or subjective basis for the description of the inhabitants as 'people', is to diminish the possibility of creating any clear and coherent rules to determine who are a 'people' entitled to the right. It could also foster abuse of the term 'peoples' and of the right of self-determination as other States and groups apply these legal concepts to any situation with little regard for the actual circumstances.

The whole of the United Kingdom's practice in this area shows a very broad definition of 'peoples' who are entitled to the right of self-determination. It has applied the term to non-self-governing and other colonial territories, no matter the number of inhabitants, the size, or the uncertain status, of the territory. It has taken actions which show that it accepts that more than one 'people' do exist within States, including within its own borders. While its inclusion of the inhabitants of Northern Ireland as a 'people' can be criticized for not being legally coherent, the consequence is that it makes any action by the United Kingdom in Northern Ireland which is contrary to the right of self-determination subject to international scrutiny. This wide application of the term 'peoples' by the United Kingdom means that more groups would be protected from abuse of the right of self-determination and there is less State restriction as to who is entitled to this protection. After all, as the United Kingdom has confirmed, the right of self-determination

> is, as the Charter and the two International Covenants expressly declare, a right of peoples. Not States. Not countries. Not governments. Peoples.[79]

III. The Application of the Right Beyond the Colonial Context

(a) *Colonial Territories*

While the debate was still in progress about whether self-determination should be included as a right within the two International Human Rights Covenants, the first major General Assembly resolution dealing expressly with the 'right of self-determination' was passed: the Declaration on Granting of Independence to Colonial Countries and Peoples of 1960.[80] The intention of that resolution was 'the necessity of bringing to a speedy and unconditional end colonialism in all its forms and manifestations'.[81] It urged States to take immediate steps 'in Trust and Non-Self-Governing Territories or all other territories which have not yet

[79] Statement by the UK Representative (H. Steel) to the UN Commission on Human Rights, 9 February 1988: UKMIL, this *Year Book*, 59 (1988), p. 441.

[80] GA Resolution 1514 (XV), 14 December 1960.

[81] Preamble.

attained independence, to transfer all powers to the peoples of those territories, . . . in accordance with their freely expressed will and desire'.[82] The United Kingdom abstained on this Declaration.[83]

The movement for decolonization put pressure on the United Kingdom and other colonial powers to give self-government to the people of their colonies. The success of this pressure can be seen in the increased membership of the United Nations, with the United Kingdom noting that,

> since General Assembly Resolution 1514 (XV) was adopted at the end of 1960, [by 1982] we have brought to sovereign independence and membership of [the United Nations] no less than 28 States.[84]

This decolonization process is now acknowledged by the United Kingdom to have been an exercise by the peoples of its colonies of their right of self-determination, as

> those that are no longer on the list [of non-self-governing territories] are now independent, sovereign States or have chosen some other future. They have benefited from Article 73 and the exercise of their right of self-determination.[85]

Indeed, general State practice has been so conclusive that the right of self-determination applies to non-self-governing territories that the ICJ in the *Namibia* case concluded, as was seen above, that

> the subsequent development of international law in regard to non-self-governing territories, as enshrined in the Charter of the United Nations, made the principle of self-determination applicable to all of them.[86]

(b) *Non-Colonial Territories*

While it is clear that, by customary international law, the right of self-determination applies to non-self-governing territories, it has not been certain that it applies to other territories. United Kingdom practice has been valuable in resolving this uncertainty. From the earliest discussions about the ambit of the right of self-determination, the United Kingdom sought to stress that the right was applicable to all territories and within

[82] Para. 5.

[83] There were 89 votes for the Declaration, none against and 9 abstentions (UK, Australia, Belgium, Dominican Republic, France, Portugal, South Africa, Spain, United States).

[84] Loc. cit. above (n. 1). The importance of this GA resolution as the basis for the decolonization process is expounded by the ICJ in the *Western Sahara* case, *ICJ Reports*, 1975, p. 12, at para. 57.

[85] Statement by the UK Permanent Representative (Sir John Thomson) to the GA, 2 November 1982, UKMIL, this *Year Book*, 53 (1982), p. 378.

[86] Loc. cit. above (n. 37). This decision was confirmed by the ICJ in the *Western Sahara* case, loc. cit. above (n. 84), at para. 54. In that latter case, Judge Dillard noted (at p. 121) that 'the pronouncements of the Court thus indicate, in my view, that a norm of international law has emerged applicable to the decolonisation of those non-self-governing territories which are under the aegis of the United Nations'.

State borders.[87] This action was probably a tactic to defuse support for the right and to move the focus from colonialism. Nevertheless, once the right became part of international law, the United Kingdom continued to argue strongly that it applied beyond the colonial context, on the basis that

> it is not only peoples suffering occupation by a foreign power which are deprived of their right of self-determination. We are all aware of appalling violations of the right of self-determination, accompanied by equally appalling violations of many other fundamental rights, perpetrated against peoples by their own countrymen. Amin's atrocities in Uganda and Pol Pot's in Cambodia are perhaps the most glaring contemporary examples. But they are by no means the only ones.[88]

In consequence, the United Kingdom has applied the right of self-determination to non-colonial situations, such as Palestine,[89] not only by its statements and by its votes in the UN but also by ratifying treaties to that effect. For example, it ratified (together with three of the other four Permanent Members of the UN) the Treaty on the Final Settlement with respect to Germany, 1990, in which it was expressly mentioned that the

> German people, freely exercising their right of self-determination, have expressed their will to bring about the unity of Germany as a State,[90]

despite the fact that neither East nor West Germany was a colony.[91] The United Kingdom was also closely involved in the recognition of new States arising from the break-up of the former USSR and Yugoslavia, and was a party to statements in which the right of self-determination was directly referred to.[92]

This practice by the United Kingdom in applying the right to all peoples in all territories is consistent with all major international instruments dealing with the right of self-determination since the

[87] In the statement by the UK representative (Mr Hoare) to the Third Committee of the GA, 642nd meeting (1954), p. 90, para. 15, he wondered 'whether even States having no colonies were indeed prepared to face the consequences of assuming a legal obligation to promote the right of self-determination within their borders'.

[88] Statement by UK representative to Third Committee of the GA (Edna Young) on 11 October 1985, UKMIL, this *Year Book*, 56 (1985), p. 400.

[89] The Foreign Secretary (Francis Pym) said that the right of self-determination 'applies equally to the Palestinians as it does to the people of the Falkland Islands': HL Debs., vol. 25, col. 189, 9 June 1982, UKMIL, this *Year Book*, 53 (1982), p. 372.

[90] Preamble to the Treaty, *International Legal Materials*, 29 (1990), p. 1186. Self-determination is also referred to in Articles 1 and 7 of the Treaty.

[91] The Foreign Secretary (Douglas Hurd) stated that 'we have made clear our long-standing support for German unity on the basis of free self-determination': HC Debs., vol. 172, col. 177, 9 May 1990, UKMIL, this *Year Book*, 61 (1990), p. 507.

[92] European Community's (EC) Declaration on the Guidelines on the Recognition of New States in Eastern Europe and in the Soviet Union of 16 December 1991, *European Journal of International Law*, 4 (1993), p. 72. The EC criteria were essentially followed by the United States: United States Department of State *Dispatch*, vol. 13, no. 3 (13 April 1992), at p. 287.

Declaration on Granting of Independence to Colonial Countries and Peoples in 1960. For example, common Article 1 of the two International Human Rights Covenants applies the right to all States, '*including* those having responsibility for the administration of [colonial] Territories',[93] without any restriction as to their status, and Article 20(2) of the African Charter on Human and Peoples' Rights (ACHPR) refers to both 'colonized *or* oppressed peoples' as having the right.[94] Indeed, India's reservation to common Article 1, in which it stated that the right did not apply 'to sovereign independent States or to a section of a people or nation',[95] was objected to by other States as being 'incompatible with the object and purpose of the Covenants' and 'contrary to the clear language' of Article 1.[96]

In its General Comment on common Article 1, the HRC supports this wider application of the right beyond colonial territories, as it states that

> the obligations [under Article 1] exist irrespective of whether a people entitled to self-determination depends on a State party to the Covenant or not. It follows that all States parties to the Covenant should take positive action to facilitate realization of and respect for the right of peoples to self-determination.[97]

In other words, the obligation to protect the right of self-determination exists irrespective of whether the people are in a dependent (i.e. colonial) relationship with a State. The HRC has confirmed this approach during its consideration of States' reports as its members have asked questions of States about issues of the right of self-determination in non-colonial territories.[98] State practice beyond these treaties also supports the United Kingdom's position,[99] as seen in the widespread acceptance that the right of self-determination applies to non-colonial territories such as Palestine,[100] Namibia,[101] Afghanistan[102] and Cambodia,[103] and also in the

[93] Art. 1(3) (emphasis added). The words 'including those' were adopted (without objection) by the Third Committee expressly to make it clear that Art. 1(3) applied to all peoples: UN Doc. A/C.3/L.495/Rev. 2 and A/C.3/SR.676, para. 17; M. Nowak, *United Nations Covenant on Civil and Political Rights: A Commentary* (1993), at p. 12.

[94] Emphasis added.

[95] *Multilateral Treaties Deposited with the Secretary-General*, op. cit. above (n. 14), at p. 116.

[96] Ibid., pp. 119–20; objections by Germany and the Netherlands.

[97] General Comment 12(21), para. 6, UN Doc. A/39/40 (1984), p. 143.

[98] See for example, questions to Japan about Palestine and Namibia (First Report of Japan, UN Doc. A/37/40 (1982), para. 57); questions to Chile about Nicaragua and El Salvador (Second Report of Chile, UN Doc. A/39/40 (1984), para. 453); and questions to Iraq about the Kurds (Third Report of Iraq, UN Doc. A/47/40 (1992), paras. 194–5).

[99] See further R. McCorquodale, 'Self-Determination Beyond the Colonial Context and its Potential Impact on Africa', *Revue africaine de droit international et comparé*, 4 (1992), p. 592.

[100] For example, GA Resolutions 2787 (XXVI) of 6 December 1971, 3089D (XXVIII) of 7 December 1973 and 3210 (XXIX) of 14 October 1974; and the Commission on Human Rights Resolution 2 (XXXIV) of 14 February 1978.

[101] For example, GA Resolution 2145 (XXI) of 27 October 1966, and the ICJ decision in the *Namibia* case, loc. cit. above (n. 37).

[102] For example, GA Resolution 36/34 of 18 November 1981.

[103] For example, GA Resolutions 36/5 of 21 October 1981 and 46/18 of 20 November 1991.

opinions of the Badinter Arbitration Commission set up by the European Commission (EC) to consider issues arising from the former Yugoslavia.[104]

(c) *Within States*

The United Kingdom has also stressed that the right of self-determination applies within a State's borders (often known as 'internal self-determination'). As seen in section II(c) above, it considers that the right applies within its own territory, at least to the Scots, the Welsh and the Northern Irish. Moreover, the United Kingdom has signed documents arising from the Conference on Security and Co-operation in Europe (CSCE—now OSCE) which uphold internal self-determination[105] and make it clear that the right applies within States.[106] It has justified this position by noting that

> many peoples today are deprived of their right of self-determination, by elites of their own countrymen and women: through the concentration of power in a particular political party, in a particular ethnic or religious group, or in a certain social class.[107]

Much of the discussion in the section above about the application of the right of self-determination to non-colonial territories is appropriate to support the United Kingdom's position concerning the application of the right within States, including the response to India's reservation to common Article 1 set out in the section above. There has also been other practice showing the application of the right within States, as it has been applied to the blacks within South Africa[108] and to the blacks within Southern Rhodesia.[109] This development in the application of the right

[104] Opinion no. 2, *European Journal of International Law*, 3 (1992), pp. 183–4. However, in its opinion no. 1 (ibid., pp. 182–3), there is no reference to the right of self-determination and all its opinions were very brief and did not fully legally analyse the situation.

[105] Principle VIII of the Helsinki Final Act 1975 includes: 'by virtue of the principle of equal rights and self-determination of peoples, all peoples have the right, in full freedom, to determine, when and as they wish, their *internal and external* political status, without external interference, and to pursue as they wish their political, economic, social and cultural development' (emphasis added). This is confirmed in, for example, Principle 1(6) of the Document of the Copenhagen Meeting of the Conference on the Human Dimension of the CSCE, 1990, and the principle on 'Friendly Relations among Participating States' in the Charter of Paris for a New Europe, 1990.

[106] In a statement to the Third Committee of the GA on 12 October 1984, the UK representative (R. Fursland) said that 'the majority of South Africa's people are denied any effective role in running the society in which they live. That is, they are denied the right of self-determination': UKMIL, this *Year Book*, 55 (1984), p. 431.

[107] Statement by UK representatives to Third Committee of the GA on 12 October 1984 (R. Fursland), UKMIL, this *Year Book*, 55 (1984), p. 432, and on 11 October 1985 (Edna Young), UKMIL, this *Year Book*, 56 (1985), p. 400.

[108] For example, GA Resolution 31/6 of 26 October 1976, and SC Resolutions 417 and 418 of 4 November 1977. See further R. McCorquodale, 'South Africa and the Right of Self-Determination', *South African Journal on Human Rights*, 10 (1994), p. 4.

[109] SC Resolutions 216 and 217 of 12 November 1965, and 232 of 16 December 1966.

of self-determination is also consistent with the position that human rights are now a matter not solely within a State's domestic jurisdiction.[110] Thus the early warnings by the United Kingdom of the potentially wide applications of the right have been borne out in practice.

IV. Determining the Wishes of the People

(a) *Non-Self-Governing and Colonial Territories*[111]

In the *Western Sahara* case, the ICJ

> confirm[ed] and emphasize[d] that the application of the right of self-determination requires a free and genuine expression of the will of the peoples concerned.[112]

The method by which the wishes of the peoples were to be determined was not set out in that case, and no single method has emerged from practice. Yet the United Kingdom has adopted one main method for ascertaining the freely expressed will of the peoples in its territories: it has insisted that 'the way of genuinely determining what the population of a territory wanted was to hold elections'.[113] Thus, the United Kingdom concludes that

> the peoples of our remaining dependent territories exercise their right to self-determination every time they go to the polls.[114]

This practice is justified on the basis that, at periodic elections,

> both the electorate and candidates [have] the opportunity to express their views on constitutional change, including the constitutional link with the United Kingdom and the question of independence.[115]

Occasionally other methods are undertaken by the United Kingdom, such as reliance on comments by Prime Ministers of these territories on

[110] See n. 78, above. Also in the Concluding Document from the Moscow Conference on the Human Dimension of the CSCE (*International Legal Materials*, 30 (1991), p. 1670), the States involved 'categorically and irrevocably declare that the commitments undertaken in the field of the human dimension of the CSCE are matters of direct and legitimate concern of all participating States and do not belong exclusively to the internal affairs of the State concerned'. See also A. Bloed, 'Human Rights and Non-Intervention', in A. Bloed and P. van Dijk (eds.), *Essays on Human Rights in the Helsinki Process* (Nijhoff, Dordrecht, 1985), p. 57, and W. M. Reisman, 'Sovereignty and Human Rights in Contemporary International Law', *American Journal of International Law*, 82 (1990), p. 866.

[111] For the discussion on the distinction (or lack of distinction) between non-self-governing and colonial territories, see section II(b), above.

[112] Loc. cit. above (n. 84), at para. 55.

[113] Statement by the UK representative to the HRC (Mr Fearn) on the Second Report, UN Doc. CCPR/C/SR.856, p. 8, para. 34.

[114] UK Representative to the UN (T. Richardson) speaking to the GA, 20 November 1990, UN Doc. A/45/PV, p. 72, UKMIL, this *Year Book*, 61 (1990), p. 509.

[115] Loc. cit. above (n. 113), at p. 5, para. 17.

their visits to London, information received on visits to dependent territories by British Ministers,[116] or by referenda, but the main one has been elections.

In accordance with this practice, the United Kingdom has relied on elections in most of its territories to gauge the will of the people there. Thus, in regard to the Falkland Islands, the United Kingdom concluded that

> the Falkland Islanders have made clear in free and fair elections their wish to remain British and to keep their present way of life.[117]

In contrast, while the people of Gibraltar have a significant degree of self-government and have regular elections, the United Kingdom held a referendum in September 1967 to determine their wishes. The referendum presented two options: to retain Gibraltar's present status under United Kingdom administration, or to transfer to Spanish sovereignty. In a 95% turn-out, 12,138 voters chose the former, with only 44 voters choosing the latter.[118] In regard to Hong Kong, the United Kingdom has confirmed that it must determine the wishes of the people by consulting them, because 'any arrangement [on the future of Hong Kong] must be acceptable to the population'.[119] No reliance could be placed on elections, as there is a very limited democratic electoral system (with the first elections in 1991 being for only 18 out of the 60 seats), but the United Kingdom has chosen not to use a referendum. Instead it claimed that there was 'an extensive consultation exercise to ascertain the views of the population' of Hong Kong.[120]

The United Kingdom is correct in insisting that it must consult the people of a territory in order to determine their wishes. However, to rely on elections as the primary means of determining their free and genuine wishes is fraught with difficulty. It is impossible to prove from election results on what particular issue or issues a voter casts her/his vote, when there will invariably be other issues besides self-determination which are raised during an election campaign. In any event, for the United Kingdom to rely on elections when there are very few elected representa-

[116] The visit by the Special Committee to the Cayman Islands was criticized by the UK and 'the people [of the Cayman Islands] had asked [the UK] never to subject them to that kind of experience again': Response of the UK representative to the HRC (Mr Stratton) on the First Report, UN Doc. CCPR/C/SR.164, p. 183, para. 12.

[117] Letter dated 13 April 1982 from the UK Permanent Representative to the UN (Sir Anthony Parsons) to the President of the SC, UN Doc. S/14973, UKMIL, this *Year Book*, 53 (1982), p. 368.

[118] Second Report, UN Doc. CCPR/C/32/Add. 14, p. 47, Annex E, para. 3. Bermuda also held a referendum on independence. The referendum proposing independence, put to the vote on 15 and 16 August 1995, was defeated—in a 58.8% voter turnout—by 16,369 votes (73.6%) to 5,714 votes (25.7%): *Bermuda Sun*, 18 August 1995.

[119] Statement by the UK representative to the HRC (Mr Beamish) on the Third Report, UN Doc. CCPR/C/SR.1046, pp. 9–10, para. 42.

[120] Statement by the UK representative to the HRC (Mr Fearn) on the Second Report, UN Doc. CCPR/C/SR.856, p. 5, para. 18.

tives (or population) in a dependent territory such as the Falkland Islands seems disingenuous.[121]

Referenda have been the preferred method used by the United Nations—for example, as proposed in Western Sahara—because referenda allow the people to vote directly on the right of self-determination, particularly if all possible options of exercise of the right are put before the people and sufficient education about these options occurs.[122] The lack of these latter aspects in the Gibraltar referendum must raise the possibility that the referendum was not a full ascertainment of the people's wishes.[123] Other options such as free association, different forms of integration, or independence, were not offered, because the United Kingdom considered that they were merely 'speculation'[124] or were excluded by a treaty.[125] In this context, despite the acceptance by the United Kingdom that the right is a right of peoples not of governments,[126] the United Kingdom itself decided what options the people of Gibraltar had to exercise their right.[127] Further, no referendum has taken place in Gibraltar about its sovereignty since 1967, despite the fact that Spain is now a liberal democracy and a member of the European Union. Indeed, the elections in 1992 in Gibraltar seemed to indicate that the people of Gibraltar now consider independence to be a possible option,[128] but this has not been acted upon by the United Kingdom.

[121] Until 1985 the Executive Council was largely appointed. This was changed by the Falkland Islands Constitutional Order 1985.

[122] Referenda do not resolve the issues of who can vote and what account should be taken of deliberate population transfers, as can be seen in the Western Sahara situation; see J. Chopra, *United Nations Determination of the Western Saharan Self* (Norwegian Institute of International Affairs, Oslo, 1994).

[123] The referendum was declared invalid by the GA (for other reasons): see section VI(a), below.

[124] Response of the UK representative to the HRC (Mr Fearn) to the Second Report, UN Doc. CCPR/C/SR.856, p. 11, at para. 54.

[125] 'Independence is excluded by the 1713 Treaty of Utrecht [between the UK and Spain], which stated that, if the UK gave up its sovereignty over those territories, Spain would exercise its rights': response of the UK representative to the HRC (Mr Fearn) to the Second Report, UN Doc. CCPR/C/SR.856, p. 8, at para. 33. See further Section VI(b), below.

[126] See text at n. 79, above.

[127] Too often the UK seeks to impose its own (as against the people's) views on the exercise of the right; for example, it considers that the Tibetans cannot seek independence (Minister of State, FCO (Lord Reay), HL Debs., vol. 526, col. 964, 26 February 1991, UKMIL, this *Year Book*, 62 (1991), p. 574, and Minister of State, FCO (Baroness Chalker), HL Debs., vol. 542, col. 5, 1 February 1993, UKMIL, this *Year Book*, 64 (1993), p. 609); and that the Kashmiri people can only choose between India and Pakistan (Under-Secretary of State, FCO (Tim Sainsbury), HC Debs., vol. 177, col. 210, 23 July 1990, UKMIL, this *Year Book*, 61 (1990), p. 507). France may be no different from the UK in its practice in this respect, as France did not allow the option of integration with Morocco (or retrocession as claimed by Morocco) to be put to the people of Mauritania: I. Brownlie, *African Boundaries: A Legal and Diplomatic Encyclopaedia* (Hurst, London, 1979).

[128] See the comments by the Chief Minister of Gibraltar in J. Bossano, 'Self-Determination in Gibraltar', *New European Quarterly Review*, vol. 5, no. 6 (1992), p. 10, at p. 12, and the address by the Chief Minister of Gibraltar to the Special Committee, 14 July 1993, UKMIL, this *Year Book*, 64 (1993), p. 609.

It is in regard to determining the wishes of the people of Hong Kong that the United Kingdom practice is seen to be most incompatible with international law. International law requires that the people of a non-self-governing (or colonial)[129] territory must be consulted when any change in sovereignty is involved, even if the change could be by means of integration with a neighbouring State. As Judge Nagendra Singh stated in the *Western Sahara* case:

the consultation of the people of a territory awaiting decolonization is an inescapable imperative. . . . Thus even if integration of territory was demanded by an interested State, as in this case, it could not be had without ascertaining the freely expressed will of the people—the very *sine qua non* of all decolonization.[130]

While the United Kingdom has accepted this obligation by seeking to consult the people of Hong Kong, its method of determining the wishes of the people of Hong Kong was not to have a referendum, even though it was practically feasible; rather, it was to establish

an assessment office, manned by local civil servants, . . . to collect opinions and pronounce judgement on the people's views. Potential respondents were warned, however, that the [Joint Declaration] had to be considered as a whole, that it could not be amended in part, and that the alternative to its acceptance was a unilateral plan for the future of the territory drawn up by the Chinese government.[131]

This was a 'take it or else' method of determining the wishes of the people of Hong Kong. No options were presented other than to accept (or reject if the dire warning was ignored) the Joint Declaration proposal.[132] The canvassing of views was very limited and relied on the self-motivation of individuals and organizations to come forward.[133] Indeed, the wishes of the people were only sought after the Joint

[129] See section II(b), above.

[130] Loc. cit. above (n. 84), at p. 81.

[131] I. Scott, *Political Change and the Crisis of Legitimacy in Hong Kong* (1989), quoted in R. McGee and D. Lam, 'Hong Kong's Option to Secede', *Harvard International Law Journal*, 33 (1992), p. 427, at p. 429. In fact the UK stated in the introduction to the draft of the Joint Declaration: 'The choice is therefore between reversion of Hong Kong to China under agreed, legally binding international arrangements or reversion to China without such arrangements. This is not a choice which Her Majesty's Government have sought to impose on the people of Hong Kong. It is a choice imposed by the facts of Hong Kong's history': UK White Paper, *A Draft Agreement on the Future of Hong Kong*, Cmnd. 9352 (HMSO, London, 1984), Introduction, p. 10.

[132] Joint Declaration of the Government of the UK and the Government of China on the Question of Hong Kong, 19 December 1984 ('Joint Declaration'), *International Legal Materials*, 23 (1984), p. 1366.

[133] Out of the six million population of Hong Kong, only 1,815 individuals, 249 groups of individuals and 430 organizations responded to the Assessment Office: International Commission of Jurists, *Countdown to 1997: Report of a Mission to Hong Kong*, op. cit. above (n. 54), at p. 59.

Declaration had already been agreed. This cannot be seen as a genuine (or efficient) ascertainment of the wishes of the Hong Kong people.[134]

The wishes of the people of Hong Kong about the transfer of sovereignty to China have never been accurately ascertained. Nevertheless, if the usual practice of the United Kingdom is followed then some understanding of their views may be inferred from the (limited) elections they have been allowed. In 1991, when the first directly elected members of the Legislative Council were elected, 17 of the 18 seats were won by individuals critical of the Joint Declaration arrangements. The Hong Kong legislature, even though a largely United Kingdom appointed body, rejected the Basic Law (which is the future legislative framework for Hong Kong)[135] after the United Kingdom had stated that 'the views of the Hong Kong people on [the Basic Law] are of crucial importance'.[136] In addition, public opinion polls since 1984 (and particularly since the Tiananmen Square massacre in June 1989) have consistently shown that a significant majority of the Hong Kong people do not wish to become part of China in the way proposed by the Joint Declaration.[137] This evidence is in marked contrast to the results of the supposedly '*extensive* consultation exercise to ascertain the views of the population' adopted by the United Kingdom.[138]

The unsatisfactory consultation exercise by the United Kingdom was not improved by any involvement of Hong Kong people in the negotiations between the United Kingdom and China, as the role of the Hong Kong officials was largely formal and their advice was generally ignored.[139] Nor could the United Kingdom claim to represent equally both its interests and those of Hong Kong in the negotiations, despite the assurance by the then United Kingdom Prime Minister (Margaret Thatcher) that

[134] Many members of the HRC considered that there had been no genuine consultation: see questions by Mr Zielinski, Mr Mavrommatis and Mr Dimitrijevic on the Second Report, UN Doc. CCPR/C/SR.856, p. 5, para. 21, p. 6, para. 25, p. 7, para. 27, and Mrs Chanet and Mr Aguilar on Third Report, UN Doc. CCPR/C/SR.1045, p. 8, para. 21, and SR.1046, p. 13, para. 58.

[135] The Basic Law of the Hong Kong Special Administrative Region of the People's Republic of China, 4 April 1990, referred to in Art. 1 of Annex I of the Joint Declaration ('Basic Law').

[136] Third Report, Annex F: Hong Kong, para. 18. This rejection by the legislature was largely an action without substantive effect, as the Basic Law is enacted by the Chinese National People's Congress (a legislature in which the people of Hong Kong are not represented).

[137] Only about 15% are in support of the Joint Declaration proposal: see, for example, poll results in J. Chen, *Hong Kong in Search of a Future* (OUP, Hong Kong, 1984), p. 85, and newspaper polls subsequently, such as that by the *Sunday Morning Post* on 30 June 1991 showing 29% in favour of full independence and a further 19% in favour of self-government within the Commonwealth. See also question by Mr Wako during consideration of the UK's Third Report, UN Doc. CCPR/C/SR.1046, p. 14, para. 61.

[138] See text at n. 120, above.

[139] See R. Cottrell, *The End of Hong Kong* (John Murray, London, 1993), pp. 104–5, 152–3 and 155–6.

in conducting these talks [with China], I shall speak not only for Britain, but for Britain's moral responsibility and duty to Hong Kong.[140]

While the United Kingdom certainly had a responsibility and duty to Hong Kong, no United Kingdom official, and no Hong Kong official because of the lack of elections there, could speak as a credible representative of the Hong Kong people. The Chinese were well aware of this as they noted that

the relationship between the British government and the Chinese residents of Hong Kong is like that between a colonial ruler and its subjects. Therefore in the present talks, Britain is not qualified to be their representative.[141]

The realities of the situation with China may have meant that the options available for the exercise of the right of self-determination of the people of Hong Kong were limited.[142] But the crucial issue is not whether Hong Kong should or could become independent—since other options existed such as a free association with China or integration on the basis of equality[143]—but that the wishes of the people of Hong Kong about exercising their right of self-determination were never freely and genuinely sought or given. If a referendum had been held at the time of the Joint Declaration, it is likely that the people of Hong Kong would have recognized the geo-political realities in their decision and endorsed the terms of the Joint Declaration and so given some legitimacy to the actions of the United Kingdom (and China). But at no stage was there any genuine ascertainment of the wishes of the people of Hong Kong. Indeed, the International Commission of Jurists concluded in its report on Hong Kong:

We regard it as intolerable for the British Government to transfer British citizens in Hong Kong to the jurisdiction of the People's Republic of China

[140] Speech to Hong Kong's Chamber of Commerce, 27 September 1982, as reported in R. Cottrell, ibid., p. 92.

[141] Beijing *People's Daily* (the newspaper of the Communist Party Central Committee), 20 September 1983, as reported in R. Cottrell, op. cit. above (n. 139), pp. 122–3. This point was also made firmly by the International Commission of Jurists, *Countdown to 1997: Report of a Mission to Hong Kong*, op. cit. above (n. 54), at p. 54.

[142] There is some evidence that at one stage the UK contemplated that independence for Hong Kong could have been an option: see speech by the UK Minister of State for Foreign Affairs (Mr Ormsby Gore) to the GA on 28 November 1960, where he said: 'the United Kingdom is doing all it can to hurry on the processes of self-government as fast as possible, but it would surely be a betrayal of the whole spirit of Chapter XI of the Charter for us to say that the people of, for example the Seychelles Islands, or the Gilbert Islands, should decide immediately what form they wish their ultimate independence to take; or, to take another example, the peoples of Basutoland or Hong Kong': Report of the Proceedings of the 15th Session of the GA, Cmnd. 1456 (HMSO, 1961), p. 124. All these peoples, except for Hong Kong, have now attained independence.

[143] See E. Amberg, 'Self-Determination in Hong Kong: A New Challenge to an Old Doctrine', *San Diego Law Review*, 22 (1985), p. 839, especially at p. 858.

without their own consent and without any opportunity having been given to them to participate in deciding on their own future.[144]

Thus United Kingdom practice in regard to determining the wishes of the peoples within its territories has not been helpful in establishing any coherent rules or particular methods of action.

(b) *Within States*

Consistent with its position that the right of self-determination applies within States, the United Kingdom has reiterated that peoples within a State must be able freely to express their wishes. The justification for this position is that

self-determination is not a one-off exercise. It cannot be achieved for any people by one revolution or one election. It is a continuous process. It requires that peoples be given continuing opportunities to choose their governments and social systems, and to change them when they so choose.[145]

In applying this view, the United Kingdom has pressed for democratic systems across the world[146] and it has accepted that it must ascertain the will of the peoples within its own territory. As with its dependent territories, its primary method is by periodic elections:

the right of self-determination in the United Kingdom itself is exercised primarily through the electoral system . . . The British system of parliamentary government is sustained by an electorate casting its votes in free and secret ballots at periodic elections which offer a choice between rival candidates, usually representing organised political parties of different views . . . All elections in Northern Ireland continue to produce an overall majority of the electorate voting for Unionist policies, i.e. continuing as part of the United Kingdom.[147]

However, the United Kingdom has very occasionally sought to ascertain directly the wishes of the peoples within its territory by means of a referendum. This has occurred on four occasions since 1945: by the people of Northern Ireland (in 1973) about remaining in the United Kingdom (called a 'Border Poll'); by the people of each of Scotland and Wales (in 1979) on devolution; and by all the people of the United

[144] *Countdown to 1997: Report of a Mission to Hong Kong*, op. cit. above (n. 54), at p. 56. The International Commission of Jurists suggested that the right of residence in the UK be granted to all Hong Kong residents as a means of compensation for the UK's breach of the right of self-determination.

[145] Statement by the UK representative to Third Committee of the GA (R. Fursland) on 12 October 1984, UKMIL, this *Year Book*, 55 (1984), p. 432. See also statement to the same effect by the Under-Secretary of State, Foreign and Commonwealth Office (FCO) (Timothy Eggar), to the UN Commission on Human Rights: UKMIL, this *Year Book*, 58 (1987), p. 519.

[146] See, for example, the statement by the UK Representative (H. Steel) to the UN Commission on Human Rights, 9 February 1988, UKMIL, this *Year Book*, 59 (1988), p. 442.

[147] Third Report, paras. 18–20.

Kingdom (in 1975) on membership of the EC. In each of these referenda, two options were placed before the relevant people. In addition, there is the likelihood of a referendum in Northern Ireland arising from the Downing Street Declaration. In that case, the United Kingdom has stated that

> the wish of the greater number of the people of Northern Ireland would be determined by a numerical majority of those validly voting in a poll fairly and explicitly organised for this purpose.[148]

As well as the difficulty in principle of expecting elections to be able to show the wishes of the people, as was discussed in the section above, the United Kingdom electoral system is particularly problematic as there is no proportional representation electoral system (other than in EC and local elections in Northern Ireland). It has a 'first-past-the-post' electoral system, where the winner of a constituency seat is the person who polls the most votes, however few, which means that the winner of the election may very often not reflect the views of the majority of voters.[149] There is an additional difficulty with a 'first-past-the-post' system if it is the sole means to determine the wishes of the people in Northern Ireland because of the divided nature of its society. As the Gardiner Committee on Northern Ireland noted: 'in a plural society such as this, the normal conventions of majority rule will not work'.[150] This comment could also be applied to a referendum, if the result of a referendum was determined by a simple majority as has been suggested by the United Kingdom,[151] because if the result is

> used to justify bigotry and discrimination, [then] it loses the legitimacy it might otherwise acquire as a mechanism to ensure basic rights to equality and participation in government.[152]

If the United Kingdom does proceed to a referendum of the people of Northern Ireland and the result is based solely on a simple majority, without any minority protections built in, then there must be the risk that further infringements of human rights will occur.[153]

By offering only two options in each referendum within its territory, the United Kingdom's practice can be criticized, as it was in the section

[148] *The Guardian*, 20 May 1994, p. 11.

[149] The UK electoral system has been criticized by some members of the HRC as failing to comply with Article 1: see question by Mr Mavrommatis on the Third Report, UN Doc. CCPR/C/SR.1046, p. 14, at para. 62.

[150] *Report of a Committee to consider, in the context of Civil Liberties and Human Rights, Measures to deal with Terrorism in the United Kingdom*, Cmnd. 5847 (1975), para. 4(*c*). See also the Opsahl Report on Northern Ireland, discussed in *Public Law*, 1993, pp. 588–95.

[151] See text at n. 148, above.

[152] H. Hannum, *Autonomy, Sovereignty and Self-Determination: The Accommodation of Conflicting Rights*, op. cit. above (n. 72), p. 246.

[153] For further discussion, see S. Bailey, *Human Rights and Responsibilities in Britain and Ireland* (Macmillan, London, 1988), pp. 88–90, and C. Palley, *The United Kingdom and Human Rights* (Stevens, London, 1991), pp. 139–40.

above, for restricting the wishes of the people to the options chosen by the United Kingdom. For example, in the Scottish and Welsh referenda, the possible exercises of the peoples' right of self-determination were limited to either a particular type of devolution or maintaining the status quo, despite the range of possible exercises identified by the Royal Commission on the Constitution:

the two extremes would be separatism for Scotland, even for Wales and England . . . or for maintaining the status quo. Between these poles are a range of possibilities for decentralizing government: a federal or quasi-federal solution under which the powers of the Westminster parliament would be limited and Assemblies in the nations or regions would have some exclusive powers, or . . . devolution [with] a choice of the transfer of legislative and executive powers to 'Assemblies' below Westminster in the constitutional hierarchy, or the transfer of executive powers only.[154]

In Northern Ireland many possible options exist other than integration with either the United Kingdom or with Ireland, including different sovereignty over various aspect of life; for example, Ireland could have sovereignty over communications and the United Kingdom could have sovereignty over foreign policy but there could be joint sovereignty over fisheries.[155] In addition, because of the limited opportunity for the peoples of Northern Ireland, Scotland and Wales to be directly involved in issues concerning them—as seen by the largely bureaucratic system of central government of those regions described above[156]—an option which allowed for more involvement in (an accountable) regional government by these peoples may be a more appropriate method of exercising their right of self-determination. Creating such a system could also lead to the 'continuing opportunities to choose their governments and their social systems' advocated by the United Kingdom,[157] rather than relying on very occasional referenda. After all, as the United Kingdom itself acknowledges, the right of self-determination is 'a continuous process' and is 'not a one-off exercise achieved by one revolution or one election',[158] or, presumably, by one referendum. Even if it is accepted that the referendum result was a genuine expression of the wishes of the

[154] Cmnd. 5460 (1973).

[155] See also K. Boyle and T. Hadden, *Northern Ireland—The Choices*, op. cit. above (n. 77). G. Gottlieb, *Nation Against State* (CFRP, New York, 1993), pp. 52–8, suggests that there would be a 'national home' for the whole of the island of Ireland in addition to the existing Ireland and Northern Ireland, so leaving UK-Northern Ireland links unimpaired. Each identity would have differentiated forms of political participation and different rights, as chosen by the people themselves.

[156] See section II(*c*), above.

[157] See text at n. 145, above.

[158] Ibid.

Scottish and Welsh people at the time,'[159] it does not mean that having had a referendum in 1979 is all the United Kingdom has to do from that date to determine the wishes of those peoples. Finally, if the option of independence is to be put to any of these peoples, then some protection against infringing the rights of the other peoples within the United Kingdom, including the right of self-determination, should occur,[160] and any referendum should only be held after a period of debate and broad-based education about the options.[161]

As a consequence of the comments above, it is evident that the United Kingdom practice within its territory has been as unhelpful in clarifying the issue of how to determine the wishes of the peoples within that territory as was its practice in its other territories.

V. How the Right can be Exercised

(a) *External Self-Determination*

In marked contrast to its practice in determining the wishes of the people—where it was very restrictive—the United Kingdom has adopted an approach to the exercise of the right which stresses the unlimited types of exercise that exist. It has made this very clear when it has been dealing with 'external' self-determination, where the right of self-determination potentially effects changes in the external relations of a State, usually through territorial boundary alterations. In these situations it has affirmed that the right 'does not give every distinct group or territorial sub-division within a State the right to secede from it'.[162] Rather, it has stated that the right can be exercised in different ways, even in colonial situations, as 'we remind the [General] Assembly once again that the right to self-determination does not necessarily mean full independence'.[163]

[159] In fact, the majority of those who voted in the referendum in Scotland favoured devolution but, owing to the requirement (s. 85 Scotland Act 1978) that more than 40% of the entire electorate had to vote in favour of the proposed devolution, the referendum was not passed. For the reasons for this requirement, see C. Turpin, *British Government and the Constitution* (Weidenfeld and Nicolson, 2nd edn., 1990), pp. 250–2. Also it seems from recent election results and opinion polls that both devolution and independence are preferred to the status quo: see Liberty, *Democracy and Human Rights in the UK* (NCCL, London, 1994), p. 35, and D. Oliver, *Government in the United Kingdom* (Open University Press, Milton Keynes, 1991), pp. 96–8.

[160] Where the option of independence/secession is being voted on there is some State practice to indicate that the wishes of the rest of the inhabitants of the State must be considered as their rights need to be taken into account, though some protection against overriding the wishes of the smaller group needs to occur: see G. Marchildon and E. Maxwell, 'Quebec's Right of Secession under Canadian and International Law', *Virginia Journal of International Law*, 32 (1992), p. 583.

[161] See D. Oliver, *Government in the United Kingdom*, op. cit. above (n. 159), pp. 108–9.

[162] Minister of State, FCO, HL Debs., vol. 446, cols. 93–4, 12 December 1983, UKMIL, this *Year Book*, 54 (1983), p. 409.

[163] UK Representative to the UN (T. Richardson) speaking to the GA, 20 November 1990, UN Doc. A/45/PV, p. 72, UKMIL, this *Year Book*, 61 (1990), p. 509.

The United Kingdom's approach to its territories is set out in its Second Report to the HRC, where it stated that

it has been the policy of successive British Governments to give every help and encouragement to those dependent territories which wish to become independent, and where independence is feasible, while not forcing independence on those which do not wish it. Wherever independence is an option, we will seek to create the conditions which will make it a realistic and desirable objective.[164]

There are now very few United Kingdom territories which are likely to choose the option of independence as their exercise of the right of self-determination, with a debate on independence only occurring in Bermuda and in the Turks and Caicos Islands.[165] Of the remaining territories, each has a population of less than 25,000—Pitcairn has less than 100—and a small economy. Therefore, the United Kingdom has noted (somewhat paternally) that

there are many factors, different in every case, which may cause their people to hesitate about separate independence. They may be isolated geographically, with an economy barely sufficient to meet the expanding needs of their people. These people may have no wish to sacrifice the economic and social progress to which they are entitled in order to assume responsibility for maintaining the expensive apparatus of a modern independent State. Alternatively, in some cases the people of these territories feel—justly or unjustly— threatened by a large and powerful neighbour. They fear that their independence may not long endure and that they might, unprotected, lose the political freedom which they now enjoy.[166]

While the issue of what 'political freedom' is enjoyed in these territories will be discussed in the next section, it is clear that the United Kingdom takes the position that there is a range of possible exercises of the right of self-determination, with independence or secession now being a rare form even for non-self-governing territories.

The United Kingdom does not exclude the possibility of the exercise of the right by secession from an independent State, as even in 1964 the United Kingdom was aware that

[164] Second Report, Part II, para. 6 (UN Doc. CCPR/C/32/Add. 3).

[165] The people of Bermuda voted on 15 and 16 August 1995 on a referendum proposing independence. The proposal was defeated, in a 58.8% turnout (being 22,236 of 37,841 eligible voters) by 16,369 votes (73.6%) to 5,714 votes (25.7%): *Bermuda Sun*, 18 August 1995. In the Third Report, Annex J, para. 2, there is the implication that independence may occur in the Turks and Caicos Islands in 1998, though the 1993 Constitution only gives greater autonomy and not independence: see D. Taylor, 'Democratic Spirit: Self-Determination for a British Dependency', *The Parliamentarian*, 75 (1994), p. 103.

[166] Speech to the GA by the Minister of State for Foreign Affairs (Mr Ormsby Gore) on 28 November 1960, Report of the Proceedings of the 15th Session of the GA, Cmnd. 1456 (HMSO, 1961), p. 123. In a statement by the UK representative to the HRC (Mr Stratton) on the First Report, he said that 'there may well prove to be certain Territories, for example St Helena, which might never be able to achieve independent status on their own': UN Doc. CCPR/C/SR. 164, p. 2.

if a 'right' of self-determination were held to exist it could be . . . held to authorize the secession of a province or other part of the territory of a sovereign independent state.[167]

Indeed, its attitude to secession within its own territory is shown by its response to the potential exercises of the right by the people of Northern Ireland:

Northern Ireland is free to determine its own future . . . If the majority of the people in Northern Ireland wish not to be [part of the United Kingdom], obviously we would honour their wish, whether it was to be independent or to join up elsewhere. Northern Ireland is part of the United Kingdom because of the wish of the majority of its people.[168]

Therefore, in general, the United Kingdom would appear to accept a wide variety of modes of exercise of external self-determination both within and outside a State's territorial boundaries.

The United Kingdom's practice in this area is consistent with the international instruments dealing with the right of self-determination. From as early as 1960, the General Assembly acknowledged that alternatives to independence were accepted as forms of exercise of the right.[169] This was confirmed and clarified by the Declaration on Principles of International Law 1970, where it provided that

[t]he establishment of a sovereign and independent State, the free association or integration with an independent State *or the emergence into any other political status* freely determined by a people constitute modes of implementing the right of self-determination by that people.[170]

So independence is seen as only one possible, and often not the most appropriate, mode of exercising the right, even in the context of non-self-governing territories. Indeed, when considering the self-determination of small territories, the Special Committee does not now always push for independence but urges the administering State to strengthen the local economy and to encourage local political leadership.[171] The Special Committee also said, in deciding on types of exercise of the right of self-determination of the people of Pitcairn Island, that the people should take into account

the Territory's tiny size, its small and decreasing population, mineral resources and dependence on postage stamps for the bulk of its revenue.[172]

[167] Submission by the UK Government, 22 September 1964 during consideration of the drafting of the Declaration on Principles of International Law, UN Doc. A/5725/Add.4 (1964), p. 74.

[168] Statement by the then Prime Minister (Margaret Thatcher) in an interview in *Newsweek*, 16 May 1983, as quoted in A. Guelke, 'International Legitimacy, Self-Determination, and Northern Ireland', *Review of International Studies*, 11 (1985), p. 37, at p. 37.

[169] GA Resolution 1541 (XV), passed on 15 December 1960, loc. cit. above (n. 40).

[170] Loc. cit. above (n. 20) (emphasis added).

[171] UN Doc. A/31/23/Rev.1 (1977), vols. 3 and 6, pp. 193–4 and 161–71 respectively.

[172] UN Doc. A/9623/Add.5 (Part III) (1974), pp. 6–7.

Thus by stressing the alternatives to independence as a mode of exercising the right of self-determination, the United Kingdom could be acting in the best interests of the people of many territories and it could reduce potential conflict by restricting the legitimacy of the demand for independence/secession often made by elites in a territory, who are seeking more power rather than acting in the best interests of the people of the territory. At the same time, the acknowledgement by the United Kingdom that there may be situations where secession from an independent State could occur is consistent with the notion that any human right must be constantly protected and cannot be available once and only once.[173]

(b) *Internal Self-Determination*

It has been shown that the United Kingdom has been very active in pressing for the application of the right of self-determination internally, so that the right includes the choice by people within a State of the form of their government and their political and social institutions. In fact, in relation to a couple of its territories it has included a general statement within the 'constitutions' of those territories concerning a commitment to promote and respect the right of self-determination.[174] It has generally fostered self-government in its territories, as is demonstrated by the large percentage of its territories which have become independent, and its actions in its remaining territories, with direct elections for all or most of the government occurring in many of them, shows a continuing attempt to provide for some exercise of internal self-determination.[175]

The position of Hong Kong is quite at odds with the general practice of the United Kingdom as regards internal self-determination of its territories. Until 1988 not a single seat in Hong Kong's Legislative Council was decided in a direct election by the people of Hong Kong, and even by 1997 it seems that the United Kingdom will not have provided for a fully elected government in Hong Kong. The United

[173] This position is consistent with the rejection of India's reservation to the International Human Rights Covenants, where it had sought to rule out the possibility of the right of self-determination being exercised by secession from an independent State: see text at nn. 95 and 96, above.

[174] e.g. Falkland Islands Constitutional Order 1985, Chapter 1, preamble, and Montserrat Constitutional Order 1989, Chapter 4, preamble.

[175] When the Falkland Islands Constitutional Order 1985 was introduced, it was said to be 'designed, in accordance with art. 73 of the Charter of the United Nations, to develop the Islanders' political institutions. For example, it will provide for the abolition of nominated members of the Executive Council, an increase in the number of elected members in both Legislative and Executive Councils, and the removal of the right to vote from the two ex officio members of each Council': letter from the UK Permanent Representative to the UN (Sir John Thomson) to the UN Secretary-General, 13 March 1985, UKMIL, this *Year Book*, 56 (1985), p. 397. In Gibraltar, the 1969 constitution 'sets out the division of powers between the elected Government of Gibraltar and the British Government. It bestows an appropriate level of self-government for domestic matters while preserving British sovereignty and reserving necessary powers to Britain': answer by the Minister of State, FCO (Mr Tristan Garel-Jones), HC Debs., vol. 182, WA, col. 189, 6 December 1990.

Kingdom has sought to explain this anomaly by noting that 'for various geographical and historical reasons, the situation in Hong Kong was special',[176] and it has made a reservation to Article 25 of the ICCPR (right of participation) in respect of Hong Kong, namely:

> the government of the United Kingdom reserve the right not to apply sub-paragraph (*b*) of article 25 [voting at genuine periodic elections] in so far as it may require the establishment of an elected Executive or Legislative Council in Hong Kong[177]

Despite the possible overlap between Article 25(*b*) and Article 1 in aspects of internal self-determination,[178] neither the United Kingdom nor the HRC has taken the view that this reservation directly affects the United Kingdom's legal obligations under Article 1 of the ICCPR, and so the United Kingdom regularly reports on internal self-determination in Hong Kong. The United Kingdom has gone further and expressly reported on the wishes of the people of Hong Kong for more self-government,[179] and in 1984 it stated that it

> fully accept[ed] the legitimate concerns which have been expressed that we should develop a solidly based democratic administration in Hong Kong in the period up to 1997.[180]

It is worth noting that, after pressure from the HRC and in response to the expression of concerns by the people of Hong Kong, the United Kingdom did introduce a Bill of Rights in Hong Kong in 1991.[181] The stated purpose was to incorporate the ICCPR into Hong Kong law; however, this is subject to the existing reservations.[182] The right of self-determination protected by Article 1 of the ICCPR is not included in the

[176] Statement by the UK representative to the HRC (Mr Stratton), First Report, UN Doc. CCPR/C/SR. 164, p. 183, at para. 5.

[177] *Multilateral Treaties Deposited with the Secretary-General*, op. cit. above (n. 14), at p. 132.

[178] R. Higgins, *Problems and Process: International Law and How We Use It* (OUP, Oxford, 1994), at pp. 120–1, explains that the two articles are complementary as 'Article 25 is concerned with the *detail* of how free choice (necessarily implied in Article 1) is to be provided' (her emphasis).

[179] For example, response of the UK representative to the HRC (Mr Martin) to Second Report, UN Doc. CCPR/C/SR.856, p. 10, at para. 47; response of the UK representative to the HRC (Mr Beamish) to Third Report, UN Doc. CCPR/C/SR.1045, p. 4, at para. 12. Since the time of the Third Report, the Governor of Hong Kong has announced widespread changes to increase (or create) elected representatives of district boards, municipal councils and the Legislative Council: C. Patten, *Our Next Five Years: Governor's Annual Address to the Legislative Council* (7 October 1992), reported in *The Independent*, 8 October 1992, p. 12. The Legislative Council is to have 20 directly elected members, 30 elected by functional constituencies and 10 by an election committee. This should allow about 2.7 million people to vote, as against fewer than 700,000 in 1991. These changes have been supported by the UK House of Commons Foreign Affairs Committee: *Relations between the UK and China in the period up to and beyond 1997*, First Report (HMSO, 1994), paras. 312 and 318.

[180] Minister of State for the FCO (Baroness Young), HL Debs., vol. 458, col. 85, 10 December 1984.

[181] Bill of Rights Ordinance 1991, enacted on 8 June 1991.

[182] Section 2 of the Bill of Rights. Section 13 incorporates the reservation to Article 25(*b*) of the ICCPR.

Bill of Rights, but no comment about this omission has been made by the United Kingdom.

A clear indication of the extent to which the United Kingdom's practice on internal self-determination in Hong Kong is not in keeping with international law is that Article 68 of the Basic Law, which is Hong Kong's effective constitution from 1997, declares that

the ultimate aim is the election of all members of the Legislative Council by universal suffrage.[183]

This Basic Law was drafted, not by the United Kingdom or by elected representatives of the Hong Kong people, but by a committee appointed by China's National People's Congress with a majority of Hong Kong members on it, none of whom were elected.[184] The unsatisfactory, slow and piece-meal steps by the United Kingdom towards allowing the exercise of internal self-determination by the people of Hong Kong was highlighted by the Governor of Hong Kong (Christopher Patten) when he noted that

it is extraordinary that people should argue that the tenth most successful trading nation in the world contains a population who are not capable of deciding who should collect their dustbins.[185]

In regard to internal self-determination within its own territory, the United Kingdom has the difficulty that it has an unwritten constitution with no entrenched fundamental rights; a rule of law in which Parliament is supreme; a hereditary monarchy; an unelected upper house of Parliament; a 'first-past-the-post' electoral system; and a highly centralized government, to mention but a few of the aspects of its system which could be considered as limiting internal self-determination.[186] It relies on

[183] Loc. cit. above (n. 135). See, further, M. Kelly, 'Sino-British Discord over Hong Kong', *New Zealand Law Journal*, 1994, p. 18. Prime Minister Lee Kuan Yew of Singapore has stated that 'I do not think a democratically elected government in Hong Kong can be a guarantee of Hong Kong's rights under the [Chinese Special Administrative Region] Constitution': L. Zaoboa, *Lee Kuan Yew on China and Hong Kong after Tiananmen* (Shinglee, Singapore, 1990), p. 48.

[184] Of 59 members, only 23 were from Hong Kong, and this number was reduced by resignations, expulsions and deaths, without replacements. For a particular view of the Basic Law, see M. Davis, *Constitutional Confrontation in Hong Kong: Issues and Implications of the Basic Law* (Macmillan, London, 1989).

[185] Reported in *The Guardian*, 25 February 1994, p. 12. Mr. Wako of the HRC, in discussing the UK's Third Report, said that 'Hong Kong was far more developed, economically, socially and in other ways, than some African countries had been in the 1960s, and yet those countries, at the time of independence, had established universal suffrage': UN Doc. CCPR/C/SR.1046, p. 5, para. 18.

[186] See further, for example, R. Brazier, *Constitutional Reform* (1991); B. Hadfield, 'Whither the House of Lords?', *Northern Ireland Legal Quarterly*, 35 (1984), p. 313; Liberty, *Democracy and Human Rights in the UK* (NCCL, London, 1994); M. Loughlin, *Local Government in the Modern State* (London, 1986); D. Oliver, op. cit. above (n. 159); J. Zecca, 'Avoiding "Electoral Dictatorship" in the United Kingdom: Debate on Constitutional and Electoral Reform through Proportional Representation', *Hastings International and Comparative Law Review*, 16 (1993), p. 425; and, more generally, G. Fox, 'The Right to Political Participation in International Law', *Yale Journal of International Law*, 17 (1992), p. 539; and H. Steiner, 'Political Participation as a Human Right', *Harvard Human Rights Yearbook*, 1 (1988), p. 77.

periodic elections (and very occasional referenda) to enable the peoples in its territory to exercise their internal self-determination,[187] and it gives some special protection to peoples in the regions: for example, the voters in Scotland and Wales elect a larger number of Members of Parliament than their population would be entitled to if strict proportionality in constituency seats were observed.

It has been cogently argued that the political system in the United Kingdom is now one of a largely centralized government, in which affairs of the regions are handled by unelected and unrepresentative central government departments with minimal direct accountability to the people.[188] Others consider that this centralization could cause a feeling of oppression amongst the peoples of the regions and foster claims for more extreme forms of exercise of the right of self-determination, such as secession,[189] especially as the wishes of the elected representatives of these areas can also easily be overridden by the majority of Parliament, who are from English constituencies.[190] It would certainly seem that there are few ways in which the peoples of Northern Ireland, Scotland and Wales can participate in government and have their views heard on regional, social and cultural matters (such as matters of language and education) which affect them as a people.[191] So United Kingdom practice concerning internal self-determination has been inconsistent and selective.

(c) *The United Kingdom within Europe*

Membership by the United Kingdom of the EC (now the European Union (EU)) has had an effect on the peoples within the United Kingdom and their internal self-determination. This is particularly apparent with the trend towards regional or sub-national government by virtue of the principle of 'subsidiarity' and the development of the idea of 'a Europe of the Regions'.[192] For example, a European Committee of the

[187] See section IV(b), above.

[188] Liberty, *Democracy and Human Rights in the UK* (NCCL, London, 1994), pp. 32–3 and p. 43, and Liberty, *Broken Covenants* (NCCL, London, 1993), p. 184. The authors also criticize the method of passing laws for Northern Ireland by Orders in Council, incapable of amendment by Parliament, and the lack of serious consideration of Scottish and Welsh affairs by Parliament. S. Livingstone, 'The House of Lords and the Northern Ireland Conflict', *Modern Law Review*, 57 (1994), p. 333, raises the issue of the level of justice given to those in Northern Ireland by the UK judicial House of Lords; and see also A. Scott, J. Peterson and D. Millar, 'Subsidiarity: A "Europe of the Regions" *v.* the British Constitution', *Journal of Common Market Studies*, 32 (1994), p. 47.

[189] See M. Loughlin, op. cit. above (n. 186), p. 201.

[190] See H. Rawlings, 'The Redistribution of Parliamentary Seats', *Public Law*, 1987, p. 324.

[191] See discussion in section IV(b), above.

[192] For a detailed discussion, see A. Scott, J. Peterson and D. Millar, 'Subsidiarity: A "Europe of the Regions" *v.* the British Constitution', *Journal of Common Market Studies*, 32 (1994), p. 47; G. Berman, 'Subsidiarity and the European Community', *Hastings International and Comparative Law Review*, 17 (1993), p. 97; and A. Toth, 'Is Subsidiarity Justiciable?', *European Law Review*, 19 (1994), p. 268.

Regions has been created to provide formal representation in the EU for sub-national governments, especially on education, regional development and environment policies, and Scotland and Wales have established representative offices in Brussels.[193] Indeed, a survey of the debates within the EU concluded that, despite resistance by the United Kingdom,

> each line of argument involves a more prominent role for the regions . . . The European future may be uncertain but one point is clear: in one form or another it will involve a greater role for local and regional authorities and, as a result, conflict with national governments.[194]

It is conceivable that these developments within the EU will not only assist in the clarification of the application of the right of self-determination in the United Kingdom by identifying people's wishes more specifically, but will also extend the possible exercises of internal self-determination. For example, the people of Scotland may decide that their exercise of the right in regard to education could be best achieved by participation in an EU body. Therefore, the United Kingdom's relationship with the EU could be beneficial as a basis for building a new set of relationships with and within the United Kingdom and so lead to the increased protection of the rights of peoples within the United Kingdom.

VI. The Impact of Territorial Claims by Other States on the Exercise of the Right

The right of self-determination may be limited in certain situations to protect the rights of others (including other people's right of self-determination) and/or to protect the general interests of society.[195] The ICJ acknowledged this in its advisory opinion in the *Western Sahara* case:

> the validity of the principle of self-determination, defined as the need to pay regard to the freely expressed will of peoples, is not affected by the fact that in certain cases the General Assembly has dispensed with the requirement of consulting the inhabitants of a given territory. Those instances were based either on the consideration that a certain population did not constitute a 'people'

[193] Opened in early 1992: see *The Guardian*, 27 February 1992 and 8 March 1994, p. 12.

[194] R. Rhodes, 'The Europeanisation of Sub-central Government: The Case of the UK', *Staatswissenschaften und Staatspraxis*, vol. 2, no. 3, Jahrgang, p. 272, at p. 280, quoted in A. Scott, J. Peterson and D. Millar, loc. cit. above (n. 192), p. 65.

[195] For a detailed discussion of the limitations on the right of self-determination, see R. McCorquodale, 'Self-Determination: A Human Rights Approach', *International and Comparative Law Quarterly*, 43 (1994), p. 857.

entitled to self-determination or on the conviction that a consultation was totally unnecessary, in view of special circumstances.[196]

The General Assembly relied on 'special circumstances' when it dispensed with consultation of the people of West Irian about integration with Indonesia upon the completion of the UN interim administration at the end of Dutch colonial rule.[197] However, the General Assembly has not decided that any of the populations of the United Kingdom's territories do not constitute a 'people' entitled to self-determination.[198] Although these people are entitled to the right of self-determination, there have been some instances where it has been claimed that the exercise of their right must be limited by 'special circumstances'. The territories affected by these claims include the Falkland Islands, Gibraltar, Hong Kong and, previously, Belize. For each of these territories the United Kingdom has had to consider the effect of competing territorial claims by other States. The principal limitations which have been raised are: infringement of territorial integrity, acting contrary to treaty obligations and illegal acquisition of the territory.

(a) *Infringement of Territorial Integrity*

The Declaration on the Granting of Independence to Colonial Countries and Peoples, General Assembly Resolution 1514(XV), upholds the right of self-determination in paragraph 2.[199] But paragraph 6 of that Declaration provides:

any attempt aimed at the partial or total disruption of the national unity and the territorial integrity of a country is incompatible with the purposes and principles of the Charter of the United Nations.

This provision was affirmed in the Declaration on Principles of International Law, 1970, which provides that the right of self-determination shall not

be construed as authorizing or encouraging any action which would dismember or impair, totally or in part, the territorial integrity or political unity of sovereign and independent States.[200]

Although the later Declaration seems to limit the applicability of the limitation of territorial integrity to circumstances where internal self--

[196] *Western Sahara* case, loc. cit. above (n. 84), para. 59.

[197] See GA Resolutions 1752 (XVII) of 21 September 1962 and 2504 (XXIV) of 19 November 1969. The (somewhat dubious) view was taken that the Dutch East Indies (Indonesia) and West Irian were one colonial territorial unit.

[198] See discussion above in sections II(a) and II(b), especially in regard to the population of the Falkland Islands.

[199] Loc. cit. above (n. 80).

[200] Loc. cit. above (n. 20).

determination has not been exercised,[201] there is the potential for conflict between the exercise of the right of self-determination by the people of a colonial territory and the territorial integrity of a neighbouring independent State. At the same time, the General Assembly has affirmed

> the necessity of scrupulously respecting the national unity and territorial integrity of a colonial territory at the time of its accession to independence.[202]

These competing issues of territorial integrity and self-determination have been at the heart of disputes concerning a few of the United Kingdom's territories.

Generally, the United Kingdom has considered that the right of self-determination of peoples in its non-self-governing or colonial territories is pre-eminent and absolute. In 1983 it proclaimed:

> If we as the administering Power accept that the interests of the inhabitants of the Falkland Islands are paramount, how can we negotiate with another Government about transferring sovereignty when that is manifestly contrary to what the people of the Islands see as their interests? The administering Power cannot move in direct contradiction to the wishes of the people of the Territories concerned. How can we say that their interests and their wishes stand in direct opposition to one another? Administering Powers accept 'as a sacred trust the obligation to promote to the utmost [their] well-being'.[203]

This stress on the paramount nature of the right of self-determination in the face of competing territorial claims of other States has been repeated in relation to, for example, Belize[204] and Gibraltar, with the United Kingdom stating that its commitment to the exercise of the right of self-determination of people of Gibraltar

> is clear and as solid as the Rock of Gibraltar. The preamble to the [Gibraltar] constitution . . . says this, 'Her Majesty's Government will never enter into arrangements under which the people of Gibraltar would pass under the sovereignty of another State against their freely and democratically expressed wishes'. Nothing could be clearer than that.[205]

The United Kingdom has ignored the territorial integrity of a colony if it perceives that the wishes of the people of the colony indicate another

[201] The words following those quoted are: 'conducting themselves in compliance with the principle of equal rights and self-determination of peoples as described above and thus possessed of a government representing the whole people belonging to the territory without distinction as to race, creed or colour'.

[202] GA Resolution 34/91, *GAOR*, Supplement No. 46, UN Doc. A/34/46 (1976), at p. 82.

[203] Statement by the UK Permanent Representative to the UN (Sir John Thomson) at the GA's Decolonization Committee, 2 September 1983, UN Doc. A/AC.109/PV.1238, UKMIL, this *Year Book*, 54 (1983), p. 403.

[204] The UK Colonial Secretary (I. Macleod) stated in 1961 that Belize could become independent whenever its people wished: J. Zammit, *The Belize Issue* (Latin American Bureau, London, 1978), at p. 19.

[205] Statement by the Foreign Secretary (Lord Carrington), HL Debs., vol. 416, col. 766, 28 January 1981. Repeated, nearly verbatim, by the Prime Minister (Margaret Thatcher), HC Debs., vol. 72, col. 744, 5 February 1985.

solution. For example, it accepted that British Togoland could be integrated into the new State of Ghana, that the colonies of British and Italian Somaliland could become the one independent State of Somalia and that the non-self-governing territory of the Gilbert and Ellice Islands could be separate States on independence. The United Kingdom was a party to the recognition of separate States in Yugoslavia, the basis for that recognition being, *inter alia*, an exercise of the right of self-determination, despite the strong claim in favour of territorial integrity.[206]

In the case of Belize, the United Kingdom appears to have succeeded in persuading the General Assembly of the correctness of its position, despite Guatemala's claim of territorial integrity and *uti possidetis* (the maintenance of colonial boundaries). In both 1975 and 1980, the General Assembly passed resolutions upholding 'the inalienable right of the people of Belize to self-determination and independence',[207] with the 1980 resolution urging that Belize should become an independent State before the end of 1981.[208] Belize became independent in September 1981.

The United Kingdom was not so successful in regard to the Falkland Islands, though it was able to maintain its position.[209] However, in 1967 the General Assembly adopted a resolution rejecting the right of self-determination of the people of Gibraltar in favour of supporting the territorial integrity of Spain. The General Assembly resolved that

> any colonial situation which partially or completely destroys the national unity or territorial integrity of a country is incompatible with the purposes and principles of the Charter of the United Nations, and specifically with paragraph 6 of General Assembly resolution 1514 (XV).[210]

The resolution went further and declared invalid the referendum held in Gibraltar earlier that year.[211] This was the first time that the General Assembly had subordinated the right of self-determination to a pre-colonial sovereignty claim based on historical links. The resolution implied that the exercise of the right of self-determination by the people of Gibraltar was limited by the Spanish claim of territorial integrity and

[206] EC Declaration on the Guidelines on the Recognition of New States in Eastern Europe and in the Soviet Union, loc. cit. above (n. 92).

[207] GA Resolution 3432 (XXX), 8 December 1975, adopted by 110 votes to 9, with 16 abstentions; and GA Resolution 35/20 (XXXV), 11 November 1980, adopted by 139 votes to 0, with 7 abstentions (Guatamala refused to participate in the voting).

[208] Ibid., para. 2. See further J.R. Maguire, 'The Decolonization of Belize: Self-Determination *v.* Territorial Integrity', *Virginia Journal of International Law*, 22 (1982), p. 850, and T. Franck and P. Hoffman, 'The Right of Self-Determination in Very Small Places', *New York University Journal of International Law and Politics*, 8 (1976), p. 331, at pp. 358–69.

[209] See section VI(c), below.

[210] Resolution 2353 (XXII), *GAOR*, 22nd Session, Supplement No. 16, at p. 53, UN Doc. A/6716 (1967) (73 to 19 with 27 abstentions). Paragraph 6 of GA Resolution 1514 (XV) is set out at p. 320, above.

[211] See section IV(a), above.

so any exercise of that right which retained the present links with the United Kingdom would be excluded as a breach of Spain's territorial integrity. The United Kingdom has rejected the resolution, with its Commonwealth Secretary saying:

> I frankly regard the adoption of Resolution 2353 . . . as little short of disgraceful . . . [I]t does great damage to the reputation of the General Assembly as the guardian of the rights of colonial peoples.[212]

The United Kingdom has maintained this stance ever since. Most of the negotiations between the United Kingdom and Spain to resolve the issue have not included the active involvement of elected representatives from Gibraltar, and these negotiations are made more problematical by matters arising from the EU, such as deciding where are the boundaries of the EU and which State ensures compliance by Gibraltar with EU law.

It could be argued that the General Assembly resolution concerning Gibraltar was passed before the increased application of the right of self-determination, before the ratification by Spain and the United Kingdom of the International Human Rights Covenants upholding the right of self-determination, and before the possible identification of the right of self-determination for non-self-governing territories as part of *jus cogens*.[213] It has also been considered that paragraph 6 of Resolution 1514 was not intended to limit the right of self-determination of the peoples of colonial territories, but was intended to indicate that the exercise of the right of self-determination only occurred 'within the established boundaries of colonies, rather than sub-regions' within a State.[214] But the resolution does create, at the very least, a presumption against the United Kingdom practice of deciding that the wishes of the people of Gibraltar are paramount over the Spanish claim.

The practice of the United Kingdom of supporting the right of self-determination of the peoples in its territories, even in the face of competing—sometimes generally accepted—claims, appears, at least, consistent. But this appearance is made false by the United Kingdom's actions in Hong Kong. Here the United Kingdom has been quite prepared to negotiate for a transfer of sovereignty to China irrespective of the wishes of the people of Hong Kong[215] on the simple basis of Hong

[212] George Thomson, HC Debs., vol. 764, col. 271, 7 May 1968.

[213] See section VI(b), below.

[214] T. Frank and P. Hoffman, 'The Right of Self-Determination in Very Small Places', loc. cit. above (n. 208), at p. 370. This view is based on the debates within the United Nations at the time of the passing of the resolution and the juxtaposition of these debates with events in the former Belgian Congo, where Katanga sought to secede.

[215] In fact, no genuine attempt was made to discover what those wishes were: see section IV(a), above.

Kong's 'unique situation' in relation to China's claims, including China's claim of territorial integrity (in regard to Hong Kong Island and Kowloon).[216] China's claims of territorial integrity[217] do not differ in principle from the claims of Guatemala, Argentina or Spain. Each claim relies on pre-existing historical links prior to the British colonial administration of the territory, and the territory concerned is very small and either surrounded by an independent State or relatively close to it (often called a 'colonial enclave').[218] While the General Assembly has not provided any clear guidelines as to whether the people of a 'colonial enclave' cannot exercise their right of self-determination when there is a competing territorial claim, it may be, as one jurist comments,

> less to do with [the territory's] factual characteristics and more to do with the political reactions to the particular situation of member States of the United Nations.[219]

If this comment is accurate, then it may be the only explanation why the United Kingdom supports the right of self-determination of a population of 30,000 on a territory of less than six square kilometres (Gibraltar), which is economically linked with the claimant State (though ethnically distinct), while it ignores the right of self-determination of a population of about six million on a territory of 1074 square kilometres (Hong Kong), which has great economic strength and has separate representation in international organizations.[220]

Legally, the practice of the United Kingdom in regard to the exercise of the right of self-determination in Hong Kong is inconsistent and incoherent in relation to its general practice. The mere fact that there is a competing sovereignty claim about a territory does not mean that the exercise of the right of self-determination of its people is automatically

[216] Statement by UK representative (Mr Beamish) on the Third Report, UN Doc. CCPR/C/SR. 1046, p. 9, para. 41.

[217] For China's other claims, see section VI(b), below.

[218] See J. Crawford, *The Creation of States in International Law* (Clarendon, Oxford, 1979), at p. 384. Even though the Falkland Islands are about 350 miles distant from Argentina, they could be placed in the same category as Gibraltar: see D. Greig, 'Reflections on the Role of Consent', *Australian Yearbook of International Law*, 12 (1988–9), p. 125, at pp. 155–6.

[219] D. Greig, loc. cit. above (n. 218), pp. 156–7.

[220] Hong Kong is treated as a separate territory within the General Agreement on Tariffs and Trade (GATT) and the UN Conference on Trade and Development (UNCTAD), is a member of the UN Economic and Social Commission for Asia and the Pacific, and Organization of Economic Cooperation and Development (OECD) and the Asian Development Bank, and has signed international agreements: see R. Mushkat, 'The International Legal Status of Hong Kong under Post-Transitional Rule', *Houston Journal of International Law*, 10 (1987), p. 1, at pp. 3–4; R. Mushkat, 'Jurisdictional Issues in a "Highly Autonomous Region"—The Case of Hong Kong', *International and Comparative Law Quarterly*, 42 (1993), p. 11; and UKMIL, this *Year Book*, 60 (1989), pp. 594–5.

limited.[221] An administering State must, at the very least, ensure that there is a free and genuine ascertainment of the wishes of the people of the territory it is administering. To do otherwise, as the United Kingdom has done in Hong Kong by not ascertaining the wishes of the people of Hong Kong, could be an infringement of the right of self-determination of the people of the territory. In fact, there are very few instances of peaceful, negotiated transfers of sovereignty of non-self-governing or colonial territories where the right of self-determination has not been exercised, in that consultation with the people of that territory has been totally dispensed with. Therefore, the practice of the United Kingdom in this area has not clarified the limitation of territorial integrity on the exercise of the right of self-determination, as that practice has been inconsistent and incoherent, and, possibly, a breach of international law.

(b) *Acting Contrary to Treaty Obligations*

In the case of both Gibraltar and Hong Kong there exist treaties which deal with the territory without regard to the wishes of the inhabitants. As far as Gibraltar is concerned, Article 10 of the Treaty of Utrecht 1713, between the United Kingdom and Spain, provides:

> in any case it shall hereafter seem meet to the Crown of Great Britain to grant, sell or by any means to alienate therefrom the propriety of the said town of Gibraltar, it is hereby agreed and concluded, that the Preference of having the same shall always be given to the Crown of Spain before any others.[222]

Both the United Kingdom and Spain interpret this provision to mean that 'if the United Kingdom gave up its sovereignty over those territories, Spain would exercise its rights' to take sovereignty.[223] So they agree that Spain would have sovereignty over Gibraltar as soon as the United Kingdom relinquishes its sovereignty. This position becomes incompatible with the right of self-determination only if the wish of the people of Gibraltar is for independence, integration with a State other than the United Kingdom or Spain, or some other exercise of the right

[221] In the *Western Sahara* case, *ICJ Reports*, 1975, p. 68, Judge Gros noted (at p. 71) that a transfer of sovereignty of a colonial territory without the consent of the people, at least where such transfer was based on historical ties with the 'acquiring' State, 'would have been without any legal effect in the international sphere'. The majority of the ICJ gave a similar indication at para. 162. J. Crawford, *The Creation of States in International Law*, op. cit. above (n. 218), at p. 380, also takes the view that the right of self-determination is a fundamental right and the need to protect territorial integrity only affects the form and procedure by which the right may be exercised, and not its substance, as otherwise, if there was a straight choice between the right and territorial integrity in each case, then it would reduce 'both to procedural policies or processes'.

[222] *Consolidated Treaty Series*, vol. 28 (1713–14).

[223] Response of the UK representative to the HRC (Mr Fearn) to the Second Report, UN Doc. CCPR/C/SR.856, p. 8, at para. 33. See also the statement by the Minister of State, FCO (Mr Cranley Onslow), HC Debs., vol. 40, col. 1100, 15 April 1983.

by which sovereignty of the United Kingdom ends.[224] So the commitment by the United Kingdom to protect the right of self-determination of the people of Gibraltar[225] only extends to certain exercises of the right by the people, which is justified on the basis that one form of exercise of the right is limited by a treaty.

The difficulty in upholding this practice is that since 1713 not only has international law governing territorial sovereignty developed but common Article 1 of the International Human Rights Covenants has come into effect with both Spain and the United Kingdom parties to them. Both States were aware of the dispute over Gibraltar when they ratified these treaties. Article 1(3) obliges the United Kingdom, as administrator of a non-self-governing territory, and Spain, as a signatory of the treaties,[226] to

> promote the realization of self-determination, and [to] respect that right, in conformity with the provisions of the Charter of the United Nations.

The treaty obligations under Article 1 of the Covenants must prevail because where two treaties (or the provisions within two treaties) are inconsistent then the latter treaty prevails, and where one treaty is general and one specific, then the specific treaty qualifies the general.[227] In addition, if the right of self-determination represents a norm of *jus cogens*, which it may be at least to the extent of non-self-governing territories[228] (such as Gibraltar), then, as one jurist notes:

> it is clear that a particular treaty [or treaty provision] may override others if it represents a norm of *jus cogens*.[229]

The United Kingdom acknowledges that it has obligations to the people of Gibraltar under Article 73 of the UNC,[230] which include obligations to 'develop self-government [and to] take due account of the political aspirations of the peoples'.[231] Article 103 of the UNC provides that UNC obligations override other treaty obligations—which is a rule the United

[224] The UK takes the view that independence is only an option for Gibraltar if Spain agrees: see answer by the Minister of State, FCO (Mr Tristan Garel-Jones), HC Debs., vol. 182, WA, col. 189, 6 December 1990.

[225] See text at n. 205, above.

[226] See text at nn. 97–8, above.

[227] Article 30, Vienna Convention on the Law of Treaties, 1969 (to which both the UK and Spain are parties).

[228] Supporters of the view that the right of self-determination is probably part of *jus cogens* include I. Brownlie, *Principles of Public International Law* (4th edn., OUP, Oxford, 1991), p. 513; A. Cassese, *International Law in a Divided World* (OUP, Oxford, 1986), p. 136; id., *Self-Determination of Peoples: A Legal Reappraisal* (Cambridge University Press, 1995), p. 140; and H. Gros Espiell, *The Right to Self-Determination, Implementation of United Nations Resolutions* (United Nations, 1978), para. 85.

[229] I. Brownlie, *Principles of Public International Law*, op. cit. above (n. 228), p. 625.

[230] On 1 December 1993, Baroness Chalker, Minister of State, FCO, agreed that 'in addition to the rights and responsibilities in the Treaty of Utrecht, [we have] rights and responsibilities in the Charter of the United Nations, in particular those in Chapter XI': HL Debs., vol. 550, WA, col. 20.

[231] Article 73(*b*).

Kingdom relies on in its reservation to the International Human Rights Covenants[232]—and the UNC obligations (as clarified by the Declaration on Principles of International Law) include the obligation to protect the right of self-determination.[233] These obligations under the UNC do not include any express limit on the exercise of the right if there is an earlier treaty concerning a territory. Thus the practice by both the United Kingdom and Spain in limiting the possible exercises of the right of self-determination by the people of Gibraltar because of an eighteenth century treaty does not seem consistent with international law.

In the case of Hong Kong, a number of treaties are involved which gave the United Kingdom title in perpetuity over Hong Kong Island and Kowloon and title for 99 years over the New Territories, in particular the Convention of Peking 1898 (concerning the latter title). China claims that this was an 'unequal treaty', being one where

> the circumstances in which it was negotiated were inconsistent with the sovereignty and equality of both contracting parties and its burdens and advantages were non-reciprocal.[234]

The United Kingdom has not expressly accepted that the treaty was unequal. Nevertheless, the possibility of the inequality of the treaty may have added to its willingness to transfer sovereignty of all parts of Hong Kong to China without the genuine ascertainment of the wishes of the people of Hong Kong.[235] The transfer of all the territory of Hong Kong—rather than just the New Territories—was justified by the United Kingdom on the basis that Hong Kong Island 'would not be viable without the New Territories'.[236] Yet this justification is inconsistent with the justification given by the United Kingdom in relation to the Falkland Islands, that the size of a territory and its economic viability are irrelevant to the right of self-determination, at least in relation to non-self-governing territories.[237]

Despite some arguments in favour, there is no international consensus that inequality is a ground of invalidity of a treaty in international law.[238] Also 'an international instrument has to be interpreted and applied

[232] See section I(b), above.

[233] Loc. cit. above (n. 20).

[234] P. Wesley-Smith, *Unequal Treaty 1898–1997: China, Great Britain and Hong Kong's New Territories* (OUP, Hong Kong, 1980), at p. 184. For a summary of the legal history of Hong Kong, see H. Hannum, *Autonomy, Sovereignty and Self-Determination: The Accommodation of Conflicting Rights*, op. cit. above (n. 72), chapter 7, and International Commission of Jurists, *Countdown to 1997: Report of a Mission to Hong Kong*, op. cit. above (n. 54), chapter 2.

[235] See section IV(a), above.

[236] FCO memorandum submitted to the UK House of Commons Foreign Affairs Committee, 22 March 1989, UKMIL, this *Year Book*, 60 (1989), p. 595.

[237] See section II(a) above. The Special Committee has consistently expressed the view that factors such as territorial size, geographical location, size of population and scarce natural resources should not delay the speedy exercise of the right of self-determination of non-self-governing territories, e.g., UN Doc. A/41/23 (1986), in regard to Anguilla and the Cayman Islands.

[238] See I. Brownlie, *Principles of Public International Law*, op. cit. above (n. 228), pp. 615–16.

the framework of the entire legal system prevailing at the time of the interpretation'.[239] Whilst China is a party to the UNC (one purpose of which is to uphold the 'principle of equal rights and self-determination of peoples'[240]), it is not a party to any other treaty which expressly upholds the right of self-determination. However, customary international law does apply to China and the right of self-determination is a rule of customary international law, at least with respect to non-self-governing territories.[241] Even if China does not consider Hong Kong to be a non-self-governing territory, it does consider Hong Kong to be a colony of the United Kingdom (even if unlawfully acquired) as it has stated that the relationship between the United Kingdom and the people of Hong Kong is 'like that between a colonial ruler and its subjects'.[242] The lack of any distinction between a colony and a non-self-governing territory for the purposes of the right of self-determination has already been demonstrated,[243] in that

> a colony or other Non-Self-Governing Territory has . . . [a] separate and distinct status . . . [which] shall exist *until* the people of the colony or other Non-Self-Governing Territory have exercised their right of self-determination.[244]

Thus, until the people of Hong Kong exercise their right of self-determination they remain a colony no matter what the treaties between the United Kingdom and China may provide and whether or not any treaty was unequal. So, whatever the legality of the nineteenth century treaties between the United Kingdom and China concerning Hong Kong, the exercise of the right of self-determination of the people of Hong Kong is not limited by them.

There is an additional element in this conclusion. Because there has been no exercise yet of the right of self-determination by the people of Hong Kong, after 1997 China will become primarily responsible for allowing the right to be exercised.[245] This position is reinforced by the Joint Declaration—where China 'resume[s] the exercise of sovereignty over Hong Kong with effect from 1 July 1997'[246]—although the right of self-determination is not expressly referred to. In this treaty with the

[239] *Namibia* case, loc. cit. above (n. 37), p. 31. See also *Minquiers and Ecrehos* case *(France* v. *UK), ICJ Reports*, 1953, p. 47, at p. 56, and R. Mushkat, 'The International Legal Status of Hong Kong under Post-Transitional Rule', *Houston Journal of International Law*, 10 (1987), p. 1, at p. 2.

[240] Article 1(2).

[241] See section I(b), above. In the *East Timor* case, *ICJ Reports*, 1995, the ICJ considered that the right of self-determination had an *erga omnes* character (at para. 29).

[242] Loc. cit. above (n. 141).

[243] See section II(b), above.

[244] Declaration on Principles of International Law, 1970, loc. cit. above (n. 20) (emphasis added).

[245] The people of Hong Kong may exercise their right by, for example, seeking significant autonomy within China.

[246] Loc. cit. above (n. 132), Article 1.

United Kingdom,[247] China has expressly accepted that the legal obligations of both International Human Rights Covenants will continue to apply to Hong Kong after 1997.[248] So under both treaty and customary international law, the right of self-determination of the people of Hong Kong is not limited by any treaty. Indeed, the action of the United Kingdom in entering into a treaty with China without allowing the people of Hong Kong to exercise their right of self-determination is a breach of the United Kingdom's treaty obligations (under the International Human Rights Covenants) to protect the right of self-determination.[249] Because common Article 1 requires all States at all times to 'facilitate realization of and respect for the right of peoples to self-determination',[250] irrespective of the dependency of those people on that State, the United Kingdom retains a legal obligation to the people of Hong Kong in regard to their right of self-determination after 1997.

(c) *Illegal Acquisition of Territory*

The issue of whether the manner in which the United Kingdom acquired a territory should limit the right of self-determination of the inhabitants of that territory arises in regard to the Falkland Islands. Argentina claims that the Falkland Islands were historically part of Argentina but were forcibly acquired by the United Kingdom. Thus, Argentina argues, to allow the people of the Falkland Islands to decide conclusively if there is to be any change in sovereignty over that territory would mean that there was a legitimization of an illegal acquisition of territory by a colonial power.[251] Consequently, Argentina considers that the Falkland Islands is a special and unique exception to the rule that the people's wishes are paramount. The United Kingdom strongly disputes the allegation of illegal occupation and, in any event, states that 'the administering Power cannot move in direct contradiction to the wishes of

[247] The Joint Declaration is a treaty binding on both parties, despite its characterisation: see answer by the UK representative to the HRC (Mr Beamish) on Third Report, UN Doc. CCPR/C/SR.1046, p. 10, para. 44.

[248] Art. XIII of Annex I.

[249] Moreover, if the right of self-determination forms part of *jus cogens*, then the Joint Declaration would be void as breaching the right: Art. 53, Vienna Convention on the Law of Treaties, 1969. It would become void under Art. 64 of that Convention if it is later established that the right is *jus cogens*.

[250] HRC, General Comment 12(21), para. 6, UN Doc. A/39/40 (1984), p. 143.

[251] The use of force to acquire territory is now unlawful in international law: Article 2(4) of the Charter of the UN prohibits the use of force by a State, and the Declaration on Principles of International Law, loc. cit. above (n. 20), provides that 'no territorial acquisition resulting from the threat or use of force shall be recognized as legal'. The SC applied this principle when it declared the forcible acquisition of Kuwait by Iraq to be illegal: SC Resolution 662 (1990). For a detailed discussion of the claims made by Argentina and the UK, see M. Sanchez, 'Self-Determination and the Falkland Islands Dispute', *Columbia Journal of Transnational Law*, 21 (1983), p. 557, especially at pp. 561–77, and D. Greig, 'Sovereignty and the Falkland Islands', *Australian Yearbook of International Law*, 8 (1983), p. 20.

the people of the Territories concerned'.[252] Indeed, the United Kingdom refuses to negotiate with Argentina on sovereignty over the Falkland Islands until the right of self-determination is on the agenda.[253]

To some extent the General Assembly, over the objections of the United Kingdom, was persuaded by Argentina's arguments. Its resolutions dealing with the Falkland Islands conflict invite the United Kingdom and Argentina to find a peaceful solution to the dispute '*bearing in mind* . . . the interests of the population of the Falkland Islands (Malvinas)'.[254] Thus, in the view of the majority of the General Assembly, any expressed wishes of the people of the Falkland Islands (such as to remain with the United Kingdom) must merely be borne in mind and are not decisive in the determination of sovereignty over that territory.[255]

It would seem from this resolution that the right of self-determination may be limited by an unlawful acquisition of territory, perhaps in the same way as the people in the Turkish Republic of Northern Cyprus are not considered to be able to exercise the right.[256] However, the United Kingdom rejects any suggestion of illegality in its acquisition of the Falkland Islands and, even if the territory was acquired by force, the United Kingdom could rely on the principle of intertemporal law in asserting that its actions were not illegal at the time.[257] In addition, one jurist has noted that the issue is 'on the boundary between two systems and philosophies of international law',[258] which is indicated by the likelihood that

> the General Assembly is probably more disposed to uphold the right to self-determination of a population that has been subjugated by a foreign colonial power . . . [than one which] share[s] a common ancestry with the colonial power itself.[259]

While the wishes of the people of the Falkland Islands may not be paramount in determining sovereignty over that territory, they are

[252] Loc. cit. above (n. 203).

[253] See, for example, the statement by the Minister of State, FCO, HC Debs., vol. 997, WA, col. 424, 28 January 1981.

[254] e.g. GA Resolution 2065(XX), 16 December 1965, *GAOR*, 20th Session, Supplement No. 14, at p. 57, UN Doc. A/6014 (1965) (emphasis added). Adopted by 94 votes in favour, none against, and 14 abstentions (including the UK).

[255] The resolution is only directed to the United Kingdom and Argentina and not to the peoples of the Falkland Islands.

[256] By Resolution 541 (1983) the SC declared the Turkish Republic of Northern Cyprus 'legally invalid' and called on States not to recognize it: see J. Dugard, *Recognition and the United Nations*, op. cit. above (n. 74), pp. 108–11.

[257] On intertemporal law, see I. Brownlie, *Principles of Public International Law*, op. cit. above (n. 228), pp. 129–30.

[258] D. Greig, 'Sovereignty and the Falkland Islands Crisis', *Australian Yearbook of International Law*, 8 (1983), p. 20, at p. 69.

[259] M. Sanchez, 'Self-Determination and the Falkland Islands Dispute', *Columbia Journal of Transnational Law*, 21 (1983), p. 557, at p. 573.

certainly relevant and must be taken into account. Thus any solution to the dispute must include an ascertainment of the wishes of the people of the Falkland Islands, in exercise of their right of self-determination.

VII. Conclusion

This review of the practice of the United Kingdom in regard to the right of self-determination has clarified a number of the aspects of the right which have a wider significance for the protection of the right in international law.

1. The right of self-determination is a human right and must be protected by all States.
2. In defining the 'peoples' entitled to the right of self-determination a very flexible, practical definition is required.
3. The right of self-determination now applies to all peoples in all territories—including those within a State—who are subject to oppression by subjugation, domination or exploitation.
4. The peoples of a territory must be consulted about any change of sovereignty over that territory. The general reliance by the United Nations on referenda to determine the wishes of peoples is a far better method than by elections alone.
5. The right of self-determination can be exercised in many ways, with independence or secession now rarely appropriate. This position may reduce the automatic demands for independence which can arise in situations where the right is being infringed, and may aid the peaceful settlement of disputes.
6. There are limitations on the exercise of the right of self-determination. However, the right generally has priority over competing claims of territorial integrity.
7. Any change of sovereignty over a territory without any exercise of the right of self-determination by the peoples of that territory does not absolve the old or the new sovereign of the responsibility to protect the right of self-determination of the people of that territory.

Finally, the United Kingdom has confirmed the importance of the right of self-determination in international law in asserting that:

> Self-determination is . . . of a different order of importance and generality to the rights and wrongs of particular territorial disputes. Self-determination is not a matter for negotiation.[260]

[260] Statement by the UK Permanent Representative to the UN (Sir John Thomson) to the GA, 27 September 1985, UN Doc. A/40/PV.93, pp. 13–15, UKMIL, this *Year Book*, 56 (1985), p. 403.

THE EUROPEAN COMMUNITY ARBITRATION COMMISSION ON YUGOSLAVIA*

By MATTHEW C. R. CRAVEN‡

1. Introduction

At a meeting in Brussels on 27 August 1991, the European Community and its Member States agreed to convene an International Conference for Peace in Yugoslavia with a view to finding a permanent and pacific solution to the crisis within the Socialist Federal Republic of Yugoslavia (SFRY) which had resulted in conflict.[1] Those to attend the opening session in The Hague were the Federal Presidency and Federal Government of Yugoslavia, the Presidents of the six Republics, the President of the EC Council and representatives of the EC Commission and EC Member States.[2] With a view to finding 'a peaceful accommodation of the conflicting aspirations of the Yugoslav peoples', it was decided that an Arbitration Commission should be created 'in the framework of the Conference'[3] to which 'the relevant authorities will submit their differences'.[4]

The Arbitration Commission so created delivered ten 'opinions' between December 1991 and July 1992.[5] Opinions 1–3 and 8–10 were delivered in response to questions formulated by the Chairman of the EC peace conference, and Opinions 4–7 on the initiative of the Council of Ministers of the EC. It also rendered an 'interlocutory decision' prior to its eighth opinion following Serbia and Montenegro's challenge to its

‡ Lecturer in Law, University of Leicester.

[1] Joint Statement, 28 August 1991, *Bulletin of the EC*, 24 (1991), no. 7/8, p. 115, s. 1.4.25. It was stated (p. 116): 'The Community and its member States cannot stand idly by as the bloodshed in Croatia increases day by day. An agreement on the monitoring of the cease-fire and its maintenance should allow the Community and its Member States to convene a peace conference and establish an arbitration procedure.'

[2] Ibid.

[3] Joint Statement, 3 September 1991, *Bulletin of the EC*, 24 (1991), no. 9, p. 63, s. 1.4.1. The idea of creating a European Court of Conciliation and Arbitration had been advanced earlier by Robert Badinter, President of the French Constitutional Court: see note, *La Monde*, 21 June 1991.

[4] Joint Statement, loc. cit. above (n. 1).

[5] In total, the Commission issued fifteen opinions: Opinion No. 1, *International Legal Materials*, 31 (1992), p. 1494; Opinion No. 2, ibid., p. 1497; Opinion No. 3, ibid., p. 1499; Opinion No. 4, ibid., p. 1501; Opinion No. 5, ibid., p. 1503; Opinion No. 6, ibid., p. 1507; Opinion No. 7, ibid., p. 1512; Opinion No. 8, ibid., p. 1521; Opinion No. 9, ibid., p. 1523; Opinion No. 10, ibid., p. 1525.

competence.[6] In January 1993 the Arbitration Commission was 'reconstituted', its composition and terms of reference being revised and clarified.[7] In that form, the Arbitration Commission delivered a further five opinions (Opinions 11–15).[8] Since 1993, although the Conference of Yugoslavia has still been operating,[9] the Commission has not been asked to deliver any further opinions on matters arising.

The fifteen opinions delivered by the Arbitration Commission represent an important and unusual range of opinions on a variety of questions of international law relating to statehood and succession. Rarely has it been the case that a body of legal experts has been asked to deliver a series of apparently abstract opinions on the international legal dimensions of the dismemberment of a single State. In a formal sense, the opinions of the Arbitration Commission are not binding on any of the States concerned. The Commission was not created in virtue of an international arbitration agreement between disputing parties, and had no treaty base. Rather, it was an executive creation on the part of the EC and its Member States acting through the medium of the Conference on Yugoslavia. Its opinions were directed not to the parties concerned but to the Conference itself, and were delivered in a consultative capacity.[10] Nevertheless, as has been made clear with respect to the International Court of Justice (ICJ), advisory opinions delivered by independent judicial bodies have considerable moral and political authority, and while not having the effect of *res judicata* may be declaratory of general international law.[11] Even if the Arbitration Commission cannot strictly be seen as an 'independent judicial body', it was certainly independent of the disputing parties, it attempted to conduct its activities in a broadly judicial manner, and it sought to found its opinions in general international law. As such, its opinions may be treated as non-binding but authoritative statements of the relevant law.

Ultimately, the significance of the Arbitration Commission's opinions may be appreciated in two ways. First, the opinions served to provide a

[6] Interlocutory Decision, ibid., p. 1518.

[7] *International Legal Materials*, 32 (1993), p. 1572.

[8] Opinion No. 11, ibid., p. 1586; Opinion No. 12, ibid., p. 1589; Opinion No. 13, ibid., p. 1591; Opinion No. 14, ibid., p. 1593; Opinion No. 15, ibid., p. 1595.

[9] See Reports of Co-Chairmen of the Steering Committee of the International Conference on the Former Yugoslavia, S/1994/1074, 19 September 1994; S/1994/1124, 3 October 1994; S/1994/1246, 3 November 1994; S/1994/1372, 1 December 1994; S/1994/1454 29 December 1994; S/1994/811, 8 July 1994; S/1994/83, 26 January 1994; S/1995/175, 2 March 1995; S/1995/302; S/1995/6, 5 January 1995. Reports of the Secretary-General on the International Conference on Yugoslavia: S/24795, 11 November 1992; S/25015, 24 December 1992; S/25050, 6 January 1993; S/25100, Annex, 14 January 1993; S/25221, 2 February 1993; S/25708, 30 April 1993; S/25709, 3 May 1993.

[10] Below, nn. 78–85.

[11] See separate opinion of Judge Azevedo in the *Peace Treaties* case, *ICJ Report*, 1950, p. 79, at p. 80. In the same case Judge Zoricic noted that 'in practice, an advisory opinion given by the Court in regard to a dispute between States is nothing else than an unenforceable judgment': ibid., p. 101. Cf. Article 38(1)(*d*), Statute of the ICJ.

legal rationalization for elements of State practice that were otherwise contradictory or incoherent. For example, its view that in the dismemberment of the SFRY the principle of *uti possidetis juris* should be applied to 'internationalize' former administrative boundaries[12] essentially followed earlier statements of the EC Member States to the effect that they would 'never recognize changes of [former internal] frontiers which have not be brought about by peaceful means and by agreements'.[13] Secondly, the Commission's opinions also had a proactive dimension, in that they provided a legal framework for the development of subsequent State practice. For example, the EC and its Member States, in refusing to accept the new Federal Republic of Yugoslavia (FRY) as the sole successor to the former Socialist Federal Republic of Yugoslavia (SFRY), expressly referred to the Arbitration Commission's conclusions in Opinion No. 10.[14] The view that the SFRY underwent a process of dismemberment[15] was also undoubtedly influential as regards the United Nations' determination that the FRY should not continue automatically the membership of the former SFRY in the UN.[16] In fact the influence exerted by the opinions of the Arbitration Commission became a point of issue as far as the FRY was concerned, which complained that in practice the advisory opinions 'were taken as judgments and served as a basis for making concrete decisions on relevant issues concerning the Yugoslav crisis'.[17]

It should be noted, however, that the opinions of the Arbitration Commission were not entirely determinative of State practice. Despite its findings to the contrary, EC Member States proceeded to recognize Croatia as an independent State and at the same time refused to give diplomatic recognition to the Republic of Macedonia.[18] As will be seen, however, this was largely due to the fact that on the issue of recognition, the Arbitration Commission was acting as a fact-finding body and its opinions were treated merely as a matter of information. In any case, it is apparent that the main elements of the Commission's opinions broadly corresponded with State practice and provided a legal framework for the precarious territorial and political settlement that was ultimately imposed upon the former Yugoslavia.

[12] Below, n. 307.

[13] Joint Statement, loc. cit. above (n. 1). While the principle outlined by the EC might have been acceptable as regards existing international frontiers, it was highly unusual in so far as it referred to a situation which was at the time prima facie internal. See Weller, 'The International Response to the Dissolution of the Socialist Federal Republic of Yugoslavia', *American Journal of International Law*, 86 (1992), p. 569, at pp. 575–6.

[14] Statement of EC Member States, 22 September 1992, this *Year Book*, 63 (1992), p. 658.

[15] Opinion No. 8, loc. cit. above (n. 5), p. 1523.

[16] SC Resn. 777, 19 September 1992.

[17] Letter from the Deputy Prime Minister and Minister for Foreign Affairs of the FRY addressed to the ICFY Co-Chairmen, 2 July 1993, *International Legal Materials*, 32 (1993), p. 1584.

[18] Below, nn. 257–8.

2. The Arbitration Commission[19]

2.1. *Membership*

Under its initial mandate, the Arbitration Commission was to consist of five members, three of whom were to be appointed by the EC and its Member States, and the other two by the Yugoslav Federal Presidency.[20] The EC and its Member States accordingly designated the President of the French *Conseil Constitutionnel* (Robert Badinter), the President of the German Federal Constitutional Court (Roman Herzog) and the President of the Italian Constitutional Court (Aldo Corasaniti). The Yugoslav Federal Presidency, however, was unable to come to a unanimous agreement on the proposed candidates. This possibility had been specifically foreseen in the Commission's terms of reference, which had provided that where no agreement was possible on the appointment of the Yugoslav members, they would be chosen by the other three members.[21] Accordingly the final two members were appointed, and were the President of the Spanish Constitutional Court (Francisco Tomas y Valiente) and the President of the Belgian *Cour d'Arbitrage* (Irène Petry). At its first session, M. Badinter was appointed as the President of the Commission, and it was decided that the Commission would continue to sit in Paris. It also adopted a set of rules of procedure which were not made public.[22]

When the EC Arbitration Commission was reconstituted in January 1993 its composition was similarly changed. As previously, it was determined that the Arbitration Commission should be composed of five permanent members: three to be designated by the Council of Ministers of the EC from among incumbent Presidents of Constitutional Courts of the existing Member States or from members of the highest courts of

[19] See generally Pellet, 'Note Sur la Commission d'Arbitrage de la Conférence Européenne Pour la Paix en Yugoslavie', *Annuaire français de droit international*, 37 (1991), p. 329; id., 'L'Activité de la Commission d'Arbitrage de la Conférence Européenne Pour la Paix en Yugoslavie', ibid., 38 (1992), p. 220; id., 'L'Activitié de la Commission d'Arbitrage de la Conférence Européenne Pour la Paix en Yugoslavie', ibid., 39 (1993), p. 286; Regazzi, 'Introductory Note', *International Legal Materials*, 31 (1992), p. 1488.

[20] Joint Statement, loc. cit. above (n. 1).

[21] Ibid.

[22] Pellet describes the working methods as follows:

'cette procédure est demeurée extrêmement souple, informelle et discrète. Sur chaque problème, un rapporteur a été assuré par l'envoi . . . à chacune des parties intéressées des documents émanant des autres parties. En revanche, la Commission a refusé de donner suite aux demands d'audience qui lui ont été transmises, et, bien qu'elle ait envisagé la possibilité de désigner des délégués mandatés collectivement pour se rendre sur place à fin d'information et d'instruction, elle n'a jamais utilisé cette procédure.

De même, bien qu'elle eût prévu que ses recommandations seraient adoptées à la majorité simple des voix sans possibilité d'abstention ni indication sur le sens du vote des members qui, cependant, pourraient publier, le cas échéant, des opinions dissidentes, elle a arrêté ses positions par consensus.'

(Loc. cit. above (n. 19) (1991), p. 332.)

those States;[23] the fourth member was to be designated by the President of the ICJ from among the former members of that Court or persons possessing the qualifications required by Article 2 of the Statute of the Court; the final member was to be a member of the European Court of Human Rights, designated by the President of that Court. It was further stipulated that no two members were to have the same nationality and that each member 'is to serve as long as he or she holds the office on the basis of which the designation is made'.[24] In addition to the permanent members of the Arbitration Commission, it was provided that in contentious proceedings, the contending parties would each be entitled to appoint an *ad hoc* member to the Commission. The *ad hoc* members should either be incumbent members of Constitutional Courts or highest courts in existing Member States of the CSCE or qualify in the same manner as the fourth and fifth permanent members of the Commission.

Pursuant to the terms of reference of the Commission, and in light of the responses provided by the Presidents of the ICJ and European Court of Human Rights, the initial composition of the Commission was as follows: Robert Badinter (President of the Constitutional Court of France), Francisco Paolo Casavola (President of the Constitutional Court of Italy), Roman Herzog (President of the Constitutional Court of Germany), Elizabeth Palm (Judge of the European Court of Human Rights), Jose Maria Ruda (former President of the ICJ). The Arbitration Commission's competence with respect to contentious proceedings was never invoked and therefore no *ad hoc* members were ever appointed to sit upon the Commission.

2.2. *The Constitution of the Arbitration Commission*

The legal basis of the Arbitration Commission is to be found initially in the EC Declaration of 27 August 1991. In that Declaration the EC and its Member States, together with the various parties to the Yugoslav crisis, resolved to create an arbitral procedure 'in the framework of the peace Conference' with a view to considering 'differences' submitted by '[t]he relevant authorities'.[25] It was further resolved that '[t]he relevant authorities will submit their differences to an arbitration Commission of five members'.[26]

These initial terms of reference fall considerably short of what one would usually expect of an arbitral procedure. As the International Law Commission's Model Rules on Arbitral Procedure suggest, the terms of

[23] It was understood that initially those members were to be those from France, Germany and Italy.

[24] Ibid.

[25] Joint Statement, loc. cit. above (n. 1), p. 116.

[26] Ibid.

a *compromis* should indicate as a minimum '(*a*) the undertaking to arbitrate according to which the dispute is to be submitted to the arbitrators; (*b*) the subject-matter of the dispute and, if possible, the points on which the parties are or are not agreed; (*c*) the method of constituting the tribunal and the number of arbitrators'.[27] In addition, it suggested that a number of other provisions deemed desirable by the parties might be indicated, such as the rules of law to be adopted by the tribunal, the procedure to be followed, the majority required for the award, the time limit within which the award should be made and the languages to be employed in the proceedings.[28] As far as the Arbitration Commission was concerned, all that was made utterly clear was the composition of the Commission. In terms of the undertaking to arbitrate, the identity of the parties to the dispute, and the subject-matter(s) covered by the procedure, there remained a number of questions to be resolved. Before addressing such questions, it is worth considering what might have been intended by the parties concerned in specifically creating what they termed to be an 'Arbitration Commission'.[29]

Arbitration is traditionally understood as meaning 'the settlement of disputes between States by judges of their own choice and on the basis of respect for law'.[30] The two dimensions of arbitration highlighted by this definition, which set it apart from other forms of international dispute settlement, are, on the one hand, the need for the consent of States at every stage of the arbitration process (including the right to choose their own judges[31]) and, on the other hand, the legal nature of the award.[32] Arbitration may thus be distinguished from other forms of diplomatic settlement such as conciliation,[33] mediation[34] or negotiation,[35] in virtue

[27] *General Assembly Official Records*, 13th Session, Supplement No. 9, Doc. A/3859, pp. 5–8 (1958).

[28] Ibid., Article 2.

[29] It should be noted, nevertheless, that denomination alone cannot be determinative. That a body is specifically referred to as an 'Arbitration Commission' does not necessitate that it is to engage in arbitration in the proper sense.

[30] Article 15, Hague Convention 1899; Article 37, Hague Convention 1907. The International Law Commission similarly defined arbitration as 'a procedure for the settlement of disputes between States by a binding award on the basis of law and as a result of an undertaking voluntarily accepted': *Yearbook of the ILC*, 1953, vol. 2, p. 202.

[31] Johnson, 'The Constitution of an Arbitral Tribunal', this *Year Book*, 30 (1953), p. 152.

[32] See Fox, 'Arbitration', in *International Disputes: The Legal Aspects* (1972), p. 101, at pp. 101–2.

[33] Merrills describes conciliation as: 'a method for the settlement of international disputes of any nature according to which a commission set up by the parties, either on a permanent basis or an ad hoc basis to deal with a dispute, proceeds to the impartial examination of the dispute and attempts to define the terms of a settlement susceptible of being accepted by them or affording the Parties, with a view to its settlement, such aid as they may have requested': *International Dispute Settlement* (2nd edn., 1991), p. 59. It is clearly open for judicial tribunals, such as the ICJ, to undertake a conciliatory function: see *North Sea Continental Shelf* cases, *ICJ Reports*, 1969, p. 3. See also Fox, 'Conciliation', in *International Disputes: The Legal Aspects* (1972), p. 93.

[34] Darwin, 'Mediation and Good Offices', in *International Disputes: The Legal Aspects* (1972), p. 83.

[35] Darwin, 'Negotiation', in *International Disputes: The Legal Aspects* (1972), p. 77.

of the fact that in cases of arbitration, the parties are obliged to accept the award as binding.[36] That arbitration is essentially a legal task has certain consequences for the composition and functioning of the arbitral body. The arbitral body must proceed strictly within its terms of reference and must respect the rules of natural justice. The judicial character of the body was stressed, for example, by the PCIJ in the *Interpretation of Article 3, Paragraph 2, of the Treaty of Lausanne* case, where it found that because of its political composition it was 'impossible, properly speaking, to regard the Council, acting in its capacity of an organ of the League of Nations . . . as a tribunal of arbitrators'.[37] Despite the similarities in function, arbitration is also usually distinguished from judicial settlement. As has frequently been noted, however, no clear-cut distinction can be made, the differences lying more in terms of typological characteristics[38] such as the relative permanence of the tribunal[39] and the degree of control exercised by the disputing parties over its composition and procedure.[40]

Given that the Arbitration Commission was to be composed of jurists appointed by the EC and its Member States on the one hand, and the Yugoslav Federal Presidency on the other, one might assume that the Commission was created to arbitrate on disputes arising between those parties. That of course was never the intention, it being clear from the fact that the Arbitration Commission was created within the framework of the Conference on Yugoslavia that the disputes to which it would address itself were those arising from the conflict within the SFRY following the attempted secession of Croatia and Slovenia. This raises a number of significant problems as regards both the characterization of the procedure and the application of legal principle.

The first, and most obvious, problem relates to the legal status of the disputing parties. Even on the most optimistic analysis,[41] the statehood of Croatia and Slovenia can only clearly be established once the three-month suspension of their declarations of independence came to an end

[36] Article 37 of the 1907 Hague Convention adds to the defiinition: 'Recourse to arbitration implies an engagement to submit in good faith to the award'.

[37] Advisory opinion, *PCIJ*, Series B, No. 12, at p. 26 (1925).

[38] Brownlie cites the following factors as being influential in designating a tribunal as an 'arbitral tribunal': (i) if the compromis is likely to allow settlement on extra-legal principles; (ii) if the agency of decision is designated as an 'arbitral tribunal'; (iii) if the tribunal consists of an odd number and includes representatives from the disputing States; (iv) if the tribunal is merely created to deal with a particular dispute, or class of disputes; (v) if there is flexibility in the procedures: Brownlie, *Principles of Public International Law* (4th edn., 1990), p. 710.

[39] Merrills, op. cit. above (n. 33), p. 80.

[40] Schwarzenberger notes that 'the only difference between arbitration and judicial settlement lies in the method of selecting the members of these judicial organs. While, in arbitration proceedings, this is done by agreement between the parties, judicial settlement presupposes the existence of a standing tribunal with its own bench of judges and its own rules of procedure which parties to a dispute must accept': *Manual of International Law* (6th edn., 1976), p. 195.

[41] Below, nn. 252–61.

on 8 October 1991.[42] As regards the other Republics, their acquisition of statehood occurred somewhat later (up to nine months later in the case of the Federal Republic of Yugoslavia).[43] Accordingly, it appears that the Arbitration Commission was not intended to arbitrate on differences between 'States' as such, but rather, non-State actors.[44] This much, at least, was implicitly recognized in the terms of its mandate, which referred opaquely to the 'relevant authorities' between which the Commission was to arbitrate.[45] Having said that, it cannot have been far from the minds of those involved in the creation of the Commission that at least some of the Republics were likely to acquire independent statehood in the foreseeable future and that questions of public international law were therefore likely to arise.

The very real difficulty facing the Conference was therefore providing a legal basis for the jurisdiction of the Commission. Arbitration, as a procedure for settling disputes in national or international law, is always constructed on the basis of a *compromis*—a binding agreement between two parties (either on an *ad hoc* or a general basis[46]) to submit a dispute to the jurisdiction of an arbitrator or an arbitration tribunal. If the agreement were solely founded in Yugoslav law, it would not sufficiently deal with matters relating to the acquisition of statehood and subsequent issues of statehood. Similarly, if the agreement were founded in international law, it could only bind the Republics themselves in so far as they were deemed to have international personality as States *in statu nascendi*,[47] and only to the extent that they were deemed to have consented to the procedure.

In the event, the agreement on arbitration was essentially contained in the Declaration adopted by the Conference on Yugoslavia. Although it was approved by all the participants of the Conference, it cannot readily be seen as a treaty or other form of binding commitment. Rather, it

[42] See Opinion No. 11, loc. cit. above (n. 8), p. 1588.

[43] This assumes, of course, that the FRY is not the continuation of the SFRY: below, nn. 224–32.

[44] That, at the time of the creation of the arbitration procedure, the situation was essentially internal to the SFRY, was in some respects reflected in the composition of the Arbitration Commission. The Arbitration Commission in the first instance contained judges from constitutional courts across Europe, suggesting that the *lex arbitri* was intended to be Yugoslav law and that the Commission was to enquire *inter alia* into the legitimacy and effects of the secession of Slovenia and Croatia under the Yugoslav Constitution.

[45] It was open to question whether the leaders of the Serbian enclave within Croatia (which had constituted itself as the Serbian Autonomous Republic of Krajina) could have been considered 'relevant authorities' for the purposes of the dispute settlement procedure.

[46] The difference between *ad hoc* and general *compromis* is that in the latter case, States agree to submit all or definite classes of disputes to a tribunal (usually an arbitral institution). In the latter case, there is usually the need for a further 'special agreement' or 'implementing *compromis*' to outline the details of the procedure to be adopted and the issues that the tribunal is to deal with. See Oellers-Frahm, 'Compromis', in *Encyclopaedia of Public International Law*, vol. 1 (1991), p. 712.

[47] See Crawford, *The Creation of States in International Law* (1979), pp. 391–6; Brownlie, op. cit. above (n. 38), p. 79.

appears to be in the form of a 'gentleman's agreement' incorporating a declaration of intention or preliminary agreement to submit disputes to arbitration. As Pellet suggests of the Declaration creating the Commission, '[i]l s'agit . . . d'un acte concerté non conventionnel sans valeur juridique obligatoire'.[48] Thus, although there was nothing to prevent the EC creating an Arbitration Commission pursuant to the Declaration, the 'relevant parties' were in no sense obliged to submit their differences to it.[49] Indeed, it is likely that were they to do so, a further 'implementing *compromis*' would be necessary in order to lay down the details of the procedure to be followed, or at least the expression of *ad hoc* consent.

The initial terms of reference of the Arbitration Commission were supplemented in a joint statement of 3 September 1991, which specified that the Chairman of the EC Peace Conference would transmit to the Arbitration Commission the issues submitted for arbitration, and that the results of the Commission's deliberations would then be returned to the Peace Conference through its chairman.[50] The intercession of the Chairman of the Peace Conference in the arbitration procedure would not be significant if he merely represented a channel of communication. It would, however, significantly alter the nature of the procedure if the Chairman were to involve himself, as he later did, in determining the questions that were ultimately to be addressed by the Commission.[51] In the latter case, the Commission would find itself in the position not of arbitrating between two parties, but rather of delivering a legal opinion to the Conference as an advisory organ.

In fact, of its first ten opinions, six resulted from references to the Commission by the Chairman of the Peace Conference (Lord Carrington), two of which had been initiated by Serbia but were redrafted by the Chairman. The other four (relating to the conditions for recognition) were referred to the Commission by the Council of Ministers of the EC. That the Commission considered itself obliged to respond to the request of the Council to deliver opinions on the diplomatic recognition of the Republics lends some ambiguity as to the States or institutions to which it was responsible. Indeed, what serves to confuse matters is that the creation of the Commission was in effect initiated under the auspices of the EC in an extraordinary ministerial meeting of the Council of

[48] Pellet, loc. cit. above (n. 19) (1991), p. 331.

[49] This is the case irrespective of the fact that the Declaration provides that the relevant authorities '*will* submit their differences' to the Arbitration Commission (emphasis added): Joint Statement, loc. cit. above (n. 1).

[50] Interlocutory Decision, loc. cit. above (n. 6), p. 1520.

[51] Cf. Schwebel, 'Was the Capacity to Request an Advisory Opinion Wider in the Permanent Court of International Justice than it is in the International Court of Justice?', this *Year Book*, 62 (1991), p. 77.

Ministers[52] and that it was funded primarily from the EC budget.[53] It would appear nevertheless that the Commission was not intended to be an organ of the Community, but rather one of the Peace Conference as a separate entity. Its response to the request of the EC for opinions may presumably be explained by the fact that the EC and its Member States were members of the Conference. As will be seen below, however, many of the confusions that attached to the Arbitration Commission's initial terms of reference were subsequently remedied when its constitution was revised and clarified on 27 January 1993.[54] That initiative was undoubtedly prompted by the first of two challenges that were raised by the FRY against the jurisdiction of the Commission.

2.3. *The First Challenge to Jurisdiction*[55]

The competence of the Commission to render 'opinions' on issues put before it by the Chairman of the Commission and the Council of Ministers of the EC went unchallenged for the first seven of its fifteen opinions. When it came to deal in detail with issues relating to the terms of succession in June 1992, however, its competence was challenged by Serbia and Montenegro. The Chairman of the Arbitration Commission was informed by the Presidents of Montenegro (Momir Bulatovic) and Serbia (Slobodan Milosevic) that they challenged the Commission's competence to give an opinion on the latest three questions (which were to form Opinions 8–10) submitted to it by the Chairman of the Conference for Peace in Yugoslavia.[56] They contended that: (i) the questions did not fall within the mandate given to the European Community under the terms of the Brioni agreement; (ii) that outstanding matters between the various Republics should be resolved by

[52] The Community and its Member States convened the Conference 'under their aegis'. They agreed to 'ensure the Chairmanship of the Conference' and stipulated that the proceedings would be 'conducted on their behalf by a Chairman on the basis of a mandate from them': Joint Statement, loc. cit. above (n. 3).

[53] Pellet notes that '[d]ès sa première réunion, la Commission décida d'ailleurs que "le relevé des frais engagés (voyages, traductions, fais de téléphone et de télécopie) serait centralisé à Paris et transmis ultérieurement à fins de remboursement à l'organe compétent de la Communauté", en l'espèce la Présidence'; Pellet, loc. cit. above (n. 19) (1991), p. 332.

[54] Note on Composition and Terms of Reference, *International Legal Materials*, 32 (1993), p. 1573.

[55] The terms 'jurisdiction' and 'competence' have been used loosely in the practice of the ICJ. Here, the approach advocated by Fitzmaurice will be used, namely, to use 'jurisdiction' as a term associated with the tribunal's entire jurisdictional field *ratione materiae, personae* or *termporis*; and 'competence' as the tribunal's capacity to determine a particular case: see Fitzmaurice, 'The Law and Procedure of the International Court of Justice', this *Year Book*, 34 (1958), p. 5, at pp. 8–9. Cf. Rosenne, *The Law and Practice of the International Court* (2nd edn., 1985), pp. 296–304; Pratap, *The Advisory Jurisdiction of the International Court* (1972), pp. 113–15.

[56] Interlocutory Decision, loc. cit. above (n. 6), p. 1518.

means of an overall agreement; and (iii) that those questions that could not be resolved by agreement should be submitted to the ICJ.[57]

These points were addressed by the Commission in what was termed an 'interlocutory decision' before going on to consider the questions that became the subject of Opinions 8 to 10. The first issue to be dealt with by the Commission in its interlocutory decision was whether it was in fact able to pronounce upon its own competence in the case at hand (the *compétence de la compétence*). This matter had been specifically contested by Serbia and Montenegro[58] which apparently considered that the jurisdiction of the Commission had to be determined by the parties to the arbitration proceedings rather than by the Commission itself.[59] The Commission initially pointed out that it had been established, not as Serbia and Montenegro had suggested under the Brioni Agreement of 7 July 1991,[60] but by the joint statement on Yugoslavia adopted on 27 August 1991.[61] It also noted that the arrangements set out in that document, although summary in nature, had been accepted by the six Yugoslav Republics. Moreover, it was clear 'from the terminology used and even the composition of the Commission that the intention was to create a body capable of resolving on the basis of law the differences which were to be submitted to it by the parties'.[62] This, as the Commission argued, 'precisely constitutes the definition of arbitration' as defined by the ICJ in the *Arbitral Award of 31 July 1989* case (1991).[63] It followed that since the Commission was an arbitral tribunal properly so-called, it was therefore competent to determine its own jurisdiction. Recalling the dicta of the ICJ in the *Nottebohm* case (*Preliminary*

57 Ibid., p. 1519.

58 Ibid.

59 There is some evidence in the Commission's decision that Serbia's objection on this point was itself the subject of objections by other Republics, the Commission considering it necessary to ascertain its competence 'independent of any dispute on this point' and without considering the 'admissibility of [the] preliminary objections': ibid. See also Pellet, loc. cit. above (n. 19) (1992), p. 223.

60 The Brioni Agreement, brokered by the EC, provided *inter alia* for the withdrawal of JNA forces from Slovenia in return for the suspension of the implementation of Croatia's and Slovenia's declarations of independence for a period of three months: *Keesing's Record of World Events* (hereinafter *Keesing's*), vol. 37, p. 38374 (1991).

61 The source of Serbia and Montenegro's confusion on the point is unclear: the Brioni Agreement itself made no mention of the Conference on Yugoslavia, let alone the Arbitration Commission that was later to be set up.

62 Interlocutory Decision, loc. cit. above (n. 6), p. 1519.

63 *ICJ Reports*, 1991, p. 50. In that case the ICJ made the following point:

'. . . when states sign an arbitration agreement, they are concluding an agreement with a very specific object and purpose: to entrust an arbitration with the task of settling a dispute in accordance with the terms agreed by the parties, who define in the agreement the jurisdiction of the tribunal and determine its limits. In the performance of the task entrusted to it, the tribunal "must conform to the terms by which the Parties have defined this task".'

(Ibid., p. 70.) It may be noted that this definition is not 'precisely' that advanced by the Arbitration Commission, in that it makes no mention of the legal nature of the issues to be decided.

Objection),[64] the Commission noted that this was a principle of international law that had been generally accepted in the field of arbitration 'since the Alabama case'.[65]

On this initial point the reasoning of the Commission is largely opaque and even confused. Although it is generally accepted that international tribunals have an inherent power to determine their own jurisdiction,[66] it is doubted whether the reasoning pursued by the Commission to establish this point is sound. The Commission suggested that this competence derived from its position as an arbitral tribunal. It is clear, as the ICJ suggested, that in cases where parties to a dispute refer the matter to arbitration by means of a *compromis*, the tribunal must be deemed to possess, *de minimis*, the competence to interpret the terms of the *compromis* unless specifically excluded from doing so.[67] If it were otherwise, the very object of arbitration would be defeated.[68] However, as suggested above, the Commission's initial mandate was not so much a *compromis* agreed between disputing States, with binding force under international law, as a declaration of intention on the part of the participating entities. In the absence of a further agreement between the disputing parties to submit the matter to the Commission for arbitration, it cannot be said that the Commission based its jurisdiction on the consent of the parties concerned. In fact, as the Commission later came to recognize, its role was rather one of delivering advisory opinions to the Conference from its position as a consultative organ.[69]

The Arbitration Commission, having established its power to determine jurisdictional issues, turned to examine its competence as regards the three questions submitted to it by the Chairman of the Peace Conference. In doing so, the Commission advanced two arguments in

[64] *ICJ Reports*, 1953, p. 4.

[65] Ibid., p. 119.

[66] See Fitzmaurice, loc. cit. above (n. 55), pp. 25–8. The competence of the ICJ in this regard is founded in Article 36(6) of the Statute of the ICJ, which provides that a dispute as to whether the Court has jurisdiction shall be settled by the Court. This is applicable to advisory cases by virtue of Article 68 of the Statute. See Pratap, op. cit. above (n. 55), p. 117.

[67] In doing so, an arbitral tribunal may consider both the intentions of the parties and the rules of law to be applied: *Rio Grande Irrigation and Land Co.* case (1923), *Reports of International Arbitral Awards*, vol. 6, p. 131. The competence of an arbitration tribunal to determine jurisdictional questions is, however, generally limited by the principle *extra compromissum arbiter nil facere potest*. See Schlochauer, 'Arbitration', in *Encyclopaedia of Public International Law*, vol. 1 (1991), p. 215, at p. 224.

[68] See Johnson, loc. cit. above (n. 31), p. 160.

[69] This point was alluded to by the Arbitration Commission in its interlocutory decision in so far as it referred to the full passage in the *Nottebohm* judgment which included the following passage: '[the principle that an international tribunal has the right to decide as to its own jurisdiction] assumes particular force when the international tribunal is no longer an arbitral tribunal constituted by virtue of a special agreement between the parties for the purpose of adjudicating on a particular dispute, but is an institution which has been pre-established by an international instrument defining its jurisdiction and regulating its operation': *Nottebohm (Preliminary Objection)*, *ICJ Reports*, 1953, p. 119. There are, however, difficulties with viewing the position of the Arbitration Commission as being analogous to that of the ICJ in this respect: see below, nn. 113–15.

favour of it performing the functions requested. First, it asserted that its competence derived from the consent of the parties as expressed in their participation in the work of the Commission.[70] Secondly, and implicitly recalling the opinion of the ICJ in the *Interpretation of Peace Treaties* case,[71] it argued that its competence derived from its position as an organ of the Conference, in which guise it was under an obligation to deliver an opinion when so requested by the Chairman.[72] As to the first point, the Commission relied upon the 'practice followed by the Conference . . . and by the responsible authorities in the various Yugoslav Republics'.[73] In that respect it noted that the Republic of Serbia had earlier taken the initiative of submitting three questions to the Conference (two of which had been considered by the Commission and formed Opinions 2 and 3), and that none of the Republics had challenged the Commission's competence in that respect. It thereby concluded that the Republics had recognized the Commission's competence 'in consultative issues as well'.[74]

In relying upon the imputed consent of the Republics as expressed by their participation in its procedures to ground its competence in the case before it, the Commission apparently comes close to invoking the doctrine of *forum prorogatum*[75] as operated in the context of the compulsory jurisdiction of the ICJ.[76] It would seem unlikely, however, that this doctrine could be invoked in the circumstances as the sole basis for the competence of the Commission. First, it is clear that although the Republic of Serbia had actively sought the opinions of the Commission in earlier cases, it had in no way signalled its willingness or desire for the Commission to exercise its competence with respect to the particular issues in hand.[77] Secondly, given that the Republic of Montenegro did not participate to the same extent in the early proceedings of the Commission, it may be questioned whether the FRY could be deemed to be bound by any commitments undertaken by Serbia in that regard. In reality, however, it would appear that the Arbitration Commission was not actually attempting to establish consent to its competence in the case before it, but rather more generally in relation to its role and activity as

[70] Interlocutory Decision, loc. cit. above (n. 6), p. 1520.

[71] *Interpretation of Peace Treaties with Bulgaria, Hungary and Romania*, *ICJ Reports*, 1950, p. 65, at p. 71.

[72] Interlocutory Decision, loc. cit. above (n. 6), p. 1521.

[73] Ibid., p. 1520.

[74] Ibid.

[75] See *Corfu Channel* case (*UK* v. *Albania*), *ICJ Reports*, 1948, p. 15; H. Lauterpacht, *The Development of International Law by the International Court* (1958), pp. 103–4; Rosenne, op. cit. above (n. 55), pp. 344–63.

[76] See Pellet, loc. cit. above (n. 19) (1992), p. 224.

[77] Cf. case concerning *Application of the Convention on the Prevention and Punishment of the Crime of Genocide (Bosnia and Herzegovina* v. *Yugoslavia (Serbia and Montenegro))*, *ICJ Reports*, 1993, p. 3, at pp. 17–18.

a consultative body. In that respect, it is the Commission's second argument that is crucial.

In its second argument, the Arbitration Commission noted that 'it was established in the framework of the Conference for Peace as a body of this Conference' and that '[r]eplying to the questions put by the Chairman of the Conference constitutes Commission participation in the work of the Conference, of which it is a body, and it would require conclusive reasons to bring it to refuse such a request'.[78] It accordingly considered that in the case at hand, it could see 'no reason to refuse to perform its functions'.[79] With respect to this point, it is very clear that the Arbitration Commission had in mind[80] the dicta of the ICJ in the *Peace Treaties* case.[81] In that case, the ICJ had stated that:

> [t]he consent of States, parties to a dispute, is the basis of the Court's jurisdiction in contentious cases. The situation is different in regard to advisory proceedings even where the Request for an Opinion relates to a legal question actually pending between States. The Court's reply is only of an advisory character: as such, it has no binding force. It follows that no State, whether a Member of the United Nations or not, can prevent the giving of an Advisory Opinion which the United Nations considers to be desirable in order to obtain enlightenment as to the course of action it should take.[82]

With this passage in mind, it can be assumed that the Commission considered that the apparent lack of consent on the part of the FRY was essentially irrelevant to the exercise of its competence in the case before it.[83] At the same time, it is clear that the Arbitration Commission considered itself to have a certain discretion as to whether or not it should exercise its competence: it suggested, in particular, that it might refuse to offer an opinion if there were 'conclusive reasons' for it not to do so.[84] This, however, appears to be primarily a question of propriety rather than one of jurisdiction.[85]

[78] Interlocutory Decision, loc. cit. above (n. 6), p. 1521.

[79] Ibid.

[80] This point was later made explicit by the Commission: see Reactions of the Members of the Arbitration Commission of the ICFY to the Statement made by the FRY Government on its Competence, *International Legal Materials*, 32 (1993), p. 1582, at p. 1583.

[81] In the *Interpretation of Peace Treaties with Bulgaria, Hungary and Romania, ICJ Reports*, 1950, p. 65.

[82] Ibid., p. 71; *Reservations to the Convention on Genocide, ICJ Reports*, 1951, p. 15, at pp. 19–20.

[83] *Peace Treaties* case, ibid, p. 70. See also *Western Sahara* case, *ICJ Reports*, 1975, p. 12. The Arbitration Commission accordingly appears to have adopted the position of the ICJ with respect to jurisdiction, rather than that of the PCIJ: see *Eastern Carelia* case, *PCIJ*, Series B, No. 5 (1923). See generally Rosenne, op. cit. above (n. 55), pp. 698–716; Pomerance, *The Advisory Function of the International Court in the League and UN Eras* (1973), pp. 279–95; Pratap, op. cit. above (n. 55), pp. 150 ff. On the position with respect to the Inter-American Court, see Buergenthal, 'The Advisory Practice of the Inter-American Human Rights Court', *American Journal of International Law*, 79 (1985), p. 1.

[84] Interlocutory Decision, loc. cit. above (n. 6), p. 1521.

[85] Pratap, op. cit. above (n. 55), p. 142. He notes later, however, that in the *Peace Treaties* case, questions of propriety and jurisdiction were somewhat confused: ibid., p. 148.

As far as the ICJ is concerned, the exercise of its discretion under Article 65 of the Statute is determined by a number of interrelated *desiderata* relating to its role as the principal judicial body of the United Nations. Broadly speaking, the main considerations are: (i) that the court should confine its opinions to questions of an essentially legal nature;[86] (ii) that it should not offer an opinion if to do so would circumvent the principle that a State is not obliged to allow its disputes to be submitted to judicial settlement without its consent;[87] and (iii) that it should only respond to a request if it relates to matters that fall properly within the field of competence of the requesting organ.[88] In that the Arbitration Commission clearly considered its advisory jurisdiction to be analogous to that of the ICJ, it is not surprising to find that it addressed some of these points.

As regards the first point, the Commission confirmed that the questions that had been put to it were essentially legal questions and that as such, 'far from constituting an obstacle to the Arbitration Commission's exercising its competence, [it] is, on the contrary, a justification: as the arbitral body of the Conference, the Commission can give a judgement only in law, in the absence of any express authorization to the contrary from the parties, it being specified that in this case it is called upon to express opinions on the legal rules applying'.[89] There is little doubt that the Commission was correct on this point. The questions to which it was asked to respond, while certainly having a political dimension, essentially related to the issues of statehood (the expiration of the SFRY and the emergence of the FRY) and to the principles of succession, and were susceptible to judicial determination. This conclusion is not necessarily affected by the somewhat abstract nature of the questions asked. The Commission might have reached a different conclusion, however, had the point at issue been the substance of Opinions 4–7, in which the Arbitration Commission had acted primarily as a fact-finding body for the EC and its Member States (in determining whether the four Republics had fulfilled the necessary conditions for recognition).

As regards the second point, it was undoubtedly clear to the Arbitration Commission that the questions it was asked to address related to a legal dispute between States (even possibly to the merits of that

[86] *Conditions of Admission of a State to Membership in the UN*, *ICJ Reports*, 1947–8, p. 57, at p. 61; *Certain Expenses* case, *ICJ Reports*, 1962, p. 151. See generally Greig, 'The Advisory Jurisdiction of the International Court and the Settlement of Disputes between States', *International and Comparative Law Quarterly*, 15 (1966), p. 325.

[87] *Western Sahara* case, *ICJ Reports*, 1975, p. 12. Cf. *Eastern Carelia* case, *PCIJ*, Series B, No. 5 (1923), where it was stated that 'no State can, without its consent, be compelled to submit its disputes with other States either to mediation or to arbitration, or to any other kind of pacific settlement': p. 27.

[88] *ILO Administrative Tribunal* case, *ICJ Reports*, 1956, pp. 83–4; Fitzmaurice, loc. cit. above (n. 55), p. 139. See also Fitzmaurice, 'The Law and Practice of the International Court of Justice: International Organizations and Tribunals', this *Year Book*, 29 (1952), p. 1, at pp. 45–55.

[89] Interlocutory Decision, loc. cit. above (n. 6), p. 1521.

dispute[90]), and that the FRY had certainly not explicitly consented to its competence on the point. As suggested above, however, the Commission did appear to consider that some form of consent could be imputed to the FRY in virtue of its participation in the activities of the Commission at an earlier stage. One may recall in this regard that a significant consideration in the *Eastern Carelia* case had been the fact that Russia was not a Member of the League of Nations nor a party to the Statute of the Permanent Court. As far as the ICJ was concerned, this was a major point of distinction, such that in the *Western Sahara* case it noted that 'Spain is a Member of the United Nations and has accepted the provisions of the Charter and Statute; it has thereby in general given its consent to the exercise by the Court of its advisory jurisdiction'.[91] If there is sufficient basis for an analogy being drawn between the role of the ICJ and that of the Arbitration Commission (a point which is somewhat doubtful), it may be argued that the FRY's participation in the work of the Commission and the Conference can be assimilated to prior consent.[92]

With respect to the third point, the Commission noted that the Conference for Peace in Yugoslavia had a mission 'to reestablish peace for all in Yugoslavia and to achieve lasting solutions which respect all legitimate concerns and legitimate aspirations'.[93] The Commission considered that in attempting to enlighten the Conference on the legal aspects of problems encountered it was acting entirely within the role entrusted to it by the EC, its Member States, and the six Republics. It might be questioned, however, whether the Arbitration Commission had really done enough to establish the institutional interest in the case at hand. Certainly, Serbia had participated in the Conference on Yugoslavia and had accepted the creation of the Arbitration Commission, but whether that participation is sufficient to establish a legitimate interest on the part of the Conference in the status of the FRY under international law is open to question. Further, it is doubtful whether a strict analogy can be drawn with the position of the ICJ as the principal judicial organ of the UN, in so far as the role of the ICJ is set out in the UN Charter, which is ratified by Member States, and which defines in concrete terms the purposes of the organization itself. These matters come into focus in

[90] The *Eastern Carelia* case has been distinguished on a number of occasions on the basis that the question to be addressed did not address the merits of the dispute: see *Peace Treaties* case, *ICJ Reports*, 1950, p. 65, at p. 70; *Interpretation of Article 3, Paragraph 2, of the Treaty of Lausanne* case, *PCIJ*, Series B, No. 12.

[91] *Western Sahara* case, *ICJ Reports*, 1975, p. 12. That Spain was only said to have given its consent 'in general' may suggest that in certain circumstances consent may not be imputed from membership alone.

[92] Pomerance, op. cit. above (n. 83), p. 295. The fact that the PCIJ Statute was not organically linked to membership of the League of Nations is often cited as one of the reasons for the more tentative approach that was apparently adopted by the PCIJ: see Rosenne, op. cit. above (n. 55), pp. 60–70.

[93] Ibid.

the second challenge directed against the jurisdiction of the Arbitration Commission.[94]

2.4. *The Second Challenge to Jurisdiction*

The FRY launched a second assault upon the jurisdiction of the Commission on 30 April 1993. On this occasion the challenge related to the Commission's competence to deliver opinions relating to the division of the assets and liabilities of the SFRY, and to deliver advisory opinions on the principles by which the succession of States to the SFRY would be effected.[95] In doing so, the FRY made a number of inter-related points. First, it considered 'unacceptable' the idea that the Commission should discuss the principles upon which succession should be determined 'prior to any substantial discussion of these principles within the Succession Group of the Conference on Yugoslavia'.[96] Secondly, recalling its earlier challenge to the Commission, it argued that the Commission 'was not established or composed for arbitration purposes' and that its work within the Conference on Yugoslavia 'has been seriously in breach of both the law and procedure and implementation of material law'.[97] Thirdly, it reiterated that all disputes arising as regards the division of assets and liabilities 'should be referred by agreement either to the Permanent Court of Arbitration . . . or to an *ad hoc* arbitration court'.[98] In that regard it pointed out that it considered arbitration proceedings as being 'proceedings before a court of law in the sense of general international law and not as proceedings before the Arbitration Commission presided by Mr Badinter'.[99] Finally, it was argued that the opinions of the Commission were 'doctrinary in the sense of article 38(d) of the Statute of the International Court of Justice, which do not constitute a legal ground for any valid decision'. Accordingly, the FRY determined that it 'shall consider null and void and non-binding any

[94] The Commission did not comment on the final two points raised by Serbia and Montenegro, namely that the questions should be resolved by the parties concerned, and that outstanding disputes should be referred to the ICJ. It may be presumed that the Commission considered these issues not to be relevant given its assumption of competence in the matter at hand. It is worth noting, nevertheless, that the ICJ did not consider this statement sufficient to establish a prima facie basis for its jurisdiction in the *Genocide* case: case concerning *Application of the Convention on the Prevention and Punishment of the Crime of Genocide, ICJ Reports*, 1993, p. 3. It was considered that the statement did not make clear whether it was intended as an immediate commitment to accept unconditionally the unilateral submission of a wide range of legal disputes; or as a commitment solely to submit the three questions raised by the Chairman of the Commission; or as 'no more than the enunciation of a general policy of favouring juidicial settlement': ibid., p. 18.

[95] Statement of 30 April 1993 by the Government of the Federal Republic of Yugoslavia, *International Legal Materials*, 32 (1993), p. 1581.

[96] Ibid.

[97] Ibid.

[98] Ibid.

[99] Ibid., p. 1582.

opinion of the Commission adopted in the procedure to which it has not agreed'.[100]

These objections were contained in a 'Statement' issued by the FRY issued to the Steering Committee of the Conference on Yugoslavia. While they were not directly addressed to the Commission itself (a fact that might be explained by the FRY's contention that the Commission did not have the power to determine its own jurisdiction[101]), the Arbitration Commission 'considered it an appropriate opportunity to set out the scope and limits of its competence'. Nevertheless, the document containing the Commission's response was not entitled, as in the earlier case, an 'interlocutory decision', but rather merely 'Reactions of the members of the Arbitration Commission'.[102] Further, it was made clear that the document reflected the opinions of 'members of the Arbitration Commission' rather than of the Commission as a whole, and that it 'in no way prejudges . . . the competence of the Commission in this matter if it is challenged on grounds which they deem justified'.[103] In other words, the document was an informal response issued by the individual members acting *ex officio* and in a collective capacity, which did not in any way prejudice the ability of the Commission to address other matters that merited an official response. Why the Commission took the unusual step of issuing only an informal response is unclear. Although it had not been directly asked to respond to the statement issued by the FRY, it might have been appropriate for the Commission to have addressed the issues while acting *proprio motu*.[104] Equally, the suggestion that it should only respond officially in cases where the challenge is 'justified' would appear to entail an unwarranted element of prejudgment.

By this stage, the constitution of the Arbitration Commission had been placed on a new footing. Its composition and terms of reference had been re-defined in a document dated 27 January 1993 issued by the Steering Committee of the Conference on Yugoslavia.[105] Although the document did not provide any firmer legal foundation for the Arbitration Commission, it did specifically lay down the terms of the Commission's contentious and advisory jurisdiction, and altered its terms of member-

[100] Ibid.

[101] Above, nn. 56–8.

[102] Reactions of the members of the Arbitration Commission, *International Legal Materials*, 32 (1993), p. 1582.

[103] Ibid.

[104] As Judge McNair noted, 'An International tribunal cannot regard a question of jurisdiction solely as a question *inter partes*. That aspect does not exhaust the matter. The Court itself, acting *proprio motu*, must be satisfied that any State which is brought before it by virtue of such a Declaration has consented to the jurisdiction': *Anglo-Iranian Oil Co.* case, judgment of 22 July 1952, *ICJ Reports*, 1952, p. 93, at p. 116 (separate opinion). See also Judge Cordova, dissenting opinion in *ILO Administrative Tribunal* case, *ICJ Reports*, 1956, p. 163.

[105] *International Legal Materials*, 32 (1993), p. 1573.

ship.[106] According to paragraph 3 of that document, the Commission is competent to:

(*a*) Decide, with binding force for the parties concerned, any dispute submitted to it by the parties thereto upon authorization by the Co-Chairmen of the Steering Committee of the Conference;
(*b*) Give its advice as to any legal question submitted to it by Co-Chairmen of the Steering Committee of the Conference.[107]

The Commission pointed out that the six questions relating to the principles of succession had been referred to it for the purpose of receiving an advisory opinion according to the terms of paragraph 3(*b*). The implications of this were twofold. First, the competence of the Commission as an advisory body stemmed 'not from the consent of the parties concerned but from the mere fact of referral to it by the Co-Chairmen of the Conference'.[108] The opinions constituted the Commission's participation in the work of the Conference and therefore were to be given not to the States concerned but to the Co-Chairman 'in order to furnish them with the information needed to take decisions'.[109] Secondly, the opinions were essentially advisory in nature and possessed, in the words of the ICJ, 'no binding force'.[110] However, they did constitute a 'subsidiary means for the determination of rules of law' according to the terms of Article 38, paragraph 1(*d*), of the Statute of the ICJ. The Commission noted, in the manner of a parenthesis, that if the parties were not able to reach an agreement in their negotiations, it was open for them to refer the matter to the Arbitration Commission under paragraph 3(*a*) or to any other adjudicatory or arbitral body of their choice.[111]

[106] Ibid. Pursuant to Article 4 of the terms of reference, the Arbitration Commission adopted a set of Rules of Procedure, ibid., p. 1575. The Rules stipulate, *inter alia*, that the members of the Commission shall be 'completely independent and impartial' (rule 1.1) and that they shall maintain 'absolute secrecy in respect of the proceedings of the Commission' (rule 1.4); that the permanent members shall elect one of their number to be Chairperson for a three-year term of office (rule 2.1.); that it should be supported by a Secretariat with the necessary staff (rule 3.1.); that the Commission should meet in Paris unless otherwise decided (rule 4.1); that 'proceedings shall be as informal as possible' (rule 5.1.) and should be confidential until the opinion has been disclosed (rule 5.4); that in advisory proceedings the proceedings should normally be exclusively in writing (rule 7.1) and that in exceptional circumstances the Commission may decide to hear representatives of the parties concerned or other persons (rule 7.4); that decisions and opinions shall be adopted by majority vote, abstentions not being permitted (rule 8.1) but that no record of the number of votes constituting the majority should be made (rule 8.3.1.); that decisions and opinions shall state the grounds on which they are given (rule 8.2) and that any member in the minority may attach to the decision a brief dissenting opinion (rule 8.3.2); that while decisions shall be addressed to the parties concerned (rule 8.4.2.), opinions shall be addressed to the Co-Chairmen of the Steering Committee of the Conference and shall not be made public except on authority of the Co-Chairmen (rule 8.4.2.).

[107] Ibid.

[108] Reactions, loc. cit. above (n. 102), p. 1583.

[109] Ibid.

[110] *Interpretation of Peace Treaties* case, *ICJ Reports*, 1950, p. 65, at p. 71.

[111] Reactions, loc. cit. above (n. 102), p. 1583.

Although considerable problems remained, the reactions of the Commission to these points were considerably clearer and less objectionable than those produced following the first challenge. Not only was its mandate much more precise, making clear that it had both a contentious and an advisory jurisdiction, but it did not confuse matters by characterizing its activities as essentially those of an arbitral body. A question that might be raised, however, is whether the FRY could be deemed to have tacitly accepted the consultative jurisdiction of the Arbitration Commission as established in January 1993 in virtue of its participation in the work of the Conference on Yugoslavia. Although the Commission had been reconstituted, it was still only a creation of the Conference and lacked any treaty basis. At the same time it is difficult to argue, given the fact that the Commission was officially reconstituted in 1993 with a new mandate and a different composition, that the Republic's initial approval of the work of the Conference and its organs still had any significance. Indeed, since June 1992, the FRY had consistently opposed the work of the Arbitration Commission and therefore, as at April 1993, it could be assimilated to a third party, or a non-consenting member of the organization. If that is the case, it is arguable that its position was analogous to that of Russia in the *Eastern Carelia* case. In that case the PCIJ considered that, owing to the fact that the dispute involved a non-Member of the League, the exercise its advisory jurisdiction 'could take place only by virtue of their [Russia's] consent'.[112]

Although the ICJ has not followed the practice of the PCIJ as regards the exercise of its advisory jurisdiction, a number of considerations point towards taking a somewhat stricter line on the question of consent in the context of the Conference than that adopted by the ICJ. Whereas the UN exists under a constituent treaty defining its objects and purposes and enjoys a 'large measure of international personality',[113] the same cannot be said of the Conference for Peace in Yugoslavia. It has no constituent instrument, possesses only an ill-defined set of 'organs',[114] and does not prescribe the rights and obligations of the participating States. It is one thing for States to accept, by treaty, limitations on their sovereignty through membership in an organization where the purposes and powers of the organization are clearly set out,[115] and where the rights and

[112] *Eastern Carelia* case, *PCIJ*, Series B, No. 5 (1923), p. 27. Cf. *Western Sahara* case, *ICJ Reports*, 1975, p. 12, para. 30.

[113] *Reparation for Injuries Suffered in the Service of the United Nations* case, *ICJ Reports*, 1949, p. 174.

[114] The only 'organs' as such that might be associated with the Conference are the Secretariat, the four Working Groups (Succession Issues; Institutions; Minorities Rights; and Economic Relations), the Arbitration Commission, and the Steering Committee.

[115] Lauterpacht could see no 'reason why the sovereignty of States should be protected from a procedure to which they have consented in advance as members of the United Nations, of ascertaining the law through a pronouncement which, notwithstanding its authority, is not binding on them': Lauterpacht, op. cit. above (n. 75), pp. 357–8. Fitzmaurice points out, however, that the consent is in itself only to a permissive jurisdiction, loc. cit. above (n. 55), pp. 142–3.

obligations of the States *vis à vis* the organization are defined in advance. It is quite another for such limitations to be imputed to a State in virtue of its 'participation' in an organization with an ill-defined and open-ended mandate.

This argument is not displaced by the fact that the opinions of the Arbitration Commission are not binding. As the Commission noted itself, its opinions can nevertheless be treated as an authoritative statement of the law and would thereby be likely to affect the interests of the parties concerned when, and if, they came to negotiate on the matter.[116] This point was not lost on the FRY, which later declared its intention of discontinuing its participation in the Working Group on Succession Issues, ostensibly because: '[i]n practice the opinions of the Commission, as an advisory body of the International Conference on the Former Yugoslavia, on the basis of which the Yugoslav participants at the Conference were to adopt relevant decisions by consensus taking also into account the Commission's opinion, were taken as judgements and served as a basis for making concrete decisions on relevant issues concerning the Yugoslav crisis'.[117] The FRY evidently objected to the activities of a 'quasi-judicial' organ exercising jurisdiction over matters subject to dispute without its consent, and on the basis that there was some organizational interest on the part of the Conference.

3. The Opinions of the Commission

The Arbitration Commission issued a total of fifteen 'opinions' in its consultative capacity dealing with a range of issues including questions of statehood, recognition, self-determination and succession. It is not intended to consider in detail the opinions delivered to the EC Council of Ministers relating to the application of the Community Guidelines on Recognition (Opinions 4–7).[118] In those opinions, the Commission did not attempt to interpret or apply general principles of international law, but rather acted as a fact-finding body in assessing whether the various Republics had fulfilled the criteria for recognition laid down in the Guidelines. As such, they are of less interest than the other opinions in

[116] On the status of advisory opinions of the ICJ, see Pratap, op. cit. above (n. 55), pp. 227–34; Rosenne, op. cit. above (n. 55), pp. 744–7; Greig, loc. cit. above (n. 86), pp. 360–5; Hambro, 'The Authority of the Advisory Opinions of the International Court of Justice', *International and Comparative Law Quarterly*, 3 (1954), p. 2.

[117] Letter of 2 July 1993, *International Legal Materials*, 32 (1993), p. 1584.

[118] See generally Warbrick, 'Recognition of States: Part 2', *International and Comparative Law Quarterly*, 42 (1993), p. 433; Rich, 'Recognition of States: The Collapse of Yugoslavia and the Soviet Union', *European Journal of International Law*, 4 (1993), p. 36; Weller, 'The International Response to the Dissolution of the Socialist Federal Republic of Yugoslavia', *American Journal of International Law*, 86 (1992), p. 569.

which the Arbitration Commission offered its own interpretation of international law in the context of the dismemberment of the SFRY. Rather than follow the pattern of the opinions entirely in sequence, it is intended to address the issues that arise under three general headings: statehood (secession/dismemberment), self-determination, and succession.

3.1. *Statehood (Secession/Dismemberment)*

The first question addressed by the Arbitration Commission arose from a difference in opinion between the Republics as to the legal nature of the crisis within the SFRY. On the one hand, Serbia contended that the Republics which had proclaimed, or intended to proclaim, independence were in fact seeking to secede from the SFRY, whose international personality would nevertheless continue.[119] The other Republics (Croatia, Slovenia, Macedonia and Bosnia-Herzegovina) considered that there was 'no question of secession', but rather one of the 'disintegration or breaking-up of the SFRY as the result of the concurring will of a number of Republics'.[120] Accordingly the personality of the SFRY would be extinguished and the six Republics would be considered equal successors in title.

The position adopted by the Arbitration Commission to this first question was significant in so far as it formed the basic framework for the later opinions. Although the question was formulated in terms of the identity and continuity of the SFRY, its significance essentially lay in the field of State succession. Traditional doctrine in the law of succession has tended to differentiate between cases of 'total' and 'partial' succession.[121] If the Republics were to be seen as seceding from the Federation, the personality of the Federation would remain intact and it would continue to remain bound by existing international obligations and would retain its membership in international organizations.[122] If, on the other hand, the new Republics emerged as a result of the general disintegration, or dismemberment[123] of the SFRY, succession would be 'total' in the sense that each of the Republics would be an equal successor in title. While this does not necessarily entail that there would be a corresponding total or partial succession to the legal relations of the previous sovereign,[124] the

[119] Opinion No. 1, loc. cit. above (n. 5), p. 1494.

[120] Ibid.

[121] See O'Connell, *State Succession in Municipal Law and International Law* (1967), vol. 1, pp. 3–4; Jennings and Watts, *Oppenheim's International Law*, vol. 1 (9th edn., 1992), pp. 208–9.

[122] Below, n. 239.

[123] The term 'disintegration' was used by the Chairman of the Peace Conference in the first question addressed to the Arbitration Commission, to describe the breaking-up of the SFRY. By contrast, the Commission used the term 'dismemberment'. Although the latter term appears to have more 'active' connotations, it is clear that neither is a legal term of art, and that both describe the same process.

[124] O'Connell, op. cit. above (n. 121), p. 4.

evidence points towards a greater degree of succession in cases of dismemberment than in cases of revolutionary secession.[125] Indeed in cases of dismemberment there would, by necessity, have to be a reapportionment of the assets and liabilities of the parent State.[126] Thus issues of succession were inevitably predicated upon an understanding as to the issue of continuity or otherwise of the State. Before turning to the question of personality, however, it is worthwhile briefly considering the interrelationship between principles of continuity and succession.

3.1.1. *Succession and identity/continuity*

The traditional distinction between the identity or continuity of the State, and State succession, is both artificial,[127] and marked by confused terminology.[128] The issue arose historically with the abstraction of the concept of sovereignty in the eighteenth and nineteenth centuries when a distinction came to be drawn between the legal consequences that attach to changes in government on the one hand, and changes in sovereignty on the other.[129] It has become clear, however, that the notion of statehood itself is not sufficiently precise as to determine clearly in all cases where a change in the condition of a State has occurred, whether or not the personality of the State is affected (i.e. whether or not it 'continues'). Difficulties have arisen, for example, in distinguishing between cases of lawful annexation or union,[130] and between cases of

[125] With respect to conventional obligations, a number of cases point to the application of the clean slate doctrine in cases of revolutionary secession: e.g., secession of the Spanish American Colonies; secession of Texas, 1840; secession of Cuba, 1898; secession of Finland, 1919. See generally O'Connell, *State Succession in Municipal Law and International Law* (1967), vol. 2, pp. 88–100.

[126] This is particularly the case with respect to immovable property located in the territory of third States: see Article 18(1)(*b*), Vienna Convention on Succession of States in Respect of State Property, Archives and Debts 1983, *International Legal Materials*, 22 (1983), p. 306.

[127] See e.g., Brownlie, op. cit. above, (n. 38). He comments: 'Unfortunately the general categories of "continuity" and "state succession", and the assumption of a neat distinction between them, only make a difficult subject more confused by masking the variations of circumstance and the complexities of the legal problems which arise in practice. "Succession" and "continuity" are levels of abstraction unfitted to dealing with specific issues': pp. 82–3.

[128] 'Continuity' as a term has been used both with respect to the personality of a State and as regards the rights and obligations assumed by successor States. See, e.g., O'Connell, op. cit. above (n. 121), pp. 9–25. This assimilation, however, was central to his thesis that the boundary between change of sovereignty and change of government in terms of their legal consequences should be reassessed: ibid., p. 6. Similarly, the term 'succession' is not infrequently used in reference to territorial entities which retain the personality of the parent State in the face of dramatic changes in its condition, e.g., announcement of Finland in relation to Russia, 30 December 1991, cited in Broms, 'The Agreement on the Foundations of Relations between the Republic of Finland and the Russian Federation', *Finnish Yearbook of International Law*, 3 (1992), p. 615, at p. 620.

[129] O'Connell, op. cit. above (n. 121), p. 5. For an early view that admitted no such distinction, see Grotius, *De jure belli et pacis* (1625), book II, xiv, p. 11; Vattel, *Le Droit des gens* (1758), book II, xii, p. 191. For the modern view, see Wright, 'The Status of Germany and the Peace Proclamation', *American Journal of International Law*, 46 (1952), p. 299, at p. 307; Crawford, op. cit. above (n. 47), pp. 28–9.

[130] e.g. unification of Italy, 1848–1870.

secession or dismemberment.[131] In each category, the factual circumstances may well be similar, the conclusion as to continuity being derived from extraneous elements of procedure or assertion. The view that the unification of Italy, for example, came about through a process of annexation by the Kingdom of Sardinia in the period 1848–70, rather than through a union of independent States, appears to be more a matter of perception and emphasis than one of fact.[132] Similarly, on the facts alone, the break-up of Austria-Hungary can equally plausibly be argued either as a case of dismemberment involving the extinction of the personalities of Austria and Hungary, or as a case of the dissolution of the union and the corresponding secession of several national groups.[133] Ultimately, while the facts upon which statehood is premised are always relevant, they are not necessarily sufficient as the sole determining considerations of continuity.

In most cases, questions of personality and succession go hand in hand and for that reason tend to become entangled. It is undoubtedly the case that the characterization of a particular situation as one of continuity or discontinuity will be heavily influenced by the respective claims made by interested parties. These claims themselves will necessarily reflect the interests of the States concerned as regards questions of succession. For example, in the case of Austria in 1919, the difference in opinion arose primarily in relation to the issue of reparations; Austria denied continuity in order to avoid liability for reparations; the Allies, by contrast, wanted to establish continuity for converse reasons.[134] Similarly, the contention advanced by the USSR in 1919 that it did not represent the continuation of the Russian State may be attributed, in part at least, to the desire to avoid liability for the debts of its Tsarist predecessor.[135]

Whatever their interrelationship in practice there are, however, several reasons for clearly maintaining the distinction between identity and succession. First, on an abstract level, issues of identity and succession should be distinguished in so far as the former relate to the existence and identification of the legal subject, and the latter to the rights and duties that are to be assumed by a legal subject once it comes into existence or

[131] e.g. dismemberment of Austria, 1918; secession of Pakistan, 1947; dismemberment of Mali Federation, 1959; dismemberment of United Arab Republic, 1961.

[132] Anzilotti argued in favour of Union: *Rivista di diritto internazionale*, 6 (1912); see also *Costa* v. *Military Service Commission of Genoa* (1939), *Annual Digest*, vol. 9, No. 13. For the view that it was a case of annexation, see Marek, *Identity and Continuity of States in Public International Law* (1954), pp. 191–8.

[133] See generally Feilchenfeld, *Public Debt and State Succession* (1931), pp. 431–755; Udina, *L'estinzione dell'imperio Austro-Ungarico nel diritto internazionale* (1933); Borchard, 'Sequestered Private Property and American Claims—The Treaties of Versailles and Berlin', *American Journal of International Law*, 19 (1925), pp. 358–9; Anzilotti, loc. cit. above (n. 132), p. 86; Marek, op. cit. above (n. 132), pp. 199–236.

[134] See generally Marek, op. cit. above (n. 132), pp. 199–236.

[135] See, Oppenheim, op. cit. above (n. 121), p. 205.

when it takes over responsibility for a new piece of territory.[136] As such, the problem of State succession only arises once a conclusion is reached as to the issue of State personality.[137] Secondly, it can be seen that problems of succession and personality do not always coincide. For example, if island State A were to lose permanently the entirety of its territory as a result of some natural occurrence (such as a rise in the sea level), the only question involved would be that of personality; the issue of succession would simply not be relevant.[138] Finally, it has to be admitted that whatever arguments might be put forward for eliminating the distinction between continuity and succession (or between 'succession of States' and 'succession of governments'),[139] as long as the law of succession is premised upon the distinction, it will have to be maintained.[140]

3.1.2. *The dismemberment of the SFRY*

On 8 October 1991, when the suspension of their declarations of independence came to an end, Croatia and Slovenia purported to secede from the Federation.[141] The question facing the Arbitration Commission, however, was whether the various acts of independence had, when

[136] As Marek comments, '[w]hereas the problem of State identity and continuity bears on the *identity of the subject* . . . the problem of succession relates to the identity of certain rights and obligations between *different subjects*': op. cit. above (n. 132), p. 10 (original emphasis). Article 2 of the Vienna Conventions on the Succession of States 1978 and 1983 defines succession as 'the replacement of one State by another in the responsibility for the international relations of territory'. It notably assumes that the question of personality has already been determined. See Crawford, 'The Contribution of Professor D.P. O'Connell to the Discipline of International Law', this *Year Book*, 51 (1980), p. 2, at p. 32.

[137] Hall, *International Law* (8th edn., 1924), p. 114; Crawford, op. cit. above (n. 47), p. 29.

[138] No doubt significant legal problems might arise from such an occurrence (e.g. in relation to the disposal of debts, the rights of former nationals in third States, and any interest in property held on the territory of third States). But these problems would not be resolved by reference to principles of succession.

[139] O'Connell advocated a return to the 18th century position (in which no distinction was made between succession of States or governments) overtly in order to ensure greater certainty (and arguably greater continuity) and suggested that the touchstone should be the degree of political, economic and social disruption: op. cit. above (n. 121), p. 25. Cf. O'Connell, 'Independence and Problems of State Succession', in O'Brien (ed.), *The New Nation in International Law and Diplomacy* (1965), p. 7, at p. 11.

[140] See Crawford, op. cit. above (n. 47), pp. 29–30; Marek, op. cit. above (n. 132), pp. 9–13.

[141] Croatia and Slovenia initially declared their independence on 25 June 1991 (*Keesing's*, vol. 38, p. 38274 (1991)). In its 'Declaration of Independence' Slovenia declared that '[o]n the basis of the right of the Slovene nation to self-determination . . . the people of the Republic of Slovenia have decided to establish an independent State, the Republic of Slovenia, which will no longer be part of the Socialist Federal Republic of Yugoslavia': Blaustein and Flanz (eds.), *Constitutions of the Countries of the World*, Release 92–6, p. 55.

Croatia issued both a 'Declaration on the Establishment of the Sovereign and Independent Republic of Croatia' and a 'Constitutional Decision on the Sovereignty and Independence of the Republic of Croatia'. In the latter it was declared that, '[p]roceeding from the inalienable . . . right of the Croatian nation to self-determination, including the right of disassociation', Croatia was to establish herself as a 'sovereign and independent State'. Further, '[b]y this act Croatia initiates proceedings for disassociation from the other republics and from the SFRY': Blaustein and Glanz, ibid, Release 92–3, pp. 119, 123.

taken in conjunction, affected the continuing sovereignty of the SFRY to the extent that it could be said to have become extinct as a legal person. Dismemberment, as a term descriptive of a set of circumstances in which a State has ceased to exist by virtue of the disassociation of its various territorial elements, stands alongside other 'categories' of extinction such as merger,[142] absorption[143] and (formerly) annexation.[144] It is not a term of art, however, and is analytically useful only in so far as the range of situations it encompasses are analogous so as to form a coherent corpus of practice. In terms of actual (or posited) cases of dismemberment in the past century, most may be distinguished from that of the SFRY. A number of cases of dismemberment involved failed unions of pre-existing States (such as the United Arab Republic 1960,[145] the Union between Norway and Sweden 1905, and possibly the Mali Federation 1960[146]) and for that reason, the problems of disassociation were considerably less acute. Others were accompanied by an agreement between the parties concerned (USSR 1991,[147] and Czechoslovakia 1993[148]), and have more in common with cases of devolution or cession than of dismemberment. The best analogy is that of Austria-Hungary in 1918, but there the divergencies in views and practice as to the continuation or otherwise of Austria deprive it of much decisive value as a precedent.[149]

The approach adopted by the Arbitration Commission was on the face of it uncontroversial. As its starting point, it merely stated that 'the existence or disappearance of the State is a question of fact',[150] and in that respect the State is 'commonly defined as a community which consists of a territory and a population subject to an organized political authority'

[142] e.g. the union of Tanganyika and Zanzibar to create Tanzania in 1964. The union of Syria and Egypt to form the United Arab Republic was also intended to have extinguished the independent personalities of the two States (according to Arts. 1 and 58 of the Provisional Constitution of the UAR): see Cotran, 'Some Legal Aspects of the Formation of the United Arab Republic and the United Arab States', *International and Comparative Law Quarterly*, 8 (1959), p. 346.

[143] e.g. absorption of Congo Free State into Belgium in 1908; absorption of Montenegro into the Serb-Croat-Slovene State in 1919.

[144] Acquisition of territory by conquest is no longer permissible under international law; see Oppenheim, op. cit. above (n. 121), p. 699. For a more circumspect approach, see O'Connell, *International Law* (2nd edn., 1970), pp. 431–2.

[145] See generally Cotran, loc. cit. above (n. 142); Young, 'The State of Syria: Old or New?', *American Journal of International Law*, 56 (1962), p. 482.

[146] See generally Cohen, 'Legal Problems Arising from the Dissolution of the Mali Federation', this *Year Book*, 36 (1960), p. 375; Gandolfi, 'Naissance et mort sur le plan international d'un état éphémère: la Fédération du Mali', *Annuaire français de droit international*, 6 (1960), p. 881; Shaw, *Title to Territory in Africa* (1986), pp. 213–4.

[147] Agreement establishing the Commonwealth of Independent States, Alma Ata, 21 December 1991, *International Legal Materials*, 31 (1992), p. 138. The USSR was technically not a case of dismemberment in that Russia was deemed to continue the personality of the USSR: see generally Mullerson, 'The Continuity and Succession of States by Reference to the Former USSR and Yugoslavia', *International and Comparative Law Quarterly*, 42 (1993), p. 473.

[148] See Malenovsky, *Annvaire français de droit international*, 39 (1993), p.305.

[149] See Marek, op. cit. above (n. 132), p. 205.

[150] Opinion No. 1, loc. cit. above (n. 5), p. 1495.

and which is 'characterized by sovereignty'.[151] While the conditions outlined by the Arbitration Commission closely reflect the classical criteria for statehood,[152] its approach could be subject to two qualifications. First, strictly speaking, a State is not a 'fact' in the same way as other material objects, but is rather a legal construction in which significance is attached to the existence of a certain state of affairs.[153] The question is, therefore, a mixture of fact and law[154] and is one which may be subject to modification in virtue of the existence or emergence of other fundamental legal principles.[155] Secondly, even if it is accepted that these factors generally govern the extinction as well as the creation of States, they assist little in determining the position in cases where the elements of Statehood are not extinguished *in toto*, but are rather merely altered or adjusted. In other words the real question is how far a State can survive fundamental changes to its condition even when it nominally continues to possess all the material elements of statehood.

Traditionally, scholars have sought to explain the 'continuity' of the State in face of changes in its condition, and have tended to ignore the more fundamental question of when the State itself may cease to exist. This, in part, has been moved by the perception that the existence of the State is a meta-legal phenomenon embracing historical and political facts which the law can only presuppose.[156] Thus the notion of continuity has

[151] Ibid.

[152] Ibid. Clear reference is made in this regard to the Montevideo Convention on the Rights and Duties of States, 1933, *League of Nations Treaty Series*, vol. 165, p. 19. Article 1 stipulates that '[t]he State as a person of international law should possess the following qualifications: (*a*) a permanent population; (*b*) a defined territory; (*c*) government; and (*d*) capacity to enter into relations with other States'. Although the Convention refers to 'the capacity to enter into relations with other States', this has generally been treated as meaning 'independence': see, e.g., Harris, *Cases and Materials on International Law* (4th edn., 1991), p. 105, Crawford, op. cit. above (n. 47), pp. 47–8.

'Sovereignty' is more convincingly appreciated as a function of statehood and not a precondition: see Rousseau, *Droit international public*, vol. 2 (1974), pp. 55–93; Crawford, op. cit. above (n. 47), p. 71; Oppenheim, op. cit. above (n. 121), p. 122. As has been noted: 'sovereignty in the relations between States signifies independence. Independence in regard to a portion of the globe is the right to exercise therein, to the exclusion of any other State, the function of a State': *Island of Palmas* arbitration, *Reports of International Arbitral Awards*, vol. 2, p. 829, at p. 838 (*per* Huber). Cf. also *Austro-German Customs Union* case, advisory opinion, *PCIJ*, Series A/B, No. 41 (1931), *per* Judge Anzilotti.

[153] That is not to say that the State is created by law. As Marek notes: 'International law does not "create" States, just as State law does not "create" individuals. But it is international law and international law alone which provides the legal evaluation of the process, determines whether an entity is in fact a State, delimits its competences and decides when it ceases to exist': op. cit. above (n. 132), p. 2.

[154] Waldock, 'General Course on Public International law', *Receuil des cours*, 106 (1962–II), p. 5, at p. 146.

[155] Crawford, op. cit. above (n. 47), p. 4. One might note, in that respect, the prohibition of the use of force and the principle of self-determination which have been seen as operative principles in the acquisition of Statehood; below, nn. 183–4.

[156] See e.g., Quadri, *Diritto Internazionale Pubblico* (1960). Charles de Visscher conceives of the factual basis of States as being distinct from the legal order. The historical facts which found the State are, in his words, 'des donées pré-juridiques'. He continues: 'L'ordre juridique international ne fond pas l'Etat; il présuppose son existence': *Théories et réalitiés en droit international public* (1970), pp. 184–5.

been expressed in terms of the continuity of socio-political factors (such as population or territory)[157] or the continuity of the national legal order[158] (sometimes expressed in the form of sovereignty or its basic legal norm[159]). While these considerations serve to construct the identity of States, in the sense of distinguishing between them, none of them sufficiently addresses the fundamental issue of a State's existence or its demise.

A good example of what might be termed the 'existence-identity paradox' is provided by the work of Marek. Marek appears to consider that in order to evaluate whether State A_1 is the same as or different from State A, which existed at an earlier time on the same territory, the central question is one of 'identity'. Rather than referring to the factual elements of statehood (which in an abstract sense all States by definition possess equally), she defines the identity of a State in terms of the identity of its rights and obligations.[160] Continuity, as such, is the 'dynamic predicate'[161] of a State's identity and expresses its extension on the temporal plane.[162] The answer, therefore, to whether there is continuity between State A_1 and State A at different times, is determined by whether or not its rights and obligations remain relatively constant. There are two clear problems with this approach. First it introduces an unworkable level of relativism into the issue of identity[163] in that it allows little scope for distinguishing between on the one hand, differences in the rights and duties of a State at two different points in time, and on the other hand, differences between two separate States. Secondly, as Crawford points out, it appears to suggest that the possession of rights and duties by an entity is a condition for statehood, rather than being an attribute of statehood.[164]

What is interesting about the work of Marek, however, is that when she comes to determining the criterion by which the 'identity' of a State might be preserved, she returns to more familiar territory. Marek relies first upon the notion of independence,[165] which she considers to be 'chiefly, but not exclusively, expressed in the delimination of the legal order of the State, that is, in its basic norm',[166] and secondly upon the

[157] e.g. Verdross, *Völkerrecht* (1950), p. 79.
[158] Kelsen, *Principles of International Law* (2nd edn., 1966), p. 382.
[159] Marek, op. cit. above (n. 132), p. 186.
[160] Ibid., p. 5.
[161] Ibid.
[162] Cf. Kelsen, *Principles of International Law* (2nd edn., 1966), pp. 307–84. He remarks that '[a] State exists . . . not only in space but also in time': pp. 381–2.
[163] Marek admits that '[a]ny definition of identity is, to some extent, relative': op. cit. above (n. 132), p. 5.
[164] Crawford, op. cit. above (n. 47), pp. 401–2. It might be added, however, that this criticism assumes that Marek was actually concerned with the question of acquisition of statehood. It is arguable, in fact, that her test for identity was concerned with a different set of issues, namely, the distinguishing criteria of States.
[165] Marek, op. cit. above (n. 132), p. 186.
[166] Ibid.

extent of territorial and political changes.[167] Ultimately, recognizing there to be a certain interdependence of principles, Marek argues that the extinction of a State only occurs when both the legal order and the territorial and personal delimitation of the State experience substantial changes.[168]

What this brief excursus indicates is two things. First, that far from being an issue of 'continuity' or 'identity' in the terms expressed, the issue is essentially one of the 'existence' or 'extinction' of the State.[169] The identity of a State may be posited in a number of ways—according to its social, cultural, political, territorial or legal delimitation—but none of these expresses the terms by which the State is said to exist as a legal person. The rules for the existence of a State are external, abstract, rules and do not stipulate the need for a particular form of government, possession of a particular piece of territory or control over a particular section of the population. In other words, the notion of identity thus constructed is by definition too particularized for it to be determinative of a State's existence. Secondly, as the specific rules developed in Marek's work indicate, there is in fact less disagreement as regards the basic criteria by which the extinction of the State is to be determined than might at first be imagined: however posited, they appear to be little more than subtle applications of the basic requirements of statehood (territory, population, government and independence).

To conclude, it is clear that the factual predicates for a State's existence only provide broad parameters by which the existence of a State may be determined. For example, mere loss of territory (even if quite extensive)[170] will not affect the legal personality of the State,[171] nor will a political transformation in the State.[172] Indeed, it has been accepted that in the context of belligerent occupation, complete lack of government does not extinguish the sovereignty of the State.[173] While

[167] Marek argues that 'international law provides for the identity and continuity of a State in case of revolution on condition that the validity of the new revolutionary order corresponds more or less to the pre-revolutionary territorial and personal delimitation of that State': ibid., p. 63.

[168] Ibid., p. 186.

[169] Kunz, 'Identity of States under International Law', *American Journal of International Law*, 49 (1955), p. 68, at pp. 71–2.

[170] Guggenheim argues that the principle that territorial changes will not affect the identity of a State is subject to an exception where territorial change is 'quantitatively very considerable': *Beiträge zur Völkerrechtlichen lehve vom Staatenwechsel* (1925), p. 19. Hall similarly argues that territorial change must leave 'a part of the territory which can be recognized as an essential portion of the old State': *A Treatise on International Law* (7th edn., 1917), p. 22. Kunz notes, however, that these are 'tautological statements, telling us that territorial changes do not affect the identity of the State, except when they do': *The Changing Law of Nations* (1964), p. 289.

[171] Turkey, for example, was considered the continuation of the Ottoman Empire, *Ottoman Debt* arbitration, *Annual Digest*, vol. 3, No. 57.

[172] Protocol of London, 19 February 1831, Martens, *Nouveau recueil des traités*, vol. 10, p. 197, at pp. 197–9. With respect to Russia, see *Lazard Bros. & Co.* v. *Midland Bank Ltd.*, *Annual Digest*, vol. 6, No. 69.

[173] Crawford, op. cit. above (n. 47), pp. 49, 418–19.

this does not necessarily mean that 'there are no fixed criteria of State extinction',[174] it does suggest that a more synthetic approach is needed, taking into account both a combination of factual considerations and the assertions of all parties concerned, including those of other members of the international community (as might be expressed, for example, through the medium of diplomatic recognition).

As far as the Arbitration Commission was concerned, however, recognition had little formal significance: in its own words, 'the effects of recognition by other States are purely declaratory'.[175] Without entering into the extensive and rather sterile debate over whether the function of diplomatic recognition is either declaratory or constitutive,[176] it could be said that such a categorical position appears overstated. To say that recognition is 'purely' declaratory is to admit rather too easily the idea that the existence of international law is somehow independent of the appreciation of individual States. This is not to say that diplomatic recognition is therefore 'constitutive' in the sense that recognition becomes a *sine qua non* for the existence of international rights and duties, but rather that States have an active role in the construction, application and appreciation of norms of international law.[177] For example, where there is some doubt as to the identity of a State, the position adopted by other members of the international community is highly significant.[178]

The Arbitration Commission subsequently qualified its rather dogmatic stance in respect of recognition in its later opinions. First, in

[174] Marek op. cit. above (n. 132), p. 9.

[175] Opinion No. 1, loc. cit. above (n. 5), p. 1495.

[176] See generally, H. Lauterpacht, *Recognition in International Law* (1947); Dugard, *Recognition and the United Nations* (1987); Chen, *The International Law of Recognition* (1951); Oppenheim, op. cit. above (n. 121), pp. 126–203; Crawford, op. cit. above (n. 47), pp. 10–25; O'Connell, op. cit. above (n. 144), pp. 127–65; Brownlie, op. cit. above (n. 38), pp. 87–106. For support for the 'declaratory' view of recognition, see *Deutsche Continental Gas-Gesellschaft* v. *Polish State* (1929), *Annual Digest*, vol. 5, No. 5; *Tinoco* arbitration (1923), *Reports of International Arbitral Awards*, vol. 1, p. 369 (as regards recognition of governments). The principal problems with the constitutive theory of recognition are: (i) that it may lead to 'degrees of legal personality' according to how many States have recognized an entity; (ii) that unrecognized entities will not be burdened by any duties under international law; (iii) that it does not conceive of the possibility of illegal recognition. See Brierly, *The Law of Nations* (6th edn., 1963), pp. 138–40; Crawford, op. cit. above (n. 47), pp. 18–20.

[177] As has been noted, an act of recognition is more than merely one of cognition, or knowledge that an entity possesses the factual elements of statehood. Recognition indicates, in addition, a willingness to bring about the legal consequences of that acknowledgement. See O'Connell, op. cit. above (n. 144), p. 128. Cf. Alexandrowicz, 'The Quasi Judicial Function in Recognition of States and Governments', *American Journal of International Law*, 42 (1952), p. 631. Statehood may thus be said to be opposable as regards the recognizing State: Charpentier, *La Reconnaissance internationale et l'évolution du droit des gens* (1956), pp. 217–25.

[178] Brierly comments that the 'primary function of recognition is to acknowledge as a fact something which has hitherto been uncertain, namely the independence of the body claiming to be a state, and to declare the recognizing state's readiness to accept the normal consequences of that fact, namely the usual courtesies of international intercourse': op. cit. above (n. 176), p. 139.

Opinion No. 8, it noted that 'while recognition of a state by other states has only declaratory value, such recognition, along with membership of international organizations, bears witness to these states' conviction that the political entity so recognized is a reality and confers on it certain rights and obligations under international law'.[179] Secondly, and more controversially, in Opinion No. 10 it asserted that 'while recognition is not a prerequisite for the foundation of a state and is purely declaratory in its impact, it is nonetheless a discretionary act that other states may perform when they choose and in a manner of their own choosing, subject only to compliance with the imperatives of general international law, and particularly those prohibiting the use of force in dealings with other states or guaranteeing the rights of ethnic, religious or linguistic minorities'.[180] It is generally accepted that the formal act of 'recognition' is a discretionary one, and that there is no duty to accord recognition to a State even if it happens to fulfil the requisite criteria.[181] There is also some practice to suggest that there is a general duty of non-recognition[182] where the emergence of a State is associated with some illegality, such as the prohibition on the use of force,[183] or a violation of the right of self-determination.[184] It is highly unusual, however, for it to be suggested

[179] Opinion No. 8, loc. cit. above (n. 5), p. 1523.

[180] Opinion No. 10, ibid., p. 1526.

[181] The US Government has taken the position that '[i]nternational law does not require a state to recognize another entity as a state, it is a matter of judgment of each state whether an entity merits recognition as a state': *US Digest*, 1976, p. 19. This statement is to some extent a response to the position espoused by both Lauterpacht and Chen that there is an international legal obligation on the part of States to recognize entities as States when they have fulfilled the necessary criteria: Lauterpacht, op. cit. above (n. 176), p. 61; Chen, op. cit. above (n. 176), pp. 50–4.

[182] In analysing early State practice, O' Connell was sceptical about the existence of a 'custom of non-recognition': op. cit. above (n. 144), p. 147. Oppenheim notes, however, that a gradual change in attitude may be discerned: op. cit. above (n. 121), p. 185. Although in practice duties of non-recognition have mainly been identified in cases where the Security Council has so ordered (e.g. Southern Rhodesia, Namibia), it is considered that the duty exists independently of Security Council action. For the view that an obligation not to recognize a situation created by the unlawful use of force is 'self-executory', see Skubiszewski (dissenting opinion), case concerning *East Timor* (*Portugal* v. *Australia*), judgment of 30 June 1995, paras. 125, 129–30.

It should be noted, however, that this duty is arguably an imperfect one: recognition of an illegal situation is not necessarily forbidden by international law as States may well choose to waive the interest they have in the observance of the rule in question in order to give recognition to the factual existence of the entity. Indeed over time, such a choice may become inevitable: *ex factis jus oritur*, e.g. recognition of Ethiopia; Australian recognition of Indonesian control of East Timor, case concerning *East Timor*, ibid., para. 17. That a State is ultimately recognized, however, does not serve to remedy the earlier illegality, but rather affirms, in spite of it, the fact of effective government: Lauterpacht, op. cit. above (n. 176), p. 412; Crawford, op. cit. above (n. 47), pp. 121–3.

[183] The cases of Northern Cyprus (1974–) and Manchukuo (1932–45) support the view that States will not recognize entities created following the illegal use of force. See Lauterpacht, op. cit. above (n. 176), p. 420.

[184] e.g., Southern Rhodesia in 1965, when the Security Council adopted a resolution calling on all States 'not to recognize this illegal racist minority regime': SC Resn. 216 (12 November 1965). The Security Council later repeated this demand and went on to declare the declaration of independence as having no legal validity: SC Resn. 217 (22 November 1965). See generally Fawcett, 'Security

that a putative breach of the rights of minorities should also prohibit recognition. The Commission's approach on this point is undoubtedly related to its view that the rights of ethnic, religious or linguistic minorities have the status of norms of *jus cogens*. If so, the Commission would also appear to suggest that norms of *jus cogens* apply to the question of statehood. This matter will be discussed in more detail below.[185]

These points aside, it is perhaps relevant to point out that recognition has only an indirect role in the extinction of States. States will not necessarily withdraw recognition from a State on its demise;[186] more often than not, the withdrawal of recognition will merely be implied by the recognition of the succeeding State(s). For example, the UK withdrew recognition from Abyssinia in 1939, not explicitly, but implicitly by recognizing *de jure* its annexation by Italy.[187] Such practice is inevitable given that States need to be assured that they will not legally put themselves at risk in the period between the demise of one State and the emergence of its successor. Even taking into account the broadly declaratory nature of recognition, what this suggests is that it is unrealistic to assert the demise of one State before its successors have been clearly identified.

The main element of the Commission's first opinion was the legal construction it placed upon the facts before it. It noted that although 'the form of internal political organization and the constitutional provisions are mere facts', they need to be taken into consideration 'in order to determine the Government's sway over the population and the territory'.[188] Accordingly, it argued that in 'a federal-type State, which embraces communities that possess a degree of autonomy and, moreover, participate in the exercise of political power within the framework of

Council Resolutions on Rhodesia', this *Year Book*, 41 (1965–6), p. 102. In 1970, the SecurityCouncil called upon Member States to 'take appropriate measures, at the national level, to ensure that any act performed by officials and institutions of the illegal regime in Southern Rhodesia shall not be accorded any recognition': SC Resn. 277 (18 March 1970). The Security Council also declared the independence of Transkei to be 'invalid' and called upon governments to 'deny any form of recognition to the so-called independent Transkei': GA Resn. 31/6A (1976), endorsed in SC Resn. 402 (1976). These cases have been interpreted in two main ways: either as an affirmation that self-determination is an additional criterion for statehood (Crawford, op. cit. above (n. 47), pp. 81, 102–6); or as evidence of self-determination as a norm of *jus cogens* serving to vitiate an otherwise established case of statehood, (Dugard, op. cit. above (n. 176), p. 147). For a moderate position, see Greig, 'Recognition and the United Nations', *Australian Yearbook of International Law*, 12(1992), p. 296.

[185] Below, nn. 283–97.

[186] The Montevideo Convention of 1933 provides that 'Recognition is unconditional and irrevocable': loc. cit. above (n. 152), p. 19. Practice suggests, however, that recognition may be withdrawn upon a State's demise: see, e.g., US withdrawal of recognition from Montenegro, *US Foreign Relations*, 1921, vol. 2, p. 946.

[187] See *Haile Selassie* v. *Cable and Wireless Ltd. (No. 2)*, [1939] Ch. 182. On the question of Abyssinia, see Marek, op. cit. above (n. 132), pp. 331–7. On current UK practice as regards recognition of governments, see Talmon, 'Recognition of Governments: An Analysis of the New British Policy and Practice', this *Year Book*, 63 (1992), p. 231, at p. 263.

[188] Opinion No. 1, loc. cit. above (n. 5), p. 1495.

institutions common to the Federation, the existence of the State implies that the federal organs represent the components of the Federation and wield effective power'.[189] Turning then to the position of Yugoslavia, the Commission noted that four of the six Republics had indicated their desire for independence, and that the 'composition and workings of the essential organs of the Federation' no longer met 'the criteria of participation and representatives [sic] inherent in a federal state'.[190] Consequently, it came to the conclusion that the SFRY was 'in the process of dissolution'[191] and that therefore the Republics were to settle such problems of State succession as may arise in keeping with the principles and rules of international law, 'with particular regard for human rights and the rights of peoples and minorities.'[192]

As to the factual basis for the Commission's assessment, there is little with which to disagree. By the time of its decision, Slovenia and Croatia had both actively asserted their independence from the Federation,[193] Macedonia had held a referendum on independence,[194] and the Parliament of Bosnia-Herzegovina had adopted a resolution on sovereignty. The Republics of Slovenia, Croatia and Macedonia had also withdrawn their representatives from participation in the Presidency[195] and other federal organs[196] following a dispute over the nomination of a representative for Kosovo,[197] and the Serbian rejection of the incoming Croatian

[189] Ibid.

[190] Ibid.

[191] It was later made clear in Opinion No. 8 that this did not mean the immediate expiry of the personality of the SFRY—'the SFRY was at that time still a legal international entity': loc. cit. above (n. 5), p. 1522.

[192] Ibid.

[193] Slovenia initially made moves towards autonomy in 1989 when it included in its constitution a provision declaring it to be 'an independent, sovereign and autonomous State': *Keesing's*, vol. 35, pp. 36899–36900 (1989). On 23 December 1990 it held a referendum in which 94.6% of votes were cast in favour of secession: *Keesing's*, vol. 36, p. 37790 (1990). Croatia held a referendum on independence on 19 May 1991 in which 92.2% of voters favoured secession: *Keesing's*, vol. 37, p. 38204 (1991). Both Croatia and Slovenia initially declared their independence on 25 June 1991: *Keesing's*, vol. 38, p. 38274 (1991). See above, n. 141. They subsequently agreed, in Brioni, to a three month moratorium on their independence: *Keesing's*, vol. 37, p. 38374 (1991). See generally Weller, loc. cit. above (n. 13); Zametica, 'The Yugoslav Conflict', *Adelphi Paper* No. 270 (1992); Thompson, *A Paper House: The Ending of Yugoslavia* (1992); Glenny, *The Fall of Yugoslavia* (1993); Glenny, *The Rebirth of History* (2nd edn., 1993); Malcolm, *Bosnia: A Short History* (1994); Magas, *The Destruction of Yugoslavia* (1993); *The United Nations and the Situation in the Former Yugoslavia* (UN publication, 1995).

[194] *Keesing's*, vol. 37, p. 38420 (1991).

[195] The remaining Republics formed a 'Rump Presidency' which assumed the powers of the full Presidency, but without constitutional authority: *Keesing's*, vol. 37, p. 38513 (1991).

[196] *Keesing's*, vol. 37, pp. 38420, 38559 (1991): Magas, op. cit. above (n. 193), p. 295.

[197] In March 1991 the representative of Kosovo to the Presidency was replaced by an appointee of the Serbian Assembly (Bajramovic). Magas comments: 'Without a functioning assembly, Kosovo representatives in the Federal Assembly and on the Federal presidency became illegitimate, and with them also the work of these bodies': op. cit. above (n. 193), pp. 291–2.

President, Stipe Mesic.[198] At the same time, although the Federal Presidency had initially sent federal troops into Slovenia,[199] by September 1991 it was clear that the federal organs no longer had direct control over the conflict.[200] As the Commission itself noted, the authorities of the Federation and the Republics showed themselves to be 'powerless to enforce respect for the succeeding ceasefire agreements concluded under the auspices of the European Communities or the United Nations'.[201]

Even if the Commission's assessment of the facts is accurate, one may question the conclusions it draws from them. The first point is the emphasis it apparently placed upon the internal structure of the Federation as a basis for asserting the dismemberment of the Federation. As a general proposition, the criteria governing the legal existence of a State do not vary according to the type of political or social system that is operated. As the ICJ noted in the *Western Sahara* case, 'no rule of international law, in the view of the Court, requires the structure of the State to follow any particular pattern, as is evident from the diversity of the forms of State found in the world today'.[202] Even if it is accepted that self-determination has become an additional criterion for statehood,[203] requiring accordingly a certain level of representativity, as Crawford noted, '[t]his principle does not—at this stage of the development of international law and relations—constitute a principle of law with respect to existing States'.[204] Nevertheless, it appears that the Commission was not directly asserting that the criteria for statehood differed according to the internal structure of the State, but rather that the system

[198] *Keesing's*, vol. 37, pp. 38203–4 (1991). The Federal Presidency had eight members, one from each of the six republics and the two autonomous provinces. Each of the representatives was to be elected by secret ballot in the appropriate provincial assembly. The President was elected by the Presidency according to a strict rota each year. In 1989 the post was held by Slovenia (Janez Drnovsek), in 1990 by Serbia (Borisav Jovic), and it was due to go to Croatia (Stipe Mesic) in 1991. The constitutional deadlock continued until June 30 when Mesic was eventually proclaimed President: *Keesing's*, vol. 37, p. 38275 (1991).

[199] *Keesing's*, vol. 38, p. 38275 (1991).

[200] On 12 September, the Defence Minister, Veljko Kadijevic, rejected an order to withdraw JNA troops to barracks. Mesic, in response, called upon JNA soldiers to desert: *Keesing's*, vol. 37, p. 38421 (1991).

[201] Opinion No. 1, loc. cit. above (n. 5), p. 1497.

[202] *ICJ Reports*, 1975, p. 12, pp. 43–4.

[203] Fawcett argues, in light of the Southern Rhodesia case, that 'to the traditional criteria for the recognition of a regime as a new State must now be added the requirement that it shall not be based upon a systematic denial in its territory of certain civil and political rights, including in particular the right of every citizen to participate in the government of his country, directly or through representatives elected by regular, equal and secret suffrage': op. cit. above (n. 184), p. 112. For a different view see Dugard, op. cit. above (n. 176), pp. 128–31; Devine, 'The Requirements of Statehood Re-examined', *Modern Law Review*, 34(1971), p. 410.

[204] Crawford, op. cit. above (n. 47), p. 105. It is considered, however, that no distinction can be made between new and existing States. The personality of a State, premised by certain conditions of fact and law, is an enduring phenomenon and must be seen to be a test for the continued existence of States as much as their creation. Cf. Arbitrator Huber, *Island of Palmas* case (1928), *Reports of International Arbitral Awards*, vol. 2, p. 829. Accordingly, if self-determination is not an operative criterion as regards existing States, it cannot be so with respect to new States.

of government had to be taken into account for the purposes of determining its effectiveness. While this may be presumptively more consistent, it still suggests that the test of effectiveness may differ according to the type of government established within a State.

The Arbitration Commission's appreciation that the effectiveness of a State is conditioned by a degree of participation and representativity may be considered too strict for normal unitary States. It is certainly true that the representatives of the organs of the State may well influence the credibility of a government's claim to wield effective authority over a portion of its territory in face of an act of secession, but it cannot be accepted that as a general proposition the personality of a State is extinguished merely by lack of representativity or participation in government itself. What needs to be distinguished is the notion of control on the one hand, which concerns the *de facto* authority exercised by the government over the people, and the notion of participation on the other, which serves as a legitimizing principle, but which traditionally has no significance with respect to a State's personality. Much as the EC Member States and other members of the international community conditioned their recognition policy upon a requirement of a referendum and the institution of minority guarantees,[205] it has to be accepted from State practice that so long as a government continues to wield power over its territory, any lack of representativity will be of little consequence as far as its continuity is concerned.

Although international law does not formally recognize any distinction between unitary and federal States in terms of their personality, it may be argued that the test of effectiveness in the case of federal States is different. Federations have been thought to be characterized by a constitutionally guaranteed division of power between central and regional government in which both forms of government exercise, at the same time, independent and direct control over the population.[206] Although it is the federal State that will generally have full (although not necessarily exclusive[207]) authority over foreign affairs,[208] and will be considered the person in which the sovereignty of the State is vested in terms of international law,[209] sovereignty, in terms of competence over functions of the State, is divided between the federal and constituent governments. Even if the variety of forms of federations and unions precludes the identification of universal principles, it might be argued

[205] EC guidelines on recognition, *European Journal of International Law*, 4 (1993), p. 72.

[206] Bernier, *International Aspects of Federalism* (1973), p. 5.

[207] e.g. Byelorussia and Ukraine under the 1977 Constitution of the USSR. Article 80 provided that 'a Union Republic shall have the right to enter into relations with foreign States, conclude treaties with them and exchange diplomatic and consular representatives, and participate in the work of international organizations'. See generally Dobrin, *Transactions of the Grotius Society*, 30 (1944), pp. 260–83.

[208] See Stoke, *The Foreign Relations of the Federal State* (1931).

[209] Montevideo Convention, 1933, Art. 2, *League of Nations Treaty Series*, vol. 165, p. 19.

that in cases such as that of Yugoslavia where the constituent Republics possess a high degree of autonomy,[210] the only real test of effectiveness for the federal government is the extent to which the constituent entities participate in its organs. It is considered, however, that even in these circumstances the test appears too rigid and inflexible. Effectiveness should not be calculated in a mathematical fashion merely by reference to the number of constituent Republics that continue to participate in the federation. Rather, it should be determined by effectiveness on the ground, namely by reference to population and territory over which the government continues to hold sway. This may not render a radically different conclusion to the case in hand, but it avoids the conclusion that federal States, in virtue of their devolved systems of government, are necessarily more fragile as legal persons.

Even if it is accepted, considering the matter purely as one of control, that the federal government could not be said to be effectively 'governing' the territories in question, whether or not this is sufficient to conclude that the SFRY was in the process of dismemberment, and one might presume extinction, appears somewhat doubtful. Prior to these events, there was much concurrence in the view that a strong presumption existed in favour of the continuity of an established State.[211] Statehood would not be affected merely by a change in government or territory.[212] Indeed, as Crawford notes, '[e]xtinction is thus, within broad limits, not affected by more or less prolonged anarchy within the State'.[213] A case in point is that of Austria-Hungary where, despite the extensive territorial changes and the change in government, certain States persisted in the view that the personality of Austria continued intact.[214] Even if this was not a universally accepted view, it

[210] The Federation of Yugoslavia consisted of six Federal Republics (Slovenia, Croatia, Bosnia-Herzegovina, Montenegro, Serbia and Macedonia) and two Autonomous Regions (Kosovo, Vojvodina). Each of the six Republics essentially represented the territorial 'home' of one of the Yugoslav nations (Serbs, Croats, Solvenes, Muslims, Macedonians and Montenegrins), although only Slovenia was ethnically homogenous (90% Slovene). The 'nations' of Yugoslavia were considered sovereign in that they were deemed to have entered into the federation through a process of 'free association', retaining a right to self-determination and secession: 1974 Yugoslav Constitution, Basic Principles 1(1). See generally Ramet, *Nationalism and Federalism in Yugoslavia 1963–1983* (1984), pp. 20–84; Bagwell, 'Yugoslavian Constitutional Questions: Self-Determination and Secession of Member Republics', *Georgia Journal of International and Comparative Law*, 21 (1991), p. 489. The Federation was highly decentralized, the constituent Republics enjoying complete freedom of economic management and a high degree of political autonomy: Lapenna, 'Main Features of the Yugoslav Constitution 1946–1971', *International and Comparative Law Quarterly*, 21 (1972), p. 209. In virtue of the constitutional amendments of 1969 the Republics were awarded the right to participate autonomously in the foreign policy of the Federation by directly engaging in contacts with foreign States: Ramet, op. cit. above, p. 81.

[211] Marek, op. cit. above (n. 132), p. 548; Crawford, op. cit. above (n. 47), p. 417.

[212] Above, nn. 170–2.

[213] Crawford, op. cit. above (n. 47), p. 417. Cf. Somalia, 1994.

[214] This was the view taken by the Allies, support for which is found in the Treaty of St Germain, 1919. Austria lost nearly 75% of its pre-war territory and over 75% of its population: Marek, op. cit. above (n. 132), pp. 199–236.

clearly points to the fact that the extinction of a State cannot be lightly presumed. Turning to the case of Yugoslavia then, even though four of the Republics had indicated their desire for greater independence, only Slovenia and Croatia had actually issued a declaration of independence by December 1991 and had taken steps to assert that independence. Macedonia had only held a referendum on the question,[215] and Bosnia-Herzegovina had merely adopted a sovereignty resolution within its Parliament. In fact, neither of the latter States had entirely dismissed the possibility of continued participation in Yugoslavia within a loose union of sovereign States,[216] and neither had at that stage secured their borders or required the removal of federal forces.[217] Equally, although some of the Republics had withdrawn from participation in the organs of the Federation, the Federation continued to operate in the form of the Rump Presidency with two of the six Republics still participating in the Federation. This being the case, one might question whether the opinion of the Commission was not premature.

It is apparent that the Arbitration Commission appreciated the difficulty of merely declaring the dismemberment of the Federation, in that it attempted to mitigate the force of its statement by remarking that the Federation was 'in the process of' dismemberment.[218] One might question, however, whether the idea of a 'process of dismemberment' has any legal meaning. Dismemberment, as was noted above, is merely descriptive of a form of extinction following the disassociation of various territorial units. As such, it can only really be attributed to a situation *ex post facto* once the lack of continuity of the State has been finally determined. If the issue is simply whether or not a State continues to exist, it makes no sense to speak of dismemberment as a process. Indeed the Commission later made clear that, at the time of its first opinion (December 1991), the SFRY was 'still an international entity'. If that was the case, one can only understand the Commission's finding as a prediction about events of which it could only guess, and in which case it should properly have refrained from offering its opinion.

However premature the Commission's first opinion, subsequent evidence suggests that the dismemberment of the SFRY has since been effected. On 18 May 1992, the Chairman of the Conference for Peace in Yugoslavia, Lord Carrington, asked the Arbitration Commission *inter alia* whether the process of dissolution, to which it had previously

[215] Above, n. 194.

[216] *Keesing's*, vol. 37, p. 38420 (1991). It would appear, nevertheless, that Macedonia and Bosnia-Herzegovina were only willing to continue their association within Yugoslavia if both Croatia and Serbia were also involved. When it became clear that the international community would recognize Croatia as an independent State, their departure became inevitable.

[217] An agreement was eventually reached as to the withdrawal of forces from Macedonia by April 1992; *Keesing's*, vol. 38, pp. 38779, 38833 (1992).

[218] Opinion No. 1, loc. cit. above (n. 5), p. 1496.

referred, could be regarded as complete.[219] The Commission began by noting, rather belatedly it seems, that as 'the dissolution of a state means that it no longer has legal personality', and that it has 'major repercussions in international law', there was a need for 'the greatest caution'.[220] It went on to state that 'the existence of a federal state, which is made up of a number of separate entities, is seriously compromised when a majority of these entities, embracing a greater part of the territory and population, constitute themselves as sovereign states with the result that federal authority may no longer be effectively exercised'.[221] Recalling, *inter alia*,[222] the fact that 'the former national territory and population of the SFRY are now entirely under the sovereign authority of new states', and that 'the common federal bodies on which all the Yugoslav republics were represented no longer exist', the Commission concluded that 'the process of dissolution of the SFRY . . . is now complete and that the SFRY no longer exists'.[223]

In coming to the conclusion that the SFRY was extinct as a State, the Commission made three important assertions: first, that a majority of the constituent entities of the Federation had sought independence from the Federation; secondly, that all the territory occupied by the SFRY was under the control of new sovereign States (ie. that all the Republics had acquired statehood); and thirdly that the newly formed FRY (Serbia and Montenegro) could not be considered the continuation of the SFRY.[224] With respect to the first issue, it has already been noted that, according to general principles, the personality of the SFRY cannot be considered extinct merely by reference to the level of participation of the constituent Republics.[225] In this later opinion, however, it is significant that the Commission also takes note of the fact that the Republics attempting to disassociate themselves constituted 'the greater part of the territory and population'.[226] This observation is arguably crucial in the context of Yugoslavia in so far as it provides a partial basis for distinguishing between it and the case of the USSR, the personality of which was deemed to continue in the form of Russia. The Russian Republic's territory constituted 76% of the total territory of the USSR (22.4 million km^2) and 51% of the total population (148 million). The territory of the FRY, by contrast, comprises 40% of the territory of the SFRY, and its population, 45% (10.5 million). Although it would be wrong to place too

[219] Opinion No. 8, loc. cit. above (n. 5), p. 1519.

[220] Ibid., p. 1522.

[221] Opinion No. 8, loc. cit. above (n. 5), p. 1522.

[222] The Arbitration Commission first noted that a referendum held in Bosnia during February and March 1992 had found a large majority in favour of independence, and that Serbia and Montenegro had 'constituted a new state, the "Federal Republic of Yugoslavia", and on 27 April adopted a new constitution': ibid., p. 1523.

[223] Ibid., p. 1523.

[224] Ibid.

[225] Above, nn. 202–10.

[226] Opinion No. 8, loc. cit. above (n. 5), p. 1523.

much emphasis upon such considerations, they are significant when combined with other factors such as the reactions of other members of the international community (the concurrence of the other former Soviet States being highly determinative in the case of Russia).

As to the second question, the Commission noted that Bosnia-Herzegovina, Croatia and Slovenia had each been recognized by all the Member States of the EC and 'numerous other states',[227] and had been admitted to membership of the UN. Lest it be argued that the diplomatic recognition of the various Republics does not conclusively demonstrate their statehood, the Commission noted that recognition, whilst being merely declaratory, 'bears witness to these States' conviction that the political entity so recognized is a reality and confers on it certain rights and obligations under international law'.[228] What the Commission did not mention was the fact that neither the FRY nor the Republic of Macedonia had attracted diplomatic recognition by the time of its opinion. It may be excused, however, for considering such matters as irrelevant.[229] The failure of the international community to recognize Macedonia was more out of deference to Greek sensibilities than any material factor that operated to disqualify Macedonia from acquiring statehood.[230] At that time, Greece and Macedonia were in dispute over the latter's name which was said to be an appropriation of Greek heritage and a threat to the territorial integrity of Greece.[231] As regards the FRY, in claiming to be the continuation of the former SFRY, it had not in fact sought international recognition at all. Indeed, when it came to consider the position of the FRY in its tenth opinion, the Arbitration Commission considered that 'within the frontiers constituted by the administrative boundaries of Montenegro and Serbia in the SFRY, the new entity meets the criteria of international public law for a State'.[232]

The third assumption upon which the Commission based its opinion was that the personality of the SFRY did not continue in the form of the

[227] Ibid.

[228] Ibid.

[229] Macedonia was only recognized after its admission into the UN in April 1993 under the name 'the former Yugoslav Republic of Macedonia': SC Resn. 817 (1993); *Keesing's*, vol. 39, pp. 39428, 39698, 39785 (1993). The UK considered its support for the application for UN membership by the Republic as an act of recognition: see HC Debs., vol. 223, WA, col. 241, 22 April 1993.

[230] The Arbitration Commission had previously opined that the Republic of Macedonia complied with the EC guidelines on recognition: Opinion No. 6, loc. cit. above (n. 5), p. 1512. See generally Craven, 'What's in a Name? The Former Yugoslav Republic of Macedonia and Issues of Statehood', *Australian Yearbook of International Law*, 15 (1995), p. 1.

[231] *Keesing's*, vol. 38, p. 38734 (1992); vol. 39, p. 39328 (1993). Statement of Greek Government Spokesperson, 17 April 1992, cited in Ioannou, *The Question of Recognition of Skopje* (1992), p. 77. See generally Perry, 'Macedonia: From Independence to Recognition', *RFE/RL Research Reports*, 3 (1994), p. 118.

[232] Opinion No. 10, loc. cit. above (n. 5), p. 1526.

FRY.[233] It noted, in that respect, that UN Security Council Resolutions 752 and 757 (1992) contained references to 'the former SFRY'.[234] More important, however, was the fact that in Resolution 757 (1992), the Security Council noted that 'the claim by the Federal Republic of Yugoslavia (Serbia and Montenegro) to continue automatically (the membership) of the former Socialist Federal Republic of Yugoslavia (in the United Nations) has not been generally accepted'.[235] This point was reinforced in Opinions 9 and 10. In Opinion 9 the Commission, in outlining the basis upon which the succession of States should be based, noted that the European Council had demonstrated its conviction that the FRY should not be considered the sole successor (or what should properly be regarded as the continuation) of the SFRY. It recalled in particular the Council's Lisbon declaration, in which it was stated that:

> the community will not recognize the new federal entity comprising Serbia and Montenegro as the successor State of the former Yugoslavia until the moment that decision has been taken by the qualified international institutions. They have decided to demand the suspension of the delegation of Yugoslavia at the CSCE and other international fora and organizations.[236]

It followed, as was made clear in Opinion 10, that the FRY does not *ipso facto* enjoy the recognition enjoyed by the SFRY and that it is therefore for other States to recognize it as a State under international law.[237] It added that with respect to EC Member States, recognition would be conditioned upon its compliance with the requirements laid down in the Guidelines of 16 December 1991.[238]

The position adopted by the Arbitration Commission in these later opinions flowed inexorably from its findings in its first opinion. As soon as the Commission had declared the SFRY to be 'in the process of dismemberment', unless some extraordinary reversal of events had subsequently taken place, it followed that the extinction of the SFRY would occur, that the FRY could not thereby claim to be its continuation, and that so long as it fulfilled the necessary conditions it would have to be considered a new State under international law. That it has neither received nor sought recognition does not affect this conclusion, as the Arbitration Commission appeared to admit.

The Arbitration Commission's views have since been mirrored in the

[233] At the time of the proclamation of the FRY on 27 April 1992 a declaration was issued proclaiming the FRY to be the continuation of the SFRY: see case concerning *Application of the Convention on the Prevention and Punishment of the Crime of Genocide (Bosnia-Herzegovina* v. *Yugoslavia (Serbia and Montenegro))*, *ICJ Reports*, 1993, p. 3, at p. 15.

[234] Opinion No. 8, loc. cit. above (n. 5), p. 1523.

[235] Ibid.

[236] Opinion No. 9, loc. cit. above (n. 5), p. 1524.

[237] Opinion No. 10, loc. cit. above (n. 5), p. 1526.

[238] Ibid.

practice of the UN. In Resolution 777 (1992) the Security Council noted that 'the State formerly known as the Socialist Federal Republic of Yugoslavia has ceased to exist' and that the 'Federal Republic of Yugoslavia (Serbia and Montenegro) cannot continue automatically the membership of the former Socialist Federal Republic of Yugoslavia in the United Nations; and therefore *recommends* to the General Assembly that it decide that the Federal Republic of Yugoslavia (Serbia and Montenegro) should apply for membership in the United Nations and that it shall not participate in the work of the General Assembly'.[239] The General Assembly responded by adopting Resolution 47/1, in which it noted that 'the Federal Republic of Yugoslavia (Serbia and Montenegro) cannot continue automatically the membership of the former Socialist Federal Republic of Yugoslavia in the United Nations', and resolved that it should not participate in the work of the General Assembly.[240]

The UN Legal Counsel explained the implications of General Assembly Resolution 47/1 in the following terms:

> the only practical consequence that the resolution draws is that the Federal Republic of Yugoslavia (Serbia and Montenegro) shall not *participate* in the work of the General Assembly. It is clear, therefore, that representatives of the Federal Republic of Yugoslavia (Serbia and Montenegro) can no longer *participate* in the work of the General Assembly, its subsidiary organs, nor conferences and meetings convened by it.
>
> On the other hand, the resolution neither terminates nor suspends Yugoslavia's *membership* in the Organization. Consequently, the seat and nameplate remain as before, but in Assembly bodies representatives of the Federal Republic of Yugoslavia (Serbia and Montenegro) cannot sit behind the sign 'Yugoslavia'. Yugoslav missions at United Nations Headquarters and offices may continue to function and may receive and circulate documents. At Headquarters, the Secretariat will continue to fly the flag of the old Yugoslavia as it is the last flag of Yugoslavia used by the Secretariat. The resolution does not take away the right of Yugoslavia to participate in the work of organs other than Assembly bodies. The admission to the United Nations of a new Yugoslavia under Article 4 of the Charter will terminate the situation created by resolution 47/1.[241]

As the ICJ noted, the solution adopted by the UN 'is not free from legal difficulties'.[242] Apart from the limited scope of the resolution, a matter which was later rectified by an additional resolution excluding the FRY

[239] SC. Resn. 777 (1992), 19 September 1992.

[240] GA Resn. 47/1, *General Assembly Official Records*, 47th Session, Agenda Item 8, UN Doc. A/47/L.1 and Add. 1 (1992).

[241] UN Doc. A/47/485.

[242] Case concerning, *Application of the Convention on the Prevention and Punishment of the Crime of Genocide (Bosnia-Herzegovina* v. *Yugoslavia (Serbia and Montenegro)), ICJ Reports*, 1993, p. 3, at p. 14. See Gray, 'Application of the Convention on the Prevention and Punishment of the Crime of Genocide (Bosnia and Herzegovina v. Yugoslavia (Serbia and Montenegro))', *International and Comparative Law Quarterly*, 43 (1994), p. 704, at pp. 707–10.

from participation in ECOSOC,[243] it appears to allow for the continued existence of an extremely ambiguous situation.[244] If, as the Legal Counsel suggests, the membership of Yugoslavia in the UN is retained, one may question whether that implies that the SFRY continues to exist as a State in a manner reminiscent of India after the secession of Pakistan.[245] Certainly for operational purposes that appears to be the case,[246] but it is otherwise inconsistent with the non-participation of the FRY. Similarly, although the opinion suggests that the admission of a 'new Yugoslavia' would terminate the situation created by Resolution 47/1, that itself is open to question. If the FRY were to be admitted to the UN under Article 4, one may wonder why that would affect the (admittedly fictitious) membership of the SFRY, unless, contrary to what has been asserted, it was indeed the continuation of the SFRY. If, on the other hand and against all odds, Yugoslavia were to recreate itself, one would assume that, as in the case of Syria in 1962,[247] it would resume its membership without having to re-apply. In the final analysis, the matter would be clarified only if the membership of Yugoslavia in the UN were to be officially terminated and the participation of the FRY completely eliminated.

Whatever the residual ambiguities in the position adopted by the UN, it is difficult to see practice as showing anything other than the extinction of the legal personality of the SFRY. To some extent, that situation was determined by the Arbitration Commission, which saw fit to proclaim

[243] GA Resn. 47/229 (1993), 29 April 1993, pursuant to SC Resn. 821 (1993), 28 April 1993.

[244] See Blum, 'UN Membership of the "New" Yugoslavia: Continuity or Break?', *American Journal of International Law*, 86 (1992), p. 830; Lloyd, 'Succession, Secession, and State Membership in the United Nations', *New York University Journal of International Law and Politics*, 26 (1994), p. 761.

[245] On that occasion the General Assembly First Committee agreed to the following formulation to govern the question of admission:

'1. That as a general principle, it is in conformity with legal principles to presume that a State which is a member of the organization of the United Nations does not cease to be a member simply because its constitution or its frontier have been subjected to changes, and that the extinction of the State as a legal personality recognized in the international order must be shown before its rights and obligations can be considered thereby to have ceased to exist;

2. That when a new State is created, whatever may be the territory and the populations which it comprises and whether or not they formed part of a State member of the United Nations, it cannot under the system of the Charter claim the status of a member of the United Nations unless it has been formally admitted as such in conformity with the provisions of the Charter;

3. Beyond that, each case must be judged according to its merits.'

(UN Doc. A/C.1/212, 11 October 1947.) See generally Schachter, 'The Development of International Law through the Legal Opinions of the United Nations Secretariat', this *Year Book*, 25 (1948), p. 91.

[246] The Secretariat has resisted the complete expulsion of the FRY from the organization because of the practical consequences it might have for the peace initiatives and other deliberations within the Conference on Yugoslavia: see UN Doc. A/48/847 (1993).

[247] Syria was able to revive its United Nations membership on seceding from the UAR without the need for readmission: Young, loc. cit. above (n. 145). Crawford argues, however, that in so far as the existence of Syria had been expunged by mutual consent on its entry into the UAR, its subsequent assertion of identity 'takes on decidedly fictional overtones': op. cit. above (n. 47), p. 408.

the dissolution of the Federation in December 1991 and which laid the ground for the subsequent recognition of the emergent Republics by other members of the international community. The determinants of dismemberment outlined by the Commission were arguably somewhat superficial and were applied in an unnecessarily formulaic manner. Little consideration was given to the formal continuance of the Federation and its organs (albeit in a mutilated form), or to their claim to sovereignty over the territory. Similarly, in the early stages, the absence of diplomatic recognition was effectively overlooked, it being considered to be strictly declaratory and therefore irrelevant to any determination as to a State's existence or demise. In the circumstances, this was patently unrealistic. The facts in question were never sufficiently clear to render any opinion as to the legal situation beyond doubt. The fact of diplomatic recognition was undoubtedly highly 'constitutive' as regards Bosnia-Herzegovina and also perhaps Croatia. Having said that, as a case of dismemberment, the significant factors in the case of Yugoslavia (that perhaps distinguish it from the USSR) appear to have been the extent of territory and population lost in virtue of the disassociation of the various Republics, the fact that the Federation and its organs had to be legally reconstituted as a result, and the widespread conviction that the FRY could not automatically assume the membership of the SFRY in international organizations.

3.1.3. *Dismemberment and the statehood of the emergent Republics*

As a brief comment before considering the Arbitration Commission's approach to the acquisition of statehood by the Yugoslav Republics, it is worth noting that in established doctrine, although a necessary link is made between the expiry of one State and the rights and obligations that arise for the emergent entities, it has rarely been recognized that there should be any necessary interrelationship between the legal extinction of one State and the acquisition of personality by another in its place. Crawford, for example, although briefly considering the question of extinction,[248] does not directly address the implications of dismemberment on the acquisition of personality by the emergent entities. Rather he refers exclusively to two main processes—devolution and secession—both of which apparently assume the continued existence of the parent State.[249] Marek, by contrast, considers in depth the question of dismemberment, but does not address whether that fact has any impact upon the acquisition of statehood by an emergent entity.[250]

One does not have to go too far to find an explanation. Generally speaking, unless an explicit process of devolution is at work, the process

[248] Crawford, op. cit. above (n. 47), pp. 417–20.

[249] Ibid., pp. 215–70.

[250] Marek, op. cit. above (n. 132), *passim*.

by which an entity acquires or loses statehood is shrouded by doubt, both as regards the relevant factual circumstances and as to their legal significance. It is therefore only when nascent entities come to be recognized as States by other members of the international community that these issues will be presumptively resolved. Accordingly, the demise of one State and the emergence of another in its place involve a single set of events which cannot be conceptually separated. At the same time, as a matter of policy it is not convenient to admit the possibility of an 'interregnum', or a discontinuity in responsibility for a piece of territory, as might emerge between the extinction of one entity and the emergence of another in its place, not least because the rights and duties of third States might be put at risk during the intervening period. It is therefore the practice that the extinction of a State will only be signalled once a view has been taken as to its presumptive successors.[251]

The Arbitration Commission, by force of circumstances one might presume, appeared to reverse this natural sequence of events by identifying the dissolution of the Federation (albeit in the form of a process) before the acquisition of statehood of the emergent entities could clearly be established beyond doubt.[252] It subsequently attempted to rationalize the decision by retroactively dating the time of succession (and *a fortiori* the date of acquisition of statehood) of most Republics some time before their recognition by the international community.[253] This is certainly consistent with the declaratory approach to recognition, which the Commission itself endorsed, in which the date of commencement of statehood is to be divined by reference to the existence of factual criteria and not to the discretionary acts of the recognizing States. On this view, even if 'retroactivity' has no place in the context of statehood (to the extent that late recognition of an entity is essentially superfluous[254]), it may serve to give legal recognition to a factual situation which was only concretized by subsequent events. As Crawford notes:

> [A]n entity whose status is doubtful at a particular time may well, if it becomes definitively established or generally recognized as a State, be regarded as having been a State also at that earlier time: in such cases, subsequent events are capable of giving form to a state of affairs which would otherwise have been equivocal.[255]

[251] This is consistent with the view that States tend not to withdraw recognition from States (as distinct from governments) but rather merely to recognize the successor State: above, n. 251.

[252] It is suggested that the 'doubt' was only removed once Croatia and Slovenia were recognized by the EC Member States on 15 January 1992: *Keesing's*, vol. 38, p. 38703 (1992).

[253] Opinion No. 11, loc. cit. above (n. 8), p. 1589. Although it might be considered that the Arbitration Commission was creating problems for itself by identifying specific dates of succession, as indeed it recognized itself (ibid., p. 1588), it is nevertheless considered an undertaking that is suited to judicial determination: see Chen, op. cit. above (n. 176), pp. 176–7. See, e.g., decision of International Commission of Jurists in the *Aaland Islands* case, *League of Nations Official Journal*, 1920, Special Supplement No. 3.

[254] Brownlie, op. cit. above (n. 38), p. 95.

[255] Crawford, op. cit. above (n. 47), p. 389.

As Crawford explains, it is the 'relatively conservative' operation of rules relating to the acquisition of statehood by secession which have encouraged international tribunals to date the commencement of the State from the 'earliest date at which it could be said to have been effectively in control of its territory'.[256] What is clear from the Yugoslav situation, however, is that the 'conservative' rules regarding secession were not applied, not least because there remained considerable doubt about the effectiveness of the control exercised by the Croatian and Bosnia-Herzegovinian Governments even at the time of their recognition.[257] Only in the case of Macedonia, which was recognized following its admittance to the United Nations in April 1993, is there a strong case for retroactivity.[258]

The problems posed by the Commission's chronology are compounded by the fact that when the dates of succession provided by the Commission are analysed, they are not entirely consistent with the conclusions posited in its first opinion. According to the Commission, Croatia and Slovenia acquired statehood on 8 October 1991, Macedonia on 17 November 1991, Bosnia-Herzegovina on 6 March 1992, and Serbia-Montenegro on 27 April 1992.[259] As it also determined that the process of disintegration started on 29 November 1991,[260] it is difficult to view Croatia's and Slovenia's declarations of independence as anything other than acts of secession. Indeed, ironically enough, it also appears that Macedonia's independence is the result of an act of secession. Only Bosnia-Herzegovina and the FRY can be seen to have emerged once the process of dismemberment was under way. Such problems underline the arbitrary and reductive nature of legal chronologies and demonstrate the difficulties of differentiating between cases of secession and dismemberment. That the Commission was apparently indifferent to the problems of chronology may be understandable, but its insistence on

[256] Ibid., p. 390. He cites as an example the practice of mixed arbitral tribunals of holding that the various States formed after the World War I came into existence prior to the relevant peace treaties, e.g. *Deutsche Continental Gas-Gesellschaft* v. *Polish State* (1920), *Annual Digest*, vol. 2, No. 5.

[257] The EC Member States recognized Croatia on 15 January 1992: *Keesing's*, vol. 38, no. 1, p. 38703 (1992). At that time, the Serbian Republic of Krajina (formerly the two Autonomous Regions of Krajina and Slavonia, Baranja and Western Srem), which amounted to approximately one third of Croatian territory, was effectively entirely independent. It was recognized by Serbia on 20 December 1991: *Keesing's*, vol. 37, p. 38685 (1991). Similarly Bosnia-Herzegovina was recognized on 6 April 1992, despite the existence of the self-proclaimed Republic of the Serbian People of Bosnia-Herzegovina: *Keesing's*, vol. 38, pp. 38704, 38833 (1992).

[258] In Opinion No. 6, the Arbitration Commission opined that FYROM had fulfilled the necessary requirements for recognition: loc. cit. above (n. 5), p. 1512. Although it was concerned primarily with compliance with the EC recognition guidelines, one might suppose that no such recommendation would be given if the Republic did not fulfil the basic criteria for statehood. FYROM was admitted to the UN on 8 April 1993 under a provisional name: *Keesing's*, vol. 39, p. 39442 (1993).

[259] Opinion No. 11, loc. cit. above (n. 8), p. 1589.

[260] Ibid., p. 1587.

different dates for accession to independence undoubtedly complicates the issues of succession that arise.[261]

Leaving aside the Commission's asserted chronology of events, it may be argued that the significance of identifying the process as one of dismemberment was that it enabled the statehood of the Republics to be established with considerably greater ease. According to traditional doctrine, the normal requirements for statehood are applied more strictly in cases of secession, where the emergent entities have to show considerably higher levels of effectiveness, than would be required in a case of devolution.[262] The primary distinguishing feature in cases of devolution is the consent of the parent State, which serves to confer territorial sovereignty upon the new entity and provides it with a prima facie right to govern its territory as a State.[263] Thus, in 1960, the Congo was admitted to membership of the UN primarily on the basis of the agreement of Belgium and despite the fact that its government was struggling to prevent the Katangese secession and can hardly be said to have been in effective control of the territory.[264] Where no such agreement is evident, the seceding entity has to struggle to establish effective control in face of a presumption in favour of the integrity and effectiveness of the parent State.[265] For example, in the cases of Katanga and Biafra, even though the secessionist units exercised significant control over the disputed territory, the majority of States refused to accord them recognition out of deference to the sovereignty of the respective parent States (the Congo and Nigeria).[266] Indeed, as Lauterpacht noted, in cases of secession, recognition will only be legitimate once it is clear that the parent State is unlikely to be able to reassert control.[267]

The emergence of the new States in Yugoslavia cannot be seen as the result of a process of devolution in that, throughout the operative period, the Federation consistently opposed the intended secession of the various

[261] Below, n. 369.

[262] Devolution can be either 'partial' or 'universal'. The former involves the 'consensual' secession of a territorial unit, leaving the State otherwise intact. The latter involves the voluntary unification of two States or the separation of a whole State (as opposed to merely parts of a State) to form a new international person, e.g., the merger of Egypt and Syria to form the United Arab Republic in 1958; the merger of the People's Democratic Republic of Yemen and the Yemen Arab Republic to form the Republic of Yemen in 1990; the separation of Czechoslovakia into the Czech and Slovak Republics on 1 January 1993.

[263] Crawford, op. cit. above (n. 47), pp. 44, 218. He identifies a number of exceptions to this rule, however, particularly as regards grants of independence in violation of the principle of self-determination: ibid, pp. 219–22.

[264] See Shaw, op. cit. above (n. 146), pp. 202–8.

[265] Ibid., pp. 214–16.

[266] Biafra was recognized only by Tanzania, Gabon, the Ivory Coast and Zambia. Even then, recognition appears to have been accorded for 'humanitarian' reasons: see Shaw, ibid., pp. 209–10. Similarly, the General Assembly condemned the attempted secession of Mayotte as a violation of the sovereignty and territorial integrity of the Comoros: GA Resn. 31/4, 21 October 1971; GA Resn. 45/11, 11 November 1990.

[267] Lauterpacht, op. cit. above (n. 176), p. 45.

Republics.[268] Equally, although the Constitution of the SFRY did explicitly embody a right to secession,[269] that it served to provide legitimacy for the acts of the various Republics is extremely doubtful. Strictly speaking the constitutional right to self-determination and secession belonged to the respective 'nations' rather than to the Republics themselves.[270] As none of the constituent Republics (with the possible exception of Slovenia) was nationally homogenous, it was questionable whether the right devolved upon the Republics themselves. Moreover, there was never any agreement as to the precise implication of the right to secession,[271] there being doubt, for example, as to whether or not it could have been exercised by means of a unilateral act.[272]

Given the non-consensual nature of the acts of independence, one might have expected that a presumption would be operated in favour of the effectiveness of the federal government, and correspondingly against that of the seceding Republics. Nevertheless, the international community was willing to afford diplomatic recognition to Slovenia, Croatia, and Bosnia-Herzegovina at an early stage and in spite of an obvious lack of effectiveness in the latter two cases.[273] To some extent, the advice of

[268] On 24 June 1991 the Yugoslav Prime Minister warned that the 'Federal Government will use all means available to stop the republics' unilateral steps towards independence': cited in Weller, loc. cit. above (n. 13), p. 570. The FRY did eventually recognize Slovenia in 1992: *Keesing's*, vol. 38, p. 39036 (1992).

[269] The 1974 Yugoslav Constitution provided (Basic Principles I, para. I): 'The nations of Yugoslavia, proceeding from the right of every nation to self-determination, including the right to secession, on the basis of their will freely expressed in the common struggle of all nations and nationalities . . . have, together with the nationalities with which they live, united in a federal republic of free and equal nations and nationalities and founded a socialist federal community of working people—the Socialist Federal Republic of Yugoslavia'.

[270] This also excludes a right of secession on behalf of 'nationalities' (i.e. the Albanians in Kosovo and the Hungarians in Vojvodina): see Rich, loc. cit. above (n. 118), pp. 38–9. Serbia adopted the position that the proper subjects of any political settlement are not the republics or provinces, but rather the South Slav nations. Accordingly, it considered the internal borders of Yugoslavia to be administrative rather than political, and therefore claimed the right to represent Serbs irrespective of where they lived. Serbia officially committed itself to the annexation of parts of Croatia, Bosnia-Herzegovina and Macedonia in the event of the federation being replaced by a looser State structure: Magas, op. cit. above (n. 193), pp. 275–6.

[271] The right to secede was set alongside a duty to ensure the 'unity of the political system' (Art. 244). As Singleton comments: 'The legal theory behind the federal structure is that the separate South Slav peoples voluntarily acceded to the [SFRY] and have the right of self-determination . . . [However] the possibility that any of them should exercise the right to secession is politically unthinkable': *A Short History of the Yugoslav Peoples* (1985), p. 210. It is pertinent to note that Article 1 of the 1946 Yugoslav Constitution, which is the predecessor of the 1974 Constitution, described the Federal Republic as 'a community of peoples equal in rights who, on the basis of the right to self-determination, including the right of separation, have expressed their will to live together in a federative State'. This apparently reflects the idea that self-determination has already been exercised in the creation of the Federation.

[272] See generally Bagwell, 'Yugoslavian Constitutional Questions: Self-Determination and Secession of Member Republics', *Georgia Journal of International and Comparative Law*, 21 (1991), p. 489; Iglar, 'The Constitutional Crisis in Yugoslavia and the International Law of Self-Determination: Slovenia's and Croatia's Right to Secede', *Boston College International and Comparative Law Review*, 15 (1992), p. 213, at pp. 218–21.

[273] Above, n. 257.

the Arbitration Commission was ignored on this point. Despite the Arbitration Commission's concern that Croatia had not fully incorporated the provisions on the 'special status' of minorities,[274] the EC Member States proceeded to afford it recognition.[275] Similarly, although the Republic of Macedonia was found to have fulfilled the EC Guidelines on recognition,[276] it was refused recognition by the EC Member States on the basis that 'more important issues' had to be resolved.[277] That being said, it is clear that considerable deference was given to the Commission's view that the federation was in the process of dismemberment. Indeed, it may be directly as a result of that finding that the precipitous recognition of Bosnia-Herzegovina and Croatia is to be explained. If this reasoning is accepted, it could be suggested that once an entity asserts its independence as against a State which shows itself to be in the process of dismemberment (in virtue of the effective, simultaneous, disassociation of the majority of the constituent territorial units), no presumption will operate in favour of the sovereignty of the parent State and the nascent entity will be able to establish its statehood with relative ease. Such a case might in practice be assimilated to one in which the parent State had specifically consented to the act of independence, or perhaps even one in which the principle of self-determination was operative.[278]

3.2. *Self-Determination*

The fact that the various Republics attained statehood following acts of independence which recalled in no uncertain terms the principle of self-determination[279] has prompted a number of commentators to consider the applicability of self-determination to the situation of Yugoslavia,[280] and more generally to consider its relevance in the post-colonial

[274] Opinion No. 2, loc. cit. above (n. 5), p. 1505.

[275] Croatia was recognized by the EC Member States on 15 January 1992: *Keesing's*, vol. 38, p. 38703 (1992). It was admitted to the UN on 22 May 1992: *Keesing's*, vol. 38, p. 38918 (1992). Weller suggests that recognition was accorded because the EC's insistence on constitutional guarantees exceeded the standard adopted among many EC Member States: loc. cit. above (n. 13), p. 593.

[276] Opinion No. 6, loc. cit. above (n. 5), p. 1511.

[277] *Keesing's*, vol. 38, p. 38704 (1992). Macedonia was ultimately admitted to the UN in April 1993 under the provisional name 'the Former Yugoslav Republic of Macedonia': *Keesing's*, vol. 39, pp. 39328, 39422 (1993). Six States of the EC established diplomatic relations with Macedonia in December: *Keesing's*, vol. 39, p. 39785 (1993).

[278] The only obvious exception on this point being the case of Macedonia. It is considered, however, that Macedonia should be treated as having acquired independent Statehood in early 1992, the delay in recognition being solely due to Greek intransigence on the question of its name. Above, n. 258.

[279] Above, n. 141.

[280] See, e.g., Mullerson, *International Law, Rights and Politics* (1994), pp. 58–91; Iglar, loc. cit. above (n. 272); Franck, 'Fairness to "Peoples" and their Right to Self-Determination', *Recueil des cours*, 240 (1993–III), p. 125; Koskenniemi, 'National Self-Determination Today: Problems of Legal Theory and Practice', *International and Comparative Law Quarterly*, 43 (1994), p. 241.

era.[281] The Arbitration Commission did not directly consider the applicability of the principle of self-determination in relation to the acts of independence of the various Republics. Indeed, it appears to have implicitly rejected the relevance of self-determination as a determining factor in the acquisition of statehood. It did, however, make a number of broad pronouncements upon the subject which were a mixture of the cautious and the controversial.

In its first opinion, while discussing the question of the dismemberment of the SFRY, the Commission obliquely referred to self-determination by asserting that all successor States to the Federation would be bound by 'the peremptory norms of general international law and, in particular, respect for the fundamental rights of the individual and the rights of peoples and minorities'.[282] Leaving aside the question of fundamental individual rights and the rights of minorities, both of which raise specific problems with respect to their status as 'peremptory norms', the first issue is what is meant by 'the rights of peoples'. Although a number of rights, such as the right to peace, the right to development and the right to a clean environment, have all been posited in the category of 'peoples' rights', it has rarely been suggested that they also have the status of norms of *jus cogens* to which the Commission referred. One can only assume that the Arbitration Commission specifically had in mind the right to self-determination for which there is greater, albeit somewhat equivocal, support as a norm of *jus cogens*. If this is the case, however, one might wonder why the Commission was not specific on the point.

The existence of a category of norms having the status of *jus cogens*, although relatively recent, is now widely accepted.[283] Its classical statement is found in Article 53 of the Vienna Convention on the Law of Treaties, which provides:

[281] See, e.g., Cassese, *Self-Determination of Peoples: A Legal Reappraisal* (1995); McCorquodale, 'Self-Determination: A Human Rights Approach', *International and Comparative Law Quarterly*, 43 (1994), p. 857.

[282] Opinion No. 1, loc. cit. above (n. 5), p. 1496.

[283] See generally Verdross, '*Jus dispositivum* and *jus cogens* in International Law', *American Journal of International Law*, 60 (1966), p. 55; Virally, 'Réflexions sur le "jus cogens" ', *Annuaire français de droit international*, 12 (1966), p. 5; Onuf and Birney, 'Peremptory Norms of International Law: Their Source, Function and Future', *Denver Journal of International Law and Policy*, 4 (1974), p. 187; Hannikainen, *Peremptory Norms (Jus Cogens) in International Law* (1988). The International Law Commission's commentary notes: 'The view that in the last analysis there is no rule of international law from which states cannot at their own free will contract out has become increasingly difficult to sustain . . . The Commission pointed out that the law of the Charter concerning the prohibition of the use of force in itself constitutes a conspicuous example of a rule in international law having the character of jus cogens. Moreover, if some governments in their comments have expressed doubts as to the advisability of the article . . . only one questioned the existence of rules of jus cogens in the international law of today': *Yearbook of the ILC*, 1966, vol. 2, p. 247. For a sceptical view, see Schwarzenberger, 'International "Jus Cogens"?', *Tulane Law Review*, 43 (1965), p. 455.

> A treaty is void if, at the time of its conclusion, it conflicts with a peremptory norm of general international law. For the purposes of the present Convention, a peremptory norm of general international law is a norm accepted and recognized by the international community of States as a whole as a norm from which no derogation is permitted and which can be modified only by a subsequent norm of general international law having the same character.[284]

Without entering into a detailed discussion of the nature of norms of *jus cogens*, it is generally considered that the main difficulty attached to the notion is that of its content and field of application.[285] This is nowhere more evident than in the debate over self-determination.[286] A number of commentators have asserted the peremptory nature of self-determination,[287] support for which is found in the work of the International Law Commission[288] and the separate opinion of Judge Ammoun in the *Barcelona Traction* case.[289] However, even if it is accepted that self-determination operates as a peremptory norm in the context of decolonization,[290] it is not yet clear whether its application outside that limited

[284] Vienna Convention on the Law of Treaties (1969). Article 64 also provides: 'If a new peremptory norm of general international law emerges, any existing treaty which is in conflict with that norm becomes void and terminates'. See Sztucki, *Jus Cogens and the Vienna Convention on the Law of Treaties* (1974); Rosenne, *The Law of Treaties* (1970), pp. 290–3; Sinclair, *The Vienna Convention on the Law of Treaties* (2nd edn., 1984), pp. 203–41.

[285] The ILC felt constrained to mention just three examples of *jus cogens* norms: '(*a*) a treaty contemplating an unlawful use of force contrary to the principles of the Charter, (*b*) a treaty contemplating the performance of any other act criminal under international law, and (*c*) a treaty contemplating or conniving at the commission of acts, such as trade in slaves, piracy or genocide, in the suppression of which every state is called upon to co-operate': *Yearbook of the ILC*, 1966, vol. 2, p. 248.

[286] The 'legal' basis of the right to self-determination is founded in a range of legal texts including: UN Charter, Art. 1, para. 1; International Covenant on Civil and Political Rights, Art. 1; International Covenant on Economic, Social and Cultural Rights, Art. 1; Helsinki Final Act 1975, Part VIII, *International Legal Materials*, 14 (1975), p. 59; African Charter on Human and Peoples' Rights 1981, Art. 20; GA Resn. 1514, *General Assembly Official Records*, 15th Session, Supplement No. 16, p. 66, UN Doc. A/4684 (1960); GA. Resn. 2625, ibid., 25th Session, Supplement No. 28, p. 121, UN Doc. A/8028 (1970). The ICJ has also recognized the right to self-determination: see advisory opinion on the *Legal Consequences for States of the Continued Presence of South Africa in Namibia (South West Africa) notwithstanding Security Council Resolution 276 (1970) (Namibia* case), *ICJ Reports*, 1971, p. 16, at p. 31, and *Western Sahara* case, *ICJ Reports*, 1975, p. 12, at p. 31. See generally Cristescu, *The Right of Self-Determination: Historical and Current Development on the Basis of United Nations Instruments* (1981).

[287] Cassese, *Self-Determination of Peoples* (1995), pp. 133–40, 169–74; Gros Espiel, 'Self-Determination as *Jus Cogens*', in Cassese (ed.), *UN Law/Fundamental Rights* (1979), p. 168; Dugard, *Recognition and the United Nations* (1987), pp. 158–62; Hannikainen, op. cit. above (n. 283), pp. 421–4; Salo, 'Self-Determination: An Overview of History and Present State with Emphasis on the CSCE Process', *Finnish Yearbook of International Law*, 2 (1991), p. 307.

[288] *Yearbook of the ILC*, 1966, vol. 2, p. 248; ibid., 1976, vol. 2, part 2, p. 95.

[289] *ICJ Reports*, 1970, p. 3, at pp. 304, 312. Judge Ammoun again referred to the 'imperative character of the right of peoples to self-determination' in the *Namibia* case, *ICJ Reports*, 1971, p. 16, at pp. 72–5.

[290] The approach of the international community with respect to Southern Rhodesia, for example, might be considered to provide evidence that self-determination, as a norm of *jus cogens*, serves to vitiate statehood in cases where it is asserted in violation of an applicable principle of representativity: see Dugard, op. cit. above (n. 287), pp. 123–63; Hannikainen, op. cit. above (n. 283),

context can be said to be peremptory in nature.[291] This problem may be addressed either by severely limiting the definition of the entitlement holders (i.e. the 'peoples' to which the principle refers) or by accepting that it is an umbrella principle embodying a range of subsidiary rights and principles each of which might have differential status in international law (customary, conventional or peremptory). If the latter is the case, it is perhaps better to start speaking of discrete forms of self-determination, rather than using it as an all-encompassing notion.

As far as the Commission was concerned, in its first opinion it referred to self-determination as an operative principle for all successor States to the SFRY. As such, it was not apparently referring to self-determination as a principle governing the creation or modification of existing States or their borders, but rather to what has been termed the 'internal' dimension of self-determination[292] which requires the creation, and operation, of participatory and representative mechanisms of government.[293]

pp. 357–424. *Contra*, Crawford, op. cit. above (n. 47), pp. 81–2. The principal problem in this context is whether or not the field of application of *jus cogens* is wider than the specific context of treaties: see Hannikainen, op. cit. above (n. 283), p. 9; Sztucki, op. cit. above (n. 284), pp. 67–9.

Crawford argues that self-determination is 'controversial even as *jus dispositivum*' and therefore the suggestion that it constitutes a norm of *jus cogens* is 'difficult to accept': op. cit. above (n. 47), p. 81; Sinclair, op. cit. above (n. 284), p. 217, n. 75; Pomerance, *Self-Determination in Law and Practice* (1982), pp. 63–72. It is considered that such caution is no longer warranted. In the case concerning *East Timor*, the ICJ noted that the right of peoples to self-determination had an '*erga omnes* character' (loc. cit. above (n. 182), para. 29). While this suggests that it is more than merely part of the *jus dispositivum*, it does not resolve the question of its status as *jus cogens*. In terms of its scope of application, the court merely referred to self-determination 'as it evolved from the Charter and from United Nations practice' (ibid). This may argue in favour of its being limited broadly to the context of decolonization.

[291] Judge Dillard, e.g., in analysing the *Namibia* case concluded that self-determination as a norm of international law was 'applicable to the decolonisation of those non-self-governing territories which are under the aegis of the United Nations': *Western Sahara* case, *ICJ Reports*, 1975, p. 12, at p. 121. Principle IV of GA Resn. 1541 (XV) defines non-self-governing territories as 'a territory which is geographically separate and is distinct ethnically and/or culturally from the country administering it'. Crawford identifies the following as units to which the principle of self-determination applies: (*a*) Trust and mandated territories, and non-self-governing territories under Chapter XI of the Charter; (*b*) States, excluding those parts of States which are themselves self-determination units; (*c*) (possibly) other territories forming distinct political-geographical areas, whose inhabitants do not share in government with the result that they become non-self-governing; (*d*) all other territories or situations to which self-determination is applied by the parties as an appropriate solution or criterion: op. cit. above (n. 47), p. 101.

[292] See Cassese, 'Political Self-Determination—Old Concepts and New Developments', in Cassese (ed.), *UN Law/Fundamental Rights* (1979), p. 137; Higgins, *Problems and Process* (1994), pp. 111–28.

[293] Principle VIII of the Helsinki Final Act, 1975 provides: 'By virtue of the principle of equal rights and self-determination of peoples, all people always have a right, in full freedom, to determine, when and as they wish, their internal and external political status, without interference, and to pursue as they wish their political, economic, social and cultural development': *International Legal Materials*, 14 (1975), p. 1292. The Friendly Relations Declaration (GA Resn. 2625 (XXV), 24 October 1970) implicitly defines a self-determined State in a savings clause as one which is 'possessed of a government representing the whole people belonging to the territory without distinction as to race, creed or colour'. There is a possible connection here between the Commission's approach to self-determination and its opinion as to the criterion of effectiveness in the context of federal States: above, nn. 205–10. It can also be seen to have recognition in the EC guidelines on recognition: above, n. 205.

Although this reflects an increasing preoccupation in the international community with the application of democratic principles both in terms of human rights treaty norms[294] and more broadly in the practice of international relations,[295] it may be questioned whether there is, as yet, sufficient evidence to suggest that a rule of internal self-determination is peremptory in nature. Such a conclusion is to some extent dependent upon the particular construction of *jus cogens* adopted. For example, it is probably not too difficult to accept the proposition that States must not derogate from a norm of internal self-determination in their conventional relations *inter se*.[296] The suggestion that any derogation from the principle of internal self-determination is not only unlawful (as part of the *jus dispositivum*) but also amounts to an international crime,[297] however, appears unsubstantiated in practice.

The Arbitration Commission came to consider the question of self-determination more directly in its second opinion.[298] There, it was asked whether the Serbian population of Croatia and Bosnia-Herzegovina, 'as one of the constituent peoples of Yugoslavia', had the right to self-determination.[299] The implications of this question were significant. At the time, Serbian populations in both Croatia and Bosnia-Herzegovina had declared their independence and had set up 'Serbian Autonomous Republics' in Krajina and Bosnia-Herzegovina, and like the other Republics were seeking international recognition as independent States.[300] Although the Commission had decided that the SFRY was in the process of dismemberment, it had not identified how the new territorial entities were to be defined. In such circumstances, it was clearly the position of the Serbs that the principle of national self-determination should be the governing criterion and that it should be applied irrespective of the existing internal boundaries of the Federation. The Commission's response to this issue is in some respects quite remarkable.

Although it initially declared that 'international law as it currently stands does not spell out all the implications of the right to self-determination',[301] the Commission went on to make two broad assertions

[294] e.g. Articles 1 and 25 of the International Covenant on Civil and Political Rights, 1966, *UN Treaty Series*, vol. 999, p. 171.

[295] See Crawford, 'Democracy and International Law', this *Year Book*, 64 (1993), p. 113.

[296] Such a conclusion, however, is dependent upon acceptance of 'internal self-determination' as part of the *jus dispositivum*. For the argument that this is the proper understanding of self-determination, see Higgins, op. cit. above (n. 292), pp. 118–21.

[297] It is in virtue of the distinction between 'crimes' and 'delicts' in international responsibility, that commentators have justified the application of *jus cogens* beyond the confines of treaty law: see Dugard, op. cit. above (n. 287), pp. 141–7. Cf. ILC Draft Articles on State Responsibility (Article 19), *Yearbook of the ILC*, 1976, vol. 2, pp. 95–122.

[298] Opinion No. 2, loc. cit. above (n. 5).

[299] Ibid., p. 1498.

[300] *Keesing's*, vol. 37, p. 38685 (1991).

[301] Ibid.

applicable respectively to the external and internal dimensions of self-determination. First, the Commission stated that 'whatever the circumstances, the right to self-determination must not involve changes to existing frontiers at the time of independence (*uti possidetis juris*) except where the States concerned agree otherwise'.[302] Secondly, and by contrast, the Commission argued that in virtue of Article 1 of the two International Covenants on Human Rights, the right to self-determination entailed a right of every individual 'to belong to whatever ethnic, religious or language community he or she wishes'.[303] Neither of these assertions can be accepted in an unqualified form.

3.2.1. *External self-determination and* uti possidetis

As regards the first point, the Commission's line of thought is largely unexplained. Its argument that self-determination must not involve changes to existing frontiers at the time of independence can easily be accepted as regards established international borders. Most recent enunciations of self-determination have been accompanied by a corresponding confirmation of the integrity of existing international borders,[304] and there is little practice to suggest that the application of self-determination has justified the non-consensual re-drawing of such borders. In the context of Yugoslavia, for example, it was never suggested that the borders between Yugoslavia and Greece or Bulgaria could or should be redrawn on the basis of self-determination claims by peoples within Yugoslavia. One may note in that respect the considerable deference given to the Greek complaint that the Republic of Macedonia had irredentist designs over Northern Greece. The real question related to what were formerly the internal borders within the SFRY that demarcated the various Republics for administrative purposes. This matter was taken up by the Arbitration Commission in its third opinion (issued on the same day), in which it specifically addressed the question whether the internal boundaries between Croatia and Serbia and between Bosnia-Herzegovina and Serbia could be regarded as frontiers in terms of public international law.[305] Expressly relying on the principles and rules of public international law, the Commission began by declaring that all external frontiers must be respected in line with the principle laid down in the UN Charter, in General Assembly Resolution 2625 (XXV) and in

[302] Ibid.

[303] Ibid.

[304] Resolution 1514 (XV) provides that 'any attempt at the partial or total disruption of the national unity and the territorial integrity of a country is incompatible with the purposes and principles of the Charter of the UN': loc. cit above (n. 286). Resolution 2625 (XXV) provides that '[n]othing in the foregoing paragraphs shall be construed as authorizing or encouraging any action which would dismember or impair, totally or in part, the territorial integrity or political unity of sovereign and independent States': loc. cit. above (n. 286).

[305] Opinion No. 3, loc. cit. above (n. 5).

the Helsinki Final Act.[306] It went on to state that the internal boundaries that were the subject of the question 'may not be altered except by agreement freely arrived at', and that they had become 'frontiers protected by international law'.[307] In reaching this conclusion, the Commission invoked the principle of *uti possidetis juris* (which it took to be a general principle of international law) and quoted at length from the decision of the ICJ in the *Burkina Faso and Mali Frontier Dispute* case.[308] In that case the Court had stated that the principle *uti possidetis juris* 'is a general principle, which is logically connected with the phenomenon of the obtaining of independence, wherever it occurs. Its obvious purpose is to prevent the independence and stability of new States being endangered by fratricidal struggles.'[309] The Commission considered that this principle applied all the more readily to the Republics since Article 5(2) and (4) of the Constitution of the SFRY stipulated that the Republic's territories and boundaries could not be altered without their consent.

The decision of the Arbitration Commission on this point represents a novel extension of the *uti possidetis* principle outside the context of decolonization. *Uti possidetis juris* has arguably undergone a number of subtle changes in its evolution.[310] As it was originally applied in the context of South America (a context to which some considered it to be restricted[311]), it was a means of establishing title to territory and of fixing boundaries in the unexplored hinterlands without having to wait for title to accrue through prescription.[312] This was recognized in the *Beagle Channel* arbitration,[313] where it was noted that *uti possidetis* encompassed two broad principles: first, a presumption that all territory is deemed to have been part of one of the former administrative divisions of colonial rule and that therefore that no territory would have the status of *res nullius*; and secondly, that the title to any given locality is deemed automatically to rest in whatever State took over the former administrative division in which it was situated.[314] Accordingly it had a narrow

[306] Ibid., p. 1500. It noted that this principle also underlies Article 11 of the Vienna Convention on the Succession of States in respect of Treaties. That article provides that 'A succession of States does not as such affect: (*a*) a boundary established by a treaty . . .': *American Journal of International Law*, 72 (1978), p. 971.

[307] Ibid.

[308] *ICJ Reports*, 1986, p. 554.

[309] Ibid., p. 556.

[310] The principle originated in Roman Law in which it was used to denote an edict of the praetor used to preserve an existing state of possession pending litigation: see Fisher, 'The Arbitration of the Guatemalan-Honduran Boundary Dispute', *American Journal of International Law*, 27 (1933), p. 403, at p. 415. For its development in decolonization, see Frank, 'Fairness to "Peoples" and their Right to Self-Determination', *Receuil des cours*, 240 (1993–III), p. 125, at pp. 129–34; Klabbers and Lefeber, 'Africa: Lost Between Self-Determination and Uti Possidetis', in Brolmann, Lefeber and Zieck (eds.), *Peoples and Minorities in International Law* (1993), p. 37.

[311] Jessup, 'Diversity and Uniformity in the Law of Nations', *American Journal of International Law*, 58 (1964), p. 341, at p. 347.

[312] O'Connell, op. cit. above (n. 125), p. 426.

[313] *Beagle Channel* arbitration (*Argentina* v. *Chile*), 52 ILR 121.

[314] Ibid., p. 125.

application in cases where the newly independent States had not in fact fully established effective control over the totality of the area of the former administrative division, and where the principle was used to prevent possible future conflict by laying down title to boundaries in advance.[315] Even within this framework, however, problems arose with respect to the identification of the boundaries that were to be frozen. For example, in the *Guatemala/Honduras* arbitration the arbitrators were presented with two possible approaches, each advocated by one of the parties to the dispute. One party advocated the application of *uti possidetis juris* which relied upon the formal delimitation of frontiers by the colonial administrators; the other party advocated *uti possidetis de jure* which established title in virtue of actual possession as demonstrated in administrative practice.[316] Although in that case greater emphasis was placed upon the fact of actual possession rather than the formal devolution of title, it is clear that practice in Latin America was not consistent on this point.[317]

In its application outside the Latin American context, the principle of *uti possidetis* (or what has been regarded as such) has taken on a number of different forms. On some occasions, it has been applied in the form of a doctrine of State succession to boundary treaties;[318] on other occasions, it has been interpreted as reinforcing the notion of territorial integrity.[319] Strictly speaking, both of these forms may be distinguished from the original notion of *uti possidetis* as employed in the process of decolonization, in which the existing administrative boundaries were transformed into boundaries protected by international law.[320] That being said, it is clear that in Africa, the former colonial administrative borders have been largely preserved intact and have served to define the shape of subsequent independent States.[321]

[315] Cf. the defensive purpose and prevention purpose outlined by Abi-Saab (separate opinion) in *Frontier Dispute* case, loc. cit. above (n. 308), p. 659.

[316] *Reports of International Arbitral Awards*, vol. 2, p. 1352. See Bloomfield, *The British Honduras-Guatemala Dispute* (1955); Fisher, loc. cit. above (n. 310).

[317] See De Lapradelle, *La Frontière* (1928), who, in light of the inconsistent practice, argues for the total abandonment of the concept. Hyde comments that 'the term uti possidetis was in reality a description of the practice that was being roughly followed. The Latin American States of Spanish origin did not at that time regard the phrase, despite its significance in Roman law or its place in the law of war, as expressive of a legal principle to which they owed deference or were endeavouring to conform in the establishment of new frontiers': *International Law: Chiefly as Interpreted and Applied by the United States* (1945), p. 501.

[318] e.g. *Guinea/Guinea-Bissau Maritime Delimitation* case, 77 ILR 635, where it was stated that the 1886 boundary delimitation treaty 'remained in force between France and Portugal and became binding between the successor states by virtue of the principle of uti possidetis': p. 657; OAU Resolution on Border Disputes among African States,OAU Doc. AHG/Res. 16(1). Cf. Article 11, Vienna Convention on State Succession in Respect of Treaties (1978).

[319] e.g. as expressed in Article III(3) of the Charter of the OAU, 1963, *UN Treaty Series*, vol. 479, p. 39; Principle IV, Helsinki Final Act (1975).

[320] *Frontier* case, loc. cit. above (n. 308), p. 566.

[321] See generally Shaw, op. cit. above (n. 146).

As far as the Arbitration Commission was concerned, in order to justify applying the principle *uti possidetis* in the context of Yugoslavia, it relied heavily upon the dictum of the ICJ in the *Frontier* case, to the effect that the principle was a general one 'logically connected with the phenomenon of obtaining of independence, *wherever it occurs*' (emphasis added).[322] It should be noted, however, that however broadly-stated the proposition, the ICJ did not necessarily have in mind the application of *uti possidetis* to a situation such as that in Yugoslavia. Rather, its concern was merely to affirm that the principle was 'not a special rule which pertains solely to one specific system of international law', and could therefore apply to cases of decolonization other than those in Spanish America. In fact, later in the same judgment, when the Court reiterated the point, it specifically used the word 'decolonization' rather than the looser terms 'independence'.[323] That some question remained as to whether *uti possidetis* was to be conceived properly as a principle of universal application is indicated in the separate opinion of Judge Luchaire, who warned that '[i]n legal discourse, the term "decolonization" should be used only with great caution and must above all not be confused with accession to independence'.[324] He continued: 'the colonial process must be regarded as finally over once the inhabitants of a colony have been able to exercise this right of self-determination'.[325]

However the judgment of the Court in the *Frontier* case is viewed, it is clear that the Arbitration Commission's determination that *uti possidetis* should apply to the case of Yugoslavia is significant and tends to reinforce a more expansive view of the principle's field of application. As a question of policy, there is a strong case for arguing that the application of *uti possidetis* to the Yugoslav situation was preferable, in the short term at least, to the delimitation of boundaries on the basis of unstable and shifting forces of nationalist sentiment, or on the basis of a strict application of the principle of effectiveness. One may question, nevertheless, whether in the long term it is a legal technique which will provide a permanent and pacific settlement to the underlying territorial disputes.

As a separate question of legal coherence, *uti possidetis* is only understandable when it is operated within an identifiable time-frame and with respect to identifiable units of statehood. As the Court in the *Frontier* case noted, '[i]t applies to the State as it is, ie. to the "photograph" of the territorial situation then existing. The principle of *uti possidetis* freezes the territorial title; it stops the clock, but does not

[322] *Frontier* case, loc. cit. above (n. 308), p. 565.
[323] Ibid., p. 566.
[324] Ibid., p. 652.
[325] Ibid.

put back the hands.'[326] In this regard, there are two particular problems that arise from its application in the context of Yugoslavia. First, the dismemberment of the SFRY as described by the Arbitration Commission did not, of itself, identify the units of government which were to be the presumptive States in the new territorial settlement. That would only be the case if the process were one of devolution or secession. Secondly, even if the original 'photograph of the territorial situation' were to be taken at the moment the Federation was proclaimed to be 'in the process of dissolution', that only effectively addresses the problem of border disputes that might arise between the various Republics. If *uti possidetis* is to apply to all cases of 'independence' there is nothing to preclude its further application within each of the Republics even after their statehood has been established.

Ultimately, two different processes are at work in each case. First, the identification of presumptive units of statehood, whether that be in virtue of the principle of effectiveness or self-determination, and secondly the determination of boundaries within which those entities are to be confined.[327] The principle of *uti possidetis*, in its original guise, only serves to address the second question and does not provide a coherent basis for establishing the statehood of the emergent entities. The manner in which the Arbitration Commission addressed the issue, however, was to use *uti possidetis* as a tool for establishing the presumptive statehood of the entities to emerge from the dismemberment of the SFRY and to deny the autonomous Serbian Republics the benefit of that presumption.

If the Commission's first opinions are taken together as a coherent whole (which is not unreasonable given the fact that the first three were delivered on the same day), one is left with the view that owing to a collapse in central government the SFRY fell into a process of dismemberment in which, through application of the principle of *uti possidetis*, the succeeding entities were presumptively deemed to be the six Republics. This being the case, it is clear that the principle of self-determination had little overall influence on the territorial settlement. First, in terms of ethnicity, while Slovenia was relatively homogenous, all of the other Republics had significant ethnic minorities within their territorial borders which generally opposed the territorial settlement that

[326] Ibid., p. 568. Cf. Claims of Morocco over Western Sahara, *Western Sahara* case, *ICJ Pleadings*, CR 75/8, pp. 11–16.

[327] This distinction is evident in the fact that in order to acquire statehood it is not necessary for the entity concerned to have its borders strictly determined, but rather that it should merely be in control of territory in an abstract sense. See *Deutsche Continental Gas-Gesellschaft* v. *Polish State*, *Annual Digest*, vol. 5, p. 11, at p. 15. It is arguable, however, that territory should not be 'excessively fragmented' as, e.g., in the case of Bophuthatswana: see UK position, *Hansard*, HC Debs., vol. 105, col. 100 (2 November 1986).

emerged.[328] Secondly, in so far as the FRY and, to a lesser extent, Bosnia-Herzegovina and Macedonia were unwilling partners in the dismemberment process, it is difficult to assert that they determined their own status; rather, their independence appears to have been thrust upon them by the fact of dismemberment. It is also apparent that in the view of the Arbitration Commission the principle of effectiveness had only a subordinate role—it being suggested that in virtue of the internationalization of their borders, each of the constituent Republics of the former SFRY enjoyed prima facie statehood irrespective of the effectiveness of their government. Ultimately, the principle of *uti possidetis* was employed *a priori*, to protect the integrity of the constitutionally-defined territorial units which were then, and only then, able or entitled to exercise some form of self-determination, whether that be full independence, or integration into a confederation of States. In other words, a principle of boundary delimitation was used as the primary determining tool not only of the shape of the new territorial entities, but also for their international personality as States.

3.2.2. *Internal self-determination*

The Arbitration Commission, perhaps aware of the limits of imposing a strict territorial settlement upon an ethnically diverse population where strong forces of nationalism were at work, sought to mitigate its effect by developing the substance of the internal dimension of self-determination. The first step in its argument was to assert that '[w]here there are one or more groups within a State constituting one or more ethnic, religious or language communities, they have the right to recognition of their identity under international law'.[329] Further, the Commission argued that the rights of the minorities so recognized had the status of peremptory norms of international law.[330] Therefore, the Serbian population in Bosnia-Herzegovina and Croatia 'must be afforded every right accorded to minorities under international conventions as well as national and international guarantees consistent with the principles of international law and the provisions of Chapter II of the draft Convention of 4 November 1991, which has been accepted by those Republics'.[331]

The position adopted by the Commission in this respect is quite ambitious. Although certain individual rights, and perhaps the right of

[328] Apart from the Serbian populations in Croatia and Bosnia-Herzegovina, the Republic of Macedonia has a significant Albanian population and Bosnia-Herzegovina has a sizeable Croatian population. Albanians dominate Kosovo and Hungarians, Vojvodina. See generally Rusinow, 'Nationalities and the National Question', in Ramet (ed.), *Yugoslavia in the 1980's* (1985), p. 131.

[329] Opinion No. 3, loc. cit. above (n. 5), p. 1498.

[330] Ibid., p. 1498. In this matter, the Commission referred back to its first opinion where it had first posited that the rights of minorities had the status of *jus cogens*.

[331] Ibid.

self-determination, may have the status of *jus cogens*,[332] it has rarely been suggested that the rights of minorities have that status. The ILC, for example, has frequently discussed the possible contenders for the category of norms of *jus cogens*, but has never even considered that the rights of minorities might be included.[333] While it is commonly accepted that rules prohibiting slavery, genocide, and perhaps racial discrimination are peremptory norms, it is not easy to extend that reasoning to the whole corpus of human rights.[334] Having said that, as a category of human rights, minority rights have a long pedigree dating back to before the creation of the United Nations[335] and have recently been the subject of considerable attention on the international plane. One may note, in particular, the recent European Framework Convention for the Protection of National Minorities[336] and the UN Declaration on the Rights of Persons Belonging to National or Ethnic, Religious, or Linguistic Minorities.[337] Much as these developments might suggest that the rights of minorities are developing into rules of customary international law, it is undoubtedly too early to suggest that they are now *jus cogens* norms. Two specific problems may attach to such a proposition. First, in conceiving of minority rights as norms of *jus cogens*, questions might arise as to the validity of certain individual human rights treaty norms (not having the status of *jus cogens*) that preserve interests which appear to conflict with those of minority groups. For example, the cultural practices of minority groups may well be incompatible with the right to non-discrimination on the grounds of sex. While much is dependent upon how the essence of the peremptory norm is defined, the differential status of the norms concerned will undoubtedly render more difficult the resolution of any inherent tensions and may ultimately undermine the very integrity of human rights in general.

A second difficulty with the Commission's approach is that although it advised that the Serbian population should be afforded 'every right accorded to minorities under international conventions', at the time of speaking there was no specific human rights convention dedicated to minority rights. The only universal human rights treaty that specifically

[332] Above, nn. 286–91.

[333] See *Yearbook of the ILC*, 1966, vol. 2, p. 248.

[334] But see Verdross, '*Jus Dispositivum* and *jus cogens* in International Law', *American Journal of International Law*, 60 (1966), p. 55, at p. 59.

[335] See Capotorti, 'Study on the Rights of Persons Belonging to Ethnic, Religious and Linguistic Minorities', UN Doc. E/CN.4/Sub.2/1979/384/Rev.1; Thornberry, *International Law and the Rights of Minorities* (1991), pp. 25–54. Cf. *Minority Schools in Albania*, *PCIJ*, Series A/B, No. 64, p. 4.

[336] *International Human Rights Reports*, 2 (1995), p. 217. This was opened for signature on 1 February 1995 and therefore post-dates the Commission's opinion.

[337] GA Resn. 47/135, 18 December 1992, *International Legal Materials*, 32 (1993), p. 912.

contained an article referring to minorities was the International Covenant on Civil and Political Rights (Article 27).[338] However, the thrust of that article, as with the later Convention and Declaration, is upon the rights of individual members of minority groups rather than upon the rights of the minority *per se*, the two not being co-terminous.

What is interesting about the Arbitration Commission's approach is that it was not specifically asked to consider the question of minority rights, but rather to spell out the implications of the right to self-determination for the Serbian population in Croatia and Bosnia-Herzegovina. That it considered the question of minority rights to be relevant is indicative of its view that there could be some effective assimilation of the concepts.[339] This it proceeded to make clear later in the same opinion. The Commission referred to common Article 1 of the two International Covenants on human rights (the International Covenant on Civil and Political Rights[340] and the International Covenant on Economic, Social and Cultural Rights[341]) which, in its opinion, establishes that the 'principle of the right to self-determination serves to safeguard human rights'.[342] According to the Commission, by virtue of Article 1, 'every individual may choose to belong to whatever ethnic, religious or language community he or she wishes'.[343] It continued by asserting that one possible consequence of this principle might be that the Serbian population of Bosnia-Herzegovina and Croatia should have the 'right to choose their nationality'.[344]

In general terms, there might be a case for arguing for a more synthetic approach to various categories of human rights (individual rights, group rights and people's rights) by drawing the necessary parallels between them and identifying their common elements. It is clear, for example, that certain minority rights can be framed in individual terms (like Article 27 ICCPR), and that individual rights themselves may be enjoyed on equal terms by members of minorities. Equally, it is apparent that the

[338] Article 27 reads: 'In those States in which ethnic, religious or linguistic minorities exist, persons belonging to such minorities shall not be denied the right, in community with the other members of their group, to enjoy their own culture, to profess and practise their own religion, or to use their own language'. See generally Thornberry, op. cit. above (n. 335), pp. 141–247.

[339] Cf. Cassese, op. cit. above (n. 287), pp.348–59.

[340] *UN Treaty Series*, vol. 999, p. 171 (1966).

[341] Ibid., vol. 993, p. 3 (1966).

[342] Article 1(1) of each Covenant reads: 'All peoples have the right of self-determination. By virtue of that right they freely determine their political status and freely pursue their economic, social and cultural development.' There is no mention here of the function that self-determination has with respect to 'safeguarding' other human rights.

[343] Opinion No. 3, loc. cit. above (n. 5), p. 1498. One may wonder at the language employed in this phrase—is there, for example, a difference between the 'right to belong' to a particular community and the 'right to choose to belong' to a particular community?

[344] Ibid., p. 1499.

internal dimension of self-determination may be reinforced by individual rights, such as the rights to take part in the conduct of public affairs and to vote, and be elected, at genuine periodic elections (Article 25 ICCPR). There are limits to the extent of assimilation, however, which are dictated by the independence and integrity of the rights themselves: the very existence of minority rights and people's rights assumes that the interests they preserve extend beyond those that may be expressed in individual terms.[345]

As far as the Arbitration Commission was concerned, it went beyond the traditional understanding of Article 1 of the Covenants as interpreted by the Human Rights Committee[346] and the Committee on Economic, Social and Cultural Rights,[347] in that it drew from self-determination an individual right, namely, the right to choose to belong to whatever ethnic, religious or language community he or she wishes. It is not clear, however, what was intended by the Commission in this assertion. If it is taken as meaning a right not to be arbitrarily excluded from the benefits of membership in a particular ethnic, religious or language community, it might be acceptable as a general principle.[348] If, on the other hand, it entails an unqualified right on the part of an individual to join a community irrespective of the needs or interests of the community itself, it is deeply problematic.

In several cases pertaining to Article 27 ICCPR, the Human Rights Committee has come to consider the problems involved in maintaining a right of individual membership in minority communities. First in the *Lovelace* case,[349] and later in the *Kitok* case,[350] complainants argued that they had been deprived of their rights under Article 27, namely the right to enjoy their own language or culture in community with other members of their group. In each case, the question related to the existence of legislation aimed at protecting the interests of a minority group which was defined in a way that excluded the individual complainant from enjoying the benefits of membership in that group. The general principle applied by the Human Rights Committee was the same in each case, namely, that 'a restriction upon the right of an individual member

[345] Cf. Higgins, op. cit. above (n. 292), pp. 120–1.

[346] See McGoldrick, *The Human Rights Committee* (1991), pp. 247–58; Cassese, 'The Self-Determination of Peoples', in Henkin (ed.), *The International Bill of Rights* (1987), p. 92.

[347] The CESCR has made remarkably few comments in relation to self-determination. See generally Craven, *The International Covenant on Economic, Social and Cultural Rights* (1995).

[348] Cf. Article 27 ICCPR, above, n. 338.

[349] *Selected Decisions* (1985), p. 83. See generally Bayefsky, 'The Human Rights Committee and the Case of Sandra Lovelace', *Canadian Yearbook of International Law*, 20 (1982), p. 244.

[350] HRC Report, *General Assembly Official Records*, 44th Session, Supplement No. 40, p. 221 (1989).

of a minority must be shown to have a reasonable and objective justification and to be necessary for the continued viability and welfare of the minority as a whole'.[351] In the *Lovelace* case, the Committee considered the exclusion of a female member of the Maliseet Band from the Tobique Indian Reserve on the basis that she had previously been married to a non-Indian was neither reasonable nor 'necessary to preserve the identity of the tribe'.[352] On the other hand, in the *Kitok* case, although the Committee did have reservations about the compatibility of certain provisions of the Swedish Reindeer Husbandry Act with Article 27, it did not consider the impediment suffered by the applicant sufficiently grave to outweigh the interests of the minority as a whole as protected by the legislation.[353] What is clear from both of these cases is that an unqualified right of membership in minority groups is unsustainable if the minority interest is to be maintained intact. Minorities, by their nature, need to have some control over the conditions for membership even if those conditions are subject to other human rights principles such as non-discrimination on the grounds of sex.[354] Ultimately, a balance needs to be maintained between the need for a minority to maintain its own identity and the legitimate interests of individual members of that group.

The second principle attributed to the right to self-determination by the Arbitration Commission was that individual members of the minorities in Yugoslavia must be afforded 'the right to choose their nationality'.[355] Here, the Commission was somewhat more cautious: this, it suggested was merely 'one possible consequence' of recognizing the right of individuals to choose to belong to whatever community they wish,[356] and was a principle that should be applied only 'where appropriate'.[357] The reason for the Commission's caution is plain: not only does it involve the issue of whether there exists a right of expatriation in international law, but it also concerns a prior question as to whether the inhabitants of a territory will succeed to the nationality of the successor State. In general, practice suggests that in cases of State succession, the

[351] Ibid., p. 230, para. 9.8.

[352] Loc. cit. above (n. 349), p. 87, para. 16.

[353] It was noted that although the statute restricted reindeer breeding to members of the Sami villages, the applicant (who was not a villager for the purposes of the Act) was nevertheless able to graze and farm his reindeer and to hunt and fish: loc. cit. above (n. 350), para. 9.8.

[354] Although the HRC did not consider it necessary to go into the question of non-discrimination in the *Lovelace* case, it is apparent that one of the major considerations was the fact that the law applied differentially to men and women: see, e.g., individual opinion of Mr Bouriri, loc. cit. above (n. 349), p. 87.

[355] Opinion No. 3, loc. cit. above (n. 5), p. 1499.

[356] Ibid., p. 1498.

[357] Ibid., p. 1499.

affected population will automatically acquire the nationality of the successor State.[358] The only substantial difference in opinion is as to whether this occurs *ipso jure* under the rules of succession[359] or whether it has merely been general practice as regards a matter which is otherwise exclusively a question for municipal law.[360] It is considered that even if nationality should be considered primarily a matter within the domestic jurisdiction of the State, that does not preclude the operation of a rule of succession that requires the granting of nationality to residents of the territory concerned provided some genuine connection can be established.[361] It is particularly clear in the context of Yugoslavia that the territorial settlement would be severely undermined were the Republics to deny nationality to sections of the population on the basis of ethnic origin. In light of that it may be said *de lege ferenda* that the granting of nationality should not be discriminatory on the basis of racial, religious, ethnic or political grounds.[362] What is more doubtful, however, is whether in cases of succession the affected population have a right of option,[363] or perhaps a right of expatriation.[364] Although there is a certain amount of treaty practice in which a right of option has been provided for,[365] it is perhaps too early to suggest that international law imposes a duty upon the successor State to permit the inhabitants of the territory to opt for an alternative nationality.[366] Nevertheless, this principle may well be suited to the specific context of the Yugoslav situation in which a number of the minorities have ethnic affiliations with one of the other Republics or neighbouring States.

358 See generally Weis, *Nationality and Statelessness in International Law* (1956); Brownlie, op. cit. above (n. 38), pp. 555–9.

359 See Brownlie, who comments:

'Sovereignty denotes responsibility, and a change of sovereignty does not give the new sovereign the right to dispose of the population concerned at the discretion of the government. The population goes with the territory: on the one hand, it would be illegal, and a derogation from the grant, for the transferor to try to retain the population as its own nationals, and, on the other hand, it would be illegal for the successor to take any steps which involved attempts to avoid responsibility for conditions on the territory, for example, by treating the population as *de facto* stateless or by failing to maintain order in the area': op. cit. above (n. 38), p. 664.

360 In the *Nationality Decrees in Tunis and Morocco* case, *PCIJ*, Series B, No. 4, p. 24 (1923), it was stated that 'in the present state of international law, questions of nationality are . . . in principle within the reserved domain' of a State's domestic jurisdiction. See also O'Connell, op. cit. above (n. 125), vol. 2, pp. 497–506; Weis, op. cit. above (n. 358), p. 149; Jones, *British Nationality Law* (1956), pp. 20–6; Oppenheim, op. cit. above (n. 121), p. 219.

361 Cf. *Nottebohm* case (*Liechtenstein* v. *Guatemala*), *ICJ Reports*, 1955, p. 4.

362 Cf. UN Convention on Reduction of Statelessness, 1961, Article 9.

363 See Kaufmann, 'Règles générales du droit de la paix', *Recueil des cours*, 54 (1935–IV), p. 373.

364 Article 15 UDHR provides that 'No one shall be arbitrarily deprived of his nationality nor denied the right to change his nationality'. The ICCPR provides somewhat less directly for a right to liberty of movement and freedom to choose one's residence, and a right to leave any country, including one's own (Article 12).

365 e.g. Brest-Litowsk, 1918. For practice until 1918, see Kunz, 'L'Option de Nationalité', *Recueil des cours*, 31 (1930–I), p. 112.

366 See generally O'Connell, op. cit. above (n. 125), pp. 529–36.

3.3. *Succession of States*

The majority of the Arbitration Commission's opinions related in some manner at least to the question of succession. As noted above, the approach adopted by the Commission in its first opinion essentially established the framework for all its subsequent opinions. This is particularly true with respect to the question of succession. The Arbitration Commission initially outlined the broad principles upon which problems of succession should be solved in its ninth opinion. Following that, the Co-Chairmen of the Steering Committee of the ICFY submitted a further six questions to the Arbitration Commission on 20 April 1993 which were addressed in Opinions 11–15.[367] It is beyond the scope of this article to address all the issues raised in the depth necessitated by a complex and difficult area of law, and for that reason, the general elements of the Commission's approach will be outlined and a number of issues selected for discussion. It is notable to begin with that the Commission was only called upon to address directly questions of succession to State property, archives and debts. In consequence, the issues of succession to membership in international organizations[368] and

[367] The six questions were as follows:

'1) In light of the inventory in the report by the Chairman of the Working Group on Economic Issues, what assets and liabilities should be divided between the successor States to the former Socialist Federal Republic of Yugoslavia during the succession process?

2) On what date(s) did succession of States occur for the various States that have emerged from the Socialist Federal Republic of Yugoslavia?

3a) What legal principles apply to the division of State property, archives and debts of the Socialist Federal Republic of Yugoslavia in connection with the succession of States when one or more of the parties concerned refuse(s) to cooperate?

b) In particular, what should happen to property

— not located on the territory of any of the States concerned, or

— situated on the territory of the States taking part in the negotiations?

4) Under the legal principles that apply, might any amounts owed by one or more parties in the form of war damages affect the distribution of State property, archives and debts in connection with the succession process?

5a) In view of the dissolution of the Socialist Federal Republic of Yugoslavia, is the National Bank of Yugoslavia entitled to take decisions affecting property, rights and interests that should be divided between the successor States to the Socialist Federal Republic of Yugoslavia in connection with the succession of States?

b) Have the central banks of the States emerging from the dissolution of the Socialist Federal Republic of Yugoslavia succeeded to the rights and obligations of the National Bank of Yugoslavia deriving from international agreements concluded by the latter, in particular the 1988 Financial Agreement with foreign commercial banks?

6a) On what conditions can States, within whose jurisdiction property formerly belonging to the Socialist Federal Republic of Yugoslavia is situated, oppose the free disposal of that property or take other protective measures?

b) On what conditions and under what circumstances would such States be required to take such steps?' (*International Legal Materials*, 32 (1993), p. 1580).

[368] See generally Blum, loc. cit. above (n. 244); Lloyd, loc. cit. above (n. 244); Williams, 'State Succession and the International Financial Institutions: Political Criteria v. Protection of Outstanding Financial Obligations', *International and Comparative Law Quarterly*, 43 (1994), p. 776.

succession to treaties (especially human rights treaties),[369] although raising a number of interesting questions in the context, will not be considered here.

3.3.1. *The Vienna Conventions*

Throughout its opinions on succession, the Commission took as its starting point the 'principles of international law embodied in the Vienna Conventions of 23 August 1978 and 8 April 1983'.[370] The two Vienna Conventions were drafted as a result of the perceived lack of consistency in State practice and in particular the fear that such practice as existed gave 'undue prominence to the interests of the major imperial powers and not enough to those of the newer members of the international community'.[371] The initial drafts of the Conventions were compiled by the International Law Commission in 1974[372] and 1981,[373] the final text being completed at two conferences held in Vienna in 1977 and 1983. It is clear, however, that neither Convention has acquired the 15 ratifications or accessions necessary for them to enter into force and there is no prospect of their doing so in the near future. In that respect, one might question the Arbitration Commission's reliance upon the principles embodied therein.

Two factors might go to explain the position of the Commission on this point. The first, rather weak, justification is that the SFRY was one of the few States at that time to have ratified the two Vienna Conventions. It is abundantly clear, however, that the SFRY was not strictly bound by the terms of the Conventions before their entry into force,[374] and that even then, their application in the present situation was dependent either upon their having passed to the succeeding States in virtue of the rules of succession which they embody, or by reason of their embodying operative rules of customary international law. Secondly, and somewhat more significantly, all the Republics had agreed that the

[369] On this point see Shaw, 'State Succession Revisited', *Finnish Yearbook of International Law*, 6 (1995), p. 34; Mullerson, 'The Continuity and Succession of States by reference to the Former USSR and Yugoslavia', *International and Comparative Law Quarterly*, 42 (1993), p. 473; id., 'New Developments in the Former USSR and Yugoslavia', *Virginia Journal of International Law*, 33 (1993), p. 299; Williams, 'The Treaty Obligations of the Successor States of the Former Soviet Union, Yugoslavia and Czechoslovakia: Do they Continue?', *Denver Journal of International Law and Policy*, 23 (1994), p. 1; Schachter, 'State Succession: The Once and Future Law', *Virginia Journal of International Law*, 33 (1993), p. 253; Williamson and Osborn, 'A US Perspective on Treaty Succession and Related Issues in the Wake of the Breakup of the USSR and Yugoslavia', ibid., p. 261; Martins, 'An Alternative Approach to the International Law of State Succession', *Syracuse Law Review*, 44 (1993), p. 1019.

[370] Vienna Convention on Succession of States in respect of Treaties, 1978, *American Journal of International Law*, 72 (1978), p. 971; Vienna Convention on Succession of States in respect of State Property, Archives and Debts, 1983, *International Legal Materials*, 22 (1983), p. 306.

[371] Oppenheim, op. cit. above (n. 121), p. 236.

[372] *Yearbook of the ILC*, 1974, vol. 2, part 1, p. 174.

[373] Ibid., 1981, vol. 2, part 2, p. 20.

[374] Cf. Article 18 of the Vienna Convention on the Law of Treaties, 1969, *UN Treaty Series*, vol. 1155, p. 331.

Conventions should form the 'foundation for discussions between them on the succession of states at the Conference for Peace in Yugoslavia'.[375] Whilst this falls considerably short of an agreement to be bound by the terms of the Conventions, it is entirely appropriate for the Conventions then to be used by the Arbitration Commission as the starting point for its consideration of the issues.

It is interesting to note that the Commission's appreciation of the precise status of the rules embodied by the Vienna Conventions appears to change through its opinions. In its first opinion it speaks of the Conventions having 'drawn inspiration' from the general principles of international law.[376] Later, in its eighth and ninth opinions, it refers to the general principles that are embodied in the Conventions, but stops short of defining the provisions to which it refers.[377] By the time it came to deliver its thirteenth opinion in July 1993, the Commission clearly took a more circumspect view. There, it noted that 'there are few well-established principles of international law that apply to State succession' and that application of those principles 'is largely to be determined case by case, depending on the circumstances proper to each form of succession'. In that respect, it suggested, rather lamely, that the Vienna Conventions 'do offer some guidance'.[378] It is undoubtedly the case that some provisions of the Vienna Conventions do reflect customary international law: one might suggest, *inter alia*, Articles 11, 15(*a*), 16, 24(1) of the 1978 Convention and Articles 12, 14(2)(*a*), 15(1)(*a*), 17(1)(*a*) and 18(1)(*d*) of the 1983 Convention.[379] On the other hand a number of provisions, and especially those relating to 'newly independent States',[380] do not draw upon established State practice and are therefore more in the nature of norms aimed at the progressive development of international law.[381] What was perhaps overlooked by the Arbitration Commission in its reliance upon the Vienna Conventions was their limited scope. There are undoubtedly a number of questions that might arise in the context of succession on which the Vienna Conventions have nothing to say. It is clear, for example, that the Vienna Convention of 1983 does not deal with State debts owed to private individuals as distinct from other States, nor with questions or nationality, currency, or criminal, as opposed to

375 Opinion No. 8, loc. cit. above (n. 5), p. 1524.

376 Opinion No. 1, loc. cit. above (n. 5), p. 1495.

377 Opinion No. 8, loc. cit. above (n. 5), p. 1523; Opinion No. 9, loc. cit. above (n. 5), p. 1525.

378 Opinion No. 13, loc. cit. above (n. 8), p. 1592.

379 These are no more than examples—there are clearly a number of other provisions about which there would be little disagreement.

380 e.g. Articles 15, 28, 38, Vienna Convention, 1983.

381 The preambles of both Conventions refer to 'the need for the codification and *progressive development* of the rules relating to succession of States' (emphasis added). It was clearly acknowledged by members of the ILC that their role in drafting the Vienna Conventions was more legislative than codificatory: see Ago, *Yearbook of the ILC*, 1973, vol. 1, pp. 101–2.

contractual, responsibility.[382] One may only assume that the Commission considered that the broad principles it outlined would be equally operative in these areas.

3.3.2. *Broad principles*

The Commission dealt with the broad principles on which the succession of the various Republics should be based initially in its ninth opinion.[383] There, it had been asked to outline 'on what basis and by what means should the problems of the succession of states arising between the different states emerging from the SFRY be settled'. According to the Commission, '[t]he chief concern is that the solution adopted should lead to an equitable outcome, with the states concerned agreeing procedures subject to compliance with the imperatives of general international law and, more particularly, the fundamental rights of the individual and of peoples and minorities'.[384] From this rather brief statement of principle, the Commission then outlined a number of more detailed conclusions. The two main elements of its opinion were that, first, the successor States (of whom none could claim to be the sole successor) should settle all aspects of succession by agreement.[385] Failing agreement, they must settle all disputes peacefully, 'in line with the principle laid down in the United Nations Charter' and in particular by means of inquiry, mediation, conciliation, arbitration or judicial settlement.[386] Secondly, the successor States should try to achieve an equitable solution by drawing on the principles in the Vienna Conventions and general international law, taking into account the principle of equality of rights and duties between States.[387] It noted, in particular, that the assets and debts of the SFRY, together with its property located in third countries, must be divided equitably between the successor States.[388]

3.3.3. *The obligation to negotiate, non-cooperation, and third States*

In its twelfth opinion,[389] the Commission came to address an issue which had primarily arisen from the non-participation of the FRY in the Conference Working Group on Succession which was attempting to deal with the complex issues of dividing assets and debts. It was asked, in particular, to outline what principles were to apply to the division of State property, archives and debts in the face of a State's refusal to

[382] The earlier title of the Vienna Convention of 1983 referred broadly to 'matters other than treaties'; this was changed in recognition of the narrow scope of the Convention: ibid., 1981, vol. 2, p. 21.

[383] Opinion No. 9, loc. cit. above (n. 5), p. 1523.

[384] Ibid.

[385] Ibid.

[386] Ibid., p. 1525. Cf. Article 33, UN Charter.

[387] Ibid.

[388] Ibid.

[389] Opinion No. 12, loc. cit. above (n. 8).

co-operate, and what protective measures could, and should, be taken by the remaining States.[390]

In response to the questions, the Commission reiterated its broad position that it was for the States concerned to achieve an equitable result by negotiation and agreement *inter se*. If a State refused to co-operate to that end, it would be in breach of that obligation and would be liable internationally for any loss suffered as a result. In such a case, the Commission considered that it would be open to those States sustaining such a loss to take non-forcible counter-measures 'in accordance with international law'.[391] It added, however, that the fact of non-cooperation does not relieve the other States of their obligation to consult with each other to achieve a comprehensive equitable result whilst reserving the rights of the non-cooperating State(s). Any agreement arrived at by the remaining parties is *res inter alios acta* in relation to all third parties[392] (including both third States upon which property of the SFRY is located and non-cooperating States), which are therefore not bound by its terms unless they specifically consent to be so bound. Finally, the Commission noted that third States may take such interim measures as may be necessary to safeguard interests of the successor States and that they would be under an obligation to do so if a competent international agency had so declared.[393]

It is generally appreciated that the allocation of assets and debts among successor States should ideally be achieved by agreement among the parties concerned, and that the rules embodied in the Vienna Convention are generally operable only where no such agreement has been reached. It is less clear, however, whether it can be said that there is in fact an obligation to negotiate. The fact that in many cases States have resorted to negotiation to settle questions of succession[394] does not in itself provide evidence of any necessary obligation in that regard. It might be said, nevertheless, that such an obligation might flow from the fact that the issues involved relate not only to the rights and duties of successor States, but also to those of third parties, and that negotiation is a *sine qua non* for the equitable resolution to the problems. It is pertinent to note, as the Commission made clear, that even if a State should choose not to co-operate in the division of assets and liabilities, it would not lose the interest it had over the property concerned; it would merely be internationally liable for any loss incurred from its non-cooperation.

As regards its remarks on counter-measures, the Arbitration Commission was undoubtedly correct in asserting initially that States sustaining

[390] Ibid., pp. 1589–90.

[391] Ibid., p. 1590.

[392] Ibid. Cf. Article 34, Vienna Convention on the Law of Treaties.

[393] Ibid., p. 1591.

[394] e.g., Agreement on partition of debt of Czechoslovakia, 1939; Agreement on distribution of debt of Yugoslavia, 1941; see O'Connell, op. cit. above (n. 125), vol. 2, pp. 389–90.

loss would be entitled to take non-forcible measures. In stressing that counter-measures could be taken 'in accordance with international law', it appears that the Commission had in mind the requirement that they be essentially 'proportionate' to the loss suffered and should be aimed at the restoration of equality between the parties.[395] Although there might be some difficulty in determining the nature of the loss involved in absence of an agreement to that effect, the States affected are entitled to take some otherwise illegal measures to induce the non-cooperating party to return to negotiations.[396]

The Arbitration Commission appears to state this principle in too broad a manner, however, when it refers to the right of third States to take interim measures of protection in order to protect the interests of the successor States.[397] As Pellet notes, this appears to give recognition to a form of 'collective counter-measures' that would only be conceivable in relation to obligations *erga omnes*.[398] In essence, it is only those States that have suffered loss as a result of an illegal act by another State that are competent under international law to take counter-measures. In the circumstances, this might be the case with respect to third States which possess a financial interest in the property that has yet to be divided among the successor States. Third States, upon whose territory property relating to the succession of States is located, would not by that account suffer loss, and as such would not be entitled to take counter-measures. But in so far as they possessed an interest in the general settlement they might thereby be entitled to take retorsionary measures. This, however, falls considerably short of the 'interim measures of protection' envisaged by the Arbitration Commission.

3.3.4. *The division of assets and liabilities*

In its fourteenth opinion,[399] the Arbitration Commission was asked to indicate, in light of the inventory that had been drafted by the Working Group on Economic Issues, what assets and liabilities should be divided between the successor States to the SFRY. It is quite understandable that, in light of the continuing negotiations and the highly complex nature of the issues involved, the Arbitration Commission confined itself to stating the broad principles that were to apply. It noted first that the Working Group had divided the items on the inventory into two sections: agreed terms and non-agreed items.[400] With respect to the

[395] *Air Services Agreement* case (1978), *Reports of International Arbitral Awards*, vol. 18, p. 416. It might also be suggested that counter-measures are illegitimate in cases where procedures for peaceful settlement have already been agreed: *Yearbook of the ILC*, 1979, vol. 2, part 2, p. 118.

[396] Cf. Article 30, ILC Draft Articles on State Responsibility, *Yearbook of the ILC*, 1980, vol. 2, part 2, p. 33.

[397] See, Pellet, loc. cit. above (n. 19) (1993), pp. 298–9.

[398] Ibid.

[399] Opinion No. 14, loc. cit. above (n. 8).

[400] Ibid., p. 1593.

former, the Commission considered that they should be divided between the successor States. As regards the non-agreed items, the Arbitration Commission felt that it did not have sufficient information on which to base a decision and that in any case, it was not the type of issue it could readily resolve in its capacity as a consultative body.[401] It therefore resolved to confine itself to 'determining the general principles to be applied'.

The Commission proceeded to outline the applicable principle as follows:

3. The Commission would nevertheless draw attention to the well-established rule of state succession law that immovable property situated on the territory of a successor State passes exclusively to that State. Subject to possible compensation if such property is divided very unequally between the successor States to the SFRY, the principle of the *locus in quo* implies that there is no need to determine the previous owner of the property: public property passes to the successor State on whose territory it is situated. The origin or initial financing of the property and any loans or contributions made in respect of it have no bearing on the matter.
4. As regards other State property, debts and archives, a commonly agreed principle to be found in several provisions of the Vienna Convention of 8 April 1983 on the Succession of States in Respect of State Property, Archives and Debts requires that they be divided between the successor States to the SFRY if, at the date of succession, they belonged to the SFRY, and the question of the origin and initial financing of the property, debts and archives, or of any loans or contributions made in respect of them, is irrelevant.
5. To determine whether the property, debts and archives belonged to the SFRY, reference should be had to the domestic law of the SFRY in operation at the date of succession—notably to the 1974 Constitution.[402]

The first point to be made here is that the Commission did not explicitly determine how the property, archives and debts should be divided, but rather confined itself to identifying which pieces of property should be so divided.[403] In doing so, it clearly excluded from division immovable public property situated in the territory of the successor State. That such property should in principle pass to the successor State upon whose territory it is located appears an inevitable conclusion and may as such be considered to be declaratory of customary international law.[404] Rather

[401] Ibid., p. 1594.

[402] Ibid., p. 1594.

[403] The ILC notes: 'the basic principle may be stated that in general, State property passes from the predecessor State to the successor State. It is through the application of a material criterion, namely, the relation which exists between the territory and the property by reason of the nature of the property or where it is situated, that the principle of the passing of State property can be deduced': *Yearbook of the ILC*, 1981, vol. 2, part 2, p. 29.

[404] Treaty between Netherlands and Belgium, 1839, Art. 15; Agreement between Pakistan and India, 1947. See also Articles 14, 15(1)(*a*), 16, 17, 18, Vienna Convention, 1983; *Yearbook of the ILC*, 1981, vol. 2, part 2, pp. 33–6; O'Connell, op. cit. above (n. 125), vol. 1, pp. 199–200, 204, 220.

more controversially, the Arbitration Commission proceeds to suggest that the principle of the *locus in quo* can be applied to all public property found on the State in question; in other words that any movable property found on a successor State's territory would automatically pass to that State. Here the Commission departs somewhat from the terms of the Vienna Convention, which provides that only 'movable State property of the predecessor State connected with the activity of the predecessor State in respect of the territory to which the succession of States applies shall pass to the successor State'.[405] What appears to be the main thrust of the Convention qualification is that property only accidentally located on the territory of a particular State should not pass to that State, but rather should move to the State with whose territory the property has some connection.[406] In that sense, the Arbitration Commission's rule would appear too broad. However, from a pragmatic point of view, given the problems that might be associated with defining what property is 'connected with the activity of the predecessor State',[407] the approach adopted by the Arbitration Commission, with the qualification that compensation may be payable if the rule results in the very unequal (or perhaps inequitable) division of property, would appear to be a more workable approach.

With respect to all other property (property, whether movable or immovable, located in territory abroad), debts, and archives, the Arbitration Commission determined that they should be divided among the successor States, but gave little indication as to the principles that should govern their division. All that it suggested was that the division should be broadly equitable and should not take into account the origin or initial financing of the property, debts, archives or any loans or contributions made in respect of them.

As regards the principle of equitable apportionment,[408] which clearly draws upon the notion of equity as employed in the context of maritime delimitation,[409] the Commission noted that Articles 18, 31 and 41 of the Vienna Convention 'do not require that each category of assets or

[405] See Article 17, also Articles 14(2)(*b*), 15(1)(*d*), 18(1)(*c*). O'Connell defines the principle in the following manner: 'only such property as is destined specifically for local use is acquired by the successor State': op. cit. above (n. 121), vol. 1, p. 204.

[406] The ILC stated in its commentary that 'the mere fact that movable State property is situated in the territory to which the succession of States relates should not automatically entitle the successor State to claim such property': *Yearbook of the ILC*, 1981, vol. 2, part 2, p. 29. Cf. Oppenheim, op. cit. above (n. 121), p. 220, n. 7.

[407] Problems would clearly arise with respect to items such as railway rolling-stock, other forms of public transport and military supplies.

[408] Crawford notes that this concept may owe something to the notion of 'unjust enrichment' utilized by O'Connell: Crawford, loc. cit. above (n. 136), p. 46.

[409] The ILC explicitly drew upon the notion of equity as an 'autonomous source of law'. It referred in that context to the *North Sea Continental Shelf* cases, *ICJ Reports*, 1969, p. 3, where it was stated that 'it is not a question of applying equity simply as a matter of abstract justice, but of applying a rule of law which itself requires the application of equitable principles': *Yearbook of the ILC*, 1981, vol. 2, part 2, p. 20

liabilities be divided in equitable proportions but only that the overall outcome be an equitable division'.[410] There is some evidence from State practice that in cases of dismemberment, public property held abroad should be divided proportionately among the successors,[411] as should the public debt.[412] There is less evidence from practice that this should be strictly 'equitable'. As the ILC noted: '[e]quity cannot be assigned the main role, because there is also a material criterion concerning the connection between the property and the activity of the predecessor State in the territory. In fact, the principle of equity is more a balancing element, a correlative factor designed to preserve the "reasonableness" of the linkage between the movable State property and the territory.'[413] With respect to State archives, for example, the position is complex in so far as some archives will have especial relevance to a particular portion of territory or its administration, while others will retain their historical and cultural validity only by being maintained intact. As such, the 'equitable apportionment' principle could only be applied in a very general manner.[414] Ultimately, while the 'equitable apportionment' principle would appear to be broadly sound, there is a need to establish the denominators that influence the application of equity in a particular context.[415] In the apportionment of debt, for example, the relevant considerations might be the proportion of territory or population taken up by each State, the capacity to honour the debts,[416] or even the extent to which the successor had already contributed to the debt.[417]

Nevertheless, in the division of property, debts or archives, it would appear to be the case, as the Arbitration Commission asserts, that their origin and financing are broadly irrelevant.[418] The one exception pro-

[410] Opinion No. 13, loc. cit. above (n. 8), p. 1592. Cf. *North Sea Continental Shelf* cases, *ICJ Reports*, 1969, p. 3, where it was stated that '[e]quity does not necessarily imply equality'.

[411] e.g., division of diplomatic property abroad on dissolution of the Federation of Rhodesia and Nyasaland, 1963: O'Connell, op. cit. above (n. 12), vol. 1, p. 231; *Yearbook of the ILC*, 1981, vol. 2, part 2, pp. 46–7.

[412] e.g., dissolution of Union of Colombia, 1829; dismemberment of Yugoslavia, 1941; dissolution of Federation of Rhodesia and Nyasaland, 1963: O'Connell, op. cit. above, (n. 121), vol. 1, pp. 388–94. Also dismemberment of Austria-Hungary, Treaty of St Germain, Art. 203. The key to apportionment is unclear and appears to have varied in each case. See generally Feilchenfeld, op. cit. above (n. 133), pp. 205–7, 219–599; *Yearbook of the ILC*, 1981, vol. 2, part 2, pp. 72–113.

[413] *Yearbook of the ILC*, 1981, vol. 2, part 2, p. 19.

[414] Cf. State practice in *Yearbook of the ILC*, 1981, vol. 2, part 2, pp. 68–71.

[415] Cf. dissenting opinion of Judge Gross in the *Gulf of Maine* case, *ICJ Reports*, p. 246, at p. 386.

[416] This was considered to be a particularly important factor in debt apportionment, but was excluded from the text of the draft Convention for fear that it might be considered the only relevant consideration: *Yearbook of the ILC*, 1981, vol. 2, part 2, p. 113.

[417] Cf. Article 14(1)(*f*), Vienna Convention.

[418] Some State practice does point to the relevance of financing, however: see Agreement between Norway and Sweden, 1906, Article 6, cited in *Yearbook of the ILC*, 1981, vol. 2, part 2, p. 46. Cf. dispute over the application of principles of *locus in quo* or financial contribution in case concerning *Cession of Vessels and Tugs for Navigation on the Danube* (1921), *Reports of International Arbitral Awards*, vol. 1, pp. 97–212.

vided by the Vienna Convention of 1983 is that in the case of 'Newly Independent States' both movable and immovable property situated outside the territory of the State 'shall pass to the successor State in proportion to the contribution of the dependent territory'.[419] It is clear, however, that this is a controversial provision and that in any case the former Yugoslav Republics do not fall within the category of 'Newly Independent States' as defined by the Convention.[420]

The Arbitration Commission was faced with two problems in this context that related to the particular characteristics of the SFRY. The first, arising from the federal structure of the Yugoslav State, was that the 1974 Constitution transferred to the constituent Republics ownership of many items of property. These items of property, according to the Arbitration Commission, cannot be held to have belonged to the SFRY 'whatever their origin or initial financing'.[421] What is confusing about the Arbitration Commission's position on this point is that it either appears to distinguish between public property held by the Federation and public property held by the various Republics; or it assumes that once property is handed over to the Republics it becomes private property for the purposes of succession.[422] Neither position appears particularly satisfactory: the first option assumes that despite the dismemberment of the SFRY, there was some *de jure* continuity of sovereignty at a regional level; the second option distorts reality by suggesting that the various Republics were essentially non-governmental or private entities during the life of the Federation. What the Arbitration Commission clearly had in mind was the fact that if property could be clearly attributed to a particular piece of territory, it should presumptively pass to the State which assumes responsibility for that territory. As such, it might have been better for the Commission to suggest that such property would pass to the successors by virtue of the *locus in quo* principle, rather than to exclude it *a priori*.

The second problem confronting the Arbitration Commission was that the SFRY had possessed a 'particularly highly developed' concept of 'social ownership' in which certain items of what might be considered 'public' property, debts and archives were held by 'associated labour organizations'—bodies with their own legal personality. With respect to those organizations that operated exclusively within the jurisdiction of one Republic, the Commission took a territorial approach in asserting that 'their property, debts and archives are not to be divided for the

[419] Article 15.

[420] Article 2(1)(*e*) defines 'newly independent States' as successor States 'the territory of which immediately before the date of the succession of States was a dependent territory for the international relations of which the predecessor State was responsible '. See *Yearbook of the ILC*, 1974, vol. 2, pp. 175–6.

[421] Opinion No. 14, loc. cit. above (n. 8), p. 1594.

[422] Cf. the distinction between State debt, local debt, and localized debt: see *Yearbook of the ILC*, 1981, vol. 2, part 2, pp. 74–5; O'Connell, op. cit. above (n. 121), vol. 1, pp. 416 ff.

purposes of state succession: each successor state exercises its sovereign powers in respect of them'.[423] In relation to those organizations that operated 'social ownership' at a federal level, or in two or more republics, the position was a little more complex. The Commission determined that where the organizations 'exercised public prerogatives on behalf of the SFRY or of individual republics' their property, debts and archives should be divided between the successors.[424] On the other hand, 'organizations operating at a federal level or in two or more republics but not exercising such prerogatives should be considered private-sector enterprises to which state succession does not apply'.[425]

Essentially, this was a classic example in which resort to the municipal law of the predecessor State failed to clarify for the purposes of succession whether the property in question was either public or private.[426] The Arbitration Commission resorted therefore to a functional division in which the test was whether or not the organization concerned exercised 'public prerogatives' on behalf of the SFRY or individual republics. This test appears to be an appropriate and pragmatic response to a question which cannot easily be resolved by resort to rules of universal application.[427]

The Arbitration Commission came to address a similar problem in its fifteenth opinion in which it was asked to consider, first, whether the National Bank of Yugoslavia (NBY) was entitled to take decisions relating to property, rights and interests that should be divided among the successor States; and secondly, whether the central banks of the successor States succeeded to the rights and obligations of the NBY deriving from international agreements with the latter.[428] The Commission began by noting that '[a]lthough municipal laws are merely facts in international law (*Certain German Interests in Polish Upper Silesia*, 1926 PCIJ, Ser. A, No. 7, 12), account must nevertheless be taken of the structure and responsibilities of the NBY as set out in the SFRY Constitution of 21 February 1974 and in the NBY Statute of November 1989'.[429] It then confirmed that '[a]s the bank of issue of the SFRY, the NBY participated in the exercise of the prerogatives of sovereignty' and was responsible for carrying out common currency issue, credit and foreign exchange policy as a 'composite of banking institutions'. As the NBY 'partook of the State power of the SFRY', and as its collective

[423] Opinion No. 14, loc. cit. above (n. 8), p. 1594.
[424] Ibid.
[425] Ibid., p. 1595.
[426] Cf. Article 8, Vienna Convention, 1983.
[427] Cf. *Peter Pázmány University* case, PCIJ, Series A/B, No. 61, p. 237. It should be noted that many treaties specifically provide definitions of State property, e.g. Annexes to Treaty of 1960 establishing the Republic of Cyprus. Cf. also GA Resn. 388(V), 15 December 1950 (in respect of Libya); GA Resn. 530 (VI), 29 January 1952 (in respect of Eritrea).
[428] Opinion No. 15, loc. cit. above (n. 8), pp. 1595–6.
[429] Ibid., p. 1596.

structure subsequently disintegrated with the SFRY, none of its organs 'can take legitimate decisions in respect of property, rights and interests that should be divided between the successor States of SFRY'. The Arbitration Commission added that the only legitimate role for the NBY in such circumstances would be as a 'coordinating agency' acting on behalf of the central banks of the successor States for the purposes of '*jurisdictio inter volens* to effect—rather than obstruct—the division of the property, rights and interests of the former SFRY'.

As regards the second question, the Arbitration Commission distinguished between those rights and obligations that attach to the NBY as an organ of the SFRY, and those which it has assumed 'acting as a bank with its own legal personality'. The former are subject to State succession but 'do not pass automatically to the central banks of the States emerging from the dissolution of the SFRY' in that 'it is for each of the successor States to determine, by virtue of its sovereign constitutional powers, how these rights are to be exercised and these obligations discharged'. On this point, the Arbitration Commission clearly had in mind the doctrine of 'acquired rights' that underlies the notion of succession in the Vienna Convention,[430] namely that rights and obligations are not 'inherited' as in municipal law, but rather that the interests they embody are 'acquired' in virtue of the succession. As the Vienna Convention points out, '[t]he passing of State debts entails the extinction of the obligations of the predecessor State and the arising of the obligations of the successor State in respect of the State debts which pass to the successor State'.[431] Accordingly, debts, property, and archives, are 'transferred' to, or 'assumed' by, the successor State, which merely inherits a state of fact over which it, or another party, has an equitable interest.[432] As the ILC explained:

> Succession of States in respect of State debts can create a relationship between the predecessor State and the successor State with regard to debts which linked the former to the third State, but . . . it cannot, in itself, establish any direct legal relationship between the creditor third State and the successor State, should the latter 'assume' the debt of the predecessor.[433]

It follows that although the third parties retain their legal interest in the property formerly held by the NBY, they cannot enforce that interest *vis-à-vis* the successor States in virtue of the original agreement.[434] By the same token the successor States, while not 'inheriting' any rights and obligations under the original agreement, are obliged under international

[430] The question of 'acquired rights' was particularly controversial in the work of the ILC: see *Yearbook of the ILC*, 1969, vol. 2, p. 69.

[431] Vienna Convention, 1983, Article 34. Cf. also Articles 9 and 21.

[432] O'Connell, op. cit. above (n. 121), vol. 1, pp. 237–9.

[433] *Yearbook of the ILC*, 1981, vol. 2, part 2, p. 81.

[434] Ibid., p. 83.

law to discharge any obligations owed to third parties to which they have succeeded.

As regards the ordinary commitments undertaken by the NBY 'acting as a bank with its own legal personality', the Arbitration Commission offered no direct opinion—it merely asserted that any such rights and obligations do not pass to the successor State. The matter is also left open by the Vienna Convention of 1983, which specifically provides that nothing in the Convention should be considered 'as prejudging in any respect any questions relating to the rights and obligations of natural or juridical persons'.[435] The position adopted by the Arbitration Commission may be interpreted in two ways: either that private rights and obligations became *bona vacantia* with the extinction of the SFRY, or that they remained intact, entirely unaffected by the change in sovereignty. It has to be assumed, given the palpable need for stability and certainty in legal relations, that the Arbitration Commission considered the second interpretation to be the case.

3.3.5. *War damages*

In one of the more straightforward questions, the Commission was asked whether any amounts owed by one or more parties in the form of war damages should affect the distribution of State property, archives and debts in connection with the succession process.[436] The Commission began by pointing out that the rules applicable to State succession were distinct from those relating to State responsibility.[437] Accordingly, the division of assets and liabilities of the SFRY must be effected without the question of war damages being allowed to interfere in the matter of State succession. However, it admitted that 'the possibility cannot be excluded . . . of setting off assets and liabilities to be transferred under the rules of State succession on the one hand against war damages on the other'.[438]

In essence the Commission was probably correct in suggesting that in the equitable apportionment of the assets and liabilities of the SFRY, it would not be appropriate to bring into account the question of responsibility of one Republic *vis-à-vis* another. It might well be asked, however, whether it is correct to distinguish categorically between the principles relating to State succession and those of State responsibility. In that respect one might recall the definition adopted by the Arbitration Commission in its first opinion, namely that succession entails the 'replacement of one State by another in the *responsibility for the international relations* of territory' (emphasis added).[439] On one view at least,

[435] Vienna Convention, 1983, Article 6.
[436] Opinion No. 13, loc. cit. above (n. 8).
[437] Ibid., p. 1592.
[438] Ibid.
[439] Opinion No. 1, loc. cit. above (n. 5).

questions of State succession can be seen to be merely a specific species of problems that lie within the genus of issues of State responsibility. The point of distinction to which the Arbitration Commission appeared to refer is that whereas State responsibility primarily concerns the existence and consequence of illegal acts in international law, State succession is concerned with the 'transfer' of that responsibility or its 'assumption' by a successor State. When looked at from the point of view of successor States, however, one might question whether there is a great difference between the attribution of responsibility following a rule of succession and its attribution directly in virtue of the principle of *pacta sunt servanda* or other principles of customary international law.

The obvious point in the context of war damages was whether, and to what extent, the various Republics were responsible for the damage caused in the months of conflict that started in mid-1991 and continued thereafter. Although it was clearly preferable, from a pragmatic point of view, to separate the question of war damages from that of the more general question of succession, in so far as the identity of the various parties in that period was unclear the question would clearly arise as to whether any one of the Republics could be held responsible for the tortious acts committed in the name of the SFRY. That this is not merely a remote possibility is highlighted by the fact that the SFRY was not, in the opinion of the Arbitration Commission at least, defunct until July 1992, by which time a considerable amount of fighting had already taken place. A point that the Arbitration Commission might have made, however, is that it is a general principle in the law of succession that a successor State is not liable for the delicts of its predecessor.[440] Accordingly, if the claims for war damages in question were of a strictly unliquidated nature, even if they were attributable to an act of the SFRY itself, they would not pass to the successor State and would therefore not be relevant as regards the division of assets and liabilities. In essence, this would render the same conclusion as that offered by the Arbitration Commission, but would achieve it by a more consistent line of reasoning.

4. Conclusions

It is undoubtedly the case that the opinions of the Arbitration Commission, taken as a body, represent a unique and important examination of the legal issues that attach to the dismemberment of a State. It has rarely been the case that an independent body of legal experts has been asked to consider the whole range of issues relating to statehood,

[440] *Robert E. Brown* case, *Annual Digest*, vol. 2, No. 35. There is some doubt whether the principle can be strictly applied: see *Lighthouses* arbitration, 23 ILR 81; O'Connell, op. cit. above (n. 121), vol. 1, pp. 482–6.

recognition, self-determination, territorial integrity, and succession, in relation to the break-up of a single State, and to map their development as events unfold. It is equally rare for a quasi-judicial body to play such an active part in the process of dismemberment itself. As has been noted, even if the opinions of the Arbitration Commission were delivered in a consultative capacity (a point which was not entirely clear in the early stages) and for that reason are not to be regarded as *res judicata*, they nevertheless played an influential part in creating the necessary framework within which subsequent State practice developed. It is particularly clear, for example, that the Arbitration Commission's first opinion, in which it found the SFRY to be 'in the process of dissolution', not only set the scene for the subsequent recognition of the emergent Republics, but also provided the impetus for the subsequent exclusion of the FRY from automatic membership in international organizations.

The precise role and terms of reference of the Arbitration Commission was particularly unclear in the early stages of its work. It was created pursuant to an agreed statement adopted at the opening session of the International Conference for Peace in Yugoslavia, at which it was determined that an arbitral procedure should be established to which the relevant authorities would be competent to submit their differences. Thereafter, however, it did not undertake a normal process of arbitration: no *compromis* was agreed for the submission of disputes to the Commission, and no awards were delivered. Instead, the Commission delivered a series of 'opinions' as an advisory, or consultative, body to the Chairman (or later the Steering Committee) of the Conference. It also delivered a number of opinions relating to questions of recognition that had been submitted to it by the Council of Ministers of the EC.

Although its terms of reference were later revised and made more explicit, the jurisdiction of the Arbitration Commission was still challenged on two occasions by the FRY. On each occasion, the Arbitration Commission dismissed the challenge and continued to deliver the opinions as requested. In doing so, it drew heavily upon the case law of the ICJ in respect of its advisory jurisdiction. It has been argued that there are cogent reasons for distinguishing between the advisory jurisdiction of the ICJ and that of the Arbitration Commission or other bodies similarly positioned. With respect to all permanent tribunals which operate an advisory jurisdiction as part of their participation in the activities of the Organization to which they are responsible, it is clear that that jurisdiction is materially related to the object and purpose of the Organization as a whole. If, as in the case of the ICJ, there is a close, 'organic', relationship between the Court and the Organization, it is acceptable to presume that member States have consented to the jurisdiction of the Court to the extent to which the role of the Court is concerned with the purposes of the Organization. If, however, there is no clear organic relationship (as in the case of the PCIJ), or the object and purpose of the organization (or indeed the tribunal itself) are obscure, the chain of consent cannot lightly be presumed. In other words, it would be highly inappropriate for an institutional tribunal to offer an opinion on a question that related to the substance of a dispute between States without their explicit consent, unless it was apparent that consent could be imputed through the existence of a clear institutional interest. Whether or not that is the case is dependent both upon the terms of the constituent instrument and the extent to which the organization has international personality in its own right in which its interest may be developed. In the case of the Arbitration Commission, it is doubtful whether the independent interest of the Conference could be materially demonstrated as regards questions relating to the statehood of the FRY, particularly in so far as the distinct identity of the Conference could scarcely be discerned.

Notwithstanding the possible doubts regarding its jurisdiction, the Arbitration Commission produced a series of opinions which have important implications for the development of public international law. Some of the main points that can be drawn from an analysis (and in some instances a development) of its conclusions are as follows:

1) When a State loses the majority of its population and territory through the involuntary disassociation of one or more territorial units, so that the remaining entity is forced to reconstitute itself constitutionally, it may be presumed to have suffered dismemberment. Despite the suggestions of the Arbitration Commission, it is considered that the determinants of this process do not (and should not) change according to the type of government that is exercised over the territory, whether that be unitary or federal. Equally, it is considered that whether or not the material facts point towards the dismemberment or continuation of the State may ultimately be confirmed or denied by the individual appreciation of the States concerned, and that of other members of the international community. It cannot be sustained, particularly in light of the case of Bosnia-Herzegovina, that the legal function of diplomatic recognition is 'purely' declaratory.

2) If a State is identified as being in the process of dismemberment (i.e. that a majority of the constituent territorial units, which embody the majority of the population, have undertaken to disassociate themselves from the parent State), no presumption will be operated in favour of the continued effectiveness of the parent State. Accordingly, the entities that emerge therefrom will be able to establish their sovereignty and statehood with greater ease than would be the case if they had merely seceded. Whilst this does not mean that the parent State has technically transferred its sovereignty over the territory concerned to the emergent entities, it may otherwise be assimilated to a case of devolution, at least as far as the emergent States are concerned.

3) Whereas in cases of secession, the identity of the nascent State will be relatively clear, that is not necessarily the case with respect to dismemberment which, as a process, does not identify *per se* the presumptive units for future statehood. That, however, is to be determined not by resort to the principle of self-determination, nor by a strict application of the principle of effectiveness, but rather in virtue of the principle of *uti possidetis juris*. In this context, *uti possidetis* operates not merely to seal the boundaries of the emergent entities, but also serves to distinguish between those entities that have a right to territorial sovereignty and those that do not. In other words, independent territorial units that exist within the borders of a former administrative unit have to establish their statehood as against the presumptive effectiveness of the unit as a whole. This rule is not affected by the application of the principle of self-determination.

4) All successor States are bound by peremptory norms of international law relating to the rights of peoples, individuals and (possibly) minorities, and the principle of self-determination requires all successor States to allow every individual a right to choose to belong to the ethnic, religious or language community of his or her choice (subject to the necessary interests of the community). More doubtfully, it may also entail a right of individual members of minorities to choose their nationality.

5) All States emerging from a process of dismemberment are equal successors in title, and *a fortiori*, none of them can be considered to be the continuation of the former parent State. All successor States are under an obligation to enter into negotiations with a view to achieving an equitable distribution of the assets and liabilities of the parent State. Failure to co-operate to that end may invoke the international responsibility of the State concerned, and any State suffering loss is entitled to take non-forcible counter-measures in accordance with international law.

6) In the distribution of assets and liabilities, immovable property on the territory of the successor States is subject to the principle of the *locus in quo*. This is also, but more doubtfully, the case in respect of movable property. As regards other State property, archives and debts, including that on the territory of third States, they should be distributed among the successor States according to the principle of equitable apportionment. That principle itself does not require division according to equal proportions, but merely that the division should be broadly equitable.

These broad principles, which form the heart of the Arbitration Commission's opinions, are by no means without their problems and in places are obscured by some of the Commission's own reasoning. The approach of the Commission, on occasion, tended to be excessively rigid and deterministic, particularly as regards its findings in respect to statehood. On other occasions it adopted an over-ambitious approach, as for example in its views in respect of the content of *jus cogens*. In many instances, however, the Commission was attempting to deal with the very difficult and specific problems that arose in relation to the events in Yugoslavia, and for that reason, even if its views cannot always be accepted as general, and universal, propositions, they may nevertheless provide an indication as to the direction in which the various aspects of international law are developing.

THE CONCEPT OF A 'CONTINUING VIOLATION' OF AN INTERNATIONAL OBLIGATION: SELECTED PROBLEMS*

By JOOST PAUWELYN‡

For legal purposes, the most useful way to define a continuing violation is in descriptive terms, i.e. on the basis of its distinguishing features. The definition would then read as follows: *a continuing violation is the breach of an international obligation by an act of a subject of international law extending in time and causing a duration or continuance in time of that breach.*

A study of this concept does not involve the usual examination of the substantive rules of international law restricting the conduct of States. Instead, it focuses on the procedural and substantive consequences of having breached such norms. At first sight these consequences seem to be of minimal and technical importance only. The objective of this article, however, is to prove that these technicalities are of vital importance: in many cases they determine whether or not a substantive norm can be enforced against a State.

As will be discussed in section 2, to distinguish continuing from instantaneous violations will be crucial in the application of time limits and jurisdictional limitation clauses *ratione temporis*; it will determine the applicable law and influence areas such as reparation and enforcement. However, before examining these practical consequences, it will be necessary to enter the more abstract and, at first sight, purely academic discussion of how to distinguish these violations (section 1). Some tentative suggestions will be put forward to facilitate this task.

Special attention will be devoted to the continuing violations caused by an act of a State against one or more individuals. It will be argued that in some instances these violations should be subject to specifically tailored rules.

As in any attempt to establish the rules of international law related to a particular concept, Article 38(1) of the Statute of the International Court of Justice (ICJ), which sums up the sources of international law, has to be kept in mind. With respect to the concept of a continuing violation, it will become clear that 'general principles of law' (Article

‡ Lic.Jur. (Leuven), M. Juris (Oxon.); Associate, De Bandt, van Hecke & Lagae, Brussels.

38(1)(*c*)) occupy a central place. This justifies the references made below to various national legal systems and, in particular, French and Belgian criminal law where the concept of a continuing violation is highly developed. However, at the same time, it will be argued that in this specific area these 'general principles' should not be uncritically transposed to international law.

Another crucial source in establishing the concept is the work of the International Law Commission (ILC). In its reports on a Draft Convention on State Responsibility, the ILC and its Special Rapporteurs have produced an invaluable examination of the problem of continuing violations.[1] With respect to case law, special reference will be made to the International Court of Justice and the institutions established under the European Convention on Human Rights. Other international tribunals (such as the European Court of Justice and the Inter-American Commission and Court of Human Rights) have until now not dealt with the concept of continuing violation.

1. The Concept of a 'Continuing Violation'

At the origin of each continuing violation lies an act or series of acts which extend over a period of time coinciding with both the period during which the international obligation concerned is breached *and* the period the continuing violation is in existence (see figure 1).[2]

FIGURE 1. PERIOD OF COMMISSION OF THE BREACH OF AN INTERNATIONAL OBLIGATION

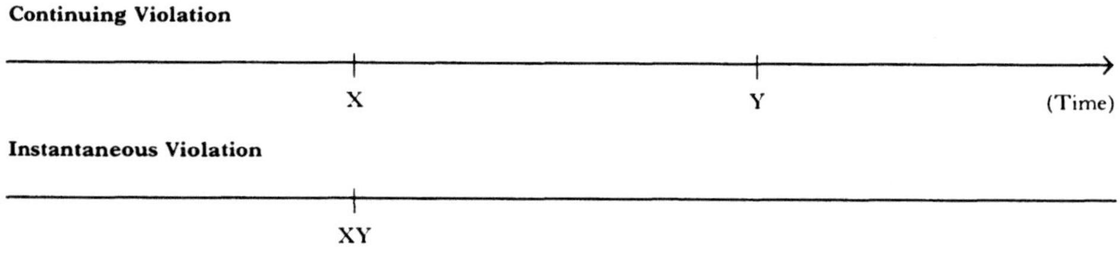

XY = period of commission of the breach

[1] See the Fifth, Sixth and Seventh Reports of Roberto Ago on State Responsibility, respectively in: *Yearbook of the ILC*, 1976, vol. 2, part 1, pp. 14–24; ibid., 1977, vol. 2, part 1, pp. 3–43, and ibid., 1978, vol. 2, part 1, pp. 31–52 (hereafter referred to as the 5th, 6th or 7th Report of Ago); the Reports of the ILC on its 28th, 29th and 30th Sessions respectively in: *Yearbook of the ILC*, 1976, vol. 2, part 2, pp. 87–122; ibid., 1977, vol. 2, part 2, pp. 11–50, and ibid., 1978, vol. 2, part 2, pp. 81–98 (hereafter referred to as ILC Report on its 28th, 29th or 30th Session), and the Preliminary Report of Arangio-Ruiz of 18 May 1988, UN Doc. A/CN.4/416 and Addenda (hereafter referred to as the Report of Arangio-Ruiz).

[2] See Brownlie, *System of the Law of Nations: State Responsibility (Part I)* (Oxford, 1983), pp. 193–8.

In respect of most continuing violations the existence of the breach of the obligation in question can be determined prior to and without considering the element of time. This category of continuing violations will be dealt with in section 1.1. For other continuing violations, the element of time (that is, duration or repetition) forms a constitutive element of the obligation, to be fulfilled before it can be breached. These violations are examined in section 1.2.

1.1. *Continuing violations caused by a continuing act*

1.1.1. *Instantaneous acts versus continuing acts*

**Continuing acts*. Many breaches of law arise from so-called continuing acts and cause a continuing violation of the obligation in question. Some examples in international law are: maintenance in effect of legislation incompatible with a State's international obligations, unlawful detention of a foreign official, unlawful occupation of part of the territory of another State, unlawful blockade of foreign coasts or ports, etc.[3] Similar examples exist in internal law: illegal restraint, unlawful possession of others' property, receipt of stolen goods, illegal possession of weapons, etc. In Belgian and French law, these continuing violations are called '*infractions continus ou successives/voortdurende misdrijven*'; in English and American law 'continuing wrongs'.[4]

Examples of such continuing violations can readily be found in the international case law. In the case concerning *US Diplomatic and Consular Staff in Teheran*,[5] for example, the detention of US diplomatic and consular staff constituted a continuing violation of Iran's international obligations towards the US. In the case concerning *Military and*

[3] As already discussed in the earliest works on the subject: Triepel, *Völkerrecht und Landesrecht* (Leipzig, 1899), p. 289, and Ago, 'Le Délit international', *Recueil des cours*, 68 (1939–II), p. 520.

[4] See, for Belgium: Hennau and Verhaegen, *Droit pénal général* (Bruxelles, 1991), p. 49, and Dupont and Verstraeten, *Handboek Belgisch Strafrecht*, Boekdeel I (Leuven, 1989), pp. 198–206; for France: Pradel, *Droit pénal général*, tome 1 (9th edn., Paris, 1994) pp. 400–7, and Stéfani, Levasseur and Bouloc, *Droit pénal général* (15th edn., Paris, 1995), pp. 186–93; for England: Brazier, *Street on Torts* (9th edn., London, 1993), p. 558; for the US: Harper, James and Gray, *The Law of Torts*, vol. 1 (2nd edn., Boston, 1986), pp. 26–30, and pp. 120–2. See also Solnar, 'La Notion de l'infraction continue sur la base du droit pénal comparé', *En hommage à J. Constant* (Paris, 1971), pp. 329 ff. In the US continuing wrongs, as defined in this paper, take the form of what is confusingly defined as 'temporary' nuisance or trespass (said to continue day by day, creating a new action for every unit of time that it continues). In the US, this 'temporary' nuisance or trespass is distinguished from what is called 'permanent' nuisance or trespass. In the latter case only the *effects* of the wrong continue, not the wrong itself, and only one cause of action arises. In French law, this category of wrongs is sometimes defined as '*infractions permanentes*'. Since these 'permanent' wrongs are submitted to exactly the same rules as instantaneous wrongs, one ought to abolish this confusing and superfluous category and merely distinguish continuing from instantaneous wrongs; this division is adopted in this article.

[5] *ICJ Reports*, 1980, p. 3.

Paramilitary Activities in and against Nicaragua[6] the US was held to be in a continuing breach of its obligations towards Nicaragua. In the *Rainbow Warrior* case (arbitral award of 30 April 1990[7]), France was held to be in continuing violation of its obligations towards New Zealand (for a specific period in the past only) by refusing to return its two agents (who assisted in the sinking of the ship *Rainbow Warrior*) to the Island of Hao. This was in breach of the agreement reached between France and New Zealand which provided that the two French agents, at that time convicted prisoners in New Zealand, should be transferred to the Island of Hao and remain there for three years.

Article 25(1) of the ILC's Draft on State Responsibility (hereafter referred to as 'the ILC's Draft') declares that, in the event of such continuing violations, 'the breach . . . *occurs* at the moment when that [continuing] act begins. Nevertheless, the *time of commission* of the breach [and thus the continuing violation] extends over the entire period during which the act continues and remains not in conformity with the international obligation' (emphasis added; see figure 2).

FIGURE 2. CONTINUING VIOLATION CAUSED BY A CONTINUING ACT

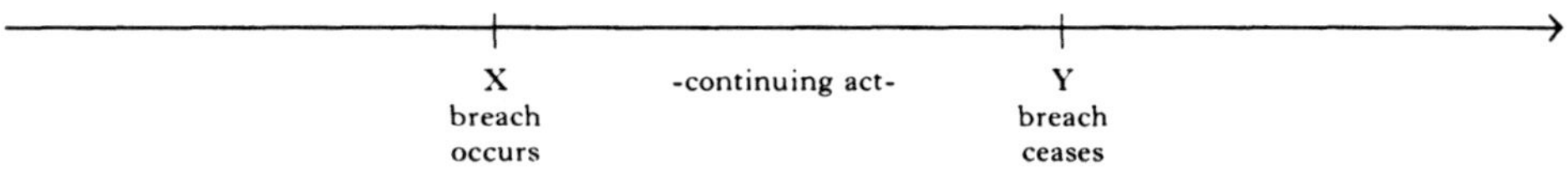

XY = period of commission of the breach

**Instantaneous acts*. Apart from continuing acts, breaches of the law can also arise from what will be called, for the sake of convenience, 'instantaneous' acts and cause an 'instantaneous' violation only (see figure 1). Examples of these are, in international law: the shooting down by one State of aircraft of another State lawfully flying over the former's territory; in domestic law: murder or the burning of others' property. The fact that the *completion* of these acts might take some time is irrelevant. Only the extension in time of the *violation* (not of the material act as such) is determinate: even though it might take hours, for example, to murder someone, the crime of murder, by its very nature, remains an 'instantaneous' crime.

**The difference*. How then can continuing acts be distinguished from instantaneous acts? Abstract definitions may readily be found. The ILC, for example, defines a continuing act as one 'which proceeds unchanged over a given period of time: in other words, an act which, after its

[6] *ICJ Reports*, 1986, p. 14.
[7] 82 ILR 499.

occurrence, continues to exist as such and not merely in its effects and consequences', and an instantaneous act as 'an act that does not extend in time, i.e. an act that ends as soon as it is committed; where the breach having occurred also automatically ceases to exist'.[8]

In practice, however, it will often be difficult to make the distinction, especially between a continuing act and an instantaneous act *having lasting effects*. The idea of a continuing violation implies that the act as such, and not merely its injurious effects, should continue to exist.

In the *Phosphates in Morocco* case (*Italy* v. *France*), for example, the Italian Government claimed that both the decision of the Department of Mines depriving Mr Tassara, an Italian citizen, of his vested property rights and the establishment of a monopoly in the exploitation of phosphates mines by means of legislation were contrary to the international obligations of France, and that both constituted continuing acts. This was because, Italy argued, these acts (respectively, the decision of the Department of Mines and the legislation) 'extend over a period of time, so that when they have become complete, in the sense that all their constituent elements are present, they do not thereby cease to exist but continue remaining identical with a permanent character'.[9]

The Permanent Court unanimously decided that the decision to dispossess Mr Tassara constituted a so-called 'instantaneous act with lasting effects' since only its harmful consequences, and not the act itself, had remained in existence after the decision was taken.[10] The qualification of the alleged monopoly was more controversial. The Court took the view that the monopolization was also caused by an instantaneous act since it 'cannot be considered separately from the legislation of which it is the result . . . [In this legislation] are to be sought the essential facts constituting the alleged monopolisation'.[11] Judges Cheng Tien-Hsi and Van Eysinga (dissenting) and most subsequent doctrine, on the contrary, considered the monopolization as an alleged continuing violation caused by a continuing act. To quote Judge Cheng:

> The monopoly, though instituted by the legislation of 1920, is still existing today. If it is wrongful, it is wrongful not merely in its creation but in its continuance . . . this prejudice does not merely continue from an old existence but assumes a new existence every day, so long as the legislation that first created it remains in force.[12]

[8] ILC Report on its 30th Session, p. 90.

[9] Observations and submissions submitted by the Italian Government, *PCIJ*, Series C, No. 84, p. 494.

[10] *PCIJ*, Series A/B, No. 74, p. 28, and confirmed in the two dissenting opinions at pp. 33 and 36; also in ILC, Report on its 30th Session, p. 89; 7th Report of Ago, p. 41, and Report of Arangio-Ruiz, p. 12.

[11] Series A/B, No. 74, p. 25.

[12] Ibid., p. 36.

Another controversial example is the act of confiscation of property by legislation (to be distinguished from dispossession by an administrative decision). Ago and the ILC consider any act of confiscation as an instantaneous act with lasting effects since 'the act of the State as such ends as soon as the confiscation has taken place, even if its consequences are lasting'.[13] According to Arangio-Ruiz, however, confiscation by legislation constitutes a continuing act, not terminated with the legislation but lasting as long as the measure stands.[14]

Three useful, but not always decisive, tools to solve these dilemmas, taking into account the particular circumstances of each case, can be proposed.

Firstly, the focus should be on the definition of the international obligation itself, rather than on the act breaching it and its effects. Indeed, one should examine whether the obligation in question is targeting a (possibly continuing) *situation* or, on the contrary, a given and instantaneous *fact*. In most domestic legal systems this examination of the legislator's abstract definition of the offence constitutes one of the decisive criteria.[15] However, in international law, and customary international law in particular, the obligations imposed on States are often only 'general principles' and cannot always be formulated verbatim. This will often make it impossible to examine any abstract definition of the obligation concerned. A second requirement to be fulfilled in most domestic regimes, in order to have a continuing act, is proof of a reiterated intention of the perpetrator to confirm or perpetuate the wrongful act or situation during the period of the alleged continuing violation.[16] A transposition of the latter requirement into international law would be inappropriate. Indeed, it seems to be absurd in theory and practically impossible to examine or prove the specific intentions behind State actions. This would require extensive examination of a State's motives and decision-making process, a task not appropriate for international tribunals.

Secondly, reference should be made to the problem of reparation and, especially, the question whether *after* the act first occurred the remedy of cessation is still of any use or the only possible reparation, or whether restitution in kind or compensation suffices to provide reparation both for the past and the future.[17] Only in the former case should a continuing violation be established.

[13] ILC Report on its 28th Session, para. 21, *in fine*.

[14] Report of Arangio-Ruiz, p. 14.

[15] See, for example, in Belgian law, Hennau and Verhaegen, op. cit. above (n. 4), p. 50, and in French law, Tsarpalas, *Le Moment et la durée des infractions pénales* (Paris, 1967), and Stéfani, Levasseur and Bouloc, op. cit. above (n. 4), pp. 187–8.

[16] Ibid.

[17] See Graefrath, 'Responsibility and Damages Caused', *Recueil des cours*, 185 (1984–II), p. 22, and below, section 2.3 on reparation.

Applying this second test to the problem cases mentioned above, one should examine the legal effect of the repeal of the legislative or administrative act. In the case of a monopoly established by legislation, the monopoly will cease to exist. In other words, the repeal of the act will constitute the 'cessation' of the violation. Moreover, in these cases, *only* 'cessation' can provide reparation for the future. Therefore, the violation itself is a *continuous* violation.

The repeal of an expropriation law, on the other hand, will not necessarily cause the return of the property to its original owner. In this sense, the repeal of the act does not constitute the 'cessation' of a violation. Indeed, one could argue that, in these cases, restitution in kind or compensation provides adequate reparation for both past *and future* which makes the need for 'cessation' obsolete. Therefore, some will conclude, unlawful expropriation constitutes an *instantaneous* violation.

Finally, one should assess whether as a legal fiction the act complained of can be said to be repeated, in its entirety, each day since it has been passed (and therefore is a continuing act), or whether only the effects or consequences of the act, which as such has only been passed once (and thus is an instantaneous act), remain intact. In other words, if the act affects the legal status of a person during a certain period in time, it should be regarded as a continuing act.

1.1.2. *The case law developed under the European Convention on Human Rights*

The case law under the European Convention on Human Rights seems to follow the lines of the approach developed above. However, one peculiarity, based on the special legal context in which it operates, can be distinguished. From the outset, one of the decisive elements in the Commission's decision on whether a continuing situation exists has been whether the position in which the victim is placed represents a continuing situation in violation of the Convention or, on the contrary, a violation of its rights and freedoms which clearly dates from the past (i.e. an instantaneous fact). In other words, the Commission focuses on the *effects* on the *victim* of the act (*in casu* the individual), taking into account all relevant circumstances of the case, rather than on the objective qualification of the *act* as such or the subjective intentions of its *author* (*in casu* the State). In this sense all rights and freedoms protected by the Convention can be the object of a continuing violation.

This approach is in sharp contrast with the one generally adopted in domestic criminal law. There the assessment is made from the point of view of the author of the offence (*in casu* the accused). The internal judge will primarily examine whether the allegedly wrongful situation results from different acts or omissions based on similar reiterated delictual intentions (forming a continuing situation), or from one single act or omission based on one single delictual intention (forming an instantaneous act).[18] As argued above, to transpose this subjective approach (which examines the intentions of the author) to international law would prove to be practically impossible.

The first continuing situation acknowledged by the Commission was in the landmark *De Becker* case. There the applicant complained that as a result of a conviction in 1946, Article 123 *sexies* of the Belgian Penal Code became applicable and *ipso facto* deprived him for life of certain rights, including the right to exercise his profession as a journalist (contrary to Article 10). The applicant argued that the judgment merely marked the beginning of a state of affairs whereby his right to freedom of expression was being repeatedly and perpetually violated, and stressed that the purpose of his application was not to appeal against an isolated decision but against legislation permanently in conflict with the Convention.[19] The Commission confirmed these arguments and added that 'it therefore appears that the Applicant finds himself in a continuing situation in respect of which he claims to be the victim of a violation of Article 10'.[20] The circumstances here (legislation allegedly contrary to an international obligation) are similar to those of the alleged monopolization in the *Phosphates in Morocco* case, where the PCIJ reached the opposite conclusion. In these cases the Commission's approach should be preferred.

In the *De Becker* case, the claim had primarily been called into existence by a legal provision. In other cases, however, where the claim was directed more against a judicial decision or a decision of the executive, the Commission refused to recognize a continuing situation. In the case of *X* v. *Belgium*, for example, the Commission came to this conclusion since

> the complaint would not appear to relate solely to a legal provision that has created a permanent situation . . . [it] also, and perhaps primarily, concerns a judicial sentence, i.e. a specific act which did not bring this provision automat-

[18] See, for example, in French law, Merle and Vitu, *Traité de droit criminel*, tome I (5th edn., Paris, 1984), p. 573; in Belgian law, Kuyl, 'Over de eenheid van opzet', *Rechtskundig Weekblad*, 1978–9, pp. 545–60.

[19] *Yearbook of the European Convention on Human Rights*, 2 (1958–9), p. 214, at pp. 230–1.

[20] Ibid., p. 231. The UN Human Rights Committee adopted the same concept of 'continuing violations' with respect to the International Covenant on Civil and Political Rights. Its case law bears a striking resemblance to the one adopted by the European Commission. See, e.g., Communication No. 1/1976, HRC Selection I, p. 17, and Communication No. 457/1991, HRC 1992 Report, p. 439; see also the discussion in Zwart, *The Admissibility of Human Rights Petitions, The Case Law of the European Commission of Human Rights and the Human Rights Committee* (*International Studies in Human Rights*, vol. 36, Dordrecht, 1994), pp. 130–4.

ically into play for an indefinite period but maintained it for a limited time only and could have terminated its application.[21]

This distinction, between legislation and administrative or judicial acts, seems to be based on the assumption that the latter are pronounced at a clearly defined moment and that the resulting consequences are of a temporary nature.

This view is open to criticism since legislative measures, too, are taken at a specific moment and the legal consequence envisaged therewith may also be of a temporary nature.[22] After all, the decisive question should be whether the State prohibits the individual from exercising his/her rights and freedoms under the Convention during a certain period, and this on an ongoing basis. In other words, whether the individual risks a conviction at any time during this period if s/he exercises these rights or freedoms. If this is the case, a continuing violation would be established. This argument gains added weight in light of the Commission's point of view generally taken, namely that of the victim, for whom the source or author of the situation in violation of the Convention will be of the least importance.

In the event of confiscation or expropriation by legislation allegedly contrary to Protocol No. 1, Article 1, to the Convention, the Commission has refused to recognize a continuing situation. In the case of *X* v. *United Kingdom*, for example, where the applicant complained of an Act of Parliament abolishing the rights of landowners whose property adjoined that of British Railways and which had deprived him of his property, the Commission decided that the applicant experienced rather 'the enduring effects of an act occurring at a given point in time' (i.e. an instantaneous act with lasting effects).[23] In the case of *Spörrong and Lönnroth* v. *Sweden*, however, the Commission found a continuing violation of the same Article 1. There the applicants complained of the effects on their ownership of properties caused by long-term expropriation permits accompanied by the prohibition of construction (which had been effective during a period of 23 and 12 years). A decision of the Municipality of Stockholm to make use of the expropriation permits was still pending. The Commission found a continuing violation since, rather than being caused by one decision or act, 'the grievances result more gradually with

[21] *Yearbook of the European Convention on Human Rights*, 4 (1961), p. 324, at p. 334. See also in *X and Y* v. *Portugal*, *Decisions and Reports of the European Commission of Human Rights* (hereafter *Decisions and Reports*), vol. 16, p. 209.

[22] Supporting this criticism are, *inter alios*, van Dijk and van Hoof, *Theory and Practice of the European Convention on Human Rights* (Deventer, 1991), pp. 103–4; Sorensen, 'Le Problème intertemporel dans l'application de la Convention européenne des droits de l'homme', in *Mélanges P. Modinos* (Paris, 1968), p. 315, and Antonopoulos, *La Jurisprudence des organes de la convention européenne des droits de l'homme* (Leyde, 1967), p. 29, at pp. 35–6.

[23] *Decisions and Reports*, vol. 8, p. 211, at p. 212. See also *X* v. *Denmark*, ECHR, *Yearbook of the European Convention on Human Rights*, 1 (1955–7), pp. 241–8, and *X* v. *Federal Republic of Germany*, ibid., pp. 157–9.

the passing of time from the accumulation of renewed delays of expropriation . . . which affect the applicants as property owners'.[24]

Therefore, with respect to Article 1, First Protocol, the Commission distinguishes *de facto* from *de jure* expropriation: only the former can constitute a continuing violation. In view of the consequences attached to continuing violations (see below), this distinction is open to criticism. It seems unfair that persons expropriated *de jure*, and thus already in practice worse off than those expropriated *de facto*, should also be legally disadvantaged before the Commission. A more neutral solution could be to regard both *de facto* and *de jure* expropriation as a *status* attributed to the applicant for a period in time (i.e. the status of being wrongfully interfered with in one's property rights) and therefore leave the option open to consider all expropriations as continuing violations according to the specific circumstances at hand. This would be more in line with the view of Arangio-Ruiz, but contrary to the approach taken by the ILC, Ago and the PCIJ.[25] However, it could be particularly justified here on the basis of the importance attached in human rights violations to the situation in which the *victim* is placed.

One could then argue that, according to this view, all human rights violations can be considered as continuing violations since they all affect the victim's 'status'. However, even though, by their very nature, all human rights violations (as much as each loss or damage) affect the victim's status *sensu lato*, not all continue to affect that status during a period in time (i.e. affect their status *sensu stricto*). Murder clearly affects the victim's 'status' but only instantaneously; whereas deprivation of property by legislation or administrative act could be said to influence your status continuously, as long as the measure stands. On this ground one could also distinguish damage or loss as an effect of an instantaneous violation from continuing deprivation of property, itself constituting the violation of an international obligation.

To illustrate that in principle all rights accorded under the Convention can be the object of a continuing violation,[26] one can mention the crucial decisions and reports of the Commission in the case of *Cyprus* v. *Turkey* (Application No. 8007/77), where a series of continuing violations by Turkey against Greek Cypriots had been established. On the basis of Article 8 (right to family life), for example, the Commission found that 'by the refusal to allow the return of more than 170,000 Greek Cypriot refugees to their homes in the North of Cyprus, Turkey did not act, and

[24] *Decisions and Reports*, vol. 15, p. 15, at pp. 20–1; see also Application No. 14807/89, *Human Rights Law Journal*, 13 (1992), p. 320.

[25] See nn. 10, 13 and 14, above, and the discussion on the issue under the second of the three tests advocated above to distinguish continuing from instantaneous violations.

[26] The establishment of a continuing violation under the Convention is no legal curiosity: in the indices of the *Decisions and Reports of the European Commission of Human Rights* between 1975–89, 25 such cases are explicitly summed up.

was continuing not to act, in conformity with Article 8 of the Convention'.[27] The same conclusion was reached on the basis of Protocol No. 1, Article 1.[28]

1.2. *Continuing violations where the element of duration or repetition is part of the content of the international obligation breached*

Contrary to the more frequent continuing violations examined above, where a decision on the existence of the breach can be made *without* referring to the element of time, in the more complicated cases falling under this section, such a decision can only be made *after* consideration of the time factor. This factor, *in casu* the element of duration (section 1.2.1.) or repetition (section 1.2.2.), forms a constitutive element of the international obligation in question. What is important here is not the question whether this substantive requirement of duration or repetition has been fulfilled, but the determination of the moment and duration of the breach once it *has* been proved that this breach exists.[29]

1.2.1. *The period of time under consideration falls outside the period of commission of the breach: the continuing violation only starts once this period of time has elapsed (see figure 3)*

In these cases, the lapse of a period of time forms a constitutive element of the breach of the international obligation in question. The latter generally targets only one individual case.

An example can be found in Article 5(3) of the European Convention on Human Rights, requiring States to try persons in detention on remand within a *reasonable time*. Other examples are Article 6 of the Convention (right to a hearing by a tribunal within a *reasonable time*) and Article 3 of its Protocol No. 1 (obligation to hold free elections at *reasonable intervals*). Similar provisions can be found in internal law. In Belgian and French law,[30] for example, a person who is under an obligation to pay alimentary pensions commits the criminal offence of

[27] Report of the Commission of 4 October 1983, *Decisions and Reports*, vol. 72, pp. 5–117, at p. 41. See also the Commission's decision of 10 July 1978 on admissibility, ibid., vol. 13, p. 85, at pp. 153–4; *X* v. *Switzerland*, ibid., vol. 6, p. 124; and *X* v. *United Kingdom*, ibid., vol. 7, p. 102.

[28] Ibid., p. 7. See also the case of *Chrysostomos and others* v. *Turkey*, *Decisions and Reports*, vol. 68, p. 216.

[29] See Brownlie, op. cit. above (n. 2), pp. 197–8.

[30] Respectively in Article 391 *bis* and Article 257 of their Penal Codes. In Belgium the offence is correctly defined as a *délit continue* (see Dupont and Verstraeten, op. cit. above (n. 4), p. 199); in France, however, most case law and authors mistakenly regard it as a *délit instantané* (see Stéfani, Levasseur and Bouloc, op. cit. above (n. 4), p. 217, with some references to the contrary in n. 9).

'abandon de famille/familieverlating' if he has not abided by the terms of his obligation for more than two months.

In these cases, the continuing violation only starts when the prescribed time period has elapsed and the obligations thereto attached are *not* abided by (for example, after X days of detention without trial or release). The breach comes to an end at the date the obligations attached to the lapse of time are fulfilled (for example the day the person is put to trial).[31] However, during the period of commission of the breach, the continuing violation is caused by a continuing act (as defined in section 1.1.1.). Figure 3 tries to illuminate this position.

FIGURE 3. CONTINUING VIOLATION WHERE ELEMENT OF DURATION IS PART OF CONTENT OF THE INTERNATIONAL OBLIGATION

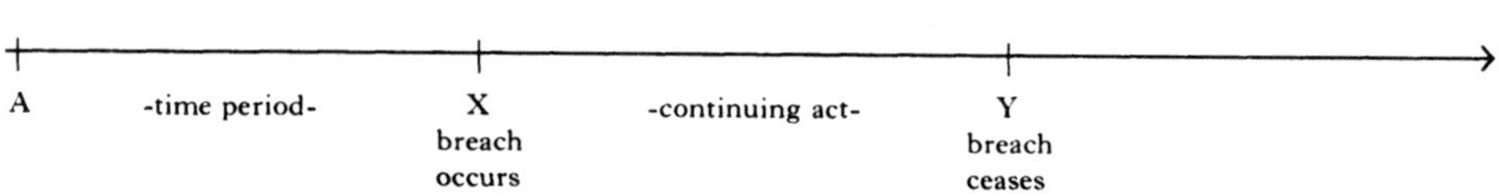

AX = (reasonable) time period to elapse before obligation can be breached

XY = period of commission of the breach

1.2.2. *The period of time under consideration falls within the period of commission of the breach: the continuing violation itself starts at the date this period of time begins (see figure 4)*

These cases generally involve a series of individual cases which in the aggregate constitute a so-called 'composite act', mostly a practice or pattern, contrary to the international obligation in question. The time factor, namely the element of repetition required in order to have a practice, forms an integral part of the content of the obligation concerned.

In this event, Article 25(2) of the ILC's Draft declares that 'the breach . . . occurs at the moment when that act or omission of the series is accomplished which establishes the existence of the composite act. Nevertheless, the time of commission of the breach extends over the entire period from the first of the actions or omissions constituting the composite act . . . and so long as such actions or omissions are repeated' (see figure 4).

[31] See, *inter alia, de Courcy* v. *United Kingdom*, decision of the Commission, *Yearbook of the European Convention on Human Rights*, 10 (1967), p. 382, and *Roy and Alice Fletcher*, decision of the Commission, *Collection of Decisions*, No. 25, 1968, p. 76.

FIGURE 4. CONTINUING VIOLATION CAUSED BY A COMPOSITE ACT

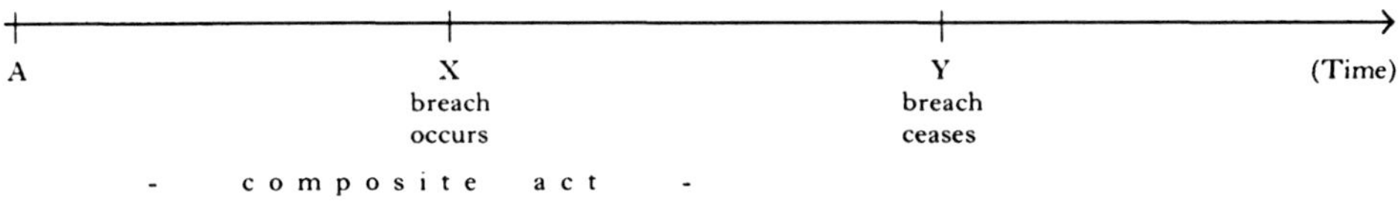

A: first individual act of the series of acts constituting the composite act or practice
X: ultimate individual act required to establish the composite act or practice
Y: last individual act part of the series

AY = period of commission of the breach

These continuing violations can take three different forms.

Firstly, one can distinguish those continuing violations where the individual acts, taken separately, are lawful and only the composite is unlawful. A frequently cited example is the breach of an international obligation prohibiting a State from adopting a 'discriminatory practice' in regard to the access of aliens from a particular country to the exercise of an activity or a profession. This obligation can only be breached if a *series* of rejections of applications from nationals of the latter has been established. One isolated rejection does not breach the obligation in question. Examples of such continuing violations can also be found in internal law. In Belgian and French law, for example, these are called *'infractions d'habitude/gewoontemisdrijven'*.[32]

A second category contains those continuing violations where not only the composite act but also each individual case as such is unlawful. An example can be deduced from the practice of the institutions of the United Nations where the '*consistent* violation of human rights and fundamental freedoms' has come to be established as a breach of an international obligation in its own right, distinct from the breach caused by an isolated violation of such rights and freedoms.[33] Here the individual human rights violations, as well as the composite act of *consistently* violating human rights, are contrary to an international obligation.

A third, and last category, is formed by those continuing violations where the composite act as such does not constitute a violation distinct from the violations caused by the individual acts composing it. In

[32] See, *inter alia*, Article 380 *bis*(4) of the Belgian Penal Code, making a criminal offence of the habitual exploitation of prostitution of others and the offence of illegal exercise of medicine in French law (Art. L.372, *C. santé public*). In English law one could refer to the Habitual Drunkards Act 1879.

[33] See ILC Report on its 30th Session, p. 93, and Brownlie, *Principles of Public Interntional Law* (4th edn., Oxford, 1990), p. 646. Another, and perhaps more obvious, example is the crime of genocide which, as a composite unlawful act, can be constituted of a series of acts (such as individual murders) which are, taken in isolation, also contrary to international law.

this event, the establishment of a continuing violation depends to a considerable degree on the formulations employed by the applicant. The judgment of the European Court of Human Rights in the case of *Ireland* v. *United Kingdom* offers a good example.[34] Instead of alleging individual violations of Article 3 of the Convention (prohibiting torture and inhuman or degrading treatment or punishment), Ireland requested the Court to censure a *practice* contrary to Article 3. The Court confirmed its competence to adjudicate on an alleged practice, examined a series of individual cases and concluded that in specific places and at specific times such a practice had been established. The Court, however, explicitly stated that the practice as such did not constitute a violation of the Convention different from the violation in each individual case (on which it did not have to adjudicate) brought before the Court as evidence of this practice.

A rather different, but nevertheless controversial, form of continuing violation is that introduced in Article 25(3) of the ILC's Draft. This refers to violations caused by a 'complex act of the State consisting of a succession of actions or omissions by the same or different organs of the State in respect of the same case'. These so-called complex acts are the collective outcome of all the actions or omissions by State organs at successive stages in a given case and represent the position taken by the State in that case. According to Article 25(3) the breach only occurs 'at the moment when the last constituent element of that complex act is accomplished'. However, it is added that 'the time of commission of the breach extends over the entire period between the action or omission which initiated the breach and that which completed it' (see figure 5).

FIGURE 5. CONTINUING VIOLATION CAUSED BY A COMPLEX ACT

A: original position or act taken by the State
X: date final position taken by the State (i.e. date domestic remedies are exhausted)

AX = period of commission of the breach

These rules proposed by the ILC are highly debatable.[35] It suffices to note here that in the event that the ILC's approach is correct, a

[34] Judgment of the Court, Series A, No. 25, p. 64, at para. 159.

[35] See, *inter alios*, Wyler, 'Quelques réflections sur la réalisation dans le temps du fait internationalement illicite', *Revue générale de droit international public*, 95 (1991), p. 881, at pp. 904–8; Salmon, 'Le Fait étatique complexe: une notion contestable', *Annuaire français de droit international*, 28 (1982), pp. 709–38.

continuing violation would be established which exists during the entire period the State needed in order to take a final decision on a specific case, even though the obligation is only breached at the end of that period (see figure 5).

2. The Practical Importance of a 'Continuing Violation'

Once the concept of a continuing violation has been examined, it is necessary to turn to the legal consequences which can be drawn from the factual determination that a breach of an international obligation extends over a certain lapse of time.

Even though both have confirmed the legal principles examined below, it should be kept in mind that the ICJ and the legal bodies established under the European Convention on Human Rights operate in a different legal context and have completely different tasks. The ICJ is commonly considered as a *juge d'exception* whose powers of *ad hoc* dispute settlement are by far the most successful in terms of actual effectiveness of the Court.[36] Besides, it only deals with disputes between States. Private parties have no standing or intervention rights. The European Commission and Court of Human Rights, on the other hand, mostly deal with claims of individuals against a State and supervise a specific 'public order of Europe'.[37] The enforcement of the Convention does not depend on the *ad hoc* consent of the member parties. Indeed, as was noted in the Explanatory Report to Protocol No. 11, 'full acceptance of the supervisory mechanism established by the convention has become, *de facto*, a condition for admission to the Organisation'.[38] The Special Rapporteur to the ILC, Arangio-Ruiz, came to a similar conclusion when he remarked that the European institutions are more municipal adjudicating bodies, concerned with acts of national authorities towards individuals *within* a municipal legal system, rather than an international tribunal considering the complex wrongful act of a State in its *external* relations with another State.[39] These considerations should be taken into account in the discussion of the case law below.

Without any intention to be exhaustive, two specific problems will be examined: the admissibility problem (section 2.1) and the intertemporal

[36] See Janis, 'The International Court', in Janis (ed.), *International Courts for the Twenty-first Century* (Dordrecht, 1992), p. 20.

[37] This was explicitly stated in the case of *Austria* v. *Italy*, *Yearbook of the European Convention on Human Rights*, 4 (1961), p. 116, at p. 141.

[38] Published in *Human Rights Law Journal*, 15 (1994), pp. 91–102, at p. 98.

[39] Report of Arangio-Ruiz, n. 27 at pp. 28–9.

problem (section 2.2). In a final section, some other practical consequences of having established a continuing violation will be summarized.

2.1. *Determination of the competence of an international tribunal: the admissibility problem*

In order to establish the competence of each court or tribunal, national or international, certain conditions *ratione temporis* have to be fulfilled. These conditions generally fall within the questions to be determined, namely:

(1) has the claim been introduced within the prescribed time limits, i.e. within the period of time allowed to elapse between the alleged breach (or some other specific date) and the introduction of the claim? (section 2.1.1).
(2) especially applicable to international tribunals, does the present claim concern a dispute, or 'acts' or 'situations' giving rise to a dispute, which occurred subsequent to the date mentioned in the clause limiting the jurisdiction of the court or tribunal *ratione temporis*? (section 2.1.2).

What then are the rules to be applied if these time-related restrictions come into play in a case where a continuing violation has been established?

2.1.1. *Time-limits*

2.1.1.1. *Explicit time limits versus extinctive prescription*

The first set of time-related restrictions, the so-called time limits, can be activated in two instances:[40] firstly, where time limits are explicitly inserted in the legal instrument or provision conferring jurisdiction on the tribunal. An example in international law is the six months' period to be observed after the exhaustion of domestic remedies in Article 26 of the European Convention on Human Rights. In domestic law, one can mention the two and three months' time limit to be observed in procedures for judicial review in, respectively, Belgian and European Community law,[41] and English law.[42] These time limits are created at the discretion of the legislature.

A second category of time limits emerges in the operation of the rules of general international law related to the doctrine of extinctive prescription. According to this doctrine the right of a State (or individual) to

[40] See King, 'Prescription of Claims in International Law', this *Year Book*, 15 (1934), pp. 82–97, and Brownlie, op. cit. above (n. 33), pp. 504–5.

[41] Article 19, *Coordinated Statutes on the Council of State*; Article 173(5), Treaty on European Union.

[42] Order 53, rule 4(1), of the rules of the Supreme Court.

invoke responsibility for an internationally wrongful act committed against it by another State, may lapse by prescription even if no explicit time limit has been provided. This concept of prescription relates to substance and aims at justice in every case. A recent example falling under this category can be found in the case concerning *Certain Phosphate Lands in Nauru (Preliminary Objections)*, where the Court recognized the principle of extinctive prescription, but rejected Australia's objection that Nauru's claim was inadmissible on the ground that it had not been submitted within a 'reasonable time'.[43]

As these two categories show, lapse of time may operate to defeat claims in two distinct ways: it may operate as a defence in itself (as in the first category) or as part of a more general defence, such as waiver or estoppel, where lapse of time is said to operate by way of acquiescence (as in the second category).

2.1.1.2. *Principles to be applied in case of a continuing violation*

Even though it is necessary to keep in mind the distinction made above, the principles to be applied in case of a continuing violation are generally the same. In that event, both categories give rise to two types of cases: firstly, cases where the breach still continues at the time of the proceedings; secondly, cases where the breach has ceased to exist before that date.

**The principle*. The general principle is that a claim can only be *in*admissible on the ground of lapse of time *once the breach has ceased to exist*, that being the earliest date from which any time limit can possibly start to run (see figure 6.1).

FIGURE 6.1. TIME LIMITS IN GENERAL

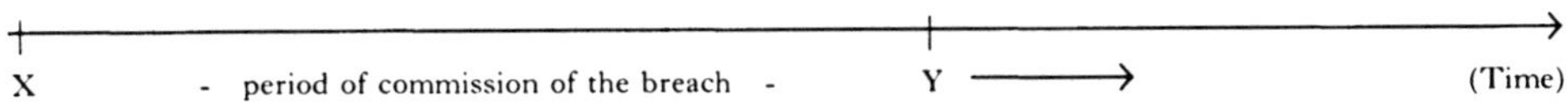

Y = first day time limit can possibly start to run

In this respect the case law under Article 26 of the European Convention is particularly instructive. According to this provision, the Commission may only deal with a matter after all domestic remedies have been exhausted and 'within a period of six months from the date on which the final decision was taken'. Applying this Article in the *De Becker* case the Commission decided that:

> when the Commission receives an application concerning . . . a permanent state of affairs . . . the problem of the six months period [within which the application has to be filed] specified in Article 26 can arise only after this state of affairs *has ceased to exist*; whereas in the circumstances, it is exactly as though

[43] *ICJ Reports*, 1992, p. 240, at p.253.

the alleged violation was being repeated daily thus preventing the running of the six months period.[44]

In the case of *Cyprus* v. *Turkey*, the Commission phrased this in other terms:

the rule requiring the exhaustion of domestic remedies [provided in Article 26] does not apply to complaints the object of which is to determine the compatibility with the Convention of legislative measures and administrative practices, except where specific and effective remedies against legislation exist.[45]

In domestic law, the same principle has been applied to continuing violations. In Belgian criminal law, for example, it is common cause that 'le délai de préscription de l'infraction continue . . . commence a courir le jour ou *cesse* cette situation'.[46] In English law, for example, section 76 of the Sex Discrimination Act 1975 provides a time limit of three months 'beginning when the act complained of was done'. There, as well, subsection 7(*b*) specifies that 'any act extending over a period shall be treated as done *at the end of that period*'.[47]

The ILC came to the same conclusion: 'in the case of a "continuing" wrongful act, however, this *dies* [*a quo* of the time limit] can be established only *after* the end of the time of commission of the wrongful act itself'.[48]

**Cases where the breach still continues*. If *a priori* the breach still continues to exist at the time of the proceedings, no problem of a lapsed time limit can occur. Indeed, since a time limit serves to make acts or decisions from the past unassailable after a given period, it does not commence as long as the continuing situation exists. In these cases, the question of whether or not there is a continuing violation becomes of vital importance.

**Cases where the breach has ceased to exist*. From these principles, one can deduce that when the breach ceased to exist *before* the claim has been brought to the court, the relevant time limit has to be calculated starting from either the day the breach ceased to exist (and not from the moment the breach came into existence), or from the date of the final decision obtained in the process of exhaustion of domestic remedies.

Again, reference can be made to the case law under Article 26 of the European Convention. In these circumstances, Article 26 can give rise to three results.

[44] *Yearbook of the European Convention on Human Rights*, 2 (1958–9), p. 214, at p. 244 (emphasis added); see nn. 19–20, above.

[45] Decision of 10 July 1978, *Decisions and Reports*, vol.13, p. 85, at p. 152.

[46] Hennau and Verhaegen, op. cit. above (n. 4), para. 270. The same view is taken in French law: see, *inter alios*, Pradel, op. cit. above (n. 4), p. 401.

[47] Emphasis added. This also reflects the approach generally taken in English law (see Brazier, op. cit. above (n. 4), p. 558) and US law (see Harper, James and Gray, op. cit. above (n. 4), vol. 1, pp. 120–2).

[48] ILC Report on its 30th Session, p. 91, n. 437 (emphasis added).

Firstly, according to the generally recognized rules of international law,[49] there *are* domestic remedies available but these have *not* been exhausted: the application will be declared inadmissible (see figure 6.2, 1st*). In deciding whether these remedies have been exhausted, a particular problem arises in respect of a continuing violation: should the applicant exhaust all local remedies available against every single 'act' of the series of acts causing the continuing violation? From the so-called 'detention cases', where a violation of Article 5(3) (prescribing trial within reasonable time) is alleged, one can conclude that the answer should be negative. If not, the Commission remarked in the *Stögmuller* case,

it would lead to the conclusion that a person held in detention while on remand would have to make incessant applications in order to exhaust the domestic remedies with respect to the whole period of his detention: such a large number of applications would not only be likely to be considered as an obstruction of the normal course of criminal procedure, but even an abuse of the right of appeal.[50]

In this respect it is interesting to note the Court's decision in the case of *Ireland* v. *United Kingdom*, already mentioned above.[51] In an elaboration on the rule of exhaustion of domestic remedies as contained in Article 26, the Court decided that

this rule does *not* apply where the applicant State complains of a practice as such with the aim of preventing its continuation or recurrence, but does *not* ask the Commission or Court to give a decision on each of the cases put forward as proof or illustration of that practice.[52]

Secondly, according to the same rules all domestic remedies have been exhausted: the application will be declared admissible only if the claim is made within six months starting from the date when the 'final decision' was obtained (see figure 6.2, 1st*). Again, a particular problem can arise when dealing with a continuing violation. If the applicant *has* exhausted all domestic remedies for several individual 'acts' of the series of acts constituting the continuing violation, should the six months' time limit apply separately to each of the final decisions thereby obtained? Once more, the answer seems to be in the negative. In the *Neumeister* case, another detention case, the Court noted:

it would be excessively formalistic to demand that an applicant denouncing such a [continuing] situation should file a new application with the Commission after each final decision rejecting a request for release. This would pointlessly involve

[49] See, *inter alios*, Brownlie, op. cit. above (n. 33), pp. 494–504, and Trindade, *The Application of the Rule of Exhaustion of Local Remedies in International Law* (Cambridge, 1983), especially chapter 5 (pp. 213–49).

[50] Judgment of the Court, 27 June 1968, Series A, No. 9, p. 38, para. 7.

[51] See n. 34, above.

[52] Judgment of the Court, Series A, No. 25, p. 64, para. 159.

both the Commission and the Court in a confusing multiplication of proceedings which would tend to paralyse their working.[53]

Thirdly, according to the aforementioned rules, no effective domestic remedies are available (for example, if the claim concerns an Act of Parliament). How then is Article 26 to be applied? In the *De Becker* case[54] the Commission decided that the term 'final decision', from which the six months' period starts to run, refers exclusively to the final decision concerned in the exhaustion of domestic remedies. However, in the case of *X* v. *United Kingdom*, it came to the view that 'where no domestic remedy is available, the act or decision complained of must itself normally be taken as the "final decision" for the purposes of Article 26'.[55] Applying this to a series of acts constituting a continuing violation, the date of the 'final decision' will be the date of the last act complained of, i.e. the date the continuing breach ceased to exist (see figure 6.2, 2nd*). This was confirmed in the case of *X* v. *Sweden*. On the applicant's complaint that he had not been entitled to have the lawfulness of his detention (a continuing situation) determined by a court contrary to Article 5(4), the Commission decided that in the absence of an effective local remedy, the applicant must submit such a complaint to the Commission within six months from the date of his release, i.e. the date the alleged continuing violation ceased to exist.[56]

FIGURE 6.2. ARTICLE 26 OF THE EUROPEAN CONVENTION ON HUMAN RIGHTS

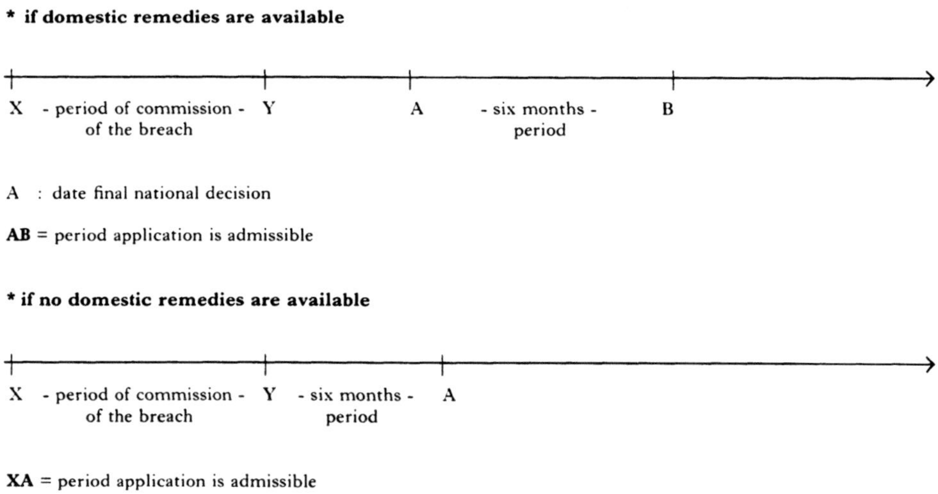

[53] Judgment of the Court, 10 November 1969, Series A, No. 8, p. 38, para. 7.

[54] *Yearbook of the European Convention on Human Rights*, 2 (1958–9), p. 214, at p. 242.

[55] *Decisions and Reports*, vol. 8, pp. 211–13; see also *Cyprus* v. *Turkey* (Appl. No. 8007/77), decision of 10 July 1978, ibid., vol. 13, p. 85, at pp. 153–4, para. 43.

[56] *Decisions and Reports*, vol. 32, p. 303, at pp. 304–5.

Therefore, in all three solutions obtained under Article 26, the impact of having established a continuing violation can only have positive effects for the applicant: the requirements of exhaustion of domestic remedies and the six months' rule apply less strictly (if they apply at all), and the date the six months' period starts to run is postponed from the day the breach came into existence to the day the breach ceased to exist.

2.1.2. *Jurisdictional limitation clauses* ratione temporis

2.1.2.1. *Principles to be applied in case of a continuing violation*

A second set of time-related restrictions on the competence of an international tribunal refers to the operation of jurisdictional limitation clauses *ratione temporis*. Here, the so-called critical date is the date indicated in the limitation clause subsequent to which disputes, situations or facts should arise in order for the international tribunal to have jurisdiction *ratione temporis*.

No difficulties arise if the period during which the breach of the relevant international obligation occurred (i.e. the 'situation' giving rise to the dispute) elapses in its *entirety* either before the critical date or after that date. In the former case, the international tribunal has no jurisdiction to decide on the alleged breach;[57] in the latter case,[58] it can exercise its jurisdiction and take account of the entire period of the breach for all relevant purposes.

One set of problematic cases remains: those where the period during which the relevant international obligation is allegedly breached starts *before* the critical date (subsequent to which 'acts' or 'situations' will fall under the general or specific jurisdiction of the tribunal), but ends only *after* that date, or still continues at the time of the proceedings. The general rule is that in these cases the international tribunal will be allowed to exercise jurisdiction over the alleged breach for the period which continues to elapse after the critical date, even though the breach came into existence before that date (see figure 7.2).

This principle has been confirmed by the ICJ, the European Commission of Human Rights (both illustrated below) and the UN Human Rights Committee (HRC). Indeed, in *Lovelace* v. *Canada* a claim was held admissible by the HRC even though it arose *before* 19 August 1976 i.e. the critical date the Covenant entered into force with respect to Canada.[59] The HRC declared that it had no jurisdiction to adjudicate on

[57] As in the *Phosphates in Morocco* case: see n. 65, below.

[58] As in the *Right of Passage* case (*Merits*), *ICJ Reports*, 1960, p. 6, at pp. 33–6, and the *Electricity Company of Sofia and Bulgaria* case, *PCIJ*, Series A/B, No. 77, p. 82.

[59] Decision of 29 December 1977, *Human Rights Law Journal*, 2 (1981), p. 158. For cases where the HRC declared complaints inadmissible on the ground that they related to events which occurred prior to the date on which the Covenant and the Optional Protocol entered into force for the State concerned, see, e.g., Communication No. 6/1977, HRC 1980 Report, p. 131, and Communication No. 499/1992, HRC 1993 Report, vol. 2, p. 236.

original cause of the action (*in casu* loss of the legal status of Maliseet Indian under the Indian Act due to marriage in 1970) but recognized that 'the situation may be different if the alleged violations, although relating to events occurring before 19 August 1976, continue, or have effects which themselves constitute violations, after that date'.[60] Consequently, it confirmed its jurisdiction to decide on the altered legal status as of 19 August 1976 and found that Canada had violated Article 27 of the Covenant (right of persons belonging to minorities to enjoy own culture, religion and language) by denying Mrs Lovelace legal status as an Indian.

2.1.2.2. *First illustration: the Statute of the International Court of Justice*

Under Article 36(2) and (3) of the Statute, a contracting State can accept the compulsory jurisdiction of the Court 'unconditionally or on condition of reciprocity . . . or for a certain time'.[61] For present purposes, two categories of declaration should be distinguished.

**Declarations without reservations* ratione temporis *(figure 7.1)*. Firstly, declarations where no reservations *ratione temporis* have been made. In this event, the declaration has retroactive effect: it covers not only future disputes, but also disputes which have arisen before the declaration was made. This principle has been confirmed by the PCIJ in the *Mavrommatis Palestine Concessions* case.[62] Therefore, whether a claim concerns an instantaneous act or a continuing situation, or whether it arose before, after or before *and* after the date the declaration was made, it cannot be defeated on the ground of lack of jurisdiction *ratione temporis*.

FIGURE 7.1. JURISDICTIONAL LIMITATION CLAUSES WITHOUT RESERVATION *RATIONE TEMPORIS*

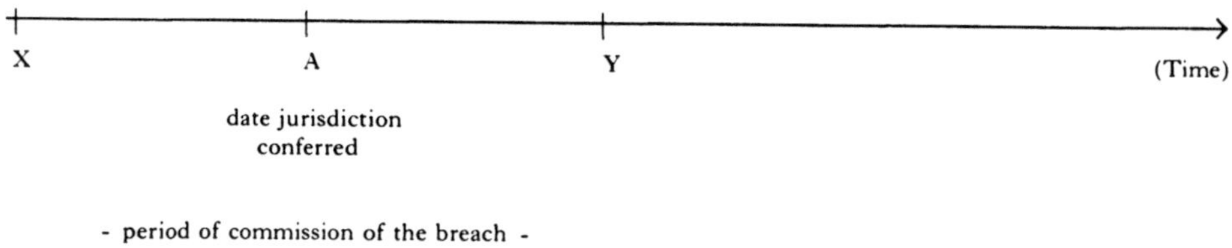

XY = period over which court or tribunal has jurisdiction
(if at X obligation is in force for State concerned)

[60] *Human Rights Law Journal*, 2 (1981), p. 158, at p. 166.

[61] On this issue see, *inter alios*, Szafarz, *The Compulsory Jurisdiction of the ICJ* (Dordrecht, 1993).

[62] *PCIJ*, Series A, No. 2, p. 35; see also Maus, *Les Réserves dans les déclarations d'acceptation de la jurisdiction obligatoire de la Cour International de Justice* (Geneva, 1959), p. 82.

**Declarations with reservations* ratione temporis *(figure 7.2)* Secondly, where the declaration does contain reservations *ratione temporis*, it will generally be formulated in two ways:[63] either the reservation excludes *disputes* prior to a critical date (for instance the date of the deposit of the declaration[64]), or it excludes disputes which have arisen from *facts or situations* existing before that date.

In these cases, the jurisdiction of the Court will depend primarily on the interpretation given to the declaration in question and the factual determination of the date of the dispute or of the facts or situations giving rise to the dispute. For this reason, the case law on the issue concerns more the problem of interpreting a specific declaration of acceptance of jurisdiction, rather than a discussion on the principles attached to the distinction between continuing and instantaneous violations.

Nevertheless, in the *Phosphates in Morocco* case, already discussed above,[65] the general rule to be applied in the event of a continuing violation (as set out in section 2.1.2.1) seems to be impliedly confirmed. There, the French declaration accepting the Court's compulsory jurisdiction was limited to disputes which arose with regard to situations or facts subsequent to 7 September 1931. As mentioned above, Italy claimed that the monopolization of the Moroccan phosphates constituted a continuing violation accomplished between 1920 and 1934. Therefore, it argued, the violation continued to exist *after* the critical date and thus, the application fell within the Court's jurisdiction *ratione temporis*.[66] However, as discussed above, the PCIJ regarded the monopoly as a mere result of legislation passed in 1920, i.e. a 'fact' prior to the critical date,

FIGURE 7.2. JURISDICTIONAL LIMITATION CLAUSES WITH RESERVATION *RATIONE TEMPORIS*

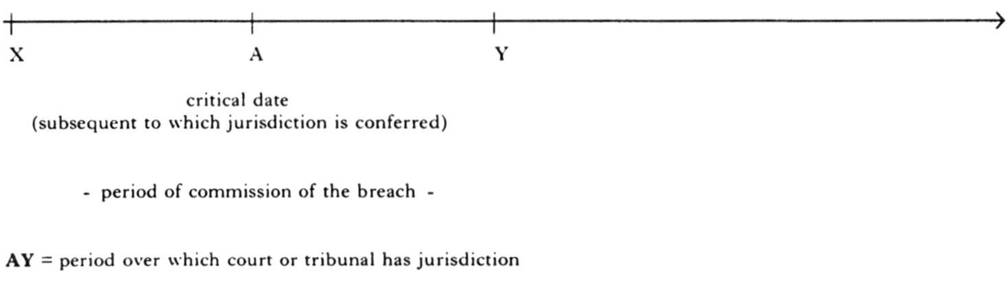

and decided it had no jurisdiction to adjudicate on the dispute. Nevertheless, the principle put forward by the Italian Government (which corresponded to the general rule set out in section 2.1.2.1) was not

[63] See Rosenne, *The Law and Practice of the ICJ* (1965), vol. 1, pp. 489–99. These declarations have to be distinguished from the formal conditions, including time limits, relating to the duration, modification and termination of the declaration itself *qua* legal act.

[64] As in the US declaration at issue in the *Interhandel* case, *ICJ Reports*, 1959, p. 6, at p. 22.

[65] *PCIJ*, Series A/B, No. 74 (1938); see section 1.1.1, above.

[66] Ibid., p. 23.

rejected and was explicitly confirmed in the dissenting opinions of Judges Van Eysinga and Cheng Tien-Hsi.[67]

2.1.2.3. *Second illustration: the European Convention on Human Rights*

The European Convention contains three optional clauses to be activated by a unilateral declaration: under Article 46 a State can accept the compulsory jurisdiction of the Court; under Article 63 a State can accept that the Convention extends to the territories for whose international relations it is responsible[68] and under Article 25 it can accept the competence of the Commission to deal with individual applications. However, once Protocol No. 11 to the Convention enters into force (which requires the ratification of all contracting parties to the Convention), the Commission as an institution will be abolished and only one single Court will remain with mandatory jurisdiction over inter-State as well as individual applications. In this event, the optional clauses in Article 25 and 46 will disappear.

The jurisdiction of the Commission to deal with inter-State applications, on the other hand is derived directly from Article 24, which becomes effective from the date the Convention enters into force with respect to the State concerned. Therefore, Article 24 can be activated at different times for different States, depending on the date the Convention came into force for each of them. In the case of *Austria* v. *Italy*,[69] where different dates applied, the Commission decided that no requirement of reciprocity *ratione temporis* exists since the obligations under the Convention establish a 'public order of Europe'. Therefore, even though the object of the claim dated from before the entry into force of the Convention with respect to Austria (applicant), the claim was admissible, since at that time the Convention was already in force with respect to Italy (respondent). This approach is in clear contradiction with the ICJ's case law, where reciprocity *ratione temporis* between declarations made under the Optional Clause is required.[70]

Declarations made under Article 46 may be 'unconditionally or on condition of reciprocity . . . or for a specified period'; those under Article 25 'may be made for a specific period'. Again, two forms of declarations can be distinguished.

The first category includes those *without* reservations *ratione temporis.* In this case, like similar declarations under Article 36 of the ICJ's Statute, both declarations under Article 46 and 25 have retroactive effect

[67] Ibid., pp. 35 and 37.

[68] See, for example, the case of *X* v. *United Kingdom, Decisions and Reports*, vol. 7, p. 102, which concerned the declaration made by the UK with respect to the Island of Jersey.

[69] *Yearbook of the European Convention on Human Rights*, 4 (1961), p. 116.

[70] See, *inter alia*, the *Anglo-Iranian Oil Co.* case, *ICJ Reports*, 1952, p. 93, at p. 107. This difference in interpretation between the European Convention and the Statute of the ICJ is due to the different legal context and objectives of the two instruments, as explained in the introduction to section 2, above.

from the moment of ratification of the Convention by the State concerned[71] (see figure 6.1). Therefore, even though a claim has to be brought before the Commission or Court *after* the date when the declaration was made, it may also refer to an alleged (continuing) violation of the Convention which took place entirely *before* that date but *after* the date when the Convention came into force for the State in question.

In this respect, it is interesting to note that, contrary to the case law developed by the ICJ and the European Commission, the UN Human Rights Committee has decided that ratification of the Optional Protocol (by which the ratifying State *inter alia* recognizes the power of the HRC to decide on individual applications) has no retroactive effect. The HRC declared itself incompetent *ratione temporis* to consider an alleged violation which took place after the entry into force of the Covenant, but before the entry into force of the Optional Protocol.[72] It is suggested that this is an erroneous decision, since the moment at which the State undertakes to respect and ensure the provisions of the Covenant is decisive, not the moment at which the procedure, laid down in the Optional Protocol for examining the conduct of that State, becomes applicable. The ratification of the Optional Protocol merely results in the recognition of one of the ways in which violations of the Covenant can be considered by an international organ. It has no influence on whether or not the Covenant itself is breached.[73]

A second category of declarations are those *with* reservations *ratione temporis* (see figure 7.2). In this event the principle defended in section 2.1.2.1 (that in case of a continuing violation, jurisdiction can only be established for the period *after* the critical date) has been confirmed by the Commission. It did so for the first time in the *De Becker* case. There, the Commission decided that, according to the generally recognized principle in international law that treaties and conventions are not retrospective in effect, the Convention only applies to facts subsequent to the date of its entry into force in respect of the respondent State. In the *De Becker* case, the critical date was the date on which the Convention came into force in respect of Belgium, 14 June 1955. The Commission concluded that 'the applicant cannot legally claim, for the period in question [the period prior to 14 June 1995] to have been the victim of a violation of the rights guaranteed by the Convention, even if the state of

[71] See, *inter alia*, *X* v. *France*, *Decisions and Reports*, vol. 29, pp. 238–9, and *Bozano* v. *France*, ibid., vol. 39, p. 143. In the same sense van Dijk and van Hoof, op. cit. above (n. 22), pp. 10 and 101.

[72] Communication No. 310/1988, HRC 1991 Report, p. 285; also in Communication No. 499/1992, HRC 1993 Report, vol. 2, p. 236.

[73] This criticism is shared by Bossuyt ('Le Règlement intérieur du Comité des Droits de l'Homme', *Revue belge de droit international*, 14 (1978–9), p. 136), Nowak (*CCPR-Kommentar* (Kehl, 1989), pp. 724–5; *CCPR Commentary* (Kehl, 1993), pp. 679–80) and Zwart (op. cit. above (n. 20), pp. 135–8).

affairs complained of is of a permanent nature . . . ', but that 'the application, in so far as it concerns this continuing situation extending after 14 June 1955 is not inadmissible *ratione temporis*'.[74]

Later, the Commission adopted the same approach when the critical date was the date mentioned in the declaration made under Article 25, only subsequent to which the State concerned recognized the competence of the Commission to deal with individual applications. In the case of *Roy and Alice Fletcher* v. *United Kingdom*,[75] for example, the applicants complained they had not been brought to trial within a reasonable time. There, the critical date, inserted in the UK's declaration accepting individual applications was 13 January 1966. Again, the Commission rejected the complaint relating to the period *before* the critical date *ratione temporis* but confirmed its competence to examine the period *after* that date. In the end, however, it concluded that for the latter period no violation could be detected and dismissed the application on the merits.

In conclusion, the establishment of a continuing violation, in cases where a jurisdictional limitation clause *ratione temporis* can be invoked, is of major importance. If the applicant can prove a continuing violation which existed *subsequent* to the critical date, the international tribunal will confirm its jurisdiction even though the violation dates back or started *before* that critical date. If, on the contrary, the tribunal decides in these circumstances that a claim only concerns an instantaneous act, even one with lasting effects, the claim will necessarily be defeated *ratione temporis*.

2.2. *Determination of the applicable rule: the intertemporal problem in public international law*

2.2.1. *General principles of law*

In the determination of the rules to be applied to the issue concerned, the perennial problem to be solved when faced with a continuing violation arises as a result of changes in the course of time of the rules of international law and of the obligations laid on States by those rules. Different rules for a specific problem can exist at different times.

The basic principle, proclaimed in Article 18(1) of the ILC's Draft, is that 'an act of the State which is not in conformity with what is required of it by an international obligation constitutes a breach of that obligation

[74] *Yearbook of the European Convention on Human Rights*, 2 (1958–9), p. 214, at p. 234. The same conclusion was reached in, *inter alia, X and Y* v. *Switzerland*, decisions of 8 October 1976, *Decisions and Reports*, vol. 6, p. 107; *X* v. *Switzerland*, decision of 12 July 1976, ibid., p. 124, and *X* v. *Belgium*, decision of 3 December 1979, *Decisions and Reports*, vol. 18, p. 250.

[75] Decision of the Commission, *Collection of Decisions*, No. 25, 1968, p. 76.

only if the act was performed at the time when the obligation was in force for that State'.[76] Therefore, in the event that the applicable rule at the time of the State *conduct* is different from the rule to be applied at the time of the *proceedings*, the former should always take precedence.

This has been confirmed by the Institute of International Law (IIL)[77] and, more recently, by the ICJ in the case concerning *Phosphate Lands in Nauru (Preliminary Objections)*.[78] There, Australia argued that the case was inadmissible on the ground that the termination of the trusteeship by the UN, *before* the date of the proceedings, precluded the making at the time of the proceedings of allegations of breaches of the Trusteeship Agreement. The Court, however, rejected this objection and implicitly stated that it would apply the provisions of the Trusteeship Agreement in its decision on the merits even though, at the time of the proceedings, this Agreement was no longer in force.

This basic principle of State responsibility is deduced from the general principle of law which prohibits retroactivity and is reflected in the adage *nullum crimen sine lege praevia*. In internal law, however, this rule is not absolute. In Belgian law, for example, the legislature may generally speaking deviate from the principle of non-retroactivity[79] and, as in most countries, retroactive application of the criminal law is only prohibited if it works to the detriment of the accused (principle of retroactivity *in mitius* or *moneat lex priusquam feriat*[80]).

In international law, however, especially in the relations between States, these exceptions should not be easily transposed.

Firstly, where the obligation alleged to have been breached entered into force for the State at a time subsequent to the State conduct complained of, it has been argued that no exceptions at all should be allowed, even if the new law prohibiting such acts henceforth is a rule of *jus cogens*. Roberto Ago, for example, noted in his Fifth Report on State Responsibility that allowing such exceptions would have 'an effect of such magnitude hardly acceptable to the legal conscience of members of the international community'.[81]

Secondly, where the obligation is in force at the time the wrongful conduct is adopted, but subsequently ceases to exist, the ILC allowed the following exception:

> conduct of a State which, although wrongful at the time of its adoption would, in the light of contemporary international law, be judged not only lawful, but

[76] ILC Report on its 28th Session, pp. 87 ff. (emphasis added).

[77] In para. 1 of its Resolution on the Intertemporal Problem in Public International Law, adopted in 1975: *Annuaire de l'Institut de Droit International*, 56 (1975), pp. 537 ff.

[78] Judgment of 26 June 1992, *ICJ Reports*, 1992, p. 240, at pp. 250–3; see also *Island of Palmas* case, arbitral award of 4 April 1928, *UN Reports of International Arbitral Awards*, vol. 2, p. 845, and *Northern Cameroons* case, *ICJ Reports*, 1963, p. 32.

[79] Alen, *Treatise on Belgian Constitutional Law* (Deventer, 1992), p. 43.

[80] See, for example, Article 2 of the Belgian Penal Code.

[81] 5th Report of Ago, p. 20.

legally required under a peremptory rule of that law, does not entail the international responsibility of that State.[82]

In other words, if the obligation breached at the time of the conduct has been transformed into a prohibition of *jus cogens* at the time of the proceedings, the original breach will be wiped out.

Finally, if the State conduct complained of was adopted at a time the obligation was in force, but this obligation is no longer binding on the State at the time of the proceedings, it has been argued that the exception allowed in most domestic criminal law systems (i.e. the principle of retroactivity *in mitius*) should not be applied. Indeed, this exception can only be justified in a relationship where the individual is opposed to society or the State (as in domestic criminal law) and seems out of place in a relationship where one State is opposed to another State. There, to apply the most favourable law to a State which commits an offence would mean applying the most unfavourable law to the State which is injured by the offence.

However, this argument does not seem to be applicable to international law cases where a State is accused of having committed an international crime against one or more individuals. Indeed, one could argue that there the most favourable law should *a priori* be applied to the individual: in municipal criminal law the individual benefits from the principle as the accused; therefore in international human rights law, where the individual is the victim of the crime, s/he should *a priori* be able to invoke the most favourable law. This argument could then be used to plead in favour of retroactive effect for rules of *jus cogens*, involving individuals as victims, more favourable to the individual (contrary to Ago's and the ILC's opinion quoted above[83]). Once more, the distinction to be drawn between general international law and international human rights law (and their respective enforcement institutions) becomes apparent.

2.2.2. *Principles to be applied in case of a continuing violation*

In the event of a continuing violation, the applicable rule can vary during the period between the date the breach came into existence, the date the breach ceased to exist and the date of the proceedings. If this is the case, which rule has to be applied? Logically applying the above mentioned principles to a continuing violation, the following solutions can be deduced.

No difficulties arise where continuing conduct or a continuing situation falls wholly within the period for which the obligation was in force, or conversely, took place entirely outside that period. In the former case a breach can be established (and this during the whole period the

[82] Article 18, para. 2, of the Draft Convention.

[83] See n. 81, above.

continuing situation took place); in the latter, no breach can be detected.

However, difficulties of application arise if the continuing conduct coincides only partly with the period during which the obligation is in force for the State concerned. In this event, there will be a breach only in so far as, and only for the period during which, the continuance of the act of the State and the existence of the obligation incumbent on it are simultaneous (see figure 8.1). This will be the case even if the continuing situation started before the obligation entered into force or continued after the obligation ceased to exist. Whether or not the newly imposed obligation is more stringent for the respondent State involved is irrelevant.[84]

FIGURE 8.1. THE GENERAL RULE

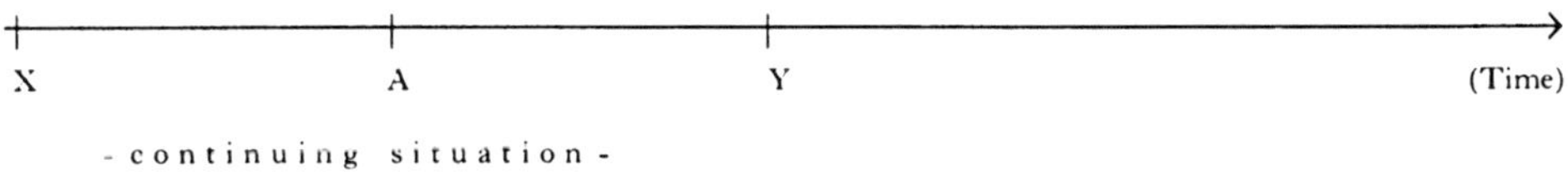

if A = date obligation enters into force: **AY** = period of the breach
if A = " " ceases to exist: **XA** = " "

This is the approach adopted by the ILC, the Institute of International Law and the European Commission of Human Rights[85] and confirmed in the arbitral award of 30 April 1990 in the *Rainbow Warrior* case.[86] In that case, even though the obligation of France to keep its two agents on the Island of Hao had ceased to exist before the time of the proceedings, France was held responsible for its decision (constituting a continuing situation still being upheld at the time of the award) not to return them to Hao during the period the obligation was in force. In other words, France was in breach of its international obligation for the period during which this obligation was incumbent on it, even though this obligation had ceased to exist at the time of the award.

[84] Even if the principle of retroactivity *in mitius* were applied to international law (as was advocated above, with respect to the victim-individual of international crimes committed by a State, where the most favourable law to the individual should apply), this position would not be altered. Indeed, in the domestic regimes where the principle applies to the accused, even a new, more stringent, law which entered into force during the period the continuing wrong was committed will be applicable. However, in the event the wrong was committed instantaneously, a law passed after the wrong occurred will not be applied unless the new law is more favourable to the accused. In this respect, to prove, in domestic law, that the alleged wrong was instantaneous will have advantageous consequences for the accused. See, for example, in Belgian law: Dupont and Verstraeten, op. cit. above (n. 4), p. 200, no. 320, and, in French law, Stéfani, Levasseur and Bouloc, op. cit. above (n. 4), p. 189, no. 220.

[85] Respectively in Article 18(3) of the ILC's Draft, and the 5th Report of Ago, p. 22; para. 2 of the IIL's Resolution, loc. cit. above (n. 77), pp. 537–8; and the *De Becker* case, loc. cit. above (n. 19).

[86] 82 ILR 499–590.

2.2.3. *Continuing violations where duration or repetition is a substantive element of the international obligation breached (see section 1.2)*

For these continuing violations, whose characteristics have been discussed above, further complications related to the very *existence* of a breach arise. Suppose that only part of the period of the alleged breach occurred while the obligation was in force and part before that obligation came into force or after it ceased to exist. Can the latter part then be taken into consideration as proof of the element of duration or repetition, i.e. to determine whether the obligation has at all been breached? This at first sight technical problem from the past will certainly re-emerge before the European Commission of Human Rights owing to the recent adoption of the Convention by many Eastern European States.

**Obligation requiring element of duration (see section 1.2.1)*. As mentioned above, an illustration of this kind of international obligation can be found in Article 5(3) of the European Convention, requiring trial after detention within a reasonable time. However, the principles defended below should be applied to all international obligations with an element of duration.

Agreement has been reached that, if Article 5(3) should cease to exist with respect to a State, the extension of the detention *after* that date would not constitute an internationally wrongful act.[87] In other words the Court will only be able to take into account the period of detention *prior* to the extinction of Article 5(3) with respect to that State in order to determine whether a reasonable time has elapsed between the imprisonment and the trial of the applicant.

Imagine, however, the opposite case where the obligation had entered into force at a time when detention had already commenced, such as where the applicant had already been detained before the European Convention was binding on the State concerned. To determine whether the detention has exceeded a reasonable time, should the court then also take into account the period of detention which elapsed before the Convention applied to the respondent State (hereafter referred to as 'the first period'), or only consider the period after that date (hereafter referred to as 'the second period')?

Whereas most doctrine prefers the latter solution[88] (the Court can only consider the second period), Roberto Ago and impliedly the ILC adopted the former[89] (the Court can consider both the first and the second period). The latter solution implies that exceptions to the general

[87] See, *inter alia*, the 5th Report of Ago, p. 22, n. 103; Sorensen, loc. cit. above (n. 22), p. 309; and Wyler, loc. cit. above (n. 35), pp. 896–7.

[88] See, *inter alia*, Sorensen, loc. cit. above (n. 22), p. 309; Wyler, loc. cit. above (n. 35), p.897; Bindschedler-Robert, 'De la rétroactivité en droit international public', *Mélanges P. Guggenheim* (Geneva, 1965), p. 188; and para. 2(*d*) of the Resolution of the IIL, loc. cit. above (n. 77), p. 538.

[89] Ago's 5th Report, p. 22, n. 103, *in fine*.

rule, elaborated in section 2.2.2, are possible. The approach of the European Commission is not entirely clear. In Application 342/57[90] it decided that, according to the principles outlined in section 2.1.2.1, the first period of detention, i.e. the detention prior to the date when the Convention entered into force, was inadmissible *ratione temporis*. However, it did not have the opportunity to consider the merits of the case (i.e. whether the detention as such exceeded reasonable time and whether the first period should then be taken into account in the assessment of the second). This was on the ground that for the second period the domestic remedies were not exhausted. Even Sorensen (an advocate of the court only taking into account the second period) noted that the decision to declare the first period inadmissible 'ne signifie pas que . . . la détention d'une personne avant l'entrée en vigueur de la Convention ne pourrait pas imposer une certaine rigueur dans l'appréciation de la periode subséquente considerée séparément'.[91]

In the view of the present writer a continuing violation of Article 5(3) should be established if three conditions are met: firstly, the international tribunal has jurisdiction over the case (even if only over the second period); secondly, the element of duration is fulfilled and this irrespective of the period during which this happened (before or after or before *and* after the date at which the Convention entered into force); thirdly, the obligation for the State concerned which is attached to the fulfilment of the element of duration (namely the obligation to try the detainee) has *not* been abided by at a date *subsequent* to the entry into force of the obligation in question.

If one accepts these conditions, and if these conditions are fulfilled, one should support the view that the court is allowed to take into account both the first and second period of detention. This is illustrated in figure 8.2. The continuing violation will then start on the date the reasonable time limit expired (i.e. at point X; see also figure 3). If, however, at that date the Convention is not yet in force, i.e. if A_2 is the date the obligation enters into force, the continuing violation will only start at the latter date (i.e. at point A_2). Thus, even though in both cases the first period has been taken into account, no exception to the principle of non-retroactivity will be made since the breach in both cases only occurs at a date when the obligation is in force. In both cases, the violation will only end

[90] *Yearbook of the European Convention on Human Rights*, 2 (1958–9), pp. 455 ff.

[91] Sorensen, loc. cit. above (n. 22), p. 310. In this respect, it is interesting to note the Commission's case law on Article 6 of the Convention: where a national court delivers a judgment *after* the entry into force of the Convention in respect of the State in question, the Commission is competent *ratione temporis* to ensure that the proceedings which this judgment concludes comply with the Convention (even though they date *prior* to the entry into force of the Convention), since the final decision is deemed to embody any defects in the preceding procedure. Therefore, in this area, the Court also takes into account facts (*in casu* proceedings) dating *prior* to the entry into force of the Convention (see, e.g., Application No. 6916/75, *Decisions and Reports*, vol. 6, p. 111, and Application No. 9453/81, ibid., vol. 31, p. 209). This approach was confirmed by the HRC (see, e.g., Communication No. 72/1980, HRC, Selection I, p. 26). On this issue see Zwart, op. cit. above (n. 20), pp. 124–6.

on the date at which the obligation attached to the lapse of the reasonable time limit (i.e. the obligation for the State to try or release the detainee) has been fulfilled (i.e. at point Y).

However, it should be stressed that the first period of detention can in any event only be taken into account to determine whether the detention exceeded a reasonable time (i.e. to determine whether the obligation is at all breached) and not, for example, in the decision on the award of compensation (since only damages caused during the commission of the breach, i.e. during the second period of detention, can be compensated).

FIGURE 8.2. ILLUSTRATION OF THE EXCEPTION: ARTICLE 5(3) EUROPEAN CONVENTION ON HUMAN RIGHTS

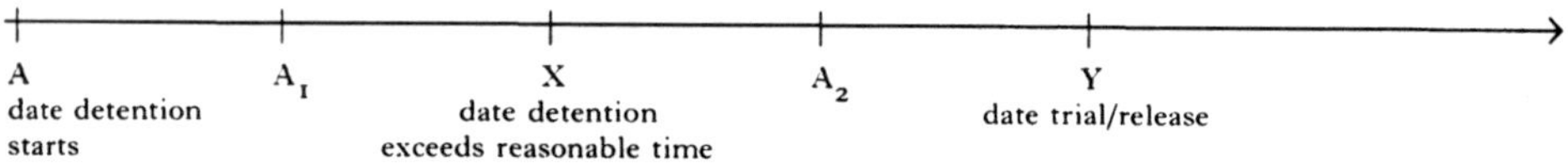

AY = period of detention to be taken into account

in case date obligation enters into force is A_1 : A_1Y = period over which court has jurisdiction
XY = period of commission of the breach
in case date obligation enters into force is A_2 : A_2Y = period over which court has jurisdiction
A_2Y = period of commission of the breach

**Obligation requiring element of repetition (see section 1.2.2)*. In other international obligations a certain degree of repetition or a so-called practice is required before it can be breached. In these cases the general rule, outlined in section 2.2.2, should be applied. This is illustrated in figure 8.3: only those individual cases or acts which occurred *after* the obligation came into force can be taken into account to determine whether the obligation in question has at all been breached, i.e. whether, for example, a 'discriminatory practice' or 'consistent violation' has been established.[92]

FIGURE 8.3. CONFIRMATION OF THE GENERAL RULE: CONTINUING VIOLATIONS CAUSED BY A COMPOSITE ACT

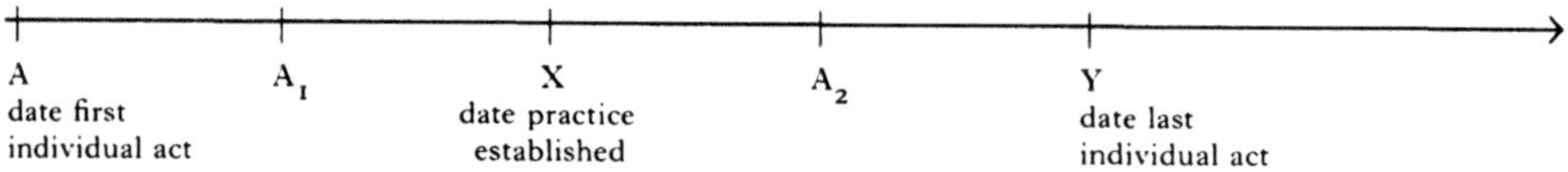

The date the obligation enters into force is A_1 or A_2
A_1 Y or A_2 Y = period over which court or tribunal has jurisdiction
= period to be taken into account to determine whether practice has been established
= period of commission of breach (if and only if during this period a practice has been established at which date only the breach as such occurs)

[92] This is confirmed in Article 18, para. 4, of the ILC's Draft.

Indeed, once it has been determined that the 'composite act' breaches the obligation, the breach will necessarily operate retroactively and start from the date of the first act of the series of acts taken into account (see figure 4). Therefore if the court took into account acts *prior* to the date of entry into force of the obligation and found that a practice has been established, it would automatically act contrary to the principle of non-retroactivity since the breach would then start on a date at which the obligation was not yet in force (see figure 8.3). This is contrary to the breach of an obligation involving an element of duration, discussed above, where the breach only occurs at the *end* of the prescribed period of time.

2.3. *Other practical consequences*

There are at least five other aspects on which the establishment of a continuing violation may have a direct bearing.

2.3.1. *Reparation*

The obligation to make reparation *lato sensu* may be discharged in two ways:[93] firstly, by way of restitution in kind, compensation or satisfaction (reparation *stricto sensu*); secondly, by way of cessation of a wrongful act having a continuing character. In this respect, having established a continuing violation is crucial.

Firstly, in order to determine the reparation *stricto sensu* the tribunal needs to consider the injury caused during *the entire period of the breach* on which it can adjudicate.[94] This also means that if the breach is still continuing at the time of the judgment, the tribunal will be reluctant to assess the amount and form of reparation due. In the case concerning *US Diplomatic and Consular Staff in Teheran*, for example, the ICJ found that Iran committed continuing breaches of the obligations laid upon it and that it, therefore, 'is under an obligation to make reparation to the United States for the injury caused to the latter by the events of 4 November 1979 *and what followed from these events*'.[95] Nevertheless, it concluded that 'since however Iran's breaches of its obligations are still continuing, the amount of such reparation cannot be determined at the present time'.[96]

Secondly, an order of cessation can be granted if, and only if, a continuing violation has been established *and* still exists at the time of the

[93] See, *inter alia*, Nagry, 'The Problem of Reparation in International Law', in *Questions of International Law*, vol. 3 (1986), pp. 178 ff.; Dominicé, *Observations sur les droits de l'Etat victime d'un fait international illicit* (Cours et travaux publiés par l'IHEI, Paris, 1982), pp. 127 ff., and Report of Arangio-Ruiz, pp. 9 ff.

[94] See, *inter alia*, ILC Report on its 30th Session, pp. 87 and 94.

[95] *ICJ Reports*, 1980, p. 3, at p. 45 (emphasis added).

[96] Ibid., p. 42.

proceedings. This was explicitly stated in the *Rainbow Warrior* case, where the Tribunal found that 'the delivery of such an order [of cessation] requires two essential conditions intimately linked, namely that the wrongful act has a continuing character and that the violated rule is still in force at the time in which the order is issued'.[97] Since, in this case, the obligation in question was found to be no longer in force,[98] the Tribunal was forced to reject the request.

As mentioned above (section 1.1.1), an *a contrario* interpretation of this rule (that cessation can only be ordered if the violation still continues) offers a useful criterion to determine whether a *continuing* violation exists at all. Indeed, the remedy of cessation is only of any use if the violation is a continuing one.

2.3.2. *Nationality of the claim and complicity*

According to the position adopted in practice,[99] a State will only be entitled to intervene for the purpose of the diplomatic protection of an individual if the national character of a claim exists from the moment of the commission of the internationally wrongful act injurious to that individual until the moment when the claim is submitted. Therefore, in case of a *continuing* violation, this character must exist during the entire period of commission of the breach. If the defendant can contradict this, the claim will be defeated.

Moreover, the determination of the nationality of the claim and of the appropriate respondent States(s) can further be complicated in the event of a continuing violation. This will be due to the fact that participation, co-operation, or complicity in general, in the commission of the breach, is possible *during the entire period of commission of the breach.*[100] The same principle applies in most domestic systems.[101]

2.3.3. *Criminal jurisdiction of national courts and non-applicability of the adage* non bis in idem

The principle of international law that the national court of the place where the crime is committed may exercise jurisdiction (the so-called

[97] 82 ILR 499, at p. 570. For cases where an order of cessation was granted, see the *Hostages* case at pp. 44–5 and the *Nicaragua* case at p. 148 (references at nn. 5–6, above).

[98] See above, section 2.2.2, n. 86.

[99] See, *inter alia*, ILC Report on its 30th Session, pp. 87 and 94.

[100] A potential example can be found in the International Convention on the Suppression and Punishment of the Crime of Apartheid (1973). Art. II defines the crime of apartheid as a *continuing* violation (i.e. 'inhuman acts committed for the purpose of establishing *and maintaining* domination by one racial group of persons over any other racial group of persons and *systematically* oppressing them', emphasis added). Art. III then specifies that international responsibility also applies to all individuals or organizations 'participating, encouraging or co-operating' in the commission of these crimes. Following the principle defended above, such acts of complicity will be punishable during the *entire period of commission* of the crime of apartheid.

[101] See, for example, the position in Belgian law: Dupont and Verstraeten, op. cit. above (n. 4), p. 200, no. 320.

territorial principle) has received universal recognition.[102] In the case of an alleged *continuing* violation, it is conceivable that the violation took place in different States (the breach can occur in one State, but can be continued in another). According to the territorial principle, the national courts of all States in which the violation took place will then be allowed to exercise jurisdiction over the crime.[103] In this event, a further complication in the realm of conflict of laws will arise since there will also be more than one *lex loci*. The above-mentioned principles also apply in most domestic regimes.[104]

Where a national court or international tribunal has adjudicated upon a continuing violation and it is subsequently alleged that the same violation has continued *after* the judgment thereby obtained, the principle of *non bis in idem* or *res judicata* will not apply. The court or tribunal should be allowed to exercise jurisdiction over the period of the breach *subsequent* to the first judgment obtained. The same rule applies in most national legal systems.[105]

2.3.4. *Seriousness of the act*

The determination of the duration of the breach may also be important at times in assessing the seriousness of the wrongful act in question in order to decide whether it may be defined as an act constituting an 'international crime' under Article 19 of the ILC's Draft on State Responsibility[106] or a 'systematic or mass violation of human rights' as defined in Article 21 of the ILC's Draft Code of Crimes against the Peace and Security of Mankind.[107] Besides, as the European Commission noted

[102] See, *inter alios*, Brownlie, op. cit. above (n. 33), p. 300.

[103] A possible example can be found in the Convention on the Prevention and Punishment of the Crime of Genocide (1948). Art. II specifies that the crime of genocide includes 'deliberately inflicting on the [national, ethnical, racial or religious] group *conditions of life* calculated to bring about its physical destruction in whole or in part' (emphasis added). Committing this crime will constitute a *continuing* violation and it is not inconceivable that, during the time of commission, it may occur in more than one State (reference could be made to the persecution of the Jews during the Second World War or, more recently, the Kurds in Turkey and Iraq). Applying the territorial principle to this continuing violation (a principle explicitly confirmed in Art. VI of the Convention), the criminal courts of *all* States in which this crime of genocide occurred will then have jurisdiction to adjudicate on the matter. Another example can be found in the Hague Convention for the Suppression of Unlawful Seizure of Aircraft (1970), which *inter alia* deals with the continuing violation of unlawfully exercising control over aircraft, an offence which can be committed, and therefore tried, in more than one State.

[104] In French law, see, *inter alios*, Pradel, op. cit. above (n. 4), p. 404, no. 372; in Belgian law, see Dupont and Verstraeten, op. cit. above (n. 4), p. 200, no. 320.

[105] See, in French law, Pradel, op. cit. above (n. 4), p. 401, no. 367; in Belgian law, Dupont and Verstraeten, op. cit. above (n. 4), p. 200, no. 320. In domestic law, this principle also entails that the accused will not be allowed to invoke a statute granting an amnesty to an offence which continued after the promulgation of that statute.

[106] See, *inter alia*, ILC Report on its 30th Session, pp. 87 and 94. Art. 19 of the Draft provides a non-exhaustive list of international crimes, repeatedly using the words 'serious' breach of specific international obligations or breach on a 'widespread scale' of the international obligations in question.

[107] Reproduced in *International Legal Materials*, 30 (1991), p. 1589.

in its second report on the case of *Cyprus* v. *Turkey* (Application No. 8007/77), 'the continuation of situations [contrary to the Convention] . . . is an *aggravating factor*'[108] of the violation as such.

2.3.5. *Enforcement*

Finally, the existence of continuing violations, especially of fundamental human rights, also influences the international legal community in its decision to take action against violations of international law. An example can be found in the practice of the Commission on Human Rights of the Economic and Social Council of the United Nations.[109] In 1967 the Economic and Social Council authorized the Commission to 'make a thorough study of situations which reveal a *consistent pattern* of violations of human rights . . . and report, with recommendation thereon, to the Economic and Social Council.'[110] On this basis, all communications (including those of individuals) received by the Secretary-General in this connection may now be considered by the Commission if they 'appear to reveal a consistent pattern of gross and reliably attested violations of human rights'.[111] Reference may also be made to the language of resolutions adopted by the General Assembly or Security Council of the UN, which frequently refer to 'systematic', 'constant' or 'persistent' practices or to practices involving 'massive', 'gross' or 'flagrant' violations of fundamental human rights and freedoms.[112]

[108] Report of 4 October 1983, *Decisions and Reports*, vol. 72, pp. 5–117, at p. 6 (emphasis added).

[109] See for example Brownlie, op. cit. above (n. 33), p. 646, and ILC Report on its 28th Session, p. 110.

[110] Resolution 1235 (XLII) of 6 June 1967 (emphasis added).

[111] Economic and Social Council Resolution 1503 (XLVIII) of 27 May 1970.

[112] See, for example, General Assembly Resolutions 2144 (XXI) of 26 October 1966 and 2547 B (XXIV) of 15 December 1969.

REVIEWS OF BOOKS

Conserving Europe's Natural Heritage. Edited By GRAHAM BENNETT. Dordrecht: Graham & Trotman/Martinus Nijhoff, 1994. xvi + 334 pp. £55.

In November 1993, 270 participants from 31 European States and 26 international organizations converged on Maastricht to debate the conservation of Europe's natural heritage, in particular the establishment of a European ecological network or 'EECONET'. This book is the product of four days of debate at Maastricht, though the brevity of the contributions suggests that the intent is to mark the event with a brief *aide-mémoire* rather than comprehensively to address within its covers all of the issues involved in conserving Europe's natural heritage. Undoubtedly the main product of the conference was not this book, nor even the 'EECONET Declaration' reproduced therein, but rather the opportunity for the 270 participants to share common concerns regarding the scope and functioning of a European Ecological Network.

The volume comprises 35 contributions of varying length grouped according to the five substantive sessions of the conference, namely: (1) introduction; (2) threats and challenges to conserving Europe's natural heritage; (3) the value and role of a European Ecological Network (EECONET); (4) developing and managing EECONET; and (5) a European Biodiversity Strategy and EECONET. There follow seven very short workshop reports, concluding remarks and an EECONET Declaration. Given the breadth of subject matter (biological and landscape diversity) and of geographic coverage (pan-European, reflecting Dutch-Hungarian collaboration in the organization of the conference), it is perhaps unsurprising, if none the less disappointing, that a comparatively short volume can only touch on some of the issues raised in respect of nature conservation in Europe.

Moreover, the range of contributions makes it possible only to convey the flavour of the proceedings and of the breadth of participation in them. Certain chapters stand out, such as those on the implementation of EECONET through national and international programmes (Opschoor and Gleichman-Verheijen), the role of the Council of Europe (Ribaut) and of the EC (Stuffmann), and the vital question of financing an ecological network (Muntingh). Holdgate and Bennett also make worthwhile contributions. Other contributions, varying in usefulness, cover such topics as the role of site managers, of private landowners and of NGOs in developing and managing an ecological network, and the role of an ecological network in the conservation strategy for grasslands, forests and coastal areas. Tucker's contribution on the conservation of birds may at first glance appear to be of the old-fashioned species-conservation school rather than of the more fashionable school of biodiversity and ecosystem oriented conservation. But he makes the valid point that as components of ecosystems, species may represent the most convenient unit for measuring biodiversity and, perhaps more importantly, may be of greater practical usefulness in an era of scarce resources by focusing attention on the need for resources to protect habitat and maintain functional ecosystems.

The overwhelming impression conveyed by the proceedings is the diversity of individuals and organizations concerned with nature conservation in Europe, making some form of overall co-ordination imperative to ensure that environmental action does not fail because of the 'mosquito' or 'pin prick' factor. A persistent theme is the need to combine protected areas status with associated buffer zones, corridors and even 'stepping stones'. The latter is rather an elegant way of conveying the image of pockets of biological diversity in Europe, important both in terms of conserving Europe's distinctive contribution to global biological diversity as well as conserving habitat for migratory species. The stress placed in a number of contributions on the need for buffer zones and a general land management strategy is reflected in the focus on nature conservation outside of protected areas in the Council of Europe's designation of 1995 as 'European Year of Nature Conservation'. In keeping with this theme, Imboden in his chapter on detecting threats to Europe's natural heritage suggests that the rather porous 'EECONET' should be replaced by an all encompassing 'Eco-Blanket'.

Most of the contributors are officials of government or of international organizations. Perhaps inevitably, this is both a strength and a weakness. Whilst it leads to some useful practical points on the establishment of an ecological network and on the practical difficulties of nature conservation and co-ordination of conservation efforts in Europe, some of the contributions lack substance or duplicate points made elsewhere in the volume. A heavier editorial hand, allowing some contributors additional space at the expense of others (welcoming remarks and the obligatory after dinner speech by royalty, for example), would go far to improve the collection and its long-term usefulness. On the whole then, this book is not for those searching for a primer on biodiversity conservation in Europe, nor a manual for the implementation of EECONET. Rather, it is a snapshot of the major issues facing environmental actors in Europe following the United Nations Conference on Environment and Development and the conclusion of the Convention on the Conservation of Biological Diversity. It serves as a timely reminder that biodiversity exists not only in tropical rainforests but also in the wetlands, grasslands, forests, coastal areas and flora and fauna of Europe, much of which is presently under threat from human activities.

CATHERINE REDGWELL

The New International Law of Fisheries: UNCLOS 1982 and Beyond. By WILLIAM T. BURKE. Oxford: Clarendon Press, 1994. xxvii + 382 pp. £60.

It has been apparent for some time that the United Nations Convention on the Law of the Sea, adopted as recently as 1982, has not succeeded in providing an adequate international regime for the conservation and allocation of marine fisheries. As Professor Burke points out in this important new work, the UN regime is unsatisfactory both in relation to the fishing of coastal species in the extended 200-mile exclusive economic zone (EEZ) and in relation to fishing in the high seas beyond.

So far as the EEZ is concerned, the Convention certainly offered the opportunity for coastal States to introduce and regulate effectively a rational fisheries regime in the 200-mile zone over which they may now claim unitary control. Regrettably, the evidence suggests that the opportunity has so far been squandered. Burke cites (p. 85) a status review of United States living marine resources as showing that 42 per cent of the species assessed are overutilized, and it is clear from an FAO appraisal that there is still massive overcapitalization in fisheries by States which now enjoy full control over their EEZ fisheries.

As regards the high seas fisheries, the problem is much more fundamental. The provision made in Part VII, Section 2, of the Convention for the co-operative conservation and management of the living resources of the high seas is drafted in notoriously general terms and based on the assumption that high seas fishing remains one of the classic freedoms of the high seas.

The two regimes (for the EEZ and the high seas) are of course inevitably interlinked, as the recent Grand Banks conflict between Canada and Spain has demonstrated. As the distant-water fleets have been driven from traditional fishing grounds following the introduction of EEZ legislation, so they have tended to concentrate their attention on the straddling stocks in the areas seaward of the EEZ limit. Moreover, as Burke points out (p. 350), if national administrations do succeed in reducing fishing efforts within national zones, this too will lead to greater pressure on straddling and high seas stocks.

There are no easy answers to the management problems currently plaguing marine fisheries, as has been shown by the difficulties experienced by the recently concluded UN Conference on Straddling Stocks and Highly Migratory Fish Stocks. This conference, convened in response to a recommendation made by the UN Conference on Environment and Development (UNCED), eventually succeeded in adopting an Agreement in August 1995. Regrettably, it came too late to be subjected to Professor Burke's keen analytical scalpel, and his readers will look forward to the prospect of a supplement devoted to an assessment of the new Agreement. In the meantime, there is more than enough food for thought in the present book. Following a historical account of the evolution of extended national jurisdiction in Chapter 1 and an analysis in Chapter 2 of the consequential regime governing coastal species, the author then deals in separate chapters with high seas fisheries, andromous species, highly migratory species, marine mammals and the crucial question of enforcement. In a concluding chapter, Professor Burke reviews the 'variety of new concepts and approaches towards improved regulation' (p. 349) which have been spawned in recent years, some of which have indeed found their way into the new Agreement. Whether his pessimistic assessment of the prospects for reaching a viable new regime will have been altered by the adoption of the 1995 Agreement remains to be seen.

As might be expected, coming from the pen of one of the world's leading exponents of international fisheries law, this is a major contribution to the literature which will be indispensable reading for anyone wishing to gain new insights into a complex area of international law. It is greatly enhanced by a scholarly apparatus of footnotes and a first-class bibliography.

E.D. BROWN

Essays in International Litigation and the Conflict of Laws. By LAWRENCE COLLINS. Oxford: Clarendon Press, 1994. lii + 466 pp. £50.

This book comprises a series of essays written over the last 30 years. Most have previously appeared in periodicals such as the *Journal of Business Law*, the *Law Quarterly Review*, and the *International and Comparative Law Quarterly*; one first appeared in a *Festschrift*. Some forty per cent of the collection consists of the course of lectures on 'Provisional and Protective Measures in International Litigation' found in *Recueil des Cours*, 234 (1992–III), p. 9, which developed out of the author's interest in this topic first expressed in *Yearbook of European Law*, 1 (1981), p. 249. The articles are accompanied by brief introductions which mention developments since these pieces were first published. It might have been helpful to have a conclusion at the end of the older writings giving Dr Collins's present views.

Many of the articles stem in part from the author's concern, as a partner in a well-known firm of City solicitors, with English conflict of laws procedure, as is evidenced by essays such as those on US anti-trust jurisdiction, the extra-territoriality of *Mareva* injunctions, service out of the jurisdiction and the rise of the doctrine of *forum non conveniens* in English common law, discovery, and negative declarations given in a *forum* less *conveniens* than the natural forum. The *Hague Recueil* monograph considers, for example, the lawfulness of *Anton Piller* orders when judged against the norms of the European Convention on Human Rights. Some articles are well known, such as '*Harris v. Taylor Revived*', and those on 'Exemption Clauses, Employment Contracts, and the Conflict of Laws' and 'Interaction between Contract and Tort in the Conflict of Laws'. Others such as that on the *Marc Rich* case may be new to some readers. The article on 'Contractual Obligations—The EEC Preliminary Draft Convention on Private International Law' (i.e. on what became the Rome Convention 1980) has been superseded by, for example, those essays which appear in P.M. North (ed.), *Contract Conflicts* (1982), and indeed by Dr Collins's own chapter in the twelfth edition of Dicey and Morris, *The Conflict of Laws* (1993), which is under the general editorship of the author. A similar comment applies to '*Harris* v. *Taylor Revived*', which has been superseded in England but not in every common law country by statute.

A persuasive justification for this collection is that many of the essays deal with aspects of cross-border litigation not normally considered in depth in the principal authorities: hence the title, which is not restricted to 'the Conflict of Laws' but extends to matters of international disputes practice, which deserves study in its own right. The outstanding monograph on provisional and protective measures concerns a topic which is not to the fore of academic study, yet freezing assets, agreeing on which court shall have jurisdiction and the obtaining of evidence in foreign law districts are matters of supreme importance to practitioners, and study of them demonstrates how far litigators will go to influence the resolution of disputes. All this occurs before the case reaches court, yet emphasis traditionally remains on choice of law issues. The resolution of interlocutory issues is often of more importance than final judgments in both national and transnational lawsuits. The author's conclusions in the Hague Lectures can be seen as an agenda for research: how far are the merits taken into account when courts are considering provisional remedies; to what extent are plaintiffs in international cases aided by measures taken in other countries; and how far is the jurisdiction of municipal tribunals limited by principles of fundamental human rights found in instruments such as the European Convention?

The book is very well produced and has tables of Conventions, legislation and cases and an index. The reviewer was surprised to see statutes and cases from the different territories within the United Kingdom placed under the same heading, and would have liked the Rules of the Supreme Court placed separately from Anglo-Welsh legislative measures, but these criticisms are slight. In sum the collection is a worthwhile one, full of live issues and ideas for their resolution.

MICHAEL JEFFERSON

International Law Anthology. Edited by ANTHONY D'AMATO Cincinnati: Anderson Publishing Company, 1994. 419 pp. No price stated.

The professed aim of this collection is to bring together extracts from some of the most provocative, stimulating and insightful writings on international law. Together these extracts, from over one hundred and thirty different authors, are intended to form the basic materials—the backbone—of an understanding of the science of international law. It is a book for students and teachers alike and the editor envisages that it will last 'for years and years' and will be the sort of book that international lawyers will want to carry with them and refer to wherever they go.

While such claims can be dismissed as over-enthusiastic self-promotion, there are things here to appreciate. The production of a single volume containing extracts from some of the seminal contributions to international legal scholarship, covering much of the realm of international law, is to be welcomed for its own sake. Many of these materials are, of course, available in full in their original form, but for the student or the overwhelmed lecturer this volume provides an effective short cut. Likewise, there are some extracts here from articles and books that are not so easily accessible, at least in the majority of universities in the United Kingdom. However, the claims of the editor go beyond this, for he would have us use this anthology as our basic textbook—the nuts and bolts for our undergraduate course in public international law. This is an unrealistic and unrealized goal. This is a book to dip into, for reassurance, for information, for ideas, but definitely for the reader already familiar with the concepts and problems of international law. Students starting with this volume will get lost. They will possess a series of intricate, finely detailed maps to parts of the system of rights and obligations called international law, but they will not find a large-scale map to guide them from 'the beginning' to 'the end'. This is a jigsaw whose pieces do not make a picture. The editor is obviously aware of this problem and has tried to tie the contributions together by including some of his own work specially written for this anthology, as well as choosing extracts by other writers of an introductory nature. As indicated, this is not altogether successful. First, the task the editor has set himself is gargantuan. To impose a methodology and structure on a work so diverse, where the various contributions are often at odds with each other, while at the same time appearing so persuasive, is a task that would defeat the most clear sighted and penetrative of scholars. Secondly, I found the impact of D'Amato's own contributions to be lessened by the peculiarities of his written style. This is admittedly a personal view, but others too may be unhappy with the informal, chatty, style of written exposition that mirrors the verbal exposition of the lecture hall and in which the form sometimes obscures the substance.

Fortunately, however, the fact that most of the extracted pieces are of high quality goes a long way to redeem these structural defects. The book is divided into four Parts: Introduction to International Law, Professional Tools, Substantive Law and Theory, and The Normative Dimension. Most of the usual topics are covered, with 'Professional Tools' dealing with sources of international law and 'The Normative Dimension' tackling such concepts as 'justice', 'democracy' and the future of international law. Not surprisingly, a majority of the contributions are extracted from the works of North American authors, but there is a liberal sprinkling of writings from non-American scholars which for the UK reader gives the book a freshness and diversity not always found elsewhere. Of particular note was the section on the 'intellectual history of the law of nations', an area of international law neglected in many standard works. I could spot no glaring omissions in the choice of extracts for topics that were selected for exposition, save that there seems little reason to restrict an analysis of the lawfulness of the use of force to those situations involving protection of human rights or as an adjunct to a discussion on the sources of law. There also seems to be an under-representation of views from what one might loosely call the 'positivist' school of international law. Conversely, there were too many extracts whose main thesis was to expound the 'values' or 'goals' that international law should achieve, rather than measuring the nature and extent of such rules as do exist by reference to the recognized sources of international law. Perhaps more of this second type of contribution could have been included at the expense of some less than central matters. 'International Sports Law' is possibly not one of the core subjects on most courses of public international law, and the editor would be hard pressed to explain why 'Elephants' and 'Whales: Their Emerging Right to Life' should take precedence in an intended textbook over, say, an extract from Brownlie's *International Law and the Use of Force by States* or Denza's *Diplomatic Law*, both topics which are hardly mentioned despite their relevance in the modern world.

As an anthology containing some of the most influential writings on international law, this book should command the attention of teachers and students of international law. As such, it has a value all of its own and deserves to be widely read. For the reasons given earlier, however, it cannot be recommended as a stand-alone text.

MARTIN DIXON

The International Legal Order. By INGRID DETTER. Aldershot: Dartmouth, 1994. 563 pp. £25 paperback.

The way in which legal rules develop is probably one of the most fascinating aspects of the study of law. To the international lawyer it is, more often than not, at the heart of any discussion. Throughout the twentieth century the international lawyer has needed to broaden the horizons within which to seek the sources and evidences of rules of law. In an earlier book, *The Concept of International Law* (1987), Professor Detter set out to show that the time-honoured methodology in seeking rules of customary international law was outdated and not in keeping with the realities or the needs of the late twentieth century. She now extends many of these ideas in a textbook of international law intended for use by students of both international law and international relations. The changes in the political complexion of international society which has seen a realignment of competing ideologies in the last decade also, she points out, calls for a reassessment of the whole system of international law.

She identifies twenty types of subject who may claim input into international law-making. The influence of international organizations, NGOs, multinationals, international companies and individuals in modern international law is well recognized. The fashions and ideologies of history must necessarily mean that influences vary and that priorities change. For instance, as Professor Detter points out, the influence of class, intrinsic in Marxist doctrine, has declined, whilst the importance of such bodies as the Holy See and International Orders can be seen to have waxed and waned throughout the centuries. The actors on the international scene have undoubtedly increased and this change has obviously had an impact on the nature of international law-making. The author points out that the international relations scholar has long abandoned the extreme State paradigm, but not the international lawyer. She is forced to admit, however, that the former is now moving towards a more State-centred model. The challenge of showing that the nature of law-making has fundamentally changed, rather than adapted to new influences, is not satisfactorily sustained in the ensuing chapters.

It is perhaps in the area of soft law that the influence of new players is most evident, but in an excellent analytical chapter devoted to this topic the conclusions are, it is disappointing to note, extraordinarily conservative.

The book certainly presents some challenging ideas; Professor Detter is not timid in being provocative—indeed she probably enjoys it. Nevertheless, it may be that the book's claim to be a student text is undermined by the framework into which much of the exposition is fitted. The author's background means that Swedish and other Scandinavian jurisprudence is constantly referred to, and this is a refreshing addition to the standard textbook. Similarly, a chapter which attempts to place the conflict of laws in the context of international law is to be welcomed, although perhaps the treatment it receives turns out to be less exciting than other parts of the text.

The disappointing aspects of the book are its inaccuracies. Typographical and stylistic infelicities distract the reader's attention but, more importantly, if the book is to be acceptable as a student text, some of the statements on the law itself need to be corrected or explained in greater detail if they are not to be misleading. For example, it is scarcely correct to say that the *rules* laid down in the European Convention on Human Rights now form part of the law of the European Community (p. 301), and it is certainly not the case that as European law the Convention becomes part of the applicable law of courts in the Member States. In similar fashion, to say that passage of warships through the territorial sea is subject to authorization or to prior notification, citing the United States' memorial to the 1910 *North Atlantic Fisheries* arbitration, without reference to the 1989 US/USSR Joint Statement on Innocent Passage (*International Legal Materials*, 28 (1989), p. 144) seems to neglect not only the reader's needs, but the purpose of the book as an analysis of contemporary law-making.

RALPH BEDDARD

Mutual Assistance in Criminal and Business Regulatory Matters. By WILLIAM C. GILMORE. Cambridge: Cambridge University Press, 1995. 421 pp. £55.

This is the second collection of materials edited by Dr Gilmore to appear in the *Cambridge International Documents Series*. That series has concentrated on collections of documents related to particular crises, those involving Kuwait, Liberia, or the former Yugoslavia, but Dr Gilmore's volumes have assembled materials which illustrate developing international practice in combating international criminal activity. Dr Gilmore is not only a leading academic authority in this field but has made an important practical contribution: the first of his volumes, *International Efforts to Combat Money Laundering*, was prepared while he was serving as Director of the Commercial Crime Unit of the Commonwealth Secretariat.

This second volume covers a wider field, some 300 pages being devoted to mutual assistance in criminal matters generally and 100 to the newly emerging practice of mutual assistance between business regulatory authorities. It is an immensely useful collection of material. Readers with access to relatively well-stocked law libraries might consider a few of the documents reproduced to be readily available. Examples are the United Nations Convention against Illicit Trafficking in Narcotic Drugs and Psychotropic Substances 1988 and the Model Treaty on Mutual Assistance in Criminal Matters prepared by the United Nations in 1990. But few libraries will have the regional variants of those instruments such as the South Asian Association for Regional Co-operation's Convention on Narcotic Drugs and Psychotropic Substances, or the Economic Community of West African States' Convention on Mutual Assistance in Criminal Matters. Neither of those conventions contains much that breaks new ground, but they may prove influential in the development of practice in the relevant region.

An impressive feature of the collection is its global nature. There are documents originating from the United Nations, the Commonwealth Secretariat, and from regional organizations such as the Council of Europe and the Organization of American States. It can be surprisingly difficult to track down material from even the largest of international organizations, especially when this takes the form of reservations by individual parties. At that level alone, Dr Gilmore serves his readers well. Even more elusive are bilateral agreements, and the pace of developments in this field is such that it really is no use waiting the appropriate number of years for a treaty to appear in the *UN Treaty Series*. The volume contains a well-chosen selection of such agreements, for example those concerning the United States and the Cayman Islands which served as models for a number of other agreements. It also publishes the model negotiating texts used by the Australian and Canadian Governments in developing their networks of bilateral treaties, and the United Kingdom's model agreements on the restraint and confiscation of the proceeds and instrumentalities of crime. Wherever possible, official explanatory reports on the various documents are also reproduced.

In the area of securities and business regulation there is as yet little in the way of treaty or comparable material; the Council of Europe Convention on Insider Trading stands as an exception. For the most part, mutual assistance is provided under the terms of memoranda of understanding or administrative agreements. A useful selection is reproduced, together with some documents emanating from the International Organization of Securities Commissions.

Dr Gilmore provides a valuable introduction to the volume, concise but thoughtful and packed with up-to-date information as to national legislative activity. It ends by quoting from a United Nations survey of the impact of organized crime: 'As Governments succeed in co-ordinating their preventative efforts through increased co-operation . . . organized crime will find that the best response is to tighten its own co-operative efforts around the globe'. It is too much to hope that those efforts will be enshrined in publishable documents, but there is little doubt that international organizations and individual Governments will have to refine their own instruments. We look to Dr Gilmore and the Cambridge University Press to continue their invaluable service in making the resulting documentation available in so convenient a form.

DAVID MCCLEAN

Child Soldiers—The Role of Children in Armed Conflict. By GUY GOODWIN-GILL and ILENE COHN. Oxford: Oxford University Press, 1994. 181 pp. + Annex. £25 hardback; £10.95 paperback.

During the Gulf War I took my daughter, then aged five, for a walk in the park. She heard a plane passing overhead and asked if it was going to drop some bombs. I thought it sad that one so young should ever have had to respond to the sound of a plane with anything other than wonderment. There is little that children miss. Notwithstanding this, the most immediate perception from the UK of the phenomenon of 'child soldiers' is possibly no more than of a young person sent to patrol the streets of Northern Ireland. When the tour is over, more normal military life can be resumed: strict, disciplined, and professional, but with regular breaks to rejoin family, friends and civilian life. Chapters 1 and 2 of this short but interesting work quickly destroy any such perception. For many children in the world, being a soldier is part of daily life. To fight is the most natural option in life. Rebellion is the only life they have ever known. It is their normality. There is no other life for them to step into. Their only heritage comes from the 'generational transmission of adult hatreds' (p. 36).

The limitations on the application of international humanitarian law are clearly set out in Chapter 3. The crucial importance of what the ICRC can achieve informally is rightly noted. However, this is not just a legal work. In Chapters 3–5 it looks at children's experiences, feelings, motivations, ideologies, indoctrinations, developmental processes, empowerment, security, culture, psychosocial and physical consequences of participation, capacities to evaluate and to decide in an existence where the only objectivity is subjective. Much of the supporting evidence is empirically based from conflicts around the world. Practical and constructive suggestions and ideas are offered to respond to these socio-cultural issues. There is much emphasis on reinforcing such family and community structures as still exist, community-based rather than institution-based strategies, education and vocational training. The provisions of the UN Convention on the Rights of the Child (1989) are frequently drawn on to provide support. Chapters 6–7 consider how the applicable international law needs updating and reinforcing, and the roles that international organizations and non-governmental organizations can play.

This book makes salutary reading. It rightly points out that 'The number of active child participants is always less than that of the children victims of war' (p. 132). It cries out as a warning against legitimizing more armed conflicts by an expansive interpretation of the concept of self-determination. Such interpretations do little service to the children of the world. Very young children often say that books without pictures are boring. This book has some forty-five pictures of child soldiers, usually carrying enormous guns or weapons.

The book is superbly presented and designed.

DOMINIC MCGOLDRICK

The Contemporary Law of Armed Conflict. By L.C. GREEN. Manchester: Manchester University Press, *Melland Schill Monographs in International Law*, 1994. xviii + 374 pp. £16.99.

This is a welcome addition to the literature on the law of armed conflict, written by someone whose work will be well-known to those specializing in this area of international law. The book has, in the words of the author, 'grown out of the *Manual of Armed Conflict Law* prepared for the Canadian Department of National Defence'. This provenance seems to pervade the book. There is, for instance, often only limited reference in the footnotes to the writings of other academics, which deprives the reader of the opportunity to explore the issues raised in the text in more detail elsewhere. There is, however, abundant use made of factual examples to illustrate principles of law under discussion and a number of cases decided in the English courts are also cited. The book deals with all the major topics likely to be needed in a manual for use by members of the armed forces, including separate chapters on land, maritime and air warfare and the rights and duties of neutrals.

Although the preface gives the date of completion of the work as October 1992, the author has been able to include developments occurring by mid-1993. It was, perhaps, unfortunate that the establishment by the Security Council of the *ad hoc* Tribunal to try those alleged to have committed war crimes in the territory of the former Yugoslavia was one such recent development. Professor Green has been able to add references to the Tribunal in various places (see p. 300, although the paragraph in which it is contained was obviously written when there were merely theories as to how a tribunal might be established). It might have been added also at p. 312. The Statute of the Tribunal and the Rules of Procedure and Evidence, however, came too late for inclusion. The Tribunal is likely to have such an effect on the laws of war that the book may be prematurely dated by the author's inability to discuss the Statute and the various charges available to the prosecutor. Professor Green does draw upon the Bosnian conflict in many passages of the book and, with some justification, appears to be unsure whether that particular conflict is an international or a non-international one. His position at pp. 58 and 299, where the conflict is considered to be a non-international one, may be contrasted with the example given in footnote 73 on p. 288, where he applies Article 49 of Geneva Convention IV of 1949 (transfer by the occupying power of the population out of the territory), which could only apply during an international armed conflict.

Other important developments occurring in 1993 have not been included. Thus there is no mention of the UN Convention on the Prohibition of the Development, Production, Stockpiling and Use of Chemical Weapons and on their Destruction, or of the review conference concerned with strengthening the Conventional Weapons Convention of 1981, especially in regard to the use of anti-personnel mines, or of the draft resolution put to the Twenty-Sixth International Conference of the Red Cross and Red Crescent on the interpretation of Article 13 of Geneva Convention III of 1949, concerning the photographing of prisoners of war, or of the fact that the United Kingdom has expressed an intention to ratify the 1977 Additional Protocols. A more detailed treatment of the protection of the environment during an armed conflict would also have been welcome. There is, for instance, no mention of the various arguments put forward for an extension of the laws of war to provide further protection for the environment, such as the proposal to draw up a new Geneva-style convention. Although Professor Green draws attention to the destruction of oil wells in Kuwait by Iraqi forces, he does not refer to Article 23(*g*) of the Hague Regulations 1907 (particularly relevant since Iraq was not a party to Additional Protocol I), nor to the 1976 Convention on the Prohibition of Military or any other Hostile Use of Environmental Modification Techniques.

There are a number of statements in the book with which not all international lawyers would be likely to agree. It is difficult, for instance, to accept that the legality of the sinking of the Argentinian cruiser, *Belgrano*, had anything to do with 'excessive' loss of life, given that it was a military objective, the effect of whose destruction must be gauged in the light of facts known at the time (p. 331), or that airborne troops in civilian clothing or enemy uniform are not entitled to combatant status (p. 144). They surely would be if in civilian clothing and they complied with Article 44(3) of Additional Protocol I. There is no authority for stating that a combatant loses his combatant status (as opposed to committing a war crime), merely by wearing the uniform of the enemy (see Article 39(2) of Protocol I and, for the pre-existing law, the *Skorzeny* trial).

Taking the book as a whole, Professor Green is to be congratulated on producing an account of the contemporary law of armed conflict which students trying to gain a real understanding of the limits of the laws of war will find extremely useful.

PETER ROWE

Problems and Process: International Law and How We Use It. By ROSALYN HIGGINS. Oxford: Clarendon Press, 1994. xxvii + 274 pp. £25.

Rosalyn Higgins's new book, her General Course in International Law given at The Hague in 1991, explains how the author was at first intimidated by the prospect of trying to condense 'the corpus of international law in fifteen lectures'. The advice of Sir Robert Jennings showed the way: 'one should never lose sight of the fact that one was not writing the definitive treatise on the entirety of international law, but rather lecturing to students about the ideas underlying international law'. Her 'job would not be to summarize or synthesize all that had ever been said on a given theme, but rather to offer my own perspectives and ideas' (p. v). The result is a wonderful book, albeit equally difficult to summarize or synthesize.

The fifteen lectures or chapters are ordered in a sensible way for an introduction to international law: the nature and function of international law, sources of international law, participants in the international legal system, jurisdiction, immunities, human rights, self-determination, natural resources, State responsibility, the United Nations, dispute settlement and the International Court of Justice, the role of national courts in the international legal process, equity and proportionality, and the use of force by individual States and the United Nations. The substance of the chapters, however, neither is meant to be nor is in fact a standard introduction to the discipline. Instead, each chapter takes several doctrinal problems and provides a personal commentary. The presumption is that the reader already has at least an acquaintance with the subject. For example, Chapter 12 on the role of national courts in the international legal process transforms the usual debate between monist and dualist theories into a very interesting discussion of how the cultures of different national legal systems and the varying perspectives of their judges and lawyers make for very different approaches to the use of international law in municipal courts (pp. 205–218).

Just as its commentary accounts for the word 'problems' in the book's title, so an underlying jurisprudential preference accounts for the term 'process'. Professor Higgins argues 'that there is an essential and unavoidable choice to be made between the perception of international law as a system of neutral rules, and international law as a system of decision-making directed towards the attainment of certain declared values' (p. vi). However, with all respect, this reviewer is not persuaded that the choice is quite so definite. It is difficult nowadays to identify any prominent international lawyer so black-letter as to maintain either that all international legal rules are perfectly neutral, or that there is little importance to international legal process. Moreover, it is equally difficult to identify a McDougalian who has abandoned interest in pursuing an arguably objective identification of international legal rules for at least some purposes, for example, as rules of decision in municipal or international judicial proceedings. Indeed, Professor Higgins, as her recent election to the International Court emphasizes, is herself a skilled and persuasive international lawyer in this formalistic respect. As the battle between naturalists and positivists once yielded a 'mixed' or 'Grotian' philosophy of the law of nations, so now has the policy process school blended so much into our ordinary philosophy of international law that most international lawyers display an appreciation for aspects of both formalism and process.

M.W. JANIS

The European Convention on Human Rights and the Protection of National Minorities. By C. HILLGRUBER and M. JESTAEDT. Cologne: Verlag Wissenschaft und Politik, 1994. 124 pp. DM 28.

This short but densely footnoted study of the Convention and minority rights was published at a time of active discussion in the Council of Europe. Since the book was written, the Council has produced its Framework Convention for the Protection of National Minorities, which relates to the European Convention in a number of its provisions. This linkage may serve to enhance the value of the present volume rather than diminish it—since all studies 'date' in some sense or other at a time of active legal and political development. The problem for a study of this kind is that the European Convention is not commonly regarded as an instrument of the highest relevance to minority rights. Certainly, judged in terms of the recent developments in international law (and domestic law, notably in Central and Eastern Europe), the Convention has, on a cursory reading of the rights, something of the appearance of a legal dinosaur. Minorities make an appearance in the Convention but only in Article 14 on non-discrimination—impermissible on the grounds, *inter alia*, of 'association with a national minority'. The burden of the Convention towards members of minorities is discharged in an indirect manner, through working out the implications of generalized 'rights for all' for the interests of members of minorities.

A certain reverence for the European Convention on Human Rights is perfectly in order. In this respect, while the authors do not quite offer an uncritical paean of praise for the Convention, they come close with the claim that '[T]he review system established by the Convention has already brought about effective minority protection' (p. 102). As many have realized, this is not the case, hence the scramble over the last five years in the European organizations and the UN to provide appropriate standards of rights which address the specifics of minority claims. The legal strategy represented by the European Convention—and by much of the post-war canon of human rights law—is an inadequate strategy and should be recognized as such. The authors implicitly understand this, as can be seen from the space they devote to proposals for reform.

There are many good things in the book. The reflections on the origins of concern in Strasbourg about national minorities are instructive, as are many of the substantive discussions on the implications of particular articles of the Convention. The discussion of the difficulties of presenting applications to the organs of the Convention on behalf of minorities is particularly illuminating. Occasionally, perhaps on account of the manner in which the Convention dominates their perceptions, a rigid dogmatism is maintained by the authors who, for example, 'cannot regard roadsigns law as part of human rights' but only as part of the right of self-administration by a regional authority (p. 95). Why 'cannot', in view of the subsequent inclusion of such a provision in the Framework Convention for the Protection of National Minorities? And why must the primary mechanisms in minority protection be 'judicial' (p. 100)?

Overall, the study is extremely useful on what the Convention can contribute (and, at least to this reader, what it cannot) to the protection of minorities. The level of detail is helpful and there is evidence of considerable scholarship. While the present author does not share many of the authors' conclusions, the study is to be recommended as forcefully articulating a particular viewpoint on what is essential and useful in legal approaches to minority rights.

PATRICK THORNBERRY

The Termination and Revision of Treaties in the Light of New Customary International Law. By N. KONTOU. Oxford: Clarendon Press, 1995. xvii + 157 pp. + 12 pp. bibliography and index. £35.

The purpose of this book—something of which the rather ambiguous title does not do enough to put one on notice—is to answer two questions: first, whether a treaty is automatically revised or terminated in the event that, subsequently to its conclusion, customary law changes in such a way as to take on a content which is incompatible with what the treaty provides; and, secondly, if neither of these things occurs, whether such a development causes a right to vest in each of the parties to the treaty to require that steps be taken with a view to procuring its revision and, if these fail, to effect its termination. Broadly speaking, the answers proffered are, respectively, 'no' and 'yes'.

These conclusions may be right; but little of what is said is calculated to convince the reader that they are, particularly as far as the second is concerned. A number of interesting precedents are described and a tour is made of the jurisprudence. However, the analysis of each incident, judgment or award is minimal or even non-existent, such that one is either left unsure of the proposition for which it is meant to 'stand' or feeling that there are so many questions left unanswered that one is not happy to accept that it does 'stand' for what it is said to.

More disappointing still is the almost total lack of examination of appropriate legal policy. This is arguably one of the most important parts of any legal work; but, whatever one's legal philosophy may be, it undoubtedly calls for sustained study in a field such as the present, where the legal materials are so under-determinative. Yet only two-thirds of a page is dedicated to this issue and that at the very end of the book. (Even then, most of what is said is off the point.) The *mélange* that is Chapter Two—only in part and sporadically the 'Review of the Literature' which is promised—contains some pertinent observations; but these tend to be downgraded to mere 'practical considerations', preference being given to consideration of aprioristic precepts or postulates concerning the organization of international society. (This, together with the thorough-going voluntarist analysis, gives the book a rather old-fashioned flavour.) One is left puzzled as to why the author argues for the conclusions which she does and, more importantly, why one should even consider entertaining them. This puzzlement is only increased by the author's failure adequately to articulate the detailed mechanics of the operation of the right which is argued for in answer to the second of the two questions.

Frustrating also is the failure to follow up the line of enquiry, which is hinted at on the first page and occasionally thereafter, that the most appropriate responses to the two questions might well vary depending upon the nature of the treaty concerned. Treaties which 'are intended to' establish 'special regimes'—that is, which 'are intended to' derogate from custom, whatever custom may be or may become—are identified as meriting special treatment; but that is all. Next to nothing is said about how to tell whether or not a treaty falls within this category. The possibility that further categories of treaties should be subject to rules of their own remains unexplored.

Another major shortcoming is that neither the conclusions argued for nor even the questions asked are satisfactorily related to other principles of law which regulate the effects on a treaty of changes in 'background' customary law. A reasonable amount is said about desuetude, the doctrine of fundamental change of circumstances and the precept that relevant rules of customary law need to be taken into account in the interpretation of a treaty. Clear conclusions are advanced regarding the ways in which at the least the first two of these three legal devices might lead either to the termination of a treaty or else to its modulated application in the light of supervening inconsistent custom. One is left unsure, though, as to whether all of the various propositions advanced are capable of working together as a harmonious whole. Perhaps they can; but little attempt is made to show this to be so. The answer depends largely upon the philosophies which underlie and justify the propositions in question; but these remain unexplored. Certainly, no picture emerges of any coherent system by which the law takes account of and deals with changes in custom which may occur subsequently to a treaty's conclusion.

These failings, together with the failure to analyse in any depth the key notion of the 'incompatibility' of a new customary rule with a treaty provision—which idea forms, after all, the very premiss of this work—, raise the question whether this book should have been published, at least in its present form. One certainly would not wish every new monograph to endeavour to be 'definitive' or to have considered each possible argument, all the 'angles', every piece of relevant legal material. There is undoubtedly a place for books which examine only certain aspects of a larger problem or which advance conclusions which are tentative only, perhaps because all of the pertinent data has not been analysed or because the area of law in which the topic arises is a large one and its thorough study would be a large enterprise. Indeed, it can be argued that there are not enough books of this type. However, the shortcomings which characterize this work are such that it cannot be said to fall into this category. The value which it does have is as a convenient reference-point for the pertinent precedents and as a starting-point for thought; and it is these qualities which may, in the end, serve to justify its publication.

DAVID HUTCHINSON

Destruction by Design. Housing Rights Violations in Tibet. By SCOTT LECKIE. The Netherlands: Centre on Housing Rights and Evictions (COHRE), 1994. 199 pp. $15 hardback; $7 paperback.

The reviewer was initially unsure of how to deal with this book in the context of a journal of international law. The title suggests the nature of the problem in referring to 'violations' of rights. Clearly, any reviewer must be on guard and recognize that 'objective' legal analysis may not be the guiding spirit of this production. There is the question of purpose. Is the book devoted to description, analysis, explanation, raising consciousness, or condemnation of the Tibet situation, or to a combination of some or all of these? There is the question of audience. The bold cover and the large format of the book would certainly stand out on the shelves of the university library or store bookshelf, but who would stock it? And would the reader of texts on international law or human rights go straight to a book on 'housing rights', including the reader acquainted with some aspects of the macro-political and international situation of Tibet?

In spite of doubts, readers may warm to this book and recognize the commitment, dedication and scholarship of the author. The book contains many reflections on international law, with a comprehensive human rights perspective. The Chinese practice in Tibet is assessed in the light of international standards, including the developing concern at the UN and elsewhere about the global implications of housing rights deprivations. There are 20 recommendations to the Government of China on protecting the housing rights of the Tibetan people, and a critical discussion of possible international remedies to deal with the situation as perceived by the author. The author knows his way around the UN system and the sense of involvement with the internationalization of the issues is palpable.

Many such books are currently offered by NGOs. Most display high commitment to exploring and analysing a particular practice which is an abuse of rights, or revealing details of a situation in a particular country involving a complex of alleged abuses. They are not to be underestimated by academics and practitioners devoting themselves to more 'abstract' analytical concerns. NGOs are the cutting edge of human rights. The best—and those who act as consultants or researchers on their behalf—do not engage in one-sided allegations, but back up criticism with refined legal analysis and practical detail. The present book fits into the latter category. If only half of what the book asserts were true, there would still be serious questions about the harsh treatment of a whole people, about the ultimate intentions of those who rule China and preside over Tibet, and ample cause for sadness and justified anger.

PATRICK THORNBERRY

National Treaty Law and Practice. Edited by MONROE LEIGH and MERRITT R. BLAKESLEE. *Studies in Transnational Legal Policy*, No. 27. Washington DC: The American Society of International Law, 1995. xiv + 267 pp. $25.

As the number and scope of treaties signed by States increase exponentially, so the importance ascribed to these treaties within the domestic legal system of States grows. This leads inevitably to a developing focus first upon the role played by such treaties within municipal law in practice, in other words, the domestic incorporation of international law, and secondly, upon the constitutional mechanisms by which such treaties are signed and ratified, and effect given to them.

This book trains the light of several very distinguished international lawyers upon the latter concern. It seeks to combine a description of the constitutional relationship of the State as a whole to international treaties with an attempt to draw some comparative conclusions. The former predominates rather than the latter, but at least a start is made by the mechanism of a common structure to the essays.

The work comprises essays upon France, Germany, India, Switzerland, Thailand and the UK—an interesting collection of developed and developing countries, reflecting both the common law and civil law systems and the unitary and federal State structures. This fascinating array of States is examined in the light of an agreed pattern containing four general sections: first, an introduction to the constitutional structure of the country concerned; secondly, a discussion of the treaty law and practice of the country; thirdly, a documentary annex, including the relevant constitutional and statutory documents, as well as important exemplary instruments, and finally, a bibliography on the treaty law and practice of each country chosen. The book also includes a rather short but extremely interesting introduction by the editors in which they point to some comparative conclusions, following upon an examination of the relevant law and practice of the six countries concerned.

It is interesting, but not really surprising, to read that in all six countries covered, it is the executive body that has the responsibility for negotiating, signing, ratifying and terminating treaties, although the extent to which the executive may commit the State internationally without parliamentary approval varies. In the case of Switzerland, at the one extreme, authorization is obtained from the Federal Assembly before any treaty can be ratified, while at the other end the executive in India may negotiate, sign and ratify a treaty without any prior legislative authorization. For the other countries, some form of legislative authorization is required for at least some kinds of treaties, although both the form and substance of this varies. The role of the legislature with regard to treaties differs from country to country, while the widest gap between the countries lies with regard to practice concerning the domestic status of treaties, or what in American parlance is regarded as the self-executing/non-self-executing treaty distinction.

It is the unusual that is particularly appreciated in works such as this which attempt to provide basic descriptions of situations, and one read with great pleasure, for example, of the long history of treaty relations in Thailand. It is always good to be reminded that international law did not start, develop and reach fruition solely in the West.

The chapter on the UK is, as one would expect from a piece authored by Sir Ian Sinclair (here writing together with Susan Dickson), elegantly and clearly written. It lays down with great clarity the essence of British treaty practice and it would certainly be no disadvantage for British constitutional lawyers to be aware of this particular piece.

The strength of this work lies in the description of the national systems for signing and ratifying treaties and the domestic provisions for incorporating them within the local legal order. It is not easy to find elsewhere a book that contains the information that is here provided in such a convenient and clearly written form. The inclusion of extracts from the relevant laws is especially helpful. In addition, the provision of examples of particular documents such as those stipulating full and simple powers enabling particular individuals to sign particular international agreements, instruments of ratification and official promulgations of treaties is particularly valuable in bringing to life what is often seen as a rather dry and dull area of international law.

The introduction notes that the essays contained in the work are to be supplemented by further volumes of essays concerning other countries' laws and practices that will ultimately be republished in a hardback as a reference manual on treaty law and practice. That is indeed a worthy enterprise. The only substantive comment that one would care to make would be to express the hope that the comparative analysis briefly undertaken in the introduction will be developed and extended. It would be useful to have a serious overview of national treaty rules and procedures that noted similarities where none had been really pointed out before and to identify and explain essential and characteristic differences.

MALCOLM N. SHAW

Basic Principles of Modern International Law. By V.S. MANI. New Delhi: Lancers Books, 1993. x + 440 pp. Rs 425.

The United Nations and the Principles of International Law. Essays in Memory of Michael Akehurst. Edited by VAUGHAN LOWE and COLIN WARBRICK. London and New York: Routledge, 1994. 266 pp. £45.

On 24 October 1970, the twenty-fifth anniversary of the founding of the United Nations, the General Assembly adopted without a vote Resolution 2625 (XXV), the Declaration on Principles of International Law concerning Friendly Relations and Co-operation among States in accordance with the Charter of the United Nations. The Declaration proclaimed seven principles: non-use of force, peaceful settlement of disputes, non-intervention, co-operation, self-determination, sovereign equality and good faith. These two books, published as the organization approached its fiftieth anniversary, provide a timely reconsideration of the Declaration and its importance.

Much of Dr Mani's book is a study of the *travaux préparatoires* of the Declaration. The first seven chapters trace in considerable detail, in relation to each of the principles, the history of the debates in the Special Committee appointed to draft the Declaration and in the General Assembly itself. The author has attempted 'to present a representative cross-section of the positions adopted by diverse delegations', highlighting the contributions of delegations of some of the Third World States, and on the whole he succeeds in producing a balanced account of the issues at stake. This part of the book is undoubtedly a useful reference tool, but it makes somewhat turgid reading, and the text engenders a sense of being locked in a time-warp: references to 'the present tendency on the part of States . . . to resort to force indirectly' or to 'recent international conflicts' have to be read in their late 1960s context. Of greater general interest is the final chapter, running to almost 100 pages, in which Dr Mani summarizes the discussions in the previous chapters, pointing out the main features of the Declaration on each principle and the principal areas of disagreement, and then assesses the Declaration's impact on subsequent General Assembly debates and resolutions. The Declaration itself and twelve other resolutions, culminating in the Declaration of 1991 on Fact-Finding by the United Nations in the Field of the Maintenance of International Peace and Security (Resolution 46/59), are reproduced as Annexes.

It is a matter for regret that Dr Mani has not been better served by his publishers and printers. Printing errors abound, the index is inadequate and unreliable, and of the ten page numbers in the table of contents, only two are correct. A scholarly work deserves higher standards of production.

A more forward-looking treatment of the Declaration is to be found in *The United Nations and the Principles of International Law*, a volume of essays by friends and colleagues of the late Professor Michael Akehurst. The volume opens with a discussion by Sir Ian Sinclair of the significance of the Declaration, in which he analyses the legal effect of General Assembly resolutions and criticizes the ICJ's excessive concentration, in the *Nicaragua (Merits)* case (*ICJ Reports*, 1986, p. 14), on the Declaration as evidence of *opinio juris*, at the expense of analysis of State practice, in relation to the principle of non-use of force. This principle receives more detailed treatment from Christine Gray, who points out that many controversial issues, such as the scope of the right of self-defence, were 'resolved by omission' from the Declaration on the Non-Use of Force of 1987 (General Assembly Resolution 42/22), as they had been in the Declaration on Friendly Relations itself and the Definition of Aggression of 1974 (Resolution 3314 (XXIX)).

J.G. Merrills surveys developments in dispute settlement since 1970, including the innovations of the Law of the Sea Convention of 1982 and the CSCE process. Two essays on the principle of non-intervention follow. Vaughan Lowe considers the use of force, contrasting the formulation of the principle with post-Charter practice, but arguing that 'the international community no longer regards an absolute prohibition on intervention as desirable even in theory'. He suggests, perhaps a trifle optimistically, that the time may be approaching when it will be possible to distinguish between justifiable and unjustifiable intervention (the protection of human life being an example of the former), but that intervention by an international or regional organization is to be preferred to unilateral action. Dominic McGoldrick studies the principle from the standpoint of human rights, discussing the very considerable developments both within and outside the United Nations system, and showing more enthusiasm than either Sinclair or Gray for use of the Declaration as evidence of customary international law.

The principle of co-operation is the subject of three essays. Alan E. Boyle discusses protection of the environment, a matter to which the 1970 Declaration made no reference. Subsequent treaty and recommendatory provisions for the most part lack teeth and are heavily dependent on consensus and co-operation for their effectiveness. David Freestone considers the prevention and punishment of terrorism, arguably one of the success stories of the Declaration, since it has been followed by a body of multilateral treaties under which States undertake to extend their jurisdiction so as to deal more effectively with various forms of terrorism. Alan James gives an account of United Nations peace-keeping (as opposed to enforcement action), which depends for its success on co-operation by the member States in authorization, provision of personnel and financing, and in particular on the attitude of the potential or actual host State.

Patrick Thornberry traces the history of the principle of self-determination from President Woodrow Wilson's principles to the present day, pointing to the shift of attention from the 'external dimension', most associated with decolonization, to the 'democratic or internal dimension', and the change in the content of human rights towards group rights such as a right to development—a subject on which his views may be too progressive to secure universal approval. Colin Warbrick contributes an interesting survey of the principle of sovereign equality, dealing with issues which have assumed recent prominence such as the position of micro-States, the right of a State to deal with its own natural resources, and the exploitation of the deep sea-bed, and concluding robustly that 'States maintain the right to decide to what obligations they should be subject and resist the imposition of duties on them which they have not clearly assumed'. The volume ends with an essay by Gillian White on the principle of good faith and its application in various contexts, especially the conclusion, interpretation and performance of treaties.

Michael Akehurst, in whose memory the volume was compiled, was the author of two major works, *The Law Governing Employment in International Organizations* (1967) and *A Modern Introduction to International Law* (six editions, 1970–87), and was also a distinguished contributor to this *Year Book*. Of his seven *Year Book* articles, those on jurisdiction (volume 46 (1972–3), p. 145) and customary international law (volume 47 (1974–5), p. 1, supplemented by a pithy note at p. 173 of the same volume on the hierarchy of the sources of international law) have acquired particular authority and respect for their rigorous analysis and cogent arguments. From volume 42 (1967) to volume 59 (1988) he provided the annual survey of decisions of the Court of Justice of the European Communities, and his final contribution to the *Year Book*, a note entitled 'Parliamentary Sovereignty and the Supremacy of Community Law' (volume 60 (1989), p. 351), was published after his untimely death in 1989 at the age of 49. Michael Akehurst expected from others the high standards of scholarship which he set for himself. He would have been pleased and touched by this fine tribute from his fellow international lawyers.

C.A. HOPKINS

Essays in Private International Law. By PETER NORTH. Oxford: Clarendon Press, 1993. xxviii + 263 pp. including index. £35.

The influence of Peter North, now Vice-Chancellor of the University of Oxford, on the conflict of laws is formidable in both academic and practical terms. As a Law Commissioner and negotiator of the Rome Convention on the Law Applicable to Contractual Obligations 1980, which became part of United Kingdom law by the Contracts (Applicable Law) Act 1990, he exerted himself to restate and reform the 'dismal swamp', as W.L. Prosser famously put it in reference to private international law. Indeed, North uses the phrase as part of the title of his essay on choice of law in tort. At the time of writing, the Private International Law (Miscellaneous Provisions) Bill is before Parliament. It will enact three Law Commission Reports (No. 124, Foreign Money Liabilities, 1983; No. 146, Polygamous Marriages, 1985; and No. 193, Choice of Law in Tort and Delict, 1990). By the time of the last named Report, North had left the Commission, and perhaps for that reason he feels free to criticize the proposals in an essay in this collection.

The nine essays comprise North's major contributions to scholarly writing on conflict of laws over the last two decades. They have all appeared before in journals, *Festschriften* or series of essays and some, such as 'Contract as a Tort Defence', are very well-known: some, however, are in obscure sources and it is good to have them gathered together in one place. All except the most recent one are published with helpful new introductions bringing the essays up to date, and some amendment has been made to the footnotes to point out recent changes which have affected the text. Even the essay without an introduction is not untouched: it has been substantially revised since its first publication in 1992. The style is felicitous. The author is appropriately critical of proposed changes which fail to enhance uniformity and predictability (see, for example, the criticism of the Law Commission's recommendations on choice of law in tort and on contractual terms as defences to tort claims, and especially his attack on rule-selecting theories on pp. 111–27).

The essays reflect North's main concerns: the integration of Anglo-Welsh law into the European Community scheme (he notes that the Brussels Convention on Jurisdiction and the Enforcement of Judgments in Civil and Commercial Matters 1968 did not originally deal with trusts, and Article 17 was defective from an English commercial viewpoint because it did not apply to many common jurisdiction clauses), the reform of choice of law in tort, and the policy issues underlying family law in tort. Four of the essays are concerned with problems of harmonization across the EC and through Hague Conventions, including the attempt in the late 1970s to negotiate a Convention between the UK and the USA for the reciprocal enforcement of judgments in civil matters as an escape mechanism from the Brussels Convention. Three treat of choice of law in contract and tort, one deals with family law (though the omission of the final chapter from the original source, the Hague *Recueil*, makes the ending as here printed abrupt), and one considers methods by which parties can directly or indirectly affect the outcome of litigation such as party autonomy in contract and failure to plead foreign law.

The introductions and essays contain several criticisms of the English courts or of the Government. For example, why did the Court of Appeal in *Re Harrods (Buenos Aires) Ltd.*, [1992] Ch. 72, not refer to the European Court of Justice the question whether or not the doctrine of *forum non conveniens* survived the incorporation of the Brussels Convention into UK law? He rightly condemns the uncertainty surrounding the place of the tort, uncertainty which it may require judicial determination to remedy. He inquires into the failure of the Contracts (Applicable Law) Act to apply to arbitration and choice of forum clauses, to contractual capacity, and to insurance contracts. He is properly critical of some aspects of EC law such as the use of supervening factors in determining the applicable law and the dilatoriness of the ECJ. North provides some interesting sidelights on the position of the British Government in relation to mandatory rules in the Rome Convention and to the decision not to make references from the House of Lords: see the Protocols on the Interpretation of the Rome Convention by the European Court in *Official Journal*, 1989, L48, not yet in force. He also raises important issues, for example, should the parties be free to choose English pre-1991 common law for a contract governed by the 1990 Act? And how do the different articles on mandatory rules in the Rome Convention interrelate?

A series of essays by one hand suffers from the same defects as a collection by many hands. There is some repetition (capacity to contract, void contracts, and presumptions under the Rome Convention), and there are *lacunae* created by the form of essays: by their very nature an incomplete picture is given. Cheshire and North, *Private International Law* (12th edn., 1992), may be needed to fill the gaps. Finally, the reviewer had one or two minor quibbles. *Pepper* v. *Hart*, [1993] AC 593, on the use of *Hansard* in court could have been mentioned on p. 20, and the footnotes were missing on p. 70 of my copy. However, the book, which is otherwise well-produced, is a fine contribution to English ideas on the conflict of laws.

MICHAEL JEFFERSON

The Tokyo Trial and Beyond: Reflections of a Peacemonger. By R.V.A. RÖLING, edited and with an introduction by A. CASSESE. Cambridge: Polity Press, 1993. ix + 142 pp. £19.50.

In 1971, when writing about the Tokyo Trial, Richard Minear stated that his avowed aim was, to 'demolish the credibility of the [Tokyo] trial and its verdict' (*Victor's Justice; The Tokyo War Crimes Trial*, by Richard M. Minear, New Jersey: Princeton University Press, 1971, p. ix). The gist of his case was that not only was the Tokyo Trial a bad precedent, bad enough to 'cast doubt upon the Nuremberg precedent' (p. xi), but also one which merited a return to the international law of the period before 1945. On both counts specifically, and upon the development and form of international law more generally, the interviews collated in this short monograph with the eminent Dutch jurist, the late Bert Röling, comprehensively yet soberly refute these claims and judgements.

This book is unusual in that it consists of a series of interviews focused upon the Tokyo Trial and its aftermath conducted by Cassese with Röling during the course of 1977. The subsequent genesis of the work proved painfully slow, and this in part accounts for both its strengths and weaknesses. During the course of 1978 Cassese suggested a widening of the overall theme to 'offer a general outlook on a progressive approach to international law and society' (p. viii). Röling's counter-suggestion was to change the format of the work in the direction of a Socratic dialogue ranging over the development of an appropriate form of international law to meet the challenge of a world order in the process of a transformation into a system of mass democracy. Unfortunately this more ambitious project never materialized and, owing to the vagaries of time and the exigencies of academic production, the manuscript lay dormant for the next eight years. The fact that a further six years elapsed before the final version appeared in print does not alter the basic question—how to evaluate and judge the work upon its essential merits.

Despite the additional interviews and dialogue in the later chapters (two, three and four), the core of the work is the extended interview with Röling where he sets out his considered views upon the Tokyo Trial (where he served as the Dutch judge) and its aftermath. This section covers some two-thirds of the narrative and is very much the seminal part of the whole discourse. Although Röling admits that his overall assessment and evaluation must be adjudged '*provisional*' (see p. 91), his considered verdict is that the judgment in Tokyo represented an 'an important step towards criminalizing aggressive war' (p. 68). It is this emphasis upon the need to develop an international law adequate to meet the challenge posed to the modern world by the threat of aggressive war in the nuclear age which provides the *leitmotif* linking Röling's views on the Tokyo Trial with the subsequent interviews and arguments developed in the latter part of the book. The insights provided into the need to reconceptualize international law and of the changing role of the international lawyer preoccupied Röling throughout the rest of his distinguished academic and diplomatic career. The insights this book provides are all the more tantalizing for their brevity, and it is this fact which suggests a shortcoming in the overall substance of the case presented. (See, for example, the discussion on the scope of international criminal law and its limits (at pp. 96–8.) It is also a danger of the format adopted in this monograph that its very immediacy may run the danger of degenerating into a '*petite histoire*' of the trial (see p. 31)—an insider view purportedly eliciting the 'real reason why things happened' (p. 31). However, Röling is far too wise a scholar to present such a form of sophisticated voyeurism. The Tokyo Trial represents far more than the foibles and idiosyncrasies of the individual *dramatis personae*. In his view the trial had and has a continuing historical significance, and whilst it may be premature to present a final verdict, this fact must not be lost upon subsequent generations. Despite all the subsequent criticisms levelled against both the Nuremberg and Tokyo Trials, Röling stands by his verdict that the trials were 'major events in international life, with consequences for people's perception of what they could and could not do with impunity' (p. 90).

A key insight into Röling's approach and philosophy is provided by his remark that essentially 'international law functions in an [environment lacking] . . . a legislator, without a judge, without a central power, a society in which relations are more horizontal than vertical' (p. 29). It was this insight which allowed Röling to develop a sophisticated approach to the issue of Japanese aggression by encompassing in his analysis and understanding a degree of realism countering any tendency to an excessive legalism—a charge he, in effect, levelled at some of his fellow judges on the Tribunal. Thus, whilst the majority of the bench were prepared to indict the Japanese leaders for pursuing a policy amounting to a conspiracy to wage aggressive war from 1 January 1928, Röling's interpretation of the events was that, under international law even in 1945, waging aggressive war was a crime *in statu nascendi* only (p. 66). He then elaborated upon a conceptualization of an international crime as being more akin to the nature of a 'political' crime under domestic law, i.e. an act where the 'criminal is considered an enemy rather than a villain and where the punishment reflects a necessary political measure rather than an expression of retribution' (p. 66). Judged at the bar of history, the Japanese leaders had been found wanting, thus meriting and at once entitling the victors to take political measures 'necessary for the preservation of peace' (p. 66). Having discarded 'values cherished by the world [those leaders] had violated basic rules of human behaviour' (p. 88), and rather than pass over such acts or resort to exemplary or summary execution, their committal to trial before a legal tribunal was both 'feasible and desirable' (p. 66). It was on these grounds, rather than procedural legal grounds, that Röling felt the ultimate justification for the trial should be constructed.

The resort to the judicial process was thus seen, to quote the words of Justice Jackson, 'as one of the most significant tributes that Power has ever paid to Reason' (p. 67). However, to vindicate the validity and legality of judicial proceedings it behoves the victors to proceed with circumspection, ensuring that above all such proceedings are both fair and just. It is on this score that Röling has many critical points to make of the conduct of the trial notwithstanding his overall vindication of it. His reasoning here is revelatory of his developing conception of international law—which, in effect blossomed into a re-conceptualization of international law appropriate to the rapidly changing world situation post-1945. Thus, he is critical of the attitudes of his fellow judges for their relative inability to see the case in its true international context, and for their propensity to allow the trial procedure to be dominated by common law principles and practice (especially regarding the formal rules of evidence). However, by situating the case in the context of international law he is able to provide a more than adequate rebuff to those critics of both Nuremberg and Tokyo who levelled the charge that the tribunals applied *ex post facto* or retrospective law. According to Röling, both tribunals did so unequivocally, but at that time the principle of retrospectivity was not a principle contained within international law (pp. 68–70). Ultimately what led Röling to an overall positive assessment of the trials, despite his reservation that the Tokyo Trial was in itself 'somewhat unfair' (p. 88), was the contribution made to the continuing transformation and development of international law, in particular, 'to the outlawing of war' (p. 89).

In Röling's view the trials initiated the beginning of a new era in international law, signalling the end of the colonial system, the emergence of human rights law and the gradual democratization of the international legal order. The concomitant 'Eurocentric' and essentially positivistic outlook of many international lawyers is undermined by such developments—the law does not 'exist in a total vacuum' (p. 137)—but nevertheless international law 'remains in a miserable state' (p. 139) according to Röling, in spite of the fact that the corner had been turned at Nuremberg and Tokyo.

In the present state of international law after the Cold War, Röling's analysis of the shortcomings of international law would suggest that it is not the law *per se* which is at fault but the contemporary stage of development of the international community. The brief but incisive insights revealed in the dialogue with Röling, however, give hope for the future and point the way for a wholly positive role for the 'new international law' (p. 138).

TONY RICHARDSON

United Nations Legal Order. Volumes 1 and 2. Edited by O. SCHACHTER and C. JOYNER. Cambridge: Co-publication of the American Society of International Law and Grotius Publications, 1995. 1166 pp. £120.

1995 is the fiftieth anniversary of the United Nations Organization. The anniversary has occurred just five years after the collective response to the Iraqi invasion of Kuwait, which has been regarded by many legal and political commentators as the first indication of the Organization's ability to use the powers bestowed upon it by the Charter more effectively after the termination of the Cold War. These events have led predictably to a number of assessments of the evolving role of the Organization within the international legal order since the end of World War II.

United Nations Legal Order is an impressive addition to this literature. The two volumes it comprises are the outcome of a three-year multidimensional project sponsored by the American Society of International Law and funded by the Ford Foundation. The project's objective was 'to examine, explain and appraise contributions made by the United Nations System to international law and the law-creating process'. Although Security Council powers under Chapter VII are perhaps the most high-profile and widely discussed provisions of the Charter, the specialized agencies and other UN bodies have developed complex regulatory regimes for the management of international affairs across a broad spectrum of activities. Accordingly, this objective is pursued through detailed examination of these regimes. The work is divided into three Parts: the UN System as a source of law; substantive law in a number of key areas (force and arms, human rights, self-determination, refugees and migration, women, labour, economic relations and development, education, science, culture and information, environment, the sea, shipping, outer space, posts and telecommunications, aviation, health, food and agriculture, international crimes and the unification of private law); and the internal law of the Organization.

The contributors are primarily American international lawyers, including many who have been predominant in American international legal thinking and practice in the era spanned by the UN. A broad array of practical and academic experience is captured in these volumes, and especially illuminating are chapters by contributors who have worked within the various agencies they discuss.

The first chapter, by Oscar Schachter, draws the themes of the book together. In his characteristically elegant way he presents the UN through an architectural metaphor. He describes it as a three-level structure: State actions take place on the ground floor; on the second floor are the activities of a legal character; and on the third floor one finds the broad policy goals that influence the relevant participants. There is continuous movement between these floors as the development of the international legal order is influenced from both above and below. Perhaps Schachter should have included a basement for the increasing activities of international non-governmental organizations. NGOs add to the 'bottom-up' process through their lobbying of States, and also seek access to the third floor to add their voices to the formulation of policy. Recent UN documentation (for example, Agenda 21, 1992, the Vienna Declaration of Human Rights and Programme of Action, 1993, the Beijing Platform for Action, 1995) recognizes the importance of NGO involvement in international law-making. One of the challenges the State-based UN faces at the end of its first half-century is to accommodate the diverse demands of international civil society as expressed through NGOs.

The chapters on general law-making (by Szasz, Kirgis, Sohn and Fleischhauer) look at the innovative techniques used by UN institutions in formulating normative standards and expectations of compliance. Kirgis compares the practices of various specialized agencies to highlight some of the more effective methodologies. He also explores the tension between the need for legal regulation by specialist bodies, especially in technical matters or those where State boundaries are increasingly irrelevant (for example, health, the environment) and the desire of States to retain their control over the law-making processes and to limit institutional autonomy. Both Kirgis and Szasz emphasize the importance of the broad range of soft-law techniques and dispute the myth that a formally binding instrument necessarily ensures greater compliance. These chapters provide practical illustrations of the argument presented in a number of more theoretical works that there is no definitive delimitation between international law and non-law. There is rather a spectrum of instruments and modalities for inducing change that States, and other actors, respond to in varying ways. Other chapters in the second part of the book provide further illustrations of this point (for example, those on food and agriculture, health). The chapter by the recently elected ICJ Judge, Carl-August Fleischhauer, is a reprint (and update) of his paper to the ASIL in 1991. It therefore does not combine his new judicial experience with his UN Secretariat knowledge, which would have been especially valuable in the context of inducing compliance.

The chapters in Part II covering substantive law are generally historical and descriptive rather than theoretical. They evaluate the main issues presented in Part I, that is, normative standard-setting and monitoring and implementation techniques, in specific areas of law. In some cases there is also an emphasis on formal and informal dispute resolution processes and their place in the development of substantive law (for example the chapters on aviation and shipping). Many of the chapters show how dramatic advances in technology have changed the scope of the work and underlying assumptions of the role of legal regulation in specific areas (for example, posts and telecommunications, outer space, aviation, health). Some chapters focus on summarizing the most significant instances of law-making (for example, the chapters on self-determination, UNESCO, shipping, food and agriculture, unification of private law), while others adopt a more thematic approach (for example, the chapters on labour, economic relations and development, outer space, health), although inevitably the two approaches merge into each other. One of the most successful of the latter is, unsurprisingly, Bernard Oxman's contribution on the law of the sea. Oxman provides a remarkably concise assessment of the major influences in the evolution of the law of the sea from the time of Grotius, and of the ways these influences have played out in State practice and treaty-making. His analysis of the interplay between customary international law and conventional law is an especially useful contribution to achieving the book's objective. Another approach chosen by some contributors is that of case studies. Effective examples are those by Louis Sohn on the interpretation by the General Assembly and Security Council of UN Charter, Article 2(7), and by John Murphy on the UN response to Iraqi aggression. What emerges from a study of Parts I and II is an understanding of the diversity of contemporary international law-making and the breadth of international legal regulation. At the same time there is a reaffirmation of the prevailing limits on international law-making through international institutions.

Part III on the internal legal regulation of the UN is the shortest section of the book with only two chapters, on the international civil service and financial responsibility. The former summarizes the influence of the incumbent on the exercise of the implied powers of the Secretary-General from the time of the League of Nations onwards and the development of an independent international civil service with formalized conditions of work. The final chapter examines the financial responsibility of Member States to the UN and its specialized agencies. Alvarez rejects Member States' justifications for failure to meet their financial obligations based upon treaty law and the doctrine of State responsibility, and considers the intractable question of how the Organization can enforce the duty to pay. Part III perhaps does not fit so readily into the objectives of the project as Parts I and II. Nevertheless, these chapters show that the UN legal order embraces both law-making by the Organization and legal order within the Organization.

It is always easy to quibble over omissions from such a work, but for this reviewer perhaps the most regrettable exclusion is that of any contribution by one of the 'new stream' international lawyers (for example Martii Koskiennemi, David Kennedy or Philip Allott). An analysis rooted in the critical tradition, especially if combined with the institutional experience of some of the 'new approaches' lawyers, would have added another dimension to the examination of 'how United Nations institutions have made the law, what law has been made and the extent to which that law has been accepted by and evidenced in contemporary state practice'.

A substantive omission is consideration of how indigenous persons have worked through the UN agencies to achieve substantive recognition of their concerns. Virginia Leary discusses how ILO Conventions 107 and 169 on indigenous populations were criticized both for going beyond the mandate of the ILO and for their 'assimilationist' approach, but otherwise such peoples remain invisible in this work. On the other hand, the inclusion of a chapter by Rebecca Cook on the UN and women is an encouraging acknowledgment of the need to counter-balance the traditional silence about women in international legal scholarship, but the silence is largely continued throughout the other chapters. A number of examples where explicit reference to women would have been relevant can be given. Various discussions of the erosion of the domestic jurisdiction exclusion do not draw attention to its continuing force with respect to the national treatment of women. Despite the fact that the majority of the world's refugees are women and children, the chapter on refugees makes no reference to the particular problems women face in claiming refugee status under the current definition, nor the growing literature by academics and UNHCR workers on women refugees. The chapter on human rights consigns the Convention on the Elimination of All Forms of Discrimination Against Women to a footnote. While Hurst Hannum justifies this on the ground that the book contains a separate chapter on women, this did not prevent him from providing brief accounts of refugee law and the attack on apartheid within the UN, both of which are also covered elsewhere. More importantly, the omission of any discussion of CEDAW from this chapter continues the separation of women's rights and human rights that has impeded adequate guarantees of the former and has formed an important part of recent debates on human rights law.

Inevitably the current rate of change and development within the UN means that some chapters are already dated. There is also inconsistency in the cut-off date across different chapters. This is probably unavoidable in a work with so many contributors and inevitably different submission dates. Nevertheless the chapter by Szasz does not go beyond 1992, while Fleischhauer and Murphy have incorporated the 1993 establishment of the Tribunal for Prosecution of War Crimes in Former Yugoslavia, and Oxman notes the important 1994 developments in the law of the sea. The number of ratifications of the United Nations Human Rights Covenants given by Hannum is for the end of 1990, although the chapter was prepared in January 1992 and the corresponding date for the Race Convention is December 1992. This chapter also states that no State has ratified the International Covenant on Civil and Political Rights without also ratifying the International Covenant on Economic, Social and Cultural Rights, which is precisely what the United States did in 1992. This surely could have been updated by the author or editors. The inconsistency in dating would have been less relevant in a more theoretical work on the role of the UN, but given the extremely rapid rate of change in so many areas since 1990 it reduces the coherence of the overall work.

Perhaps surprisingly, there is little mention of the UN conferences that have been such a visible feature of the UN in the nineties and instrumental in creating new understandings of the law in specific areas. There is some discussion of the 1992 Earth Summit (UNCED) in Rio de Janeiro in the chapter by Paul Szasz, including some useful comments on the influence of the media and NGOs in the creation of law, and a fuller analysis in the chapter by Ved Nanda on the environment. But the chapter on human rights does not refer to the 1993 Vienna Conference on Human Rights which was being planned by 1992 and is surely a significant event in the UN development of human rights law. This omission may be another consequence of the different cut-off dates across the chapters but is unfortunate in a book with a publication date of 1995.

It is plainly impossible to review separately all the contributions to a work of over one thousand pages. These two volumes have drawn together a wealth of material across the range of activities of the UN and its agencies. The chapters show how integral the work of the UN is to the modern international legal order. They are an essential reference tool for teachers, scholars and practitioners of international law. They are effectively edited to avoid irritating overlap and repetition, include useful, albeit generally brief, bibliographies for each chapter and are extremely well-presented. The American Society of International Law is to be congratulated on conceiving and carrying through this project.

CHRISTINE CHINKIN

The Charter of the United Nations: A Commentary. Edited by BRUNO SIMMA. Oxford: Clarendon Press, 1994. xlix + 1258 pp. £140.

Ten years ago, a French-language article-by-article collective commentary on the United Nations Charter was published to commemorate its fortieth anniversary (Cot and Pellet, *La Charte des Nations Unies*, currently 2nd edn., 1991). Now with a similar concept, but written entirely in English, comes a fiftieth birthday present to the United Nations from the German-speaking international legal profession and a contribution to the United Nations Decade of International Law. Professor Simma is the co-ordinating editor with Professors Mosler, Randelzhofer, Tomuschat and Wolfrum as principal co-editors. The aim of the work is, in the editor's words, 'to render more than 45 years of UN practice accessible to practitioners and academics alike, in a comprehensive and scholarly fashion'. A work of similar title, written entirely in German, had appeared in 1991, but the present book, though conceptually derived from that work, is not a mere translation of it. So much has happened in the United Nations in the last five years that the earlier work has been completely refashioned by an expanded team of contributors, sixty in all, who, though all German-speaking, submitted their contributions in English. Although there is a scattering of proof-reading errors, very little criticism can be directed at the general standard of what Professor Simma humorously refers to as 'German English'.

Two general contributions, on the history of the United Nations and on the interpretation of the Charter, precede the commentaries on individual articles. The contribution on interpretation, by Professor Ress, is in particular a stimulating and concise analysis.

Thereafter, each successive article of the Charter, together with the preamble, is treated in a standard form. The relevant text is printed at the head of the item followed by a select bibliography. These bibliographies, as might be expected, refer to many books and articles in the German language, thereby illustrating the fact that there is a large relevant literature in this language, which is often ignored in works published in English or French. A commentary on the article then follows which usually consists of the drafting history of the text, its application in the practice of the organs of the United Nations, including the International Court of Justice, its relevance within the Charter as a whole and any particular problems of interpretation or application to which it has given rise. Each commentary carries a detailed set of footnoted references. There are two subject-based contributions in addition to the sequential article-by-article commentaries: first, self-determination of peoples is discussed by the late Professor Doehring as a discrete subject in the context of Article 1(2); secondly, prior to the discussion of the articles contained in Chapter VII, Professor Bothe has written an extensive note on peace-keeping. The work concludes by reproducing the Rules of Procedure of the General Assembly. There is an extensive subject index.

It is not practicable to make other than brief remarks on a few of the contributions to this massive work. Of the United Nations' public activities in recent years its peace-keeping and enforcement efforts have been the most prominent. As already mentioned, the work includes a general discussion on peace-keeping by Bothe which complements the commentaries in particular on Articles 24 and 25 (Delbrueck), Articles 39–43 (Frowein) and Article 51 (Randelzhofer). Other sets of distinguished contributions are by Ermacora on Article 2(7), Hailbronner/Klein and Fleischauer on the functions and powers of the General Assembly contained in Articles 10–13, Mosler on the Chapter XIV articles concerning the International Court of Justice, and Fiedler on the Chapter XV articles concerning the Secretariat.

In summary, this work contains a feast of information and opinion. Its editors, contributors and publishers are to be congratulated on the production of such a fine birthday present.

GEOFFREY MARSTON

Regional Peace-keeping and International Enforcement: The Liberian Crisis. Edited by M. WELLER. Cambridge: Cambridge University Press, 1994. xxv + 465 pp. £50.

In the Foreword to the sixth volume of the *Cambridge International Documents Series* Professor Lauterpacht writes:

> During the same period as the attention of the world has been concentrated on the dreadful internecine struggle in Yugoslavia, barely 2000 miles away—no distance in terms of modern communications—a no less bestial conflict has been taking place in Liberia. It is painful to ask, and even more painful to be unable satisfactorily to answer, the question why it is that the conscience of the international community is so rightly (albeit insufficiently) exercised over the first of these episodes and is so relatively unconcerned with, to the extent that it is aware of, the horrors of the second. (p. ix)

One might suggest that the frenetic period of immediate post-Cold War peace-keeping operations authorized by the UN, which did span the world and help to solve seemingly intractable conflicts in Namibia, Nicaragua and Cambodia, has given way to a much more narrowly focused, Western-centred, Security Council. The result has been several half-hearted, and so far unsuccessful, peace-keeping operations, particularly in Africa (for example Angola and Western Sahara), while in Liberia the increasingly overburdened UN has been willing to let a regional organization take responsibility.

Although it is the case that regional organizations ought to share the burden of peace-keeping with the UN, the lead should come from the well-established and well-resourced institutions such as the EU and the OAS, which, to date, have only been peripherally involved in peace-keeping. In the case of Liberia, a little-known, and much weaker, organization, the Economic Community of West African States (ECOWAS), has attempted to solve the civil war.

The documents in this volume chart ECOWAS' involvement, and the subsequent, somewhat reluctant, concern of the UN. Given the difficulty of finding even the most basic ECOWAS documents, this volume is essential for anyone involved, or interested, in collective security. The volume raises numerous contentious issues relating to the law of international organizations, most of which are highlighted in the helpful Introduction. A few of these issues will be reviewed here as illustrations of the usefulness of this volume.

The legal basis of ECOWAS' military involvement in Liberia, commencing in 1990, is the 1981 ECOWAS Protocol Relating to Mutual Assistance on Defence (pp. 19–24). Although this provides for collective security as well as collective self-defence (p. xx), it is debatable whether it permits military intervention in an internal armed conflict (Article 18(2)), unless the conflict is 'engineered and supported actively from outside' (Article 4(*b*), also Article 18(1)). Another limitation on military intervention by ECOWAS is contained in Article 15(1), which states that intervention is only 'justified by the legitimate defence of the territories of the Community'.

Although there are numerous documents concerning the issue of whether the conflict in Liberia is 'internal' or 'international', they are characterized, in the main, by accusation and counter-accusation (pp. 32–5), with very little objective fact-finding. This is not a criticism of the editor, it is simply a fundamental problem of international law, particularly acute in the area of armed conflict when so much turns on whether the conflict is international or not.

Nevertheless, ECOWAS' original intention was to create a peace-keeping force to monitor a cease-fire (pp. 67–9) agreed to by the parties. The creation of a truly neutral and consensual peace-keeping force can be seen as a necessary implied power of an international organization concerned with collective security, applying the opinion of the World Court in the *Expenses* case. Peace-keeping is not a use of force contrary to Article 2(4) of the UN Charter, nor is it enforcement action requiring the authorization of the

UN Security Council by the terms of Article 53(1) of the UN Charter. Genuine peace-keeping by a regional organization whose remit includes collective security is lawful.

However, it is clear that the ECOWAS Cease-Fire Monitoring Group (ECOMOG) was not consented to by all the factions, and it immediately became involved in the fighting (p. 87). The National Patriotic Front of Liberia (NPLF), which virtually controlled the whole country, treated ECOMOG as an enemy faction (p. 87, p. 94). In response, ECOMOG launched an offensive against the NPLF alongside another of the factions (p. 99). Although there was an agreement for a cessation of hostilities in November 1990 (p. 114), the conflict fully erupted again in April 1991.

During the lull in hostilities, the UN Security Council approved of the ECOWAS actions in a Presidential Statement (p. 128). Whether, at this stage, the Council was able to hide behind the fiction that it was simply rhetorically supporting a 'peace-keeping' operation was soon to become irrelevant as ECOWAS imposed economic sanctions against the NPLF in October 1992 (p. 226), and then explicitly confirmed the obvious fact that ECOMOG was taking military enforcement action in Liberia (p. 341). In Resolution 788 of November 1992 (p. 273), the Security Council retrospectively endorsed these decisions as well as imposing an arms embargo of its own on Liberia (with the exception of ECOMOG).

This resolution seems to be a recognition of the increasing autonomy of regional organizations to take enforcement action in the absence of prior Security Council authorization, despite the literal wording of Article 53 of the Charter. Regional organizations have developed this autonomy as regards economic enforcement action, evidenced by the recent OAS sanctions against Haiti, imposed prior to the Security Council embargo and retrospectively approved by the UN General Assembly. Autonomy in military intervention is less clear, though Liberia is a precedent in that direction.

However, despite this encouragement from the UN, it became clear that ECOWAS was unable to solve the crisis on its own and so the UN became more heavily involved, negotiating a now typical UN package of peace-keeping and peaceful settlement in the form of elections, the accords to be implemented by a joint ECOMOG/UN peace-keeping operation (p. 412).

It can be seen how the UN has reluctantly become involved in Liberia, its attempts at leaving the matter to a regional organization, albeit one badly equipped, resulting in failure. In so doing, and in turning a blind eye to enforcement action in an attempt to encourage regional peace-keeping, the UN has perhaps created a dangerous precedent, giving the green light to stronger regional institutions wishing to take enforcement action, but not wanting, for political or military reasons, to seek Security Council authorization. Furthermore, the UN's failed gamble will seem even more costly if its operation in Liberia is unsuccessful, for it could result in a further restriction of UN peace-keeping on pragmatic grounds.

This brief survey of some of the issues raised by this excellent collection illustrates its tremendous importance as a teaching and research tool.

N.D. WHITE

REVIEW ARTICLE

JAPANESE DECONSTRUCTIONS OF THE GROTIAN TRADITION IN INTERNATIONAL LAW*

By ANTHONY CARTY‡

A Normative Approach to War: Peace, War and Justice in Hugo Grotius. Edited by YASUAKI ONUMA. Oxford: Clarendon Press, 1993. xvi + 421 pp. £40.

This work might well be characterised as an anti-*Festschrift*,[1] written to question the place of honour accorded to Grotius in international law. It is not exactly another refutation of the thesis that Grotius is the father of international law as much as it is a mark of disaffection with the ancestor-worship which is a main characteristic of the discipline of international law. It could usefully be read alongside another production of Oxford University Press, *Hugo Grotius and International Relations*. This latter work does not make the literal mistake of treating Grotius as the founder of the discipline,[2] but it does treat him as a spiritual father. Each contributor reflects on the, as it were, *sacred* writings of Grotius and is thereby stimulated to thoughtfully expressed concerns about *the present state of the world.* The tone is quite different in the volume put together by the Japanese Research Group on the Fundamental Theory of International Law headed by Yasuaki Onuma, Professor of International Law in the University of Tokyo. If the remarks which follow in this review are at times rather strong, they do no more than enter into the spirit in which this book has been written, a spirit which the reviewer very much welcomes.

From an Appendix, 'Eurocentrism in the History of International Law', which Onuma has added to the book, it may be possible to gain a better understanding of the aim of a work whose object is not otherwise altogether clearly stated. For instance, at the beginning of the Conclusion the same author disavows an intention to offer an annotated commentary, albeit the study is presented, justifiably, as a close reading of the text (p. 333). Onuma argues that since it was European States which established the global colonial system and European international law which came to regulate inter-State relations, we have to explore the structure of this system. It is only by understanding this system,

‡ LL M (London), Ph. D (Cantab.); Eversheds Professor of International Law, University of Derby.

[1] A German word signifying a collection of papers written by distinguished international lawyers to honour a more aged member of their circle.

[2] Edited by Hedley Bull, Benedict Kingsbury and Adam Roberts (1990), esp. at pp. 2–3: Kingsbury treats this issue as long since recognized as badly posed.

and not by arbitrarily inventing a 'non-European' perspective, or by over-estimating the influence of such non-European factors, that we can liberate ourselves from Eurocentrism (p. 373).[3]

A sympathetic interpretation of this exercise is given by Robert Chu. He describes the book as signalling the arrival of outsiders—Japanese scholars—at the centre: ' . . . All of a sudden, the table is turned : Grotius, that father figure, the head of our family, has become the inscrutable "other". And international law is now the "culture" which has to be deciphered and represented.'[4] This may help to explain the recurrent demonstration of contradiction in the text of Grotius, which entitles (?) the authors to be characterized as critical legal scholars, engaged in a close reading of the text which is intended to turn it against itself. The supreme attack on Eurocentric international law would be to reduce its founding master to illogicality and even unintelligibility.

Hence there is a restless desire on the part of the authors to undo any ancestry attributed to Grotius. For instance, in a chapter on *temperamenta*, Tanaka Tadashi objects to the remark by Wheaton and Lawrence, leading figures of nineteenth century international law literature, that Grotius's more moderate and humanitarian principles concerning the laws of war, i.e. *temperamenta*, were supported by Vattel and unanimously adopted by international law scholars in the nineteenth century. Tanaka Tadashi objects that although Wheaton traces the process by which the severity of war was mitigated, he does not identify any direct link with Grotius. He merely speaks of correspondence or coincidence. This is the most that can be generally said of the 'influence' of Grotius, whatever the individual detail of influence (pp. 304–5). Again, Yanagihara Masasharu attacks the notion that Grotius is the 'Father of Private Law Theory Based on Natural Law' (p. 167). The author says this judgement cannot be sustained. One reason is that the concern of Grotius is to enumerate the just causes of war and not to develop theories of ownership, contract, etc. The reason why he discusses marriage and succession in such detail is that they were major causes of war. He did not discuss, for instance, the requirements for the assignment of property or specific forms of will, although they are important in the field of private law (p. 168). Secondly, Grotius did not distinguish clearly between the public and private law concept of *dominium*. It is only with Hegel that the political character of *dominium* disappears (pp. 169–70).[5]

The primary attack on Grotius's fatherhood of international law in general comes from Onuma in his critique of past studies. This claim of parentage has been long disputed, as he acknowledges. Haggenmacher emphasizes the pre-

[3] Onuma means by Eurocentrism an exclusivist style of thinking and not an unfair handling of non-European questions. The latter issue appears to interest the authors only marginally. Maybe this is why they do not consider Kingsbury's quite extensive consideration of this question, op. cit. above (n. 2), pp. 42–50. For very important recent work which edits Grotius's actual sources, i.e. his footnotes or references, see *Hugo Grotius, de jure belli ac pacis*, edited by R. Feenstra and C. E. Persenaire (Scientia Verlag, 1993).

[4] Robert Chu, 'Grotian Encounters', *Harvard International Law Journal*, 35 (1994), p. 595, at p. 596.

[5] Furukawa Terumi also objects that Grotius's work does not deserve to be considered to mark the first appearance of the idea of criminal law in the modern theory of natural law, merely because—in the same vein—it was not conceived with a view to constructing a self-contained theory of punishment but merely to providing a preliminary to advocating punishment as one of the just causes of war. However, this criticism is levelled against a fellow-Japanese (p. 221).

modernity of Grotius. That is, Grotius's work, which is mainly about the doctrine of just war, is a culmination of a medieval scholastic tradition, which depended upon a medieval and classical Greek concept of natural law. The central feature of this doctrine is that *man* is embedded in society and in the Cosmos.[6] von Kaltenborn, not cited by Onuma, but in the general bibliography, also defended the same thesis in a work published in 1848 (p. 358).[7] Onuma remarks that simplistic views of Grotius as an advocate of modern natural law, i.e. of the *rights of man* as preceding society or as a theorist of modern international law, are no longer held, at least not by experts (p. 358). Onuma leaves this statement at rather a general level, but it can easily be taken to mean that Grotius did not develop a modern concept of the sovereign State as the virtually exclusive actor in international relations upon whose free consent the main body of international law had to rely for its validity.[8]

If one brings Onuma's general argument to a specific issue such as the question of the binding nature of agreements, the style of reasoning runs as follows. Had Grotius intended to establish a general theory of the binding force of agreements applicable to all agreements and promises—and Onuma acknowledges that he is regarded by such major figures as Pothier, Wieacker, Gierke and Arnaud as having a role in the birth of modern contract theory (p. 174)—that general theory should have constituted the basis of the binding force of State contracts, slave contracts, feudal contracts, etc. Consent was treated as the basis of associations such as the State and marriage, and the law of nations was considered to be based on agreement between nations. However, the binding force of these specific agreements is not demonstrated in any coherent way. Yet this is not to say that no account is given of why such agreements are binding. In the Prologue, Grotius states that it is necessary that among men there be some method of obligating themselves to one another, and no other natural method can be found than promising (pp. 214–15). So it appears that the argument comes full circle and no more is said than that Grotius marked a transition stage between the medieval motley of feudal entities, all of which concluded agreements of some sort, and the crisp modernity of exclusivist sovereign States, which concluded what are now called international treaties.[9] At another point Onuma makes rather clearer what he is trying to argue when he says that Grotius was far from a pure voluntarism in his theory of contract, and that he (Onuma) can understand Wieacker's insistence that Grotius's contract theory follows the Aristotelian tradition, which requires *aequalitas* as the touchstone of the justness of contracts (p. 197).

This type of criticism marks the entire book. It may be read as a *critical turning* of the text, or, alternatively, as failure to detach explanatory exposition from analysis. However, in the present writer's view, it has more to do with the

[6] P. Haggenmacher, *Grotius et la doctrine de la guerre juste* (Paris, 1983).

[7] C. von Kaltenborn, *Die Vorlaufer des Hugo Grotius auf dem Gebiete des ius naturae et gentium* (Leipzig, 1848, rep. Frankfurt am Main, 1965).

[8] A recent major study of the doctrine of international law from Grotius to Vattel takes this as its major thesis, making Vattel the *father* of international law: Emmanuelle Tourme-Jouannet, *L'Émergence doctrinale du droit international classique, Emer De Vattel et l'école du droit de la nature et des gens* (Thèse pour le doctorat de l'Université de Paris II, 1993).

[9] This thesis—the question of who are the subjects of international law in the work of Grotius—is thoroughly considered in Chapters 4 and 5 of the book : see below.

radically problematic nature of international law as a discipline, which means that each would-be historian of the subject finds the parameters of his investigation contestable.[10] In so far as the concerns of the authors are primarily theoretical and not historical, it is possible to read their work much more as a criticism of Grotius where he is expected to meet certain absolute standards.

So another and more promising way to read the book may be as a user's guide to Grotius for those international lawyers interested in theory,[11] i.e. concerned about the confused and incomplete nature of the discipline at present and wondering about whether an understanding of the 'fundamentals' of Western or any other legal culture can afford an answer. An example of a theoretical problem might be whether it makes any conceptual sense in international law to set up an international criminal tribunal to try individuals for crimes against humanity committed in Bosnia-Herzegovina, while at the same time engaging in political negotiations with those finally responsible for committing these crimes. This is not simply a function of the liberal principle that equals have no authority to judge one another.[12] It is also a function of the political power diffusion in international society which makes the outcome of war dependent not on its supposed character as legal procedure but on the material power and competence of the protagonists.[13]

If one could leave aside the question whether many criminal lawyers are right to regard Grotius as their 'father', it can only be interesting, with the above stated problem in mind, to explore the close treatment of this theory of punishment by Furukawa Terumi. He points out that Grotius proposed the theory of the fictitious superior. An offender by his very criminal act may be considered to have made himself inferior to *everybody else* who has not committed a similar crime. Consequently, all other persons who have not committed a similar crime stand above the offender and anyone may punish him (p. 224). Grotius overrides arguments about equal status and even arguments about the exclusivity of State jurisdiction which had appealed to the scholastics such as Vitoria (one trembles at the thought whether this makes Grotius modern rather than pre-modern, or primitive, or whatever). Where the power of the State does not function, natural freedom may still exist in its original form in kings, peoples, etc., because they do not fall under a common jurisdiction. The right of punishment comes to those who have not themselves been injured, etc. (p. 232). Grotius's anxiety to minimize the wholesale mayhem which such a

[10] For instance the three most extensive recent attempts at a history of international law have not succeeded in becoming accepted as standard works. They are E. Reibstein, *Völkerrecht : Eine Geschichte seiner Ideen in Lehre und Praxis* (2 volumes, 1958 and 1963); Verzijl, *International Law in Historical Perspective* (12 volumes, Leiden, 1968–); and W. Grewe, *Epochen der Völkerrechtsgeschichte* (Baden-Baden, 1984). The first two treat historical precedents as sources for contemporary institutions of international law with bizarre consequences for historical chronology. The third embeds illustrations of legal information in a general diplomatic history which follows the schema of epochs (hence the title) of the Great Powers, each of which had the chance to force the agenda of international law in the modern era. A student textbook following closely on Grewe is K. H. Ziegler, *Völkerrechtsgeschichte* (Munchen, 1994).

[11] Which is at least suggested by the title since there is now a distinctive *normative* approach to international relations.

[12] This is an outcome of Vattel's theory of sovereignty. See the reception of Vattel in this sense in J. L. Brierly, *The Law of Nations* (6th edn., by H. Waldock, Oxford, 1963).

[13] See R. Aron, *Paix et guerre entre les nations avec une présentation inédite de l'auteur* (Paris, 1962, 1984), pp. 704–12, esp. pp. 710–11.

theory could provoke led him to devise criteria for limiting the initiative—the right to intervene—to those who could be taken to be relatively more impartial, and confining the *casus*—of intervention—to extreme cases of crimes which are both atrocious and evidently wrong (pp. 233–4).[14] While Furukawa cannot resist attacking Vollenhoven for treating Grotius as the forerunner of modern collective security ideas (p. 236), he none the less provides an important beginning to a critique of Grotius by saying that he treats crime as a misuse of reason, somehow external to man, rather than as a destructiveness (Furukawa says evil elements) integral to all human experience (p. 241). One thinks of the Christian saying, let he who is without sin throw the first stone, and then looks again at Furukawa's treatment of how Grotius separates his theory of punitive war from any notion of divine authority, using instead the concept of the fictitious superior (p. 233). This approach demonstrates that a major virtue of the book is to serve as a warning against a facile or superficial use of Grotius as a support for a solution to contemporary problems.

None the less, a use of the book as a guide to theory cannot exhaust its purpose which is also historical. So one has to investigate, above all, Onuma's claim that Grotius was relying upon the common sense and social consciousness of his time in his method of legal argument, an undertaking which Grotius executed successfully. Onuma states that Grotius gave specific form to the idea of justice by introducing common sense, i.e. concrete ideas, senses and emotions shared by his contemporaries, thereby enhancing the persuasiveness of his argument (p. 120). In reality Onuma does not engage in historical research but confines himself to an internal debate within the international law profession, and, in particular, with Haggenmacher. The latter is taken as right in recognizing that while in principle Grotius aspired to an independence of law from religion, in reality he used Christian concepts as societal norms, although Haggenmacher is apparently prone to underestimate the theoretical independence of law from religion (p. 76). This argument is presented in a context in which Onuma claims that Grotius is addressing the social class to which readers of the *JBP* were intended to belong, those with direct control over issues of peace and war and not the ideas generally shared by the masses (ibid.). When Onuma maintains the argument that Grotius relied upon precepts shared by his European contemporaries and capable of regulating human behaviour in the secular context of his time, he means that, for instance, Christian precepts will be drawn upon in so far as they are societal norms, and it is this style of argument by Grotius which was supposedly crucial in the widespread acceptance of the book by his contemporaries.[15] In this context, that is to say where the Christian religion is expected to exert a considerable social power, the strongest impression of Grotius's style of persuasion or argument may come across especially in Tanaka Tadashi's chapter on *temperamenta* (Chapter 9), where there are expositions of the rather brutal State practice on the conduct of war and arguments for its moderation, through multi-faceted calls for constraint. At this point one might add Onuma's criticism of ethnocentricity. Grotius speaks of the universality of norms,

[14] For Kingsbury's treatment of the same issue, see *Hugo Grotius and International Relations*, op. cit. above (n. 2), pp. 38–42.

[15] p. 76.

whereas all he means is the concept of law generally applied in Christendom. A main theme of the book is to question this enthnocentricity.[16]

Precisely because for Onuma key partners for dialogue are present members of the international law profession—*the real ethnocentricity*—Onuma does not undertake any historically serious investigation of who were Grotius's contemporaries. His approach does not entail a naive overestimation of the influence of Grotius. The *JBP* could not have such a great influence on contemporaries because it is so difficult to limit war, but if the book had not been so evenly balanced in its arguments it could not even have exercised the influence it did. The difficulty remains that Onuma confines himself to speculation already current within the discipline. So he refers to the opinion of Falk that Grotius encouraged the European rulers of the day to reconcile their practical pursuits as statesmen with their spiritual heritage, thereby filling the vacuum caused by the weakening, if not collapse, of the Roman Church as a source of international unity.[17]

The root of this type of analysis lies in a strength as well as a weakness. Onuma is determined, as are the other authors of the book, to place Grotius not only alongside other 'classical' international lawyers, but also alongside political theorists such as Hobbes, Locke and Rousseau.[18] Yet how this method of comparative political theory is used is problematic when it amounts to a statement of the significance of Grotius's work even for his legal contemporaries.[19] So Tanaka Tadashi argues that since the *JBP* is based upon man's social and rational nature, and since this was fundamentally challenged by Hobbes within decades, what remained of Grotius's work was a motley collection of specific legal rules and regulations. What then brought Grotius the title 'father of international law' cannot have been his 'system', which had collapsed, but the acceptance of the rules and principles he set out as valid among nations on essentially empirical grounds.[20] Tanaka is assuming that history is a linear textbook evolution of political theorists each of which effectively refutes his predecessor, and that such an evolution permeates the minds of the 'practitioners' of international law who are in the grip of some kind of *Zeitgeist*.

Where the interdisciplinary (legal/political theory) approach works most successfully is in the chapters directly concerned with the theory of the State. The two chapters on 'State and Governing Power' and '*dominium* and *imperium*' display the function and strength of the book at its best. This is *Grotius* scholarship, including an immense erudition, especially in the German and Japanese languages. The authors are firmly convinced that there are periods and epochs in history, the pre-modern and the modern. Grotius is pre-modern because he fails to think abstractly concerning the nature of political community,

[16] pp. 6 and 1 respectively.

[17] pp. 76–7.

[18] p. 2.

[19] This is a weakness shared by international relations theorists such as Hedley Bull in *Grotius and International Relations*, pp. 65–93. Grotius is presented as a paradigm of international society without any serious investigation of the historical specificity of that society. A particularly vague part of Bull's piece is the section on the 'Doctrines' (a sacred word *par excellence*) and the Peace of Westphalia: op. cit., pp. 74–6.

[20] pp. 55–6.

i.e. he does not abstract individuals from society or the State and then reconstruct them from first principles, as does Hobbes.[21] He is opposed to a right of resistance against a ruler and indeed treats the relation between ruler and ruled (the question of legitimacy) as a matter of political theory, while he, Grotius, as a jurist is concerned with the association of law and governing power.

At the same time the weight of textual treatment of Grotius is to treat his work as another treatise on the State, to object, for instance, that Grotius confuses the problem of legitimacy of power with that of forms of government and develops his criticism of popular sovereignty—which would bring with it the power to punish rulers who abuse their power—by confining his interest to the actual state of affairs in particular communities, where people do voluntarily subject themselves to other rulers, do find themselves conquered in just wars, do find that some governments are not in fact constituted for their benefit. The objection is made that thereby Grotius confuses the issue.[22] Yet it is recognized that his aim is the pacifist one to opt for justice over peace, the Netherlands' War of Independence being justifiable as a war of secession based upon necessity rather than as a rebellion.[23]

Tanaka Tadashi is working towards the idea that, notwithstanding his pre-modern character as a thinker, Grotius effectively accepted the autonomy of law in its consideration of State power. He concludes by saying that the theory of sovereignty played a major role in removing from the agenda of lawyers questions of the legitimacy of the State—not merely questions of the justness of causes of war, but also questions of the political character of the State. They slipped away in favour of a purely formal concept of the State. For this proposition Jellinek is cited, writing in Germany in the years preceding 1914. Yet Grotius is distinguished from Bodin, a predecessor, for not having adopted a doctrine of absolute and indivisible sovereignty.[24] Instead, one has to await Pufendorf's theory, systematized in *de jure naturae et gentium*, the outstanding successor to Grotius and Hobbes, for such a theory.[25]

These arguments are immensely stimulating. They highlight a major conceptual weakness of international law since it is most destabilized by wars of secession and civil wars with respect to which international lawyers have no settled contribution to make at present. The service the author renders is to highlight the difficulties which Grotius faced but—indeed it may be a mark of the respect shown towards Grotius by the author—the text is treated entirely as a work which has to stand as a contribution to theory in which the author intervenes on every line, without explaining either his own standpoint or how it was that a thinker as apparently confused as Grotius could have had any influence. The difficulty is simply that the concerns of the contemporary legal

[21] p. 130, a chapter by Tanaka Tadashi.
[22] p. 138.
[23] pp. 143–4.
[24] p. 135.
[25] p. 146.

theorist predominate over the historian. While this makes the argument difficult to follow, it is worth the effort.[26]

Where this dominance of the historical text by the theoretical author (in the next case, Yanagihara Masaharu) becomes insufficient is in the discussion of the question whether Grotius gave a satisfactory account of and solution for the main causes—one might have thought pretexts—for war in his time, wars about succession, disputed questions of inheritance. How the author treats this question may be seen in the following. Grotius explicitly states that the rule that the eldest child is given preference if patrimonial kingdoms are indivisible is based on the law of nations. In usufructuary kingdoms it is not the king but the people who decide succession. Yet Grotius is admonished for not making the distinction between the two cases clear. He says that some kings come to hold *imperium* with *dominium plenum* when they have acquired their kingdom in a just war, or when a people have subjected themselves without reservation to avoid some other disaster.[27] At the same time the author follows up Grotius's recognition that if a dispute arises over succession there is no one authorized to render a final decision on such disputes, in particular between a king and a people. The author concludes, not surprisingly, that it is doubtful whether Grotius's standards could effectively solve actual problems.[28] Surely the reader is entitled to ask what is going on here. The author has begun this section by arguing that Grotius is here trying to offer solutions to what are the causes of most contemporary wars, although for this major proposition he does no more than cite a chapter by Trevor-Roper in *The New Cambridge Modern History* along with a fellow Japanese colleague, Naruse.[29] The analysis acquires an iconoclastic tone which is entertaining in itself. It does correspond with the aim of 'killing the father'. However, the author could have invoked Tanaka's assertion that Grotius works with too close an association of law and governing power (p. 145) and then have asked why Grotius did not see, at this point, the need for a theory of the State which might resolve the question of legitimacy. Alternatively, Masaharu could have praised the illogicalities in Grotius, as marking a reflection of the practice of States such that he was able to offer a pragmatic solution to succession problems which responded so much to common sense as to reduce the likelihood of conflict to a minimum, his (Grotius's) main goal (the tendency of Onuma's argument).

However, it is at this point that impatience with the lack of reference by the authors to actual State practice reaches breaking-point. What is lacking is even the simplest hard historical fact. For instance, the official history of the French foreign office states categorically that although Grotius was in France as Swedish Ambassador for an extended period after the publication of his *JBP*, it never constituted a ground for legal advice at the French Court. The latter only came to take legal advice at all with the acquisition of eastern territories within

[26] As already noted, Tourme-Jouannet also provides a very lucid account of the same conceptual developments.

[27] p. 163, by Yanagihara Masaharu.

[28] p. 164.

[29] p. 161.

the Empire, and then only in terms of the need to know what these territories entailed in terms of entanglements within the Empire.[30]

Such an apparent inability to pose scientifically the question of Grotius's impact on his contemporaries is an inevitable outcome of feeling one has to accept as a starting-point for an investigation of Grotius more general questions put by contemporary international lawyers and specialists in legal philosophy and political theory. This is simply not possible. There are no clear standards to be found by appealing to theory at present to see whether the theory invoked by Grotius was sound. The disastrous consequences of this course can be seen in Tanaka Tadashi's Chapter 2 on Grotius's concept of law. The author says that Grotius completely fails to consider the possibility of right becoming separated from law. For Grotius, municipal law contrary to natural right was not law, but, at the same time, this did not accord a right of resistance to attain natural rights in the sense of the Age of Revolution (p. 36). Tanaka Tadashi goes on to note that it was the inherent connection between justice and law that made possible the revival of natural law and the development of neo-naturalism (p. 37). For this proposition the French catholic international lawyer of the inter-war period, Le Fur, is cited. Without explaining the distinction, if any, between neo-naturalism and natural law, the author argues that, if the assumption that anyone endowed with reason can agree on what is just does not hold, the identification of justice with law turns out to be ideology, for which proposition Kelsen is simply cited. The author then cites Austin and Hart as separating justice and law in order to meet the criticism that all law is not necessarily just. Finally, legal positivism is taken as concerned only with positive law and does not provide a higher standard to judge it—hence there has been a revival of natural law after the experiences of Nazism, Fascism and Japanese militarism, for which proposition McCoubrey is cited. The difficulty is that the close commentary of the Grotius text is built upon an equally close contextualisation of legal theory which takes on encylopaedic proportions without being complete and without being brought back to an exegis of the text itself. This is a type of dense theoretical erudition which may lead pragmatic international lawyers to feel that they can dispense with theory.

It is necessary to break a disciplinary *umblical cord* to begin to locate the work of Grotius in terms of its contemporary place and impact. This means embarking upon a history of mentalities, at this time primarily a history of *court literature*. The question is important because, if Grotius was the father of no one and contradicted himself on most matters, one is left wondering whether his fame is attributable to anything other than the institutional memory of international lawyers, most of whom are demonstrated by the authors of this text to have misread him. Once one leaves the discipline of international law, the cold wind of criticism can be very bracing indeed. For instance, consider the following well-known comments of Kant on the international law tradition:

For while Hugo Grotius, Pufendorf, Vattel and others whose philosophically and diplomatically formulated codes do not and cannot have the slightest legal force (since nations do not stand under any common external constraints) are always piously cited in

[30] Jean Baillou, *Les Affaires étrangères et le corps displomatique français* (CNRS edition, 1984), vol. 1, pp. 119–21, drawing on André Gros's article on legal affairs and the Ancien Regime in *Mélanges Troltabas* (Paris, LGDJ, 1970), pp. 187–95.

justification of a war of aggression (and who therefore provide only cold comfort), no example can be given of a nation having foregone its intention (of going to war) based upon the arguments provided by such important men . . . [31]

To whom did Grotius dedicate his book? Did this person read it? Where did he write his book, in whose library? What were some of the most pressing issues of his time—concerning the use of violence—and how did his approach to these questions compare to those actually adopted? It is suggested that these questions have to be posed before international lawyers can be convinced that a knowledge of Grotius does not belong exclusively with an esoteric clique of international law so-called theorists. The question is urgent for international lawyers, as for all other lawyers, because a creative role for legal doctrine is becoming more and more problematic as lawyers have become reduced to offering their services for sale predicting the behaviour of legal institutions. However confused may have been the humanistic learning of Grotius (Onuma, p. 352), it is not as wafer-thin as what we possess now.[32]

In *Le Roi de guerre: Essai sur la souveraineté dans la France du Grand Siècle*,[33] Joel Cornette presents an exhaustive account of how war was understood normatively in the France and the United Provinces of Grotius's time. The question then is whether and how far Grotius penetrated this world. His *JBP* was dedicated to Louis XIII and was written in part near Senlis in the property of Jean-Jacques de Mesmes, President of the Parlement of Paris, put at his disposal after his flight from Holland.[34] It was published at a time when (1625) Denmark had entered the war, and war could be said to be feeding on war.[35] Grotius is singled out as concerned at the recklessness with which conflicts are taken up and then conducted without regard for any human standards. The motivation for the work is compared to that of Hobbes. Cornette accepts that Grotius's work is in the tradition of the just war and very much follows Haggenmacher.[36] He does not argue for or against the relevance of Grotius. However, the overall framework of Cornette's book places Grotius on the margin.

[31] Immanual Kant, 'Perpetual Peace' in *Perpetual Peace and Other Essays*, translated by T. Humphrey Hackett Publishing Company, 1982), p. 355, following the enumeration of *Kant's gesammelte Schriften*. Kingsbury and Bull also make a collection of unfavourable comments on Grotius by Voltaire, the British King James I, Vico and Rousseau: op. cit. above (n. 2), pp. 36, 61–2 and 70. These two authors also simply collect opinions about Grotius and do not investigate the more tedious historical question of what use contemporaries of his did or—which is much more difficult—did not make of his work. The cited persons simply disagree with his opinions and do so in the context in which one is searching for so-called traditions (the Grotian, the Kantian etc., esp. p. 57), an inevitable concomitant of scholarship as ancestor-worship.

[32] One view is that Kelsen's *pure theory of law*, with its rigorous distinction between law and morality, justice or politics, has left the jurist with no other function but to systematize the work of legal, particularly judicial, decision-makers. In a world of technically interventionist institutional law, the modern would-be theorist has no independent stock of legal culture upon which to draw, independent of his own subjective preferences and prejudices : see Annick Perrot, 'La Doctrine et l'hypothèse du déclin du droit ', in *La Doctrine Juridique* (Centre d'histoire du droit et de recherches inter-normatives de Picardie, Paris, 1993), p. 181, at pp. 199–200.

[33] Payot, Paris, 1993.

[34] Ibid., p. 77.

[35] p. 68.

[36] pp. 125–7, 142–3.

The primary cause of the extent of the mayhem in the conduct of the Thirty Years War or the Wars of Religion so-called is that war was conducted between '*chefs de guerre*', hired by contract with a Prince but not under his control. They engaged in random killing and plunder to sustain themselves. This resignation of the political power signified a virtual autogestion of violence, which entailed a scorched earth policy. As Cornette puts it:

> . . . Ainsi les combats qui avaient pour terrain principal le Saint-Empire prirent peu à peu la forme d'un conflit autogénéré, les troupes pratiquant le *dégast* d'un espace à un autre, changeant de territoire dès que celui-ci voyait ses ressources épuisées . . . .[37]

Cornette relies upon contemporary descriptions of the spirals of violence among the soldiers given over to every conceivable licence in a course which usually led to their own self-destruction. Very few survived this anarchy:

> . . . En un mot, porter partout le dommage, la ruine et la mort, être exposé soi-même à ces maux, telle était l'occupation et la vie de ces hommes . . . [38]

The solution for which the France of Louis XIII, Cardinal Richelieu and Louis XIV was a model, closely followed by the United Provinces and England, was to strengthen the authority of the sovereign monarch, characterized by his power to wage war, encouraged to do so to maintain internal order, bringing—*inter alia*—the *chefs de guerre* under firm monarchical control.[39] This course of events, the consolidation of the monarchical State, signified literally a language of absolutism, the absolution of rulers from law. Because they were above and beyond law they could do whatever they had to do to maintain and restore order within their domains. The most effective device to achieve this end was to export violence abroad, the deliberate channelling of especially aristocrats' useless energies abroad. Such structural developments could be counted to reduce violence in so far as it became restricted to a deliberate policy of State. The restoration of internal order was then structurally linked to an increase in international violence since France, above all, attained a momentum rooted in the fact that its sovereign was a sovereign of war. Hence, a major cause of the inhumanity of warfare was structural and not moral. An improvement in the organization of armies reduced indiscriminate violence, itself unfavourable to military discipline.

In this context it is inevitable that it should be Hobbes, not Grotius, who is the key thinker:

> . . . *Le Leviathan* a en quelque sorte cristallisé en un organisme unique les pulsions primitives et brutales, partagées à l'origine par tous les hommes. Et c'est ainsi que la violence proclamée légitime s'est installée au coeur même de l'État. Au prince de savoir la gérer, la canaliser dans des guerres exportées, loin du territoire enfin pacifié par la loi . . . [40]

A key literary contribution was Cardin Le Bret's *De la souveraineté du roi* which appeared in 1632 at the beginning of successful French expansion in alliance with Sweden. A central feature of such Court literature was to present the process and outcome of war not as a legal procedure but as providential,

[37] pp. 68–9.

[38] p. 75.

[39] On the tendency in Holland in the course of the seventeenth century, see Chapter 2, 'Quand une république fait naître un roi de guerre'.

[40] p. 79.

attaching itself to a French tradition of religious-State triumphalism going back to the crusades, which, in appealing to Providence (*le tribunal de dieu*), recognized the unpredictable, hazardous quality of any conflict. The rightness of the French cause was taken to have been confirmed by the God of armies. In this sense, ' . . . Forgé au feu de la guerre juste, l'alliance de la raison de Dieu et de la raison d'État ne pouvait que fortifier l'État royal . . . '.[41]

There existed a vast literature concerning war coming from France, Austria and Spain, to mention some of those countries engaged in the wars of the seventeenth century, which Cornette characterizes as propaganda. He reckons that the most successful and celebrated juridical legitimation of the interventions and royal conquests in the east of the Kingdom of France was published in 1632 and dedicated to Richelieu by Jacques de Cassan, counsellor of the King and '*premier avocat au presidial de Beziers*'. The work is *La Recherche des droits du roy et de la couronne de France etc.*, providing plenty of annexationist possibilities.[42] A central feature of the literature in France was the revival of the claims of Charlemagne to reconquer Germany. This provoked innumerable responses, among which the most celebrated was by Baron de Lisola, ambassador and plenipotentary of the Emperor, *Le Bouclier d'estat et de justice contre le dessein manifestement découvert de la monarchie universelle sous le vain pretexte des prétentions de la reyne de France*, first published in 1667. Cornette reports that this study made direct use of the scholastic tradition of the just war culminating in Grotius, to characterize the expansionist, imperialist qualities of the France of Louis XIV. He considers that works of this genre, essentially pamphlets, did contribute to creating the 'légende noire' of Louis XIV.[43]

Indeed, it is probably only in this sense that one can talk of Grotius enjoying a brief life as the father of international law. Stolleis traces his influence on legal literature within the Empire, in German universities. Here Grotius contributed weight to the founding of chairs in international law. His work could attract attention as a most complete survey of the literature within a particular, i.e. just war, tradition.[44] France was on the offensive from 1630 until well into the eighteenth century, while the Empire was on the defensive. Hence it would not be surprising that it could be argued that Grotius had little influence in France, but quite a widespread audience in Germany. These remarks are merely tentative. Cornette remarks about what he calls the patient work of juridical legitimacy done by French lawyers concerning the territories they claimed bordering on France. These correspond to the provinces which were attached to France from 1659 till 1792. This analysis by Cornette would suggest that Grotius served a propaganda function in the hands of powers or States wishing

[41] pp. 130, 132–3. In this context Grotius's secular project was clearly not simply a reflection of the common sense of his contemporaries, and his concept of war as a legal process ignored, as the so-called international law tradition always has, the fortunes of arms.

[42] pp. 139–40.

[43] p. 142.

[44] Michael Stolleis, *Geschichte des öffentlichen Rechts in Deutschland*, Erster Band, 1600–1800 (Munchen, 1988), pp. 195–6, attributing the development of a specific academic discipline of international law literature in German universities from the middle of the seventeenth century to Grotius. International law flourished as a discipline in German universities precisely because it was the so-called cabinet wars which preoccupied the innumerable small States of Europe in the seventeenth and eighteenth century.

to maintain the status quo against expansionist powers who claimed special universalist authority.

Two final points need to be made to point to a realistic assessment of Grotius's significance. Returning to Carden Le Bret, he is taken by Cornette to contribute concretely to the development of the notion that the 'good of the State' or the 'common good' attaches to the fact that the King is '*absolu*' *des lois*. When necessity and justice require, the King may change any law whatever in his absolute discretion.[45] In other words, built into the structural development of international society is a lawlessness at an international level which is felt essential to the preservation of legality at an internal level. Indeed, the only alternative would be to allow States to interfere in one another's internal affairs, the logical implication of the notion that one State could have authority over another. This notion of *raison d'état* remains a constant of international law until the present time.[46] One variation of this problematic is whether international law is binding, or whether the State owes its existence as a legal entity to international law.[47] Here it has to be said that it does matter that Grotius is pre-modern and fails to develop a theory of the State. Cornette does accredit Grotius with the capacity to talk of a state of nature and to suppose that individuals do implicitly contract to accept what is agreed by the majority.[48] Grotius opposes any right of resistance, a point which the book discusses very effectively. However, he does not develop theoretically, as does Hobbes, the significance of the inevitable lawlessness of the State, not bound by any superior institution. This is Kant's reason for being dismissive of the whole international law tradition. It is submitted that this weakness of Grotius cannot be exposed through working within the tradition. The only outcome will be the great difficulty in appraising the significance and impact of Grotius which the Japanese scholars experience here. If international lawyers are to have any impact on their environment, they have to find some way of seeing that environment in terms which are other than a reflection on their own ways of thinking.[49]

This brings one to a second point. The text has raised the question that Grotius does not have a convincing theory of evil. For him morality is abstract and he does not face the possibility that evil/destructiveness may be built into or inherent in human nature. A history of international law which is not within the grip of international lawyers may benefit from a final observation which Cornette makes. The symbiotic relation between violence and the State, the inherent link between the sovereign and the right to make war, did come to be

[45] p. 320.

[46] See, for instance, John Norton Moore et al., *National Security Law* (Carolina Academic Press, 1990).

[47] Kelsen undertakes his most extensive criticism of the German representative of this standard perspective: Georg Jellinek, in *Das Problem der Souveranität und die Theorie des Völkerrechts* (Tubingen, 1922).

[48] Cornette, op. cit. above (n. 33), p. 78, citing him from the first pages, to be exact, p. 12.

[49] Niklas Luhmann notwithstanding. This person's theory of so-called autopoesis, expounded most recently in *Das Recht der Gesellschaft* (Frankfurt, 1993), is that the genius of law is that it incorporates what it wishes into its own categories and rejects what it does not find useful—as do all other categories of thought. Luhmann himself recognizes that this presents a fragmented picture of so-called disciplines of knowledge none of which have to account either to one another or to anyone or anything else.

questioned in the Europe of the Enlightenment, not because of the genius of Grotius in appealing to the common sense of elites, but because of the general discredit which the waging of war suffered particularly after Louis XIV's sacking of the Palatinate in the years 1688 and 1689. This scorched earth policy led eventually to such influential works as Voltaire's *Le Siècle de Louis XIV*, the Abbé de St Pierre's *Projet pour rendre la paix perpétuelle* and Johnathan Swift's *The Conduct of the Allies*.[50] Such a culture of criticism was to have uncertain repercussions. Because a monarchy such as the Bourbon in France had its *raison d'être* in war, its adoption of pacifism would have its problematic aspect.

[50] Op. cit. above (n. 33), pp. 324–7.

DECISIONS OF BRITISH COURTS DURING 1995 INVOLVING QUESTIONS OF PUBLIC INTERNATIONAL LAW*

International organization—recognition in domestic law—law governing constitution and representation of the organization

Case No. 1. Westland Helicopters Ltd. v. *Arab Organization for Industrialization*, [1995] QB 282, [1995] 2 WLR 126, [1995] 2 All ER 387, [1994] 2 Lloyd's Rep. 608, QBD (Colman J). Following the decision of the House of Lords in *Arab Monetary Fund* v. *Hashim (No. 3)* (the *AMF* case),[1] it is settled that in the absence of applicable legislation, the legal personality of an international organization of which the United Kingdom is not a member will be recognized in English law, provided that it has been recognized under the municipal law of at least one of its member States. The present case raised a related issue of the law to be applied by domestic courts to determine matters pertaining to the constitution and representation of an international organization that has been so recognized.

The Arab Organization for Industrialization (AOI) was established in 1975 by a treaty between the United Arab Emirates, Qatar, Saudi Arabia and Egypt, which provided that the organization's headquarters was to be in Cairo. In accordance with the treaty's provisions, the organization was given legal personality by legislation in each of its four member States. In 1979, following the conclusion of the peace treaty between Egypt and Israel, a political and economic boycott was imposed on Egypt by other members of the Arab League. It was announced that the other three members of the organization had decided that the organization's existence was to be terminated, and that a liquidation committee was to be established. However, the position of Egypt was that under the terms of the treaty it was not open to the three member States alone to terminate the organization's existence, and that the liquidation committee had been invalidly set up. A decree law was issued by the Egyptian President, which provided that the AOI continued to enjoy juristic personality in accordance with Egyptian law. The law recognized the other three member States as having determined to withdraw irrevocably from the membership of the organization, but provided that this was not to affect its juristic personality, the continuance of its activities, its rights and obligations towards third parties, or the statutes of companies in which it was a participant. That law and a subsequent law also made certain changes to the constitution of the AOI, under which the high committee of the organization was to consist solely of Egyptian ministers and officials.

In 1978, AOI had entered into a contract with Westland Helicopters Ltd. ('Westland') to establish a joint venture company to undertake the manufacture

[1] [1991] 2 AC 114, this *Year Book*, 62 (1991), pp. 433–7.

of helicopters in Egypt. The other three States informed Westland that co-operation between Westland and the AOI would cease, and invited Westland to present its claims for compensation to the liquidation committee in Riyadh. On the other hand, the chairman of the entity now existing under Egyptian law ('the Cairo body') informed Westland that it would perform all of AOI's contracts and joint ventures. Westland's view was that its contractual relationships with AOI had come to an end, and it presented a claim to the liquidation committee in Riyadh. When no settlement was reached, it subsequently submitted to the International Chamber of Commerce a formal request for arbitration. Westland's position, which the arbitrators in Geneva accepted, was that the Cairo body was not a party to the arbitration, and that the representatives of that body could not act for the AOI, which was the respondent in those proceedings. In 1993, the arbitrators made an award under which the AOI was to pay damages to Westland.[2] Westland then obtained leave of the High Court to enforce the award in England.[3] The Cairo body intervened in these enforcement proceedings, claiming that it was the same entity as the judgment debtor, and the owner of the bank deposits against which the award was to be enforced. It sought to have the leave to enforce the award set aside.

The preliminary issue before the court was thus whether the Cairo body was the same entity that had been established by the 1975 treaty and was a party to the contracts with Westland. As a matter of Egyptian law, it appeared that it was.[4] For the Cairo body, it was argued that matters relating to the existence, constitution and representation of the AOI were governed by the law of Egypt, its headquarters State and the State in which it had its 'centre of gravity' or domicile. Colman J did not agree with the argument that this was implicit in the decision in the *AMF* case.[5] In that case, the House of Lords had made it clear that although the Arab Monetary Fund had been incorporated in the domestic law of 21 different States, there was none the less only a single organization with its domicile and residence in the United Arab Emirates, and that only the one duly authorized director-general of that organization could bring an action to recover its funds in any part of the world.[6] However, Colman J did not think that the House of Lords had thereby decided that the law of the organization's State of domicile was its governing law.[7] He considered the question of which system of law governs an international organization to be entirely at large, and to be approached from first principles.

[2] The award was made on 28 June 1993. An order and two interim awards of the arbitrators made in 1982, 1984 and 1985 are reproduced in 80 ILR 596. Decisions of the Court of Justice of Geneva and the Swiss Federal Supreme Court in 1987 and 1988 relating to the arbitration are reproduced in 80 ILR 622.

[3] Under RSC, Order 73, rule 10(1).

[4] See [1995] QB at 310C–G.

[5] Loc. cit. above (n. 1).

[6] Ibid., at 162C–E.

[7] See the discussion at [1995] QB at 294G–303A. As Colman J put it (at 299C–D), this passage in the *AMF* case only established that where an organization has been accorded legal capacity under the law of more than one State, this 'does not mean that there is more than one international organisation for the English courts to recognise, but merely that there is more than one factual basis upon which recognition can be accorded to the same organisation'.

In his view, the question could not be resolved by analogy with the private international law rule that matters relating to the constitution of a corporation are governed by the law of the place of incorporation.[8] He said:

> Where . . . a foreign friendly state has clothed an international organisation with legal personality and has thereby 'created' a foreign corporation in the special sense of that word used by Lord Templeman in the *A.M.F.* case, fundamentally different considerations apply. The international organisation may have been clothed with legal personality by such a state, but the body thus clothed is no ordinary domestic entity but an international body created by treaty. Questions as to the meaning, effect and operation of its constitution in so far as they arise between the parties to the treaty are issues which, in the eye of public international law, can only be determined by reference to the treaty and to the principles of public international law. Once the material issues are inter-state issues, they can no longer be resolved by any body of domestic law.[9]

He considered that to apply the domestic law of any one member State to determine matters relating to the constitution of an international organization or its representation would be a potential affront to all other member States whose domestic law was thereby ignored, and would be inconsistent with the principle that an international organization is a creature exclusively of international law.[10] That was particularly clear in this case, given that the treaty establishing the AOI expressly provided that the organization was 'not subject to the laws and systems in effect in the participating states'. To apply the law of any one State would thereby involve ignoring the express terms of the treaty. Colman J referred to *In re International Tin Council*,[11] in which it was held that provisions of the Companies Act 1985, despite the generality of their wording, were not to be construed as authorizing the winding up of an international organization, as this would be incompatible with international law. In that case, Millett J had said that, where States decide to carry on a collective enterprise through the medium of an international organization,

> no one member state, by executive, legislative or judicial action, can assume the management of the enterprise and subject it to its own domestic law. For if one could, then all could; and the independence and international character of the organization would be fragmented and destroyed.[12]

Colman J noted that in that case, it had not been regarded as relevant that England was the seat of the organization.[13] He agreed that if the constitution of an international organization were treated as governed by the law of the seat State, then it 'would, in the eyes of English law, be at the mercy of the government of the seat state'. This he considered to lead 'inexorably to the

[8] e.g. *Dicey and Morris on the Conflict of Laws* (12th edn., 1993), vol. 2, pp. 1111–6 (Rule 156(2)).

[9] [1995] QB at 303E–F.

[10] Ibid., at 303G–304B.

[11] [1987] Ch 419, this *Year Book*, 58 (1987), pp. 406–18.

[12] [1987] Ch. at 452D–E. Millett J referred in that case to Jenks, *The Proper Law of International Organizations* (1962), pp. 3 and 8–9. Colman J observed that the Court of Appeal had described the reasoning of Millett J in that case as 'unanswerable' in *In re International Tin Council*, [1989] Ch 309, 330F. Colman J also quoted (at 296E) from the dissenting judgment of Bingham LJ in the *AMF* case ([1991] 2 AC at 140G–H), who said that 'it would not of course be acceptable for one sovereign state, party to an international treaty, to hijack an organisation to which it and other states had given birth and subject it (contrary to the treaty terms) to its own domestic jurisdiction'.

[13] See the discussion at [1995] QB at 304G–307G.

wholesale rejection of the domestic law of the seat state as the proper law'.[14] Invoking the general rule that where questions of common law are at large, they should be decided in a manner consistent with international law in the absence of some controlling common law principle to the contrary,[15] he said that he had 'no doubt whatever that the proper law governing the existence, constitution and authority of its officers to represent the A.O.I. is public international law'.[16]

The Cairo body also argued that even if the applicable law was public international law, the Egyptian legislation was consistent with international law. It was argued that the other three States had committed a material breach of the treaty by their decision no longer to participate, and that Egypt's actions were a justifiable response, on grounds of necessity, to avoid the paralysis of the organization. Colman J found that the difficulty with this argument was that the principle of non-justiciability articulated in the *Buttes* case[17] prevented an English court from deciding whether or not the other three States had acted in breach of the treaty, or whether or not Egypt's response was justifiable under international law.[18] He found, contrary to the argument for the Cairo body, that in these proceedings the burden of proof was on it to establish that under international law it was the same entity as the original AOI. As it could not do so without reliance on non-justiciable matters, Colman J ordered that it be struck out of the proceedings.

The conclusion that matters pertaining to the constitution of an international organization are governed by public international law and not the domestic law of any of its member States seems obvious,[19] although it highlights the artificiality of recognizing an international organization's legal personality in domestic law by reference to its incorporation under the law of another State.[20] On the other hand, it seems unsatisfactory that although English law will recognize the legal existence of an international organization, the English courts may in some cases be unable to determine who, for the purposes of domestic law,

[14] Ibid., at 308E–310B. Colman J was of the view that under established principles of private international law, if the law of the seat State was the applicable law, there would be no basis for refusing to recognize laws of that State seeking to take control of the organization in violation of its constituent treaty. However, he added that even if such laws could be refused recognition on grounds of public policy, this would force the English courts 'into the position of sitting in judgment between the seat state and the rest of the organisation'. See also at 304G–305A.

[15] [1995] QB at 307G–308A, 310A, referring to *Oppenheimer* v. *Cattermole*, [1976] AC 249, 278, and to *Trendtex Trading Corporation* v. *Central Bank of Nigeria*, [1977] QB 529, 553, this *Year Book*, 48 (1976–7), pp. 353–62.

[16] [1995] QB at 308C.

[17] *Buttes Gas and Oil Co* v. *Hammer*, [1982] AC 888, this *Year Book*, 53 (1982), pp. 259–68.

[18] [1995] QB at 292D–294F, 310G–311F.

[19] See, e.g., Jenks, 'The Legal Personality of International Organizations', this *Year Book*, 22 (1945), p. 267, at pp. 270–1; Mann, 'International Corporations and National Law', this *Year Book*, 42 (1967), p. 145, especially at pp. 154–7; Seidl-Hohenveldern, *Corporations In and Under International Law* (1987), pp. 104–8. See also Mann, 'International Organisations as National Corporations', *Law Quarterly Review*, 107 (1991), p. 357, at p. 359. In respect of the AOI, this was also the view expressed by the Geneva arbitrators in their interim award of 5 March 1984 (see 80 ILR 596, at 610–12), and by the Swiss Federal Supreme Court in *Arab Organization for Industrialization and others* v. *Westland Helicopters Ltd. and others* (19 July 1988), 80 ILR 622, at 657 ('One can agree . . . that the AOI . . . is a legal entity, an organism under public international law. Instead of referring to the domestic law of a State to determine the status and legal structure of this organism it is a matter of looking at the provisions of the instrument or treaty which is at the base of its creation').

[20] See the discussion in this *Year Book*, 62 (1991), pp. 436–7.

is the legal representative of the organization. The reality is that in a case such as the *AMF* case, in which an international organization is permitted to bring an action in the English courts, the court necessarily decides (tacitly if not expressly) that those bringing the action on behalf of the organization are entitled to represent it.[21] It might be sought to distinguish the *AMF* case on the basis that there the authority of the director-general was not in question, unlike the present case where the authority of the intervener to represent the AOI could only be resolved by actually deciding questions of international law on which there was disagreement between the member States. However, it is questionable whether a clear distinction can be maintained between the two types of cases. Suppose that in proceedings brought on behalf of an international organization the defendant raised an issue as to which organ of the organization was required to authorize the bringing of the proceedings. If the answer to the question was obvious from the terms of its constituent treaty, the court might treat this as a 'matter of fact'.[22] If the answer was not clear from the treaty, the court would be faced with the choice either of undertaking its own interpretation of the treaty (which Colman J thought a court cannot do), of dismissing the proceedings on the ground that the authority to bring them on behalf of the organization is non-justiciable and thus cannot be established (which would clearly be undesirable), or of finding some other solution.[23] The logical effect of this decision might even be to render illusory the ability of such international organizations to sue and be sued in England. In cases where the organization sues on a contract, the defendant could deny the organization's capacity under its constituent treaty to enter into the contract. Where the organization itself is sued, it could similarly deny its own capacity to enter into the contract.[24] In either case, if the issue of the organization's capacity under the treaty were considered non-justiciable, the action would presumably fail.[25]

In the present case, the practical effect of the decision that the intervener could not discharge the burden of proving its identity with the original AOI was a decision by default that its representatives were *not* to be treated under English law as the representatives of the AOI. It would surely have been preferable for the issue to have been decided by legal principle, rather than by the fortuitous circumstance of where, because of the nature of the particular proceedings, the burden of proof lay under domestic law. The question is whether any other solution would have been possible. Analogous problems of recognition have arisen in cases where two rival governments of a foreign State have claimed the right to control the assets of that State located in the United Kingdom. The courts have in the past dealt with such questions by requesting an executive

[21] e.g., in the *AMF* case the House of Lords thought it clear that no one could bring an action to recover the money of that organization anywhere in the world 'except the one duly authorised director-general' ([1991] 2 AC at 162E).

[22] Cf. [1995] QB at 294E; *J.H. Rayner (Mincing Lane) Ltd.* v. *Department of Trade and Industry*, [1990] 2 AC 418, 500H–501A.

[23] Similar issues might also arise, even in cases where the legal personality of an international organization under domestic law has been given legislative recognition.

[24] Cf. Berg, 'International Organizations and Non-Justiciability', *International Financial Law Review*, January 1996, p. 32, at p. 34.

[25] Cf. Mann, 'International Corporations and National Law', this *Year Book*, 42 (1967), p. 145, at pp. 167–9, for the view that domestic courts should determine such questions of capacity themselves, and should not defer to the opinion of the organization.

certificate stating which of the two is recognized by the British Government as the government of that State.[26] Since the 1980 decision of the British Government no longer to accord recognition to governments, it has been left to the courts to answer such questions by other means.[27] It may be that a similar approach could be devised in relation to international organizations.

State immunity—validity of service of writ of summons—immunity of a separate entity of a State—whether act 'in the exercise of sovereign authority'—State Immunity Act 1978, sections 3, 12(1), 14(2)

Case No. 2. Kuwait Airways Corporation v. *Iraqi Airways Co.*, [1995] 1 WLR 1147, [1995] 3 All ER 694, [1995] 2 Lloyd's Rep. 317, HL. The House of Lords in this case allowed in part an appeal against the decision of the Court of Appeal which was noted in the previous volume of this *Year Book*.[28] The proceedings involved an action by the Kuwait Airways Corporation ('KAC') against the Iraqi Airways Co. ('IAC') and the Republic of Iraq, for damages in respect of the loss of or damage to ten civilian airliners. Following the invasion of Kuwait by Iraq in August 1990, the aircraft belonging to KAC had been removed from Kuwait airport to Iraq by IAC pilots and engineers pursuant to a direction from the Iraqi Minister for Transport and Communications. Subsequently, a resolution of the Revolutionary Command Council of Iraq (RCC Resolution 369) was expressed to dissolve KAC and to transfer all of its assets to IAC. The aircraft were incorporated into the IAC fleet, although only limited use was made of them because of the almost complete cessation of international flights to and from Iraq. In March 1991, following Iraq's agreement to comply with United Nations Security Council Resolution 686, the Revolutionary Command Council passed a further resolution under which its earlier decisions relating to Kuwait were deemed rescinded. Proceedings were commenced in England by KAC against IAC and the Republic of Iraq, in which KAC obtained default judgments. However, the validity of the service of the writs and jurisdiction of the court were subsequently challenged. Evans J at first instance allowed the action to proceed against IAC, but held that there had not been effective service on the Republic of Iraq. The Court of Appeal held that IAC enjoyed immunity from jurisdiction under section 14(2) of the State Immunity Act 1978 and had not submitted to the jurisdiction. KAC appealed against this decision.

The first issue considered by the House of Lords was whether service on IAC and the Republic of Iraq had been effective. Lord Goff (with whom Lord Jauncey and Lord Nicholls agreed, and with whom Lord Mustill and Lord Slynn agreed on this point) found that the writ had been validly served on the former, but not on the latter. In the case of IAC, the writ had been served at the London office of IAC on the employee in charge. Evans J at first instance had found that IAC fell within the definition of an 'oversea company' in section 744 of the Companies Act 1985, and that the writ had been validly served by virtue

[26] e.g., *The Arantzazu Mendi*, [1939] AC 256.

[27] See, e.g., *Republic of Somalia* v. *Woodhouse Drake & Carey (Suisse) SA*, [1993] QB 54, this *Year Book*, 63 (1992), pp. 501–5.

[28] *Kuwait Airways Corporation* v. *Iraqi Airways Company and Republic of Iraq*, [1995] 1 Lloyd's Rep. 25, this *Year Book*, 65 (1994), pp. 496–500.

of section 695(2) of that Act.[29] Lord Goff considered that even if IAC was not an 'oversea company' (a question which was not decided), service was effective under RSC, Order 65, rule 3(1).[30] As to the Republic of Iraq, it appeared that the documents for service were sent by the Senior Master to the Secretary of State for service in accordance with section 12(1) of the State Immunity Act 1978.[31] At that time there was no British diplomatic presence in Baghdad, nor was any other country representing British interests in Iraq. However, the Embassy of Iraq in London was still functioning. The Foreign and Commonwealth Office sent the documents to the Embassy, with a letter requesting that they be forwarded to the Ministry of Foreign Affairs in Baghdad, but on the evidence this was not done. The House of Lords agreed that service on the Embassy in London was not service on the Ministry of Foreign Affairs of Iraq for the purposes of section 12(1), but at best a request to the Embassy to forward the documents to the Ministry of Foreign Affairs. Service on the Republic of Iraq had thus not been effected.[32] Although the question of the effectiveness of service on the Republic of Iraq was straightforward, it does provide an example of the difficulties which may be encountered in practice in complying with the service requirements of section 12(1).[33]

The second issue was that of State immunity. In view of the finding that there had been no valid service on the Republic of Iraq, only the question of the immunity of IAC needed to be decided. As it was not doubted that IAC was a 'separate entity' of the Republic of Iraq for the purposes of the Act, that depended on the application of section 14(2) of the Act, which provides that:

> A separate entity is immune from the jurisdiction of the courts of the United Kingdom if, and only if—
> (*a*) the proceedings relate to anything done by it in the exercise of sovereign authority; and
> (*b*) the circumstances are such that a State . . . would have been so immune.

Lord Goff, with whom Lord Jauncey and Lord Nicholls agreed, treated the principal question as being whether the acts of IAC complained of by KAC were performed 'in the exercise of sovereign authority' within the meaning of section

[29] In relevant circumstances, this provision allows for service by leaving a document at 'any place of business established by the company in Great Britain'.

[30] This rule states that where provision is not otherwise made for personal service of a document on a body corporate, this may be effected by serving it on 'the mayor, chairman, or president of the body, or the town clerk, clerk, secretary, treasurer or other similar officer thereof'. It was found, as a question of fact, that the person on whom the writ was served (a clerk who was left in charge of the London office when the manager was transferred to Baghdad) fell within the definition of 'other similar officer'. See [1995] 1 WLR at 1152G–1155A.

[31] Section 12(1) provides that 'Any writ or other document required to be served for instituting proceedings against a State shall be served by being transmitted through the Foreign and Commonwealth Office to the Ministry of Foreign Affairs of the State and service shall be deemed to have been effected when the writ or document is received at the Ministry'.

[32] See [1995] 1 WLR at 1155A–1156D. Reference was made to Lewis, *State and Diplomatic Immunity* (3rd edn., 1990), pp. 78–9. Section 12(1) of the Act may be contrasted with section 24 of the Foreign States Immunities Act 1985 (Australia), which similarly makes provision for service through the diplomatic channel, but was designed to be flexible enough to allow service upon the foreign State's mission in Australia or even upon a mission of a third State looking after the interests of the defendant State in Australia, as well as on the foreign ministry in the State concerned. See Australian Law Reform Commission, Report No. 24, *Foreign State Immunity* (1984), pp. 91, 137.

[33] For another example, see *Westminster City Council* v. *Government of the Islamic Republic of Iran*, [1986] 1 WLR 979, this *Year Book*, 57 (1986), pp. 423–6.

14(2)(*a*). He considered that these words were to be construed in accordance with the accepted meaning of *acta iure imperii*,[34] and said that in accordance with the decision in *I Congreso del Partido*,[35] 'the ultimate test of what constitutes an act jure imperii is whether the act in question is of its own character a governmental act, as opposed to an act which any private citizen can perform'.[36] He thought that in the case of a separate entity of a State, it was not enough that the entity acted on the directions of the State, or that the purpose or motive of the act was to serve the purposes of the State. However, he added that even where it is not entitled to immunity, where a separate entity acts at the direction of the State, it may be able to plead a substantive defence such as *force majeure*.[37]

In this case, Lord Goff found that the essential acts of IAC which were the subject of the claim were, first, the removal of the aircraft from Kuwait airport to Iraq, and secondly, the treatment of the aircraft by IAC as part of its fleet after the coming into force of RCC Resolution 369. Like Evans J and the Court of Appeal, he had no doubt that the removal of the aircraft from Kuwait constituted an exercise of the governmental power by the State of Iraq. He did not think that IAC acted as a mere carrier, performing the mundane task of preparing and flying the aircraft, but rather that IAC 'was closely involved with the State of Iraq in the last stage of an enterprise which entailed both the seizure of the aircraft and their removal to Iraq to be used for such purposes as the Government of Iraq should direct'.[38] He similarly thought that the acts of IAC in looking after the aircraft after their arrival in Iraq until the coming into effect of RCC Resolution 369 were sufficiently related to the act of seizure of the aircraft by Iraq to amount to *acta iure imperii*.[39] However, he thought that the position changed after RCC Resolution 369 came into effect. He said:

> Certainly, . . . the fact that Resolution 369 was itself a governmental act by the State of Iraq could not of itself render I.A.C.'s consequent retention and use of the aircraft a governmental act. Plainly, a separate entity of a state which receives nationalised property from the state cannot ipso facto claim sovereign immunity in respect of a claim by the former owner, though it may well be able to plead, by way of defence, that its actions were not unlawful. Nor can it be said . . . that the acts done by I.A.C. after 17 September 1990 were mere outward manifestations of a denial of title which occurred at the time of seizure of the aircraft. . . . Then, does it make any difference that, in the present case, the state entity was at an earlier stage involved in the seizure of the property from the former owner in the exercise of sovereign authority? I for my part cannot see that the

[34] [1995] 1 WLR at 1159–1160A. He referred to the statement of Lord Diplock in *Alcom Ltd.* v. *Republic of Colombia*, [1984] AC 580, 600, that section 14(2) of the Act comes close to adopting 'the straightforward dichotomy between acta jure imperii and acta jure gestionis'.

[35] [1983] 1 AC 244.

[36] [1995] 1 WLR at 1160A. Lord Goff referred to *Arango* v. *Guzman Travel Advisors Corporation*, 621 F 2d 1371 (1980), as an example of a case involving a governmental act by a separate entity of a State. In that case, a State-owned airline was held to be immune from a suit relating to the 'involuntary rerouting' of a passenger after immigration officials of that State had refused the passenger permission to enter the country. There the court found that the airline had been 'impressed into service . . . by Dominican immigration officials' and had 'acted merely as an arm or agent of the Dominican government'.

[37] [1995] 1 WLR at 1160A–F, referring to *C. Czarnikow Ltd.* v. *Centrala Handlu Zagranicznego Rolimpex*, [1979] AC 351.

[38] [1995] 1 WLR at 1163A–B.

[39] Ibid., at 1164A–B.

characterisation as an act jure imperii of the earlier involvement by the entity in the act of seizure can, on the facts of the present case, be determinative of the characterisation of the subsequent retention and use of the property by the state entity following the formal vesting of the property in the entity by a legislative act of the state'.[40]

It followed that IAC could not claim immunity in respect of its conduct after RCC Resolution 369 was adopted.

On this last point, Lord Mustill and Lord Slynn disagreed with Lord Goff. Lord Mustill said that the real substance of the complaint was the allegation that IAC had wrongfully remained in possession of the aircraft, thus causing KAC to lose their entire value. He considered that the Republic of Iraq would have enjoyed immunity in respect of such a claim as it did not fall within the 'commercial activity' exception under section 3 of the Act, so that section 14(2)(*b*) was satisfied.[41] He acknowledged that section 14(2)(*a*) imposed an additional requirement for immunity, and was not simply an 'echo' of section 3, so that section 14 assumed that a State may be immune in circumstances where a separate entity is not. In his view, to be an act 'in the exercise of sovereign authority' for the purposes of section 14(2)(*a*), it was necessary that the act, 'although not done by the sovereign, is a manifestation of the sovereign's authority'. He said that it was 'not enough to show that a sovereign act was an essential preliminary to the conduct by the entity of which the plaintiff complains, for the sovereign quality of the train of events may have died away by the time that the entity comes to play its part'. However, in the present case, he could not 'detect any change in the character of the successive events', and he thought that at all relevant times IAC was 'not acting autonomously, but in harness with the Republic of Iraq, and under the shadow of the sovereign authority by which the latter itself was acting, so that its acts were a manifestation of that authority'.[42]

Lord Slynn was of a similar view. He considered that the Republic of Iraq had acted throughout in exercise of its sovereign authority, and did not consider that IAC at any time played an independent role.[43] He said that the intention all along was that the aircraft should be used for civil aviation purposes in Iraq, and that fine distinctions could not be made as to the moment at which IAC was acting independently of Iraq, since the nature of IAC's acts remained the same throughout. He did not consider that this was a case where the separate entity had broken the 'chain of causation' by going right outside the exercise of sovereign authority and acting autonomously. He also thought it clear that if RCC Resolution 369 had vested title to the aircraft in the Republic of Iraq rather

[40] Ibid., at 1163C–F.
[41] Ibid., at 1170F–1171F.
[42] Ibid., at 1171G–1172E.
[43] He said that Iraq was 'not being sued for carelessly flying an aircraft or running a commercial airline in such a way as to cause damage to people or property', and that in this case there was 'not in any sense the kind of commercial transaction contemplated by the restricted immunity doctrine' (ibid., at 1175F).

than IAC, the Republic of Iraq would have enjoyed immunity in respect of the same acts.

However, even though IAC was found by the majority not to have immunity in so far as the claim related to the period after RCC Resolution 369 was adopted, a third question was whether the issues arising in the claim against IAC were non-justiciable in the English courts. It was argued for IAC that determination of these issues would be inconsistent with the principle in the *Buttes* case,[44] in that it would involve adjudication on transactions of Iraq in the conduct of its foreign affairs, and on the legislative acts of Iraq with respect to property in its own territory.[45] Lord Goff disagreed with Evans J at first instance, who had said that the principle of non-justiciability did not preclude jurisdiction in cases where immunity from jurisdiction was denied under the State Immunity Act. However, although Lord Goff considered that the defence of non-justiciability was potentially applicable, he thought that it was not possible to determine this at the present stage of the proceedings. There was no agreement between the parties whether RCC Resolution 369 had been rescinded *ab initio* or simply repealed in 1991, nor was it clear what other actions of the Iraqi Government IAC might invoke as part of its case. In the circumstances, the House of Lords considered that the proper course was to remit the proceedings to the Commercial Court to deal with those parts of the claim against IAC in respect of which IAC did not enjoy immunity.[46] That court could then decide, in the light of the pleadings and submissions of the parties, how to deal with the justiciability issue. The ultimate disposition of the claim in this case therefore remains to be decided.[47]

The disagreement between the majority and minority in this case on the question of State immunity was not so much on the test to be applied, but on the application of the test to the facts of the case. This illustrates yet again the

[44] Loc. cit. above (n. 17).

[45] [1995] 1 WLR at 1164E–1168B. Reference was made also to *Duke of Brunswick* v. *King of Hanover*, (1848) 2 HL Cas. 1, 21–2, and *Underhill* v. *Hernandez*, 168 US 250, 252 (1897).

[46] Although the issue of non-justiciability was not decided by the House of Lords, some indication of the differing views of the parties was given. It appeared to be the argument of counsel for KAC that RCC Resolution 369 could be refused recognition in England on grounds of public policy, and that the court could look at binding United Nations resolutions for the purpose of ascertaining public policy. This was challenged by counsel for IAC. See [1995] 1 WLR at 1165H–1166H (Lord Goff), referring also to *Anglo-Iranian Oil Co. Ltd.* v. *Jaffrate (The Rose Mary)*, [1953] 1 WLR 246; *In re Claim by Helbert Wagg & Co. Ltd.*, [1956] Ch. 323, 346–9; *Oppenheimer* v. *Cattermole*, [1976] AC 249, 277–8; *Banco Nacional de Cuba* v. *Sabbatino*, 376 US 398 (1964). Without entering into these issues, Lord Goff did observe (at 1166A–B) that the principle of non-justiciability could not only be pleaded as a defence, but raised a question of jurisdiction 'in the sense that the English court will decline to adjudicate as a matter of judicial restraint or abstention'. He also observed (at 1167C–G) that unlike State immunity, the principle of non-justiciability is not one which a defendant is precluded from invoking by virtue of having submitted to the jurisdiction.

[47] A further argument, which had been advanced in the Court of Appeal, was that IAC had submitted to the jurisdiction, for the purposes of section 2 of the State Immunity Act: see this *Year Book*, 65 (1994), at pp. 499–500. As argument was not addressed on this point before the House of Lords, it was not prepared to depart from the decision of the Court of Appeal on this point: see [1995] 1 WLR at 1164C–D.

inherent difficulty in applying general concepts of 'sovereign' and 'non-sovereign' acts to determine questions of immunity.[48]

Refugees—exclusion from the definition of 'refugee'—'serious non-political crime'—exception to the principle of non-refoulement*—'danger to the security' of the country of refuge—Geneva Convention relating to the Status of Refugees 1951, Articles 1F(b), 33(2)*

Case No. 3. R. v. *Secretary of State for the Home Department, ex parte Chahal*, [1995] 1 WLR 526, [1995] 1 All ER 658, CA. *Case No. 4. T* v. *Secretary of State for the Home Department*, [1995] 1 WLR 545, [1995] 2 All ER 1042, CA. These two cases concerned the application in the United Kingdom of provisions of the 1951 Geneva Refugees Convention[49] relating to the exclusion of certain persons from the protection of that Convention.

In *Chahal*, the applicant was an Indian national who had been in the United Kingdom since 1971, and who had indefinite leave to remain. In 1990, pursuant to section 3(5)(*b*) of the Immigration Act 1971, the Secretary of State made a deportation order against him on the ground that his continued presence in the United Kingdom would not be conducive to the public good 'for reasons of national security and other reasons of a political nature, namely the international fight against terrorism'. The applicant then claimed asylum on the ground that if he returned to India he was likely to be killed because of his strong religious and political beliefs. The claim for asylum was refused by the Secretary of State, and the applicant sought judicial review of this decision, as well as of the deportation order.[50] One issue was whether the applicant came within the scope of Article 33(2) of the Convention.[51] Article 33(1) contains the general prohibition of expulsion or return ('*refoulement*') by a contracting State of refugees within its territory. However, Article 33(2) provides:

> The benefit of the present provision may not, however, be claimed by a refugee whom there are reasonable grounds for regarding as a danger to the security of the country in which he is, or who, having been convicted by a final judgment of a particularly serious crime, constitutes a danger to the community of that country.

[48] In another recent case, the Employment Appeal Tribunal considered whether it should exercise its power to grant a foreign State an extension of time to appeal against a decision that it did not have immunity in an unfair dismissal claim: *United Arab Emirates* v. *Abdelghafar*, [1995] ICR 65. The employer State had not appeared at the hearing on the question of immunity. Mummery J noted the obligation under section 1(2) of the State Immunity Act to give effect to the immunities under the Act even if the defendant State does not appear in the proceedings to claim them. He said that 'If the tribunal in the original proceedings has not given effect to the immunity conferred by the Act, then it must be the duty of the appeal tribunal to give effect to it by correcting the error'. As the employer State had shown that there was a reasonably arguable case that the law of State immunity had not been applied correctly, an extension of time to appeal was granted.

[49] Convention relating to the Status of Refugees (Cmd. 9171), as modified by the 1967 New York Protocol (Cmnd. 3906).

[50] The procedural history of the case is described by Staughton LJ, [1995] 1 WLR at 529–30.

[51] This issue arose for determination as a matter of domestic administrative law by virtue of paragraph 161 of the Statement of Changes in Immigration Rules, which provides that 'Where a person is a refugee full account is to be taken of the provisions of the Convention and Protocol relating to the Status of Refugees. Nothing in these rules is to be construed as requiring action contrary to the United Kingdom's obligations under these instruments.'

For Staughton LJ, the major issue was whether Article 33(2) requires the threat to life or freedom referred to in Article 33(2) to be balanced against the danger to the security of the contracting State referred to in Article 33(2). He decided that it did. He referred to writers indicating that under Article 33(2), there may be cases where the danger to a refugee outweighs the menace to public security,[52] or that in the application of Article 33(2), the principle of proportionality operates.[53] He said:

> Despite the literal meaning of article 33, it would seem to me quite wrong that some trivial danger to national security should allow expulsion or return in a case where there was a present threat to the life of the refugee if that took place.[54]
>
> . . .
>
> In an extradition case this country would be reluctant to send back someone who was likely to face death on arrival, without charge or trial. Consideration should in my view be given to such circumstances even in a case of deportation, and weighed against any risk to national security if the person remains here.[55]

Staughton LJ appeared to consider that even without relying on the Convention, he would have been led to the same conclusion by paragraphs 162 and 167 of the Statement of Changes in Immigration Rules.[56] He left open the further possibility that a decision to deport a refugee without undertaking such a balancing exercise might be amenable to judicial review on grounds of unreasonableness.[57]

Nolan LJ expressed his full agreement with the other members of the Court,[58] although in his separate reasons he added also that in balancing the risks to the United Kingdom against the risks to the individual, 'the scales might properly be weighted in favour of the former'.[59] He also emphasized that the balancing requirement arose under paragraphs 164 and 167 of the Statement of Changes in Immigration Rules, and said that this requirement was not 'displaced' by the provisions of the Refugees Convention and Protocol,[60] apparently thereby assuming that Article 33(2) itself imposes no such requirement. Neill LJ seemed to be of the same view. He said that the balancing requirement was imposed by paragraphs 162 and 167 of the Statement of Changes in Immigration Rules, 'notwithstanding article 33(2) of the Convention'.[61]

However, all members of the court also concluded that in the circumstances of this case, the Secretary of State had carried out this balancing exercise, or at

[52] [1995] 1 WLR at 533B, referring to Robinson, *Commentary on the Convention Relating to the Status of Refugees* (1953), p. 164 (who in turn refers to the *travaux préparatoires*).

[53] [1995] 1 WLR at 533B–C, referring to Goodwin-Gill, *The Refugee in International Law* (1983), p. 96; *Plender's International Migration Law* (2nd edn., 1988), p. 427.

[54] [1995] 1 WLR at 533C–D. He thus disagreed with a contrary view which was expressed by Neill LJ in *NSH* v. *Secretary of State for the Home Department*, [1988] Imm. AR 389, 399. See also [1995] 1 WLR at 544 (Neill LJ).

[55] [1995] 1 WLR at 534E–F.

[56] Ibid., at 533D–E. The effect of these paragraphs is to require 'compassionate circumstances' to be included in the matters to be taken into account in deportation decisions.

[57] [1995] 1 WLR at 534B–E, referring to *R* v. *Secretary of State for the Home Department, ex parte Brind*, [1991] 1 AC 696, 748–9.

[58] [1995] 1 WLR at 537C.

[59] Ibid., at 538H–539A.

[60] Ibid., at 539A–B.

[61] Ibid., at 544E–545B.

least, that it had not been shown that he had failed to do so. The appeal was thus dismissed.[62]

In *T* v. *Home Secretary*, the appellant was an Algerian national who applied for asylum in the United Kingdom after being detected as an illegal entrant. The request for asylum was rejected by the Secretary of State, and subsequent appeals were rejected by a special adjudicator and the Immigration Appeals Tribunal. This further appeal was then taken to the Court of Appeal. The special adjudicator accepted that the appellant, a member of the Islamic Salvation Front (FIS), had a well-founded fear of being persecuted if returned to Algeria, and therefore prima facie fell within the Convention definition of a refugee under Article 1A. However, the special adjudicator and the Immigration Appeals Tribunal were of the view that he was excluded from the definition under Article 1F(*b*), as there were serious reasons for considering that he was involved in an FIS bomb attack on an airport in Algeria, in which ten people were killed, and in a raid on an army barracks.[63] The relevant part of Article 1F provides:

> The provisions of this Convention shall not apply to any person with respect to whom there are serious reasons for considering that: . . . (*b*) he has committed a serious non-political crime outside the country of refuge prior to his admission to that country as a refugee . . .

The Court of Appeal was of the view that the application of Article 1F did not require a 'balancing' test of the kind referred to in *Chahal*. The Court said that it could:

> find nothing in the Convention which supports the view that, in deciding whether a non-political crime is 'serious' and therefore within article 1F, the Secretary of State or the appeal tribunal is obliged to weigh the threat of persecution if asylum be refused against the gravity of the crime.[64]

Despite the literal wording of Article 1F(*b*), this seems a surprising conclusion, given that it is directly contradicted by the *UNHCR Handbook*[65] in a paragraph quoted by the court,[66] as well as by commentators on the Convention.[67]

The court did not doubt that the supposed crimes in this case were 'serious'. The question was whether they could be characterized as 'non-political' for the

[62] Ibid., at 534–537 (Staughton LJ), 539C–540A (Nolan LJ), 544H–545B (Neill LJ).

[63] The question of the application of the Convention arose for determination in domestic law because of section 8(1) of the Asylum and Immigration Appeals Act 1993, which provides that 'A person who is refused leave to enter the United Kingdom under the . . . [Immigration Act 1971] may appeal against the refusal to a special adjudicator on the ground that his removal in consequence of the refusal would be contrary to the United Kingdom's obligations under the [1951 Refugees] Convention'.

[64] [1995] 1 WLR at 555A–B.

[65] Office of the United Nations High Commissioner for Refugees, *Handbook on Procedures and Criteria for Determining Refugee Status* (re-edited 1992), at para. 156 (' . . . it is also necessary to strike a balance between the nature of the offence presumed to have been committed by the applicant and the degree of persecution feared. If a person has a well-founded fear of very severe persecution, e.g. persecution endangering his life or freedom, a crime must be very grave in order to exclude him').

[66] [1995] 1 WLR at 554G.

[67] Hathaway, *The Law of Refugee Status* (1991), pp. 224–5; Goodwin-Gill, *The Refugee in International Law* (1983), pp. 61–2; and cf. Grahl-Madsen, *The Status of Refugees in International Law* (1966), pp. 297–8.

purposes of Article 1F.[68] In answering that question, the court relied primarily on English cases dealing with the definition of 'political offences' in the context of extradition,[69] in particular on the speech of Lord Diplock in *R* v. *Governor of Pentonville Prison, ex parte Cheng*.[70] The Court also referred to paragraph 152 of the *UNHCR Handbook*,[71] which states that:

> In determining whether an offence is 'non-political' or is, on the contrary, a 'political' crime, regard should be given in the first place to its nature and purpose i.e. whether it has been committed out of genuine political motives and not merely for personal reasons or gain. There should be a close and direct causal link between the crime committed and its alleged political purpose and object. The political element of the offence should also outweigh its common-law character. This would not be the case if the acts committed are grossly out of proportion to the alleged objective. The political nature of the offence is also more difficult to accept if it involves acts of an atrocious character.

The Court of Appeal considered that the first two sentences of that paragraph clearly accorded with the earlier English authorities referred to, as did the remainder of the paragraph, if less obviously so. The court said that the 'common thread' running through the whole of paragraph 152 of the *UNHCR Handbook* was that:

> before any crime can be said to have a genuinely political purpose it must in some coherent sense be calculated to promote that purpose. That will simply not be so if the crime is wholly disproportionate to the purpose to be served. The more atrocious it is, the more gratuitous violence it involves, the more likely it is to be disproportionate. The more disproportionate it is, the more difficult will it be to establish the close and direct causal link that must exist between the crime and its suggested political object.[72]

Applying that test to the present case, the court said:

> After anxious consideration and not without some initial hesitation, we would answer this question in the same way as the tribunal did, namely, by holding that . . . [the supposed crimes] are indeed non-political. We, too, think in inappropriate 'to characterise indiscriminate bombings which lead to the deaths of innocent people as political crimes.' Our reason is not that all terrorists acts fall outside the protection of the Convention. It is that it cannot properly be said that these particular offences qualify as political. In our judgment the airport bombing in particular was an atrocious act, grossly out of proportion to any genuine political objective. There was simply no sufficiently close or direct causal link between it and T.'s alleged political purpose. It offends commonsense to suppose that F.I.S.'s cause of supplanting the government could be directly advanced by such an offence.[73]

[68] A further question which was argued but not decided by the court was whether it is the applicant for refugee status or the Secretary of State who has the burden of proving that Article 1F is applicable: see [1995] 1 WLR at 552F–553A.

[69] *In re Castioni*, [1891] 1 QB 149; *R* v. *Governor of Brixton Prison, ex parte Schtraks*, [1964] AC 556; *R* v. *Governor of Pentonville Prison, ex parte Cheng*, [1973] AC 931; *R* v. *Governor of Winson Green Prison, ex parte Littlejohn*, [1975] 1 WLR 893. Reference was made also to Stephen, *History of the Criminal Law of England* (1883), vol. 2, pp. 70–1.

[70] Loc. cit. above (n. 69).

[71] Loc. cit. above (n. 65).

[72] [1995] 1 WLR at 558H–559A.

[73] Ibid., at 559G–560A.

This approach of equating the concept of a political crime under Article 1F(*b*) with the concept of a political offence for the purposes of extradition is one which has been supported by commentators as being the intention of the Convention.[74] However, the court's conclusion that paragraph 152 of the *UNHCR Handbook* was 'consistent with' the English extradition cases on political offences is curious. These extradition cases are not entirely coherent,[75] and the test applied in this case is in fact more in line with what has been described as the 'Swiss approach' than with the United Kingdom approach.[76] This case may thus also signal a development in the political offence exception in British extradition law.[77,78]

[74] Hathaway, op. cit. above (n. 67), pp. 221–6; Grahl-Madsen, op. cit. above (n. 67), pp. 298–9. See also Goodwin-Gill, op. cit. above (n. 67), pp. 35–8, 60.

[75] See, e.g., Gilmore, 'Extradition and the Political Offence Exception: Reflections on United Kingdom Law and Practice', *Commonwealth Law Bulletin*, 18 (1992), p. 701, at pp. 704–9.

[76] See Gilbert, *Aspects of Extradition Law* (1991), pp. 120–4, 128–9, 130–1; Van den Wijngaert, *The Political Offence Exception to Extradition* (1980), pp. 111–16, 126–32.

[77] However, in the area of extradition, any such approach would be subject to the effect of treaties such as the 1977 European Convention on the Suppression of Terrorism (*UK Treaty Series*, No. 93 (1978), Cmnd. 7390) and the 1972 Supplementary Treaty concerning the Extradition Treaty between the United States and the United Kingdom (Cmnd. 9565 and 9915), in cases where they are applicable.

[78] A number of other recent cases have dealt with the interpretation and application of particular treaty provisions. On Article 7 of the International Convention for the Unification of Certain Rules relating to the Arrest of Sea-going Ships 1952 (*UN Treaty Series*, vol. 439, p. 193; *UK Treaty Series*, No. 47 (1960)), see *The Anna H*, [1995] 1 Lloyd's Rep. 11, CA. On Articles 13 and 14 of the International Convention on Salvage 1989, see *Semco Salvage and Marine Pte. Ltd.* v. *Lancer Navigation Co. Ltd. (The Nagasaki Spirit)*, [1995] 2 Lloyd's Rep. 44, QB (Com. Ct.). On the Hague-Visby Rules, see *Mediterranean Freight Services Ltd.* v. *BP Oil International Ltd.*, [1994] 2 Lloyd's Rep. 506, CA. On the Convention on the Contract for the International Carriage of Goods by Road 1956 (*UN Treaty Series*, vol. 399, p. 189; *UK Treaty Series*, No. 90 (1967)), see *Shell Chemicals UK Ltd.* v. *P & O Roadtanks Ltd.*, [1995] 1 Lloyd's Rep. 297, CA. On the Warsaw Convention for the Unification of Certain Rules Relating to International Carriage by Air 1929 (*League of Nations Treaty Series*, vol. 137, p. 11; *UK Treaty Series*, No. 11 (1933)), as amended by the 1955 Hague Protocol (*UN Treaty Series*, vol. 478, p. 371), see *Antwerp United Diamond BVBA* v. *Air Europe*, [1995] 3 WLR 396, CA. On the Brussels Convention on Jurisdiction and the Enforcement of Judgments in Civil and Commercial Matters 1968 (Cmnd. 3795), see *IP Metal Ltd.* v. *Ruote OZ SpA (No. 2)*, [1994] 2 Lloyd's Rep. 560, CA; *The Anna H*, [1995] 1 Lloyd's Rep. 11, CA; *Ocarina Marine Ltd.* v. *Marcard Stein & Co.*, [1994] 2 Lloyd's Rep. 524, QB (Com. Ct.); *Grupo Torras SA* v. *Sheikh Fahad Mohammed Al-Sabah*, [1995] 1 Lloyd's Rep. 374, QB (Com. Ct.); *Qingdao Ocean Shipping Co.* v. *Grace Shipping Establishment Schiffahrtskontor GmbH (The Xing Su Hai)*, [1995] 2 Lloyd's Rep. 15, QB (Com. Ct.); *Atlas Shipping Agency (UK) Ltd.* v. *Suisse Atlantique Société d'Armement Maritime SA*, [1995] 2 Lloyd's Rep. 188, QB (Com. Ct.). On that Convention and the Lugano Convention, see *Société Commerciale de Réassurance* v. *Eras International Ltd. (No. 2)*, [1995] 2 All ER 278, QB (Com. Ct.). On the Hague Convention on the Civil Aspects of International Child Abduction 1980 (*UK Treaty Series*, No. 66 (1986), Cm 33), see *In re F (A Minor) (Abduction: Custody Rights Abroad)*, [1995] Fam. 224, CA (in which it was decided that the removal of a child from the State of habitual residence could be a 'wrongful removal' under the Convention even if not actually illegal under the law of that State); *In re N (Child Abduction: Jurisdiction)*, [1995] Fam. 96, Fam. D (in which it was held that a court may make orders in respect of a child expected to be brought to the United Kingdom before the child's arrival); *R* v. *R (Residence Order: Child Abduction)*, [1995] Fam. 209, Fam. D (meaning of 'notice of a wrongful removal or retention' in Article 16); *In re A (Minors) (Child Abduction: Habitual Residence)*, [1996] 1 WLR 25, Fam. D (in which it was decided that the 'habitual residence' of a child living on a United States naval base in Iceland was not the United States but Iceland, which was not a contracting State).

Extradition—admissibility of evidence in extradition proceedings—Extradition Act 1989, Schedule 1, paragraphs 6(1), 7(1)

Case No. 5. R v. *Governor of Belmarsh Prison, ex parte Francis*, [1995] 1 WLR 1121, [1995] 3 All ER 634, DC (McCowan LJ and McKinnon J). *Case No. 6. R* v. *Governor of Belmarsh Prison, ex parte Martin*, [1995] 1 WLR 412, [1995] 2 All ER 548, DC (McCowan LJ and Gage J). Under the Extradition Act 1989, it is unnecessary to establish a prima facie case against an accused person whose extradition is sought, if the relevant extradition treaty and Order in Council so provide.[79] In the absence of such provision in the treaty and Order in Council, it remains a requirement under the 1989 Act, as under the former Extradition Act 1870, that the magistrate be satisfied that there is evidence that would be sufficient to justify the accused person's trial if the extradition crime had been committed in England and Wales.[80] These two cases concerned questions of the admissibility of certain types of evidence in cases where a prima facie case must be established. The applicant in each case had been committed to custody, to await the Secretary of State's decision as to his return to the United States of America.[81] In each case it was argued in habeas corpus proceedings that reliance had been placed on inadmissible evidence.

In *Francis*, the evidence against the applicant consisted mainly of the testimony of eight alleged accomplices who had pleaded guilty in the United States pursuant to a 'plea agreement' with the United State authorities. It was argued for the applicant that it was a term of the plea agreement that those concerned would be given substantially reduced sentences of imprisonment in return for giving evidence against the applicant and others. The applicant argued that this evidence should have been excluded pursuant to section 78 of the Police and Criminal Evidence Act 1984. That section gives the courts a discretion to refuse to admit prosecution evidence in criminal proceedings 'if it appears to the court that, having regard to all the circumstances, including the circumstances in which the evidence was obtained, the admission of the evidence would have such an adverse effect on the fairness of the proceedings that the court ought not to admit it'. The magistrate had held that that provision did not apply to extradition proceedings. The Divisional Court, dismissing the application for habeas corpus, was of the same view.[82] McCowan LJ (with whom McKinnon J agreed) observed that a number of previous decisions had proceeded on the basis that section 78 did apply to extradition proceedings,[83]

[79] Extradition Act 1989, sections 4, 9(4) and (8).

[80] Extradition Act 1989, section 9(8)(*a*) and Schedule 1, paragraph 7(1). The wording of these provisions has since been amended by the Criminal Justice and Public Order Act 1994, section 158(5) and (8). (The Extradition Act 1870 was repealed and replaced by the Extradition Act 1989. However, the regime of the 1989 Act applies only to new treaties entered into and implemented by Orders in Council under the new Act. The substantive provisions of the 1870 Act are reproduced in Schedule 1 to the 1989 Act, and apply to those Orders in Council made under section 2 of the 1870 Act which remain in force: see sections 1(3) and 4 of the 1989 Act.)

[81] The extradition treaty between the United Kingdom and the United States is implemented by an Order in Council made under the former Extradition Act 1870. See n. 80, above.

[82] The Divisional Court was also of the view that the decision of the magistrate to admit the evidence was justifiable in any event, since the alleged accomplices had given the evidence *after* they had been sentenced: see [1995] 1 WLR at 1125H–1126F.

[83] e.g., *R* v. *Governor of Pentonville Prison, ex parte Chinoy*, [1992] 1 All ER 317, this *Year Book*, 63 (1992), pp. 516–18.

although the question had been left open in at least one case,[84] and there was no appellate authority on the point. The argument of the applicant relied on the general principle of private international law that questions of procedure (including questions as to the admissibility of evidence) are governed by the *lex fori*.[85] This general principle was said to be reflected in the Extradition Act. Paragraph 6(1) of Schedule 1 provided that the magistrate 'shall hear the case in the same manner . . . as near as may be' as if the person had been charged with an indictable offence committed in England or Wales. Paragraph 7(1) of Schedule 1 required the production of such evidence as would, 'according to the law of England and Wales, justify the committal for trial of the prisoner'.[86]

However, the court considered that there were clear distinctions between domestic committal proceedings and extradition proceedings. McCowan LJ observed that in extradition proceedings there is no opportunity to challenge evidence, there is no abuse of process jurisdiction,[87] and the Judges' Rules and Code that replaced them do not apply.[88] McCowan LJ quoted from the judgment of Ognall J in *R* v. *Governor of Pentonville Prison, ex parte Lee*,[89] who said:

> It is of course right to observe that the law of extradition proceeds upon the fundamental assumptions that the requesting state is acting in good faith and that the fugitive will receive a fair trial in the courts of the requesting state. If it were otherwise, one may assume that our government would not bind itself by treaty to such process. But that is not to say that it is the duty of our courts to inquire into the adequacy or otherwise of the procedural safeguards afforded to a defendant before those courts. Our courts have consistently resisted attempts to import the requirements of domestic criminal procedure into extradition proceedings.[90]

In that case, Ognall J had quoted from the judgment of McLachlin J in *Kindler* v. *Canada (Minister of Justice)*,[91] who said that the extradition process differs from the criminal trial process in the factors which render it fair, extradition procedure being 'founded on the concepts of reciprocity, comity and respect for differences in other jurisdictions'.

In *Martin*, the applicant argued that the magistrate should have excluded evidence of telephone conversations between the United States and Ireland that had been intercepted by United States agents in the United States. For the applicant, it was argued that as it could not be proved that the calls had not been routed through the United Kingdom, the evidence was inadmissible by virtue of section 9 of the Interception of Communications Act 1985, which provides that no evidence shall be adduced which 'tends to suggest' that an offence under the Act has been or is to be committed. Subject to specified exceptions, that Act makes it an offence, *inter alia*, to intercept a telephone call to or from the British

[84] *In re Davison*, Divisional Court, 1 July 1994, unreported.

[85] Dicey and Morris, op. cit. above (n. 8), vol. 1, pp. 169 and 175–6.

[86] See n. 80, above. The wording of these provisions has since been amended by the Criminal Justice and Public Order Act 1994, section 158(8).

[87] [1995] 1 WLR at 1125E, referring to *In re Schmidt*, [1995] 1 AC 339, this *Year Book*, 65 (1994), pp. 500–2.

[88] Ibid., referring to *R* v. *Governor of Ashford Remand Centre, ex parte Beese*, [1973] 1 WLR 1426.

[89] [1993] 1 WLR 1294.

[90] Ibid., at 1300.

[91] (1991) 84 DLR (4th) 438, 488.

Islands which is to be or has been transmitted by means of a public telecommunication system licensed under that Act.[92] A number of specific arguments were advanced concerning the construction of provisions of that Act. However, the court was of the view that the provisions of the Act simply had no application in this case. In accordance with general principles, it was held that this Act did not create an offence triable in the United Kingdom in respect of an act of a non-resident committed outside the United Kingdom.[93] The court also rejected an argument that the evidence was inadmissible by virtue of paragraph 7(1) of Schedule 1 to the Extradition Act 1989.[94] Because no offence had been committed against the Interception of Communications Act, section 9 of that Act did not prevent the evidence being adduced in any proceedings in the United Kingdom, whether extradition proceedings or otherwise.[95]

'Disguised extradition'—discretion of the court to stay prosecution on grounds of abuse of process—execution of Scottish warrant in England

Case No. 7. R v. *Commissioner of Police of the Metropolis, ex parte Bennett*, [1995] QB 313, [1995] 2 WLR 598, [1995] 3 All ER 248, DC (Rose LJ and Potts J). This case provides a postscript to the decision of the House of Lords in *R* v. *Horseferry Road Magistrates' Court, ex parte Bennett*.[96] The applicant in the present case, a New Zealand citizen, claimed that as a result of collusion between the English and South African police, he had been forcibly removed from South Africa to England without recourse to lawful extradition procedures. The House of Lords decided, as a preliminary issue, that a committing magistrate has the power to stay a prosecution as an abuse of process and order the release of the accused if he is satisfied that the accused has been forcibly brought within the jurisdiction in disregard of available extradition procedures by a process to which English authorities have been a knowing party. The case was then remitted to the Divisional Court, which decided that the accused had been brought to England in defiance of extradition procedures as a result of collusion between the English and South African authorities, and the indictment against him was quashed.[97]

However, a warrant for the applicant's arrest had also been issued in Scotland. Unlike the Divisional Court, the High Court of Justiciary in Scotland found that the Lord Advocate was entitled to reject the allegation of collusion between the South African and English authorities, and concluded that it would not be an abuse of process for the Scottish courts to enforce the warrant. The present proceedings were brought to challenge the decision of the English police to execute the Scottish warrant in England. The Divisional Court held, however, that it had no jurisdiction to restrain the execution of the Scottish warrant, because of Article XIX of the Union with Scotland Act 1706. That article provides that 'the courts of Chancery, Queen's Bench, Common Pleas, or any

[92] See [1995] 1 WLR at 415A–417A for the relevant provisions.

[93] [1995] 1 WLR at 418F–421A. Reference was made to *Macleod* v. *Attorney-General for New South Wales*, [1891] AC 455; *Cox* v. *Army Council*, [1963] AC 48; and *Air-India* v. *Wiggins*, [1980] 1 WLR 815.

[94] See text to n. 86, above.

[95] [1995] 1 WLR at 421B–422B.

[96] [1994] 1 AC 42, this *Year Book*, 64 (1993), pp. 447–52.

[97] *R* v. *Horseferry Road Magistrates' Court, ex parte Bennett (No. 2)*, [1995] 1 Cr.App.R 147.

other court in Westminster Hall . . . shall have no power to cognosce, review or alter the acts or sentences of the judicatures within Scotland, or stop the execution of the same'. The Divisional Court rejected an argument that the word 'execution' in this article was confined to execution in Scotland. It also rejected an argument that execution of the warrant would amount to an abuse of the process of the English courts, since no proceedings in the English courts were necessary to render the warrant enforceable in England. If any process was arguably abused, it could only be Scottish process, and this was not a matter for the English courts.

Unimplemented treaty—relevance in domestic law—judicial review—European Convention for the Protection of Human Rights and Fundamental Freedoms

Case No. 8. R v. *Secretary of State for the Home Department, ex parte McQuillan*, [1995] 4 All ER 400, QBD (Sedley J). *Case No. 9. R* v. *Ministry of Defence, ex parte Smith*, [1995] 4 All ER 427, DC (Simon Brown LJ and Curtis J). Although the European Convention for the Protection of Human Rights and Fundamental Freedoms ('the European Convention')[98] may be referred to by English courts for a variety of purposes,[99] it is clear from the decision of the House of Lords in *Brind*[100] that inconsistency with the Convention is not a ground of judicial review of administrative action. Nevertheless, the possibility was not excluded that the Convention may have some role to play in administrative law cases, a matter which was further considered in these cases.

In *McQuillan*, the applicant, who lived in Northern Ireland,[101] sought judicial review of an 'exclusion order', prohibiting him from entering Great Britain on the ground that the Home Secretary was satisfied he was or had been concerned in acts of terrorism.[102] The Home Department declined to give more detailed reasons for the making of the order, because it considered that this might lead to the discovery of sources of information which could compromise police operations and put the lives of informants at risk. The applicant denied having ever been involved in terrorist activities, and said that his life and the lives of his family were in danger if they continued to live in Northern Ireland. In these proceedings, reliance was placed on Articles 2 and 3 of the European Convention.[103]

[98] *United Nations Treaty Series*, vol. 213, p. 221; *UK Treaty Series*, No. 71 (1953), Cmd. 8969.

[99] See Cunningham, 'The European Convention on Human Rights, Customary International Law and the Constitution', *International and Comparative Law Quarterly*, 43 (1994), p. 537, esp. at pp. 553–67; and this *Year Book*, 64 (1993), pp. 455–63.

[100] *R* v. *Secretary of State for the Home Department, ex parte Brind*, [1991] 1 AC 696, this *Year Book*, 62 (1991), pp. 437–40.

[101] The applicant was a national of both the United Kingdom and the Republic of Ireland.

[102] The order was made under section 5 of the Prevention of Terrorism (Temporary Provisions) Act 1989. Sedley J described this power to make exclusion orders as a 'draconic measure adopted . . . in response to a grave emergency' which amounted to 'what has been known in other parts of the world as internal exile or banishment': [1995] 4 All ER at 422a.

[103] Article 2 provides that 'Everyone's right to life shall be protected by law'. Article 3 provides that 'No-one shall be subjected to torture or to inhuman or degrading treatment or punishment'. Reference was made to *Vilvarajah* v. *United Kingdom*, (1991) 14 EHRR 248, 292; *W* v. *United Kingdom* (Application 9348/81), (1983) 5 EHRR 504; and *Soering* v. *United Kingdom*, (1989) 11 EHRR 439.

On the relevance of the Convention, Sedley J noted that its principles now inform the law of the European Union and he considered that 'the principles and standards set out in the convention can certainly be said to be a matter of which the law of this country now takes notice in setting its own standards'.[104] He then said:

> Once it is accepted that the standards articulated in the convention are standards which both march with those of the common law and inform the jurisprudence of the European Union, it becomes unreal and potentially unjust to continue to develop English public law without reference to them. Accordingly, and without in any way departing from the ratio decidendi of *Brind*, the legal standards by which the decisions of public bodies are supervised can and should differentiate between those rights which are recognised as fundamental and those which, though known to the law, do not enjoy such a pre-eminent status. Once this point is reached, the standard of justification of infringements of rights and freedoms by executive decision must vary in proportion to the significance of the right which is at issue. . . . Whether this in itself is a doctrine of proportionality I do not now pause to ask; if it is, the House of Lords has long since contemplated its arrival with equanimity.[105]

He said that if in this case the evidence available to the Home Secretary when making the exclusion order had been before the court,

> it would be my task to balance both sides with great care in order to decide whether the Secretary of State's judgment lay within the band of rational decisions available in a case which potentially called the right to life in question; and to this end I consider that it would be right to measure rationality by, among other things, asking whether in the light of its impact the exclusion order could reasonably be considered an expedient response by a Home Secretary who has given proper weight to the fundamental right thereby put at risk.[106]

However, Sedley J added that special issues arose in the area of national security, and he considered himself bound by existing authorities to hold that in this case the interests of national security had been sufficiently invoked to preclude any further enquiry by the court into the legitimacy of the Home Secretary's conclusion.[107] The application for judicial review on this ground was therefore unsuccessful.[108]

Smith involved a challenge to the blanket policy of the Ministry of Defence not to permit homosexual men and women to serve in the armed forces. The four applicants, who had been administratively discharged under this policy,

[104] [1995] 4 All ER at 422e–f.

[105] [1995] 4 All ER at 422h–423a. He indicated that his reasoning reflected that in an extracurial article by Laws J, 'Is the High Court the Guardian of Fundamental Constitutional Rights?', *Public Law*, 1993, p. 59.

[106] [1995] 4 All ER at 423d–e.

[107] See [1995] 4 All ER at 411–15, 423–4. He indicated that had he not been bound by authority, he would have concluded that the court itself should decide in this case whether the interests of justice called for disclosure of the information by the Home Secretary, notwithstanding the possible effects on informants.

[108] This case also raised a question whether the exclusion order was consistent with European Community law, including Article 8*a*(1) of the EC Treaty ('Every citizen of the Union shall have the right to move and reside freely within the territory of the Member States, subject to the limitations and conditions laid down in this Treaty and by the measures adopted to give it effect'). Sedley J found that in this respect the case raised issues on which English courts had referred questions to the European Court of Justice in two other cases. He therefore stayed these proceedings, pending answers by the European Court on those questions.

challenged the legality of their discharge on the ground that the policy was irrational. Both Simon Brown LJ and Curtis J agreed that the challenge was justiciable (notwithstanding that it involved the defence interests of the State), and that the ordinary *Wednesbury* principles provided the standard of review.

Simon Brown LJ said that in cases where fundamental human rights are being restricted, the Minister will need to show that there is an important competing public interest which he or she could reasonably judge sufficient to justify the particular restriction. He thought that in cases involving fundamental rights the judicial review process might be more intensive, with the courts showing a greater readiness to intervene, and being less inclined to overlook minor flaws in the decision-making process or to exercise their discretion to withhold relief. However, he considered that even in such cases 'the threshold of unreasonableness' is not lowered, and it remained the responsibility of the Minister and not the court to exercise the primary judgment as to whether the competing public interest justifies the restriction. He considered that the court was only entitled to exercise a secondary judgment by asking whether a reasonable minister, on the material before him or her, could reasonably make that primary judgment. Furthermore, because the European Convention is not part of English law, in his view it was not necessary for a minister exercising a discretion to act in conformity with it, or even to have regard to its provisions.[109]

Simon Brown LJ was overtly critical of the challenged policy,[110] and suggested it would be difficult to defend under the European Convention.[111] However, he ultimately decided, 'albeit with hesitation and regret', that the Minister's stance could not be held to be unlawful. He said that although the justification for the ban 'may to many seem unconvincing', there was no present uniformity of outlook on this issue and there was still room for two views. For the court to intervene would be to exercise a primary judgment, rather than a merely secondary judgment.[112]

On the other hand, Curtis J concluded, without reference to the Convention, that the challenged decision, 'ha[d] been taken for rational reasons, the relative weight of which is not for this court'.[113] He then added that the decision in *Brind* made it clear that the applicants could not rely on the Convention, and this being so, he questioned why it should be alluded to at all. He said that in any event, the only relevant breach of the Convention would be Article 8(1), and in his view Article 8(2) would be applicable in this case.[114] He stated also that he did not

[109] [1995] 4 All ER at 443h–445g (quoting from the judgment of Neill LJ in *National and Local Government Officers Association* v. *Secretary of State for the Environment*, [1992] CA Transcript 1141), 448.

[110] See, e.g., [1994] 4 All ER at 440h ('The tide of history is against the ministry . . . It seems to me improbable, whatever this court may say, that the existing policy can survive for much longer').

[111] Ibid., at 448g–449c. He thought that the decision of the Commission in *B* v. *United Kingdom*, (1983) 34 D & R 68, was distinguishable, and observed that whatever the Commission may have decided in 1983, the Convention had to be interpreted 'in the light of present-day conditions': *Tyrer* v. *United Kingdom*, (1978) 2 EHRR 1, 10. He said that 'I for my part strongly suspect that so far as this country's international obligations are concerned, the days of this policy are numbered'.

[112] Ibid., at 448a–f.

[113] Ibid., at 452d.

[114] Ibid., at 452g–j. Article 8(1) of the Convention deals with the right to respect for private and family life. Article 8(2) permits derogations 'in accordance with the law' on a number of specified grounds, including 'national security'.

hold the opinion that the decision of the armed forces was 'necessarily wrong'.[115,116]

The three judgments in these two cases are not consistent, and the precise role of the Convention in administrative law cases remains unclear. While Sedley J envisaged that the Convention could be relied upon to define standards of reasonableness, Simon Brown LJ thought that the Convention could not be used to lower the 'threshold of unreasonableness', while Curtis J doubted the relevance of the Convention at all.[117] Furthermore, the result in both cases suggests that whichever approach is correct, in practice there will be limits on the direct influence of the Convention in judicial review proceedings.[118]

CHRISTOPHER STAKER

[115] Ibid., at 453b. Both Simon Brown LJ and Curtis J were unpersuaded by further arguments that the policy was inconsistent with Council Directive (EEC) 76/207 ('Council Directive on the implementation of the principle of equal treatment for men and women as regards access to employment, vocational training and promotion, and working conditions'), or Commission Recommendation (EEC) 92/131 on the Protection of the Dignity of Men and Women at Work. Simon Brown LJ said (at 450) that these instruments were concerned only with discrimination on grounds of gender, and not sexual orientation.

[116] The decision of the Divisional Court in this case was subsequently affirmed by the Court of Appeal: *R* v. *Ministry of Defence, ex parte Smith*, [1996] 2 WLR 305. Sir Thomas Bingham MR said (at 339H–340E) that the European Convention was relevant as 'background to the complaint of irrationality', but noted that its provisions were not enforceable by the courts, and that the failure of a decision-maker to take account of Convention obligations was not of itself grounds for judicial review. Henry LJ was of a similar view (at 345). All members of the Court declined to answer the question whether the policy was consistent with the Convention (at 340, 345, 346), although Thorpe LJ found the argument that there was a breach of Article 8 'very persuasive'.

[117] It is of interest to compare these cases with the recent decision of the High Court of Australia in *Minister for Immigration and Ethnic Affairs* v. *Teoh*, (1995) 183 CLR 273, in which an international treaty was accorded much greater significance in judicial review proceedings. The court in this case held by a majority that the ratification by Australia of the United Nations Convention on the Rights of the Child gave rise to a legitimate expectation that administrative decision-makers would act in conformity with the Convention. For a discussion, see Allars, *Sydney Law Review*, 17 (1995), p. 204; Walker and Mathew, *Melbourne University Law Review*, 20 (1995), p. 236.

[118] For another recent example of a case in which the European Convention was (unsuccessfully) relied upon in argument, see *R* v. *Radio Authority, ex parte Bull*, [1995] 3 WLR 572, DC. In that case, judicial review was sought of a decision of the Radio Authority that radio advertising by Amnesty International (British Section) was unacceptable under rule 8(*a*) of the Radio Authority Advertising Code and section 92(2)(*a*)(i) of the Broadcasting Act 1990, on the ground that the organization was 'a body whose objects are wholly or mainly of a political nature'. It was argued that, having regard to the freedom of expression under Article 10 of the European Convention, the term 'political' in section 92(2)(*a*)(i) of the Broadcasting Act should be construed narrowly. In dismissing the application, the court did not accept that the Radio Authority's interpretation was inconsistent with Article 10: see [1995] 3 WLR at 585C–F (Kennedy LJ), 591E–592B (McCullough J). See also *R* v. *Mid Glamorgan Family Health Services Authority, ex parte Martin*, [1995] 1 WLR 110, CA, especially at 118G–119A (Evans LJ); *In re D (Minors) (Adoption Reports: Confidentiality)*, [1995] 3 WLR 483, HL, at 495C–F (Lord Mustill).

DECISIONS ON THE EUROPEAN CONVENTION ON HUMAN RIGHTS DURING 1995*

Following the scheme which was adopted for the first time in the 1994 volume of the *Year Book*, this survey is divided into four parts. Part One contains full notes on the more important decisions in the period under review. Part Two contains summaries of other cases which were decided on the merits. Part Three lists those cases in which the only issue was that of just satisfaction under Article 50. And Part Four lists those which were removed from the list following a friendly settlement, or where there was no decision on the merits for some other reason. Within each part the decisions are in chronological order.

Part One: Selected Decisions

Freedom of expression (Article 10)—seizure and forfeiture of a film—the scope for protecting religious feelings under Article 10(2)—the margin of appreciation

Case No. 1. Otto-Preminger-Institut case.[1] In this case, which concerned the seizure and confiscation of a film in Austria, the Court held by 6 votes to 3 that there had been no violation of Article 10 of the Convention.

The applicant in this case was an association which ran a licensed cinema in Innsbruck where it intended to show a controversial film entitled *Das Liebeskonzil* (Council in Heaven) in May 1985. Three days before the intended screening the public prosecutor, on the prompting of the local diocese of the Roman Catholic Church, instituted criminal proceedings against the applicant's manager for the attempted offence of 'disparaging religious precepts' under the Austrian criminal code. Moreover, two days later the regional court ordered seizure of the film, so preventing it from being shown. In October 1985 the criminal proceedings were discontinued and proceedings for forfeiture of the film substituted. In October of the following year forfeiture was ordered on the ground that the provocative attitude taken in the film represented a gross interference with religious feelings which was not outweighed by its artistic merits. An attempt to challenge this decision in the Austrian courts was unsuccessful.

In its application to the Commission in October 1987 the association complained that the seizure of the film and subsequent forfeiture constituted interferences with its right to freedom of expression as guaranteed by Article 10. In its report in January 1993 the Commission expressed the opinion that this

 I wish to express my thanks to the Registrar of the Court for his co-operation in making material available to me for the preparation of these notes. Cases decided towards the end of 1995, which appeared too late for inclusion in the present survey, will be covered in the next issue of the *Year Book*.

[1] European Court of Human Rights (ECHR), judgment of 20 September 1994, Series A, No. 295A, decided by a Chamber.

provision had been violated on both counts. The Commission then referred the case to the Court.

After rejecting a preliminary objection from the Government,[2] the Court turned to the main issue, Article 10, which lays down that:

1. Everyone has the right to freedom of expression. This right shall include freedom to hold opinions and to receive and impart information and ideas without interference by public authority and regardless of frontiers. This Article shall not prevent States from requiring the licensing of broadcasting, television or cinema enterprises.
2. The exercise of these freedoms, since it carries with it duties and responsibilities, may be subject to such formalities, conditions, restrictions or penalties as are prescribed by law and are necessary in a democratic society, in the interests of national security, territorial integrity or public safety, for the prevention of disorder or crime, for the protection of health or morals, for the protection of the reputation or rights of others, for preventing the disclosure of information received in confidence, or for maintaining the authority and impartiality of the judiciary.

It was conceded that both the seizure and subsequent forfeiture amounted to interferences with the applicant's exercise of its right to freedom of expression, and the Court was satisfied that these interferences were 'prescribed by law'. Accordingly, the question was whether they had a legitimate aim and, if so, whether they could be considered 'necessary in a democratic society'.

On the first point the Court recalled that in the *Kokkinakis* case[3] it had emphasized the importance of freedom of thought, conscience and religion, which is guaranteed by Article 9 of the Convention, and had indicated that whilst religious believers must accept the right of others to oppose their views, the State is entitled to repress conduct incompatible with that provision. In the present case the purpose of the measures complained of was to protect the right of citizens not to be insulted in their religious feelings by the public expression of views by other persons. In these circumstances the Court was satisfied that the impugned measures pursued a legitimate aim under Article 10(2), namely 'the protection of the rights of others'.

The crucial question was therefore whether the seizure and forfeiture were 'necessary in a democratic society' for the achievement of the above aim. This type of issue is one the Court has often had to consider, and its case law on Article 10 is particularly extensive.[4] The Court recalled that while unpopular ideas must be tolerated, the exercise of freedom of expression also involves 'duties and responsibilities'. In deciding whether measures could be justified in cases involving religious beliefs and ideas, the Court indicated that the national authorities' margin of appreciation may also be significant since, as in the case of morals, it is not possible to identify a uniform European conception of the significance of religion in society.

Applying these general principles to the specific facts, the Court explained that although access to the applicant's cinema was subject to an admission fee and an age limit, the film had been widely advertised, which was enough to cause public offence, in reaching their decision the Austrian courts had paid due

[2] The objection concerned the six-month rule contained in Article 26.

[3] ECHR, judgment of 25 May 1993, Series A, No. 260A, and this *Year Book*, 64 (1993), p. 519.

[4] See, for example, the *Casado Coca* case, Series A, No. 285, and the *Jacubowski* case, Series A, No. 291, noted in this *Year Book*, 65 (1994), at pp. 527 and 532 respectively.

regard to freedom of expression, and the overwhelming majority of Tyroleans were Roman Catholics whom the State was entitled to protect from offence. The Court therefore concluded that the seizure could be justified. It reached the same conclusion as regards the forfeiture, where the Court considered that the same factors were relevant and the measure could not be regarded as disproportionate. The overall conclusion was thus that there had been no violation of Article 10.

In a joint dissenting opinion Judges Palm, Pekkanen and Makarczyk indicated that in their view Article 10 had been infringed. Although they accepted that religious feelings can legitimately be the object of protection, they pointed out that here, unlike the *Müller* case,[5] the applicant had not acted irresponsibly and so there was little likelihood of anyone being unwittingly exposed to material he or she might find objectionable. As they did not consider that any offence which might stem from the mere knowledge that the film was being shown could justify the measures taken, they regarded the seizure and forfeiture as a disproportionate response.

Other decisions involving Article 10 in the period under review were given in the *Jersild* case (Case No. 3); the *VDSO and Gubi* case (Case No. 11); the *Prager and Oberschlick* case (Case No. 17); the *Piermont* case (Case No. 18); the *Tolstoy Miloslavsky* case (Case No. 20); and the *Vereniging Weekblad 'Bluf!'* case (Case No. 35).

Right of access to the courts (Article 6(1))—application to the system of investigating and reporting under the Companies Act 1985—the margin of appreciation

Case No. 2. Fayed case.[6] In this case, which concerned the United Kingdom, the Court held unanimously that there had been no violation of Article 6(1) of the Convention. The Court also decided that it was not necessary to examine the case under Article 13.

This case arose out of the struggle between the applicants, the three Fayed brothers who are businessmen, and Lonrho plc for control of the House of Fraser group of department stores. In 1985 the applicants acquired control of the House of Fraser over the opposition of Lonrho, who owned the *Observer* newspaper. When the takeover was criticized in the *Observer*, the applicants began proceedings for libel, while Lonrho, for its part, began proceedings against the Fayed brothers in connection with the takeover.

In 1987 the Secretary of State for Trade and Industry appointed two Inspectors under the Companies Act 1985 to investigate the affairs of the applicants' company and the takeover of House of Fraser in particular. In their report in 1988 the Inspectors concluded that the applicants had behaved dishonestly at the material time and had subsequently attempted to mislead the Inspectors. After examining the report, the authorities concluded that there was insufficient evidence to warrant a criminal prosecution. However, in March 1990 the report was published and its contents were widely reported.

[5] ECHR, judgment of 24 May 1988, Series A, No. 133, and this *Year Book*, 59 (1988), p. 389.
[6] ECHR, judgment of 21 September 1994, Series A, No. 294B, decided by a Chamber.

Soon afterwards the applicants abandoned their libel action and paid the *Observer's* legal costs of £500,000. In 1993 the applicants and Lonrho negotiated a settlement which involved the discontinuance of the remaining legal proceedings. In English law an action by the applicants against the Inspectors for libel would have been met by the defence of privilege. It was open to the applicants to seek judicial review if, for example, there had been unfairness or a breach of the rules of natural justice by the Inspectors, but not on the simple ground that their findings were mistaken.

In their application to the Commission in August 1990 the Fayed brothers relied on Article 6(1) of the Convention, which guarantees access to the courts and the right to a fair hearing, and on Article 13, which guarantees a domestic remedy. In its report in April 1993 the Commission expressed the opinion that there had been no violation of Article 6(1) and also that no separate issue arose under Article 13. The Commission then referred the case to the Court.

The relevant part of Article 6(1) of the Convention provides:

> In the determination of his civil rights and obligations, . . . everyone is entitled to a fair and public hearing . . . by an independent and impartial tribunal established by law . . . .

The applicants' argument was that the making and subsequent publication of the Inspectors' report in its entirety seriously affected their reputations, thereby damaging their civil right to honour and reputation, and that the state of English law was such as to deny them effective access to the courts to challenge the interference with that right.

As far as the investigation was concerned, the Court was satisfied that the Inspectors performed an investigative, rather than an adjudicative, function. As a result, the inquiry had not determined their right to a good reputation and so did not need to follow the requirements of a judicial procedure established by Article 6. The key issue was thus the limited nature of the proceedings available to contest the Inspector's findings.

The 'right to a court' is, of course, well established in the Court's case law, but it is also established that access to the courts is not an absolute right, but may be subject to implied limitations, provided such limitations do not impair the essence of the right, and that they pursue a legitimate aim and are proportionate.[7] Turning to the particular facts,[8] the Court noted that the system of reporting and investigating under the Companies Act 1985 had an aim which was legitimate, namely furthering the public interest in the proper conduct of public companies, and this was also the purpose of giving the Inspectors the defence of privilege.

The Court acknowledged that the Inspectors enjoyed wide freedom of action, but pointed out that the remedy of judicial review supplied considerable safeguards and that while the investigation was in progress the applicants had been given proper opportunities to furnish evidence and respond to the allegations against them. As regards the issue of proportionality, the Court

[7] See, for example, the *Lithgow* case, Series A, No. 102, para. 194, and this *Year Book*, 57 (1986), p. 462.

[8] The Government denied that Article 6(1) was applicable here, but the Court, without deciding the point, proceeded on the basis that it was: see judgment, paras. 66–8. This aspect of the case was also discussed by Judge Martens in his concurring opinion.

observed that 'the limits of acceptable criticism are wider with regard to businessmen actively involved in the affairs of large public companies than with regard to private individuals',[9] and explained that the risk of some uncompensated damage to reputation was inevitable if investigators were to have the freedom required to carry out their functions. In view of these considerations, and the respondent's margin of appreciation, the Court concluded that the limitation of the applicants' access to the courts had not involved a violation of their rights under Article 6(1).

Before the Commission the applicants had taken a further point concerning Article 6 and had also relied on Article 13.[10] However, these issues had not been pursued and so the Court held that it was unnecessary to examine them.

Many cases involving Article 6(1) were decided in the period under review, but this is the only such case to show how on occasion the Court may be concerned with issues under this provision which it encounters more frequently when considering the scope of freedom of expression under Article 10. For other decisions involving the United Kingdom see the *Boner* and *Maxwell* cases (Cases Nos. 5 and 6); the *Murray* case (Case No. 7); the *Welch* case (Case No. 12); the *McMichael* case (Case No. 15); the *Air Canada* case (Case No. 19); and the *Tolstoy Miloslavsky* case (Case No. 20).

Freedom of expression (Article 10)—application to journalist disseminating racist statements—the meaning of 'necessary in a democratic society' in Article 10(2)—just satisfaction (Article 50)

Case No. 3. Jersild case.[11] The Court held by 12 votes to 7 that the applicant's conviction and sentencing to a fine for aiding and abetting the dissemination of racist remarks in Denmark constituted a violation of Article 10 of the Convention. As just satisfaction the Government was ordered to pay the applicant 1,000 Danish kroner as compensation for pecuniary damage and a further sum to cover his costs and expenses.

The applicant in this case was a television journalist who made a documentary programme about the racist attitudes of a group of young people in Copenhagen known as 'the Greenjackets'. To make the programme the applicant interviewed members of the group over a period of five or six hours, then edited the film of the interview down to a few minutes during which three of those interviewed were shown making crude and abusive remarks about immigrants and ethnic minorities. The programme was broadcast in July 1985 and shortly afterwards criminal proceedings were brought against the three for their racist statements and against the applicant and the head of the Danish Broadcasting Corporation's news section for aiding and abetting their dissemination. In April 1987 all the defendants were convicted. Mr Jersild was fined 1,000 kroner and appeals against this decision were rejected.

In his application to the Commission in July 1989, Mr Jersild relied on Article 10 of the Convention. In its report in July 1993 the Commission by a majority

[9] Judgment, para. 75.

[10] For the text of Article 13, see Case No. 7, below.

[11] ECHR, judgment of 23 September 1994, Series A, No. 298, decided by a Grand Chamber.

expressed the opinion that this provision had been violated. The Commission and the Government then referred the case to the Court.

Article 10 of the Convention, which was quoted in Case No. 1, protects freedom of expression, but permits its limitation for *inter alia* the 'protection of the reputation or rights of others'. Since it was accepted that the applicant's right to freedom of expression had been interfered with, and that such interference was 'prescribed by law' and pursued the above aim, the only point in issue was whether the conviction and sentence of Mr Jersild were 'necessary in a democratic society'.

The Court's starting-point was the vital importance of combating racial discrimination. Referring in this context to the 1966 International Convention on the Elimination of All Forms of Racial Discrimination, the Court indicated that it considered its interpretation of Article 10 of the European Convention in the present case to be compatible with Denmark's obligations under the UN Convention. The Court pointed out that as the applicant had not made the objectionable statements himself, but disseminated them in his capacity as a journalist, the principles to be found in the case law relating to the press were relevant.[12] An important point here was the impact of the audio-visual media, but, on the other hand, it was not for the courts to proscribe particular methods of reporting.

Although the Danish courts had emphasized the applicant's initiative in preparing the feature on the Greenjackets and editing the interview, the Court did not consider that the item could be seen as intended to propagate racist views and ideas. Similarly, the item did not explicitly condemn such sentiments, but the Court considered that this was unnecessary in the circumstances. Explaining that 'news reporting based on interviews, whether edited or not, constitutes one of the most important means whereby the press is able to play its vital role of "public watchdog"', the Court observed that 'the punishment of a journalist for assisting in the dissemination of statements made by another person in an interview would seriously hamper the contribution of the press to discussions of matters of public interest and should not be envisaged unless there are particularly strong reasons for doing so'.[13] Adding that the limited nature of the fine was irrelevant, the Court indicated that the remarks in respect of which the Greenjackets were convicted did not enjoy the protection of Article 10, but that this did not justify the applicant's fine and conviction. The domestic courts did not appear to have taken into account the applicant's purpose in compiling the offending item. Their reasons were therefore insufficient to establish that the interference in question was necessary and not disproportionate. The Court therefore concluded that there had been a violation of Article 10.

The only remaining issue was that of just satisfaction. Article 50 of the Convention provides:

> If the Court finds that a decision or a measure taken by a legal authority or any other authority of a High Contracting Party is completely or partially in conflict with the obligations arising from the . . . Convention, and if the internal law of the said Party allows only partial reparation to be made for the consequences of this decision or

[12] See, for example, the *Observer and Guardian* case, Series A, No. 216, and this *Year Book*, 63 (1992), p. 542.

[13] Judgment, para. 35.

measure, the decision of the Court shall, if necessary, afford just satisfaction to the injured party.

Here the Court dismissed the applicant's claim for compensation in respect of alleged non-pecuniary damage, but held by 17 votes to 2[14] that he was entitled to reimbursement of the fine which he had paid, together with a sum in respect of his costs and expenses.

Seven members of the Court voted against the decision on Article 10, explaining in their dissenting opinions that they had done so because the applicant had failed to make it clear that the views expressed in the programme were unacceptable, or to dissociate himself from them.[15] In the light of the threat posed by racism, they were therefore prepared to regard the applicant's conviction as falling within the State's margin of appreciation. By rejecting this approach the Court reinforced its long-standing commitment to journalistic freedom, while at the same time indicating that 'hate speech' in itself enjoys no protection under the European Convention. As a means of reconciling the values of Article 10 with those contained in the UN Convention, this is a sensible position.[16]

Right to respect for family life (Article 8)—the meaning of 'family life' in Article 8(1)—positive obligations—just satisfaction (Article 50)

Case No. 4. Kroon case.[17] In this case, which concerned the Netherlands, the Court held by 7 votes to 2 that the lack of a procedure for establishing legal family ties between a child and its biological father had given rise to a violation of Article 8 of the Convention. As just satisfaction the Court by 8 votes to 1 ordered the Government to pay the applicants 20,000 guilders, less the sum already received by way of legal aid, in respect of their costs and expenses.

In 1979 the first applicant, Mrs K, married M, who subsequently disappeared. She then established a relationship with the second applicant, Z, although they did not live together, and they had four children, including the third applicant, S, who was born in 1987. In 1988 Mrs K's marriage to M was dissolved and she sought a declaration that S was not M's child. The request, however, was refused, no procedure being available in the law of the Netherlands for allowing this to be done.

In their applications to the Commission in May 1991, S, Z and Mrs K relied on Article 8 of the Convention which protects the right to respect for family life. In its report in April 1993 the Commission expressed the opinion that this provision had been violated. The Commission then referred the case to the Court.

Article 8 of the Convention provides:

[14] See the supplementary joint dissenting opinion of Judges Gölcüklü and Valticos.

[15] See the joint dissenting opinion of Judges Ryssdal, Bernhardt, Spielmann and Loizou, and the joint dissenting opinion of Judges Gölcüklü, Russo and Valticos.

[16] However, see in this connection General Recommendation XV of the Committee on the Elimination of Racial Discrimination, concerning Article 4 of the UN Convention, *International Human Rights Reports*, vol. 1, no. 3 (1994), p. 11.

[17] ECHR, judgment of 27 October 1994, Series A, No. 297C, decided by a Chamber.

1. Everyone has the right to respect for his private and family life, his home and his correspondence.
2. There shall be no interference by a public authority with the exercise of this right except such as is in accordance with the law and is necessary in a democratic society in the interests of national security, public safety or the economic well-being of the country, for the prevention of disorder or crime, for the protection of health or morals, or for the protection of the rights and freedoms of others.

The first question was whether Article 8 was applicable. This depended on whether the relationship between Z, on the one hand, and Mrs K and S, on the other, amounted to 'family life'. It is well established that this concept is not limited to marriage-based relationships,[18] but here Z and Mrs K were not living together. The Court, however, held that this was unimportant since their four children were an exceptional factor which brought them within the concept. Article 8 was therefore applicable.

The next question was therefore whether it had been complied with and specifically whether the Netherlands had failed to discharge its positive duty to enable S to be integrated into his family. The Government argued that if Z and Mrs K married, S could be made their son by a 'step-parent adoption'. Alternatively, they could apply for joint custody of S. The Court, however, was not satisfied that these were enough and held that respect for the applicants' family life required a procedure for acknowledging the biological reality, without the parents needing to marry. It therefore concluded that there had been a violation of Article 8 which called for just satisfaction in the form of a payment of the applicants' costs and expenses.

Two judges delivered dissenting opinions. Judge Morenilla pointed out that the law relating to paternity raises fundamental moral and social issues and considered that the present case fell within the respondent's margin of appreciation. Judge Mifsud Bonnici agreed with that, but would also have ruled that Article 8 was inapplicable on the ground that no 'family life' had been established. In the period under review the right to respect for family life was also in issue in *Murray* (Case No. 7); *López Ostra* (Case No. 10); *McMichael* (Case No. 15); *Hokkanen* (Case No. 25); and *Nasri* (Case No. 43).

Right to legal assistance (Article 6(3)(c))—application to criminal appeal—just satisfaction (Article 50)

Cases Nos. 5 and 6. Boner case. *Maxwell* case.[19] The Court held unanimously that there had been a violation of Article 6(3)(*c*) of the Convention when the applicants were refused legal aid for the hearing of their criminal appeals in the United Kingdom. As just satisfaction under Article 50 Mr Boner was awarded £7,500.28 in respect of his costs and expenses.

The applicants in these cases were each tried and convicted of serious offences in Scotland and sentenced to terms of imprisonment. In Mr Boner's case the charge was armed robbery and in Mr Maxwell's case assault. In both cases the

[18] See, for example, the *Keegan* case, Series A, No. 290, and this *Year Book*, 65 (1994), p. 530.

[19] ECHR, judgments of 28 October 1994, Series A, Nos. 300B and C, decided by the same Chamber.

applicants received legal aid at the trial, but were refused it on appeal on the ground that their appeals had little chance of success. As a consequence they had to present their appeals themselves and in both cases were unsuccessful.

In their applications to the Commission in March and April 1991 both applicants relied on Article 6(3)(*c*) of the Convention, which is concerned with the rights of the defence. In its reports in May 1993 the Commission expressed the opinion that this provision had been violated. Both cases were then referred to the Court by the Commission and the Government.

Article 6(3) of the Convention provides:

> Everyone charged with a criminal offence has the following minimum rights:
>
> . . .
>
> (*c*) to defend himself in person or through legal assistance of his own choosing or, if he has not sufficient means to pay for legal assistance, to be given it free when the interests of justice so require.

Since it was clear that in both cases the accused lacked the means to pay for legal assistance, the only question for the Court was whether the 'interests of justice' required such assistance to be provided.

Following the Court's decision in the *Granger* case,[20] practice in Scotland was modified to enable an appeal court to adjourn a hearing so that an appellant can obtain legal aid if it becomes evident in the course of a hearing that representation is necessary. Whilst acknowledging that this was a positive development, the Court was unconvinced by the Government's argument that the new procedure met the applicants' complaints or that their cases were distinguishable from the *Granger* case. Pointing out that both applicants had been sentenced to substantial terms of imprisonment and that the issues they wished to raise could only be effectively presented by a lawyer, the Court decided that in both cases legal assistance in the appellate proceedings had been needed. Since it had not been granted, in both cases there had been a violation of Article 6(3)(*c*).

Each applicant made various claims for just satisfaction, but only Mr Boner's claim for his costs and expenses at Strasbourg was found by the Court to be justified, and then only on a reduced basis.

In a concurring opinion in both cases, Judge De Meyer indicated that in his view legal assistance is normally required in criminal proceedings not only at first instance but also on appeal. Although the judgments in this case do not go so far, the Court's reasoning clearly moves in that direction. The Government, however, indicated that if Article 6(3)(*c*) was found to have been violated in these cases, it might need to consider ending the automatic right of appeal in Scotland,[21] a reminder that in practice liberal tendencies can sometimes be neutralized by other developments. In the period under review Article 6(3)(*c*) was also in issue in the *Lala* case (Case No. 23), below.

[20] ECHR, judgment of 28 March 1990, Series A, No. 174, and this *Year Book*, 61 (1990), p. 429.

[21] *Boner* judgment, para. 42; *Maxwell* judgment, para. 39.

Right to liberty (Article 5(1))—the meaning of 'reasonable suspicion' in Article 5(1)(c)—right to be informed 'promptly' of the reasons for arrest (Article 5(2))—right to compensation for unlawful arrest (Article 5(5))—right to respect for private and family life and the home (Article 8)—right to a remedy (Article 13)

Case No. 7. Murray case.[22] In this case, which concerned the arrest and detention of a person under emergency legislation in Northern Ireland, the Court held by 14 votes to 4 that there had been no violation of Article 5(1) of the Convention; by 13 votes to 5 that there had been no violation of Article 5(2) or of Article 5(5); and by 15 votes to 3 that there had been no violation of Article 8. The Court also decided unanimously that there had been no violation of Article 13.

The applicants in this case were Mr and Mrs M and their four children, who in 1982 lived together in the same house in Belfast. In June 1982 two of Mrs M's brothers were convicted in the United States of offences connected with the purchase of arms for the IRA. On 26 July 1982 Mrs M was arrested by the army at the family home at 7 a.m. and taken to an army screening centre for questioning. At 9.45 a.m., having been photographed, she was released without charge. The arrest was in accordance with section 14 of the Northern Ireland (Emergency Provisions) Act 1978, which authorized the army to arrest and detain a person for up to four hours, if they were honestly and genuinely suspected of having committed a criminal offence. Mrs M was suspected of collecting money to finance the purchase of arms in the United States, but at first was told only that she was being arrested under section 14. However, at the screening centre she was asked about money and about America. Attempts to challenge the arrest in the domestic courts were unsuccessful.

In their applications to Strasbourg in September 1988 the applicants relied on Article 5 of the Convention, which protects the right to liberty, Article 8, which guarantees respect for private and family life and the home, and Article 13, which guarantees an effective remedy. In its report in February 1993 the Commission expressed the opinion that Mrs M had suffered an infringement of her rights under Articles 5(1), 5(2) and 5(5), and rejected the other complaints. The Commission then referred the case to the Court.

The Court began by recalling that in previous judgments it had made the point that when interpreting and applying the Convention it must take account of 'the special nature of terrorist crime, the threat it poses to democratic society and the exigencies of dealing with it'.[23] It then addressed the specific points in issue.

The relevant parts of Article 5 of the Convention provide:

1. Everyone has the right to liberty and security of person. No one shall be deprived of his liberty save in the following cases and in accordance with a procedure prescribed by law:

. . .

(*c*) the lawful arrest or detention of a person effected for the purpose of bringing him

[22] ECHR, judgment of 28 October 1994, Series A, No. 300A, decided by a Grand Chamber. Judge Valticos, who was initially a member of the Court for this case, was unable to take part in its deliberations, which is why the Grand Chamber consisted of 18 instead of the usual 19 judges.

[23] Judgment, para. 47.

before the competent legal authority on reasonable suspicion of having committed an offence . . . ;

. . .

2. Everyone who is arrested shall be informed promptly, in a language which he understands, of the reasons for his arrest and of any charge against him.

. . .

4. Everyone who is deprived of his liberty by arrest or detention shall be entitled to take proceedings by which the lawfulness of his detention shall be decided speedily by a court and his release ordered if the detention is not lawful.

5. Everyone who has been the victim of arrest or detention in contravention of the provisions of this Article shall have an enforceable right to compensation.

The first question was whether there had been a breach of Article 5(1), since Mrs Murray argued that she had not been arrested on 'reasonable suspicion' of having committed an offence and that her arrest was not for the purpose of bringing her before a competent legal authority. The Court, however, rejected both submissions. It decided that, having regard to the difficulties of investigating terrorist crime,[24] a reasonable suspicion existed here in view of the conviction of the applicant's brothers and the fact that Mrs Murray had visited them in the United States. Likewise, the domestic courts had been satisfied that the purpose of her arrest was to investigate the offence of which she was suspected and the Court saw no reason to depart from that finding. It therefore rejected the claim based on Article 5(1).

The second question was whether Mrs Murray had been informed of the reasons for her arrest, as required by Article 5(2). The Court concluded that she had, because although the reasons for her arrest had not been sufficiently indicated when she was taken into custody, they had become clear during her interrogation. There had therefore been no violation of Article 5(2). In the light of this ruling, and the decision on Article 5(1), the Court further decided that no issue arose under Article 5(5).

The remaining claims concerned Article 8, which was quoted in Case No. 4, and Article 13, which provides.

Everyone whose rights and freedoms as set forth in this Convention are violated shall have an effective remedy before a national authority notwithstanding that the violation has been committed by persons acting in an official capacity.

As regards the former, all six applicants complained of the army's entry into and search of their home and Mrs Murray complained also of being photographed. The Court, however, decided that the measures in question could all be justified by reference to Article 8(2), being in accordance with the law, necessary for the prevention of crime, and, in view of the threat posed by organized terrorism, proportionate. As regards Article 13, the Court held that an effective remedy was available in relation to Mrs Murray's claim under Article 8 and that as she had failed to make any complaint under Article 5(4), Article 13 did not need to be considered in relation to her complaints under Articles 5(1) and 5(2). Thus the applicant's complaints under Articles 8 and 13 were also dismissed.

[24] On this point the Court also stated that it was prepared to 'attach some credence' to the Government's declaration that it had reliable but confidential information grounding the suspicion against Mrs Murray. See judgment, para. 59.

This is the latest in a line of cases concerning the emergency in Northern Ireland, all of which have proved controversial.[25] The present case is no exception and apart from the ruling on Article 13, all the points in issue divided the Court. The critical questions were whether the entry and search of the applicants' home could be justified, where three judges dissented; whether a 'reasonable suspicion' had been shown, where four judges considered that a stricter approach was required; and whether the Court had interpreted Article 5(2) too loosely, where five judges explained why they thought that it had.[26] Here, as in previous cases, the fundamental issue is the extent to which it is permissible to interpret the Convention's safeguards flexibly in the interests of fighting terrorism, a question which will, no doubt, continue to provoke disagreement.

Right to respect for private life (Article 8)—refusal of permission to change surname—non-discrimination (Article 14)

Case No. 8. Stjerna case.[27] The Court held unanimously that the Finnish authorities' refusal to allow the applicant to change his surname had violated neither Article 8 of the Convention, nor Article 14, taken in conjunction with Article 8.

The applicant, Mr Stjerna, a Finnish national and resident, wished to change his name to 'Tavaststjerna', which was an ancestral name. Under Finnish law a change of name requires official permission and so the applicant applied to the local County Administrative Board. The Board sought an opinion from the Advisory Committee on Names which made an adverse recommendation, having found that the ancestors concerned had lived more than two hundred years ago, and that the proposed name had not become 'established', the first person to bear the current name having been born out of wedlock. The County Administrative Board therefore refused Mr Stjerna's request and an attempt to challenge this decision in the Finnish courts was unsuccessful.

In his application to the Commission in March 1991 Mr Stjerna relied on Article 8 of the Convention, which guarantees the right to respect for private life, and Article 14, which covers non-discrimination, in conjunction with Article 8. In its report in July 1993 the Commission expressed the opinion that these provisions had not been violated. The Commission then referred the case to the Court.

The main issue in this case concerned Article 8.[28] The Court had no difficulty in deciding that this provision was applicable since an individual's name clearly

[25] See, for example, the *Fox, Campbell and Hartley* case, Series A, No. 182, and this *Year Book*, 61 (1990), p. 444, and the *Brogan* case, Series A, No. 145B, and this *Year Book*, 60 (1989), p. 514. Such cases provide particularly clear examples of the influence of ideological factors on judicial decision-making. For discussion of this point see Merrills, *The Development of International Law by the European Court of Human Rights* (2nd edn., 1993), pp. 238–49.

[26] Judges Loizou, Morenilla and Makarczyk voted against the judgment on all the points mentioned; Judge Jambrek on all the issues, except that of Article 8; and Judge Mifsud Bonnici on Articles 5(2) and 5(5). In all instances the judges concerned explained their votes in dissenting opinions.

[27] ECHR, judgment of 25 November 1994, Series A, No. 299B, decided by a Chamber.

[28] For the text of Article 8, see Case No. 4, above.

concerns his or her private life. The question was therefore whether Article 8 had been violated. In the Court's view this depended on whether the respondent was under a positive obligation to allow the applicant to change his name, such that its refusal to do so could be regarded as an interference with his right.[29] The Court decided that in the circumstances there had been no such interference. It relied here on the variety of practice in Europe with regard to names, which means that on this matter States enjoy a wide margin of appreciation, on the lack of a convincing justification for Mr Stjerna's wish to change his name to Tavaststjerna, and on the multitude of other possibilities available to him. The Court therefore decided that there had been no violation of Article 8.

It reached the same conclusion when it considered Article 8 in conjunction with Article 14, which provides:

> The enjoyment of the rights and freedoms set forth in this Convention shall be secured without discrimination on any ground such as sex, race, colour, language, religion, political or other opinion, national or social origin, association with a national minority, property, birth or other status.

The decisive point here was that one of the applicant's ancestors having been born out of wedlock was not the reason for refusing him permission to change his name, but was treated by the national authorities as relevant only to the point that the proposed name had not been in established use within the applicant's family. In these circumstances the Court considered that the justification for refusing Mr Stjerna's request was objective and reasonable and accordingly decided that there had been no violation of Article 14.

Right to the peaceful enjoyment of possessions (Article 1 of Protocol No. 1)—locus standi *(Article 25)—right of access to the courts (Article 6(1))—non-discrimination (Article 14)—just satisfaction (Article 50)*

Case No. 9. The Holy Monasteries case.[30] In this case, in which the applicants were eight Greek monasteries, the Court held unanimously that as regards certain of the monasteries there had been a violation of Article 1 of Protocol No. 1 to the Convention and also of Article 6(1). On the other hand, it held unanimously that in respect of all the monasteries there had been no violations of Articles 9, 11 and 13, nor of Article 14, taken together with the substantive articles. As just satisfaction the successful applicants were awarded 8,400,000 drachmas in respect of their costs and expenses.

This case concerned the ownership and management of monastic property in Greece and in particular the effect of certain laws passed in 1987 and 1988. The 1987 law vested the property of five Greek monasteries in the State, unless the monasteries concerned could prove their legal ownership in one of a specified number of ways; the law of 1988 governed the property of three other monasteries which in that year had transferred their agricultural and forest land to the State by means of an agreement.

[29] For an alternative analysis, identifying the key issue as the scope of Article 8(2), see the concurring opinion of Judge Wildhaber.

[30] ECHR, judgment of 9 December 1994, Series A, No. 301A, decided by a Chamber.

In their applications to the Commission in July 1987 and May 1988 all eight monasteries relied on Article 1 of Protocol No. 1, which guarantees the right to the peaceful enjoyment of possessions, and a number of other articles of the Convention. In its report in January 1993, however, the Commission rejected all the applicants' complaints. The Commission then referred the case to the Court.

Before dealing with the merits of the case the Court had to consider two preliminary objections raised by the Government. The first objection was that the applicants lacked standing to bring a case because they were not 'non-governmental organizations' within the meaning of Article 25,[31] but rather part of the Greek State. The Court, however, rejected this argument on the ground that the monasteries concerned were all independent. The second preliminary objection, that the applicants had not exhausted their domestic remedies, as required by Article 26,[32] was also rejected.

The main substantive issue concerned Article 1 of Protocol No. 1, which provides:

> Every natural or legal person is entitled to the peaceful enjoyment of his possessions. No one shall be deprived of his possessions except in the public interest and subject to the conditions provided for by law and by the general principles of international law.
>
> The preceding provisions shall not, however, in any way impair the right of a State to enforce such laws as it deems necessary to control the use of property in accordance with the general interest or to secure the payment of taxes or other contributions or penalties.

Dealing first with the position of the monasteries which were not parties to the 1988 agreement, the Court held that by creating a presumption of State ownership of the applicants' land, rebuttable in only a limited number of ways, the respondent had interfered with their right to the peaceful enjoyment of their possessions and that this constituted a 'deprivation' of possessions within the meaning of the second sentence of the first paragraph of Article 1. With some hesitation the Court was prepared to accept that the overall objective of the 1987 law was 'in the public interest', but ruled that the interference was disproportionate, as no compensation had been provided.[33] It therefore concluded that as regards the five monasteries which were not parties to the 1988 agreement there had been a violation of Article 1. As regards the other monasteries, however, the Court found that as they had entered into the 1988 agreement voluntarily, there had been no interference with their right of property. Their complaint was therefore dismissed.

The other substantive issue concerned Article 6(1). Here the Court had to consider whether the monasteries which were not parties to the 1988 agreement had been deprived of their 'right to a court' by the 1987 law. Finding that the

[31] Article 25 authorizes the Commission to receive petitions 'from any person, non-governmental organization or group of individuals claiming to be the victim of a violation of the Convention . . . '.

[32] Article 26 provides that the Commission 'may only deal with the matter after all domestic remedies have been exhausted, according to the generally recognized rules of international law . . . '.

[33] The bearing of compensation on claims under Article 1 of Protocol No. 1 was earlier reviewed in the *James* case, Series A, No. 98, and this *Year Book*, 57 (1986), p. 450, and the *Lithgow* case, Series A, No. 102, and ibid., p. 462.

law in question deprived the applicants of any possibility of having their property rights adjudicated in the Greek courts, the Court had no difficulty in concluding that in this respect Article 6(1) had been violated. In view of this decision it held that several other complaints relating to this provision did not need to be considered.

Various complaints relating to Articles 9, 11, and 13 were briefly considered but dismissed[34] and the Court reached the same conclusion with regard to complaints based upon Article 14, where it found that the difference in treatment between the applicant monasteries and certain others had an objective and reasonable justification.

The only remaining issue was just satisfaction under Article 50. The successful applicants sought compensation for pecuniary damage, but the Court, finding that this question was not yet ready for decision, reserved it. They were, however, awarded a substantial sum in respect of their costs and expenses.

Right to respect for private life, family life and the home (Article 8)—application to nuisance claim—prohibition of degrading treatment (Article 3)—just satisfaction (Article 50)

Case No. 10. López Ostra case.[35] The Court held unanimously that Spain was responsible for a violation of Article 8 of the Convention, though not of Article 3, on account of nuisance caused to the applicant and her family by a waste treatment plant near their home. As just satisfaction the Government was ordered to pay the applicant 4,000,000 pesetas for damage and 1,500,000 pesetas, less the sum already paid as legal aid, in respect of her costs and expenses.

In July 1988 a plant for the treatment of liquid and solid waste from local tanneries, financed by a consortium of firms in the leather industry, began to operate close to the applicant's home. Fumes from the plant immediately caused widespread health problems, the local population was temporarily evacuated and in September the relevant authorities ordered a partial shut down. After returning to her home the applicant continued to suffer ill-health from the fumes and tried unsuccessfully to take action through the courts. In February 1992 the applicant and her family moved into a flat in the town centre, paid for by the municipality. In October 1993 the plant was temporarily closed following a complaint to an investigating judge by the applicant's two sisters-in-law.

In her application to the Commission in May 1990 Mrs López Ostra relied on Article 3 (prohibition of 'degrading' treatment) and Article 8 of the Convention. In its report in August 1993 the Commission expressed the unanimous opinion that the latter provision had been violated. The Commission then referred the case to the Court.

[34] Article 9 protects freedom of thought, conscience and religion; Article 11 freedom of peaceful assembly and association; and Article 13 the right to an effective remedy.

[35] ECHR, judgment of 9 December 1994, Series A, No. 303C, decided by a Chamber.

After rejecting two preliminary objections from the Government,[36] the Court considered the main issue in the case which concerned Article 8. Observing that severe environmental pollution can affect individuals' well-being and prevent them from enjoying their home in such a way as to adversely affect their private and family life, the Court recalled that a fair balance has to be struck between the competing interests of the individual and of the community as a whole. In the present case the waste treatment plant had been built in order to solve a serious pollution problem, but had itself produced environmental degradation. Although the Council had taken certain measures, these were plainly not enough and all efforts by the applicant and others to obtain redress had been resisted. Notwithstanding the State's margin of appreciation, the Court decided that in these circumstances the necessary fair balance had not been achieved, and concluded that there had been a violation of Article 8.

The applicant also relied on Article 3, but the Court rejected this part of her claim on the ground that the conditions under which she and her family had been forced to live, though difficult, could not be characterized as 'degrading'. On the issue of just satisfaction the applicant was awarded a sum to cover pecuniary and non-pecuniary damage and the bulk of her costs before the Strasbourg institutions.

Although this is not the first case in which the Court has considered a claim under the Convention in respect of nuisance,[37] the decision is a reminder that the Contracting States' responsibilities in such matters extend beyond environmental damage caused directly by their own actions, to situations where such damage is caused by others and the authorities fail to react appropriately. As cases of the first type will probably be comparatively rare, this principle of indirect, or secondary, responsibility is likely to prove extremely important in practice.

Freedom of expression (Article 10)—application to members of the armed services—the meaning of 'necessary in a democratic society' in Article 10(2)—right to an effective remedy (Article 13)—just satisfaction (Article 50)

Case No. 11. VDSO and Gubi case.[38] In this case, which concerned Austria, the Court held by 6 votes to 3 that the first applicant had been the victim of a violation of Article 10 of the Convention and also of Article 13. As regards the second applicant, the Court held by 8 votes to 1 that there had been a violation of Article 10, but unanimously that there had been no violation of Article 13. As just satisfaction the Court ordered the Government to pay the applicants 180,000 Austrian schillings in respect of their costs and expenses.

The applicants in this case were a private association, the *Vereinigung demokratischer Soldaten Österreichs* (VDSO), the 'Association of the democratic soldiers of Austria', and Mr Gubi, who was on national service, and a member of the VDSO. The association published a journal called *der Igel* ('The

[36] The preliminary objections were based on Article 25 (requirement that the applicant be a 'victim'), and Article 26 (exhaustion of domestic remedies).

[37] See the *Powell and Rayner* case, Series A, No. 172, and this *Year Book*, 61 (1990), p. 422.

[38] ECHR, judgment of 19 December 1994, Series A, No. 302, decided by a Chamber.

Hedgehog') which discussed questions relating to the armed forces, usually in a critical manner.

In July 1987 the VDSO asked the Ministry of Defence for permission to have *der Igel* distributed in barracks, like other military magazines, but received no reply. In December Mr Gubi distributed copies of the journal in his barracks, but was ordered to stop and later informed of regulations prohibiting the distribution of periodicals without the permission of the commanding officer. In January 1988 Mr Gubi raised a complaint about this matter with the Military Complaints Board, but was unsuccessful. An attempt to appeal against the Board's decision was subsequently dismissed by the Constitutional Court, which did, however, quash a disciplinary penalty imposed on Mr Gubi for distributing *der Igel* without permission.

In their application to the Commission in June 1989 the VDSO and Mr Gubi relied *inter alia* on Articles 10 and 13 of the Convention. In its report in June 1993 the Commission expressed the view that both applicants were victims of a violation of Article 10, but that only the VDSO had also suffered a violation of Article 13. The Commission then referred the case to the Court.

The main issue in this case concerned the scope and application of Article 10 of the Convention which was quoted in Case No. 1. As regards both applicants the Court was satisfied that their right to impart information and ideas had been interfered with, but also that the interference was 'prescribed by law' and had a legitimate aim, namely maintaining order in the armed forces. The crucial issue, as in the *Otto-Preminger-Institut* case (Case No. 1) and the *Jersild* case (Case No. 3), was thus whether the limitation could be said to be 'necessary in a democratic society' to achieve the above aim. The Court agreed with the Commission that it could not. Whilst recognizing that the freedom of expression of members of the armed forces can properly be restricted,[39] the Court pointed out that since all military magazines other than *der Igel* were distributed by the Austrian authorities free of charge, a heavy burden lay on the respondent to justify its special treatment. The Government claimed that the journal was subversive and that discipline was a particular problem at Mr Gubi's barracks. The Court, however, rejected the first point on the evidence and held that problems at one barracks could not justify a general ban on distribution. It therefore decided that both applicants were victims of a violation of Article 10.

The other issue concerned Article 13 of the Convention, which, it will be recalled from Case No. 7, guarantees an effective national remedy. The VDSO claimed that it had been denied an effective remedy in respect of its grievance under Article 10 and the Court, finding that the procedures cited by the Government were all inadequate, agreed. As regards Mr Gubi, however, the Court decided that there had been no violation since the Constitutional Court had jurisdiction to hear complaints by servicemen alleging a violation of their rights to freedom of expression.

As the Court decided that it was unnecessary to consider a complaint based on Article 14 (non-discrimination), the only remaining issue was just satisfaction under Article 50. Here the Court decided that no compensation was needed for

[39] For recent treatment of this point, see the *Hadjianastassiou* case, Series A, No. 252, and this *Year Book*, 64 (1993), p. 503; and earlier the *Engel* case, Series A, No. 22, and ibid., 48 (1976–7), p. 386.

pecuniary or non-pecuniary damage, and awarded the applicants about half their claim in respect of their costs and expenses.

For the three members of the Court who dissented on the claims brought by VDSO, there had been no interference with the latter's freedom of expression because the military authorities could not be expected to distribute a journal of this type and at the same time any soldier who wished to read it was free to do so.[40] From this they held that it followed that there had also been no violation of Article 13.[41] Judge Thór Vilhjalmsson went further and held that Mr Gubi had suffered no violation of Article 10 because it was entirely reasonable to prevent him distributing *der Igel* in his barracks and no other restrictions on his freedom of action had been imposed.

Protection against retroactive law (Article 7(1))—application to confiscation order—just satisfaction (Article 50)

Case No. 12. Welch case.[42] In this case, which concerned the United Kingdom, the Court held unanimously that there had been a violation of Article 7(1) of the Convention. As just satisfaction the Government was ordered to pay the applicant £13,852.60, less the sums paid by way of legal aid in respect of his costs and expenses.

In August 1988 the applicant was tried and convicted of a number of serious drugs offences and sentenced to long terms of imprisonment. In addition, the judge made a confiscation order against him for £66,914 under the Drug Trafficking Offences Act 1986, although the Act had come into force in January 1987 which was after the dates on which the applicant's offences were committed. Under the order if the applicant did not pay he would be liable to serve a further two year prison sentence. An appeal against the sentence and the confiscation order was only partially successful.

In his application to the Commission in June 1990 Mr Welch relied *inter alia* on Article 7 of the Convention. In its report in October 1993 the Commission, with the casting vote of the President, expressed the opinion that this provision had not been violated. The Commission then referred the case to the Court.

Article 7(1) of the Convention provides:

> No one shall be held guilty of any criminal offence on account of any act or omission which did not constitute a criminal offence under national or international law at the time when it was committed. Nor shall a heavier penalty be imposed than the one that was applicable at the time the criminal offence was committed.

The only issue in the present case was whether the confiscation order was to be regarded as a 'penalty' within the meaning of the second sentence.

The Court stated that the starting-point was whether the measure was

[40] See the partly dissenting opinion of Judge Matscher, joined by Judge Bernhardt, and the dissenting opinion of Judge Thór Vilhjálmsson.

[41] This conclusion seems questionable, however. Since Article 13 requires a remedy in respect of *alleged* violations, a finding that Article 10 had not been violated should not preclude a successful claim under Article 13. See further on this point Robertson and Merrills, *Human Rights in Europe* (3rd edn., 1993), pp. 167–71.

[42] ECHR, judgment of 9 February 1995, Series A, No. 307A, decided by a Chamber.

imposed following conviction for a criminal offence, and that other factors to be taken into account were the nature and purpose of the measure, its characterization under national law, the procedures used in making and implementing it and its severity. The Court agreed with the Government and the Commission that severity in itself was not decisive, but pointed out that here various elements pointed to the order being a penalty, including the statutory presumption that property is the result of drug trafficking unless the defendant can prove otherwise, the fact that orders are not limited to actual enrichment or profit, the trial judge's discretion to take into account culpability and the possibility of imprisonment in default.

The Court therefore concluded that the confiscation was a penalty and, since it had been applied retrospectively, that Article 7(1) had been violated. As regards the issue of just satisfaction, the Court decided that since the order had not yet been enforced, the question of compensation for damage should be reserved. The applicant was, however, awarded his costs and expenses.

This is the first case in which the Court has found a violation of Article 7(1)[43] and the reasoning by which the decision was supported is convincing.[44] The question whether in cases of this type imprisonment in default can also be regarded as a penalty was considered in a later case in the period under review, the *Jamil* case (Case No. 42), below.

The presumption of innocence (Article 6(2))—application to statements by a non-judicial authority—right to trial within a reasonable time (Article 6(1))—just satisfaction (Article 50)

Case No. 13. Allenet de Ribemont case.[45] The Court held by 8 votes to 1 that there had been a violation of Article 6(2) of the Convention on account of statements by the French authorities implicating the applicant in the commission of a murder, and unanimously that there had also been a violation of Article 6(1) because compensation proceedings brought in respect of the above statements had exceeded a reasonable time. As just satisfaction the Court by 8 votes to 1 ordered the Government to pay the applicant 2,000,000 French francs as compensation for damage, and unanimously awarded him 100,000 francs, plus VAT, in respect of his costs and expenses.

In December 1976 the applicant was arrested and charged with aiding and abetting the murder of a local politician. On the same day the Minister of the Interior, assisted by two high-ranking police officers, held a press conference at which the applicant was described as the instigator of the murder. In March 1980, however, the investigating judge decided that the applicant had no case to answer. Meanwhile, in March 1977, the applicant had begun proceedings to obtain compensation for the false accusation; these ended in November 1988 when his claim was finally dismissed.

[43] In the *Lawless* case, Series A, No. 3 (1961), Article 7 was invoked by the applicant but found by the Court to be irrelevant. See Robertson and Merrills, *Human Rights in Europe* (3rd edn., 1993), p. 126.

[44] In a short concurring opinion, Judge De Meyer indicated that he thought the Court could have justified its conclusion more simply.

[45] ECHR, judgment of 10 February 1995, Series A, No. 308, decided by a Chamber.

In his application to the Commission in May 1989 Mr Allenet de Ribemont relied on Articles 6(1) and 6(2) of the Convention. In its report in October 1993 the Commission expressed the unanimous opinion that these provisions had been violated. The Commission then referred the case to the Court.

The first claim in this case concerned Article 6(2) of the Convention which provides:

> Everyone charged with a criminal offence shall be presumed innocent until proved guilty according to law.

The Government's main argument was that the presumption of innocence can only be infringed by a judicial authority and not, as here, by statements made by other authorities before the trial. Previous cases involving Article 6(2) have been concerned with judicial infringements,[46] but the Court, recalling that 'the Convention must be interpreted in such a way as to guarantee rights which are practical and effective as opposed to theoretical and illusory',[47] held that it was not so limited. Having established this important point, the Court had no difficulty in concluding that what was said at the press conference went beyond the authorities' freedom to keep the public informed and infringed the presumption of innocence. It therefore agreed with the Commission that Article 6(2) had been violated.

The other claim concerned the length of the proceedings, which had lasted in all for eleven years and eight months. The Government maintained that the legal issues were complex and that the applicant had contributed to the delay. The Court accepted both points, but found that there had been several periods of inactivity for which the authorities were responsible and also that they had constantly blocked production of a video recording which the applicant needed as evidence. In all the circumstances it was therefore satisfied that the domestic proceedings had exceeded a reasonable time, with the result that Article 6(1) had been violated.

As compensation the applicant sought a large sum for alleged pecuniary damage, but the Court rejected this claim and awarded a smaller sum for non-pecuniary loss. The award in respect of costs and expenses was also made on a reduced basis.

Right to the peaceful enjoyment of possessions (Article 1 of Protocol No. 1)—scope of the power to take measures 'to secure the payment of taxes'—effect of a title retention clause—the margin of appreciation

Case No. 14. Gasus Dosier- und Fodertechnik GmbH case.[48] The Court held by 6 votes to 3 that in seizing and subsequently selling property to which the applicant claimed ownership the tax authorities in the Netherlands had not violated Article 1 of Protocol No. 1 to the Convention.

[46] See, for example, the *Minelli* case, Series A, No. 62, and this *Year Book*, 54 (1983), p. 331, and more recently the *Sekanina* case, Series A, No. 266A, and ibid., 64 (1993), p. 538.

[47] Judgment, para. 35. See also, however, the partly dissenting judgment of Judge Mifsud Bonnici, who voted against the decision on Article 6(2) on the ground that the extended interpretation of the presumption of innocence cannot be guaranteed in a practical and effective way.

[48] ECHR, judgment of 23 February 1995, Series A, No. 306B, decided by a Chamber.

The applicant in this case was a company (the G D company) which in 1980 agreed to sell a large concrete-mixer to another company (the A company). Under the contract of sale the vendors retained ownership of the machine until the price was paid in full. The concrete-mixer was delivered and installed, but the A company went bankrupt before it was paid for. The G D company therefore sought to recover their property, but were unable to do so because the tax authorities had arranged for the assets of the A company, including the concrete-mixer, to be sold as a way of meeting the A company's tax liabilities. Attempts to challenge this action in the Netherlands courts, and to obtain compensation, were unsuccessful.

In its application to the Commission in July 1989 the G D company relied on Article 1 of Protocol No. 1, which protects the peaceful enjoyment of possessions. In its report in October 1993 a divided Commission expressed the opinion, with the casting vote of the President, that this provision had not been violated. The Commission then referred the case to the Court.

After rejecting a preliminary objection from the Government based on Article 26 (non-exhaustion of domestic remedies), the Court turned to the main issue, which concerned Article 1 of Protocol No. 1. As the Court was satisfied that there had been an interference with the applicant company's 'peaceful enjoyment of its possessions', the question was whether the interference could be justified and specifically whether it was authorized as a measure 'to secure the payment of taxes' under the second paragraph of Article 1.

The Court considered that in this area there is a wide margin of appreciation and that measures to put the tax authorities in a better position than commercial creditors are not in principle objectionable. There must, however, be a fair balance between the community interest and that of the individual, which in turn requires a reasonable relationship of proportionality between the means employed and the aim pursued.[49] Applying these principles to the facts, the Court held that since the G D company was engaged in a commercial venture and could have taken other steps to reduce the risks, the tax authorities had not acted unreasonably, especially as a procedure satisfying the requirements of Article 6(1) of the Convention was available under Netherlands law to review the exercise of their powers. The Court therefore concluded that there had been no violation of Article 1.

Three judges dissented on the ground that the legislation in question, which gave unique powers to the tax authorities while making a negligible contribution to the national finances, constituted a disproportionate interference with the applicant's rights. In their opinion it was not acceptable that 'a third party, if he is a private person, should bear the risk that the person with whom he enters into an agreement has not paid all his taxes'.[50] This is a persuasive view. However, as it was also to do in the *Air Canada* case (Case No. 19), the Court based its treatment of the right to the peaceful enjoyment of possessions in the present case on a wide view of the margin of appreciation.

[49] See, for example, the *AGOSI* case, Series A, No. 108, and this *Year Book*, 57 (1986), p. 473.

[50] See the dissenting opinion of Judge Foighel, joined by Judges Russo and Jungwiert, para. 5.

Right to a fair trial (Article 6(1))—right to respect for family life (Article 8)—access to documents in care proceedings—non-discrimination (Article 14)—just satisfaction (Article 50)

Case No. 15. McMichael case.[51] In this case, which concerned the procedure governing custody and access arrangements in Scotland, the Court held by 6 votes to 3 that there had been a violation of Article 8 of the Convention in respect of the first applicant and unanimously that there had been violations of Articles 6(1) and 8 in respect of the second applicant. Various other claims were dismissed. As just satisfaction the applicants were awarded £8,000 jointly as compensation for non-pecuniary damage.

The applicants, H and W, lived in Glasgow. In November 1987 W gave birth to a son A. The applicants were not then married and H was not named on the birth certificate as the father of the child. As W suffered from a mental illness, A was taken into care shortly after he was born. In Scotland decisions on whether a child requires compulsory measures of care, and if so what measures are appropriate, are taken by a 'children's hearing', and in A's case the children's hearing took a number of decisions the effect of which was to continue care, to place A with foster parents and to refuse H and W access. W was a party to the proceedings before the children's hearing, but H, who did not have parental rights and took no steps to claim them, was not.

On two occasions in 1988 the children's hearing had before it certain documents, including social reports on A, which, in accordance with the normal practice, were not disclosed to H and W, although they were both in attendance and were informed of the substance of the documents. In 1988 and 1989 W appealed to the Sheriff Court against decisions by the children's hearing, but in both cases documents lodged with the Court were again not made available to her.

In April 1990 H and W married and H thereby obtained parental rights. Later in the same year, however, A was freed for adoption against his parents' wishes and in 1993 the court granted an application by A's foster parents to adopt him.

In their application to the Commission in October 1989 H and W claimed that the above events had given rise to numerous violations of the Convention. After rejecting several of their claims as inadmissible, the Commission in its report in August 1993 expressed the opinion that W was the victim of a violation of Article 6(1) and Article 8 and H of a violation of Article 6(1) only. The Commission then referred the case to the Court.

The Court began by considering the applicants' claims that Article 6(1) had been violated because they had been denied access to certain documents during the care proceedings, thereby depriving them of a fair trial in the determination of their civil rights.[52] In relation to W it was agreed that Article 6(1) was applicable and had not been complied with on both occasions in 1988 before the children's hearing and subsequently before the Sheriff Court. The Court

[51] ECHR, judgment of 24 February 1995, Series A, No. 307B, decided by a Chamber.

[52] Before dealing with the substantive issues described in the text, the Court rejected an attempt by the applicants to re-open various issues declared inadmissible by the Commission.

confirmed this conclusion. As regards H, however, it decided that Article 6(1) had no application because he had not sought to obtain legal recognition of his status as A's father. As a result he had not been a party to the care proceedings which, as a consequence, had not involved the determination of any of his civil rights.

The next question concerned Article 8. Here the applicants maintained that the non-disclosure of the same documents had violated their right to respect for their family life, and the Court agreed. Although Article 8 contains no explicit procedural requirements, it is well established that any decision interfering with the exercise of the right (such as care, custody and access measures) must be fair.[53] The unfair character of the care proceedings had already been conceded. Thus the only questions were whether H, as well as W, could claim to be a victim, and whether the claim under Article 8 was sufficiently distinct from the claim under Article 6(1) to merit separate consideration. On the first point the Court decided that H had standing because he had acted in concert with W throughout, while on the second point it held that the claim under Article 8 should be considered since this provision protected a distinct interest. It therefore agreed with the Commission that as regards both applicants Article 8 had been violated.

The final substantive issue concerned Article 14. This was invoked by H, who claimed that he had been the victim of discriminatory treatment in breach of this provision, taken in conjunction with Article 6(1) and/or Article 8, on account of his lack of legal rights prior to his marriage with regard to the custody of A and in relation to the care proceedings. The Court, however, like the Commission, found the difference of treatment to have an objective and reasonable justification and so dismissed the complaint.

The applicants, who were legally aided, did not make any claim for costs and expenses. They did, however, claim damages for alleged non-pecuniary loss, which the Government disputed. The Court, finding that the applicants' inability to see the confidential documents had resulted in some loss of opportunities and caused distress, decided that a modest award under this head was appropriate.

On all issues except one the Court was unanimous, the point of disagreement being H's standing to complain of a violation of Article 8. In a joint opinion three members of the Court explained that as H was not a party to the care proceedings and had never sought to become a party, they regarded his position under Article 8 as identical to that under Article 6(1). In the context of this case the rights of H were not a crucial matter. However, the general issue here is important for, as the dissenting judges pointed out, 'Article 8 should not be so construed as to prevent the imposition of reasonable conditions, in the interests of the mother and child, on participation by natural fathers ... in care proceedings ... '.[54]

[53] See, for example, *W, B and R* v. *United Kingdom*, Series A, No. 121, and this *Year Book*, 58 (1987), p. 484.

[54] Joint partly dissenting opinion of Judges Ryssdal, Palm and Freeland, para. 4.

The meaning of 'jurisdiction' in Article 1—the validity of territorial restrictions attached to Articles 25 and 46—the validity of declarations containing invalid restrictions—the interpretation and application of restrictions ratione temporis

Case No. 16. Loizidou case *(Preliminary Objections)*.[55] The Court held by 16 votes to 2 that territorial restrictions attached to Turkey's acceptances of Articles 25 and 46 of the Convention were invalid, but that they nevertheless constituted valid acceptances of the competence of the Commission and the Court. It also decided unanimously to join to the merits a preliminary objection that the complaint related to facts and events which occurred before the Turkish acceptance of the Court's jurisdiction under Article 46.

The applicant in this case grew up in northern Cyprus where she owned certain land. In 1972 she married and moved with her husband to Nicosia, but since 1974 had been prevented from gaining access to her land in the north on account of the Turkish occupation. In March 1989 a Greek Cypriot Women's Group organized a march with the declared intention of crossing the cease-fire line. They succeeded in doing so, but then some of the women, including the applicant, were arrested by the Turkish Cypriot police, after which they were returned to Nicosia.

In her application to the Commission in July 1989 Mrs Loizidou complained of violations of Articles 3, 5(1) and 8 of the Convention and of Article 1 of Protocol No. 1. In its report in July 1993 the Commission expressed the opinion that none of these provisions had been violated. The case was then referred to the Court by the Government of Cyprus under Article 48(*b*) of the Convention,[56] in so far as it relates to the alleged interference with the applicant's property rights and home, as protected by Article 1 of Protocol No. 1 and Article 8.

The Turkish Government submitted a number of preliminary objections which were dealt with in the present judgment. The Court began by noting that the *locus standi* of the Government of Cyprus was not in doubt, that Turkey was the respondent,[57] that the scope of the case was confined to the complaints under Article 8 and Article 1 of Protocol No. 1 and that the proceedings could not be regarded as an abuse of its procedures. It then turned to the main issues, which involved objections *ratione loci* and *ratione temporis* raised by the respondent.

Turkey's objections *ratione loci* required the Court to consider whether the facts alleged by the applicant were capable of falling within the jurisdiction of Turkey under Article 1 of the Convention, and then whether Turkey could rely on territorial restrictions attached to its declarations under Articles 25 and 46. On the first point the Court decided that the matters complained of were capable of falling within Turkey's jurisdiction within the meaning of Article 1 even though they occurred outside its national territory. It emphasized, however, that at the present stage it did not have to decide whether these matters were imputable to Turkey and gave rise to State responsibility, as these questions would be decided in the merits phase.

[55] ECHR, judgment of 23 March 1995, Series A, No. 310, decided by a Grand Chamber.

[56] Article 48(*b*) enables a case to be referred to the Court by 'a High Contracting Party whose national is alleged to be a victim'.

[57] See also on this point the individual dissenting opinion of Judge Gölcüklü.

The issue of Turkey's territorial restrictions was more complex. Article 46 of the Convention provides:

1. Any of the High Contracting Parties may at any time declare that it recognises as compulsory *ipso facto* and without special agreement the jurisdiction of the Court in all matters concerning the interpretation and application of the . . . Convention.
2. The declarations referred to above may be made unconditionally or on condition of reciprocity on the part of several or certain other High Contracting Parties or for a specified period.
3. These declarations shall be deposited with the Secretary General of the Council of Europe who shall transmit copies thereof to the High Contracting Parties.

In January 1990 Turkey made a declaration accepting the jurisdiction of the Court in the following terms:

The Government of the Republic of Turkey acting in accordance with Article 46 of the European Convention for the Protection of Human Rights and Fundamental Freedoms, hereby recognises as compulsory *ipso facto* and without special agreement the jurisdiction of the European Court of Human Rights in all matters concerning the interpretation and application of the Convention which relate to the exercise of jurisdiction within the meaning of Article 1 of the Convention, performed within the boundaries of the national territory of the Republic of Turkey, and provided further that such matters have previously been examined by the Commission within the power conferred upon it by Turkey.

This declaration is made on condition of reciprocity, including reciprocity of obligations assumed under the Convention. It is valid for a period of 3 years as from the date of its deposit and extends to matters raised in respect of facts, including judgments which are based on such facts which have occurred subsequent to the date of deposit of the present Declaration.

In 1987 Turkey had made a declaration accepting the right of individual petition under Article 25 in similar terms. The validity of Turkey's restrictions has given rise to a good deal of controversy[58] and, as this kind of question has not arisen previously, was examined by the Court at some length.

Recalling that it must have regard to the special character of the Convention as a treaty for the collective enforcement of human rights and the need to interpret it as a living instrument, the Court pointed out also that in view of the object and purpose of the Convention, its provisions must be interpreted and applied so as to make its safeguards practical and effective. Explaining that if substantive or territorial restrictions were permissible under Articles 25 and 46, Contracting Parties would be free to subscribe to separate regimes of enforcement, the Court noted that this would seriously weaken the role of the Commission and the Court and diminish the Convention's effectiveness. Certain provisions permit States to limit their acceptances under Article 25,[59] but the Court found it significant that no such provisions exists in Article 25 itself, nor in Article 46.

In the Court's view subsequent practice supported a restrictive interpretation since the competence of the Commission and the Court had generally been accepted without restrictions *ratione loci* or *ratione materiae*. Finding that

[58] See, for example, Cameron, 'Turkey and Article 25 of the European Convention on Human Rights', *International and Comparative Law Quarterly*, 37 (1988), p. 887, and Robertson and Merrills, *Human Rights in Europe* (3rd edn., 1993), pp. 206–8.

[59] See, for example, Article 6(2) of Protocol No. 4 and Article 7(2) of Protocol No. 7.

neither Article 36(2) of the Statute of the International Court of Justice, nor Article 63(4) of the Convention,[60] provided appropriate analogies, the Court concluded that the restrictions *ratione loci* attached to Turkey's declarations under Articles 25 and 46 were invalid.

What was the effect of this ruling on the declarations themselves? In the Court's view the respondent Government must have been aware that the impugned clauses were of questionable validity in view of the consistent practice of States in accepting the competence of the Court and Commission unconditionally. That Turkey nevertheless filed its declarations under Articles 25 and 46 in the Court's view indicated a willingness to run the risk that the limitation clauses would be declared invalid, without this affecting the validity of the declarations. Finding that the impugned restrictions could be treated as severable, the Court concluded that the declarations of 1987 and 1990 contained valid acceptances of the jurisdiction of the Commission and the Court.

The Government's objection *ratione temporis* was dealt with more briefly. This objection was based on the limitation contained in the last sentence of Turkey's declaration under Article 46 and a similar limitation in its declaration under Article 25. The Court held that the correct interpretation and application of these restrictions *ratione temporis* and the notion of continuing violations raised difficult legal and factual questions which were closely connected to the merits and which it was not yet in a position to answer.[61] Accordingly, it decided to join this objection to the merits.

This is the first case against Turkey to come before the Court and the novel issues presented give it an obvious importance. The conclusion that limitations *ratione loci* are invalid was not unexpected, but the decision to treat the limitations concerned as severable is more questionable. Judges Gölcüklü and Pettiti dissented on this point, and the reasoning by which the Court supported its conclusion does not seem very convincing. The decision to joint the objection *ratione temporis* to the merits was unanimous, but the two dissenting judges would have taken this approach further and joined all the objections to the merits in order to give the parties 'the possibility of adducing all relevant evidence on the expression "within [the] jurisdiction" and on the way the international relations of northern Cyprus are conducted'.[62]

Freedom of expression (Article 10)—application to criticism of the judiciary—the margin of appreciation

Case No. 17. Prager and Oberschlick case.[63] In this case, which concerned Austria, the Court held by 5 votes to 4 that there had been no violation of Article 10 of the Convention and unanimously that there had also been no violation of Article 14, taken together with Article 10.

[60] Article 63(4) enables a State to accept Article 25 in relation to a territory for whose international relations it is responsible, as in the *Piermont* case (Case No. 18), below.

[61] Similar objections *ratione temporis* based on the terms of Turkey's declaration were considered and rejected by the Court soon afterwards in the *Yağci and Sargin* case and the *Mansur* case (Cases Nos. 40 and 41), below.

[62] See the joint dissenting opinion of Judges Gölcüklü and Pettiti, and also the two judges' individual dissenting opinions.

[63] ECHR, judgment of 26 April 1995, Series A, No. 313, decided by a Chamber.

In 1987 the first applicant, Mr Prager, wrote an article in which he criticized the attitudes of certain judges of Austria's criminal courts, and published it in *Forum*, a magazine owned by the second applicant, Mr Oberschlick. One of the judges named, Judge J, took exception to the article and began criminal proceedings against the applicants which resulted in both of them being fined and the second applicant being ordered to pay compensation to Judge J.

In their application to the Commission in December 1989 both applicants relied on Article 10 of the Convention and Article 14 taken in conjunction with Article 10. In its report in February 1994 the Commission expressed the opinion that neither provision had been violated. The Commission then referred the case to the Court.

It will be recalled from Case No. 1 that Article 10(1) of the Convention guarantees the right to freedom of expression, but that Article 10(2), qualifies the right by authorizing limitations which are prescribed by law and necessary 'for the protection of the reputation . . . of others' and 'for maintaining the authority . . . of the judiciary'. In the present case the Court was satisfied that the interference with the applicants' rights was prescribed by law and pursued the above aims. Thus, as in the cases on Article 10 considered earlier, the critical issue was whether the interference was 'necessary'.

The Court reiterated its previous observations on the role of the press and noted that this includes discussion of the legal system and its functioning. It added, however, that public confidence in the judiciary is also important and that this can call for protection against 'destructive attacks that are essentially unfounded',[64] especially as judges are precluded from replying. In assessing these factors the Court stressed the significance of the margin of appreciation and found that in the present case Mr Prager had made serious allegations relating to 'arrogant' and 'bullying' attitudes and displays of prejudice which he had failed to justify. In this connection the Court found that his research had been superficial and considered it relevant that he had neither attended any trials presided over by Judge J, nor given the judge an opportunity to comment on the allegations. Having regard to all the circumstances, the Court was satisfied that the interference was not disproportionate to the legitimate aim. It therefore concluded that there had been no violation of Article 10.

As the alleged violation of Article 14 in conjunction with Article 10 had not been pursued, the Court held that this point need not be examined.

This was a borderline case and four judges dissented. In their view, eloquently expressed by Judge Martens,[65] Mr Prager's article was a serious attempt to raise important issues relating to the judiciary in Austria and its treatment by the national courts was unduly restrictive. This is a persuasive view. As Judge Pettiti pointed out,[66] in so far as the article could be considered defamatory, a civil action, rather than criminal proceedings, would appear to be the best way of enabling a person in Judge J's position to protect his reputation, while still enabling the press to keep the legal system under scrutiny.

[64] Judgment, para. 34.

[65] See the dissenting opinion of Judge Martens, joined by Judges Pekkanen and Makarczyk.

[66] See the dissenting opinion of Judge Pettiti.

Right to liberty of movement (Article 2 of Protocol No. 4)—freedom of expression (Article 10)—the meaning of 'local requirements' in Article 63—restrictions on the political activities of aliens (Article 16)—just satisfaction (Article 50)

Case No. 18. Piermont case.[67] The Court held by 5 votes to 4 that administrative measures taken against a visiting member of the European Parliament in French Polynesia and New Caledonia had violated Article 10 of the Convention. However, it found unanimously that there had been no breach of Article 2 of Protocol No. 4 and that it was unnecessary to consider the case under Article 14 taken in conjunction with Article 10. As just satisfaction for the violation of Article 10 the applicant was awarded 80,000 French francs in respect of her costs and expenses.

The applicant, who was a German national and a member of the European Parliament, visited French Polynesia for about a week in 1986 at the invitation of leading figures in the local independence movement. Although asked on her arrival to show discretion in commenting on French internal affairs, she took part in an independence and anti-nuclear demonstration and made a speech. As she was about to leave she was served with an expulsion order which also banned her from re-entering the territory.

She then travelled to New Caledonia, again at the invitation of pro-independence politicians. However, on arrival she was detained at the airport for some hours until the French High Commissioner issued an order excluding her from the island, after which she left. Later in the year local courts allowed Mrs Piermont's application to have the exclusion orders set aside, but these decisions in turn were subsequently set aside by the *Conseil d'Etat*.

In applications in November 1989 Mrs Piermont complained of violations of Article 10, Article 2 of Protocol No. 4 and Article 14 taken in conjunction with Article 10. In its report in January 1994 the Commission expressed the opinion that no violations had occurred in New Caledonia, but that the exclusion from French Polynesia had violated Article 10. The Commission then referred the case to the Court.

Article 2 of Protocol No. 4 to the Convention provides:

> 1. Everyone lawfully within the territory of a State shall, within that territory, have the right to liberty of movement and freedom to choose his residence.
>
> . . .
>
> 3. No restrictions shall be placed on the exercise of these rights other than such as are in accordance with law and are necessary in a democratic society in the interests of national security or public safety, for the maintenance of *ordre public*, for the prevention of crime, for the protection of health or morals, or for the protection of the rights and freedoms of others.

The Court agreed with the Commission's view that neither in French Polynesia nor in New Caledonia had this provision been violated. As regards the former, the applicant had been able to move freely during her visit and the exclusion order had been served only when she was on the aircraft and about to leave. At that point, since French Polynesia qualified as a separate territory for the purposes of Article 2, she was no longer lawfully present and so could not rely on the Protocol. As regards New Caledonia, on the other hand, although she had

[67] ECHR, judgment of 27 April 1995, Series A, No. 314, decided by a Chamber.

landed, the Court considered that she had never lawfully been in the territory, with the result that again the Protocol did not apply. This claim too was therefore rejected.

The claim under Article 10 was more difficult. As regards French Polynesia the Court considered that Mrs Piermont's expulsion, together with the ban on re-entry, constituted an interference with her freedom of expression and so the question was whether it could be justified. The Government relied on Article 63, on Article 16 and Article 10(2), but the Court found none of its arguments convincing.

Article 63(3) provides that where the Convention has been extended to overseas territories (as here), its provisions shall be applied 'with due regard . . . to local requirements'.[68] The Court held that as the tense political situation in French Polynesia was no different from situations which could occur in France itself, this provision was irrelevant.

Article 16 of the Convention provides:

> Nothing in Articles 10, 11 and 14 shall be regarded as preventing the High Contracting Parties from imposing restrictions on the political activity of aliens.

However, the Court decided that this provision could not be raised against Mrs Piermont since she possessed the nationality of a member State of the European Union and was also a member of the European Parliament.

There remained Article 10(2). Here the Court decided that the restriction in question was prescribed by law and had legitimate aims, namely the preservation of order and territorial integrity. However, it also decided that because the applicant had been contributing to a democratic debate, which is an especially important activity for an elected representative, the restriction had been disproportionate. It therefore concluded that as regards French Polynesia there had been a violation of Article 10, and reached the same conclusion when it examined the exclusion from New Caledonia.[69]

Since the Court decided that it was unnecessary to consider the issue of Article 14, the only other issue was just satisfaction under Article 50. Mrs Piermont sought compensation for non-pecuniary damage, but the Court decided that this was unnecessary. She was, however, awarded her costs and expenses, although on a much reduced basis.

Four judges dissented on the issue of Article 10,[70] demonstrating, like the cases considered earlier, the problems in applying this provision. In their view the Court had given insufficient weight to Articles 16 and 63 and should have used these provisions to inform its approach to Article 10(2). It is worth noting finally that this is only the Court's second case on Article 2 of Protocol No. 4,[71] though this aspect of the decision was not controversial.

[68] For an earlier attempt to rely on Article 63(3), which was also unsuccessful, see the *Tyrer* case, Series A, No. 26, and this *Year Book*, 49 (1978), p. 306; discussed in Merrills, *The Development of International Law by the European Court of Human Rights* (2nd edn., 1993), pp. 146–7.

[69] Contrary to the view of the Commission, the Court was satisfied that the exclusion of the applicant from New Caledonia constituted an interference with her right to freedom of expression, but considered that it could be justified under Article 10(2).

[70] See the joint partly dissenting opinion of Judges Ryssdal, Matscher, Sir John Freeland and Jungwiert.

[71] See the *Raimondo* case, Series A, No. 281A, and this *Year Book*, 65 (1994), p. 522.

Right to the peaceful enjoyment of possessions (Article 1 of Protocol No. 1)—seizure of aircraft—right to a fair hearing (Article 6(1))—the meaning of 'criminal charge' in Article 6(1)

Case No. 19. Air Canada case.[72] The Court held by 5 votes to 4 that the seizure of a commercial aircraft by the authorities in the United Kingdom had violated neither Article 1 of Protocol No. 1, nor Article 6(1) of the Convention.

The events which gave rise to this case were unusual. In April 1987 an aircraft owned and operated by the applicant company landed at Heathrow Airport and was found to be carrying a container holding a large quantity of cannabis resin. There was nothing to implicate Air Canada in the smuggling, but as there had been previous alleged breaches of security involving the company, customs officials seized the aircraft under section 139(1) of the Customs and Excise Management Act 1979, returning it later the same day on payment by Air Canada of £50,000. Subsequently, the applicant company challenged the claim that the aircraft was liable to forfeiture, but their argument was rejected by the Court of Appeal.[73]

In its application to Strasbourg in May 1991 Air Canada relied on Article 1 of Protocol No. 1 and Article 6(1). In its report in November 1993, however, a majority of the Commission expressed the opinion that neither provision had been violated. The Commission then referred the case to the Court.

It will be recalled from Case No. 9 that Article 1 of Protocol No. 1 is in two parts and covers both deprivation of property and control of its use. In the present case, since the aircraft had been released, the Court decided that the claim fell to be considered under the second paragraph. Accordingly, the question was whether the interference with the applicant's property rights could be justified by reference to the State's right under Article 1 'to enforce such laws as it deems necessary to control the use of property in accordance with the general interest'. By the narrowest majority the Court decided that it could, relying in this regard on the need to combat drug trafficking, the applicant's poor security record, the availability of judicial review to contest the seizure and the relation between the £50,000 demanded for the aircraft's release and the quantity of drugs found. Taking these factors into account, together with the respondent's margin of appreciation, the Court therefore decided that there had been no violation of the Protocol.

The applicant's other claim concerned Article 6(1). Here it argued that it had been subjected to a criminal penalty without a trial, or, alternatively, that the seizure of the aircraft amounted to a determination of its civil rights and obligations without court proceedings. Again, however, the Court rejected the claim. Holding that the proceedings in question did not involve any criminal charge, the Court pointed out that the lawfulness of the seizure had been determined in the forfeiture proceedings, and it would also have been open to Air Canada to seek judicial review of the decision to require payment as a condition for returning the aircraft. In these circumstances the Court was satisfied that the requirements of Article 6(1) had been complied with.

[72] ECHR, judgment of 5 May 1995, Series A, No. 316, decided by a Chamber.

[73] See *Customs and Excise Commissioners* v. *Air Canada*, [1991] 2 QB 446.

This was a controversial case and four members of the Court voted against the decision on both issues.[74] In dissenting opinions they maintained that a law which allows the authorities to seize the property of an innocent person, and to return it on payment of a sum determined entirely as a matter of discretion, is effectively imposing a criminal penalty without a trial, which cannot be reconciled with the requirements of either Article 1 of Protocol No. 1, or of Article 6. This robust reliance on first principles is, it is submitted, in every way superior to the surprisingly deferential approach taken by the majority.

Freedom of expression (Article 10)—excessive award of libel damages—right of access to the courts (Article 6(1))—security for costs as a condition of appeal—just satisfaction (Article 50)

Case No. 20. Tolstoy Miloslavsky case.[75] The Court held unanimously that the size of an award of damages for libel made by a jury in the United Kingdom, taken in conjunction with the state of national law at the relevant time, had given rise to a violation of Article 10 of the Convention. However, the Court found no violation of that provision in respect of an injunction issued by the High Court. The Court also concluded by 8 votes to 1 that there had been no violation of the applicant's right of access to the courts, as guaranteed by Article 6(1), when he was ordered to provide security for the plaintiff's costs as a condition of having an appeal heard. As just satisfaction the applicant was awarded 40,000 Swiss francs and £70,000 in respect of his costs and expenses.

The applicant wrote a pamphlet which was seriously defamatory of A who successfully sued for libel. The jury awarded A £1.5 million damages and the court granted A's request for an injunction restraining the applicant from repeating the libel. When the applicant sought to appeal A applied for an order requiring the applicant to give security for A's costs should the appeal fail. This order was granted by the Court of Appeal, which decided that there was little chance of the appeal being successful and ordered the applicant to provide security for the sum of £124,900. The applicant was unable to do this within the fourteen days available and so his appeal was dismissed.

In his application to the Commission in December 1990 Count Tolstoy relied on various articles of the Convention. In its report in December 1993 the Commission expressed the opinion that there had been a violation of Article 10, but not of Article 6(1). The Commission then referred the case to the Court.

The main issue in this case concerned Article 10, which protects freedom of expression and which was quoted in Case No. 1. As regards the injunction the Court was clear that this was simply a consequence of the finding of libel and could be readily justified. A more difficult question, however, was the award of damages and specifically whether it could be regarded as 'prescribed by law' and 'necessary in a democratic society' to protect the reputation or rights of others, as Article 10(2) requires. On the first issue the Court held that the rules concerning damages for libel were formulated with sufficient precision to qualify

[74] See the dissenting opinion of Judges Walsh and Pekkanen and the dissenting opinion of Judge Martens, joined by Judge Russo.

[75] ECHR, judgment of 13 July 1995, Series A, No. 323, decided by a Chamber.

as 'prescribed by law'; on the second issue, however, it agreed with the Commission that the award was so large as to be disproportionate and pointed out that in a recent case[76] the Court of Appeal had itself recognized that the almost limitless discretion given to the jury in libel cases was hard to reconcile with Article 10. The Court therefore concluded that this provision had been violated.

The other issue in the case concerned the right of access to the courts which is guaranteed by Article 6(1). The applicant argued that this had been infringed because the requirement that he provide security for A's costs had made it impossible for him to pursue his appeal. The Court, however, held that both the order itself and the size of the security required were reasonable having regard to A's legitimate interests and the circumstances of the case. With only one dissentient[77] the Court therefore dismissed this part of the claim.

As regards the issue of just satisfaction under Article 50, the Court awarded the applicant his costs and expenses on a reduced basis, but found his claim for damages to be unjustified and his request for a declaratory judgment, reducing his liability to A, as beyond its jurisdiction.[78]

Part Two: Other Cases Decided on the Merits

Right to a hearing before 'an independent and impartial tribunal established by law' (Article 6(1))—application to disciplinary proceedings before a professional body

Case No. 21. Debled case.[79] In this case, which concerned Belgium, the Court held unanimously that there had been no violation of Article 6(1) of the Convention.

The applicant in this case was a doctor whose right to practise had been suspended by the Provincial Council of the *Ordre des médecins* on the ground that he had charged unreasonable fees. His case then came before the Appeals Board, which reduced the period of suspension, but rejected an attempt by Dr Debled to challenge its membership. In his application to Strasbourg Dr Debled complained that his case had not been heard by 'an independent and impartial tribunal established by law', as Article 6(1) requires. In the case of *Albert and Le Compte*[80] in 1983 the Court decided that medical practitioners, though elected to the Appeals Board by the Provincial Councils, act in a personal capacity, and thereby satisfy the requirement of structural impartiality which the Convention imposes. This ruling was not enough to dispose of the present case because the

[76] See *Rantzen* v. *Mirror Group Newspapers Ltd*, [1994] QB 670. In this case the Court of Appeal exercised its powers under section 8 of the Courts and Legal Services Act 1990 and the new Order 59, Rule 11(4), to develop a more searching scrutiny of large awards of damages than was possible at the time of the *Tolstoy* proceedings.

[77] Judge Jambrek dissented on this point.

[78] At the time of the Strasbourg proceedings the applicant had not yet paid any part of the award against him to A, who, for his part, had offered in 1990 to settle the case for £300,000.

[79] ECHR, judgment of 22 September 1994, Series A, No. 292B, decided by a Chamber.

[80] ECHR, judgment of 10 February 1983, Series, A, No. 58, and this *Year Book*, 54 (1983), p. 319.

applicant alleged that the disciplinary bodies of the *Ordre* did not constitute tribunals 'established by law', and also that his challenge to the membership of the Appeals Board had not been handled in a manner compatible with Article 6. The first argument, however, had not been raised before the Commission and so the Court was unable to consider it, while the second argument was rejected on the facts.

The Court therefore agreed with the Commission that there had been no violation of Article 6.

Right to the peaceful enjoyment of possessions (Article 1 of Protocol No. 1)—right to a fair trial and to trial within a reasonable time (Article 6(1))—just satisfaction (Article 50)

Case No. 22. Hentrich case.[81] The Court held by 5 votes to 4 that the pre-emption of the applicant's land by the tax authorities in France had violated Article 1 of Protocol No. 1 to the Convention, and unanimously that there had also been a violation of Article 6(1). As just satisfaction the applicant was awarded 56,075 French francs in respect of her costs and expenses, while the issue of compensation in respect of pecuniary damage was reserved.

In 1979 the applicant and her husband bought a plot of agricultural land in Strasbourg, but eight months later were informed by the Commissioner of Revenue that he intended to pre-empt the land on the ground that it had been bought too cheaply. Attempts to challenge this decision in the French courts were unsuccessful, the final decision being given in June 1987. In her application to the Commission Mrs Hentrich complained that the pre-emption amounted to an arbitrary expropriation of her property contrary to Article 1 of Protocol No. 1[82] and that the unfairness and length of the subsequent proceedings had violated Article 6(1).

The Commission accepted the applicant's arguments and the Court agreed.[83] As regards the proceedings the Court found that the applicant had been prevented from challenging the Revenue's position effectively and that the time taken to decide the case was excessive. Similarly, in relation to the applicant's property rights, the Court agreed that the absence of basic procedural safeguards meant that Article 1 had been violated. However, four judges dissented on the second point,[84] holding that as compensation had been paid, the matter should be treated as falling within the respondent's margin of appreciation.

The issue of compensation for pecuniary damage was eventually resolved in July 1995 and as Case No. 48 is described below.

[81] ECHR, judgment of 22 September 1994, Series A, No. 296A, decided by a Chamber.

[82] For the text of Article 1 of Protocol No. 1, see Case No. 9, above.

[83] A preliminary objection alleging the non-exhaustion of domestic remedies as required by Article 26 was also considered but dismissed.

[84] See the partly dissenting opinion of Judges Ryssdal and Baka and the partly dissenting opinion of Judges Pettiti and Valticos.

Right to a fair trial (Article 6(1))—right to legal assistance (Article 6(3)(c))—application to trial in absentia—*just satisfaction (Article 50)*

Case No. 23. Lala case.[85] The Court held by 8 votes to 1 that there had been a violation of Article 6(1) of the Convention, taken together with Article 6(3)(*c*), because the applicant had been tried and convicted in the Netherlands in his absence and without his counsel, who had been present at the trial, having been given the opportunity to conduct his defence.

The applicant was convicted of fraud in respect of social security benefits and sentenced to a term of imprisonment. The proceedings were held *in absentia*, as was an appeal, the applicant having refused to appear. In view of the applicant's absence his counsel was not allowed to present his defence. The result of the appeal was that the applicant's conviction was confirmed, although his sentence was reduced. A further appeal to the Supreme Court was unsuccessful. In the proceedings at Strasbourg the applicant relied on Article 6, and in particular on Article 6(1), taken in conjunction with Article 6(3)(*c*), with regard to the proceedings in the Court of Appeal.

The Commission considered that these provisions had been violated and the Court agreed. Recalling that in the *Poitrimol* case[86] it had recognized the importance of an accused appearing at his trial, the Court nevertheless decided that removing the right to be defended by counsel, although in accordance with the law of the Netherlands, could not be reconciled with the right to be defended as guaranteed by Article 6(3).[87] It therefore held that the Convention had been violated, but also ruled that in the circumstances no compensation was required.[88]

Right to a fair trial (Article 6(1))—right to legal assistance (Article 6(3)(c))—application to trial in absentia—*just satisfaction (Article 50)*

Case No. 24. Pelladoah case.[89] In this case, which concerned the Netherlands, the Court decided unanimously that there had been a violation of Article 6(1) taken in conjunction with Article 6(3)(*c*) of the Convention.

The situation in this case was very much like that in the *Lala* case (Case No. 23 above), the main differences being that here the conviction was for possessing drugs and that the accused's absence from the hearing in the Court of Appeal was accounted for by his home being in Mauritius. As in *Lala*, however, the accused's counsel was denied the right to defend him because the accused was not present, and the Court, finding the case to be covered by the principle laid

[85] ECHR, judgment of 22 September 1994, Series A, No. 297A, decided by a Chamber.

[86] ECHR, judgment of 23 November 1993, Series A, No. 277A, and this *Year Book*, 65 (1994), p. 513.

[87] For the text of Article 6(3)(*c*), see Case No. 5, above.

[88] In a short concurring opinion, Judge Ryssdal, joined by Judge Mifsud Bonnici, distinguished the situation in the present case from that in *Poitrimol*, while Judge Matscher, in a dissenting opinion, made a similar point and also explained that he saw a distinction between the situation in *Lala* and that in *Pelladoah*, Case No. 24, below.

[89] ECHR, judgment of 22 September 1994, Series A, No. 297B. This case was decided by the same Chamber as the *Lala* case.

down in its earlier decision, held that there had been a violation of the Convention, but that there was no call to award compensation.[90]

Right to respect for family life (Article 8)—application to custody dispute—just satisfaction (Article 50)

Case No. 25. Hokkanen case.[91] In this case, which concerned Finland, the Court held unanimously that the failure of the authorities to enforce the applicant's right of access to his daughter up to 21 October 1993 constituted a violation of his right to respect for family life, contrary to Article 8 of the Convention. However, it decided by 6 votes to 3 that there was no violation after that date, and that the non-enforcement of his right to custody and the subsequent transfer of custody to the daughter's maternal grandparents did not violate Article 8 either. As just satisfaction under Article 50 the Government was ordered to pay the applicant 100,000 Finnish marks in respect of non-pecuniary damage and 135,000 marks, less the sums already paid as legal aid, in respect of his costs and expenses.

The applicant in this case was involved in a long-running dispute with his wife's parents, initially over access to his daughter, Sini, and later over custody. The grandparents began looking after Sini after the death of the applicant's wife, with his agreement. However, they then refused to return her and strenuously resisted the applicant's efforts to obtain access. Eventually, the grandparents were awarded custody of Sini and on 21 October 1993 a court decided that, as the child was now ten years old, the applicant's access should depend on her consent.

At Strasbourg the applicant's complaint was based mainly on Article 8,[92] but was only partially successful. As regards the period before 21 October, the Court decided that Article 8 had been violated because the authorities had made insufficient efforts to compel the grandparents to recognize the applicant's right of access. As regards the subsequent period, however, it decided that there was no reason to question the domestic court's finding that Sini was sufficiently mature to have her views taken into account, and so there was no violation. On the issue of custody the Court decided that the reasons for the decision to transfer custody were relevant and sufficient for the purposes of Article 8(2) and that the measure could not be regarded as disproportionate, having regard to the child's interest. Here too, therefore, the conclusion was that there had been no violation of Article 8.

Disputes over parental rights are among the most difficult cases on Article 8 and frequently divide the Court.[93] In the present case three judges accepted the applicant's argument on all points on the ground that the grandparents, through

[90] As in the *Lala* case, Judge Ryssdal, joined by Judge Mifsud Bonnici, gave a short concurring opinion distinguishing the *Poitrimol* case. Judge Matscher's dissenting opinion in *Lala* (note 88 above) is also relevant to the present case.

[91] ECHR, judgment of 23 September 1994, Series A, No. 299A, decided by a Chamber.

[92] For the text of Article 8, see Case No. 4, above.

[93] See, for example, the *Eriksson* case, Series A, No. 156, and this *Year Book*, 60 (1989), p. 539, and the *Margareta and Roger Andersson* case, Series A, No. 226A, and this *Year Book*, 63 (1992), p. 559.

their unlawful action, had sought to create a *fait accompli* which it would be wrong for the Court to endorse.[94]

Right to the peaceful enjoyment of possessions (Article 1 of Protocol No. 1)—trial within a reasonable time (Article 6(1))

Case No. 26. Katte Klitsche de la Grange case.[95] In this case, which concerned building restrictions imposed on land in Italy, the Court held unanimously that there had been no violation of Article 1 of Protocol No. 1, nor of Article 6(1) of the Convention.

The applicant owned land in Italy which was subject to various restrictions on building. Wishing to develop the land he began legal proceedings in 1978 to challenge the restrictions, but after eight years of litigation was unsuccessful. At Strasbourg he claimed that the prohibition on building, for which he had received no compensation, violated his rights under Article 1 of Protocol No. 1 and that the length of the ensuing proceedings had exceeded a reasonable time, contrary to Article 6(1). Although the Commission upheld his claim on both counts, the Court reached the opposite conclusion. Whilst recognizing that the applicant's property right had been interfered with, the Court ruled that in the light of various considerations relating to the particular facts, the balance between the applicant's interests and those of the community had not been upset, with the result that the interference could be justified. As regards the length of the proceedings, the Court decided that this had not been excessive, having regard to the complexity and sensitivity of the issues. It therefore concluded that there had been no violations of the Convention.

Trial within a reasonable time (Article 6(1))—right to a hearing by an independent 'tribunal' (Article 6(1))—just satisfaction (Article 50)

Case No. 27. Beaumartin case.[96] The Court held unanimously that there had been a breach of Article 6(1) of the Convention on account of the length of proceedings in the French courts, and a further breach because the applicants' case was not heard by an independent 'tribunal', having full jurisdiction. As just satisfaction the Government was ordered to pay the applicants 100,000 French francs as compensation for non-pecuniary damage and 80,000 francs in respect of their costs and expenses.

The applicants were shareholders in a property company whose land was expropriated by the Moroccan Government. Although an agreement providing for compensation was negotiated between the Moroccan and French Governments, a dispute arose over the applicants' entitlement which took more than eight years for the French courts to resolve. Noting that there were long periods during which the proceedings in the *Conseil d'Etat* had stagnated, the Court found that the delays in resolving the matter had violated Article 6(1). The main

[94] See the partly dissenting opinion of Judge De Meyer, joined by Judges Russo and Jungwiert.

[95] ECHR, judgment of 27 October 1994, Series A, No. 293B, decided by a Chamber.

[96] ECHR, judgment of 24 November 1994, Series A, No. 296B, decided by a Chamber.

issue in the domestic litigation concerned the interpretation of the compensation agreement, and here the *Conseil d'Etat* had decided the legal point by referring it to the Minister for Foreign Affairs and treating his decision as conclusive.[97] This led the Court to conclude that there had been a further violation of Article 6(1), since by handling the matter in this way the *Conseil d'Etat* had failed to act as an independent tribunal.[98]

Right to liberty (Article 5(1))—detention to ensure accused appears for trial (Article 5(1)(c))

Case No. 28. Kemmache (No. 3) case.[99] The Court held by 8 votes to 1 that the detention of the applicant by the French authorities after his trial had been adjourned had not violated Article 5(1)(*c*) of the Convention.

The applicant, who had been at liberty, surrendered to custody the day before he was due to be tried on various counterfeiting charges. At the request of a co-defendant the trial was adjourned, but the applicant was not released until two months later and then only after payment of the first instalment of a security bond. On this, his third visit to the European Court,[100] Mr Kemmache argued that his detention had involved a violation of his right to liberty as guaranteed by Article 5(1) because it failed to meet the requirements of Article 5(1)(*c*).[101] Although the Commission had upheld his claim, the Court rejected it, finding that the applicant's detention was 'in accordance with a procedure prescribed by law' and showed 'neither abuse of authority nor bad faith nor arbitrariness'.[102] Since it was not for the Court to make its own assessment of the facts, nor to act as a court of third or fourth instance, it concluded that there had been no violation of the Convention.[103]

Right of access to the courts and right to a fair hearing (Article 6(1))—jurisdiction of the Court

Case No. 29. Ortenberg case.[104] In this case, which concerned arrangements for land use and development in Austria, the Court held that there had been no violation of Article 6(1) of the Convention and that a complaint based on Article 1 of Protocol No. 1 was beyond its jurisdiction.

The applicant, Mrs Ortenberg, owned a house in Austria and objected to a local land use plan which would lead to houses being built adjacent to her

[97] This practice has now been discontinued: see para. 20 of the judgment.

[98] Before deciding the two substantive issues, the Court rejected a submission by the Government that Article 6(1) was inapplicable. See judgment, paras. 26–8.

[99] ECHR, judgment of 24 November 1994, Series A, No. 296C, decided by a Chamber.

[100] See the Court's 1991 decision on the merits in the first *Kemmache* case, Series A, No. 218, and this *Year Book*, 63 (1992), p. 218, and its subsequent application of Article 50, Series A, No. 270B, and this *Year Book*, 65 (1994), p. 546.

[101] For the text of Article 5(1)(*c*), see Case No. 7, above.

[102] Judgment, para. 45.

[103] Judge Walsh dissented on the ground that the applicant's detention was based on a 'speculative and intuitive approach' by the French courts which could not be reconciled with the Convention.

[104] ECHR, judgment of 25 November 1994, Series A, No. 295B, decided by a Chamber.

property. When attempts to challenge the plan in the Austrian courts were unsuccessful, she took her case to Strasbourg, alleging that she had been denied her right of access to the courts, contrary to Article 6(1), and that the domestic proceedings were unfair. The Commission rejected both submissions and the Court agreed. Before the Court Mrs Ortenberg also sought to rely on Article 1 of Protocol No. 1 which guarantees a right to property. However, the Commission had ruled this complaint inadmissible, with the result that it lay outside the scope of the case referred to the Court, which therefore held that it had no jurisdiction to entertain it.

Right to a fair hearing and to trial within a reasonable time (Article 6(1))—right to the peaceful enjoyment of possessions (Article 1 of Protocol No. 1)—just satisfaction (Article 50)

Case No. 30. Stran Greek Refineries and Stratis Andreadis case.[105] In this case, which concerned a contractual dispute in Greece, the Court held unanimously that there had been a violation of Article 6(1) of the Convention in respect of the applicants' right to a fair trial, but not with respect to the length of the proceedings. A complaint based on Article 1 of Protocol No. 1 was also upheld. As just satisfaction for the breach of Article 6(1) the Government was ordered to pay the applicants 116,273,442 drachmas, 16,054,165 US dollars and 614,627 French francs, plus interest, as compensation for pecuniary damage, and £125,000 for their costs and expenses.

In 1972 the applicant, Mr Andreadis, made an agreement with the Greek military Government to build an oil refinery and operate it through the SG company. In 1977, following the restoration of democracy, the new Government terminated the contract, but after arbitration the SG company obtained an award for the costs it had incurred between 1972 and 1977. The Government challenged the award in the courts, but initially was unsuccessful. However, it then passed a law nullifying the award, as a result of which the final decision of the courts was in favour of the Government.

The applicants based their complaint to Strasbourg on Article 6(1) and Article 1 of Protocol No. 1. As regards the former, the Court agreed with the Commission that the length of the proceedings was not unreasonable, but also that the Government's legislative intervention had violated the applicants' right to a fair trial. It also agreed that by seeking to revoke a final and binding arbitration award it had deprived them of their possessions in a manner which could not be justified under Article 1. The sums awarded under Article 50 corresponded to those awarded in the arbitration.

Right to a fair trial (Article 6(1))—scope of the obligation to provide reasoned judgments—just satisfaction (Article 50)

Cases Nos. 31 and 32. Ruiz Torija case; *Balani* case.[106] In both cases, which concerned Spain, the Court decided by 8 votes to 1 that there had been a

[105] ECHR, judgment of 9 December 1994, Series A, No. 301B, decided by a Chamber.

[106] ECHR, judgments of 9 December 1994, Series A, Nos. 303A and 303B, decided by the same Chamber.

violation of Article 6(1) of the Convention. The Government was ordered to pay the applicants 1,000,000 pesetas and 997,050 pesetas respectively for their costs and expenses.

The applicants in these cases were involved in civil litigation in Spain. Mr Ruiz Torija's dispute was over a lease and Mrs Hiro Balani's case concerned a trade mark. In both cases the applicants were unsuccessful in the domestic proceedings and one of the courts which gave the decision, in one case the Madrid *Audienca Provincial* and in the other the Spanish Supreme Court, did so in a judgment which failed to deal with one of the applicant's submissions. The applicants submitted that this failure violated their right to a fair trial and the Court agreed. Although it recognized that Article 6(1) does not require the domestic courts to provide a detailed answer to every argument, the Court found that in the present cases the applicants' submissions were relevant and sufficiently important to merit an answer. It therefore concluded that the Convention had been violated.[107]

Right to a fair hearing and to trial within a reasonable time (Article 6(1))—the meaning of 'civil rights and obligations' in Article 6(1)—just satisfaction (Article 50)

Cases Nos. 33 and 34. Schouten and *Meldrum* cases.[108] The Court held unanimously that delays in confirming a social security decision in the Netherlands had violated the applicants' rights under Article 6(1) of the Convention. As just satisfaction the Government was ordered to pay each applicant the sum of 10,000 Netherlands guilders in respect of their costs and expenses.

The applicants in these cases provided specialist equipment for physiotherapists and became involved in a dispute with the social security authorities over whether the physiotherapists concerned were to be regarded as their employees. The disputes in question were eventually resolved, but only after considerable delays caused in part by the failure of one of the bodies concerned, the BVG, to confirm its decision promptly. In Mr Schouten's case the BVG's delay was for 22 months and in Mr Meldrum's case for 16 months. Finding that these periods were unreasonable, the Court held that there had been a violation of Article 6(1). A claim that the proceedings had also been unfair was rejected, however.

The interest of these cases is to be found in the preliminary decision that Article 6(1) was applicable. For these are the first cases to involve disputes concerning contributions under social security schemes, as opposed to benefits, which have been the subject of several previous decisions.[109] Following the principles laid down in its case law on the latter, however, the Court decided that

[107] Judge Bernhardt dissented in both cases on the ground that the domestic courts had impliedly rejected the applicants' arguments and nothing more was needed in the particular circumstances.

[108] ECHR, judgment of 9 December 1994, Series A, No. 304, decided by a Chamber. Although these were separate cases, involving slightly different facts, the Court dealt with the issues raised in a single judgment.

[109] See the *Feldbrugge* case, Series A, No. 99, and this *Year Book*, 57 (1986), p. 456; the *Salesi* case, Series A, No. 257E, and this *Year Book*, 64 (1993), p. 512; and the *Schuler-Zgraggen* case, Series A, No. 263, and this *Year Book*, 64 (1993), p. 530.

both cases involved 'civil rights and obligations', with the result that Article 6(1) was applicable, so further extending the scope of this provision.

Freedom of expression (Article 10)—the meaning of 'necessary in a democratic society' in Article 10(2)—just satisfaction (Article 50)

Case No. 35. Vereniging Weekblad 'Bluf!' case.[110] In this case, which concerned the Netherlands, the Court held unanimously that the withdrawal from circulation of one issue of the applicant association's periodical had infringed Article 10 of the Convention. As just satisfaction the Government was ordered to pay the applicant 60,000 guilders in respect of its costs and expenses.

The applicants in this case were an association which published a left-wing journal called *Bluf!* in the Netherlands. In 1987 they came into possession of a report prepared by the internal security service and published it in their journal. However, most of the copies of the relevant issue were seized by the authorities, and although some 2,500 copies were circulated, a court subsequently ordered the issue to be withdrawn.

The applicant's complaint was based on Article 10 of the Convention, which was quoted in Case No. 1. The Commission expressed the opinion that this provision had been violated and the Court agreed. In the latter's view the crucial point was that when the domestic court made its order, the offending issue had already been widely circulated. The Court therefore concluded that the measure could not be regarded as 'necessary in a democratic society', with the result that Article 10 had been violated.[111]

Right to be informed of the nature of a criminal charge (Article 6(3)(a))—effect of a clerical error

Case No. 36. Gea Catalán case.[112] In this case, which concerned Spain, the Court held unanimously that there had been no violation of Article 6(3)(*a*) of the Convention.

In 1986 the applicant was committed for trial on a charge of defrauding his employers. In 1988 he was convicted on the same charge and given a sentence of imprisonment. In the meantime, however, the public prosecutor, through a clerical error, had informed the applicant that the charge against him was slightly different. The applicant claimed that this confusion had violated his rights under Article 6(3) of the Convention which provides:

> Everyone charged with a criminal offence has the following minimum rights:
> (*a*) to be informed promptly, in a language which he understands and in detail, of the nature and cause of the accusation against him . . .

The Commission upheld this submission, but the Court rejected it. Finding

[110] ECHR, judgment of 9 February 1995, Series A, No. 306A, decided by a Chamber.

[111] For an earlier case on Article 10 which turned on the same point, see the *Observer and Guardian* case, Series A, No. 216, and this *Year Book*, 63 (1992), p. 542.

[112] ECHR, judgment of 10 February 1995, Series A, No. 309, decided by a Chamber.

that the error was obvious in view of the charge clearly set out in the committal order, it ruled that there had been no violation of the Convention.[113]

Right to liberty (Article 5(1))—detention with a view to extradition (Article 5(1)(f))—pre-trial detention (Article 5(3))—just satisfaction (Article 50)

Case No. 37. Quinn case.[114] In this case, which concerned detention pending extradition from France, the Court held unanimously that there had been a violation of Article 5(1) of the Convention, but not of Article 5(3). As just satisfaction the Government was ordered to pay the applicant 60,000 francs as compensation for damage and 150,000 francs in respect of his costs and expenses.

The applicant was arrested on a charge of fraud, and although a court ordered his immediate release, he was detained for a further eleven hours and was then re-arrested with a view to extradition to Switzerland. He was then detained for a further two years before an extradition order was made. Article 5(1), which was quoted in Case No. 7, protects the right to liberty, and the Court had no difficulty in deciding that the applicant's eleven hour detention, which had no legal basis, violated this provision. It also decided that a further violation had occurred when the applicant's detention with a view to extradition, which could initially be justified under Article 5(1)(*f*),[115] had exceeded a reasonable time. Before being finally extradited, the applicant was tried and convicted on the original fraud charge in France for which he had earlier spent a year in pre-trial detention. The applicant complained that this constituted a violation of his right to trial within a reasonable time under Article 5(3),[116] but the Court, finding that the authorities had acted reasonably, rejected this submission.

Right to a public hearing by a tribunal (Article 6(1))—scope of Austrian reservation—just satisfaction (Article 50)

Case No. 38. Fischer case.[117] The Court held unanimously that the lack of an oral public hearing before the Austrian Administrative Court had occasioned a breach of Article 6(1) of the Convention. However, it also decided by 8 votes to 1 that there had been no violation of this provision with regard to the applicant's right to have his case heard by a 'tribunal'. As just satisfaction for the violation

[113] Before dealing with the merits of this case the Court rejected a preliminary objection from the Government, which submitted that the case should be struck out under Rule 49(2).

[114] ECHR, judgment of 22 March 1995, Series A, No. 311, decided by a Chamber.

[115] Article 5 provides:

'1. Everyone has the right to liberty and security of person. No one shall be deprived of his liberty save in the following cases and in accordance with a procedure prescribed by law:

. . .

(*f*) the lawful arrest or detention of a person to prevent his effecting an unauthorized entry into the country or of a person against whom action is being taken with a view to deportation or extradition.'

[116] For the text of Article 5(3), see Cases Nos. 40 and 41, below.

[117] ECHR, judgment of 26 April 1995, Series A, No. 312, decided by a Chamber.

which had been found, the Government was ordered to pay the applicant 200,000 schillings in respect of his costs and expenses.

This case concerned a dispute over the revocation of a tipping licence which eventually came before the Austrian Administrative Court. At Strasbourg the applicant's first complaint was that the Administrative Court's powers of review were limited, with the result that he had been denied the 'right to a court' which Article 6(1) guarantees. The European Court, however, like the Commission, rejected this argument on the facts.[118] His second complaint was that he had been denied an oral hearing which the Convention also guarantees in certain circumstances. Here he was more successful. Holding that the issue was not covered by a reservation which Austria had made when it ratified the Convention in 1959,[119] the Court held that since the Administrative Court was the first and only judicial body to consider the applicant's case, which raised important issues, a hearing should have been granted.[120] It therefore decided that in this respect the Convention had been violated.

Trial within a reasonable time (Article 6(1))—just satisfaction (Article 50)

Case No. 39. Paccione case.[121] The Court held unanimously that the length of proceedings brought by the applicant in the Italian Court of Audit had violated Article 6(1) of the Convention.

The proceedings in this case, which concerned a claim to a pension, lasted for nearly eight years. Applying the criteria laid down in its case law, the Court concluded that this period was excessive. The applicant, however, had failed to submit his claim under Article 50 within the time limits prescribed in the Court's Rules. The Court therefore held that this part of the claim was inadmissible.

Pre-trial detention (Article 5(3))—trial within a reasonable time (Article 6(1))—jurisdiction ratione temporis*—just satisfaction (Article 50)*

Cases Nos. 40 and 41. Yağci and Sargin case. *Mansur* case.[122] In these cases, which concerned Turkey, the Court held that there had been violations of Articles 5(3) and 6(1) of the Convention on account of the length of the applicants' detention pending trial and the criminal proceedings brought against them. In the *Yağci and Sargin* case the decision was arrived at by 8 votes to 1, and the applicants were awarded 30,000 francs as compensation for damage and

[118] In a closely reasoned separate opinion, Judge Martens explained that he had voted against the judgment on this point on both methodological and material grounds. In a short concurring opinion, Judge Jambrek supported Judge Martens' methodological objections.

[119] The Court's conclusion on this point was based on the fact that the law under which the applicant was denied a hearing dated from 1982 and was therefore not in force when Austria made its reservation. The Austrian reservation was more fully examined in the separate opinion of Judge Martens at paras. 23 to 25.

[120] On the scope of the right to a public hearing generally and in Austrian law specifically, see also the concurring opinion of Judge Matscher.

[121] ECHR, judgment of 27 April 1995, Series A, No. 315, decided by a Chamber.

[122] ECHR, judgments of 8 June 1995, Series A, Nos. 319 and 321, decided by Chambers.

a similar sum in respect of their costs and expenses. In the *Mansur* case the Court was unanimous and similar sums were awarded, but with a deduction corresponding to the amount paid by the Council of Europe as legal aid.

The applicants in these cases were arrested on criminal charges in Turkey, held in detention and subsequently tried. Mr Yağci and Mr Sargin, who were charged with subversive activities, were acquitted and Mr Mansur, who was charged with drugs offences, was convicted. The applicants complained that the length of the proceedings violated their right to trial within a reasonable time, as guaranteed by Article 6(1), and that the length of their pre-trial detention violated Article 5(3), which provides:

> Everyone arrested or detained in accordance with the provisions of paragraph 1(*c*) of this Article shall be brought promptly before a judge or other officer authorized by law to exercise judicial power and shall be entitled to trial within a reasonable time or to release pending trial. Release may be conditioned by guarantees to appear for trial.

A complicating factor was that in both cases Turkey's acceptance of the Court's jurisdiction had been made during the period of pre-trial detention and was not retrospective.[123] The Government submitted that this meant that the Court lacked jurisdiction *ratione temporis*, but the argument was rejected. Holding that events after the declaration were subject to review by the Convention institutions and that in examining the complaints under Articles 5(3) and 6(1) it should take account of the state of the proceedings when the declaration came into effect, the Court decided that the periods of detention and length of the proceedings had violated the Convention in both cases.[124]

Protection against retroactive law (Article 7(1))—application to imprisonment for default—just satisfaction (Article 50)

Case No. 42. Jamil case.[125] In this case, which concerned France, the Court held that there had been a violation of Article 7(1) of the Convention. As just satisfaction the Government was ordered to pay the applicant 50,000 francs in respect of his costs and expenses.

In June 1987 the applicant was convicted of a serious drugs offence and sentenced to a long term of imprisonment and a large customs fine. Under the legislation then in force if the applicant failed to pay the fine he would be liable to a maximum of four months' further imprisonment. In December 1987 a law was passed increasing this period to two years, and in 1989 the Court of Cassation held that this applied to the applicant retrospectively.

In his application to Strasbourg Mr Jamil claimed that the above decision violated his rights under Article 7(1) of the Convention, which was quoted in

[123] For the text of Turkey's declaration, see Case No. 16, above.

[124] In the *Yağci and Sargin* case the overall length of the pre-trial detention was twenty-nine months, including three after Turkey's declaration. In the *Mansur* case the corresponding periods were six years four months and thirteen months. As regards the length of proceedings, the relevant periods were four and a half years and two years (*Yağci and Sargin* case), and eight years and one year three months (*Mansur* case). Judge Gölcüklü voted against the decision in the *Yağci and Sargin* case on the ground that the Court's approach had rendered Turkey's limitation *ratione temporis* devoid of practical effect.

[125] ECHR, judgment of 8 June 1995, Series A, No. 320, decided by a Chamber.

Case No. 12. The Government maintained that Article 7(1) had no application since imprisonment in default was not a penalty, but a sanction imposed for failure to comply with a pecuniary order. Not surprisingly, the Court rejected this argument. Following the approach adopted in the *Welch* case (Case No. 12 above), the Court found that in substance the sanction it was dealing with here was indeed a penalty. It therefore agreed with the Commission that its retrospective application had violated the Convention.

Right to respect for family life (Article 8)—application to deportation decision—just satisfaction (Article 50)

Case No. 43. Nasri case.[126] In this case, which concerned France, the Court held unanimously that there would be a violation of Article 8 of the Convention, if the decision to deport the applicant were to be implemented.

The applicant, an Algerian deaf-mute, came with his family to France in 1965 when he was five years old. By 1987 he had accumulated a substantial criminal record, including a conviction for participating in a gang rape, and in that year the Minister of the Interior ordered him to be deported, the order subsequently being confirmed by the courts. In his application to Strasbourg Mr Nasri relied on Article 8 of the Convention, which was quoted in Case No. 4 and on Article 3, which prohibits torture and 'inhuman or degrading treatment or punishment'. The main question for the European Court was whether Mr Nasri's deportation could be regarded as 'necessary in a democratic society', having regard on the one hand to his appalling criminal record, and on the other to his handicap, his illiteracy, his dependence on his family and his lack of ties with Algeria. In the light of the above special circumstances, the Court agreed with the Commission that his deportation would violate Article 8,[127] and by 7 votes to 2 decided that it was unnecessary to consider his claim under Article 3.[128] As regards the issue of just satisfaction, it held that it had no power to annul the deportation order, as the applicant had requested.

Right to take proceedings to determine the lawfulness of detention (Article 5(4))—equality of arms—just satisfaction (Article 50)

Case No. 44. Kampanis case.[129] The Court held unanimously that Article 5(4) of the Convention was violated when the applicant was denied an opportunity to participate in proceedings in the Greek courts relating to his pre-trial detention. As just satisfaction the Government was ordered to pay the applicant 1,400,000 drachmas in respect of his costs and expenses.

The applicant, a company director, was remanded in custody on a series of

[126] ECHR, judgment of 13 July 1995, Series A, No. 324, decided by a Chamber.

[127] Judges Pettiti and Wildhaber examined the scope of Article 8 further in separate opinions. For an earlier case of this type, which divided the Court, see the *Beldjoudi* case, Series A, No. 234A, and this *Year Book*, 63 (1992), p. 572.

[128] Judges De Meyer and Morenilla voted against the judgment on this point and explained their votes in partly dissenting opinions. The Commission had upheld the applicant's claim on this point.

[129] ECHR, judgment of 13 July 1995, Series A, No. 325, decided by a Chamber.

fraud charges. Various applications for release were refused, including applications made in December 1990, January 1991 and March 1991, and eventually in July 1994 he was convicted and sentenced to a term of imprisonment. In his application to Strasbourg Mr Kampanis complained *inter alia* that the handling of his requests for release had violated Article 5(4) of the Convention, which was quoted in Case No. 7.

Reviewing the facts in the light of the principles laid down in its case law, the Court rejected the claim in relation to the first and the third applications for release, but upheld it in relation to the application of January 1991, because on that occasion the applicant had not been allowed to see the prosecutor's submissions. Finding that in the circumstances of the case this amounted to a failure to respect the principle of equality of arms, the Court concluded that in relation to that set of proceedings there had been a violation of the applicant's rights under Article 5(4).

Pre-trial detention (Article 5(3))—relevance of the 'clean hands' doctrine

Case No. 45. Van der Tang case.[130] In this case, which concerned Spain, the Court held unanimously that a long period of pre-trial detention had not violated Article 5(3) of the Convention.

The applicant in this case was a Dutch lorry driver who was arrested in Spain in May 1989 when his vehicle was found to contain a large quantity of hashish and a pistol. After several unsuccessful applications for bail, he was eventually released from detention in July 1992 and then absconded to the Netherlands in violation of the conditions attached to his release. He was tried *in absentia*, along with others, in September 1993, but did not return to Spain.

At Strasbourg the applicant argued that his detention for a period of more than three years violated his rights under Article 5(3) of the Convention.[131] The Court, however, rejected the argument on the grounds that the risk of the applicant's absconding was a relevant and sufficient ground for refusing his repeated applications for release, and that the authorities' decision to join the applicant's case to a nation-wide investigation of drug-trafficking, which had delayed his trial, was not unreasonable in the circumstances. In an unusual preliminary objection the Government submitted that by absconding the applicant had forfeited his right to have his case considered at Strasbourg, but the Court, pointing out that the complaint related to the period before the applicant absconded, rejected this dubious invocation of the 'clean hands' doctrine.[132]

[130] ECHR, judgment of 13 July 1995, Series A, No. 326, decided by a Chamber.

[131] For the text of Article 5(3), see Cases Nos. 40 and 41, above.

[132] The decision on this point was by 8 votes to 1. In a separate opinion, Judge Morenilla explained that he had voted against the decision because in his view the applicant's flight had disqualified him from relying on the Convention.

Case No. 46. Kerojärvi case.[133] The Court held unanimously that the failure of the Finnish Supreme Court to make certain documents available to the applicant gave rise to a violation of his right to a fair trial, as guaranteed by Article 6(1) of the Convention. As just satisfaction the Government was ordered to pay the applicant 73,144 Finnish marks in respect of his costs and expenses, less the amount already received from the Council of Europe by way of legal aid.

The applicant, a disabled war veteran, claimed a military pension, but after investigating the matter the Insurance Court and the Finnish Supreme Court both rejected the claim. During the proceedings both bodies examined medical files and other documentation, which, in accordance with the usual practice, were not communicated to the applicant. The applicant claimed that the failure to give him access to the documentation violated his rights under Article 6(1), and the Court and the Commission agreed. Although the Convention was not in force for Finland at the time of the hearing before the Insurance Court,[134] it was in force when the case was considered by the Supreme Court. The European Court therefore decided that as the applicant's claim was covered by Article 6(1), his right to a fair trial had been violated.[135]

Part Three: Decisions on the Issue of Just Satisfaction

Case No. 47. Schuler-Zgraggen v. *Netherlands*, ECHR, judgment of 31 January 1995, Series A, No. 305A, decided by a Chamber. Compensation in respect of damage awarded by 7 votes to 2. Judges Bernhardt and Wildhaber dissented on the ground that the award of a pension to the applicant had removed the need for compensation. For the Court's decision on the merits, finding a violation of Article 14 of the Convention in conjunction with Article 6(1), see ECHR, judgment of 24 June 1993, Series A, No. 263, and this *Year Book*, 64 (1993), p. 530.

Case No. 48. Hentrich v. *France*, ECHR, judgment of 3 July 1995, Series A, No. 322, decided by a Chamber. Compensation in respect of damage awarded by 8 votes to 1, together with costs and expenses and interest unanimously. Judge Martens dissented on the ground that the Court should have obtained an expert valuation of the land in question, instead of relying on equitable considerations. For the Court's decision on the merits, finding that there had been breaches of Article 1 of Protocol No. 1 and Article 6(1) of the Convention, see Case No. 22 above.

[133] ECHR, judgment of 19 July 1995, Series A, No. 328, decided by a Chamber.

[134] The Convention entered into force for Finland in May 1990, one month before the rejection of the applicant's case by the Supreme Court.

[135] Judge Pekkanen gave a short concurring opinion.

PART FOUR: CASES IN WHICH THERE WAS NO DECISION ON THE MERITS

Case No. 49. Demai v. *France*, ECHR, judgment of 28 October 1994, Series A, No. 289C, decided by a Chamber. Application based on Article 6(1) of the Convention struck out following a friendly settlement, providing for the payment of compensation (Rule 49(2)).[136]

Case No. 50. Friedl v. *Austria*, ECHR, judgment of 31 January 1995, Series A, No. 305B, decided by a Chamber. Application based on Articles 8 and 13 of the Convention struck out following a friendly settlement providing for the payment of compensation and the destruction of photographs taken at a demonstration (Rule 49(2)).

Case No. 51. Marlhens v. *France*, ECHR, judgment of 24 May 1995, Series A, No. 317, decided by a Chamber. Application based on Article 6(1) of the Convention struck out following a friendly settlement, providing for the payment of compensation (Rule 49(2)).

Case No. 52. Kefalas v. *Greece*, ECHR, judgment of 8 June 1995, Series A, No. 318, decided by a Chamber. Application based on Article 6(1) of the Convention rejected on the ground that the Convention institutions lacked jurisdiction *ratione temporis* because, when making its declaration under Article 25, Greece had recognized the Commission's competence only in relation to acts, decisions, facts or events subsequent to 20 November 1985.

Case No. 53. Morganti v. *France*, ECHR, judgment of 13 July 1995, Series A, No. 327, decided by a Chamber. Application based on Article 5(3) of the Convention held to be inadmissible because the Government had referred the case to the Court more than three months after the Commission's report had been sent to the Committee of Ministers (Article 32(1) of the Convention requires cases to be referred 'within a period of three months').

J. G. MERRILLS

[136] Rule 49(2) provides:

'When the Chamber is informed of a friendly settlement, arrangement or other fact of a kind to provide a solution of the matter, it may, after consulting, if necessary, the Parties, the Delegates of the Commission and the applicant, strike the case out of the list.

The same shall apply where the circumstances warrant the conclusion that the applicant does not intend to pursue his complaints or if, for any other reason, further examination of the case is not justified.'

DECISIONS OF THE COURT OF JUSTICE OF THE EUROPEAN COMMUNITIES DURING 1995*

I. *Bananas—common organization of the market—import regime—assessment of validity—bananas—Article 95 of the EC Treaty—internal taxation—direct effect of provisions of the GATT and Lomé Convention—bananas—GATT—WTO—Framework Agreement on bananas—Opinion Article 228(6) of the EC Treaty—competence of the Community or one of its institutions to participate in the third decision of the OECD on national treatment—Article 113 of the Treaty—exclusive or joint competence—international relations—Former Republic of Yugoslavia—international tensions constituting threat of war—action under Article 225 of the EC Treaty*

I.1 *Case C–466/93, Atlanta Fruchthandelsgesellschaft mbH and others* v. *Bundesamt für Ernahrung und Forstwirtschaft*, 9 November 1995. Atlanta Fruchthandelsgesellschaft mbH and a number of other companies in the Atlanta group ('Atlanta') received from the Bundesamt für Ernahrung und Fortswirtschaft (the Federal Office of Food and Forestry) ('Bundesamt') provisional import quotas for third-country bananas. Atlanta who were traditional importers of third country bananas were dissatisfied with the terms of the quotas offered to them and accordingly complained. The Verwaltungsgericht of Frankfurt am Main who heard Atlanta's application against the rejection of these complaints referred two questions to the Court of Justice on the validity of Title IV and Article 21(2) of Council Regulation (EEC) No. 404/93 of 13 February 1993 on the common organization of the market in bananas.[1]

The background to this reference may be found in the opposition of the German Government and German banana importers to the adoption of Regulation 404/93. Bananas grown in the Community and those imported from ACP States are appreciably more expensive than those emanating from other sources. Under the Protocol annexed to the Implementing Convention on the Association of the Overseas Countries and Territories with the Community provided pursuant to Article 136 of the Treaty, Germany had enjoyed a special arrangement, allowing it to import an annual quota of bananas free of customs duty. That privilege was discontinued when the Regulation was adopted,[2] whereupon Germany applied to the Court of Justice for its annulment. By its judgment of 5 October 1994 in Case C–280/93, *Germany* v. *Council*,[3] the Court of Justice dismissed this application as unfounded.

In the present case, the Court of Justice found, consistently with its decision in Case C–280/93, *Germany* v. *Council*, that examination of Title IV and Article 21(2) of Regulation 404/93 had disclosed no basis upon which it could be

[1] OJ, 1993, L47, p. 1.

[2] Under Article 21(2).

[3] [1994] ECR I–4973, summarized in 'Decisions of the Court of Justice of the European Communities during 1994', this *Year Book*, 65 (1994), pp. 552–5.

declared invalid. The Court noted that most of the national court's questions had been covered by pleas relied on by Germany in its application for annulment of the Regulation. Moreover, neither the order for reference nor the observations submitted added anything to the Court's finding in its previous judgment. In particular, difficulties alleged by the applicants in applying the Regulation could not affect its validity.

The Court, however, did examine one new point. This was an alleged breach of Article 190 of the Treaty[4] on the ground that the Council did not provide an appropriate statement of reasons for raising the import duty on bananas and subdividing the tariff quota. In this respect, the Court noted that the eleventh recital in the preamble made it clear that imports not falling within the tariff quota are to be subject to sufficiently high rates of duty to permit Community production and the import of ACP bananas to take place in acceptable conditions, and that the 13th and 14th recitals to the preamble to the Regulation unequivocally demonstrated the reasons for sub-dividing the tariff quota. Accordingly, Atlanta's argument that the Regulation was invalid was rejected.

I.2 *Case C–469/93, Amministrazione delle Finanze dello Stato* v. *Chiquita Italia SpA*, 12 December 1995. The Tribunal di Trieste, Italy referred two questions to the Court of Justice under Article 177 of the EC Treaty asking, first, whether provisions of the GATT and the Lomé Convention can produce direct effects enforceable by individuals, and second, whether, if these provisions were directly effective, an Italian tax on the consumption of fresh bananas imported from non-member countries which are parties to the GATT or to the ACP-Lomé Conventions should disapplied by the national court.

The case arose as a result of two judgments of the Court of Justice in Case 193/85, *Co-Frutta* v. *Amministrazione delle Finanze dello Stato*,[5] and Case 184/85, *Commission* v. *Italy*,[6] in which the Court had held that an Italian tax on the consumption of bananas which was applicable to bananas originating in other Member States was incompatible with Article 95 of the EC Treaty. On the basis of those judgments, Chiquita Italia had sought an order from the Tribunal di Trieste declaring that it could bring into Italy consignments of bananas from Colombia, Honduras and Saint Lucia without paying the tax. The application was granted. However, subsquently, the Italian Ministry of Finance brought two actions before the Italian court seeking a declaration that the tax was lawful to the extent that it was applicable to bananas originating in other Member States or those in free circulation. Whilst proceedings before the Tribunal di Trieste were taking place, the Court of Justice delivered its judgment in Joined Cases C–228/90 to C–234/90, C–339/90 and C–353/90, *Simba and others*,[7] in which the Court held that although the Treaty did not itself prohibit discrimination in the imposition of taxes to products originating from non-member States, account must be taken of international agreements in force between the

[4] Which provides: 'Regulations, directives and decisions adopted jointly by the European Parliament and the Council, and such acts adopted by the Council or the Commission, shall state the reasons on which they are based and shall refer to any proposals or opinions which were required to be obtained pursuant to this Treaty.'

[5] [1987] ECR 2085.

[6] [1987] ECR 2013.

[7] [1992] ECR I–3713.

Community and the non-member countries which might contain clauses affecting that conclusion. The Court also held that it was a matter for the national courts after seeking, if necessary, an interpretation from the Court of Justice on the provisions of the international agreements to determine whether a Member State was prohibited from levying a duty such as the consumption tax on bananas imported directly from the non-member countries concerned.

In response to that judgment, Chiquita paid the tax in respect of bananas originating from Honduras but refused to pay the tax on Colombian and Saint Lucian bananas on the grounds that the levying of the tax was incompatible with Article III of the GATT and the provisions of the ACP-EEC Conventions.

At the beginning of its judgment, the Court of Justice clarified which of the four ACP-EEC Conventions was applicable on the facts. The Court held that since the imports which gave rise to the levying of the tax at issue took place from April 1990, the Fourth ACP-EEC Convention[8] and its Protocol No. 5 on bananas,[9] which both entered into force on 1 March 1990, applied.

The Court went on to consider whether provisions of the GATT and the Fourth ACP-EEC Convention could produce direct effects. Beginning with the GATT, the Court recalled its earlier case law[10] and concluded that the provisions of the GATT may not be invoked before the national courts of a Member State to challenge the application of national legislation. However, on the question of the direct effect of provisions of the Fourth ACP-EEC Convention, the Court came to a different conclusion, holding that the Fourth ACP-EEC Convention may contain provisions capable of producing direct effects. In this respect, the Court considered that the ACP-EEC Conventions

> are characterized by a quite appreciable imbalance in the level of obligations undertaken by the contracting parties. Their general aim is to promote the economic and social development of the non-member countries participating in them, in particular through an improvement in the conditions of access for their products to the Community market.[11]

However, relying on its earlier judgment in Case 87/75, *Bresciani* v. *Amministrazione delle Finanze*,[12] the Court concluded that the imbalance in the obligations assumed by the Community towards the Associated States which was inherent in the special nature of the Convention did not prevent some of its provisions from having direct effect.

The Court then examined whether provisions of the Fourth ACP-EEC Convention might be interpreted as prohibiting a tax on the consumption of bananas originating from EC States that are parties to that Convention.

[8] Signed at Lomé on 15 December 1989 (OJ, 1991, L229, p. 1).

[9] OJ, 1991, L229, p. 213.

[10] See Joined Cases 21/72 to 24/72, *International Fruit Company and others* v. *Produktschap voor Groenten en Fruit*, [1972] ECR 1219; Case 9/73, *Schlüter* v. *Hauptzollamt Lörrach*, [1972] ECR 1135; Case 266/81, *SIOT* v. *Ministero delle Finanze*, [1983] ECR 731; Joined Cases 267/81, 268/91 and 269/91, *SPI and SAMI*, [1983] ECR 801.

[11] At paragraph 32 of the judgment.

[12] [1976] ECR 129. This case concerned the interpretation of the Second Association Agreement between the European Economic Community and the African States and Madagascar signed at Yaoundé on 29 July 1969 (OJ, English Special Edition, Second Series, I External Relations (2)), the predecessor to the ACP-EEC Conventions.

The Court rejected arguments that the Fourth ACP-EEC Convention contained provisions having the same effect as the prohibitions contained in Articles 30 and 95 of the EC Treaty, holding:

in the absence of specific provisions relating to internal taxation, it must be held that the parties to that Convention did not intend to regulate the matter within the framework of the general trade arrangements put in place.[13]

Chiquita also argued that Article 1 of Protocol No. 5[14] constituted a 'standstill' clause capable of having direct effect. From the time that it entered into force, the clause precluded an increase in a tax such as the one in issue. Accordingly, the clause could be invoked to challenge Italian tax increases after 1 April 1976.

This argument was accepted by the Court who accordingly ruled that the ACP-EEC Conventions precluded increases in internal taxation on bananas originating in the ACP States where those increases took place after 1 April 1976 and whose effect was to put those banana exports in a situation less favourable than before, as regards access to their traditional markets and the advantages they enjoy on those markets.

I.3 *Opinion 3/94 pursuant to Article 228(6) of the EC Treaty*, 13 December 1995. Germany requested an opinion, pursuant to Article 228(6) of the Treaty,[15] on the compatibility of the Framework Agreement on Bananas concluded between the European Community and Colombia, Costa Rica, Nicaragua and Venezuela.[16]

On the substance, the German Government advanced four arguments. First, the Commission had no authority, as required under Article 228(1) of the Treaty, to negotiate the Framework Agreement; alternatively, the Commission went beyond the Council's instructions. Second, the Commission was not authorized to sign the Agreement. Third, the procedure followed was contrary to usual practice in these matters. Finally, Germany argued that the Framework Agreement contravened substantive Treaty provisions.

In its Opinion delivered on 13 December 1995, the Court of Justice declined to consider the substance of Germany's criticisms. Instead it concluded that there was no need to respond to Germany's request for the following reasons.

First, Article 228(6) was to be interpreted as precluding a request for an opinion once the Community had concluded an agreement. The Court considered that:

It would therefore be contrary to the internal logic of Article 228(6) to accept that it is appropriate for the Court to rule on the compatibility with the Treaty of an agreement

[13] At paragraph 53 of the judgment.

[14] Which provides: 'In respect of banana exports to the Community markets, no ACP State shall be placed, as regards access to its traditional markets and its advantages on those markets, in a less favourable situation than in the past or at present.'

[15] Which provides as follows: 'The Council, the Commission or a Member State may obtain the opinion of the Court of Justice as to whether an agreement envisaged is compatible with provisions of this Treaty. Where the opinion of the Court of Justice is adverse, the agreement may enter into force only in accordance with Article N of the Treaty on European Union.'

[16] Concluded on 28 March 1994. The Uruguay Round agreements, including the Community's commitments in relation to banana imorts, entered into force on 1 January 1995.

which has already been concluded, since a negative opinion would not have the legal effect prescribed by that article.[17]

Moreover, such an interpretation was consistent with the purpose of requesting an Opinion from the Court of Justice under Article 228(6), which was to forestall complications arising from the incompatibility with the Treaty of international agreements binding on the Community and not to protect the interests of the Member State or the Community institution that had requested the Opinion.[18] The preventative purpose of Article 228(6) could no longer be achieved in the case of an agreement which had already been concluded.

Finally, the Court of Justice noted that the State or Community institution which has requested the Opinion might commence proceedings seeking the annulment of the Council's decision to conclude the agreement, and could also apply for interim relief in support of such an application.

I.4 *Opinion 2/92, Third Revised Decision on National Treatment of the Council of the OECD*, 24 March 1995.[19] On 4 December 1992, the Kingdom of Belgium submitted a request for an Opinion pursuant to the second paragraph of Article 228 of the (then) EEC Treaty, first, on the legal basis to be adopted for the Council decision on participation by the Community in the Third Revised Decision on national treatment of the Council of the OECD[20] and, second, on the question whether the Community had exclusive or joint competence to participate in that decision.

The Third Revised Decision concerns, *inter alia*, the treatment to be accorded to foreign-controlled undertakings operating on the territory of OECD Member countries.[21] By the Revised Declaration,[22] the OECD countries and, so far as possible, the Community have undertaken to implement the principle of national treatment to undertakings from another OECD Member State operating in their territory.

The Council argued that the request for an Opinion was inadmissible on the grounds that a number of the questions referred related not to the question of the competence of the Community to participate in the Third Decision nor the compatibility of the Decision with the Treaty but to the quite different problem of legal base. As such, a large part of the request fell outside the scope of consultative procedure set out in Article 228. The Court of Justice rejected that argument and held that Belgium's request for an Opinion was admissible.

The Court of Justice began by considering whether participation by the Community in the Third Decision fell within the scope of the Community's exclusive competence in the field of commercial policy under Article 113 of the Treaty. In this respect, the Court noted that the national treatment rule concerned both the conditions for the participation of foreign-controlled

[17] Paragraph 13 of the judgment; see also Opinion 1/94 of 15 November 1994, [1994] ECR I–5267.

[18] See Opinion 1/75 of 11 November 1975, [1975] ECR 1355.

[19] [1995] ECR I–521.

[20] The Organization for Economic Co-operation and Development.

[21] It forms part of what is known as the Strengthened National Treatment Instrument. This is in two parts, namely the Revised Declaration on National Treatment in the 1976 Declaration on International Investment and Multi-national Enterprises, and the decisions annexed thereto, including the Third Decision.

[22] See n. 21, above.

companies in the internal economic life of the Member States as well as the conditions for trade between the Member States and non-member countries. In so far as the decision concerned conditions of trade between Member States and non-member countries, this fell within the scope of the Community's exclusive competence under Article 113. However, to the extent that the decision concerned the participation of foreign-controlled companies in intra-Community trade, such trade was governed by Community rules in the internal market and not by the common commercial policy. The Court of Justice further noted that the Third Decision covered the conditions under which foreign-controlled undertakings are involved in international transport to or from non-member countries. Such measures fell within the scope of the common transport policy and not the common commercial policy. Accordingly, the Court of Justice concluded that Article 113 did not confer exclusive competence on the Commission to participate in the Third Decision.

Next, the Court considered the Commission's argument that participation by the Community in the Third Decision could be based not only on Article 113 but also on Article 57 and, in the further alternative, on Article 100*a* of the Treaty, applying the principle laid down by the Court of Justice in the *AETR* judgment[23] and in *Opinion 1/76*,[24] according to which, in the absence of express provision in the Treaty, the external competence of the Community may be inferred. After examining the degree of internal Community legislative action in the areas covered by the Third Decision and, in particular, measures concerning the treatment to be accorded to foreign-controlled undertakings, measures empowering the institutions to negotiate with non-member countries and measures harmonizing the rules governing the right to take up activity as a self-employed person, the Court concluded that the Community did not enjoy exclusive competence to enter into international agreements covering all of the fields of activity to which the Third Decision relates. Nor could Article 235 of the Treaty in itself vest exclusive competence in the Community at Community level. Save where internal powers may only be effectively exercised in tandem with external powers,[25] internal competence may only give rise to exclusive external competence to the extent that it is exercised.

In conclusion, the Court ruled that the Community was competent to participate in the Third Revised Decision of the OECD. However, such competence was jointly shared between the Community and the Member States.

I.5 *Case C–120/94, Commission* v. *Greece*, Opinion of 6 April 1995. In April 1994, the Commission lodged an application with the Court of Justice under Article 225(2) of the Treaty seeking a declaration that the Hellenic Republic had made improper use of its powers under Article 224 of the Treaty in adopting unilateral measures on 16 February 1994, prohibiting trade in products originating in, coming from or destined for the former Yugoslav Republic of Macedonia

[23] Case 22/70, *Commission* v. *Council*, [1971] ECR 263.

[24] [1977] ECR 741.

[25] See Opinion 1/76, [1977] ECR 741, for a situation where the Court of Justice held that external competence may be based upon the Community's internal powers without the exercise of such powers by means of internal legislation being a necessary prerequisite of the exercise of that competence externally.

('FYROM'), and had breached its substantive Treaty obligations, in particular, Article 113 of the Treaty. At the same time, the Commission applied for interim measures[26] and for an order requiring the Hellenic Republic to suspend the measures adopted pending judgment in the main action. On 29 June 1994, the Court of Justice dismissed the Commission's application for interim measures.[27]

In his opinion, Advocate General Jacobs first considered whether, absent the safeguard clause contained in Article 224 of the Treaty, Greece's action would be contrary to EC law. Advocate General Jacobs considered that 'it cannot be doubted' that the embargo imposed by Greece on trade with FYROM was, in principle, incompatible with Community law, unless it fell within the scope of Article 224.

Next, Advocate General Jacobs considered whether Greece could invoke Article 224 to justify the measures taken against FYROM on the grounds that it was designed to counter 'serious internal disturbances affecting the maintenance of law and order'[28] or, alternatively, on the grounds of 'international tension constituting a threat of war'.[29] As to the first ground, the Advocate General rejected Greece's claims that the embargo was justified to counter 'serious internal disturbances'. He considered that the claims were vague and unsubstantiated, with no detail provided, and that Greece had failed to establish that the absence of a trade embargo would lead to civil disturbance on such a scale that Greece would not have sufficient means at its disposal to deal with it.

On Greece's claim that the embargo was justified on the grounds of 'international tension constituting a threat of war', however, Advocate General Jacobs came to a different conclusion. He stressed that the scope of the Court's power of review in this area was extremely limited. However, the issue for the Court of Justice to decide was whether, having regard to all the circumstances, geopolitical and historical, Greece could have some basis for considering that the strained relations between Greece and FYROM could degenerate into civil war. In this respect, the Advocate General considered that it could not be said that Greece was acting wholly unreasonably by taking the view that tension between itself and FYROM carried with it the threat of war. Accordingly, the Advocate General concluded that it would be wrong to rule that Greece could not invoke Article 224 on the grounds of serious international tension constituting a threat of war.

Finally, the Advocate General considered whether it might be alleged that Greece had made improper use of its Article 224 powers. Once more, the Advocate General stressed the limited nature of the Court of Justice's power of review under Article 225. Foreign policy was still essentially a matter for the Member State. The Advocate General further noted that the degree of autonomy left to the Member State in the field of foreign policy was in stark contrast to the integration achieved in the field of economic affairs. The sole limit placed on the autonomy of the Member State was that it must not make

[26] Pursuant to Article 186 of the Treaty.

[27] [1994] ECR I–1307; see also 'Decisions of the Court of Justice of the European Communities during 1994', this *Year Book*, 65 (1994), pp. 549–50, for a summary of the Court of Justice's ruling on interim measures in Case C–120/94.

[28] See wording of Article 224 of the Treaty.

[29] See wording of Article 224 of the Treaty.

improper use of its powers. For example, if the embargo had been imposed not to prosecute a political dispute but to protect Greece's economy or in the interests of domestic trade, such action would have been improper. However, the Advocate General concluded that there was no suggestion that these purposes had been the motivation behind the present embargo.

The Commission had also alleged that the embargo infringed the principles of equal treatment and proportionality. Advocate General Jacobs conceded that the principle of equal treatment might be applicable in principle, but rejected the Commission's argument on the facts. There was no suggestion that the ban discriminated in any way between Greek-produced goods and those produced in other Member States. As to the argument that the ban was disproportionate, the Advocate General concluded that such a view 'rests on a political analysis that the Court is ill equipped to carry out'.[30] In any event, the Advocate General concluded that the embargo was unlikely to have any perceptible impact on the competitive situation in the Community. He thus considered that Greece could not be said to have made improper use of its powers on the grounds of proportionality.

Advocate General Jacobs accordingly recommended that the Commission's application be dismissed with costs awarded against it.[31]

II. *Community law—power of national court to consider of own motion whether national law is compatible with Community law—national legislation prohibiting private undertakings from providing job placements for workers—lack of jurisdiction of the Court*

II.1 *Case C–312/93, Peterbroeck, Van Campenhout & Cie. SCS* v. *Belgian State*, 14 December 1995. Peterbroeck, Van Campenhout & Cie. SCS ('Peterbroeck') was a Belgian partnership with limited liability. A Dutch company drew an active partner's income from Peterbroeck upon which it was charged non-resident tax at the rate of 44.9%; had the income been that of a Belgian company, the tax payable would not have exceeded 42%.

Before the Brussels Cour d'Appel, Peterbroeck argued for the first time that the application to a company having its seat in the Netherlands of a rate of tax higher than that applicable to a Belgian company constituted an obstacle to the freedom of establishment guaranteed by Article 52 of the Treaty. The Belgian State contended that this plea was inadmissible because it was out of time. Under the relevant provisions of the Belgian Income Tax Code, pleas not included in the original complaint against the imposition of tax submitted to the Regional Tax Director, nor raised by the Director of his own motion, could be raised by the appellant taxpayer in its appeal to the Cour d'Appel, subject to a limitation period of 60 days running from the date of the lodging by the Director of a copy of the decision. Although these procedural rules applied to most pleas based on domestic law, Belgian case law allowed exceptions for pleas based upon a number of principles, in particular, time-bar of the right to charge tax and the force of *res judicata*.

[30] At paragraph 71 of his opinion.

[31] It is understood by the author that Case 120/94, *Commission* v. *Greece*, will be removed from the Court's register.

The Brussels Cour d'Appel considered that the raising of Article 52 of its own motion constituted a new plea. It further considered that the relevant provisions of the Belgian Income Tax Code prevented it from raising of its own motion a point which the Belgian taxpayer could no longer raise. However, doubting the compatibility with the EC Treaty of the fact that it could not consider the Article 52 plea, it made a preliminary reference to the Court of Justice under Article 177 of the EC Treaty.

The Court of Justice began its judgment by invoking the principle of co-operation set out in Article 5 of the Treaty and re-affirming its case law on the application of domestic procedural rules to rights derived by individuals from Community law,[32] that, in the absence of Community rules governing the matter, national procedural rules may be applied to safeguard rights derived from Community law as long as the application of domestic rules was non-discriminatory and did not render virtually impossible the exercise of those rights. The Court considered that the question whether a national procedural rule renders the application of national law impossible or excessively difficult:

> must be analyzed by reference to the role of that provision in the procedure, its progress and its special features, viewed as a whole, before the various national instances. In the light of that analysis the basic principles of the domestic judicial system, such as protection of the rights of defence, the principle of legal certainty and the proper conduct of procedure, must, where appropriate, be taken into consideration.[33]

The Court also noted that a rule of national law preventing a preliminary reference under Article 177 of the EC Treaty must be set aside.[34]

Applying these principles to the facts of the case, the Court concluded that, although a time limit of 60 days to lodge all pleas was not *per se* objectionable, several factors operated to make the Belgian time limit incompatible with Community law. First, the Cour d'Appel was the first court with power to make a reference under Article 177 of the EC Treaty. Second, in this case, the time limit had expired by the time that the Cour d'Appel held its hearing and thus the Court was precluded from considering the question of compatibility of its own motion. Third, no other national court subsequently hearing the proceedings could examine the issues of Community law raised. Finally, the impossibility for national courts to raise issues of Community law of their own motion did not appear to be reasonably justified by such principles as the requirement of legal certainty or the proper conduct of the procedure.

Accordingly, the Court ruled that Community law precluded a domestic procedural rule preventing a national court from considering of its own motion whether a measure of domestic law was incompatible with Community law unless that incompatibility had been invoked by the litigant within a short period.

[32] See, in particular, Case 33/76, *Rewe* v. *Landwirtschaftskammer das Saarland*, [1976] ECR 1989, paragraph 5; Case 45/76, *Comet* v. *Produktschap voor Siergewassen*, [1976] ECR 2043, paragraphs 12 to 16; Case 199/82, *Amministrazione delle Finanze dello Stato* v. *SpA San Giorgio*, [1983] ECR 3595, paragraph 12.

[33] Paragraph 14 of the judgment.

[34] Case 166/73, *Rheinmühlen* v. *Einfuhr- und Vorratsstelle für Getreide und Futtermittel*, [1974] ECR 33, paragraphs 2 and 3.

II.2 *Joined Cases C–430/93 and C–431/93, Jeroen van Schijndel* v. *Stichting Pensioenfonds voor Fysiotherapeuten, Johannes Nicolaas Cornelis van Veen* v. *Stichting Pensioenfonds voor Fysiotherapeuten*, 14 December 1995. This reference from the Hoge Raad der Nederlanden also raised issues on the power of a national court to consider of its own motion the compatibility of a rule of domestic law with Community law.

Mr van Veen and Mr Van Schijndel were both physiotherapists established in the Netherlands. They applied for exemption from compulsory membership of the Dutch occupational pension scheme for physiotherapists. Their application was refused. This decision was challenged before the Dutch courts, where, at first instance, Mr van Schijndel was successful and Mr van Veen unsuccessful. On appeal, however, the Breda Rechtbank upheld the view of the pension fund and dismissed the two appellants' claims.

Before the Hoge Raad, Mr van Schjindel and Mr van Veen contended, for the first time in the proceedings, that the Dutch appeal court should have considered, 'if necessary of its own motion', the question of the compatibility of compulsory membership of the scheme with Community law, invoking Articles 3(*f*), 5(2), 85, 86 and 90 of the EC Treaty as well as Articles 52 to 58 and 59 to 66 of the EC Treaty.

Under Dutch law, a plea in cassation excluded new arguments unless on pure points of law that did not require an examination of the facts. Moreover, although Article 48 of the Netherlands Code of Civil Procedure required a court to raise points of law, if necessary of its own motion, the principle of judicial passivity entailed that additional pleas on points of law could not require the court to go beyond the subject-matter of the dispute as defined by the parties themselves, nor rely on additional facts or circumstances. The Hoge Raad found that Mr van Veen and Mr van Schijndel were relying on facts and circumstances not established by the lower courts and not relied on by them previously. However, considering that there were doubts on the compatibility with Community law of restrictions placed upon its power to consider in cassation pleas raised for the first time based on Community law, it made a reference under Article 177 to the Court of Justice.

The Hoge Raad's first question sought to ascertain whether a national court was obliged to raise issues of Community law of its own motion. The Court of Justice's ruling was succinct: a national court was under an obligation to raise issues of Community law of its own motion if it was obliged to do so in respect of pleas based upon domestic law.

The Court then went on to consider whether such an obligation existed where the national court would be forced to abandon the passive role assigned to it by going beyond the subject matter of the dispute and by relying on matters not relied on before lower courts.

In contrast to its judgment in *Peterbroeck*, the Court ruled that the limitation on new pleas did not render the application of Community law impossible or excessively difficult and was thus not incompatible with the Treaty. The Court considered that the restriction was justified by the principle that, in a civil suit, it is for the parties themselves to take the initiative, the court being required to examine points of its own motion only in exceptional circumstances. Moreover, such a principle safeguarded the rights of the defence and ensured the proper conduct of proceedings, in particular protecting the parties from the delays caused by the examination of new pleas.

II.3 *Case C–111/94, Job Centre Coop arl*, 19 October 1995. Job Centre applied to the Tribunale Civile e Penale di Milano for confirmation of its memorandum of association in accordance with Article 2230(3) of the Italian Civil Code. The company's activities were to include serving as an intermediary on the employment market between employers and workers and the provision of temporary staff for third parties[35] both in Italy and in the rest of the Community. In Italy, the private placement and provision of temporary workers is forbidden by provisions of Italian law.[36] Job Centre considered that such a restriction was incompatible with Community law.

The Court of Justice held that it had no jurisdiction to grant the preliminary reference. An application for confirmation of a company's articles of association with a view to its registration was non-contentious. It was a purely administrative task. As such, the national court was performing a non-judicial function without being asked at the same time to settle a dispute between the parties. Only if the person seeking confirmation of a company's articles of association sought judicial review of a decision rejecting the application would the national court thus seised be regarded as exercising a judicial function, with the result that the Court of Justice would have jurisdiction to give a preliminary reference under Article 177.

III. *Competition—Article 86—abuse of a dominant position—television programme listings—copyright—Article 85 of the EC Treaty—Article 53 of the EEA Agreement—rail transport—suspension of operation of a measure—interim relief—requirement of serious and irreparable harm*

III.1 *Joined Cases C–241P and C–242/91P, Radio Telefis Eireann (RTE) and Independent Television Publications (ITP)* v. *Commission of the European Communities*, 6 April 1995.[37] This was an appeal to the Court of Justice against the judgment of the Court of First Instance of 10 July 1991 in Cases T–69/89 and T–76/89.[38] The judgment of the Court of First Instance upheld Commission Decision 89/205/EEC[39] which found, *inter alia*, that the BBC, RTE and ITP, in refusing to grant Magill TV Guide Limited licences to publish their weekly television listings in a weekly television guide, were abusing their dominant position. The decision further ordered the three organizations to put an end to that infringement by supplying third parties on request with advance weekly listings on a non-discriminatory basis and by permitting reproduction of those listings. Subsequently, by order of 11 May 1989, the President of the Court of Justice ordered suspension of the Commission decision in so far as it ordered the organizations to supply forthwith and on a non-discriminatory basis their advance weekly programme listings and ordered them to permit reproduction of the said listings.

35 In essence, it was an employment agency.
36 Law No. 264 of 29 April 1949.
37 [1995] ECR I–743.
38 [1991] ECR II–1995; [1992] 5 CMLR 302.
39 OJ, 1989, L78, p. 43.

Before the Court of Justice, RTE relied on three arguments in support of its appeal. First, it argued that the Court of First Instance had wrongly interpreted the concept of abuse of a dominant position. That argument was rejected by the Court of Justice who ruled that, contrary to the arguments advanced by RTE and Intellectual Property Owners Inc. ('IPO'), intervening, which presupposed that conduct consisting of exercise of a right classified under national law as 'copyright' could never fall within the scope of Article 86 of the Treaty, the exercise of the exclusive right granted by a 'copyright' might, in exceptional circumstances, be abusive. The Court of Justice considered that, in the present case, the appellants' refusal to provide weekly television listings in advance thus prevented the emergence on the market of a new product for which there was consumer demand, a comprehensive weekly television listings guide, and such refusal constituted an abuse under Article 86(2)(*b*) of the Treaty. Further, the Court of Justice considered that there was no objective justification for the refusal. Finally, the Court noted that by refusing to supply details of its weekly television programmes, the appellants had reserved to themselves the secondary market of weekly television guides and, accordingly, had excluded all competition on that market.

Second, RTE argued that the Court of First Instance had misapplied the concept of effects on trade between Member States. This argument too was rejected. The Court of Justice noted that the Court of First Instance found that RTE had excluded all potential competition on a geographical market consisting of one Member State (Ireland) and part of another Member State (Northern Ireland), thus affecting the structure of competition on that market. Accordingly, the Court of First Instance had been correct to find that trade between Member States must be affected.

Finally, RTE alleged that the Court of First Instance had wrongly refused to consider the effect of the Convention for the Protection of Literary and Artistic Works,[40] and, in particular Articles 9(1) and 9(2) thereof[41] as it was required to do under Article 234 of the Treaty.[42] The Court of Justice reaffirmed the finding at first instance that the Community was not a party to the Berne Convention. Further, the Court of Justice stressed that the provisions of an international agreement entered into prior to the conclusion of the Treaty or before a Member State's accession cannot be relied upon within the scope of the Treaty unless the rights of a non-member country are involved. Finally, the Paris Act, which had amended Article 9(1) and 9(2) of the Convention, had been ratified by the United Kingdom only after its accession to the Community and had still not been ratified by Ireland. Accordingly, the Court of Justice concluded that the Court of First Instance had correctly concluded that Article 9 of the Convention could not be relied upon to limit the Community's powers.

In its appeal, ITP put forward three arguments. First, it alleged for the same

[40] Concluded at Berne in 1886.

[41] Article 9(1) of the Berne Convention confers an exclusive right of reproduction on the copyright owner. Article 9(2) allows a signatory State to permit reproduction only in special circumstances provided that such reproduction does not conflict with normal exploitation of the work and does not unreasonably prejudice the legitimate interests of the author.

[42] Article 234 provides that the application of the EC Treaty may not affect rights and obligations arising from international agreements entered into by the Member States before their accession to the EC Treaty. It has been the subject of restrictive interpretation by the Court of Justice.

reasons as RTE that the Court of First Instance had wrongly characterized the concept of abuse under Article 86. In addition, it alleged that the Commission had misused its powers under Article 3 of Regulation 17[43] in ordering compulsory licensing. Finally, it argued that Article 190 of the Treaty had been infringed to the extent that the Court of First Instance held that the reasoning of the Commission decision fulfilled the conditions relating to the rights of the defence.

Both these grounds were also rejected by the Court of Justice. As to the first argument, the Court held that having found an infringement of Article 86, the Commission was entitled under Article 3 to oblige the organizations to provide the information requested. The Court of First Instance had been correct to find that such a requirement was the only way to bring the infringement to an end and had been similarly correct to find that the principle of proportionality had not been infringed As to the plea based on breach of Article 190 of the Treaty, ITP had failed to establish that the assessment of the Court of First Instance that the decision had been sufficiently reasoned to safeguard its right to a fair hearing was erroneous.

Accordingly, the Court of Justice dismissed the appeal, ordered RTE and ITP to pay the costs of the appeal lodged by them and ordered IPO, intervening, to bear its own costs and those incurred by the Commission as a result of the intervention.

III.2 *Cases T–79/95R and T–80/95R, Société Nationale des Chemins de Fer Français (SNCF) and British Railways Board (BR)* v. *Commission of the European Communities*, 12 May 1995. SNCF and BR applied to the Court of First Instance for interim measures to suspend certain conditions attached to an exemption granted to an agreement concerning rail operations in the Channel Tunnel. In 1987 SNCF and BR entered into an agreement with The Channel Tunnel Group Limited and France Manche SA ('Eurotunnel') concerning the use of the Channel Tunnel. In brief, the agreement lays down the arrangements and conditions under which BR and SNCF may use the Channel Tunnel for transit by passenger and freight trains and under which Eurotunnel may operate a shuttle train service transporting various types of vehicle and passengers. Following notification, the agreement was exempted by the Commission for a period of three years expiring on 15 November 1991.

Eurotunnel requested renewal of that exemption. By Commission Decision 94/894/EEC of 13 December 1994[44] an exemption was granted.[45] The decision listed a number of conditions attached to the grant of the exemption including a requirement that SNCF and BR surrender one quarter of their rights under the contract to use the tunnel to third-party railway undertakings. SNCF and BR have applied for annulment of the decision on the grounds, *inter alia*, that the conditions are unlawful and harmful to their interests.

[43] Regulation 17 sets out the procedural mechanism for the enforcement by the Commission of Articles 85 and 86 (OJ, 1959–1962, English Special Edition, p. 87).

[44] OJ, 1994, L354, p. 66.

[45] The Commission declared Article 85(1) of the Treaty, Article 2 of Council Regulation No. 1017/68 of 19 July 1968 applying rules of competition to transport by rail, road and inland waterway, and Article 53(1) of the EEA Agreement inapplicable to the agreement for a period of thirty years.

On the application for interim measures before the Court of First Instance, the Commission argued that the conditions were flexible, permitting BR and SNCF to use 'more than 75% of the hourly capacity if the other railway undertakings do not use the 25% of capacity remaining'. The President of the Court of First Instance accepted that the conditions were flexible but noted that it could not be ruled out that they could cause serious disadvantage to BR and SNCF in so far as they could give rise to uncertainty as to the extent and duration of the rights granted to them. Moreover, the President considered that argument advanced by BR and SNCF concerning the complex long-term planning necessary to operate services through the Channel Tunnel could not be ignored.

However, the President noted that neither the Commission nor the applicants were aware of any railway undertaking interested in obtaining the right to use part of the tunnel's capacity. In those circumstances, the President concluded that the risk of damage pleaded by BR and SNCF was too uncertain and speculative and that they had failed to demonstrate that the conditions imposed by the Commission would cause them serious and irreparable harm. Accordingly, the application for interim measures to suspend the disputed conditions was dismissed. However, the President noted that under Article 108 of the Rules of Procedure an order for interim measures may at any time be varied or cancelled if there is a change in circumstances. Consequently, should the grant of capacity occur to third party undertakings in the future, the applicants could, if the need arose, renew their application for interim measures.

IV. *Brussels Convention—interpretation of Article 5(3)—'place where harmful event occurred'—action for defamation arising from newspaper article—national legislation modelled on Brussels Convention—preliminary reference requested—lack of jurisdiction of the Court of Justice—Article 5(3)—'place where the harmful event occurred'*

IV.1 *Case 68/93, Fiona Shevill and others* v. *Press Alliance SA*, 7 March 1995.[46] In this case, the House of Lords referred several questions on the interpretation of the Brussels Convention of 27 September 1968 on Jurisdiction and the Enforcement of Judgments in Civil and Commercial Matters ('the Convention').[47] The case raised interesting issues on the interpretation of Article 5(3)[48] of the Brussels Convention which governs jurisdiction in tort claims and, in particular, the meaning of the phrase 'place where the harmful event occurred' in the context of an action for alleged defamation arising out of a newspaper article which had been distributed in several Member States.

In 1989, an article was published in the newspaper *France-Soir* concerning an operation carried out by French drug squad officers in one of the *bureaux de change* operated in Paris by Chequepoint SARL. The article mentioned the company 'Chequepoint' and also 'a young woman by the name of Fiona

[46] [1995] ECR I–415.

[47] OJ, 1972, L299, p. 32.

[48] Which provides as follows: 'Article 5. A person domiciled in a Contracting State may, in another Contracting State, be sued . . . (3) In matters relating to tort, delict or quasi-delict, in the courts for the place where the harmful event occurred.'

Shevill-Avril'. Miss Shevill, Chequepoint and a number of other companies involved considered the article defamatory in that it suggested that they were involved in the laundering of money arising from drug-trafficking. Consequently, a writ was issued in the English High Court claiming damages for libel from Press Alliance SA, publishers of *France-Soir*, in respect of copies of the newspaper distributed in France and those distributed in the other European States in which the newspaper had been distributed, including England and Wales. The pleadings were subsequently amended to delete all references to copies sold outside England and Wales.

On the question of which courts had jurisdiction to hear an action for damages for defamation in respect of a libel published in a newspaper that is distributed in several Contracting States, the Court of Justice adopted a common-sense approach. Consistent with its judgment in Case 21/76, *Bier* v. *Mines de Potasse*, and subsequent case law,[49] the plaintiff has the option of bringing its claim either in the place of the event giving rise to the damage or the place where the damage occurred.

On the facts, the Court of Justice held that the place of the event giving rise to the damage in a libel action can only be the place where the publisher of the newspaper in question was established. Moreover, the plaintiff may bring a claim in that jurisdiction in respect of the totality of harm it alleges has been suffered as a result of the libel. The Court noted that this forum will generally coincide with the general rule of jurisdiction set out at paragraph 2(1) of the Convention, that a defendant should be sued in its State of domicile.

The Court went on to consider the meaning of the phrase 'the place where the damage occurred'. On that issue, the Court held that, in the case of an international libel, damage is suffered in each place where the publication is distributed when the victim is known in those places. Accordingly, the courts in each Contracting State in which the newspaper has been distributed and in which the victim claims to have suffered damage to his reputation have jurisdiction to rule on the extent of damage suffered by the victim in that State.

The Court was also asked whether, in deciding whether it has jurisdiction under Article 5(3), a national court must apply special rules in assessing whether the event was harmful and in respect of evidence of the existence and extent of the alleged harm. On that question, the Court ruled that the court seised should apply its own substantive law under its national conflicts of law rules so long as the effectiveness of the Convention was not thereby impaired.

IV.2 *Case C–346/93, Kleinwort Benson Ltd.* v. *City of Glasgow District Council*, 28 March 1995.[50] From 1982, Kleinwort Benson and Glasgow District Council, entered into several interest rate 'swaps' contracts. In July 1991, the House of Lords ruled that local authorities lacked capacity to enter into such contracts.[51] Their action was *ultra vires* and the contracts were void *ab initio*.

Subsequently, Kleinwort Benson commenced proceedings in the English Commercial Court for restitution of monies paid by it under the void contracts.

[49] [1976] ECR 1735, paragraph 11; see also Case C–220/88, *Dumez France and Tracoba* v. *Hessische Landesbank (Helaba) and others*, [1990] ECR I–49, paragraph 17.

[50] [1995] ECR I–615.

[51] *Hazell* v. *Hammersmith and Fulham Borough Council*, [1992] 2 AC 1.

Glasgow District Council challenged the jurisdiction of the English court arguing that, under Schedule 4 of the Civil Jurisdiction and Judgments Act 1982 ('CJJA'),[52] the action should be brought in Scotland where the defendant was domiciled. In response, Kleinwort Benson argued that Glasgow District Council was being sued either 'in matters relating to a contract' or 'in matters relating to tort, delict and quasi delict' and that the English Court thus had jurisdiction under Article 5(1) or Article 5(3) of Schedule 4 to the CJJA. The matter came before the Court of Appeal who, considering that the wording of the provisions at issue was substantially identical to their counterparts under the Brussels Convention, made a reference to the Court of Justice.

The Court of Justice held that it had no jurisdiction to give the ruling requested for three reasons. First, the purpose of the ruling requested by the Court of Appeal was to determine the application of national law and not the Brussels Convention. Second, the CJJA did not contain a direct *renvoi* to the Brussels Convention but only used the Convention as a model. Therefore, the provisions could not be regarded as having been rendered applicable by national law to situations outside the scope of the Convention. Third, under the relevant provisions of the CJJA, any ruling given by the Court would not be of binding effect but merely advisory. Under the Protocol of 3 June 1971 on interpretation, the Court was only competent to give rulings that bind the national court.[53]

IV.3 *Case C–364/93, Antonio Marinari* v. *Lloyd's Bank plc and others*, 29 September 1995. This reference from the Italian Corte Suprema di Cassazione concerned once more the interpretation of Article 5(3) of the Brussels Convention as interpreted by the case law of the Court of Justice.

Mr Marinari commenced proceedings against Lloyd's Bank in the Tribunal di Pisa, Italy. Following the lodging by him of promissory notes with Lloyd's Bank in Manchester, the bank staff had notified the police and Mr Marinari had been arrested. The notes had been sequestrated. Mr Marinari claimed compensation for damage caused by the bank staff's conduct. Lloyd's Bank objected to the jurisdiction of the Italian court on the grounds that any damage suffered by Mr Marinari had occurred in England.

The Court of Justice held that, as an exception to the general principle under Article 2 of the Brussels Convention that defendants should be sued in their state of domicile, Article 5(3) and, in particular, the concept of the 'place where the damage occurred' as developed by its case law[54] could not be construed so as to grant jurisdiction to the courts of any place where a plaintiff suffered adverse consequences as a result of actual damage suffered elsewhere. Consequently, Article 5(3) did not grant jurisdiction to the courts of the place where a plaintiff

[52] This Schedule deals with the attribution of jurisdiction between England and Scotland. It substantially replicates the provisions of the Brussels Convention.

[53] The English Court of Appeal has recently itself given judgment in the case, holding that an action for restitution of monies paid under a contract that is void, owing to the fact that one of the parties lacked the capacity to enter into it, does fall within the scope of 'matters relating to a contract' under Article 5(1) of Schedule 4 to the CJJA 1982: see *Kleinwort Benson* v. *City of Glasgow District Council, The Times*, 1 February 1996.

[54] See, in particular, Case 21/76, *Bier* v. *Mines de Potasse*, [1976] ECR 1735, paragraph 11; see also Case C–220/88, *Dumez France and Tracoba* v. *Hessische Landesbank (Helaba) and others*, [1990] ECR I–49, paragraph 17.

suffered financial damage as a result of initial damage arising and suffered by him in another jurisdiction.

V. *Free movement of persons—Article 48 of the Treaty—principle of equal treatment—discrimination—taxation of the income of non-residents—Regulation (EEC) No. 1612/68—Article 12—definition of 'child'—composition of Court—decisions concerning the expulsion of nationals—Directive 64/221/EEC—decision ordering expulsion—prior opinion of the competent authority*

V.1 *Case C–279/93, Finanzamt Köln-Alstadt* v. *Roland Schumacker*, 14 February 1995.[55] Mr Schumacker lived in Belgium but worked in Germany from 15 May 1988 until 31 December 1989. His wife, who was not employed, also lived in Belgium. She drew unemployment benefit during 1988. Since 1989, however, Mr Schumacker's wages had been the household's sole income.

Mr Schumacker was liable to pay tax in Germany.[56] Under German law, workers resident in Germany were subject to taxation on all of their income but were permitted to off-set certain allowances and benefits against their liability to pay tax and, if married, were subject to special more advantageous rules of calculation. Non-resident workers were taxed only on the part of their income that arose in Germany but were not permitted the benefit of many of the deductions applicable to resident German workers. Mr Schumacker asked the German Finanzamt to calculate his tax on an equitable basis,[57] and requested that the difference between the tax that would be payable by him if he were classified as a married resident German worker and that payable by him as a non-resident worker be refunded to him.

The questions referred to the Court of Justice asked essentially whether, in a situation where a worker resident in one Member State derived his income entirely or almost exclusively from his work in another Member State and did not receive in his Member State of residence sufficient income to make him subject to direct taxation, Article 48 of the Treaty precluded the Member State in which he worked from taxing him more heavily than a resident worker, in particular, by denying him tax benefits and deductions relating to his personal and family circumstances and marital status.

The Court of Justice first considered whether Article 48 of the Treaty was capable of limiting the power of a Member State to lay down the conditions under which tax is payable by non-resident workers. The Court noted that, although at present direct taxation is not a matter regulated by the Community, the Member States must nevertheless exercise the powers retained by them in accordance with Community law. In this respect, the Court recalled its judgment in Case C–175/88, *Biehl* v. *Administration des Contributions*,[58] that the principle of equal treatment in remuneration would be rendered ineffective if it

[55] [1995] ECR I–225.

[56] Pursuant to Article 15(1) of the Double Taxation Treaty concluded between Belgium and Germany in 1967.

[57] Under paragraph 3 of the *Abgabenordnung* (the German Tax Code).

[58] [1990] ECR I–1779, paragraph 12.

could be undermined by discriminatory taxation, and also noted that under Article 7 of Council Regulation 1612/68 of 15 October 1968 on the free movement of workers within the Community,[59] workers who are nationals of a Member State must receive, in the territory of another Member State, tax benefits equivalent to national workers.

Moving on to the critical issue in the case, the Court examined whether the application of the rules at issue was discriminatory. Noting first that non-residents were, in the majority of cases, foreigners, the Court concluded that tax benefits granted only to residents of a Member State may constitute indirect discrimination on the grounds of nationality. However, the Court considered that, in the most part, the income of a non-resident worker is concentrated in the place where his personal and financial interests are centred, usually his place of residence. The situation of a resident worker was different in so far as his income was concentrated in the State where he both worked and lived. Consequently, such a difference in treatment was not discriminatory as resident and non-resident tax payers were not in a comparable situation.

The position was different, however, in the present case, where the non-resident worker derived the majority of his income in the State of his employment and not the State of his residence, with the consequence that he was unable to take advantage of tax benefits available in his State of residence as he paid no tax in that State. In such circumstances, there was no objective difference between a resident and a non-resident worker and the application of different tax rules was discriminatory, since the worker did not benefit from deductions on account of his personal and family circumstances either in his State of residence or in his State of employment.

Accordingly, the Court of Justice ruled that the application of national rules which taxed more heavily a non-resident worker than a resident worker where that non-resident worker obtained his income entirely or almost exclusively from the State of his employment was incompatible with Article 48 of the Treaty.

V.2 *Case C–7/94, Landesamt für Ausbildungsförderung Nordrhein-Westfalen* v. *Lubor Gaal*, 4 May 1995.[60] This preliminary reference from the Bundesverwaltungsgericht (Federal Administrative Court) concerned the interpretation of the word 'child' under Article 12[61] of Council Regulation 1612/68 of 15 October 1968[62] on freedom of movement for workers within the Community and, in particular, whether the interpretation to be given to 'child' was to be limited as in Articles 10(1) and 11(1) of Council Regulation 1612/68 to children under 21 years of age or dependent.

[59] OJ, English Special Edition, 1968 (II), p. 475.

[60] [1995] ECR I–1031.

[61] The first paragraph of which provides as follows: 'the children of a national of a Member State who is or has been employed in the territory of another Member State shall be admitted to that State's general educational, apprenticeship and vocational training courses under the same conditions as the nationals of that State, if such children are residing in its territory'.

[62] OJ, English Special Edition, 1968 (II), p. 475.

The Court of Justice held that the interpretation to be given to 'child' under Article 12 was not limited to children under 21 years of age or dependent.

During the oral hearing before the Court, an interesting procedural point was raised by the German Government. The German Government questioned the regularity of the composition of the Sixth Chamber of the Court[63] on the grounds that Article 165 of the EC Treaty[64] provided for Chambers of three to five judges, whereas pursuant to Decision 94/C/304/03[65] the Sixth Chamber consisted of six judges, a number for which there was no basis in the Treaty.

The objection was rejected by the Court of Justice. The Court pointed out that Article 165 was included to enable the Court to adjudicate on particular categories of cases in Chambers of three or five judges rather than sitting in plenary session.[66] However, such a provision was without prejudice to the fact that, for reasons relating to Court organization, the three or five judges assigned to determine a particular case[67] might belong to a Chamber consisting of a higher number of judges.

V.3 *Case C–175/94, The Queen* v. *Secretary of State for the Home Department, ex parte John Gallagher*, 30 November 1995. The English Court of Appeal referred two questions on Council Directive 64/221 of 25 February 1964[68] with reference to certain aspects of the procedure governing the making of expulsion orders by the Secretary of State for the Home Office under section 7(1) and (2) of the Prevention of Terrorism (Temporary Provisions) Act 1989.

Mr Gallagher had been arrested on 24 September 1991.[69] On 27 September 1991 he was served with an exclusion order on the ground that the Secretary of State was satisfied that Mr Gallagher was concerned with 'the commission, preparation or instigation of acts of terrorism connected with the affairs of Northern Ireland'. After his removal, Mr Gallagher raised objections against the exclusion order in writing to the Secretary of State.[70] Following an interview between Mr Gallagher and a person nominated by the Secretary of State at the British Embassy in Dublin, the Secretary of State reconsidered the case[71] but did not alter his decision. Mr Gallagher instituted proceedings challenging the legality of the exclusion order. On appeal, he argued in particular that his exclusion from the United Kingdom had been incompatible with Article 9 of

[63] Who decided the case.

[64] The second paragraph of which provides: 'The Court of Justice shall sit in plenary session. It may, however, form Chambers, each consisting of three or five judges, either to undertake certain preparatory inquiries or to adjudicate on particular categories of cases in accordance with rules laid down for these purposes.'

[65] Adopted by the Court on 10 October 1994 (OJ, 1994, C304, p. 1).

[66] For which a quorum of seven judges is required pursuant to Article 15 of the EEC Statute of the Court of Justice.

[67] The case at issue was decided by five judges.

[68] On the coordination of special measures concerning the movement and residence of foreign nationals which are justified on grounds of public policy, public security or public health (OJ, English Special Edition, 1963–64, p. 117).

[69] Pursuant to section 14 of the Prevention of Terrorism (Temporary Provisions) Act 1989.

[70] In accordance with paragraph 3(1) of Schedule 2 to the Act.

[71] Pursuant to paragraph 4 of Schedule 2 to the Act.

Council Directive 64/221,[72] on the grounds that he had been excluded from the United Kingdom before he could even make representations against the exclusion order or meet the person nominated by the Secretary of State. He also alleged that the person nominated to meet him was not competent to deliver the opinion required under Article 9 of the Directive.

The Court of Justice first determined which of the provisions of Article 9 it was necessary to interpret on the facts. In accordance with the Commission's submissions as accepted by the United Kingdom at the oral hearing, the Court ruled that Article 9(1) was applicable since that provision covered not only the expulsion of those persons holding a residence permit, but also the expulsion of a national of another Member State who is not required by the legislation of the host State to hold a residence permit.[73]

The first question referred to the Court of Justice asked whether the opinion of the competent authority referred to in Article 9(1) of the Directive could be delivered after the decision to expel the person had been taken. The United Kingdom had argued that the purpose of Article 9(1) of the Directive was satisfied if the persons the subject of an order are allowed to make representations to a competent authority and the Secretary of State is required, where appropriate, to reconsider his decision before the individual concerned is removed.

This argument was rejected by the Court of Justice. It stated that the distinction between Articles 9(1) and 9(2) of the Directive was that, in situations covered by Article 9(1), the opinion must be obtained before the decision is taken, whereas under Article 9(2) the opinion is obtained only after the decision is taken and if the person concerned raises objections. Accordingly, the Court of Justice ruled that Article 9(1) must be interpreted as precluding a national authority, save in cases of urgency, from taking a decision ordering expulsion before a competent authority has given its opinion.

By its second question, the Court of Appeal asked whether Article 9(1) prevented the competent authority from being appointed by the same authority that takes the decision ordering expulsion. In this respect, the Court noted that the Directive did not specify how the competent authority be appointed nor that it be appointed for a specified period. Recalling its earlier case law,[74] the Court

[72] Which provides as follows:
'1. Where there is no right of appeal to a court of law, or where such appeal may only be made in respect of the legal validity of the decision, or where the appeal cannot have suspensory effect, a decision refusing renewal of a residence permit or ordering the expulsion of the holder of a residence permit from the territory shall not be taken by the administrative authorities, save in cases of urgency, until an opinion has been obtained from a competent authority of the host country before which the person concerned enjoys such rights of defence and of assistance as the domestic law of that country provides for.

This authority shall not be the same as that empowered to take the decision refusing renewal of the residence permit or ordering expulsion.

2. Any decision refusing the issue of a first residence permit or ordering expulsion of the person concerned before the issue of the permit shall, where that person so requests, be referred for consideration to the authority whose prior opinion is required under paragraph 1. The person concerned shall then be entitled to submit his defence in person, except where this would be contrary to the interests of national security.'

[73] Irish nationals are not required to hold a residence permit to reside in the United Kingdom.

[74] Joined Cases 115/81 and 116/81, *Adoui and Cornuaille* v. *Belgium*, [1982] ECR 1665, paragraph 16; Joined Cases C–297/88 and C–197/89, *Dzodzi* v. *Belgium*, [1990] ECR I–3763, paragraph 62.

of Justice considered that, first, the competent authority was required to perform its duties in absolute independence and, second, the competent authority was required to follow a procedure enabling the person concerned to present its defence. However, it was for the national court to determine in each case whether those requirements had been fulfilled.

Finally, the Court of Justice considered formal requirements applicable to the competent authority's opinion. Although the opinion must be notified to the person concerned, the Court indicated that the opinion need not identify the members of the authority nor their professional status, since such identification was only relevant to enable the national court to determine whether the members of the authority were independent and impartial.

RICHARD PLENDER

UNITED KINGDOM MATERIALS ON INTERNATIONAL LAW 1995*

Edited by GEOFFREY MARSTON[1]

[*Editorial note*: Attention is drawn to the editorial note in UKMIL 1983, p. 361. The publication schedule of the present edition of UKMIL has permitted the citation of the definitive column references in the bound volumes of the Parliamentary Debates.]

INDEX[2]

[1] LL.M, Ph.D (Lond.): Lecturer in Law, University of Cambridge; Fellow of Sidney Sussex College. The assistance of Mr A. Aust, CMG, Legal Counsellor, Foreign and Commonwealth Office, the Treaty and News Departments, Foreign and Commonwealth Office, and the staff of the Official Publications Department, University Library, Cambridge, is gratefully acknowledged.

[2] Based on the *Model Plan for the Classification of Documents concerning State Practice in the field of Public International Law* adopted by the Committee of Ministers of the Council of Europe in Resolution (68) 17 of 28 June 1968. For a more detailed index of subject-matter, readers are referred to the general index to this volume.

Abbreviations

HC Debs	*Hansard*, House of Commons Debates (6th series)
HL Debs	*Hansard*, House of Lords Debates (5th series)
Cmnd	Command Paper (5th series)
Cm	Command Paper (6th series)
UKMIL	*United Kingdom Materials on International Law*
TS	*United Kingdom Treaty Series*
EC	European Community

EU European Union
FCO Foreign and Commonwealth Office
WA Written Answers

Part One: I. *International law in general—nature, basis, purpose*

In June 1995, the UK Government submitted a written statement to the International Court of Justice in the course of proceedings arising out of a request made by the UN General Assembly for an advisory opinion on the legality of the threat or use of nuclear weapons. The statement contained the following paragraphs:

3.3 The question addressed to the Court is whether the threat or use of nuclear weapons is in any circumstance *permitted* under international law. It is, however, axiomatic that, in the absence of a prohibitive rule opposable to a particular State, the conduct of the State in question must be permissible.[39] Properly, therefore, the question should be whether the threat or use of nuclear weapons is *prohibited* by any rule of international law. In contrast, the question as formulated is implicitly cast in terms of a presumption of illegality, rebuttable on proof that the conduct in question is permitted.

[39] This principle was recently given specific application and endorsed by the Court in the *Nicaragua* case in the following terms:

> '. . . in international law there are no rules, other than such rules as may be accepted by the State concerned, by treaty or otherwise, whereby the level of armaments of a sovereign State can be limited, and this principle is valid for all States without exception.' (*Military and Paramilitary Activities in and Against Nicaragua* (Merits), ICJ Reports, 1986, p. 14, at paragraph 269.)

The principle stated in the text flows in some measure from the often quoted statement of the Permanent Court in the *Lotus* case that international law leaves to States 'a wide measure of discretion which is only limited in certain cases by prohibitive rules' (PCIJ Reports, Series A, No. 10, at p. 19). The principle does not, however, rely thereon but draws its support from the more general proposition that the basis of international law is 'the express or tacit consent of States to the body of rules comprising international law as a whole at any particular time' (Jennings and Watts, *Oppenheim's International Law* (9th ed., 1992), vol. I, paragraph 5).

3.4 Flowing from this presumption of illegality is an almost imperceptible shifting in the burden of proof from those seeking to show that the conduct in question is prohibited to those seeking to show that it is permitted. In other words, contrary to accepted principles of international law, the formulation of the question places the burden on those seeking to show that the threat or use of nuclear weapons may in some circumstances be permissible to prove this to be the case. In the United Kingdom's view, it is for those contending for a prohibitive rule to prove that it exists and that it is opposable to other States. In the event that the Court decides to respond to the request for an advisory opinion, the correct interpretation of the question would therefore be whether the threat or use of nuclear weapons is in any circumstance *prohibited* by any rule of international law. In the absence of proof that this is so, it would follow that the conduct in question is lawful.

(Statement, pp. 21–2; text provided by the FCO)

Part One: II. D. 1. *International law in general—relationship between international law and internal law—implementation of international law in internal law—treaties*

On 25 January 1995, Lord Lester of Herne Hill moved the second reading in the House of Lords of the Human Rights Bill for the purpose of incorporating into internal law the European Convention on Human Rights, 1950, and its First Protocol. Speaking for the Government, the Minister of State, Home Office, Baroness Blatch, stated:

My Lords, the preservation and development of the rights and freedoms of the individual are central to effective and legitimate constitutional arrangements. . . . I welcome this opportunity to set out the Government's policy on a Bill which raises issues of great importance.

It may be helpful for me at the outset to summarise the Government's position. It is in three parts. First, we consider that our present arrangements, both in principle and in practice, provide properly and effectively throughout the United Kingdom for the securing of rights and freedoms, including but not exclusively, those in the European Convention on Human Rights. Secondly, the claimed advantages of incorporating the Convention into our domestic law are, in our assessment, few and arguable. Thirdly, and by contrast, we believe that the disadvantages of incorporation would be considerable and fundamental. Notably, incorporation would strike at the constitutional principle of parliamentary supremacy. The areas of public policy covered by the general principles set out in the convention have traditionally, and rightly, been the province of Parliament rather than the courts.

Turning then to the principle of our present arrangements, the Government do not consider that it is properly the role of our legislature to purport to confer rights and freedoms, such as those in the European Convention, which are in fact already enjoyed by all members of society. It is central to our position, which is the same position as that taken by successive governments before us, that the rights and freedoms recognised in international instruments to which the United Kingdom is party, including those in the ECHR, are inherent in the United Kingdom's legal systems, and are protected by them and by Parliament, unless removed or restricted by statute.

. . .

What is afforded is that all the national laws of the country, together with the rights backed by the European Convention, exist and are available to all our citizens. What we are talking about and what the debate has been about—and it is interesting to me, after listening to all the contributions—is not whether the citizens enjoy the protection, it is about the mechanisms, the efficiency and effectiveness of using the system. I shall say to the House that I think that in terms of the mechanisms and with all the protections of the ECHR, the arrangements that we have in place and the protection of our national law, the citizens of this country are not in any way disadvantaged. . . .

It is entirely consistent with this position that the Government attach great importance to the convention and take most seriously the United Kingdom's obligations under it. As we have been reminded earlier in this debate, the United Kingdom played a leading role in drafting the convention. Created very much with the horrors of the defeated war time regimes in mind, it was intended to give binding effect to the guarantee of various rights in the United Nations Declaration of Human Rights which had been adopted in December 1948. We were among the first states to ratify the convention, as long ago as 1951; and, again, we were among the first major countries to subscribe, nearly 30 years ago, to the right of individual petition to the European Commission of Human Rights, and to accept the compulsory jurisdiction of the European Court of Human Rights.

Our present arrangements already provide for our commitments under the convention to be taken into proper account in our governmental, legislative and judicial system. Our obligations under the convention are systematically and carefully taken into account by Ministers and officials in the formulation and application of government policy, and in the preparation of draft legislation.

As regards the courts, judgments of this House have made it clear that the United Kingdom's international human rights obligations are part of the legal context in which the judges consider themselves to operate. For example, the judgment in the case of *Salomon* v. *the Commissioners of Customs and Excise*, stated—if I may be permitted to quote from it: 'There is a prima facie presumption that Parliament does not intend to act in breach of international law, including therein specific treaty obligations; and if one of the meanings which can reasonably be ascribed to the legislation is consonant with the treaty obligations and another or others are not, the meaning which is consonant is to be preferred.'

Another test of the seriousness and importance which the Government attach to the convention is our record in remedying breaches of the convention where these occur. If I may, I shall address the contention that incorporation might further minimise such breaches more fully later in my remarks. Perhaps it may suffice for the moment for me to say that, in our view, non-incorporation is not the reason why the United Kingdom is from time to time found to be in breach of the convention. Instead, the answer to that lies partly in the broad and general provisions of the convention itself—which are inevitably subject to different and changing interpretations—and partly in the inevitability of flaws in any human contrivance. . . .

If and where the United Kingdom is found to be in breach of the convention by the European Court of Human Rights and the Committee of Ministers of the Council of Europe, effective arrangements are in place for remedying the matter. Any necessary changes in the law or administrative practice are made as soon as possible. The United Kingdom's record in this respect is second to none: of the 89 cases that are currently on the books of the Council of Ministers as awaiting substantive resolution under Article 54, only three arise from the United Kingdom, of which two relate to judgments given as recently as October 1994.

I come now to the second element in the Government's position; that is, our assessment of arguments made for incorporation. We have to ask in what respects, if any, incorporation would enhance the enjoyment in the United Kingdom of the rights and freedoms provided for in the convention. Any answer to this must entail a degree of speculation. But one objective test is to compare the United Kingdom's performance with that of other states party to the convention which have incorporated it into their domestic law. Information is available on which to compare both the extent to which, in the first place, states are found in breach of the convention; and the extent to which, in the second place, when such breaches are found, the necessary remedial action is taken by the countries concerned. By both these measures, the United Kingdom's record is good, and better than that of many countries which have incorporated the convention into their domestic law.

I noted that the noble and learned Lord, Lord Taylor, rather chided me on the possibility that I might introduce comparative figures. But I do not believe that we can dismiss this matter lightly. This debate has centred very much on speed, effectiveness, efficiency and justice for those at the receiving end. Such comparisons are very important.

We repeatedly hear claims (and we have heard them again in this debate) that the United Kingdom has a poor record before the convention institutions. In fact, such claims are ill-founded. In considering the figures for findings of violation, account should be taken both of the relative population size of states which are party to the convention and the date of acceptance of the right of individual petition. In the case of the United Kingdom, that was many years earlier than numerous other countries, including France, Italy, Portugal and Switzerland. Taking these factors into account, the United Kingdom is well down the so-called 'league table' for breaches of the convention. We are 15th overall, below many countries which have incorporated the convention into their domestic law, including Switzerland, Italy, Austria, Belgium, the Netherlands, Portugal, France and Finland.

Comparative information on practice in taking action to remedy breaches of the convention tells a similar story. I noted earlier that the United Kingdom has an excellent record in this regard. Information provided by the European Commission of Human Rights shows that the majority of cases in which remedial action is outstanding arise from Italy, France, Belgium, Greece and the Netherlands. What all these countries have in common is that they have incorporated the convention.

Comparative information also casts doubt on the contention that non-incorporation places citizens at a real disadvantage in seeking to remedy possible breaches of the convention. It is far from certain that being able to litigate the convention in our courts would lead to a reduction in the number of cases, or to more rapid disposal and resolution of cases overall.

Although alleged violations of the convention may be considered in the domestic courts of countries where it forms a part of the law, what happens is that a large number of those cases still find their way to the European Commission and Court of Human Rights, where they must be examined afresh. For example, in 1994 62 allegations of violation were referred to the Austrian Government; 723 allegations to the Turkish Government; 118 allegations to the French Government, and 356 allegations to the Italian Government. Those are all countries which have already incorporated the ECHR. During the same period 46 such allegations—only 46—were referred to the United Kingdom. That would suggest that incorporation is hardly a way of reducing or speeding up the handling of cases.

Finally, as regards perceived merits, the delay in securing a decision or judgment under the convention, to which advocates of incorporation also sometimes refer, affects all applicants, irrespective of whether the countries concerned have or have not incorporated the convention. These delays are a matter of concern and one on which we, with other states party to the convention, have acted. Over recent years the United Kingdom has consistently played a leading role in the discussions in the Council of Europe which have resulted in various reforms of the ECHR procedures aimed at the speedier conduct of business. That work culminated most recently in Protocol 11 to the convention which provides, among other things for the present, part-time Commission and Court to be replaced by a single permanent court. The United Kingdom signed Protocol 11 as soon as it was available for signature. That was last May. We ratified the protocol last month, making us the fourth of the 33 states party to the convention to do so.

I come now to the disadvantages of incorporation which, as I indicated, the Government find serious and conclusive. As I have already said—and I make no apology for repeating—incorporation would strike at the long-held principle of parliamentary sovereignty which lies at the heart of our system of parliamentary democracy. The areas of public policy covered by the general principles set out in the convention have traditionally, and rightly, been the province of Parliament rather than the courts. Under our constitutional arrangements, it is for Parliament to enact detailed legislation on matters affecting the rights and liberties of the individual and to decide where the often difficult balance between competing public and individual interests is to be struck. In doing so, of course, it must have regard to the United Kingdom's obligations under the convention, as indeed it must in respect of all the United Kingdom's international obligations. Nevertheless, the final decision on such matters remains with Parliament. In our view they should continue to remain with Parliament.

That is a vital merit of our present arrangements. They provide that, if and when change is needed, often in areas of keen social and public interest, it is our democratically elected and accountable Parliament which decides how and when any such changes should be made. Among other things, that helps to ensure that change carries public support and understanding.

By contrast, to incorporate the convention into domestic law would transfer that final responsibility to the judiciary. United Kingdom judges would have to decide whether provisions approved in detail by Parliament, and clear in their meaning, offended against the general principles of the convention and, if so, whether effectively the courts should strike down that legislation. The question here is whether it is desirable or appropriate for these matters to rest with judges who are not directly accountable to the people rather than with democratically elected Members of Parliament. The Government's view is that the judges are not the right and appropriate people to be left with that power.

The Government also consider that incorporation would entail serous practical problems. In particular, incorporation would, in our view, have an adverse impact on the work of our courts. We could reasonably expect that, in innumerable challenges to action by public authorities, the convention would be invoked. Each complaint reaching the courts would have to be tried by reference to the principles of the convention but without the benefit of the initial screening process carried out by the Commission which currently sifts out as unfounded a very large number of cases—in excess of 80 per cent.

Further, if incorporation took the form the noble Lord's Bill proposes, the potential for allegations of 'breach of statutory duty'—a key provision in the

Bill—would be enormous: every time someone disagreed with, say, a decision by an immigration officer or social worker, proceedings for breach of statutory duty under the Bill could be instituted. These various factors could lead to a great deal of complicated and time-consuming litigation in the courts, with an inevitable effect on the conduct of other court business and without any real and corresponding improvement to human rights in practice.

The noble Lord, Lord Lester, in a very eloquent introduction to the Bill which I enjoyed, said that the courts can already strike down provisions of United Kingdom primary legislation if they conflict with European Community law. I accept that the European Court of Justice and our domestic courts can suspend the operation of UK primary legislation where it conflicts with European Community law. There is no disagreement with us there. Such cases have, however, been vary rare indeed. The nature of the international obligations which the UK assumed on joining the European Community on the one hand, and by ratifying the European Convention on Human Rights on the other, are nevertheless different. Our obligations under European Community law tend to be narrow and well defined while those under the ECHR are broad and general in nature. In joining the European Community, the United Kingdom was obliged to accept that Community law could have the effect of suspending any national law with which it conflicted. We could not have joined without accepting that. In the case of the ECHR, however, we are under no such obligation.

The convention recognises that contracting states have a choice as to whether or not to incorporate the convention in domestic law and as to how best to implement the Court decisions. If the European Court of Human Rights decides that our law does not satisfy the requirements of the convention in a particular case, it is for Parliament to decide how our domestic law should be amended. Until it is amended, it remains in force.

I submit that it is a far more satisfactory state of affairs than that proposed under Clause 1(3) of the Bill, which would give every judge and every magistrate in the country power to decide not to enforce the law of the land if he or she, by their own judgment, formed the view that any person would thereby be deprived of any of the rights and freedoms set out in the convention. That really would represent a shift of power from the sovereignty of Parliament to the judiciary.

The noble and learned Lord, Lord Taylor, mentioned that the extension of judicial review had weakened the case against incorporation. With great respect to the noble and learned Lord, that disregards the fundamental difference between judicial review and incorporation. In considering applications for judicial review, for example, the court is not concerned with the merits of a particular decision or a particular policy. It is concerned only to ensure that the appropriate procedures were followed in reaching that decision and that the decision was within the powers given by Parliament to the public body concerned. Incorporation, as proposed in the Bill, would require the courts to address the merits of decisions made by Parliament on matters of public policy and set down in detailed legislation. It would require the courts to adopt a much wider role very different from their current function in cases of judicial review.

The noble Baroness, Lady Williams of Crosby, talked as though the citizens of the United Kingdom would not enjoy the protection of the ECHR unless the

Bill was accepted for incorporating the ECHR into United Kingdom law. I have to remind the House that it was the United Kingdom which helped to draft the European Convention on Human Rights legislation. We were one of the first countries to sign the convention. We have a very good record, as I have set out, working within it. Whether we have incorporation or not, there is no disadvantage to United Kingdom citizens—either given the mechanisms that are in place at the moment in terms of delay or in terms of effective decisions at the end of the day. Full protection is afforded to all citizens.

The noble Baroness, Lady Williams of Crosby, implored us not to stand in the way of the international conventions but to encourage and support them. We have not stood in the path of ECHR legislation. As I say, we drafted it and we have supported it. We are bound by it and, as I have said, we have a good record of operating within it. Therefore, no citizen of this land is disadvantaged by that.

It has been my aim to indicate why we consider that incorporation is not necessary to secure the rights and freedoms protected under the European Convention on Human Rights in our country. Claims that incorporation would enhance enjoyment of those rights and freedoms are arguable and are certainly not supported by the comparative performance of countries which have incorporated the convention. There are substantial objections to incorporation both of principle and practice. The fact is that whether or not the convention has been incorporated into the domestic law of a country bears no relationship to how well that country affords legal protection for its people.

The drawbacks of incorporation are not minor matters but involve major changes to existing constitutional arrangements which have developed in this country over many hundreds of years. The Government remain unconvinced that the Bill would mark an advance in the protection of human rights in the United Kingdom sufficient to justify such a major departure from our current constitutional arrangements. Over a very long time the United Kingdom has developed a careful network of arrangements to ensure good government and fairness, including parliamentary sovereignty and full participation of both our Houses, ministerial accountability and judicial review.

To elevate the convention to the status of the primary source of good government and fairness would run the risk of upsetting the balance of arrangements for doubtful advantage, if any. This is a Private Member's Bill and the Government, therefore, would not propose to vote against it. However, the Government consider that incorporation is undesirable and unnecessary both in principle and in practice and for those reasons would not be able to support this Bill.

(HL Debs., vol. 560, cols. 1163–70: 25 January 1995)

The World Trade Organisation (Immunities and Privileges) Order 1995 entered into force on 8 February 1995. An Explanatory Note attached to the Order read as follows:

This Order confers privileges and immunities on the World Trade Organisation, its officials and representatives of Members. These privileges and immunities are conferred in accordance with the Agreement Establishing the World Trade Organisation (Cm. 2571). It will enable Her Majesty's Government to give effect to that Agreement, and will come into force on the date on which that Agreement enters into force in the United Kingdom.

(Statutory Instruments 1995, No. 266; see also Part Three: II.A.1. (c), below)

During the debate in Committee in the House of Lords on the Human Rights Bill, amendments were moved to incorporate in the Bill a provision to require the courts to construe primary and secondary legislation in accordance with the principles established by the jurisprudence of the European Court of Human Rights. The Minister of State, Home Office, Baroness Blatch, stated:

I believe the amendments betoken a recognition of the force of the Government's arguments in respect of the effects of incorporation upon the carefully balanced relationship between Parliament and the courts which lies at the heart of our tradition of parliamentary supremacy. But these amendments, although preferable in many respects to the original proposals in this Bill, do not allay the Government's anxieties on this point.

The Government's concern is that, in construing parliamentary enactments, the courts should look at the words of those enactments first, and only in the case of ambiguity should they look to see which of the possible meanings is consistent with the UK's international obligations. The amendments to Clause 1 under discussion would each (albeit in slightly different ways) increase the number of occasions in which the courts would be entitled, and indeed obliged, to look at the convention before deciding how the words of an enactment should be interpreted, even if those words are clear and unambiguous. In the Government's view, where the words of Parliament are clear, they should be given effect to by our courts.

As far as subordinate legislation is concerned—a matter to which the noble and learned Lord, Lord Browne-Wilkinson, paid particular attention at Second Reading—the courts already give the most careful scrutiny to whether such delegated legislation is within the powers given by an Act of Parliament. They can, and indeed do, strike it down if it goes beyond what Parliament intended. Should the courts be permitted to go further than this and strike down subordinate legislation because, in their view, it offends against the principles of the convention even though it is within the powers given by Parliament and even though it has in all probability been approved by Parliament under either the negative or affirmative resolution procedure? In the Government's view, the courts should not have such powers.

There is a further danger in interpreting domestic legislation, old or new, by reference to the convention. The interpretation of the rights and freedoms set out in the convention and the jurisprudence of the European Court of Human Rights and the Commission is by its nature an evolving process. It is well recognised, not least by the Strasbourg court, that the interpretation of the convention will alter over time as social and political attitudes change. The noble and learned Lord, Lord Archer of Sandwell, made reference to the difficulty of making changes where the social and political attitudes change over the time. In the Government's view, it is for Parliament to decide how best to respond to those changes, not for the judges to decide that domestic enactments, whenever passed, must now be interpreted so as to accord with developments in current European social policy.

In short, the Government consider that, even with one or other of these amendments, the Bill would amount to a significant change in the current position in providing for the convention to be litigated in the courts where now it may not be. For the reasons set out in my speech at Second Reading, the Government do not consider that such a change is necessary in order to secure the rights and freedoms protected under the European Convention on Human Rights. Nor do we believe that it would enhance the enjoyment of those rights and freedoms in this country.

(HL Debs., vol. 561, cols. 773–4: 15 February 1995)

The following question was asked of Her Majesty's Government:

Whether they consider, in the light of the decisions of the Court of Session in *Kaur* v. *Lord Advocate 1981 SLT 322* and *Moore* v. *Secretary of State for Scotland 1985 SLT 38*, that the European Convention on Human Rights has the same status in the law of Scotland as in the laws of England, Wales and Northern Ireland?

The Minister of State, Scottish Office, wrote in reply:

Yes. The decisions in the cases of *Kaur* and *Moore* were to the effect that the rights conferred by the convention were not directly enforceable by the Scottish courts because the convention was not part of the domestic law of Scotland. It is thought that a similar view would be arrived at by the courts in any other part of the United Kingdom.

(HL Debs., vol. 561, *WA 104*: 2 March 1995)

The following question was then asked:

Whether they have any plans to introduce legislation to overrule the decisions of the Court of Session in *Kaur* v. *Lord Advocate 1981 SLT 322* and *Moore* v. *Secretary of State for Scotland 1985 SLT 38*, that, in the absence of legislation, the European Convention on Human Rights plays no part in Scots law; and, if not, why not?

The same Minister wrote:

No. The decisions in *Kaur* and *Moore* reflect the well known constitutional principle that an international treaty or convention to which the United Kingdom is a party does not form part of the domestic law of any part of the United Kingdom, unless and until Parliament has legislated to give effect to it. This principle was affirmed by the House of Lords in *R.* v. *Home Secretary, ex parte Brind 1991 1 AC 696* per Lord Bridge at p. 747.

(Ibid., *WA 104–5*)

The following question was later asked of Her Majesty's Government:

Whether further to the reply . . . of 2 March (*WA 104*), they consider, in the light of the decisions of the Court of Session in *Kaur* v. *Lord Advocate* 1981

SLT 322 and *Moore* v. *Secretary of State for Scotland* 1985 SLT 38, that the European Convention on Human Rights may be relied upon in Scottish courts to resolve ambiguities in domestic legislation?

In reply, the Minister of State, Scottish Office, wrote:

There does not appear to be any decision of the Scottish courts in which they have held that the European Convention of Human Rights can or cannot be relied upon, in appropriate cases, as an aid to construction of domestic legislation. It is a matter for the Scottish courts, and ultimately for the House of Lords, to decide whether Scots law adopts the same rules of statutory interpretation which have been acknowledged to exist in an English case by the House of Lords.

(HL Debs., vol. 562, *WA 50*: 15 March 1995)

During the report stage of the debate in the House of Lords on the Human Rights Bill, the Minister of State, FCO, Baroness Blatch, stated:

The Government's position is that in construing legislative provisions, the courts should look at the words of those enactments first, and only in the case of ambiguity should they then look to see which of the possible meanings is consistent with the UK's international obligations. The amendments to Clause 1 under discussion change that position: they would enable the courts to have regard to the convention even where there was no such ambiguity. It is the Government's view that, where the words of Parliament are clear, they should be given effect to by the courts. It is not for the courts to decide that domestic enactments, whenever passed, should be interpreted so as to accord with developments in current European social policy as reflected by decisions of the court in Strasbourg. That really does constitute a shift of sovereignty.

(HL Debs., vol. 562, col. 1696: 29 March 1995)

Replying for the Government during the third reading debate in the House of Lords on the Human Rights Bill, the Minister of State, Home Office, Baroness Blatch, stated:

The guiding principle of the Bill, and of the series of stimulating debates we have enjoyed during its passage through this House, is that the preservation and development of the rights and freedoms of the individual are an essential feature of effective and legitimate constitutional arrangements. The Government wholeheartedly endorse that principle and—I must stress this—take very seriously their human rights obligations under the European Convention on Human Rights and under the other international treaties to which they are party.

What we are discussing here therefore is not ends but means. The Bill now before us would incorporate the convention into the domestic law of the United Kingdom, providing for the principles set out in the convention to serve as an aid to the construction of primary and secondary legislation and to be taken into account in equity and at common law. We have debated at length various different forms of incorporation and, as the Bill now stands, some have suggested that this particular form of incorporation would be helpful in that it would clear up existing confusion over how the courts should approach the convention without impinging upon parliamentary sovereignty.

That is simply not the case. The current position in our courts is clear: under our constitutional arrangements it is for Parliament to enact detailed and specific legislation on matters affecting the rights and liberties of the individual and for the courts to apply that legislation, having regard to the convention only where there is ambiguity. This Bill would certainly change that position. It would enable the courts to interpret legislation by reference to the convention even where there is no such ambiguity and Parliament's intention is clear and specific; and, in the case of the common law, it would apparently allow the courts to overturn long established traditions in common law which would, now, be considered to be the domain of Parliament.

It is a vital merit of our present arrangements that, if and when change of this kind is needed, it is our democratically elected and accountable Parliament which decides how and when any such changes should be made. As well as assuring proper accountability for such decisions, this helps to ensure that such changes, often in areas of keen social and public interest, carry public support and understanding.

The Government's view remains that incorporation of the convention into the domestic law of the United Kingdom would do nothing in practice to improve the enjoyment of the rights or freedoms protected under the European Convention on Human Rights. As the Secretary General of the Council of Europe himself has recently observed, these rights and freedoms are already well protected under the existing arrangements in this country. The figures speak for themselves. Given the length of time that the right of individual petition has been accepted in this country, and the size of our population, the United Kingdom's record is very much better than that of many countries which have incorporated the convention.

Nor would incorporation guarantee fewer referrals to Strasbourg, as some of your Lordships have argued; nor would it minimise the cost or waste of time or effort, as is shown very clearly when we look at the records of those countries where the convention has been incorporated into their domestic law. What happens in practice is that a large number of those cases still find their way to the European Commission and Court of Human Rights where they must be examined afresh.

I should remind the House that, in 1994, 62 allegations of violation were referred to the Austrian Government; 723 to the Turkish Government; 118 allegations to the French Government; and 356 allegations to the Italian Government. What did they all have in common? All those countries had already incorporated the European Convention on Human Rights. By contrast, 46 such allegations were referred to the United Kingdom Government during the same period. I cannot see how, from these figures, it can be argued that incorporation is a way of reducing costs or speeding up the handling of cases.

I noticed that the noble Lord, Lord Lester, referred to Germany. He was mightily selective in choosing Germany. He did not choose Italy, France, the Netherlands, Belgium, Sweden, Austria or Switzerland. France, a country with a comparable size of population to the United Kingdom, has almost as many violations as the United Kingdom despite having accepted the individual right of petition only 14 years ago. Italy, which again is of similar size to the United

Kingdom, has more than twice as many violations. Of the smaller countries, which are a quarter of the size of the United Kingdom or less—the Netherlands, Austria, Switzerland, Belgium and Sweden—all have between 20 and 27 violations. That hardly suggests that the United Kingdom has the worst record in Europe.

This hardly seems a basis upon which to make changes to constitutional arrangements which have been tried and tested over many years. No citizen in this country is denied his rights under the European Convention on Human Rights. The Government's view remains that incorporation, whatever form it takes, is undesirable and unnecessary, both in principle and in practice; and accordingly, we cannot give support to the Bill. But although it is the convention that we make known our views about the Bill, I shall not be opposing the Bill.

(HL Debs., vol. 563, cols. 1283–4: 1 May 1995)

Speaking during the second reading debate in the House of Lords on the subject of the Geneva Conventions (Amendment) Bill, introduced by a private member, the Minister of State, Home Office, Baroness Blatch, stated:

My Lords, a fortnight ago the 50th anniversary of victory in Europe was commemorated throughout the country. Indeed, it was commemorated throughout the world. It was an opportunity to remember and give thanks for the spirit and sacrifice of those who fought for the democratic ideals which we all hold dear and which were so determinedly threatened during those dark days of the last war.

During that long conflict, those in the Armed Forces and their loved ones could draw some comfort from the protection afforded by the Geneva Conventions. However, the war showed that there was a need to improve and indeed extend the scope of those Conventions, which have now been replaced by the four Geneva Conventions of 1949.

The process of improvement has been taken further with the additional protocols of 1977. Through the Conventions, a humanitarian duty towards friend and foe alike is imposed upon combatant states. The Geneva Conventions are, of course, inextricably linked in history and in practice with the Red Cross whose relief work in time of war and peace cannot be commended too highly. In this, the 125th anniversary year of the British Red Cross, it is fitting that we should be discussing ratification of the additional protocols to the Geneva Conventions which extend the protection already given to combatants under the Geneva Conventions and introduce new protections for the civilian population.

Few could argue with the general principles underlying the protocols and, indeed, the Government are committed to their ratification. As my noble friend indicated in his outstanding and telling Second Reading speech in bringing forward his Bill, domestic legislation is required before ratification can take place. Such legislation is needed in order to ensure that what are defined as 'grave breaches' of the First Protocol can be dealt with under our criminal law. My noble friend's Bill, however, goes somewhat further than is strictly required in a number of areas and in so doing raises some sensitive issues. It also has some technical deficiencies, as was pointed out by the noble Lord, Lord McIntosh, which would require amendment. Indeed, the Bill requires substantial amendment.

Clause 2, for example, provides that certain contraventions of the First Protocol, such as threatening an adversary that there shall be no survivors, shall be treated as grave breaches, although the protocol itself does not treat them as such. In these circumstances it is, in the Government's view, inappropriate and inconsistent with the approach we have taken to the Geneva Conventions more generally to seek to extend the criminal law to cover those acts which are, in any event, already likely to be covered by the general criminal law or the Armed Forces' disciplinary codes.

Clause 3 also goes further than is required for ratification by seeking to make the Defence Council the sole protecting authority for emblems instead of the function being divided between the Defence Council and the Board of Trade, as is currently the case. The current arrangements reflect the fact that the misuse of the relevant emblems often arises in a trading context and raises issues which are outside the responsibility of the Defence Council.

Those are only two examples of areas in which my noble friend's Bill goes beyond what is strictly required by the protocols and raises wider issues.

(HL Debs., vol. 564, cols. 1083–4: 25 May 1995)

In July 1995, the UK Government presented to the UN Human Rights Committee its Fourth Report in respect of Hong Kong under Article 40 of the International Covenant on Civil and Political Rights. The Report contained the following passages:

Effect of human rights instruments in national law

28. In general, and as is usual in Common Law systems, treaties which apply to Hong Kong (including human rights treaties) do not themselves have the force of law and cannot be directly invoked before the courts as the source of individual rights, though the courts will, when possible, construe domestic legislation in such a way as to avoid incompatibility with the United Kingdom's international legal obligations. The usual method of giving effect to treaty obligations (when these require some change in existing laws or practice) is to enact specific new legislation—this could be an Ordinance enacted locally, such as the Crimes (Torture) Ordinance which was enacted in 1993 to give effect in Hong Kong to the Convention Against Torture and other Cruel, Inhuman or Degrading Treatment or Punishment: alternatively, it could be an Order in Council made by the United Kingdom Government—either to amend existing legislation or to adapt existing administrative practices, as the case may require. Where this results in the creation or definition of specific legal rights and these are denied or interfered with (or there is the threat of such action), a remedy will be available in the courts through the ordinary procedures of civil litigation, or the law may provide criminal sanctions.

Bill of Rights Ordinance

29. The International Covenant on Civil and Political Rights (ICCPR) and the International Covenant on Economic, Social and Cultural Rights (ICESCR) were extended to Hong Kong in 1976. The Joint Declaration guarantees that the provisions of the two Covenants as applied to Hong Kong shall remain in force after 1997. Until recently, the provisions of the ICCPR, like those of the ICESCR, were implemented in Hong Kong as described above, that is to say, through a combination of common law, particular legislation and administrative measures. However, in view of the strong support in the community for the embodiment of basic civil and political rights in a justiciable Bill of Rights, the Hong Kong Bill of Rights Ordinance (BORO) was enacted in June 1991 specifically to give effect in local law to the provisions of the ICCPR as applied to Hong Kong. It achieves this by setting out a detailed Bill of Rights whose terms substantially correspond to those of the ICCPR and by providing that all existing and future laws must, if possible, be construed so as to conform to it and that it overrides any existing law that cannot be so construed. To complement and complete these provisions, the Letters Patent (see paragraphs 2 and 3 above) were amended so as to ensure that no law can in fact be made in Hong Kong in the future that restricts the rights and freedoms enjoyed in Hong Kong in a manner which is inconsistent with the ICCPR as applied to Hong Kong. The amendment came into operation at the same time as the BORO. . . . The relevant provision of the principal Letters Patent, Article VII(3), has since been re-numbered as Article VII(5).
30. The Letters Patent will cease to apply on 30 June 1997. However, the ICCPR (the Covenant) as applied to Hong Kong will continue in force. This is provided for in the Sino-British Joint Declaration and in article 39 of the Basic Law of the Hong Kong Special Administrative Region of the People's Republic of China. Article 39 also provides that the Covenant as applied to Hong Kong shall be implemented through the laws of the Hong Kong Special Administrative Region. Since the Boro incorporates the provisions of the Covenant as applied to Hong Kong into local law, it is considered to be fully consistent with the Basic Law and in particular with article 39.
31. The BORO further provides that no proceedings shall be held to be outside the jurisdiction of any court or tribunal on the ground that they relate to the Bill of Rights. Any court or tribunal may, in any proceedings within its jurisdiction in which a violation or threatened violation of the Bill of Rights is raised or to which it is relevant, grant such remedy or relief or make such order in respect of that violation or threatened violation as it has power to make in those proceedings and as it considers appropriate and just in the circumstances. A person may take action for breach of the BORO or allege such a breach in other proceedings, whether civil or criminal. A person may also challenge a law made after the enactment of the BORO on the basis that it is inconsistent with article VII(5) of the Letters Patent. The BORO binds the Government and all public bodies.
32. The BORO contains a provision, exactly corresponding to Article 4 of the Covenant, which permits derogation from certain of the provisions of the Bill of Rights in time of public emergency.

(Text provided by the FCO)

In reply to the question whether Parliament should debate on a free vote the incorporation of the European Convention on Human Rights into internal law as a British Bill of Rights, the Minister of State, Home Office, Baroness Blatch, stated:

> . . . in the Government's view the incorporation of the covenant, the European Convention on Human Rights or, indeed, a Bill of Rights is not necessary or desirable. I fear that they would not provide significantly greater protection for the individual than is already provided in this country. Each would transfer the responsibility for determining such matters from our elected and democratically accountable Parliament to the court, eroding the principle of parliamentary sovereignty.

(HL Debs., vol. 566, cols. 1188–9: 26 October 1995)

Her Majesty's Government was asked the following question:

> Whether they intend to take action (*a*) to meet the concern expressed by the Human Rights Committee (CCPR/C/97/Add.55, of 27th July 1995) at the extent to which the implementation of the International Covenant on Civil and Political Rights is impeded by the combined effects of the non-incorporation of the covenant into domestic law, the failure to accede to the first Optional Protocol, and the absence of a constitutional Bill of Rights, and (*b*) to give effect to the committee's recommendation that the United Kingdom 'take urgent steps to ensure that its legal machinery allows for the full implementation of the Covenant' by examining the need to incorporate the covenant into domestic law or introducing a Bill of Rights, and reviewing its position under the Optional Protocol?

In reply, the Minister of State, Home Office, wrote:

> No. The Government consider that the existing arrangements in this country already allow for full compliance with the covenant.

(HL Debs., vol. 566: *WA 142*: 30 October 1995)

Her Majesty's Government was then asked the following question:

> Whether they will introduce legislation in accordance with Article 7 of the Declaration on the Elimination of All Forms of Intolerance or of Discrimination based on Religion, produced by the United Nations General Assembly Resolution 36/55, adopted on 25th November 1981, that everyone in the United Kingdom shall be able to avail himself of the rights and freedoms set forth in the declaration; and if not, why not?

In reply, the Minister of State, Home Office, wrote:

> The Government have no plans to do so. There is no evidence to suggest that existing legislation is inadequate to deal with any problems which may exist.

(Ibid.)

In moving the second reading in the House of Commons of the Chemical Weapons Bill, the Parliamentary Under-Secretary of State, Department of Trade and Industry, Mr Phillip Oppenheim, stated:

The provisions of the Bill will enable the UK to fulfil all its convention obligations. We have done our best to respond to comments and concerns expressed during a quite lengthy consultation period.

The convention was signed in 1993 after 20 years of difficult and tortuous negotiation. It is unique in the history of arms control. It is the first treaty to provide for a verifiable worldwide ban on an entire class of weapons of mass destruction. I am pleased to say that the UK has played an active part in support of the treaty throughout the negotiations. The treaty holds the promise of ridding the world of chemical weapons. The Government take it extremely seriously and support it fully. In total, 159 states have signed the convention. We hope that many others will sign in the near future.

The convention enters force six months after 65 countries have ratified it. So far, 42 have done so. It is estimated that the convention is unlikely to enter into force until the second half of next year. Two key signatories—the United States and the Russian Federation—have yet to ratify. As they hold 90 per cent. of the world's stockpile of chemical weapons, we hope sincerely that rapid UK ratification will help to encourage these two states to ratify the convention.

(HC Debs., vol. 267, col. 810: 23 November 1995)

Part Two: I. *Sources of international law—treaties*

The following question was asked of the Secretary of State for Foreign and Commonwealth Affairs:

. . . what steps he is taking to identify all those treaties and agreements to which the United Kingdom is a signatory but of which his Department has lost sight; if he will list those treaties and agreements so far identified; if he will indicate in each case the main provisions of the treaty or agreement and the action which he now proposes to take to comply with the provisions of those treaties and agreements; and if he will make a statement?

In reply, the Parliamentary Under-Secretary of State, FCO, wrote:

Treaty records, which were opened in 1835, show that the United Kingdom is now signatory to some 2,460 multilateral and 9,273 bilateral treaties.

The treaties cover a wide range of subjects and most fall to other Government Departments to administer. Each treaty would need to be researched individually to determine its present status. The information sought is not therefore readily available from treaty records and could be provided only after lengthy research at disproportionate cost.

(HC Debs., vol. 257, WA, col. *663*: 29 March 1995)

Part Two: II. *Sources of international law—custom*

(See also Part Six: I. B. (item of 20 July 1995), below)

In June 1995, the UK Government submitted a written statement to the International Court of Justice in the course of proceedings arising out of a request made by the UN General Assembly for an advisory opinion on the legality of the threat or use of nuclear weapons. The statement contained the following paragraphs:

(a) *Customary International Law on the Environment and the Threat or Use of Nuclear Weapons*

3.113 It has also been suggested that customary international law on the environment has developed a prohibition on the use of nuclear weapons. This prohibition is said to be derived from international agreements and other texts, such as resolutions of the General Assembly and other bodies. The Court has, however, made it clear that the existence of a rule of customary law will not lightly be presumed:

> 'It is, of course, axiomatic that the material of customary international law is to be looked for primarily in the actual practice and *opinio juris* of States, even though multilateral conventions may have an important role to play in recording and defining rules deriving from custom, or indeed in developing them.'[189]

---

[189] *Continental Shelf (Libyan Arab Jamahiriya/Malta)*, ICJ Reports, 1985, p. 13, at paragraph 27.

3.114 In the present case, the practice of States in environmental matters gives no hint of a rule regarding the use, or threat of use, of nuclear weapons. Treaties on the environment which contain no reference to such weapons and in which no prohibition on their use can reasonably be implied clearly cannot be relied upon as evidence of a customary rule prohibiting the threat or use of nuclear weapons. Resolutions of the General Assembly and other bodies may be relied upon as evidence of customary international law only if they command widespread and representative support, are regarded by the States voting for them as articulating a principle of customary law and are capable of normative application. Hortatory provisions with only partial support among States cannot give rise to, or change the content of, a rule of customary law.

The statement went on to discuss the Stockholm and Rio Declarations and concluded on this point:

3.116. The fact that there is no evidence of widespread and representative support for the existence of a rule of custom prohibiting *per se* the threat or use of nuclear weapons, as well as the absence of *opinio juris* on the part of States concerning the existence of such a rule, has effectively precluded the emergence of a rule of customary international law to this effect.

(Statement, pp. 70–1 (some footnotes omitted); text provided by the FCO)

On 15 November 1995, the Attorney-General, Sir Nicholas Lyell, addressed the International Court of Justice on behalf of the UK Government. After referring to certain submissions put forward by the Foreign Minister of Australia to the effect that nuclear weapons were inherently illegal, the Attorney-General went on:

That leads me, Mr President, to reflect a little on whether that elusive ingredient of customary law, the *opinio juris*, is reliably to be gathered from the speeches in the United Nations General Assembly or even from speeches before this Court. Sometimes there may be better evidence of what States actually believe the law to be. One valuable source—I don't know whether it is inherently valuable—is their military manuals, the instructions they actually issue to their armed forces for time of war. May I quote briefly from one such manual which we referred to in our Written Submissions. It is very short. Under the heading 'nuclear weapons', it says: 'Although the United Nations General Assembly has purported to condemn all nuclear weapons as illegal, the consensus of the international community is that such weapons are not prohibited *per se*.' The extract, Mr President, is from the 'Commanders' Guide' issued to its Defence Forces by the Australian Government. And the date is March 1994.

Moving on from this point, I feel obliged to make some comment on the wholly imprecise suggestions which have been made to the Court to the effect that there is a rule of customary international law, which is somehow emerging from some other source, that outlaws the use of nuclear weapons. I must emphasise that there is no State practice, there is no *opinio juris*, which could begin to support such an assertion.

A new rule of customary law cannot, contrary to what has been claimed, be derived simply from general humanitarian principles. Nor can 'general principles of humanity' be turned into rules of law by saying that they have been recognised by this Court in its previous decisions. General principles of humanity have indeed been referred to in two decisions by this Court, in the *Corfu Channel* case and in the *Military and Paramilitary Activities* case. But one cannot stop there, at the threshold, and refrain from looking at what the Court actually decided, and what it said. In both cases what the Court decided was that there was a legal obligation to notify, for the benefit of shipping, the existence of known minefields. In each case, an obligation to warn of a known danger. This is a far cry indeed from the proposed outlawing *per se* of a lawful weapon, still less a weapon of such importance in the strategic balance. In the *Corfu Channel* case the Court did not conjure up this obligation solely out of humanitarian considerations; it said explicitly that it was basing itself on several general and well recognised principles, which included considerations of humanity, but also such principles of law as the freedom of maritime communication and the obligation of every State not knowingly to allow its territory to be used for acts contrary to the rights of other States. Similarly, in the *Military and Paramilitary Activities* case, the Court did not derive its conclusion solely from free-standing 'principles of humanity', but analysed them against the background of specific treaty provisions. Moreover, when the Court went on to consider broader obligations under international humanitarian law, it did so clearly and specifically in the context of treaties in force. Therefore, while the approach now suggested seeks to borrow a handful of words and phrases previously employed by the Court, it uses them in a way which bears not the slightest relationship to how the Court has previously handled humanitarian considerations.

This Court has on many occasions set out the real requirements of custom. There must be a coherent body of State practice. That practice must be of sufficient generality to show widespread support among States. The practice must embody a positive belief that it is required by law. Support for the existence of the rule must be evident, in particular, from States whose interests are specially affected.

In the present case *none* of these criteria are satisfied. Although some States contend for the existence of a prohibitive rule, there is no widespread and uniform body of practice in support of such a contention. Moreover, whatever practice there may be does not include the practice of States whose interests are specially affected. Specifically, nuclear-weapon States and those States on whose territory such weapons are situated have, by word and deed, disavowed the existence of such a rule. The evident disagreement on this matter before the Court is itself adequate testimony to the absence of a sufficient consistency of practice on this point.

Equally, Mr President, there is no evidence of any belief on the part of States that any such practice is required by customary international law. Although some have argued that the non-use of nuclear weapons since 1945 implies a belief that such use would be illegal this contention has no merit. I have already explained that the purpose of nuclear weapons is to deter by their very existence. The fact that a weapon has not been used is not evidence of a prohibition unless the States which refrain from such use do so because they consider themselves under an obligation not to use that weapon. That is not the case here. That States with nuclear weapons have not used them and that some *other* States consider their use would be unlawful cannot be said to create a prohibitive rule.

(Text provided by the FCO)

Later in his statement, the Attorney-General said:

In the absence of State practice and *opinio juris* sufficient for the formation of a rule of custom, there can be no rule prohibiting the use of nuclear weapons. Custom is not something which can be conjured from the air or even, in 'The Tempest', from the vasty deep. It requires evidence, particularly if it is to be relied upon to overturn a body of practice that has gone to the very heart of the defence of many States over the past fifty years. It is not something which can be assumed, or deduced from appeals to general principles of humanity.

Nor can a customary prohibition on nuclear weapons be derived from the resolutions of the General Assembly of which so much has again been made in these proceedings. In some cases, it has not been a specific instrument that has been prayed in aid but the allegedly 'cumulative effect' or 'combined weight' of a number of instruments.

Mr President, such an approach lacks any solid foundation in international law. Resolutions of the General Assembly on matters such as these do not create binding obligations for United Nations Members. While they may, in certain circumstances, be evidence of custom, a rule of custom cannot lightly be presumed. As the Court has itself said, resolutions of the General Assembly may only be relied upon as evidence of custom (i) if they command widespread and representative support, (ii) if they are regarded by States voting for them as articulating a principle of customary law, and (iii) if they are capable of normative application. Provisions which are merely hortatory and which received only partial support among States cannot be relied upon to generate a new rule or to change an existing rule of custom.

Without exception the General Assembly resolutions cited in support of the existence of a prohibitive rule of custom do not meet the standards required by this Court. The voting figures in each case indicate controversy among States on the matters in issue. (The figures are given in our written submissions.) In each case, nuclear weapon States and other States whose interests were specifically affected either voted against or abstained from voting for the resolution. This fact fatally undermines any notion that the resolutions express an *opinio juris* in favour of a prohibitive rule. Moreover, the very language of the resolutions in most cases demonstrates their hortatory nature and indicates that they are unsuitable for normative application. The resolutions cannot, therefore, be evidence of a prohibitive rule of customary law.

The approach of deducing a rule of custom from various multilateral treaties is equally flawed. The treaties relied upon for this purpose are invariably treaties for the protection of the environment. As I noted a moment ago, these treaties make no mention of nuclear weapons, let alone contain a prohibition on their use. Just as these treaties cannot be read as prohibiting the use of nuclear weapons as a matter of treaty law, so we can not extract from them a rule of customary law to that effect. If a rule of custom is to be deduced from a treaty, it is surely a prerequisite that the rule in question is identifiable, first—and this was not done—first, in the treaty itself.

So, Mr President, there remains only the 'cumulative effect' argument. With due respect to its authors, this is an argument for the Court to make law, not to state the law as it finds it. If ever there was a case in which it would be inappropriate for this Court to make the law, this is it. There is no evidence to sustain a rule of custom. There is a consensus that nuclear disarmament must proceed by negotiation. As the differing views expressed in these very proceedings attest, there is no uniformity of view to which the Court can simply add its voice.

(Text provided by the FCO)

Part Two: IX. *Sources of international law—comity*

(See Part Eight: II. D. (item of December 1994), below)

Part Two: X. *Sources of international law—acquisition, retention and loss of rights*

On 27 September 1995, the Governments of the UK and Argentina signed a Joint Declaration on co-operation over offshore activities in the South West Atlantic. Paragraph 1 of the Joint Declaration reads:

1. The Government of the United Kingdom of Great Britain and Northern Ireland and the Government of the Argentine Republic agreed that the following formula on sovereignty, based on that contained in the Joint State-

ment issued at Madrid on 19 October 1989, applies to this joint Declaration and its results:

(1) Nothing in the content of the present Joint Declaration or of any similar subsequent Joint Statements and meetings shall be interpreted as:

(a) a change in the position of the United Kingdom with regard to sovereignty or territorial and maritime jurisdiction over the Falkland Islands, South Georgia and the South Sandwich Islands and the surrounding maritime areas.

(b) a change in the position of the Argentine Republic with regard to sovereignty or territorial and maritime jurisdiction over the Falkland Islands, South Georgia and the South Sandwich Islands and the surrounding maritime areas.

(c) recognition of or support for the position of the United Kingdom or the Argentine Republic with regard to sovereignty or territorial and maritime jurisdiction over the Falkland Islands, South Georgia and the South Sandwich Islands and the surrounding maritime areas.

(2) No act or activity carried out by the United Kingdom, the Argentine Republic or third parties as a consequence and in implementation of anything agreed to in the present Joint Declaration or in any similar subsequent Joint Statements and meetings shall constitute a basis for affirming, supporting, or denying the position of the United Kingdom or the Argentine Republic regarding the sovereignty or territorial and maritime jurisdiction over the Falkland Islands, South Georgia and the South Sandwich Islands and the surrounding maritime areas. The areas subject to the controversy on sovereignty and jurisdiction will not be extended in any way as a consequence of this Joint Declaration or its implementation.

This Joint Declaration does not apply to the maritime areas surrounding South Georgia and the South Sandwich Islands.

(Text provided by the FCO)

Part Three: I. A. 1. *Subjects of international law—States—international status—sovereignty and independence*

(See also Part Eight: II. A., and Part Fourteen: I. B. 6. (item of 23 January 1995), below)

In the course of a statement following the adoption of Resolution 971 (1995) concerning the United Nations Observer Mission in Georgia (UNOMIG), the UK Permanent Representative to the UN in New York, Sir David Hannay, remarked in the UN Security Council on 12 January 1995:

The overall aim of this Council's policy is to bring about a viable and lasting settlement to the Georgian-Abkhaz conflict while fully respecting the Republic of Georgia's sovereignty and territorial integrity.

. . . UNOMIG's presence is a means to an end, not an end in itself. It is contradictory that the Abkhaz authorities on the one hand declare Abkhazia to be a sovereign State while at the same time claiming to be ready to negotiate a political settlement in accordance with the Council's past decisions. That contradiction must be resolved in a manner that respects Georgia's sovereignty and territorial integrity.

(S/3488, pp. 5–6)

On 23 January 1995, the EU Presidency issued a statement which read in part:

The European Union is committed to the sovereignty and territorial integrity of Croatia within its internationally recognized borders.

(*Bulletin of the European Union*, 1995–1/2, p. 87)

On 6 February 1995, the EU Presidency issued a statement which read in part:

The European Union reiterates its attachment to the conclusion of an overall resolution of the conflicts in the former Yugoslavia guaranteeing the sovereignty and territorial integrity of all States within their internationally recognised borders.

(Ibid., p. 87; see also ibid., 1995–5, pp. 51–2 (statement of 29 May 1995))

On 30 January 1995, the EU Presidency issued a statement which read in part as follows:

The European Union is following the situation in Afghanistan particularly closely. It wishes to express its support for the peace process initiated by the United Nations and would reiterate the importance it attaches to maintaining the territorial integrity and national independence of Afghanistan.

(*Bulletin of the European Union*, 1995–1/2, p. 81)

In reply to a question relating to the Commonwealth of Independent States, the Government spokesman in the House of Lords wrote:

Our policy is based on firm support for the sovereignty and independence of all the countries of the region, including the members of the Commonwealth of Independent States. We recognise the right of those countries to decide to conclude agreements among themselves, within the Commonwealth of Independent States and outside it.

(HL Debs., vol. 561, *WA 52*: 16 February 1995)

An FCO press statement issued on 17 February 1995 stated in part:

The UK remains committed to the sovereignty, territorial integrity and stability of the Former Yugoslav Republic of Macedonia (FYROM). It is vital that all neighbouring countries respect these principles, and cooperate fully with the Macedonian authorities to maintain them.

(Text provided by the FCO)

In the course of a debate on the subject of Belize, the Minister of State, FCO, Mr David Davies, observed:

Britain's relations with Belize go back a long way. The original British settlement was established in about 1638. From then on, the main activity was logwood cutting for the European dye industry. It was not until the treaty of Paris in 1763 that Spain conceded to British settlers the rights to engage in the logwood industry. That was reaffirmed by the treaty of Versailles of 1783 and the convention of London of 1789. In 1862, Britain designated Belize as a British colony, and called it British Honduras. It has been known as Belize since 1973.

When Guatemala became independent in 1821, she claimed that she had inherited the previous Spanish title to British Honduras. However, in 1859, Guatemala signed and ratified the UK-Guatemala treaty in which she recognised the existing boundary between Guatemala and British Honduras. In 1939, however, Guatemala denounced the 1859 treaty and claimed Belize. In 1945, the Guatemalan Government wrote into its new constitution an article to the effect that Belize was an integral part of Guatemalan territory.

Although Belize had become self-governing in 1964, the Guatemalan claim delayed the setting in train of constitutional procedures leading to full independence. In 1980, the United Nations General Assembly called on Britain to convene a constitutional conference to bring Belize to early independence.

The constitutional conference was duly convened in April 1981 and, the following September, Belize became an independent state recognised by all nations except Guatemala, which maintained its claim. Following independence, a British garrison remained in Belize, with the full support of the Belizean Government, to counter any external threat to its security.

Recent years have been momentous in Belize's independent history. In 1991, the United Kingdom, our European partners and the international community as a whole welcomed recognition of Belize as a sovereign independent country by President Serrano of Guatemala. During 1992, the Guatemalan constitutional court and congress confirmed recognition of Belize. However, they did not renounce certain territorial claims on the country. That is of continuing concern to us, and we have been encouraging the two sides to reach agreement.

(HC Debs., vol. 257, col. 1284: 30 March 1995)

Speaking on 14 April 1995 in the UN Security Council during a debate on the situation in Iraq, the UK Permanent Representative to the UN in New York, Sir David Hannay, stated:

We have been compelled in this resolution to allocate between $130 million and $150 million to be spent in the three northern Governorates of Iraq by the United Nations. This is not because the Security Council does not respect the sovereignty and territorial integrity of Iraq. We do respect Iraq's sovereignty and its territorial integrity, even if Iraq itself has not always been so respectful of its obligations in this respect towards its neighbours; and we have made our respect for those principles clear in this resolution. But it is Iraq itself that imposes an economic blockade against its three northern Governorates. The provision for the North is simply intended to ensure that the inhabitants of the three northern Governorates receive an equitable share of the humanitarian goods to be purchased with the proceeds of the oil sales. It is not politically motivated. It is simply intended to ensure that all Iraqis, and not just some of them, benefit from the sale of oil provided for in this resolution.

(S/3519, p. 12)

On 2 June 1995, the EU Presidency on behalf of the EU issued a declaration on the merging of the self-proclaimed Serbian 'Republics' of Krajina and Bosnia-Herzegovina. This stated in part:

The European Union has noted the intention expressed by the 'Parliaments' in Knin and Pale to merge the self-proclaimed Serb 'Republics' of Krajina and Bosnia-Herzegovina.

It would point out that if any such decision were taken, it would be contrary to the framework established in particular by UN Security Council Resolutions 981 of 31 March 1995 and 990 of 22 April 1995, and it warns against the risk of military escalation.

Emphasizing its commitment to the territorial integrity of Croatia and Bosnia-Herzegovina and recognition of their international frontiers, the European Union considers that such a decision would be null and void.

(Text provided by the FCO)

Her Majesty's Government were asked: 'What they regard as the attributes which characterise or define a self-governing sovereign state?' In reply, the Minister of State, FCO, wrote:

Sovereignty is an attribute which under international law resides inherently in any independent state recognised as such. By virtue and in exercise of their sovereignty, states conduct dealings with one another internationally—for example, the conclusion of treaties laying down mutual rights and obligations and the exchange of diplomatic representatives.

(HL Debs., vol. 566, *WA 85*: 16 October 1995)

In reply to the question

if the Government have raised the matter of the claim on the territory of the United Kingdom by the Irish Republic with international or regional bodies of which both countries are members,

the Secretary of State for Foreign and Commonwealth Office wrote:

No. Northern Ireland's status as part of the United Kingdom is not disputed in any international organisation of which the UK and the Republic of Ireland are both members. No purpose would therefore be served in raising the matter in any of these bodies.

(HC Debs., vol. 265, col. 65: 30 October 1995)

Part Three: I. A. 2. *Subjects of international law—States—international status—non-intervention and non-use of force*

On 2 June 1994, the UK Government submitted a written statement to the International Court of Justice in the course of proceedings arising out of a request made by the World Health Assembly for an advisory opinion on the legality of the threat or use of nuclear weapons. The statement contained the following passage:

21. In the absence of a rule of international law specifically prohibiting the use of nuclear weapons, the legality of their use has to be assessed by reference to the principles of law applicable to any use of armed force. According to these principles, the use of force is lawful only if it is in circumstances in which resort to force is permissible under the principle enshrined in the United Nations Charter and if it meets the requirements of the law of armed conflict regarding the conduct of hostilities.

(Statement, p. 77; text provided by the FCO)

The following declaration was issued by the EU Presidency on behalf of the EU on 13 February 1995:

Six years after the publication of the *fatwa* condemning the British author Salman Rushdie to death and calling for his assassination, the European Union solemnly reaffirms its condemnation of this sentence.

Decided in defiance of the Universal Declaration on Human Rights and the principle of the sovereignty of States, in particular regarding the protection by the latter of their nationals, this sentence is null and void.

The European Union renews its demand to Iranian leaders to abide by international law and accept all the consequences of doing so.

(*Bulletin of the European Union*, 1995–1/2, p. 83)

Speaking on 27 November 1995 in the Third Committee of the UN General Assembly, the representatives of Spain, on behalf of the EU, stated:

We repeat our condemnation of the *fatwa* threatening the life of Salman Rushdie. The *fatwa* is a blatant breach of international law, contrary to the Universal Declaration of Human Rights and the principle of the sovereignty of states. The European Union will spare no effort to obtain from the Government of Iran assurances that the life of Salman Rushdie will not be endangered under any circumstances.

(Text provided by the FCO)

Part Three: I. A. 3. *Subjects of international law—States—international status—domestic jurisdiction*

In reply to a question concerning the use of the death penalty for British citizens found guilty of drug trafficking abroad, the Parliamentary Under-Secretary of State, FCO, wrote:

The use of the death penalty for persons found guilty of drug trafficking abroad is a matter for those countries concerned, provided that respect is shown for the provisions on the death penalty of international human rights law. Once a British national has been sentenced to death, and all local appeals for clemency have been exhausted, we consider whether, and at what level, any further appeal should be made. Intervention is considered on a case-by-case basis.

(HC Debs., vol. 252, WA, col. *498*: 18 January 1995)

In reply to a similar question relating to Pakistan, the same Minister wrote in part:

The inclusion of provision for the death penalty as the maximum sentence for the possession, import, export or transhipment of more than 100gm of heroin—or equivalent—is a matter for the Government of Pakistan, provided that respect is shown for the provisions on the death penalty in international human rights law.

(Ibid., col. *748*: 20 January 1995)

In reply to a question to the Secretary of State for Foreign and Commonwealth Affairs asking 'what evaluation he has made of the independence of the judiciary of Singapore from the Government of Singapore in relation to cases which have political or international significance', the Minister of State, FCO, wrote:

None. The independence of the Singapore judiciary is a matter for the Singapore Government.

(HC Debs., vol. 258, WA, col. *741*: 28 April 1995; see also ibid., vol. 263, WA, col. *866*: 17 July 1995)

Part Three: I. B. 1. *Subjects of international law—States—recognition—recognition of States*

During a debate on the subject of Bosnia, the Secretary of State for Foreign and Commonwealth Affairs, Mr Douglas Hurd, stated:

Historians will argue about the timing of the recognition of Croatia and Slovenia, but no one could seriously suggest that it could have been long delayed. No one could seriously suggest that we could have gone on pretending that the old Yugoslavia still existed. We must deal with realities, and the reality was that Croatia existed. Whether it should have been recognised in the autumn, which was what the Germans wanted, or at the end of the year, which is what happened, or a little later, is a matter for dispute, but it is not relevant to the present.

(HC Debs., vol. 259, col. 332: 3 May 1995)

In reply to a question, the Minister of State, FCO, wrote:

We and our EC partners recognised Bosnia-Herzegovina on 7 April 1992 following acceptance of the report of the arbitration commission attached to the EC conference on former Yugoslavia. The US Government recognised Bosnia-

Herzegovina on the same day and the Russian Government did the same on 28 April 1992. A key factor in the EC's decision was the Bosnian Government's guarantee to respect the rights of minorities.

(HC Debs., vol. 261, WA, col. *477*: 13 June 1995)

The Secretary of State for Foreign and Commonwealth Affairs was asked to 'make a statement on the (*a*) legal and (*b*) other grounds on which Her Majesty's Government recognises a territory as a national state; and to what extent these criteria had been met when Her Majesty's Government recognised Croatia as a national state'. In reply, the Minister of State, FCO, wrote:

In recognising a national state, we take into account that a country should have a clearly defined territory with a population, a Government with a prospect of retaining control and independence in its foreign relations. These criteria are always subject to interpretation in the light of circumstances on the ground. In January 1992 we and our EC partners recognised Croatia on the basis of advice from the arbitration commission that Croatia largely fulfilled the guidelines on recognition adopted in December 1991. These were that the state to be recognised should respect the United Nations charter, guarantee the rights of minorities, respect the inviolability of frontiers except by peaceful agreement, accept commitments on disarmament, nuclear non-proliferation, security and regional stability and promise to settle by agreement questions of state succession and regional disputes.

(HC Debs., vol. 261, WA, cols. *478–9*: 13 June 1995)

In reply to the question

Whether [Her Majesty's Government] intend to commission, along with other west European governments, a study of the steps by which those governments came to recognise, and to accord permanent international boundaries to, certain component parts of the Yugoslav Federation, and how those boundaries accord with the relevant CSCE provisions and with the opinions of the citizens of these areas; and if they do not intend so to do, whether and if so how they propose to ensure that such steps are avoided on other occasions,

the Government spokesman in the House of Lords wrote:

We do not intend to commission a study. Each case of the recognition of a state is considered on its own merits.

(HL Debs., vol. 567, *WA 137*: 19 December 1995)

Part Three: I. B. 5. *Subjects of international law—States—recognition—non-recognition*

In reply to a question on the subject of Indonesia's annexation of East Timor, the Minister of State, FCO, wrote:

Our policy has been consistent throughout this period. We do not recognise Indonesia's annexation of East Timor and continue to encourage Indonesia and Portugal to work together, under the auspices of the UN Secretary-General, to find a lasting and acceptable solution to the problem. We welcome the outcome of the latest round of talks on 9 January.

(HC Debs., vol. 252, WA, col. *745*: 20 January 1995; see also ibid., vol. 253, col. 1072: 1 February 1995)

In reply to an oral question, the Prime Minister, Mr John Major, stated:

. . . we have not recognised the Indonesian annexation of East Timor. That has been our position for a long time and we continue to support the efforts of the United Nations Secretary-General to find a lasting solution to the problem. However, there is neither a European Union nor a United Nations embargo on arms sales to Indonesia, nor do I believe that one would be justified.

(HC Debs., vol. 253, col. 140: 24 January 1995)

In the course of oral questions, the Minister of State, FCO, Mr Alastair Goodlad, stated:

Since 1972, this country has recognised the People's Republic of China as the sole representative of China at the United Nations. The claims of Taiwan are not so recognised.

(HC Debs., vol. 253, col. 1071: 1 February 1995)

In the course of a debate on the subject of China and Hong Kong, the Minister of State, FCO, Mr Alastair Goodlad, stated:

One consequence of our policy of not recognising Taiwan as a state is that we cannot recognise the travel documents issued there as passports. Our practice, which is by no means unique, is to place our visas on a separate certificate of identity. I do not think that that can be seen as a serious impediment to the growth of our commercial links with Taiwan, which are flourishing, as are Taiwan's links with Japan, which has the same practice on visas. That practice in no way retards the issue of visas through the British trade and cultural office in Taipei, which is normally done within 72 hours.

(HC Debs., vol. 258, col. 1072: 27 April 1995)

In reply to a question, the Minister of State, FCO, wrote:

We do not recognise the Federal Republic of Yugoslavia (Serbia and Montenegro). We will review our position in the light of developments in the peace process.

(HC Debs., vol. 263, WA, col. *260*: 5 July 1995)

In reply to a question, the Minister of State, FCO, wrote:

The United Kingdom recognised the Republics of Croatia and Slovenia on 15 January 1992, the Republic of Bosnia-Herzegovina on 7 April 1992 and the former Yugoslav Republic of Macedonia on 8 April 1993. The United Kingdom does not recognise the statehood of the Federal Republic of Yugoslavia—Serbia and Montenegro. Succession issues, such as the division of assets and liabilities, will be resolved after the conclusion of the peace process.

(HC Debs., vol. 265, col. WA, *262*: 1 November 1995)

Part Three: I. C. 4. *Subjects of international law—States—types of States—dependent States and territories*

(See also Part Three: I. E. and Part Four: VII., below)

In reply to a question, the Minister of State, FCO, wrote:

The decision not to renew the acceptance of the right of individual petition in respect of the British Virgin Islands and the Cayman Islands under Article 25 of the European Convention on Human Rights was notified to the UN Human Rights Committee in connection with the United Kingdom's Third Periodic Report under the International Covenant on Civil and Political Rights.

(HL Debs., vol. 563, *WA 18*: 5 April 1995)

On 5 May 1995, the Governments of Hong Kong and the Federal Republic of Germany made an Agreement concerning Air Services. In respect of the draft agreement, the Secretary of State for Foreign and Commonwealth Affairs, Mr Douglas Hurd, addressed a letter dated 27 February 1995 to the Governor of Hong Kong, Mr Christopher Patten, which read as follows:

Your Excellency,

I have the honour to refer to the draft Agreement for the purpose of providing the framework for air services between Hong Kong and the Federal Republic of Germany, the text of which was negotiated during the period from September 1987 to July 1990.

The United Kingdom Government remains responsible for the external relations of Hong Kong until 30 June 1997. However, the United Kingdom Government hereby entrusts to you authority:

(*a*) to conclude the said Agreement;
(*b*) in accordance with prior specific authorisation in that behalf from the United Kingdom Government, to agree and confirm amendments to the said Agreement;
(*c*) to carry into effect and to exercise the other powers conferred upon a Contracting Party by the said Agreement.

Further, with the prior agreement of the United Kingdom Government, you may terminate the said Agreement in accordance with its terms.

If action is required to be taken relating to the international conventions referred to in the said Agreement it shall be taken either by the United Kingdom Government or, as appropriate, by the Hong Kong Government acting under the authority of the United Kingdom Government.

Following the coming into force of the said Agreement, the United Kingdom Government will register it on behalf of the Hong Kong Government.

(Special Supplement No. 5 to the *Hong Kong Government Gazette*, vol. 137 (1995), p. E44)

In a television interview in Gibraltar on 19 June 1995, the Secretary of State for Foreign and Commonwealth Affairs, Mr Douglas Hurd, stated:

Britain has many clear obligations towards the people of Gibraltar and they are set out in the 1969 Constitution.

(Text provided by the FCO)

On 6 July 1995, the Governments of Hong Kong and New Zealand concluded an Agreement for the Promotion and Protection of Investments. The preamble to the Agreement contains the following recital:

The Government of Hong Kong, having been duly authorised to conclude the agreement by the Government of the sovereign State which is responsible for foreign affairs relating to Hong Kong . . .

(Special Supplement No. 5 to the *Hong Kong Government Gazette*, vol. 137 (1995), p. E97)

The following question was asked of Her Majesty's Government:

Whether it is intended that the Hong Kong Court of Final Appeal will be empowered freely to decide whether an administrative act is within the 'act of state' defence, or that the Final Court will be bound to give effect to the Chief Executive's certificate on that point?

In reply, the Minister of State, FCO, wrote:

The availability of a plea of act of state is a question of law to be determined by the court in the light of the facts of the case.

Articles 8 and 18 of the Basic Law provide that the Court of Final Appeal has jurisdiction to apply the common law except in so far as it may contravene the Basic Law itself.

Article 19 of the Basic Law obliges the court to obtain an executive certificate but only on questions of fact concerning acts of state whenever such questions arise in the course of adjudication. This is consistent with the present position in the common law, whereby certificates on questions of fact concerning acts of state are binding on the courts. But such a certificate cannot pronounce on matters of law, as opposed to fact. In so far as it purported to do so, it would not be binding on the courts. Thus, the legal consequences which flow from the facts remain a matter of law for the courts.

(HL Debs., vol. 566, *WA 86*: 16 October 1995)

In reply to a question, the Minister of State, FCO, wrote:

We have compared our practice of issuing visas with a number of other countries who, like us, do not recognise Taiwan. We have agreed, with effect from 1 December, that visas for the UK should be placed in travel documents issued by the Taiwan authorities. We regard such travel documents as no more than confirming the identity of the holder. Our change in practice does not involve recognition of Taiwan or constitute acceptance by Her Majesty's Government of a Taiwanese nationality.

(HL Debs., vol. 567, *WA* 7: 22 November 1995)

Part Three: I. E. *Subjects of international law—States—self-determination*

(See also Part Eight: II. A. (items of 22 March and 14 December 1995), below)

In reply to the question what policy the FCO has in respect of self-determination for Chechnya, the Minister of State, FCO, wrote:

> We continue to press the Russian Government to pursue a peaceful settlement which allows the Chechen people to express their identity within the framework of the constitution of the Russian Federation.

(HC Debs., vol. 255, WA, col. *279*: 23 February 1995)

In the course of a debate on the subject of Chechnya, the Government spokesman in the House of Lords, Lord Inglewood, stated:

> The question of self-determination for the Chechens was raised both by the noble Lord, Lord Hylton, and the noble Viscount, Lord Waverley. In international law the right of self-determination is recognised and specifically in international covenants on civil and political rights and on economic, social and cultural rights, both of which the United Kingdom has ratified. However, the exercise of the right must also take into account questions such as what constitutes a separate people and respect for the principle [of] territorial integrity of the unitary state. In the case of Chechnya no country has recognised President Dudayev's unilateral declaration of independence, but we have repeatedly called on the Russians to work for a political solution which would allow the Chechen people to express their identity within the framework of the Russian Federation. It is worth remembering in this context that the Russian Federation comprises 89 separate units and that the relationship of their component parts with the centre varies from one unit to another; so there is an inherent flexibility in the constitution which ought to assist in this matter.

(HL Debs., vol. 563, col. 476: 18 April 1995)

In reply to a question on the subject of self-determination for the people of Gibraltar, the Minister of State, FCO, wrote:

> Our policy has consistently been that while we support the principle or right of self-determination, reflecting the wishes of the people concerned, it must be exercised in accordance with the other principles and rights in the United Nations Charter as well as other treaty obligations. In the case of Gibraltar, the right of self-determination is circumscribed by Article X of the Treaty of Utrecht. We are willing to look at options for constitutional change, if that is what Gibraltar wants. But they have to be compatible with the Treaty of Utrecht and they have to be realistic.

(Ibid., *WA* 54: 19 April 1995)

In replying to an oral question on the subject of Gibraltar, the Secretary of State for Foreign and Commonwealth Affairs, Mr Douglas Hurd, stated in part:

We hold entirely to the undertaking given to the people of Gibraltar in the 1969 constitution that we would never enter into arrangements whereby the people of Gibraltar would pass under the sovereignty of another state against their freely and democratically expressed wishes.

(HC Debs., vol. 261, cols. 204–5: 7 June 1995)

In the course of a debate in the UN General Assembly on 27 September 1995, the UK representative, Mr. S. J. Gomersall, in exercising a right of reply to the Argentine Foreign Minister, stated in part:

On the question of the Falkland Islands, as our Foreign Secretary Douglas Hurd stated in this Assembly last year, we have no doubts about Britain's sovereignty over the Falkland Islands and other British dependencies in the South Atlantic, which rests upon firm historical foundations and upon the inalienable right of the Falkland Islanders to self-determination, which they have exercised on repeated occasions in democratic elections.

We must heed the wishes of the people concerned. The elected representatives of the Islanders, who visited the United Nations for the debate in the Committee of 24 last July, clearly expressed their view that the Argentine claim to the Falklands was unjustified and should be dropped. The Minister refers to respect for the Islanders. We should respect their right to determine their own future.

(A/50/PV.9, p. 49)

Speaking on 11 October 1995 in the Fourth Committee of the UN General Assembly, the UK representative, Mr P. T. Arkwright, stated:

The United Kingdom has 10 Dependent Territories which come under the agenda of the Fourth Committee. It is right therefore that the UK should take this opportunity, as in previous years, to make its national position known to the Committee.

The United Kingdom remains firmly committed to the principle of self-determination. The United Kingdom is however disappointed by the continued failure of the draft resolutions and decisions before us to appreciate the considerable difference between self-determination and independence. My delegation notes that in his statement to this Committee last week, the Acting Chairman of the Special Committee acknowledged that other options are open to the Non-Self-Governing Territories. He referred in particular to the conclusions of the seminar on decolonisation held this year in Trinidad and Tobago.

Despite these welcome signs that the Special Committee is beginning to face the realities of a post-colonial world, archaic and irrelevant language continues to appear in the texts. This is again apparent in the draft texts the Special Committee produced this year under agenda item 18. I should therefore like to reaffirm my government's view that it is totally incorrect to equate self-determination solely with independence. This ignores other options which are available.

(Text provided by the FCO; see also A/C.4/50/SR.6, pp. 9–10)

Speaking in explanation of vote on 6 December 1995 in the UN General Assembly, the UK Deputy Permanent Representative to the UN in New York, Mr S. J. Gomersall, stated:

Once again, I regret that my delegation has found it necessary to vote against the resolutions on the Implementation of the Declaration on the Granting of Independence to Colonial Countries and Peoples (A/49/L.45) and on Dissemination of Information on Decolonisation (A/50/23, Part II, Chapter III, para 9).

This is despite improvements in the latter text, in particular, the welcome recognition that self-determination does not automatically equate to independence and that there are other options available. The recent referendum in Bermuda illustrates this well. The people there voted against independence and to maintain their existing links with the United Kingdom.

However, my delegation cannot accept that the request for the Department of Political Affairs and Department of Public Information to publicise decolonization issues, is an effective way to spend scarce resources when the Organisation is facing a serious financial crisis.

On the resolution on the Granting of Independence to Colonial Countries and Peoples there remain unfortunately far too many examples of language that is out of touch with present-day reality. For example, we do not accept that the presence of military bases in our Dependent Territories could in any way constitute an obstacle to the granting of independence or impede them from expressing their views on self-determination.

(Text provided by the FCO; see also A/50/PV.82, p. 23)

Part Three: II. A. 1. (a) *Subjects of international law—international organizations—in general—legal status—personality*

The World Trade Organisation (Immunities and Privileges) Order 1995, which entered into force on 8 February 1995, provides in its Article 4:

The Organisation shall have the legal capacities of a body corporate.

(Statutory Instruments 1995, No. 266)

Part Three: II. A. 1. (c). *Subjects of international law—international organizations—in general—legal status—privileges and immunities*

(See also Part One: II. D. 1. (item of 8 February 1995), above)

In moving the approval in the House of Lords of the draft World Trade Organisation (Immunities and Privileges) Order, the Minister of State, FCO, Baroness Chalker, stated:

. . . the Uruguay Round of multilateral trade negotiations which took place within the framework of the General Agreement on Tariffs and Trade between 1986 and 1993 was formally concluded at Marrakesh on 15th April this year. The GATT provides a framework of agreed multilateral rules for world trade and the Uruguay Round marks an important step forward in the liberalisation of such trade. The legal vehicle for bringing the results of the round into force is the agreement establishing the World Trade Organisation—Cm 2571.

The WTO will provide an institutional structure for the operation of the various trade agreements covered by the agreement establishing the World Trade Organisation. It will provide a framework for the accession of new members, for the settlement of disputes, and for the amendment of various trade agreements and for other decisions and waivers. The secretariat will comprise the director-general and some 400 officials and will be located in Geneva.

Specifically, this debate is about the privileges and immunities accorded under the draft order which need to be conferred in order for Her Majesty's Government to fulfil their obligations under Article VIII of the Agreement Establishing the WTO (Cm 2571). This article provides that the WTO shall be accorded by each of its members such legal capacity and privileges and immunities as are necessary for the exercise of its functions. Privileges and immunities are also to be accorded to officials of the WTO and the representatives of members. In both respects these are to be similar to those provided for in the Convention on the Privileges and Immunities of the Specialised Agencies of the United Nations 1947.

However, as the World Trade Organisation will be located in Geneva, many of the privileges and immunities set out in the draft order in council will never need to be relied upon by the WTO, its officials and representatives of members. The World Trade Organisation is in practice likely only to claim refunds of VAT on goods and services purchased in the United Kingdom for the official purposes of the organisation. We will need only to accord the relevant privileges and immunities to its officials and representatives of members if they attend any WTO meetings or conferences which may be held in the United Kingdom. I would like to emphasise to the House that the privileges and immunities provided for in the order are granted in accordance with the limitations imposed by the International Organisations Act 1968, as amended, under whose provisions the order is made.

The Joint Committee on Statutory Instruments considered this draft instrument and had no comments. I commend the order to the House.

(HL Debs., vol. 559, cols. 1269–70: 13 December 1994)

The World Trade Organisation (Immunities and Privileges) Order 1995, which came into force on 8 February 1995, provides in its Articles 5–12:

5. Except in so far as in any particular case it has expressly waived its immunity, the Organisation shall have immunity from suit and legal process. No waiver of immunity shall be deemed to extend to any measure of execution.
6. The Organisation shall have the like inviolability of official archives and premises as in accordance with the 1961 Convention Articles is accorded in respect of the official archives and premises of a diplomatic mission.
7. The Organisation, its assets, income and other property shall have exemption from income tax, capital gains tax and corporation tax.
8. The Organisation shall have the like relief from rates as in accordance with Article 23 of the 1961 Convention Articles is accorded in respect of the premises of a diplomatic mission.
9. The Organisation shall have exemption from customs duties and taxes on the importation by it of goods for its official use in the United Kingdom and on the importation of publications of the Organisation imported by it, such exemption to be subject to compliance with such conditions as the Commissioners of Customs and Excise may prescribe for the protection of the Revenue.
10. The Organisation shall have exemption from prohibitions and restrictions on importation or exportation in the case of goods imported or exported by the Organisation for its official use and in the case of any publications of the Organisation imported or exported by it.
11. The Organisation shall have relief, under arrangements made by the Commissioners of Customs and Excise, by way of refund of customs duty paid on imported hydrocarbon oil (within the meaning of the Hydrocarbon Oil Duties Act 1979) or value added tax paid on the importation of such oil which is bought in the United Kingdom and used for the official purposes of the Organisation, such relief to be subject to compliance with such conditions as may be imposed in accordance with the arrangements.
12. The Organisation shall have relief, under arrangements made by the Secretary of State, by way of refund of value added tax paid on the purchase of new motor vehicles of United Kingdom manufacture and of value added tax paid on the supply of any goods or services which are used for the official purposes of the Organisation, such relief to be subject to compliance with such conditions as may be imposed in accordance with the arrangements.

The order goes on to provide for privileges and immunities for officials of the Organisation and for representatives of Members attending meetings of the Organisation in the UK.

(Statutory Instruments 1995, No. 266)

Part Three: II. A. 2. (b). *Subjects of international law—international organizations—in general—participation of States in international organizations—suspension, withdrawal and expulsion*

The Minister of State, FCO, Mr Alastair Goodlad, sent the following letter, dated 15 December 1993, to the Secretary-General of the South Pacific Commission, Noumea:

I have the honour to refer to the agreement establishing the South Pacific Commission signed at Canberra on 6 February 1947 with agreement extending the territorial scope of the South Pacific Commission to Guam and the Trust Territory of the Pacific Islands signed in Noumea on 7 November 1951, the agreement relating to the frequency of sessions of the South Pacific Commission signed at Canberra on 5 April 1954, and the agreement amending the agreement establishing the South Pacific Commission, as amended, signed at London on 6 October 1964.

In accordance with Article XIX, paragraph 61 of the agreement establishing the South Pacific Commission, I have the honour to inform you on behalf of the Government of the United Kingdom of Great Britain and Northern Ireland that the United Kingdom hereby gives notice of its intention to withdraw from the aforementioned agreements with effect from 1 January 1995.

(Text provided by the FCO)

An internal minute of the FCO dated 31 August 1995 conveyed the following additional information:

. . . in order to restrict the disruption to the SPC, we offered to phase withdrawal until 1 January 1996, as long as agreement was reached for the UK's contribution for 1995 to be reduced by 50 per cent. This condition was accepted by the SPC in May 1994.

The UK's membership of the SPC will therefore formally end on 1 January 1996. However, we have agreed to continue to represent Pitcairn, our last remaining Dependent Territory in the region and we will pay its budget contribution of 0.24 per cent of the core budget, on current rates about £12,000 per annum.

(Ibid.)

Reporting on the meeting of the Commonwealth Heads of Government in New Zealand on 10–13 November 1995, the Minister of State, FCO, wrote in part:

The meeting rightly took issue with those members of the Commonwealth, notably Nigeria, which continue to defy the principles of democratic and accountable government agreed at the CHOGM in Harare in 1991. The Commonwealth's widespread and increasing concern about the importance of an early transition to accountable democratic government in Nigeria, and the Nigerian Government's callous execution of Mr. Ken Saro-Wiwa and his eight associates, following a flawed judicial process with no formal right of appeal and no regard for the basic legal rights of defendants, gave the Commonwealth little alternative but to suspend Nigeria. This was essential if the Harare principles were to carry credibility for the future. How long Nigeria remains suspended depends on its own conduct. If the Nigerian Government show themselves willing to abide by the Harare principles, the Commonwealth will be very ready to support them. Conversely, the meeting agreed that if no democratic progress has been made within a time-frame to be stipulated, Nigeria will be expelled from the Commonwealth.

(HL Debs., vol. 567, *WA 2*: 16 November 1995)

Part Three: II. A. 3. *Subjects of international law—international organizations—in general—legal effect of acts of international organizations*

On 2 June 1994, the UK Government submitted a written statement to the International Court of Justice in the course of proceedings arising out of a request made by the World Health Assembly for an advisory opinion on the legality of the threat or use of nuclear weapons. The statement contained the following paragraphs:

15. The only documents which do treat nuclear weapons as if they were unlawful *per se* are a number of resolutions of the United Nations General Assembly, starting with Resolution 1653 (XVI) . . .

. . .

A series of subsequent resolutions[25] declared that the use of nuclear weapons would be unlawful and called upon States to adopt a convention prohibiting their use and the threat of their use.

17. These resolutions are not, of course, legally binding instruments. Moreover, there are several reasons for rejecting any suggestions that they are declaratory of a rule of customary international law forbidding all use of nuclear weapons. First, an analysis of the voting figures reveals that the resolutions were controversial. Resolution 1653 (XVI) was adopted by 55 votes to 20, with 26 abstentions. Of the nuclear powers, France, the United Kingdom and the United States voted against the resolution, while the Soviet Union voted in favour. Resolution 2936 (XXVII) was adopted by 73 votes to 4, with 46 abstentions. The Soviet Union was one of the sponsors of the resolution and voted in its favour; France, the United Kingdom and the United States abstained. The later resolutions also failed to command the general support which characterised those resolutions which have often been treated as declaratory of customary international law.[26]

18. Secondly, it is evident that many of those States which voted for the resolutions concerned did not regard them as stating such a customary law principle. In the case of Resolution 1653, the link between the assertion of the illegality of nuclear weapons in paragraph 1 and the request that the Secretary-General consult States about the conclusion of a convention to prohibit the use of nuclear weapons raises the question whether those States which voted for the resolution regarded the use of nuclear weapons as lawful in the absence of such a convention. Statements by a number of States, including some of the sponsors of the resolution, suggest that they did not take such a position.[27] The later resolutions also refer to the adoption of a convention prohibiting the use of nuclear weapons.

19. Thirdly, in Resolution 2936 the prohibition of nuclear weapons was expressly linked to the renunciation of the use of force 'in accordance with the Charter of the United Nations'. The resolution thus leaves open the possibility that nuclear weapons might lawfully be used in self-defence, since the renunciation of the use of force was clearly not intended to preclude the exercise of that right. That was made clear by the Soviet Union, one of the sponsors of the resolution,[28] whose subsequent security assurances given to the Conference on Disarmament made clear that it regarded the use of nuclear weapons as lawful where that was a necessary measure of self-defence.

20. Finally, the significance of the General Assembly resolution has to be seen in the light of State practice as a whole, including the conclusion of the agreements discussed above, the failure to adopt a convention of the kind suggested by the General Assembly, the decision not to discuss nuclear weapons at the Diplomatic Conference on the Development of Humanitarian Law and the statements and security assurances made by the nuclear powers in 1978 and in connection with the Treaty of Tlatelolco, all of which indicates that there is no consistent State practice from which a customary law prohibition of nuclear weapons might have developed.

---

[25] Resolutions 33/71B, 35/152D, 36/92I, 45/59B, 46/37D and 47/53C.

[26] 103–18–18; 112–19–14; 121–19–6; 125–17–10; 122–16–22; and 126–21–21 respectively.

[27] See, eg, the statement by Ceylon, GAOR, 17th Sess., 1st Ctee., 1288th Mtg, para 8. See also the discussion in UN Doc A/9215, vol. 1. pp. 147–54.

[28] See the statement by the Soviet Union at A/PV.2040, pp. 26–33.

(Statement, pp. 73–7; text provided by the FCO)

In June 1995, the UK Government submitted a statement to the International Court of Justice in the course of proceedings arising out of a request made by the UN General Assembly for an advisory opinion on the same subject. After making reference to certain resolutions of the General Assembly, the statement went on:

3.27 These resolutions are not, of course, legally binding instruments.[83] Moreover, there are several reasons for rejecting the suggestion that they are declaratory of a rule of customary international law forbidding all use of nuclear weapons. First, an analysis of the voting figures reveals that the resolutions were controversial. Resolution 1653 (XVI) was adopted by 55 votes to 20, with 26 abstentions. Of the nuclear powers, France, the United Kingdom and the United States voted against the resolution, while the Soviet Union voted in favour. It is evident, therefore, that, as an authoritative United Nations Report stated, this resolution demonstrated not a consensus but rather the sharp conflict of views on this issue.[84] Resolution 2936 (XXVII) was adopted by 73 votes to 4, with 46 abstentions. The Soviet Union was one of the sponsors of the resolution and voted in its favour; France, the United Kingdom and the United States abstained. The later resolutions[85] also failed to command the general support which has characterised those resolutions which have been widely regarded as declaratory of customary international law.[86]

3.28 Secondly, it is evident that many of those States which voted for the resolutions concerned did not regard them as stating such a customary law principle.

. . .

---

[83] The General Assembly has no power under the Charter to impose binding obligations upon Member States except in respect of certain internal matters. This is in contrast to the position of the Security Council the resolutions of which are, in certain circumstances, binding by virtue of Article 25 of the Charter. The criteria identified by the Court in the *Namibia* Opinion (ICJ Reports, 1971, p. 15 at p. 53) for determining whether or not such a resolution is a binding one concerned only resolutions of the

Security Council and did not, contrary to what is suggested by the Solomon Islands in its submissions regarding the WHO request for an Advisory Opinion (Written Statement of the Government of the Solomon Islands, p. 38, paragraph 3.26), suggest that resolutions of the General Assembly possess a binding character merely because they are couched in language similar to that of a Security Council resolution. The Court in the *Namibia* Opinion considered General Assembly resolutions to have a determinative effect only in certain exceptional matters, none of which are relevant in the present case.

[84] UN Secretary-General's Report on *Existing Rules of International Law concerning the Prohibition or Restriction of Use of Specific Weapons* (UN Doc.A/9215), vol. I, p. 147.

[85] Adopted by votes of 103–18–18; 112–19–14; 121–19–6; 125–17–10; 122–16–22; 126–21–21 and 120–23–34 respectively.

[86] For example Resolution 2625 (XXV) (Declaration on Principles of International Law) and Resolution 3314 (XXIX) (Definition of Aggression), which were treated by the Court in the *Case Concerning Military and Paramilitary Activities in and against Nicaragua*, ICJ Reports, 1986, p. 3 at paragraphs 188 and 195, as reflecting the content of customary international law, were both adopted without a vote, as was Resolution 3452 (XXX) (Declaration on Torture), which was regarded as declaratory of customary international law by a United States court in *Filartiga* v. *Pena-Irala* 630 F 2d 876 (1980); 77 ILR 169. The requirement that a General Assembly resolution must command wide support, including support from all the various groups of States most closely affected, if it is to be treated as declaratory of customary international law was also emphasized by Professor Dupuy as Sole Arbitrator in *Texaco/Calasiatic* v. *Libya* 53 ILR 389.

(Statement, p. 32; text provided by the FCO)

On 16 December 1995, the UK Permanent Representative to the UN in New York, Sir John Weston, speaking in a debate in the UN Security Council on the Peace Implementation Resolution for Bosnia, referred to the NATO Implementation Force (IFOR) and went on:

> IFOR is not imposing the peace settlement; but it will take the necessary action to ensure compliance. And let me at this point also make it clear should it be decided that, in the execution of its assigned tasks, IFOR should detain and transfer to the appropriate authorities any persons indicted by the Tribunal who come into contact with it in Bosnia, then the authority to do so is provided by this resolution, read together with the provisions of the Peace Agreement.

(Text provided by the FCO)

Part Four: IV. *The individual (including the corporation) in international law—minorities*

Addressing the Parliamentary Assembly of the Council of Europe on 30 June 1995, the Lord Chancellor, Lord Mackay of Clashfern, stated:

> We have good legal instruments in the Council of Europe, and we are adding to them all the time. But it also behoves us to stand back occasionally and see what we have reached in terms of signatures and ratifications of existing documents, in addition to the consideration of new ones. A case in point is the status of national minorities, where I shall permit myself a little questioning of the Assembly. There is little doubt that without the Assembly's consistent pressure, the agreements, compromises, commitments (call them what you will)

at the Vienna Summit, and in its Declaration, would in all likelihood not have been agreed—let alone translated into action. This action was eventually embodied in the Framework Convention on National Minorities. The Framework Convention is the first international legal instrument for the protection of national minorities. I must say, that I regard its negotiation in little more than a year as a remarkable achievement. This is confirmed by the fact that 27 countries, including my own, have already signed.

(Text provided by the FCO)

Part Four: VI. *The individual (including the corporation) in international law—immigration and emigration, extradition, expulsion and asylum*

In the course of a reply on the subject of asylum seekers, the Parliamentary Under-Secretary of State, Home Office, set out a number of annual tables of statistics of asylum applications. A consolidated table for the years 1990 to 1994 read as follows:

Applications[1] received for asylum in the United Kingdom, and decisions[1], including dependents, 1990 to 1994

	1990	1991	1992	1993	1994
Applications for asylum	38,195	73,400	32,300	28,000	41,100
Total Decisions[2]	6,055	9,140	59,050	36,890	28,210
Recognised as a refugee and granted asylum	1,590	800	1,900	2,860	1,380
Not recognised as a refugee but granted exceptional leave to remain	3,610	2,950	21,680	15,480	5,480
Refused asylum and exceptional leave[3]	855	5,390	35, 480	18,550	21,350

[1] Provisional figures rounded to the nearest 5.
[2] A breakdown of decisions into port and in-country is not available for 1990 and 1991.
[3] Includes refusals on safe third country grounds and those under para. 180F—para. 101 prior to 26 July 1993— of the Immigration Rules.
Removals figures for 1990 and 1991 are not available.

(HC Debs., vol. 253, WA, col. *896*: 3 February 1995)

In the course of a further debate on the same subject, the Parliamentary Under-Secretary of State, Home Office, Mr Nicholas Baker, stated:

The Government fully accept and comply with the United Kingdom's obligations under the 1951 United Nations convention on refugees.

(HC Debs., vol. 256, col. 1213: 17 March 1995)

In reply to a question, the Minister of State, FCO, wrote:

Section 15 of the Extradition Act 1989 permits special extradition arrangements to be made for the extradition of individuals to states with which the United Kingdom has no extradition arrangements. No extradition has so far taken place under this provision.

(HL Debs., vol. 562, *WA 60*: 20 March 1995)

On 18 July 1995, the Governments of the UK and Brazil signed an Extradition Treaty. Article 3 of the treaty reads as follows:

Grounds for Refusal of Extradition

(1) A person shall not be extradited if the appropriate authority in the Requested State is satisfied:

- (a) that the offence for which his extradition is requested is an offence of a political character; or
- (b) that it is an offence under military law which is not also an offence under the general criminal law; or
- (c) that the request for extradition (though purporting to be made on account of an extradition offence as is specified in Article 2) has in fact been made for the purpose of prosecuting or punishing the person sought on account of his race, religion, nationality or political opinions; or
- (d) that the person sought might, if extradited, be prejudiced at his trial or be punished, detained or restricted in his personal liberty, by reason of his race, religion, nationality or political opinions; or
- (e) that it would, having regard to all the circumstances, be unjust or oppressive to extradite the person sought:
  - (i) by reason of the trivial nature of the offence of which he is accused or was convicted; or
  - (ii) in accordance with its laws, because of the passage of time since he is alleged to have committed it or to have become unlawfully at large, as the case may be; or
  - (iii) because the accusation against him has not been made in good faith in the interests of justice; or
- (f) that, in the case of a request from the United Kingdom, a previous request based on the same facts has been made for the extradition of the person sought, and that request was denied.

(2) A person shall not be extradited if he would, if proceeded against in the territory of the Requested State for the offence for which his extradition is requested, be entitled to be discharged under any rule of law of the Requested State relating to his previous acquittal or conviction.

(3) If the Requested State does not extradite its own national on the grounds of his nationality, it shall at the request of the Requesting State submit the case to its competent authorities in order that proceedings may be taken if they are

considered appropriate. For this purpose, the file, information and exhibits relating to the offence shall be transmitted without charge by the means provided for in Article 5. The Requesting State shall be informed of the result of its request.

(Cm 2975 (instruments of ratification have not yet been exchanged))

In reply to a question, the Parliamentary Under-Secretary of State, Home Office, wrote:

With the exception of the Falkland Islands and Gibraltar, citizens of British dependent territories seeking permanent entry into the United Kingdom must meet the requirements of the Immigration Rules (HC395). I have no plans to enable entry similar to that operated by France in respect of residents of French overseas departments.

(HC Debs., vol. 264, WA, col. *337*: 19 October 1995)

In replying to a debate on the subject of Mrs Brenda Price, arrested near Dunquerque on a request for extradition made by Spain, the Minister of State, Home Office, Mr David Maclean, stated:

Mrs. Price is at present being held at the Maison d'Arrêt in Loos. Before I turn to particular concerns, it may be helpful if I explain the general background to the case.

Extradition is the mechanism for returning fugitives to the country where an alleged offence has been committed, for the fugitive to be tried in a court of law. Extradition among all European Union countries apart from Belgium is covered by the Council of Europe convention on extradition. The convention lays down a common standard and common procedures for handling extradition requests between European countries which have signed and ratified it.

Under the convention, there is no requirement for a requesting state to make a prima facie case in support of an extradition request. All that the requesting country has to provide is an authenticated copy of an arrest warrant, a statement of the offences for which extradition has been requested, a copy of the relevant laws in the requesting country, and identification evidence. This material is usually considered by a court, in England and Wales a magistrates court, before a decision is made to issue an arrest warrant.

Under the Extradition Act 1989, which implements the UK's obligations under the European convention, there is an alternative procedure which may be used in emergencies—for example, where a fugitive offender is likely to leave the country.

Under the emergency procedure, the requesting country can, through Interpol channels, request the provisional arrest of a fugitive. The requesting country must provide evidence that a case exists which is sufficient for a Bow Street magistrate to issue a provisional arrest warrant. It should be noted that a decision by a court to issue a provisional arrest warrant is not a final decision.

The requesting state has to back up the request with full supporting documents. If it does not, the arrest warrant will be discharged.

Once the fugitive is arrested, the requesting country has to provide documents in support of its extradition request within statutory deadlines. In the case of European convention countries, the documents must be provided within 40 days.

A country can issue an Interpol red notice, which alerts other countries that a person is wanted in that country to face charges, and should be arrested if located. The UK often receives such requests from other countries for British and other nationals. Indeed, the majority of requests we receive—around 70 per cent. of all cases—are initiated by an Interpol red notice and a provisional arrest.

As my hon. Friend will appreciate, extradition requests, by their very nature, involve individuals who have already crossed international boundaries. It is an essential element in the success of the fight against crime internationally that those individuals wanted in connection with criminal offences in one country can be arrested before they have a chance to escape to yet another country.

In this connection, my hon. Friend has questioned why he was not notified if the Spanish authorities had renewed their extradition request for Mrs. Price. He will appreciate that, by their very nature, extradition requests involve alleged offences against a person who has crossed international boundaries. Great care is therefore taken that the person is not alerted, in order to preclude any risk that he or she will flee the country. I make those general points by way of background, because they are pertinent to the case of Mrs. Price.

Mrs. Price was the subject of an extradition request from Spain to the UK in 1993. The request from Spain was made through the emergency procedure for Mrs. Price's provisional arrest to face charges relating to the trafficking of 940 kg of cannabis. The Spanish provided information about the drug trafficking operation, and stated that an arrest warrant for Mrs. Price and others had been issued in Spain on 8 October 1992. That information was put before the magistrate at Bow Street magistrates court, and he was invited to issue a provisional arrest warrant. He issued the warrant on 7 January 1993, and Mrs. Price was arrested on 13 January.

As is usual in such cases, the Spanish authorities were notified of Mrs. Price's arrest, and were informed that they had 40 days in which to provide documents in accordance with the European convention on extradition in support of their extradition request. However, the Spanish authorities failed to send the necessary supporting documents within the 40 days, as required under the international convention, and Mrs. Price was discharged.

I pause at this stage to make two points in answer to the concerns raised by my hon. Friend. As he is aware, the United Kingdom Government were concerned that what I have called the emergency procedure was used when there was, as it turned out, no evidence that Mrs. Price was an emergency case—that is, that she was about to flee the country—and when the Spanish authorities had not finished preparing the paperwork.

The then Home Office Minister, my hon. Friend the Member for Fylde (Mr. Jack), informed my hon. Friend by letter of those concerns in the following terms:

'We share her solicitor's concern that Mrs. Price was detained for so long in respect of an extradition request which was not pursued—although I must stress that in acting as they did the Spanish authorities did nothing that they were not entitled to do—and we will be registering this concern with them'.

We wrote to the Spanish authorities about that aspect of the case in May 1993, and received confirmation from Spain that our concerns had been noted, together with an explanation as to why the Spanish authorities had not followed up the extradition request. They decided to await the outcome of the trial of Mrs. Price's co-defendants, which took place in May 1993. Had they been found not guilty, no doubt the request for Mrs. Price would have been dropped. In fact, the four defendants were convicted and sentenced to eight years' imprisonment and fined 65 million pesetas—or £336,000 in real money.

My second point is to stress that Mrs. Price was released from custody, and the provisional arrest warrant discharged, solely because Spain did not produce the necessary documents within the time limits. At no time was the Spanish request refused, and it was open to Spain to make a second request to the United Kingdom or to any other country where Mrs. Price was found. Those points were explained to my hon. Friend at the time.

In his second reply of 22 April 1993 to letters from my hon. Friend, my hon. Friend the Member for Fylde stated:

'As you know Mrs. Price was discharged by the Metropolitan magistrate at Bow Street as the Spanish authorities decided not to pursue Mrs. Price's extradition at this time'.

I repeat and emphasise that the Spanish authorities did not drop Mrs. Price's case: they simply decided not to pursue it further at that time. I emphasise that point, because it appears from correspondence sent on behalf of Mrs. Price to the Home Office that Mrs. Price was under the misapprehension that the discharge of the provisional arrest warrant in 1993 was the end of the matter, and that the Spanish authorities had given up their intention to seek her extradition. That was and is not the case. If Mrs. Price was advised differently, I am sorry to say that she was badly advised. We, for our part, stated the matter clearly in the letter to my hon. Friend.

The Interpol red notice for Mrs. Price's arrest continued to be in force, and it was on that notice that Mrs. Price was arrested in France on 5 October this year. As her extradition was not rejected by the United Kingdom, there was no reason why that should not have occurred. The United Kingdom police were not acting on that notice, because, as is usual practice in such cases, once a provisional arrest warrant has been discharged by the authorities of a state, the requesting authority must make a request with full supporting documents the next time it seeks extradition from that state.

The French authorities were perfectly entitled to act on the Interpol red notice. Had the United Kingdom authorities been put in a similar position, they would have acted in the same way—and rightly so. It is in the nature of the emergency procedure that action must be taken on Interpol information. No consideration can, or indeed should, be expected to be given to detailed facts, such as whether a person is only on a day trip. All sorts of false stories could be given by those fleeing justice.

The procedure provides opportunities in court and, by way of representations to Ministers at a later stage, for deciding such issues. I put it to my hon. Friend that, if we were to change the procedures to accommodate those views, we would fundamentally undermine the workings of Interpol.

In Mrs. Price's case, the next stage under the convention is for the requesting state, Spain, to submit all the necessary documents to the French authorities within 40 days, and for the French authorities to consider the request. I understand that the French authorities have received some papers from Spain, and are now in the process of considering them. If, for any reason, the Spanish request cannot be complied with, no doubt Mrs. Price will be free to return to the United Kingdom.

However, I must emphasise that those matters are for the Spanish and French authorities. It is not for the United Kingdom to intervene, any more than a foreign country would attempt to intervene in or influence a request from a second country to the United Kingdom about a national of that country.

My hon. Friend the Member for Harlow has raised a number of other concerns in the past, and he did so again this evening. He is concerned that 18 months had elapsed since the date of the alleged offence to the date of the request from Spain to the United Kingdom in 1993. My hon. Friend may be aware that undue delay in making a request is a factor to which Ministers and the courts must have regard when considering whether to make an extradition order in any particular case.

However, undue delay must take into account, among other factors, the time required for the police and prosecuting authorities to pursue their inquiries and go through the proper procedures. When the crime is serious or when, as in this case, a number of individuals are involved, the time for completing those procedures may be quite lengthy. In this case, Ministers and the courts never addressed the issue, because the warrant was discharged after 40 days.

My hon. Friend has also expressed concern that Mrs. Price is being held in custody in France, and, if returned to Spain, may be held for some time in prison on remand there. The question of bail is, of course, a matter for the courts in those countries, in the same way that the decision whether to bail a French or Spanish national charged with offences in the United Kingdom or wanted for extradition would be a matter for our courts. A key issue, of course, is whether the offender will answer to that bail at the relevant time, but that is not the only issue. Courts will also have regard to the seriousness of the offence and any likely sentence if found guilty.

What is called 'Euro-bail' would be a benefit only in cases where the only reason for not granting bail is the likelihood of absconding. As such, it is of limited application, and raises more problems in relation to the harmonisation of judicial decisions across Europe than any remedy it might provide. Bail is at present a question for the French courts, and I do not believe that we should seek to interfere in their decision. We would resent it if they tried to interfere in any decision that we might make.

What the United Kingdom can do in this case—and what we are doing—is provide consular support to Mrs. Price and her family.

I hope that my hon. Friend will be satisfied, from the full and detailed explanation that I have given him, that all the proper procedures have been carried out in the United Kingdom; that we believe that Spain and France are following the procedures in the European convention; and that the British

Government, through our consulate-general's office, are giving every assistance to Mrs. Price.

(HC Debs., vol. 265, cols. 370–4: 31 October 1995)

In opening a debate on the subject of asylum and immigration, the Home Secretary, Mr Michael Howard, stated:

The Government have always attached the very greatest priority to preserving good race relations in this country, and it has consistently been our policy that fair but firm and effective immigration control is a necessary condition for doing so.

We must be prepared to respond quickly when new threats to that control emerge. This is something that successive Governments have done over the years. I have a number of proposals to announce today. All are consistent with our international obligations under the 1951 refugee convention. None will reduce in any way the rights of those who presently qualify to come to this country to live.

(HC Debs., vol. 267, col. 335: 20 November 1995)

In reply to a question, the Parliamentary Under-Secretary of State, Home Office, wrote:

All applications for asylum are considered in accordance with the criteria set out in the 1951 United Nations convention relating to the status of refugees. Decisions are based on all the relevant circumstances of individual cases as well as on an assessment of conditions in the country of origin. There is no question of our refusing to consider, or of our automatically refusing, an application because of the country of origin of the applicant.

(HC Debs., vol. 267, WA, col. *292*: 23 November 1995)

Part Four: VII. *The individual (including the corporation) in international law—protection of human rights and fundamental freedoms*

(See also Part One: II. D. 1. (material on Human Rights Bill), and Part Three: I. A. 3., above)

In reply to a question, the Parliamentary Under-Secretary of State, FCO, wrote:

With our European Union partners we have consistently deplored all abuses of human rights, including the frequent use of detention without trial. We look to the Nigerian Government to respect all their international human rights obligations.

(HC Debs., vol. 253, WA, col. *335*: 26 January 1995)

In reply to a question, the Minister of State, Home Office, wrote:

The Crown dependencies are the Channel Islands and the Isle of Man. The protection in the dependencies of the rights and freedoms recognised both in the

European Convention on Human Rights and in the United Nations Covenant on Civil and Political Rights is assured by the United Kingdom being party to the convention and to the covenant on behalf of all the Islands.

(HL Debs., vol. 561, *WA 50*: 16 February 1995)

In reply to a question on the obligations of China towards the UN international covenants on human rights, the Minister of State, FCO, wrote:

The Sino-British Joint Declaration obliges China to ensure that the provisions of the covenants, as applied to Hong Kong, remain in force. It clearly means that all the provisions of the two covenants now applied to Hong Kong, including the reporting provisions, shall continue to apply. We have made our views known to the Chinese Government as to how it may fulfil its obligations under the joint declaration. One way to implement the reporting obligations would be for China to accede to the covenants in respect of the whole of its territory. Alternatively, we believe it would be feasible for China to assume reporting obligations under the covenant in respect of Hong Kong only. We continue to discuss this question in the joint liaison group.

(HL Debs., vol. 561, *WA 75*: 23 February 1995)

In reply to the question in respect of which Crown dependencies and dependent territories has the right of individual petition been accepted under Article 63(4) of the European Convention on Human Rights, the Minister of State, FCO, wrote:

The right of individual petition has been accepted in respect of the following Crown dependencies and dependent territories:

Anguilla
Bermuda
Falkland Islands
South Georgia and the Sandwich Islands
Gibraltar
Bailiwick of Guernsey
Isle of Man
Bailiwick of Jersey
Montserrat
St. Helena
St. Helena Dependencies
Turks and Caicos

The right of individual petition has not been accepted in respect of the following dependent territories in which the convention applies:

British Virgin Islands
Cayman Islands

(HL Debs., vol. 561, *WA 29*: 14 February 1995)

In reply to a further question, addressed to the situation in respect of the British Virgin Islands and the Cayman Islands, the same Minister wrote:

We are satisfied that the obligations accepted on behalf of both territories under the convention and the covenant are fulfilled. The question of how to give further legal protection to human rights and fundamental freedoms in the Cayman Islands is currently under consideration by a Select Committee of the Cayman Islands Legislative Assembly. Such questions will also be considered by the new Legislative Council in the British Virgin Islands following the General Election on 20 February.

(Ibid., *WA* 97: 1 March 1995)

In the course of a debate in the House of Lords on the subject of human rights in Nigeria, the Minister of State, FCO, Baroness Chalker, remarked:

All members of the European Union have consistently made their views on human rights known to the Nigerian Government. Nigeria is failing to live up to its human rights obligations. Nigeria has aspirations to the highest standards and is party to many international human rights instruments. We deplore all human rights abuses and shall continue to raise specific cases with the Nigerian Government.

(HL Debs., vol. 562, cols. 202–3: 7 March 1995)

In reply to the question whether Articles 9 and 10 of the European Convention on Human Rights could be interpreted as justification for unbridled freedom of expression, the Minister of State, FCO, wrote:

Article 9 of the Convention guarantees the right to freedom of thought, conscience and religion, including the right to manifest one's religion or beliefs. Article 10 guarantees the right to freedom of expression. The enjoyment of the rights and freedoms set out in the two articles is subject to certain limitations which are specified in the Convention. These are limitations which are prescribed by law and are necessary in a democratic society in the interests of, among other things, public safety, the prevention of disorder or crime, the protection of public order, health or morals, or the protection of the reputation and rights and freedoms of others. The jurisprudence of the European Commission of Human Rights and European Court of Human Rights has shown that the Convention cannot be interpreted as permitting unbridled freedom of expression.

(HL Debs., vol. 563, *WA 125*: 4 May 1995)

In reply to the question whether Her Majesty's Government will make it their policy to support the inclusion in any treaty arising from the 1996 European Inter-Governmental Conference of a specific recognition of the role of the Council of Europe in the field of human rights, the Minister of State, FCO, wrote:

Article F of the Maastricht Treaty already contains a reference to the need for the European Union to respect fundamental rights, as guaranteed by the Council of Europe Convention for the Protection of Human Rights and Fundamental Freedoms. In addition, Article 230 of the Treaty of Rome enables the Community to establish appropriate forms of co-operation with the Council of Europe. We see no need for a further reference to the Council of Europe in the Community treaties, but will consider carefully any proposals which are made.

(HL Debs., vol. 564, *WA 46*: 19 May 1995)

The following passages are taken from a paper entitled *Britain and the UN* published by the FCO in May 1995. They are reproduced here for general interest:

Human Rights

Within the UN system, the Commission on Human Rights is the main forum for substantive discussions in this field. Its parent body is ECOSOC. The Commission considers and adopts Resolutions on a wide range of human rights issues.

The Commission's first big task was to work on the Universal Declaration on Human Rights, proclaimed by the UN in 1948. This was the first definition by the UN of what constituted human rights. It has been followed by many legally binding instruments, including the International Covenant on Civil and Political Rights, the International Covenant on Economic, Social and Cultural Rights, the International Convention for the Elimination of All Forms of Racial Discrimination, the International Convention on the Elimination of Discrimination Against Women, the Convention Against Torture, and the Convention on the Rights of the Child. Britain adheres to these Covenants and Conventions.

The Commission on Human Rights discusses a wide range of general rights issues (such as torture and racism), and also passes Resolutions condemning severe violations in individual countries. It appoints Special Rapporteurs or Working Groups to investigate and report on human rights themes and on situations in particular countries. Britain is currently a member of the Commission, and is committed to the observance and promotion of universal human rights standards throughout the world. She regularly contributes financially to UN human rights activities, for example the Voluntary Funds for Advisory Services and for the Victims of Torture, and the human rights monitoring force in Rwanda.

The UN World Conference on Human Rights, in 1993, reaffirmed, among other things, the universality of human rights, the need to promote *all* human rights (civil, political, economic, social and cultural), the centrality of the human rights of women, and that human rights are a legitimate concern of the international community, not just an internal affair. The Conference also led to the creation of the post of UN High Commissioner for Human Rights.

(Text provided by the FCO)

On 30 June 1995, the Lord Chancellor, Lord Mackay of Clashfern; addressed the Parliamentary Assembly of the Council of Europe in Strasbourg. The following extract is taken from the text of the address:

That thought has also been running through my mind over the last 24 hours in relation to the human rights work of the Council of Europe, a remarkable new home for which we inaugurated yesterday. Historically this work has been central to our common purposes of further realising human rights and fundamental freedoms, and thus protecting individuals from the oppression which gave rise to the Second World War. The European Convention on Human Rights has been the cornerstone of the Council of Europe. It established for the first time a regional enforcement mechanism to protect human rights, and has been an influence world-wide in this field. Its great innovation was to allow individuals, not just States, to lodge complaints against a government in an international forum. But the Convention, and the Commission and Court, are not merely of historical significance. The principles enshrined in the Convention which have guided the countries of Western Europe for the last 50 years are now to guide the new, wider Europe in the ways of democracy and human rights. The Convention now is as important as it has ever been, and the machinery set up under it faces a great challenge.

It is for this reason I am very pleased that, soon after the Vienna Summit which I attended, the remaining problems on Protocol 11 to the Convention were solved in a way which enabled my Government not merely to sign, but be among the first to ratify it. We did so because we believe that the enlarged Council of Europe not only needs, but must have, a more simple and speedy judicial procedure to cope with the rapid present and anticipated growth in applications under the Convention on Human Rights. The United Kingdom will, as it has offered to, play a part with the Court in trying to establish good working procedures before the new arrangements come into effect.

(Text provided by the FCO)

The following question was asked of Her Majesty's Government:

What procedures are envisaged to ensure implementation of Article 39 of the Basic Law of the Hong Kong Special Administrative Region of the People's Republic of China in view of the statement in that article that the provisions of the International Covenant on Civil and Political Rights and of the International Covenant on Economic, Social and Cultural Rights as applied to Hong Kong 'shall remain in force' after 1997?

In reply, the Minister of State, FCO, wrote:

The Basic Law, promulgated by China's National People's Congress in 1990, will replace the Letters Patent as Hong Kong's constitutional document when it comes into effect on 1 July 1997. It will entrench the ICCPR and the ICESCR as applied to Hong Kong through Article 39.

Hong Kong's Bill of Rights Ordinance, which fully reflects the provisions of the ICCPR as applied in Hong Kong, provides the vehicle for substantive rights to be justifiable in Hong Kong.

The ICESCR contains a number of objectives which States Party are committed to achieving. It does not define certain minimum rights of the individual as the ICCPR does. For this reason, no States Party have incorporated the objectives set out in the ICESCR in domestic law. For Hong Kong after 1 July 1997, as for States Party, the primary obligation will be to achieve progressively the realisation of the objectives of the ICESCR.

(HL Debs., vol. 566, *WA 101*: 23 October 1995)

The following question was put to Her Majesty's Government:

Whether they intend to give effect to the Human Rights Committee's recommendation (UN Document CCPR/C/79/Add.55 of the 27th July 1995) that the Criminal Justice and Public Order Act 1994 and the equivalent legislation in Northern Ireland be reviewed in order to ensure that the provisions which allow inferences to be drawn from the silence of accused persons do not compromise the implementation of various provisions in Article 14 of the International Covenant on Civil and Political Rights?

In reply, the Minister of State, Home Office, wrote:

The Government do not accept that the provisions of the Criminal Justice and Public Order Act 1994 on inferences from silence, or the comparable legislation in Northern Ireland, contravene in any way the provisions of the International Covenant on Civil and Political Rights.

(HL Debs., vol. 566, *WA 141*: 30 October 1995)

The following question was asked of Her Majesty's Government:

Further to the Answer . . . on 23 October 1995 (*WA 101*), whether the provisions of the International Covenant on Civil and Political Rights and of the International Covenant on Economic and Social and Cultural Rights, as applied to Hong Kong, will remain in force after 1997 in terms of the reporting obligations imposed by each covenant to ensure international supervision of the observance of the rights recognised by the covenants?

In reply, the Minister of State, FCO, wrote:

The last paragraph of Chapter XIII of Annex I to the Joint Declaration (JD 156), reflected in Article 39 of the Basic Law, obliges China to ensure that the provisions of the International Covenant on Civil and Political Rights and the International Covenant on Economic, Social and Cultural Rights, as applied to Hong Kong, remains in force. The British Government firmly believes that the Covenants, as prescribed by JD 156 and BL 39, necessarily entail continuing reporting to the UN Human Rights Committee as required by the covenants.

We have described to the Chinese Government reporting procedures under the covenants and how the United Kingdom fulfils its obligations in respect of Hong Kong under the covenants. We have also made our views known to China as to how it may fulfil its obligations under JD 156. We will continue to work for a satisfactory resolution of this question.

(HL Debs., vol. 566, *WA 169*: 2 November 1995)

In reply to a question, the Minister of State, FCO, wrote:

The European Committee for the Prevention of Torture's report on its most recent visit to Turkey in 1994 has yet to be made available. We have not yet been informed on the extent to which the committee found its earlier recommendations had been implemented. We are not aware of any new measures in Turkey designed to implement the recommendations of the UN Committee against Torture in its report to the General Assembly in 1994. We have consistently made clear to the Turkish Government that we expect them to co-operate fully with all human rights mechanisms established under international treaties and conventions to which they are parties.

(HL Debs., vol. 566, *WA 169–70*: 2 November 1995)

The following question was asked of Her Majesty's Government:

Whether they will list those States Parties to the International Covenant on Civil and Political Rights whose governments have rejected in their entirety the recommendations made by the Human Rights Committee, for the full domestic implementation of the Covenant, pursuant to Article 40 of the Convention; and

Whether they consider that their rejection of all the Human Rights Committee's recommendations (UN document CCPR/C/79/Add.55 of 27 July 1995) for full implementation in the United Kingdom of the International Covenant on Civil and Political Rights will make it more difficult for the United Kingdom to ensure that the People's Republic of China implements the Covenant in Hong Kong after the transfer of sovereignty on 1 July 1997; and

Whether they consider the Human Rights Committee to be a body of persons of high moral character and recognised competence in the field of human rights, whose views on the United Kingdom's implementation of its legal obligations under the International Covenant on Civil and Political Rights should, except for cogent and compelling reasons, be implemented.

The Government spokesman in the House of Lords wrote in reply:

Article 28(2) of the International Covenant on Civil and Political Rights (ICCPR) provides that the Human Rights Committee should possess the characteristics that the noble Lord describes. The Government respect the views of the committee, which, unlike the Covenant itself, are not legally binding. The Government have not rejected the committee's recommendations issued on 27 July 1995 concerning the United Kingdom's fourth periodic report. As my noble friend Lady Blatch said on 26 October 1995 [HL Deb, col. 1187], the Government noted the Committee's observations but do not plan any specific changes in the arrangements for the protection of human rights in the United Kingdom in the light of them. In their next periodic report, the Government will report on the measures which they have adopted to give effect to the rights recognised in the Covenant and on progress made in the enjoyment of those rights. The Government are not able to give details about the reaction of other States Parties to the comments of the committee after consideration of their reports. That is a matter for them. As far as Hong Kong is concerned, the last paragraph of Chapter XIII of Annex I to the Joint Declaration (JD 156), reflected in Article 39 of the Basic Law, obliges China to ensure that the provisions of the ICCPR, as applied to Hong Kong, shall remain in force. The committee's observations on the United Kingdom's fourth periodic report have no relevance to Hong Kong, in respect of which a separate periodic report has been submitted.

(HL Debs., vol. 566, *WA 193*: 7 November 1995)

Asked why Her Majesty's Government have not ratified Protocol No. 9 of the European Convention on Human Rights, the Government spokesman in the House of Lords wrote:

We do not believe that becoming party to Protocol 9 would significantly enhance the protection of human rights in the U.K. On the other hand, it would add considerably to the workload of and consequent delays in the Court, which Protocol 11 is designed to reduce. Protocol 9 will, moreover, be repeated when Protocol 11 comes into force.

(HL Debs., vol. 566, *WA 193*: 7 November 1995)

Speaking in the Third Committee of the UN General Assembly on 27 November 1995, the representative of Spain, on behalf of the EU, stated:

The European Union strongly condemns the execution on 10 November of Mr. Ken Saro-Wiwa and his eight co-defendants, which constituted a clear breach by *Nigeria* of its obligations under the international instruments to which Nigeria is a party. We condemn the human rights violations perpetrated by the military regime, including capital punishment and harsh prison sentences implemented after flawed judicial processes and without granting the possibility of recourse to a higher court. In this context, it expresses its particular concern at the detention without trial of political figures and the suspension of habeas corpus.

(Text provided by the FCO)

In the course of an oral answer, the Prime Minister, Mr John Major, stated:

We are certainly unhappy about some of the rulings made under the European convention on human rights. We have made that point and that we will continue to do so. We were one of the founders of the European convention on human rights which, as my hon. Friend knows, is a quite separate matter from the European Court of Justice. That does not alter the fact that we and a number of other countries have been profoundly unhappy with some of its rulings. As I have said, we have made that point clear and will continue to do so.

We have not said that we shall withdraw from the European convention on human rights. We have said that we are profoundly dissatisfied with some of the court's judgments and that we propose to take that up with the European Commission on Human Rights and deal with it in some way in the future.

(HC Debs., vol. 268, col. 488: 7 December 1995)

In reply to a question, the Minister of State, FCO, stated:

We have decided to renew for five years our acceptance of the two optional articles of the European convention on human rights which expires for the United Kingdom on 13 January 1996. Individuals will therefore continue to be able to bring cases under article 25—the right of individual petition—and the Government will continue to accept the jurisdiction of the European Court of Human Rights under Article 46. The United Kingdom first accepted these articles in 1966. They have both been renewed for consecutive periods of five years for the last 20 years.

As my right hon. Friend the Prime Minister informed the House on 7 December, *Official Report*, column 488, the Government were not satisfied with some of the rulings made under the convention by the European Court of Human Rights in Strasbourg. We will initiate discussions with other members of the Council of Europe, and representatives of its institutions, to change and improve the way in which the convention system works. We are developing specific proposals to achieve this, which we believe will be widely welcomed.

(HC Debs., vol. 268, WA, col. *645*: 13 December 1995; see also HL Debs., vol. 567, *WA 117*: 14 December 1995)

Part Five: II. *Organs of the State—ministers*

[*Editorial Note*: the following written answer by the Parliamentary Under-Secretary of State, Ministry of Agriculture, Fisheries and Food, Earl Howe, to a question relating to the decision of the House of Lords in *Pepper* v. *Hart* [1993] AC 593, is reproduced here out of general legal interest]:

An implication of the *Pepper* v. *Hart* decision is that, if legislation is ambiguous or obscure, the courts may in certain circumstances take account of statements made in Parliament by Ministers or other promoters of a Bill in construing that legislation.

Textual clarity and precision, and the avoidance of ambiguity, will continue to be high priorities in drafting legislation. Nonetheless, in the light of the ruling, administrative procedures are being put into place for avoiding or correcting any errors or ambiguities arising out of ministerial statements during the passage of legislation. In particular: speeches and speaking notes will generally be reviewed by a department's legal adviser for possible influence on interpretation; the *Hansard* record of Ministers' contributions to debates on legislation will similarly be reviewed to consider whether there is any inaccuracy; and, where it seems sensible to do so, Ministers may more frequently offer to reflect and take further advice on points of interpretation that are raised in debate.

If it does prove necessary to correct a ministerial statement, the aim will be to do this as promptly as possible at an appropriate point during the further consideration of the Bill.

(HL Debs., vol. 563, *WA 26*: 5 April 1995)

Part Five: IV. *Organs of the State—diplomatic agents and missions*

In reply to a question, the Parliamentary Under-Secretary of State, FCO, wrote:

The number of foreign nationals—that is diplomats officially accredited to missions in London—expelled from the United Kingdom since 1979 is as follows:

	Nationality	*Number*
1979	nil	—
1980	Libya	3
1981	Soviet Union	1
1982	nil	—
1983	Czechoslovakia	2
1984	Czechoslovakia	2
	Libya	2
	Soviet Union	1
1985	Soviet Union	2
1986	nil	—
1987	Bulgaria	1
	Soviet Union	1
1988	Soviet Union	1
	Cuba	2
	Vietnam	1
	Czechoslovakia	3
	Iraq	4
1989	Czechoslovakia	4
	South Africa	3
	Soviet Union	8
1990	Iraq	11
1991	Iraq	9
1992	Iran	1
1993	nil	—
1994	Iran	1
	Sudan	1

(HC Debs., vol. 252, WA, col. *500*: 18 January 1995)

In reply to a further question, the same Minister wrote:

The information you request was not centrally recorded before 1972, but the number of diplomats officially accredited to missions in London who were expelled between 1972 and 1978 is as follows:

1972: Yemen 1
1974: Cuba 1
1974: nil
1975: nil
1976: nil
1977: nil
1978: Iraq 7

(Ibid., vol. 253, WA, col. *450*: 27 January 1995)

In reply to a question, the Minister of State, FCO, wrote:

Twenty-five alleged serious offences by persons entitled to diplomatic immunity were drawn to the attention of the Foreign and Commonwealth Office in 1994. 'Serious offences' are defined in accordance with the report to the Foreign Affairs Committee *The Abuse of Diplomatic Immunities and Privileges (1985)* as offences which fall into the category which in certain circumstances attract a maximum penalty of six months' imprisonment or more: the majority involved drinking and driving and shoplifting.

Six diplomats or members of their families were withdrawn from post in Britain as a result of alleged offences, compared with one the previous year.

(HL Debs., vol. 563, *WA 110*: 2 May 1995)

Part Five: VII. *Organs of the State—armed forces*

In reply to the question what jurisdiction the Visiting Forces Act 1952 gives to American military personnel to take action against persons entering bases to make a peaceful protest, the Minister of State for the Armed Forces wrote:

The Visiting Forces Act 1952 does not give United States service personnel jurisdiction to take action against United Kingdom citizens. In accordance with article VII of the NATO status of forces agreement, however, the United States visiting forces are entitled to police premises made available to them in the United Kingdom and, with due regard to United Kingdom law, to take all appropriate measures to ensure the maintenance of order and security on such premises.

United States service personnel do not have more legal powers over United Kingdom citizens in this country than the Ministry of Defence police.

(HC Debs., vol. 253, WA, col. *286*: 25 January 1995)

Part Five: VIII. A. *Organs of the State—immunity of organs of the State—diplomatic and consular immunity*

In moving the approval in the House of Lords of the Vienna Document 1994 (Privileges and Immunities) Order 1995, the Government spokesman, Lord Chesham, stated:

My Lords, the purpose of this order is to confer privileges and immunities on observers, inspectors, evaluators and auxiliary personnel in accordance with the provisions of the 1994 Vienna Document of the Negotiations on Confidence and Security Building Measures. The Vienna Document 1994, which was adopted on 28th November 1994, integrates a new set of confidence and security building measures. These build on those adopted in the earlier Vienna Document 1992, which it supersedes and with which your Lordships will be familiar.

Agreement by the 53 states of the Organisation for Security and Cooperation in Europe to the provisions of the Vienna Document 1994 is a welcome enhancement of military transparency and predictability throughout Europe. It has a particular role to play in reducing the risk of confrontation and tension.

A necessary component in any arms control regime is the ability to monitor compliance with the regime's obligations. In the case of the Vienna Document 1994, this is done by means of observations, evaluations and short-notice on-site challenge inspections carried out by representatives of individual OSCE states. The document requires that those certain persons mentioned previously are granted during their mission privileges and immunities in accordance with the Vienna Convention on Diplomatic Relations.

The number of missions to the United Kingdom is not very high. We are liable to receive up to three inspections and two evaluation visits a year. Observations are by invitation and are linked to the size of military exercises, demonstrations of new types of military equipment and visits to combat air-bases.

This order is necessary for the United Kingdom to give effect in domestic law to these provisions on privileges and immunities. The order is being made under Section 1(2) of the Arms Control and Disarmament (Privileges and Immunities) Act 1988.

(HL Debs., vol. 567, cols. 449–50: 23 November 1995; see also HC, Third Standing Committee on Statutory Instruments etc., 1 November 1995, col. 1)

Part Five: VIII. B. *Organs of the State—immunity of organs of the State—immunity other than diplomatic and consular*

Mr A. Aust, Legal Counsellor, FCO, addressed a letter to a firm of solicitors which had enquired about the operation of the State Immunity Act 1978. The letter, which was undated but sent in the latter months of 1994, stated in part:

. . .

2. Section 21(d) of the State Immunity Act provides that a certificate issued by or on behalf of the Secretary of State shall be conclusive evidence on any question whether, and if so when, a document has been served or received as mentioned in Section 12(1) or (5). The provision merely goes to the weight which the court must give to the evidence contained in the certificate. There is nothing in the section, or elsewhere in the Act or in Order 11, Rule 5(6), which requires a certificate to be given, or as to the circumstances in which one should be given. A certificate has never before, to our knowledge, been given on the matters mentioned in section 21(d).

3. The FCO gives certificates during the course of legal proceedings in the United Kingdom, both when such certificates are envisaged by statute (as here) and when they are not. A typical example of the latter would be a certificate as to whether or not HMG recognises a particular country as a State. Since this is a question of fact which is peculiarly within the knowledge of the Secretary of State, it is appropriate for it to be certified by him rather than introduced in argument or evidence. The practice is that certificates (statutory or non-statutory) are issued only once it has been established that an issue which can

properly be certified needs to be resolved for the proper disposition of legal proceedings. This means that the FCO seldom, if ever, issue a certificate of this kind on the sole application of one party to an action. It is usually better and more convenient for a question to be formulated by the court once it has been able to form a view, with the assistance of both or all parties, whether a certificate is required in order to enable it to dispose of the issue and, if so, on what question.

(Text provided by the FCO)

In reply to a question about the need to provide information to (a) the Oslo Commission (b) the European Commission and (c) the London Dumping Convention, on disposal at sea of surplus chemical weapon munitions, redundant explosives and other military origin toxic materials, the Minister of State, Ministry of Agriculture, Fisheries and Food, wrote:

There are no requirements to report any information on disposal at sea to the European Commission. The reporting requirements of the London and Oslo conventions do not extend to military wastes which are covered by sovereign immunity. However, the UK no longer disposes such wastes at sea.

(HC Debs., vol. 261, WA, col. *377*: 12 June 1995)

In reply to the question 'what factors are taken into account when granting foreign nationals residing in the United Kingdom immunity from United Kingdom taxes', the Financial Secretary to the Treasury wrote:

Immunity from direct taxation is accorded to income and gains beneficially owned by foreign Heads of State and their Governments. This treatment has its origins in a principle of international law, which has been recognised by successive Governments in this country.

There is no immunity from Customs and Excise duties and taxes.

(HC Debs., vol. 264, WA, col. *310*: 19 October 1995)

Part Six: I. A. *Treaties—conclusion and entry into force—conclusion, signature, ratification and accession*

(See also Part Three: I.C. 4. (items of 5 May and 6 July 1995), above)

The following question was asked of Her Majesty's Government:

Whether they consider that it is a constitutional convention, contained in the so-called 'Ponsonby Rule', that the Government do not proceed to the ratification of a treaty until the treaty has lain on the table of each House of Parliament for a period of 21 sitting days, and that, in the case of important treaties, the Government submit them to each House for discussion within this period.

In reply, the Minister of State, FCO, wrote:

It has been the practice of successive Governments for the past hundred years to lay before Parliament, in the Treaty Series of Command papers, all treaties entered into by the United Kingdom, but only after their entry into force. Since 1924, it has also been the practice (known as the 'Ponsonby Rule') to lay before Parliament, before entry into force, those treaties which have been signed subject to ratification. The treaty lies on the table in the normal case for a period of 21 sitting days, after which it is ratified and published again in the Treaty Series once it has entered into force. The Ponsonby Rule, which applies as indicated only to treaties which are subject to ratification (or its equivalent), has been understood as allowing for exceptions from its operation in special cases, when other means of consulting or informing Parliament may be employed in its stead.

The above practices are not understood as precluding the Government, in appropriate cases, from proceeding to ratification (or its equivalent) without laying for 21 days or from concluding treaties which enter into force on signature.

The practice is more fully described in an affidavit sworn for the purposes of the proceedings in *R.* v. *Secretary of State for Foreign and Commonwealth Affairs, ex p. Rees-Mogg.* . . .

. . . departures from the Ponsonby rule are in practice rare.

(HL Debs., vol. 566, *WA 159–60*: 1 November 1995; see also UKMIL 1993, pp. 629–33)

In reply to the question

whether it remains part of the practice known as the 'Ponsonby Rule' (referred to in Appendix 4 to H.L. Paper 80 of Session 1990–91) that, in the case of the important treaties, the Government submit them to each House of Parliament for discussion during the period of 21 days after the treaty is laid on the table of each House,

the Minister of State, FCO, wrote:

The practice relating to the discussion of important treaties has not changed. It is for the Government of the day to determine which treaties not requiring legislation are of sufficient importance that a debate on a Motion should be held.

(HL Debs., vol. 567, *WA 38*: 28 November 1995)

In reply to a question asking for a list of the exceptions to the Ponsonby Rule, the Minister of State, FCO, wrote:

In the past, alternative procedures have occasionally been used to inform Parliament of treaties which the Government propose to ratify:

(i) by adopting a Motion;
(ii) by passing a Bill;
(iii) by making an announcement in a debate;
(iv) by adopting a Resolution or a Motion as part of the Affirmative Resolution procedure for making an Order in Council;
(v) by answering a parliamentary Question;

(vi) by consulting leaders of the Opposition and other Parliamentary parties.

However, no records are available of specific cases in which such alternative procedures have been employed during the last 15 years.

(HL Debs., vol. 567, *WA 121*: 18 December 1995)

In reply to further questions about the operation of the Ponsonby Rule, the Government spokesman in the House of Lords wrote:

General guidance is issued to government departments by the Foreign and Commonwealth Office which retains responsibility for compliance with the Ponsonby Rule and all other matters to do with the ratification of treaties. The gist of this guidance was published in the *British Year Book of International Law 1992* (volume LXIII at page 704).

(HL Debs., vol. 567, *WA 135*: 19 December 1995; see also UKMIL 1992, p. 704)

There are no fixed criteria for determining which treaties are debated in Parliament for discussion. The matter is decided case by case.

(Ibid., *WA 136*)

In reply to the question

Further to the Answer . . . on 28 November 1995 (HL Deb, col. *WA 38*), whether in determining which treaties not requiring legislation are of sufficient importance that a debate on a Motion be held, they consider themselves bound by the statement made in 1924 by the then Under-Secretary of State for Foreign Affairs, Mr. Ponsonby, that 'if there is a formal demand for discussion forwarded through the usual channels from the Opposition or any other party, time will be found for the discussion of the Treaty in question' (HC Deb, 1 April 1924, col. 2003),

the Government spokesman in the House of Lords wrote:

The Government do not consider themselves bound by a statement made over 70 years ago by a member of an Administration of a different political persuasion. However, in responding to requests for debate, the Government have regard to a wide range of considerations and give due weight to representations made by the Opposition and others.

(Ibid., *WA 152*: 20 December 1995)

The following text of a document conferring full power for the signature of a treaty is reproduced as an example of its kind:

WHEREAS, for the better treating of and arranging certain matters which have come into discussion between the Government of the United Kingdom of Great Britain and Northern Ireland and all States and the other entities referred to in Article 305 1(a), (c), (d), (e) and (f) of the United Nations Convention on the Law of the Sea of 10 December 1982 relative to the Conservation and Management of Straddling Fish Stocks and Highly Migratory Fish Stocks, it is expedient that a fit person should be invested with Full Power on the part of the

United Kingdom of Great Britain and Northern Ireland: I, Malcolm Leslie Rifkind, One of Her Majesty's Counsel learned in the Law, a Member of Her Majesty's Most Honourable Privy Council, &c., &c., Her Majesty's Principal Secretary of State for Foreign and Commonwealth Affairs, do hereby certify that David Heywood Anderson, Companion of the Most Distinguished Order of Saint Michael and Saint George, Second Legal Adviser at the Foreign and Commonwealth Office, is by these Presents named, constituted and appointed as Plenipotentiary and Representative having Full Power and Authority to sign the Agreement for the Implementation of the Provisions of the United Nations Convention on the Law of the Sea of 10 December 1982 relating to the Conservation and Management of Straddling Fish Stocks and Highly Migratory Fish Stocks, in respect of Bermuda, British Indian Ocean Territory, British Virgin Islands, Falkland Islands, Pitcairn Islands, South Georgia and the South Sandwich Islands, St Helena including Ascension Island, and Turks and Caicos Islands. Further, I do hereby certify that the provisions of the said Agreement shall, subject to Ratification by the Government of the United Kingdom of Great Britain and Northern Ireland, be agreed to, acknowledged and accepted by the said Government of the United Kingdom of Great Britain and Northern Ireland in the fullest manner.

In witness whereof I have signed these Presents and affixed hereto my Seal.

Signed and sealed at the Foreign and Commonwealth Office, London, the Thirtieth day of November, One thousand Nine hundred and Ninety-five.

MALCOLM RIFKIND

(Text provided by the FCO)

Part Six: I. B. *Treaties—conclusion and entry into force—reservations and declarations to multilateral treaties*

In reply to a question, the Government spokesman in the House of Lords wrote:

The current list of reservations entered by the United Kingdom to the United Nations Convention on the Elimination of all Forms of Discrimination against Women is as follows . . .

Declarations and reservations entered on behalf of the United Kingdom of Great Britain and Northern Ireland

(a) The United Kingdom understands the main purpose of the Convention, in the light of the definition contained in article 1, to be the reduction, in accordance with its terms, of discrimination against women, and does not therefore regard the Convention as imposing any requirement to repeal or modify any existing laws, regulations, customs or practices which provide for women to be treated more favourably than men, whether temporarily or in the longer term; the United Kingdom's undertakings under article 4, paragraph 1, and other provisions of the Convention are to be construed accordingly.

(b) The United Kingdom reserves the right to regard the provisions of the Sex Discrimination Act 1975, the Employment Protection (Consolidation) Act 1978, the Employment Act 1980, the Sex Discrimination (Northern Ireland) Order 1976, the Industrial Relations (No. 2) (Northern Ireland) Order 1976, the Industrial Relations (Northern Ireland) Order 1982, the Equal Pay Act 1970 (as amended) and the Equal Pay Act (Northern Ireland) 1970 (as amended), including the exceptions and exemptions contained in any of these Acts and Orders, as constituting appropriate measures for the practical realisation of the objectives of the Convention in the social and economic circumstances of the United Kingdom, and to continue to apply these provisions accordingly; this reservation will apply equally to any future legislation which may modify or replace the above Acts and Orders on the understanding that the terms of such legislation will be compatible with the United Kingdom's obligations under the Convention.

(c) In the light of the definition contained in article 1, the United Kingdom's ratification is subject to the understanding that none of its obligations under the Convention shall be treated as extending to the succession to, or possession and enjoyment of, the Throne, the peerage, titles of honour, social precedence or armorial bearings, or as extending to the affairs of religious denominations or orders or to the admission into or service in the Armed Forces of the Crown.

(d) The United Kingdom reserves the right to continue to apply such immigration legislation governing entry into, stay in and departure from the United Kingdom as it may deem necessary from time to time and, accordingly, its acceptance of article 15(4) and of the other provisions of the Convention is subject to the provisions of any such legislation as regards persons not at the time having the right under the law of the United Kingdom to enter and remain in the United Kingdom.

Article 1

With reference to the provisions of the Sex Discrimination Act 1975 and other applicable legislation, the United Kingdom's acceptance of article 1 is subject to the reservation that the phrase 'irrespective of their marital status' shall not be taken to render discriminatory any difference of treatment accorded to single persons as against married persons, so long as there is equality of treatment as between married men and married women and as between single men and single women.

Article 2

In the light of the substantial progress already achieved in the United Kingdom in promoting the progressive elimination of discrimination against women, the United Kingdom reserves the right, without prejudice to the other reservations made by the United Kingdom, to give effect to subparagraphs (f) and (g) by keeping under review such of its laws and regulations as may still embody significant differences in treatment between men and women with a view to making changes to those laws and regulations when to do so would be compatible with essential and overriding considerations of economic policy. In relation to forms of discrimination more precisely prohibited by other provisions of the Convention, the obligations under this article must (in the case of the United Kingdom) be read in conjunction with the other reservations and declarations made in respect of those provisions including the declarations and reservations of the United Kingdom contained in paragraphs (a)–(d) above.

With regard to subparagraphs (f) and (g) of this article the United Kingdom reserves the right to continue to apply its law relating to sexual offences and prostitution; this reservation will apply equally to any future law which may modify or replace it.

Article 9

The British Nationality Act 1981, which was brought into force with effect from January 1983, is based on principles which do not allow of any discrimination against women within the meaning of article 1 as regards acquisition, change or retention of their nationality or as regards the nationality of their children. The United Kingdom's acceptance of article 9 shall not, however, be taken to invalidate the continuation of certain temporary or transitional provisions which will continue in force beyond that date.

The United Kingdom reserves the right to take such steps as may be necessary to comply with its obligations under article 2 of the First Protocol to the Convention for the Protection of Human Rights and Fundamental Freedoms signed at Paris on 20 March 1952 and its obligations under paragraph 3 of article 13 of the International Covenant on Economic, Social and Cultural Rights opened for signature at New York on 19 December 1966, to the extent that the said provisions preserve the freedom of parental choice in respect of the education of children; and reserves also the right not to take any measures which may conflict with its obligation under paragraph 4 of article 13 of the said Covenant not to interfere with the liberty of individuals and bodies to establish and direct educational institutions, subject to the observation of certain principles and standards.

Article 10

The United Kingdom can only accept the obligations under subparagraph (c) of article 10 within the limits of the statutory powers of the central Government, in the light of the fact that the teaching curriculum, the provision of textbooks and teaching methods are reserved for local control and are not subject to central Government direction; moreover, the acceptance of the objective of encouraging coeducation is without prejudice to the right of the United Kingdom also to encourage other types of education.

Article 11

The United Kingdom interprets the 'right to work' referred to in paragraph 1(a) as a reference to the 'right to work' as defined in other human rights instruments to which the United Kingdom is a party, notably article 6 of the International Covenant on Economic, Social and Cultural Rights of 19 December 1966.

The United Kingdom interprets paragraph 1 of article 11 in the light of the provisions of paragraph 2 of article 4, as not precluding prohibitions, restrictions or conditions on the employment of women in certain areas, or on the work done by them, where this is considered necessary or desirable to protect the health and safety of women or the human foetus, including such prohibitions, restrictions or conditions imposed in consequence of other international obligations of the United Kingdom.

The United Kingdom reserves the right to apply all United Kingdom legislation and the rules of pension schemes affecting retirement pensions, survivors' benefits and other benefits in relation to death or retirement (including retirement on grounds of redundancy), whether or not derived from a social security scheme.

This reservation will apply equally to any future legislation which may modify or replace such legislation, or the rules of pension schemes, on the understanding that the terms of such legislation will be compatible with the United Kingdom's obligations under the Convention.

The United Kingdom reserves the right to apply the following provisions of United Kingdom legislation concerning the benefits specified:

(a) Social security benefits for persons engaged in caring for a severely disabled person under section 37 of the Social Security Act 1975 and section 37 of the Social Security (Northern Ireland) Act 1975;
(b) Increases of benefit for adult dependants under sections 44 to 47, 49 and 66 of the Social Security Act 1975 and under sections 44 to 47, 49 and 66 of the Social Security (Northern Ireland) Act 1975;
(c) Retirement pensions and survivors' benefits under the Social Security Acts 1975 to 1982 and the Social Security (Northern Ireland) Acts 1975 to 1982;
(d) Family income supplements under the Family Income Supplements Act 1970 and the Family Income Supplements Act (Northern Ireland) 1971.

This reservation will apply equally to any future legislation which may modify or replace any of the provisions specified in subparagraphs (a) to (d) above, on the understanding that the terms of such legislation will be compatible with the United Kingdom's obligations under the Convention.

The United Kingdom reserves the right to apply any non-discriminatory requirement for a qualifying period of employment or insurance for the application of the provisions contained in article 11(2).

Article 15

In relation to article 15, paragraph 2, the United Kingdom understands the term 'legal capacity' as referring merely to the existence of a separate and distinct legal personality.

In relation to article 15, paragraph 3, the United Kingdom understands the intention of this provision to be that only those terms or elements of a contract or other private instrument which are discriminatory in the sense described are to be deemed null and void, but not necessarily the contract or instrument as a whole.

Article 16

As regards paragraph 1(f) of article 16, the United Kingdom does not regard the reference to the paramountcy of the interests of the children as being directly relevant to the elimination of discrimination against women, and declares in this connection that the legislation of the United Kingdom regulating adoption, while giving a principal position to the promotion of the children's welfare, does not give to the child's interests the same paramount place as in issues concerning custody over children.

The United Kingdom's acceptance of paragraph 1 of article 16 shall not be treated as either limiting the freedom of a person to dispose of his property as he wishes or as giving a person a right to property the subject of such a limitation.

(HL Debs., vol. 564, *WA 30–4*: 16 May 1995)

In reply to a further question on the same subject, the spokesman wrote:

The United Kingdom's reservations to the United Nations Convention on the Elimination of All Forms of Discrimination against Women are reviewed regularly. In June 1993 the Government announced it was withdrawing part of its reservation under Article 11 on underground work and its reservation under Article 13 on tax. All changes to reservations are fully reported in the Government's periodic reports to the Convention. The next UK report is due to be published in June 1995.

(Ibid., *WA 33*: 16 May 1995)

Addressing the UN Human Rights Committee on 20 July 1995, the FCO Legal Adviser, Sir Franklin Berman, submitted written observations on the subject of the International Covenant on Civil and Political Rights. The observations read as follows:

1. The United Kingdom is of course aware that the General Comments adopted by the Committee are not legally binding. They nevertheless command great respect, given the eminence of the Committee and the status of the International Covenant on Civil and Political Rights. The issue dealt with in General Comment Number 24 (52) (reservations to the Covenant) is one of great importance, both in respect of the development of the Covenant and the Committee's role under it and in its wider ramifications. The United Kingdom is therefore grateful for the opportunity provided under Article 40(5) of the Covenant to submit to the Committee certain observations on the General Comment.

2. These will be divided into four parts: *the legal régime regulating reservations to the Covenant*; *the criteria for assessing compatibility with the object and purpose of the Covenant*; *the power to determine compatibility with the object and purpose*; *the legal effect of an incompatible reservation.*

The Legal Régime regulating Reservations to the Covenant

3. The United Kingdom shares the Committee's concern that the integrity of the Covenant's treaty régime should not be undermined by too extensive a practice of reservations formulated by States on becoming Party to them. The United Kingdom agrees also that individual reservations may on occasion be so widely drawn as to cast doubt on whether their maintenance is compatible with

being Party to the Covenant. Regrettable though it may be, such a situation is not materially different from that obtaining in other areas of international relations, and would not provide a justification for a different legal régime to regulate reservations to human rights treaties. To create such a special régime by amendment of the Covenant would be a major task. To do so as part of the development of general international law would, all other considerations aside, be undesirable if the effect was to fragment this aspect of the law of treaties which is currently under study by the International Law Commission.

4. The modern law of reservations to multilateral treaties moreover owes its origin to the Advisory Opinion of the International Court of Justice of 28 May 1951 on Reservations to the Genocide Convention. The Genocide Convention is itself (in the Committee's phrase) a human rights treaty concluded for the benefit of persons within the jurisdiction of the States Parties to it. As the International Court observed, the Genocide Convention is of a type in which 'the contracting States do not have any interests of their own; they merely have, one and all, a common interest, namely the accomplishment of those high purposes which are the raison d'être of the Convention'. It was in the light precisely of those characteristics of the Genocide Convention, and in the light of the desirability of widespread adherence to it, that the Court set out its approach towards reservations. The United Kingdom does not accordingly believe that rules different from those foreshadowed by the International Court and in due course embodied in the Vienna Convention on the Law of Treaties are required to enable the international community to cope with reservations to human rights treaties. The correct approach is rather to apply the general rules relating to reservations laid down in the Vienna Convention in a manner which takes full account of the particular characteristics of the treaty in question.

5. The argument that the existing rules of international law are inadequate to cope with human rights treaties rests in any case, as the United Kingdom sees it, on a mistaken assumption. The Committee says in paragraph 17 that the Vienna Convention's provisions on the role of State objections in relation to reservations are inappropriate to address the problem of reservations to human rights treaties. This is because such treaties 'are not a web of inter-State exchanges of mutual obligations' and because '[t]he principle of reciprocity has no place'. The United Kingdom does not find this to be an adequate account, for various reasons. In the first place, it is not the basis on which the International Court of Justice approached the Genocide Convention (paragraph 3 above). In the second place, it is not the view taken by other authoritative bodies, such as the European Court of Human Rights, which held in 1978[1] that the European Convention on Human Rights 'comprises *more than* mere reciprocal engagements between Contracting States. It creates *over and above a network of mutual bilateral understandings*, objective obligations which in the words of the preamble benefit from a "collective enforcement"' (emphasis added)[2]. In the third place, both the faculty under Article 41 of the Covenant for bringing inter-State complaints and the widespread practice of States in invoking the Covenant as against other States Parties in respect of the treatment of individuals show that in a very real and practical sense even the substantive provisions of the Covenant are indeed regarded as creating 'a network of mutual bilateral undertakings'. Finally, it must be assumed that, in respect of reservations which are clearly *compatible with* the object and purpose of the Covenant, the Committee accepts

that States Parties exercise the rights and functions assigned to them by the Vienna Convention. If so, it is not easy to discover a logical ground for ruling out these rights and functions for other reservations, including those where there is at least a reasonable measure of doubt as to whether the reservation is or is not compatible with the object and purpose of the Covenant. Given therefore that the bilateral rights and general interests of other Parties are, as indicated, directly affected, the United Kingdom regards it as a self-evident proposition that the reaction of those Parties to a reservation formulated by one of them is of direct significance both in law and in practice. In short, the legal effect of any particular reservation to a human rights treaty is an amalgam of the terms of the treaty and the terms and import of the reservation, in the light of the reactions to it by the other treaty Parties and in the light of course of any authoritative third-party procedure that may be applicable.

---

[1] Ireland v. United Kingdom.
[2] Series A, no. 25, p. 90, para. 239.

The Criteria for assessing Compatibility with the Object and Purpose of the Covenant

6. The United Kingdom shares the Committee's view that an automatic identification between non-derogability and compatibility with the object and purpose is too simplistic. Derogation from a formally contracted obligation and reluctance to undertake the obligation in the first place are not the same thing. The United Kingdom is likewise of one mind with the Committee that multi-facetted treaties like the Covenants pose considerable problems over the ascertainment of their object and purpose. The problem is one common to all lengthy treaties containing numerous provisions of coordinate status with one another.

7. The United Kingdom is however less convinced by the argument that, because human rights treaties are for the benefit of individuals, provisions in the Covenant that represent customary international law may not be the subject of reservations. It is doubtful whether such a proposition represents existing customary international law; it is not a view shared by most commentators, and States have not expressly objected to reservations on this ground. In the United Kingdom's view, there is a clear distinction between choosing not to enter into treaty obligations and trying to opt out of customary international law. Such a distinction is inherent in the Committee's recognition that reservations to Articles that guarantee customary international law rights are permitted provided that the right is not deprived of its basic purpose.

8. For broadly similar reasons, the United Kingdom does not wholly share the Committee's concern over reservations which exclude the acceptance of obligations which would require changes in national law to ensure compliance with them. The Committee's comments that 'no real international rights or obligations have thus been accepted' and that 'all the essential elements of the Covenant guarantees have been removed' miss the fact that States Parties, even while entering such reservations, do at least accept the Committee's supervision, through the reporting system, of those Covenant rights guaranteed by their national law.

The Power to determine Compatibility with the Object and Purpose

9. The United Kingdom shares the Committee's view as to the seriousness of the issue of compatibility of reservations with the object and purpose of the treaty in question. It does not however believe that this is the central issue in the law and practice of reservations to multilateral conventions. The vast majority of reservations are in practice dealt with satisfactorily through the operation of the normal rules in the Vienna Convention, it being borne in mind that another Contracting State always has the right formally to object even to a reservation which is undoubtedly admissible (except in the special case of a reservation expressly permitted by the treaty). The question of compatibility with the object and purpose is confined to a small number of extreme cases.

10. It is clear however that a legal régime of reservations that depends to any extent on the general criterion of compatibility with the object and purpose of a treaty as a whole will be uncertain in its operation in the absence of an objective method for determining whether the criterion is satisfied. The availability of binding third-party procedures could be of great importance in this respect, as the International Law Commission itself recognised at the outset. This state of affairs inevitably raises a serious question as to the proper role which the Committee itself may play, to which the Committee has given serious consideration at pp. 6–7 of the General Comment.

11. The United Kingdom shares the analysis that the Committee must necessarily be able to take a view of the status and effect of a reservation where this is required in order to permit the Committee to carry out its substantive functions under the Covenant. Thus, the Committee might find itself unable in particular cases to deliver a report under the special powers conferred upon it by Article 41 or the First Optional Protocol, except on the basis of a view as to the impact of a given reservation. Similarly, the Committee might, according to the circumstances, find it appropriate to form or express its view on a reservation for the purpose of questioning a State Party in its reports under Article 40 or for the purpose of reporting its own conclusions. Paragraph 20 of the General Comment, however, uses the verb 'determine' in connection with the Committee's functions towards the status of reservations, and does so moreover in the context of its *dictum* that the task in question is inappropriate for the States Parties. This would appear to have implications which call for comment.

12. Without wishing to take a final view on the matter, the United Kingdom would make the following points:

(a) even if it were the case (as the General Comment argues but the United Kingdom doubts: see paragraphs 3–5 above) that the law on reservations is inappropriate to address the problem of reservations to human rights treaties, this would not of itself give rise to a competence or power in the Committee except to the extent provided for in the Covenant; any new competence could only be created by amendment to the Covenant, and would then be exercisable on such terms as were laid down;

(b) no conclusion as to the status or consequences of a particular reservation could be properly *determinative* unless it were binding not only on the reserving State Party but on all the Parties to the Covenant, which would in turn automatically presuppose that the Parties had undertaken in proper form a prior legal obligation to accept it;

(c) there is a qualitative distinction between decisions judicially arrived at after full legal argument and determinations made without the benefit of a judicial process.

The Legal Effect of an Incompatible Reservation

13. The Committee correctly identifies Articles 20 and 21 of the Vienna Convention on the Law of Treaties as containing the rules which, taken together, regulate the legal effect of reservations to multilateral treaties. The United Kingdom wonders however whether the Committee is right to assume their applicability to incompatible reservations. The rules cited clearly do apply to reservations which are fully compatible with the object and purpose but remain open for acceptance or objection (see paragraph 9 above). It is questionable however whether they were intended also to cover reservations which are inadmissible *in limine*. For example, it seems highly improbable that a reservation expressly *prohibited* by the treaty (the case in Article 19(a) of the Vienna Convention) is open to acceptance by another Contracting State. And if so, there is no clear reason why the same should not apply to the other cases enumerated in Article 19, including incompatibility with the object and purpose under 19(c). The *Genocide Convention* Advisory Opinion did indeed deal directly with the matter, by stating that acceptance of a reservation as being *compatible* with the object and purpose entitles a party to consider the reserving State to be party to the treaty. In the converse case (i.e. the case where the reservation is *not* compatible with the object and purpose) the Court states plainly, 'that State cannot be regarded as being a party to the Convention'[1]. This is the approach which the United Kingdom has consistently followed in its own treaty practice.

[1] ICJ Reports 1951, at p. 29.

14. The General Comment suggests, *per contra*, that an 'unacceptable' reservation will generally be severable, in the sense that the Covenant will be operative for the reserving party as if the reservation had not been entered. The United Kingdom agrees that severability of a kind may well offer a solution in appropriate cases, although its contours are only beginning to be explored in State practice. However the United Kingdom is absolutely clear that severability would entail excising both the reservation *and* the parts of the treaty to which it applies. Any other solution they would find deeply contrary to principle, notably the fundamental rule reflected in Article 38(1) of the Statute of the International Court of Justice, that international conventions establish rules 'expressly recognized by' the Contracting States. The United Kingdom regards it as hardly feasible to try to hold a State to obligations under the Covenant which it self-evidently has not 'expressly recognized' but rather has indicated its express unwillingness to accept. The United Kingdom fears that, questions of principle aside, an approach as outlined in paragraph 20 of the General Comment would risk discouraging States from ratifying human rights conventions[1] (since they would not be in a position to reassure their national Parliaments as to the status of treaty provisions on which it was felt necessary to

reserve) or might even lead to denunciations by existing Parties who ratified against a set of assumptions different from those now enunciated in the General Comment.

---

[1] A similar point applies for example to the First Optional Protocol, to which the United Kingdom is not however a party.

15. The United Kingdom believes that the only sound approach is accordingly that adopted by the International Court of Justice: a State which purports to ratify a human rights treaty subject to a reservation which is fundamentally incompatible with participation in the treaty régime cannot be regarded as having become a party at all—unless it withdraws the reservation. The test of incompatibility is and should be an objective one, in which the views of competent third parties would carry weight. Ultimately however it is a matter for the treaty Parties themselves and, while the presence or absence of individual State 'objections' should not be decisive in relation to an objective standard, it would be surprising to find a reservation validly stigmatized as incompatible with the object and purpose of the Covenant if none of the Parties had taken exception to it on that ground. For all other reservations the rules laid down in the Vienna Convention do and should apply—except to the extent that the treaty regulates such matters by its own terms.

16. The United Kingdom wishes finally to express its gratitude to the Committee for having focussed attention on what is undoubtedly a real and serious problem and for having illuminated the underlying issues. Inasmuch as these issues go wider than the Covenant itself, or than human rights treaties in general, the United Kingdom proposes to reflect further on how international consideration of these matters can best be carried forward.

(Text provided by the FCO; see also CCPR/C/SR.1432, p. 6)

Speaking on 24 November 1995 in the Third Committee of the UN General Assembly considering the implementation of human rights instruments, the representative of Spain, on behalf of the EU, stated:

The European Union, in accordance with the recommendations of the chairpersons of the Treaty monitoring bodies, appeals to States considering ratification of international human rights instruments to avoid making it subject to wide reservations. We are particularly concerned about the abundant use of reservations by acceding states aimed at excluding the applicability of provisions that are the core of an instrument or accepting obligations only if they are consistent with domestic legislation. At their most extreme, such reservations are incompatible with the object and purpose of the instrument concerned and, as such, are not acceptable under treaty law.

The significance of national and regional particularities and various historical, cultural and religious backgrounds should not be invoked to undermine the universality of human rights instruments. We wish to reiterate that reservations are not meant to be an expedient for acquiring international respectability by purported adherence to a treaty, while ignoring in practice most of its obligations. Finally, States that have made reservations should regularly consider the possibility of withdrawing them or further limiting their scope.

(Text provided by the FCO; see also A/C.3/50/SR.38, p. 19)

Part Six: II. B. *Treaties—observance, application and interpretation—application*

During a debate on the subject of restrictions imposed by the Spanish authorities on movement in and out of Gibraltar, the Minister of State, FCO, Mr David Davis, stated:

We do not accept that the present delays at the Gibraltar frontier can be justified by the Schengen agreement. When the civil governor of Cadiz predicted problems over Easter, he implied that Spain would knowingly understaff the Gibraltar border posts. That is unacceptable. I do not know whether that policy was co-ordinated with Madrid. I have no evidence as yet that it was, and I hope that it was not to be taken seriously as an expression of Spanish Government policy. Part of the view from Cadiz appears to be that the Spain-Gibraltar frontier is an external frontier of Europe. As hon. Members know, Gibraltar is an integral part of the European Union and it must be treated as such. Article 227(4) of the European Community treaty extends the application of the treaty to Gibraltar. It states: 'the provisions of this treaty shall apply to European Territories for whose external relations a member state is responsible.'

The Schengen convention is an agreement between certain member states of the European Union but it is not a European Union agreement. It cannot supersede the rights of UK citizens, including Gibraltarians, under EC law. There should be no discrimination between Schengen and non-Schengen EU nationals at the border. We are closely monitoring the position to observe that.

(HC Debs., vol. 260, col. 306: 17 May 1995)

Part Six: II. C. *Treaties—observance, application and interpretation—interpretation*

(See also Part Eight: IV. (item of 3 November 1995), below)

On 2 June 1994, the UK Government submitted a written statement to the International Court of Justice in the course of proceedings arising out of a request for an advisory opinion made by the World Health Assembly. The statement contained the following paragraph:

13. So far as the WHO Constitution is concerned, it is a treaty which must be interpreted in accordance with the rules governing interpretation of treaties; and paramount amongst these is the principle of good faith. As expressed by one distinguished commentator

> 'Or, si le traité doit être exécutée de bonne foi, il doit nécessairement être interprété de bonne foi. L'exécution dépend de l'interprétation et, sans se confondre, ces deux opérations juridiques sont intimement liées.'[6]

It would lack good faith to interpret that Constitution now, in 1993, so as to embody in it an obligation for Member States relating to the use of nuclear weapons which was never intended and which for 45 years no Member State has ever thought to exist. Indeed, for the Court to adopt so expansive a view of those treaty obligations would be highly damaging to international institutions, for States would be wary about taking on membership when this might imply legal obligations not spelt out in the constituent treaty, and not discernible by any accepted means of treaty interpretation.

---

[6] Yasseen, 'L'interprétation de traités d'après la Convention de Vienne sur le Droit des Traités' 151 Recueil des Cours (1976–III), 221.

In June 1995, the UK Government submitted a written statement to the International Court of Justice in the course of proceedings arising out of a request by the UN General Assembly for an advisory opinion on the same subject. The statement contained the following paragraphs:

(1) General Considerations

3.88 First, it is a fundamental principle of the law of treaties that a prohibitive rule, purporting to exclude a particular activity from the scope of permissible State practice, must be clearly stated. Referring to 'the need of express terms to alter an existing rule of law', Lord McNair quotes, 'in spite of its antiquity' the principle stated by Sir Leoline Jenkins that

> '. . . Treaties . . . are not to be understood as altering or restraining the Practice generally received, unless the Words do fully and necessarily infer an Alteration or Restriction.'[168]

---

[168] McNair, *The Law of Treaties* (1961), p. 463.

3.89 As a basic proposition, one cannot, therefore, infer from general words, or a treaty of general application, a prohibitive rule of specific content that would have the effect of limiting the scope of otherwise permissible State conduct. It would be neither sound practice nor sufficient to rely upon general provisions of international law on human rights or the environment for the purpose of conjuring up a rule prohibiting the threat or use of nuclear weapons by way of legitimate self-defence. Indeed, such an approach would pose considerable dangers for the wider integrity and effectiveness of the provisions of law in question.

3.90 Secondly, both the performance and interpretation of treaties are subject to the overriding obligation of good faith. One aspect of this is that:

> '. . . it would be a breach of this obligation for a party to make use of an ambiguity in order to put forward an interpretation which it was known to the negotiators of the treaty not to be the intention of the parties.'[169]

---

[169] *Ibid.*, p. 465.

3.91 In the words of the Permanent Court of International Justice, the text of a treaty cannot

'. . . be enlarged by reading into it stipulations which are said to result from the proclaimed intentions of the authors of the Treaty, but for which no provision is made in the text itself.'[170]

[170] *Polish War Vessels in Danzig*, PCIJ Reports, Series A/B, No. 43, p. 142.

3.92 Considering this obligation in the light of the principle of effectiveness, Sir Hersch Lauterpacht noted that:

'. . . good faith requires no more than that effect be given, in a fair and reasonable manner, to the intention of the parties. This means that on occasions, if such was the intention of the parties, good faith may require that the effectiveness of the instrument should fall short of its apparent and desirable scope. The principle of effectiveness cannot transform a mere declaration of lofty purpose—such as the Universal Declaration of Human Rights—into a source of legal rights and obligations. . . . Equally, although a recommendation, which is not binding, by an organ of the League of Nations or the United Nations is of less potency than a binding decision, this does not mean that it is open to a judicial tribunal to endow with binding character an expression, however politically or morally weighty, of collective opinion.'[171]

[171] *The Development of International Law by the International Court of Justice* (1958), pp. 292–3.

3.93 Thus, the fact that a treaty *could* be construed to achieve a particular result does not mean that it *should* be so construed. Particularly in the context of a case such as that presently in issue, the construction of a treaty to achieve a purpose not within the contemplation of its authors would be inappropriate. In the context of treaties having as their express object the protection of specific aspects of the ecosystem, there is also a danger that such an approach could undermine the integrity of these conventions and impugn their normative quality more generally. It would also do great disservice to the cause of environmental protection if the prospect of judicial creativity in the interpretation and application of such treaties translated into caution on the part of States when it came to participating in such agreements in the future.

3.94 Thirdly, 'treaties must be applied and interpreted against the background of general principles of international law.'[172] This rule now finds partial expression in Article 31(3)(c) of the Vienna Convention on the Law of Treaties, 1969, which permits 'any relevant rules of international law applicable in the relations between the parties' to be taken into account for the purposes of the interpretation of treaties. On this principle, one commentator has noted that 'every treaty provision must be read not only in its own context, but also in the wider context of general international law, whether conventional or customary'.[173] A treaty cannot, therefore, be construed in a vacuum, or in the abstract, without reference to other rules of international law with which it may interact.

[172] McNair, *op. cit.*, p. 466.

[173] Sinclair, *The Vienna Convention on the Law of Treaties* (2nd ed., 1984), p. 139.

3.95 One aspect of this rule which is of particular importance in the present context is that, save to the extent expressly provided, a treaty must be construed against the background of the inherent right of self-defence. In other words, save to the extent expressly provided, a treaty cannot be construed so as to restrict the inherent right of States to act by way of legitimate self-defence.
3.96 As stated, this proposition merely reflects the fundamental and overriding character of self-defence in general international law. In the words of Judges Anzilotti and Huber in the *Wimbledon* case:

> 'The right of a State to adopt the course which it considers best suited to the exigencies of its security and to the maintenance of its integrity, is so essential a right that, in case of doubt, treaty stipulations cannot be interpreted as limiting it, even though those stipulations do not conflict with such an interpretation.'[174]

---

[174] *Case of the SS Wimbledon*, PCIJ Reports, Series A, No. 1, p. 37.

3.97 Although these comments were made in the context of a joint dissenting opinion, the text of Article 380 of the Treaty of Versailles in issue in the proceedings, and the judgment of the Court, implied that Germany would have been entitled, in the event of a war in which it was involved, to restrict access to the Kiel Canal, notwithstanding the terms of the Treaty. The dissent was therefore on the issue of Germany's rights in the case of a war in which it was not involved. In so far as is material to the present case, therefore, the proposition stated by Judges Anzlotti and Huber is not at variance with the judgment of the Court and may be regarded as of general application.
3.98 In the light of these observations, the issue before the Court in respect of the law of human rights and the law on protection of the environment is not whether the use or threat of use of nuclear weapons is, in the abstract, compatible with those laws. Rather, it is whether any of the rules of the law of human rights or the law on environmental protection can be construed, in accordance with the general principles stated above, as prohibiting the use or threat of use of nuclear weapons *when carried out by way of legitimate self-defence*.

(Statement, pp. 61–4; text provided by the FCO)

After considering certain environmental treaties, the statement concluded on this point:

In the United Kingdom's view, the relevant principle of law is that stated by the Permanent Court of International Justice in the *Polish War Vessels in Danzig* case—the text of a treaty cannot be enlarged by reading into it stipulations for which no provision is made in the text itself.'

(Statement, p. 70 (footnote omitted); text provided by the FCO)

Part Eight II. A. *State territory and territorial jurisdiction—territorial jurisdiction—territorial sovereignty*

(See also Part Two: X. and Part Three: I.E. (item of 27 September 1995), above)

The UK Government deposited with the UN Secretary-General on 4 January 1995 the following declaration concerning an objection made by the Argentine Government to the extension by the UK of the Convention on Psychotropic Substances, 1971:

> The British Government have no doubt about the sovereignty of the United Kingdom over the Falkland Islands, as well as South Georgia and the South Sandwich Islands, and have no doubt, therefore, about their right to extend the said Convention to these territories. The British Government can only reject as unfounded the claim by the Government of Argentina that these Islands are a part of Argentine territory.

(TS No. 80 (1995); Cm 3063, p. 6)

In the course of a debate on the subject of the Russian incursion into Chechnya, the Minister of State, FCO, Mr Douglas Hogg, stated:

> The suffering in Chechnya is the latest tragedy in a list of events since the collapse of the former Soviet Union that includes other conflicts in the Caucasian region. The Chechens are proud of their warrior tradition. During the 19th century, there was frequent fighting between Russia and the tribesmen of the northern Caucasus. In 1859, Chechnya became part of the Russian empire, although that did not end the conflict.
>
> Subsequently, Chechnya, together with the rest of the Russian empire, was incorporated into the Soviet Union. During the second world war, Stalin ordered the forced deportation of the Chechen people, and thousands died. The consequences of that act of barbarism are with us today.
>
> Alone among the leaders of the Russian Federation, General Dudayev was unwilling to negotiate seriously with Moscow on the republic's status within the federation. In November 1991, the general unilaterally declared independence, which received no international recognition.
>
> . . .
>
> In formulating our approach to this tragedy, we have to be clear about the status of Chechnya. Chechnya is part of the Russian Federation. That is the view of the British Government. That is the view of the international community. Against that background, we have identified three priorities.
>
> . . .
>
> For the Russians, the status of Chechnya is a matter of great importance. They emphasize that Chechnya is part of the Russian Federation and, as I have said, the international community accepts that fact.
>
> But equally, in view of the commitments that Russia has made in the OSCE, what is happening in Chechnya is a matter of legitimate international concern.

(HC Debs., vol. 252, cols. 686–7: 17 January 1995)

In reply to oral questions on the subject of the above incursion, the Government spokesman in the House of Lords, Lord Inglewood, stated:

So far as concerns the position of the Chechens in the Russian Federation, it is important that we appreciate that the Russian Federation comprises 87 different component parts. The Chechens are part of that federation which, in turn, was created by the dissolution of the old Soviet Union. They are and historically have been for some time part of Russia.

Chechnya is part of the Russian Federation. If, within the constitution of that federation, they wish to secede and that was agreed by all the parties concerned, it would be a matter for them.

(HL Debs., vol. 560, cols. 756–8, *passim*: 19 January 1995)

The following question was asked:

What is the present value in international law of the United Nations General Assembly Resolutions 181(II) of 29 November 1947, 194(III) of 11 December 1948 and 303(IV) of 9 December 1949 declaring the city of Jerusalem a *corpus separatum* under a special international régime; and what means exist, or could be envisaged, by which these resolutions might be brought into force?

In reply, the Minister of State, FCO, wrote:

We acknowledge the *corpus separatum* defined by General Assembly Resolutions 181(II) of 1947, 194(III) of 1948, and 303(IV) of 1949, which includes the city of Jerusalem and its surroundings. These resolutions of the UN General Assembly were not mandatory. According to the Declaration of Principles signed by Israel and the Palestinians, the status of Jerusalem remains to be determined in the permanent status negotiations between the parties. The outcome of these negotiations should not be prejudiced by agreements reached for the interim period.

(HL Debs., vol. 560, *WA 87–8:* 26 January 1995)

The following question was asked:

Whether any subsequent government of Israel has repudiated the statement of the then Prime Minister of that country (made on 7 April 1949 and reported in UN General Assembly Document A/838) that his government accepted without reservation an international régime for, or international control of, the Holy Places in the city of Jerusalem, but could not accept the establishment of an international régime for that city?

In reply, the Minister of State, FCO, wrote:

We know of no such repudiation by an Israeli government. To the contrary: in 1950, the Knesset declared that Jerusalem was the country's capital, although Israel held only the western sector of the city. Government institutions were progressively transferred there. Following the 1967 war, Israel annexed the old, eastern and former Jordanian sector *de facto*. In 1980, Israel enacted its 'Jerusalem law', formally proclaiming the united city to be its capital.

The UK is at one with the international community in rejecting all such claims. Our position has been repeatedly expressed in UN resolutions, in national statements and in company with our EU partners. We do not accept that commitments concerning the Holy Places alter, or are relevant to, the fact that Israel's efforts unilaterally to change the status of the city of Jerusalem contravene international law.

(Ibid., *WA 88*)

The following question was asked of the Secretary of State for Foreign and Commonwealth Affairs:

. . . what position the United Kingdom Government are taking up over the proper extent of Moroccan territorial water to be included in the EU-Morocco fishing agreement; and if he will make it his policy that no disputed territorial waters will be so included?

In reply, the Minister of State, FCO, wrote:

As with all EC fisheries agreements, the waters under the sovereignty or jurisdiction of Morocco will not be defined. The United Kingdom Government do not consider the renegotiation of the EC-Morocco fisheries agreement the appropriate place to address the issue of the sovereignty of the former Spanish Sahara.

(HC Debs., vol. 255, WA, col. *209*: 22 February 1995)

In the course of a debate on the subject of the Falkland Islands, the Minister of State, FCO, Mr David Davis, stated:

We have no doubt about the sovereignty of the islands and the right to self-determination involves respecting the wishes of the people of the Falklands.

(HC Debs., vol. 257, col. 282: 22 March 1995)

In reply to the question

what consideration Her Majesty's Government have given to making representations to the Universal Postal Union in respect of postage stamps issued by the Argentine postal authorities bearing the words 'Islas Malvinas'; and if he will make a statement,

the Minister of State, FCO, wrote:

We have not made representations to the Universal Postal Union about the stamps in question. However, we have protested to the Argentine Government about the issue, reiterating our sovereignty over the Falklands Islands, and informing the Argentines that they have no right to issue such stamps.

(HC Debs., vol. 260, WA, col. *81*: 15 May 1995)

On 27 September 1995, the Governments of the UK and Argentina signed a Joint Declaration on Co-operation over Offshore Activities in the South West Atlantic. At the same time, the UK Government issued a declaration which read in part as follows:

The Joint Declaration safeguards British sovereignty and jurisdiction over the Falkland Islands and the surrounding maritime areas. HMG have no doubts about the sovereignty and jurisdiction of the UK.

HMG are aware that Argentina proposes to enact legislation purporting to impose charges on companies working in maritime areas surrounding the Falkland Islands. HMG do not accept any Argentine claim to impose such charges on companies by reason only of their activities on the continental shelf around the Falkland Islands under Falklands licence. HMG will be working with the Falkland Islands Government in the development of the forthcoming Licensing Round. We welcome the understanding as a beneficial factor which will reassure the oil industry and improve the climate for exploration for and exploitation of hydrocarbons in a frontier area.

(Text provided by the FCO).

Speaking on 11 October 1995 in the UN Fourth Committee, the UK representative, Mr P.T. Arkwright, stated:

In his speech on behalf of the Rio Group earlier today, the distinguished representative of Ecuador expressed the wish for a solution to be found to the sovereignty dispute over the Falklands, South Georgia and the South Sandwich Islands. The position of the British Government on these matters is well known. It was set out most recently by the British Delegation in the UK right of reply to the statement to the General Assembly by the Argentine Foreign Minister on 27 September.

(Text provided by the FCO; see also A/C.4/50/SR.6, p. 12; see also Part Three: I.E. (item of 27 September 1995), above)

In reply to the question what was Her Majesty's Government's position on the future of Gibraltar, the Minister of State, FCO, wrote:

My right honourable friend the Member for Watford (Mr. Garel-Jones) made clear the Government's position in another place on 6 December 1990. It has not changed.

First, and most important, Britain stands by its commitment to the people of Gibraltar, enshrined in the 1969 constitution. The Government will not enter into arrangements under which the people of Gibraltar would pass under the sovereignty of another state against their freely and democratically expressed wishes.

Secondly, we continue to recognise the validity of the Treaty of Utrecht, which established British title to Gibraltar. Article X of the treaty gave Spain the right of 'first refusal', if Gibraltar ceased to be British. Any constitutional change would have to be compatible with the Treaty of Utrecht and sustainable in practice. Independence would only be an option for Gibraltar if Spain agreed.

Thirdly, Spain is Gibraltar's immediate neighbour. The Government recognise the importance of negotiations with Spain, including through the Brussels Process, to overcome the existing differences over Gibraltar. Our ultimate goal is to achieve a lasting solution which is acceptable to all parties and mutually beneficial.

(HL Debs., vol. 567, *WA 116*: 14 December 1995; See also UKMIL 1990 p. 558)

Part Eight: II. D. *State territory and territorial jurisdiction—territorial jurisdiction—extra-territoriality*

(See also Part Nine: VII. H., below)

In December 1994, the UK Government communicated its comments on the draft 'Antitrust Enforcement Guidelines for International Operations' issued by the US Department of Justice and Federal Trade Commission on 13 October 1994. The comments read as follows:

The Government of the United Kingdom is grateful for this opportunity to comment on the draft 'Antitrust Enforcement Guidelines for International Operations' ('the Guidelines') issued by the Department of Justice and Federal Trade Commission ('the Agencies') on 13 October 1994. The Guidelines provide a most useful statement of the Agencies' policy and of their interpretation of US law. The United Kingdom and United States have a shared interest in ensuring fair and open competition in international business. Nevertheless, the Guidelines demonstrate that there remain significant differences in the scope of the two countries' antitrust laws, the principles upon which they are based and the approach to their enforcement.

2. Although the new Guidelines recognise the importance of comity analysis and foreign sovereign compulsion in decisions on enforcement, both are narrowly construed. The UK Government is particularly concerned that insufficient weight is given to these factors in an era of increasing co-operation in enforcement of antitrust cases with international aspects. The Guidelines give an impression of increasing willingness on the part of the Agencies to take unilateral action in such cases. This approach could lead to jurisdictional conflicts which would hinder effective co-operation and enforcement to the benefit of neither party. The detailed comments on the Guidelines below reflect these concerns.

Jurisdiction

3. One of the areas of difference is our interpretation of the proper extent of jurisdiction. In support of their claims for the extent of jurisdiction under US antitrust law the Agencies state that there is increasing international recognition of the 'effects doctrine'. They cite European Community law as an example. One of the criteria governing the application of Articles 85 and 86 of the EC Treaty is that anti-competitive conduct under investigation should 'affect trade between Member States'. However, in the European Court of Justice case cited by the Agencies (Ahlstrom v. Commission), the Court accepted that there was a legitimate jurisdictional claim only because the conduct in question was implemented in the Community. The Court, therefore, distinguished 'implementation' in the Community from the 'effects' doctrine as espoused by US law. It is only under the US interpretation of the 'effects doctrine' that commercial actions that are not implemented within US territory, such as those cited in Examples C and F, are, nevertheless, regarded as falling within US jurisdiction.

4. Furthermore, certain claims to jurisdiction rest on the effect that conduct which takes place wholly outside the US would have on US export commerce. The Agencies assert that foreclosure of a foreign market or refusal to adopt US technical standards is sufficient to establish the requisite effect. Such jurisdictional claims show US antitrust law being used as an instrument of trade policy to open markets perceived as closed to US exporters. The UK Government regards this as an objectionable and inappropriate use of antitrust powers.
5. The UK Government is also concerned that the Guidelines confirm the use of US antitrust law as an instrument of domestic policy to assert jurisdiction in those instances where the US Government finances or procures goods or services outside the territory of the US. In such cases, jurisdiction should lie only with the country where the conduct took place.
6. A contrast can be drawn between the approach taken to the actions of importers trying to enter the US market and the position of US exporters trying to enter foreign markets. It seems ironic at a time when the Agencies are ever more prepared to pursue foreign cartels, as in Examples A and B, that apparently similar actions by US firms are under certain circumstances sanctioned by the Webb-Pomerene Act, as in Example M.

Enforcement: Comity, Foreign Sovereign Compulsion and Personal Jurisdiction

7. The UK Government welcomes the statement that international comity has to be taken into account in the enforcement of US antitrust law, and that the Agencies do not discriminate on the basis of the nationality of the parties. The clear statement of the factors that the Agencies will take into account in making a comity analysis is also welcome. However, it appears from this statement and the circumstances in which the defence of foreign sovereign compulsion will be available that the principles of both comity and foreign sovereign compulsion will be very narrowly construed. The Agencies have introduced the effectiveness of foreign enforcement as a new factor to be weighed in comity analysis. This indicates that they will be increasingly prepared to consider unilateral action on the basis of whether foreign Governments are prepared to take action or the perceived adequacy of remedies available in a particular jurisdiction. The Agencies' willingness to pursue unilateral action does not give appropriate recognition, in cases falling principally within the jurisdiction of foreign governments, to the law and policy of foreign governments which may include a decision not to pursue a particular case. It follows that the UK Government would object to unilateral action based solely on the Agencies' assessment of the adequacy of enforcement in other countries. The apparent absence in a given case of a conflict of enforcement does not on its own justify enforcement activity by the Agencies.
8. In addition, the Guidelines indicate that personal jurisdiction will be widely construed to make persons or foreign entities subject to the jurisdiction of US courts and that compulsory measures will be used against such persons where other efforts to secure co-operation have failed even where there is no alleged activity in the US. Personal jurisdiction will be asserted over a foreign person or entity where it 'transacts business' in the US. However, in Example I this includes foreign firms that merely purchase from US suppliers. As far as

personal jurisdiction is concerned, the UK Government maintains that this is a question of fact to be determined in the particular circumstances of any case.

9. The UK Government considers that the Agencies' approach to comity and personal jurisdiction can be expected to lead to more frequent confrontation with other sovereign states and in appropriate cases to action being taken by states to protect their national interests. In this context, the UK Government objects to the statement in the Guidelines that particular statutes might 'purport to prevent persons from disclosing documents or information for use in United States proceedings'. It is a legitimate exercise of national sovereignty for a state to act to protect its sovereignty and its trading interests. The invocation of such a statute by a foreign government would be an important indication of the degree of governmental concern and should be regarded as decisive in the Agencies' comity analysis.

Co-operation

10. While no formal bilateral co-operation agreement exists between the United States and the UK Government and competition authorities, the UK Government stands ready to develop the existing informal arrangements and contacts as fully as possible within existing legal and policy constraints.

(Text provided by the FCO. The final version of the Guidelines, issued in April 1995, was published in *International Legal Materials*, 34 (1995), pp. 1080–1114. The Guidelines include the lettered examples referred to in the above comments, which are too long to be conveniently reproduced here)

The EU Presidency issued a statement on 5 April 1995 in respect of Cuba. It read in part as follows:

The European Union once again draws the attention of the United States authorities to its serious concern regarding the possible adoption by Congress of the Bill on Liberty and Democratic Solidarity with Cuba (Bill S 381-Helms Bill and HR 927-Burton Bill).

The European Union would point out in this connection that it is opposed to the adoption of any measure having extraterritorial application and in breach of WTO rules.

(*Bulletin of the European Union*, 1995–3, p. 60)

Part Eight: IV. *State territory and territorial jurisdiction—regime under the Antarctic Treaty*

The following passages are extracted from a Background Brief entitled *Britain and Antarctica* published by the FCO in June 1995 and are reproduced here for general interest:

Since Antarctica was discovered in 1774 by the British navigator, Captain James Cook, on a voyage of scientific research and discovery, British scientists and explorers have been closely involved with the area. Britain's permanent presence there dates from 1943, when the war-time Operation Tabarin was established to provide reconnaissance and meteorological information in the South Atlantic and Antarctic. Since 1962, the British Antarctic Survey (BAS) has been responsible for the Government's scientific research in Antarctica—research which focuses on issues of global importance such as depletion of the ozone layer, atmospheric pollution, global warming and a possible attendant rise in the sea level.

British Antarctic Territory

The British Antarctic Territory (BAT) is the oldest territorial claim in the continent, although most of it is now also claimed by either Chile or Argentina. There is no indigenous population, but the BAS has four permanent research stations there and the Royal Navy maintains an ice patrol vessel, HMS Endurance, in the area. The Territory has its own legal system and legal and postal administrations, and is financially self-sufficient on revenue from income tax and the sale of postage stamps.

Antarctic Treaty system

By the 1950s, five-sixths of the continent was claimed by seven States (see map). None of the claims were recognised by non-Claimant States, however, and the Antarctic Treaty was negotiated to put in place a mechanism to defuse the escalating disputes over sovereignty. It followed the unprecedented scientific cooperation in Antarctica demonstrated by 12 countries during the International Geophysical Year, 1957–58.

Britain was the first to sign the Treaty, which entered into force in 1961. Covering the area south of 60 degrees latitude south, its objectives are:

- to keep Antarctica demilitarised, to establish it as a nuclear-free zone, and to ensure that it is used for peaceful purposes only;
- to promote international scientific cooperation in Antarctica;
- to set aside disputes over territorial sovereignty.

The Treaty provides for confidence-building procedures, including exchanges of information about Antarctic activities and on-site inspections. It also provides means of consulting on matters of common interest.

The Treaty remains in force indefinitely; it has the possibility for review after 30 years (i.e. after June 1991), but no Party has indicated a desire for such a review. It is open for accession to all Member States of the United Nations, and to others by agreement of the Treaty States. Thirty countries have now joined the original 12 . . . , and represent Claimants/non-Claimants, the developed/developing countries, and 80 per cent of the world's population.

Consultative (voting) status is open to all countries which have demonstrated their commitment to Antarctica by conducting significant scientific research there. Twenty-six, including Britain, have Consultative status; they meet at annual (previously biennial) Antarctic Treaty Consultative Meetings (ATCMs), in which non-Consultative Parties and international organisations with expertise are also invited to participate. Eighteen such meetings, held since 1961, have adopted more than 200 regulatory measures known as Recommendations. These have been largely exhortative in terms, though since 1987 an increasing number of mandatory Recommendations have been adopted. More than half of those adopted have dealt with conservation and environmental protection, while

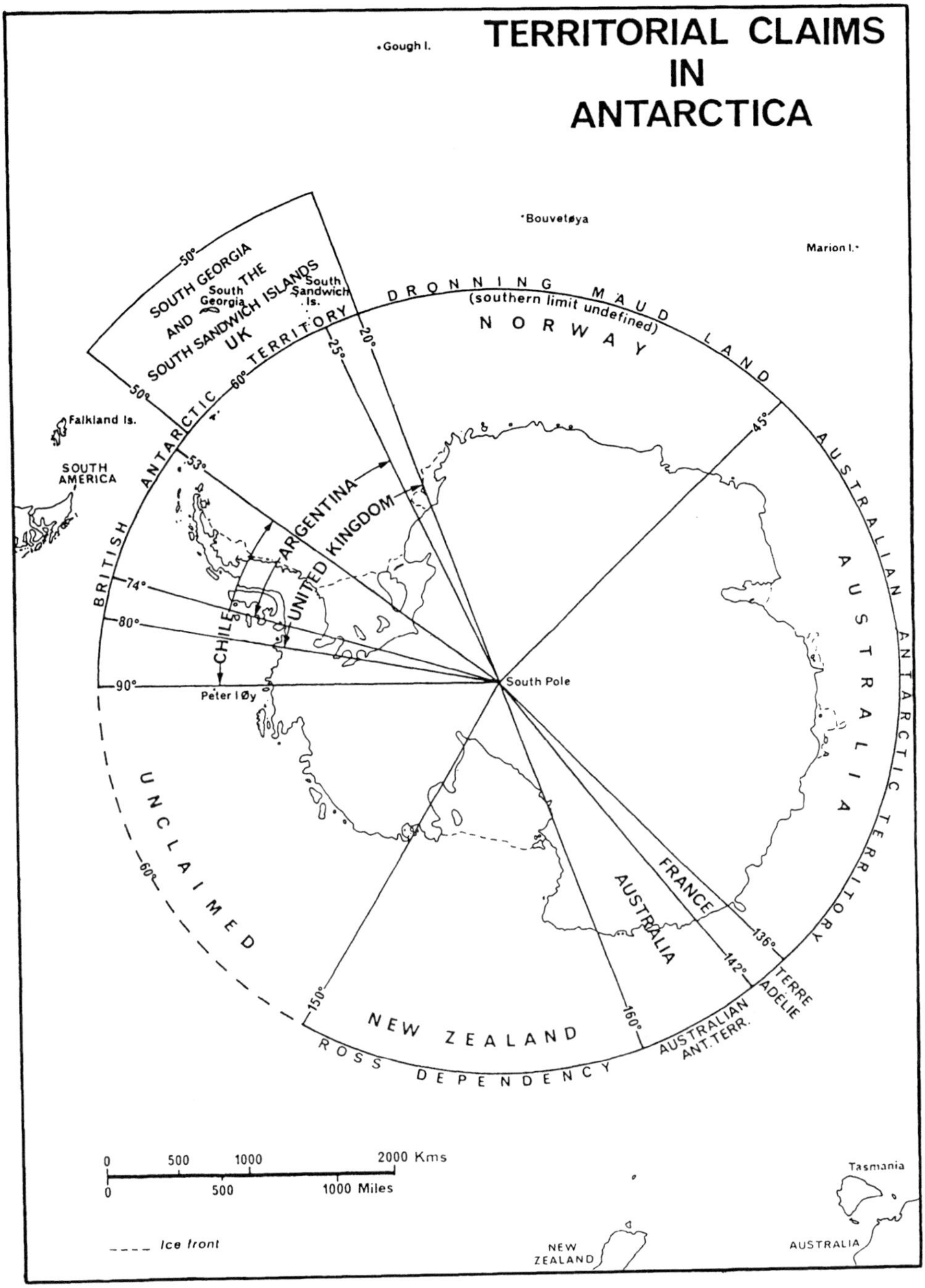
TERRITORIAL CLAIMS IN ANTARCTICA
Gough I.
Bouvetøya
Marion I.
SOUTH GEORGIA AND THE SOUTH SANDWICH ISLANDS UK
South Georgia
South Sandwich Is.
Falkland Is.
SOUTH AMERICA
BRITISH ANTARCTIC TERRITORY
DRONNING MAUD LAND
(southern limit undefined)
NORWAY
AUSTRALIAN ANTARCTIC TERRITORY
AUSTRALIA
ARGENTINA
UNITED KINGDOM
CHILE
Peter I Øy
South Pole
UNCLAIMED
FRANCE
TERRE ADÉLIE
AUSTRALIAN ANT. TERR.
NEW ZEALAND
ROSS DEPENDENCY
50°
60°
53°
25°
20°
45°
74°
80°
90°
136°
142°
150°
160°
0 500 1000 2000 Kms
0 500 1000 Miles
Ice front
Tasmania
NEW ZEALAND
AUSTRALIA

others have covered subjects such as telecommunications, postal service, air safety and meteorological cooperation. Special Consultative Meetings address issues which cannot be adequately examined at the regular gatherings.

Five separate international agreements have been negotiated which, together with the original Treaty and the Recommendations, provide the framework governing all activities in Antarctica. Collectively known as the Antarctic Treaty System, the five agreements are:

- Agreed Measures for the Conservation of Antarctic Fauna and Flora (1964);
- Convention for the Conservation of Antarctic Seals (1972);
- Convention on the Conservation of Antarctic Marine Living Resources (1982);
- Convention on the Regulation of Antarctic Mineral Resource Activities (1988) [superseded by the Environmental Protocol (see below) and unlikely to enter into force];
- Protocol on Environmental Protection to the Antarctic Treaty (1991).

(Text provided by the FCO)

The document included the map reproduced on page 673.

During the meeting of the Commission established under the Convention on the Conservation of Antarctic Marine Living Resources (CCAMLR), the delegates of Argentina, Chile and Brazil made statements about the relationship between the convention regime and the regime of the coastal States. In reply, on 3 November 1995, the Australian delegate stated:

Australia has listened carefully to the statements of Argentina, Brazil and Chile. Australia does not consider that there is any incompatibility between the exercise of coastal state jurisdiction and obligations of the Convention. The legal position is quite clear.

Subparagraphs (b) and (c) of Article IV of the Convention expressly recognise that Parties may exercise coastal state jurisdiction; and such jurisdiction may be exercised in respect of islands within the area of application of CCAMLR. In respect of those islands, CCAMLR makes provision for a modified regime. The Final Act of the Conference on the Conservation of Antarctic Marine Living Resources includes the text of a statement made by the Chairman of the Conference on 19 May 1980 ('the Chairman's Statement') regarding the application of the Convention to the waters adjacent to islands within the area to which the Convention applies. The statement set out four understandings regarding the application of the Convention to those islands. The Final Act records that no objection to the statement was made. In interpreting the Convention one must have regard to any agreement relating to it which was made between the Parties in connection with its conclusion (Vienna Convention on the Law of Treaties 1969, Article 31(2)(a)). The Chairman's Statement falls squarely within that provision.

As regards the policy adopted by coastal states, it is of course correct that CCAMLR was created for the purpose of conserving Antarctic marine living resources (which include fish) by means of international cooperation. The Convention defines 'conservation' as including 'rational use' e.g. fishing. CCAMLR, by its terms and practice, in particular Article IX, unquestionably involves regional fishing regulation. International cooperation involves not only agreeing within CCAMLR on conservation measures, but also requires that the Members of the Commission do what is necessary to ensure that conservation measures are implemented by their national legislation and enforced by national means. CCAMLR has no police force, no fisheries patrol boats. Enforcement rests primarily with those Members of the Commission whose flag vessels fish in the CCAMLR area.

However, as has been demonstrated this year, and in previous years, infringements by flag vessels of Members of the Commission continue, and are increasing despite the efforts made by flag states. Exercise of coastal state jurisdiction is a most useful additional way of seeking to ensure compliance with conservation measures (including compliance by vessels of States which are Parties to the Convention but not Members of the Commission and non-CCAMLR States).

It has been said that coastal states should only exercise their jurisdiction exceptionally when the consensus mechanism of CCAMLR has failed. Australia would not agree with that interpretation for which in our view there is no basis in the Chairman's Statement. But it is nevertheless clear that we as a Commission do not have effective enforcement of conservation measures.

Australia could not accept any suggestion that our exercise of coastal state jurisdiction is in any way inconsistent with the Convention, or its spirit.

We would be pleased to take up the offer of Argentina and Chile to take part in intersessional consultations on these matters, which would include discussion of all relevant aspects, including the question of compatibility of vessel notification systems with international law.

We would also welcome discussion at CCAMLR-XV on how best to attain the objectives of the Convention.

The report then noted: 'The Delegation of the UK strongly associated itself with each and every point in the statement of Australia'.

(Text provided by the FCO)

In reply to the question for what reasons the Antarctic Minerals Act 1989 has not fully been brought into force, the Minister of State, FCO, wrote:

The Convention on the Regulation of Antarctic Mineral Resource Activities (CRAMRA) has, in effect, been superseded by the 1991 Environmental Protocol to the Antarctic Treaty. Provisions to enable the United Kingdom to ratify the Protocol were included in the Antarctic Act 1994. The Act also repealed the Antarctic Minerals Act 1989, except for provisions relating only to the administration of justice for the British Antarctic Territory.

(HC Debs., vol. 267, WA, col. *108*: 22 November 1995)

Part Nine: I. A. *Seas, waterways, ships—territorial sea—delimitation, baselines*

In reply to a question, the Minister of State, Department of the Environment, wrote:

Under international law, territorial waters, and their accompanying jurisdiction, only extend to a maximum of 12 nautical miles from the baseline—that is, the coast or in certain circumstances a line drawn between two headlands. More limited jurisdictions can be claimed in a region up to 200 nautical miles from those baselines. With the other North Sea states, the Government set out their intention in the 1992 Paris declaration of extending jurisdiction in this way in respect of shipping. The Government therefore will make regulations under the Merchant Shipping (Salvage and Pollution) Act 1994 to extend our coastal state jurisdiction over pollution from shipping. In exercising these jurisdictions, the Government complies with the United Kingdom's obligations under the comprehensive system for the protection of the marine environment of the north-east Atlantic contained in the Oslo, Paris and OSPAR conventions and applies the policies agreed in the North Sea conferences, both to the North Sea and other UK waters.

(HC Debs., vol. 262, WA, col. *122*: 19 June 1995)

In reply to a question, the Minister of State, FCO, wrote:

The agreement with France relating to the territorial sea boundary in the Straits of Dover, Cm 733, entered into force on 6 April 1989. The territorial seas of the United Kingdom and Belgium do not meet, but there is an agreement for the delimitation of the continental shelf between the United Kingdom and Belgium, Cm 2499. The delimitation of the continental shelf between the United Kingdom and the Irish Republic is the subject of a 1988 agreement, Cm 990 and a 1992 protocol, Cm 2227.

(HC Debs., vol. 264, WA, cols. *249–50*: 18 October 1995)

In reply to the question 'how many nautical square miles of the United Kingdom's territorial seas are claimed by the Irish Republic in its constitution; and what percentage of the total United Kingdom territorial seas that represents', the Secretary of State for Foreign and Commonwealth Affairs wrote:

We do not recognise the claim by the Irish Republic to Northern Ireland or its territorial sea. No delimitation of Northern Ireland waters has taken place as the British and Irish Governments have not discussed this issue. In the circumstances the information requested is not available and cannot accurately be calculated.

(Ibid., col. *250*)

The following notice was issued by the Hydrographic Department of the Navy on 1 January 1996:

ADMIRALTY NOTICES TO MARINERS

12 NATIONAL CLAIMS TO MARITIME JURISDICTION

Former Notice 2122/95 is cancelled.

The following list shows the breadth of sea (measured from the appropriate baselines) claimed respectively as territorial sea (TS), contiguous zone (CZ), exclusive economic zone (EEZ) and fishery zone (FZ), where no EEZ is claimed, as being under the state's jurisdiction. The information is compiled from various, sometimes unofficial sources, the absence of a limit from this list indicates that the information is not held.

The claims are published for information only. Her Majesty's Government does not recognise claims to territorial seas exceeding twelve nautical miles, to contiguous zones exceeding twenty four nautical miles or to exclusive economic zones and fisheries zones exceeding two hundred nautical miles.

Country	*TS*	*CZ*	*EEZ*	*FZ*
Albania[1]	12**	—	—	12
Algeria[1]	12**	—	—	52[23]
Angola*	20	—	—	200
Antigua and Barbuda[2]*	12**	24	200	—
Argentina[1]	12	24	200	—
Australia[1]*	12[11]	24	200	—
Australian Antarctica	12	—	—	12
Bahamas[2]*	12	—	200	200
Bahrain*	12	24	—	—
Bangladesh[4]	12**	18	200	—
Barbados*	12**	—	200	—
Belgium	12	—	—	200
Belize[1]*	12[17]	—	200	—
Benin	200	—	—	200
Brazil[1]*	12**	24	200	—
Brunei	12	—	200	—
Bulgaria	12**	24	200	—
Burma[1]	12**	24	200	—
Cambodia[1]	12**	24	200	—
Cameroon*	50	—	—	—
Canada[1]	12	—	—	200
Cape Verde Islands[2]*	12	24	200	—
Chile[1]	12	24	200	—
China				
PRC[1]	12**	—	—	—
ROC (Taiwan)	12	—	—	200
Colombia[1]	12	—	200	—
Comoros[2]*	12	—	200	—
Congo	200	—	—	200

Country	*TS*	*CZ*	*EEZ*	*FZ*
Costa Rica*	12	—	200	—
Croatia[1]*	12	—	—	—
Cuba[1]*	12	—	200	—
Cyprus*	12	—	—	12
Denmark[1]	3**	—	—	200
Djibouti[1]*	12	24	200	—
Dominica*	12	24	200	—
Dominican Republic[1]	6	24	200	—
Ecuador[1]	200	—	—	200
Egypt[1]*	12**	24	200	—
El Salvador	200	—	—	200
Equatorial Guinea	12**	—	200	—
Eritrea[1]	12[13]	—	—	—
Estonia	12**[21]	—	200	—
Fiji[2]*	12	24	200	—
Finland[1]	12**[14, 21]	14	—	12[22]
France[1]	12	24	200[15]	12[15]
French Antarctica	12	—	—	—
Gabon	12	24	200	—
Gambia*	12	18	200	—
Georgia	12	—	200	—
Germany[1]*[9]	12	—	—	200
Ghana*	12	24	200	—
Greece*	6	—	—	6
Grenada*	12**	—	200	—
Guatemala	12	—	200	—
Guinea[1]*	12	—	200	—
Guinea Bissau[1]*	12	—	200	—
Guyana*	12**	—	200	—
Haiti	12	24	200	—
Honduras*	12	24	200	—
Iceland[1]*	12	—	200	—
India	12**	24	200	—
Indonesia[2]*	12	24	200	—
Iran[1]	12**	24	200	—
Iraq*	12	—	—	—
Irish Republic[1]	12	—	—	200
Israel	12[18]	—	—	—
Italy[1]*	12	—	—	12
Ivory Coast*	12	—	200	—
Jamaica*	12	—	200	—

Country	*TS*	*CZ*	*EEZ*	*FZ*
Japan	12	—	—	200
Jordan	3	—	—	3
Kenya[1]*	12	—	200	—
Kiribati[2]	12	—	200	—
Korea (North)	12**	—	200	—
Korea (South)[1]	12[6]**	—	—	—
Kuwait*	12	—	—	—
Latvia	12	—	200	—
Lebanon*	12	—	—	—
Liberia	200	—	—	200
Libya[5]	12**	—	—	20
Lithuania	12	—	200	—
Madagascar[1]	12	24	200	—
Malaysia[1]	12	—	200	—
Maldives[3]	12[3]**	—	200[3]	—
Malta[1]*	12**	24	—	25
Mauritania[1]	12	24	200	—
Mauritius[1]*	12**	—	200	—
Mexico[1]*	12	24	200	—
Monaco[3]	12	—	—	12
Morocco[1]	12	24	200	—
Mozambique[1]	12	—	200	—
Namibia*	12	—	200	—
Nauru	12	—	—	200
Netherlands[1]	12	—	—	200
Netherlands Antilles	12	—	—	12
Aruba	12	—	—	12
New Zealand	12	—	200	—
Ross Dependency	12	—	—	—
Nicaragua	200**	—	—	200
Nigeria*	30**	—	200	—
Norway[1]	4	—	200	—
Svalbard	4	—	—	200
Oman[1]*	12	24	200	—
Pakistan	12**	24	200	—
Panama	200	—	—	200
Papua New Guinea[2]	12[16]	—	200	—
Peru	200	—	—	200
Philippines[2]*[3]	12	—	200	—
Poland	12**	—	200	—
Portugal[1]	12	—	200	—

Country	*TS*	*CZ*	*EEZ*	*FZ*
Qatar	12	24	—	to median lines
Romania[1]	12**	24	200	—
Russia[1]	12	—	200	—
St. Kitts-Nevis*	12	24	200	—
St. Lucia*	12	24	200	—
St. Vincent and the Grenadines[2]*	12**	24	200	—
Sao Tome and Principe[2]*	12	—	200	—
Saudi Arabia[1]	12	18	—	—
Senegal[1]*	12	24	200	—
Seychelles*	12	24	200	—
Sierra Leone*	200	—	—	200
Singapore*	3	—	—	3
Slovenia*	12	—	—	—
Solomon Islands[2]	12	—	200	—
Somalia*	200**	—	—	200
South Africa	12	—	—	200
Spain[1]	12	24	200[15]	12[15]
Sri Lanka*	12**	24	200	—
Sudan*	12**	18	—	—
Surinam	12	—	200	—
Sweden[1]	12	—	200	—
Syria	35**	41	—	—
Tanzania[1]*	12	—	200	—
Thailand[1]	12	—	200	—
Togo*	30	—	200	—
Tonga*	12	—	200	—
Trinidad and Tobago[2]*	12	24	200	—
Tunisia[1]*	12	24	—	12[8]
Turkey[1]	12[7]**	—	200[19]	12[7]
Tuvalu	12	24	200	—
UAE[1]	12**	24	200	—
UK[1]	12	—	—	200
Anguilla	3	—	—	200
Bailiwick of Guernsey	3	—	—	12
Bailiwick of Jersey	3	—	—	3
Bermuda	12	—	—	200
British Antarctic Territory	3	—	—	3
British Indian Ocean Territory	3	—	—	200
British Virgin Islands	3	—	—	200
Cayman Islands	12	—	—	200
Cyprus (Sovereign Base Areas)	3	—	—	3
Falkland Islands[1]	12	—	—	200[10]
Gibraltar	3	—	—	3

Country	*TS*	*CZ*	*EEZ*	*FZ*
Hong Kong	3	—	—	3
Isle of Man	12	—	—	12
Montserrat	3	—	—	200
Pitcairn	3	—	200	—
St. Helena and Dependencies	12	—	—	200
South Georgia[1]	12	—	200	—
South Sandwich Islands	12	—	200	—
Turks and Caicos Islands[1]	12	—	—	200
Ukraine	12	—	200	—
Uruguay*	200[12]	—	—	200
USA	12	—	200	—
Federated States of Micronesia*	12	—	200	—
Marshall Islands*	12	24	200	—
Vanuatu[2]	12	24	200	—
Venezuela[1]	12	15	200	—
Vietnam[1]*	12**	24	200	—
Western Samoa*	12	—	200	—
Yemen*	12**	24	200	—
Yugoslavia[1]*[20]	12	—	—	12
Zaire*	12	—	—	200

Limits of dependent territories have not been listed unless they differ from those of the metropolitan state.

1 employs straight baseline systems along all or a part of the coast.
2 claims archipelago status.
3 claims waters within limits defined by geographic co-ordinates not related to distance from the coastline.
4 claims straight baseline system between points along the 18 metre isobath.
5 claims all water south of 32° 30′N. in the Gulf of Sirte as internal waters.
6 claims 3 nm in Korea Strait.
7 claims 6 nm in Aegean Sea.
8 fishery limit extends to 50 metre isobath off the Gulf of Gabes.
9 special claim extends limit to include the deep water anchorage west of Helgoland.
10 150 nm in west with a rhumb line between 52° 30′.00S, 63°19′.25W and 54° 08′.68S, 60° 00′.00W.
11 certain islands in the Torres Strait retain 3 nm territorial sea limit.
12 freedom of navigation and overflight is not curtailed beyond 12 nm.
13 jurisdiction claimed to the limit of the pearl and sedentary fishery grounds.
14 Bogskar has a 3 nm territorial sea limit.
15 does not claim an EEZ in the Mediterranean, only a 12 nm fishery limit.

[16] reduced to 3 nm in the Torres Strait area.
[17] reduced to 3 nm in the Gulf of Honduras.
[18] reduced to 3 nm off Gaza.
[19] only claims an EEZ in the Black Sea.
[20] Republic of Serbia and Montenegro.
[21] TS limit reduced in parts of the Gulf of Finland to preserve a 6 nm wide high seas corridor.
[22] to maritime boundaries in areas exceeeding 12 nm.
[23] reduced to 32 nm west of the longitude of Ras Térés.

* indicates a state which has ratified or acceded to the U.N. Convention of the Law of the Sea, which came into force on 16 November 1994.
** indicates a state which requires prior permission or notification for entry of foreign warships into territorial sea. The United Kingdom government does not recognise this requirement.

(Published in *Annual Summary of Admiralty Notices to Mariners in Force* on 1 January 1996, pp. 1–74—1–77 (with some later amendments))

Part Nine: I. B. 1. *Seas, waterways, ships—territorial sea—legal status—right of innocent passage*

In reply to the question 'what controls the Marine Safety Agency has over ships sailing in British waters which do not dock in British ports', the Parliamentary Under-Secretary of State, Department of Transport, wrote in part:

International law limits the right of coastal states to interfere with foreign-flagged ships exercising the right of innocent passage through territorial waters or transit passage through straits used in international navigation. Only if the ship has been involved in an accident or poses a threat of pollution or threatens the peace or security of the coastal state can the coastal state intervene.

The position of foreign-flagged ships anchored or operating in territorial waters, and not on innocent or transit passage, is different, and Lord Donaldson's report, 'Safer Ships, Cleaner Seas', recommended that we should extend our powers in respect of such ships to the maximum extent allowed under international law. The Department will shortly issue a consultation paper on how this can be achieved. The consultation paper will take account of changes stemming from the recent adoption of an EC directive on port state control which provides for the inspection and, if appropriate, detention of foreign-flagged vessels anchored near a port or offshore installation.

(HC Debs., vol. 258, WA, col. *502*: 25 April 1995)

On 31 January 1995, the Government of Egypt communicated to the UN Secretary-General the terms of certain declarations which should have accompanied its deposit of an instrument of accession to the Basel Convention on the Control of Transboundary Movements of Hazardous Wastes and their Disposal, of 1985. The first of the above declarations read:

First declaration: passage of ships carrying hazardous wastes through the Egyptian territorial sea

The Arab Republic of Egypt, upon acceding to the Basel Convention on the Control of Transboundary Movements of Hazardous Wastes and their Disposal, which was done on 22 March 1989 and is referred to hereafter as 'the Convention', and, in accordance with article 26 of the Convention,

Declares that:

1. In accordance with the provisions of the Convention and the rules of international law regarding the sovereign right of the State over its territorial sea and its obligation to protect and preserve the marine environment, since the passage of foreign ships carrying hazardous or other wastes entails many risks which constitute a fundamental threat to human health and the environment; and in conformity with Egypt's position on the passage of ships carrying inherently dangerous or noxious substances through its territorial sea (United Nations Convention on the Law of the Sea, 1983 [*sic*]), the Government of the Arab Republic of Egypt declares that foreign ships carrying hazardous or other wastes will be required to obtain prior permission from the Egyptian authorities for passage through its territorial sea.

2. Prior notification must be given of the movement of any hazardous wastes through areas under its national jurisdiction, in accordance with article 2, paragraph 9, of the Convention.

On 9 October 1995, the UK Government communicated the following objection to the above first declaration:

The Government of the United Kingdom of Great Britain and Northern Ireland cannot accept the first declaration of Egypt (passage of ships carrying hazardous wastes through the Egyptian territorial sea) set out in the annex to the above Notification. Not only was this declaration out of time, but like all other declarations to similar effects, it is unacceptable in substance. In this connection, the United Kingdom Government recalls its own statement upon signature confirmed upon ratification, which reads as follows:

> 'The Government of the United Kingdom of Great Britain and Northern Ireland declares that, in accordance with article 4(12), the provisions of the Convention do not affect in any way the exercise of navigational rights and freedoms as provided for in international law. Accordingly, nothing in this Convention requires notice to or consent of any State for the passage of hazardous wastes on a vessel under the flag of a party, exercising rights of passage through the territorial sea or freedom of navigation in an exclusive economic zone under international law.'

(C.N. 394, 1995. TREATIES–10)

Part Nine: I. B. 5. *Seas, waterways, ships—territorial sea—legal status—bed and subsoil*

In the course of a debate in the House of Lords on the subject of marine nature reserves, the Minister of State, Department of the Environment, Viscount Ullswater, stated:

The . . . power for the appropriate Secretary of State, following an application from the appropriate conservation agency, to establish statutory marine nature reserves, to conserve and provide opportunity for the study of marine flora and fauna and of geological and physiographical features can be found in Section 36 of the Wildlife and Countryside Act 1981. . . . the relevant Secretary of State may apply such a designation to any areas of land covered (continuously or intermittently) by tidal waters or to parts of the sea up to the seaward limits of territorial waters.

(HL Debs., vol. 564, col. 589: 17 May 1995)

Part Nine: II. *Seas, waterways, ships—contiguous zone*

(See Part Nine: I. A. (Admiralty Notice), above)

Part Nine: VII. A. 2. *Seas, waterways, ships—the high seas—freedoms of the high seas—fishery*

(See also Part Nine: VII. F., below)

In reply to a question, the Minister of State, Ministry of Agriculture, Fisheries and Food, wrote in part:

Fisheries protection and enforcement in international waters is the responsibility of the flag state.

(HC Debs., vol. 256, WA, col. 776: 17 March 1995)

In the course of a debate on the subject of the dispute between the EU and Canada over fishing in the north-west Atlantic, the Minister of Agriculture, Fisheries and Food, Mr William Waldegrave, stated:

The British Government welcome the agreement reached on Sunday between the EU and Canada, which settles the recent conflict over fisheries in the north-west Atlantic.

After protracted negotiations between the European Commission and Canadian officials an agreement was reached, which is being ratified by written procedure by the Council of Ministers. It will then be applied provisionally with immediate effect, pending full agreement by the contracting parties to the North-west Atlantic Fisheries Organisation.

The agreement is in four parts. The first element is a tough new control and enforcement regime for the high seas of the NAFO regulatory area. Neutral observers will be placed on board all vessels fishing in the area, with the task of monitoring compliance with all internationally agreed conservation measures. They will have powers to alert inspection vessels to any apparent infringements. When major offences are detected the vessel will be boarded and directed into port for enforcement action. Every vessel will also be subject to exhaustive checks on returning to port. Infringements will be subject to enforcement by the flag state. That system will be complemented by the introduction of a satellite surveillance system, applicable initially to 35 per cent. of vessels in the area.

Secondly, new conservation measures for Greenland halibut will be proposed to NAFO, including a minimum size of fish—for which there is currently no provision—and tougher by-catch limits.

Thirdly, quotas have been agreed. Hon. Members will recall that a total allowable catch of 27,000 tonnes for Greenland halibut was set for the first time last year. Agreement has now been reached on the share-out of that total allowable catch for the remainder of 1995 and future years.

Finally, Canada has agreed to delete Spain and Portugal from the scope of her legislation governing international waters, and to repay the bonds lodged for release of the Estai and her master, and to return the catch or its value to the owner.

This agreement has required both sides to make important compromises. It is a victory for good sense and negotiation, the course that the British Government have been urging throughout the conflict. Reasonable quota shares have been agreed for both sides, together with control measures which will ensure that the stock is conserved and rules are respected.

Throughout the negotiations, the United Kingdom has been determined to play a full part in using its role as a member of both the EU and the Commonwealth to further a successful outcome. There have been frequent contacts between the UK and the parties directly concerned. Her Majesty's ambassador in Madrid, David Brighty, was asked to call on Carlos Westendorp, State Secretary for European Affairs, in Madrid yesterday to discuss the EU-Canada fisheries dispute. Media reports of that meeting bear little relation to what transpired. Mr. Brighty used the opportunity to make it clear that we had throughout the dispute tried to promote a negotiated settlement favourable to conservation, involving effective enforcement of rules and acceptable to both the EU and Canada. That has now been achieved.

(HC Debs., vol. 258, cols. 19–20: 18 April 1995)

Part Nine: VII. C. *Seas, waterways, ships—the high seas—hot pursuit*

Cannabis was shipped from Morocco in m.v. *Poseidon*, registered in Kingstown, St Vincent. Pursuant to the plans of those later charged with conspiracy to import the drugs into the UK, a quantity of the cannabis was transferred on the high seas to a British-registered trawler, the *Delvan*, which had set out from the Republic of Ireland. Unknown to the accused, the *Delvan* had a crew of under-cover British customs and police officers. The transhipment was monitored by radar from a task force of British naval vessels supported by helicopters. The *Delvan* entered UK waters on 11 November 1993 and on 12 November 1993 docked at Littlehampton on the south coast of England where the drugs were unloaded and those present to receive them were arrested. The Ministry of Defence then sent a signal to the task force to stop and arrest the *Poseidon*. This was done on 13 November 1993 by customs officers winched from helicopters after a VHF radio message from a helicopter to the ship ordering it to heave to had brought no response. The location of the boarding and arrest of the crew was on the high seas more than 300 miles west of Portugal.

Six of the crew of the Poseidon, all foreign nationals, applied to the Crown Court at Croydon for a stay of the proceedings against them on the ground of abuse of process, alleged by them to consist of a wrongful arrest on the high seas in breach of international law. After legal argument in which the application and interpretation of Article 23 of the Geneva Convention on the High Seas, 1958 were lengthily debated, Judge Devonshire gave judgment in 1995, holding that the *Poseidon* 'was properly arrested in international waters under the terms of the Geneva Convention and in accordance with the provisions of the international law of the sea'. In the course of his judgment, he stated that 'the Government of St Vincent had raised no protest at the arrest of a ship registered under its flag'. He also stated:

Soon after the defendants had first been brought before the magistrates the Crown gave notice to them by letter dated 8th December 1993 that they had been arrested in international waters in exercise of the right of 'hot pursuit' contained in international law which is to be found in the Geneva Convention on the High Seas of 1958.

(*R.* v. *Mills and others*, undated judgment (text provided by the FCO). For a fuller account of the case, see W. C. Gilmore, 'Hot Pursuit: The Case of *R.* v. *Mills and others*', *International and Comparative Law Quarterly*, 44 (1995), pp. 949–58)

Part Nine: VII. E. *Seas, waterways, ships—the high seas—piracy*

In the course of a debate on the subject of international measures to combat maritime piracy in South-East Asia and the Far East, mention was made of two incidents in which ships were alleged to have been seized by crews of Chinese patrol boats. The Minister of State, FCO, Baroness Chalker, remarked:

. . . under the Law of the Sea Convention, acts of piracy committed by a government ship whose crew has mutinied and taken control of the ship are, in the words of the convention, 'assimilated to acts committed by a private ship'. We are not aware that this happened in the case that my noble friend cites. However, there is absolutely no doubt that there are occasions when boats are stopped by persons who look like officials, indeed may be officials, their cargoes snaffled, the boats held in some far off port, and no one hears any more about it. That is a problem on which the IMO is working very hard at present.

(HL Debs., vol. 566, col. 110: 18 July 1995)

In reply to a question, the Parliamentary Under-Secretary of State, Department of Transport, wrote:

During the last 12 months there has been one report of a piracy attack on the high seas against a ship registered in the UK or the Crown dependencies. This was against the UK-registered ocean-going yacht, the Longo Barda, attacked off Somalia in April 1995.

(HC Debs., vol. 264, WA, col. *580*: 24 October 1995)

Part Nine: VII. F. *Seas, waterways, ships—the high seas—conservation of living resources*

The Minister of State, Ministry of Agriculture, Fisheries and Food, Mr Michael Jack, made the following statement of Her Majesty's Government's policy on the dispute between the EU and Canada over fishing rights:

> At the heart of this dispute is a disagreement between Canada and the European Union over the division of an agreed catch quota of 27,000 tonnes of Greenland halibut in the waters regulated by the North-west Atlantic Fisheries Organisation outside the Canadian 200-mile limit. That quota was set for the first time for this fishery in NAFO last September. The European Union expected a share of the total allowable catch proportionate to its track record which, in the most recent three-year period, represented 75 per cent. of the catch, while Canadian vessels took less than 14 per cent. At a NAFO meeting in February this year, Canada did not agree and advanced an alternative distribution which would have given it 60 per cent. of the TAC and the EU 12 per cent. The EU felt that this was neither fair nor just and decided unanimously to invoke the objection procedure which is provided for in NAFO rules.
>
> Having invoked the procedure, the EU was entitled to take its preferred share of the 27,000 tonne TAC. Canada disputed the EU's use of the objection procedure, took national powers to act against EU vessels fishing outside its 200-mile limit and warned the EU that it would use those powers if the EU vessels did not leave the fishery. On Thursday last, Canada used its legislation to arrest a Spanish vessel on the high seas.
>
> The United Kingdom has no fishing vessels in the disputed fishery and is not directly involved. However, we are actively encouraging the intense diplomatic efforts which are now taking place with a view to reducing the tension and getting negotiations restarted.

(HC Debs., vol. 256, col. 563: 13 March 1995)

On 20 July 1995, the Governments of the UK and the Seychelles signed a Joint Statement on the Conservation of Fisheries which established a British-Seychelles Fisheries Commission 'to promote, facilitate and coordinate conservation and scientific research of fish stocks in an area of the Indian Ocean to be determined by mutual agreement between the two Governments'. The Joint Statement went on to mention that the Commission will have the function, *inter alia*,

> . . . in accordance with international law to recommend to both Governments possible actions for the conservation in international waters of migratory and straddling stocks and species related to them.

(Text provided by the FCO)

Part Nine: VII. G. *Seas, waterways, ships—the high seas—pollution*

In reply to a question, the Parliamentary Under-Secretary of State, Scottish Office, wrote:

The deep sea disposal of the Brent Spar buoy in the north-east Atlantic at a depth in excess of 2,000 m will not present a hazard to the environment or to other users of the sea including fishermen. Disposal in this way complies fully with our obligations under international conventions. Accordingly, Shell UK has received the necessary approval for this disposal.

(HC Debs., vol. 261, WA, col. *214*: 7 June 1995)

In the course of a debate in the House of Lords on the subject of the disposal in the open sea of disused oil platforms and other structures from the UK continental shelf, the Government spokesman, Lord Inglewood, stated:

The legal position as regards this kind of matter is complicated, but, once it has been unravelled, it is relatively straightforward. Under international law, the London Convention applies, together with the UN Convention on the Law of the Sea. As regards the North East Atlantic, the provisions of the London Convention are supplemented by the Oslo and Paris Conventions, which in turn are being subsumed in another convention which this country has ratified but not yet implemented in domestic law. I refer to the OSPAR Convention.

(HL Debs., vol. 564, cols. 1537–8: 12 June 1995)

Part Nine: VII. H. *Seas, waterways, ships—the high seas—jurisdiction*

The following question was asked:

. . . what steps are being taken to examine the implications of the decision of the Dover magistrates court not to hear the sexual harassment case brought by the Crown Prosecution Service on behalf of a British crew member on Stena Sealink's Fantasia ferry on the ground that the alleged incident occurred on a foreign registered vessel; and if he will make a statement in respect of United Kingdom citizens employed on foreign-flagged vessels?

In reply, the Parliamentary Secretary to the Lord Chancellor's Department wrote:

I understand that the case was dismissed because the court was not satisfied it had the necessary territorial jurisdiction. In general, courts will have jurisdiction for an offence committed in territorial waters, on a British ship, or if the accused is a British subject. Where the offence is committed on the high seas, the matter is likely to fall within the jurisdiction of the country with which the ship is registered.

(HC Debs., vol. 253, *WA*, col. 5: 23 January 1995)

In reply to a question on the subject of a collision between two vessels, the *Kiwi Arrow* and the *Pelander*, off the Isle of Wight, the Parliamentary Under-Secretary of State, Department of Transport, wrote in part:

At the time of the collision between Kiwi Arrow and Pelander the sea was calm and visibility was approximately five nautical miles. The Solent coastguard responded immediately to the distress call, but both ships were able to proceed to Southampton under their own power. Two surveyors from the Marine Safety

Agency carried out a port state control inspection of both ships to examine the damage.

As the incident occurred outside the United Kingdom's territorial waters and involved non-UK registered ships, the responsibility for accident investigation rests with the flag states of the Kiwi Arrow and Pelander. However, an inspector from the Marine Accident Investigation Branch visited the ships when in Southampton to obtain background information concerning the incident which has been sent to both administrations.

The flag states have been asked to advise of the outcome of an investigation into the causes of this accident. Under the provisions of the international conventions, any representations made to the International Maritime Organisation on the circumstances of this collision will be a matter for the flag states. The flag states have been asked to inform the MSA of the measures they intend to take to ensure that the ships comply with international requirements before departure. Neither ship will be permitted to leave Southampton until the MSA is satisfied that they are fit to proceed to sea.

(HC Debs., vol. 260, WA, col. *116*: 16 May 1995)

Part Nine: VIII. *Seas, waterways, ships—continental shelf*

(See also Part Nine: I. A. (item of 18 October 1995), above)

Mr M. Wood, Legal Counsellor, FCO, addressed a letter dated 20 September 1995 to the Assistant Director-General for Culture, UNESCO, Paris concerning the proposed Underwater Cultural Heritage Convention. The letter stated in part:

> I am writing in response to the invitation extended in your letter of 11 July 1995 for national experts to submit comments on the proposed Underwater Cultural Heritage Convention.
>
> The United Kingdom welcomes the opportunity to comment on the proposed Convention. As a nation with an extensive maritime history the United Kingdom is conscious of the need for protection of historic wrecks from uncontrolled treasure hunting. A Convention on Underwater Cultural Heritage could meet this need. But we should be wary of upsetting the jurisdictional package in the UN Convention on the Law of the Sea, which includes the provisions of Article 303 of the Convention.
>
> In this regard the United Kingdom notes that Article 1 of the proposed Convention foresees the creation of a Cultural Heritage Zone stretching to the edge of the continental shelf. This would be a major distortion to the finely balanced package of jurisdictions contained in the UN Convention on the Law of the Sea. It would set a bad precedent for other areas where, some states may argue, their interests are much more at stake.

(Text provided by the FCO)

Part Nine: IX. *Seas, waterways, ships—exclusive fishery zone*

(See Part Nine: I. A. (Admiralty Notice), above)

Part Nine: X. *Seas, waterways, ships—exclusive economic zone*

(See Parts Nine: I. A. (Admiralty Notice) and Nine: I. B. 1. (item of 9 October 1995), above)

Part Nine: XVII. *Seas, waterways, ships—platforms and other structures*

(See also Part Nine: VII. G., above)

On 7 July 1995, the UK and Norwegian Governments concluded an Exchange of Notes concerning the disposal of the 'Brent Spar' offshore installation which had been taken into Norwegian waters. The Note of the British Embassy in Oslo read as follows:

Note no. 61

Her Britannic Majesty's Embassy present their compliments to the Royal Ministry of Foreign Affairs and have the honour to confirm that the United Kingdom agrees to ensure that arrangements are provided for the disposal of the 'Brent Spar', whose owners accept that they have a statutory duty to provide for its satisfactory disposal, to which the usual statutory procedures will have to be applied. The 'Brent Spar' is still, and will remain, registered as a United Kingdom offshore installation. Its eventual disposal will not become a Norwegian responsibility. The United Kingdom Government will give any permits and consents necessary for the removal of the 'Brent Spar' from waters under Norwegian jurisdiction when, in accordance with the Norwegian authorities' decision, the date for temporary mooring in Norway has expired.

If the content of this Note is acceptable to the Government of Norway this Note and the reply of the Government of Norway will constitute an agreement between our two Governments.

(TS No. 65 (1995); Cm 2951)

Part Ten: III. *Air space, outer space—outer space*

The following question was asked of Her Majesty's Government:

Whether the 1967 Space Treaty gives an undoubted right, to those individual states that are capable of doing so, to conduct unlimited military espionage and target acquisition on other sovereign states, and if so whether they will cite the passages in the treaty text which allow this, in the light of Article 1 of the treaty, which states that 'exploration and use of outer space . . . shall be carried out for the benefit and in the interests of all countries, irrespective of their degree of economic and scientific development, and shall be the province of all mankind'.

In reply, the Minister of State wrote:

The Outer Space Treaty does not prohibit the use of satellites for the purposes of military observation. Such use is an accepted part of space activities.

(HL Debs., vol. 566, *WA 160*: 1 November 1995)

In reply to the question

whether the peaceful uses to which ESA's activities are restricted are all those which are permitted under the space treaty of 1967,

the Minister of State, Department of Trade and Industry, wrote:

While all activities carried out under the convention of the European Space Agency are consistent with the 1967 treaty on principles governing the activities of states in the exploration and use of outer space, including the moon and other celestial bodies, the treaty itself does not define those activities which are permitted.

(Ibid., *WA 172*: 2 November 1995)

Part Eleven: II. A. 1. *Responsibility—responsible entities—States—elements of responsibility*

(See Part Eleven: II. D. (item of 2 October 1995), below)

Part Eleven: II. A. 6. *Responsibility—responsible entities—States—reparation and other remedies*

In reply to the question what support has been given to former prisoners of war and civilian internees who are seeking compensation from the Japanese Government, the Minister of State, FCO, wrote in part:

The question of compensation was legally settled, in the Government's view, by the San Francisco peace treaty of 1951, and we are precluded from raising it formally with the Japanese Government.

(HC Debs., vol. 255, WA, col. *281*: 23 February 1995; see also ibid., vol. 263, col. *372*: 5 July 1995)

The following provisions, typical of several such agreements made in the year, appear in the Agreement between the Governments of the UK and Cuba, for the promotion and protection of investments, signed on 30 January 1995 and in force on 11 May 1995:

ARTICLE 4

Compensation for Losses

(1) Nationals or companies of one Contracting Party whose investments in the territory of the other Contracting Party suffer losses owing to war or other armed conflict, a state of national emergency, revolt, insurrection or riot in the territory of the latter Contracting Party shall be accorded by the latter Contracting Party treatment, as regards restitution, indemnification, compensation or other settlement, no less favourable than that which the latter Contracting Party accords to its own nationals or companies or to nationals or companies of any third State. Resulting payments shall be freely transferable.

(2) Without prejudice to paragraph (1) of this Article, nationals and companies of one Contracting Party who in any of the situations referred to in that paragraph suffer losses in the territory of the other Contracting Party resulting from:

(a) requisitioning of their property by its forces or authorities; or
(b) destruction of their property by its forces or authorities, which was not caused in combat action or was not required by the necessity of the situation;

shall be accorded restitution or adequate compensation. Resulting payments shall be freely transferable.

ARTICLE 5

Expropriation

(1) Investments of nationals or companies of either Contracting Party shall not be nationalised, expropriated or subjected to measures having effect equivalent to nationalisation or expropriation (hereinafter referred to as 'expropriation') in the territory of the other Contracting Party except for a public purpose related to the internal needs of that Party on a non-discriminatory basis and against prompt, adequate and effective compensation. Such compensation shall amount to the genuine value of the investment expropriated immediately before the expropriation or before the impending expropriation became public knowledge, whichever is the earlier, shall include interest at a normal commercial rate until the date of payment, shall be made without delay, be effectively realizable and be freely transferable. The national or company affected shall have a right, under the law of the Contracting Party making the expropriation, to prompt review, by a judicial or other independent authority of that Party, of his or its case and of the valuation of his or its investment in accordance with the principles set out in this paragraph.
(2) Where a Contracting Party expropriates the assets of a company which is incorporated or constituted under the law in force in any part of its own territory, and in which nationals or companies of the other Contracting Party own shares, it shall ensure that the provisions of paragraph (1) of this Article are applied to the extent necessary to guarantee prompt, adequate and effective compensation in respect of their investment to such nationals or companies of the other Contracting Party who are owners of those shares.

ARTICLE 6

Repatriation of Investment and Returns

Each Contracting Party shall in respect of investments guarantee to nationals or companies of the other Contracting Party the unrestricted transfer of their investments and returns after the payment of any taxes due in the territory of the first Contracting Party in respect of the investment. Transfers shall be effected without delay in the convertible currency in which the capital was originally invested or in any other convertible currency agreed by the investor and the Contracting Party concerned. Unless otherwise agreed by the investor transfers shall be made at the rate of exchange applicable on the date of transfer pursuant to the exchange regulations in force.

(TS No. 50 (1995); Cm 2912)

Part Eleven: II. A. 7. (a). *Responsibility—responsible entities—States—procedure—diplomatic and consular protection*

The following list was prepared by the FCO in October 1995:

UK BILATERAL INVESTMENT PROMOTION AND PROTECTION AGREEMENTS

Country	Date/Signature			Date of Entry into Force		
Albania	30	March	1994	30	August	1995
Antigua & Barbuda	12	June	1987	12	June	1987
Argentina	11	December	1990	19	February	1993
Armenia	22	May	1993	Not yet in force		
Bahrain	30	October	1991	30	October	1991
Bangladesh	19	June	1980	19	June	1980
Barbados	7	April	1993	7	April	1993
Belarus	1	March	1994	28	December	1994
Belize	30	April	1982	30	April	1982
Benin	27	November	1987	27	November	1987
Bolivia	24	May	1988	16	February	1990
Brazil	19	July	1994	Not yet in force		
Burundi	13	September	1990	13	September	1990
Cameroon	4	June	1982	7	June	1985
China	15	May	1986	15	May	1986
Colombia	9	March	1994	Not yet in force		
Congo	25	May	1989	9	November	1990
Costa Rica	7	September	1982	Not yet in force		
Côte d'Ivoire	8	June	1995	Not yet in force		
Cuba	30	January	1995	11	May	1995
Czechoslovakia	10	July	1990	26	October	1992
Dominica	23	January	1987	23	January	1987
Ecuador	10	May	1994	24	August	1995
Egypt	11	June	1975	24	February	1976
Estonia	12	May	1994	16	December	1994
Georgia	15	February	1995	15	February	1995
Ghana	22	March	1989	25	October	1991
Grenada	25	February	1988	25	February	1988
Guyana	27	October	1989	11	April	1990
Haiti	18	March	1985	27	March	1995
Honduras	7	December	1993	8	March	1995
Hungary	9	March	1987	28	August	1987
India	14	March	1994	6	January	1995
Indonesia	27	April	1976	24	March	1977
Jamaica	20	January	1987	14	May	1987

Country	Date/Signature		Date of Entry into Force	
Jordan	10 October	1979	24 April	1980
Korea	4 March	1976	4 March	1976
Kyrgyz Republic	8 December	1994	Not yet in force	
Laos	1 June	1995	1 June	1995
Latvia	24 January	1994	15 February	1995
Lesotho	18 February	1981	18 February	1981
Lithuania	17 May	1993	21 September	1993
Malaysia	21 May	1981	21 October	1988
Malta	4 October	1986	4 October	1986
Mauritius	20 May	1986	13 October	1986
Mongolia	4 October	1991	4 October	1991
Morocco	30 October	1990	Provisionally in force	
Nepal	2 March	1993	2 March	1993
Nigeria	11 December	1990	11 December	1990
Pakistan	30 November	1994	30 November	1994
Panama	7 October	1983	7 November	1983
Papua New Guinea	14 May	1981	22 December	1981
Paraguay	4 June	1981	23 April	1992
Peru	4 October	1993	21 April	1994
Philippines	3 December	1980	2 January	1981
Poland	8 December	1987	14 April	1988
* Romania	19 March	1976	22 November	1976
* (Romania	13 July	1995	Not yet in force)	
Senegal	7 May	1980	9 February	1984
Sierra Leone	8 December	1981	Not yet in force	
Singapore	22 July	1975	22 July	1975
South Africa	20 September	1994	Not yet in force	
Soviet Union	6 April	1989	3 July	1991
Sri Lanka	13 February	1980	18 December	1980
St Lucia	18 January	1983	18 January	1983
Swaziland	5 May	1995	5 May	1995
Tanzania	7 January	1994	Not yet in force	
Thailand	28 November	1978	11 August	1979
Trinidad & Tobago	23 July	1993	8 October	1993
Tunisia	14 March	1989	4 January	1990
Turkey	15 March	1991	Not yet in force	
Turkmenistan	9 February	1995	9 February	1995
Ukraine	10 February	1993	10 February	1993
United Arab Emirates	8 December	1992	13 December	1993
Uruguay	21 October	1991	Not yet in force	
Uzbekistan	24 November	1993	24 November	1993
Venezuela	15 March	1995	Not yet in force	
Yemen Arab Rep.	25 February	1982	11 November	1983
Zimbabwe	1 March	1995	Not yet in force	

* The 1976 IPPA with Romania will terminate on the entry into force of the 1995 Agreement.

(Text provided by the FCO)

In the course of a written reply on the subject of missing persons in Cyprus, the Minister of State, FCO, wrote:

Under international law British citizens with dual nationality are the responsibility of the country of their second nationality whilst in that country.

(HC Debs., vol. 265, WA, col. *375*: 2 November 1995)

Part Eleven: II. D. *Responsibility—responsible entities—individuals, including corporations*

In the course of replying to oral questions, the Parliamentary Under-Secretary of State, FCO, Mr Tony Baldry, stated:

I agree that it is imperative that everyone who is involved in war crimes is brought to trial. That is why an international criminal tribunal for Rwanda was established by a United Nations Security Council resolution last November. The United Kingdom was a co-sponsor of that resolution and we are determined that the tribunal will bring to justice as many as possible of those who were responsible for war crimes.

(HC Debs., vol. 253, col. 1079: 1 February 1995)

In reply to a question, the Parliamentary Under-Secretary of State, FCO, wrote:

The International Tribunal for Rwanda, established by Security Council resolution 955 of 8 November 1994, is in the process of being set up. It will be for the prosecutor to decide whom to bring to trial. We expect all states to comply with their obligations under SCR 955 to surrender suspects at the tribunal request.

(HC Debs., vol. 255, WA, col. *152*: 21 February 1995)

Addressing the UN *ad hoc* Committee on the establishment of an international criminal court, the UK representative stated in April 1995:

Aggression

As the ILC commentary notes, there is no treaty definition, nor is there a clearly defined customary law crime of aggression. The Charter of the Nuremberg Tribunal gave jurisdiction over 'the planning, preparation, initiation or waging of a war of aggression or a war in violation of international treaties, agreements or assurances, or participation in a common plan or conspiracy of the foregoing'. But there is no definition of a war of aggression. The General Assembly resolutions on the Friendly Relations Declaration and on the Definition of Aggression similarly contain no definition for the purpose of individual criminal responsibility.

(Text provided by the FCO)

Speaking on 28 August 1995 in the UN Security Council debating a resolution relating to events in Burundi, the UK Permanent Representative to the UN in New York, Sir John Weston, stated:

This resolution sends a clear message that those responsible for grave violations of humanitarian law will be held responsible for their actions. The British Government therefore strongly supports the establishment of a Commission of Inquiry, and my delegation is pleased to have co-sponsored the resolution which provides for this.

(S/3571, p. 11)

Speaking on 2 October 1995 in the Sixth Committee of the UN General Assembly debating measures to eliminate international terrorism, the representative of Spain, on behalf of the EU, stated:

. . . given that States have legal responsibility for the protection of human rights, the European Union is of the opinion that the violation of international instruments on the protection of human rights cannot be ascribed to illegal groups or to individuals.

(Text provided by the FCO; see also A/C.6/50/SR.6, p. 3)

In reply to a question, the Lord Chancellor, Lord Mackay of Clashfern, stated:

. . . on 12th July, 1995, the Attorney-General granted his consent to the prosecution of one case under the War Crimes Act 1991. There are no outstanding applications for consent.

(HL Debs., vol. 566, col. 575: 16 October 1995)

Speaking on 30 October 1995 in the Sixth Committee of the UN General Assembly debating the report of the *ad hoc* Committee on the Establishment of an International Criminal Court (A/50/22), the representative of Spain, on behalf of the EU, stated:

The European Union welcomes the increasing support of the international community for the creation of an appropriate and effective institution to respond to the atrocities that are repeatedly perpetrated, atrocities which, fifty years after the adoption of the United Nations Charter, still cast a shadow over an international life that should be based on the principles of the Charter. We fully share that support.

The European Union is aware of the swiftness and efficiency displayed by the United Nations in the establishment by the Security Council, pursuant to Chapter VII of the Charter, of two International Tribunals to respond to two specific situations of serious violations of International Humanitarian Law. However, these *ad hoc* Tribunals cannot be the answer in every case to crimes that affront the conscience of humankind. A permanent international court should be established, which could take care of the concerns which have led to the establishment of the *ad hoc* tribunals and at the same time draw on the experience of those tribunals.

The European Union is aware of the legal complexity of the work undertaken by the Ad Hoc Committee and the need to reconcile different procedural approaches based as much on the diversity of the legal systems of Member States as on the differences in their organisation of criminal justice.

An International Criminal Court should be an independent permanent institution with the widest participation, and closely linked to the United Nations.

We do not believe that this is the time or the place for addressing, in the detail which they deserve, the different options that have been examined in the two sessions of the Ad Hoc Committee. The European Union considers, however, that an important characteristic of the Court should be that it is complementary to national criminal justice systems. Resort would be made to it where the Court decided that national systems were not available, or were ineffective. This principle should be duly reflected in the Statute.

We are also of the view that the jurisdiction of the Court should be confined to the crimes which represent the most serious offences of concern to the international community as a whole.

Since a court should have clear and precise law to adjudicate upon and administer, there should be certainty as to the crimes within jurisdiction of the international criminal court. The Statute should also contain provisions on the general rules of criminal law applicable by the Court.

Finally, the Court must protect the rights of the accused by having proper standards of due process and there must be obligations on State Parties for cooperation with the Court which reflect effective and speedy arrangements for the transfer of individuals, taking account of existing structures of judicial cooperation.

(Text provided by the FCO)

Speaking in the Third Committee of the UN General Assembly on 27 November 1995, the representative of Spain, speaking on behalf of the EU, stated:

In *Rwanda*, the genocide, massacres and civil war have constituted one of the most tragic chapters in Africa's history. Prosecution of the perpetrators of these massive violations of human rights and humanitarian law, with full respect for legal safeguards and guaranties of due process, is a moral and legal imperative. It is also an indispensable element of national reconciliation and of political stabilization in the country as well as in the region as a whole. We are encouraged that the International Tribunal for Rwanda will soon start its proceedings and issue its first indictments. We have expressed our concern about the slow pace of setting up the Tribunal. In that context we believe that the Tribunal must be properly funded. We reiterate the legal obligation of all states under international law to cooperate in full with the Tribunal. The granting of sanctuary to perpetrators of human rights abuses is unacceptable.

(Text provided by the FCO)

Speaking at the International Conference of the Red Cross and the Red Crescent on 4 December 1995, the FCO Legal Adviser, Sir Franklin Berman, stated:

An International Criminal Court

The United Kingdom played a full part in the discussions on this important topic. The discussions in New York now point towards the establishment of a court which could be effective, efficient and universally acceptable, where national jurisdiction is not a viable option. My Government has indicated, and I repeat today, that the United Kingdom can support a court of that kind. We will play our full part in the substantial preparatory work which remains. The present Conference could send a message of its encouragement and support in the cause of implementing international humanitarian law.

(Text provided by the FCO)

Speaking in the UN Security Council on 12 December 1995, the UK Permanent Representative, Sir John Weston, observed:

It is also a matter of the greatest importance to the British Government that the perpetrators of the genocide be brought to justice. This is an important element in the return to normality in Rwanda. We note that the International Tribunal for Rwanda has now begun the significant task of identifying the perpetrators of genocide and of bringing them to justice, and only today has issued an indictment. We call on all States in the region to cooperate with the Tribunal as it goes about its work. We welcome the fact that UNAMIR will continue to assist in the coming period in providing security for the Tribunal until the arrangements worked out between the Government of Rwanda and the Tribunal are put in place. We call on all States in the region to cooperate with the Tribunal as it goes about its work.

(S/PV 3605, p. 4)

Part Twelve: II. A. *Pacific settlement of disputes—modes of settlement—negotiation*

In reply to a question on whether the Spratly Islands should be demilitarized and issues relating to their natural resources submitted to international arbitration, the Minister of State, FCO, wrote:

We continue to believe that competing claims to the Spratly Islands should be resolved peacefully by diplomatic means and not through the use of military force. All competing claimants have subscribed to the 1992 Manila ASEAN declaration on the South China Sea which prescribes the peaceful resolution of all issues relating to the conflicting claims. Where we believe this will be effective, we do not hesitate to raise critical situations in the UN or in other international bodies.

(HL Debs., vol. 561, *WA 99*: 1 March 1995)

On 2 March 1995, the EU Presidency issued a statement about the situation in the South China Sea. It read as follows:

The European Union has noted with concern the latest developments in the South China Sea, a maritime area of great importance to international traffic.

The Union welcomed the adoption in Manila in July 1992 of a declaration, endorsed by China, which committed the ASEAN countries to resolving their disputes in the South China Sea by peaceful means, encouraged the countries concerned to show restraint and invited them to adhere to the principles in the declaration. The Union reiterated its support for this declaration in September 1994 in the framework of the 11th EU-ASEAN ministerial meeting in Karlsruhe.

The Union reaffirms once again its support for the principles embodied in the Manila declaration. It calls upon all parties concerned to show restraint and to abstain from any measure which may make its implementation more difficult. It welcomes the announcement that consultations between the authorities of the Philippines and China will take place in Beijing from 13 to 15 March.

The Czech Republic, Hungary, Poland, Romania and Slovakia associate themselves with this declaration.

(*Bulletin of the European Union*, 1995–3, pp. 59–60)

In reply to a question, the Prime Minister wrote:

Britain supported, and both India and Pakistan agreed, the United Nations resolutions of 1948 and 1949, which provided the basis of a possible solution of the Kashmir disputes. Neither side fully implemented those resolutions which have, to some extent, been overtaken by events. The 1972 Simla agreement represents the most recent formal agreement between India and Pakistan on the handling of the dispute. It envisages settlement through bilateral negotiations or other peaceful means mutually agreed between them. We believe this to be the best way forward.

(HC Debs., vol. 258: WA, col. *342*: 24 April 1995)

Part Twelve: II. E. *Pacific settlement of disputes—modes of settlement—mediation*

In reply to questions about the policy of Her Majesty's Government towards the fishery dispute between Spain and Canada, the Parliamentary Secretary, Ministry of Agriculture, Fisheries and Food, Earl Howe, stated:

. . . as members of both the Commonwealth and the EU, the UK is in a unique position in this affair. Therefore, we are actively working with all parties to reduce tension, to avoid further confrontation and to encourage sensible negotiation.

. . . we took the stance that we did because Canada decided to act in a confrontational way, having taken the law into its own hands, and in seeking to impose a formula for sharing the agreed total allowable catch for Greenland halibut. In our view, that is not a sensible way in which to resolve an honest disagreement. It is now our task to mediate. We believe that we have made a useful contribution to that process.

(HL Debs., vol. 562, col. 1223: 22 March 1995)

Part Twelve: II. G. 1. *Pacific settlement of disputes—modes of settlement—arbitration—arbitral tribunals and commissions*

The following provisions appear in the Agreement between the Governments of the UK and Cuba for the promotion and protection of investments, signed on 30 January 1995 and in force on 11 May 1995:

ARTICLE 8

Settlement of Disputes between an Investor and a Host State

(1) Disputes between a national or company of one Contracting Party and the other Contracting Party concerning an obligation of the latter under this Agreement in relation to an investment of the former which have not been amicably settled shall, after a period of three months from written notification of a claim, be submitted to international arbitration if the national or company concerned so wishes.
(2) Where the dispute is referred to international arbitration, the national or company and the Contracting Party concerned in the dispute may agree to refer the dispute either to:
- (a) the Court of Arbitration of the International Chamber of Commerce; or
- (b) an international arbitrator or ad hoc arbitration tribunal to be appointed by a special agreement or established under the Arbitration Rules of the United Nations Commission on International Trade Law.

If after a period of three months from written notification of the claim there is no agreement to one of the above alternative procedures, the dispute shall at the request in writing of the national or company concerned be submitted to arbitration under the Arbitration Rules of the United Nations Commission on International Trade Law as then in force. The parties to the dispute may agree in writing to modify these Rules.

ARTICLE 9

Disputes between the Contracting Parties

(1) Disputes between the Contracting Parties concerning the interpretation or application of this Agreement should, if possible, be settled through the diplomatic channel.
(2) If a dispute between the Contracting Parties cannot thus be settled, it shall upon the request of either Contracting Party be submitted to an arbitral tribunal.
(3) Such an arbitral tribunal shall be constituted for each individual case in the following way. Within two months of the receipt of the request for arbitration, each Contracting Party shall appoint one member of the tribunal. Those two members shall then select a national of a third State who on approval by the two Contracting Parties shall be appointed Chairman of the tribunal. The Chairman shall be appointed within two months from the date of appointment of the other two members.
(4) If within the periods specified in paragraph (3) of this Article the necessary appointments have not been made, either Contracting Party may, in the absence of any other agreement, invite the President of the International Court of Justice to make any necessary appointments. If the President is a national of either Contracting Party or if he is otherwise prevented from discharging the said function, the Vice-President shall be invited to make the necessary appointments. If the Vice-President is a national of either Contracting Party or if he too is prevented from discharging the said function, the Member of the Inter-

national Court of Justice next in seniority who is not a national of either Contracting Party shall be invited to make the necessary appointments.
(5) The arbitral tribunal shall reach its decision by a majority of votes. Such decision shall be binding on both Contracting Parties. Each Contracting Party shall bear the cost of its own member of the tribunal and of its representation in the arbitral proceedings; the cost of the Chairman and the remaining costs shall be borne in equal parts by the Contracting Parties. The tribunal may, however, in its decision direct that a higher proportion of costs shall be borne by one of the two Contracting Parties, and this award shall be binding on both Contracting Parties. The tribunal shall determine its own procedure.

(TS No. 50 (1995); Cm 2912)

Article 8 in the Agreement between the Governments of the UK and Belarus for the promotion and protection of investments, signed on 1 March 1994 and in force on 28 December 1994, reads as follows:

ARTICLE 8

Reference to International Centre for Settlement of Investment Disputes

(1) Each Contracting Party hereby consents to submit to the International Centre for the Settlement of Investment Disputes (hereinafter referred to as 'the Centre') for settlement by conciliation or arbitration under the Convention on the Settlement of Investment Disputes between States and Nationals of Other States opened for signature at Washington on 18 March 1965 any legal dispute arising between that Contracting Party and a national or company of the other Contracting Party concerning an investment of the latter in the territory of the former.
(2) A company which is incorporated or constituted under the law in force in the territory of one Contracting Party and in which before such a dispute arises the majority of shares are owned by nationals or companies of the other Contracting Party shall in accordance with Article 25(2)(b) of the Convention be treated for the purposes of the Convention as a company of the other Contracting Party.
(3) If any such dispute should arise and agreement cannot be reached within three months between the parties to this dispute through pursuit of local remedies or otherwise, then, if the national or company affected also consents in writing to submit the dispute to the Centre for settlement by conciliation or arbitration under the Convention, either party may institute proceedings by addressing a request to that effect to the Secretary-General of the Centre as provided in Articles 28 and 36 of the Convention. In the event of disagreement as to whether conciliation or arbitration is the more appropriate procedure the national or company affected shall have the right to choose. The Contracting Party which is a party to the dispute shall not raise as an objection at any stage of the proceedings or enforcement of an award the fact that the national or company which is the other party to the dispute has received in pursuance of an insurance contract an indemnity in respect of some or all of his or its losses.
(4) Neither Contracting Party shall pursue through the diplomatic channel any dispute referred to the Centre unless:

(a) the Secretary-General of the Centre, or a conciliation commission or an arbitral tribunal constituted by it, decides that the dispute is not within the jurisdiction of the Centre, or
(b) the other Contracting Party should fail to abide by or to comply with any award rendered by an arbitral tribunal.

(TS No. 15 (1995); Cm 2768)

Article 8 of the similar agreement between the Governments of the UK and Swaziland, signed and in force on 5 May 1995, reads as follows:

ARTICLE 8

Settlement of Disputes between an Investor and a Host State

(1) Disputes between a national or company of one Contracting Party and the other Contracting Party concerning an obligation of the latter under this Agreement in relation to an investment of the former which have not been amicably settled shall, after a period of three months from written notification of a claim, be submitted to international arbitration if either party to the dispute so wishes.
(2) Where the dispute is referred to international arbitration, the national or company and the Contracting Party concerned in the dispute may agree to refer the dispute either to:
(a) the International Centre for the Settlement of Investment Disputes (having regard to the provisions, where applicable, of the Convention on the Settlement of Investment Disputes between States and Nationals of Other States, opened for signature at Washington DC on 18 March 1965 and the Additional Facility for the Administration of Conciliation, Arbitration and Fact-Finding Proceedings); or
(b) the Court of Arbitration of the International Chamber of Commerce; or
(c) an international arbitrator or ad hoc arbitration tribunal to be appointed by a special agreement or established under the Arbitration Rules of the United Nations Commission on International Trade Law.

If after a period of three months from written notification of the claim there is no agreement to one of the above alternative procedures, the parties to the dispute shall be bound to submit it to arbitration under the Arbitration Rules of the United Nations Commission on International Trade Law as then in force. The parties to the dispute may agree in writing to modify these Rules.

(TS No. 76 (1995); Cm 2967)

On 31 January 1995, the UK Government signed an Agreement on Illicit Traffic by Sea, implementing Article 17 of the UN Convention against Illicit Traffic in Narcotic Drugs and Psychotropic Substances. Article 34 of the Agreement reads:

ARTICLE 34

Settlement of disputes

(1) The European Committee on Crime Problems of the Council of Europe shall be kept informed of the interpretation and application of this Agreement.
(2) In case of a dispute between Parties as to the interpretation or application of this Agreement, the Parties shall seek a settlement of the dispute through negotiation or any other peaceful means of their choice, including submission of the dispute to the European Committee on Crime Problems, to an arbitral tribunal whose decisions shall be binding upon the Parties, mediation, conciliation or judicial process, as agreed upon by the Parties concerned.
(3) Any State may, at the time of signature or when depositing its instrument of ratification, acceptance, approval or accession, or on any later date, by a declaration addressed to the Secretary General of the Council of Europe, declare that, in respect of any dispute concerning the interpretation or application of this Agreement, it recognises as compulsory, without prior agreement, and subject to reciprocity, the submission of the dispute to arbitration in accordance with the procedure set out in the appendix to this Agreement.
(4) Any dispute which has not been settled in accordance with paragraphs (2) or (3) of this article shall be referred, at the request of any one of the parties to the dispute, to the International Court of Justice for decision.
(5) Any State may, at the time of signature or when depositing its instrument of ratification, acceptance, approval or accession, by a declaration addressed to the Secretary General of the Council of Europe, declare that it does not consider itself bound by paragraph 4 of this article.
(6) Any Party having made a declaration in accordance with paragraphs (3) or (5) of this article may at any time withdraw the declaration by notification to the Secretary General of the Council of Europe.

(Cm 2979)

Part Twelve: II. H. 1. *Pacific settlement of disputes—modes of settlement—judicial settlement—the International Court of Justice*

In an interview given on 23 May 1995 to a Middle East television network, the Secretary of State for Foreign and Commonwealth Affairs, Mr Douglas Hurd, was asked what was the British position on the claim of the United Arab Emirates to the Abu Musa Islands. Mr Hurd stated:

> We strongly support the decision by Sheikh Sayed [of the United Arab Emirates] to pursue this matter in the International Court. We think this was a wise proposal and we hope it can be accepted.

(Text provided by the FCO)

On 2 June 1994, the UK Government submitted a written statement to the International Court of Justice in the course of proceedings arising out of a request made by the World Health Assembly for an advisory opinion on the legality of the threat or use of nuclear weapons. The statement contained the following paragraphs:

1. It is clear that the Court is not bound to give an advisory opinion, even if the requesting organ or organisation is fully *intra vires* in requesting it: the language of Article 65 of the Statute is permissive rather than mandatory.

As the Court said in the *Interpretation of the Peace Treaties* Case:

> 'Article 65 of the Statute is permissive. It gives the Court the power to examine whether the circumstances of the case are of such a character as should lead it to decline to answer the Request . . . the Court possesses a large amount of discretion in the matter.' (Advisory Opinion of 30 March 1950, I.C.J. Rep. 1950, pp. 71–72).

The point was re-iterated by the Court in its Advisory Opinion on *Reservations to the Genocide Convention*,[1] and again in the *Certain Expenses* Case.[2]

[1] Advisory Opinion of 28 May 1951: I.C.J. Rep. 1951, at p. 19.
[2] Advisory Opinion of 20 July 1962: I.C.J. Rep. 1962, at p. 155.

2. This being said, the Court has nevertheless indicated that, as the principal judicial organ of the United Nations, its opinion on a legal question posed by an organ or specialised agency of the United Nations ought normally to be given when requested.

> 'But, as the Court also said in the same Opinion [viz. *Interpretation of the Peace Treaties*, I.C.J. Reports 1950, p. 72] "the reply of the Court, itself an 'organ of the United Nations', represents its participation in the activities of the Organisation, and, in principle, should not be refused" (ibid., p. 71). Still more emphatically, in its Opinion of 23 October 1956, the Court said that only compelling reasons should lead it to refuse to give a requested advisory opinion (*Judgment of the Administrative Tribunal of the I.L.O. upon complaints made against UNESCO*, I.C.J. Reports 1956, p. 86).'[3]

That position of principle is clearly right, and the desire of the Court to play a constructive role in assisting organs of the United Nations in the pursuit of their constitutional activities can be warmly supported. But, of course, the case would be entirely different if the request were *ultra vires*. It would also be different if a response to the request was in fact unlikely to provide any constructive assistance to the Organisation submitting the request, but, on the contrary, likely to prove detrimental to activities undertaken by the United Nations family at large. At this point the issue is one of *propriety*, rather than powers.

[3] *Certain Expenses of the U.N.*, Advisory Opinion of 20 July 1962, I.C.J. Reports 1962, at p. 155.

3. In fact the Court's own jurisprudence gives extremely useful guidance on the matter of propriety. A careful analysis reveals the categories of cases in which opinions *ought* to be given—and the reasons therefor: and also the categories of cases in which an opinion *ought not* to be given, as a matter of propriety.

(Text provided by the FCO)

In reply to a question, the Minister of State, FCO, wrote:

The Government believe that advisory opinions by the International Court of Justice at the request of the UN or a specialised agency can serve a useful purpose when they resolve legal matters on which the requesting organisation requires guidance for its current activities. Advisory opinions of the court are given careful consideration. However, they are not binding either on the requesting organisation or on its member states. The Government's attitude to particular advisory opinions depends on the terms of the opinion and the circumstances of the case.

(HC Debs., vol. 268, WA, col. *81*: 4 December 1995)

Part Thirteen: I. B. *Coercion and counter-measures short of the use of force—unilateral acts—non-forcible counter-measures*

The UK representative to the Sixth Committee of the UN General Assembly, Sir Franklin Berman, circulated a written addendum to his statement of 17 October 1995 made in the course of a debate on the subject of the annual report of the International Law Commission. The addendum contained the following general comments on State responsibility and counter-measures:

1. In the present state of international organisation, the right of an injured State to have recourse to countermeasures in response to an internationally wrongful act is an important one. The rules regulating the resort to countermeasures, their use, and what acts may not be resorted to by way of countermeasure, must (a) be practicable; (b) not unduly fetter the right; (c) be in accordance with existing international law.
2. As regards arbitral or judicial oversight of the legality of countermeasures, it is essential that the scope of such a review extend to the legality of the precipitating wrongful act.

(Text provided by the FCO)

The addendum then contained specific comments on the Commission's provisional draft Articles dealing with counter-measures. The comments read in part:

4. *Draft Article 13 (Proportionality)*. This provision adopts a negative formulation, providing that a countermeasure 'shall not be out of proportion' to the relevant criteria. It establishes two criteria by which proportionality is to be assessed: (i) the degree of gravity of the internationally wrongful act and (ii) the effects on the injured State. This formulation and the two criteria are broadly acceptable. One additional matter to which consideration might usefully be given, however, is the question of minimizing collateral damage to persons and to third States. The former is purportedly dealt with in draft Article 14(d) (see below) as a prohibited countermeasure; but this seems inappropriate. The latter does not appear to be touched on anywhere.
5. *Draft Article 14 (Prohibited countermeasures)*. It is well-recognised that there are certain limitations on what countermeasures can be taken. In principle, the UK supports the inclusion of a list of prohibited countermeasures. Such a list must, however, satisfy two fundamental criteria: it must accurately reflect State

practice and embody the requirement of legal certainty. Three items on the proposed list are problematic in these respects:

(a) The prohibition of the 'threat or use of force' by way of countermeasures is itself uncontroversial. But it is unduly and misleadingly circumscribed here by reference to the UN Charter. The commentary (paragraph 4) indicates that the Commission wished to include a general reference to the Charter as one source—but not the exclusive source—of this prohibition. This is not reflected in the draft provision. The commentary (at pp. 152–153) unnecessarily enters into the controversial question of the permissibility of recourse to self-defence under the Charter. This is inappropriate in the present context and should be discouraged.

(b) The prohibition of 'extreme economic or political coercion designed to endanger the territorial integrity or political independence' of the wrongdoing State is problematic in two respects. First, there are problems of definition. 'Economic coercion' as a concept does not lend itself to a definition that is both exact and comprehensive; the same can be said of 'political coercion'. *A fortiori* therefore for 'extreme' versions of either. Second, the focus on the severity of the measures appears to be misplaced. It would seem that the conduct aimed at is that which is intended to have the specified effects. If that is so, consideration might be given to adopting more general language prohibiting any measure intended to have these effects. This brings to the fore the question of principle as to whether such a prohibition is in conformity with existing State practice or an innovation.

(c) The prohibition of countermeasures 'derogating from human rights' (para. (d)) has a beguiling simplicity about it. But it is ill-defined and overbroad. Regard to the commentary suggests that the prohibition is intended to encompass five general propositions, i.e. a State (i) cannot breach its obligations under international humanitarian law; (ii) cannot take peacetime reprisals against individuals; (iii) cannot violate human rights regarded as *jus cogens*; (iv) cannot violate human rights which are non-derogable under treaties; and (v) must ensure that its reprisals have a minimal effect on individuals. It is clear that some of these propositions are widely accepted. Others, however, are controversial. And the last-mentioned appears misplaced. It concerns collateral effects on individuals, not measures directed against them. As such, it seems to be an aspect of proportionality. This is an instance in which it would be useful for the Commission to enumerate the various propositions it has in mind and to indicate more clearly the support they enjoy.

6. *Recourse to dispute settlement in respect of countermeasures.* The Part III dispute-settlement proposals which have been adopted impose no requirement to make recourse to dispute settlement a pre-condition of the right to take countermeasures. This is a welcome outcome. Such a constraint would be quite impracticable, for the reasons set out in the Commission's debate on the subject (at p. 141), and inconsistent with arbitral authority.

7. The proposal to make arbitration compulsory in disputes arising from the use of countermeasures (at the behest of the victim of them) (Part III, Article 5) is new. No rationale for this separate regime for countermeasures is provided in the commentary. But the debate in the Commission suggests that it is viewed as a necessary counterpart to the decision not to prohibit countermeasures, and as

a safeguard for weaker States against arbitrary action. As a matter of principle, it would seem desirable that what are, after all, otherwise unlawful acts should be subject to arbitral or judicial review. Such review must however extend to the precipitating act(s). This is envisaged in the commentary (paragraph 5) but not in the provision itself. The scope of review that is contemplated is in fact very broad indeed. It would extend to the underlying dispute which, it is recognised, may include not only issues relating to the (secondary) rules of State responsibility, but also issues relating to the (primary) rules that are alleged to have been violated. This is an interesting proposal, but a far-reaching one. Its potential implications will have to be carefully considered.

(Ibid.)

Part Thirteen: II. A. *Coercion and counter-measures short of the use of force—collective measures—regime of the UN*

The following notice was issued by the FCO on 17 October 1994:

UNITED NATIONS ACT 1946

THE HAITI (UNITED NATIONS SANCTIONS) ORDER 1994 (NO 1323)

THE HAITI (UNITED NATIONS SANCTIONS) (CHANNEL ISLANDS) ORDER 1994 (NO 1325)

THE HAITI (UNITED NATIONS SANCTIONS) (ISLE OF MAN) ORDER 1994 (NO 1326)

PURSUANT to the provisions of Article 1(2) of the above-mentioned Orders, the Secretary of State for Foreign and Commonwealth Affairs hereby gives notice that, by resolution 944 (1994) adopted on 29th September 1994, the Security Council of the United Nations decided to cancel with effect from 16th October 1994 the operation of resolutions 841 (1993) adopted by it on 16th June 1993 and 917 (1994) adopted by it on 6th May 1994, which imposed certain economic measures in relation to Haiti. Paragraph 11 of resolution 917 (1994) remains in force.

In accordance with the provisions of the said Article 1(2), the above-mentioned Orders therefore ceased to have effect as from 16th October 1994 to the extent required in the above-mentioned decision of the Security Council.

(*The London Gazette*, 1994, p. 14681)

Speaking on 18 January 1995 in respect of the Secretary-General's position paper 'Supplement to an Agenda for Peace' (S/1995/1), the UK Permanent Representative to the UN in New York, Sir David Hannay, stated in the UN Security Council:

Preventive action, peacemaking, peace-keeping—these are obviously the preferred tools: persuading, negotiating, cooling heads. But sometimes that is not enough. Aggression needs to be reversed, halted in its tracks or prevented from recurring, and support for terrorism must be halted. In these cases the Security Council has to have resort to the instruments provided by Chapter VII of the Charter. No such measures are taken lightly. Armed force should be used only as a last resort. We recognize the validity of the Secretary-General's argument that recent experience has shown that the United Nations as such is not well equipped to carry out such actions. But, short of that last resort, sanctions, to which the Secretary-General referred, remain, in our view, a valid and sometimes necessary option.

We attach importance to devising sanctions regimes that have the greatest effect on the target Government and its supporters and the least effect on innocent civilians. But we should not be blind to the ruthlessness of regimes that use sanctions to justify their own appalling treatment of the civilian population. Nor should we be seduced by what are called smart sanctions—sanctions that are partially and narrowly targeted. There may be opportunities for this sort of instrument, but in general they are notoriously hard to enforce and are therefore unlikely to have the desired effect of bringing about a change of policy.

The Secretary-General was right to point up some of the problems raised by sanctions. But the posing of paradoxes, such as the conflict between sanctions and development, is hardly a sound basis for making difficult policy decisions. Moreover, a decision to impose sanctions presupposes—because it is taken under Chapter VII—that there is a threat to international peace and security. Such threats are themselves inimical to the development objectives of both the transgressor and the victim. Is it, then, the threats and the unlawful actions that damage development, or is it the sanctions imposed to counter them? The Security Council must be able, if the international situation warrants it, to impose sanctions at short notice and without undue delay.

(S/3492, p. 5)

In reply to a question, the Minister of State, FCO, wrote:

We observe mandatory United Nations embargoes on Iraq, Libya, Somalia, Liberia, Former Republic of Yugoslavia, Federal Republic of Yugoslavia (Serbia and Montenegro), UNITA (Angola) and Rwanda; European Union embargoes on China, Burma, Zaire and Sudan; an Organisation on Security and Co-operation in Europe embargo on Armenia and Azerbaijan.

In addition we do not supply military equipment to Argentina or Iran.

We also observe the EU policy of applying a presumption of denial for new export licence applications for defence equipment for Nigeria, and the UN policy of encouraging a reduction in military expenditure by Cyprus.

(HC Debs., vol. 259, WA, col. *250*: 3 May 1995)

The following notice was issued by the FCO on 24 November 1995:

UNITED NATIONS ACT 1946

The Serbia and Montenegro (United Nations Prohibition of Flights) Order 1992 (No. 1304)

The Serbia and Montenegro (United Nations Sanctions) Order 1992 (No. 1302)

The Serbia and Montenegro (United Nations Sanctions) (Channel Islands) Order 1992 (No. 1308)

The Serbia and Montenegro (United Nations Sanctions) Order 1993 (No. 1188)

The Serbia and Montenegro (United Nations Sanctions) (Channel Islands) Order 1993 (No. 1253)

The Serbia and Montenegro (United Nations Sanctions) (Isle of Man) Order 1993 (No. 1254)

The Former Yugoslavia (United Nations Sanctions) Order 1994 (No. 2673)

The Former Yugoslavia (United Nations Sanctions) (Channel Islands) Order 1994 (No. 2675)

Pursuant to the provisions of Article 1(2) of the above-mentioned Orders and further to his Notice of 18th September 1995, the Secretary of State for Foreign and Commonwealth Affairs hereby gives notice that, by resolution 1022 (1995) adopted on 22nd November 1995, the Security Council of the United Nations has decided to suspend indefinitely (with immediate effect) the operation of the measures imposed by resolutions 757 (1992), 820 (1993), 942 (1994) and other relevant resolutions which imposed certain measures in relation to Serbia and Montenegro and the United Nations Protected Areas of the Republic of Croatia, with the exception that certain assets frozen or impounded pursuant to resolutions 757 (1992) and 820 (1993) shall remain frozen or impounded as provided in paragraph 5 of resolution 1022 (1995).

By resolution 1022 (1995) the Security Council further decided that, on the occurrence of certain event specified in the resolution, (a) the suspension would be extended to the measures imposed in relation to the areas of Republic of Bosnia and Herzegovina controlled by the Bosnian Serb forces, (b) the measures would be automatically reimposed, or (c) the measures would be cancelled. In any of these cases a further notice will be issued.

By resolution 1022 (1995) the Security Council further decides that States shall continue to ensure that there shall be no claim in connection with the performance of any contract or other transaction where such performance was affected by the measures imposed by the resolutions referred to above and related resolutions.

In accordance with the provisions of the said Article 1(2), the operation of the above-mentioned Orders was therefore suspended indefinitely to the extent required by the above-mentioned decision of the Security Council in resolution 1022 (1995), the text of which is attached.

(*The London Gazette*, 1995, pp. 16193–4 (text of resolution not reproduced); see also ibid., pp. 6139, 12735–6)

In reply to the question what steps have been taken to freeze the personal accounts or assets of members of regimes with which the UK are in dispute as part of a national or international sanctions policy, the Minister of State, FCO, wrote:

The United Kingdom has no unilateral sanctions in place against the assets or personal accounts of foreign regimes. However, we do implement the mandatory financial sanctions imposed by the UN Security Council. Such financial sanctions are in place against Iraq, in UNSCR 661—adopted on 6 August 1990—and Libya, in UNSCR 863—adopted on 11 November 1993.

The financial sanctions imposed on the Federal Republic of Yugoslavia in UNSCRs 757 and 820—adopted on 30 May 1992 and 17 April 1993, respectively—were suspended with immediate effect by UNSCR 1022—adopted on 22 November—with the exception that certain assets frozen or impounded by UNSCRs 757 and 820 shall remain frozen or impounded. A copy of UNSCR 1022 is available in the Library of the House.

(HC Debs., vol. 267, WA, col. *528*: 28 November 1995)

Part Thirteen: II. B. *Coercion and counter-measures short of the use of force—collective measures—outside the UN*

In the course of a debate in the House of Lords on the subject of human rights in Nigeria, the Minister of State, Baroness Chalker, stated:

The European Union measures against Nigeria were in response to the annulment of the 1993 election, and the later return to power of military government. We suspended military co-operation and high-level visits; restricted visas for members of the military and their dependants; reviewed all new export licence applications for defence equipment with the presumption of denial, and reviewed all new aid projects on a case-by-case basis. It was the European Union which agreed that all measures should remain in force. They will be reviewed only in the light of clear progress towards a return to civilian rule.

I am sometimes asked to consider the imposition of additional measures or sanctions. We do not rule it out. To date we have resisted appeals for wider sanctions on the grounds that we have no wish to harm the interests or the livelihoods of the ordinary people of Nigeria. They would be the first to suffer from an oil embargo or trade sanctions. By contrast, our current measures remind the Nigerian military that they are responsible for the disruption to the democratic process. I hope that we shall soon see progress towards democracy and a resumption of co-operation in every sphere.

(HL Debs., vol. 562, col. *204*: 7 March 1995)

In reply to the question what equipment Her Majesty's Government consider is covered by its ban on arms sales to China, the Minister of State, FCO, wrote:

Since 7 June 1989 the United Kingdom has enforced an embargo on the sale to China of 'weapons, and equipment which could be used for internal repression'. The EU introduced a ban on arms sales to China on 26 June 1989 but the scope of that ban has, in the absence of agreement on a common interpretation, been left for national interpretation. In the interests of clarity we have decided that henceforward the embargo will include: lethal weapons such as machine guns, large calibre weapons, bombs, torpedoes, rockets and missiles; specially designed components of the above, and ammunition; military aircraft and helicopters, vessels of war, armoured fighting vessels and other such weapons platforms; any equipment which is likely to be used for internal repression.

All applications will be considered on a case-by-case basis in the light of these criteria as well as our usual criteria governing all defence exports.

(HC Debs., vol. 257, WA, cols. *842–3*: 31 March 1995)

In reply to a question, the Minister of State, FCO, wrote:

We believe that the best way to resolve the fisheries dispute between the EU and Canada is by negotiation. There is no formal proposal to impose sanctions. A proposal under article 228a of the treaty of Rome to interrupt or reduce, in part or completely, economic relations with Canada would require the adoption of a common position or joint action according to the provisions of the treaty on European Union relating to common foreign and security policy, which would be subject to unanimity.

(HC Debs., vol. 257, WA, col. *890*: 3 April 1995)

Part Fourteen: I. A. 4. *War and other uses of force—international war and armed conflict—resort to war—limitation and reduction of armaments*

Speaking at the Non-Proliferation Treaty Review and Extension Conference on 19 April 1995, the UK representative, Sir Michael Weston, stated:

We welcome the recent agreement to establish an Ad Hoc Committee at the Conference on Disarmament to negotiate a Treaty banning the production of fissile material for nuclear weapons or for other nuclear explosive devices. We look forward to an early start to these negotiations, hopefully at the end of May. As a demonstration of our commitment to these negotiations, my Secretary of State announced yesterday that the UK has ceased the production of fissile material for explosive purposes.

. . .

The UK has also supported many other measures which contribute to the goal of general and complete disarmament. The UK took the original initiative which ultimately led to the conclusion of the Biological Weapons Convention in 1972, and played an active part in the negotiations of the Chemical Weapons Convention which was open for signature in 1993. We fully support recent efforts to strengthen the BWC following the special conference of states parties in September 1994.

At a regional level, the UK has consistently sought verifiable reductions in conventional arms in Europe, and played a full part in the negotiations which led to the CFE Treaty.

(Text provided by the FCO)

Part Fourteen: I. B. 1. *War and other uses of force—international war and armed conflict—the laws of war and armed conflict—sources and sanctions*

On 2 June 1994, the UK Government submitted a written statement to the International Court of Justice in the course of proceedings arising out of a request made by the World Health Assembly for an advisory opinion on the legality of the threat or use of nuclear weapons. The statement contained the following paragraph:

31. It has been suggested[34] that the use of nuclear weapons would violate the principle that the parties to an armed conflict do not have an unlimited choice of the methods and means of warfare, a principle stated in Article 22 of the Hague Regulations, 1907,[35] and reaffirmed in Article 35(1) of Additional Protocol I. While that principle is undoubtedly well established as part of customary international law, however, it cannot stand alone as a prohibition of a particular category of weapons. It is necessary to look outside the principle in order to determine what limitations are imposed by customary or conventional law upon the choice of methods and means of warfare. The argument thus begs the question whether there exists some other principle of international law which limits the right to choose nuclear weapons as a means of warfare.

---

[34] Singh and McWhinney, *Nuclear Weapons and Contemporary International Law* (1989), p. 115.

[35] Regulations annexed to Hague Convention No. IV, Respecting the Laws and Customs of War on Land, 1907, UKTS 9 (1910), Cd. 5030.

32. The same is true of the argument based upon the 'Martens Clause' which appeared in the preamble to Hague Convention No. IV respecting the Laws and Customs of War on Land, 1907. A most recent version of this clause appears in Article 1(2) of Additional Protocol I, 1977, which provides that:

> 'In cases not covered by this Protocol or by other international agreements, civilians and combatants remain under the protection and authority of the principles of international law derived from established custom, from the principles of humanity and from the dictates of public conscience'.

While the Martens Clause makes clear that the absence of a specific treaty provision on the use of nuclear weapons is not, in itself, sufficient to establish that such weapons are capable of lawful use, the Clause does not, on its own, establish their illegality. The terms of the Martens Clause themselves make it necessary to point to a rule of customary international law which might outlaw the use of nuclear weapons. Since the existence of such a rule is in question, reference to the Martens Clause adds little.

(Statement, pp. 83–4; text provided by the FCO)

Part Fourteen: I. B. 6. *War and other uses of force—international war and armed conflict—the laws of war and armed conflict—humanitarian law*

On 23 January 1995, the EU issued a declaration on Chechnya. It read in part:

The European Union recalls its declaration of 17 January and continues to follow developments in Chechnya with great concern. It deplores the serious violations of human rights and international humanitarian law which are still occurring there. It calls for an immediate cessation of the fighting, and for the opening of negotiations to allow a political solution to the conflict to be found. It demands that freedom of access to Chechnya and the proper convoying of humanitarian aid to the population be guaranteed.

The European Union places its action in the framework of the implementation of the principles and provisions of the OSCE, in compliance with the sovereignty and territorial integrity of Russia.

(Text provided by the FCO)

In the course of oral questions on the subject of land mines, the Minister of State for Defence Procurement, Mr Roger Freeman, stated:

The parties in the conflict in the former Yugoslavia have indiscriminately sown anti-personnel land mines. That may be in direct contravention of the United Nations weaponry convention, which we signed in 1981, and which we will ratify next month.

(HC Debs., vol. 253, cols. 842–3: 31 January 1995)

In reply to the question whether the use in South Lebanon by Israeli artillery of shells containing *fléchettes* (steel arrows three inches long) contravenes international law, the Government spokesman in the House of Lords wrote:

These weapons are not specifically prohibited by an international agreement but their use in any particular case would be subject to generally applicable rules of international humanitarian law. We deplore the use of weapons that may be deemed to be excessively injurious or to have indiscriminate effects.

(HL Debs., vol. 561, *WA 2*: 6 February 1995)

In the course of a debate on the subject of land mines, the Minister of State, FCO, Mr David Davis, stated:

It would be easy to say, 'Ban the export of all land mines.' However, the vast majority of countries, including Britain and most other western countries, accept that land mines are a legitimate means of defence, provided that they are used responsibly and in accordance with the laws of war. Frankly, we would not persuade many countries that they should give up land mines altogether.

Even more importantly, a complete ban on the export of land mines by well-meaning western countries would have little effect where it really matters. The conflicts which the hon. Member for Leyton and I have mentioned have largely been in the developing world. Land mines are a cheap weapon. In our view, it is only realistic to recognise that they will continue to be used.

Our aim should be to ensure that existing stocks are replaced as quickly as possible with self-destructing mines. That is not only a logical and realistic approach; in our view, it is the most humanitarian approach. That is why I announced last July a ban on the export of anti-personnel land mines which do not self destruct. It is our policy to support steps that represent realistic and practical progress. Our decisions at each stage reflect that.

I am pleased to be able to announce to the House an extension of the United Kingdom's policy. I am announcing a ban, with immediate effect, on the export of all types of anti-personnel land mines to those countries which have not ratified the United Nations weaponry convention. I can also announce . . . that the United Kingdom's moratorium is now extended to cover a total ban on the export of non-detectable anti-personnel land mines.

That enhanced moratorium underlines our commitment to put an end to the trade in the types of anti-personnel land mines that are the most dangerous to civilians. It adds a further safeguard by confirming our support for a complete ban on non-detectable anti-personnel land mines which are especially difficult, dangerous and expensive to clear . . . Above all, it underlines our support for the principle that land mines must be used responsibly. I hope that it shows a principled and sensible example.

We hope that our action will encourage more countries to ratify the UN weaponry convention and abide by its provisions. We hope that others which have not announced moratoriums, and most particularly those countries which produce land mines, will follow that example soon. However, we are not simply making a gesture, as I believe we were accused of doing earlier, important though it is. The United Kingdom was one of the initial signatories to the 1981 UN weaponry convention—the so-called inhumane weapons convention. That convention lays down rules for the responsible use of land mines and certain other weapons.

The hon. Member for Leyton was correct to say that we did not ratify that convention until earlier this year. However, that was a somewhat technical and legal point, because our armed forces have been trained, throughout the period since signature, to abide by the convention. They have abided by it in two wars—the Falklands war and the Gulf war. In the Gulf war, we were dealing with an adversary who had not even signed the convention, let alone abided by it. Rather more than most countries, we can demonstrate a commitment to the notion of responsible behaviour in warfare.

The weaponry convention is an important landmark in the process of establishing sound laws of war, but it is now 15 years old. It is generally accepted that its provisions need strengthening. . . . The convention will be reviewed at a conference to be held in September. We will be there, as a full state party, and we will be taking a lead.

Our objectives are to strengthen the convention and to persuade more states to ratify and abide by it. When I talk about strengthening the convention, I mean a significant expansion of its coverage; here I come to a point raised by the hon. Gentleman. We want the convention to cover not only international conflicts but civil wars and other internal conflicts. That is vital, because the majority of cases of land mine abuse are not international wars. It is important that the convention should send a signal that the use of land mines in internal conflicts should also be governed by the humanitarian laws of war.

These are important areas in which we are working for the strengthening of the convention. It is important that the convention should set down clear definitions and standards for self-destructing mines, for the reasons that I set out earlier. It should stipulate when and how minefields are to be marked to keep civilians out. It should ensure that minefields are properly mapped, both to assist mine clearance after a conflict and to protect humanitarian agencies. There should also be provision to assist those agencies when working in those areas. Those are provisions which our own armed forces are trained to adhere to strictly.

The convention should ensure that mines are detectable. There is broad agreement on that, and on banning non-detectable anti-personnel mines. We also support the proposal that the convention should introduce international controls on transfers.

(HC Debs., vol. 256, cols. 864–5: 15 March 1995)

Speaking on 10 August 1995 in the UN Security Council, the UK Permanent Representative to the UN in New York, Sir John Weston, stated:

The British Government therefore joins with others in demanding that the Bosnian Serb authorities give immediate access to the international humanitarian agencies, and cooperate fully and unreservedly with the efforts of the International Committee of the Red Cross (ICRC) and others to determine the whereabouts of those still unaccounted for. We look for the early release of those who are still detained, and we remind the Bosnian Serb authorities of their obligation under international humanitarian law to ensure the safety and well-being of those who are under their control.

(S/PV. 3612, p. 9)

Speaking at the International Conference of the Red Cross and the Red Crescent on 4 December 1995, the FCO Legal Adviser, Sir Franklin Berman, stated:

It was international concern for victims of conflict which inspired the Swiss Government's initiative in 1993 to convene an International Conference on the Protection of War Victims. My Government fully supported that initiative. Some may express disappointment that the experts' recommendations were modest. Of course they were modest: recommendations which did not command sufficient international consensus and highlighted disagreements would have had limited value: limited practical value, limited political value. But the recommendations are not as modest as they may seem, and they are a first step on which we can build. My Government therefore regards it as vital that this meeting endorse the experts' recommendations as the start of a real and concerted international effort towards securing respect for the existing rules of international humanitarian law.

(Text provided by the FCO)

Later in his speech, Sir Franklin Berman remarked:

Landmines

There is no doubting the horrendous effects on civilian populations of the indiscriminate use of anti-personnel landmines. The United Kingdom had hoped that the Weaponry Convention Review Conference which took place in

Vienna recently would strengthen the legal prohibitions and restrictions on the use and transfer of anti-personnel landmines on a global basis. We were extremely disappointed that the Conference was unable to reach agreement. Rather than accept an inadequate outcome, we agreed that it was better to adjourn the Conference and to make a further attempt next year. Those countries which blocked progress should now reconsider their positions. The United Kingdom will not give up in its efforts for an agreement which achieves real progress.

(Ibid.)

Addressing the UN Security Council on 21 December 1995, the UK Permanent Representative to the UN in New York, Sir John Weston, stated in respect of events in Bosnia:

The British Government unreservedly condemns the violations of international humanitarian law and human rights that took place.

(S/PV. 3612, p. 8)

Part Fourteen: I. B. 7. *War and other uses of force—international war and armed conflict—the laws of war and armed conflict—belligerent occupation*

In reply to a question, the Minister of State, FCO, wrote:

We consider that all settlements in the occupied territories, including east Jerusalem, are illegal and an obstacle to peace. With our EU partners, we are in frequent contact with the Israeli Government, whom we regularly remind of their obligations under the fourth Geneva convention. The EU issued a statement on 5 January which called for the total cessation of work on settlements.

(HC Debs., vol. 252, WA, col. *606*: 19 January 1995)

In reply to an oral question, the Government spokesman in the House of Lords, Lord Inglewood, stated:

. . . the building of settlements in the occupied territories is contrary to international law and is an obstacle in the way of peace. The matter of settlements is one that has been reserved under the declarations of principle of the Oslo Agreement of 1993 until issues relating to permanent status are determined. Nevertheless, the building of those settlements is in breach of international law and we believe that it is contrary to the spirit behind the declarations of principle.

The EU troika of Foreign Ministers will visit Israel next month and that matter will be brought very forcefully to the attention of the Israeli Government. Indeed, in the following month, the Prime Minister of this country is to visit Israel and he too will be bringing forward those matters.

(HL Debs., vol. 560, col. 1332: 31 January 1995)

In the course of oral questions about events in the Middle East, the Secretary of State for Foreign and Commonwealth Affairs, Mr Douglas Hurd, stated:

We believe that all settlements in occupied territories—that includes east Jerusalem—are illegal and an obstacle to peace.

(HC Debs., vol. 253, col. 1068: 1 February 1995; see also ibid., col. 1076)

Speaking on 28 February 1995 in the UN Security Council, the UK Permanent Representative to the UN in New York, Sir David Hannay, stated:

But we understand the frustration felt by the Palestinians in relation to Israeli settlement activity. The British Government's position on settlements is well known, and I reiterate it now: they are illegal, they contravene the Fourth Geneva Convention and they represent an obstacle to an overall peace.

(S/3505, p. 14)

In reply to a question, the Government spokesman in the House of Lords, Lord Inglewood, stated:

. . . we and our European Union partners have recently reaffirmed to both the Israeli Government and the United Nations Security Council our view that settlements are illegal and an obstacle to peace.

(HL Debs., vol. 563, col. 176: 5 April 1995)

Speaking on 12 May 1995 in the UN Security Council, the UK Permanent Representative to the UN in New York, Sir David Hannay, stated:

The British Government regrets that the problems caused by Israel's settlements policy have arisen again less than three months since the last time the Council discussed the subject. On that occasion, we reiterated our position that settlements in the occupied territories, including East Jerusalem, are illegal, contravene the Fourth Geneva Convention and are an obstacle to peace. That remains our view.

Our concerns about the latest decision to expropriate 131 acres of land in East Jerusalem have been raised with the Israeli authorities by European Union representatives in Tel Aviv. We consider that the decision is contrary to Security Council resolutions and in particular to resolution 267 (1969), which was adopted unanimously on 3 July 1969 and confirmed that ' . . . all legislative and administrative measures . . . taken by Israel which purport to alter the status of Jerusalem, including expropriation of land and properties thereon, are invalid . . . ' (*resolution 267 (1969), para. 4*) and called upon Israel to refrain from taking any further such measures in the future.

(S/3536, pp. 3–4)

In the course of a debate on the subject of east Jerusalem, the Minister of State, FCO, Mr Douglas Hogg, stated:

My hon. Friend the Member for Bexleyheath began by reciting the recent history of a very ancient city. He is, of course, right to say that the fourth Geneva convention applies. He emphasised the importance of an occupying power's compliance with the convention, and I entirely agree. That is fundamentally important, and from time to time we have made precisely the same point to the Israeli Government.

My hon. Friend and the hon. Member for Dundee, West also focused on the Israeli Government's recent decision to expropriate 130-odd acres of land in and around east Jerusalem. My hon. Friend advanced the arguments against that expropriation very clearly. The British Government regarded the decision as a serious development; let me make it plain that we consider the settlements in the occupied territories in east Jerusalem to be illegal, and also to constitute a serious obstacle to any peace settlement.

The decision to expropriate was roundly condemned by the international community, and the United Kingdom joined—and joins—in that condemnation. I very much welcome the decision by the Israeli Cabinet not to proceed with the expropriation. I very much hope that that proposal is not brought forward again at any time in the future.

(HC Debs., vol. 261, col. 189: 7 June 1995)

Part Fourteen: I. B. 8. *War and other uses of force—international war and armed conflict—the laws of war and armed conflict—conventional weapons*

(See also Part Fourteen: I. B. 6. (items referring to landmines), above)

On 13 February 1995, the UK Government deposited with the UN Secretary-General its instrument of ratification of the Convention on Prohibitions or Restrictions on the Use of certain Conventional Weapons which may be deemed to be Excessively Injurious or to have Indiscriminate Effects (and Protocols), 1981. Accompanying the instrument was the following declaration:

(a) *Generally*

(i) The term 'armed conflict' of itself and in its context denotes a situation of a kind which is not constituted by the commission of ordinary crimes, including acts of terrorism, whether concerted or in isolation.

(ii) The United Kingdom will not, in relation to any situation in which it is involved, consider itself bound in consequence of any declaration purporting to be made for the purposes of Article 7(4), unless the United Kingdom shall have expressly recognised that it has been made by a body which is genuinely an authority representing a people engaged in an armed conflict of the type to which that paragraph applies.

(iii) The terms 'civilian' and 'civilian population' have the same meaning as in Article 50 of the 1st Additional Protocol of 1977 to the 1949 Geneva Conventions. Civilians shall enjoy the protection afforded by this Convention unless and for such time as they take a direct part in hostilities.

(iv) Military commanders and others responsible for planning, deciding upon, or executing attacks necessarily have to reach decisions on the basis of their assessment of the information from all sources which is reasonably available to them at the relevant time.

(b) *Re: Protocol II, Article 2; and Protocol III, Article 1*

A specific area of land may be a military objective if, because of its location or other reasons specified in this Article, its total or partial destruction, capture or neutralisation in the circumstances ruling at the time offers a definite military advantage.

(c) *Re: Protocol II, Article 3*

In the view of the United Kingdom, the military advantage anticipated from an attack is intended to refer to the advantage anticipated from the attack considered as a whole and not only from isolated or particular parts of the attack.

(d) *Re: Protocol III, Article 2*

The United Kingdom accepts the provisions of Article 2(2) and (3) on the understanding that the terms of those paragraphs of that Article do not imply that the air-delivery of incendiary weapons, or of any other weapons, projectiles or munitions, is less accurate or less capable of being carried out discriminately than all or any other means of delivery.

In accordance with paragraphs 2 and 4 respectively of its article 5, the Convention and its Protocols will enter into force for each of the States concerned six months after the date of deposit of the instrument, i.e. for Italy on 20 July 1995, for Belgium on 7 August 1995 and for the United Kingdom on 13 August 1995.

(C.N. 48. 1995. TREATIES–1)

Speaking on 17 August 1995 at the Conference on Disarmament and Arms Control, the UK representative, Mr R. Smith, stated:

Nor must we forget about conventional weapons. Nuclear, biological and chemical weapons are potential weapons of mass destruction, but now, today, it is conventional weapons which are the actual weapons of mass destruction. One has only to think of the large numbers of people killed and maimed by the sadly all too commonplace landmine. Like a number of other states, we have introduced an extensive national moratorium on the export of anti-personnel landmines. We urge others to do so too. We also believe that we must take full advantage of the UN Weaponry Convention Review Conference next month. Our main objectives will be to broaden adherence to the Convention and to see its provisions on the use of landmines considerably strengthened and extended. We also remain committed to making progress on the Landmine Control Programme—the initiative launched in June at Budapest with a view to restricting the production, stockpiling and transfer of anti-personnel landmines—in a way which will complement the revised UN Weaponry Convention.

But landmines are only one of the many forms of conventional weapon. It is very important not to forget all the others, and I wish to emphasise our hope that all states will submit returns for 1994 to the UN Register of Conventional Arms. Completion of these annual returns is not a demanding step for states to take, but in the past too many have not taken it. It is also our strong view that this Conference should continue to give thoughtful attention to the problems posed by conventional weapons, including by reestablishing its Ad Hoc Committee on Transparency in Armaments. The issues posed by conventional weapons require attention. It is no more right for this Conference to ignore these issues than it would be for it to ignore nuclear issues.

(Text provided by the FCO)

Part Fourteen: I. B. 9. *War and other uses of force—international war and armed conflict—the laws of war and armed conflict—nuclear, bacteriological and chemical weapons*

(See also Part One: I., Part One: II. D. 1. (item of 23 November 1995), Part Two: II., and Part Three: I. A. 2. (item of 2 June 1994), above and Part Fourteen: V., below)

On 2 June 1994, the UK Government submitted a written statement to the International Court of Justice in the course of proceedings arising out of a request made by the World Health Assembly for an advisory opinion on the legality of the threat or use of nuclear weapons. The statement contained the following paragraph:

1. The question asks the Court whether the use of nuclear weapons by a State in war or other armed conflict would be a breach of that State's obligations under international law, including the WHO Constitution. Despite the terms in which it is framed, this question does not admit of a simple answer. In particular, there is no foundation for the view that the use of nuclear weapons would automatically contravene international law. The international community has never adopted in binding form any general prohibition on the use of nuclear weapons. Indeed, those treaties which have been adopted regarding nuclear weapons presuppose that there are circumstances in which such weapons might lawfully be used. Moreover, an examination of the principles of international law governing the use of force and the conduct of hostilities reveals that, while nuclear weapons (like all methods and means of warfare) are subject to limitations on their use, those limitations are not such as to render the use of nuclear weapons unlawful *per se*.

(Statement, p. 62; text provided by the FCO)

In its final submissions, the statement read:

3. As regards the principles of law raised by the question, it is submitted that:

(i) the use of nuclear weapons would not involve a breach of States' obligations under the WHO Constitution;

(ii) there is no rule contained in either customary international law or treaty which expressly prohibits all use of nuclear weapons. Moreover, State practice regarding the possession of nuclear weapons necessarily implies that the use of nuclear weapons would be lawful in proper circumstances;

(iii) the legality of the use of nuclear weapons must therefore be assessed in the light of applicable principles of international law regarding the use of force and the conduct of hostilities, as for other methods and means of warfare;

(iv) the use of nuclear weapons will not be contrary to the Charter of the United Nations if it meets the criteria for the exercise of the right of self-defence. Whether the use of nuclear weapons meets those criteria will depend upon the circumstances of each individual case; and

(v) nuclear weapons are not prohibited *per se* by the law of armed conflict. Their use will be lawful provided that it complies with the general principles of the law regarding unnecessary suffering and the protection of the civilian population. Their use in circumstances which would otherwise be illegal may moreover be lawful if it constitutes a legitimate belligerent reprisal.

(Statement, pp. 96–7; text provided by the FCO. See also statement of June 1995, pp. 74–5)

In the course of his oral statement to the International Court of Justice on 15 November 1995, the Attorney-General, Sir Nicholas Lyell, said:

So far as the customary law of war is concerned, the United Kingdom has always accepted that the use of nuclear weapons is subject to the general principles of the *jus in bello*. But to say that a weapon is *subject* to the law does not mean that it must be *prohibited* by that law. There is no doubt that the customary law of war does prohibit *some* uses of nuclear weapons, just as it prohibits some uses of *all* types of weapons. But again, it is assumption not argument to say that it prohibits *all* uses of nuclear weapons, without regard to the circumstances.

(Text provided by the FCO)

In reply to questions, the Minister of State, FCO, wrote:

The United Kingdom's Positive and Negative Security Assurances, announced in 1968 and 1978, have always been applied to non-nuclear weapons States Parties to the Non-Proliferation Treaty (NPT) or States Parties to other internationally binding commitments not to manufacture or acquire nuclear explosive devices. Under the Negative Security Assurance the United Kingdom undertakes not to use nuclear weapons against such states except in the case of an attack on the United Kingdom, its dependent territories, its armed forces or its Allies by such a state in association or alliance with a nuclear weapon state.

This has not changed.

(HL Debs., vol. 560, *WA 64*: 23 January 1995)

An FCO press statement issued on 13 February 1995 read in part:

The UK Permanent Representative to the United Nations in New York yesterday deposited the UK's instrument of ratification of the 1981 United Nations Weaponry Convention. The Convention provides a legal framework for prohibitions and restrictions on the use of non-detectable fragments, mines and booby traps, and incendiary weapons, covered in three separate Protocols. The UK will be bound by all three Protocols.

(Text provided by the FCO)

The following statement was issued by the EU Presidency on behalf of the EU on 28 February 1995:

The European Union welcomes the fact that Argentina has deposited on 10 February its instrument of accession to the Treaty on the Non-proliferation of nuclear weapons as a non-nuclear weapon State. This accession confirms Argentina's firm commitment to contribute towards international nuclear non-proliferation efforts, as already demonstrated by the quadripartite agreement concluded between Argentina, Brazil, the ABACC and the IAEA and the Treaty of Tlatelolco ratified by Argentina on 18 January 1994.

The European Union takes this opportunity to underscore its belief in universal adherence to the NPT and calls upon States which have not yet done so to accede to the NPT as non-nuclear weapon States.

The Central and Eastern European countries associated with the Union align themselves to this statement.

(Text provided by the FCO)

In reply to questions, the Minister of State, FCO, wrote:

The nuclear non-proliferation treaty is the cornerstone of the nuclear non-proliferation regime. It has established an international norm against the spread of nuclear weapons and provides for effective International Atomic Energy Agency safeguards to verify compliance. We are working hard to secure the treaty's indefinite and unconditional extension at the review and extension conference in April and May.

We are committed to article VI of the nuclear non-proliferation treaty, whereby we undertake to pursue negotiations in good faith on effective measures relating to cessation of the nuclear arms race at an early date and to nuclear disarmament and on a treaty on general and complete disarmament under strict and effective international control.

(HC Debs., vol. 256, WA, col. *196*: 8 March 1995)

The following answers were given by the Minister of State, FCO, to questions put to Her Majesty's Government:

Q. In what circumstances they consider Article 4 of the Non-Proliferation Treaty, which refers to the 'inalienable right' of parties to the treaty to the civil use of nuclear energy, may be abrogated, and whether recent Israeli or other statements that Iran has a nuclear weapons programme, which have not been confirmed by the IAEA, can provide such circumstances?

A. Article IV preserves the right of all states parties to the treaty to use nuclear energy for peaceful purposes in conformity with Articles I and II; in the case of non-nuclear-weapon states, Article II provides that they will not manufacture, or seek assistance in the manufacture, of nuclear weapons. Therefore concerns about a country's compliance with Articles I and II are a relevant factor in considering their position under Article IV.

Q. What limitations they see to the rights of non-weapons power signatories to the civil use of nuclear energy, which are enshrined in Article 4 of the Non-Proliferation Treaty as 'inalienable', and whether they believe that Russia should not be completing a nuclear power station under IAEA safeguards for Iran?

A. Article IV of the Nuclear Non-Proliferation Treaty (NPT) recognises the rights of all states parties to use nuclear energy for peaceful purposes. But it also provides that they should be in conformity with their obligations under Article I and II of the treaty concerning the transfer or acquisition of nuclear weapons. Article III of the treaty also includes a commitment by non-nuclear-weapon states to accept International Atomic Energy Agency safeguards to prevent diversion of nuclear energy from peaceful uses to nuclear weapons. We are concerned about the potential proliferation risk of Russian plans to provide nuclear technology and equipment to Iran because of reports that Iran may have a nuclear weapons development programme.

(HL Debs., vol. 562, *WA 23–4*: 8 March 1995)

Speaking at the Non-Proliferation Treaty Review and Extension Conference on 19 April 1995, the UK representative, Sir Michael Weston, stated:

For its part, the UK takes its non-proliferation obligations under Article I very seriously. It has not transferred to any recipient whatsoever nuclear weapons or other nuclear explosive devices or control over such weapons or explosive devices, directly or indirectly. Nor has it in any way assisted, encouraged or induced any non-nuclear weapon state to manufacture or otherwise acquire nuclear weapons or other nuclear explosive devices, or control over such weapons or explosive devices. The UK has in place—as we believe we are bound to if we take our responsibilities under the Treaty seriously—a system of export controls designed to ensure that exports of nuclear items to non-nuclear weapon states can be made only for legitimate non-explosive uses.

. . .

. . . the UK is fully committed to practical disarmament and non-proliferation measures, and we believe that much has been achieved. In a statement to the Conference on Disarmament on 6 April, the UK, together with France, US and Russia, solemnly reaffirmed our commitments, as stated in Article VI, to pursue negotiations in good faith on effective measures relating to nuclear disarmament, which remains our ultimate goal. We believe that, if we are to build further on the momentum created by recent disarmament successes, we must ensure that the essential framework of stability and predictability provided by the Treaty is made permanent. The Treaty has enabled us to make much progress. Making it permanent will enable us to make more.

(Text provided by the FCO)

Speaking at the same Conference on 24 April 1995, the UK representative, Mr C. Hulse, stated:

There are of course some constraints to technology transfer, not least those imposed by the NPT itself. The UK is a trading nation. We take the view that, in general, goods should be traded freely. But almost all nuclear technology for civil nuclear power can be used in ways which could also constitute a proliferation threat. Some technologies pose a greater threat than others. Some states give rise to genuine concerns about their intentions on proliferation. And this freedom to trade widely in nuclear technology has to be set in a framework which helps us to prevent those transfers which, if allowed to proceed, would put us in breach of our obligations under Articles I and III.2 of the Treaty.

(Ibid.)

The Secretary of State for Foreign and Commonwealth Affairs, Mr Douglas Hurd, remarked during a debate on the subject of the Nuclear Non-Proliferation Treaty:

For 25 years, the non-proliferation treaty has helped prevent the spread of nuclear weapons. It is one of the essential foundations of our security. On 11 May the parties to the treaty decided unanimously to extend the treaty indefinitely. That decision is excellent news. A permanent treaty, properly applied, will make the world a safer place. It will provide the stability and predictability essential to continuing efforts towards disarmament and to the peaceful use of nuclear energy.

The conference also agreed by consensus a number of important texts, copies of which will be placed in the Library. The declaration on principles and objectives for nuclear non-proliferation and disarmament calls upon states not party to the treaty, in particular those with unsafeguarded nuclear facilities, to join it as a matter of urgency. It affirms the support of all states parties for the safeguards regime administered by the International Atomic Energy Agency and for efforts to increase the agency's capability to detect undeclared nuclear activities.

(HC Debs., vol. 260, col. 151: 16 May 1995)

In reply to a question, the Minister of State, FCO, wrote:

There is no requirement under the treaty on European Union or the Community treaties—including the EURATOM treaty—for a member state to give notification of plans to carry out nuclear weapons tests. A Member state could if it wished give such notification in the context of the Common Foreign and Security Policy. None has been given in recent years.

(HC Debs., vol. 263, WA, col. *395*: 10 July 1995)

In reply to a question on the subject of the French nuclear testing in the South Pacific, the Minister of State, FCO, Baroness Chalker, stated:

The French testing is consistent with the Non-Proliferation Treaty. There is no comprehensive test ban in force. France is not in breach of the NPT or any other international treaty obligations. The French Government have made it absolutely clear that they will limit the number of tests to the minimum, that they will give up testing when a comprehensive test ban treaty has been concluded, and that the current tests are designed to put France in a position to sign the comprehensive test ban treaty in 1996.

. . .

As regards whether or not France provides information about the tests to other authorities, I should point out that there is no legal requirement upon it to do so.

(HL Debs., vol. 566, cols. 1107–8: 25 October 1995)

Part Fourteen: III. *War and other uses of force—self-defence*

In reply to a question, the Minister of State, FCO, wrote:

The Turkish Government have explained that their operations in northern Iraq are temporary and aimed solely at destroying PKK capability to mount attacks against Turkey from northern Iraq. There has been no determination by the UN of whether the incursion is a violation of Article 2(4) of the United Nations Charter.

(HL Debs., vol. 563, *WA 35*: 6 April 1995)

In June 1995, the UK Government submitted a written statement to the International Court of Justice in the course of proceedings arising out of a request by the UN General Assembly for an advisory opinion on the legality of the threat or use of nuclear weapons. The statement contained the following paragraphs:

3 The United Nations Charter and the Right of Self-Defence

3.33 The use of force is not prohibited by Article 2(4) of the United Nations Charter if it is duly authorized by the competent organ of the United Nations, or if it is in the exercise of the right of self-defence. Although for Member States of the United Nations Article 51 of the Charter recognizes their right to self-defence, Article 51 is not the source of that right. Indeed, the use of the word 'inherent' in Article 51 was intended to mark the pre-existence of this right, based on customary international law.[95] There had been no reference to self-defence in the Dumbarton Oaks Proposals and the view of Committee I at the San Francisco Conference was that the prohibition of the use of force, contemplated as a core provision of the new UN Charter, would leave the use of arms in self-defence unimpaired.[96] The same view had been taken earlier in relation to the Covenant of the League and the 1928 Pact of Paris. The decision to make express reference to the right of individual or collective self-defence came largely as a response to the demand of regional organizations, such as the Organization of American States and the Arab League, that the legitimacy of their arrangements for collective self-defence should be expressly recognized.

---

[95] See *Case Concerning Military and Paramilitary Activities in and Against Nicaragua*, Judgment of 27 June 1986, ICJ Reports 1986, paragraph 176.

[96] See Bowett, *Self-defence in International Law* (1958), pp. 182–184.

(1) The Terms and Effects of Article 51

3.34 The terms of Article 51 are well known:

'Nothing in the present Charter shall impair the inherent right of individual or collective self-defence if an armed attack occurs . . . '

On its face, therefore, the effect of this provision is to safeguard the right of Member States to take such action as would be permissible in self-defence independently of the United Nations Charter. In other words, if action by a

State meets all the requirements of legitimate self-defence under traditional, customary international law, such action is not impaired or prohibited by anything contained in the Charter. Such measures must, however, be reported to the Security Council.

3.35 The elaboration of this provision at San Francisco in 1945 did not in fact turn on a discussion of different types of weapons, and certainly there is nothing in the *travaux préparatoires* to suggest that any particular type of weapon was, *per se*, incapable of use in self-defence. It follows, therefore, that discussion of the legality of the use or threat of use of nuclear weapons in the exercise of the right of self-defence must centre on whether such use of nuclear weapons would meet the traditional criteria for lawful self-defence.

(2) The Conditions of Lawful Self-defence

3.36 As an inherent, customary law right of States, recognized by Article 51 of the Charter, self-defence is permitted under certain conditions. These conditions are, in particular, that it is necessary to act in self-defence and that the steps taken by way of self-defence are proportionate. These principles are equally applicable to the use of nuclear weapons in self-defence as to the use of any other type of weapon in self-defence. Moreover, it would be entirely arbitrary to exclude *ex hypothesi* the right of a State to rely on nuclear weapons as a means of defence against a conventional attack.

(a) The necessity to react in self-defence

3.37 The notion has long been accepted that States should only use force in self-defence as a matter of last resort. This is inherent in the concept of self-defence. The burden of showing necessity would exist whether the weapons used are nuclear or conventional.

3.38 In this context the theory of nuclear 'deterrence' falls to be considered. For the past forty or so years States have relied upon their possession of nuclear weapons, or on alliance with nuclear-weapon States, and even their targeting of another nuclear-weapon State, as a necessary means of deterring an attack by the latter. Whatever the theoretical criticisms voiced of the idea of deterrence, the fact is, first, that it has worked and, second, that for many years a number of States have based their self-defence upon that idea, in the belief that the possession of nuclear weapons, and the threat to use them in self-defence, is legitimate.

(b) The Proportionality of the Reaction

3.39 It has always been accepted that self-defence must be proportionate. The controversy has been over the question of what the measures of self-defence have to be proportionate to: to the scale of the attack or to the extent to which the target State is jeopardised?

3.40 The former view has its adherents,[97] but, as Ago wrote as Rapporteur of the I.L.C. on State responsibility:

> 'It would be mistaken . . . to think that there must be proportionality between the conduct constituting the armed attack and the opposing conduct. The action needed to halt and repulse the attack may well have to assume

dimensions disproportionate to those of the attack suffered. What matters in this respect is the result to be achieved by the "defensive" action, and not the forms, substance and strength of the action itself.'[98]

Thus, on this argument, there can be no easy assumption that the use of nuclear weapons can never be justified in response to a conventional attack, because there is 'disproportion' between the two. The question to be posed is whether, in the actual circumstances of the attack, the use of the particular nuclear weapon was necessary in order to defend the victim State.[99]

---

[97] See, for example, Singh, 'The right of self-defence in relation to the use of nuclear weapons' 5 *Indian Yearbook of International Affairs* (1956), vol. 3, pp. 32–34.

[98] Ago, 'Addendum to Eighth Report on State Responsibility' 1980 II (i) I.L.C.Y.B., 13 at p. 69.

[99] For a discussion of this question, see Dinstein, *War, Aggression and Self-Defence* (2nd ed., 1994) pp. 230–236.

3.41 The answer to that question may depend upon a host of factors: the nature, scale and location of the attack, the means of defence available to the victim State; the extent to which the defensive means chosen (nuclear or non-nuclear) will minimise the danger to non-military targets; whether the damage is caused on the territory of the aggressor or the victim State, and so on.

(Statement, pp. 36–8; text provided by the FCO)

Part Fourteen: IV. A. *War and other uses of force—use of force under collective measures—regime of the UN*

Her Majesty's Government were asked:

Whether in their view United Nations Security Council Resolution No. 949 permits the use of force in the event of Iraq redeploying its armed forces 'towards the south' without further reference to the Security Council?

In reply, the Government spokesman in the House of Lords wrote:

Resolution 949 does not as such authorise the use of force.

(HL Debs., vol. 561, *WA 3*: 6 February 1995)

In reply to a question, the Minister of State, FCO, wrote:

The Unified United Nations Command, which was established in 1950, remains legally in existence. Its prime purpose is to oversee the 1953 Armistice Agreement on behalf of the United Nations. It was to this Command that 16 members of the United Nations, including the UK, sent forces in 1950 to repel the North Korean invasion of South Korea. The Command has no forces of its own; should it require them, it would in the first instance draw on those of the US-Republic of Korea Combined Forces Command, which was established in 1978.

(HL Debs., vol. 563, *WA 33*: 6 April 1995)

Part Fourteen: V. *War and other uses of force—use of force other than international war, civil war and self-defence*

On 2 June 1994, the UK Government submitted a written statement to the International Court of Justice in the course of proceedings arising out of a request made by the World Health Assembly for an advisory opinion on the legality of the threat or use of nuclear weapons. The statement contained the following paragraphs:

Reprisals

45. Even if a particular use of nuclear weapons is contrary to the laws of armed conflict, it remains necessary to consider whether that use might be justified as a belligerent reprisal. A belligerent reprisal is an action, taken by a party to a conflict, which would normally constitute a violation of the laws of armed conflict but which is lawful because it is taken in response to a prior violation of that law by an adversary. To be lawful, a belligerent reprisal must meet two conditions. First, it must not be directed against persons or objects against which the taking of reprisals is specifically prohibited. Secondly, it must meet the criteria for the regulation of reprisals, namely that it is taken in response to a prior wrong, is proportionate, is undertaken for the purposes of putting an end to the enemy's unlawful conduct and for preventing future illegalities, and is a means of last resort.

46. The Geneva Conventions of 1949 prohibit the taking of reprisals against persons or objects protected by the Conventions.[51] That, however, would have little relevance here, since it is difficult to conceive of the use of nuclear weapons against such persons or objects.[52] The Conventions do not preclude the taking of reprisals against the enemy's civilian population or civilian objects in enemy territory.

[51] Convention No. I, Article 46, Convention No. II, Article 47, Convention No. III, Article 13, Convention No. IV, Art. 33.

[52] See section (d) above.

47. Additional Protocol I, on the other hand, prohibits the taking of reprisals against the civilian population (Article 51(6)), civilian objects (Article 52(1)), historic monuments (Article 53(c)), objects indispensable to the survival of the civilian population (Article 54(4)), the natural environment (Article 55(2)) and works and installations containing natural forces (Article 56(4)). Again, however, these provisions are widely regarded as innovative and thus as inapplicable to the use of nuclear weapons.[53]

[53] Kalshoven, note 33 above, p. 283. The ICRC Commentary, note 6 above, does not include the reprisals provisions in the list of provisions which it expressly regards as applicable to nuclear weapons, p. 595.

48. So far as the second condition for the conduct of lawful reprisals is concerned, it has been argued that the use of nuclear weapons could never satisfy the requirements of proportionality and preventiveness. This argument, however, suffers from the same flaws as the argument that the use of nuclear

weapons could never satisfy the requirements of self-defence. Whether the use of nuclear weapons would meet the requirements of proportionality cannot be answered in the abstract; it would depend upon the nature and circumstances of the wrong which prompted the taking of reprisal action. Nor can it be ruled out that the retaliatory use of nuclear weapons might have the effect of putting a stop to a series of violations of the law by an adversary.

(Statement, pp. 93–4; text provided by the FCO. See also statement of June 1995, pp. 58–60)

APPENDICES

I. Multilateral Agreements Signed by the United Kingdom in 1995[1]

Title	*Place and Date*	*UK Signature*	*Text*[2]
Convention on Customs Treatment of Pool Containers used in International Transport	Geneva, 21.1.1994	13.4.1995	
Fifth Additional Protocol to the Constitution of the Universal Post Union	Seoul, 14.9.1994	14.9.1994	
Amendment to the Agreement Relating to the International Telecommunications Satellite Organization, 'INTELSAT', done at Washington on 20.8.1971	Margarita Island, Venezuela, 26.10.1994	26.10.1994	
Final Act of the 1994 Conference of Parties to the International Convention for the Prevention of Pollution from Ships 1973, as modified by the Protocol of 1978 relating thereto	London, 3.11.1994	3.11.1994	
Amendments to the Convention on the International Maritime Satellite Organization (INMARSAT)	London, 9.12.1994		
Amendment to the Operation Agreement on the International Maritime Satellite Organization (INMARSAT)	London, 9.12.1994		

[1] Information supplied by the Foreign and Commonwealth Office. The table includes some agreements signed by the United Kingdom before 1995, where information was not previously available. The information is correct as at January 1996, although in some cases information available since that time has been included.

[2] Publication is in various series of UK Command Papers, including European Communities Series (EC), Miscellaneous Series (Misc.), and Treaty Series (TS). Cm = Command Paper number.

Title	*Place and Date*	*UK Signature*	*Text*[2]
Convention on the Safety of United Nations and Associated Personnel	New York (UN), 9.12.1994		
1994 Amendments to the International Convention for the Safety of Life at Sea 1994 (Resolution MSC 42(64))	London, 9.12.1994		
Energy Charter Treaty	Lisbon, 17.12.1994	17.12.1994	Misc. No. 6 (1995) (Cm 2952)
Energy Charter Protocol on Energy Efficiency and Related Environmental Aspects	Lisbon, 17.12.1994	17.12.1994	Misc. No. 6 (1995) (Cm 2952)
Agreement on Illicit Traffic by Sea, implementing Article 17 of the United Nations Convention Against Illicit Traffic in Narcotic Drugs and Psychotropic Substances	Strasbourg, 31.1.1995	31.1.1995	Misc. No. 8 (1995) (Cm 2979)
Framework Convention for the Protection of National Minorities	Strasbourg, 1.2.1995	1.2.1995	Misc. No. 7 (1995) (Cm 2953)
Agreement on the establishment of the Korean Peninsula Energy Development Organization	New York, 9.3.1995		
Convention drawn up on the Basis of Article K.3 of the Treaty on European Union, on Simplified Extradition Procedure between the Member States of the European Union	Brussels, 10.3.1995	10.3.1995	EC No. 5 (1995) (Cm 2958)
WEU Security Agreement	Brussels, 28.3.1995	28.3.1995	Misc. No. 9 (1995) (Cm 2971)
1995 Amendments to the International Convention for the Safety of Life at Sea 1974 (Resolution MSC 46 (65))	London, 16.5.1995		

Title	*Place and Date*	*UK Signature*	*Text*[2]
Convention drawn up on the Basis of Article K.3 of the Treaty on European Union, on the Use of Information Technology for Customs Purposes	Brussels, 26.7.1995		
Convention drawn up on the Basis of Article K.3 of the Treaty on European Union, on the Protection of the European Communities Financial Interests	Brussels, 26.7.1995		
Convention based on Article K.3 of the Treaty on European Union, on the Establishment of a European Police Office (Europol Convention)	Brussels, 26.7.1995	EC No. 13 (1995) (Cm 3050)	
Agreement for the Implementation of the Provisions of the United Nations Convention on the Law of the Sea of 10 December 1982 relating to the Conservation and Management of Straddling Fish Stocks and Highly Migratory Fish Stocks	New York, 4.12.1995	4.12.1995	Misc. No. 12 (1995) (Cm 3125)

II. European Communities Agreements Signed by the United Kingdom in 1995[1]

Title	*Place and Date*	*UK Signature*	*Text*[2]
Exchange of Letters between the European Community and the Republic of Bulgaria amending the Interim Agreement on Trade and Trade-related Matters between the European Economic Community and the European Coal and Steel Community, of the one part, and the Republic of Bulgaria, of the other part, and the Europe Agreement establishing an Association between the European Communities and their Member States, of the one part, and the Republic of Bulgaria, of the other part, both as amended by the Additional Protocol signed on 21.12.1993	Brussels, 30.6.1994		EC No. 11 (1995) (Cm 3122)
Agreement on Free Trade and Trade-related Matters between the European Community, the European Atomic Energy Community and the European Coal and Steel Community, of the one part, and the Republic of Estonia, of the other part, together with the Final Act thereto	Brussels, 18.7.1994		

[1] Information supplied by the Foreign and Commonwealth Office. The table includes some agreements signed by the United Kingdom before 1995, where information was not previously available. The information is correct as at January 1996, although in some cases information available since that time has been included.

[2] Publication is in the European Communities Series of UK Command Papers (EC). Cm = Command Paper Number.

Title	*Place and Date*	*UK Signature*	*Text*[2]
Agreement on Free Trade and Trade-related Matters between the European Community, the European Atomic Energy Community and the European Coal and Steel Community, of the one part, and the Republic of Latvia, of the other part, together with the Final Act thereto	Brussels, 18.7.1994		
Agreement on Free Trade and Trade-related Matters between the European Community, the European Atomic Energy Community and the European Coal and Steel Community, of the one part, and the Republic of Lithuania, of the other part, together with the Final Act thereto	Brussels, 18.7.1994		
Partnership and Co-operation Agreement between the European Communities and their Member States and the Republic of Moldova, including Exchanges of Letters, with Declarations and Final Act	Brussels, 28.11.1994	28.11.1994	EC No. 3 (1995) (Cm 2863)
Agreement in the form of an Exchange of Letters between the European Communities and the Republic of India on the Guaranteed Prices for Cane Sugar for 1993/1994	Brussels, 7.12.1994		
Agreement in the form of an Exchange of Letters concerning the Amendment to the Agreement on Fisheries between the European Economic Community, on the one hand, and the Government of Denmark and	Brussels, 19.12.1994		

Title	*Place and Date*	*UK Signature*	*Text*[2]
the local Government of Greenland, on the other hand			
Third Protocol laying down the Conditions relating to Fishing provided for in the Agreement on Fisheries between the European Economic Community, on the one hand, and the Government of Denmark and the local Government of Greenland, on the other hand	Brussels, 19.12.1994		
Agreement in the form of an Exchange of Letters extending the Adaption to the Agreement between the European Community and Uruguay on Trade in Mutton, Lamb and Goatmeat	Brussels, 20.12.1994		
Agreement in the form of an Exchange of Letters extending the Adaption to the Agreement between the European Community and Hungary on Trade in Mutton, Lamb and Goatmeat	Brussels, 21.12.1994		
Agreement in the form of an Exchange of Letters extending the Adaption to the Agreement between the European Community and Slovakia on Trade in Mutton, Lamb and Goatmeat	Brussels, 21.12.1994		
Agreement in the form of an Exchange of Letters extending the Adaption to the Agreement between the European Community and Argentina on Trade in Mutton, Lamb and Goatmeat	Brussels, 22.12.1994		
Agreement in the form of an Exchange of Letters extending	Brussels, 22.12.1994		

Title	Place and Date	UK Signature	Text[2]
the Adaption to the Agreement between the European Community and Poland on Trade in Mutton, Lamb and Goatmeat			
Agreement in the form of an Exchange of Letters between the European Communities and the Kingdom of Morocco on the Regime for Imports into the Community of Tomatoes and Courgettes originating in and imported from Morocco	Brussels, 22.12.1994		
Second Additional Protocol to the Europe Agreement between the European Communities and their Member States, of the one part, and Romania, of the other part, and to the Interim Agreement on Trade and Trade-related Matters between the European Economic Community and the European Coal and Steel Community, of the one part, and Romania, of the other part	Brussels, 22.12.1994	22.12.1994	EC No. 2 (1996) (Cm 3082)
Agreement in the form of an Exchange of Letters extending the Adaption to the Agreement between the European Community and Bulgaria on Trade in Mutton, Lamb and Goatmeat	Brussels, 22.12.1994		
Agreement in the form of an Exchange of Letters extending the Adaption to the Agreement between the European Community and Poland on Trade in Mutton, Lamb and Goatmeat	Brussels, 22.12.1994		

Title	*Place and Date*	*UK Signature*	*Text*[2]
Exchange of Letters between the European Community and Barbados, Belize, the Republic of the Congo, Fiji, the Co-operative Republic of Guyana, the Republic of Côte d'Ivoire, Jamaica, the Republic of Kenya, the Republic of Madagascar, the Republic of Malawi, the Republic of Mauritius, the Republic of Suriname, St Kitts and Nevis, the Kingdom of Swaziland, the United Republic of Tanzania, the Republic of Trinidad and Tobago, the Republic of Uganda, and the Republic of Zimbabwe on the guaranteed prices for cane sugar for 1993/1994 delivery period	Brussels, 22.12.1994		
Agreement in the form of an Exchange of Letters extending the Adaption to the Agreement between the European Community and Czech Republic on Trade in Mutton, Lamb and Goatmeat	Brussels, 28.12.1994		
Second Additional Protocol to the Europe Agreement between the European Communities and their Member States, of the one part, and Romania, of the other part, and to the Interim Agreement on Trade and Trade-related Matters between the European Economic Community and the European Coal and Steel Community, of the one part, and Bulgaria, of the other part	Brussels, 30.12.1994	23.1.1995	EC No. 4 (1995) (Cm 2900)
Partnership and Co-operation Agreement between the European Communities and	Brussels, 23.1.1995	23.1.1995	EC No. 6 (1995) (Cm 2966)

Title	Place and Date	UK Signature	Text[2]
their Member States and the Republic of Kazakhstan, with Protocol, including Declarations and Final Act			
Agreement in the form of an Exchange of Letters extending the Adaption to the Agreement between the European Community and Australia on Trade in Mutton, Lamb and Goatmeat	Brussels, 8.2.1995		
Partnership and Co-operation Agreement between the European Communities and their Member States and the Republic of Kazakhstan, with Protocol, including Declarations and Final Act	Brussels, 23.2.1995	9.2.1995	EC No. 8 (1995) (Cm 2969)
Agreement in the form of an Exchange of Letters extending the Adaption to the Agreement between the European Community and New Zealand on Trade in Mutton, Lamb and Goatmeat	Brussels, 27.2.1995		
Partnership and Co-operation Agreement between the European Communities and their Member States and the Republic of Belarus, with Protocol, including Declarations and Final Act	Brussels, 27.2.1995	6.3.1995	EC No. 7 (1995) (Cm 2972)
Exchange of Letters concerning the provisional application of the Protocol establishing, for the period from 1.1.1994 to 31.12.1995, the fishing rights and financial compensation provided for in the Agreement between the European Community and the Government of the Republic of Guinea on fishing off the Guinea coast	Brussels, 17.3.1995		

Title	*Place and Date*	*UK Signature*	*Text*[2]
Agreement between the European Community and Austria on a tariff quota of 5000 head for cows and heifers	Brussels, 10.4.1995		
Interim Agreement on Trade and Trade-related matters between the European Community, the European Coal and Steel Community and the European Atomic Energy Community, of the one part, and Ukraine of the other part	Brussels, 1.6.1995		
Protocol on Financial and Technical Co-operation between the European Community and the Republic of Cyprus	Luxem-bourg, 12.6.1995		
Europe Agreement establishing an Association between the European Communities and their Member States, of the one part, and the Republic of Estonia, of the other part	Luxem-bourg, 12.6.1995		EC No. 7 (1996) (Cm 3187)
Europe Agreement establishing an Association between the European Communities and their Member States, of the one part, and the Republic of Latvia, of the other part, including Exchanges of Letters, with Declarations and Final Act	Luxem-bourg, 12.6.1995		EC No. 8 (1996) (Cm 3238)
Additional Protocol to the Europe Agreement establishing an Association between the European Communities and their Member States, of the one part, and Romania, of the other part	Brussels, 30.6.1995		EC No. 1 (1996) (Cm 3081)

Title	Place and Date	UK Signature	Text[2]
Additional Protocol to the Europe Agreement establishing an Association between the European Communities and their Member States, of the one part, and Hungary, of the other part	Brussels, 13.7.1995		EC No. 5 (1996) (Cm 3085)
Additional Protocol to the Europe Agreement establishing an Association between the European Communities and their Member States, of the one part, and Poland, of the other part	Brussels, 17.7.1995		EC No. 4 (1996) (Cm 3084)
Euro-Mediterranean Agreement establishing an Association between the European Communities and their Member States, of the one part, and the Republic of Tunisia, of the other part, with Final Act	Brussels, 17.7.1995		EC No. 6 (1996) (Cm 3159)
Additional Protocol to the Europe Agreement establishing an Association between the European Communities and their Member States, of the one part, and Bulgaria, of the other part	Brussels, 20.7.1995		EC No. 10 (1995) (Cm 3124)
Additional Protocol to the Agreement between the European Economic Community and the Kingdom of Norway consequent on the Accession of the Republic of Austria, the Republic of Finland and the Kingdom of Sweden to the European Union	Brussels, 25.7.1995		

Title	*Place and Date*	*UK Signature*	*Text*[2]
Additional Protocol to the Europe Agreement establishing an Association between the European Communities and their Member States, of the one part, and the Czech Republic, of the other part	Brussels, 24.8.1995		EC No. 3 (1996) (Cm 3083)
Protocol of Correction to the Partnership and Co-operation Agreement between the European Communities and their Member States and Ukraine, signed at Luxembourg on 14.6.1994, including Final Act and Declaration by the French Government	Brussels, 27.9.1995		

III. Bilateral Agreements signed by the United Kingdom in 1995[1]

Country and Title	*Place and Date*	*Text*[2]
ALGERIA		
Exchange of Notes concerning the UK/Algeria Debt Agreement No.1 (1994)	Algiers, 7.12.1994	TS No. 55(1995) (Cm 2939)
ARGENTINA		
Agreement in the form of an Exchange of Letters extending the Adaption to the Agreement between the European Community and Argentina on Trade in Mutton, Lamb and Goatmeat	Brussels	

[1] Information supplied by the Foreign and Commonwealth Office. The table includes some agreements signed by the United Kingdom before 1995, where information was not previously available. The information is correct as at January 1996, although in some cases information available since that time has been included.

[2] Publication is in various series of UK Command Papers, including European Communities Series (EC), Miscellaneous Series (Misc.), and Treaty Series (TS). Cm = Command Paper number.

Country and Title	*Place and Date*	*Text*[2]
AUSTRALIA		
Agreement in the form of an Exchange of Letters extending the Adaption to the Agreement between the European Community and Australia on Trade in Mutton, Lamb and Goatmeat	Brussels	
AUSTRIA		
Agreement between the European Community and Austria on a tariff quota of 5000 head for cows and heifers	Brussels	
BELARUS		
Partnership and Co-operation Agreement between the European Communities and their Member States and the Republic of Belarus, with Protocol, including Declarations and Final Act	Brussels, 6.3.1995	EC No. 7(1995) (Cm 2972)
Convention for the Avoidance of Double Taxation and the Prevention of Fiscal Evasion with respect to Taxes on Income and Capital	London, 7.3.1995	
Exchange of Notes terminating the Agreement constituted by an Exchange of Notes between the Government of the UK and the Government of the Union of Soviet Socialist Republics concerning the Mutual Abolition of Consular Fees on Visas signed at Moscow on 13.4.1964, as between the Governments of the UK and the Republic of Belarus	Minsk, 24.7.1995	
Agreement on Co-operation in the Fields of Education, Science and Culture	Minsk, 25.7.1995	
BOLIVIA		
Convention for the Avoidance of Double Taxation and the Prevention of Fiscal Evasion with	La Paz, 3.11.1994	

Country and Title	*Place and Date*	*Text*[2]
respect to Taxes on Income and Capital, with Exchange of Notes		
Exchange of Notes amending the UK/Bolivia Debt Agreement No. 5 (1995) (The UK/Bolivia Debt Agreement No. 5 (1995) Amendment)	La Paz, 22/23.8.1995	TS No. 105 (1995) (Cm 3117)
BULGARIA		
Agreement in the form of an Exchange of Letters extending the Adaption to the Agreement between the European Community and Bulgaria on Trade in Mutton, Lamb and Goatmeat	Brussels	
Exchange of Notes between the European Communities and the Republic of Bulgaria amending the Interim Agreement on Trade and Trade-related Matters between the European Economic Community and the European Coal and Steel Community, of the one part, and the Republic of Bulgaria, of the other part, and the Europe Agreement establishing an Association between the European Communities and their Member States, of the one part, and the Republic of Bulgaria, of the other part, both as amended by the Additional Protocol signed on 21.12.1993	Brussels, 30.6.1994	EC No. 11 (1995) (Cm 3122)
Second Additional Protocol to the Europe Agreement between the European Communities and their Member States, of the one part, and Romania, of the other part, and to the Interim Agreement on Trade and Trade-related Matters between the European Economic Community and the European Coal and Steel Community, of	Brussels, 23.1.1995	EC No. 4 (1995) (Cm 2900)

Country and Title	*Place and Date*	*Text*[2]
the one part, and Bulgaria, of the other part		
Additional Protocol to the Europe Agreement establishing an Association between the European Communities and their Member States, of the one part, and Bulgaria, of the other part	Brussels, 20.7.1995	EC No. 10 (1995) (Cm 3124)
Agreement for the Promotion and Protection of Investments	London, 11.12.1995	
BRAZIL		
Extradition Treaty	London, 18.7.1995	Brazil No. 1 (1995)(Cm 2975)
CANADA		
Exchange of Notes concerning the Consolidated Arrangements on Social Security	Ottawa, 11.10.1994	Canada No. 1 (1995)(Cm 2859)
Exchange of Notes amending the Convention providing for the Reciprocal Recognition and Enforcement of Judgments in Civil and Commercial Matters	London, 7.11.1994/ 17.2.1995	TS No. 36 (1996) (Cm 3226)
CHILE		
Agreement concerning Mutual Assistance in relation to Illicit Trafficking in Narcotic Drugs and Psychotropic Substances	London, 1.11.1995	
CONGO, REPUBLIC OF		
Exchange of Notes concerning Certain Commercial Debts (The UK/Congo Debt Agreement No. 3 (1994))	Kinshasa/ Brazzaville, 5.12.1994	
COTE D'IVOIRE		
Exchange of Notes concerning Certain Commercial Debts (The UK/Côte d'Ivoire Debt Agreement No. 7 (1994))	Abidjan, 10.1.1995	TS No. 67 (1995) (Cm 2955)
Agreement for the Promotion and Protection of Investments	London, 8.6.1995	Côte d'Ivoire No. 1 (1994)(Cm 2585)
CUBA		
Agreement for the Promotion and Protection of Investments	London, 30.1.1995	TS No. 50 (1995) (Cm 2912)

Country and Title	*Place and Date*	*Text*[2]
CYPRUS		
Protocol on Financial and Technical Co-operation between the European Community and the Republic of Cyprus	Luxembourg	
CZECH REPUBLIC		
Agreement in the form of an Exchange of Letters extending the Adaption to the Agreement between the European Community and the Czech Republic on Trade in Mutton, Lamb and Goatmeat	Brussels	
Additional Protocol to the Europe Agreement establishing an Association between the European Communities and their Member States, of the one part, and the Czech Republic, of the other part	Brussels	
DENMARK		
Agreement in the form of an Exchange of Letters concerning the Amendment to the Agreement on Fisheries between the European Economic Community, on the one hand, and the Government of Denmark and the local Government of Greenland, on the other hand	Brussels	
Third Protocol laying down the Conditions relating to Fishing provided for in the Agreement on Fisheries between the European Economic Community, on the one hand, and the Government of Denmark and the local Government of Greenland, on the other hand	Brussels	
ECUADOR		
Agreement for the Promotion and Protection of Investments	Quito, 10.5.1994	TS No. 18 (1996) (Cm 3076)

Country and Title	*Place and Date*	*Text*[2]
Exchange of Notes concerning the UK/Ecuador Debt Rescheduling Agreement (1994)	London, 24.6.1994	
Exchange of Notes concerning the UK/Ecuador Debt Agreement No. 6 (1994)	London, 23.12.1994/ 13.1.1995	TS No. 106 (1995)(Cm 3114)
Exchange of Notes concerning the British School, Quito	Quito, 9.6.1995	TS No. 73 (1995) (Cm 2982)
EGYPT		
Exchange of Notes concerning Certain Commercial Debts (UK/ Egypt Debt Agreement No. 2 (1991))	Cairo/London, 13.4.1992	
ESTONIA		
Agreement on International Road Transport of Investments	Tallinn, 16.8.1995	Estonia No. 1 (1995)(Cm 3105)
Agreement on Free Trade and Trade-related Matters between the European Community, of the one part, and the Republic of Estonia, of the other part, together with the Final Act thereto	Brussels	
Europe Agreement establishing an Association between the European Communities and their Member States, of the one part, and the Republic of Estonia, of the other part	Luxembourg	
GEORGIA		
Agreement for the Promotion and Protection of Investments	London, 15.2.1995	TS No. 41 (1995) (Cm 2882)
GREENLAND		
Agreement in the form of an Exchange of Letters concerning the Amendment to the Agreement on Fisheries between the European Economic Community, on the one hand, and the Government of Denmark and the local Government of Greenland, on the other hand	Brussels	

Country and Title	*Place and Date*	*Text*[2]
Third Protocol laying down the Conditions relating to Fishing provided for in the Agreement on Fisheries between the European Economic Community, on the one hand, and the Government of Denmark and the local Government of Greenland, on the other hand	Brussels	
GRENADA		
Agreement concerning Mutual Assistance in relation to Drug Trafficking	St George's, 6.2.1995	
GUINEA		
Exchange of Letters concerning the provisional application of the Protocol extablishing, for the period from 1.1.1994 to 31.12.1995, the Fishing Rights and Financial Compensation provided for in the Agreement between the European Community and the Government of the Republic of Guinea for Fishing off the Guinea coast	Brussels	
HUNGARY		
Agreement in the form of an Exchange of Letters extending the Adaption to the Agreement between the European Community and Hungary on Trade in Mutton, Lamb and Goatmeat	Brussels	
Additional Protocol to the Europe Agreement establishing an Association between the European Communities and their Member States, of the one part, and Hungary, of the other part	Brussels	
INDIA		
Agreement in the form of an Exchange of Letters between the European Communities and the Republic of India on the	Brussels	

Country and Title	*Place and Date*	*Text*[2]
Guaranteed Prices for Cane Sugar for 1993/1994		
Exchange of Notes further amending the Air Services Agreement done at New Delhi on 1.12.1951	New Delhi, 14.12.1994	TS No. 39 (1995) (Cm 2875)
INDONESIA		
Exchange of Notes concerning the Proposed Export of Uranium by AEA Technology to the Government of the Republic of Indonesia's BATAN Nuclear Fuel Element Centre	Jakarta, 5.5.1995	TS No. 96 (1995) (Cm 3127)
Exchange of Notes concerning the Proposed Export by AEA Technology to the National Atomic Energy Agency, Indonesia, of 33 Kilograms of Uranium Oxide Powder	Jakarta, 7/8.11.1995	TS No. 34 (1996) (Cm 3195)
Exchange of Notes concerning the Proposed Export by AEA Technology to the National Atomic Energy Agency, Indonesia, of Technical Data concerning the Recovery of Highly Enriched Uranium	Jakarta, 7/8.11.1995	TS No. 35 (1996) (Cm 3196)
KAZAKHSTAN		
Partnership and Co-operation Agreement between the European Communities and their Member States and the Republic of Kazakhstan, with Protocol, including Declarations and Final Act	Brussels, 23.1.1995	EC No. 6 (1995) (Cm 2966)
Exchange of Notes terminating the Agreement constituted by an Exchange of Notes between the Government of the UK and the Government of the Union of Soviet Socialist Republics concerning the Mutual Abolition of Consular Fees on Visas signed at Moscow on 13.4.1964, as between the Governments of the	Almaty, 31.7.1995	

Country and Title	*Place and Date*	*Text*[2]
UK and the Republic of Kazakhstan		
Agreement for the Promotion and Protection of Investments	London, 23.11.1995	TS No. 30 (1996) (Cm 3176)
KYRGYZSTAN		
Partnership and Co-operation Agreement between the European Communities and their Member States and the Republic of Kyrgystan, with Protocol, including Declarations and Final Act	Brussels, 9.2.1995	EC No. 8 (1995) (Cm 2969)
LAOS		
Agreement for the Promotion and Protection of Investments	Vientiane, 1.6.1995	TS No. 112 (1995)(Cm 3054)
LATVIA		
Agreement on Free Trade and Trade-related Matters between the European Community, the European Atomic Energy Community and the European Coal and Steel Community, of the one part, and the Republic of Latvia, of the other part, together with the Final Act thereto	Brussels	
Europe Agreement establishing an Association between the European Communities and their Member States, of the one part, and the Republic of Latvia, of the other part, including Exchanges of Letters, with Declarations and Final Act	Luxembourg	
Agreement on Co-operation in the fields of Education, Science and Culture	Riga, 22.11.1995	
LITHUANIA		
Agreement on Free Trade and Trade-related Matters between the European Community, the European Atomic Energy Community and the European Coal and Steel Community, of the one part, and the Republic of	Brussels	

Country and Title	*Place and Date*	*Text*[2]
Lithuania, of the other part, together with the Final Act thereto		
MALTA		
Convention on Social Security	London, 19.10.1995	
MAURITANIA		
Exchange of Notes concerning the UK/Mauritania Debt Agreement No. 6 (1995)	Rabat, 24.11.1995	
MOLDOVA		
Partnership and Co-operation Agreement between the European Communities and their Member States and the Republic of Moldova, including Exchanges of Letters, with Declarations and Final Act	Brussels, 28.11.1994	EC No. 3 (1995) (Cm 2863)
MOROCCO		
Agreement in the form of an Exchange of Letters between the European Communities and the Kingdom of Morocco on the Regime for Imports into the Community of Tomatoes and Courgettes originating in and imported from Morocco	Brussels	
MOZAMBIQUE		
Exchange of Notes concerning Certain Commercial Debts (The UK/Mozambique Debt Agreement No. 4 (1993) Amendment)	Maputo, 4.7.1995	
NETHERLANDS		
Exchange of Notes extending the European Convention on Extradition of 13.12.1957 to the Netherlands Antilles and Aruba	London, 24.11.1994	
Protocol amending the Convention for the Avoidance of Double Taxation and the Prevention of Fiscal Evasion with respect to Taxes on Estates of Deceased Persons and Inheritances and on	London, 7.9.1995	

Country and Title	*Place and Date*	*Text*[2]
Gifts, signed at The Hague on 11.12.1979		
NEW ZEALAND		
Agreement in the form of an Exchange of Letters extending the Adaption to the Agreement between the European Community and New Zealand on Trade in Mutton, Lamb and Goatmeat	Brussels	
NICARAGUA		
Exchange of Notes concerning the UK/Nicaragua Retrospective Terms Adjustment Agreement 1994	Managua, 15.3.1995	TS No. 56 (1995) (Cm 2940)
NIGER		
Exchange of Notes concerning Certain Commercial Debts (The UK/Niger Debt Agreement No. 8 (1994))	Abidjan/ Niamey, 4.8.1994	
NORWAY		
Additional Protocol to the Agreement between the European Economic Community and the Kingdom of Norway consequent on the Accession of the Republic of Austria, the Republic of Finland and the Kingdom of Sweden to the European Union	Brussels	
Agreement in the form of an Exchange of Notes concerning the Export of Uranium to Norway	Oslo, 14.12.1994	TS No. 35 (1995) (Cm 2862)
Exchange of Notes amending the Agreement relating to the Exploitation of the Statfjord Field Reservoirs and the Offtake of Petroleum therefrom, signed at Oslo on 16.10.1979	Oslo, 24.3.1995	TS No. 57 (1995) (Cm 2941)
Exchange of Notes concerning the Export of Uranium to Norway	Oslo, 12.5.1995	TS No. 98 (1995) (Cm 3131)

Country and Title	*Place and Date*	*Text*[2]
Exchange of Notes concerning the Disposal of the 'Brent Spar' Offshore Installation	Oslo, 7.7.1995	TS No. 65 (1995) (Cm 2951)
Exchange of Notes concerning the Export of Uranium to Norway	Oslo, 1/10.11.1995	TS No. 33 (1996) (Cm 3194)
OMAN		
Agreement for the Promotion and Protection of Investments	Muscat, 25.11.1995	
PERU		
Exchange of Notes concerning the UK/Peru Retrospective Terms Agreement 1995	Lima, 27.1.1995	TS No. 23 (1996) (Cm 3144)
POLAND		
Agreement in the form of an Exchange of Letters extending the Adaption to the Agreement between the European Community and Poland on Trade in Mutton, Lamb and Goatmeat	Brussels	
Additional Protocol to the Europe Agreement establishing an Association between the European Communities and their Member States, of the one part, and Poland, of the other part	Brussels	
ROMANIA		
Second Additional Protocol to the Europe Agreement between the European Communities and their Member States, of the one part, and Romania, of the other part, and to the Interim Agreement on Trade and Trade-related Matters between the European Economic Community and the European Coal and Steel Community, of the one part, and Romania, of the other part	Brussels, 22.12.1994	
Additional Protocol to the Europe Agreement establishing an Association between the European Communities and their Member States, of the one part, and Romania, of the other part	Brussels	

Country and Title	*Place and Date*	*Text*[2]
Agreement concerning Air Services	London, 28.3.1995	
Agreement for the Promotion and Protection of Investments	London, 13.7.1995	
RUSSIAN FEDERATION		
Exchange of Notes concerning Certain Commercial Debts (The UK/Russian Federation Debt Agreement No. 2 (1994))	London, 28.2.1995	TS No. 72 (1995) (Cm 2963)
Denunciation of the Agreement constituted by an Exchange of Notes concerning the Mutual Abolition of Consular Fees on Visas signed at Moscow on 13.4.1964	Moscow, 26.7.1995	
SENEGAL		
Exchange of Notes concerning Certain Commercial Debts (The UK/Senegal Debt Agreement No. 10 (1994))	Dakar, 25.11.1994	TS No. 103 (1995)(Cm 3107)
SIERRA LEONE		
Exchange of Notes concerning Certain Commercial Debts (The UK/Sierra Leone Debt Agreement No. 6 (1994))	Freetown, 13.12.1994	TS No. 68 (1995) (Cm 2956)
SLOVAKIA		
Agreement in the form of an Exchange of Letters extending the Adaption to the Agreement between the European Community and Slovakia on Trade in Mutton, Lamb and Goatmeat	Brussels	
SOUTH AFRICA		
Agreement on Co-operation in Science and Technology	Cape Town, 27.2.1995	TS No. 62 (1995) (Cm 2959)
SWAZILAND		
Agreement for the Promotion and Protection of Investments	London, 5.5.1995	TS No. 76 (1995) (Cm 2967)
TOGO		
Exchange of Notes concerning Certain Commercial Debts (The UK/Togo Debt Agreement No. 9 (1992))	Lomé, 20.9.1995	

Country and Title	*Place and Date*	*Text*[2]
TUNISIA		
Euro-Mediterranean Agreement establishing an Association between the European Communities and their Member States, of the one part, and the Republic of Tunisia, of the other part, with Final Act	Brussels	
TURKMENISTAN		
Agreement concerning Air Services	Ashgabat, 9.2.1995	
Agreement for the Promotion and Protection of Investments	Ashgabat, 9.2.1995	Turkmenistan No. 1 (1995)(Cm 2976)
Agreement on Co-operation in the Fields of Education, Science and Culture	Ashgabat, 9.2.1995	Turkmenistan No. 2 (1995)(Cm 3121)
UKRAINE		
Interim Agreement on Trade and Trade-related matters between the European Community, the European Coal and Steel Community and the European Atomic Energy Community, of the one part, and Ukraine of the other part	Brussels	
Protocol of Correction to the Partnership and Co-operation Agreement between the European Communities and their Member States and Ukraine, signed at Luxembourg on 14.6.1994, including Final Act and Declaration by the French Government	Brussels	
Exchange of notes regarding the proposed Transfer by the British Antarctic Survey of their Research Station at Faraday in the British Antarctic Territory to the Antarctic Research Centre at the National Academy of Sciences of Ukraine	London, 20.7.1995	TS No. 15 (1996) (Cm 3060)
Agreement on International Road Transport	London, 13.12.1995	

Country and Title	*Place and Date*	*Text*[2]
UNITED STATES OF AMERICA		
Agreement concerning the Facilitation of Air Navigation Services	London, 11.5.1995	TS No. 63 (1995) (Cm 2986)
URUGUAY		
Agreement in the form of an Exchange of Letters extending the Adaption to the Agreement between the European Community and Uruguay on Trade in Mutton, Lamb and Goatmeat	Brussels	
VENEZUELA		
Agreement for the Promotion and Protection of Investments	London, 15.3.1995	
VIETNAM		
Exchange of Notes concerning the UK/Vietnam Debt Agreement No. 1 (1993)	Hanoi, 1.12.1994	TS No. 58 (1995) (Cm 2942)
ZIMBABWE		
Agreement for the Promotion and Protection of Investments	Harare, 1.3.1995	Zimbabwe No. 1 (1995)(Cm 2968)

IV. United Kingdom Legislation During 1995 Concerning Matters of International Law[1]

The European Communities (Finance) Act (1995 c. 1) amends and extends the definition of 'the Treaties' and 'the Community Treaties' in section 1(2) of the European Communities Act 1972 so as to include the Council decision of 31 October 1994 on the Communities' system of own resources.

The Geneva Conventions (Amendments) Act (1995 c. 27) amends the Geneva Conventions Act 1957 to enable effect to be given to the 1977 Protocols additional to the Geneva Conventions of 1949 on the protection of victims of armed conflicts. (See Part One: II.D.1., above.)

The Merchant Shipping Act (1995 c. 21) consolidates provisions from various earlier statutes on matters relating to merchant shipping, includ-

[1] Compiled by C. A. Hopkins.

ing, *inter alia*, registration of ships, collisions, pollution, liability of shipowners, salvage and wreck.

The Private International Law (Miscellaneous Provisions) Act (1995 c. 42) provides in Part I for the award in England and Wales of interest on judgment debts and arbitral awards expressed in a currency other than sterling. Part II provides for the validity under the law of England and Wales and the law of Scotland of marriages which are actually monogamous but which were entered into under a law which permits polygamy. Part III provides for the choice of the law to be applied where an action is brought in part of the United Kingdom in respect of a tort or delict (excluding defamation) committed abroad or in another part of the United Kingdom.

The Proceeds of Crime Act (1995 c. 11), *inter alia*, provides in section 14 for the enforcement in the United Kingdom of overseas forfeiture and restraint orders, and amends the Terrorism (Temporary Provisions) Act 1989 and the Criminal Justice (International Co-operation) Act 1990.

The Shipping and Trading Interests Protection Act (1995 c. 22) consolidates provisions from the Merchant Shipping Acts 1974 and 1988 on retaliatory measures open to the Secretary of State to be taken against foreign discriminatory actions against United Kingdom shipping or trading interests (sections 1–4), and on prohibition by the Secretary of State of coastal shipping in United Kingdom waters by shipping services not permanently based in the British Islands (sections 5 and 6).

The South Africa Act (1995 c. 3) modifies certain statutes in order to take account of the readmission of South Africa as a member of the Commonwealth on 1 June 1994.

TABLE OF CASES[1]

[1] The figures in heavier type indicate the pages on which cases are reviewed.

INDEX

Printed in the United Kingdom
by Lightning Source UK Ltd.
132652UK00007B/45/P

9 780198 258827